ANNUAL REVIEW OF MICROBIOLOGY

ANNUAL REVIEW OF MICROBIOLOGY

MORTIMER P. STARR, *Editor*
University of California, Davis

JOHN L. INGRAHAM, *Associate Editor*
University of California, Davis

A. BALOWS, *Associate Editor*
Center for Disease Control, Atlanta

VOLUME 31

1977

ANNUAL REVIEWS INC. 4139 EL CAMINO WAY PALO ALTO, CALIFORNIA 94306

ANNUAL REVIEWS INC.
Palo Alto, California, USA

International Standard Book Number: 0-8243-1131-0
Library of Congress Catalog Card Number: 49–432

REPRINTS

The conspicuous number aligned in the margin with the title of each article in this volume is a key for use in ordering reprints. Available reprints are priced at the uniform rate of $1 each postpaid. The minimum acceptable reprint order is 10 reprints and/or $10.00, prepaid. A quantity discount is available.

PRINTED AND BOUND IN THE UNITED STATES OF AMERICA

DEDICATED TO

CORNELIS BERNARDUS VAN NIEL

WITH AFFECTION, ADMIRATION, AND GRATITUDE

ON HIS EIGHTIETH BIRTHDAY

4 NOVEMBER 1977

CONTENTS

A "PURE" ORGANIC CHEMIST'S DOWNWARD PATH, *Michael Heidelberger* 1

BIOSYNTHESIS OF POLYENE MACROLIDE ANTIBIOTICS, *Juan-Francisco Martín* 13

BIOLOGY OF THE MARINE ENTEROBACTERIA: GENERA *BENECKEA* AND *PHOTOBACTERIUM*, *Paul Baumann and Linda Baumann* 39

BEHAVIOR OF MIXED CULTURES OF MICROORGANISMS, *A. G. Fredrickson* 63

THE SPIROCHETES, *Russell C. Johnson* 89

MICROBIAL ECOLOGY OF THE GASTROINTESTINAL TRACT, *Dwayne C. Savage* 107

THE INACTIVATION OF MICROBIAL ENZYMES IN VIVO, *Robert L. Switzer* 135

NOCARDIOFORM BACTERIA, *M. Goodfellow and D. E. Minnikin* 159

ION CURRENTS AND PHYSIOLOGICAL FUNCTIONS IN MICROORGANISMS, *F. M. Harold* 181

BACTERIAL PHYTOTOXINS, *Gary A. Strobel* 205

PHOTOTROPHIC PROKARYOTES: THE CYANOBACTERIA, *R. Y. Stanier and G. Cohen-Bazire* 225

PHOTOTROPHIC GREEN AND PURPLE BACTERIA: A COMPARATIVE, SYSTEMATIC SURVEY, *Norbert Pfennig* 275

ANTIFUNGAL AGENTS: RECENT DEVELOPMENTS, *George S. Kobayashi and Gerald Medoff* 291

BIOGENESIS OF METHANE, *R. A. Mah, D. M. Ward, L. Baresi, and T. L. Glass* 309

EFFECT OF PRIMARY METABOLITES ON SECONDARY METABOLISM, *Stephen W. Drew and Arnold L. Demain* 343

THE GENOME OF HEPATITIS B VIRUS, *William S. Robinson* 357

OIL TANKERS AND POLLUTION: A MICROBIOLOGICAL APPROACH, *David L. Gutnick and Eugene Rosenberg* 379

BACTERIAL FLAGELLA, *Michael Silverman and Melvin I. Simon* 397

RECENT PROGRESS IN EPSTEIN-BARR VIRUS RESEARCH, *M. A. Epstein and B. G. Achong* 421

THE ROLE OF OPPORTUNISTIC BACTERIA IN HUMAN DISEASE, *Alexander von Graevenitz* 447

TANDEM GENETIC DUPLICATIONS IN PHAGE AND BACTERIA, *R. Philip Anderson and John R. Roth* 473

PHAGOCYTE LYSOSOMES: INTERACTIONS WITH INFECTIOUS AGENTS, PHAGOSOMES, AND EXPERIMENTAL PERTURBATIONS IN FUNCTION, *Mayer B. Goren* 507

BEHAVIORAL GENETICS OF *PHYCOMYCES*, *Enrique Cerdá-Olmedo* 535

BACTERIAL BIOLUMINESCENCE, *J. Woodland Hastings and Kenneth H. Nealson* 549

CELL DIFFERENTIATION IN *NAEGLERIA GRUBERI*, *Chandler Fulton* 597

INDEXES

AUTHOR INDEX 631

SUBJECT INDEX 661

CUMULATIVE INDEX OF CONTRIBUTING AUTHORS, VOLUMES 27–31 688

CUMULATIVE INDEX OF CHAPTER TITLES, VOLUMES 27–31 690

OTHER REVIEWS OF MICROBIOLOGICAL INTEREST

From the *Annual Review of Biochemistry,* Volume 46 (1977):

Kurland, C. G. *Structure and Function of the Bacterial Ribosome*

Fareed, G. C., Davoli, D. *Molecular Biology of Papovaviruses*

Storm, D. R., Rosenthal, K. S., Swanson, P. E. *Polymyxin and Related Peptide Antibiotics*

From the *Annual Review of Ecology and Systematics,* Volume 8 (1977):

Cohen, J. E. *Mathematical Models of Schistosomaisis*

Nahmias, A. J., Reanney, D. C. *Evolution of Viruses*

From the *Annual Review of Genetics,* Volume 11 (1977):

Doi, R. H. *Genetic Control of Sporulation*

Eisenstark, A. *Genetic Recombination in Bacteria*

Iino, T. *Genetics of Structure and Function of Bacterial Flagella*

Low, K. B., Porter, R. *Modes of Gene Transfer and Recombination in Bacteria*

Nomura, M., Morgan, E. A., Jaskunas, S. R. *Genetics of Bacterial Ribosomes*

Parkinson, J. S. *Behavioral Genetics in Bacteria*

Weisberg, R., Adhya, S. *Illegitimate Recombination in Bacteria and Bacteriophage*

From the *Annual Review of Medicine,* Volume 28 (1977):

Eickhoff, T. C. *The Current Status of BCG Immunization Against Tuberculosis*

Hersh, E. M., Gutterman, J. U., Mavligit, G. M. *BCG as Adjuvant Immunotherapy for Neoplasia*

DuPont, H. L., Portnoy, B. L., Conklin, R. H. *Viral Agents and Diarrheal Illness*

Klein, P. A., Smith, R. T. *The Role of Oncogenic Viruses in Neoplasia*

From the *Annual Review of Phytopathology,* Volume 15 (1977):

Hopkins, D. L. *Diseases Caused by Leafhopper-Borne, Rickettsia-Like Bacteria*

Maxwell, D. P., Armentrout, V. N., Graves, L. B. Jr. *Microbodies in Plant Pathogenic Fungi*

Chakravorty, A. K., Shaw, M. *The Role of RNA in Host-Parasite Specificity*

ANNUAL REVIEWS INC. is a nonprofit corporation established to promote the advancement of the sciences. Beginning in 1932 with the *Annual Review of Biochemistry,* the Company has pursued as its principal function the publication of high quality, reasonably priced Annual Review volumes. The volumes are organized by Editors and Editorial Committees who invite qualified authors to contribute critical articles reviewing significant developments within each major discipline.

Annual Reviews Inc. is administered by a Board of Directors whose members serve without compensation.

Annual Reviews are published in the following sciences: Anthropology, Astronomy and Astrophysics, Biochemistry, Biophysics and Bioengineering, Earth and Planetary Sciences, Ecology and Systematics, Energy, Entomology, Fluid Mechanics, Genetics, Materials Science, Medicine, Microbiology, Nuclear Science, Pharmacology and Toxicology, Physical Chemistry, Physiology, Phytopathology, Plant Physiology, Psychology, and Sociology. The *Annual Review of Neuroscience* will begin publication in 1978. In addition, two special volumes have been published by Annual Reviews Inc.: *History of Entomology* (1973) and *The Excitement and Fascination of Science* (1965).

Michael Heidelberger

Ann. Rev. Microbiol. 1977. 31:1–12

A "PURE" ORGANIC CHEMIST'S DOWNWARD PATH ❖1694

Michael Heidelberger
Emeritus Professor of Immunochemistry, Columbia University, New York, New York 10032 and Adjunct Professor of Pathology (Immunology), New York University School of Medicine, New York, New York 10016

> We attribute to "pure chance" (automaton) all those events which are such as ordinarily admit to a telic explanation, but which happened on this occasion to have been produced without any reference to the actual result. The word "luck" (tyche), on the other hand, is restricted to that special type of chance events which (1) are possible objects of choice, and (2) affect persons capable of exercising choice.
>
> Aristotle, as translated by Wheelwright (22)

I begin with this appearance of profundity because chance and luck have been frequent determinants along my way. And I add obstinacy, because I was known as an obstinate child and, having made up my mind at the age of eight that I wanted to be a chemist, though without knowing why, I stuck to it and became one.

I was born on East 127th Street in New York City on April 29, 1888. My grandparents were Jewish Germans who emigrated between 1840 and 1850, apparently because of the greater opportunities in the United States. I know little of my father's parents, except that his father, Michael, died in Silver City, Idaho. David, my father, was born in Philadelphia and left school early to earn a living. He became a partner in a firm that made carriage robes, but with the advent of automobiles, he went "on the road" almost six months of the year selling lace curtains for another manufacturer. My maternal grandparents settled in Norfolk, Virginia, and sent their oldest daughter, Fanny, my mother, to a young lady's finishing school, where she learned to play the piano. They also shipped her off to relatives in Nürnberg for a year. She and my father were married in 1884. Their first child died before I was born and I was followed in two years by a brother, Charles. My parents were devoted to each other, but the necessarily long absences of my father gave my mother much responsibility and resulted in a strictness that she herself characterized as "Spartan."

As a consequence of her year abroad, Charles and I were required to speak German at the table and were accompanied to Central Park two afternoons a week by a governess who would tolerate nothing but French. We hated both burdens, and it was only years later, when these languages became essential, that I realized what a head start I had had.

Charles and I wandered in safety all over Central Park and knew several of its policemen by name. We ranged over many more distant parts of the city with the help of one or two friendly drivers of delivery wagons, this without the knowledge of our parents. We also gravitated often to the Metropolitan Museum of Art and the Museum of Natural History. All of these excursions were possible because my mother taught us all the primary school subjects in an hour or two each day, leaving the remainder for reading (I read *David Copperfield* and was taken to opera and concerts when I was eight years old), wanderings such as those above, and playing in the street with other children just out of school.

Later, when one of my teachers at public school, a Mr. Curtis, was invited to dinner, he was told that I wanted to become a chemist. "Buy him Cooley's 'Physics,' " he said, "he ought to know physics before chemistry, and if that doesn't discourage him, maybe he will really go on to be a chemist." I skimmed rather superficially through the book and was not frightened off. The real introduction to science followed in the eighth grade at the Workingman's School of the Ethical Culture Society, with a beautiful course in botany by Dr. Henry A. Kelly, followed in the Ethical Culture High School by his tour through zoology and well-taught courses in physics and chemistry by William E. Stark, with many hours in the laboratory. These led to my first research, an unpublished venture with Mr. Stark. Late in 1904, the Seventh Avenue-Broadway subway was about to open and the newspapers contained dire predictions of mass suffocation in the soon-to-be crowded trains. During the Christmas holiday, we lugged a five-gallon demijohn of water about a quarter of a mile to the nearest subway platform, emptied it there, replacing the water with air, and bore the stoppered demijohn back in triumph to the laboratory. There we exploded a small portion of the air with hydrogen in a eudiometer. Something went wrong, however, and we found only five percent of oxygen!

At the Ethical, I also learned to write good English from Percival Chubb and was taught higher mathematics, even trigonometry, by Matilda Auerbach, a superb but very strict teacher. As a freshman at Columbia, I started with an exciting course in qualitative chemical analysis, given for the first time according to the ionic theory by a young instructor, Hal T. Beans, against the wishes of the old-fashioned head of the department, a Professor Wells. He had Beans brought up on charges before the president, Nicholas Murray Butler, but Butler said Beans was right to teach in the most modern way possible. Another memorable course was Charles F. Chandler's Industrial Chemistry, which consisted mainly of personal anecdotes ranging far and wide. Quantitative analysis, the next year, with Floyd J. Metzger, led eventually to an offer of a fellowship if I would go on to a Ph.D. with him, but by that time I had tasted the joys of organic chemistry and decided on that for my doctoral work. I did get a master's degree, with Metzger, and we published two small papers together (17, 18). The second was rejected by W. A. Noyes, Senior, at that time the peppery editor and sole referee of the *Journal of the American Chemical Society,* on the ground that we did not know how to standardize potassium permanganate. Metzger, who had been watching me like a hawk, sent the paper back, saying that if Noyes didn't take it he would send it to the *Zeitschrift für analytische Chemie* with a note explaining why. Noyes took the paper.

Organic chemistry was taught by Marston Taylor Bogert and John M. Nelson (affectionately called Pop Nelson), both excellent teachers. After the preliminaries, Bogert would write two unrelated compounds on the board and ask you to synthesize one from the other. All around the room, a handful of us at each session would be racking our brains at the blackboard, while the rest of the class looked on in grim amusement, knowing their turn would come, too. I became interested in organophosphorus compounds as a subject for my thesis and Bogert wisely let me have a fling at the ones in the chemical museum. However, they were difficult to handle and sometimes caught fire in the air, and before long I was ready to join the other grads and work on quinazolines, with which one could figure out everything on paper and all compounds were nicely crystalline. An earlier student had made a quinazolone phthalone as a brown powder with hopefully useful properties as a yellow dye, and this topic was assigned to me. The more I purified the phthalone, the paler it became, so I added bromine to a derivative of it, hoping to intensify the color. Uncooperatively, the last traces of color disappeared. This intrigued me, and with Nelson's coaching I found that oxidative splitting had occurred (1). But this took time and I obstinately stuck to it, and at the end of two years I had only twenty new compounds instead of the forty traditionally required. Incidentally, one of my fellow students had his forty new compounds but was never able to do a C and H combustion correctly, also a requirement. Both of us were finally recommended for the Ph.D. degree, and guess to what eminence my colleague rose: a Professorship of Organic Analysis at a large, well-known university!

As for me, the question was "what next?" A part-time, older, German-American laboratory instructor named Hoffman had often pointed out the deficiencies of chemical, especially organic chemical, teaching and insisted that at least a year in a European laboratory under one of the recognized masters was a prerequisite to a successful career. My parents were willing to stake me to this, and I was selfish enough to accept what I knew was a sacrifice. But first they wished me to seek advice from old Dr. Samuel Meltzer, who had listened with his massive head against my chest as our family physician throughout my boyhood and had then become the distinguished head of Physiology at the Rockefeller Institute for Medical Research. He tried, wisely, I think, to discourage me, saying a scientific career was nothing for a poor man's son, but he gave it up and turned me over to the chemists, who would know the best person under whose direction to work. Thus, I had the luck to meet P. A. Levene, Walter A. Jacobs, and D. D. Van Slyke at tea that same afternoon. I had thought of going to Emil Fischer, with whom all three had worked, but they said he was aging and assigning his students to his assistants. On the other hand, Richard Willstätter was much younger, very able, and doing outstanding research on alkaloids and chlorophyll. Again, luck was with me, for Willstätter was willing to have me come.

That September, 1911, I boarded the French cabin liner "Chicago" (off-season rate, $50, for an outside cabin to myself, good food, and 11 days to Le Havre) and soon found myself fighting hard not to fall in love, for I had been brought up with the now strange notion that that was taboo until one could support a wife. My struggle was a result of a remarkable, attractive, and intelligent girl on her way to the Sorbonne for a Ph.D. (which she won) and who could read a whole page at a glance. Anyhow, we enjoyed being together and even renewed our friendship forty years later when we were both living alone and she was Professor of English Literature at a leading women's college. But I did fall in love with Paris during a week with as few hours as possible in a little back room on the top floor of a small, still existent hotel. Shortly after, Willstätter received me kindly and hopefully at the Federal Polytechnic Institute in Zurich. I became one of about twenty students to whose laboratory tables the Professor came twice a day. His first assistant was Arthur Stoll, who became the guiding spirit of the Sandoz Company of Basel, and his second assistant was Laszlò Zechmeister, with whom an abiding friendship developed and who came to the United States many years later as Professor of Organic Chemistry at the California Institute of Technology. I wanted to work on chlorophyll, but Willstätter said that would take two years—one to learn methods and another to penetrate further into its structure. But he had a one-year problem, a study of cycloöctatetraene, which had been synthesized in the laboratory by Ernst Waser, who then left for a job in industry. It would be an expensive problem, starting with a rare alkaloid, pseudopelletierine, and requiring much silver nitrate to remove nitrogen atoms by the Hofmann degradation (24). One had to pay for all materials, and when I doubted that my father, who was footing the bill, could afford it, Willstätter proposed that he and I should alternate in buying, whereupon he presented me with 500 grams of alkaloid and saw to it that it was always his turn when we had to buy silver nitrate and my turn for acetic acid or the like. I started with a practice degradation of a less-valuable alkaloidal derivative, and while I was watching the steam distillation, the mixture suddenly crystallized but fortunately remained fluid. Watching this unexpected happening intently, I did not hear Willstätter come up behind me. Suddenly, an arm with a pointing finger shot past my head and a voice hissed in my ear: "Was-s-s is-s-st das-s-s?" I was so startled I could not answer, and only later did I realize that sodium hydroxide had crystallized temporarily from the hot alcoholic solution. I am sure this made Willstätter realize that his new American student was very inexperienced in the handling of the unexpected or of a difficult problem, but that was precisely why I had come to him. Cycloöctatetraene, as made from the alkaloid, had the unpleasant habit of throwing bridges across the 8-carbon span, so that in addition to the final steps of preparation one had to do all necessary experiments with the product as rapidly as possible. This meant starting at 8 AM and working steadily until 3 the next morning. Not only did all details have to be thought out and all apparatus have to be readied for the appointed time, but there were difficulties unknown to the modern research worker. I mention one: the only way to obtain solid CO_2 was to invert a tank of the compressed gas on a diagonal wooden frame and blow the gas into a leather bag. Yields were low, and around midnight it was necessary to cross the street to the convenient pub, Café Friedegg (still there), and shoulder one of the tanks supplying the beer pumps. I had three of these nineteen-hour workdays, and the next day I was fit only for cleaning up.

There were also diversions. I played clarinet in the student orchestra, and in the middle of the overlong annual concert we played the Mozart quintet—the only time I have had a musical criticism in a daily paper, the "Züri Zietig," as the Neue Zürcher Zeitung was popularly called. Then there were fine operas and also concerts, for which one could borrow a regular student's card and be admitted for almost nothing. At these I heard Fritz Kreisler and Percy Grainger for the first time, and even the clarinetist, Mühlfeld, for whom Brahms wrote so superbly. I also had long Sunday walks with Hugh Clark, my English neighbor in the lab, a ten-day memorable trip at Easter to Italy, and, at the end of the academic year, the Professor's excursion up the lake to a fine restaurant, where, after dinner, I played a few selections and Zechmeister, with great seriousness, read a beautiful paper on "hippopotamuric acid."

Through all this I was worried about the future, and though offered an assistantship by Professor Eugen Bamberger at the Polytechnic, I wrote letters to a score of universities in the United States, proffering my services as instructor in organic chemistry. Not only was I turned down by all but the very last, but most of the answers bore only two cents postage instead of the then required five. The Swiss imposed a double penalty, so that being refused was expensive as well as discouraging. In the end, I received an appointment at the University of Illinois. After writing up the year's work with Willstätter for publication (23) (I asked him for a letter of recommendation and he said "Shall I write it the way I think, or the way you wish?"), I started for home, intending to see something of Germany and England on the way.

At Nürnberg, where I stayed a few days with relatives of my mother, a cable came from my father stating that I could have a job at the Rockefeller Institute if I returned at once and was approved by its director, Dr. Simon Flexner. As I had liked the Institute's chemists who had given me such good advice, I took an upper berth, second class, on the steamer that could get me back the fastest, the "Provence." Here, pure chance, as defined by Aristotle, was operative, or was it luck, since it aided in the choice? Getting into a compartment at random on the boat train from Paris to Le Havre, I found myself in the company of two professors from the University of Illinois and their wives, pleasant and interesting people, but with a lack of enthusiasm for their university that made me all the more inclined to accept the appointment at Rockefeller if I passed muster. This position was to assist Dr. W. A. Jacobs in synthesizing drugs for the cure of poliomyelitis, as part of the study of the disease by Dr. Flexner himself, and I started in September, 1912, as a Fellow of the Institute at a salary of $1200 a year.

One of the first things my father insisted upon after my return was for me to add up my expenses. I wondered at that, for he was not interested in details not mentioned in my letters, only in the total. I soon found out, for when I had calculated it as somewhat over $800, he immediately wrote out a check to my brother for the same amount. Alas, this benefitted Charles very little, for a sequel to an earlier attack of rheumatic fever, endocarditis, caused his death the following spring. Early in his illness, the Health Department of the City of New York immunized a horse with the strain of *Streptococcus viridans* isolated from Charles' blood. This first contact with immunology was not encouraging, for large injections of the horse's serum failed to help.

The Rockefeller Institute was rather small in 1912, with two buildings containing laboratories and another for the hospital. There were a few tables in a small lunchroom, a very necessary adjunct, as the nearest eating places were quite distant. Jacobs proved to be a very shy, kindly person and a keen organic chemist with original ideas. He made it clear that I was an essential part of the laboratory and that my name would be on every paper published, as my work would give him time for additional syntheses. He also taught me, when, for example, a reaction had to be refluxed for several hours, to start something else so that I could carry forward a number of syntheses simultaneously, keep working steadily, and not get things mixed up, all by his own example. He and his wife, Laura, were very hospitable and I was often at their home in Mt. Vernon, where Walter played the pianola very temperamentally. He had perforated rolls of all of Beethoven's piano works and of arrangements of the symphonies for the piano. At first we went to the lunch room of the Institute together, but as he always led me to the table at which the other chemists sat, I soon realized that I was missing much of the life of the Institute. After a month or so of this, I plucked up enough courage to ask if he would mind if I went to lunch at my own convenience. He did not, and then I began to meet men such as Jacques Loeb, Peyton Rous, Alexis Carrel, Hideyo Noguchi, and John Auer, all of whom would linger at the table and talk with young, unknown beginners like myself. I became an authority on Jacobs, often being asked questions about him, as he was scarcely known to the rest of the Institute because of his shyness and his habit of always lunching with the chemists.

For the chemotherapy of polio, Jacobs chose as his lead the slight therapeutic effect of hexamethylenetetramine, several quaternary salts of which had been made. He foresaw that a large number of such salts could be prepared from the almost limitless choice of chloro, bromo, and iodo compounds, both aliphatic and aromatic. We bought what we could, synthesized large amounts of others, and combined them with hexamethylenetetramine (11, 11a, 14, 15). Some of the new salts were highly bactericidal. One or two even seemed to delay the death of monkeys infected with the virus, but this was found to be the result of a loss of virulence of the virus itself.

At this juncture, with Dr. Flexner's encouragement, we turned to African sleeping sickness, or trypanosomiasis, which was making whole regions of that continent uninhabitable. Atoxyl, para-acetaminophenyl-arsonate, widely used by Thomas in its treatment (20), was dangerously toxic and not very effective. As Jacobs and I began to synthesize new and hopefully better arsenicals, we were joined by Drs. Wade H. Brown and Louise Pearce, who were to test our compounds for efficacy against trypanosomes in animals. Paul Ehrlich of Frankfort, the great pioneer of modern chemotherapy, had started on the same quest but it had led to "606" or Salvarsan, a cure for syphilis, instead. His most active synthetic against trypanosomiasis was the trivalent, highly toxic, and therefore unusable para-arseno-phenylglycine. Jacobs thought that the inactivity against trypanosomes of the less poisonous pentavalent para-phenylglycine arsonic acid might be a result of its highly reactive carboxyl group, which could combine with many components of tissues rather than with the parasites. He proposed masking the –COOH by converting it into $-CONH_2$, the amide, a grouping common to tissues, and this substance, sodium para-phenylglycinamide arsonate, our first and simplest arsenical, was more active than the many others that we synthesized in attempts to improve upon it. Dr. Flexner named it "Tryparsamide" and it was patented for purposes of control (10). A large batch was prepared by Powers, Weightman, and Rosengarten, a Philadelphia pharmaceutical concern, and when World War I was over, Louise Pearce conducted a field test in the Belgian Congo. She found Tryparsamide to be superior to the previously used drugs, and tests in this country showed it to be useful in the treatment of tertiary syphilis as well.

The value of Tryparsamide was eventually recognized by the Belgian government by bestowing upon us (and Thomas, who had introduced Atoxyl) the Order of Leopold II and monetary awards. Louise Pearce was given the lion's share deservedly, for she had risked her life and handled the field tests beautifully. I was angry, though, that Brown, who had merely tested our drugs on animals, received twice as much money as Jacobs, whose brilliant idea led to Tryparsamide, while I, the lowest in the group, was given as much as Jacobs. I immediately protested to the Belgian consul general and to the ambassador, but they claimed that nothing could be done after the king had signed the decree. Walter never complained, but my blood pressure still goes up as I write this.

Supplies of Salvarsan were very meager after the onset of World War I, and such difficulties were encountered in attempts to manufacture it here that Ehrlich was accused of deliberately omitting some essential step in his application for a patent. This was not true, however, for Jacobs and I, who were used to handling arsenicals, had no trouble in making the substance. By this time, I was a 1st lieutenant in the Sanitary Corps of the Army, assigned to U.S. Laboratory No. 1, the Rockefeller Institute, much of which was given over to training Army physicians in laboratory techniques. Jacobs and I thought we could improve upon Salvarsan and actually synthesized an analogue that was at least as active and less toxic. After exhaustive tests in animals by Brown and Pearce, it was tried with good results on about 100 human cases of syphilis. However, a second batch inexplicably resulted in several dangerous cases of dermatitis and we withdrew the drug.

In the early summer of 1915, when it appeared that we might soon be at war, I enrolled in a six-week officer's training course at Plattsburg, New York, to learn something of military life and soon found out how easy it was to acquire the art of killing. After that, armed with a Marksman's button and a commission as 1st lieutenant in a volunteer army that was quickly found to be utterly useless, I went cross-country to a summer camp at Center Lovell, on Lake Kezar in Maine, where I had my own canoe. The first evening, while I was playing Pergolese's "Nina" with my friend Stanley Ries at the piano, the door opened and a startlingly lovely girl walked in. Stanley stopped playing and said, "Meet Nina!" Would Aristotle have called this "chance" or "luck?" Companionship with Nina Tachau was a joy, and the following June we were married. Our son, Charles, was born in 1920; his mother died of cancer in 1946: we had been comrades for 31 years and had helped each other in our respective careers, for Nina was a writer and later became a frequent speaker for the American Association for the United Nations and chairman on foreign policy for the New York City League of Women Voters. While on this personal note, I might as well tell of living alone for the next nine years, bouyed by the excitement of the laboratory, the encouragement of warm friends, and visits to my son and his growing family. A good friend, Nellie Doogan, who had been in the family for years, came in daily to cook breakfast and clean; another, Anna Greene, cooked dinners two or three times a week. Then, one evening, I was invited to play the Mozart trio for clarinet, viola, and piano by Vally Weigl, widow of Karl Weigl, the composer. The violist was Charlotte Rosen, an outstanding musician and a cheerful, outgiving woman who had been a concert violinist in her native Germany and whose husband, a dermatologist, had died several years before. Though she lived in the same apartment house I did, I had never seen her, as she went to the second floor via the stairs while I used the elevator to the tenth. We walked home together, and again chance or luck and music brought companionship that ripened into marriage. With two happy marriages in one lifetime, I count myself among the most fortunate.

One of my duties as 1st Lieutenant at U.S. Laboratory No. 1 in 1917–18 was to march the visiting medical captains, majors, and lieutenant-colonels up and down while teaching them the Sanitary Detachment Drill, which I had learned at Plattsburg. This was also the year of a severe epidemic of influenza, at that time thought to be caused by an influenza bacillus. Dr. Martha Wollstein, of the Institute, prepared a vaccine from this bacillus and I persuaded all of my close relatives to receive injections of it. None of us caught the viral disease! Chance, once more!

At the close of the war, Jacobs and I decided that we had had enough of pure synthetic organic chemistry, but Dr. Flexner, an ardent believer in chemotherapy, insisted that we tackle bacterial infections, notably pneumococcal and streptococcal diseases. Lloyd D. Felton joined us for the testing in animals, and we started to synthesize increasingly active bactericides, including a number of cinchona alkaloidal derivatives (8–8b) more potent in vitro than Optochin (12), which had been used with some success against local pneumococcal infections. However, the combination "drug and bug" usually killed the test mice more quickly than the drug alone. One of the intermediates that we converted into such useless substances was para-aminophenyl sulphonamide, or Sulfanilamide, which the Tréfouels, Nitti & Bovet (21) found to be the active portion of the purple dye for which Domagk received the Nobel Prize in 1939. That so simple a substance could cure bacterial infections by a mechanism other than direct killing of the microorganisms never occurred to us. If it had, we might have saved hundreds of thousands of lives in the twenty years before Domagk, the Tréfouels, Nitti, and Bovet made their discoveries. I always told this story in lecturing on chemotherapy in the course on biochemistry at the College of Physicians and Surgeons of Columbia University and begged the students never to allow themselves to become slaves of an idea.

After nine and a half years of chemotherapy, Walter and I were still good friends but were eager to go on to something else, and, we agreed, independently. Dr. Flexner finally consented to our dropping out of chemotherapy, Felton went to the U.S. Public Health Service, and Walter went ahead with structural studies on cardiac-active glycosides, which we had started together (13), and related alkaloids. I wanted to find the active principles of several ancient Chinese drugs that had attracted notice in Western medicine, but Dr. Flexner did not consider that worth equipping a new laboratory and sent me over to Van Slyke, who was then chemist to the hospital of the Institute, to learn some biochemistry "so we can find you a job more easily somewhere else."

The hospital, devoted to research on a limited number of diseases and to the care and treatment of patients with these diseases, was directed by Dr. Rufus Cole, who also headed the team studying pneumonia. Van Slyke had a group actively probing the functions of the kidneys, and in 1921, when I started work with him, he had just begun a study of the equilibrium between oxygen and hemoglobin with Dr. A. Baird Hastings. They were having trouble obtaining enough purified oxyhemoglobin with intact oxygen-carrying power for their tonometric experiments. It devolved upon me to eliminate the trouble, and as this was primarily an organic chemical problem, I was soon making many grams at a time of crystalline equine oxyhemoglobin with virtually 100% oxygen-carrying power (4). This involved keeping the materials at low temperatures, so we put a No. 2 International centrifuge into a cold room. Eventually, my laboratory helper was threatened with a nervous breakdown as a result of the many colds caught from the necessary sudden changes in his working temperatures. Accordingly, I asked the president of the centrifuge company, then a frequent visitor to laboratories using his centrifuges, to build me one with an insulated brine coil around it, as the hospital had circulating brine to cool the banks of refrigerators and the cold rooms. The new instrument fulfilled its purpose and, thus, was the first refrigerated centrifuge invented and operated. Many of the visitors to the laboratory immediately ordered copies, as the wonder was how such a machine, so essential to the development of modern biochemistry, microbiology, and, indeed, molecular biology, had not been devised earlier. Thousands of refined, improved models are now in use throughout the world—my financial profit was $50 for writing the International Company's first descriptive booklet.

During the two years that I was making oxyhemoglobin and learning biochemistry, several more instances of good luck occurred. Dr. Karl Landsteiner, the famous Austrian pathologist and immunologist, became a Member of the Rockefeller Institute, and as he was interested in the immunological properties of hemoglobin, we were soon collaborating (9, 16) and I was learning my first immunological techniques from a great master. Then, Dr. Walter W. Palmer, head of the Department of Medicine at the Presbyterian Hospital, spent some months working with Van Slyke. Acquaintance with him was later to prove of crucial importance to me. And last, but not least, Dr. Oswald T. Avery, microbiologist of the pneumonia team, would come in from time to time with a small vial of brownish powder to say, "When can you work on this, Michael? The whole secret of bacterial specificity is in this vial." Eventually, the need for oxyhemoglobin ended and I was transferred to the pneumonia group, although "Van" generously let me continue to use the same laboratory. Thus began my career as a microbiologist.

In 1917, Dochez & Avery had published their discovery of the serologically type-specific "soluble specific substance" of pneumococcus (3), and five years had elapsed before a chemist undertook its characterization. In the meantime, Dochez had left the Institute, leaving Avery, or "the Fess," as he was affectionately called, to carry the study forward. At that time, there were only three "fixed types" of Pneumococcus, type I, Neufeld's "typical Pneumococcus," and types II and III, all other serological variants having been relegated to "group IV." Fess said we had better not start with type III, which formed the largest capsules, because some people called it *Streptococcus mucosus,* nor was type I a favorable prospect because its capsules were very small. That left only type II with its capsules of intermediate size. I needed type II antiserum with which to identify serologically active fractions, so Fess took me down to the cold room where there were shelves of large bottles of therapeutically used, type-specific horse sera. I spied a bottle of type II serum half filled with mold and, to Avery's horror, took it along for the chemical tests, sterility being unnecessary for rapid, qualitative precipitin tests. Another innovation that he was dubious about was centrifuging weak precipitin tests that did not settle rapidly by themselves, but he was soon convinced by a series of adequate control tubes.

In our initial studies, we concentrated batches of meat-infusion broth cultures on a large steam bath in a hood until we had accumulated the concentrate from 300 liters. Precipitation with alcohol and centrifugation gave a three-layer separation, with the active material in the gummy middle layer. The more we purified this, the less nitrogen it contained, which surprised us, as all immunologically active substances were supposed to be proteins. Finally, when it was virtually nitrogen free, Fess said, "Could it be a carbohydrate?" So I boiled a bit with acid and got a strong test for reducing sugars, one of which was shown to be glucose (5, 5a). An acidic component was recognized, but its identification as D-glucuronic acid and the finding of L-rhamnose were accomplished much later (2, 19). One must remember that our work was done before the introduction of paper chromatography, when one had to isolate the sugar itself or a characteristic derivative and the relatively large amounts of purified material required were not easy to obtain. The conclusive test that we had the "soluble specific substance" was to precipitate some with two liters of outdated antiserum and recover essentially the same polysaccharide from the washed, proteolytically digested precipitate. To test the resistance of the type II substance (SII) to carbohydrate-splitting enzymes, Fess suggested that we write to Peterson and Fred in Wisconsin for some of their thermophilic cellulose-splitting bacteria. These microbiologists obligingly sent us a culture, and we seeded it into a slurry of filter-paper pulp made up in a 1:20,000 nutrient broth solution of SII and put it into an incubator at 55°C to stew overnight. Next morning the filter paper was gone, but the culture was still 1:20,000 as to SII!

As soon as we started to purify our first batch of the "soluble specific substance" of type III, I knew it would be different chemically from SII, as it formed dense fibers when precipitated by alcohol. Moreover, SII was dextrorotatory whereas SIII was levorotatory. Both were almost nitrogen free and contained glucose, but obviously in a different combination. SII was a weaker acid than SIII.

From the products of hydrolysis of the latter, Dr. Walther F. Goebel, who had joined us, and I isolated a glucuronoglucose, which we termed an "aldobionic acid" (7, 7a) instead of the more correct "aldobiouronic acid." Such acidic bioses were later found to occur in enormous tonnage in the hemicelluloses and gummy exudates of trees and plants, but the first discovery of this combination of sugars was in the microscopic capsule of Pneumococcus type III.

Only after isolating SII and SIII did we turn our attention to type I, which immediately confirmed Fess's wisdom and unerring intuition in not working on it first, as its number, I, would have suggested. Not only were the yields small, but SI turned out to be an amphoteric polyelectrolyte and I threw the first batch down the sink, thinking it was nucleoprotein, while Zinsser and Mueller actually recorded their analogous "residue antigen" from type I as a polypeptide. It soon developed, however, that SI contained a large proportion of galacturonic acid, defining it as a third immunologically active, chemically different, type-specific polysaccharide (7b).

By this time, Avery's imagination, which always ranged far and wide, led him to the belief that if bacteria possessed immunologically reactive polysaccharides others should exist "free in nature." We accordingly bought the few plant gums then available, and lo!, gum arabic precipitated our type II antisera. While purifying a batch, I let it stand overnight in fairly strong hydrochloric acid. When I precipitated it next day with alcohol, pentose had been split off, exposing more chemical groups common to SII, so that the degraded substance reacted at a 150-fold higher titer than the native gum (6).

During all this period, I had to keep my eyes open for a job elsewhere, for although I was happy and satisfied, Dr. Flexner probably wisely insisted that as long as I stayed my work would be known as someone else's and that I should go elsewhere and stand on my own feet. Accordingly, when Dr. Samuel Bookman retired as Chemist to Mt. Sinai Hospital in New York after forty years of faithful service and the post was offered to me, I accepted it.

The year 1927–28 at Mt. Sinai was a very busy, interesting, and instructive one, with its close contact with medicine. It was necessary to reorganize the chemical laboratories, introduce new methods of analysis, and eliminate parallel determinations yielding the same information. This sometimes led to friction with the Medical Board. Although my associate, Dr. David J. Cohn, provided able assistance with the supervision of the vast amount of chemical routine, there was little sustained time for research. Accordingly, when Dr. Walter W. Palmer, Professor of Medicine at the College of Physicians and Surgeons of Columbia University, proposed that I join him as the first full-time chemist in a department of medicine, I was glad to accept. With me, from Mt. Sinai, went my technician, Check M. Soo Hoo, who was to serve ably and faithfully in that capacity for thirty-five years.

This brings me to the end of one epoch and to the start of others: twenty-seven years of ideal working conditions at P. and S. and "retirement," the story of which I hope to relate elsewhere.

Editors note: The story of Michael Heidelberger's career will be continued in the prefatory chapter of Volume 48 of the Annual Review of Biochemistry, scheduled for publication in July 1979.

Literature Cited

1. Bogert, M. T., Heidelberger, M. 1912. *J. Am. Chem. Soc.* 34:183–201
2. Butler, K., Stacey, M. 1955. *J. Chem. Soc.*, pp. 1537–41
3. Dochez, A. R., Avery, O. T. 1917. *J. Exp. Med.* 26:477–93
4. Heidelberger, M. 1922. *J. Biol. Chem.* 53:31–40
5. Heidelberger, M., Avery, O. T. 1923. *J. Exp. Med.* 38:73–79

5a. Heidelberger, M., Avery, O. T. 1924. *J. Exp. Med.* 40:301–16

6. Heidelberger, M., Avery, O. T., Goebel, W. F. 1929. *J. Exp. Med.* 49: 847–57
7. Heidelberger, M., Goebel, W. F. 1926. *J. Biol. Chem.* 70:613–24

7a. Heidelberger, M., Goebel, W. F. 1927. *J. Biol. Chem.* 74:613–18

7b. Heidelberger, M., Goebel, W. F., Avery, O. T. 1925. *J. Exp. Med.* 42: 727–45

8. Heidelberger, M., Jacobs, W. A. 1919. *J. Am. Chem. Soc.* 41:817–33

8a. Heidelberger, M., Jacobs, W. A. 1920. *J. Am. Chem. Soc.* 42:2278–86

8b. Heidelberger, M., Jacobs, W. A. 1922. *J. Am. Chem. Soc.* 44:1098–107

9. Heidelberger, M., Landsteiner, K. 1923. *J. Exp. Med.* 38:561–71
10. Jacobs, W. A., Brown, W. H., Heidelberger, M., Pearce, L. 1918. *U.S. Patents No. 1280119–24 and No. 1280126*
11. Jacobs, W. A., Heidelberger, M. 1915. *J. Biol. Chem.* 20:659–84; 685–94

11a. Jacobs, W. A., Heidelberger, M. 1915. *J. Biol. Chem.* 21:103–43; 145–52; 403–37; 439–53; 455–64; 465–75

12. Jacobs, W. A., Heidelberger, M. 1919. *J. Am. Chem. Soc.* 41:1581–87; 1587–600; 1834–40
13. Jacobs, W. A., Heidelberger, M. 1922. *J. Biol. Chem.* 54:253–61
14. Jacobs, W. A., Heidelberger, M., Amoss, H. L. 1916. *J. Exp. Med.* 23:569–76
15. Jacobs, W. A., Heidelberger, M., Bull, C. G. 1916. *J. Exp. Med.* 23:577–99
16. Landsteiner, K., Heidelberger, M. 1923. *J. Gen. Physiol.* 6:131–35
17. Metzger, F. J., Heidelberger, M. 1909. *J. Am. Chem. Soc.* 31:1040–45
18. Metzger, F. J., Heidelberger, M. 1910. *J. Am. Chem. Soc.* 32:642–44
19. Record, B. R., Stacey, M. 1948. *J. Chem. Soc.*, pp. 1561–67
20. Thomas, H. W. 1905. *Br. J. Med.* 1:1140–43
21. Tréfouel, J., Tréfouel, T. J., Nitti, F., Bovet, D. 1935. *C. R. Soc. Biol.* 120: 756–58
22. Wheelwright, P. 1951. *Aristotle*, pp. 29–35. New York: Odyssey. 336 pp.
23. Willstätter, R., Heidelberger, M. 1913. *Ber. Dtsch. Chem. Ges.* 46:517–27
24. Willstätter, R., Waser, E. 1911. *Ber. Dtsch. Chem. Ges.* 43:3423–45

Ann. Rev. Microbiol. 1977. 31:13–38

BIOSYNTHESIS OF POLYENE MACROLIDE ANTIBIOTICS

❖1695

Juan-Francisco Martín

Instituto de Microbiología Bioquímica, CSIC, Departamento de Microbiología, Facultad de Ciencias, Universidad de Salamanca, Salamanca, Spain

CONTENTS

INTRODUCTION 13
Mode of Action and Medical Relevance 14
BIOSYNTHESIS OF THE MACROLIDE RING 16
Precursors of the Macrolide Ring 16
Polyketide Synthesis and Fatty Acid Synthesis 17
Acyl-CoA Pool and Acyl-CoA Carboxylases in Polyene Macrolide Synthesis 20
Precursor Condensation 23
Chain Elongation and Ring Cyclization 23
Effect of Fatty Acids on Polyene Macrolide Synthesis 25
BIOSYNTHESIS OF THE AROMATIC MOIETY 26
Precursors of the Aromatic Moiety 26
Aromatic Moieties as Polyketide Starters 28
Regulation by Aromatic Amino Acids of the Synthesis of Aromatic Polyene Macrolides 28
BIOSYNTHESIS OF THE MACROLIDE AMINOSUGARS 30
Aminosugars in Polyene Macrolides 30
Precursors of the Aminosugar Moiety 31
Sugar Nucleoside Diphosphate Derivatives as Intermediates 31
Attachment of the Aminosugar Moiety to the Macrolide Ring 32
SUMMARY AND FUTURE OUTLOOK 34

INTRODUCTION

The polyene macrolide antibiotics are a large group of antifungal agents, including more than 90 different members discovered since the early 1950s. Compilations of the polyene macrolides were made by Vining (150), Oroshnik & Mebane (113), Hamilton-Miller (41), and Martin & McDaniel (88). However, the identity of many of these compounds remains questionable and caution should be taken in considering all of them as different (88). A summarized list of the polyene macrolide antibiotics that are better characterized or more relevant medically is included in Table 1, along with the producer strains.

The polyene antibiotics are a subgroup of the class of macrolide antibiotics. The structures of the macrolide antibiotics consist of macrocyclic rings closed by a lactone bond (the so-called lactone ring), usually with one or more sugars attached glycosidically to the macrolide ring. The polyene subgroup is characterized by a lactone ring of 26 to 38 atoms, a polyene chromophore consisting of a series of four to seven alternating double bonds that form part of the macrolide ring, and usually one aminosugar moiety. Neutral sugars do not occur in polyene macrolides, although neutral sugars are frequent components of nonpolyene macrolides (18). One free carboxylic group exists in some polyenes as a side group of the macrolide ring. The lactone ring is larger than that of nonpolyene macrolides. Thus, amphotericin B, one of the best known polyene macrolides, has a 38-membered ring that is much larger than that of erythromycin (14-membered lactone), a typical nonpolyene macrolide (31, 101). Recently, however, Bianchi et al (9) described a new class of nonpolyene macrolides, the axenomycins, with large 34-membered rings.

The polyene chromophore gives a rigid planar character to one part of the macrolide ring, which contrasts with the polyhydroxylated hydrophilic region of the rest of the molecule. This amphipathic character accounts for the physicochemical properties (low water solubility, photolability, etc) and biological activites (interactions with membranes and sterols). According to the number of alternating double bonds in the chromophore, the polyene macrolides have been traditionally divided into tetraenes, pentaenes, hexaenes, and heptaenes (Table 1). The chemistry of these compounds has been reviewed in detail by Oroshnik & Mebane (113) and by Mechlinski (99).

Mode of Action and Medical Relevance

All the polyene antibiotics are essentially antifungal agents in contrast to the nonpolyene macrolides, which are antibacterial. Initial work summarized by Lampen (60) and Kinsky (56) established the membrane sterols of sensitive organisms as the binding sites of the polyene macrolides. The biochemical evidence for this interaction has been proved by using biophysical techniques such as fluorescence (4, 21, 105, 137, 143) and fluorescence polarization (12). Considerable insight into the mode of action of polyene macrolides has been gained recently by studying the sterol-polyene interactions in monolayers of lipid mixtures (23) and in stable lipid bilayer films (147). Although the theory that polyenes form pores in membranes remains open to discussion (28), the polyene-induced distortion of selective membrane permeability is well established. This distortion results in leakage of potassium and magnesium ions followed by decreased protein and RNA synthesis (65, 66). For detailed information on the mode of action of polyene antibiotics, the extensive reviews of Kinsky (57) and Hamilton-Miller (42) are suggested.

Polyene macrolides traditionally have been used in the treatment of external, subcutaneous, and systemic mycoses in animals and humans. Because of their effect on membrane permeability, some polyenes have been found to potentiate the effect

Table 1 Some of the more representative polyene macrolide antibiotics

Name (alternate name)	Producer strain	Chromophore subgroup	Aminosugar moiety	Aromatic moiety
Etruscomycin (lucensomycin)	*Streptomyces lucensis*	Tetraene	Mycosamine[a]	None
Pimaricin (tennecetin)	*S. natalensis* *S. chattanoogensis* *S. gilveosporus*	Tetraene	Mycosamine	None
Tetrin A, B	*Streptomyces* sp.	Tetraene	Mycosamine	None
Rimocidin	*S. rimosus*	Tetraene	Mycosamine	None
Nystatin (polifungin)	*S. noursei* *S. albulus*	Tetraene	Mycosamine	None
Chainin	*Chainia* sp.	Methylpentaene	None	None
Filipin (durhamycin)	*S. filipensis*	Methylpentaene	None	None
Fungichromin (moldcidin B) (pentamycin) (lagosin)	*S. cinnamoneus* *S. roseoluteus* *S, cellulosae* *S. pentaticus*	Methylpentaene	None	None
Eurocidin A, B	*S. eurocidicus* *S. albireticuli*	Pentaene	Mycosamine	None
Flavofungin (mycoticin A)	*S. ruber* *S. flavofungini*	Carbonylpentaene	None	None
Mycoticin B	*S. flavofungini*	Carbonylpentaene	None	None
Candihexin A, B	*S. viridoflavus*	Hexaene	Mycosamine	None
Candihexin E, F	*S. viridoflavus*	Hexaene	None	None
Flavacid	*S. flavus*	Hexaene	None	None
Dermostatin	*S. viridogriseus*	Carbonylhexaene	None	None
Ascosin	*S. canescus*	Aromatic heptaene	Mycosamine	*p*-Aminoacetophenone
Ayfactin (aureofacin)	*S. aureofaciens* *S. viridofaciens*	Aromatic heptaene	Mycosamine	*p*-Aminoacetophenone
Aureofungin	*S. cinnamoneus*	Aromatic heptaene	Mycosamine	*p*-Aminoacetophenone
Candicidin	*S. griseus*	Aromatic heptaene	Mycosamine	*p*-Aminoacetophenone
Hamycin	*S. primprina*	Aromatic heptaene	Mycosamine	*p*-Aminoacetophenone
Heptafungin A	*S. longisporolavendulae*	Aromatic heptaene	Mycosamine	*p*-Aminoacetophenone
Levorin	*S. levoris*	Aromatic heptaene	Mycosamine	*p*-Aminoacetophenone
Trichomycin	*S. hachijoensis*	Aromatic heptaene	Mycosamine	*p*-Aminoacetophenone
DJ-400 B_2	*S. surinam*	Aromatic heptaene	Mycosamine	*p*-Aminoacetophenone
DJ-400 B_1	*S. surinam*	Aromatic heptaene	Mycosamine	N-methyl-*p*-aminoacetophenone
Perimycin (fungimycin)	*S. coelicolor*	Aromatic heptaene	Perosamine[b]	N-methyl-*p*-aminoacetophenone
Amphotericin B	*S. nodosus*	Nonaromatic heptaene	Mycosamine	None
Candidin	*S. viridoflavus*	Nonaromatic heptaene	Mycosamine	None
Mycoheptin	*Streptoverticillium mycoheptinicum* *S. netropsis*	Nonaromatic heptaene	Mycosamine	None

[a] 3-Amino-3,6-dideoxy-D-mannopyranose.
[b] 4-Amino-4,6-dideoxy-D-mannopyranose.

of other drugs (5, 58, 102, 144). Synergism of polyenes with other agents may have clinical implications permitting the use of lower doses of other drugs.

In addition to their use as antifungal agents, polyene macrolides have been used in recent years in the treatment of prostatic hypertrophy (37, 55, 112). An anti-cholesterolemic effect of polyene macrolides, resulting from their sterol-binding ability, has also been reported in polyene-treated animals (136). However, therapy is limited because of the considerable toxicity and poor water solubility of most polyene macrolides. New water-soluble derivatives have been reported that might be of clinical interest (100).

In spite of the medical usefulness and industrial production of several polyene macrolide antibiotics (88), there has been a paucity of studies on biosynthesis and metabolic regulation. Industrial studies have centered on isolation of higher-yielding strains without a detailed study of the mechanisms involved in antibiotic biosynthesis. Little is known at the enzymatic level of the biochemical steps involved in biosynthesis. Even the role of antibiotics in the producer cells is completely unknown (22)

BIOSYNTHESIS OF THE MACROLIDE RING

To study the biosynthesis of polyene macrolides I consider separately the biosynthesis of the macrolide ring, the origin of the aromatic moiety, and the formation of the aminosugar moiety. In a simplified form, the biosynthesis of the polyene macrolide can be divided into three sections. The first section includes the formation of acetyl-CoA and other precursors from glucose. The second part includes the carboxylation of acetyl-CoA and propionyl-CoA to malonyl-CoA and methylmalonyl-CoA, respectively, the condensation of the precursors, and cyclization of the ring. The third section refers to later transformations of the macrolide ring, including sugar attachment.

Precursors of the Macrolide Ring

The macrolide ring of polyene antibiotics is formed basically from acetate and propionate. Initial studies by Birch et al (10) showed that [1-, 2-, and 3-^{14}C]propionate and [1-^{14}C]acetate were incorporated into the nystatin aglycone (nystatinolide), whereas negative results were obtained with [2-^{14}C]mevalonic acid and [*methyl*-^{14}C]methionine, indicating the absence of terpenoid or C_1 precursor units. Degradation studies of labeled nystatin suggested that acetate was the primer (i.e. starter) unit from which the chain is extended. Similar precursor incorporations were observed in the biosynthesis of the polyene macrolides lucensomycin (74), amphotericin B (64, 117), candicidin (67, 81, 85), levorin (8), and fungimycin (68). The lack of incorporation of methyl groups was also described by Perlman & Semar (117) in amphotericin B and Liu et al (67) in candicidin. Thus, neither methionine nor formate are precursors of the side chain methyl groups derived from the C_1 methyl group of propionate units.

Birch and co-workers (10) suggested that the nystatinolide ring is synthesized by condensation of 3 propionate and 16 acetate units (Figure 1). The aglycone of lucensomycin arises from 2 propionate units and 12 acetate units (74), and that of amphotericin B seems to be derived from 3 propionate and 16 acetate units (64). In lucensomycin, one propionate unit provides the chain-initiating primer whereas the second propionate unit, involved in chain elongation, undergoes oxidation at its methyl group to the free carboxyl group of the aglycone (74). This is also the case in nystatin where the free carboxyl group arises by oxidation of the methyl group of one propionate unit, whereas the lactone carbonyl was originally an acetate carboxyl group. Martin & Liras (85), by using phosphate-limited resting cells of *Streptomyces griseus*, have found that [^{14}C]propionate is incorporated into candicidin to a much greater extent than is [^{14}C]acetate. The degree of incorporation of propionate carbons 1, 2, or 3 into candicidin is not the same. [2-^{14}C]propionate yields candicidin of higher specific activity than does [U-^{14}C]propionate or [1-^{14}C]propionate (85). Similar results have been reported with amphotericin B (64) and are probably due to the loss of radioactivity from the carbon 1 of propionate during the condensation process. The labeling of levorin with a mixture of [^{14}C]acetate and [^{14}C]propionate was higher than that obtained with each precursor alone (8). This indicates that both acetate and propionate participate in the polymerization process and that there is no significant interconversion of these two precursors. Incorporation of propionate units, and the methyl side groups derived from them, is much more extensive in nonpolyene than in polyene macrolides. In fact, some of the nonpolyene macrolides (e.g. erythromycin) are synthesized exclusively from propionate units.

As observed in Figure 1, straight side chains of 4 to 6 carbon atoms exist in the polyenes filipin, chainin, and etruscomycin, which might represent direct introduction of preformed 6 to 8 carbon fatty acids. Whether or not this is the case has not been proved, although in any case such fatty acids would be formed by previous condensation of acetate units. Pimaricin, a relative of lucensomycin with a methyl instead of an *n*-butyl side chain, represents a lower biosynthetic homologue in which the starter propionate unit is lacking and chain development is initiated by an acetate unit instead. Similarly, the starter units of mycoticin A (syn. flavofungin) and mycoticin B differ in one methyl group. There is no firm evidence for or against the direct utilization of 4-carbon precursors such as butyrate or succinate in the biosynthesis of polyene macrolides. Butyrate does stimulate the synthesis of candicidin by resting cells of *S. griseus* (87). Butyrate is in effect a precursor of the nonpolyene macrolides magnamycin (108), maridomycin (111), and tylosin (109), and succinate appears to be incorporated in the biosynthesis of the macrotetrolide nonactin (115). Malonate and methylmalonate are stimulatory for candicidin biosynthesis and might be biosynthetic intermediates (see below) (87). Some lower alcohols, especially 1-propanol, propanediol, and isopropanol, are also stimulatory to candicidin biosynthesis. 1-Propanol is even more stimulatory than is propionate (87). Since there have been no incorporation studies with labeled propanol, it is assumed to be oxidized to propionate. Although acetate and propionate are incorporated into macrolide aglycones, they usually support antibiotic production to a lesser degree than glucose (75, 79, 87). The reason is that glucose is a better precursor of the aromatic and aminosugar moieties (see below).

Polyketide Synthesis and Fatty Acid Synthesis

The biosynthesis of the macrolide rings (aglycones) of the polyene antibiotics occurs via the polyketide pathway by repeated head-to-tail condensation of acetate and propionate units. The term polyketide (polyacetate) pathway was introduced to indicate the formation of a β-polyketo chain by condensation of acetate units, which

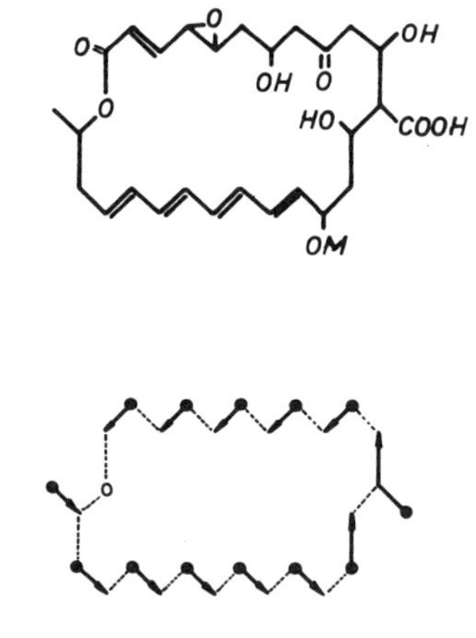

PIMARICIN (TENNECETIN)

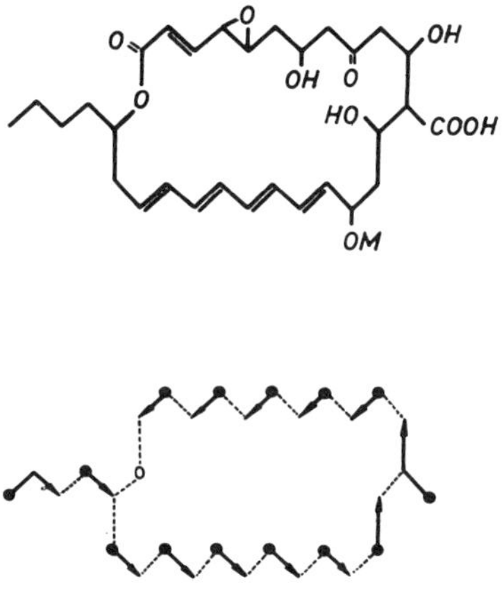

ETRUSCOMYCIN (LUCENSOMYCIN, ARENOMYCIN)

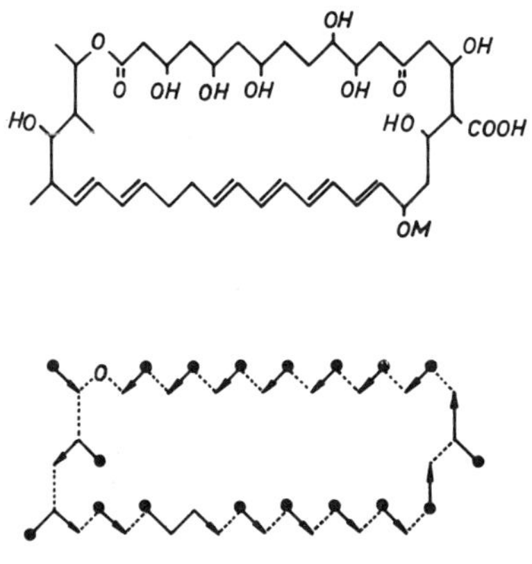

NYSTATIN
(FUNGICIDIN, POLIFUNGIN)

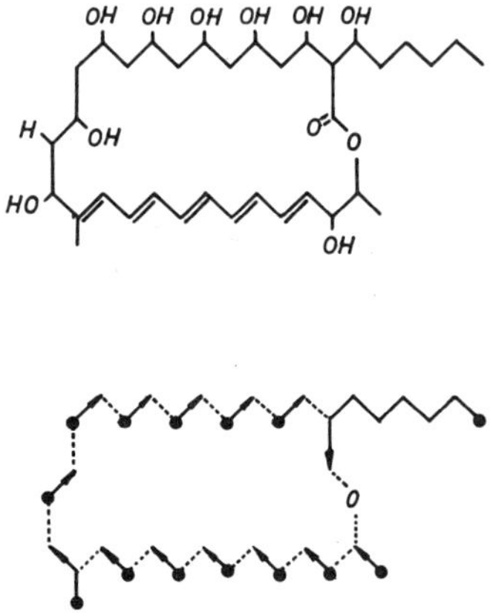

FILIPIN

Figure 1 Chemical structure and building units of some polyene macrolide antibiotics. The circles indicate the methyl group of acetate or propionate units, and the arrow indicates the

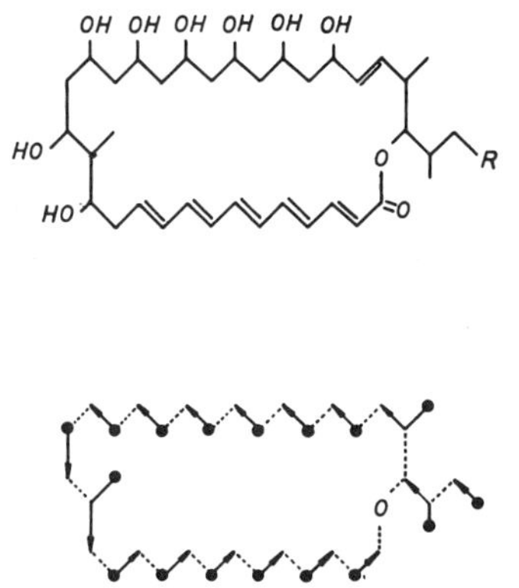

MYCOTICIN A (FLAVOFUNGIN)
(R = H)

MYCOTICIN B (R = CH_3)

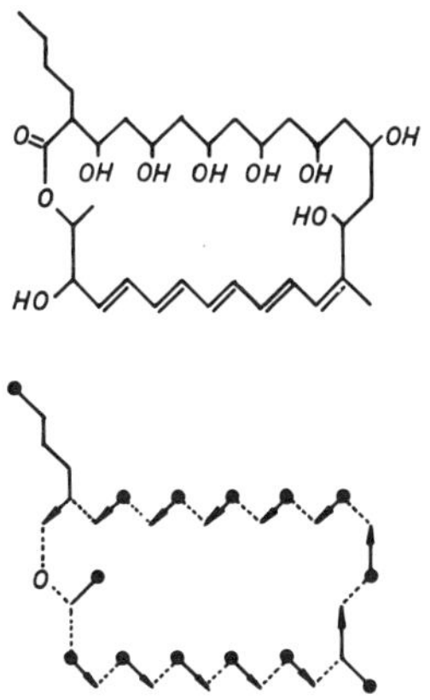

CHAININ

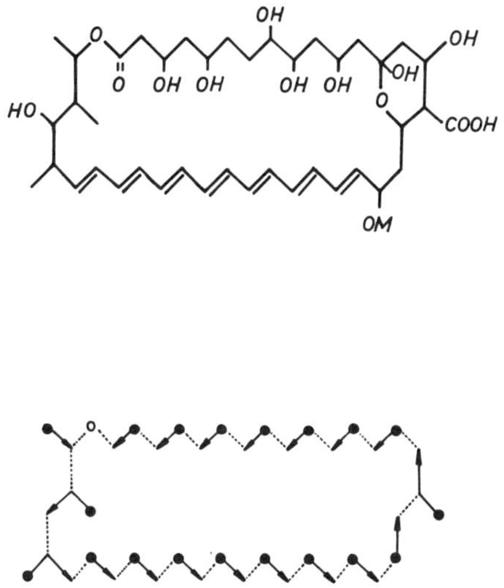

AMPHOTERICIN B

carboxylic acid group of the same units. M represents the aminosugar mycosamine (see text for explanation).

is involved in the biosynthesis of a large number of plant and microbial metabolites (17, 62, 145). Two types of lipid products, fatty acids and polyketides, are derived from acetate and malonate. Fatty acids are synthesized by a specific pathway in which a single acetate (or propionate) starter unit and a small number of malonate units (7–12) are joined together. Polyketides are formed by nonspecific pathway in which one starter unit (acetate or some other compound) and a highly variable number of malonate or methylmalonate units are similarly attached together. In fatty acid synthesis, the β-keto group introduced at each condensing step is modified by reduction, dehydration, and hydrogenation prior to the next condensation step (152). In polyketide synthesis, the β-keto group formed at each chain-extending step may or may not be retained. Successive condensation steps result in the formation of a polyketide chain of the general type R–CO-CH_2-CO-CH_2-CO–CH_2-CO-CH_2-CO-SCoA, where R indicates the radical of different starter units, e.g. methyl or ethyl as in the macrolides, malonamyl in the tetracyclines (6, 119), acetyl in the 2-acetyl-2 decarboxyamidotetracyclines (104), or aromatic moieties (see below).

In fatty acid synthesis, reduced NADPH is required as a cofactor in the reduction and hydrogenation steps. The requirement for NADPH is lower in the biosynthesis of the polyenes since some of the keto groups are maintained in the final structure and most of them are simply reduced to hydroxyl groups without undergoing subsequent dehydration and hydrogenation (see Figure 2).

The microbial synthesis of fatty acids uses acetate (starter) and malonate (elongator) in their activated forms, acetyl-CoA and malonyl-CoA, respectively. Activation occurs by an ATP-mediated formation of thiol esters either with CoA or with pantetheine. Activated acetyl-CoA is carboxylated to malonyl-CoA, the actual elongation unit. The synthesis of fatty acids occurs through the formation of β-keto esters that remain attached to the pantetheinyl protein, a component of the fatty acid synthase.

There is only partial evidence to support a similar mechanism of condensation in the synthesis of macrolides. The following discusses such evidence.

Acyl-CoA Pool and Acyl-CoA Carboxylases in Polyene Macrolide Synthesis

The cellular pools of acetyl-CoA and propionyl-CoA are important in the synthesis of polyene macrolides. The acyl-CoA pool is up to 30-fold higher in a high-producing strain of polifungin (syn. nystatin) than in a low producer. The oxidation of pyruvate to acetyl-CoA by the action of pyruvate dehydrogenase (EC 1.2.1.4) is important in the formation of acetyl-CoA since there are a large number of other enzymes competing for pyruvate. The activities of the enzymes involved in the formation of the acyl-CoA (acetyl-CoA synthase and propionyl-CoA synthase) and its degradation (thioesterases) have been studied in the polifungin producer *Streptomyces noursei.* In this species, formation of CoA derivatives of short fatty acids by the activity of acyl-CoA synthases is a two-step process involving sequentially two enzymes: a kinase (phosphotransferase ATP:acetate, EC 2.7.2.1); and an acetylphosphotransferase (acetyl-CoA:orthophosphate acetyltransferase, EC 2.3.1.8) (124). The yield of polifungin is not related to the activity of the total system synthesizing acyl-CoA. The specific activity of acetyl-CoA and propionyl-CoA

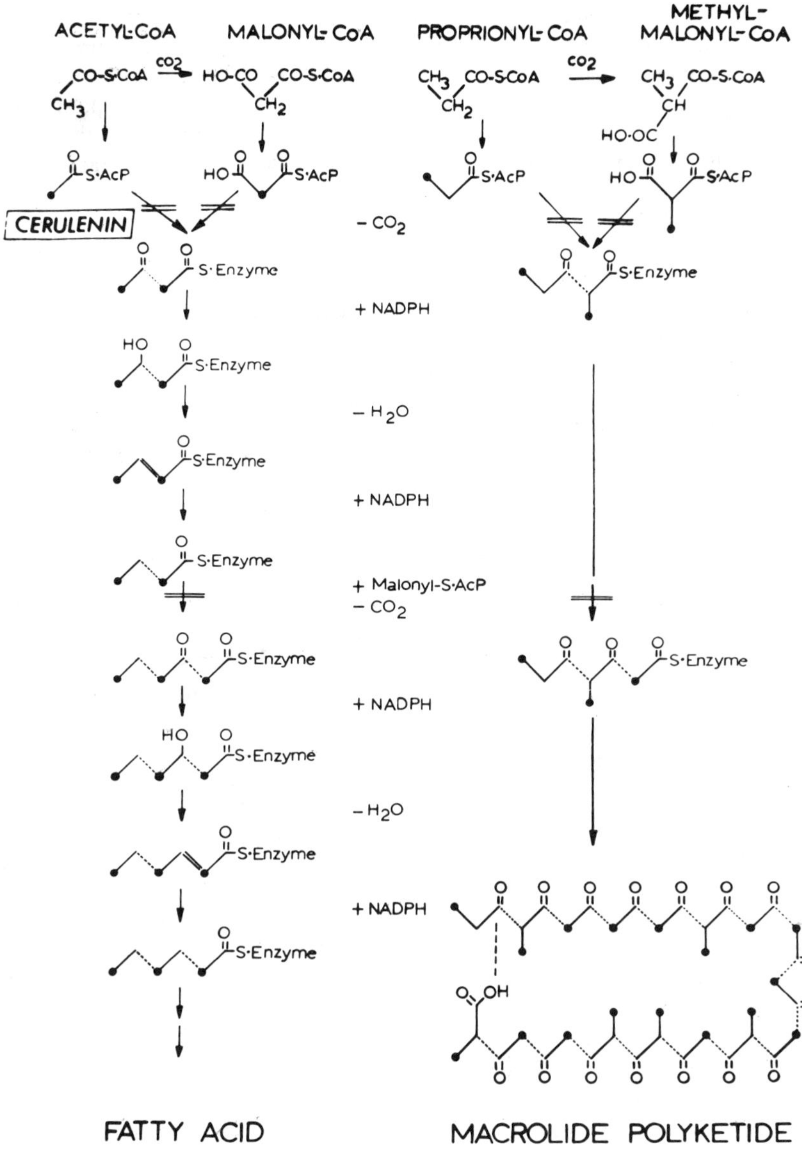

Figure 2 Condensation of precursors and chain elongation in fatty acid synthesis and macrolide synthesis. Acetyl-CoA and other activated precursor units (e.g. aromatic moieties) are used in addition to propionyl-CoA as starters of macrolide synthesis. Cerulenin inhibits the condensation reactions (⧧). From Martin & McDaniel (81). (Reprinted with permission from Elsevier, North Holland.)

synthases do not differ in high- and low-producing strains of the antibiotic. Rather, the acyl-CoA pool seems to be regulated by the thioesterases. High-producing strains containing a high pool of acyl-CoA show a very low thioesterase activity toward acetyl-CoA and propionyl-CoA. On the other hand, in a low-producing strain, the deacylation system has a high specific activity. Not only the activity but also the substrate affinity of thioesterases is higher in low-producing strains (120, 127).

Two carboxylating systems have been reported in the biosynthesis of polifungin: a nonspecific ATP and magnesium-dependent acetyl-CoA carboxylase (acetyl-CoA:carbon dioxide ligase, EC 6.4.1.2) that utilizes carbon dioxide for carboxylation; and a carboxyltransferase (methylmalonyl-CoA:pyruvate carboxyltransferase, EC 2.1.3.1), which uses oxalacetate as a carboxyl group donor. In addition, a third carboxylase, the phosphoenolpyruvate carboxylase (EC 4.1.1.31), also plays a role in the biosynthesis of polyene macrolides (Table 2).

The antibiotic-synthesizing activity of *S. noursei* mutants is associated with increased lipogenesis. A direct correlation between levorin biosynthesis and lipogenesis has also been found in *Streptomyces levoris* (7). Carboxylation of acetyl-CoA and propionyl-CoA has been correlated with the synthesis of polifungin (131) and turimycin (38). The specific activities of acetyl-CoA and propionyl-CoA carboxylases are almost double in a high-producing strain as compared to the initial strain. The time course of activity of acetyl-CoA and propionyl-CoA carboxylases indicates that the maximum activity occurs at the onset of antibiotic synthesis decreasing threefold during the phase of antibiotic production. This decrease has been taken to indicate participation of additional carboxylating systems in antibiotic biosynthesis.

The role of carboxyltransferases in the formation of precursor units of polyene macrolides has been studied by Raczynska-Bojanowska and co-workers (120, 122, 125, 126). The carboxyltransferase system of *S. noursei* as well as the acetyl-CoA carboxylase system are nonspecific. Purified preparations carboxylate acetyl-CoA and propionyl-CoA with equal efficiency (128). Both enzymes have been purified about 50-fold. The ratio of carboxylase activity towards acetyl-CoA and propionyl-CoA is 1.0 at all steps of purification and that of the carboxyltransferase is 1:1.5, indicating a lack of substrate specificity (128). However, the carboxyl transferase is about 100 times more active than the carboxylase (126). The activities of both

Table 2 Carboxylating systems of *Streptomyces noursei* involved in nystatin (polifungin) synthesis

Acetyl–CoA + ATP + CO_2 + H_2O = malonyl–CoA + ADP + phosphate [Acetyl–CoA carboxylase (acetyl–CoA ligase), EC 6.4.1.2]
Propionyl–CoA + oxalacetate = methylmalonyl–CoA + pyruvate [Carboxyltransferase (methylmalonyl–CoA:pyruvate carboxyltransferase), EC 2.1.3.1]
Phosphoenolpyruvate + CO_2 = oxalacetate (Phosphoenolpyruvate carboxylase, EC 4.1.1.31)

carboxylating systems are associated with higher antibiotic synthesis in a series of mutants (131).

Also associated with antibiotic production is a high activity of the anaplerotic enzyme phosphoenolpyruvate carboxylase, which supplies oxalacetate to the Krebs cycle. The work of the transcarboxylation system depends on the availability of oxalacetate, which is under control of the enzymes synthesizing and metabolizing this dicarboxylic acid. The oxalacetate pool is replenished via carboxylation of phosphoenolpyruvate by phosphoenolpyruvate carboxylase (EC 4.1.1.31). Phosphoenolpyruvate itself is synthesized from pyruvate and ATP. Oxalacetate has been postulated as the limiting intermediate in the biosynthesis of polyene macrolides. Oxalacetate pools are higher in a series of high-producing mutants of polifungin in parallel with higher activity of phosphoenolpyruvate carboxylase and lower activities of malate dehydrogenase (EC 1.1.1.37) and citrate synthase (EC 4.1.3.7), which decrease the pool of oxalacetate (125, 126). The general significance of oxalacetate in the biosynthesis of other polyene macrolides remains questionable.

The existing evidence does not explain the need for two carboxylating systems to maintain the pool of malonyl-CoA and methylmalonyl-CoA. It may be assumed that acetyl-CoA carboxylase is associated with fatty acid synthesis, whereas methylmalonyl-CoA carboxyltransferase may cooperate in the hypothetical "oxalacetate cycle," thus providing malonyl-CoA and methylmalonyl CoA for biosynthesis of the lactone ring of polyene macrolide antibiotics (128).

Precursor Condensation

Polymerization of activated precursor units in polyene macrolide biosynthesis seems to occur much in the same way as condensation of acetyl-CoA during fatty acid biosynthesis. This was demonstrated by the use of cerulenin, a 12-carbon fatty acid amide, (2S) (3R)-2,3-epoxy-4-oxo-7,10-dodecadienoyl amide, which is an inhibitor of fatty acid synthesis (36, 107a). It is a noncompetitive inhibitor of both the multienzyme fatty acid synthase complex of yeast and the non-associated fatty acid synthase of *Escherichia coli* (146). Cerulenin specifically inhibits the β-ketoacyl-acyl carrier protein synthase subunit of the fatty acid synthase, the enzyme catalyzing the condensation of fatty acyl-acyl carrier protein with malonyl-acyl carrier protein (see Figure 2). Cerulenin inhibits the synthesis of the polyene candicidin without affecting protein synthesis or precursor uptake (81, 82). The cerulenin concentration required for 50% inhibition of candicidin synthesis is similar to that required for 50% inhibition of fatty acid synthesis (81). Cerulenin also inhibits the synthesis of the nonpolyene macrolide leucomycin (110) and the polyketide-derived 6-methylsalicylic acid (107), which are synthesized by entirely similar mechanisms. The specific inhibition of candicidin synthesis by cerulenin suggests that the condensing enzyme acting in polyene macrolide synthesis is similar to that of fatty acid synthesis.

Chain Elongation and Ring Cyclization

As in the biosynthesis of fatty acids, no free oligoketide intermediates have ever been found. Synthetic polyketide intermediates are rather labile, and it is suggested that attachment to the synthases stabilizes them. Circumstantial evidence suggests that a multienzyme complex of enzymes (the macrolide synthase analogous to the fatty acid synthase) carries out the synthesis of macrolides. The existence of oxygen atoms and olefinic bonds in the structures of polyenes suggests that oxygen removal processes of the synthase complex may not be functional. Corcoran & Chick (18) have suggested that the presence of methyl side groups introduced from 2-methylmalonate as the chain extending unit is one of the reasons for this malfunction. Although it can be understood why the presence of repeated methyl side groups in the polyketide chain as in erythromycin would pose a stereochemical hindrance to the action of hydrogenases and dehydrases, it is not clear why long segments of the polyhydroxylated chains of some polyene macrolides that lack methyl side groups would not be fully reduced (Figure 1). The suggestion also does not explain the selective formation and constant length of the chromophore (four to seven double bonds) of each particular polyene. The chromophore regions of the macrolide correspond to a fragment formed by exclusive condensation of acetate units usually flanked by propionate-derived units or the attachment point of the aminosugar. The formation and control of the length of the chromophore remains one of the most intriguing problems in the biosynthesis of polyene macrolides. The length of the chromophore is strictly defined. Only one mutant is known in which this length is altered: it is from *Streptomyces viridoflavus* and produces a hexaene instead of a heptaene chromophore (76, 98).

One factor that may explain the conservation of oxygen functions in the macrolide ring is the relative lack of NADPH during the antibiotic-producing phase. The $NADPH/NADP^+$ ratio decreases about threefold between 24 and 48 hr in cultures of *S. noursei,* even though the total amount of NAD increases up to 72 hr. The decrease in the ratio of $NADPH/NADP^+$ occurs at the initial stage of antibiotic biosynthesis and remains unchanged during the antibiotic-producing phase (121). However, the ability to synthesize polyene macrolides in *S. noursei* mutants is not strictly correlated with the activities of NADP-dependent dehydrogenases, although these activities are lower in nonproducing mutants (132). Low levels of reduced nucleotides seem to be limiting for fatty acid biosynthesis. Lynen and co-workers (24a, 160) observed formation of triacetic acid lactone from acetyl-CoA and malonyl-CoA by bakers yeast fatty acid synthase when NADPH was not available. Fatty acid synthesis in this case was blocked at the stage of the acetoacetyl-acyl carrier protein intermediate. The same occurs in *E. coli* where the condensing enzyme (purified free of the β-keto-acyl reductase) produces triacetic acid lactone even in the presence of NADPH (15). According to Gatenbeck & Hermodsson (33), the cellular content of NADPH plays a regulatory role in determining the fate of acetyl-CoA and malonyl-CoA in polyketide synthesis. When extracts of *Alternaria tenuis* that form the polyketide-derived alternariol were supplied with NADPH, radioactive acetyl-CoA was largely incorporated into lipids, whereas in the absence of NADPH the incorporation was mainly into the polyketide alternariol. This result, if confirmed with in vitro systems from a polyene producer, would explain the differential synthesis of fatty acids or polyene macrolides.

Retention of hydroxyl groups may play a role in ring cyclization via an intramolecular lactonization. The termination of chain growth followed by lactonization probably occurs when the length of the chain is such that a strain-free lactone ring can be formed. The rigid portion of the chromophore seems to increase the number of chain members needed to favor ring closure (18). Although this theory explains the much larger ring size of polyene macrolides than of nonpolyene macrolides, it does not explain the large 34-membered ring size of the recently discovered nonpolyene macrolide axenomycins.

Effect of Fatty Acids on Polyene Macrolide Synthesis

Since both fatty acids and macrolides are synthesized by the same cell, we may ask the following questions. Are the fatty acid synthase and macrolide synthase one single enzyme or two different entities? What are the effects of fatty acids on polyene macrolide synthesis? Studies on the biosynthesis of the polyketide-derived 6-methylsalicylic acid have demonstrated that the oligoketide synthase involved is a multienzyme complex, similar to but physically different from fatty acid synthase (24, 24a, 63). The synthases have been separated by gel filtration and sucrose density gradient centrifugation. The purified methylsalicylic acid synthase shares several biochemical properties with fatty acid synthase. It is inhibited by iodoacetamide and N-ethylmaleinimide and has a molecular weight of $1.1–1.5 \times 10^6$. Preliminary evidence on the biosynthesis of erythromycin indicates that this macrolide is also synthesized by a multienzyme synthase complex (20). The erythromycin synthase and fatty acid synthase of *Streptomyces erythreus* differ in substrate specificity. In fact, the substrate of erythromycin synthase 2-methylmalonate is a competitive inhibitor of the fatty acid synthase. It is interesting to note that the erythromycin producer *S. erythreus* differs from other bacteria in possessing a multienzyme fatty acid synthase complex, a biochemical characteristic of yeasts and molds (130).

Long-chain fatty acids are not precursors of macrolides (39). Martín & McDaniel (81) described that exogenous fatty acids were unable to support candicidin biosynthesis when endogenous condensation of acetyl-CoA units was prevented by cerulenin. Fatty acids, however, do affect polyene macrolide synthesis. In some instances, fatty acids stimulate polyene macrolide production (16, 97), whereas in other cases, they are inactive (14) or even inhibitory (82). The nutritional and regulatory roles of fatty acids are discussed in detail by Martín & McDaniel (88). Several recent reports emphasize a regulatory role of fatty acids in the biosynthesis of macrolides. Fatty acids and polyene macrolides are end products of a branched pathway competing for the utilization of precursor units. Fatty acids do not support the synthesis of candicidin by resting cells of *S. griseus* in the absence of another carbon source and they inhibit candicidin synthesis when added to a glucose-based medium (82). The biosynthesis of levorin is inhibited by oleic and linoleic acids (143a). Rafalski & Raczynska-Bojanowska (128) described recently that the in vitro activity of purified carboxylase and carboxyltransferase is strongly inhibited by 0.1–0.01 mM butyrate or C_{14}–C_{18} fatty acids, whereas medium-length fatty acids are ineffective at the same concentration. Ten times as much fatty acid is required to inhibit the carboxyltransferase than the acyl-CoA carboxylase. An in vivo feedback regulatory effect of fatty acids on polyene biosynthesis is probable as the intracellular concentration of long-chain fatty acids in *S. noursei* is of the same order (0.1mM) as the reported in vitro inhibitory concentration. Similarly, feedback inhibition of fatty acid synthesis by palmitoyl-CoA and other long-chain acyl-CoA derivatives has been described in many cases (11, 29, 72, 134), although the specificity of this feedback inhibition is controversial (152). By contrast, neither glycolytic intermediates (fructose-1,6-diphosphate, glycerol-3-phosphate) nor Krebs cycle acids such as 2-ketoglutarate or fumarate affect the biosynthesis of polifungin. Citrate, a known activator of acetyl-CoA carboxylase in mammals, is equally inactive (87, 128). Polifungin does not exhibit end-product inhibition of the carboxylases.

BIOSYNTHESIS OF THE AROMATIC MOIETY

Several polyenes belonging to the heptaene subgroup (ascosin, aureofungin, ayfactin, azacolutin, candicidin, hamycin, heptamycin, levorin, trichomycin, and antibiotics known only as Sch 16656 and DJ-400B2) have an aromatic *p*-aminoacetophenone moiety. Other heptaenes including candimycin, DJ-400B1, and perimycin have an aromatic N-methyl-*p*-aminoacetophenone moiety.

Precursors of the Aromatic Moiety

Two biosynthetic routes have been described for the formation of aromatic rings existing in the natural products of microorganisms: the aromatic pathway, which is also used in the biosynthesis of the aromatic amino acids, and an alternative polyketide-derived route, which is used in the formation of the rings of tetracycline (19). The *p*-aminoacetophenone and N-methyl-*p*-aminoacetophenone moieties of polyene macrolides are synthesized from glucose via the aromatic pathway. 4-Aminobenzoic acid (PABA) has been identified as the immediate precursor of the aromatic moiety of candicidin. The intact ring and the carboxyl group of PABA are incorporated into candicidin as concluded from the quantitative incorporation of [ring UL-^{14}C]PABA and [7-^{14}C]PABA, the latter labeled in the carboxyl group (67). A high-specific incorporation of PABA into candicidin was observed in phosphate-limited resting cells of *S. griseus* (85). Most (98%) of the radioactivity of PABA-labeled candicidin was located in the aromatic moiety after hydrolysis. A very low incorporation of acetate into the aromatic moiety rules out a polyketide-derived biosynthesis of *p*-aminoacetophenone. Intermediates of the aromatic pathway such as shikimic acid are also incorporated into the aromatic moiety of polyene macrolides although with much lower efficiency of incorporation than PABA. This indicates that PABA is a closer biosynthetic precursor of the aromatic moiety than other aromatic intermediates. The branching point (Figure 3) of the pathway giving rise to the *p*-aminoacetophenone moiety appears to be chorismic acid (35). Initial studies on the biosynthesis of PABA suggested that it was formed from shikimate-5-phosphate and that glutamine was the precursor of the amino group (138, 154). Further studies with blocked mutants indicated that chorismate was converted to PABA in the presence of L-glutamine (34). Genetic mapping studies of PABA-requiring mutants of *Neurospora crassa* and *E. coli* suggest that at least two reactions are involved in the branch pathway specific for PABA (44, 48). Biochemical evidence obtained with cell-free extract of yeasts supports the two-step pathway, although no intermediate between chorismic acid and PABA has ever been isolated.

The PABA synthase of several microorganisms is composed of nonidentical subunits (1, 2, 47, 135). The PABA synthase of *Bacillus subtilis* is an aggregate of two nonidentical subunits. The crude enzyme catalyzes the formation of PABA in the presence of chorismate and either glutamine (acting as amido-transferase) or ammonia (acting as aminase). Subunit A of the enzyme has aminase but not amido-transferase activity. The second subunit, X, which is also a component of the anthranilate synthase complex, has no PABA synthase activity itself but complexes with subunit A to give an aggregate with amidotransferase activity (53). The close relationship between the synthesis of PABA and that of anthranilic (2-aminobenzoic) acid (an intermediate in tryptophan biosynthesis) is interesting because of the inhibitory effect of tryptophan on the biosynthesis of candicidin (see below). So far, there is no evidence supporting a role of anthranilic acid as an intermediate in the biosynthesis of aromatic polyenes. We have isolated several mutants of *S. griseus* blocked in the biosynthesis of candicidin (86). One of these mutants requires PABA to synthesize candicidin, and preliminary experiments suggest that it is unable to produce candicidin when supplemented with anthranilic acid. This argues against anthranilic acid being an intermediate and would suggest that the branch point of the candicidin pathway is at chorismic acid. Other mutants of *S. griseus* blocked

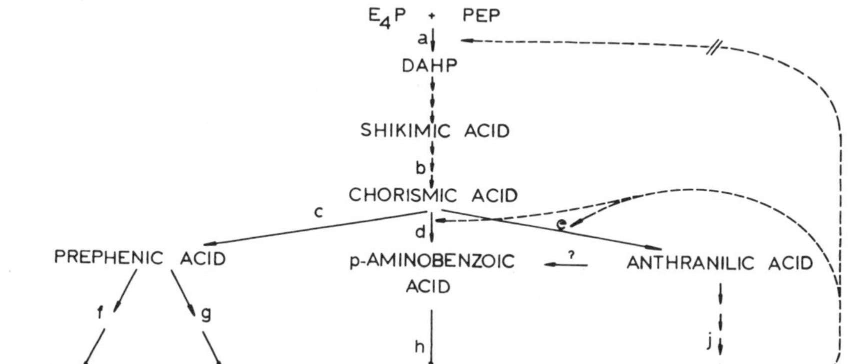

Figure 3 The aromatic amino acid pathway with the branch synthesizing PABA and the aromatic moiety of candicidin. Regulation of candicidin synthesis by tryptophan may be due to feedback regulation of anthranilate synthase or PABA synthase (dotted lines.) (*a*) DAHP synthase. (*b*) Chorismate synthase. (*c*) Chorismate mutase. (*d*) PABA synthase. (*e*) Anthranilate synthase. (*f*) Prephenate dehydratase and phenylalanine transaminase. (*g*) Prephenate dehydrogenase and tyrosine transaminase. (*h*) Candicidin synthase. (*j*) Anthranilate phosphoribosyl transferase, phosphoribosyl-anthranilate isomerase, indoleglycerol phosphate synthase, and tryptophan synthase.

in the biosynthesis of candicidin require shikimic acid for candicidin production. This confirms the participation of the aromatic pathway in the biosynthesis of the aromatic moiety of polyene macrolides.

Similar results on incorporation of precursors were obtained in the study of the biosynthesis of the N-methyl-*p*-aminoacetophenone moiety of perimicin (syn. fungimycin) (68). The N-methyl group of the methyl-*p*-aminoacetophenone is derived from the methyl group of L-methionine. However, it is not clear whether the *p*-aminoacetophenone moiety is methylated before or after attachment to the macrolide ring.

Aromatic Moieties as Polyketide Starters

Are the aromatic moieties used as starters or elongation units of the macrolide rings or are they attached after the macrolide ring is formed? There is evidence from biosynthetic studies of several polyketide-derived products with aromatic moieties indicating that aromatic rings are used as primer (starter) units in polyketide formation. Unfortunately, none of this work has been done with polyene producers. However, the chemical structure of the aromatic heptaenes (13, 25) indicates that the aromatic moiety is covalently linked to the carbon atom of the macrolide ring that supports the lactone bond. This suggests that cyclization occurs after the polyketide chain started by the aromatic ring has achieved the adequate length. Light (62) described several examples in which an aromatic cinnamoyl starter unit produces several compounds of the chalcone or the stilbene series by addition of malonyl-CoA units. A cerulenin-sensitive chalcone synthase that has been purified and characterized recently forms the flavanone naringenin from a *p*-coumaroyl-CoA primer and stepwise elongation by several malonyl-CoA units (59). Another well-known example of an aromatic moiety being a starter in the synthesis of aromatic antibiotics is the macrolactam antibiotic rifamycin. Recent studies at the Lepetit Laboratories, Milan, Italy, have established that rifamycin is synthesized from a single polyketide chain initiated by a seven-carbon aromatic amino unit. Starting with this unit, the polyketide chain is formed by a linear condensation in the appropriate sequence of eight methylmalonates and two malonates (54, 158, 159). Further studies on the origin of the seven-carbon primer unit suggest that it is formed by condensation of phosphoenolpyruvate and erythrose-4-phosphate in common with the pathway of aromatic amino acids (157).

Supporting a starter function of the aromatic moiety in polyene macrolide biosynthesis is the fact that cerulenin, a specific inhibitor of polyketide synthesis, rapidly inhibits incorporation of PABA into candicidin (81). Inhibition of PABA incorporation into candicidin would not be expected, if PABA is attached after the macrolide ring is formed, until the pool of macrolide ring is depleted. In light of the existing evidence, the pathway of Figure 4 is proposed for the biosynthesis of the aglycone of the aromatic polyene macrolides.

Regulation by Aromatic Amino Acids of the Synthesis of Aromatic Polyene Macrolides

The aromatic pathway is a complex, multibranched, diverging pathway leading to the biosynthesis of the aromatic amino acids and quantitatively minor metabolic

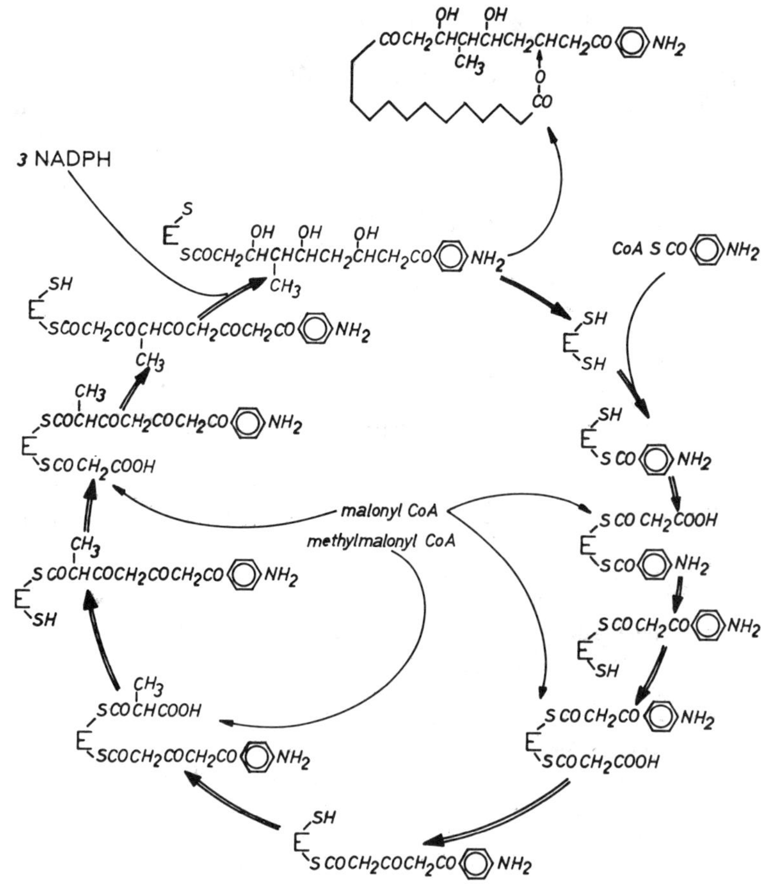

Figure 4 Aromatic moieties as starters of aromatic polyene macrolide synthesis. A *p*-aminobenzoyl-CoA starter unit is condensed with malonyl-CoA and methyl-malonyl-CoA elongation units.

products such as PABA, 4-hydroxybenzoic acid, and 2,3-dihydroxybenzoate (Figure 3) (43). In strains producing aromatic polyene macrolides under conditions of active antibiotic synthesis, the branch to PABA is very active. The aromatic biosynthetic pathway is common to all microorganisms but different patterns of regulation have evolved in different microorganisms. Feedback inhibition is exerted on the first enzyme specific for the synthesis of aromatic amino acids, i.e. 3-deoxy-D-arabino-heptulosonate-7-phosphate synthase (DAHP synthase) (35). The different types of feedback inhibition exerted include isoenzyme feedback inhibition in *E. coli*, sequential feedback inhibition in *Bacillus*, concerted feedback inhibition in *Rhodomicrobium*, and cumulative feedback inhibition in *Hydrogenomonas*. There are some genera of microorganisms, including *Streptomyces* and *Micromonospora*, that lack feedback inhibition of the DAHP synthase (51).

In addition to DAHP synthase, the first enzyme of each aromatic branch is subject to feedback inhibition by its respective end product. The sequences from chorismate to tryptophan, from prephenate to phenylalanine, and from prephenate to tyrosine can be considered simple pathways with normal feedback regulation. Thus, anthranilate synthase is inhibited by tryptophan, and prephenate dehydrogenase and prephenate dehydrase are inhibited by tyrosine and phenylalanine, respectively. The modulation of these branches is in fact more complicated, with some aromatic amino acids acting as activators or inhibitors of enzymes of other branches (35, 40).

Liu et al (67) first reported that the biosynthesis of candicidin, an aromatic heptaene, was inhibited by a mixture of L-tryptophan, L-tyrosine, and L-phenylalanine. Inhibition (50%) of candicidin synthesis was produced by 5 mM aromatic amino acid mixture. To avoid a complicating effect on growth, these experiments were repeated with resting cells (J. F. Martín, unpublished data). It was found that the inhibition of candicidin biosynthesis by the aromatic amino acids mixture is due exclusively to L-tryptophan. These results suggest that PABA synthesis and therefore candicidin production is subject to end-product regulation by tryptophan. The specific inhibition by tryptophan, and the identity of some of the protein subunits of anthranilate synthase and the PABA synthase (see above), suggest that tryptophan inhibits the PABA synthase of *S. griseus* rather than DAHP synthase. In support of this is the fact that tryptophan inhibits anthranilate synthase in a wide variety of microorganisms, whereas DAHP synthase is insensitive to tryptophan in at least seven *Streptomyces* species (51). A similar branched aromatic pathway involved in the biosynthesis of the antibiotic chloramphenicol has been described in *Streptomyces* species 3022 (155). As in other *Streptomyces*, the DAHP synthase of this microorganism is insensitive to end-product inhibition or repression (52, 69, 70). Mutants of the candicidin producer *S. griseus* resistant to 5-fluoro-tryptophan and 6-fluoro-tryptophan have been obtained. Such mutants seems to be deregulated in tryptophan regulation of candicidin biosynthesis and are candicidin overproducers (J. Kreidberg and J. F. Martín, unpublished data).

BIOSYNTHESIS OF THE MACROLIDE AMINOSUGARS

Aminosugars in Polyene Macrolides

Two unique aminosugars, mycosamine and perosamine, have been described so far as components of most of the polyene macrolides. Mycosamine (3-amino-3,6-dideoxy-D-mannopyranose) is the aminosugar component of most polyenes. The structure and stereochemistry of this aminosugar were elucidated by the group of Dutcher (26, 133). It is attached by a β-glycosidic bond to the aglycone. Perosamine (4-amino-4,6-dideoxy-D-mannopyranose), the aminosugar of perimycin, is an isomer of mycosamine, with the amino group in C-4 position (61, 142). A new tetraene antifungal antibiotic, barodamycin, contains an aminosugar different from mycosamine (32); it is not known whether or not it is perosamine. There are also several polyenes that lack an aminosugar, most of which belong to the methylpentaene and carbonylpentaene subgroups (88). Mycosamine and perosamine are closely related to the aminosugars of nonpolyene macrolides, e.g. mycaminose (3-dimethylamino-3,6-dideoxy-D-glucose), desosamine (3-dimethylamino-3,4,6-trideoxy-D-xylohexose), and forosamine (4-dimethylamino-2,3,4,6-tetradeoxyhexose). Similar aminosugars exist also in several anthracycline antibiotics, e.g. rhodosamine (3-dimethylamino-2,3,6-trideoxyhexose) (149) and daunosamine (3-amino-2,3,6-trideoxy-L-lixohexose) (3). It is also of interest that D-perosamine is a component of the lipopolysaccharide of *Vibrio cholerae* (129). Similarly, 4-amino-4-deoxy-L-arabinose is a constituent of *Salmonella* lipopolysaccharide (151) and the D-gluco and D-galacto derivaties are found in the lipopolysaccharides of *E. coli* strains (50). Several 2-amino-2,6-dideoxyhexoses have been identified as components of bacterial polysaccharides: 2-amino-2,6-dideoxy-D-galactose (fucosamine), 2-amino-2,6-dideoxy-D-glucose (chinovosamine), 2-amino-2,6-dideoxy-L-mannose (rhamnosamine), 2-amino-2,6-dideoxy-L-galactose, and 2-amino-2,6-dideoxy-L-talose (pneumosamine) (118, 156). Viosamine (4-amino-4,6-dideoxy-D-glucose) is present in *Chromobacterium violaceum* (140). The sugar constituents of antigenic lipopolysaccharides of enterobacteriaceae have been reviewed by Lüderitz and co-workers (71). The enzymatic synthesis of antigenic polysaccharides occurs through lipid-linked intermediates in which the lipid acts as carrier of the polymerizing sugar (71). A similar role of the macrolide ring of polyene macrolides acting as lipid carrier of the aminosugar moieties has not been considered before but seems probable in light of current information.

Precursors of the Aminosugar Moiety

Although no in vitro study has been carried out specifically on the biosynthesis of the aminosugar moieties of polyene macrolide antibiotics, the similarity with the biosynthesis of aminosugars of nonpolyene macrolides and bacterial lipopolysaccharides provides some data on the probable biosynthetic pathway. Birch et al (10) suggested that the carbon skeleton of nystatin is formed directly from glucose. The sugars of erythromycin are derived from an uncleaved glucose skeleton (148). Glucose isotopically labeled in different carbons is incorporated into the macrolide sugars giving specifically labeled sugars without extensive randomization of label (18).

Sugar Nucleoside Diphosphate Derivatives as Intermediates

Since the 1960s, it has been known that the aminodideoxyhexoses in gram-negative bacteria are formed from hexoses without cleavage of the sugar chain. The biosynthetic transformations occur while the sugars are in the form of nucleoside diphosphate derivatives. UDP, TDP, CDP, and GDP derivatives are all involved in the biosynthesis of different sugars. In all cases, the corresponding 4-keto-6-deoxy-sugar nucleoside diphosphate has been described as an intermediate (71). Thus, TDP-4-keto-6-deoxy-D-glucose has been described as an intermediate in the biosynthesis of 4-amino-4,6-dideoxy-D-glucose. Stevens and co-workers (139, 141) isolated from *E. coli* strains TDP-4-keto-6-deoxyglucose as an intermediate in the biosynthesis of TDP-4-acetamido-4,6-dideoxy-D-glucose and TDP-4-acetamido-4,6-dideoxy-D-galactose. GDP-4-keto-6-deoxymannose is an intermediate in the interconversion of mannose to the sugars fucose and colitose (27). CDP-glucose is converted to CDP-ascarylose, CDP-abequose, CDP-paratose, and CDP-tyvelose, and in all cases, CDP-4-keto-6-deoxyglucose is an intermediate (71). The same intermediate has been found in the biosynthesis of sugars of antibiotics. dTDP-4-keto-6-deoxyglucose is an intermediate in the biosynthesis by *S. griseus* of dTDP-dihydrostreptose, a precursor of streptomycin (114). A cell-free extract from *Streptomyces rimosus* catalyzes the formation of TDP-mycarose from TDP-D-glucose. TDP-4-keto-6-deoxy-D-glucose is an intermediate in the reaction (116).

The first step in the biosynthesis of all the deoxyhexoses, therefore, is the conversion of a nucleoside diphosphate hexose to the corresponding 4-keto-5-deoxyhexose derivative. The formation of 4-keto-6-deoxyhexose nucleoside diphosphate from dTDP-glucose or CDP-glucose is catalyzed by NAD-dependent dTDP-glucose oxidoreductase or CDP-glucose oxidoreductase (103). From extracts of *S. rimosus*, the producer of the macrolide tylosin, TDP-D-glucose oxidoreductase was purified and the product of enzymatic reaction was characterized as TDP-4-keto-6-deoxy-D-glucose (94). The oxidoreductase activity, which is stimulated by NAD, increases during the stationary phase together with the tylosin synthesizing system. The action of NAD-requiring oxidoreductases proceeds through an intramolecular oxidation-reduction mechanism with removal of water in which the C-4 of glucose is oxidized while C-6 is reduced (see Figure 5). Transfer of tritium from C-4 of glucose to C-6 of 4-keto-6-deoxy-D-glucose has been described (30).

The following step is the conversion of TDP-4-keto-6-deoxy-D-glucose to TDP-4-amino-4,6-dideoxy-D-glucose. It is carried out by a pyridoxal phosphate-requiring transaminating enzyme that catalyzes the transfer of an amino group from L-glutamate (95). The enzyme that catalyzes the reaction, TDP-4-keto-6-deoxy-D-glucose + L-glutamate $\xrightarrow{\text{(pyridoxal phosphate)}}$ TDP-4-amino-4,6-dideoxy-D-glucose + α-ketoglutarate, has been purified from *E. coli.* Similar enzymes from *Salmonella* and *Pasteurella* catalyze the synthesis of the aminosugar nucleotide with the D-galacto configuration (96, 106).

In light of this evidence, the pathway of Figure 5 is proposed for the synthesis of the aminosugar moieties of polyene macrolides. The intermediate TDP-4-amino-4,6-dideoxy-D-glucose may be converted into TDP-perosamine by an epimerization. Several epimerases are involved in the biosynthesis of the 3,6-dideoxy sugar of gram-negative bacteria. An epimerase has also been described in the conversion of the intermediate TDP-4-keto-6-deoxy-D-glucose to dihydrostreptose in the biosynthesis of streptomycin (153). A similar biosynthetic process seems probable in the formation of the polyene aminosugar mycosamine except that isomerization of the keto group is required. TDP-3-keto-3,6-dideoxy-D-glucose could be formed by internal enediol formation, as indicated in Figure 5 (18).

Attachment of the Aminosugar Moiety to the Macrolide Ring

The attachment of the aminosugar to the macrolide ring and the possible reversible character of the glycosidic bond are important since non-glycosylated derivatives are usually much less active antibiotics. The aglycones of a number of macrolides

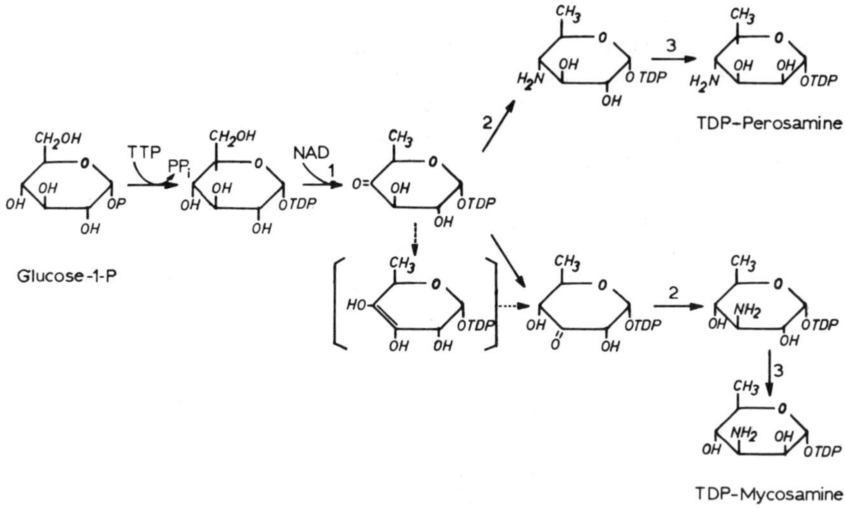

Figure 5 Proposed pathway of biosynthesis of the aminosugar moieties of polyene macrolide antibiotics. The compound inside brackets is a hypothetical intermediate in the rearrangement through enediol formation. (*1*) NAD-dependent dTDP glucose oxidoreductase. (*2*) Pyridoxal phosphate-requiring transaminase. (*3*) Epimerase.

have been identified as fermentation products (49). Work on the biosynthesis of the nonpolyene macrolide, erythromycin, indicates that glycosilation is one of the last steps in macrolide biosynthesis (89–92). In the polyene macrolide group, mutants of *S. noursei* are known that synthesize the aglycone of polifungin but not the aminosugar moieties (131). These aglycone compounds are antibiotically inactive even though they show a normal polyene chromophore. The lack of aminosugar moiety in these mutants may be related to the lower mycelial pool of total sugars when grown in lipid substrates as compared to the high sugar pool of producing strains. Martin & McDaniel described that candidin and candihexin can be resolved into a mixture of chemically related components (77). Two of the components of the candihexin complex produced by *S. viridoflavus* strain $18A_2$ lack the mycosamine moiety and are also inactive against yeasts or filamentous fungi (80). Studying the biosynthesis of the glycosylated and non-glycosylated components, it was observed that the intracellular antibiotic consists exclusively of non-glycosylated inactive components, whereas the excreted antibiotic contains a mixture of glycosylated and non-glycosylated components (78). Very little is known about the timing of or the site in the cell where binding of the aminosugar to the macrolide ring occurs. The absence of intracellular glycosylated candihexin components suggests that glycosylation takes place during secretion of the polyene macrolide. This evidence is consistent with the theory that the macrolide ring acts as a lipid-soluble carrier of the aminosugar during the secretion process. Late glycosylation of the macrolide aglycone is supported by the work of Vanek et al (149) in which glycosylation of the aglycone pyrromycinone occurred when it was externally added to cells of mutant strain B-96 of *Streptomyces aureofaciens.* This strain is a producer of the tetracene glucoside aureovacin and has the ability to glycosylate a variety of aglycones. Since the uptake of the intact exogenous pyrromicinone seems very unlikely because of its high molecular weight, it was concluded that glycosylation takes place by membrane-bound (or extracellular) enzymes and is probably one of the final steps in macrolide biosynthesis. Similar results have been reported with *Streptomyces narboensis,* which can transform exogenous aglycones narbonolide and picronolide to the corresponding macrolides narbomycin and picromycin (73).

The glycosylation process seems quite nonspecific. Vanek and co-workers (45, 149) have used mutant strain B-96 of *S. aureofaciens* to glucosidate a variety of aglycones of the hydroxyanthraquinone group (46, 93). The partially purified glucosidating enzyme catalyses the transfer of glucose from UDP-glucose to several 1,2-dihydroxyanthraquinones.

The final assembly of the polyene macrolide antibiotics requires regulation of the rate of lactone formation as well as the rate of synthesis of the sugar moiety. The stimulatory effects of propanol, propionate, and acetate on candicidin synthesis (87) and of propanol in erythromycin synthesis (123) suggest that the biosynthesis of the macrolide ring is rate limiting. This seems to be generally true as only minor amounts of aglycone are excreted into the culture broth except in mutants unable to glycosylate.

SUMMARY AND FUTURE OUTLOOK

A good deal of knowledge has been gained in the last few decades on the precursor and biosynthetic pathways involved in macrolide biosynthesis. Unfortunately, in many of these cases the reported studies have not proceeded. Some new aspects (e.g. regulatory studies of polyene macrolide biosynthesis) are starting to be studied. The results on regulation of the biosynthesis of aromatic polyene macrolides by aromatic aminoacids have been reviewed in the text. Other aspects of the problem, such as the regulation of macrolide synthesis by phosphate (68a, 83, 84), have been left out of this review to avoid increasing the length of the manuscript. The utilization of the techniques of biochemical genetics and enzymological studies of cell-free preparations will bring a better understanding of the biosynthesis of polyene macrolides and antibiotics in general in the next few years.

Acknowledgments

I thank Arnold L. Demain and Lloyd E. McDaniel for editing the manuscript and Julio R. Villanueva for continuous help and encouragement. I also acknowledge the help of my wife, P. Liras, in preparing the manuscript.

Literature Cited

1. Altendorf, K. H., Bacher, A., Lingens, F. 1969. *FEBS Lett.* 3:319–21
2. Altendorf, K. H., Gilch, B., Lingens, F. 1971. *FEBS Lett.* 16:95–98
3. Arcamone, F., Cassinelli, G., Franceschi, G., Orezzi, P., Mondelli, R. 1968. *Tetrahedron Lett.* 1968:3353–56
4. Archer, D. B. 1975. *Biochem. Biophys. Res. Commun.* 66:195–201
5. Aszalos, A. 1975. *Antimicrob. Agents Chemother.* 7:754–57
6. Behal, V., Podojil, M., Hostalek, Z., Vanek, Z., Lynen, F. 1974. *Folia Microbiol.* 19:146–50
7. Belousova, I. I., Lishnevskaya, E. B., Elgart, R. E., Tereshin, I. M. 1970. *Antibiotiki* 15:224–29
8. Belousova, I. I., Lishnevskaya, E. B., Elgart, R. E. 1971. *Antibiotiki* 16: 684–87
9. Bianchi, M., Cotta, E., Ferni, G., Grein, A., Julita, P., Mazzoleni, R., Spalla, C. 1974. *Arch. Microbiol.* 98:289–99
10. Birch, A. J., Holzapfel, C. W., Rickards, R. W., Djerassi, C., Suzuki, M., Westley, J., Dutcher, J. D., Thomas, R. 1964. *Tetrahedron Lett.* 1964:1485–90
11. Birnbaum, J. 1970. *J. Bacteriol.* 104: 171–76
12. Bittman, R., Fischkoff, S. A. 1972. *Proc. Natl. Acad. Sci. USA* 69:3795–99
13. Bohlmann, F., Dehmlow, E. V., Neuhahn, H. J., Brandt, R., Bethke, H. 1970. *Tetrahedron* 26:2199–207
14. Brewer, G. A., Frazier, W. R. 1962. *Antimicrob. Agents Chemother.* 1961: 212–17
15. Brock, D. J. H., Bloch, K. 1966. *Biochem. Biophys. Res. Commun.* 23: 775–80
16. Brock, T. D. 1956. *Appl. Microbiol.* 4:131–33
17. Bulock, J. D. 1967. *Essays in Biosynthesis and Microbial Development.* New York: Wiley
18. Corcoran, J. W., Chick, M. 1966. In *Biosynthesis of Antibiotics,* ed. J. F. Snell, 1:159–201. New York: Academic
19. Corcoran, J. W., Darby, F. J. 1970. In *Lipid Metabolism,* ed. S. J. Wakil, pp. 431–79. London: Academic
20. Corcoran, J. W. 1974. In *Genetics of Industrial Microorganisms,* ed. Z. Vanek, Z. Hostalek, J. Cudlin, 2: 339–51. Prague: Academia
21. Crifo, C., Strom, R., Santoro, A. S., Mondovi, B. 1971. *FEBS Lett.* 17: 121–26
22. Demain, A. L. 1974. *Ann. N.Y. Acad. Sci.* 235:601–12
23. Demel, R. A., Van Deenen, L. L. M., Kinsky, S. C. 1965. *J. Biol. Chem.* 240:2749–53
24. Dimroth, P., Ringelmann, E., Lynen, F. 1976. *Eur. J. Biochem.* 68:591–96

24a. Dimroth, P., Walter, H., Lynen, F. 1970. *Eur. J. Biochem.* 13:98–110

25. Dutcher, J. D. 1968. In *Encyclopedia of Chemical Technology,* ed. R. E. Kirk, D. F. Othmer, 16:133–43. New York: Interscience Publ.
26. Dutcher, J. D., Walters, D. R., Wintersteiner, O. 1963. *J. Org. Chem.* 28:995–99
27. Elbein, A. D., Heath, E. C. 1965. *J. Biol. Chem.* 240:1926–31
28. Finkelstein, A., Holz, R. 1973. In *Membranes 1973: Lipid Bilayers and Antibiotics,* ed. G. Eisenman, pp. 377–408. New York: Dekker
29. Flick, P. K., Bloch, K. 1975. *J. Biol. Chem.* 250:3348–51
30. Gabriel, O., Lindquist, L. C. 1968. *J. Biol. Chem.* 243:1479–84
31. Ganis, P., Avitabile, G., Mechlinski, W., Schaffner, C. P. 1971. *J. Am. Chem. Soc.* 93:4560–64
32. Ganju, P. L., Rengaraju, S., Lyengar, M. R. S. 1976. *Abstr. 5th. Int. Ferment. Symp. Berlin,* p. 220.
33. Gatenbeck, S., Hermodsson, S. 1965. *Acta Chem. Scand.* 19:65–71
34. Gibson, F., Gibson, M., Cox, G. B. 1964. *Biochim. Biophys. Acta* 82:637–38
35. Gibson, F., Pittard, J. 1968. *Bacteriol. Rev.* 32:465–92
36. Goldberg, I., Walker, J. R., Bloch, K. 1973. *Antimicrob. Agents Chemother.* 3:549–54
37. Gordon, H. W., Schaffner, C. P. 1968. *Proc. Natl. Acad. Sci. USA.* 60:1201–8
38. Graefe, U., Bocker, H., Thrum, H. 1975. *Z. Allg. Mikrobiol.* 13:115–29
39. Grisebach, H. 1967. *Biosynthetic Patterns in Microorganisms and Higher Plants,* pp. 32–65. New York: Wiley
40. Hagino, H., Nakayama, K. 1975. *Agric. Biol. Chem.* 39:351–61
41. Hamilton-Miller, J. M. T. 1973. *Bacteriol. Rev.* 37:166–96
42. Hamilton-Miller, J. M. T. 1974. *Adv. Appl. Microbiol.* 17:109–34
43. Haslam, E. 1974. *The Shikimate Pathway.* New York: Halsted. 316 pp.
44. Hendler, S., Srinivasan, P. R. 1967. *Biochim. Biophys. Acta* 141:656–58

45. Hovorkova, N., Cudlin, J., Mateju, J., Blumauerova, M., Vanek, Z. 1974. *Collect. Czech. Chem. Commun.* 39:662–667
46. Hovorkova, N., Cudlin, J., Mateju, J., Blumauerova, M., Vanek, Z. 1974b. *Collect. Czech. Chem. Commun.* 39: 3568–72
47. Huang, M., Gibson, F. 1970. *J. Bacteriol.* 102:767–73
48. Huang, M., Pittard, J. 1967. *J. Bacteriol.* 93:1938–42
49. Hung, P. P., Marks, C. L., Tardrew, P. L. 1965. *J. Biol.Chem.* 240:1322–26
50. Jann, B., Jann, K. 1967. *Eur. J. Biochem.* 2:26–31
51. Jensen, R. A., Rebello, J. L. 1970. *Dev. Ind. Microbiol.* 11:105–21
52. Jones, A., Westlake, D. W. S. 1974. *Can. J. Microbiol.* 20:1599–611
53. Kane, J. F., O'Brien, H. D. 1975. *J. Bacteriol.* 123:1131–38
54. Karlsson, A., Sartori, G., White, R. J. 1974. *Eur. J. Biochem.* 47:251–56
55. Keshin, J. G. 1973. *Int. Surg.* 58: 116–22
56. Kinsky, S. C. 1967. In *Antibiotics,* ed. D. Gottlieb, P. D. Shaw, 1:122–41. Berlin: Springer-Verlag
57. Kinsky, S. C. 1970. *Ann. Rev. Pharmacol.* 10:119–42
58. Kobayashi, G. S., Medoff, G., Schlessinger, D., Kwan, C. N., Musser, W. E. 1972. *Science* 177:709–10
59. Kreuzaler, F., Hahlbrock, K. 1975. *Eur. J. Biochem.* 56:205–13
60. Lampen, J. O. 1969. *Am. J. Clin. Pathol.* 52:138–46
61. Lee, C. H., Schaffner, C. P. 1966. *Tetrahedron Lett.* 1966:5837–40
62. Light, R. J. 1970. *J. Agric. Food Chem.* 18:260–67
63. Light, R. J., Hager, L. P. 1968. *Arch. Biochem. Biophys.* 125:326–33
64. Linke, H. A. B., Mechlinski, W., Schaffner, C. P. 1974. *J. Antibiot.* 27:155–60
65. Liras, P., Lampen, J. O. 1974. *Biochim. Biophys. Acta* 372:141–53
66. Liras, P., Lampen, J. O. 1974. *Biochim. Biophys. Acta* 374:159–63
67. Liu, C. M., McDaniel, L. E., Schaffner, C. P. 1972. *J. Antibiot.* 25:116–21
68. Liu, C. M., McDaniel, L. E., Schaffner, C. P. 1972. *J. Antibiot.* 25:187–88
68a. Liu, C. M., McDaniel, L. E., Schaffner, C. P. 1975. *Antimicrob. Agents Chemother.* 7:196–202
69. Lowe, D. A., Westlake, D. W. S. 1971. *Can. J. Biochem.* 49:448–55
70. Lowe, D. A., Westlake, D. W. S. 1972. *Can. J. Biochem.* 50:1064–73
71. Lüderitz, O., Staub, A. M., Westphal, O. 1966. *Bacteriol. Rev.* 30:192–255
72. Lust, G., Lynen, F. 1968. *Eur. J. Biochem.* 7:68–72
73. Maezawa, I., Hori, T., Kinumaki, A., Suzuki, M. 1973. *J. Antibiot.* 26:771–75
74. Manwaring, D. G., Rickards, R. W., Gaudiano, G., Nicolella, V. 1969. *J. Antibiot.* 22:545–50
75. Martín, J. F., McDaniel, L. E. 1974. *Dev. Ind. Microbiol.* 15:324–37
76. Martín, J. F., McDaniel, L. E. 1974. *J. Antibiot.* 27:610–19
77. Martín, J. F., McDaniel, L. E. 1975. *J. Chromatogr.* 104:151–60
78. Martín, J. F., McDaniel, L. E. 1975. *Antimicrob. Agents Chemother.* 7: 208–14
79. Martín, J. F., McDaniel, L. E. 1975. *Biotechnol. Bioeng.* 17:925–38
80. Martín, J. F., McDaniel, L. E. 1975. *Antimicrob. Agents Chemother.* 8:200–8
81. Martín, J. F., McDaniel, L. E. 1975. *Biochim. Biophys. Acta* 411:186–94
82. Martín, J. F. 1976. *Dev. Ind. Microbiol.* 17:223–31
83. Martín, J. F. 1976. In *Microbiology 1976,* ed. D. Schlessinger, pp. 548–52. Washington, D. C.: Am. Soc. Microbiol.
84. Martín, J. F., Demain, A. L. 1976. *Biochem. Biophys. Res. Commun.* 71: 1103–9
85. Martín, J. F., Liras, P. 1976. *J. Antibiot.* 29:1306–9
86. Martín, J. F., Liras, P., Gil, J. A. 1976. *Abstr. Int. Symp. Gen. Actinomycetales Borstel*
87. Martín, J. F., McDaniel, L. E. 1976. *Eur. J. Appl. Microbiol.* 3:135–44
88. Martín, J. F., McDaniel, L. E. 1977. In *Advances in Applied Microbiology,* ed. D. Perlman, New York: Academic 21: 2–52
89. Martín, J. R., Egan, R. S., Goldstein, A. W., Mueller, S. L., Hirner, E. A., Stanaszek, R. S. 1974. *J. Antibiot.* 27:570–72
90. Martín, J. R., Egan, R. S., Perun, T. J., Goldstein, A. W. 1973. *Tetrahedron* 29:935–40
91. Martín, J. R., Perun, T. J., Girolami, R. L. 1966. *Biochemistry* 5:2852–56
92. Martín, J. R., Rosenbrook, W. 1967. *Biochemistry* 6:435–40
93. Mateju, J., Cudlin, J., Hovorkova, N., Blumauerova, M., Vanek, Z. 1974. *Folia Microbiol.* 19:307–16

94. Matern, H., Brillinger, G. U., Pape, H. 1973. *Arch. Mikrobiol.* 88:37–48
95. Matsuhashi, M., Strominger, J. L. 1964. *J. Biol. Chem.* 239:2454–63
96. Matsuhashi, M., Strominger, J. L. 1966. *J. Biol. Chem.* 241:4738–44
97. McCarthy, F. J., Fisher, W. P., Charney, J., Tytell, A. 1955. *Antibiot. Ann.* 1954:719–23
98. McDaniel, L. E. 1976. *J. Antibiot.* 29:195–96
99. Mechlinski, W. 1973. In *CRC Handbook of Microbiology,* ed. H. A. Lechevalier, A. Laskin, 3:93–107. Cleveland: CRC Press
100. Mechlinski, W., Schaffner, C. P. 1972. *J. Antibiot.* 25:256–58
101. Mechlinski, W., Schaffner, C. P., Ganis, P., Avitabile, G. 1970. *Tetrahedron Lett.,* pp. 3873–76
102. Medoff, G., Kobayashi, G. S., Kwan, C. N., Schlessinger, D., Venkov, P. 1972. *Proc. Natl. Acad. Sci. USA* 69:196–99
103. Melo, A., Elliott, W. H., Glaser, L. 1968. *J. Biol. Chem.* 243:1467–74
104. Miller, M. W., Hochstein, F. A. 1962. *J. Org. Chem.* 27:2525–28
105. Norman, A. W., Demel, R. A., de Kruyff, B., Van Deenen, L. L. M. 1972. *J. Biol. Chem.* 247:1918–29
106. Ohashi, H., Matsuhashi, M., Matsuhashi, S. 1971. *J. Biol. Chem.* 246:2325–30
107. Ohno, H., Ohno, T., Awaya, J., Omura, S. 1975. *J. Biochem.* 78:1149–53
107a. Omura, S. 1976. *Bacteriol. Rev.* 40: 681–97
108. Omura, S., Nakagawa, A. 1975. *J. Antibiot.* 28:401–33
109. Omura, S., Nakagawa, A., Takeshima, H., Miyazawa, J., Kitao, C., Piriou, F., Lukacs, G. 1975. *Tetrahedron Lett.,* pp. 4503–6
110. Omura, S., Takeshima, H. 1974. *J. Biochem.* 75:193–95
111. Ono, H., Harada, S., Kishi, T. 1974. *J. Antibiot.* 27:442–48
112. Orkin, L. A. 1974. *Urology* 4:80–84
113. Oroshnik, W., Mebane, A. D. 1963. *Prog. Chem. Org. Natl. Prod.* 21:17–79
114. Ortman, R., Matern, U., Grisebach, H., Stadler, P., Sinnwell, V., Paulsen, H. 1974. *Eur. J. Biochem.* 43:265–71
115. Pape, H. 1972. *Arch. Mikrobiol.* 82: 254–64
116. Pape, H., Brillinger, G. U. 1973. *Arch. Mikrobiol.* 88:25–35
117. Perlman, D., Semar, J. B. 1965. *Biotechnol. Bioeng.* 7:133–37
118. Perry, M. B., Daoust, V. 1973. *Can. J. Biochem.* 51:1335–39
119. Podojil, M., Vanek, Z., Behal, V., Blumauerova, M. 1973. *Folia Microbiol.* 18:415–17
120. Raczynska-Bojanowska, K. 1974. *Postepy Hig. Med. Dosw.* 28:499–514
121. Raczynska-Bojanowska, K., Gaworowska-Michalik, J., Midak, B. 1971. *Acta Biochim. Pol.* 18:199–207
122. Raczynska-Bojanowska, K., Rafalski, A., Ostrowska-Krysiak, B. 1970. *Acta Biochim. Pol.* 17:331–38
123. Raczynska-Bojanowska, K., Ruczaj, Z., Ostrowska-Krysiak, B., Roszkowski, J., Gaworowska-Michalik, J., Sawnor-Korszynska, D. 1970. *Acta Microbiol. Pol. Ser. B* 2:103–10
124. Raczynska-Bojanowska, K., Ruczaj, Z., Sawnor-Korszynska, D., Rafalski, A. 1973. *Antimicrob. Agents Chemother.* 3:162–67
125. Rafalski, A., Raczynska-Bojanowska, K. 1972. *Acta Biochim. Pol.* 19:71–87
126. Rafalski, A., Raczynska-Bojanowska, K. 1973. *Acta Microbiol. Pol. Ser. B.* 5:87–93
127. Rafalski, A., Raczynska-Bojanowska, K. 1975. *Acta Biochim. Pol.* 22:257–61
128. Rafalski, A., Raczynska-Bojanowska, K. 1975. *Acta Biochim. Pol.* 22:311–17
129. Redmond, J. W. 1975. *FEBS Lett.* 50:147–48
130. Rossi, A., Corcoran, J.W. 1973. *Biochem. Biophys. Res. Commun.* 50:597–602
131. Roszkowski, J., Kotiuszko, D., Rafalski, A., Morawaska, H., Raczynska-Bojanowska, K. 1972. *Acta Microbiol. Pol. Ser. B* 4:9–22
132. Roszkowski, J., Ruczaj, Z., Kotiuszko, D., Sawnor-Korszynska, D., Morawaska, H., Siejko, D., Raczynska-Bojanowska, K. 1971. *Acta Microbiol. Pol. Ser. B* 3:97–106
133. Saltza, M. von, Dutcher, J. D., Reid, J., Wintersteiner, O. 1963. *J. Org. Chem.* 28:999–1004
134. Satyanarayana, T., Klein, H. P. 1973. *J. Bacteriol.* 115:600–6
135. Sawula, R. V., Crawford, I. P. 1973. *J. Biol. Chem.* 248:3573–81
136. Schaffner, C. P., Gordon, H. W. 1968. *Proc. Natl. Acad. Sci. USA* 61:36–41
137. Schroeder, F., Holland, J. F., Bieber, L. L. 1972. *Biochemistry* 11:3105–11
138. Srinivasan, P. R., Weiss, B. 1961. *Biochim. Biophys. Acta* 51:597–99
139. Stevens, C. L., Blumbergs, P., Daniher, F. A., Strominger, J. L., Matsuhashi, M., Dietzler, D. N., Suzuki, S., Okazaki, T., Sugimoto, K., Okazaki, R. 1964. *J. Am. Chem. Soc.* 86:2939–40

140. Stevens, C. L., Blumbergs, P., Daniher, F. A., Wheat, R. W., Kujomoto, A., Kollins, E. L. 1963. *J. Am. Chem. Soc.* 85:3061
141. Stevens, C.L., Blumbergs, P., Otterbach, D. H., Strominger, J. L., Matsuhashi, M., Dietzler, D. N. 1964. *J. Am. Chem. Soc.* 86:2937–38
142. Stevens, C. L., Gupta, S. K., Glinski, R. P., Taylor, K. G., Blumbergs, P., Schaffner, C. P., Lee, C. H. 1968. *Carbohydr. Res.* 7:502–4
143. Strom, R., Crifo, C., Santoro, A. S. 1973. *Biophys. J.* 13:581–93
143a. Tereshin, I. M. 1976. *Polyene Antibiotics. Present and Future.* Tokyo: Univ. Tokyo. 144 pp.
144. Titsworth, E., Grunberg, E. 1973. *Antimicrob. Agents Chemother.* 4:306–8
145. Turner, W. B. 1971. *Fungal Metabolites.* London: Academic. 446 pp.
146. Vance, D., Goldberg, I., Mitsuhashi, O., Bloch, K., Omura, S., Nomura, S. 1972. *Biochem. Biophys. Res. Commun.* 48:649–56
147. Van Zutphen, H., Van Deenen, L. L. M., Kinsky, S. C. 1966. *Biochem. Biophys. Res. Commun.* 22:393–98
148. Vanek, Z., Majer, J. 1967. In *Antibiotics. II. Biosynthesis,* ed. D. Gottlieb, P. D. Shaw, 2:154–88. Berlin: Springer-Verlag. 466 pp.
149. Vanek, Z., Tax, J., Cudlin, J., Blumauerova, M., Steinerova, N., Mateju, J., Komersova, I., Stajner, K. 1976. In *Second International Symposium on Genetics of Industrial Microorganisms,* ed. K. D. McDonald, pp. 473–95. London: Academic. 636 pp.
150. Vining, L. C. 1960. *Hind. Antibiot. Bull.* 3:37–54
151. Volk, W. A., Gålanos, C., Lüderitz, O. 1970. *Eur. J. Biochem.* 17:223–29
152. Volpe, J. J., Vagelos, P. R. 1973. *Ann. Rev. Biochem.* 42:21–60
153. Wahl, H. P., Matern, U., Grisebach, H. 1975. *Biochem. Biophys. Res. Commun.* 64:1041–45
154. Weiss, B., Srinivasan, P. R. 1959. *Proc. Natl. Acad. Sci. USA* 45:1491–94
155. Westlake, D. W. S. 1969. *Biotechnol. Bioeng.* 11:1125–34
156. Wheat, R., Rollins, E. L., Leatherwood, J. 1964. *Nature* 202:492–93
157. White, R. J., Martinelli, E. 1974. *FEBS Lett.* 49:233–36
158. White, R. J., Martinelli, E., Gallo, G. G., Lancini, G., Beynon, P. 1973. *Nature* 243:273–77
159. White, R. J., Martinelli, E., Lancini, G. 1974. *Proc. Natl. Acad. Sci. USA* 71:3260–64
160. Yalpani, M., Willecke, K., Lynen, F. 1969. *Eur. J. Biochem.* 8:495–502

Ann. Rev. Microbiol. 1977. 31:39–61

BIOLOGY OF THE MARINE ENTEROBACTERIA: GENERA *BENECKEA* AND *PHOTOBACTERIUM*

❖1696

Paul Baumann and Linda Baumann
Department of Bacteriology, University of California, Davis, California 95616

CONTENTS

INTRODUCTION 39
AFFINITY OF THE MARINE FACULTATIVE ANAEROBES TO THE TERRESTRIAL ENTEROBACTERIA 40
THE Na^+ REQUIREMENT OF MARINE ENTEROBACTERIA 41
TAXONOMIC CHARACTERIZATION OF THE MARINE ENTEROBACTERIA 42
Methods of Speciation 42
Generic Assignments 43
THE GENUS *BENECKEA* 47
General Properties 47
Flagellation 48
Species of the Genus Beneckea 52
B. harveyi DNA homology group 52
B. splendida DNA homology group 53
Other species of Beneckea 53
Miscellaneous strains of Beneckea 54
THE GENUS *PHOTOBACTERIUM* 54
General Properties 54
P. phosphoreum DNA Homology Group 55
P. fischeri DNA Homology Group 55
DISTRIBUTION OF LUMINOUS SPECIES OF MARINE ENTEROBACTERIA 56
METHODOLOGICAL CONSIDERATIONS 56
RELATION OF *BENECKEA* TO *LUCIBACTERIUM* AND *VIBRIO* 57

INTRODUCTION

Facultatively anaerobic eubacteria, able to grow on common laboratory media supplemented with a seawater base, can be readily isolated from ocean waters as well as from the surfaces and intestinal contents of fish and other marine animals (8, 65, 80). Morphologically, these organisms resemble other gram-negative bacteria in that they are straight or curved rods, are motile by means of flagella, and have a typical gram-negative cell wall (1, 8, 20, 35, 59, 81, 112). Until recently the interest of most investigators has focused on two conspicuous properties common to a few species —the ability to emit light and the capacity to cause disease in man. The property of bacterial luminescence is a striking attribute prompting numerous studies dealing with its physiology and biochemistry (21, 44, 45); a comprehensive review of these topics by Hastings & Nealson (46) is included in this volume. The most extensively studied pathogenic marine species, *Beneckea parahaemolytica,* is the causative agent of a severe form of human gastroenteritis contracted upon consumption of contaminated seafood; it is of particular importance in the Orient where raw seafood products are a frequent component of the diet. The extensive literature dealing with the medical aspects of *B. parahaemolytica* has been amply reviewed in a number of recent publications (3, 17, 40). During the last several years, a number of studies have appeared in which not only luminous bacteria and species of medical importance were considered but also other physiologically related marine organisms. It is the aim of this review to bring together these diverse findings to provide a broad perspective on the biology of this important group of microorganisms.

AFFINITY OF THE MARINE FACULTATIVE ANAEROBES TO THE TERRESTRIAL ENTEROBACTERIA

Considerable evidence has accumulated indicating that in bacteria the pattern of regulation of key enzymes in biosynthetic pathways is a stable character conserved during evolution. This conclusion is based on the fact that large groups of microorganisms, which appear to be related by a number of independent physiological attributes, often share a common regulatory pattern (5, 7, 19, 54). Comparative studies of the regulation of enzyme activity, therefore, may be useful in establishing or confirming broad evolutionary affinities. This is particularly well illustrated in studies dealing with the regulation of aspartokinase, an activity that initiates the pathway responsible for the biosynthesis of amino acids of the aspartate family. A number of distinct regulatory patterns for this enzyme activity have been found in bacteria (5, 7, 19). The large and ecologically diverse assemblage of terrestrial organisms, commonly referred to as the enterobacteria (101) or the enteric group (99) (which includes the genera *Escherichia, Salmonella, Enterobacter, Serratia, Proteus, Erwinia,* and *Aeromonas*), has a complex and unique regulatory mechanism involving three isofunctional aspartokinases (19). A similar regulatory pattern is found in the marine facultative anaerobes (5). In all these microorganisms, aspartokinases I and III are subject to feedback inhibition by L-threonine and L-lysine, respectively, whereas aspartokinase II has no allosteric effectors. Enzyme II is repressed by L-methionine and enzyme III by L-lysine. In addition, as in the case of *Escherichia coli* (105), aspartokinases I and II from marine facultative anaerobes appear to be associated with homoserine dehydrogenase activity. The presence of this complex pattern of regulation in both the terrestrial enterobacteria and the marine facultative anaerobes suggests a common evolutionary origin and justifies the use of the designation "the marine enterobacteria" for the latter organisms (5).

An additional important finding in support of an evolutionary relationship between marine and terrestrial enterobacteria comes from work on the organization of the genes coding for enzymes of tryptophan biosynthesis. By using a transducing phage for the tryptophan region (60), Crawford & Nealson (23) found that the order of these genes in the marine species *Beneckea harveyi* is identical to that found in the terrestrial enterobacteria (22). Furthermore, evidence was presented suggesting that in *B. harveyi,* as in the terrestrial enterobacteria, these genes are contained within a single operon (23).

A number of less distinctive physiological properties are also shared by the terrestrial (39, 99) and marine enterobacteria. The latter organisms have been found to catabolize D-glucose by means of a phosphotransferase system (66, 69) and a constitutive Embden-Meyerhof pathway and D-gluconate via an inducible Entner-Doudoroff pathway (11, 32, 81); the utilization of D-fructose involves an inducible phosphotransferase and an inducible 1-phosphofructokinase (41). When grown anaerobically, these organisms perform a mixed acid fermentation of D-glucose, with some species producing gas (CO_2 and H_2) and/or acetoin and 2,3-butylene glycol (8, 11, 28, 71, 81).

THE Na^+ REQUIREMENT OF MARINE ENTEROBACTERIA

The marine enterobacteria differ from the terrestrial species in having a specific and relatively high requirement for Na^+ (49, 83). The concentration of Na^+ necessary for an optimal growth rate and yield varies in different species and strains, ranging from 70–460 mM (83). In some cases, the requirement for Na^+ can be reduced by the addition of Mg^{2+} and Ca^{2+} to the medium at concentrations considerably higher (50 and 10 mM, respectively) than that used for the cultivation of terrestrial organisms. A specific requirement for Na^+ is not unique to the marine enterobacteria but appears to be found in all gram-negative marine bacteria (49, 67, 68, 83). Thus far, a detailed analysis of the physiological basis for the Na^+ requirement has been restricted to one aerobic species, *Alteromonas haloplanktis* (10, 82). MacLeod and his collaborators have shown that Na^+ is required in this organism for a number of complex and essential cellular functions, which include the following: the operation of permease systems involved in the uptake of galactose, amino acids, tricarboxylic acid cycle intermediates, orthophosphate, and K^+ (34, 102–104, 115); the maintenance of cell wall integrity (37); and the retention of solutes within the cell (116). The first of these conclusions has been extended to the marine species *Photobacterium fischeri* (29, 115). The complexity of the Na^+ requirement of marine bacteria suggests that this is a stable character that would not be lost as a consequence of a few mutations. The stability of this requirement, as well as the relatively high Na^+ concentrations needed for the growth and survival of marine bacteria, would severely restrict their ability to colonize most terrestrial habitats. With the exception of some ecologically specialized groups that inhabit environments with relatively constant Na^+ concentrations [such as the moderate and extreme halophiles (38, 62), as well as the rumen bacteria (16)], most gram-negative terrestrial strains do not appear to have a specific requirement for Na^+. Where a requirement has been demonstrated, it has usually been found to be considerably lower than that observed in marine bacteria (61, 83) and is often dependent on the conditions of cultivation (75, 76). A number of studies suggest that terrestrial gram-negative bacteria do not survive in the marine environment (53, 72, 74). This observation, together with the high ionic requirement of marine strains, may account for the ecological separation of marine and terrestrial bacteria.

TAXONOMIC CHARACTERIZATION OF THE MARINE ENTEROBACTERIA

Methods of Speciation

The general approach that we have taken in the characterization of the marine enterobacteria is similar to that used by Stanier, Doudoroff, Palleroni, and their collaborators for the characterization of the terrestrial pseudomonads (77, 78, 100). A total of about 530 strains from a variety of sources (Table 1) was subjected to an extensive phenotypic characterization, which included a screening of 150 organic

Table 1 Sources of some strains of the marine enterobacteria

Strains	Sources
Beneckea harveyi	Coastal seawaters; samples from surfaces of fish; sources include Massachusetts, Bermuda, Puerto Rico, Portugal, Israel, Salton Sea (California), Hawaii, and New Guinea
B. campbellii	Open ocean waters off Hawaii; samples obtained at depths ranging from 7.5–1,300 m
B. parahaemolytica	Cases of gastroenteritis in Japan and Maryland; contaminated seafoods; localized tissue infections
B. alginolytica	Coastal waters off Hawaii; localized tissue infections
B. natriegens	Mostly from coastal waters off Hawaii
B. vulnifica	Wounds or other infections
B. splendida I	Coastal waters off Massachusetts and Holland
B. splendida II	Open ocean waters off Hawaii; samples obtained at depths ranging from 7.5–800 m
B. pelagia I and II, *B. nereida*, *B. nigrapulchrituda*	Coastal waters off Hawaii
B. anguillara	Salmon and other marine fish
Photobacterium phosphoreum, *P. leiognathi*	Luminous organs of fish and squid; surfaces of fish, squid, and octopus (obtained by enrichment); intestinal contents of fish; open ocean waters
P. angustum	Open ocean waters off Hawaii; samples obtained from depths ranging from 7.5–1,300 m

compounds for their ability to serve as principal sources of carbon and energy (6, 8, 9, 11, 81, 84). These data were submitted to a numerical analysis that grouped the strains according to their phenotypic similarity. To avoid a proliferation of species names, the following conservative rule was applied: only those clusters with the largest number of strains phenotypically distinguishable from other clusters were given species designations. In practice, such clusters were usually formed at similarity values of 70–80% when the complete linkage method was used (8, 11). In several cases it was recognized that the species contained phenotypically distinguishable subclusters that, upon further study, might deserve separate species or biotype rank. To gain further insight into the relationships of these organisms to one another, strains representative of the various species and subclusters were selected for a study of their DNA homology using the in vitro DNA/DNA competition technique (85). The application of this method confirmed and refined our previous speciation and showed that, in general, strains assigned to a single species on the basis of phenotypic similarity were related by homologies greater than 80%. A similar observation has been made by Brenner (13), whose extensive studies have indicated that most of the species of terrestrial enterobacteria have internal DNA homologies of over 80% (89). The results of the numerical analysis of the marine enterobacteria (slightly rearranged in view of the genetic relationships of the strains) are shown in Figure 1. A table presenting the phenotypic differences between the various species and groups has been published (85). A number of these species contained strains related to other species by DNA homology values of over 35% and on this basis were assigned to one of four homology groups. The relationship among these homology groups, as well as among the remaining species, was below 30%. A summary of these results is presented in Figure 2.

Generic Assignments

In our initial studies on the marine enterobacteria, species were assigned to the genera *Beneckea* and *Photobacterium* on the basis of differences in structure and the mol% guanine + cytosine (GC) contents of their DNAs (8, 81). Some distinguishing properties of *Beneckea* and *Photobacterium* and a list of their constituent species are given in Table 2. This subdivision is in overall agreement with the studies of other investigators, which have been mainly concerned with the marine luminous bacteria (18, 47). Electron micrographs showing the flagellation of representative species are presented in Figure 3*a–d*. Two traits, the production of amylase and the ability to utilize D-alanine, are present in most species of *Beneckea* but are absent in *Photobacterium*; these readily determinable traits can be useful for a preliminary distinction between these two genera.

Members of *Beneckea* resembled the type species of *Vibrio* (*V. cholerae*) in a number of general physiological and structural properties, as well as in the GC content of their DNAs. The exclusion of marine strains from *Vibrio* rested primarily on the differences in the ionic requirements and habitats of these organisms. *V. cholerae,* unlike the marine bacteria, has been found to grow in a medium without added Na^+ (contaminating levels = 0.068 mM), although its growth rate and yield were stimulated approximately twofold in the presence of NaCl, with an optimum

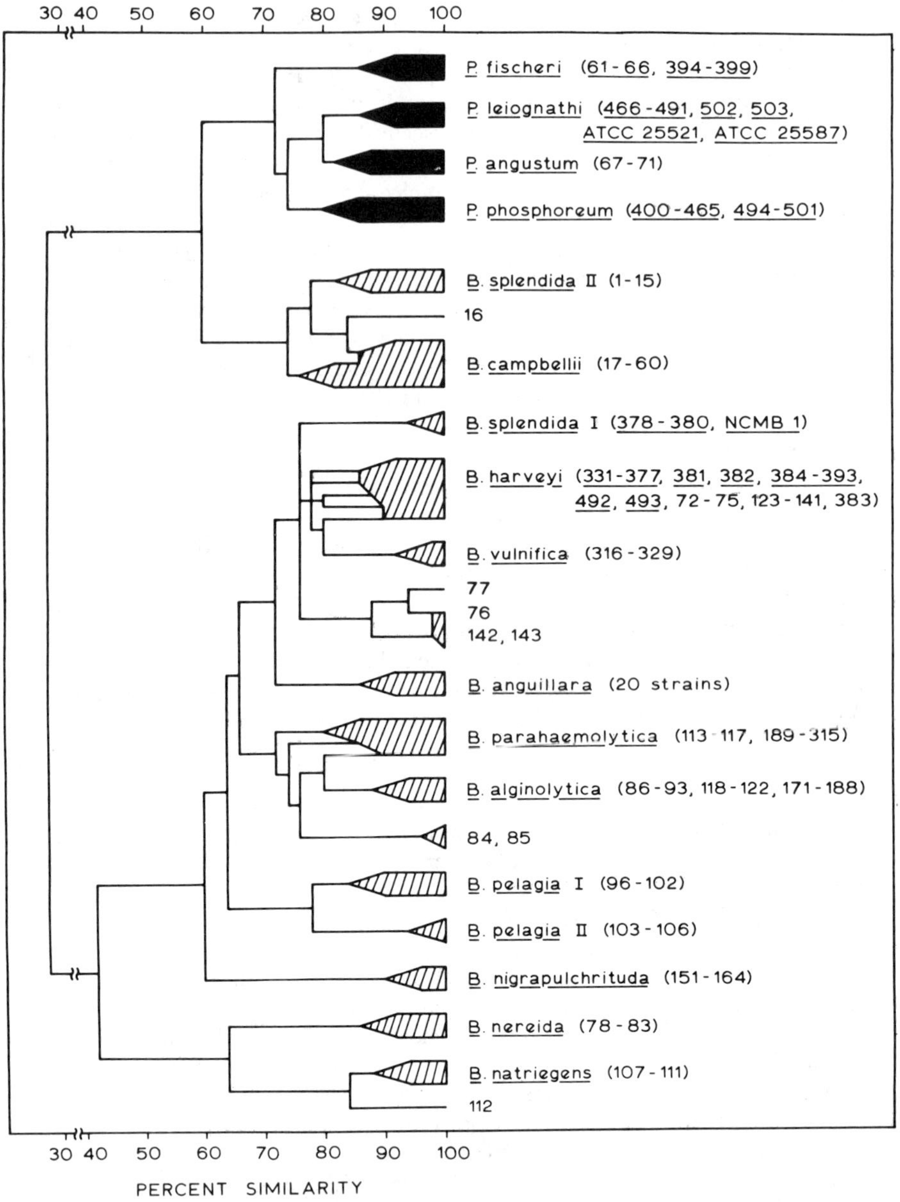

Figure 1 Results of a numerical analysis that grouped strains into clusters on the basis of their phenotypic similarities. Solid wedges indicate species of *Photobacterium*; all other species and strains belong to the genus *Beneckea*. Numbers refer to the strain designations used in our publications (8, 9, 11, 81, 84, 85).

achieved at 2.5–5.0 mM. The physiological complexity of the Na^+ requirement of marine bacteria as well as the ecological consequences of this requirement suggested that a generic separation between *V. cholerae* and the marine isolates was warranted (8, 81, 83). On the basis of these and other considerations, several investigators have arrived at a similar conclusion with respect to these organisms (88, 106) as well as to the fresh water and marine spirilla (52). The choice of the genus *Beneckea* was based on the overall morphological, physiological, and ecological similarity between most of our marine isolates and the species described by Campbell (see 8, 12). Unfortunately, no strains of his species were found in culture collections and attempts to assign our isolates to previously described species of *Beneckea* on the basis of phenotypic similarity were unsuccessful (8).

To base our generic assignments on some degree of natural relationship, we studied the homology of genes coding for rRNA in species of *Beneckea, Photobacterium, V. cholerae,* and selected terrestrial enterobacteria by using the in vitro DNA/rRNA hybridization technique (7a). The underlying principle of this method is based upon the observation that the nucleotide sequences coding for rRNA are conserved to a greater degree in the course of evolution than are other regions of the genome (26, 30). Consequently, an application of this method should permit a natural grouping of species having little or no DNA homology as detected by hybridization experiments; such groupings have been established in *Pseudomonas* (79) and *Clostridium* (57). A summary of our rRNA hybridization studies, using three reference strains of *Beneckea* and a strain of *V. cholerae,* is presented in Figure 4. These results supported the generic separation of *Beneckea, Photobacterium,* and *V. cholerae,* suggested an evolutionary divergence between marine and terrestrial enterobacteria, and indicated that *V. cholerae* is more closely related to marine than to terrestrial enterobacteria. The evolutionary divergence between the marine and

Table 2 Major subdivisions of the marine enterobacteria

Genus	Mol % GC contents of DNAs	Flagellation	Constituent species and groups
Beneckea	45–54	In liquid medium single, polar, sheathed flagellum; on solid medium may have additional unsheathed, peritrichous flagella	*B. harveyi,*[a] *B. campbellii, B. parahaemolytica, B. alginolytica, B. natriegens, B. vulnifica, B. splendida,*[a] *B. pelagia, B. nigrapulchrituda, B. anguillara, B. proteolytica,* group E-3
Photobacterium	39–44	1–3 unsheathed, polar flagella	*P. phosphoreum,*[a] *P. leiognathi,*[a,b] *P. angustum*
		2–11 sheathed, polar flagella	*P. fischeri,*[a] ATCC 15382

[a]Species that contain luminous strains.
[b]Formerly *P. mandapamensis* (84).

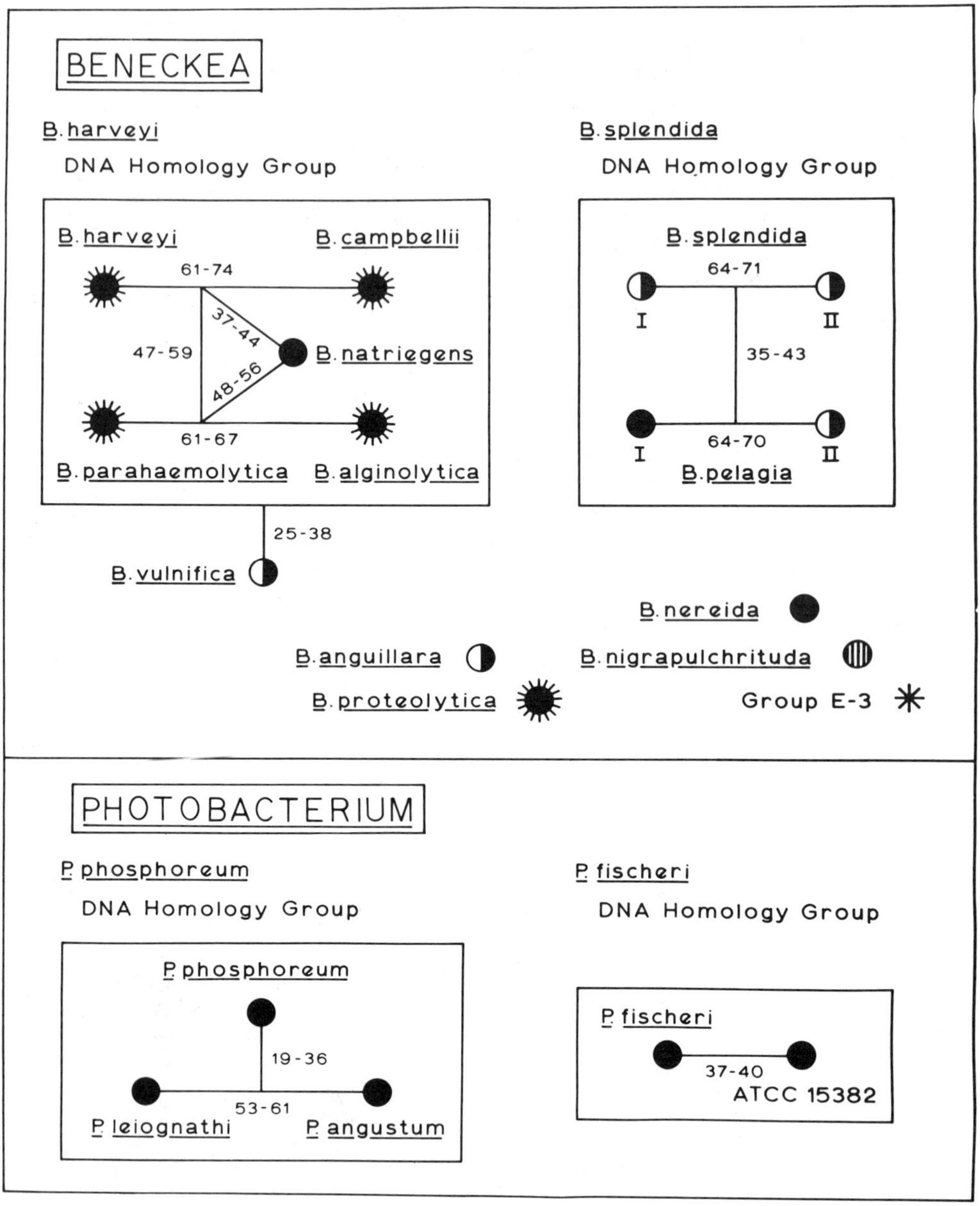
BENECKEA
B. harveyi
DNA Homology Group
B. harveyi
B. campbellii
61-74
37-44
47-59
B. natriegens
48-56
61-67
B. parahaemolytica
B. alginolytica
25-38
B. vulnificus
B. splendida
DNA Homology Group
B. splendida
64-71
I
II
35-43
64-70
I
II
B. pelagia
B. nereida
B. anguillara
B. nigrapulchrituda
B. proteolytica
Group E-3
PHOTOBACTERIUM
P. phosphoreum
DNA Homology Group
P. phosphoreum
19-36
53-61
P. leiognathi
P. angustum
P. fischeri
DNA Homology Group
P. fischeri
37-40
ATCC 15382

terrestrial enterobacteria is consistent with the previously discussed ecological separation of these organisms (see section on Na^+ requirement). The finding that *V. cholerae* was more closely related to marine rather than to terrestrial enterobacteria is of considerable interest since it suggests that this human pathogen may have evolved from a marine ancestor (for a discussion see section on relation of *Beneckea* to *Lucibacterium* and *Vibrio*).

THE GENUS *BENECKEA*

General Properties

Species of the genus *Beneckea* (6, 8, 9, 11, 81, 85) are composed of oxidase-positive, straight or curved rods, which produce acid but no gas during the fermentation of D-glucose; *B. alginolytica, B. anguillara,* and *B. proteolytica* also make acetoin and 2,3-butylene glycol. All of the species and strains of *Beneckea* grow at 20 and 30°C; the majority do not grow at 4°C and none has been found to grow at 45°C. Growth at 40°C is restricted to some strains of *B. harveyi* and *B. nereida,* all strains of *B. alginolytica, B. natriegens,* and the two pathogenic species *B. parahaemolytica* and *B. vulnifica.* With the exception of *B. nigrapulchrituda,* which makes a water-insoluble, blue-black pigment, none of the strains is pigmented. From 18–67 organic compounds can be used by different species of *Beneckea* as sole sources of carbon and energy, including pentoses, hexoses, disaccharides, sugar alcohols and acids, tricarboxylic acid cycle intermediates, and amino acids. Production of extracellular enzymes is common among members of this genus; most strains synthesize an extracellular amylase, gelatinase, lipase, and chitinase, and a few strains also make an alginase. Four species (*B. splendida* biotype I, *B. nereida, B. anguillara,* and *B. proteolytica*) are able to convert arginine to ornithine under anaerobic conditions by way of a constitutive arginine dihydrolase system. *B. natriegens, B. nereida,* and some strains of *B. nigrapulchrituda* have the ability to accumulate poly-β-hydroxybutyrate as an intracellular reserve product. Strains able to utilize *p*-hydroxybenzoate and/or quinate degrade protocatechuate by means of a *m* cleavage. With the exception of the GC contents of group E-3 and *B. proteolytica,* which are 53.6 and 50.5 mol%, respectively, the GC contents of the species of *Beneckea* are very similar, ranging from 45–48 mol%.

Figure 2 Summary of in vitro DNA homologies among marine enterobacteria (85). Dots indicate that the strains within the species or biotype are related by DNA homologies of over 80%. The internal DNA homology of the two strains of group E-3 (denoted by an asterisk) has not been determined. Numbers refer to the percent DNA homologies by which the various species or biotypes are related. Species and groups not interconnected are related by DNA homologies of less than 30%. Solid dots indicate that over 83% of the strains of the species or biotype are straight rods; dots with spikes indicate that over 86% of the strains have peritrichous flagella when grown on solid medium; and sectored dots indicate that 60% or more of the strains are curved rods. The striped dot designating *B. nigrapulchrituda* indicates that the strains are straight rods during exponential phase but become curved in early stationary phase.

Flagellation

All species of *Beneckea* have a single, sheathed polar flagellum when grown in a liquid medium (Figure 3*b*); however, about half of the species are able to synthesize additional, peritrichous flagella (Figure 3*a*) when transferred to solid medium (1, 6, 8, 9, 11, 42, 70, 73, 81, 111). This is true for over 86% of the strains of *B. parahaemolytica, B. alginolytica, B. campbellii,* and *B. harveyi,* as well as for the single available strain of *B. proteolytica* and some strains of *B. splendida* biotype II (85, 117). The polar flagellum, present in cells grown in liquid or solid medium, has a diameter of 24–30 nm and consists of a core (14–16 nm) surrounded by a sheath. The peritrichous flagella are unsheathed and have a diameter of 14–15 nm (1). The wavelength of the polar flagellum of *B. alginolytica* has been reported to be 1.5 μm, whereas the peritrichous flagella of this species have a wavelength of 0.9 μm (24).

The initial observation that cells of *B. harveyi* had a thick polar flagellum and thin peritrichous flagella when harvested from solid medium was made by Johnson et al (56) in one of the early studies of bacterial morphology that made use of the electron microscope. Hendrie et al (47) showed that the polar flagellum in this species was sheathed. The shift from polar to peritrichous flagellation upon transfer from liquid to solid media, as well as a difference in the wavelength of the polar and peritrichous flagella, had been previously observed in a number of marine facultative anaerobes (64, 65). Buttiaux & Voisin (15) isolated a strain of *Beneckea,* found that it had both a thick polar and thin peritrichous flagella, and noted that the presence of peritrichous flagella was affected by NaCl and agar concentrations. Although the advantage of a shift from polar to peritrichous flagellation upon transfer from liquid to solid medium is not clear, some evidence suggests that polarly flagellated bacteria move faster in liquid medium than on solid medium whereas the reverse holds true for peritrichously flagellated organisms (63).

Recently, Shinoda and his collaborators have shown the presence of two flagellins in the flagella of *B. parahaemolytica* grown on solid medium (73, 92, 94, 95). Both flagellins had a molecular weight of about 40,000 but differed in their antigenicity, amino acid composition, and chromatographic properties on hydroxyapatite columns. Final proof that one flagellin came from the polar and the other from the peritrichous flagella was obtained with ferritin-conjugated antibodies (92). The addition of antibodies specific for each flagellin to cells harvested from solid medium indicated that one of the antibodies reacted with only the polar flagellum (which presumably had been stripped of its labile sheath), whereas the other antibody

Figure 3 Electron micrographs of representative species of marine enterobacteria. Markers indicate 0.5 μm. (*a*) *Beneckea alginolytica* with a thick, sheathed polar flagellum and unsheathed peritrichous flagella when grown on solid medium (24). (*b*) *B. alginolytica* with only the sheathed polar flagellum when grown in liquid medium (42). (*c*) *Photobacterium fischeri* with a tuft of sheathed polar flagella (81). (*d*) *Photobacterium angustum* with unsheathed polar flagella (1). All micrographs reproduced with permission from *Netherlands Journal of Sea Research* (*a,b*), *Archives for Microbiology* (*c*), and *Journal of Bacteriology* (*d*).

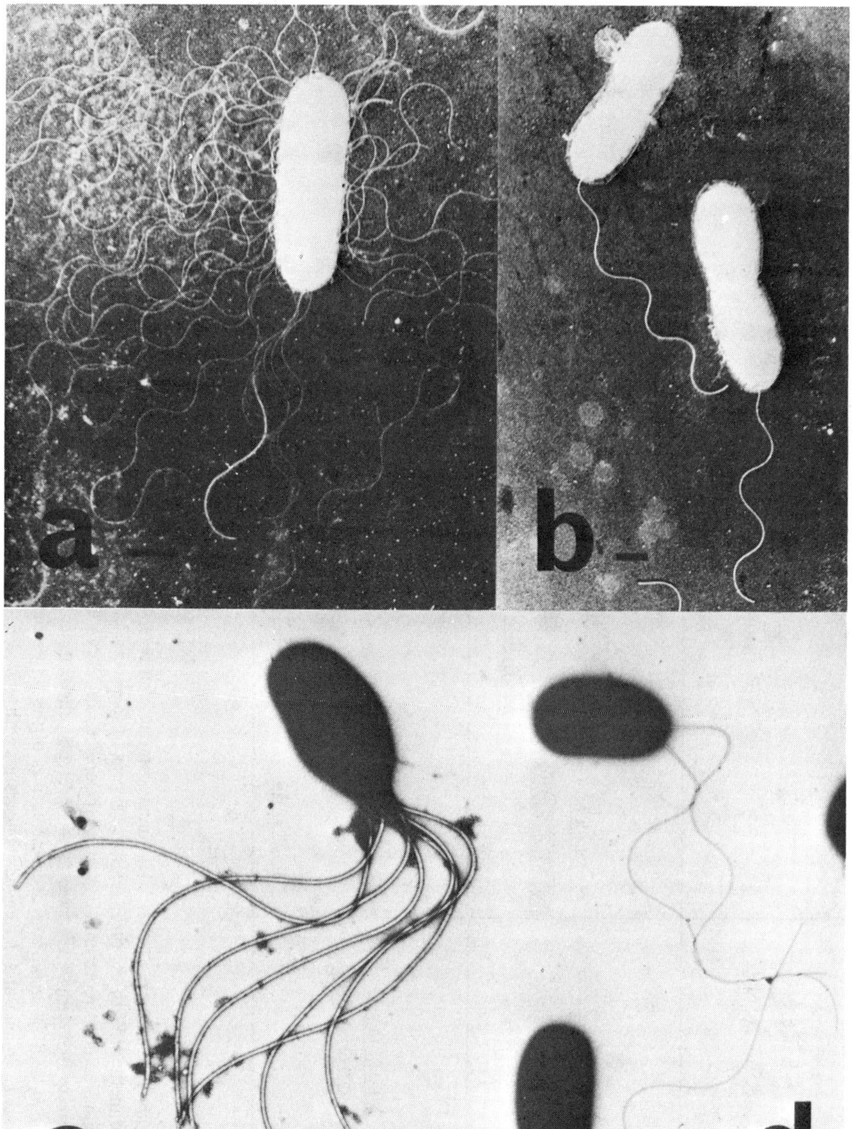
a
b
c
d

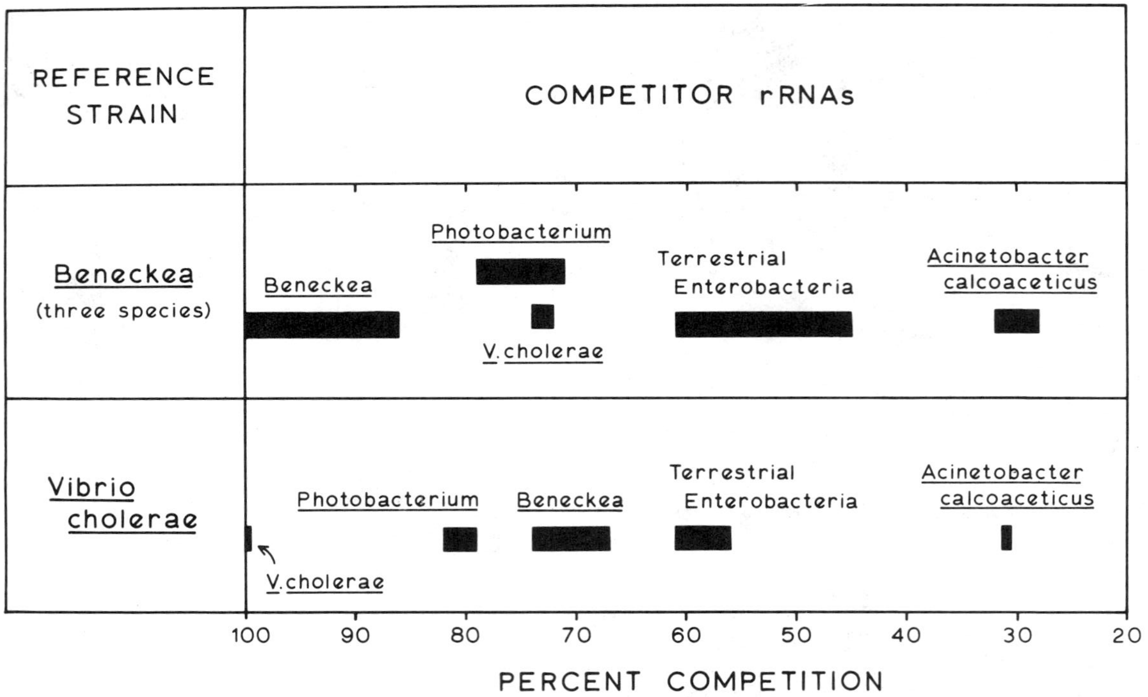

Figure 4 Summary of rRNA homologies among marine and terrestrial enterobacteria using the in vitro DNA/rRNA competition method. With the three reference strains of *Beneckea* (*B. parahaemolytica, B. alginolytica,* and *B. pelagia*), the competitor strains included representatives of all the species and DNA homology groups presented in Figure 2 as well as a representative of group E-3; with *V. cholerae* as the reference, the competitor strains of *Beneckea* were *B. parahaemolytica, B. splendida, B. pelagia,* and *B. anguillara.* Representatives of the terrestrial enterobacteria consisted of species of *Escherichia, Enterobacter, Serratia, Proteus,* and *Aeromonas.* The results with *Acinetobacter calcoaceticus* are indicative of values obtained with an organism unrelated to the enterobacteria.

reacted specifically with the peritrichous flagella. An extension of these studies to other species of *Beneckea* indicated that the flagellins from the polar flagella of *B. parahaemolytica, B. alginolytica, B. harveyi, B. campbellii, B. natriegens, B. pelagia* biotype I, *B. nereida,* and *B. anguillara* had a common antigenic structure (93). Similar antigenic determinants were found in the flagellin of the more distantly related species, *V. cholerae.* An additional interesting observation was that the peritrichous flagella, unlike the polar flagella of different species, could have different antigenic properties. The flagellins from the peritrichous flagella of *B. harveyi* and *B. campbellii* were antigenically distinct from each other as well as from *B. parahaemolytica* and *B. alginolytica,* whereas those from the latter two species were antigenically related.

In his studies of bacterial flagellation, Leifson (64) noted a correlation between swarming and the ability to form peritrichous flagella on complex solid media. Although it is true that two peritrichously flagellated species of *Beneckea* (*B. alginolytica* and the single available isolate of *B. proteolytica*) are vigorous and consistent swarmers on complex solid medium, most of the strains of *B. campbellii, B. harveyi,* and *B. parahaemolytica* fail to swarm, despite the fact that they form peritrichous flagella (6, 8, 11, 81). There are a few exceptional strains in the latter two species that are able to swarm, especially on complex media containing Tween 80 (polyethylene sorbitan monooleate). All of the vigorous swarmers have been seen to form the concentric circles characteristic of swarming colonies of *Proteus* (48) (P. Baumann and L. Baumann, unpublished observations). As in the case of *Proteus,* the edges of the swarming colonies of *B. parahaemolytica* and *B. alginolytica* contain long swarmer cells with large numbers of flagella (108, 111); these cells have also been observed in swarming strains of *B. harveyi* and *B. proteolytica* (P. Baumann and L. Baumann, unpublished observations). Although swarming usually occurs only on complex media, Ulitzur (109) has succeeded in inducing *B. alginolytica* to swarm on minimal medium by using concentration gradients of diethylmalonic ester, propionate, or isovalerate. Futhermore, nonswarming strains of *B. parahaemolytica* were able to swarm on complex solid medium that had been pretreated with H_2O_2 (108). An observation that suggested the involvement of a volatile compound(s) in the swarming response was the failure of *B. alginolytica* to swarm on complex solid medium in the presence of alkali-saturated filter paper (109). A number of additional physical and chemical parameters affecting the synthesis of peritrichous flagella and swarming in *B. alginolytica* have been the subject of recent investigations (24, 25, 110). Temperatures above 28°C inhibited both the formation of peritrichous flagella and swarming; the effect of temperature was reversed by increasing the NaCl concentration. On complex media containing 4% agar swarming was inhibited although the cells remained peritrichously flagellated; at agar concentrations below 0.75%, the number of flagella was greatly reduced. Inclusion of boric acid or aluminum hydroxide in liquid medium containing yeast extract resulted in the formation of a few peritrichous flagella by some of the cells (25).

A number of nonswarming mutants of *B. alginolytica* have been obtained that could be subdivided into two major classes (109). One class consisted of polarly flagellated cells unable to form peritrichous flagella on solid media and incapable of being induced to swarm by compounds produced during growth of the wild type or mutants. The second class consisted of mutants either devoid of peritrichous flagella or having only 10–15 flagella on solid medium. This latter class of mutants could be induced to swarm by compounds produced during the growth of either the wild type or mutants of the first class; swarming cells of the mutants resembled the wild type in that they contained a large number of flagella (>100 per cell). Although the complexity of the factors determining flagellar synthesis and swarming is indicated by the phenotypic properties of the mutants, the results suggest that swarming, as in the case of *Proteus* (48), is dependent upon the formation of long cells with large numbers of flagella.

Species of the Genus Beneckea

B. HARVEYI DNA HOMOLOGY GROUP The *B. harveyi* DNA homology group is composed of the closely related species *B. harveyi, B. campbellii, B. parahaemolytica,* and *B. alginolytica,* as well as the more distantly related species *B. natriegens* and *B. vulnifica* (Figure 2); the considerable genetic and phenotypic similarity between *B. parahaemolytica* and *B. alginolytica* has been previously established by several investigators (2, 43, 90, 91, 98). *B. harveyi,* the oldest named species of this group (55), consists of both luminous and nonluminous isolates with a high genotypic and phenotypic similarity that justifies their inclusion into one species (81, 85). As previously noted, *B. parahaemolytica* is an important pathogen causing gastroenteritis in man. A number of strains of this species as well as of *B. alginolytica* and *B. vulnifica* have been isolated from infected tissues; strains of the latter species have also been implicated in several cases of fatal septicemia (11, 51, 86, 107). The existence of human pathogens among common marine species poses a potential public health problem, since a localized increase in the organic carbon and nitrogen content of seawater (e.g. due to pollution) would cause an increase in the indigenous marine flora, including the potential pathogens.

Studies concerned with the frequency and distribution of *B. parahaemolytica* in the marine environment have been hampered by a lack of information concerning the properties of other common, phenotypically similar organisms [for a discussion of this problem see (11)]. As a result it has not been clear whether the diagnostic scheme used to identify strains of this species in stool samples of gastroenteritis patients is valid when applied to strains obtained from marine sources. A beginning in the resolution of this problem has been made by the extensive phenotypic and genotypic characterization of a number of common marine bacteria. A diagnostic table for all of the characterized species has recently been published (85). From this table traits useful for the identification of pathogenic species of *Beneckea* can be readily extracted. An example of the usefulness of these studies is the finding that the traits most commonly used for the identification of *B. parahaemolytica,* namely the ability to grow at 40°C and the inability to utilize sucrose (90, 91), are shared by *B. vulnifica* and a number of strains of *B. harveyi.* In view of this fact, studies concerned with the ecology of *B. parahaemolytica,* where this species has been identified primarily on the basis of these two traits, must be regarded with considerable caution (11, 58).

B. natriegens is the most nutritionally versatile species of *Beneckea* in that it is able to utilize 65–67 organic compounds as sole sources of carbon and energy (8). Unlike the remaining species of this genus, this organism is able to utilize L-rhamnose, betaine, hippurate, benzoate, and *p*-hydroxybenzoate; the degradation of the latter compound involves a *m* cleavage of the intermediate protocatechuate. Radiosperimetric experiments have provided evidence that *B. natriegens* utilizes D-glucose and D-gluconate via the Embden-Meyerhof pathway and the Entner-Doudoroff pathway, respectively (32). Recently, extensive studies on the respiratory chain of this organism have indicated the presence of cytochromes of the *a, b,* and *c* types, as well as a cytochrome *o* (113, 114). *B. natriegens* has one of the fastest recorded growth rates; at 37°C in a complex medium the doubling time of this species is 9.8 min (31).

B. SPLENDIDA DNA HOMOLOGY GROUP The two species of the *B. splendida* DNA homology group, *B. splendida* and *B. pelagia,* have each been divided into two biotypes (Figure 2). Although the strains within these biotypes are related by competition values over 80%, they were not assigned species designations since two of the biotypes contained a relatively small number of strains, and it was felt that additional isolates should be studied before proposing species names. *B. splendida* biotype I consists of four curved, luminous strains that have a constitutive arginine dihydrolase (85). Although these strains are genetically related to biotype II of *B. splendida* (Figure 2), they have a greater phenotypic similarity to the genetically unrelated species *B. harveyi* (Figure 1). A similar situation exists for *B. campbellii* and *B. splendida* biotype II, which share a number of phenotypic properties although they have a low genetic relationship.

OTHER SPECIES OF BENECKEA Four species of *Beneckea, B. nereida, B. nigrapulchrituda, B. proteolytica,* and *B. anguillara,* are phenotypically and genotypically distinct from one another as well as from the members of the *B. harveyi* and *B. splendida* DNA homology groups (Figures 1 and 2). With the exception of some strains of *B. vulnifica* (51, 85), *B. nigrapulchrituda* is the only species that readily utilizes lactose (9); the former species appears to acquire this ability by mutation. Another distinctive property of *B. nigrapulchrituda* is its ability to produce a blue-black, water-insoluble pigment that crystallizes within the colony and in the surrounding medium; production of the pigment is enhanced by growing the organism on a minimal medium. The single strain designated *B. proteolytica* (71) resembles *B. alginolytica* in a number of traits, which include the formation of unsheathed peritrichous flagella, the ability to swarm on solid medium, and the production of 2,3-butylene glycol during the fermentation of D-glucose (1, 8, 70, 71). This strain, however, is readily distinguishable from *B. alginolytica* on the basis of a number of phenotypic properties, as well as of the higher GC content of its DNA (50.5 mol%).

B. anguillara is generally considered to be a pathogen of fish and eels (96, 97). In the past, its description has been inadequate and its status has been complicated by the fact that in a commonly used diagnostic scheme *B. anguillara* was a repository for those strains that could not be identified as either *B. parahaemolytica* or *B. alginolytica* (11, 90, 91). This unfortunate situation has been clarified by Anderson & Ordal (2), who showed that a group of strains isolated from fish (including the neotype of *B. anguillara*) had an internal DNA homology of over 80% and was genetically distinct from both *B. parahaemolytica* and *B. alginolytica.* A phenotypic characterization of *B. anguillara* has indicated that this species is distinguishable from the other marine enterobacteria (Figure 1) (see also 85). The neotype of this species and the reference strain used by Anderson & Ordal (2) were shown to have low or no significant DNA homology to other species of *Beneckea* (Figure 2). Studies dealing with the effect of NaCl on the growth rate and cell yield of these two strains have indicated that an optimum was attained at about 55 mM NaCl (J. L. Reichelt, unpublished observations), a concentration somewhat lower than that observed with most other marine bacteria (83).

MISCELLANEOUS STRAINS OF BENECKEA Included in the dendrogram of Figure 1 are a number of strains which have properties of the genus *Beneckea* but are phenotypically and genotypically different from the species presented in Figure 2. Among these organisms is strain 16 with a DNA homology of 56–62% to *B. splendida* biotypes I and II, strain 77 with 41–55% homology to *B. parahaemolytica* and *B. alginolytica,* and strain 112 with 72% homology to *B. natriegens.* Two groups (strains 84 and 85 and strains 76, 142, and 143) with internal homologies over 92% were related by DNA homologies of less than 30% to each other as well as to species of *Beneckea.* In a similar category were the two strains of group E-3, which had a GC content of 53.6 mol%; their internal DNA homology has not been determined. The assignment of species or possibly biotype status to these strains must await the characterization of additional isolates.

THE GENUS *PHOTOBACTERIUM*

General Properties

Members of the genus *Photobacterium* are usually straight rods with a GC content of 39–44 mol% that utilize 7–22 organic compounds as sole or principal sources of carbon and energy (8, 81, 84, 85). Most of the strains make an extracellular chitinase; two species produce an extracellular lipase. On the basis of structural properties (Table 2), as well as of DNA homologies (85), species of the genus *Photobacterium* can be subdivided into two groups designated the *P. phosphoreum* and *P. fischeri* DNA homology groups (Figure 2). In spite of these differences, a generic separation of these two groups was not justified since the results of the DNA/rRNA hybridization experiments indicated that they were related by rRNA homologies of over 90% (7a).

P. phosphoreum DNA Homology Group

The organisms comprising the *P. phosphoreum* DNA homology group have GC contents in their DNAs ranging from 41–43 mol% and include the luminous species *P. phosphoreum* and *P. leiognathi* and one nonluminous species, *P. angustum* (Figure 1). The DNA homology between *P. leiognathi* and *P. angustum* is considerably higher than the homology between either of these species and *P. phosphoreum* (Figure 2). Motile strains of all three species have one to three unsheathed polar flagella (Figure 3d) with a diameter of 14–16 nm (1, 47, 50, 81). Bizarre involution forms are frequently observed in some strains, especially when the culture reaches stationary phase. All three species accumulate poly-β-hydroxybutyrate as an intracellular carbon reserve but are unable to utilize extracellular β-hydroxybutyrate as a substrate for growth (8, 33, 81, 84, 85); this combination of properties is unusual since a large number of species found to accumulate poly-β-hydroxybutyrate utilize the extracellular monomer (8–10, 78). *P. angustum* is distinctive in that, despite its low nutritional versatility, it is the only species of marine enterobacteria able to utilize D-xylose. Approximately two thirds of the strains of *P. phosphoreum* require L-methionine (either alone or in combination with other amino acids); this requirement is not generally found in other species of *Photobacterium* (27, 81, 84). None of the strains of *P. angustum,* a few strains of *P. leiognathi,* and most of the strains of *P. phosphoreum* produce gas and 2,3-butylene glycol during the fermentation of D-glucose (8, 81, 85). A positive Voges-Proskauer reaction is given by many strains of the latter two species and, consequently, cannot be used to differentiate *P. phosphoreum* from *P. leiognathi* as has been suggested by some investigators (47). The oxidase test, which appears to determine the presence of cytochrome *c* (100), presents problems when applied to the genus *Photobacterium;* both positive and negative reactions may be obtained with different strains of a single species. Some oxidase-negative strains give a positive reaction if the cells are treated with toluene prior to the addition of the oxidase reagent. Both oxidase-positive and -negative strains of *P. phosphoreum, P. leiognathi,* and *P. angustum* have been found to contain low levels of cytochromes of the *b* and *c* types (81, 85). *P. angustum* and *P. phosphoreum* share the ability to grow at 4°C. A relatively specific enrichment for the latter species consists of incubating fish, squid, or octopus, half submerged in seawater, at 10–15°C. The luminous spots usually evident after an overnight incubation are generally due to the growth of *P. phosphoreum* (81).

P. fischeri DNA Homology Group

The *P. fischeri* DNA homology group consists of the luminous species *P. fischeri* and a single nonluminous strain ATCC 15382 (81). The latter strain is related to *P. fischeri* by a DNA homology of 37–40%, suggesting that it constitutes a distinct species within *Photobacterium* (Figure 2). A substantiation of this conclusion must await the isolation and characterization of additional strains. Members of the *P. fischeri* DNA homology group have a GC content of 39–41 mol%, are oxidase positive, and ferment D-glucose without the production of gas (81). Unlike other

Photobacterium species, they are unable to accumulate poly-β-hydroxybutyrate as an intracellular reserve product. All strains produce a light orange, cell-associated pigment that becomes especially apparent in 3- to 5-day-old cultures grown on complex solid media. Johnson et al (56) noted that *P. fischeri* had tufts of polar flagella of varying thickness. These flagella were subsequently shown to be sheathed (1), with the thickness of the flagella dependent on the presence or absence of the fragile sheath. The number of flagella in the polar tuft varies from two to eleven (Figure 3c) and their diameter is 24–30 nm, similar to the diameter of the sheathed polar flagellum of *Beneckea* (1, 50, 81).

DISTRIBUTION OF LUMINOUS SPECIES OF MARINE ENTEROBACTERIA

Strains of all the luminous species have been isolated from seawater (Table 1) (81, 85). A seasonal variation in the numbers of luminous strains of *Beneckea* has been found off the coast of LaJolla, California (E.G. Ruby and K. H. Nealson, personal communication). This variation correlates well with the temperature of the seawater; greater numbers are observed during the summer months and lesser numbers during the winter. Three species, *B. harveyi, P. phosphoreum,* and *P. leiognathi,* have also been isolated from the surfaces of marine animals and, in the case of the latter two species, from the intestinal contents of fish (Table 1). All the luminous strains in our collection obtained from the luminous organs of fish and squid were found to belong to either *P. phosphoreum* or *P. leiognathi* (81, 85). Since only a few strains of *P. fischeri* were studied, no conclusions concerning the distribution of this species could be made (81, 85). Recently, Ruby & Nealson (87; K. H. Nealson, personal communication) found that *P. fischeri* can be readily isolated from seawater off the coast of La Jolla and that this bacterium is the sole species in the luminous organ of the fish *Monocentris japonica.* The apparent absence of luminous species of *Beneckea* in the luminous organs of fish or squid suggests that the potential to colonize these organs is restricted to *P. phosphoreum, P. leiognathi,* and *P. fischeri.*

B. harveyi consists of genetically related luminous and nonluminous strains; nonluminous isolates of the remaining luminous species have not been obtained (85). The absence of such strains may simply reflect the fact that the criterion for the isolation of these organisms has been luminescence.

METHODOLOGICAL CONSIDERATIONS

In view of our phenotypic and genotypic characterization of a considerable number of marine isolates, some generalizations concerning the methodology can be made. From the results of the in vitro DNA/DNA hybridization experiments and the numerical analysis (Figures 1 and 2), it is apparent that most clusters with a phenotypic similarity of 70–85% consist of strains related by a DNA homology of over 80%. There have been some exceptions to this generalization, yet in these exceptions a definite segregation of phenotypically and genotypically related strains was apparent (Figure 1). Therefore, an extensive phenotypic characterization based primarily upon nutritional properties (if applicable to the organisms studied), followed by a numerical analysis of the data, is of considerable value as a first step in studying the taxonomy of a group of organisms. Subsequently, selected strains representative of the various clusters may be used for studies of genetic relationships. One problem occasionally encountered in our numerical analyses was a high linkage of single strains (which were the sole representatives of phenotypically distinct species) to clusters of unrelated organisms. This problem was usually alleviated when the number of strains of the poorly represented species was increased. It should be emphasized that the major practical result of such an approach [derived from that used for the pseudomonads (77–79, 100)] is the expected finding that genotypically different species can generally be distinguished by a number of unrelated phenotypic traits, thereby providing a simple and generally reliable means of identification.

RELATION OF *BENECKEA* TO *LUCIBACTERIUM* AND *VIBRIO*

In the 8th edition of *Bergey's Manual of Determinative Bacteriology,* the species we have designated *B. harveyi* is placed in the genus *Lucibacterium,* whereas the species *B. parahaemolytica* is assigned to the genus *Vibrio* (14). The genus *Lucibacterium* was created to accommodate peritrichously flagellated luminous strains whereas the genus *Vibrio* is restricted to polarly flagellated organisms. The major flaw in this taxonomic treatment is the failure to recognize that both *B. parahaemolytica* and *B. harveyi* undergo a shift from polar to peritrichous flagellation upon transfer from liquid to solid medium. The generic assignments of these species to *Lucibacterium* and *Vibrio* are based on the fact that the flagellation of *B. harveyi* was determined in cells harvested from solid medium, whereas in the case of *B. parahameolytica* the cells were harvested from liquid medium. According to this taxonomic scheme, a species may shift genera with different conditions of cultivation. The generic separation of *B. parahaemolytica* and *B. harveyi* is also untenable due to the results of DNA/DNA hybridization studies, which indicate that *B. harveyi* and *B. parahaemolytica* are related by a homology of 47–59% (Figure 2). This somewhat bizarre situation is further complicated by the fact that the commonly accepted species *alginolytica* is given biotype status within the species *parahaemolytica* (14). Since in vitro DNA/DNA hybridization studies indicate that these two species, as well as *campbellii* and *harveyi,* are related to each other by 47–74% homology (Figure 2), assignment of biotype rank to *alginolytica* forces the same status upon *campbellii* and *harveyi.* Furthermore, since the oldest epithet among these four species is *harveyi,* this name has priority over *parahaemolytica.* A considerably simpler solution is the retention of species rank for *harveyi, campbellii, parahaemolytica,* and *alginolytica,* which are generally accepted as distinct species by most investigators. With respect to generic assignments, *Beneckea* has priority over *Lucibacterium,* and the results of DNA/rRNA homology studies support a generic separation between *V. cholerae* (the type species of *Vibrio*) and *Beneckea* (Figure 4). Although the latter conclusion deserves further substantiation by other methods, it at least has the merit of having an experimental basis.

The closer relationship of *V. cholerae* (by rRNA homology) to the marine than to the terrestrial enterobacteria (Figure 4) suggests the possibility that this species may have evolved from a marine organism (7a). As previously discussed, the high Na^+ requirement of marine bacteria is a physiologically complex attribute involving a number of different functions and would not be expected to be greatly reduced or lost as a result of a single mutational event. A gradual reduction and subsequent loss of the Na^+ dependence of a number of functions might be possible, however, if an organism was able to sequentially adapt to environments with lower Na^+ concentrations. The selective pressures leading to such a loss could be envisioned in the course of the evolution of an accidental marine pathogen into a successful human intestinal pathogen. A potentially pathogenic marine organism may have gained access to the intestine by means of heavily contaminated seafood consumed by a potential human host. Since the concentration of Na^+ in the small intestine is about 15–35% of that found in seawater (36), the establishment and survival of this organism in the intestine may have involved a relatively small number of adaptive changes. A further decrease in the Na^+ requirement would have been essential for the transmission of this pathogen to susceptible hosts by means of fresh water contaminated with fecal material. In this way, the selective pressures leading to the establishment and dissemination of a successful pathogen may have resulted in the gradual loss of its original Na^+ requirement. Such an evolutionary sequence might also have rendered the pathogen incapable of surviving in its former habitat so that it became ecologically separated from its marine ancestors. This difference in habitat could account for the evolutionary divergence between *V. cholerae* and the physiologically and morphologically similar species of *Beneckea.* The recent evidence suggesting that the sole reservoir of *V. cholerae* is the human intestine—the microorganism persisting in subclinical cases (4)—is consistent with these speculations.

Acknowledgments

We wish to acknowledge our indebtedness to the late M. Doudoroff, as well as to R. Y. Stanier and N. J. Palleroni whose extensive and elegant studies on the genus *Pseudomonas* served as a guide for our own investigations. For many helpful suggestions and criticisms of the manuscript, we would like to express our appreciation to J. Macy and M. Woolkalis.

Work from this laboratory was supported by Public Health Service Grants FD 00520 and FD 00626 from the division of the Environmental Health Sciences.

Literature Cited

1. Allen, R. D., Baumann, P. 1971. *J. Bacteriol.* 107:295–302
2. Anderson, R. S., Ordal, E. J. 1972. *J. Bacteriol.* 109:696–706
3. Barrow, G. I. 1974. *Postgrad. Med. J.* 50:612–19
4. Barua, D., Burrows, W. 1974. *Cholerae.* Philadelphia: Saunders. 458 pp.
5. Baumann, L., Baumann, P. 1973. *Arch. Mikrobiol.* 90:171–88
6. Baumann, P., Baumann, L. 1973. *J. Milk Food Technol.* 36:214–19
7. Baumann, L., Baumann, P. 1974. *Arch. Mikrobiol.* 95:1–18

7a. Baumann, L., Baumann, P. 1977. *Microbios Lett.* In press

8. Baumann, P., Baumann, L., Mandel, M. 1971. *J. Bacteriol.* 107:268–94
9. Baumann, P., Baumann, L., Mandel, M., Allen, R. D. 1971. *J. Bacteriol.* 108:1380–83
10. Baumann, L., Baumann, P., Mandel, M., Allen, R. D. 1972. *J. Bacteriol.* 110:402–29
11. Baumann, P., Baumann, L., Reichelt, J. L. 1973. *J. Bacteriol.* 113:1144–55
12. Breed, R. S., Murray, E. G. D., Smith, N. R. 1957. *Bergey's Manual of Determinative Bacteriology.* Baltimore: Williams & Wilkins. 1094 pp. 7th ed.
13. Brenner, D. J. 1973. *Int. J. Syst. Bacteriol.* 23:298–307
14. Buchanan, R. E., Gibbons, N. E., eds. 1974. *Bergey's Manual of Determinative Bacteriology.* Baltimore: Williams & Wilkins. 1246 pp. 8th ed.
15. Buttiaux, R., Voisin, C. 1958/1959. *Ann. Inst. Pasteur Lille* 10:151–58
16. Caldwell, D. R., Hudson, R. F. 1974. *Appl. Microbiol.* 27:549–52
17. Chichester, C. O., Graham, H. D. 1973. *Microbial Safety of Fishery Products.* New York: Academic. 334 pp.
18. Chumakova, R. I., Vanyushin, B. F., Kokurina, N. A., Vorob'eva, B. F., Medvedeva, S. E. 1972. *Microbiology USSR* 41:613–20
19. Cohen, G. N., Stanier, R. Y., Le Bras, G. 1969. *J. Bacteriol.* 99:791–801
20. Colwell, R. R. 1970. *J. Bacteriol.* 104:410–33
21. Cormier, M. J., Lee, J., Wampler, J. E. 1975. *Ann. Rev. Biochem.* 44:255–72
22. Crawford, I. P. 1975. *Bacteriol. Rev.* 39:87–120
23. Crawford, I. P., Nealson, K. 1976. *Fed. Proc.* 35:1546 (Abstr.)
24. de Boer, W. E., Golten, C., Scheffers, W. A. 1975. *Nether. J. Sea Res.* 9:197–213
25. de Boer, W. E., Golten, C., Scheffers, W. A. 1975. *Antonie van Leeuwenhoek J. Microbiol. Serol.* 41:385–403
26. Doi, R. H., Igarashi, R. T. 1965. *J. Bacteriol.* 90:384–90
27. Doudoroff, M. 1942. *J. Bacteriol.* 44: 451–59
28. Doudoroff, M. 1942. *J. Bacteriol.* 44: 461–67
29. Drapeau, G. R., Matula, T. I., MacLeod, R. A. 1966. *J. Bacteriol.* 92:63–71
30. Dubnau, D., Smith, I., Morell, P., Marmur, J. 1965. *Proc. Natl. Acad. Sci. USA* 54:491–98
31. Eagon, R. G. 1962. *J. Bacteriol.* 83: 736–37
32. Eagon, R. G., Wang, C. H. 1962. *J. Bacteriol.* 83:879–86
33. Eberhard, A., Rouser, G. 1971. *Lipids* 6:410–14
34. Fein, J. E., MacLeod, R. A. 1975. *J. Bacteriol.* 124:1177–90
35. Felter, R. A., Kennedy, S. F., Colwell, R. R., Chapman, G. B. 1970. *J. Bacteriol.* 102:552–60
36. Fordtran, J. S., Ingelfinger, F. J. 1968. In *Handbook of Physiology,* ed. C. F. Code, Sect. 6, Vol. 3. Baltimore: Williams & Wilkins. 1570 pp.
37. Forsberg, C. W., Costerton, J. W., MacLeod, R. A. 1970. *J. Bacteriol.* 104:1338–53
38. Forsyth, M. P., Kushner, D. J. 1970. *Can. J. Microbiol.* 16:253–61
39. Fraenkel, D. G., Vinopal, R. T. 1973. *Ann. Rev. Microbiol.* 27:69–100
40. Fujino, T., Sakaguchi, G., Sakazaki, R., Takeda, Y. 1974. *International Symposium on Vibrio parahaemolyticus.* Tokyo: Saikon. 261 pp.
41. Gee, D. L., Baumann, P., Baumann, L. 1975. *Arch. Microbiol.* 103:205–7
42. Golten, C., Scheffers, W. A. 1975. *Nether J. Sea Res.* 9:351–64
43. Hanaoka, M., Kato, Y., Amano, T. 1969. *Biken J.* 12:181–85
44. Harvey, E. N. 1952. *Bioluminescence.* New York: Academic. 649 pp.
45. Hastings, J. W. 1968. *Ann. Rev. Biochem.* 37:597–630
46. Hastings, J. W., Nealson, K. H. 1977. *Ann. Rev. Microbiol.* 31:549–95
47. Hendrie, M. S., Hodgkiss, W., Shewan, J. M. 1970. *J. Gen. Microbiol.* 64: 151–69
48. Henrichsen, J. 1972. *Bacteriol. Rev.* 36:478–503

49. Hidaka, T., Sakai, M. 1968. *Bull. Misaki Mar. Biol. Inst. Kyoto Univ.* 12:125–59
50. Hodgkiss, W., Shewan, J. M. 1968. *Advan. Microbiol. Sea* 1:127–66
51. Hollis, D. G., Weaver, R. E., Baker, C. N., Thornsberry, C. 1976. *J. Clin. Microbiol.* 3:425–31
52. Hylemon, P. B., Wells, J. S., Krieg, N. R., Jannasch, H. W. 1973. *Int. J. Syst. Bacteriol.* 23:340–80
53. Jannasch, H. W. 1968. *Appl. Microbiol.* 16:1616–18
54. Jensen, R. A., Rebello, J. L. 1970. *Dev. Ind. Microbiol.* 11:105–21
55. Johnson, F. H., Shunk, I. V. 1936. *J. Bacteriol.* 31:585–93
56. Johnson, F. H., Zworykin, N., Warren, G. 1943. *J. Bacteriol.* 46:167–85
57. Johnson, J. L., Francis, B. S. 1975. *J. Gen. Microbiol.* 88:229–44
58. Kaneko, T., Colwell, R. R. 1973. *J. Bacteriol.* 113:24–32
59. Kennedy, S. F., Colwell, R. R., Chapman, G. B. 1970. *Can. J. Microbiol.* 16:1027–31
60. Keynan, A., Nealson, K., Sideropoulos, H., Hastings, J. W. 1974. *J. Virol.* 14:333–40
61. Kodama, T., Tanaguchi, S. 1976. *J. Gen. Microbiol.* 96:17–24
62. Larsen, H. 1962. *The Bacteria,* ed. I. C. Gunsalus, R. Y. Stanier, 4:297–342. New York: Academic. 459 pp.
63. Leifson, E. 1960. *Atlas of Bacterial Flagellation,* p. 10. New York: Academic. 171 pp.
64. Leifson, E. 1963. *J. Bacteriol.* 86: 166–67
65. Leifson, E., Cosenza, B. J., Murchelano, R., Cleverdon, R. C. 1964. *J. Bacteriol.* 87:652–66
66. Lin, P., Saier, M. H., Nealson, K. H. 1976. *Fed Proc.* 35:1361 (Abstr.)
67. MacLeod, R. A. 1965. *Bacteriol. Rev.* 29:9–23
68. MacLeod, R. A. 1968. *Advan. Microbiol. Sea* 1:95–126
69. Matsumoto, K., Iuchi, S., Fujisawa, A., Tanaka, S. 1974. *J. Bacteriol.* 119: 632–34
70. McCarthy, D. H. 1975. *Can. J. Microbiol.* 21:902–4
71. Merkel, J. R., Traganza, E. D., Mukerjee, B. B., Griffin, T. B., Prescott, J. M. 1964. *J. Bacteriol.* 87:1227–33
72. Mitchell, R., Morris, J. C. 1969. *Advances in Water Pollution Research,* ed. S. H. Jenkins, pp. 811–17. Oxford: Pergamon. 946 pp.
73. Miwatani, T., Shinoda, S., Fujino, T. 1970. *Biken J.* 13:149–55
74. Moebus, K. 1972. *Mar. Biol.* 15:81–88
75. O'Brien, R. W., Frost, G. M., Stern, J. R. 1969. *J. Bacteriol.* 99:395–400
76. O'Brien, R. W., Stern, J. R. 1969. *J. Bacteriol.* 99:389–94
77. Palleroni, N. J. 1975. *Genetics and Biochemistry of Pseudomonas,* ed. P. H. Clarke, M. H. Richmond, pp. 1–36. London: Wiley. 366 pp.
78. Palleroni, N. J., Doudoroff, M. 1972. *Ann. Rev. Phytopathol.* 10:73–100
79. Palleroni, N. J., Kunisawa, R., Contopoulou, R., Doudoroff, M. 1973. *Int. J. Syst. Bacteriol.* 23:333–39
80. Pfister, R. M., Burkholder, P. R. 1965. *J. Bacteriol.* 90:863–72
81. Reichelt, J. L., Baumann, P. 1973. *Arch. Mikrobiol.* 94:283–330
82. Reichelt, J. L., Baumann, P. 1973. *Int. J. Syst. Bacteriol.* 23:438–41
83. Reichelt, J. L., Baumann, P. 1974. *Arch. Microbiol.* 97:329–45
84. Reichelt, J. L., Baumann, P. 1975. *Int. J. Syst. Bacteriol.* 25:208–9
85. Reichelt, J. L., Baumann, P., Baumann, L. 1976. *Arch. Microbiol.* 110:101–20
86. Rubin, S. J., Tilton, R. C. 1975. *J. Clin. Microbiol.* 2:556–58
87. Ruby, E. G., Nealson, K. H. 1976. *Biol. Bull. Woods Hole Mass.* In press
88. Rüger, H.-J. 1972. *Veröff. Inst. Meeresforsch. Bremerhaven* 13:239–54
89. Sakazaki, R. 1968. *Jpn. J. Med. Sci. Biol.* 21:359–62
90. Sakazaki, R., Iwanami, S., Fukumi, H. 1963. *Jpn. J. Med. Sci. Biol.* 16: 161–88
91. Sanderson, K. E. 1976. *Ann. Rev. Microbiol.* 30:327–49
92. Shinoda, S., Honda, T., Takeda, Y., Miwatani, T. 1974. *J. Bacteriol.* 120:923–28
93. Shinoda, S., Kariyama, R., Ogawa, M., Takeda, Y., Miwatani, T. 1976. *Int. J. Syst. Bacteriol.* 26:97–101
94. Shinoda, S., Miwatani, T., Fujino, T. 1970. *Biken J.* 13:241–47
95. Shinoda, S., Miwatani, T., Honda, T., Takeda, Y. See Ref. 37, pp. 193–97
96. Sinderman, C. J. 1970. *Principal Diseases of Marine Fish and Shellfish.* New York: Academic. 369 pp.
97. Smith, I. W. 1961. *J. Gen. Microbiol.* 24:247–52
98. Staley, T. E., Colwell, R. R. 1973. *Int. J. Syst. Bacteriol.* 23:316–32
99. Stanier, R. Y., Adelberg, E. A., Ingraham, J. L. 1976. *The Microbial*

World. Englewood Cliffs, N.J.: Prentice-Hall. 871 pp.

100. Stanier, R. Y., Palleroni, N. J., Doudoroff, M. 1966. *J. Gen. Microbiol.* 43: 159–271
101. Starr, M. P., Chatterjee, A. K. 1972. *Ann. Rev. Microbiol.* 26:389–426
102. Thompson, J., Costerton, J. W., MacLeod, R. A. 1970. *J. Bacteriol.* 102:843–54
103. Thompson, J., MacLeod, R. A. 1973. *J. Biol. Chem.* 248:7106–11
104. Thompson, J., MacLeod, R. A. 1974. *J. Bacteriol.* 117:1055–64
105. Truffa-Bachi, P., Cohen, G. N. 1968. *Ann. Rev. Biochem.* 37:79–108
106. Tubiash, H. S., Colwell, R. R., Sakazaki, R. 1970. *J. Bacteriol.* 103: 271–73
107. Twedt, R. M., Spaulding, P. L., Hall, H. E. 1969. *J. Bacteriol.* 98:511–18
108. Ulitzur, S. 1974. *Arch. Microbiol.* 101: 357–63
109. Ulitzur, S. 1975. *Arch. Microbiol.* 104: 67–71
110. Ulitzur, S. 1975. *Arch. Microbiol.* 104: 285–88
111. Ulitzur, S., Kessel, M. 1973. *Arch. Mikrobiol.* 94:331–39
112. Unemoto, T., Hayashi, M., Kozuka, Y., Hayashi, M. 1974. In *Effect of the Ocean Environment on Microbial Activities,* ed. R. R. Colwell, R. Y. Morita, p. 53. Baltimore: University Park. 587 pp.
113. Weston, J. A., Collins, P. A., Knowles, C. J. 1974. *Biochim. Biophys. Acta* 368:148–57
114. Weston, J. A., Knowles, C. J. 1974. *Biochim. Biophys. Acta* 333:228–36
115. Wong, P. T. S. 1969. *Studies on the mechanism of Na^+ dependent transport in marine bacteria.* PhD thesis. McGill Univ., Montreal. 218 pp.
116. Wong, P. T. S., Thompson, J., MacLeod, R. A. 1969. *J. Biol. Chem.* 244:1016–25
117. Yabuuchi, E., Miwatani, T., Takeda, Y., Arita, M. 1974. *Jpn. J. Microbiol.* 18:295–305

Ann. Rev. Microbiol. 1977. 31:63–87

BEHAVIOR OF MIXED CULTURES OF MICROORGANISMS

❖1697

A. G. Fredrickson

Department of Chemical Engineering and Materials Science, University of Minnesota, Minneapolis, Minnesota 55455

CONTENTS

INTRODUCTION 63
Experimental Apparatus and Techniques 64
Conceptual Apparatus and Techniques 65
CLASSIFICATION OF BINARY POPULATION INTERACTIONS 66
INDIRECT INTERACTIONS BETWEEN TWO POPULATIONS 67
Competition 67
Other Antagonistic Indirect Interactions 70
Commensalism 71
Mutualism and Protocooperation 73
DIRECT INTERACTIONS BETWEEN TWO POPULATIONS 75
Predation 75
Parasitism 79
INTERACTIONS BETWEEN THREE POPULATIONS 82
Competition Between Two Phagotrophic Populations for a Common Prey 82
The Effects of a Common Predator on Two Competing Prey Populations 82
CHANGES IN GENETIC COMPOSITIONS OF INTERACTING POPULATIONS 83
CONCLUDING REMARKS 84

INTRODUCTION

G. F. Gause (37) was the first biologist to try to isolate the "elementary processes" of the "struggle for existence." In laboratory apparatus, he put together inocula from two to four different but identified populations of microorganisms and he measured numbers or volumes of each of the populations at frequent intervals thereafter. He made painstaking efforts to "eliminate the complicating influence of numerous secondary factors, and to employ a technique of cultivation as would enable one to form a perfectly clear idea as to the nature of the factor limiting growth" of each population. He saw that "experimental researches will enable us to understand the mechanism of the elementary process[es] of the struggle for existence," and he thought that once this had been accomplished the next step was to "express these processes mathematically." He realized that "a rational study of the struggle for existence . . . can be begun only after the questions of the multiplication of organisms have undergone a thoroughly exact quantitative analysis" so that one "must therefore begin by analyzing the laws of growth of homogeneous groups consisting of individuals of one and the same species . . ."

Gause's prescription for studying the elementary processes (population interactions) of the struggle for existence (the dynamics of ecosystems) was not immediately seized upon by other workers in ecology or microbiology. One reason for this may have been the lack of experimentally verified laws of growth for individual microbial populations. Gause had found, for instance, that the Lotka-Volterra generalization of the logistic growth equation could not describe the results of his experiments on microbial predation. By the late 1950s, however, researches on pure cultures of microorganisms—particularly those of Monod (65, 66) and Herbert and his colleagues (45, 46)—had shown that some of the more important aspects of microbial growth could be described with considerable accuracy by simple mathematical equations. In 1958, Powell (77) published a mathematical analysis of competition between two microbial populations that has stood the test of experiment; Powell's analysis was based on Monod's model of growth. The catalytic effect of his contribution is difficult to judge, but papers employing Gause's methodology and Monod's model, or modifications and extensions of it, began to appear with increasing frequency in the microbiological and biochemical engineering literature during the 1960s.

This article is a review of the literature on mixed populations that has appeared since Gause's book was published (1934). The review is limited to those works in which an attempt, deliberate or otherwise, to follow Gause's methodology was made. Thus, studies in which populations were unidentified, or in which essential knowledge about medium composition was unobtained or unobtainable, are not ordinarily considered. Earlier reviews on behavior of mixed population, perhaps not quite so restricted, have been published by the Bungays (15), Veldkamp & Jannasch (109), Meers (61), and Jannasch & Mateles (49). Knowledge in the field of microbial ecology, of which the present review covers only a small part, is summarized in the books of Brock (11) and Alexander (2).

Experimental Apparatus and Techniques

Experimental studies on microbial population interactions can be conducted by observing the developments of the populations in a batch of medium. The range of phenomena that occur in such studies is usually quite limited because development soon stops, owing to depletion of nutrients or accumulation of staling products. A wider range of phenomena can occur, hence, more searching tests of hypotheses can be made, if provisions are made to add nutrients and to remove staling products along with a portion of the new organisms formed during the course of the observation period. Gause made such provisions by periodically replacing the medium with fresh medium. This technique is laborious, not easily automated, and introduces transients that may have unsuspected effects on system dynamics. Consequently, much recent work has made use of growth apparatus of the chemostat type (109,

110, 112); presumably, this kind of apparatus minimizes the difficulties that accompany Gause's technique. Williams (112) writes that "... the chemostat is the best laboratory idealization of nature for population studies. It is a dynamic system with continuous energy and material inputs and outputs, thus modeling the open system character and temporal continuity of nature. The input and removal of nutrients analogs the continuous turnover of nutrients in nature. The washout of organisms is formally equivalent to non-age-specific death, predation, or emigration which always occur in nature." Many ecologists would probably object to this statement because the analogies between the chemostat and nature are much less than perfect. A less controversial view of the chemostat, and the one adopted here, is that it is the best tool available for studying population interactions under controlled conditions.

Chemostat devices are often modified to provide a more controlled chemical environment. Thus, devices to control pH and dissolved oxygen level, etc, are often employed. One must remember that such auxiliary systems are themselves dynamic and that their interaction with the culture can produce spurious results. Sinclair et al (90) point out that these devices can produce oscillations of system variables in pure cultures, and there is little doubt that they can do the same in mixed cultures. Therefore, proposals to use controls, such as Bungay's (13), should be viewed with some reserve. Other factors that can cause spurious phenomena in chemostat cultures include incomplete mixing (33, 46, 89), evaporation (53), entrainment (39), attachment of cells to walls (56, 102), concentration of cells in foams (38), dropwise addition of medium (62), and size selectivity of washout.

An additional consideration of importance concerns the question of apparatus size. Gause's experiments with the *Didinium-Paramecium* predator-prey system showed that the outcome of predation was a matter of chance if the initial numbers of organisms were small (37). Similarly, Luckinbill (59) found that the mean time required for *Didinium* to consume all the paramecia in a growth vessel was greatly prolonged by increasing the initial numbers of the organisms, even though the initial population densities (numbers per unit volume of culture) were the same. I believe that the primary explanation of these results is to be found in the randomness of behavior of individual organisms. If this is correct, and if we wish to correlate data with the usual deterministic models (such as Monod's), then the numbers of individual organisms employed must be large enough so that individual cell randomness is a negligible factor in the behavior of the system.

Conceptual Apparatus and Techniques

Gause emphasized the importance of constructing mathematical models of population interactions. He thought that this could be done once experiments had revealed the mechanisms involved; that is, when they had shown which population-changing processes (growth, reproduction, maintenance, product formation, death, lysis, motility, morphologic change, attachment of cells to other cells or to solid surfaces, sedimentation, etc) were occurring at significant rates. Mathematical models of the kinetics of the population-changing processes are simply formulas that express the dependences of the rates of the processes on environmental variables, such as medium composition and temperature. When Gause wrote his book, no models for these processes were available, but contemporary workers do have reasonably reliable models available for several of them. Such models are discussed in a number of reviews (34, 35, 73, 104, 108). Fredrickson et al (34) and Williams (113) should be consulted for discussions of the approximations and idealizations that are usually made in constructing models.

It should be noted here that it is often convenient to reverse the order of two of the steps in Gause's methodology. In many cases, we may have some a priori knowledge that leads us to suspect that certain population-changing processes will be prominent when two specified populations are grown together. We can construct a model of the interaction based on the postulate that only the suspected processes occur, and from the model we can construct a set of experiments designed to test our postulates. This is in fact the procedure H. M. Tsuchiya and I have used in most of our joint work on mixed populations.

CLASSIFICATION OF BINARY POPULATION INTERACTIONS

Recent summaries (2, 11, 15, 61) of population interaction studies classify an interaction on the basis of its effects, beneficial or detrimental, on the populations. Beneficial generally means stimulatory to growth, whereas detrimental generally means inhibitory to growth or stimulatory to death, lysis, or maintenance requirement. Here, I use the terms *positive* and *negative* in place of beneficial and detrimental, respectively.

The foregoing classification does not have a mechanistic basis, which leads to the unsatisfactory feature that things occupying the same place in the taxonomic system can exhibit quite different behavior. For example, the situation in which population A is supplied with a required growth factor by the activities of population B is called commensalism, as is the situation in which the activities of population C stimulate the growth of population D by removing a staling factor produced by the growth of D. The dynamic properties of these two situations are bound to be somewhat different, but the usual classification scheme does not reflect this.

Classification based on the effects of interactions is established, logical, and useful, so it will be retained here; however, a higher-order taxonomic level that has a mechanistic basis will also be used. In particular, an interaction will be called *direct* if it necessarily involves physical contact of individuals from the two populations. It will be called *indirect* if physical contact is not a necessary part of the interaction and if, instead, the nonliving environment is a necessary intermediary between the two populations. Borderline cases will arise of course.

There are two primary reasons for using this additional taxonomic level. First, the usage emphasizes the role played by the nonliving environment, particularly in indirect interactions. This role enters what may be called classical models of population interactions—those based on generalizations of the Lotka-Volterra predator-prey and competition equations—only in an indirect and ad hoc fashion, i.e. through altered values of carrying capacity, intrinsic rate of increase, and interaction coefficients. However, alteration of the chemical composition of the medium in which microorganisms live has observable and measurable effects on their activities, and this fact ought to be incorporated explicitly into models of interactions. As Henrici put it (44): "Where these [mathematical models of growth] are not interpreted in terms of organisms, substrate, products of metabolism or other definite factors, they do not seem to be very helpful to an understanding of the phenomena to one who is not mathematically minded." This tongue-in-cheek comment is still appropriate today.

Second, the usage emphasizes the point that it is impossible, from pure culture studies alone, to predict or to understand the dynamics of two populations that interact directly. This is so obvious as to appear trivial if one thinks only of the direct interactions of predation and parasitism. However, other interactions, such as commensalism, mutualism, or competition, may also have an element of directness, and if so, their dynamics cannot be predicted from pure culture studies either.

One further remark on classification is necessary. Populations often interact in more than one way, even in laboratory situations. For instance, two populations may compete for a common substrate and one of them may produce a factor that stimulates the growth of the other. Rather than inventing some new term for this situation, I simply combine existing terms and call it *competition plus commensalism.* The same procedure will be used for other combinations of interactions.

INDIRECT INTERACTIONS BETWEEN TWO POPULATIONS

Indirect interactions ordinarily do not have the degree of specificity that often characterizes direct interactions. It may be, therefore, that indirect interactions have been somewhat neglected by biologists, for to them the specificity of an interaction is often its most interesting aspect. One can hardly deny the practical and theoretical importance of specificity, but that fact should not inhibit the study of interactions that are not specific. Indirect interactions are of importance in many natural systems (11) and they will also prove to be of importance in many large-scale mixed culture applications.

Competition

Indirect interactions that have a negative effect on both populations are called resource-type competition, or simply competition, if each population removes from the common environment substances needed by the other for growth; they are called interference-type competition (72) if each population excretes into the common environment substances that are inhibitory or toxic to the other. Antagonism would be a better term than interference-type competition, but it is already used for any interaction in which at least one population experiences a negative effect.

In discussing competition, we assume that the substances competed for are chemical species dissolved in the growth medium. Competition of phagotrophic predators for common prey is likely to be dynamically more complex because the prey population may also be growing.

Two populations of microorganisms with similar nutrient requirements will compete for a number of common, required nutrients when grown together. Competition will have observable effects on the dynamics of the system if and only if at least one of the nutrients competed for is present at a concentration that is rate limiting for the vital processes of one or both populations. Hence, competition as used here will refer only to situations in which at least one nutrient is present at such a concentration.

Competition in a batch culture results in a reduction of extent and perhaps also of rate of growth of both populations. The interaction can look like amensalism if one population grows much faster than the other. The effects of competition in a chemostat are more pronounced, for the continual removal of cells with the overflow exerts a strong selective pressure. This selective pressure makes the chemostat a particularly useful tool for studies on mutation and enrichment, and it was in connection with such studies that the first mathematical analyses of microbial competition were made (47, 76, 77, 80, 87).

The analysis of microbial competition in a chemostat is straightforward if it can be assumed: that a single nutrient determines the growth rate of both competitors, that no inhibitory effects are associated with this or any other nutrient, that mixing is perfect within the chemostat, that the flow rate is constant, and that no attachment of cells to its walls occurs (the last three hypotheses, and others such as constant temperature, define an ideal chemostat). Analysis shows that, if population A grows faster than population B at all concentrations of the rate-limiting nutrient less than its concentration in the feed to the chemostat, population B will eventually be excluded from the chemostat no matter what dilution rate is used. On the other hand, if the curves of specific growth rate vs concentration of the rate-limiting nutrient for the two organisms cross (say at concentration s_c and specific growth rate μ_c), the outcome of competition will depend on the dilution rate (D) used. If D exceeds μ_c, the population that grows more slowly at concentrations of the rate-limiting nutrient greater than s_c must eventually be excluded, whereas the other population must be excluded if D is less than μ_c. Whether or not either population can establish itself in the chemostat depends on D and the concentration of the rate-limiting nutrient in the feed (s_f); the dilution rate must not exceed its specific growth rate at concentration s_f of the rate-limiting nutrient if a population is to remain in the chemostat. These relations are conveniently summarized on an operating diagram, which is a graphic device that shows the effect of operating conditions (D, s_f) on the outcome of competition (or of any other interaction for that matter). An operating diagram for competition is given (35).

Several studies of competition in the chemostat verify the applicability of the foregoing analyses (41, 47, 48, 51, 60, 63, 101). The experiments of Jannasch (47), Meers (60), and Harder & Veldkamp (41) are particularly significant, for they show that alteration of the dilution rate can change the identity of the competitor that eventually predominates. In addition, Harder & Veldkamp (41) showed that altering the temperature could reverse the effect of dilution rate on the outcome of competition, just as allowed by their observations on the differential effects of temperature on the growth curves of the competitors.

Continued coexistence of competitors is theoretically possible if the value of s_f exceeds s_c and if the dilution rate is held exactly at value μ_c. The concentrations of the biomasses of the populations, x_A and x_B, are not uniquely determined for this coexistence steady state, although stoichiometry requires that $Y_A Y_B(s_f - s_c) = Y_B x_A + Y_A x_B$, where Y_A and Y_B are the yield coefficients of the populations. Hence, the values of x_A and x_B in the coexistence steady state would be dependent upon how the system was started.

In practice, it would be impossible to maintain the dilution rate exactly at μ_c; a slight but persistent deviation from this value would lead to a slow but persistent decline in the population density of one of the competitors. A dilution rate that fluctuates periodically or randomly around μ_c would probably have the same effect.

Analysis of competition becomes considerably more complex when the rate-limiting nutrient competed for has inhibitory effects at high concentrations (R. Aris, personal communication); a full analysis of this situation has not yet appeared in the literature, although thoughts and experimental data have been given (107, 109, 114).

Discussion to this point has presumed that only one substance competed for has a rate-limiting effect on both populations. Taylor & Williams (100) analyzed a case where two substances have such an effect. Their analysis shows that a steady state of coexistence of competitors should be possible over a range (not just a single value) of dilution rates if two nutrients have rate-limiting effects. The analysis also suggests that n competing populations should be able to coexist in a steady state for a range of dilution rates if the growth rate of each population is limited by the same set of at least n nutrients. Similarly, an analysis by Schuelke (87a) shows that two competing populations can coexist in a steady state if two nutrients have rate-limiting effects on both populations but if there is only one common rate-limiting nutrient. Both of these analyses are based on a model of multiple substrate limitation (multiplicative effects) that is not well established (5, 63, 91), but an alternate model (threshold effects) (83, 99) would probably yield the same qualitative results. These predictions from mathematical models certainly need experimental testing, but they do suggest that two competitors can coexist in an ideal chemostat if the medium is minimal with respect to at least two substances. They also provide an alternative to the explanation proposed by Titman (101) for his observation of coexistence of two species of diatoms in semicontinuous culture.

There are a number of circumstances that can allow competitors to coexist in a chemostat even when only one substance in the feed has a rate-limiting effect on the populations. First, the occurrence of an interaction with a positive effect on at least one of the populations, in addition to the competitive interaction, can allow coexistence. Mathematical models of commensalism plus competition (63) and of mutualism plus competition (64) predict stable or partially stable steady states of coexistence. The prediction of coexistence by the commensalism-plus-competition model was verified experimentally with a yeast-*Lactobacillus*-glucose-riboflavin system (63), and that of the mutualism-plus-competition model was verified experimentally with a *Streptococcus-Lactobacillus*-glucose-folic acid-L-phenylalanine system by Meyer (63a). Second, preferential attachment to the walls of the chemostat of the population that is at a competitive disadvantage in the liquid phase of the system should allow competitors to coexist. The Bungays (15) state that "adherence to the walls of the vessel can be a key factor in competition," but they give no details of the experiments nor do they give calculations on which this statement is based. The wall growth model of Topiwala & Hamer (102), perhaps generalized to account for competition for space on the wall, might serve as a basis for a model study of this situation. Third, the existence of a third population that preys on both competing populations has been shown (51) to allow coexistence under conditions of dilution rate that are fatal to one of the competitors in the absence of the predators. The coexistence here is not a steady state; rather, it appears to be a sustained oscillation of population densities.

Finally (although it does not exhaust the possibilities) [see Veldkamp & Jannasch (109)], the ecological literature often cites temporal variation of some external factor that influences the ecosystem as a means whereby coexistence of competitors can be brought about. An experimental example of this from the microbial world is provided by the work of van Gemerden (106). He found that two species of purple sulfur bacteria that did not coexist when grown in a continually illuminated chemostat with sulfide being rate limiting could coexist if the chemostat was subject to alternate periods of light and dark. A mathematical example is provided by the work of Koch (54). He showed that periodic, nonselective harvesting of two competing populations growing in a chemostat (according to Monod's model) could lead to coexistence in a perpetually transient state.

This discussion of competition shows that the interaction has a strong tendency to result in exclusion of one of the competitors. However, it also shows that many mitigating circumstances can be present, so that competition does not inevitably result in an exclusion. This seems to me an appropriate statement of the so-called competitive exclusion principle (42). If one accepts it, one would not be surprised to find two competitors coexisting, but on the other hand, one would certainly be stimulated to look for the circumstances that make coexistence possible. Thus, the principle would have served a useful purpose.

Other Antagonistic Indirect Interactions

Certain microbial populations (such as the myxobacteria) obtain essential nutrients by secreting enzymes that lyse and digest cells of another population; the degradation products are then utilized by the enzyme-secreting population. Since the effects of this interaction are positive on one population and negative on the other, it is of the type that includes parasitism and predation. Thus, some authors use one or the other of these terms when describing the interaction. I believe that "parasitism" and "predation" should be reserved for positive-negative effect interactions that are direct and that some other term should be used for the interaction now being considered. Alexander (2) calls the interaction "lysis," but this word already has a generally accepted, and different, meaning in biology. Since a brief term is needed, I use *indirect parasitism,* a contraction of Brock's (11) "parasitism without cell contact." This is done by default however; a better term is needed.

Amensalism, interference-type competition, and indirect parasitism have a common feature: at least one of the interacting populations releases into the medium material that has a negative effect on the other. In amensalism and interference-type competition, the negative effect may be simply an inhibition of growth of the affected population, but in indirect parasitism the negative effect must involve lysis. Thus, construction of mathematical models of indirect parasitism that are even minimally adequate requires models for the kinetics of extracellular enzyme formation, of the action of lytic enzymes, and of the action of enzymes that degrade products of lysis. The literature contains a great deal of information about each of the processes mentioned, but there is at present no generally accepted mathematical model for the kinetics of any of them. In view of this deficiency and the obvious experimental difficulties that would be encountered, it is not surprising to find that neither models nor experimental data that could be used for model construction exist for this kind of parasitism. The same comments also apply to amensal and interference-type competition interactions in which antagonistic substances released into the medium are antibiotics. Studies of these antagonistic interactions by using the Gause technique should be undertaken in spite of the difficulties, because the interactions are certainly important in some medical and industrial applications and they are probably also important in a number of ecological situations (2, 61).

Cases of amensalism and interference-type competition in which the antagonistic substances released into the medium are neither enzymes nor antibiotics might sometimes be handled by existing simple models, such as those used by Aiba & Shoda (1) and Wilkinson et al (111).

Commensalism

Although antagonistic interactions are important in many situations of interest to the microbial ecologist, probably positive (as opposed to antagonistic) interactions will prove to be more important in industrial or laboratory situations where one aims to use the activities of a mixed culture to perform some productive task. The rationale behind this prediction is simply that antagonistic interactions apparently tend always to reduce the diversity of an ecosystem, and such reduction is clearly undesirable if all members of a community are required to accomplish the task. Of course, a fermentation engineer realizes that amensalism and competition can be important factors in maintaining the purity of his cultures, but here we are considering overtly mixed cultures.

Various mechanisms can give rise to a commensal interaction. Production by the host population of substances essential for the growth of the commensal population and removal by the host (the word seems strange here) population of inhibitors of the commensal population are the two most commonly cited mechanisms. Commensalism of the first type mentioned may be an important factor in successions of microbial communities and in the contamination of cultures.

A number of chemostat studies involving commensalism have been reported (8, 21, 24, 58, 63, 88).[1] Although it was clear in each case that commensalism was involved, it was equally clear in several cases that other interactions, not well defined, were occurring. For instance, Meers (61) points out that competition was a likely complicating interaction in the experiments performed by Shindala et al (88), and Chao & Reilly (21) stated that a feedback by which the commensal

[1]The reference to Bergter & Noack (8) is from Meers (61); I have not seen this paper.

population affected the host population was present in their experimental system. Reilly (79) later constructed some mathematical models that predicted dynamic behavior like that observed by Chao & Reilly (21).

Megee et al (63) reported results of experiments in which commensalism was complicated by a second interaction and also by the physiology of the host population. The complications were identified, however, and it was possible to handle them in the mathematical model of the system that was constructed.

The system used by these workers consisted of *Saccharomyces cerevisiae* and a riboflavin assay strain of *Lactobacillus casei.* When riboflavin was not present in the feed to the chemostat, the bacteria were dependent upon the riboflavin produced by the yeast. In addition, the populations competed for glucose, which was present in minimal quantities in the feed. Although *S. cerevisiae* had a somewhat larger maximum specific growth rate than *L. casei,* the competitive advantage nevertheless lay with the latter. This occurred primarily because its growth rate saturated at a much lower glucose concentration than that required to saturate the growth rate of *S. cerevisiae;* also, there was a substantial death rate of *S. cerevisiae* under the starvation conditions in the chemostat. Calculations showed, and experiments confirmed, that the superior ability of the bacteria to compete for glucose would cause the yeasts to be washed from the chemostat if riboflavin were present in the feed at a sufficiently high concentration. However, when no riboflavin was present in the feed, the existence of the commensal interaction counteracted the influence of competition, and the populations coexisted over a wide range of chemostat dilution rates.

Meers (61) states that "commensalism involving organic growth factors . . . may often be associated with competition. To set up a situation in which true commensalism occurs in a defined medium may require careful contrivance." I would have agreed with this statement before Lee et al described the system: *Lactobacillus plantarum, Propionibacterium shermanii,* and glucose-minimal medium (58). The association of these two organisms is not contrived; it is an important part of Swiss cheese manufacture.

Inoculation of a batch of medium containing glucose but no lactic acid with the foregoing organisms results initially in a competition for glucose. This competition does not continue, however. As soon as *L. plantarum* starts to grow, lactic acid formed as a by-product of its metabolism is released into the medium. *P. shermanii* can obtain energy by fermenting either glucose or lactic acid, but if both energy sources are present it utilizes lactic acid preferentially (57). Thus, initial competition is quickly replaced by commensalism, with lactic acid the coupling substance. Preferential utilization of lactic acid by *P. shermanii* also occurs in chemostat cultures, and so competition is replaced by commensalism in such cultures also. The growth characteristics of *P. shermanii* and *L. plantarum* on glucose are such that, were it not for the preferential utilization of lactic acid by *P. shermanii,* competition for glucose would lead to exclusion of *P. shermanii* from chemostat cultures operated at high dilution rates, whereas *L. plantarum* would be excluded at low dilution rates. In fact, the two populations were found to coexist in a steady state for a wide range of chemostat dilution rates.

Mutualism and Protocooperation

The terms mutualism and protocooperation are used for interactions that have positive effects on both populations. In *mutualism* the interaction is obligatory for both populations; in *protocooperation* it is not (72). *Obligatory,* as used here, has no connotation of specificity but means simply necessary for survival in the habitat. The foregoing definition of protocooperation is ambiguous in that it could refer to interactions that were obligatory to neither population, or to interactions that were obligatory to one of the populations but not to the other. I believe that the distinction is important in the sense that the two situations would have different dynamic behavior. Therefore, it is desirable to use "protocooperation" for interactions that are obligatory to neither population and to use a new term for interactions that are obligatory to just one population. I do not have a new term to suggest, however, so *protocooperation* will refer to any mutually positive interaction not obligatory to both populations. The term "symbiosis" is sometimes used in place of mutualism or protocooperation, but it should be reserved for highly specific direct interactions.

MUTUALISM Mutualism between two populations can arise in different ways, but one of the most obvious is the production and release into the medium of a substance or set of substances [here called a coupling substance(s)] by one partner that the other needs but cannot produce by itself. The interaction need not be specific; all that is required is that the metabolisms of partners be complementary (syntrophic). The interaction can be reduced to commensalism, or destroyed completely, by supplying all of the growth requirements of one or both partners with the medium.

Placing two populations known to have complementary metabolisms into a medium deficient in coupling substances but not in any other substance needed by either population will not necessarily result in significant growth, even though sufficient amounts of coupling substances are present to start growth. Additional quantitative conditions must be met, which can be shown by simple mathematical analysis.

If the coupling substances are growth-associated products, and if death, maintenance requirements for the coupling substances, etc, are negligible, then the minimal set of equations describing the interaction between populations A and B are (64) $dx_A/dt = -Dx_A + \mu_A x_A$, $dx_B/dt = -Dx_B + \mu_B x_B$, $ds_1/dt = -Ds_1 - Y_{A1}^{-1}\mu_A x_A + \alpha_B \mu_B x_B$, and $ds_2/dt = -Ds_2 + \alpha_A \mu_A x_A - Y_{B2}^{-1}\mu_B x_B$, where s_1 and s_2 are the concentrations of the coupling substances, Y is the yield coefficient for growth, α is the amount of coupling substance produced per unit amount of growth, D is the dilution rate, and μ is the specific growth rate of the population. The specific growth rates are not constants but depend on s_1, on s_2, and on the concentrations of other substances present in the medium if they are rate limiting; I assume that the specific growth rates are positive.

Analysis of these equations for a batch system ($D = 0$) shows that s_1 and s_2 will (i) increase with time if $Y_{A1}Y_{B2} > (\alpha_A\alpha_B)^{-1}$; (ii) remain constant if $Y_{A1}Y_{B2} = (\alpha_A\alpha_B)^{-1}$; and (iii) decrease with time if $Y_{A1}Y_{B2} < (\alpha_A\alpha_B)^{-1}$. Similar analysis of the equations for a chemostat culture ($D > 0$) shows that a mutualistic steady state cannot exist unless $Y_{A1}Y_{B2} > (\alpha_A\alpha_B)^{-1}$. Thus, a necessary condition for a mutualistic interaction to sustain itself in chemostat culture, or to produce increasing concentrations of the coupling substances in batch culture, is that $Y_{A1}Y_{B2} > (\alpha_A\alpha_B)^{-1}$; if this condition is met by a pair of populations with complementary metabolisms, the situation is called *supercritical,* in analogy with the terminology of nuclear physics. Similarly, the situations $Y_{A1}Y_{B2} = (\alpha_A\alpha_B)^{-1}$ and $Y_{A1}Y_{B2} < (\alpha_A\alpha_B)^{-1}$ are called critical and subcritical, respectively. Evidently, many pairs of populations potentially capable of forming a mutualistic system in a chemostat would not, in fact, do so, because their metabolisms do not satisfy the requirement for supercriticality. Thus, demonstration by using batch culture experiments that two populations mutually stimulate growth does not of itself guarantee that these populations can be propagated in a chemostat fed with medium deficient in all coupling substances.

A mutualistic steady state in a chemostat in which the only rate-limiting factors are the availabilities of the coupling substances is unstable; any perturbation of this steady state will cause either wash-out of both populations or the establishment of a new situation in which at least one additional factor is rate limiting (64). Meyer et al (64) present analyses of two possible cases. In their first case, the availability of a substrate introduced with the feed and required by both populations is assumed to be an additional rate-limiting factor, whereas in their second case, inhibitory effects of the coupling substances on the populations that consume them are assumed to be additional rate-limiting factors. In addition, M. Defreitas and A. G. Fredrickson (unpublished results) analyzed a case where inhibitory effects of the coupling substances on the populations that produce them were assumed to be additional rate-limiting factors.

The mutualistic steady states of all three of the situations described above are only partially stable. That is, analyses show that they can always recover from perturbations that are small, but large perturbations can lead to washout of both populations. This suggests that mutualistic steady states may be achievable in chemostat cultures only if the chemostats are started from a restricted set of initial conditions.

The first case analyzed by Meyer et al (64) is mutualism plus competition; the second case is mutualism plus interference-type competition. It should be noted that addition of the mutualistic interaction partially stabilizes the coexistence steady states of these antagonistic interactions.

Experimental studies of mutualism done in the spirit of Gause are rare. Probably, this is due to difficulties in identifying coupling substances, in determining their modes of action, and in counting populations composed of similar cells. Yeoh et al (116) present a study that satisfies some of Gause's protocols. The coupling substances for the populations of *Proteus vulgaris* and *Bacillus polymyxa* they studied appeared to be niacin and biotin. However, the syntrophism of this system seemed to be complicated by the production by *P. vulgaris* of proteinaceous substances that had inhibitory effects on *B. polymyxa.* These may have been responsible for the oscillations of population densities that occurred. The interaction scheme proposed by Yeoh et al (116) has not been analyzed (64), and Yeoh et al made no model of their scheme; hence, it is not certain that the scheme can account for the oscillations observed. A model of the scheme should be made, to see if it does predict oscillations. Meyer (63a) studied a system developed by Nurmikko (71). Meyer was able to grow the mixed populations in a chemostat on a defined feed medium that would not support growth of either pure culture. However, the organisms involved, particularly the *Lactobacillus* sp., were so sensitive to moderate changes in environmental conditions that it was impossible to apply any simple mathematical model to the data obtained. The two studies cited here do establish the supercriticality of the systems used however.

PROTOCOOPERATION Wilkinson et al (111) discovered what seems to be an interesting example of protocooperation in the course of their studies on production of single-cell protein from methane. The postulated interaction involves the production of methanol by the methane-utilizing *Pseudomonas* sp. in their mixed culture and the consumption of methanol by the *Hyphomicrobium* sp. present. Methanol is strongly inhibitory to the growth of the *Pseudomonas* sp., but even low concentrations of it support rapid growth of the *Hyphomicrobium* sp. Presumably, the *Pseudomonas* sp. could survive alone in the medium used (albeit in a strongly autoinhibited state); thus the interaction is properly called protocooperation. It should be noted, however, that the authors were not able to grow the *Pseudomonas* sp. in pure culture. Whether this was due to strong autoinhibitory effects of methanol or to the absence of the *Acinetobacter* and *Flavobacter* spp. that were present in the mixed culture studies is not clear. The authors postulate that the *Acinetobacter* and *Flavobacter* populations remove "complex biological products of growth or cell lysis" of the *Pseudomonas-Hyphomicrobium* system; they also note that growth of the *Pseudomonas-Hyphomicrobium* system was "not comparable" to that of the crude system containing all four populations (111).

The mathematical model proposed by Wilkinson et al (111) for the interaction they studied is an interesting one, but unfortunately they did not give a full analysis of it. The effects of changed operating conditions are not summarized by an operating diagram and nothing is said about the stability of the washout steady state. Presentation of this material would have allowed one to compare the dynamics of mutualistic and protocooperative interactions.

A protocooperative interaction with the same pattern as that described by Wilkinson et al seems to be involved in the association of the two organisms formerly designated as *Methanobacillus omelianskii* (12). One of the components of this association utilizes ethanol and produces acetic acid and hydrogen; the latter substance is strongly autoinhibitory. The other component, which does not compete for ethanol, uses hydrogen and carbon dioxide to form methane and water.

DIRECT INTERACTIONS BETWEEN TWO POPULATIONS

Predation

Salt (85) points out that Gause's work (37) has had a very strong influence on the way most ecologists think about predation. "Even the most recent [ecological] textbooks illustrate predation by citing Gause's work along with perhaps one other." This is not to say that "Gause's findings are an incorrect representation of predation, but that they are incomplete. There is more to the process than is demonstrated in his experiments." Salt might have said "much more" because, as we shall see, the literature on microbial predation contains many seemingly contradictory findings and there are not very many facts that are generally agreed upon.

One fact about which agreement does prevail is that the growth and feeding rates of a population of protozoans are saturated at sufficiently high densities of their prey population. Monod's model handles the saturation phenomenon and it is therefore a candidate for a model of predation. However, Monod's model assumes that the ratio of the predator's specific growth rate (or specific reproduction rate if number instead of biomass is measured) to its specific feeding rate is constant and that specific growth rate shows a hyperbolic (as opposed to, say, a sigmoidal) dependence on the prey population density. Whether or not a given predator-prey system satisfies these conditions must be answered by experiment.

Phenomena observed in predator-prey experiments will generally be more complicated if both predators and prey are growing. These complications are not necessarily undesirable, but they are often removed by adjusting conditions to prevent growth of the prey. Thus, Proper & Garver (78) grew the ciliate *Colpoda steinii* on stationary-phase cells of *Escherichia coli* in batch cultures. Monod's model fitted the data obtained but batch culture experiments are not very searching tests of a model. Hamilton & Preslan (40) used chemostats in their study of predation; nongrowing bacteria were fed from a reservoir into a chemostat in which the ciliates were growing. Monod's model—with biomass of ciliates replaced by numbers of ciliates—gave a reasonable description of the results obtained, although washout that the model did not predict was observed under certain conditions (long holding times, low bacterial densities in the feed). It should be noted that prediction of conditions leading to washout is quite sensitive to the value of the Michaelis constant used, and Hamilton & Preslan (40) could not determine this quantity with precision. Of course, variation of the Michaelis constant could be taken as evidence against the Monod model.

Consider now the situation in which both predator and prey populations are growing in a single chemostat. If Monod's model describes the growth of both populations, then the model equations (equation 1) will be $dn_A/dt = -Dn_A + (\nu_m x_B n_A) / (L + x_B)$, $dx_B/dt = -Dx_B + (\mu_m s x_B) / (K + s) - (1/X)[(\nu_m x_B n_A) / (L + x_B)]$, and $ds/dt = D(s_f - s) - (1/Y)[(\mu_m s x_B) / (K + s)]$, where n_A is the population density of the predators, s is the concentration of the (nonliving) substrate that limits the prey growth rate, and ν_m, μ_m, L, K, X, and Y are the parameters of Monod's model for the two populations. These equations were published independently by the Bungays (15) and by Drake et al (30). Canale (16, 17) reported detailed analyses of the behavior of solutions of these equations, and Jost et al gave an operating diagram (52) for this set of equations.

Equation 1 predicts that a steady state of coexistence of predators and prey can be obtained if operating conditions are appropriate; under most feasible operating conditions, however, it predicts a perpetually transient state of oscillations of the variables n_A, x_B, and s. These oscillations are independent of the initial values of n_A, x_B, and s that are used and, therefore, are of the type called limit cycle by the mathematicians (28). Graphs showing such oscillations have been calculated by numerical integration of equation 1 and may be found in papers by Canale (17), Curds (25), and Tsuchiya et al (103). The Lotka-Volterra predation equations predict oscillations of population densities at all operating conditions, and moreover, the oscillations predicted are dependent upon the initial values of n_A and x_B used and so are not of limit cycle type.

Equation 1 never predicts extinction of one or both populations when operating conditions are such that their solutions are limit cycles. That is, the equation predicts that no matter how small n_A or x_B becomes the system will eventually recover. In reality, however, recovery may not occur and the predicted recovery may be simply an artifact of the approximations made in developing the mathematical model. That is, the model does not recognize that the number of organisms present in a system must be an integer nor does it take into account the increasing importance of chance events as the total number of organisms present becomes smaller and smaller. Bonomi & Fredrickson (9) have considered the problem of extinction in a qualitative fashion, and they show from equation 1 that conditions that tend to increase the probability of extinction are enrichment (increase of s_f), increase of holding time, and decrease of total volume of culture.

A number of experimental studies of predation in a chemostat, where both populations were growing, have been reported (6, 7, 18, 24, 51, 98, 103, 105). In most of these, oscillations of population densities, either sustained or damped, were observed. Remarkably, none of the studies has addressed the question of whether or not the oscillations are independent of initial conditions. Substantial discrepancies between observations and the predictions of Equation 1 occur in almost all of the studies. Only the system *Dictyostelium discoideum-Escherichia coli* used by Tsuchiya et al (103) was well described by these equations, and even here, there was always an abrupt and unexplained change from a state of undamped oscillations to a steady state after the system had gone through a number of oscillations.

Various explanations for discrepancies between data and model predictions have been offered. One class of explanations is based on the postulate that processes in addition to those accounted for by equation 1 are occurring. Examples are provided by the papers of Canale et al (18) and van den Ende (105).

A second class of explanations is based on the postulate that the properties of the populations, particularly those of the predator population, change in response to the changes of environmental conditions that are continually occurring during predator-prey oscillations. Thus, Jost et al (51) observed that predation of *T. pyriformis* on *Escherichia coli* or *Azotobacter vinelandii* seemed to become less effective at very low densities of the prey, and in a subsequent paper (52), they proposed that this was due to a shift in the relative numbers of predators in the various stages of the predator life cycle, as the availability of prey changed. On this basis, they proposed that the Monod factor $\nu_m x_B/(L + x_B)$ of equation 1 should be replaced everywhere by the multiple saturation factor $\nu_m x_B^2/(L_1 + x_B)(L_2 + x_B)$. This change did indeed remove the discrepancy—that Monod's model effectively predicted extinction of the prey followed by extinction of the predators, whereas no extinction was observed—and in addition it predicted that increase of holding time should change the observed state of sustained oscillations of population densities into a stable steady state of coexistence of predator and prey. This was in fact observed when the experiments were done (51). However, I now believe that the multiple saturation equation derived by Jost et al (52) is incorrect. One, but not the only, reason for this belief is that the "inconvenient variables" p', p'', and p''' (see 52) in the model were eliminated by applying the pseudo steady-state hypothesis to two of these, with the choice of the two completely arbitrary. If a different choice had been made, a different result would have been obtained. Furthermore, the multiple saturation model is not necessary to explain the discrepancies noted. Bonomi & Fredrickson (9) showed that retention of Monod's model for the kinetics of predation and addition of the Topiwala & Hamer (102) terms for wall growth of the prey to equation 1 would remove the discrepancy and, moreover, that these predict that increased holding time would turn sustained oscillations of population densities into a stable steady state. Unfortunately, the explanation based on wall growth has not been tested; variation of the ratio of chemostat wetted surface area to culture volume should be an important part of future studies on microbial predator-prey relations.

Here I criticized an explanation of a discrepancy based on an assumed shift of the distribution of states within a population and proposed that it be replaced by an explanation based on the occurrence of an additional process (wall growth). I do think, however, that we shall eventually have to consider internal changes in the structure of populations. This opinion is based on observations of cell size and other reported changes of protozoan predators (26, 29, 40, 86).

Curds & Cockburn (26) and Salt (86) observed marked changes in the mean size of predator cells during transient chemostat situations, even though the specific reproduction rate remained essentially constant (i.e. proliferation was exponential). In both cases the average feeding rate per predator cell decreased with time (population density of predators increasing but population density of prey decreasing), although at a given specific reproduction rate the feeding rate per unit volume of ciliate biomass appeared to remain constant in the experiments of Curds & Cockburn (26). A variable feeding rate per predator during exponential proliferation is not consonant with Monod's model, at least not with Monod's model written in terms of numbers rather than biomass, so the foregoing results call for modifications of the model.

What form will such modifications take? The experimental evidence is contradictory. Curds & Cockburn (26) found that the mean size of predator cells decreased with time, whereas Salt (86) found that it increased with time in his experiments. One might argue that Salt used a different system than did Curds & Cockburn; however, if this proves to be true, it will be difficult to construct any general model of microbial predation. Again, I have calculated mean feeding rates per cell from the steady-state data of Hamilton & Preslan (40), and I am not convinced that these show any significant tendency to decline with increased predator population density, even though this was varied by a factor of nearly 400; this contradicts both of the findings mentioned above. Furthermore, there exist such puzzling features as the finding of Curds & Cockburn (26) that the specific reproduction rate of *Tetrahymena pyriformis* in a chemostat experiment tends to maintain itself nearly at the dilution rate imposed on the chemostat, even though the situation is a transient one, with both population density and cell size changing with time. Why should this be so, and why should the transient period last for so many generations?

The modification of Monod's model proposed by Curds & Cockburn (26) is to write the specific reproduction rate of the predators as $\nu'_m x_B/(K' + m x_B)$, where m is the mean biomass of a predator cell, instead of as $\nu_m x_B/(K + x_B)$ as in equation 1. Similarly, Salt (85) suggested that the specific feeding rate of a protozoan predator is a function of the densities of the prey and predator populations, with the actual nature of that function determinable from experiments of the type described in his paper. I do not believe that either of these suggestions has validity outside of the specific experimental situation from which they were developed, for the following reason. One expects (34) transient situations of the type encountered here to be described by sets of autonomous differential equations that express the rates of change of system state variables as functions of the instantaneous values of those state variables. Population densities and mean cell sizes are examples of some of the state variables involved, but others that are not measured may be important also. Integration of these equations for a specific experimental situation would allow us to express each of the state variables as an explicit function of time. We could then eliminate time from two or more of these relations and so obtain correlations between two or more state variables. These correlations would differ with experimental conditions, even though there is an underlying unity, i.e. the set of differential equations mentioned above, connecting all of them.

Finally, a few remarks on two additional processes, encystment and excystment, that may complicate predation by protozoans need to be made. Bader et al (6) found that inoculation of growing chemostat cultures of the blue-green alga *Anacystis nidulans* with *Colpoda steinii* resulted eventually in episodes of encystment of *Colpoda.* Salt (84) reported earlier that encystment complicated predation of *Woodruffia metabolica* on *Paramecium aurelia*; he found that the population densities of predator and prey at the onset of encystment episodes were strongly and positively correlated. Bader et al (6) found that the densities of *Colpoda* and *Anacystis* at the onset of encystment episodes were similarly correlated, provided that the densities of both populations were neither very high nor very low. However, low densities of the alga and high densities of the ciliate seemed to result in encystment of the latter, regardless of the density of the other population under these conditions. This phenomenon, if real, must surely result in drastic reduction of predator effectiveness under the conditions noted (4) and in turn stabilize the predator-prey relation. In fact, Bader et al (6) did not observe sustained oscillations of population densities in the *Colpoda-Anacystis* system even though incident irradiation intensity and chemostat dilution rate were both widely varied. Instead, this system tended to approach a steady state of coexistence following several episodes of encystment.

Parasitism

Predation is a direct interaction, but most of the concepts that have been used in describing its dynamics have their origins in studies on pure cultures of saprotrophic microorganisms. Thus, the prey population is generally treated as a substrate, and Monod's model is assumed to apply to the growth of the predator on this substrate. As pointed out above, it may be necessary to modify this simple view to make models agree with data, but the modifications suggested again involve concepts that are familiar from pure culture studies on saprotrophs.

Parasitism of one microbial form upon another is different however. The researches of physiologists have provided much information about the mechanics of the parasitism of viruses and *Bdellovibrio* on bacteria (27, 93, 95), and attempts to formulate mathematical models of microbial parasitism from this information do not involve such reassuringly familiar concepts as Monod's model. In addition, the models that have been proposed for parasitism are usually considerably more complex than models proposed for predation.

Consider first the dynamics of infection of a bacterial population by a strain of virulent bacteriophage. Numerous models for this situation have been proposed, and I include a representative but not exhaustive list (10, 19, 20, 22, 36, 92, 115). Some of these models, such as Yassky's (115), deal with only one aspect of the infection (attachment of virions to bacterial cells). Others, which treat all aspects of infection as stochastic processes (which of course they are), lead to formidable mathematical difficulties, and it seems more appropriate to me to stick to more tractable though less exact deterministic models of phage infections.

Perhaps the best model for infection by virulent bacteriophages is that of Chen et al (22). Although this model was developed for RNA phages, it can probably be used for DNA phages also, provided that some obvious modifications in terminology are made. The model reproduces some but by no means all of the salient features of virulent phage infections. Its authors suggest that dependence of model parameters on the physiological state of the host cells is the source of most discrepancies noted. This may be true, but I think that problems raised by multiplicity of infection may also cause discrepancies. The authors assume, for example, that fission produces viable host cells without phages attached at rate $\mu(X + X_a)$ and that it produces no viable cells with phages attached. In their notation, μ is the specific reproduction rate of the host, and X and X_a are the densities of host cells without and with phages attached, respectively. If, however, one assumes that host cells with small numbers of phages attached, but with no viral RNA injected [Chen et al (22) were dealing with RNA phages], reproduce at the same rate as cells with no phages attached, then fission would produce host cells with no phages attached at rate μ $(X_0 + X_1 + 1/2X_2 + 1/4X_3 + \ldots)$, and it would produce host cells with one phage attached at rate $\mu(X_2 + 3/4X_3 + \ldots)$, etc, where X_i is the density of viable host cells with i phages attached but with no viral RNA injected. These results follow from the fact that fission of a cell with j phages attached will produce on the average $j!/2^{j-1}i!(j-i)!$ daughter cells with i phages attached if the distribution of phages between the two daughter cells is random. In addition, Chen et al (22) make the standard virological assumption that the distribution of attached phage particles among the host cells is of Poisson type. Yassky's kinetic equations for adsorption (115) do indeed predict that the Poisson distribution should obtain during the initial stages of adsorption of free phage particles to host cells in situations not complicated by lysis, reproduction of the host, or washout. But, in general, these complications must be considered, and Yassky's ideas ought to be incorporated into the model proposed by Chen et al.

One further remark on this model needs to be made. The model as written assumes that the specific growth rate of the uninfected cells is constant. In a dynamic host-parasite situation in a chemostat, one expects oscillations of population densities to occur, and such oscillations have been observed by Paynter & Bungay (74).[2] Change of environmental conditions and so change of growth rate of the host occur concomitantly with oscillations of the host population density, and thus the model of Chen et al (22) cannot be applied to such situations.

Consider next the dynamics of a population of lysogenic bacteria. This situation is even more complex because the intracellular mechanism that represses lysis of host cells must be considered. Apparently Noack (67–69) is the only author who has attempted to construct models of this situation. These models take account of the fact that the reproduction rate of the host will vary with changes in the concentration of its rate-limiting nutrient. They predict steady-state behavior rather than host-parasite oscillations for chemostat cultures. They also make the interesting prediction that there should be a range of dilution rates over which the steady state of coexistence of hosts and parasites is not unique. Noack (69) and Paynter & Bungay (75) provide some experimental evidence for the existence of two stable steady states at a given dilution rate.

Noack's arguments for multiple steady states in chemostat cultures of lysogenic bacteria are not convincing. In two of his models, he assumes that the specific rate of induction of lysogenic cells is dependent upon the degree of superinfection of lysogenic cells. I cannot accept his proposal that the quantity R/L be used as a measure of superinfection [L = number of lysogenic cells containing one prophage; R = number of injected DNA molecules present in all cells, whether or not those cells have been induced (see his balance equation for the quantity R)]. Noack's models should be redone, and an appropriate measure of superinfection should be used. In addition, Noack's models make no distinction between attachment of phages and injection of macromolecules into host cells, as in the model of Chen et al (22); this distinction might be incorporated into revised version of Noack's models. It is not clear that such revisions would still lead to predictions of multiple steady states in chemostat cultures.

Finally, consider the dynamics of infection of a bacterial population by *Bdellovibrio.* A mathematical model for this situation has been published by Sterkin & Samoilenko (94). The model is similar to those for virus parasitism discussed above in that it assumes the existence of a host-parasite complex, but it differs in that it recognizes no intermediate stages between formation of the complex and lysis of infected host cells. Unfortunately, the authors do not consider the complicating

[2]The situation investigated by Paynter & Bungay was complicated by the appearance of a phage-resistant mutant and they thought that competition of the sensitive and resistant strains of the host for nutrient was important in their system. If so, this is another mitigating factor —selective parasitism—that can allow competing populations to coexist.

effects of reproduction of the host cells in their model, because they were interested in the experimental situation in which host cells from a parasite-free chemostat are fed to a second chemostat containing the parasites. This situation is an excellent one for studying the effects of changed physiological state of the host cells on the kinetics of infection, but of course reproduction of the host must also be included in any general host-parasite model.

INTERACTIONS BETWEEN THREE POPULATIONS

Electronic counting devices such as the Coulter counter have stimulated interest in mixed population studies, but almost all of the work done has been with binary systems in which cells from the two populations have quite different sizes (31). Jost et al (51) used the Coulter counter to count three populations, but rapid progress in the study of interactions of three or more populations probably awaits the development of automatic counting devices that do not rely on size differences for discriminating among populations. Hence, not much can be said about experimental studies involving more than two populations.

Competition Between Two Phagotrophic Populations for a Common Prey

Competition between two phagotrophic populations for a common prey has not been investigated experimentally, but Koch (55) has published an interesting model study of it. He assumes that reproduction and feeding of both phagotrophic populations follow Monod's model and that reproduction and death of the prey not caused by predation follow the logistic equation. Thus, his model contains only three dependent variables—the densities of the three populations—instead of the four that it would contain if he had assumed that growth of the prey also followed Monod's model.

Koch did not analyze the foregoing model; he simply presented the results of numerical integrations of the model equations. These reveal that coexistence of the competing populations of phagotrophs can occur under certain conditions. The coexistence is not a steady state but one of perpetual oscillations.

Koch's prediction of coexistence of the predators is a surprising one and I am skeptical of it. I would take the prediction more seriously if it had followed from a model in which Monod's model was used for the growth of all three populations.

The Effects of a Common Predator on Two Competing Prey Populations

The effects of a common predator on two competing prey populations were studied experimentally by Jost et al (51). They showed first that competition between *Escherichia coli* and *Azotobacter vinelandii* for glucose in a chemostat led to continued decline of the *Azotobacter* population. They then showed that addition of the ciliate *Tetrahymena pyriformis,* which feeds on both species of bacteria, led to coexistence of all three populations. The coexistence was not a steady state but was a state of oscillations of the population densities with a period of about 5 days. Unfortunately, these experiments had to be terminated after slightly more than one complete cycle of change because an "explosive onset" of wall growth became apparent (51).

Formulation of mathematical models for the feeding of a phagotrophic population on two or more prey populations raises a number of interesting questions. Bungay (14) has presented some useful thoughts on these. He points out that consumption of cells from different prey populations will provide different amounts of the nutrient that is rate limiting for the predator population, and he shows how to generalize Monod's model to account for this. His suggested generalization does assume, however, that the predator exercises no preference in feeding. He also mentions the possibility of double nutrient limitation of the predators. An extremely interesting case of this would be indicated if it were possible to grow a population of phagotrophs on a mixture of two prey populations but not on the individual prey populations. Studies of the type conducted by Sudo & Aiba (96, 97) on *Vorticella* populations should be expanded to see if this phenomenon can be detected.

The assumption of lack of food preference may be best for bacteria-consuming protozoans like *Tetrahymena* or *Colpoda.* Large particles are immune to ingestion by these organism, but other mechanisms for food selection are not evident, and recent studies on uptake rates of yeast cells and latex particles by *Tetrahymena* indicate that the rates reflect the ratio of particle densities in the medium (81). Similarly, Coleman (23) found earlier that the rumen ciliate *Entodinium caudatum* took up two bacterial species at rates that stood in the ratios of the population densities in the medium.[3] On the other hand, other protozoans may exhibit very strong food preferences. For instance, Gause's predator (84) *Didinium nasutum* is a "nearly obligate predator on species of *Paramecium*." The feeding of *Didinium* is quite different from that of *Tetrahymena.* Jennings (50) summarized the process by saying that *Didinium* "proves all things and holds fast to that which is good." How it knows what is "good" is an unanswered question.

Food preference, or lack of it, could be studied in a three-chemostat system if means could be found for counting three populations in a mixture. Pure cultures of the prey would be grown in two of the chemostats, the overflows of which would be fed to the third chemostat, containing predators. Counting should be based on some means of population discrimination other than size, for one would like to see if factors in addition to size were important in food preference.

CHANGES IN GENETIC COMPOSITIONS OF INTERACTING POPULATIONS

Workers who have taken a mathematical approach to the problems of microbial population interactions have largely ignored the possibility that changes in the genetic composition of the populations occur. Honorable exceptions are Renneboog-Squilbin (80) and Heineken & O'Connor (43), who published mathematical papers dealing with competition between a wild-type population and its mutant. But implicit in all other models discussed above is the hypothesis that populations are

[3]Ricketts' study (81) may go a long way toward explaining reports of food selectivity in *Tetrahymena* and similar organisms. Some of these, however, such as the report of Elliott & Clemmons (32) on exclusion of colloidal gold particles and the preferential uptake of bacteria, remain puzzles.

genetically homogeneous and not subject to mutation, or that inhomogeneity in the genetic composition of a population is not expressed in ways that affect the rates of the population's vital processes.

Several experimental papers make it clear that the foregoing hypothesis is by no means generally applicable. The importance of mutation and selection in parasitism has been demonstrated by Anderson (3) and Northrop (70), and Paynter & Bungay (74) suggest that they were important in their study as well. van den Ende (105) and possibly also Tsuchiya et al (103) report similar findings for predation. These reports, and biological common sense, suggest that considerably more thought should be expended on the role of mutation and genetic inhomogeneity in population interactions.

CONCLUDING REMARKS

Consideration of the material presented above leads me to think that research along a number of lines could be pursued with profit by those interested in the behavior of mixed microbial populations. First, work already done has led to a number of unsolved problems that need to be clarified. These problems include the nature of the mitigating factors that allow competing populations to coexist, the role played by attachment of organisms to surfaces in predator-prey [and host-parasite (82)!] relations, and the nature of the relation between feeding rate, cell size, and population densities in protozoan-bacterial associations. Qualitative speculations about these problems should be checked by the construction and analysis of suitable mathematical models, and the models should, in turn, be checked by experiments.

Second, interesting phenomena predicted by plausible mathematical models of interactions should be searched for experimentally. Such phenomena include the existence of multiple chemostat steady states in the relation between a temperate phage and its host, mitigation of the competitive exclusion tendency by various time- or space-dependent conditions, and the "switching" phenomenon predicted by Meyer et al (64) from their model of mutualism.

Third, many different modes of indirect population interaction can lead to commensalism, mutualism, etc, and quantitative studies are available for only a few of these modes. Mathematical models of different mechanisms of interaction should be constructed and analyzed, and appropriate experimental systems should be set up to test the applicability of the models.

Fourth, more attention should be paid to indirect antagonistic interactions that are not primarily resource-type competition. That is, amensalism, interference-type competition, and indirect parasitism should be studied both mathematically and experimentally, since the sum total of quantitative knowledge concerning these interactions is near zero.

Fifth, examples of interactions other than predation or parasitism that have elements of directness should be sought in the library and in the laboratory, and models should be constructed and tested for any examples so found. The dialysis culture technique used by Nurmikko (71) in his study of mutualism may be helpful in deciding whether or not an interaction is direct.

Sixth, models for the interaction of three or more populations should be constructed and tested. Preliminary studies have been made on systems involving one predator and two competing prey or one prey and two competing predators, and these could form a point of departure for additional studies on multiple population interactions. Emphasis on competition and predation is often overdone, however, and I recommend that some future work on multiple population situations should include some interactions that are positive.

Seventh, much more attention needs to be paid to the possible effects of mutation and selection in all dynamic situations.

Eighth, new and improved mathematical models, techniques for estimating parameters in models, techniques for testing models, and techniques for finding the solutions of model equations need to be developed or applied. No emphasis has been placed on these aspects of research in this review, but the applied mathematician or statistician who studies the papers referred to will certainly find much that is disturbing and much work to do.

Finally, new methods of counting mixed populations that do not involve size as a basis for discrimination should be developed. The appearance of the Coulter counter in the 1960s markedly aided mixed population studies, and the appearance of a new automated counting system would do so again.

Literature Cited

1. Aiba, S., Shoda, M. 1969. *J. Ferm. Techol. Jpn.* 47:790–94
2. Alexander, M. 1971. *Microbiol. Ecology.* New York: Wiley. 511 pp.
3. Anderson, S. E. 1957. In *Microbial Ecology,* ed. R. E. O. Williams, C. C. Spicer, pp. 189–217. Cambridge: Cambridge Univ. Press. 388 pp.
4. Bader, F. G., Fredrickson, A. G., Tsuchiya, H. M. 1976. In *Modeling Biochemical Processes in Aquatic Ecosystems,* ed. R. P. Canale, pp. 257–79. Ann Arbor: Ann Arbor Sci. 389 pp.
5. Bader, F. G., Meyer, J. S., Fredrickson, A. G., Tsuchiya, H. M. 1975. *Biotech. Bioeng.* 17:279–83
6. Bader, F. G., Tsuchiya, H. M., Fredrickson, A. G. 1976. *Biotech. Bioeng.* 18:311–32
7. Bader, F. G., Tsuchiya, H. M., Fredrickson, A. G. 1976. *Biotech. Bioeng.* 18:333–48
8. Bergter, F., Noack, D. 1966. *Stud. Biophys.* 1:257
9. Bonomi, A., Fredrickson, A. G. 1976. *Biotech. Bioeng.* 18:239–52
10. Bourgin, D. G. 1974. *Math. Biosci.* 20:179–84
11. Brock, T. D. 1966. *Principles of Microbial Ecology.* Englewood Cliffs, N.J.: Prentice-Hall. 306 pp.
12. Bryant, M. P., Wolin, E. A., Wolin, M. J., Wolfe, R. S. 1967. *Arch. Mikrobiol.* 59:20–31
13. Bungay, H. R. 3rd. 1972. In *Fermentation Technology Today,* ed. G. Terui, pp. 117–20. Osaka: Soc. Fermentation Technol. 890 pp.
14. Bungay, H. R. 3rd. See Ref. 4, pp. 377–82
15. Bungay, H. R. 3rd., Bungay, M. L. 1968. *Adv. Appl. Microbiol.* 10:269–90
16. Canale, R. P. 1969. *Biotech. Bioeng.* 11:887–907
17. Canale, R. P. 1970. *Biotech. Bioeng.* 12:353–78
18. Canale, R. P., Lustig, T. D., Kehrberger, P. M., Salo, J. E. 1973. *Biotech. Bioeng.* 15:707–28
19. Chang, M. L., Chang, T. S. 1969. *Math. Biosci.* 5:9–18
20. Chang, M. L., Chang, T. S., Conolly, B. W. 1969. *Math. Biosci.* 4:403–10
21. Chao, C.-C., Reilly, P. J. 1972. *Biotech. Bioeng.* 14:75–92
22. Chen, M. S. K., Nagai, S., Humphrey, A. E. 1971. *Biotech. Bioeng.* 13:257–70
23. Coleman, G. S. 1964. *J. Gen. Microbiol.* 37:209–23
24. Contois, D. E., Yango, L. D. 1964. *Abstr. Papers Am. Chem. Soc. 148th Meet.,* p. 17Q

25. Curds, C. R. 1971. *Water Res.* 5:793–812
26. Curds, C. R., Cockburn, A. 1971. *J. Gen. Microbiol.* 66:95–108
27. Davis, B. D., Dulbecco, R., Eisen, H. N., Ginsberg, H. S., Wood, W. B. Jr., McCarty, M. 1973. *Microbiology,* 2nd. ed. Hagerstown, Md.: Harper & Row. 1562 pp.
28. Davis, H. T. 1962. *Introduction to Nonlinear Differential and Integral Equations,* pp. 269, 331–36. New York: Dover. 566 pp.
29. Dive, D. 1975. *J. Protozool.* 22:545–50
30. Drake, J. F., Jost, J. L., Fredrickson, A. G., Tsuchiya, H. M. 1968. In *Bioregenerative Systems,* ed. J. F. Saunders, pp. 87–95. Washington, D.C.: NASA Sp–165. 153 pp.
31. Drake, J. F., Tsuchiya, H. M. 1973. *Appl. Microbiol.* 26:9–13
32. Elliott, A. M., Clemmons, G. 1966. *J. Protozool.* 13:311–23
33. Fan, L. T., Erickson, L. E., Shah, P. S., Tsai, B. I. 1970. *Biotech. Bioeng.* 12:1019–68
34. Fredrickson, A. G., Megee, R. D. III, Tsuchiya, H. M. 1970. *Adv. Appl. Microbiol.* 13:419–65
35. Fredrickson, A. G., Tsuchiya, H. M. 1977. In *Chemical Reactor Theory: A Review* ed. N. R. Amundson, L. Lapidus, Chap. 7. Englewood Cliffs, N.J.: Prentice-Hall. In press
36. Gani, J. 1965. *Biometrics* 21:134–39
37. Gause, G. F. 1934. *The Struggle for Existence.* Baltimore: Williams and Wilkins. 163 pp.
38. Grieves, R. B., Wang, S.-L. 1967. *Biotech. Bioeng.* 9:187–94
39. Hamer, G. 1972. *Biotech. Bioeng.* 14: 1–12
40. Hamilton, R. D., Preslan, J. E. 1970. *J. Exp. Mar. Biol. Ecol.* 5:94–104
41. Harder, W., Veldkamp, H. 1971. *Antonie van Leeuwenhoek J. Microbiol. Serol.* 37:51–63
42. Hardin, G. 1960. *Science* 131:1292–97
43. Heineken, F. G., O'Connor, R. J. 1972. *J. Gen. Microbiol.* 73:35–44
44. Henrici, A. T. 1928. *Morphologic Variation and the Rate of Growth of Bacteria,* p. 20. Springfield, Ill.: Thomas. 194 pp.
45. Herbert, D. 1958. In *Continuous Culture of Microorganisms, A Symposium,* ed. I. Malék, pp. 45–52. Prague: Czechoslovak Acad. Sci. 234 pp.
46. Herbert, D., Elsworth, R., Telling, R. C. 1956. *J. Gen. Microbiol.* 14:601–22
47. Jannasch, H. W. 1967. *Arch. Mikrobiol.* 59:165–73
48. Jannasch, H. W. 1968. *Appl. Microbiol.* 16:1616–18
49. Jannasch, H. W., Mateles, R. I. 1974. *Adv. Microb. Physiol.* 11:165–212
50. Jennings, H. S. 1906. *Behavior of the Lower Organisms,* p. 186. New York: Columbia Univ. Press. 366 pp.
51. Jost, J. L., Drake, J. F., Fredrickson, A. G., Tsuchiya, H. M. 1973. *J. Bacteriol.* 113:834–40
52. Jost, J. L., Drake, J. F., Tsuchiya, H. M., Fredrickson, A. G. 1973. *J. Theoret. Biol.* 41:461–84
53. King, W. R., Sinclair, C. G., Topiwala, H. H. 1972. *J. Gen. Microbiol.* 71:87–92
54. Koch, A. L. 1974. *J. Theoret. Biol.* 44: 373–86
55. Koch, A. L. 1974. *J. Theoret. Biol.* 44: 387–95
56. Larsen, D. H., Dimmick, R. L. 1964. *J. Bacteriol.* 88:1380–87
57. Lee, I. H., Fredrickson, A. G., Tsuchiya, H. M. 1974. *Appl. Microbiol.* 28:831–35
58. Lee, I. H., Fredrickson, A. G., Tsuchiya, H. M. 1976. *Biotech. Bioeng.* 18:513–26
59. Luckinbill, L. S. 1974. *Ecology* 55: 1142–47
60. Meers, J. L. 1971. *J. Gen. Microbiol.* 67:359–61
61. Meers, J. L. 1973. *CRC Crit. Rev. Microbiol.* 2:139–84
62. Megee, R. D. III. 1970. *Interactions between dissimilar microbial populations and their environment.* PhD thesis. Univ. Minn., Minneapolis. 359 pp.
63. Megee, R. D. III, Drake, J. F., Fredrickson, A. G., Tsuchiya, H. M. 1972. *Can. J. Microbiol.* 18:1733–42
63a. Meyer, J. S. 1975. *Dynamics of mixed populations having complimentary metabolisms.* PhD thesis. Univ. Minn., Minneapolis. 227 pp.
64. Meyer, J. S., Tsuchiya, H. M., Fredrickson, A. G. 1975. *Biotech. Bioeng.* 17:1065–81
65. Monod, J. 1942. *Recherches sur la Croissance des Cultures Bactériennes.* Paris: Hermann. 210 pp.
66. Monod, J. 1950. *Ann. Inst. Pasteur* 79:390–410
67. Noack, D. 1968. *J. Theoret. Biol.* 18: 1–8
68. Noack, D. 1968. *Z. Allg. Mikrobiol.* 8:161–63
69. Noack, D. 1969. In *Continuous Cultivation of Microorganisms, Proc. 4th. Symp. Prague,* ed. I. Málek, K. Beran,

Z. Fencl, V. Munk, J. Ričica, H. Smrčková, pp. 233–41. Prague: Academia. 651 pp.
70. Northrop, J. H. See Ref. 69, pp. 243–46
71. Nurmikko, V. 1956. *Experientia* 12:245–49
72. Odum, E. P. 1971. *Fundamentals of Ecology,* 3rd ed. Philadelphia: Saunders. 574 pp.
73. Painter, P. R., Marr, A. G. 1968. *Ann. Rev. Microbiol.* 22:519–48
74. Paynter, M. J. B., Bungay, H. R. 3rd. 1969. In *Fermentation Advances,* ed. D. Perlman, pp. 323–35. New York: Academic. 909 pp.
75. Paynter, M. J. B., Bungay, H. R. 3rd. 1970. *Biotech. Bioeng.* 12:347–51
76. Pfennig, N., Jannasch, H. W. 1962. *Ergeb. Biol.* 25:93–135
77. Powell, E. O. 1958. *J. Gen. Microbiol.* 18:259–68
78. Proper, G., Garver, J. 1966. *Biotech. Bioeng.* 8:287–96
79. Reilly, P. J. 1974. *Biotech. Bioeng.* 16:1373–92
80. Renneboog-Squilbin, C. 1967. *J. Theoret. Biol.* 14:74–101
81. Ricketts, T. R. 1971. *Exp. Cell Res.* 66:49–58
82. Roper, M. M., Marshall, K. C. 1974. *Microb. Ecol.* 1:1–13
83. Ryder, D. N., Sinclair, C. G. 1972. *Biotech. Bioeng.* 14:787–98
84. Salt, G. W. 1967. Ecol. Monogr. 37: 113–44
85. Salt, G. W. 1974. *Ecology* 55:434–39
86. Salt, G. W. 1975. *J. Protozool.* 22: 112–15
87. Schlegel, H. G., Jannasch, H. W. 1967. *Ann. Rev. Microbiol.* 21:49–70
87a. Schuelke, L. M. 1976. *Stability analysis of various chemical engineering systems by a method of decomposition.* MS thesis. Univ. Minn. Minneapolis. 131 pp.
88. Shindala, A., Bungay, H. R. 3rd., Krieg, N. R., Culbert, K. 1965. *J. Bacteriol.* 89:693–96
89. Sinclair, C. G., Brown, D. E. 1970. *Biotech. Bioeng.* 12:1001–17
90. Sinclair, C. G., King, W. R., Ryder, D. N., Topiwala, H. H. 1971. *Biotech. Bioeng.* 13:451–52
91. Sinclair, C. G., Ryder, D. N. 1975. *Biotech. Bioeng.* 17:375–98
92. Srinivasan, S. K., Rangan, A. 1970. *Math. Biosci.* 8:295–305
93. Starr, M. P., Huang, J. C.-C. 1972. *Adv. Microb. Physiol.* 8:215–61
94. Sterkin, V. E., Samoilenko, V. A. 1972. *Mikrobiologiya* 41:408–12
95. Stolp, H., Starr, M. P. 1965. *Ann. Rev. Microbiol.* 19:79–104
96. Sudo, R., Aiba, S. 1971. *Jpn. J. Ecol.* 21:140–46
97. Sudo, R., Aiba, S. 1972. *Water Res.* 6:137–44
98. Sudo, R. Kobayashi, K., Aiba, S. 1975. *Biotech. Bioeng.* 17:167–84
99. Sykes, R. M. 1972. *J. Water Pollut. Control Fed.* 45:888–95
100. Taylor, P. A., Williams, P. J. LeB. 1975. *Can. J. Microbiol.* 21:90–98
101. Titman, D. 1976. *Science* 192:463–65
102. Topiwala, H. H., Hamer, G. 1971. *Biotech. Bioeng.* 13:919–22
103. Tsuchiya, H. M., Drake, J. F., Jost, J. L., Fredrickson, A. G. 1972. *J. Bacteriol.* 110:1147–53
104. Tsuchiya, H. M., Fredrickson, A. G., Aris, R. 1966. *Adv. Chem. Eng.* 6:125–206
105. van den Ende, P. 1973. *Science* 181: 562–64
106. van Gemerden, H. 1974. *Microb. Ecol.* 1:104–19
107. van Gemerden, H., Jannasch, H. W. 1971. *Arch. Mikrobiol.* 79:345–53
108. van Uden, N. 1969. *Ann. Rev. Microbiol.* 23:473–86
109. Veldkamp, H., Jannasch, H. W. 1972. *J. Appl. Chem. Biotechnol.* 22:105–23
110. Veldkamp, H., Kuenen, J. G. 1973. *Bull. Ecol. Res. Comm. NFR Statens Naturvetensk. Forskningsrad.* 17:347–55
111. Wilkinson, T. G., Topiwala, H. H., Hamer, G. 1974. *Biotech. Bioeng.* 16: 41–59
112. Williams, F. M. 1971. In *Systems Analysis and Simulation in Ecology,* ed. B. C. Patten, 1:198–267. New York: Academic. 607 pp.
113. Williams, F. M. 1972. *Trans. Conn. Acad. Arts Sci.* 44:397–426
114. Yang, R. D., Humphrey, A. E. 1975. *Biotech. Bioeng.* 17:1211–35
115. Yassky, D. 1962. *Biometrics* 18:185–91
116. Yeoh, H. T., Bungay, H. R. 3rd., Krieg, N. R. 1965. *Can. J. Microbiol.* 14: 491–92

Ann. Rev. Microbiol. 1977. 31:89–106

THE SPIROCHETES

❖1698

Russell C. Johnson
Department of Microbiology, University of Minnesota, Minneapolis, Minnesota 55455

CONTENTS

INTRODUCTION 89
STRUCTURAL FEATURES 90
General Description 90
Slime Layer 90
Outer Envelope 90
Flagella 91
Peptidoglycan Layer and Cytoplasmic Membrane 91
Perimural Fibrils and Microfibrils 92
Cytoplasmic Tubules 92
Cytoplasm, Nuclear Areas, and Cytoplasmic Inclusions 93
LIPID COMPOSITION 93
DISTRIBUTION 94
Free-Living Spirochetes 94
Host-Associated Nonpathogenic Spirochetes 95
Host-Associated Pathogenic Spirochetes 97
NUTRITION AND GROWTH REQUIREMENTS 101
ISOLATION TECHNIQUES 102
CONCLUDING REMARKS 103

INTRODUCTION

Spirochetes have a unique morphology and motility that sets them apart from other bacteria. These flexible, helically shaped bacteria, although grouped together because of basic structural similarities, are very heterogenous in regard to other characteristics. Within the group the cell dimensions vary from diameters of 0.09–0.75 μm to lengths of 3–500 μm. Their habitats are diverse. Spirochetes can establish themselves in environments such as mud, sewage, the digestive tract of mollusks, and the convoluted tubules of the mammalian kidney.

In addition to their unusual cell structure and their intriguing flexing, translocational movements, the spirochetes are of interest because of the propensity of some to cause disease. Most noteworthy among these is *Treponema pallidum,* the etiological agent of one of man's oldest social diseases, syphilis. This anthropophilic treponeme has successfully eluded efforts to control its transmission and to cultivate it in vitro.

STRUCTURAL FEATURES

General Description

All the spirochetes share the following basic morphological features. Enclosing the cell is a multilayered membrane referred to as the outer envelope or outer membrane. The peptidoglycan layer and the cytoplasmic membrane, which surround the cytoplasmic contents of the cell, are located beneath the outer envelope. The cellular components underlying the outer envelope are collectively referred to as the protoplasmic cylinder. The cytoplasm contains ribosomes, mesosomes, vacuoles, and nuclear areas. Between the outer envelope and the peptidoglycan layer lie the flagella, which are attached bipolarly in a subterminal position and extend toward the opposite end of the cell.

Slime Layer

A surface or slime layer has been observed occasionally on some of the spirochetes (63–65, 128). The serological non-reactivity of freshly isolated *Treponema pallidum* has been postulated to be caused by the presence of such a layer (22). Aging or treatment with heat, lysozyme, trypsin, or papain restores the serological reactivity of the spirochete (52, 117).

Outer Envelope

A three- (61, 64, 65, 67, 70, 81, 123, 125, 129) to five- (2, 11, 104, 127) layered membrane or envelope surrounds the spirochete cell. The viability of spirochetes is dependent on an intact outer envelope (OE). Damage of the leptospiral OE mediated by the action of antibody and complement results in the loss of intracellular components and cell death (2, 80). The elastic OE is fragile, and when cells are exposed to certain adverse conditions, or during the stationary phase of growth, it frequently separates from the protoplasmic cylinder and a blebing of the cell surface occurs.

Spirochetes differ in their response to variations in the osmolarity of their environment. Hypertonic conditions cause the leptospire OE to separate from the protoplasmic cylinder and to assume the shape of a sphere. Within this sphere is the protoplasmic cylinder that maintains its helical form (4). In contrast, the *Treponema* retain their spiral shapes when exposed to high salt concentrations, but when presented with a hypotonic environment, they convert to the spherical form (53). Spirochetal cells with a fully distended OE are nonviable.

Leptospires, when exposed to low concentrations of the detergent sodium dodecyl sulfate (SDS, 0.7 mM), will maintain their viability for at least 8 hr. However, if the cells are first rendered nonviable by exposure to 1 M NaCl, the OE is solubilized by 0.7 mM SDS within minutes (4). Outer envelopes of nonviable *Treponema* and *Borrelia* are also rapidly solubilized by low concentrations of SDS (84, 97). Dialysis of the SDS-solubilized leptospiral OE against distilled water results in its reaggregation into trilayered membranelike structures (4). The solubilized OE of *B. hermsii* responds in a similar manner to the dialysis treatment (97). The treponemal OE reaggregation differs in that divalent or trivalent cations are required for its reassembly (84). The lipid, protein, and carbohydrate (%) composition of several spirochetal OE are *L. interrogans* serovar *canicola,* 35.7, 48.8, and 6 (3); serovar *pomona,* 22.5,

46.6, and 27 (167); *T. phagedenis* biotype *Kazan 5,* 4–5, 60–73, and 1–2 (161); and *B. hermsii,* 23, 62.5, and 4 (97).

The OE of the leptospire is the primary target for the antibody-complement bactericidal reaction (2). The same is probably true for the pathogenic *Borrelia* and *Treponema* since they are also immobilized and/or killed by the antibody-complement system. The immunogenicity of the leptospiral OE has been evaluated in small animals and demonstrated to be a potent immunogen (4, 9, 42). Similar studies have not been conducted with the OE of the *Borrelia* or *Treponema.*

Flagella

Because the axial filaments of spirochetal cells are structurally and chemically similar to the external flagella of other bacteria, it is recommended that they be referred to as flagella (Subcommittee on the Taxonomy of the *Spirochaetales,* unpublished data). The spirochete flagella and other bacterial flagella consist of three structural components: the filament, the hook, and the basal body (10, 27, 61, 68, 71, 123). A sheath surrounds the filament of the *Leptospira, Treponema,* and *Spirochaeta* but is not present on the *Borrelia* filament (65). The flagella of *Treponema* (10, 62, 71), *Spirochaeta* (61), and *Borrelia* (65) have basal bodies with a single pair of rings and resemble the flagella of gram-positive bacteria (27). The flagella of the *Leptospira* (123) have a basal body with a series of disks that are similar to the two pair of rings present on flagella of gram-negative bacteria (27). The spirochete flagella are attached subterminally at each cell end and extend toward the opposite pole of the cell. The flagella of *Treponema, Spirochaeta,* and *Borrelia* overlap at the cell center. In contrast, overlapping of the leptospiral flagella does not occur (2, 11). The number of flagella per spirochetal cell ranges from two to hundreds. The number of flagella inserted at each end of various spirochetal cells are *Leptospira,* 1; *Spirochaeta,* 1; pathogenic treponemes, 3; cultivable treponemes (nonpathogenic), 1–8; *Borrelia,* 15–20; and *Cristispira,* >100.

The flagella of the spirochetes are presumed to be responsible for their motility (72) even though there is no direct evidence for this function. The following model for leptospiral motility was proposed by Cox & Twigg (24) and confirmed by Kaiser & Doetsch (90). Nontranslational movement in free liquid gives the organism the appearance of spinning, rotating on its axis. However, it does not spin; the body remains relatively stationary with contrarotation of the hooked ends. Translational movement is effected by helical waves traveling for a short distance near the trailing end of the cell. The broad hook at the trailing end waves in a direction opposite to the propulsive helical wave to prevent rotation of the whole body. For this movement to be possible, the flagella must extend along the axis of the body and not be wound helically around the body of the cell. The leptospiral flagella have been observed to be free against one side of the cell (2).

Peptidoglycan Layer and Cytoplasmic Membrane

The triple-layered-appearing membranous structure that encloses the cytoplasmic and nuclear components has been referred to as the peptidoglycan-cytoplasmic membrane complex. This term was used because of the difficulty in delineating the peptidoglycan layer from the cytoplasmic membrane. The presence of a peptidoglycan layer was suggested by Ginger (41), who detected muramic acid in *Leptospira* and *Borrelia* cells. The cellular location of this layer was ascertained from several observations. Chemical analyses of *Leptospira* (4), *Treponema* (161), and *Borrelia* (97) established the absence of muramic acid in the OE and its presence in the protoplasmic cylinder. In accordance with this finding was the observation that intact leptospiral cells were resistant to the action of lysozyme. However, if the leptospiral OE was damaged by the antibody-complement system, it permitted lysozyme to act on the wall of the protoplasmic cylinder (2). Thus, morphological evidence for the location of a peptidoglycan-containing structure of these spirochetes was obtained, and it is this structure that is responsible for the helical form of the cell. The protoplasmic cylinders of *Treponema* (70) and *Spirochaeta* (89) were also found to be sensitive to lysozyme. Anderson & Johnson (2) observed that the outer electron-dense layer of the triple-layered peptidoglycan-cytoplasmic membrane complex was thicker than the innermost layer and suggested it may contain peptidoglycan. The excellent studies of *Leptospira, Treponema,* and *Borrelia* by Hovind-Hougen et al (11, 65, 67) demonstrated the presence of the thicker outer layer of this structure, and they also suggested that it was the location of the peptidoglycan layer. The exacting work of Joseph et al (89) with *Spirochaeta* established that this thick layer was actually two layers and the thin outermost electron-dense layer consisted of peptidoglycan. Thus, it would appear that the *Spirochaeta, Leptospira, Treponema,* and *Borrelia* have a triple-layered cytoplasmic membrane surrounded by a thin peptidoglycan layer. This structural arrangement is the same as that seen in *Escherichia coli* (122) and correlates with the gram-negative staining characteristics of the spirochetes.

Chemical analyses of the peptidoglycan of *Leptospira* (5), *Treponema* (5, 154), and *Spirochaeta* (89) reveal that they are similar in containing muramic acid, glucosamine, alanine, and glutamic acid as major amino acids and amino sugar components. The diamino acid present in the *Leptospira* peptidoglycan is γ, ϵ-diaminopimelic acid (5), whereas the cell wall of *Treponema* (5, 154) and *Spirochaeta* (89) contain ornithine. Muramic acid, glucosamine, and ornithine have also been identified in whole cell preparations of *Borrelia* (97). *Leptospira* and *Treponema* cell walls contain 90% or more polysaccharide as compared to 2–5% peptidoglycan (5).

Perimural Fibrils and Microfibrils

Perimural fibrils (164) and microfibrils (165) have been reported to be associated with the surface of the leptospiral cell wall. The significance of these structures is unknown at the present time.

Cytoplasmic Tubules

Cytoplasmic tubules are unique structures present in some of the spirochetes. These tubules have diameters of about 7.5 nm and are seen as two bundles of six to eight tubules, one bundle originating at each end of the cell. They lie close to the innermost layer of the cytoplasmic membrane and overlap at the middle of the cell (68). Cytoplasmic tubules are present in all the *Treponema* examined with the exception of *T. genitalis* (66, 67). They have not been observed in the *Borrelia* (65) and *Spirochaeta* (61, 89). Within the genus *Leptospira,* cytoplasmic tubules have been seen in serovar *illini* (128). These structures were absent in all other leptospires examined (128). The function of the cytoplasmic tubules has not been determined.

Cytoplasm, Nuclear Areas, and Cytoplasmic Inclusions

The cytoplasm, nuclear areas, and cytoplasmic inclusions of the spirochetes appear to be similar to that of most bacteria (160). The *Cristispira* may have as many as 80 inclusions of unknown composition, which, in stained preparations, give the cell a striated appearance (132).

LIPID COMPOSITION

The spirochetes are relatively rich in lipids, which comprise approximately 20% of the cell dry weight (3, 78, 79, 107). Studies on the lipid composition and metabolism of *Leptospira, Treponema, Borrelia,* and *Spirochaeta* suggest that this type of information may have taxonomic value. The *Spirochaeta* are fully capable of synthesizing complex polar lipids and all their essential fatty acids de novo (88). The fatty acids varied in chain length from 12–18 carbons with branched 15-carbon fatty acids predominating (88, 107). In contrast, the *Leptospira, Treponema,* and *Borrelia* do not have this biosynthetic capability and long-chain-saturated and unsaturated fatty acids are required for their growth (75, 85, 94). Because of their inability to chain elongate fatty acids, the leptospires and treponemes require fatty acids containing at least 15 carbons (75, 85). Fatty acids are chain shortened and desaturated by the *Leptospira* but not by the *Treponema* (78, 79). The fatty acid composition of these spirochetes largely reflects those present in the culture medium or host animal tissues and consists of long-chain-saturated and -unsaturated acids (78, 79). However, the leptospires do form the unusual positional isomer of hexadecenoic acid, *cis*-11-hexadecenoic acid (109). Although the leptospires and treponemes are deficient in fatty acid biosynthesis, they are able to synthesize their complex polar lipids. Significant differences exist in the polar lipid composition of the *Spirochaeta, Leptospira,* and *Treponema.* The *Spirochaeta* and *Treponema* lipids consist of phospholipids and glycolipids (106, 107, 118). The major phospholipids of the *Treponema* are phosphatidylcholine (PC) and phosphatidylethanolamine (PE). The *Spirochaeta* do not have these phospholipids but instead have phosphatidylglycerol and cardiolipin predominating (107). Both the *Spirochaeta* and the *Treponema* contain the glycolipid monoglycosyl diglyceride (106, 107, 118). However, variation in the hexose content of the glycolipid occurs from species to species (107). Only the monoglycosyl form of the glycolipid was present in these spirochetes. No glycolipid or PC was present in the leptospires and PE was their major phospholipid (78). Several spirochetes isolated from the human oral cavity and from pig feces have lipid compositions intermediate between the *Treponema* and the free-living *Spirochaeta.* These host-associated spirochetes, which require the short-chain isobutyric and valeric acids for growth, contain the glycolipid monoglycosyl diglyceride but do not have the nitrogenous phospholipids PC or PE that are present in the *Treponema* and

Leptospira (108). The lipid composition of *Borrelia* is similar to that of the treponemes with PC and the glycolipid monogalactosyl diglyceride as the major constituents (B. P. Livermore, R. F. Bey, and R. C. Johnson, unpublished information).

DISTRIBUTION

Spirochetes are present in diverse environments such as mud (18), brine shrimp tissues (158), and the convoluted tubules of the mammalian kidney (49). They range from the free-living *Spirochaeta* to the human pathogen *Treponema pallidum.*

Free-Living Spirochetes

Spirochaeta is the only genus in the order *Spirochaetales* that does not contain parasitic spirochetes. Members of this genus are present in H_2S-containing fresh water and seawater mud. Most species are nonpigmented obligate anaerobes. Recently, a pigmented halophilic, facultative anaerobic organism, *S. halophila,* was isolated from a high-salinity pond in Israel (44, 45). This spirochete and *S. aurantia* (14), a facultative anaerobe found in fresh waters, are the only pigmented spirochetes known at the present time. The synthesis of the carotenoid pigments occurs under aerobic conditions and they are the type found in gliding bacteria (44, 45).

The genus *Leptospira* is presently represented by a single species, *L. interrogans* (156). However, within the genus two "complexes" exist, the biflexa complex, representing the free-living or saprophytic leptospires, and the parasitic complex, which contains the pathogenic leptospires.

Members of the biflexa complex are frequently referred to as the water leptospires because of their association with this environment. Although they are most frequently found in fresh surface waters, several halophilic isolates have been obtained from saline waters (23). In addition to being in surface waters, these leptospires have been isolated from frog kidney (28), turtles (159), bovine urine (50), and equine kidney tissue (119). None of these isolates are capable of causing infection in experimental animals. The distribution of biflexa leptospires in a natural environment in Minnesota was examined by using an enrichment culture technique (83) and specific immunofluorescence staining coupled with the contact (buried) slide technique (58). The frequency of isolation for a 1-year period was as follows: streams, 100%; lake, 65%; spring, 28%; bog lake, 5%; marsh, 0% (the greatest number of isolations occurred during the warmer months). The soil associated with lake, spring, and bog yielded leptospires more frequently than the water. Moreover, when water samples from the ice-covered lake were negative, leptospires were isolated from the adjacent soil, suggesting their primary habitat is soil rather than water. Soil with high moisture ($>$65%) and organic content yielded leptospires more frequently than sandy soils. The year-around isolation of leptospires from the stream is thought to be due to the leaching of these spirochetes from the soil (57). Kidneys and body fluids of frogs, turtles, mud puppies, salamanders, and fish obtained from areas known to contain leptospires were culturally negative for these organisms, and these animals could not be experimentally infected with fresh leptospiral isolates (57). The resistance of these animals to infection by these spirochetes may be related to the antibody-mediated antileptospiricidal activity of their blood (21).

Members of the biflexa complex have been isolated from municipal water (29). Because of the ubiquitous nature of these leptospires, coupled with their ability to pass through 0.22-μm-pore-size filters, they must be considered potential contaminants of filter-sterilized media containing deionized water. Contamination of bacteriologic and tissue culture media with leptospires has been reported (12, 155).

Host-Associated Nonpathogenic Spirochetes

The digestive tract of insects, especially the wood-eating types such as termites, contains spirochetes (13). Frequently they are attached to the surface of protozoa present in the insect gut. The spirochetes have an end-on attachment fitting into depressions in the protozoan plasma membrane that gives them a cilia-like appearance. Moreover, it has been established that those spirochetes actually serve a vital role in propelling the flagellate, *Mixotricha paradoxa,* by producing a series of metachromal waves of undulations (6). Spirochete-like organisms have also been observed in flies, fleas, mosquitoes, keds, gnats, and butterflies (13).

A crustacean host of a spirochete-like organism is the brine shrimp. Approximately 3% of the *Artemia salina* examined contained a microorganism with spirochete ultrastructural features. The spirochetes were present both intracellularly and intercellularly in the maxillary glands and did not appear to have an adverse effect on the brine shrimp (158).

The spirochetes in the genus *Cristispira* derive their name from the presence of a spirally wound crest that extends almost the entire length of the organism. Crista are not seen in freshly isolated *Cristispira* but develop after the cells undergo degenerative changes. The so-called crista are bundles of flagella loosened from the protoplasmic cylinder lying beneath the distended outer envelope (98, 132). *Cristispira* are present as commensals in the digestive tracts of many marine and fresh water mollusks and largest numbers are found associated with the intact crystalline style (13, 98). When the mollusks are under unfavorable conditions, the crystalline style dissolves and *Cristispira* rapidly decrease in number. These spirochetes may occur in other animals such as the echinodermes and tunicates (13, 98). *Cristispira* can survive for short periods outside the host, which provides a mechanism for their transmission (13). *Cristispira* have not been cultivated in vitro (98).

The first compartment of the multichambered stomach of ruminants may contain as many as 10^{10} bacteria per ml. In this anaerobic, densely populated environment, spiral-shaped bacteria are present and may reach a population density of 10^8 per ml. Several rumen spirochetes have been isolated and characterized (15, 38, 166), but the role of spirochetes in the rumen remains unknown.

Spirochetes are also present in the digestive tracts of nonruminant mammals. Earlier morphological observations on spiral-shaped organisms in the large intestine were not in sufficient detail to differentiate between spirilla and spirochetes. However, recent ultrastructural studies have established a close association of spirochetes with the epithelial cells of large intestines of humans (150), monkeys (150, 151), swine (54), dogs (99), rats (26), and mice (135). Few, if any, spirochetes are located in the small intestines. The number of spirochetes present varies with the animal species and its state of health. Intestinal spirochetes are more common in the rhesus monkey (28%) as compared to humans (2–10%) (100, 150). In the human large intestine, spirochetes were strictly limited to the brush border (microvilli layer) of the surface epithelium and extended only for a short distance into the crypts (glands of Luberkuhn). It is unlikely that human intestinal spirochetosis has any serious pathological importance (100). The monkey intestinal spirochetes are intimately associated with a polarly flagellated microbe and both spiral-shaped organisms are exclusively localized in the brush border of the colonic epithelial cells. These microbes penetrate the epithelial cells and structurally alter the upper three cytocomponents, whereas the remaining cell structure remains unchanged (151). This is in contrast to the spirochetes of the mouse colon, which frequently are located close to the brush border but do not penetrate it or cause structural alterations (135). The intestinal spirochetes of the pig, dog, rat, and possibly the mouse are in highest numbers in the intestinal crypts (glands). Because large numbers of spirochetes are present in diarrheal stools, they have been implicated as the etiological agent of this intestinal dysfunction. An alternative explanation for this observation is that normally the majority of spirochetes remain within the crypts of the large intestine with small numbers being shed into the feces. However, as a result of the inflammation and excessive mucous secretion that frequently accompany diarrhea, large numbers of spirochetes are displaced from the crypts and appear in the feces (99). Experimental evidence to support this interpretation is the presence of large numbers of spirochetes in the feces of rats (99) and swine (32) with artificially induced diarrhea. Moreover, attempts to induce canine diarrhea by the oral administration of spirochetes have been unsuccessful (54).

Several morphologically distinct spirochetes are located in swine large intestines. One of these, *Treponema hyodysenteriae* (54), appears to be pathogenic and is associated with swine dysentery (54, 153). The oral administration of pure cultures of this spirochete will produce dysentery in normal pigs but not in germ-free pigs unless other bacteria are also introduced (54). *Treponema hyodysenteriae* invades intestinal epithelial and globlet cells but does not penetrate beyond the lamina propria (54).

The human oral flora begins to develop shortly after birth, and with the eruption of teeth it closely resembles that of the adult (40). For reasons unknown, spirochetes and *Bacteriodes melaninogenicus* do not colonize the gingival crevices until approximately puberty (40). The oral spirochetes that have been cultivated are oxygen-sensitive anaerobes (111) requiring an oxidation-reduction potential of approximately −180 mV (114, 145). The gingival crevice (in particular the subgingival plaque) provides a very reduced environment (95, 124) and the spirochetes are essentially restricted to this location (103). In the absence of tooth brushing, plaque accumulates, with gingivitis developing within 10–21 days (110), and the spirochete portion of the microbial population of the subgingival plaque increases from 0.6–17% (137) The distribution of the spirochetes in this plaque is not random. Rather, they grow preferentially at the external surface of the subgingival plaque in close contact with gingival tissue (103). The excessive accumulation of plaque results in periodontal disease, which is a chronic inflammation of tooth-supporting tissues, resulting in tissue destruction and eventual tooth loss. It has been suggested (103) that, because of the strategic location of the spirochete layer on the subgingival plaque, these organisms may play an important role in the etiology of periodontal disease.

Spirochetes may also be involved in acute necrotizing ulcerative gingivitis (ANUG, trench mouth), a painful infection most commonly seen in young individuals under physical, nutritional, or psychological stress (43). Numerous spirochetes and fusobacteria are associated with ANUG and were believed to play a role in its etiology. This role was questioned when it was reported that *B. melaninogenicus* alone could cause abscess formation (113, 114). However, this experimentally induced lesion resembles that caused by a bite wound rather than ANUG (47, 131). In ANUG spirochetes are seen invading viable tissue and they are the only plaque bacteria known to possess this property (60, 101).

Oral spirochetes have been divided into three groups based on size and number of flagella (105, 144). The small spirochetes can be cultivated and, of these, *T. denticola, T. macrodentium,* and *T. oralis* have been well characterized (101). These spirochetes have a protoplasmic cylinder with a diameter of 100–250 nm and one to two pair of flagella. The only intermediate-size spirochete that has been cultivated is *T. (Borrelia) vincentii.* These spirochetes have a protoplasmic cylinder diameter of 200–500 nm and 3–20 pair of flagella. None of the large-size spirochetes (protoplasmic cylinder diameter, 500 nm; 12 to >20 pair of flagella) have been isolated. It is the intermediate and large spirochetes that are seen invading viable gingival tissue (102).

Host-Associated Pathogenic Spirochetes

Diseases caused by the pathogenic treponemes are collectively referred to as the treponematoses. The human treponematoses—syphilis, endemic syphilis (bejel), yaws, and pinta—are chronic, granulomatous diseases. The treponemes responsible for these diseases cannot be distinguished from one another morphologically (69, 163) or immunologically (7, 163). Information is lacking on their physiology and chemical composition due to the inability to routinely cultivate the pathogenic treponemes in vitro. Accordingly, the treponemes are separated into species based on clinical and epidemiologic characteristics (51, 136, 163).

Treponema pallidum is the etiological agent of syphilis (the great pox), and this disease is omnipresent, infecting people in all parts of the world. With the exception of congenital syphilis, the disease is transmitted by sexual contact. In contrast, bejel (endemic syphilis), which is probably also caused by *T. pallidum* (51), is a nonvenereal disease. This disease is acquired in childhood and is now largely restricted to primitive populations of less developed, arid, and tropical and subtropical areas (25, 162). The infectious lesions are usually present in the oral cavity and transmission probably most frequently occurs through the use of common drinking vessels. Endemic syphilis is a milder disease than venereal syphilis. Cardiovascular and neural involvement are uncommon, and since the disease occurs in childhood, the congenital form of endemic syphilis does not occur. Persons who have recovered from this disease have immunity to venereal syphilis (25, 162). It is a rapidly disappearing disease because of improvements in the standards of living and the use of penicillin (25, 162).

Yaws is also a nonvenereal treponematosis, which is restricted to rural populations located in tropical countries. This disease is characterized by destructive lesions of the skin and bones in the late stages of infection. It is rarely fatal, but it is a debilitating disease if untreated. The etiological agent of yaws is *Treponema pertenue.* This disease is thought to have originated in the Afro-Asian area and to have been transported to the Americas by African slaves (46). As a result of this, its distribution in South America is restricted to persons of African ancestry who largely inhabit the coastal areas. Non-human primates in yaws-prevalent areas show a high incidence of treponemal antibodies, and treponemes have been isolated from the lymph nodes of a baboon and from a skin lesion of a monkey (51). The isolated treponemes are thought to be *T. pertenue.*

Pinta, which may be the oldest of the treponematoses (46), is caused by *Treponema carateum.* This is a nonvenereal disease of adolescents and young adults that is restricted to populations located in remote, primitive areas of tropical Central and South America that live under unhygienic conditions. This treponeme produces dyschromic skin lesions. The early skin lesions are usually red, then change to a dark blue to black color, and eventually become depigmented. Lesions are most common on uncovered areas of the body, especially those exposed to the sun. Other tissues are not involved in this infection. Thus, pinta is disfiguring rather than debilitating and the major consequence of this disease is social since the afflicted are frequently ostracized. The treponemes are shed from exuding lesions, and transmission requires close personal contact permitting the organisms to enter through abrasions of the skin and mucous membranes. The cross immunity to venereal syphilis provided by endemic syphilis and yaws is not known to occur with pinta.

The nonvenereal treponematoses have rapidly decreased in incidence because of improved hygienic conditions (the use of soap) and large-scale treatment programs. However, these relatively mild diseases, endemic syphilis and yaws, provide protection against the more serious disease, venereal syphilis. As a result of the success of the eradication programs, venereal syphilis is now being found in urban and rural areas of developing countries where it formerly was not present (25).

Rabbits have a naturally occurring mild venereal disease caused by *Treponema paraluis-caniculi.* The infected rabbits appear normal except for the presence of erythematous lesions with crusted edges, which are most commonly associated with the genitalia but which also occur around the face, ears, nose, and extremities. The reported incidence of rabbit syphilis varies from 0.3–60% (143). It is readily transmitted from rabbit to rabbit by natural means and is worldwide in distribution. However, it is difficult to maintain this treponeme in the rabbit by intratesticular passage as is so easily accomplished with *T. pallidum. T. paraluis-caniculi* is not known to be transmitted to humans from infected rabbits. The inoculation of two human volunteers with a rich emulsion of the treponemes did not produce an infection (37). This treponeme is similar to those that cause the human treponematoses in that it cannot be cultivated in vitro.

Treponemes have also been associated with skin ulcers, lung abscesses, and infections of the digestive tract. Since it has not been firmly established that they are the etiological agents responsible for these infections, they will not be covered in this review.

Louse-borne or epidemic relapsing fever is caused by a single species of *Borrelia, B. recurrentis.* The human louse, *Pediculus humanus humanus,* becomes infected by feeding on a spirochetemic patient. A sufficient number of borreliae survive the passage through the louse esophagus to the midgut to penetrate the gut epithelium into the hemolymph where they multiply. The spirochetes are restricted to the hemolymph and the central ganglion of the louse and, therefore, are not transmitted to a new host via the bite of the louse nor are they maintained in the louse population transovarially. Humans become infected by scratching the area of the louse bite, thereby crushing or injuring the louse, allowing borreliae from the released hemolymph to enter the broken skin (17, 33). Clinically, the disease is characterized by recurrent fevers separated by afebrile periods (134). Spirochetes are present in the blood during febrile periods and are absent during the afebrile interval. *Borrelia* are destroyed by antibodies and the relapses are related to antigenic changes in the spirochete during the course of the disease (33). Since the human louse prefers a 37°C environment, it leaves the febrile patient in search of a new host, which accounts for the rapid spread of this disease during epidemics (17). Humans are the reservoir for this disease since they are not transmitted transovarially in the louse, and although the louse is infected for its life span this is very short, 10–61 days (17, 33). Overcrowding and poor personal hygiene favor the multiplication and transfer of *P. humanus humanus.* These conditions are associated with wars, earthquakes, famines, and floods, as is epidemic relapsing fever. The scantier-clothed population of hot, humid areas rarely experience louse-borne relapsing fever.

In the past, large epidemics have occurred in Europe, Africa, Asia, and America (33). It is estimated that during World War II and its aftermath 10 million people were infected with *B. recurrentis,* with a fatality rate of 5% (16). Since 1967 louse-borne relapsing fever has been reported primarily from Ethiopia and Sudan (152). This disease has disappeared from the U.S.

A number of *Borrelia* species are responsible for tick-borne or endemic relapsing fever. *Ornithodoros,* the soft ticks, carry the relapsing fever spirochetes and become infected when obtaining a blood meal from a spirochetemic animal. The spirochetes invade all tissues of the tick and are maintained within the tick population by transovarial transmission. Ticks transmit borreliae to humans and animals via infectious saliva or the coxal fluid, which is excreted during or after feeding (17, 33). The borreliae-transmitting ticks generally do not have a painful bite and are mostly nocturnal, fast feeders (5–20 min). In contrast to the body louse, the tick does not have to be damaged to transmit spirochetes. Thus, a single tick can infect a different person or animal at each feeding (33). The ticks spend most of their time in places such as rodent burrows, caves, and crevices of old, fallen trees, and between the logs of rodent-infested cabins. Adult ticks have the ability to survive long periods of starvation. They have been stored in the laboratory for as long as 15 years without feeding (17). Foci of tick-borne borreliae are quite restricted, being limited to burrows, nests, and caves, with the borreliae being maintained between the tick vector and animal hosts. Humans are accidental hosts and become infected when they invade the habitat of the tick. The two major outbreaks of endemic relapsing fever in the U.S. occurred in people occupying tick-infested log cabins (17). The major agents of American tick-borne relapsing fevers are *Borrelia hermsii, Borrelia turicatae,* and *Borrelia venezuelensis.* Endemic centers of tick-borne relapsing fever occur throughout the world with the exception of Australia, New Zealand, and Oceania. East African relapsing fever is caused by *Borrelia duttonii.* The vector of this spirochete is *Ornithodoros moubata,* which, in contrast to the other borreliae-carrying ticks, has become a domestic ectoparasite. Humans are believed to be the major reservoir for *B. duttonii.* Because of frequent exposure to this spirochete, the natives have a degree of immunity to this disease, and they associate this with the presence of ticks. In certain areas natives transfer ticks from old to new dwellings and, when traveling to other areas, carry a good luck tick along in a matchbox allowing them to feed regularly on their skin (39). Tick-borne relapsing fever tends to be less severe than the louse-borne disease but otherwise the clinical syndromes are similar (134).

Avian species are also infected by *Borrelia.* The causative agent of avian borreliosis is *B. anserina,* and the primary vectors are ticks of the genus *Argas.* No relapses of the disease have been observed (34).

The pathogenic members of the genus *Leptospira* comprise the interrogans complex. At least 160 serovars have been isolated from various parts of the world (157). Leptospirosis, the disease resulting from infection with these spirochetes, is one of the most widespread of the zoonoses. The major reservoirs for the pathogenic leptospires are rodents and domestic animals (92). The natural habitat for these helically shaped bacteria is within the proximal convoluted tubules of the mammalian kidney. The leptospires multiply in this area and are shed into the urine, sometimes reaching cell densities of 10^7 per ml. The period of shedding varies with the host and the infecting serovar. Leptospiruria has been observed for as long as 3.5 months in cattle (149), 11 months in humans (73) and swine (139), and over 4 years in dogs (116); it is believed that some rodents may shed leptospires throughout their lifetime (49). Transmission of the disease involves direct contact with the urine of leptospiruric animals or indirectly by contact with contaminated soil and water. The jungle environment with its warm temperature, abundance of animal life, surface waters, and moist organic soil may be one of the most important natural foci of leptospirosis (115). The isolation of 1424 strains (29 serovars) of pathogenic leptospires from natural waters and wet soils in Malaysia (1) was consistent with the infection by diverse serovars in troops who had operated in this area (115). Leptospires excreted in the urine of animals survive up to 15 days in humid soil under natural conditions (91). In the U.S. the dog has superceded the rodent as the major source of human leptospirosis (92). Human-to-human transmission of this infection occurs rarely. Leptospires usually enter the host through broken or altered skin and the mucous membranes. The major site of multiplication is the liver and other visceral tissues. With the development of antibodies that are leptospiricidal in the presence of complement (80), the leptospires are eliminated from the host, with the exception of the kidney, eyes, and brain where they may persist for extended periods of time. Abortion is a common sign of leptospirosis in cattle and swine. Recurrent uveitis (moon blindness) of horses is associated with this infection (121).

NUTRITION AND GROWTH REQUIREMENTS

Since they have not been successfully cultivated in artificial media, little is known about the growth requirements of *Treponema pallidum* (venereal and endemic syphilis), *T. pertenue* (yaws), *T. carateum* (pinta), *T. paraluis-cuniculi* (rabbit syphilis), the *Cristispira,* and *Spirochaeta plicatilis.*

The *Spirochaeta* are anaerobic with the exception of *S. aurantia* and *S. halophila,* which are facultatively anaerobic (18, 45). When these spirochetes are grown in the presence of oxygen, a carotenoid pigment is synthesized resulting in colonies with a yellow-orange or red color (13, 45). The other *Spirochaeta* are nonpigmented. These spirochetes have a fermentative metabolism with carbohydrates serving as their source of energy. Most of the *Spirochaeta* that have been cultured grow well in media of appropriate osmolarity containing a fermentable carbohydrate, yeast extract, peptone, mineral salts, and reducing agents. *Spirochaeta litoralis,* a marine mud isolate, has been grown in chemically defined media containing glucose, NH_4Cl, or amino acids, sulfide, NaCl, vitamins, coenzyme A, and inorganic salts (59). The optimal temperature range for *Spirochaeta zuelzerae, Spirochaeta halophila,* and *Spirochaeta stenostrepta* is 35–40°C whereas 30°C is optimal for *S. litoralis* and *Spirochaeta aurantia* (18, 45).

The treponemes that have been cultivated are anaerobic and fermentative. Amino acids and/or carbohydrates serve as sources of energy (141, 142). Good treponemal growth is obtained in media containing glucose, yeast extract, peptone, reducing agents, and serum or short-chain fatty acids. A defined medium for *Treponema phagedenis,* biotype Reiter, has been formulated that contains amino acids, glucose, a pyrimidine, vitamins, serum albumin, and inorganic salts (147). The majority of the host-associated treponemes grow best at 37°C (141). The pathogenic treponemes that have not been cultivated are propagated in laboratory animals (e.g. *T. pallidum* by intratesticular inoculation of rabbits). The feasibility of utilizing tissue culture for the cultivation of *T. pallidum* is under investigation (35, 36, 87, 133). The one pathogenic treponeme, *Treponema hyodysenteriae,* that can be cultivated grows well in Trypticase soy broth containing 10% fetal calf serum (96).

In 1971 the first satisfactory medium for the cultivation of the relapsing fever borreliae was described by Kelly (93). This medium was suitable for the growth of *Borrelia hermsii, B. parkeri,* and *B. turicatae,* the American tick-borne relapsing fever borreliae (94). The louse-borne *B. recurrentis* could be isolated in this medium but could not be subcultured in it (30). Recently, Kelly formulated two additional media that will support the growth and successful subculture of *B. recurrentis* and

B. hispancia (94). These media are relatively complex, containing glucose, peptones, yeast extract, pyruvate, citrate, cystine, N-acetylglucosamine, asparagine, glutamine, choline, ascorbic acid, gelatin, bovine albumin, rabbit serum, and inorganic salts (94). The *Borrelia* are fermentative spirochetes. In contrast to the *Spirochaeta* and *Treponema,* which produce a number of acids as end products of fermentation, the *Borrelia* only produce lactic acid from glucose (94). *Borrelia* cultures are incubated at 35°C (93, 94). Stoenner (148) reported that Kelly's medium was excellent for supporting the growth of adapted strains of *B. hermsii* but somewhat inefficient for isolating the spirochete from blood.

The *Leptospira* are probably the most readily cultivated of all the spirochetes. They are aerobic and their nutritional requirements are simple. Leptospires cannot use amino acids (82) or carbohydrates (74) as major sources of energy. Instead, long-chain fatty acids are beta-oxidized to provide their energy needs (56, 78, 85). Ammonium salts effectively provide the leptospiral nitrogen requirements (76) whereas amino acids do not (82). Serum-containing media have been replaced largely by media containing bovine albumin, fatty acids, ammonium chloride, vitamins B_1 and B_{12}, and inorganic salts (31, 77). The addition of pyruvate to these media augments the initiation of leptospiral growth from small inocula (86). Several chemically defined media have been proposed (55, 126, 138, 146). Generally, these media will only support the growth of a limited number of leptospiral strains and inconsistency in their growth-promoting capacity is frequently encountered.

ISOLATION TECHNIQUES

The small, thin spirochetes possess several characteristics that facilitate their isolation. Their narrow diameter, flexibility, shape, and unique motility permit them to pass through 0.1- to 0.45-μm-pore-size filters and to migrate through solid media containing as much at 1% agar. With the exception of thin spirilla and small vibrios, most bacteria do not have these capabilities. An isolation method has been described that utilizes both the filterability and migration ability of the spirochetes (112, 140). The test material is introduced onto a membrane filter placed on the surface of an agar medium and incubated under the appropriate conditions. Spirochetes will pass through the filter into the medium and multiply. Spirochetal growth is visualized as a haze in the medium (subsurface growth veil) that extends toward the periphery of the plate. If the medium is not nutritionally adequate or the spirochetes are not actively motile, their multiplication will be restricted to the area beneath the filter. The filtration technique and the migration in agar method, separately or in combination, have been used for the isolation of *Treponema* (48, 112, 141), *Spirochaeta* (14, 19, 20), and *Leptospira* (8, 57, 130, 140). The isolation of leptospires from contaminated materials is augmented by the addition of the antibacterial pyrimidine analogue 5'-fluorouracil to the isolation media (83). The insensitivity of leptospires to this analogue is due to their inability to utilize exogenously supplied pyrimidines (82). Nalidixic acid (57) and neomycin (120) have also been used for the isolation of leptospires. Several antibiotics have been incorporated into isolation media for *Treponema* (48, 141).

CONCLUDING REMARKS

A great deal has been learned about the spirochetes, especially during the past 15 years, and it is readily apparent that much remains to be known about this group of bacteria. Many intriguing questions concerning the basic biology of the spirochetes remain to be answered. Limited information is available for their classification. Differentiations are based on a few characteristics, some of which are essentially quantitative. Properties reflecting genotype need to be analyzed in greater depth. Spirochetal diseases remain an important public health problem throughout the world, and there are obvious gaps in our understanding of these diseases. The use of a vaccine to control syphilis needs to be explored but is hindered by our inability to cultivate *Treponema pallidum* in sufficient numbers. Progress in this area will depend to a great extent on a multidisciplinary and coordinated approach. Leptospirosis and the relapsing fevers are frequently misdiagnosed and affect more people than reports indicate. These rather complex zoonoses are maintained in natural foci and small outbreaks will continue to occur with possibly increasing frequency due to greater utilization of wilderness areas. Unfortunately, the competency to investigate these problems is rapidly being lost on a worldwide basis because of the lack of interest and support.

Acknowledgments

I have been supported by Public Health Service Grants AI 06589, AI 08124, and AI 12978 from the National Institute of Allergy and Infectious Diseases.

Literature Cited

1. Alexander, A. D., Evans, L. B., Baker, M. F., Baker, H. J., Ellison, D., Marriapan, M. 1975. *Appl. Microbiol.* 29: 30–33
2. Anderson, D. L., Johnson, R. C. 1968. *J. Bacteriol.* 95:2293–99
3. Auran, N. E. 1972. *Morphologic, antigenic and immunogenic aspects of Leptospira.* PhD thesis. Univ. Minn., Minneapolis. 112 pp.
4. Auran, N. E., Johnson, R. C., Ritzi, D. M. 1972. *Infect. Immun.* 5:968–75
5. Azuma, I., Taniyama, T., Yamamura, Y., Yanagihara, Y., Hattori, Y., Yasuda, S., Mifuchi, I. 1975. *Jpn. J. Microbiol.* 19:45–51
6. Ball, G. H. 1969. In *Research in Protozology,* ed. T.-T. Chen, 3:565–718. New York: Pergamon. 745 pp.
7. Balows, A., Feeley, J. C., Jaffe, H. 1976. In *The Biology of the Parasitic Spirochetes,* ed. R. C. Johnson, pp. 201–8. New York: Academic. 410 pp.
8. Baseman, J. B., Henneberry, R. C., Cox, C. D. 1966. *J. Bacteriol.* 91: 1374–75
9. Bey, R. F., Auran, N. E., Johnson, R. C. 1974. *Infect. Immun.* 10:1051–56
10. Bharier, M. A., Eiserling, F. A., Rittenberg, S. C. 1971. *J. Bacteriol.* 105: 413–21
11. Birch-Andersen, A., Hovind-Hougen, K., Borg-Petersen, C. 1973. *Acta Pathol. Microbiol. Scand.* 81:665–76
12. Brendle, J. J., Alexander, A. D. 1974. *Appl. Microbiol.* 28:505–6
13. Breznak, J. A. 1973. *Crit. Rev. Microbiol.* 2:457–89
14. Breznak, J. A., Canale-Parola, E. 1969. *J. Bacteriol.* 97:386–95
15. Bryant, M. P. 1952. *J. Bacteriol.* 64:325–35
16. Bryceson, A. D. M., Parry, E. H. O., Perine, P. L., Warrell, D. A., Vukotich, D., Leithead, C. S. 1970. *Q. J. Med.* 39:129–70
17. Burgdorfer, W. See Ref. 7, pp. 191–200
18. Canale-Parola, E. 1974. In *Bergy's Manual of Determinative Bacteriology,* ed. R. Buchanan, N. Gibbons, pp. 168–71. Baltimore: Williams and Wilkins. 1246 pp.

19. Canale-Parola, E., Holt, S. C., Udris, Z. 1967. *Arch. Mikrobiol.* 59:41–48
20. Canale-Parola, E., Udris, Z., Mandel, M. 1968. *Arch. Mikrobiol.* 63:385–97
21. Charon, N. W., Johnson, R. C., Muschel, L. H. 1975. *Infect. Immun.* 12:1386–91
22. Christiansen, S. 1963. *Lancet* 1:423–25
23. Cinco, M., Babudieri, B. 1974. *Folia Fac. Med. Univ. Comenianae Bratisl.* 12: (Suppl.) 147–55
24. Cox, P. J., Twigg, G. I. 1974. *Nature* 250:260–61
25. Cutler, J. C. See Ref. 7, pp. 365–73
26. Davis, C. P., Mulcahy, D., Takeuchi, A., Savage, D. C. 1972. *Infect. Immun.* 6:184–92
27. DePamphilis, M. L., Adler, J. 1971. *J. Bacteriol.* 105:384–95
28. Diesch, S. L., McCulloch, W. F., Braun, J. L., Ellinghausen, H. C. 1966. *Nature* 209:939–40
29. Dimitroff, V. T. 1927. *J. Infect. Dis.* 40:508–15
30. Dodge, R. W. 1973. *Appl. Microbiol.* 25:935–39
31. Ellinghausen, H. C., McCullough, W. G. 1965. *Am. J. Vet. Res.* 26:45–51
32. Eriksen, L., Andersen, S. 1970. *Nord. Veterinaermed.* 22:161–73
33. Felsenfeld, O. 1971. *Borrelia, Strains, Vectors, Human and Animal Borreliosis,* pp. 3–98. St. Louis: Warren H. Green. 180 pp.
34. Felsenfeld, O. See Rcf. 33, pp. 139–42
35. Fitzgerald, T. J., Miller, J. N., Sykes, J. A. 1975. *Infect. Immun.* 11:1133–40
36. Fitzgerald, T. J., Miller, J. N., Sykes, J. A., Johnson, R. C. See Ref. 7, pp. 57–64
37. Fribourg-Blanc, A., Mollaret, H. H. 1968. *WHO Vener. Dis. Treponematoses Res.* 68:135–36
38. Fulghum, R. S., Moore, W. E. 1963. *J. Bacteriol.* 85:808–15
39. Geigy, R. 1968. In *Infectious Blood Diseases of Man and Animals,* eds. D. Weinman, M. Ristic, 2:175–216. New York: Academic. 576 pp.
40. Gibbons, R. J., van Houte, J. 1975. *Ann. Rev. Microbiol.* 29:19–44
41. Ginger, C. D. 1963. *Nature* 199:159
42. Glosser, J. W., Johnson, R. C., Sulzer, C. R., Auran, N. E. 1974. *Am. J. Vet. Res.* 35:681–84
43. Goldhaber, P., Giddon, D. B. 1964. *Int. Dent. J.* 14:468–96
44. Greenberg, E. P., Canale-Parola, E. 1975. *J. Bacteriol.* 123:1006–12
45. Greenberg, E. P., Canale-Parola, E. 1976. *Arch. Microbiol.* 110:185–94
46. Hackett, C. J. 1963. *Bull. WHO* 29: 7–41
47. Hampp, E. G., Mergenhagen, S. E. 1961. *J. Infect. Dis.* 109:43–61
48. Hanson, A. W. 1970. *Br. J. Vener. Dis.* 46:303–6
49. Hanson, L. E. See Ref. 7, pp. 295–306
50. Hanson, L. E., Tripathy, D. N., Evans, L. B., Alexander, A. D. 1974. *Int. J. Syst. Bacteriol.* 24:355–57
51. Hardy, P. H. See Ref. 7, pp. 107–19
52. Hardy, P. H., Nell, E. E. 1955. *J. Exp. Med.* 101:367–82
53. Hardy, P. H., Nell, E. E. 1961. *J. Bacteriol.* 82:967–78
54. Harris, D. L., Glock, R. D., Kinyon, J. M. See Ref. 7, pp. 277–93
55. Henneberry, R. C., Baseman, J. B., Cox, C. D. 1970. *Antonie van Leeuwenhoek J. Microbiol. Serol.* 36:496–501
56. Henneberry, R. C., Cox, C. D. 1970. *Can. J. Microbiol.* 16:41–45
57. Henry, R. A. 1972. *Ecological studies on the genus Leptospira.* PhD thesis. Univ. Minn., Minneapolis. 168 pp.
58. Henry, R. A., Johnson, R. C., Bohlool, B. B., Schmidt, E. L. 1971. *Appl. Microbiol.* 21:953–56
59. Hespell, R. B., Canale-Parola, E. 1970. *Arch. Mikrobiol.* 74:1–18
60. Heylings, R. T. 1967. *Br. Dent. J.* 122:51–56
61. Holt, S. C., Canale-Parola, E. 1968. *J. Bacteriol.* 96:822–33
62. Hovind-Hougen, K. 1972. *Acta Pathol. Microbiol. Scand.* 80:297–304
63. Hovind-Hougen, K. 1974. *Acta Pathol. Microbiol. Scand.* 82:329–44
64. Hovind-Hougen, K. 1974. *Acta Pathol. Microbiol. Scand.* 82:495–507
65. Hovind-Hougen, K. 1974. *Acta Pathol. Microbiol. Scand.* 82:799–809
66. Hovind-Hougen, K. 1975. *Acta Pathol. Microbiol. Scand.* 83:91–99
67. Hovind-Hougen, K. See Ref. 7, pp. 7–18
68. Hovind-Hougen, K., Birch-Andersen, A. 1971. *Acta Pathol. Microbiol. Scand.* 79:37–50
69. Hovind-Hougen, K., Birch-Andersen, A., Jensen, H. S. 1976. *Acta Pathol Microbiol. Scand.* 84:101–8
70. Jackson, S., Black, S. H. 1971. *Arch. Mikrobiol.* 76:308–24
71. Jackson, S., Black, S. H. 1971. *Arch. Mikrobiol.* 76:325–40
72. Jahn, T. L., Bovee, E. C. 1965. *Ann. Rev. Microbiol.* 19:21–58
73. Johnson, D. W. 1950. *Med. J. Aust.* 2:724–31

74. Johnson, R. C. 1965. *Bacteriol. Proc.* 65:54 (Abstr.)
75. Johnson, R. C., Eggebraten, L. M. 1971. *Infect. Immun.* 3:723–26
76. Johnson, R. C., Gary, N. D. 1962. *J. Bacteriol.* 83:668–72
77. Johnson, R. C., Harris, V. G. 1967. *J. Bacteriol.* 94:27–31
78. Johnson, R. C., Livermore, B. P., Jenkin, H. M., Eggebraten, L. 1970. *Infect. Immun.* 2:606–9
79. Johnson, R. C., Livermore, B. P., Walby, J. K., Jenkin, H. M. 1970. *Infect. Immun.* 2:286–91
80. Johnson, R. C., Muschel, L. H. 1966. *J. Bacteriol.* 91:1403–9
81. Johnson, R. C., Ritzi, D. M., Livermore, B. P. 1973. *Infect. Immun.* 8:291–95
82. Johnson, R. C., Rogers, P. 1964. *Arch. Biochem. Biophys.* 107:459–70
83. Johnson, R. C., Rogers, P. 1964. *J. Bacteriol.* 87:422–25
84. Johnson, R. C., Wachter, M. S., Ritzi, D. M. 1973. *Infect. Immun.* 7:249–58
85. Johnson, R. C., Walby, J. K. 1972. *Appl. Microbiol.* 23:1027–31
86. Johnson, R. C., Walby, J. K., Henry, R. A., Auran, N. E. 1973. *Appl. Microbiol.* 26:118–19
87. Jones, R. H., Finn, M. A., Thomas, J. J., Folger, C. 1976. *Br. J. Vener. Dis.* 52:18–23
88. Joseph, R. 1972. *J. Bacteriol.* 112: 629–31
89. Joseph, R., Holt, S. C., Canale-Parola, E. 1973. *J. Bacteriol.* 115:426–35
90. Kaiser, G. E., Doetsch, R. N. 1975. *Nature* 255:656–57
91. Karaseva, E. V., Chernukha, Y. G., Piskunova, L. A. 1973. *J. Hyg. Epidemiol. Microbiol. Immunol.* 17:339–45
92. Kaufmann, A. F. See Ref. 7, pp. 177–89
93. Kelly, R. 1971. *Science* 173:443–44
94. Kelly, R. See Ref. 7, pp. 87–94
95. Kenney, E. B., Ash, M. M. 1969. *J. Periodontol.* 40:630–33
96. Kinyon, J. M., Harris, D. L. 1974. *Vet. Rec.* 95:219–20
97. Klaviter, E. C. 1975. *The biology of the relapsing fever causing Borrelia.* PhD thesis. Univ. Minn., Minneapolis. 80 pp.
98. Kuhn, D. A. See Ref. 18, pp. 171–74
99. Leach, W. D., Lee, A., Stubbs, R. P. 1973. *Infect. Immun.* 7:961–72
100. Lee, F. D., Kraszewski, A., Gordon, J., Howie, J. G. R., McSeveney, D., Harland, W. A. 1971. *Gut* 12:126–33
101. Listgarten, M. A. 1965. *J. Periodontol.* 36:328–39
102. Listgarten, M. A., Lewis, D. W. 1967. *J. Periodontol.* 38:379–86
103. Listgarten, M. A., Mayo, H. E., Tremblay, R. 1975. *J. Periodontol.* 46:10–26
104. Listgarten, M. A., Socransky, S. S. 1964. *J. Bacteriol.* 88:1087–1103
105. Listgarten, M. A., Socransky, S. S. 1965. *Arch. Oral Biol.* 10:127–38
106. Livermore, B. P., Johnson, R. C. 1970. *Biochim. Biophys. Acta* 210:315–18
107. Livermore, B. P., Johnson, R. C. 1974. *J. Bacteriol.* 120:1268–73
108. Livermore, B. P., Johnson, R. C. 1975. *Can. J. Microbiol.* 21:1877–80
109. Livermore, B. P., Johnson, R. C., Jenkin, H. M. 1969. *Lipids* 4:166–67
110. Löe, H., Theilade, E., Jensen, S. B. 1965. *J. Periodontol.* 36:177–87
111. Loesche, W. J. See Ref. 7, pp. 261–75
112. Loesche, W. J., Socransky, S. S. 1962. *Science* 138:139–40
113. MacDonald, J. B., Gibbons, R. J., Socransky, S. S. 1960. *Ann. NY Acad. Sci.* 85:467–78
114. MacDonald, J. B., Socransky, S. S., Gibbons, R. J. 1963. *J. Dent. Res.* 42:529–45
115. McCrumb, F. R. Jr., Stockard, C. R., Robinson, L. H., Turner, L. H., Levis, D. G., Maisey, C. W., Kelleher, M. F., Gleiser, C. A., Smadel, J. E. 1957. *Am. J. Trop. Med. Hyg.* 6:238–56
116. McIntyre, W. I. M., Seiler, H. E. 1953. *J. Hyg.* 51:330–39
117. Metzger, M., Podwinska, J. 1966. *Arch. Immunol. Ther. Exp.* 14:594–601
118. Meyer, H., Meyer, F. 1971. *Biochim. Biophys. Acta* 231:93–106
119. Meyers, D. M. 1976. *J. Clin. Microbiol.* 3:548–55
120. Meyers, D. M., Varela-Diaz, V. M. 1973. *Appl. Microbiol.* 25:781–86
121. Morter, R. L., Williams, R. D., Bolte, H., Freeman, M. J. 1969. *J. Am. Vet. Med. Assoc.* 155:436–42
122. Murray, R. G. E., Steed, P., Elson, H. E. 1965. *Can. J. Microbiol.* 11:547–60
123. Nauman, R. K., Holt, S. C., Cox, C. D. 1969. *J. Bacteriol.* 98:264–80
124. Onisi, M., Kondo, W., Horiuchi, I., Uchiyama, Y. 1960. *Bull. Tokyo Med. Dent. Univ.* 7:161–66
125. Ovchinnikov, N. M., Delektorskii, V. V. 1969. *Br. J. Vener. Dis.* 45:87–116
126. Phibbs, P. V. Jr., Van Eseltine, W. P. 1968. *J. Infect. Dis.* 118:197–205
127. Pillot, J., Ryter, A. 1965. *Ann. Inst. Pasteur Paris* 108:791–804
128. Ritchie, A. E. See Ref. 7, pp. 19–37
129. Ritchie, A. E., Ellinghausen, H. C. 1965. *J. Bacteriol.* 89:223–33

130. Rittenberg, M. B., Linscott, W. D., Ball, M. G. 1958. *J. Bacteriol.* 76: 669–70
131. Rosebury, T. 1962. *Microorganisms Indigenous to Man,* pp. 186–221. New York: McGraw-Hill
132. Ryter, A., Pillot, J. 1965. *Ann. Inst. Pasteur Paris* 109:552–62
133. Sandok, P. L., Knight, S. T., Jenkin, H. M. 1976. *J. Clin. Microbiol.* 4:360–71
134. Sanford, J. P. See Ref. 7, pp. 307–15
135. Savage, D. C., McAllister, J. S., Davis, C. P. 1971. *Infect. Immun.* 4:492–502
136. Sazerac, R., Levaditi, C. 1922. *C. R. Soc. Biol.* 173:128–31
137. Schultz-Haudt, S., Bruce, M. A., Bibby, B. G. 1954. *J. Dent. Res.* 33:454–58
138. Shenberg, E. 1967. *J. Bacteriol.* 93: 1598–606
139. Sleight, S. D., Lundberg, A. M. 1961. *J. Am. Vet. Med. Assoc.* 139:455–56
140. Smibert, R. M. 1965. *Can. J. Microbiol.* 11:743–44
141. Smibert, R. M. 1973. *Crit. Rev. Microbiol.* 2:491–544
142. Smibert, R. M. See Ref. 7, pp. 175–84
143. Smith, J. L., Pesetsky, B. R. 1967. *Br. J. Vener. Dis.* 43:117–27
144. Socransky, S. S., Listgarten, M., Hubersak, C., Cotmore, J., Clark, A. 1969. *J. Bacteriol.* 98:878–82
145. Socransky, S. S., Loesche, W. J., Hubersak, C., MacDonald, J. B. 1964. *J. Bacteriol.* 88:200–9
146. Stalheim, O. H. V., Wilson, J. B. 1964. *J. Bacteriol.* 88:48–54
147. Steinman, H. G., Eagle, H., Oyama, V. I. 1952. *J. Bacteriol.* 64:265–69
148. Stoenner, H. G. 1974. *Appl. Microbiol.* 28:540–43
149. Sullivan, N. D. 1972. *Aust. Vet. J.* 48:388–90
150. Takeuchi, A., Jervis, H. R., Nakazawa, H., Robinson, D. M. 1974. *Am. J. Clin. Nutr.* 27:1287–96
151. Takeuchi, A., Zeller, J. A. 1972. *Infect. Immun.* 6:1008–9
152. Tarizzo, M. L. 1973. *Pan. Am. Health Organ. Sci. Publ.* 263:50–59
153. Taylor, D. J., Alexander, T. J. L. 1971. *Br. Vet. J.* 127:58–61
154. Tinelli, R., Pillot, J. 1966. *C. R. Acad. Sci. Paris* 263:739–41
155. Tumilowicz, J. J., Alexander, A. D., Stafford, K. 1974. *In Vitro* 10:238–42
156. Turner, L. H. See Ref. 18, pp. 190–92
157. Turner, L. H. See Ref. 7, pp. 95–106
158. Tyson, G. E. 1970. *J. Invertebr. Pathol.* 15:145–47
159. Van der Holden, J. 1966. *Ann. Soc. Belge. Med. Trop.* 46:171–72
160. VanEseltine, W. P. 1972. In *The fine Morphology of Spirochaetas,* ed. B. Babudieri, pp. 63–75. Rome: Leonardo Edizioni Scientifiche. 210 pp.
161. Wachter, M. S., Johnson, R. C. 1976. *Proc. Soc. Exp. Biol. Med.* 151:97–100
162. Willcox, R. R. 1974. *Br. J. Vener. Dis.* 50:169–78
163. Willcox, R. R., Guthe, T. 1966. *Treponema pallidum.* A bibliographical review of the morphology, culture and survival of *T. pallidum* and associated organisms. *Suppl. Bull. WHO* 169 pp.
164. Yanagawa, R., Faine, S. 1966. *Nature* 211:823–26
165. Yanagihara, Y., Mifuchi, I. 1968. *J. Bacteriol.* 95:2403–6
166. Yokoyama, M. T., Davis, C. L. 1971. *J. Bacteriol.* 107:519–27
167. Zeigler, J. A., VanEseltine, W. P. 1975. *Can. J. Microbiol.* 21:1102–12

Ann. Rev. Microbiol. 1977. 31:107–33

MICROBIAL ECOLOGY OF THE GASTROINTESTINAL TRACT

❖1699

Dwayne C. Savage
Department of Microbiology and School of Basic Medical Sciences, University of Illinois, Urbana, Illinois 61801

CONTENTS

INTRODUCTION 107
MICROBIAL ECOLOGY AS APPLIED TO THE GASTROINTESTINAL TRACT 108
MICROBIAL HABITATS IN THE MAMMALIAN GASTROINTESTINAL TRACT 110
COMPOSITION AND LOCALIZATION OF CLIMAX COMMUNITIES IN ADULTS 111
Some Comments on Methods 111
The Stomach (Esophagus) 112
The Small Bowel 115
The Large Bowel 116
The Feces 118
SUCCESSION IN BABIES 119
FACTORS INFLUENCING COMPOSITION OF THE MICROBIOTA 121
Forces Exerted by the Host and Its Diet and Environment 121
Forces Resulting from Activities of the Microbes Themselves 126
HOW MICROBES IN THE BIOTA MAKE THEIR LIVING (NICHES) 127
SUMMARY AND CONCLUSIONS 129

INTRODUCTION

The adult human organism is said to be composed of approximately 10^{13} eukaryotic animal cells (27). That statement is only an expression of a particular point of view. The various body surfaces and the gastrointestinal canals of humans may be colonized by as many as 10^{14} indigenous prokaryotic and eukaryotic microbial cells (70). These microbes profoundly influence some of the physiological processes of their animal host (49, 103). From another point of view, therefore, the normal human organism can be said to be composed of over 10^{14} cells, of which only about 10% are animal cells.

The vast majority of the microbial cells in that mass reside someplace in the gastrointestinal tract (70). In this review, I examine some evidence derived from studies of various aspects of the gastrointestinal microbiota of nonruminant mammals, evaluating that evidence in terms of some simplified concepts of ecological theory. In so doing, I present my opinion of the current level of understanding of the ecology of the gastrointestinal tract and attempt to illustrate some possible directions for experimental attempts to further that understanding. Emphasis is placed upon comparing the biotas of different mammalian species, including the human.

Much information on the microbiota of the human gastrointestinal tract has been summarized in recent books (29, 30). Therefore, discussion of the human biota will be limited primarily to findings published since 1970, which can be used in comparing the human microflora with that of other mammalian species. In developing this review, I drew heavily from information given in the proceedings of four symposia on intestinal microecology held at Columbia, Missouri, in 1970 (40), 1972 (71), 1974 (41), and 1976 (72), and I acknowledge with gratitude my debt to the conveners of those symposia.

MICROBIAL ECOLOGY AS APPLIED TO THE GASTROINTESTINAL TRACT

In 1965, Dubos et al attempted to organize around ecological principles information available at the time on the gastrointestinal microbiota (31). They hypothesized that the gastrointestinal microflora, which they called the "indigenous flora," of any given animal species is made up of microorganisms present during evolution of the animal (the autochthonous microbiota), those so ubiquitous in the animal's community that they establish in all its members (the normal microbiota), and true pathogens that have been accidentally acquired and are capable of persisting in the system. These ideas provided a rational basis for research and a useful theoretical framework within which both old and new observations could be organized.

These concepts give some problems, however, when they are considered in reference to ecological theory as applied more recently to microorganisms (3). As described in its simplest form, a microbial ecosystem is the complex of microbes in a specified environment and the surroundings with which the organisms are associated (3). Any given ecosystem contains habitats and niches for the microbes in it. Habitats, physical spaces in the system, are occupied normally by climax communities of autochthonous (indigenous) microbes. The way in which any such organism makes its living in its habitat defines its niche in the ecosystem. Pristine habitats first made available to the microbial world, such as the gastrointestinal tract of a newborn baby, are colonized by microbes in characteristic successions. The types of microbes that colonize any given habitat and niche are influenced by forces exerted by the environment (allogenic succession) and by changes in the environment induced by the microbial colonizers themselves (autogenic succession) (3).

Allochthonous (nonindigenous) microbes might be found in any given habitat in any given system. Normally, these latter organisms contribute little to the local economy (3). They are not characteristic of the habitat and may be present only in dormant form. In habitats, in flowing streams, such as the gastrointestinal canal, allochthonous microbes may be just passing through. Such transient microbes may, on occasion, fill a niche in a habitat when it is vacated for some reason by its autochthonous inhabitants. Presumably, however, an autochthonous species would vacate its niche only if the system were perturbed in some abnormal way and would reoccupy it, evicting the allochthonous species, once the system returned to normal.

Dubos et al (31) recognized that microbial types found in the gastrointestinal tract of animals can be differentiated into two major groups: autochthonous and normal biotas. Their definitions of these two biotas does not conform, however, to the concepts of autochthony and allochthony as presented above. As described in those concepts, autochthonous and indigenous are synonyms. So an indigenous biota can be composed only of populations of autochthonous microbial types. The key to the problem lies in how Dubos et al regarded the microbes they called "normal biota." They did not regard them as transients or allochthonous microbes as such but as "so ubiquitous in a given community, they become established in practically all its members. . . ." (31). That these microbes could "establish" in the tracts of animals in a given community requires that habitats and niches exist there for them. Normally, however, such would not be the case for allochthonous microbes. In a well-functioning gastrointestinal ecosystem, all available habitats and niches would be occupied by indigenous microbes (3). Any allochthonous species found in a given habitat, then, would not be established (implying that they had colonized and were multiplying) but would just be passing through, having arrived in the habitat in food, in water, from another habitat in the gastrointestinal tract, or from elsewhere on the animal's body. As noted, however, allochthonous microbes might colonize habitats vacated by their autochthonous inhabitants in a perturbed gastrointestinal ecosystem. Under such circumstances, the allochthonous organisms might be thought incorrectly to be members of the indigenous biota. I shall return later to this problem.

Gastrointestinal ecosystems are open, integrated, interactive units containing many microbial habitats. In the normal adult animal, each of these habitats is colonized by a microbial community consisting of one, and usually more, autochthonous (indigenous) microbial species. Each of these species occupies a niche in the habitat and thereby contributes in some way to the economy of the whole system. At any given time, allochthonous microbes may be found in any given habitat. Such microbes may derive from food, water, soil, air, and habitats on the skin, mouth, and upper respiratory membranes. In addition, they can derive from habitats in the alimentary system above the one in which they are identifiable as allochthonous, or even below it as in coprophagous animals (121). That is, a particular microbial species may be autochthonous to one habitat in the gastrointestinal canal but allochthonous to another, which it normally transits after it is shed from its native home.

The critical distinction is that an autochthonous microbe colonizes the habitat natively, whereas an allochthonous one cannot colonize it (i.e. multiply in it) except under abnormal circumstances. As shall be discussed subsequently, this concept has important implications for studies of the structure and organization of the interrelationships in the gastrointestinal ecosystem. As a consequence, in such studies, microbes autochthonous to a given habitat must be distinguished from those found in the habitat that are allochthonous to it (103).

Criteria for determining autochthony of microbes isolated from the gastrointestinal canal have been developed from analysis of the findings of several investigators (3, 31, 103). These criteria stipulate that autochthonous gastrointestinal microorganisms (i) can grow anaerobically, (ii) are always found in normal adults, (iii) colonize particular areas of the tract, (iv) colonize their habitats during succession in infant animals, (v) maintain stable population levels in climax communities in normal adults, and (vi) may associate intimately with the mucosal epithelium in the area colonized. They undoubtedly are incomplete and may have to be revised again and again as new discoveries emerge. As presently constituted, however, they have been useful when indigenous microbes must be distinguished from nonindigenous ones in studies of the mechanisms of interactions between microbes in the gastrointestinal tract and their animal hosts (103). As shall be demonstrated subsequently, they are useful also to investigators developing and evaluating studies of the composition, localization, and succession of microbial communities in the gastrointestinal ecosystem.

MICROBIAL HABITATS IN THE MAMMALIAN GASTROINTESTINAL TRACT

The gastrointestinal tract of a mammal has five major areas: esophagus, stomach, small intestine, cecum, and large intestine (119). Depending upon the animal species, any of these areas may be further compartmentalized or divided into subareas. Three fundamental variations on the overall theme can be recognized, i.e. ruminant, cecal, and "straight tube." The first two variations are seen in animals exclusively or predominantly herbivorous. Both involve adaptations of the tract in which coarse, fibrous food is delayed in transit and exposed to microbial degradation from which the animal derives nutritional benefit.

In the ruminant, the stomach is enlarged and ramified into compartments, the first of which is essentially a fermentation vat (58). Microbes in the vat have first approach to the animal's food. In the main, the adult ruminant is dependent for its nutrition upon the microbes and their metabolic end products (58). By contrast, a cecum is a blind sac extending from the side of the otherwise straight intestinal canal at the end of the small intestine and beginning of the large (119). Animals with a cecum have first approach to their own food and, thus, by virtue of the action of their own digestive enzymes, derive from it a large (but variable, depending upon the species and the food) proportion of its nutrient value. Nevertheless, in some such animal species, microbial activity in the cecum may provide as much as 25–35% of the animal's nutritional needs (76, 77).

Animals with straight-tube intestinal canals are omnivores or meat eaters. Such animals consume comparatively little material indigestible by their own enzymes. As a consequence, during evolution they either never developed or diminished in size and complexity the modified stomach or cecum needed to slow the passage of the food to allow for microbial degradation. Such an animal is the human (119).

The structure of the gastrointestinal tract dictates the localization of the microbiota and, to some extent, the composition of the microbiota as well. As noted, this review concerns current knowledge of the biotas of nonruminant mammals, meaning therefore mammals with a cecum or a straight tube. It must be noted, however, that knowledge of the ruminant biota has contributed significantly to current understanding of that of the other animal types. Moreover, as is becoming more and more evident, the biotas of the rumen, cecum, and large bowels of man and other animals have striking similarities (15, 126).

In all three types of tracts, microbial habitats may exist in any area from the esophagus to the anus. Some of these habitats may cover visible areas of the mucosal epithelium, others may be of microscopic dimension, i.e. microhabitats. They may occur in any major area of the tract, in the lumen, on an epithelial surface, or deep in the crypts of Lieberkuhn in the mucosa (105). The lumen[1] can be colonized by microbes in any area of the tract but may be colonized normally only in areas of relative stasis, such as the rumen, cecum, and large intestine, where the flow rate of the contents does not exceed the doubling rate of the microbial population levels. The epithelial surface also can be colonized in any area by characteristic biotas and, as shall be seen, frequently is, depending upon the animal species. Similarly, in some animal species, the mucosal crypts may possess microbiotas distinct from either the lumenal or epithelial biotas. Each of these general types of habitat apparently provided for its microbial colonizers a different type of environmental or nutritional challenge (3). Unfortunately, as shall be seen, little detailed evidence is available on this point.

COMPOSITION AND LOCALIZATION OF CLIMAX COMMUNITIES IN ADULTS

Some Comments on Methods

For most of the years during which the science of microbiology developed, *Escherichia coli* was thought by most persons concerned to be the chief inhabitant of the animal bowel. As is now well known, *E. coli* is actually a minority inhabitant of most gastrointestinal ecosystems. This confusion arose primarily because until about the mid-1960s the methods now in use for culturing oxygen-intolerant anaerobic bacteria either were not used or were not available. Once investigators studying the intestinal microbiota of monogastric animals used such methods, especially those developed for culturing ruminant bacteria (58), they quickly found that in most systems in adults the strict anaerobes outnumbered the facultative microbes such as *E. coli* by as much as 1000 to 1 (50, 66, 107).

[1]The lumen of any region of the tract can be regarded as a habitat only in the sense that microbes can colonize material found in it. In many cases, the true habitats of microbes in the lumen may be the surfaces of particles of solid material such as food stuffs (2).

Advances have been made in methods for culturing anaerobic bacteria, particularly in techniques for avoiding exposure of natural samples and the microbes themselves to oxygen and oxidized environments (39, 71, 85). Nevertheless, many microbial forms that can be seen with microscopes in various habitats in the gastrointestinal tracts of several mammalian species have not been cultured in recognizable form (6, 20–22, 106, 122). Moreover, in most studies, the investigators' estimate based upon viable count of the total of the individual population levels of all microbial types cultured, for example, from human feces (54, 85), is rarely more than two thirds of the total level of all types present based upon microscopic clump count. Thus, some technical problems remain to be solved in methods of culturing microbes from the gastrointestinal tract.

Even if all such problems can be solved and all microbial types present in a given gastrointestinal habitat can be cultured, an investigator still will be faced with the problem of determining whether or not a particular microbial type is indigenous to that habitat or merely a transient passing through the area. Such a determination is compounded in difficulty if the animals are housed conventionally so that they are exposed continuously to exogenous microbes from air, soil, water, food, and other sources. Allochthonous microbes entering the alimentary tract from such sources may be isolatable from habitats in the tract (101). A large number of microbial types may be involved. Moreover, in an ecosystem perturbed by intestinal disease, such as is likely to exist in an animal housed conventionally, allochthonous microbes may further confuse the issue by actually colonizing habitats vacated by their autochthonous inhabitants.

Animals can be housed under conditions in which they are protected from air, nutrients, and water containing microbes other than those from their own bodies (31, 109, 110). This procedure simplifies the study of the composition of the biota by reducing the number of exogenous species that appear in the system. Unfortunately, this example has not been followed in all investigations and is virtually impossible to follow in studies in which humans and some other primates are subjects. Nevertheless, if followed, the procedures facilitate the studies by simplifying decisions about autochthony or allochthony of microbial species isolated from the system. Because the model has not been adopted more widely, however, interpretation of the findings from many studies is most difficult. These difficulties will become clear during the discussion to come.

The Stomach (Esophagus)

Microorganisms of various types have been isolated from the contents of the stomachs of nonruminant mammals including the human (Table 1). The microbial types isolated and their population levels vary to some extent, depending upon the diets and environments of the animals, the microbiological methods used, and, especially when humans are the subjects, the geographical locale of the investigation. Indeed, results from studies of the composition of the gastric microbiota in humans have varied to such an extent that the stomach is reported to be free of communities of indigenous microbes. Any microbes isolated from gastric contents are considered

Table 1 Microorganisms isolated from the stomachs of nonruminant mammals[a]

Microbial type	Animal type yielding microbe					
	Human	Baboon	Swine	Rat	Mouse	Hamster
Lactobacilli	9, 86[b]	127	24, 25, 31, 125	31, 61, 90, 91, 93, 99, 100, 102	31, 103, 106, 107	61
Streptococci	30, 86	127	24, 25	61, 91, 98	31	61
Bifidobacteria	30			93		
Clostridia	86		24, 25	102		
Veillonella	86		125	61, 98		
Coliforms	86		24, 25, 125	61, 91, 98		61
Other bacterial types[c]	86		125	91, 98, 102		
Candida	52, 112		125			
Torulopsis	112			97, 103, 104	97, 103, 104	
Unidentified yeasts	86	127				61

[a]To be cited, in general a microbial type had to be isolated at an estimated population level exceeding 10^3 microbes/g of wet gastric content from a large proportion of the total number of individuals examined in the study.

[b]Reference.

[c]*Peptostreptococcus, Bacteroides, Staphylococcus, Actinobacillus.*

transients, either having passed down from habitats above the stomach or having been present in ingested materials (30).

Some nonruminant mammals, however, do have in their stomachs microorganisms believed to be indigenous to habitats in that region (103, 105). Unlike the human stomach, the stomach in rodents and certain other types of mammals is incompletely separated into at least two compartments, of which one is lined with stratified squamous epithelium and the other is lined with columnar secreting epithelium. In rodents, the stratified squamous epithelium is usually colonized by lactic acid bacteria (61, 107, 120, 124), whereas the columnar secreting epithelium may be colonized by yeasts, often of the genus *Torulopsis* (61, 97, 103–105). In some such animals, lactobacilli may also colonize the stratified squamous epithelium of the esophagus (107). Lactobacilli and yeasts also colonize the squamous epithelium of the pars oesophagia and the columnar epithelium of the stomachs of swine (125). Lactobacilli are known as well to colonize the squamous epithelium of the crops of chickens (13).

Microbial types other than lactic acid bacteria and yeasts have been found in the contents of the stomachs of both rodents and swine (Table 1). Nevertheless, only the lactic acid bacteria and yeasts are consistently reported to be present. Moreover, only these latter microbial types are known to associate with epithelial surfaces in the region (105), a characteristic that undoubtedly is critical for the maintenance of microbial communities in regions of the tract where the rate of passage of the contents exceeds the rate of multiplication of the microbes.[2] Many allochthonous microbial types can enter the gastric contents in materials ingested by animals housed under conventional conditions and fed nonsterile food and water. Coprophagic animals, such as rodents and swine, ingest in feces enormous numbers of microbes that are allochthonous to habitats in their stomachs. Similarly, allochthonous microbes may pass into the stomach from habitats above, either in secretions or in ingested materials. Lactobacilli and yeasts are known to be sufficiently aciduric to grow at high hydrogen ion concentrations (114, 118) such as are found in the stomach (43, 62). Any other microbial types found in the area must be regarded only as transients in the region until they can be shown to satisfy criteria for autochthony (see above) for habitats in that area.

The human stomach contains no stratified squamous epithelium and is lined throughout with columnar secreting epithelium (119). Nevertheless, lactic acid bacteria are commonly isolated from the human gastric contents (Table 1), especially when good anaerobic techniques are used (86). Moreover, *Candida* and some other yeast species are also often isolated from such contents (Table 1) when special effort is made to detect such microbes (52, 112). Thus, under proper conditions, communities of indigenous microbes may colonize habitats in the human stomach or esophagus. These communities may associate with epithelial surfaces on the gastric mucosa.

Microbes closely associated with an epithelium, especially if they are physically attached to the epithelial cells, may be isolatable only with difficulty from sampled contents. Even if they can be isolated from the contents, the estimates of their population levels may be unrealistically low. Estimates per unit weight of material of the population levels of microbes attached to an epithelial surface made from samples of the mucosa itself have been found to be higher than estimates made from lumenal content in the region (31). Thus, because of the methods they must use, investigators sampling the lumenal content of human stomachs may be underestimating the size or even misinterpreting the composition of gastric microbial communities.

Of course, such communities indeed may not be present in human stomachs sampled in most studies. In laboratory rodents, the communities of lactobacilli and yeast in the stomach disappear when the animals are starved or decline markedly in population level when diets of the animals are altered dramatically (123). Likewise, in swine (25), the types of lactic acid bacteria in the stomach reflect the type of diet the animals are consuming. Perhaps investigators fail to isolate microbes from the stomachs of humans in many studies because the individuals involved have been eating diets and living under conditions inappropriate for their species. In this sense then, the gastric ecosystem in humans in many areas of the world might be

[2]Stomachs may retain their contents long enough for microbes to grow in them, but they also can be empty for prolonged periods if the animal does not have continuous access to food. Thus, the only microbes that can remain in the region, undoubtedly, are those that attach to epithelial surfaces.

considered a perturbed one in which the microbial communities that should colonize surfaces there are simply not normally constructed in most individuals. Such a concept could help explain why results vary in studies of gastric biota from place to place in the world. Only further research, both microbiological and nutritional, can resolve these issues.

The Small Bowel

The mammalian small bowel can be divided into the upper, mid, and lower areas, called the duodenum, jejunum, and ileum, respectively (119). Microorganisms are isolated frequently from the contents taken from all regions of the small intestine of nonruminant mammals of several types (Table 2). The population levels are usually estimated to be highest in the lower portion (30).

Such findings are difficult to interpret. Any microbes isolated from small bowel content could just be passing down the bowel with digesting food, either from habitats above the small intestine or from outside of the body. In the lower part of the ileum, they could be microbes from the rich biota of the cecum (see below), finding their way by the ileocecal valve into the small intestine (30). In either case, the organisms would be only transients in the lumen of the small intestine and not indigenous inhabitants. This problem is difficult to resolve. The contents of the small intestine normally flow rapidly, possibly becoming static for any appreciable period only in the distal ileum (30). Thus, if any indigenous microbes colonize lumenal habitats in the small bowel, they probably do so only in the distal ileum in nonruminant mammals of most types.

In some animals, however, microbes that are undoubtedly indigenous to the habitat have been found colonizing the epithelial surface of most of the mid and

Table 2 Microorganisms isolated from the small bowels of nonruminant animals[a]

Microbial type	Animal type yielding microbe									
	Human		Baboon		Swine		Rat		Mouse	
	U[b]	L[b]	U	L	U	L	U	L	U	L
Lactobacilli	26, 30, 68, 86[c]	30, 86,	127	127	25, 93	25, 93	91, 102	91, 102	103	31, 103, 107
Streptococci	26, 30	30, 48, 74, 86	127	127	25	25, 93	102	91, 102		31
Bifidobacteria		74			93	93				
Clostridia	86	86		127				102		
Coliforms		30, 48, 74		127	25, 93	25, 93		91, 102		
Bacteroides	74	30, 74								
Veillonella	26	86								
Other bacterial types[d]	86	30, 86	127	127		25		91		
Yeasts	26		127	127		93	102	102	103	103

[a]To be cited, in general a microbial type had to be isolated at an estimated population level exceeding 10^3 microbes/g of intestinal content from a large proportion of individuals examined in the study.
[b]U, Upper (duodenum, upper jejunum); L, lower (lower jejunum, ileum).
[c]Reference.
[d]Gram-positive nonsporing anaerobes; other unidentified anareobes, *Staphylococcus, Actinobacillus.*

lower small bowel (22, 23, 103, 105). The microbes involved are segmented, filamentous prokaryotes (22) and are unique in that they attach to intestinal epithelial cells via a segment on one of their ends that inserts into an invagination in the membrane of the epithelial cell. These microbes have yet to be cultured in identifiable form and are known to colonize the epithelial habitat in adult rodents (22), dogs (20), and chickens (105) only because they have been seen in preparations examined by various microscopic techniques. Nevertheless, their population levels, as judged in microscope examinations, may be quite high (22).

Such microbes have yet to be reported to be present in the human small intestine. In this case, technical limitations severely hamper efforts to detect any microbes associated with epithelia. Humans cannot be sacrificed to the purposes of the experiment as can animals of other types. Intestinal biopsies taken with capsules from living persons may not yield satisfactory results because the sampled area is small relative to the total surface area. Moreover, the number of persons sampled must be large to give confidence in the results. Even biopsies taken at surgery are unsatisfactory because the patients usually have had their diets manipulated in some way or have been treated with antimicrobial drugs. The microbes attached to the epithelium in the rodent small bowel are known to disappear if the animals are starved for a period (123) or are treated orally with antibiotics (23). Thus, undoubtedly, the best source of information about such microbes in the human small intestine is samples taken from individuals killed in accidents (86). Problems arise even here, however, because the samples must be taken immediately after death and the number of individuals sampled must still be quite large. Only much further research can resolve this problem.

The Large Bowel

In all adult mammals examined, including humans, the large bowel, including the cecum and colon, harbors complex microbiotas composed undoubtedly of both indigenous and allochthonous microorganisms. Many different microbial types can be cultured at high population levels from the contents of these areas (Table 3). As with the stomach and small bowel, however, problems of interpretation remain concerning which of the microbes are truly indigenous to habitats in the region and which are merely transients. Microbes in food are known to pass at high population levels into human feces (101). Microbes from habitats above the large bowel certainly pass down into the lumen of that region. Therefore, many of the microbes found in the contents of the large bowel are undoubtedly allochthonous to the region. However, the population levels of these transients probably do not contribute significantly to the total level in the region. In the main, microbes occupying habitats above the large bowel are present at population levels much lower than those of the chief inhabitants of the large bowel (Tables 1, 2, and 3).

Enormous microbial populations can develop in the lumen of the large bowel, and especially in that of the cecum, because these are areas of relative stagnation in the flowing stream that is the gastrointestinal tract. In these areas, the passage rate of lumenal content does not exceed the doubling times of bacteria. In most mammals, including humans, these lumenal populations are composed in the main of oxygen-intolerant anaerobic bacteria of various types. Many genera, and in some cases

Table 3 Microorganisms isolated from the large bowels of nonruminant animals[a]

Microbial type	Animal type yielding microbe				
	Human[b]	Baboon	Swine	Rat[c]	Mouse[c]
Lactobacilli	30[d]	127	25, 93	19, 91, 98, 102	31, 50
Streptococci	30	127	25, 93	91, 98, 102	31, 50
Bifidobacteria			93	19	
Clostridia		127			50, 124
Eubacterium					50, 53
Propionibacterium					50
Coliforms	30	127	25, 93	19, 91, 98	31
Bacteroides	30	127	93	91	31, 53
Veillonella			93	98	
Fusobacterium					50, 53, 66, 108
Other bacterial types[e]			25	19, 91, 98, 102	50, 65, 66, 108
Yeasts		127	93	98, 102, 103	103

[a]To be cited, in general a microbial type had to be isolated at an estimated population level exceeding 10^6 microbes/g of wet colonic or cecal content from a large proportion of individuals examined in the study. The levels of strictly anaerobic bacterial types often exceed 10^{10} bacteria/g.

[b]The colonic biota of humans is thought to be essentially identical in composition to the fecal biota (see table 4) (85, 86).

[c]Microbes may have been isolated from cecum or colon.

[d]Reference.

[e]Staphylococci, *Bacillus* sp., unidentified anareobes, *Actinobacillus*, staphylococci, spiral-shaped microbes.

hundreds of bacterial species (86), can be isolated (Table 3). The lumenal community, therefore, is extremely complex. It is similar in that respect to the microbial communities in the rumen (15, 58) and the stomachs of certain monkeys (96). Indeed, the lumenal community in the cecum of many mammalian types much resembles the ruminant community in many characteristics, including types of microbial species involved and their nutritional, fermentative, and symbiotic activities (15).

Microbial communities other than lumenal ones have also been detected in the large bowels of monogastric animals of a number of types (103, 105). Oxygen-intolerant anaerobic bacteria, spirochetes, and other spiral-shaped microbes colonize habitats on the cecal and colonic epithelium of rats, mice, dogs, and other animals. Spirochetes of several types can be found in communities in crypts of Lieberkuhn in the cecal mucosa of rats (103) and dogs (63). Spirochetes and spiral-shaped bacteria colonize the epithelium of the colons of rhesus monkeys (122). Spirochetes have been found colonizing the colonic epithelium in presumably normal humans (67, 78). Complex microbial communities similar in composition to some found on the epithelial surfaces in the large bowels of monogastric animals have also been seen on the epithelium of the sheep rumen (6). Most of these communities have been described only because they have been seen microscopically. Few of the microbial types have been cultured in vitro. Thus, almost none of the organisms have been shown to satisfy criteria of autochthony for their habitats. Microbes in communities associated with the epithelium in the colons and cecums of mice and rats are probably indigenous to their habitats (103, 105). Evidence permitting such a conclusion about the microbes in other animals is not available.

The Feces

Feces are processed waste. They result from complex interactive biological processes that may begin in the food even before it passes the lips of the animal. These activities include microbial growth in the food before it is eaten (101); the digestive and absorptive functions of the animal host, and the biochemical activities of millions of microbial cells in different parts of the entire alimentary canal including the mouth. Up to 40% of the bulk of feces consists of wet microbial cells (85). These cells presumably have collected in the thing called feces, having shed from all possible habitats above the anus. Some of the cells will have traveled far, as from the mouth. Some may have entered from habitats on the epithelium of the esophagus, stomach, small intestine, or large intestine (103, 105). Those populations that had far to come may have been reduced markedly in level by the combined effects of the animal's digestive processes, competition for nutrients with the host and the microbial natives, and toxic substances produced by those natives in the habitats through which the transients pass on the way to the dump.

All of the microbes in feces are exposed to the influences of the dehydrating and concentrating mechanisms of the colon and rectum and intense biochemical activity of the microbes living in the material. In short, feces are a complex microbial habitat in their own right, with untold numbers of niches to be filled by microorganisms able to fill them. Therefore, the levels of microbial populations in feces, and indeed the types of microbes themselves, may not always be indicative of the composition of communities in the gastrointestinal tract.

Nevertheless, the composition of the microbiota of the feces of humans (Table 4) has been said to be indicative of the composition of communities in the colonic lumen (85). Studies in which only feces are sampled, however, can never reveal the composition and localization of epithelial and cryptal communities anywhere in the tract. Likewise, such studies probably reveal little about the composition of lumenal communities in any area except perhaps the large bowel. Even for lumenal communities in the large bowel, the fecal biota would be unlikely to reveal the extent to which microbes associate with particles of digesta in the lumen. Thus, on balance, the fecal microbiota can never be a good index of the true character of the gastrointestinal microbial ecosystem. In some cases (for example, when humans and certain other precious primates are the experimental subjects), feces only can be sampled practically. Whenever that burden is placed on the experimental system, however, the investigators must be cautious about attempting to describe the ecosystem in terms of their findings and should endeavor where possible to amplify the findings by examining samplings taken from all areas of the system. Fortunately, such attempts have been (30) and are being (86) made with humans.

Table 4 Microorganisms isolated from the feces of nonruminant animals[a]

Microbial types	Human
Lactobacilli	39, 54, 55, 79, 81, 82, 84[b]
Streptococci	39, 54, 55, 74, 79, 82, 84
Peptostreptococcus	39, 54, 79, 82, 84
Peptococcus	39, 54, 84
Bifidobacterium	39, 54, 74, 79, 80, 82, 84
Clostridium	1, 39, 54, 55, 79, 82, 84, 92
Eubacterium	39, 54, 55, 84
Propionibacterium	54
Ruminococcus	39, 54, 55, 84
Gemminger	51, 54
Coprococcus	54, 55, 84
Catenabacterium	79, 82, 84
Coliforms	39, 54, 79, 84
Bacteroides	39, 54, 55, 74, 79, 82, 84
Fusobacterium	39, 54, 84
Veillonella	75, 79, 82
Other bacterial types[c]	39, 54, 74, 82, 84
Yeasts	39

[a] To be cited, in general a microbial type had to be isolated from the feces at an estimated population level exceeding 10^9 microbes/g of wet (or dry) feces from most individuals examined in the study. In most cases, the levels of the strictly anaerobic bacterial types exceed 10^{10} per/g of material.

[b] Reference.

[c] *Acidaminococcus, Staphylococcus, Succinivibrio, Butyrivibrio,* spiral-shaped bacteria, *Megasphaera, Bacillus* sp.

SUCCESSION IN BABIES

As is well known, the gastrointestinal tract is sterile in the normal fetus up to the time of birth (49). During normal birth, however, the baby picks up microbes from the vagina and external genitalia of the mother and any other environmental source to which it is exposed (30). Thus, the pristine habitats of the infant's gastrointestinal ecosystem are exposed first to a hodgepodge of microbial types derived from a variety of sources. Many of these microbes are not able to colonize habitats in the neonatal tract and disappear from it soon after birth. Other microbial types are the pioneers, however, that will produce the offspring that eventually form the climax communities in the adult.

When the pioneers land in the once sterile habitats, a sequence of events begins that is characteristic of the animal type and to some extent its diet. This process can be interpreted as the successional colonization of the various habitats by indigenous microbes until all of the habitats are occupied by climax communities (3). In such a succession in a given animal type, the habitats are colonized in a characteristic sequence dependent upon the age of the animal. Particularly profound transitions in the sequence may take place when the animal begins to consume solid food.

The succession of the biota has been examined in numerous animal types. Problems of interpretation arise, however, if the data describing any particular succession have been derived from studies in which only feces were sampled. Moreover, whether or not the entire tract is sampled, if autochthonous microbial types are not differentiated from allochthonous ones in any habitat, then the significance of any particular type in the succession is still difficult to interpret. This problem is especially acute when the succession is studied in animals housed under conventional conditions and drinking water and food containing living microbes.

In most studies of succession, animals housed conventionally have been used, and only feces have been sampled. In a few cases, the entire system has been examined. In only rare cases, however, have efforts been made to differentiate indigenous microbes from transient ones. Therefore, on balance, current understanding of succession in the gastrointestinal ecosystem of most animals is weak at best. Nevertheless, some understanding of the overall processes may be gained from a comparative overview of information published about each system.

Soon after birth, in most suckling infants, the biota is composed primarily of lactic acid bacteria. Populations of *Lactobacillus* sp. predominate in most animals and in human babies drinking formulas (18, 25, 30, 75, 79–81, 107, 109, 115, 116), whereas *Bifidobacterium* sp. predominate in breast-fed humans (30, 75, 80). In species examined, this gram-positive biota can be detected soon after birth and quickly reaches high population levels. In infant rodents (107, 109) and swine (25), at least, the bacteria colonize throughout the tract, but especially in the stomach where they colonize habitats on the gastric epithelium (107, 125).

Usually shortly after birth as well, populations of facultative anaerobes, such as *Escherichia coli* and *Streptococcus faecalis,* can be detected along with the lactic acid bacteria. In some animal species, these bacterial types may achieve high population levels after they are detected initially (107, 109, 115, 116) and may be found at these high levels in all regions of the tract including the stomach (107, 109). In laboratory mice, when their population levels are high, usually during the second week after birth, microcolonies of these facultatives can be seen in the mucus coating the colonic epithelium (21, 107).

Once the animals begin to sample solid food, strict anaerobes can be detected (18, 21, 64, 75, 94, 107, 109, 115, 116), usually in the large intestine (64, 107, 109). The population levels of these bacteria increase progressively. By the time the animals are weaned, their populations are at adult climax levels, completely dominating all other microbial populations in the large bowel. As the levels of the populations of strict anaerobes increase, the levels of facultatives, such as *E. coli* and *S. faecalis,* may decline concomitantly (64, 107, 109, 115, 116). At weaning time, the climax populations of the facultatives may be quite low and will remain at those low levels unless the ecosystem is perturbed in some drastic way, such as by antimicrobial drugs (104) or starvation (123). Interestingly, this succession is essentially reproduced in baby rodents born to ex-germfree mothers colonized by a defined microbiota (36), the components of which colonize the different regions of the tract in a way essentially identical to that described already for the biota of animals colonized naturally (34).

Some components of the indigenous microbiota may colonize their habitats only after weaning. In mice and rats (104, 105), the yeasts that colonize the epithelium of the stomach and the segmented, filamentous microbes that colonize the epithelium of the small bowel (22) can be detected only after the animals are weaned. Thus, in these cases at least, the succession of the biota is not completed until after weaning.

Many microbial types other than those subsumed in the major groups mentioned here (for example, *Bacillus* sp.) have been recovered from the feces and bowel contents of animals during successions (115, 116). In most cases, however, the animals were being housed under conventional conditions. Therefore, whether or not such microbes are significant in succession cannot be affirmed.

As shall be discussed in more detail shortly, successional events involve complex sequential interactions between the animals, their diet and environments, and the various microbial types. These interactions influence the localization and make-up of the developing microbial communities and, in the end, dictate their climax composition. Given stability in an animal's health, diet, and environment, only changes associated with aging should influence the composition of the biota. In certain animals, the composition may change with age (79, 80). Such changes are difficult to evaluate, however, unless the diets and environments of the animals have been controlled throughout the life spans of the subjects. For technical reasons, those factors are nearly impossible to maintain in a steady state during the full life spans of most animals, including laboratory rodents. Therefore, studies of the influence of aging on the biota may remain difficult to interpret for some time.

FACTORS INFLUENCING COMPOSITION OF THE MICROBIOTA

The population levels and types of microbes in the many climax communities in the gastrointestinal ecosystem, and the successions of those communities, are regulated by multifactorial processes. Some of the regulatory forces in these processes are exerted by the animal host. Some are exerted by the microbes themselves (29, 30, 44, 104, 128, 129). Some microbial communities can exert direct influences to exclude other microbes from their habitats and niches. Some can effect changes in the functions of the host that regulate the biota and thus exert indirect influences on its composition and geographic distribution (104).

Forces Exerted by the Host and Its Diet and Environment

Some forces generated by the host influence the composition of the biota in particular areas of the tract (Table 5). Hydrogen ion concentration is a major factor dictating what types of microbes can colonize habitats in the stomach (43, 62, 73). Peristalsis is a strong influence preventing microbial communities from developing in the lumen of the upper and middle regions of the small bowel (30, 104). Other forces exerted by the animal influence the composition in all regions of the tract.

Table 5 Conditions imposed by the animal that may influence the composition of the indigenous microbiota in the various regions of the gastrointestinal tract[a]

Factor	Stomach	Small intestine	Large intestine	Ref.
Temperature	37°C	37°C	37°C	
pH	acidic	neutral to alkaline	neutral to alkaline	see text
Stasis	periodic	periodic, but only in lower part	prolonged, especially in cecum	see text
Oxygen	?[b]	?	little, if any	95, 130
Oxidation reduction potential	?	?	very low when microbiota present	see text
Vitamin B_{12} (intrinsic factor)	?	upper portions	?	30
Enzymes (proteins)	?	pancreatic enzymes	?	see text
Bile acids	little	conjugated	deconjugated	see text
Epithelial turn-over	all areas; requires replacement of attached microbes; sluffed cells may become microbial nutrients			see text
Urea	?	?	in cecum	87
Mucin	all areas; may act as microbial nutrient; contribute to viscous environment			see text
Diet	all areas; act as microbial nutrients; habitats			see text
Drugs	all areas			16, 23, 74, 128
Antibodies	?	?	?	see text
Phagocytic cells	?	in Crypts of Leiberkuhn	?	see text

[a] Any of these conditions may be altered by the microbiota itself to be either more or less effective in influencing the composition of the microbial communities (44,104).
[b] ?, Evidence is insufficient even to suggest that factor may operate in this region.

A temperature optimum for growth of about 37°C is undoubtedly an asset to microbes colonizing any habitat in the bowel. Likewise, the ability to grow anaerobically is an advantage to microbes colonizing habitats in any location in the tract, as mentioned earlier (95, 130). In most cases, however, the influence of any particular factor on the composition of the biota in any habitat is not so clear.

For example, repeated attempts have been made to demonstrate that bile acids are important forces regulating the biota in the small bowel. Some microbial types commonly isolated from human feces are inhibited in growth in vitro by certain unconjugated bile acids at low concentrations (10). Nevertheless, in vivo, the impact of bile acids on the composition of the microbiota in the small bowel is less well defined. The human small bowel rarely contains appreciable quantities of unconjugated bile acids (74). Thus, several experimental attempts have been made to demonstrate that bile acids as they appear in the small bowel, i.e. in conjugated form, regulate the composition of microbial populations in intestinal fluids (30, 74). Efforts have even been made to follow the fate of individual microbial species in the small intestine in individuals who increased their bile acid pools by consuming conjugated bile acids (136). None of these efforts have yielded convincing evidence, however, that bile acids in any form influence the population levels of indigenous microbes in the small intestine.

If conjugated bile acids do exert an influence on the composition and localization of microbial communities in the small intestine, then they probably do so by inhibiting growth of microbes not normally found in the intestines. Allochthonous species in ingested materials or from habitats above (mouth, stomach, etc) that enter the small bowel could find conjugated bile acids inhibitory to their growth. Direct evidence on this point must await experimental efforts in which the investigators distinguish indigenous from nonindigenous microbes isolated from the various areas examined in their study. Deconjugated bile acids, which can be found normally in the contents of the large bowel, may function in some way in regulating the composition of the biota in that region. If so, the influence is obscure.

Similar comments can be made about the current state of understanding of other substances produced by the animal that may regulate the composition of the biota in various habitats. Some microbial types in the gastrointestinal ecosystem may utilize mucins as carbon and energy sources. Various bacterial species isolated from the gastrointentinal canals of humans and other animals produce enzymes that hydrolyze mucins (56). Germfree animals excrete in their feces more mucin than do conventional animals (49). Mucins on the epithelial surfaces and possibly also in lumens are colonized by various indigenous microbial types in several regions of the tracts of laboratory rodents (20, 105, 107). Thus, these substances may influence the composition of the microbiota in different habitats. Unfortunately, little direct evidence supports such a speculation.

Likewise, little evidence supports an hypothesis that an animal's immunological responses affect the composition of the indigenous microbiota. At least some bacterial inhabitants of the gastrointestinal tract can induce antibodies detectable in the serum (88) and intestinal secretions (14) or as produced by spleen cells (8) of their hosts. At present, such evidence must be evaluated with care because investigators conducting the studies have rarely confirmed that the microbes they used are truly autochthonous to habitats in the gastrointestinal canal of the animal species with which they worked. When such care is taken, not uncommonly, as predicted in 1965 (31), the microbe proves to be poorly or totally (8, 42, 88) without capacity to induce antibodies, especially when present only in the gastrointestinal canal. When checked, such microbes often share antigens with the mucus or mucosa of the gut in which they normally occupy a habitat (42).

These and other similar findings concerning antigenic similarities between intestinal microorganisms and their animal hosts suggest that such microbes have evolved to a close immunological relationship with the animal. At least, the surfaces of the microbes that contact the animal's cells must be sufficiently related to the host's antigens so as to render them recognizable as "self" by the animal's immunological system (42). Being recognized as self would give indigenous microbes enormous advantage in colonizing their habitats. In this context, then, it would be rational if bacteria from the feces of human secretors of blood group-specific glycoproteins differed in antigenic type depending upon the secretor type of the individual (57). Future work may reveal that such glycoproteins do influence the antigenic types of other microbial species, especially strictly anaerobic ones.

Certain allochthonous microorganisms such as *Vibrio cholerae* colonize temporarily the epithelial surface of the small intestine. Such pathogens induce antibodies that circulate in the serum and also enter the intestinal tract (44). Under certain conditions, these antibodies prevent increases in population levels of *V. cholerae* in the murine intestine, in part at least by preventing the microbe from attaching to the intestinal epithelium (44). Thus, if an animal's immunological system influences at all the composition of the microbiota in the gastrointestinal canal, the main effect of that influence may be to prevent allochthonous species from colonizing habitats in the system.

Nevertheless, immunological mechanisms do not obviously influence succession in infant mice (8, 35). This finding may be explained by the discovery that immunological mechanisms operating in the intestine to repress growth of *V. cholerae* do so in synergism with microbial interference exerted by the indigenous microbiota (113). Microbial interference in the gastrointestinal ecosystem will be discussed again later. It is mentioned at this time, however, because such interference mechanisms probably do not operate efficiently in baby mice before succession of the microbiota, especially its strictly anaerobic components, is essentially complete (64). However, this specific problem needs further study. In addition, much more investigation is needed on the general problem of how antibodies operate, if at all, in regulating the composition or localization of the microbiota in the gastrointestinal ecosystem.

Similarly, little is known concerning whether or not phagocytosis is an important mechanism in such regulation. Macrophages and polymorphonuclear leukocytes can be found in the lamina propria of the intestinal mucosa (49). If such cells could enter and function in the environment of the lumen of the tract, especially by scavenging epithelial surfaces for unwelcome microbial guests, then they would be powerful factors regulating the composition of the biota. Direct evidence for such phenomena are not available.

Interestingly, some cells in the epithelium itself function as phagocytes. Paneth cells in the epithelium at the bases of the crypts of Leiberkuhn in the small intestines of rats have been identified both functionally and structurally as active phagocytes (38). These cells may function to clear the crypts of microbes that progress too deeply into those areas where the epithelial cells are actively dividing (38). The influence of these particular cells in regulating the indigenous microbiota is not known at this time. However, microbes are not commonly seen at the bases of the crypts in small intestines. Therefore, Paneth cells may be important in limiting where microbes can localize in that region.

Some evidence suggests that certain influences in the environment of an animal may alter the composition of the microbiota. Stimuli that induce strong emotions in humans may alter the composition of their fecal biota (54). Air pressure as altered during changes in altitude may change the composition of the fecal biota in humans and mice (47). Such factors undoubtedly alter animal physiology, which in turn then alters the composition of the microbial communities. The precise physiological mechanisms that might be affected are unknown. Any physiological change that would increase or decrease peristaltic rate, the amount of HCl secreted in the stomach or perhaps even mucus secreted anywhere in the tract, could conceivably alter the microbial communities in local habitats. Evidence for such hypotheses are lacking.

A controversy surrounds the issue whether or not the diet of the animal is an important factor regulating the composition of indigenous microbial communities in monogastric animals. This issue is an important one, because in man diets of certain composition are linked to the etiology of cancer of certain types, especially that of the large bowel (30). The linkage may be mediated in some way by microbes in the intestines (30, 85). Early information, largely from one source (30), indicated that diet does alter the composition of the populations of microbes in the feces of man. More recent evidence, gained through careful comprehensive study (39, 85), runs counter to the hypothesis. These conflicting results are difficult to reconcile, unless, as has been suggested (85), the earlier studies suffered from some technical problems.

The controversy will be a difficult one to resolve. Changes in diet may differ in their influence on the composition of microbial populations in the large bowels, depending upon the animal species. Hibernating ground squirrels, presumably eating little, if at all, experience only minor changes in the types of microbes present in the biotas in their cecal lumens (5). Humans eating so-called "absorbable" diets, free of nondigestible bulk, experience little change in the composition of their fecal biota (4, 11). Therefore, in humans and ground squirrels at least, even drastic changes in diet have little obvious influence on the composition of the biota of the large bowel.

In pigs (89), however, starvation does alter the fecal biota. In mice, starvation (123) or other dietary manipulation (135) alters the composition of the communities, especially those associated with epithelial surfaces in all areas of the tract. Likewise, diet influences the types of microbes that can colonize the large, as well as small, bowels and stomachs of gnotobiotic (ex-germfree) rodents associated with indigenous microbes (32, 37). Therefore, diet may yet be found to have subtle influences upon the composition of microbiota in the large bowel of man. Some of these influences may be difficult to detect when feces only are sampled, however, because they involve populations of microbes that are actually allochthonous to habitats in the large bowel and are present in the lumen in that region and in feces only because they are shedding from habitats above.

That hypothesis would be testable only if microbial types autochthonous to habitats in the large bowel could be distinguished from allochthonous ones. But such an effort may not be worth taking. The important influence of diet on the biota in the large bowel may be to induce changes in the biochemical activities of the microbes (85, 133). Changes in biochemical activity may be detectable by methods that do not rely upon estimates of population levels of the indigenous microbes involved (132). Only much more research can resolve this difficult problem.

Forces Resulting from Activities of the Microbes Themselves

Microbial populations in established climax communities undoubtedly exert strong direct forces to maintain the stability of the structure of their communities. The practical effect of those forces would be to exclude allochthonous microbes from niches in the habitat occupied by the community. Such forces may include bacteriocins (104) and antibiotics (33), nutritional competition (45, 104), toxic metabolic end products such as volatile fatty acids (46, 64) and H_2S (45; R. Freter, personal communication), and maintenance of low oxidation-reduction potentials (17, 60).

Evidence is mixed for some of these possibilities. Certainly some enteric microbial types do produce bacteriocins (104). Such substances could operate in restricting access of alien microbial types to habitats occupied by indigenous microbes of similar types. However, evidence presently available does not assure such a function in the gastrointestinal tract (104). Likewise, practically little direct evidence is available on whether or not nutritional competition operates in the gastrointestinal ecosystem. Populations of *E. coli* in the cecums of mice may be limited in part by nutritional competition with other microbial types present (45). However, such populations are undoubtedly limited also by volatile fatty acids (64) and other toxic substances produced by strictly anaerobic bacteria (128). Thus, the relative importance of nutritional competition is difficult to assess.

Volatile and nonvolatile short-chain fatty acids are found in the tract wherever microbial communities are found (83). These compounds are known to be toxic for some allochthonous bacterial types that enter the mammalian gastrointestinal tract (46). They are especially antimicrobial at the low oxidation-reduction potentials maintained in areas of the bowel colonized by microbial communities (130). Thus, they are undoubtedly important factors protecting those communities from invasion by outsiders.

In addition, such acids may be important factors in autogenic succession of the biota in baby animals. During succession in suckling mice, volatile fatty acids produced by anaerobic bacteria may repress the population levels of facultative bacteria during the changeover from predominantly facultative to predominantly strictly anaerobic populations that takes place during the second week after birth (64). Recently, however, H_2S produced by anaerobic bacteria was indicated to be a factor in the repression of the population levels of *E. coli* by the anaerobes (45; R. Freter, personal communication). If these findings are confirmed, then further work will be necessary to reveal the relative contributions of these factors in regulating succession, as well as in maintaining the integrity of climax communities. Whichever factor is the most important, there is now strong evidence that strictly anaerobic bacteria are pivotal in regulating composition of communities in the bowel (45, 104, 129, 131).

As noted earlier, microbes in the gastrointestinal ecosystem contribute to the regulation of the composition and localization of their communities not only directly but also by altering physiological responses of the host that may be involved in the regulatory processes (104). Intestinal microbes deconjugate and otherwise alter bile acids (30) and induce immunological responses in the host (44) that may be factors regulating the composition of the biota. The biota also stimulates peristalsis, which influences colonization by microbes in all areas of the tract but especially in the small intestine (104). Intestinal microbes influence numerous other physiological properties of their host animals (Table 5). Little is known, however, about the impact of such factors on the composition of the biota.

As mentioned earlier, regulation of the composition and localization of microbial communities in the gastrointestinal tract is a multifactorial process where any or all of these many forces may come into play. For any given community, the factors must balance delicately to maintain the structure of the community. This delicate balance can be perturbed by forces such as antimicrobial drugs (104) and possibly other more subtle influences, such as emotion (54). Humans and domestic animals exposed to drugs and other influences may be constantly experiencing perturbation of their gastrointestinal ecosytem. The long-term physiological consequences of such perturbation, for example on the aging of the animal (49), are unknown.

HOW MICROBES IN THE BIOTA MAKE THEIR LIVING (NICHES)

The niche of every microbial species in the gastrointestinal ecosystem may never be defined with precision. Too many species can be isolated from the system, especially from habitats in the large bowel. Over 300 different bacterial species have been isolated from human feces (85). Up to 40% of the mass of feces is microbial cells (85). Thus, the ways the microbes make their living in most cases may never be studied directly but will have to be inferred from information about their growth in media in vitro, what types of microbial nutrients may be present in the general region of the tract they occupy, the types of end products they produce, and some facts about the stability of their communities in the habitats they occupy.

Most estimates of the growth rates of microbes in the gastrointestinal tract indicate that the microbes grow slowly, at generation times of 10 hr or more (12, 104). Such figures must be interpreted with care. Some of them are estimates of the growth rates of allochthonous microbes (104). All of them are essentially average rates estimated from data taken over relatively long periods. Such data reveal little about the true growth rates of indigenous microbes in their niches when substrates are not limited. Much more research is required on this problem.

As noted earlier, a microbe must be able to grow anaerobically to be considered autochthonous to some gastrointestinal habitat. Thus, by this definition, every indigenous microbe must have the capacity to generate energy by mechanisms not involving O_2 as a terminal electron acceptor. In the main, most species involved do this by fermentation, although some generate energy while fixing H_2 into CO_2 to form methane (15, 111). The latter process requires exceedingly low oxidation-reduction potentials and therefore may take place normally only in the large bowel in monogastric animals (15). Some bacterial types commonly found in the human bowel may generate energy by anaerobic respiration with sulfate as the terminal electron acceptor (28). If so, however, such a process has not been studied in detail, although anaerobic bacteria able to reduce sulfate have been isolated from human feces (7).

Some indigenous microbes, such as *E. coli* and some yeasts, do have the capacity to generate energy by aerobic oxidative phosphorylation (118). Thus, these microbes may occupy habitats in vivo in which oxygen offers some ecological advantage. Such habitats could be ones in close proximity to epithelial cells where O_2 molecules might pass from the blood through the epithelium to the microbes attached to it (105). By assimilating such molecules, *E. coli* may be important in developing during succession (104, 107) and maintaining in climax communities the O_2-free conditions and low oxidation-reduction potential favoring strict anaerobes in the large bowel. Direct evidence for this speculation is not available.

Since most indigenous microbial types produce energy as fermenters, they must find substrates for fermentation in their habitats. Some of these substrates derive obviously from the animals diet; some derive from products produced by the animal. As noted earlier gastrointestinal mucin produced by the animal may be an important carbon and energy source in all regions of the bowel, but especially the large bowel where it may contribute to the stability of the communities even when the animal is eating little or no food.

Some microbial types able to hydrolyze cellulose have been isolated from the feces or cecal contents (15) of some monogastric animals. The microbes involved often prove to be species that are found also in rumens (58). In animals with cecums, cellulose may be an important substrate for microbial fermentation (76, 77). In animals with straight-tube digestive systems, cellulose may be less important than mucin as a microbial carbon and energy source. This area needs more research.

Amino acids may be important carbon and energy sources and also important nitrogen sources for indigenous microbes, both in the small and large bowels (15). These compounds could derive from proteolysis of dietary proteins consumed and enzymatic proteins produced by the host and from epithelial cells extruded into the lumen during normal processes of turnover of the epithelium (104, 134). Pancreatic and other enzymes and desquamated epithelial cells could provide a significant source of macromolecules to microbes, particularly in the lower tract, and may, along with mucin, contribute to stability of the communities in that region.

Ammonia is undoubtedly an important source of nitrogen in the microbial communities in the gastrointestinal canals of monogastric animals just as it is in ruminant animals (15, 58). This compound could derive from ureolysis (87) and deamination of amino acids (15). Ammonia produced by intestinal microbes enters the blood stream of the animal host, however, and can exert harmful physiological effects (30).

Some microbial types isolated from rat ceca require long-chain fatty acids for their growth (90). Desquamated epithelial cells, as well as the host's diet, may be a significant source of such compounds. Little direct evidence supports that concept.

As noted earlier, one or more types of volatile and nonvolatile fatty acids can be found in any region of the tract colonized by microbes (83). These substances produced as end products of the microbes' fermentations contribute to the nutrition of the host animal (76, 77). They serve as well, undoubtedly, as carbon and energy sources for many microbial types. Such a phenomenon is likely to be quite common in the gastrointestinal ecosystem where the end products of the metabolism of a microbe oxidizing monosaccharides, some of which are derived from hydrolysis of polysaccharides, serve as nutrients for other species (59). However, little direct evidence supports this hypothesis for monogastric animals.

Many such interactions may take place in each habitat in the tract. Along with microbe-host interactions, these microbe-microbe interactions dictate how energy flows through the system to keep it operating. Only guesses can be made about this energy flow because of its enormous complexity. The animal takes in food, which then serves directly and indirectly its requirements for energy and molecules, and also those of the microbiota. The food serves the animal's requirements directly as mediated by its own digestive processes and indirectly as mediated by microbial processes yielding end products that are then absorbed and utilized by the animal. The food serves the microbiota's requirements directly largely because the animal ingests some things it cannot or does not digest before the microbes utilize them, and indirectly through substances such as enzymatic proteins, mucins, and desquamated epithelial cells that are utilized by the microbes. In no case is information available to allow a detailed comparison by species of this food chain.

SUMMARY AND CONCLUSIONS

The gastrointestinal ecosystems of monogastric animals are complex, open, interactive systems involving the animal's environment and diet, the animal itself, and many microbial species. In adult animals, the microbes are organized into climax communities occupying many niches in habitats distributed geographically throughout the gastrointestinal tract. The habitats are distributed horizontally from the center of the lumen to the depths of the crypts, and vertically from the esophagus to the anus. Depending upon the animal species any or all habitats may be occupied. In the main, few of these habitats have been defined well in any animal species.

The microbial communities occupying the habitats are composed normally of autochthonous (indigenous) microbes. A sample from any given habitat at any given time may yield allochthonous (nonindigenous) microbes as well as the indigenous ones. The allochthonous microbes derive from the animals ingesta (food, water, feces) or from habitats above the one in question. Efforts to distinguish autochthonous from allochthonous microbes for any given habitat are rarely made in studies of the composition of the indigenous microbiota.

In babies, sterile before birth, the microbial communities develop in the many habitats according to complex successions influenced by many factors. In the main, few of these successions are well characterized, in part because the habitats and autochthonous inhabitants of them are poorly defined for most systems. Much more attention must be given to these complex events.

Complex interactive mechanisms involving the animal, its environment and diet, and the microbes themselves regulate the course of the successional events and the population levels and geographic distribution of the climax communities once they are formed. On balance, little is known about these mechanisms. Likewise, little is known about how specific microbial types make their living in their niches in the many habitats.

Much attention should be given to these processes. The gastrointestinal microbiota interacts profoundly with its animal host influencing its early development, quality of life, aging, and resistance to infectious diseases (49). Some components of the biota induce disease when given an opportunity to do so, for example, when they are injected into normally sterile areas of the body during surgery or when host resistance mechanisms fail (30). Likewise, the biota may be involved in the etiology of some chronic degenerative diseases, such as certain forms of cancer (30, 85). Such processes grow in danger as microbes in the bowel accumulate (69) and exchange genetically (16, 117) mechanisms of resistance to antimicrobial drugs. In the main, little is known about the mechanisms of these microbe-animal interactions. They may remain unknown until the structure and biochemistry of the ecosystem itself is better understood.

ACKNOWLEDGMENTS

The findings cited herein were derived from research supported by grant AI 11858 from the National Institute of Allergy and Infectious Diseases.

Literature Cited

1. Akama, K., Otani, S. 1970. *Jpn. J. Med. Sci. Biol.* 23:161–75
2. Akin, D. E. 1976. *Appl. Environ. Microbiol.* 31:562–68
3. Alexander, M. 1971. *Microbial Ecology*, pp. 3–21. New York: Wiley
4. Attebery, H. R., Sutter, V. L., Finegold, S. M. 1972. *Am. J. Clin. Nutr.* 25: 1391–98
5. Barnes, E. M., Burton, G. C. 1970. *J. Appl. Bacteriol.* 33:505–14
6. Bauchop, T., Clarke, R. T. J., Newhook, J. C. 1975. *Appl. Microbiol.* 30: 668–75
7. Beerens, H. 1977. *Am. J. Clin. Nutr.* In press
8. Berg, R. D., Savage, D. C. 1975. *Infect. Immun.* 11:320–29
9. Bernhardt, H. 1974. *Zentralbl. Bakteriol. Parasitenkd. Infektionskr. Hyg. Abt. 1 Orig.* 226:479–90
10. Binder, H. J., Filburn, B., Floch, M. 1975. *Am. J. Clin. Nutr.* 28:119–25
11. Bounous, G., Devroede, G. J. 1974. *Gastroenterology* 66:210–14
12. Brock, T. D. 1971. *Bacteriol. Rev.* 35:39–58
13. Brooker, B. E., Fuller, R. 1975. *J. Ultrastruc. Res.* 52:21–31
14. Brown, W. R., Savage, D. C., Dubois, R. S., Alp, M. H., Mallory, A., Kern, F. Jr. 1972. *Gastroenterology* 62:1143–52
15. Bryant, M. P. 1974. *Am. J. Clin. Nutr.* 27:1313–19
16. Burt, S. J., Woods, D. R. 1976. *J. Gen. Microbiol.* 93:405–9
17. Celesk, R. A., Asano, T., Wagner, M. 1976. *Proc. Soc. Exp. Biol. Med.* 151: 260–63
18. Craven, J. A., Barnum, D. A. 1971. *Can. J. Comp. Med.* 35:324–31
19. Davis, C. P. 1976. *Appl. Environ. Microbiol.* 31:304–12
20. Davis, C. P., Balish, E., Yale, C. E. 1976. *Abstr. Annu. Meet. Assoc. Gnotobiotics, 1976*, p. 25
21. Davis, C. P., McAllister, J. S., Savage, D. C. 1973. *Infect. Immun.* 7:666–72
22. Davis, C. P., Savage, D. C. 1974. *Infect. Immun.* 10:948–56
23. Davis, C. P., Savage, D. C. 1976. *Infect. Immun.* 13:180–88
24. Decuypere, J., Henderickx, H. K., Vervaeke, I. 1973. *Zentralbl. Bakteriol.*

Parasitenkd. Infektionskr. Hyg. Abt. 1 Orig. 223:348–55
25. Decuypere, J., Van Der Heyde, H. 1972. *Zentralbl. Bakteriol. Parasitenkd. Infektionskr. Hyg. Abt. 1 Orig.* 221: 492–510
26. Dickman, M. D., Chappelka, A. R., Schaedler, R. W. 1976. *Am. J. Gastroenterol.* 65:57–62
27. Dobzhansky, T. 1971. *Genetics of the Evolutionary Process,* Vol. 1. New York: Columbia Univ.
28. Doelle, H. W. 1975. *Bacterial Metabolism,* pp. 188–92. New York: Academic. 2nd ed.
29. Drasar, B. S. 1974. *The Normal Microbial Flora of Man,* ed. F. A. Skinner, J. G. Carr, pp. 187–96. London: Academic
30. Drasar, B. S., Hill, M. J. 1974. *Human Intestinal Flora,* pp. 1–263. London: Academic
31. Dubos, R., Schaedler, R. W., Costello, R., Hoet, P. 1965. *J. Exp. Med.* 122:67–76
32. Ducluzeau, R., Dubos, F., Raibaud, P. 1971. *Ann Inst. Pasteur Paris* 121: 777–94
33. Ducluzeau, R., Dubos, F., Raibaud, P., Abrams, G. D. 1976. *Antimicrob. Agents Chemother.* 9:20–25
34. Ducluzeau, R., Raibaud, P. 1969. *Ann. Inst. Pasteur Paris* 116:370–82
35. Ducluzeau, R., Raibaud, P. 1973. *Can. J. Microbiol.* 19:1021–30
36. Ducluzeau, R., Raibaud, P., Ladire, M. 1974. *Ann. Microbiol. Paris* 125(A): 57–68
37. Ducluzeau, R., Raibaud, P., Ladire, M., Riottot, M., Chopin, A. 1973. *Ann. Microbiol. Paris* 124(B):517–32
38. Erlandson, S. L., Chase, D. B. 1972. *J. Ultrastruct. Res.* 41:296–318
39. Finegold, S. M., Flora, D. J., Attebery, H. R., Sutter, V. L. 1975. *Cancer Res.* 35:3407–17
40. Floch, M. H., Gorbach, S. L., Luckey, T. D. 1970. *Am. J. Clin. Nutr.* 23:1425–609
41. Floch, M. H., Hentges, D. J., eds. 1974. *Am. J. Clin. Nutr.* 27:1265–487
42. Foo, M. C., Lee, A. 1974. *Infect. Immun.* 9:1066–69
43. Franklin, M. A., Skoryna, S. C. 1971. *Can. Med. Assoc. J.* 105:380–86
44. Freter, R. 1974. *Am. J. Clin. Nutr.* 27:1409–16
45. Freter, R. 1975. *Microbiology–1975,* ed. D. Schlessinger, pp. 154–57. Washington, D.C.: Am. Soc. Microbiol.
46. Freter, R., Abrams, G. D. 1972. *Infect. Immun.* 6:119–26
47. Gillmore, J. D., Gordon, F. B. 1975. *Appl. Microbiol.* 29:358–67
48. Gorbach, S. L., Plaut, A. G., Nahas, L., Weinstein, L. 1967. *Gastroenterology* 53:856–67
49. Gordon, H. A., Pesti, L. 1971. *Bacteriol. Rev.* 35:390–429
50. Gordon, J. H., Dubos, R. 1970. *J. Exp. Med.* 132:251–60
51. Gossling, J., Moore, W. E. C. 1975. *Int. J. Syst. Bacteriol.* 25:202–7
52. Gracey, M., Stone, D. E., Suharjona, Sunoto. 1974. *Am. J. Clin. Nutr.* 27:345–49
53. Harris, M. A., Reddy, C. A., Carter, G. R. 1976. *Appl. Environ. Microbiol.* 31:907–12
54. Holdeman, L. V., Good, I. J., Moore, W. E. C. 1976. *Appl. Environ. Microbiol.* 31:359–75
55. Holdeman, L. V., Moore, W. E. C. 1974. *Int. J. Syst. Bacteriol.* 24:260–77
56. Hoskins, L. C., Boulding, E. T. 1976. *J. Clin. Invest.* 57:63–73
57. Hoskins, L. C., Boulding, E. T. 1976. *J. Clin. Invest.* 57:74–82
58. Hungate, R. E. 1966. *The Rumen and Its Microbes,* pp. 1–553. New York: Academic
59. Iannotti, E. L., Kafkewitz, D., Wolin, M. J., Bryant, M. P. 1973. *J. Bacteriol.* 114:1231–40
60. Koopman, J. P., Janssen, F. G. J., Van Druten, J. A. M. 1975. *Proc. Soc. Exp. Biol. Med.* 149:995–99
61. Kunstyr, I. 1974. *Zentralbl. Veterinaermed.* 21:553–61
62. Kunstyr, I., Peters, K., Gartner, K. 1976. *Lab. Anim. Sci.* 26:166–70
63. Leach, W. D., Lee, A., Stubbs, R. P. 1973. *Infect. Immun.* 7:961–72
64. Lee, A., Gemmell, E. 1972. *Infect. Immun.* 5:1–7
65. Lee, A., Gordon, J., Dubos, R. 1968. *Nature* 220:1137–39
66. Lee, A., Gordon, J., Lee, C.-J., Dubos, R. 1971. *J. Exp. Med.* 133:339–52
67. Lee, F. D., Kraszewski, A., Gordon, J., Howie, J. G. R., McSeveney, D., Harland, W. A. 1971. *Gut* 12:126–33
68. Lerche, M., Reuter, G. 1962. *Zentralbl. Bakteriol. Parasitenkd. Infektionskr. Hyg. Abt. 1 Orig.* 185:446–81
69. Levy, S. B., Fitzgerald, G. B., Macone, A. B. 1976. *New Engl. J. Med.* 295:583–88
70. Luckey, T. D. 1972. *Am. J. Clin. Nutr.* 25:1292–95

71. Luckey, T. D., Floch, M. H. 1972. *Am. J. Clin. Nutr.* 25:1291–494
72. Luckey, T. D., Hentges, D. J. 1977. *Am. J. Clin. Nutr.* In press
73. Maffei, H. V. L., Nobrega, F. J. 1975. *Gut* 16:719–26
74. Mallory, A., Savage, D., Kern, F. Jr., Smith, J. G. 1973. *Gastroenterology* 64:34–42
75. Mata, L. J., Carrillo, C., Villatoro, E. 1969. *Appl. Microbiol.* 17:596–602
76. McBee, R. H. 1970. *Am. J. Clin. Nutr.* 23:1514–18
77. McBee, R. H. 1971. *Ann. Rev. Ecol. Syst.* 2:165–76
78. Minio, F., Tonietti, G., Torsoli, A. 1973. *Rend. Gastroenterol.* 5:183–95
79. Mitsuoka, T., Hayakawa, K. 1972. *Zentralbl. Bakteriol. Parasitenkd. Infektionskr. Hyg. Abt. 1 Orig.* 223:333–42
80. Mitsuoka, T., Hayakawa, K., Kimura, N. 1974. *Zentralbl. Bakteriol. Parasitenkd. Infektionskr. Hyg. Abt. 1 Orig.* 226:469–78
81. Mitsuoka, T., Hayakawa, K., Kimura, N. 1975. *Zentralbl. Bakteriol. Parasitenkd. Infektionskr. Hyg. Abt. 1 Orig.* 232:499–511
82. Mitsuoka, T., Ohno, K., Benno, Y., Suzuki, K., Namba, K. 1976. *Zentralbl. Bakteriol. Parasitenkd. Infektionskr. Hyg. Abt. 1 Orig.* 234:219–33
83. Moore, W. E. C., Cato, E. P., Holdeman, L. V. 1969. *J. Infect. Dis.* 119:641–49
84. Moore, W. E. C., Holdeman, L. V. 1974. *Appl. Microbiol.* 27:961–79
85. Moore, W. E. C., Holdeman, L. V. 1975. *Cancer Res.* 35:3418–20
86. Moore, W. E. C., Ryser, M., Holdeman, L. V. 1975. *Abstr. Annu. Meet. Am. Soc. Microbiol. 1975,* p. 61
87. Moreau, M.-C., Ducluzeau, R., Raibaud, P. 1976. *Infect. Immun.* 13:9–15
88. Morishita, Y., Mitsuoka, T. 1973. *Jpn. J. Microbiol.* 17:181–87
89. Morishita, Y., Ogata, M. 1970. *Jpn. J. Vet. Sci.* 32:19–24
90. Morotomi, M., Kawai, Y., Mutai, M. 1976. *Appl. Environ. Microbiol.* 31:475–80
91. Morotomi, M., Watanabe, T., Suegara, N., Kawai, Y., Mutai, M. 1975. *Infect. Immun.* 11:962–68
92. Nakagawa, M., Nishida, S. 1969. *Jpn. J. Microbiol.* 13:133–37
93. Ogata, M., Morishita, Y. 1969. *Jpn. J. Vet. Sci.* 31:71–82
94. Ogata, M., Morishita, Y., Tanaka, Y., Shinjo, T., Uchida, K. 1968. *Jpn. J. Vet. Sci.* 30:281–87
95. Onderdonk, A. B., Johnston, J., Mayhew, J. W., Gorbach, S. L. 1976. *Appl. Environ. Microbiol.* 31:168–72
96. Ohwaki, K., Hungate, R. E., Lotter, L., Hofmann, R. R., Maloiy, G. 1974. *Appl. Microbiol.* 27:713–23
97. Parle, J. N. 1957. *J. Gen. Microbiol.* 17:363–67
98. Raibaud, P., Dickinson, A. B., Sacquet, E., Charlier, H., Mocquot, G. 1966. *Ann. Inst. Pasteur Paris* 110:861–76
99. Raibaud, P., Galpin, J. V., Ducluzeau, R., Mocquot, G., Oliver, G. 1973. *Ann. Microbiol. Paris* 124(A):83–109
100. Raibaud, P., Galpin, J. V., Ducluzeau, R., Mocquot, G., Oliver, G. 1973. *Ann. Microbiol. Paris* 124(A):223–35
101. Reuter, G. 1965. *Zentralbl. Bakteriol. Parasitenkd. Infektionskr. Hyg. Abt. 1 Orig.* 197:468–87
102. Sacquet, E., Raibaud, P., Garnier, J. 1971. *Ann. Inst. Pasteur Paris* 120:501–24
103. Savage, D. C. 1972. *Am. J. Clin. Nutr.* 25:1372–79
104. Savage, D. C. 1972. *Microbial Pathogenicity in Man and Animals,* ed. H. Smith, J. H. Pearce, pp. 25–57. Cambridge: Cambridge Univ.
105. Savage, D. C. 1975. *Microbiology–1975,* ed. D. Schlessinger, pp. 120–23. Washington, D.C.: Am. Soc. Microbiol.
106. Savage, D. C., Blumershine, R. V. H. 1974. *Infect. Immun.* 10:240–50
107. Savage, D. C., Dubos, R., Schaedler, R. W. 1968. *J. Exp. Med.* 127:67–76
108. Savage, D. C., McAllister, J. S., Davis, C. P. 1971. *Infect. Immun.* 4:492–502
109. Schaedler, R. W., Dubos, R., Costello, R. 1965. *J. Exp. Med.* 122:59–66
110. Schaedler, R. W., Dubos, R., Costello, R. 1965. *J. Exp. Med.* 122:77–82
111. Scheifinger, C. C., Linehan, B., Wolin, M. J. 1975. *Appl. Microbiol.* 29:480–83
112. Schonebeck, J. 1968. *Scand. J. Gastroenterol.* 3:351–54
113. Shedlofsky, S., Freter, R. 1974. *J. Infect. Dis.* 129:296–303
114. Shifrine, M., Phaff, H. J. 1958. *Antonie van Leeuwenhoek J. Microbiol. Serol.* 24:193–209
115. Smith, H. W. 1962. *J. Appl. Bacteriol.* 24:235–41
116. Smith, H. W. 1965. *J. Pathol. Bacteriol.* 90:495–513
117. Smith, H. W. 1969. *Lancet* 1:1174–76
118. Stanier, R. Y., Adelberg, E. A., Ingraham, J. 1976. *The Microbial World,* p. 679. Englewood Cliffs, N.J.: Prentice-Hall. 4th ed.

119. Stevens, C. E. 1977. *Comparative Physiology of the Digestive System.* Ithaca: Cornell Univ.
120. Suegara, N., Morotomi, M., Watanabe, T., Kawai, Y., Mutai, M. 1975. *Infect. Immun.* 12:173–79
121. Syed, S. A., Abrams, G. D., Freter, R. 1970. *Infect. Immun.* 2:376–86
122. Takeuchi, A., Zeller, J. A. 1972. *Infect. Immun.* 6:1008–18
123. Tannock, G. W., Savage, D. C. 1974. *Infect. Immun.* 9:591–98
124. Tannock, G. W., Savage, D. C. 1976. *Infect. Immun.* 13:172–79
125. Tannock, G. W., Smith, J. M. B. 1970. *J. Comp. Pathol.* 80:359–67
126. Terada, A., Uchida, K., Mitsuoka, T. 1976. *Zentralbl. Bakteriol. Parasitenkd. Infektionskr. Hyg. Abt. 1 Orig.* 234: 362–70
127. Uphill, P. F., Wilde, J. K. H., Berger, J. 1974. *J. Appl. Bacteriol.* 37:309–17
128. van der Waaij, D. 1968. *J. Infect. Dis.* 118:32–38
129. van der Waaij, D., Berghuis-de Vries, J. M., Lekkerkerk-van der Wees, J. E. C. 1971. *J. Hyg.* 69:405–11
130. Walden, W. C., Hentges, D. J. 1975. *Appl. Microbiol.* 30:781–85
131. Wensinck, F., Ruseler-van Embden, J. G. H. 1971. *J. Hyg.* 69:413–21
132. Wheeler, L. A., Carter, J. H., Soderberg, F. B., Goldman, P. 1975. *Proc. Natl. Acad. Sci. USA* 72:4607–11
133. Wheeler, L. A., Soderberg, F. B., Goldman, P. 1975. *Cancer Res.* 35:2962–68
134. Whitt, D. D., DeMoss, R. D. 1975. *Appl. Microbiol.* 30:609–15
135. Wilkins, T. D., Long, W. R. 1971. *Abstr. Annu. Meet. Am. Soc. Microbiol. 1971,* p. 113
136. Williams, R. C., Showalter, R., Kern, F. Jr. 1975. *Gastroenterology* 69:483–91

Ann. Rev. Microbiol. 1977. 31:135–57

THE INACTIVATION OF MICROBIAL ENZYMES IN VIVO

❖1700

Robert L. Switzer
Department of Biochemistry, University of Illinois, Urbana, Illinois 61801

CONTENTS

INTRODUCTION 135
DEFINITIONS AND SCOPE OF THIS REVIEW 136
EXAMPLES OF THE INACTIVATION OF MICROBIAL ENZYMES IN VIVO 137
PHYSIOLOGICAL CONDITIONS LEADING TO ENZYME INACTIVATION 137
Shifts in Carbon and Nitrogen Metabolism 142
Differentiation 143
Why Inactivation? 144
MECHANISMS OF INACTIVATION 144
Physical Mechanisms 144
Chemical Mechanisms 145
Degradative Inactivation: The Role of Proteolysis and Turnover 145
Unknown Mechanisms 147
METHODS FOR STUDYING INACTIVATION PROCESSES 147
General Characterization 147
Effects of Inhibitors 149
Use of Mutant Strains 149
Reactivation In Vivo and In Vitro 151
Following the Fate of the Enzyme Protein During Inactivation 151
Reconstruction In Vitro 153
CONCLUDING COMMENTS 154

INTRODUCTION

Two mechanisms for the regulation of enzyme activity in microbes have been generally recognized and extensively studied. These are control of enzyme levels through regulation of the rate of enzyme synthesis and control of enzyme activity through the effects of noncovalent binding of ligands. In recent years it has become appreciated that another mode of enzyme regulation is generally found in microbes, namely, the control of enzyme activity by selective inactivation. Early experiments demonstrating that most bacterial proteins are completely stable in exponentially growing cells, even in the absence of inducing metabolites (51, 67, 83, 106), gave rise to the widespread view that the inactivation of enzymes either did not occur in microbes or was of minor importance. However, a considerable body of experimental evidence has accumulated, which documents the occurrence of selective protein turnover in microbes (reviewed in 36, 37, 95). Reversible covalent modification of enzymes has been shown to serve as an important control mechanism in bacteria and fungi (54, 120). There are numerous reports in the literature of selective inactivation—often by as yet unknown mechanisms—of microbial enzymes under specific physiological conditions. It is the purpose of this review to collect and critically analyze these reports. To my knowledge this subject has not been reviewed previously, although Thurston (129) and Holzer (52) have discussed aspects of the subject in short articles. We will be led to the conclusion that enzyme inactivation is a quite general regulatory mechansim. The role of enzyme inactivation in the physiology of microbes will be considered. The known mechanisms of enzyme inactivation and generally useful methods for studying the mechansim of inactivation processes will be examined.

DEFINITIONS AND SCOPE OF THIS REVIEW

For the purposes of this review, *inactivation* will be defined as the irreversible loss in vivo of catalytic activity in the physiologically significant reaction of an enzyme. I have considered only cases where there was clear evidence that the inactivation occurred under physiological conditions in the living cell; inactivation processes that have been studied only in vitro were not reviewed. The term "irreversible loss" deserves further comment. Thc intention is to distinguish between inactivation and inhibition through the relatively loose, noncovalent binding of inhibitory metabolites. It is presumed that the latter is readily reversible by dilution or dialysis of cell extracts but that a true inactivation is not reversed by such treatments.[1] Inactivation processes reversed in vivo by a shift in the metabolism of the cell, such as occurs in the case of reversible covalent modification of enzymes, are included in the general class. The term inactivation is intended to include both modification inactivation, in which the enzyme protein remains intact but loses activity either through a change in physical state or the attachment of a covalent modifying group, and degradative inactivation, in which at least one peptide bond of the protein is cleaved as part of the inactivation process or subsequently to it. Degradative inactivation is taken to be distinct from *turnover,* which is defined as cleavage of a protein to the constituent amino acids, the more complex process in which degradative inactivation could serve as the first step.

[1]It must be conceded that the inactivation of yeast ornithine transcarbamylase by arginase, which has been included in this review, would have been excluded by this criterion. In this case the inactivation after addition of arginine could be detected when cells were rendered permeable by treatment with nystatin but not in cell-free extracts (141). The inactivation could be reconstructed in vitro if sufficiently high protein concentrations were used.

Since the product of a modification inactivation sometimes leads to the formation of an enzyme that still has catalytic activity [as in the γ-glutamyl transferase activity of adenylylated glutamine synthetase of *Escherichia coli* (120)], there is the restriction that the physiologically significant reaction of the enzyme must be totally (operationally $> 95\%$) lost. Since it often is difficult to ascertain whether a given activity is totally lost or whether some enzyme remains in the unmodified state, this quantitative restriction has not been rigorously applied in this review. Enzyme modification processes in which the physiologically significant reaction is altered but not lost [e.g. modification of fructose bisphosphate aldolase in *Bacillus cereus* (107) or interconversion of glycogen phosphorylase (27, 35, 128) and glycogen synthetase (55) by phosphorylation and dephosphorylation in eukaryotic microbes] are not included as inactivation processes.

It is intended in this review to discuss instances of the inactivation of enzymes, defined as above, that occur in prokaryotic and eukaryotic microbes. Many casual reports of the loss of enzyme activity from microbial cells exist, but I have attempted to concentrate on those cases in which the inactivation process itself was a focus of attention. Cases of the inactivation of enzymes in phage-infected bacteria (29, 47, 81, 99, 109, 131) and in differentiating slime molds (2, 43, 64, 125) have not been included because of space limitations and because of their specialized nature.

EXAMPLES OF THE INACTIVATION OF MICROBIAL ENZYMES IN VIVO

Table 1 lists 41 examples of reasonably well-characterized inactivation processes occurring in microbes that were found in a survey of the literature from about 1945 to mid 1976. It is possible that a few examples belonging in this list have escaped my attention, for which I apologize, but the number and variety of cases in Table 1 serves to document the generality of enzyme inactivation. It is likely that these examples represent only a small fraction of the actual number of inactivation processes that remain to be discovered.

PHYSIOLOGICAL CONDITIONS LEADING TO ENZYME INACTIVATION

Enzyme content, as measured by assay of specific catalytic activity in crude extracts, generally remains constant during exponential growth of microbial cells in batch culture. This constancy usually represents a uniform rate of synthesis rather than a balance between synthesis and inactivation, although a low level of protein turnover is known to occur in exponentially growing bacteria (36, 37, 67, 95, 143). Even when the inducing metabolite is removed, most inducible enzymes are stable in exponentially growing cells (51, 97). These observations have tended to obscure the significance of enzyme inactivation as a regulatory mechanism in microbes. But it should be recognized that exponential growth under constant culture conditions would hardly be expected to initiate major changes in metabolic fluxes. Such condi-

Table 1 Examples of the inactivation of microbial enzymes in vivo

Enzyme inactivated	Organism(s)	Culture conditions leading to inactivation	Proposed mechanism of inactivation	Reactivation in vivo without protein synthesis	Ref.
Aminoacyl-tRNA synthetases	*Escherchia coli*	stationary phase owing to amino acid starvation	unknown	no	144
δ-Aminolevulinic acid synthetase	*Rhodopseudomonas spheroides*	transfer of derepressed cells to highly aerobic conditions, addition of δ-aminolevulinate	unknown	?	11, 70, 71
Aspartate transcarbamylase	*Bacillus subtilis*	stationary phase, starvation	unknown; energy dependent; cross-reactive protein disappears	no	7, 16, 126, 138
Aspartokinase	*B. licheniformis*	stationary phase, starvation for carbon	unknown	?	5, 42, 121
Aspartokinase, lysine sensitive	*E. coli*	stationary phase	unknown; cross-reacting protein disappears; adenylylation reported	?	89a, 127a
Aspartokinase	*Myxococcus xanthus*	glycerol-induced myxospore formation	unknown	?	105
Citrate lyase	*R. gelatinosa*	exhaustion of citrate during anaerobic growth in light	enzymic removal of acetyl group from a sulfhydryl group on the enzyme	yes, by enzymic and (in vitro) chemical acetylation	6, 32–34, 40
Diaminopimelate decarboxylase	*B. cereus*	stationary phase	unknown	?	41
Endonuclease I	*E. coli*	end of exponential growth on certain media	unknown	?	115
Fructose bisphosphatase	*Saccharomyces* and *Candida* spp.	addition of glucose to acetate-grown cells	unknown; proteolysis demonstrated in vitro	no	30, 86, 136
Galactozymase	*S. cerevisiae*	addition of glucose to or shift to aerobiosis of galactose grown cells	unknown; probably energy dependent	?	119

Table 1 *(Continued)*

β–1, 3–Glucanase (extracellular)	Basidiomycete QM806	addition of glucose to derepressed cells	unknown; involves extracellular inactivating system and protein synthesis	no	28
Glucose-6-phosphate dehydrogenase	*Bacillus cereus*	germination and outgrowth of endospores	unknown; energy dependent	?	93
Glucose transport system II	*Neurospora crassa*	addition of high glucose to derepressed cells	unknown	no	111
α-Glucosidase	*S. cerevisiae*, *Candida stellatoidea* (?)	suspension in absence of inducer	unknown	?	3, 8, 39, 104
Glucoside 3–dehydrogenase	*Agrobacterium tumefaciens*	transfer to C– and N–free or certain N–free media	unknown	no	69
Glutamate dehydrogenase, NAD dependent	*C. utilis*, *S. cerevisiae*	transfer of glutamate grown cells to NH_4^+ or media lacking N	unknown; energy dependent	yes; also in vitro	48, 49
Glutamate dehydrogenase, NADP dependent	*C. utilis*, *Aspergillus nidulans*	transfer of derepressed cells to media lacking glucose	unknown; energy dependent	no	59, 65 (B. A. Hemmings, personal communication)
Glutamine synthetase	*C. utilis*	addition of NH_4^+ to cells grown under nitrogen limitation	ligand-induced conformational change, followed by dissociation	no	21, 116
Glutamine synthetase	*E. coli*, *Salmonella*, *Klebsiella*, *Shigella*	addition of NH_4 to cells grown under nitrogen limitations, or growth on excess N	enzymatic adenylylation of a specific tyrosine residue; cascade control of adenylylating and deadenylylating enzymes involving uridylylation	yes; by phosphorolytic deadenylylation	54, 120
Glutamine PRPP amidotransferase	*B. subtilis*	stationary phase, starvation	oxidation of enzyme bound Fe^{2+}	?	126, 134, 135
Glycerol dehydrogenase	*Aerobacter aerogenes*	transfer of induced cells to medium containing energy sources and high O_2 tension	unknown; energy dependent	no	76

Table 1 *(Continued)*

Enzyme inactivated	Organism(s)	Culture conditions leading to inactivation	Proposed mechanism of inactivation	Reactivation in vivo without protein synthesis	Ref.
Glycerol kinase	*N. crassa*	shift of cold-induced cells to 26°C; evidence suggests continuous inactivation	unknown	no	90
Isocitrate dehydrogenase	*E. coli*, *K. aerogenes*, *Salmonella typhimurium*, *Serratia marcescens*	addition of acetate to cells under growth conditions requiring operation of the glyoxalate cycle	apparently involves covalent attachment of a phosphate containing group	yes, under conditions where operation of glyoxalate cycle is not required	4 (H. C. Reeves, personal communication)
Isocitrate lyase	*Chlorella pyrenoidosa*, *C. fusca*	addition of glucose to acetate grown cells, especially when N starved	unknown; enzyme protein disappears; inactive protein accumulates in presence of 2,4–dinitrophenol	no	62, 130
Isocitrate lyase	*M. xanthus*	induction of myxospore formation by glycerol addition	unknown; energy dependent	?	94
α-Isopropylmalate synthase	*S. cerevisiae*	addition of glucose to acetate or lactate grown cells	unknown	no	10
Lysine decarboxylase	*B. cadaveris*	transfer of induced cells to medium containing glucose and cadaverine	loss of pyridoxal phosphate (?)	?	82
Malate dehydrogenase (cytoplasmic)	*Saccharomyces* spp. *Schizosaccharomyes pombe*	addition of glucose to acetate grown cells	unknown; cross-reactive protein disappears	no	19, 22–24, 87, 88, 137
Maltose permease	*S. cerevisiae* and *S. carlsbergenis*	suspension of maltose grown cells in glucose containing medium	unknown	no	39, 104, 137

Table 1 *(Continued)*

Nitrate reductase (assimilatory)	*N. crassa, Ustilago maydis, A. nidulans*	addition of NH_4^+ to derepressed cells, or suspension without N source	unknown; enzyme protein disappears; may involve pyridine nucleotides	no	13, 18, 58, 74, 118, 124, 139
Nitrate reductase (assimilatory)	*Chlorella* spp., *Chlamydomonas reinhardii, Cyanidium caldarium*	addition to NH_4^+ to NO_3^- grown cells in the light	appears to involve reduction by NADH and (in *C. vulgaris*) binding of CN^- to the enzyme	yes; also in vitro	77, 78, 103, 117
Nitrogen-fixing activity	*Rhodospirillum rubrum, Azotobacter vinelandii*	addition of NH_4^+, glutamine, or asparagine to N_2-fixing cells; stationary phase	unknown	?	66, 89
Ornithine transcarbamylase (biosynthetic)	*S. cerevisiae, Saccharomyces* spp. *B. subtilis*	addition of arginine to cells grown in minimal medium	specific binding of arginase, which is induced by arginine, to the enzyme in the presence of arginine	yes; in vitro	60, 141
Phosphomonesterase (acid)	*Euglena gracilis*	addition of P_i to derepressed cells	unknown	no	75, 100
Phosphoenolpyruvate carboxykinase	*S. cerevisiae*	addition of glucose to derepressed cells	unknown	no	31, 44
Protein synthesis initiation factor IF-3	*E. coli*	stationary phase	unknown; cross-reactive proteins disappears	?	109a
Pyruvate dehydrogenase	*N. crassa*	?	enzymatic phosphorylation by ATP	yes; in vitro by phosphatase action	142
Ribulose-1,5-diphosphate carboxylase	*Hydrogenomonas* spp., *Chromatium*	starvation of derepressed cells for carbon source (fructose)	unknown; energy dependent	?	57, 68
Threonine dehydratase (biosynthetic)	*B. licheniformis*	stationary phase, exhaustion of nutrients	unknown	?	5, 72
Threonine dehydratase (biodegradative)	*E. coli*	addition of glucose, certain keto or amino acids to derepressed cells	binding of pyruvate, followed by dissociation	yes; in vitro but not in vivo	20

tions represent only a part of the various physiological states to which a microbe must be able to respond. So important a regulatory event as inactivation of an enzyme would be much more likely to occur as an organism adapts to a major metabolic transition in which continued activity of a given enzyme becomes unnecessary or harmful in a new physiological state.

Shifts in Carbon and Nitrogen Metabolism

Perhaps the clearest situation calling for regulation by enzyme inactivation is one in which there is a shift in the nature of the carbon or nitrogen source such that the continued operation of an enzyme involved in utilization of the original metabolite creates a futile cycle during growth on a new nutrient. An example of this occurs following the anaerobic growth of *Rhodopseudomonas gelatinosa* in the light on citrate (32, 33). During citrate utilization acetate accumulates in the medium; when citrate is exhausted the cells must switch from citrate catabolism to citrate synthesis for the purpose of glutamate synthesis. The first enzyme of citrate catabolism, citrate lyase, has been shown to be inactivated under these conditions, presumably to prevent a futile cycle between citrate synthesis and citrate breakdown. This interpretation is strengthened by the finding that the inactivating enzyme, S-acetyl citrate lyase deactylase, is specifically inhibited by L-glutamate (34). A similar explanation may be applied to the inactivation of phosphoenolpyruvate carboxykinase (31, 44), fructose 1,6-bisphosphatase (30), and cytoplasmic malate dehydrogenase (19, 22), which is observed when glucose is added to acetate-adapted *Saccharomyces cerevisiae* cells. Each of these enzymes is involved in gluconeogenesis from acetate, a process that must be blocked to prevent futile cycling in glucose-fermenting yeast cells. Holzer (52) has described this phenomona of glucose-induced inactivation of yeast enzymes in detail and has proposed the term "catabolite inactivation" for it. Another example is the inactivation of the biosynthetic ornithine transcarbamylase in *S. cerevisiae* by arginase, which is induced when excess arginine is added to cells growing on minimal medium (141). The result is to prevent a futile cycle between arginine synthesis and arginine catabolism. One can imagine many other situations in which an organism is capable of both de novo biosynthesis and catabolism of an essential cellular component that might call for regulatory inactivation to prevent futile cycles; these should provide fertile territory for searching for new inactivation processes.

Enzyme inactivation also serves to divert a metabolite at a branch point from one pathway to another. For example, inactivation of isocitrate dehydrogenase in enteric bacteria is provoked by conditions, such as a shift from growth on glucose to growth on acetate, that require utilization of isocitrate in the glyoxalate cycle instead of catabolism through the citric acid cycle (4).

Even more common than the situations calling for enzyme inactivation to prevent futile cycles or to regulate branch points are those in which a shift in carbon source renders an enzyme unnecessary. In these cases the continued activity of the enzyme may be wasteful to the cell but not directly harmful. Examples are the inactivation of aspartate transcarbamylase (16, 138), aspartokinase (42, 121), glutamine phosphoribosyl-1-pyrophosphate amidotransferase (134, 135), and threonine dehydratase (72) in bacilli when these cells enter stationary phase prior to endospore formation. Such cells appear to be capable of supplying nucleotides and amino acids for spore synthesis from turnover of endogenous RNA and protein. Thus, inactivation of enzymes of de novo synthesis presumably spares metabolites and energy. Some members of the group of enzymes subject to catabolite inactivation in yeast (52) and bacteria (20) are enzymes utilizing such secondary catabolites as galactose, maltose, and threonine. These enzymes are inactivated when a preferred catabolite —glucose, fructose, or mannose—is available.

The examples of inactivation of enzymes involved in nitrogen metabolism in Table 1 accord well with the generalizations just made. A futile cycle between glutamate synthesis and catabolism in certain yeasts and fungi appears to be prevented by inactivation of NADP- and NAD-dependent glutamate dehydrogenases. NAD-dependent glutamate dehydrogenase is induced by growth on glutamate as a nitrogen or nitrogen and carbon source and probably functions in glutamate catabolism (48, 49). If *Candida utilis* cells are shifted from growth on glutamate to NH_4^+, to other nitrogen sources that lead to NH_4^+, or even to nitrogen starvation, the NAD-dependent glutamate dehydrogenase is rapidly inactivated (48, 49). The inactivation is stimulated by readily utilizable carbon sources, such as glucose. These observations can be explained by suggesting that the cells are suddenly required to switch from glutamate breakdown to glutamate synthesis under these conditions and that a futile cycle is prevented by inactivation of the dehydrogenase. The reciprocal situation has also been observed; that is, the key enzyme of NH_4^+ utilization in yeast and fungi, NADP-dependent glutamate dehydrogenase, is rapidly inactivated in *Aspergillus nidulans* (59, 65) and *C. utilis* (B. A. Hemmings, personal communication) when cells grown on glucose and NH_4^+ are switched to glutamate as a sole carbon and nitrogen source. The absence of glucose is essential for this inactivation, which suggests that futile cycling between glutamate catabolism and glutamate synthesis is most likely to occur in carbon-starved cells.

The inactivations of glutamine synthetase in bacteria (54, 120) and yeast (21, 116), nitrate reductase (13, 58, 74, 77, 78, 103, 118, 124), and enzymes of nitrogen fixation (66, 89) after the addition of NH_4^+ or other rich nitrogen sources provide examples of the sparing of metabolic energy by the rapid switching off of reactions that have become unnecessary.

Differentiation

It is likely that the inactivation of enzymes will prove to be associated with microbial differentiation or morphogenesis. Examples from Table 1 are found in bacterial endospore formation (5, 16, 41, 42, 72, 121, 126, 134, 138), endospore germination and outgrowth (93), and myxospore formation (94, 105). Protein degradation and inactivation of specific proteins during ascospore formation in yeast have been described by Betz & Weiser (5a). Examples from differentiating slime molds have been reviewed elsewhere (2, 43, 64, 125). In the instances cited the differentiation is generally elicited by a change in the carbon or nitrogen metabolism, however, and the involvement of enzyme inactivation in an event specifically concerned with microbial morphogenesis has not been proven.

Why Inactivation?

What advantages are conferred in microbial systems by enzyme inactivation? Why is inactivation found in place of or in addition to repression of enzyme synthesis and inhibition of enzymes by metabolites? The answers must be speculative at this time, but the following considerations seem important. In the case of covalent modification-inactivation the modification is catalyzed by inactivating and reactivating enzymes, which are subject to allosteric control and, in at least one case (120), a cascade control involving yet another covalent modification. The advantages of such systems have been discussed by Stadtman & Ginsburg (120) and by Holzer & Duntze (54). Clearly important among these advantages is the increased sensitivity or multiplier effect obtained when the regulatory metabolite acts on an inactivating catalyst rather than directly on the enzyme to be inactivated. Furthermore, involvement of another protein can provide more effector binding sites. If inactivation of the degradative type is found to involve specific proteins, similar advantages would apply to these systems. Simple repression of a harmful or wasteful enzyme is inadequate to block its effects, especially in cells that are not able to synthesize new proteins rapidly, as is often the case during the various metabolic transitions in Table 1. Inhibition of an enzyme by an appropriate metabolite clearly can and does function to switch off enzyme activity in many situations like those described above. During a major metabolic shift, however, a microbe is often starved until it completes adaptation to the new growth condition. In such cases degradative inactivation can serve not only to block a wasteful reaction but to provide amino acids for the synthesis of new enzymes and catabolites for metabolic energy. Selective degradation would provide a far more efficient means of doing this than a general random proteolysis.

Modification inactivation does not irreversibly commit a cell to a new metabolic situation since the inactivated enzyme can usually be reactivated quickly without new protein synthesis. Inactivation of the degradative type lacks this flexibility, although resynthesis of the inactivated enzyme is possible under appropriate conditions. It is not yet clear whether the two types of inactivation processes are predictably distributed in various physiological situations, but the somewhat longer time and protein synthesis required for reversal of degradative inactivation imposes some restrictions on the situations in which it can occur.

MECHANISMS OF INACTIVATION

The development of this field is insufficiently advanced to permit a comprehensive survey of the biochemical mechanisms of enzyme inactivation. Only a few mechanisms, all of the modification type, are adequately understood. Nonetheless, the variety already found suggests that living systems have evolved many different mechanisms for enzyme inactivation.

Physical Mechanisms

Included in the physical mechanism group are all mechanisms of the modification type that result from physical changes in the enzyme, generally as the result of tight binding of a molecule or dissociation of the enzyme, in the absence of covalent bond formation or breakage. Inactivation as the result of very tight binding of a low-molecular-weight inhibitor occurs in the inactivation of nitrate reductase upon addition of NH_4^+- to NO_3^--grown algae cells in the presence of light (77; see also 78). In this case CN^- is produced in small quantities, which inactivates the enzyme by binding very tightly to it. The tight binding of pyruvate has been implicated in inactivation and dissociation of the biodegradative threonine dehydratase from *E. coli* (20), but it is not yet known whether the pyruvate is noncovalently or covalently attached to the enzyme. The binding of a macromolecule, arginase, to biosynthetic ornithine transcarbamylase has been shown to be responsible for inactivation of the latter enzyme in yeast (141). Ligand-induced conformational changes, followed by dissociation to inactive or labile subunits, was proposed as the mechanism for NH_4^+-induced inactivation of glutamine synthetase from *C. utilis* (116).

Chemical Mechanisms

Inactivation mechanisms that result from chemical modifications without cleavage of peptide bonds are the best understood group of inactivation processes. Glutamine synthetase from enteric bacteria is inactivated by attachment of AMP in phosphodiester linkage to the phenolic hydroxyl of a specific tyrosyl residue of the protein (120). This modification reaction is catalyzed by an allosteric enzyme system, which is itself subject to regulation by reversible uridylylation of one of the necessary proteins. Because this remarkable system has been thoroughly described elsewhere (54, 120), it is not discussed in detail here. Inactivation of the citrate lyase from *R. gelatinosa* by enzymatic cleavage of acetate from a sulfhydryl group on the enzyme has been demonstrated (32–34). The enzyme responsible for this reaction is under appropriate allosteric control (34). A reactivating activity that catalyzes ATP-dependent attachment of an acetyl group has been described but is not yet fully characterized (33). ATP-dependent phosphorylation and inactivation of the pyruvic dehydrogenase complex from *Neurospora crassa,* as well as enzyme reactivation by a phosphatase, have been reported (142). This system strongly resembles the regulation of mammalian pyruvic dehydrogenase by a simlar phosphorylation mechanism. Another probable instance of inactivation by phosphorylation has been discovered in studies of the isocitrate dehydrogenase of *E. coli* (H. C. Reeves, personal communication). It is likely that the inactivation of NAD-dependent glutamate dehydrogenase from *C. utilis* involves a reversible covalent modification, but its nature is not yet known (48, 49).

Inactivation by chemical changes involving nonprotein prosthetic groups is a possible mechanism in two cases in this review. Mandelstam (82) has proposed that the inactivation of lysine decarboxylase in *Bacillus cadaveris* results from loss of the pyridoxal phosphate cofactor. Turnbough & Switzer proposed (135) that the oxygen-dependent inactivation of glutamine phosphoribosylpyrophosphate aminotransferase in *B. subtilis* is the result of oxidation of tightly bound Fe^{2+}.

Degradative Inactivation: The Role of Proteolysis and Turnover

One of the most interesting and least understood of inactivation mechanisms is the degradative type. Although the general phenomenon of protein turnover in microbes has been well studied, there are only a few instances in which evidence has been offered for the disappearance of specific enzyme proteins as part of in vivo inactivation processes. These are the inactivation of aspartate transcarbamylase from *B. subtilis* (7, 126; M. R. Maurizi, J. S. Brabson, R. L. Switzer, unpublished data), isocitrate lyase of *Chlorella* (62, 130), cytoplasmic malate dehydrogenase of *S. cerevisiae* (88), NADP-dependent glutamate dehydrogenase of *C. utilis* (B. A. Hemmings, personal communication), lysine-sensitive aspartokinase of *E. coli* (127a), protein synthesis initiation factor IF-3 of *E. coli* (109a), and the assimilatory nitrate reductase of *Neurospora* (118). It is very likely that others of the examples listed in Table 1 belong in this category and that many undiscovered examples exist. The difficulty in describing mechanisms of this class is that none of them is well understood in biochemical terms. It is not known whether inactivation results directly from a peptide bond cleavage or whether degradation occurs subsequent to another physical or chemical modification, such as those described in the previous paragraphs. The particular proteinases that are involved in vivo have not been identified. The molecular basis of the regulation of the inactivation is not known. It is clear in at least one case (126, 138) that the protein does not turn over continuously. The degradation and turnover of an enzyme must involve many individual steps, but no intermediates have been identified from in vivo studies. Clearly the solution to these problems is one of the most important challenges in this field.

Some progress has been made in characterizing the proteolytic enzymes of some microbes in which inactivation processes occur in vivo (reviewed in 53). Although there is a substantial gap between our knowledge of the action of these proteinases in vitro and our ability to assign roles to them in inactivation or turnover processes in vivo, it is certain that proteinases are involved at some stage in degradative inactivation. The proteolytic system of yeast is perhaps the most thoroughly studied. The various proteinases, their specific protein inhibitors, the subcellular compartmentalization of these proteins, and cultural conditions governing their levels in cells have all been described (53). The participation of two of these proteinases in the inactivation of tryptophan synthetase in vitro has been demonstrated (108), but this process appears to proceed rather slowly in vitro (46). Two of the enzymes subject to catabolite inactivation in yeast have been shown to be proteolyzed by yeast proteinases (63, 86, 87), and there is evidence that one of these, malate dehydrogenase, is degraded in vivo during inactivation (88). Yet the specificity of the proteinases in vitro does not account for the selectivity and regulation of the catabolite inactivation process. Inactivation of enzymes of this group can be induced by glucose in yeast spheroplasts (84), but no such regulation can be demonstrated in lysed spheroplasts (H. Matern and H. Holzer, personal communication). The possibility that the selectivity of catabolite inactivation in yeast is actually imposed at the level of transport into the vacuole, where the proteinases are concentrated, has been put forward by Holzer (52). This mechanism cannot account for the selectivity of the degradative inactivation of aspartate transcarbamylase in *B. subtilis,* however, because no such subcellular compartments exist in this organism.

The proteinases of *B. subtilis* have been characterized by biochemical and genetic techniques (17, 45, 98, 102, 127). There is at present, however, no evidence linking these proteinases to an inactivation process. Evidence obtained with proteinase-deficient mutant strains argues against their involvement in the primary step of inactivation of aspartate transcarbamylase or glutamine phosphoribosyl-1-pyrophosphate amidotransferase (16, 134, 138).

Unknown Mechanisms

Although it is likely that most inactivation mechanisms will be found to fit into one or a combination of the above categories, the discovery of other mechanistic types or major new mechanistic features must not be excluded. At least six of the examples in Table 1 present unknown biochemical mechanisms in which the inactivation process requires metabolic energy. This requirement generally has been demonstrated with the use of inhibitors. Its meaning in biochemical terms is obscure. Such a requirement could represent (i) a direct involvement of ATP or reducing equivalents in a covalent modification, (ii) a requirement for energy for protein or nucleic acid synthesis, which has been generally excluded by use of inhibitors, (iii) a requirement for energy to maintain a pool of regulatory or "signaling" metabolites, or (iv) a requirement for energy for transport of the protein into a subcellular compartment. Particularly intriguing in this regard is the report of Thurston et al (130) that the inactivation of isocitrate lyase in *Chlorella* is not inhibited by 2,4-dinitrophenol, but the disappearance of the protein is. A portion of protein turnover in microbial and mammalian systems is known to be energy dependent (36, 37, 50, 95, 110, 122). Generally, it has not been possible to demonstrate this energy dependence in cell-free systems (9, 36–38, 56, 95, 96). Curiously, failure to demonstrate inactivation in vitro has also been reported in several of the energy-dependent systems (52, 93, 138). Although these observations may be coincidental, there is a possibility that the phenomena of energy dependence of inactivation, energy dependence of protein turnover, and the difficulty of reconstructing both in vitro are mechanistically linked. If so, these systems offer experimental objects for the study of an important area of regulatory biochemistry.

METHODS FOR STUDYING INACTIVATION PROCESSES

General Characterization

The characterization of a suspected enzyme inactivation process must include experiments to establish that a true inactivation takes place. (i) It must be demonstrated that a loss in total activity occurs, i.e. that the specific activity of the enzyme decreases faster than can be accounted for by cessation of synthesis and dilution by the increase of cellular protein. (ii) Extreme care must be taken to demonstrate the stability of the enzyme in question during cell extraction and assay or at the very least to demonstrate that there is no change in the stability of the enzyme in extracts of cells harvested at various times during the apparent inactivation. This is important because the content of stabilizing or destabilizing metabolites or of degradative enzymes often changes during metabolic transitions of the kinds that induce enzyme inactivation. An example of the extreme care that may be required to avoid artifacts in the assay of an unstable enzyme that is stabilized by metabolites and increases in protein concentration is given in the studies of pyruvate kinase from *Bacillus licheniformis* (133), an enzyme that earlier had been reported to be inactivated in the stationary phase of growth (5). The appearance of proteinase activities in starved cells is a particularly troublesome problem. Recently, we were able to show that the apparent inactivation of IMP dehydrogenase in sporulating *B. subtilis* cells is an artifact caused by proteinase activity during preparation of cell extracts (85). Some methods of detecting and avoiding such artifacts were presented. (iii) Because the intracellular concentration of some enzymes appears to be regulated by excretion in the differentiating slime molds (43, 64, 91), one must determine whether an enzyme that disappears from microbial cells can be found in the growth medium and, when findings are negative, demonstrate that the enzyme in question could have been detected at the expected levels in the culture medium by the assay used. At least one instance of inactivation of an extracellular enzyme by an extracellular protein, possibly a proteinase, is known (28). (iv) Inactivation of an enzyme can be mimicked by transfer of the enzyme to a subcellular compartment that is impermeable to assay reagents or discarded during preparation of extracts. A fraction of the soluble glycogen synthetase of *Dictyostelium discoideum* undergoes such an association with insoluble cell wall material during culmination (43, 64). Therefore it is necessary to examine unfractionated extracts, cell debris, and extracts prepared by a variety of rupture methods to ensure detection of any enzyme rendered cryptic by transfer to a subcellular compartment. (v) In some cases of modification-inactivation systems the altered enzyme shows major changes in cation specificity, pH optimum, Michaelis constants for substrates, and sensitivity to metabolic effectors (48, 54, 120). Hence, it is necessary to determine these kinetic parameters on enzyme samples taken before, during, and near the end of a suspected inactivation process. Except in the case of selective inactivation of isozymes, the finding of such shifts in kinetic properties provides tentative evidence for an inactivation of the modification type (or possibly a modification that is not true inactivation) and argues against degradative inactivation. (vi) A major change in the activity of an enzyme in crude extracts could result from loss of an activator or accumulation of an inhibitor as the cells undergo a metabolic transition. For this reason it is desirable to determine whether dialysis or gel filtration has effects on the activity of extracts of cells harvested before, during, and after a suspected inactivation. The definition I have applied to enzyme inactivation excludes inhibition or loss of activation by dialyzable metabolites, but such phenomena are obviously of interest in the overall regulation of a given enzyme. Experiments in which extracts of cells harvested before the inactivation are mixed with extracts from cells harvested during or after the inactivation also aid in identifying possible activators, inhibitors, or inactivating enzymes that may be responsible for an apparent inactivation process. In this case effectors of any molecular size will be detected if they are present in excess of the enzyme or act catalytically. The cases of most direct interest are those in which an inactivating protein is found. In view of the possible artifacts in such experiments it is essential to develop criteria for establishing that any inactivation in vitro is the same as that which occurs in vivo.

The general characterization of an inactivation process should also include experiments that define the range of conditions in which inactivation occurs, the specificity of nutritional effectors, and the situations in which the enzyme reappears. Such studies often define a probable physiological function for the inactivation and may provide clues as to the metabolites that are required for the inactivation to occur.

Effects of Inhibitors

Further analysis of an inactivation process is usually aided by use of metabolic inhibitors. The general principle is to determine the biochemical requirements of an inactivation process by adding inhibitors of specific metabolic sequences prior to the inactivation, while the inactivation is in progress, and prior to a manipulation that leads to reappearance of the activity, if one can be found. For studies of a requirement for RNA and protein synthesis, rifampin and chloramphenicol, respectively, have found extensive application with bacterial systems, actinomycin D and cycloheximide with eukaryotic systems. A requirement for metabolic energy has been revealed by use of anaerobiosis, uncouplers, and inhibitors of electron transport (e.g. 30, 48, 68, 93, 94, 119, 130, 138). Such inhibitors are most useful if they are used under conditions in which the cells are totally dependent on oxidative metabolism for energy generation, i.e. when fermentative pathways cannot function. The use of inhibitors of glycolysis has proven less satisfactory in experiments with whole cells. The proteinase inhibitor phenylmethylsulfonyl fluoride (PMSF) has been used to test the involvement of proteolysis in inactivation in vivo (10, 94), but in view of a report that PMSF has pronounced effects on energy metabolism in bacteria (114) caution in interpretation of results is required. This last observation points out a serious problem in the use of metabolic inhibitors, namely, few of them are fully specific in their action. Cycloheximide, in particular, has been shown to affect overall metabolism in yeast cells (22). Rifampin may have unknown side effects since this antibiotic has been shown to kill *B. subtilis* cells rather than act as a bacteriostatic agent (12). Hence, it is desirable to document the effectiveness and specificity of action of a given inhibitor whenever possible. A range of concentrations should be examined. In addition, it is advisable to test a variety of inhibitors and to supplement inhibitor studies with the use of appropriate mutant strains.

Use of Mutant Strains

Although mutant strains have not been extensively used in the characterization of inactivation processes, their use is one of the greatest potential advantages in studying inactivation in microbes. Mutant strains with a defect in a given metabolic sequence can be used in physiological studies to define the requirements for inactivation or reappearance of an enzyme in much the same way as specific inhibitors are used but without many of the disadvantages of inhibitors. For example, mutant strains defective in enzymes of the tricarboxylic acid cycle were used to define the requirement for energy metabolism in the inactivation of aspartate transcarbamylase in *B. subtilis* (138). Duntze et al (19) used a yeast tryptophan auxotroph to show that protein synthesis was not required for catabolite inactivation of malate dehydrogenase but was required for reappearance of enzyme activity. Mutant strains can be used to test for involvement of metabolites in situations where no specific inhibitors are known. *Rel*$^-$ mutant strains have been used to demonstrate that an inactivation does not require a functional stringent response (138), for example, a conclusion that would be difficult to reach in other ways. Mutant strains deficient in specific intracellular proteinases (45, 127) have also proven useful in probing possible involvement of these proteinases in inactivation of particular enzymes (16, 134, 138). This use of proteinase-deficient mutants has several uncertainties: the possibility of pleiotropic effects in the mutant strains; the fact that most strains are not totally lacking in the proteinase activity; and the overlapping specificity of multiple proteinases in the species examined.

With the exception of the detailed genetic studies of the inactivation of glutamine synthetase by Magasanik and his colleagues (15, 25, 26, 61, 80, 101, 123), very few attempts to isolate mutant strains defective in inactivation or reappearance processes have been reported. The results of the genetic studies with glutamine synthetase in *Klebsiella aerogenes* point the way to a general and powerful method for analyzing enzyme inactivation systems, at least those involving specific inactivating enzymes. In the case of glutamine synthetase, glutamine auxotrophy will result not only from mutations in the structural gene for glutamine synthetase (*gln*A) but also from defects in the enzymes that reactivate the enzyme by catalyzing removal of the adenylyl group (*gln*B, *gln*D). Another class of mutations (*gln*E) was isolated from revertants of the *gln*B class; these were shown to be defective in the adenylylating enzyme. The effectiveness of the use of glutamine auxotrophy as a selective phenotype was reinforced in this case by the fact that adenylylated glutamine synthetase is not only inactive but serves to repress synthesis of glutamine synthetase. The discovery of roles for adenylylated and deadenylylated forms of glutamine synthetase in regulation of transcription of certain genes coding for enzymes involved in nitrogen metabolism was an important additional contribution from these studies (79).

The application of the approach developed by Magasanik and colleagues in the study of glutamine synthetase to other inactivation systems that involve reversible modification inactivation should be straightforward and fruitful as long as mutant strains that are defective in the activity of the enzyme that is inactivated can be selected easily. In the case of enzymes subject to degradative inactivation, there is no precedent to guide our thinking. Since in such cases reappearance of the enzyme results from new synthesis, defects in reactivating enzymes cannot be expected. Rather one would expect mutations in the structural gene of the target enzyme rendering it hypersensitive to the inactivating system, and mutations in the inactivating system so that it has lost its normal selectivity and destroys the target enzyme at inappropriate times. Genetic mapping and analysis of the properties of appropriate diploid strains should be valuable adjuncts to biochemical characterization of such mutant strains.

An interesting alternative approach was taken by van de Poll et al (136), who isolated a mutant strain of *S. cerevisiae* that was unable to grow on glucose but was able to grow on glycerol or ethanol. This strain is incapable of carrying out the inactivation of fructose 1,6-bisphosphatase that normally follows addition of glucose to derepressed cells (30, 86). Catabolite inactivation of maltose permease (104) is normal in the mutant cells, but the inactivation of cytoplasmic malate dehydrogenase and phosphoenolpyruvate carboxykinase is also blocked (31). The mutant cells are capable of normal glucose uptake, and no defects in the enzymes of glycolysis or gluconeogenesis have been detected (K. W. van de Poll, personal communication). The intracellular levels of ATP drop sharply in the mutant strain (unlike the wild type) when glucose is added to glycerol-grown cells. This result suggests that failure to carry out the normal catabolite inactivation results in an ATP-splitting futile cycle between glycolysis and gluconeogenesis. The nature of the biochemical defect in this interesting mutant strain remains to be defined; its identification might yield valuable clues to the nature or regulation of the catabolite inactivation process in yeast. The general approach to selecting mutant strains defective in inactivation processes adopted by van de Poll et al, namely, selecting for the nutritional limitations imposed by failure to inactivate an enzyme under given conditions, should be applicable to other situations.

Reactivation In Vivo and In Vitro

Culture conditions generally can be found under which the activity of an inactivated enzyme returns to the cells. If one can determine whether this reaction requires de novo synthesis of the enzyme, one can distinguish between inactivation processes of the modification type and of the degradative type. Most investigators have approached this problem by exposing cells to reactivating conditions in the presence of antibiotic inhibitors of RNA or protein synthesis. Restoration of activity in the presence of inhibitors implies reactivation of already existing, inactive enzyme molecules. It is necessary to document the effectiveness of the inhibitory conditions used. The converse result, failure to observe restoration of activity, may indicate that the inactivation is of the degradative type and that restoration requires de novo synthesis. This is a crude criterion, however, because protein synthesis could also be required for formation of a reactivating enzyme and because the inhibitors may have secondary effects on metabolism.

Reactivation of an inactivated enzyme in cell extracts, incubated under conditions where cell-free protein synthesis is excluded, provides strong evidence that an inactivation is of the modification type and is often a valuable technique for learning the biochemical nature of the inactivation process. For example, the activity of adenylylated glutamine synthetase can be restored by treatment of the enzyme with phosphodiesterase (120). Reactivation of citrate lyase was accomplished chemically by treating the inactivated enzyme with acetic anhydride (32). The inactivation of the NAD-dependent glutamate dehydrogenase from *C. utilis* appears to result from a covalent modification, although the nature of this modification has not yet been defined (48, 49). The inactivated enzyme can be readily reactivated in vitro; a reactivating protein has been separated from the dehydrogenase (48, 49).

Following the Fate of the Enzyme Protein During Inactivation

Biochemical analysis of an enzyme inactivation occurring in vivo or in crude cell extracts suffers from the difficulty that the experimenter has only one tool for following the inactivation, namely, assay of catalytic activity. More can be learned about the biochemical nature of an inactivation and events subsequent to it if one has a specific means of following the fate of the enzyme protein independently of its loss of catalytic activity. Is the protein accumulated in an inactive form or is it degraded? If an inactive protein is accumulated, what physical and/or chemical changes has it undergone? Several approaches to this problem have been used, the most general of which is immunochemical. It is unlikely that loss of catalytic activity in a modification inactivation will result in loss of all the antigenic determinants of the enzyme protein. For example, adenylylated glutamine synthetase is immunochemically identical to the unmodified form (132). Hence, antibodies specifically directed against the native enzyme can be used in such cases to identify the accumulation of inactive cross-reactive material. On the other hand, if the enzyme is extensively degraded during or after inactivation, it will not be detected by antibodies directed against the native enzyme. There are some uncertainties in this last conclusion. One does not know a priori how extensive the denaturation or degradation of an enzyme must be for it to escape detection by immunochemical techniques. Loss of native quaternary and tertiary structure is often associated with a marked decrease in antigenicity of globular proteins, although peptide fragments of enzymes retain the ability to react with antibodies in many cases (14). Thus, detection of modified, denatured, or degraded products of enzyme inactivation processes should be possible in some cases, but failure to detect such products does not permit one to conclude that degradation and turnover of the enzyme has occurred. An approach deserving further study is the use of denatured enzyme as the antigen as a possible means of obtaining antibody directed against sequential determinants rather than conformational determinants (14). The methods used for detection and quantitation of antigen-antibody complex formation can lead to contradictory conclusions, so it is desirable to use more than one method. In our own research on the inactivation of aspartate transcarbamylase in *B. subtilis* (7, 126; M. R. Maurizi & R. L. Switzer, unpublished experiments), we have assayed immunoprecipitation by Coomassie Blue staining and densitometry of immunoprecipitates after electorphoresis on sodium dodecyl sulfate-polyacrylamide gels and by counting gel slices after electrophoresis of immunoprecipitates from cells labeled with radioactive amino acids. These methods were useful because the aspartate transcarbamylase subunit is well resolved from the immunoglobulin chains and because fragments derived from dragradation of the enzyme that were precipitable by the antibody would have been detected. The results showed clearly that immunoprecipitable protein disappears from the cells in parallel with catalytic activity. A more commonly used immunochemical technique is to use the ability of the antibody to inhibit the enzyme to be assayed as a measure of the antigen present in an extract (72, 88, 118). This approach assumes that an inactive, cross-reactive protein will also adsorb antibody, so that an accumulation of inactive material will result in an increase in the quantity of antibody required to inhibit a unit of catalytic activity. In our experiments with aspartate transcarbamylase, this method also indicated that inactive, cross-reactive material did not accumulate. A potential difficulty with this approach is the possibility that the technique measures the effects of only that subclass of antibody molecules that bind at or near the active site. Since the active site is probably altered during inactivation, failure of this subclass to interact with the active site could possibly lead one to conclude incorrectly that all antigenic sites had disappeared. Other techniques such as microcomplement fixation (73, 140) or indirect immunoprecipitation (113) have promise as methods for following the fate of inactivated proteins, because these methods can detect soluble antigen-antibody complexes.

Another technique of potentially general usefulness for determining whether degradation and synthesis occur simultaneously is the density shift technique used by Williams & Neidhardt (144) to demonstrate the turnover of aminoacyl tRNA synthetases in *E. coli* cells. The cells were grown on 80% deuterium oxide until the proteins were uniformly labeled with deuterium, then they were transferred to normal medium under the conditions of interest. Enzyme synthesized before the shift (density = 1.33) can be separated from newly synthesized enzyme (density = 1.30) by centrifugation on isopycnic CsCl gradients and quantitated by enzymatic assay. As described, the method would not determine whether an inactivated protein accumulates in the cell, but a simple variation could be used to learn whether an inactive, density-labeled enzyme regains activity during transfer to normal medium under reactivating conditions. Unfortunately, Brown et al (10) were unable to use this technique in studies with yeast cells because of failure of the cells to grow in deuterium oxide medium.

Other approaches to following the fate of enzyme protein during an inactivation process are less general. In favorable cases, one may be able to separate the protein in question from all other proteins in the cell by electrophoresis or combined electrophoretic and isoelectric focusing techniques. As methods for reproducible separation of complex protein mixtures are more highly developed (e.g. 1, 92) this approach may become quite useful. I am aware of only two instances in which electrophoretic isolation of an enzyme protein was used to characterize an inactivation process. When *Chlorella* cells are adapted to growth on acetate as a sole carbon source, isocitrate lyase is produced to a level of about 7% of the total cell protein. This protein is readily identified as a discrete band after polyacrylamide gel electrophoresis of cell extracts, so that the fate of the enzyme protein can be followed independently of enzyme activity (62, 130). This technique has been used to show that the enzyme is normally degraded during or subsequent to glucose-induced inactivation of the enzyme, but that 2,4-dinitrophenol apparently protects the inactivated enzyme from degradation (130). An electrophoretic separation was also used by Orlowski & Goldman to determine the fate of ^{35}S-labeled glucose-6-phosphate dehydrogenase during inactivation that occurs during germination of *B. cereus* spores (93). They concluded that the enzyme was not degraded during inactivation. This conclusion is dependent on the assumption that the enzyme band, which was located on polyacrylamide gels by an activity stain, was free of other cellular proteins. This assumption was not documented in the paper, however.

Reconstruction In Vitro

A satisfactory understanding of any enzyme inactivation process cannot be achieved until it has been reconstructed in vitro from highly purified components in such a fashion that its physiological operation and regulation can be reproduced by appropriate manipulation. This goal is nearly reached in the modification inactivation of glutamine synthetase (112, 120). Progress toward this goal has been made in several other cases, all of the modification-inactivation type. For those systems involving degradative inactivation the current status is much less satisfactory. Problems in reconstruction of catabolite inactivation in yeast have been discussed above, as have those dealing with energy-dependent systems. In all cases it is necessary to demonstrate that the reconstructed process faithfully reproduces the inactivation that occurs in vivo. This means that biochemical equivalents for the physiological requirements and regulation of the inactivation must be shown for the in vitro process.

CONCLUDING COMMENTS

It has been the purpose of this review to show that the selective inactivation of enzymes is a general and important regulatory mechanism in microbes and to review what is known concerning the mechanisms of inactivation. Unlike other major types of regulation, inactivation processes do not appear to possess an appealing mechanistic unity. Perhaps for this reason the importance of this class of regulatory processes has been slow in achieving recognition. The systems involving reversible covalent modification of enzymes, all of which were unknown a decade ago, are the best studied and have greatly expanded our understanding of metabolic regulation in microbes. The magnitude of the biochemical challenge lying ahead for this field can be readily appreciated by simply noting the number of inactivation processes of unknown mechanisms listed in Table 1. Particularly challenging are those mechanisms that appear to involve the degradation of enzymes and the participation of metabolic energy. The elucidation of the molecular details of these processes—particularly the basis of the selectivity of degradation—could very well provide insight into the problem of protein turnover in all living systems.

Acknowledgments

A major portion of this review was prepared while I was a Fellow of the John Simon Guggenheim Memorial Foundation and a guest in the laboratory of Helmut Holzer, Biochemisches Institut, University of Freiburg, Germany. I am grateful to Prof. Holzer and his colleagues for their hospitality and many stimulating discussions of the subjects reviewed. My own research in this area has been supported by grant AI 11121 from the National Institutes of Health.

Literature Cited

1. Ames, G. F. 1974. *J. Biol. Chem.* 249: 634–44
2. Ashworth, J. M. 1971. *Symp. Soc. Exp. Biol.* 25:27–49
3. Bell, R. G. 1969. *Can. J. Biochem.* 47:677–84
4. Bennett, P. M., Holms, W. H. 1975. *J. Gen. Microbiol.* 87:37–51
5. Bernlohr, R. W., Gray, B. H. 1969. In *Spores IV,* ed. L. Campbell, pp. 186–195. Bethesda, Md.: Am. Soc. Microbiol. 335 pp.

5a. Betz, H., Weiser, U. 1976. *Eur. J. Biochem.* 62:65–76; 70:385–95

6. Beuscher, N., Mayer, F., Gottschalk, G. 1974. *Arch. Microbiol.* 100:307–28
7. Brabson, J. S., Switzer, R. L. 1975. *J. Biol. Chem.* 250:8664–69
8. Bradley, S. G., Creevy, D. C. 1961. *J. Bacteriol.* 81:303–10
9. Brostrom, C. O., Jeffay, H. 1970. *J. Biol. Chem.* 245:4001–8
10. Brown, H. D., Satyanarayana, T., Umbarger, H. E. 1975. *J. Bacteriol.* 121: 959–69
11. Bull, M. J., Lascelles, J. 1963. *Biochem. J.* 87:15–28
12. Coote, J. G., Wood, D. A., Mandelstam, J. 1973. *Biochem. J.* 134:263–70
13. Cove, D. J. 1966. *Biochim. Biophys. Acta* 113:51–56
14. Crumpton, M. J. 1974. In *The Antigens,* ed. M. Sela, 2:1–78. New York: Academic. 568 pp.
15. DeLeo, A. B., Magasanik, B. 1975. *J. Bacteriol.* 121:313–19
16. Deutscher, M. P., Kornberg, A. 1968. *J. Biol. Chem.* 243:4653–60
17. Doi, R. H. 1972. In *Current Topics in Cellular Regulation,* ed. B. L. Horecker, E. R. Stadtman, 6:1–20. New York: Academic. 334 pp.
18. Dunn-Coleman, N. S., Pateman, J. A. 1975. *Trans. Biochem. Soc.* 3:531–33
19. Duntze, W., Neumann, D., Holzer, H. 1968. *Eur. J. Biochem.* 3:326–31
20. Feldman, D. A., Datta, P. 1975. *Biochemistry* 14:1760–67
21. Ferguson, A. R., Sims, A. P. 1974. *J. Gen. Microbiol.* 80:173–85
22. Ferguson, J. J., Boll, M., Holzer, H. 1967. *Eur. J. Biochem.* 1:21–25
23. Flury, U., Heer, B., Fiechter, A. 1974. *Arch. Microbiol.* 97:141–48
24. Flury, U., Heer, B., Fiechter, A. 1974. *Biochim. Biophys. Acta* 341:465–83
25. Foor, F., Janssen, K. A., Magasanik, B. 1975. *Proc. Natl. Acad. Sci. USA* 72: 4844–48
26. Foor, F., Janssen, K. A., Streicher, S. L., Magasanik, B. 1975. *Fed. Proc.* 34(3):514 (Abstr.)
27. Fosset, M., Muir, L. W., Neilsen, L. D., Fischer, E. H. 1971. *Biochemistry* 10: 4105–13
28. Friebe, G., Holldorf, A. W. 1975. *J. Bacteriol.* 122:818–25
29. Friedberg, E. C., Ganesan, A. K., Minton, K. 1975. *J. Virol.* 16:315–21
30. Gancedo, C. 1971. *J. Bacteriol.* 107: 401–5
31. Gancedo, C., Schwerzmann, N. 1976. *Arch. Microbiol.* 109:221–25
32. Giffhorn, F., Beuscher, N., Gottschalk, G. 1972. *Biochem. Biophys. Res. Commun.* 49:467–72
33. Giffhorn, F., Gottschalk, G. 1975. *J. Bacteriol.* 124:1046–51
34. Giffhorn, F., Gottschalk, G. 1975. *J. Bacteriol.* 124:1052–61
35. Gold, M. H., Farrand, R. J., Livoni, J. P., Segel, I. H. 1974. *Arch. Biochem. Biophys.* 161:515–27
36. Goldberg, A. L., Dice, J. F. 1974. *Ann. Rev. Biochem.* 43:835–69
37. Goldberg, A. L., St. John, A. C. 1976. *Ann. Rev. Biochem.* 45:747–803
38. Goldspink, D. F., Goldberg, A. L. 1973. *Biochem. J.* 134:829–32
39. Görts, C. P. M. 1969. *Biochim. Biophys. Acta* 184:299–305
40. Gottschalk, G., Giffhorn, F., Beuscher, N. 1974. *Abstr. Ann. Meet. Am. Soc. Microbiol.* p. 148
41. Grandgenett, D. P., Stahly, D. P. 1968. *J. Bacteriol.* 96:2099–109
42. Gray, B. H., Bernlohr, R. W. 1969. *Biochim. Biophys. Acta* 178:248–61
43. Gustafson, G. L., Wright, B. E. 1972. *CRC Crit. Rev. Microbiol.* 1:453–78
44. Haarasilta, S., Oura, E. 1975. *Eur. J. Biochem.* 52:1–7
45. Hageman, J. H., Carlton, B. C. 1973. *J. Bacteriol.* 114:612–17
46. Hasilik, A., Müller, H., Holzer, H. 1974. *Eur. J. Biochem.* 48:111–17
47. Haslam, E. A., Roscoe, D. H., Tucker, R. G. 1967. *Biochim. Biophys. Acta* 134:312–26
48. Hemmings, B. A. 1975. *The control of glutamate metabolism in yeast.* PhD thesis. Univ. East Anglia, Norwich, England, 301 pp.
49. Hemmings, B. A. 1976. *Abstr. Int. Congr. Biochem. 10th* p. 411
50. Hershko, A., Tomkins, G. M. 1971. *J. Biol. Chem.* 246:710–14

51. Hogness, D. S., Cohn, M., Monod, J. 1955. *Biochim. Biophys. Acta* 16:99–116
52. Holzer, H. 1976. *Trends in Biochemical Sciences* 1:178–81
53. Holzer, H., Betz, H., Ebner, E. 1975. In *Current Topics in Cellular Regulation,* ed. B. L. Horecker, E. R. Stadtman, 9:103–56. New York: Academic. 241 pp.
54. Holzer, H., Duntze, W. 1971. *Ann. Rev. Biochem.* 40:345–74
55. Huang, K.-P., Cabib, E. 1974. *J. Biol. Chem.* 249:3851–57
56. Huisman, W., Bouma, J. M. W., Gruber, M. 1973. *Biochim. Biophys. Acta* 297:93–97
57. Hurlbert, R. E., Lascelles, J. 1963. *J. Gen. Microbiol.* 33:445–58
58. Hynes, M. J. 1973. *J. Gen. Microbiol.* 79:155–57
59. Hynes, M. J. 1974. *J. Gen. Microbiol.* 81:165–70
60. Issaly, I. M., Issaly, A. S. 1974. *Eur. J. Biochem.* 49:485–95
61. Janssen, K. A., Streicher, S. L., Foor, F., Magasanik, B. 1975. *Abstr. Ann. Meet. Am. Soc. Microbiol.* p. 101
62. John, P. C. L., Thurston, C. F., Syrett, P. J. 1970. *Biochem. J.* 119:913–19
63. Jusic, M., Hinze, H., Holzer, H. 1976. *Hoppe-Seyler's Z. Physiol. Chem.* 357: 735–40
64. Killick, K. A., Wright, B. E. 1974. *Ann. Rev. Microbiol.* 28:139–66
65. Kinghorn, J. R., Pateman, J. A. 1974. *Mol. Gen. Genet.* 128:95–98
66. Kleiner, D., Kleinschmidt, J. A. 1976. *J. Bacteriol.* 128:117–22
67. Koch, A. L., Levy, H. R. 1955. *J. Biol. Chem.* 217:947–57
68. Kuehn, G. D., McFadden, B. A. 1968. *J. Bacteriol.* 95:937–46
69. Kurowski, W. M., Fensom, A. H., Pirt, S. J. 1975. *J. Gen. Microbiol.* 90:191–22
70. Lascelles, J. 1960. *J. Gen. Microbiol.* 23:487–98
71. Lascelles, J. 1968. *Adv. Microbiol. Physiol.* 2:1–42
72. Leitzmann, C., Bernlohr, R. W. 1968. *Biochim. Biophys. Acta* 151:461–72
73. Levine, L., Van Vunakis, H. 1967. *Methods Enzymol.* 11:928–36
74. Lewis, C. M., Fincham, J. R. S. 1970. *J. Bacteriol.* 103:55–61
75. Liedtke, M. P., Ohmann, E. 1969. *Eur. J. Biochem.* 10:539–48 (in German)
76. Lin, E. C. C., Levin, A. P., Magasanik, B. 1960. *J. Biol. Chem.* 235:1824–29
77. Lorimer, G. H., Gewitz, H. S., Voelker, W., Solomonson, L. P., Vennesland, B. 1974. *J. Biol. Chem.* 249:6074–79
78. Losada, M. 1974. In *Metabolic Interconversion of Enzymes 1973,* ed. E. Fischer, E. Krebs, H. Neurath, E. Stadtman, pp. 257–70. New York: Springer-Verlag. 399 pp.
79. Magasanik, B. 1976. *Prog. Nucleic Acid Res. Mol. Biol.* 17:99–115
80. Magasanik, B., Prival, M. J., Brenchley, J. E., Tyler, B. M., DeLeo, A. B., Streicher, S. L., Bender, R. A., Paris, G. G. 1974. In *Current Topics in Cellular Regulation,* ed. B. L. Horecker, E. R. Stadtman, 8:119–38. New York: Academic. 350 pp.
81. Mahadik, S. P., Dharmgrongartama, B., Srinivasan, P. R. 1974. *J. Biol. Chem.* 249:1787–91
82. Mandelstam, J. 1954. *J. Gen. Microbiol.* 11:426–37
83. Mandelstam, J. 1958. *Biochem. J.* 69: 110–19
84. Matern, H., Holzer, H. 1976. *Abstr. Int. Congr. Biochem. 10th,* p. 412
85. Maurizi, M. R., Switzer, R. L. 1975. *J. Bacteriol.* 123:1269–72
86. Molano, J., Gancedo, C. 1974. *Eur. J. Biochem.* 44:213–17
87. Neeff, J. 1973. *Untersuchungen zur Glucosabhängigen Inaktivierung der Malatdehydrogenase in Saccharomyces cerevisiae.* Doctoral thesis. Freiburg Univ., German Federal Republic. 101 pp. (in German)
88. Neeff, J., Mecke, D. 1976. *Abstr. Int. Congr. Biochem. 10th,* p. 419
89. Neilson, A. H., Nordlund, S. 1975. *J. Gen. Microbiol.* 91:53–62
89a. Niles, E. G., Westhead, E. W. 1973. *Biochemistry* 12:1715–22, 1723–29
90. North, M. J. 1974. *J. Bacteriol.* 120: 741–47
91. O'Day, D. H. 1973. *J. Bacteriol.* 113: 192–7
92. O'Farrell, P. H. 1975. *J. Biol. Chem.* 250:4007–21
93. Orlowski, M., Goldman, M. 1975. *Biochem. J.* 148:259–68
94. Orlowski, M., White, D. 1974. *J. Bacteriol.* 118:96–102
95. Pine, M. J. 1972. *Ann. Rev. Microbiol.* 26:103–26
96. Pine, M. J. 1975. In *Intracellular Protein Turnover,* ed. R. T. Schimke, N. Katunuma, pp. 65–76. New York: Academic. 348 pp.
97. Pollock, M. R. 1958. *Proc. R. Soc. London Ser. B* 148:340–52
98. Prestidge, L., Gage, V., Spizizen, J. 1971. *J. Bacteriol.* 107:815–23
99. Price, A. R., Frato, J. 1975. *J. Biol. Chem.* 250:8804–11

100. Price, C. A. 1962. *Science* 135:46
101. Prival, M. J., Brenchley, J. E., Magasanik, B. 1973. *J. Biol. Chem.* 248: 4334–44
102. Reysset, G., Millet, J. 1972. *Biochem. Biophys. Res. Commun.* 49:328–34
103. Rigano, C. 1971. *Arch. Microbiol.* 76:265–76
104. Robertson, J. J., Halvorson, H. O. 1957. *J. Bacteriol.* 73:186–98
105. Rosenberg, E., Filer, D., Zafriti, D., Kindler, S. H. 1973. *J. Bacteriol.* 115: 29–34
106. Rotman, B., Spiegelman, S. 1954. *J. Bacteriol.* 68:419–29
107. Sadoff, H. L., Celikkol, E., Engelbrecht, H. L. 1970. *Proc. Natl. Acad. Sci. USA* 66:844–49
108. Saheki, T., Holzer, H. 1974. *Eur. J. Biochem.* 42:621–26
109. Sakaki, Y., Karu, A. E., Linn, S., Echols, H. 1973. *Proc. Natl. Acad. Sci. USA* 70:2215–19
109a. Scheps, R., Revel, M. 1972. *Eur. J. Biochem.* 29:319–25
110. Schlessinger, D., Ben-Hamida, F. 1966. *Biochim. Biophys. Acta* 119:171–82
111. Schneider, R. P., Wiley, W. R. 1971. *J. Bacteriol.* 106:487–92
112. Segal, A., Brown, M. S., Stadtman, E. R. 1974. *Arch. Biochem. Biophys.* 161:319–27
113. Shapiro, D. J., Taylor, J. M., McKnight, G. S., Palacios, R., Gonzalez, C., Kiely, M. L., Schimke, R. T. 1974. *J. Biol. Chem.* 249:3665–71
114. Shechter, Y., Rafaeli-Eshkol, D., Hershko, A. 1973. *Biochem. Biophys. Res. Comm.* 54:1518–24
115. Shortman, K., Lehman, I. R. 1964. *J. Biol. Chem.* 239:2964–74
116. Sims, A. P., Toone, J., Box, B. 1974. *J. Gen. Microbiol.* 80:485–99
117. Solomonson, L. P., Jetschmann, K., Vennesland, B. 1973. *Biochim. Biophys. Acta* 309:32–43
118. Sorger, G. J., Debanne, M. T., Davies, J. 1974. *Biochem. J.* 140:395–403
119. Spiegelman, S., Reiner, J. M. 1947. *J. Gen. Physiol.* 31:175–93
120. Stadtman, E. R., Ginsburg, A. 1974. In *The Enzymes*, ed. P. D. Boyer, 10: 755–807. New York: Academic. 886 pp. 3rd ed.
121. Stahly, D. P., Bernlohr, R. W. 1967. *Biochim. Biophys. Acta* 146:467–76
122. Steinberg, D., Vaughan, M. 1956. *Arch. Biochem. Biophys.* 65:93–105
123. Streicher, S. L., Bender, R. A., Magasanik, B. 1975. *J. Bacteriol.* 121:320–31
124. Subramanian, K. N., Sorger, G. J. 1972. *J. Bacteriol.* 110:538–46
125. Sussman, M., Sussman, R. 1969. *Symp. Soc. Gen. Microbiol.* 19:403–35
126. Switzer, R. L., Turnbough, C. L., Brabson, J. S., Waindle, L. M. 1975. In *Spores VI*, ed. P. Gerhardt, R. N. Costilow, H. L. Sadoff, pp. 327–34. Washington, DC: Am. Soc. Microbiol. 619 pp.
127. Szulmajster, J., Keryer, E. See Ref. 126, pp. 271–78
127a. Tecson, E. M., Westhead, E. W. 1974. *Fed. Proc.* 33(5):1345 (Abstr.)
128. Tellez-Inon, M. T., Torres, H. N. 1970. *Proc. Natl. Acad. Sci. USA* 66:459–63
129. Thurston, C. F. 1972. *Process Biochem.* 7:18–20
130. Thurston, C. F., John, P. C. L., Syrett, P. J. 1973. *Arch. Microbiol.* 88:135–45
131. Tomita, F., Takahashi, I. 1975. *J. Virol.* 15:1073–80
132. Tronick, S. R., Ciardi, J. E., Stadtman, E. R. 1973. *J. Bacteriol.* 115:858–68
133. Tuominen, F. W., Bernlohr, R. W. 1971. *J. Biol. Chem.* 246:1733–45
134. Turnbough, C. L., Switzer, R. L. 1975. *J. Bacteriol.* 121:108–14
135. Turnbough, C. L., Switzer, R. L. 1975. *J. Bacteriol.* 121:115–20
136. van de Poll, K. W., Kerkenaar, A., Schamhart, D. H. J. 1974. *J. Bacteriol.* 117:965–70
137. van Rijn, J., van Wijk, R. 1972. *J. Bacteriol.* 110:477–84
138. Waindle, L. M., Switzer, R. L. 1973. *J. Bacteriol.* 114:517–27
139. Wallace, W. 1975. *Biochim. Biophys, Acta* 377:239–50
140. Wasserman, E., Levine, L. 1961. *J. Immunol.* 87:290–95
141. Wiame, J. M. 1971. In *Current Topics in Cellular Reguation*, ed. B. L. Horecker, E. R. Stadtman, 4:1–38. New York: Academic. 268 pp.
142. Wieland, O. H., Hartmann, U., Siess, E. A. 1972. *FEBS Lett.* 27:240–44
143. Willetts, N. S. 1967. *Biochem. J.* 103:453–61
144. Williams, L. S., Neidhardt, F. C. 1969. *J. Mol. Biol.* 43:529–50

Ann. Rev. Microbiol. 1977. 31:159–80

NOCARDIOFORM BACTERIA

✤1701

M. Goodfellow
Department of Microbiology, The Medical School, University of Newcastle upon Tyne, Newcastle upon Tyne, NE1 7RU, England

D. E. Minnikin
Department of Organic Chemistry, University of Newcastle upon Tyne, Newcastle upon Tyne, NE1 7RU, England

CONTENTS

INTRODUCTION 159
TAXONOMY 161
Numerical Phenetic Studies 161
Chemotaxonomic Studies 162
Wall and whole-cell sugar composition 162
Lipid analysis 163
DNA Analysis and Genetic Studies 168
Serology 169
THE CURRENT SITUATION—*NOCARDIA* REVISITED 170
THE TYPE SPECIES OF *NOCARDIA* 173
OCCURRENCE, DISTRIBUTION, AND PARASITISM 174
CONCLUDING REMARKS 175

INTRODUCTION

Nocardioform actinomycetes are branching bacteria that reproduce by fragmentation of all, or more or less accidently involved, parts of their hyphae into bacilli and coccoid elements (141, 143, 144, 146). The remaining actinomycetes reproduce by spores formed on or in definite parts of the mycelium. In the seventh edition of *Bergey's Manual* (20), nocardioform bacteria were classified in the genera *Nocardia* (182) and *Actinomyces* (72), which at that time formed the family Actinomycetaceae. However, it was widely recognized that the genus *Nocardia* was poorly defined and contained bacteria that had little in common (95, 99, 142).

In the past few years, much effort has been directed towards establishing a better classification of the actinomycetes, established genera have been revised and given tighter definitions, new genera have been proposed to clarify the taxonomy, and many nomenspecies have been reduced to synonyms of well-described taxospecies.

Unfortunately, many of the improvements in the classification of *Nocardia* and related taxa came too late, or were not included, in the eighth edition of *Bergey's Manual* (23), so the section on the family Nocardiaceae (112) is sadly out of date and does not do justice to present views. However, in a classification based primarily on morphological, chemical, and spore characters, actinomycetes have been classified into over 30 genera and 10 families (29, 52). On this basis, nocardioform bacteria can be classified into 20 genera and 7 families (Table 1).

Table 1 Classification of nocardioform actinomycetes[a]

Family	Genus	Earlier designation/Synonyms
Actinomycetaceae	*Actinomyces* (72)	*Odontomyces*
	Agromyces (43)	
	Arachnia (137)	*Actinomyces propionicus*
	Bacterionema (42)	*Leptothrix buccalis*
		Leptotrichia buccalis
		L. dentium
	Bifidobacterium (133)	*Lactobacillus bifidus*
	Rothia (37)	*Actinomyces dentocariosus*
		Nocardia dentocariosus
		N. salivae
Dermatophilaceae	*Dermatophilus* (193)	
	Geodermatophilus (107)	
Frankiaceae	*Frankia* (22)	
Mycobacteriaceae	*Mycobacterium* (105)	
Nocardiaceae	*Micropolyspora* (103)	
	Nocardia (182)	
	Rhodococcus (49)	*Gordona*
		Jensenia
		Mycobacterium rhodochrous
		"*rhodochrous*" complex
	Saccharopolyspora (91)	
Streptomycetaceae	*Intrasporangium* (79)	
	Nocardioides (145)	
Thermomonosporaceae	*Actinomadura* (99)	*Micromonospora rubra*
		Nocardia dassonvillei
		N. madurae
		N. pelletieri
		Streptomyces luteofluorescens
		Thermopolyspora flexuosa
	Nocardiopsis (114)	*Actinomadura dassonvillei*
		Nocardia dassonvillei
Not assigned	*Oerskovia* (148)	*Nocardia turbata*
	Promicromonospora (83)	

[a] Based on the classification of Cross & Goodfellow (29).

This review is concerned mainly with the recent taxonomic developments and current status of the genera *Nocardia* (182) and *Rhodococcus* (49), and with their relationship to one another and to allied taxa. The biological properties of the genus *Nocardia sensu* Waksman (194) and the biology of the anaerobic and microaerophilic nocardioform bacteria have been the subject of recent books (50, 167) and will not be considered here. Further studies are required to determine the taxonomic status and importance of the genera *Agromyces* (43), *Frankia* (22), *Micropolyspora* (103), *Nocardioides* (145), *Nocardiopsis* (114), and *Promicromonospora* (83).

TAXONOMY

Modern taxonomic methods provided the criteria needed for the reclassification of *Nocardia sensu* Waksman (194). Numerical phenetic surveys (55) built upon the pioneering studies of Gordon and her colleagues (57, 58, 62–66) and the advances made have been extended and consolidated in chemical (118), serological (106), and genetical studies (19). There is substantial agreement between Gordon's intuitive approach and numerical classifications (169, 170), but the latter have the advantage that they quantify the relationships between taxa, highlight the degree of variation within them, and allow representative strains for detailed study to be chosen objectively.

Numerical Phenetic Studies

Numerical taxonomy has been used to good effect in the classification of some actinomycete and coryneform taxa. The impact of numerical phenetic surveys on the classification of *Nocardia sensu* Waksman (194) and *Mycobacterium* has been considered in detail (15, 55, 85, 169, 170, 187), and only the overall picture and latest findings will be considered here. In general, there is good agreement between the results of the various analyses, and the aerobic nocardioform bacteria fall into several aggregate clusters now considered to represent distinct genera.

1. *Nocardia sensu stricto* (29) includes both the well-described taxa *Nocardia asteroides, Nocardia brasiliensis, Nocardia caviae* (*Nocardia otitidis-caviarum*), and *Nocardia farcinica* (group Kyoto-1) (48, 183) and the less-well-studied *Nocardia amarae* (100), *Nocardia carnea, Nocardia salmonicida, Nocardia transvalensis* (164), and *Nocardia vaccinii* (48). There is little agreement on the internal structure of *N. asteroides,* although the taxon is clearly heterogeneous, with two (164, 183), four (87, 132), and five (48) subclusters recognized. Since few strains are common to all of these investigations, it is difficult to determine whether or not, and to what extent, defined groups overlap though *N. farcenica* (183). Schaal's cluster 11 are comparable. The status of the type species *N. farcinica* has not been resolved and will be considered later.
2. Numerical surveys have consistently shown that the soft-growing nocardiae or rhodochrous strains form a heterogeneous taxon equivalent in rank to *Nocardia sensu stricto* and to *Corynebacterium sensu stricto* and *Mycobacterium* (15). On the basis of these and other data, Goodfellow & Alderson (49) proposed that the

genus *Rhodococcus* be resurrected to accommodate bacteria variously classified as *Gordona* (184), *Jensenia* (12), *Mycobacterium rhodochrous* (63), the "*rhodochrous*" complex (17), and the "*rhodochrous*" taxon (54). Nine species are recognized in addition to the type species *Rhodococcus rhodochrous* (see Table 3).

3. The genus *Oerskovia* (148), proposed for strains previously classified as *Nocardia turbata* (29), forms a tight cluster that shows some affinity to *Corynebacterium sensu stricto* and related taxa but is distinct from both *Nocardia* and *Cellulomonas* (68, 78). A second species, *Oerskovia xanthineolytica*, has been proposed (94) and there is evidence that *Nocardia cellulans* (48, 78) should be included in the genus.
4. The monotypic genus *Rothia* (37), created to accommodate actinomycetes classified as *Actinomyces dentocariosus* (129, 130), *Nocardia dentocariosus* (159, 160), and *Nocardia salivae* (34), forms a cluster clearly distinct from phena containing aerobic and anaerobic bacteria (74).
5. The genus *Actinomadura* (99) was designed to encompass strains classified and described as *Nocardia dassonvillei* (62), *Nocardia madurae* (58), and *Nocardia pelletieri* (58). Goodfellow (48) recovered *Actinomadura madurae* and *Actinomadura pelletieri* in an aggregate cluster, which included *Actinomadura dassonvillei* at the periphery, equivalent in rank to phena associated with *Nocardia sensu stricto, Oerskovia,* and *Rothia.* In a recent numerical phenetic analysis (92), *A. dassonvillei, A. madurae,* and *A. pelletieri* from clinical sources formed good clusters, whereas isolates from grain and barley were recovered in two additional clusters. These clusters, provisionally labeled A and B, can be separated from one another and from other *Actinomadura* species by carbohydrate utilization, substrate degradation, and antibiotic sensitivity patterns.

All of the taxa derived from *Nocardia sensu* Waksman (194) can be separated from allied taxa such as *Mycobacterium, Corynebacterium sensu stricto* (78), and *Arthrobacter* (48, 53, 54). Numerical phenetic analyses have also helped to highlight the heterogeneity of the genus *Corynebacterium,* and it would seem that this taxon should be restricted to *Corynebacterium diphtheriae* and related types, including *Microbacterium flavum* and the saprophytic *Corynebacterium glutamicum* (14, 15, 78).

Numerical relationships between *Nocardia* and allied taxa may be distorted by different rates of growth or metabolic activity or by test error (170). The introduction of vigor and pattern statistics (168) provides a means of dealing with growth rate problems associated with nocardioform bacteria (49), and the development of standard reproducible tests will eventually reduce anomalies arising from test error.

Chemotaxonomic Studies

WALL AND WHOLE-CELL SUGAR COMPOSITION The walls of nocardiae and related bacteria have a complex structure that consists of a peptidoglycan, lipid constituents, and other polysaccharide or polypeptide compounds (115). The advent of wall, sugar, and amino acid analyses (32, 33, 101) led to a reappraisal of the classification of actinomycetes and coryneform bacteria. These organisms can now be divided into several chemotypes on the basis of the major sugars and amino acids found in their walls (52, 80, 95, 98). *Nocardia sensu stricto, Mycobacterium, Rhodococcus, Corynebacterium sensu stricto, Saccharopolyspora,* and a number of other genera (Table 2) have a wall chemotype IV, i.e. strains contain major amounts of *meso*-diaminopimelic acid (DAP) and arabinose and galactose. The decision to erect the genera *Actinomadura* (99), *Oerskovia* (148), and *Rothia* (37) was partly a result of data from wall composition studies; rothiae and oerskoviae contain major amounts of lysine and aspartic acid (chemotype VI), whereas actinomadurae have *meso*-DAP but no characteristic sugar (chemotype III). Whole organism hydrolysates of many *Actinomadura* species contain a characteristic sugar madurose (3-O-methyl-D-galactose), which is lacking in *Actinomadura africana, A. dassonvillei,* and *Actinomadura longispora* (92).

It is not always necessary to prepare and analyze wall preparations from nocardioform actinomycetes to determine to which chemotype they belong. Thus, chemotypes I–IV can be conveniently determined indirectly by analysis of whole-organism hydrolysates for the isomer of DAP and types of sugars present (95). Wall and whole-organism analyses have been used to identify actinomycetes and coryneform bacteria from clinical sources and natural habitats (9, 80, 132, 174), and there is some evidence that the diagnostic characters are not markedly influenced by growth conditions (31, 176).

It seems likely that more detailed structural studies on walls may provide additional chemical characters and highlight flaws in earlier work. For instance, some strains of *Streptomyces mediterranei* were reclassified in the genus *Nocardia* as they were found to have a wall chemotype IV (149, 181). More precise studies of *S. mediterranei* walls showed some structural differences with the walls of true nocardiae (13, 115). Thus, the peptide moiety of the peptidoglycan is monoaminated on DAP, but in nocardiae it is diaminated on DAP and on glutamic acid. Again, in *Nocardia asteroides, Nocardia caviae, Nocardia kirovani,* and some mycobacteria, the muramic acid residues of the peptidoglycan are N-glycolated and not N-acetylated as in *S. mediterranei* and other actinomycete taxa (13, 15, 192).

LIPID ANALYSIS Lipid analyses are also proving to be of value in the classification and identification of nocardioform and coryneform bacteria (116). Analyses of mycolic acids (120), fatty acids (118), isoprenoid quinones (117), polar lipids (119), and lipid-soluble, iron-binding compounds (152) are providing useful information, but it must be emphasized that the reliability of these characters needs substantiation.

Fatty acids Mycolic acids, long-chain 2-alkyl-branched-3-hydroxy-acids, are found only in bacteria with a wall chemotype IV (Table 2), and structural details (102, 120) support their separation into the genera *Bacterionema* (4), *Corynebacterium sensu stricto* (51), *Nocardia sensu stricto,* and *Mycobacterium* (3, 29, 118,

Table 2 Distribution of chemical characters in *Nocardia* and allied taxa

Taxon	Wall[a] chemotype	%G + C[a] ratio	Fatty[b] acids	Mycolic[c] acids (no. of carbons)	Phospholipids[d] DPG	PG	PE	PI	PDM	PDD	Glycolipids[d]	Menaquinones[e]
Bacterionema	IV	55-57	S,U(I)	30-36(12-18)	+	+	-	+	+	-	+	MK-*8* (H_2), MK-*9* (H_2)
Corynebacterium	IV	48-59	S,U(I,T)	30-36(14-18)	+	±	-	+	+	+	+	MK-*8* (H_2), MK-*9* (H_2)
Micropolyspora brevicatena[f]	IV	ND	ND	46-56(16-18)			ND				ND	MK-*6* (H_4), MK-*8* (H_4)*
M. faeni	IV	ND	ND	–			ND				ND	MK-*9* (H_4*,H_6,H_8)
Mycobacterium	IV	62-70	S,U,(I),T	60-90(22-26)	+	±	+	+	+	+[g]	+	MK-*8* (H_2), MK-*9* (H_2)*
Nocardia	IV	64-68	S,U,(I),T	46-60(12-18)	+	±	+	+	+	+[h]	+	MK-*6* (H_4), MK-*8* (H_4)*
Pseudonocardia	IV	79.3	ND	–			ND				ND	ND
Rhodococcus	IV	59-69	S,U,(I,T)	34-66(12-18)	+	±	+	+	+	+	+	MK-*8* (H_2), MK-*9* (H_2)
Saccharomonospora	IV	ND	ND	–			ND				ND	ND
Saccharopolyspora	IV	ND	ND	–			ND				ND	ND
Actinomadura	111A[i]	65-77	S,U,(I)	–	+	-	-	+	+	-	-	MK-*9* (H_4,H_6*,H_8)
"Nocardiopsis"	111B[j]	ND	S,U,I	–	+	+	±	±	–	±	±	MK-*10* (H_2,H_4*,H_6)
Oerskovia	VI	70-75	S,U,I	–	+	+	–	+	+?	+?	ND	MK-*9* (H_2,H_4*)
Rothia	VI	65-70	S,I	–			ND				+	ND
Streptomyces	I	69-77	S,I	–	+	?	+	–	+?	+?[k]	+	MK-*9* (H_4,H_6*,H_8)

[a] Data from Cross & Goodfellow (29), Lechevalier (95), and Lechevalier et al (101). ND, Not determined.

[b] Data from Alshamaony et al (4), Mininikin & Goodfellow (118), and Pandhi & Hammond (135). S, Straight-chain; U, unsaturated; I, iso- and anteiso; T, tuberculostearic acid. Parentheses indicate a low proportion or variability of appearance.

[c] Data fron Alshamaony et al (4), Minnikin & Goodfellow (118), Minnikin et al (120; unpublished data), and Lechevalier et al (102). Parentheses show number of carbons in fatty acids released on pyrolysis.

[d] Data from Minnikin & Goodfellow (118, 119). DPG, Diphosphatidylglycerol; PG, phosphatidylglycerol; PE, phosphatidylethanolamine; PI, phosphatidylinositol; PDM, phosphatidylinositol dimannoside monoacylated; PDD, phosphotidylinositol dimannoside diacylated.

[e] Data from Collins et al (27), M.D. Collins, M. Goodfellow, and D. E. Minnikin (unpublished data); Minnikin et al (117). MK-*n* (H_x), Menaquinone with *n* isoprene units and x additional hydrogens; * signifies main component.

[f] *Micropolyspora fascifera* also reported to contain mycolic acids (172).

[g] Also contains phosphatidylinositol pentamannosides.

[h] Phosphatidylcholine was detected in *Nocardia coeliaca* (200) and in strains of *Actinomadura dassonvillei* (122).

[i] *Actinomadura madurae* and *Actinomadura pelletieri.*

[j] *Nocardiopsis* has been proposed for *Actinomadura dassonvillei* strains (114).

[k] Exact nature and numbers of phosphatidylinositol mannosides uncertain.

119). The overall picture appears to be that mycolic acids of nocardiae are centered around 52 carbons; those of bacterionemae and corynebacteria are centered around 32 carbons, with mycobacteria having over 60 carbon units. *Micropolyspora brevicatena* contain mycolic acids closely similar to those of nocardiae, but *Micropolyspora faeni* lacks mycolic acids (27); a strain of *Micropolyspora fascifera* also contains mycolic acids (172). In preliminary studies on very few strains, *Rhodococcus* strains have been found to show considerable variation in the chain lengths of their mycolic acids (3, 5, 120). The three species previously assigned to the genus *Gordona* (184) have larger mycolic acids than those of all the other species, with the exception of *Rhodococcus rubropertinctus,* which forms a discrete phenon (49). The mycolic acids of *Rhodococcus erythropolis* are slightly smaller than those of *Rhodococcus rhodnii* and slightly larger than those of the remaining species, *Rhodococcus coprophilus, Rhodococcus equi, Rhodococcus rhodochrous,* and *Rhodococcus rubrus* (120). Additional studies are required to confirm these very provisional data. *Actinomadura, Oerskovia,* and *Rothia* strains do not contain mycolic acids (118; Table 2).

The different types of mycolic acids can be distinguished by pyrolysis gas chromatography and by mass spectroscopy (118, 120). The characteristic breakdown of mycolic esters (35) on pyrolysis to yield straight-chain esters and long-chain aldehydes has been developed into a gas chromatographic method that allows the mycolic esters from mycobacteria to be distinguished from those of all other taxa (97, 102). The fatty acid esters released on pyrolysis gas chromatography from mycobacterial mycolic esters contain 22–26 carbon atoms, whereas those from nocardiae, bacterionemae, corynebacteria, and rhodococci have 12–18 carbon atoms. A convenient procedure (116), involving thin-layer chromatographic analysis of whole-organism methanolysates, allows a rapid, preliminary analysis of mycolic acid composition. Methanolysates of mycobacteria produce a multispot pattern of mycolic esters in contrast to the single spot formed by strains of other taxa. This method also provides a way of distinguishing true corynebacteria from nocardiae, as the two produce mycolates of different chromatographic mobility, and from coryneforms, which do not contain mycolic acids (51). A number of poorly studied strains with a wall type IV, including *Nocardia mediterranei,* do not contain mycolic acids (118, 138).

The simple, long-chain fatty acids of the mycolic acid-containing taxa are all very similar in pattern, with mixtures of straight-chain unsaturated and 10-methyloctadecanoic (tuberculostearic) common (118; Table 2). Iso- and anteiso methyl branched fatty acids are only occasionally found in mycolic acid-containing bacteria, but these acids are more characteristic of other actinomycete taxa such as *Micromonospora* (6, 177), *Streptomyces, Microbispora, Thermomonospora, Thermoactinomyces,* and the Actinoplanaceae (6). Certain nocardioform bacteria whose classification is not clearly established also contain high proportions of iso- and anteiso acids. Good examples are *Nocardia coeliaca* (200), *Nocardia gardneri* (93), *Nocardia leishmanii* (201), *N. mediterranei,* and *Oerskovia turbata* (138); further studies should be made on the classification of these isolates. Fatty acid differences similar to those outlined above have also been found to be valuable in the classification of actinomadurae and coryneform bacteria (2, 16, 118).

Polar lipids Less attention has been paid to the value of polar lipids as taxonomic markers. The main polar lipid types in bacteria are phospholipids and glycolipids (44, 166), although other less common types such as ornithine and lysine amides have a limited distribution (118). Complicated mixtures of polar lipid types are found in actinomycetes, and their distribution has been reviewed in detail (118, 119). The most common polar lipids occurring in nocardioform and related bacteria are diphosphatidylglycerol (DPG), phosphatidylinositol (PI), and phosphatidylinositol mannosides (PIMs). Phosphatidylethanolamine (PE) is also encountered but phosphatidylglycerol (PG), widespread in many bacteria (44, 166), and phosphatidylcholine (PC) are uncommon.

In representatives of *Mycobacterium, Nocardia sensu stricto,* and *Rhodococcus* DPG, PE, PE, and PIMs may be expected (Table 2), but PE is absent in extracts of *Bacterionema* and *Corynebacterium sensu stricto* (82, 121). Organisms labeled *Corynebacterium equi* and *Corynebacterium fascians* were found (82) to contain PE in accordance with their recent reclassification (49) as *Rhodococcus equi* and *Rhodococcus rubropertinctus.* The very variable proportions of PE detected in *Nocardia* and *Rhodococcus* (121) make this lipid an unreliable chemical marker.

The most characteristic lipids of the actinomycetes and related bacteria are the PIMs. Since PIMs are uncommon in bacteria other than actinomycetes, corynebacteria, and propionibacteria, it is possible that they have a special role in the envelopes of these bacteria and may be obligatory components. The balance of evidence suggests that phosphatidylinositol dimannosides (119), rather than monomannosides, are characteristic lipids of the mycolic acid-containing taxa. Mono- and diacyl phosphatidylinositol dimannosides are present in *Nocardia sensu stricto, Mycobacterium, Corynebacterium sensu stricto, Rhodococcus,* and *"Gordona" aurantiaca,* whereas *Bacterionema matruchotii, Rhodococcus bronchialis, Rhodococcus rubrus,* and *Rhodococcus terrae* contain only a monoacylated phosphatidylinositol dimannoside (121). The only well-authenticated examples of the occurrence of phosphatidylinositol monomannosides are in the lipids of *Corynebacterium aquaticum* (70) and *Propionibacterium shermanii* (21).

The phospholipid composition of strains labeled *Nocardia coeliaca, Nocardia leishmanii,* and *Nocardia mediterranei* questions their retention in the genus *Nocardia. N. coeliaca* contains high proportions of phosphatidylcholine (81, 200), and *N. leishmanii* has PG and two PEs, one of which incorporates hydroxy fatty acids (201). *N. mediterranei* contains PE, DPG, and PIM but lacks PI (139).

The polar lipid patterns of *Actinomadura dassonvillei, Actinomadura madurae, Actinomadura pelletieri* (122), and *Oerskovia* (139) are distinct from those of *Nocardia sensu stricto* and related bacteria (Table 2). *A. madurae* and *A. pelletieri* have a simple pattern consisting essentially of DPG, PI, and monoacylphosphatidylinositol dimannoside, whereas *A. dassonvillei* contains DPG, PG, a lipid that cochromatographs with PC, and a chromatographically mobile, unknown phospholipid (122). The absence of PE in oerskoviae (139) adds some weight to the view (78) that they may be more closely related to coryneform bacteria than to actinomycetes.

The distribution of polar glycolipids in nocardioform and related bacteria has not been systematically studied (118). A strain of *Nocardia polychromogenes* contained a diglucosyl diacylglycerol (81), *Rothia dentocariosa* had a dimannosyl diacylglycerol (135), and *Actinomyces viscosus* produced a monogalactosyl diacylglycerol (202). A strain of *Micromonospora* contained an acylated trehalose (177) and *N. coeliaca* had an unidentified glycolipid (200). An unusual acidic glycolipid was found in a strain of *Nocardia caviae* (138, 140) and two acidic glycolipids characterized from a *Streptomyces* strain (7, 10). A variety of unidentified glycolipids were present in extracts of *A. dassonvillei* (122) and *Nocardia* and in other mycolic acid-containing taxa (121).

Isoprenoid quinones Menaquinones are the characteristic isoprenoid quinone type found in nocardioform and related bacteria, and the distribution of their various structural forms is proving valuable in classification (Table 2) (27, 117). In particular, menaquinone analyses distinguish *Nocardia sensu stricto,* which appear to contain a mixture of tetrahydromenaquinones with six and eight isoprene units, abbreviated as MK-*6* (H_4) and MK-*8* (H_4) from *Bacterionema, Corynebacterium, Mycobacterium,* and *Rhodococcus.* Mycobacteria, including *Nocardia farcinica* NCTC 4524, have MK-*9* (H_2) as the major isoprenologue. Representatives of some animal corynebacteria have Mk-*8* (H_2) as their main menaquinone component, but others have MK-*9* (H_2) as the major isoprenologue; the significance of these differences awaits further study. It also appears probable that menaquinone patterns will be of value in the classification of actinomycetes, which lack mycolic acids. Similar patterns to those of the streptomycetes (Table 2) are found in representatives of *Actinomadura madurae, Actinomadura pelletieri, Oerskovia turbata,* and *Micropolyspora faeni,* but the proportions of MK-*9* are different (27). In contrast, *A. dassonvillei* contains MK-*10* (H_2, H_4, H_6).

Nocobactins and related compounds Mycobacteria produce a family of lipid-soluble, iron-binding compounds, the mycobactins, which are thought to occur in all mycobacteria with the exception of species such as *Mycobacterium paratuberculosis* that require them as growth factors (196). The mycobactins show minor variations in structure, which offer a means of distinguishing mycobacteria at the species level (152, 171). Analogous but chemically distinct compounds, the nocobactins, are produced by nocardiae and can be divided into three readily distinguishable types that correspond to *Nocardia asteroides, Nocardia brasiliensis,* and *Nocardia caviae* (152, 153). In preliminary studies (49, 151), small amounts of analogous compounds were detected in *Rhodococcus* species *R. bronchialis, R. corallinus,* and *R. coprophilus* but not in *R. erythropolis, R. rhodochrous, R. rubrus,* or *R. rubropertinctus.* Studies in additional strains and taxa are required to determine whether the nocobactins and related compounds can provide good characters for the classification of nocardioform taxa.

Miscellaneous lipids In addition to the lipid classes discussed in previous sections, a limited amount of work has been performed on the analysis of pigments, acylglycerols, and mycolic esters of trehalose.

Pigmentation is not a very stable character for the identification of actinomycetes (101), but chemical analysis of pigments may prove valuable as an aid to classification. Carotenoid pigments are found in strains of *Mycobacterium, Nocardia,* and *Corynebacterium,* and a degree of structural variation has been found (128, 158, 179, 180, 191, 195). A strain labeled *Nocardia corallina* was found to have a partially characterized red nitrogeneous pigment (175). Prodiginine pigments are potentially useful for the classification of strains of *Actionomadura* and *Streptomyces.* Strains of *Actinomadura madurae* may contain nonyl- and cyclononylprodiginines, but in strains of the closely related species *Actinomadura pelletieri* undecyl- and methylprodiginines are encountered (38–40). These pigments are, so far, the only chemical characters capable of distinguishing these two species of *Actinomadura.* Related but structurally distinct prodiginine pigments have been found in *Streptomyces* and *Streptoverticillium* strains (41). Phenazine pigments have been isolated from strains of *Microbispora* species, *Streptosporangium amethystogenes,* and *Actinomadura dassonvillei* (101).

Mono- and diacylglycerols are commonly encountered in extracts of most bacteria, but since they may be breakdown products of complex lipids their occurrence may vary widely. Triacylglycerols, however, are limited in their occurrence to eukaryotic organisms and to actinomycete and related taxa. The distribution of triacylglycerols in nocardioform and related bacteria has not been systematically studied, but from preliminary studies they appear to be commonly encountered (118).

Mycolic esters of trehalose, the so-called cord factors, have been isolated from all mycolic acid-containing taxa specifically investigated for their presence (104, 118). Cord factors are 6,6'-mycolyl trehaloses, and since the nature of the mycolic acid residues may vary according to the source of the lipid (104), systematic studies of their structure may prove valuable in classification. For example, a strain of *"Nocardia" rhodochrous* had similar mycolic acids in its walls and cord factor, but the lipid from *Nocardia asteroides* contained mycolic acids of much lower (C_{32}–C_{36}) molecular weight than those found in the walls (C_{50}–C_{58}) (76).

DNA Analysis and Genetic Studies

The chemical composition of chromosomal DNA can be analyzed in several ways to yield data of taxonomic value. DNA base composition studies represent the first stage in the application of molecular biological methods to bacterial classification, and detailed lists of results have been compiled for *Nocardia* and *Rhodococcus* (125, 126). All actinomycetes are rich in guanine (G) plus cytosine (C) and fall within the same broad %G + C range (Table 2). However, bacteria with a wall chemotype IV can be divided into two groups on the basis of base determination analyses. Thus, *Bacterionema* and *Corynebacterium sensu stricto* have a lower G + C content than *Nocardia sensu stricto, Mycobacterium,* and *Rhodococcus* (124). There is some evidence that base composition analyses may be of value in the classification of *Rhodococcus* species (19, 124), whereas most *Nocardia* strains have a narrow G + C range (125).

Although only a few DNA:DNA reassociation assays have been carried out, preliminary data show that *Nocardia sensu stricto* and *Rhodococcus* have little genetic affinity either with one another or with *Actinomadura, Mycobacterium,* or *Streptomyces* (19, 127). Pairing studies are of particular value in distinguishing between closely related taxa, and they played an invaluable part in elucidating the structure of the *Rhodococcus* taxon (49, 127). Preliminary data suggest that reassociation assays will also help to clarify the structure of *Nocardia asteroides*; at least three homology groups can be recognized within this taxon (19, 36, 125, 126). Good congruence has been observed between nucleotide sequence homology and numerical phenetic data in *Mycobacterium* (69), *Rhodococcus* (49), and *Nocardia* (164).

Nocardioform actinomycetes, like other bacteria, are sensitive to phage. There is conflicting evidence on the value of phage sensitivity studies in actinomycete taxonomy (144), although phage sensitivity was used to delineate the nocardioform genus *Nocardioides* (145). Host-range studies have also been of value in the classification of *Nocardia*; Prauser & Falta (147) were able to subdivide *Nocardia* Trevisan *sensu* Waksman (194) into sensitivity groups corresponding to *Nocardia sensu stricto* (29), *Actinomadura* (99), and *Oerskovia* (148). In subsequent phage host-range work, Prauser (144) distinguished between *Nocardia, Nocardioides, Oerskovia, Promicromonospora,* and *Streptomyces,* and once again he stressed that, although phages could only attack bacteria of a given wall chemotype, a particular phage did not necessarily attack every strain with the same wall type. Phages have been reported to be of value in the tentative identification of fresh isolates (144) and in clarifying the classification of poorly defined nocardioform taxa (150).

Genetic recombination between rhodococci of heterologous origin has been demonstrated and reviewed (1). It seems likely that the taxa *Rhodococcus erythropolis* and *Rhodococcus rhodochrous* represent the genospecies known in earlier studies as *Nocardia erythropolis,* or *Nocardia corallina,* and *Nocardia rubra* (26).

Serology

Although *Nocardia* and allied taxa have been the subject of many serotaxonomic studies (15, 97, 106, 110, 170), the overall picture remains unclear and complex. Some of the confusion can be attributed to technical and interpretation difficulties, and in other instances it arises from poor strain selection. It is also evident that different serological techniques and antigens give serological specificities that range from highly species specific (110) to genus specific (162), or that exhibit even wider specificity (89).

Cummins (31) used slide agglutination tests to analyze the antigenic structure of walls of *Nocardia, Mycobacterium, Corynebacterium,* and allied taxa for comparison with chemical analysis. A comon antigenic component was found in all isolates with arabinose and galactose as major wall constituents but not in *Actinomadura pelletieri* strains that lack these components. Subsequent studies, employing a variety of serological techniques, have shown that the genera *Nocardia sensu stricto, Mycobacterium, Corynebacterium sensu stricto,* and *Rhodococcus* have antigens in common (15, 106), and it seems likely that the common wall arabinogalactan is responsible for many of the cross-reactions.

Several workers have shown that it is possible to distinguish between the mycolic acid-containing genera and other actinomycete taxa by serological methods (24, 54, 110, 154, 156, 162). Thus, Ridell & Norlin (156) found three antigens, α, pα (partial alpha), and β, that distinguished *Nocardia sensu stricto* and *Rhodococcus.* Strains of *Nocardia sensu stricto* had the α precipitinogen and rarely the β antigen, whereas most rhodococci had β or pα but never α. By the indirect fluorescent antibody technique and by using solvent-extracted cells as antigens, Schaal (162) obtained genus-specific antisera for *Nocardia sensu stricto, Mycobacterium, Corynebacterium sensu stricto, Bacterionema, Streptomyces, Actinomyces,* and *Arachnia.* However, cross-staining has been observed between *Nocardia asteroides, Corynebacterium diphtheriae, Actinomadura madurae,* and *Streptomyces somaliensis* by using the indirect fluorescent antibody technique (106).

González-Ochoa & Vasquez-Hoyos (47), by using gel diffusion, and Schneidau & Shaffer (165), by using slide agglutination, were able to distinguish *A. madurae* and *Actinomadura pelletieri* from *N. asteroides, Nocardia brasiliensis,* and *S. somaliensis* serologically. In contrast, the extensive immunodiffusion studies of Kwapinski and his colleagues (88–90) have done little to clarify the relationship between *Nocardia* and allied taxa, although antigenic mosaics of great complexity have been demonstrated. It has been suggested (170) that the antigens in this system could be mainly nonspecific ones, as cross-reactions between prokaryotes and eukaryotes exist (90).

By using extracellular antigens, Pier & Fichtner (136) confirmed serologically the heterogeneity of the *N. asteroides* taxon when they recognized four serotypes and two type mixtures. Essentially similar results were found in comparative intradermal sensitin tests (110), which can also be used to distinguish strains of *N. brasiliensis* and *Nocardia caviae.* In fact, skin tests with sensitins on immunized guinea pigs seem to be especially useful in the delineation of *Mycobacterium* (109) and *Nocardia* species (110). Preliminary results show that *Rhodococcus* species can be distinguished by immunodiffusion analyses (56, 154). Ridell (155) has also reported that strains received as *Nocardia farcinica* fall into two serological groups, one of which shows a close serological relationship to *Nocardia* and the other to *Mycobacterium.*

Additional serological analyses on well-chosen strains will undoubtably help to clarify the taxonomy of *Nocardia, Mycobacterium, Corynebacterium, Rhodococcus,* and allied taxa. An improved understanding of the serological relationships between these taxa should also help in the development of specific reagents for use in diagnostic skin tests and in the provision of amended methods for serological identification.

THE CURRENT POSITION—*NOCARDIA* REVISITED

The taxonomy of *Nocardia sensu* Waksman (194) has been radically altered by the application of modern taxonomic methods. There are now good grounds for accepting the genera Actinomadura, Oerskovia, Rhodococcus, and *Rothia*; only the latter was thus blessed in the current edition of *Bergey's Manual* (23). Although rapid progress has undoubtably been made, problems remain, and more detailed work is required to establish relationships within and between the new genera and related taxa.

Thus, although *Rothia* is homogeneous on numerical phenetic (74), chemical (29), and serological grounds (71), further work is necessary for a better understanding of the affinity of this genus to other taxa containing oral-filamentous bacteria. The taxonomic position of *Oerskovia* also is not clear. In their classification of the actinomycetes, Cross & Goodfellow (29) considered *Oerskovia* to be a genus in search of a family, and there are very preliminary data that suggests that the coryneform group of bacteria (157) might provide an appropriate niche. Oerskoviae seem to share a higher affinity with coryneform bacteria than with actinomycete (78), contain isoprenoid quinones similar to those of propionibacteria (27), and show a similar polar lipid pattern to *Corynebacterium* and *Bacterionema* (121). The removal of *Bacterionema* from the family Actinomycetaceae to the coryneform group of bacteria has been proposed mainly on the basis of chemical components and biochemical properties (4).

The status and composition of strains classified in the genus *Actinomadura* (99) have been reviewed in depth (92). The validity of the genus is supported by numerical phenetic (48, 92), chemotaxonomic (51, 95, 119), and phage sensitivity studies (144), but it has become evident that the genus description needs strengthening to prevent it from becoming a repository for species of uncertain affinity and to differentiate it clearly from other genera. Many of the 18 *Actinomadura* species described since 1970 can only be distinguished by minor characters, and there are preliminary data that suggest that some of these may be merely nomenspecies (92). It also appears that the genus *Actinomadura* may be heterogeneous, with *A. dassonvillei* differing from *A. madurae* and *A. pelletieri* in a number of properties. *A. dassonvillei* can be distinguished from the other two species on the basis of spore morphology (114, 197) and on the basis of madurose (96), fatty acid (2), pigment (101), polar lipid (122), and isoprenoid quinone (27) content. The genus *Nocardiopsis* (114) has been proposed to accommodate *A. dassonvillei* strains.

In the last edition of *Bergey's Manual, Gordona* (184) and *Jensenia* (12) are listed as genera *incertae sedis,* and rhodochrous strains are classified as *Nocardia* species *N. calcarea, N. corallina, N. erythropolis, N. globerula, N. opaca, N. restricta, N. rubra, N. rubropertincta,* and *N. salmonicolor* (112). Goodfellow & Alderson (49) recovered *Gordona* and rhodochrous strains in a heterogeneous cluster that they considered merited generic status. The name *Rhodococcus* (203) was thought to have priority over the earlier names *Proactinomyces* (77), *Jensenia* (12), and *Gordona* (184), and an emended genus description was given (49). A minidefinition of *Rhodococcus* is proposed: aerobic, nonsporing actinomycetes that are pleomorphic but often form a primary mycelium that soon fragments into rod and coccoid elements. A secondary mycelium is not produced but strains contain mycolic acids and have a wall chemotype IV, and the G + C content of their DNA ranges from 59–69%. On the basis of these properties, the genus was classified in the family Nocardiaceae (49). At present, 10 species of *Rhodococcus* can be recognized (Table 3). Further work needs to be done to establish the relationship between *Nocardia kirovani, Nocardia opaca* (3, 5), *Gordona aurantiaca* (188), and *Rhodococcus.*

Table 3 Composition of the genus *Rhodococcus* (203) [Goodfellow & Alderson (49)]

Species	Previous designation
R. bronchialis, Tsukamura (184) emend. Tsukamura (186)	*Gordona bronchialis*, Tsukamura (184)
R. coprophilus, Rowbotham & Cross (161)	L spi strains (large, spored, pink, irregular), Willoughby (198)
R. corallinus, Bergey et al (11), comb. nov.	*Gordona rubra*, Tsukamura (184)
R. erythropolis, Gray & Thornton (68), comb. nov.	*Jensenia canicruria*, Bisset & Moore (12) *Nocardia calcarea*, Metcalf & Brown (113) *Nocardia erythopolis*, Gray & Thornton (68) *Nocardia globerula*, Gray (67) Phenon 14D, Goodfellow (48) Phenon F3, Jones (78)
R. equi, Magnusson (108), comb. nov.	*Corynebacterium equi*, Magnusson (108) *Nocardia restrictus*, Turfitt (190) Phenon 1c, Goodfellow et al (54)
R. rhodnii n. sp.	
R. rhodochrous, Overbeck (134), Tsukamura (186)[a]	*Gordona rhodochroa*, Tsukamura (186) *Gordona rosea*, Tsukamura (185) *Gordona rubropertincta*, Tsukamura (185) *Nocardia rubra*, Bradley (17) Phenon 14B, 14C, Goodfellow (48) Phenon 1a, Goodfellow et al (54)
R. rubrus, Kruse, (84), Tsukamura (186), comb. nov.	*Gordona lentifragmenta*, Tsukamura et al (189) *Nocardia pellegrino*, Mordarska et al (123) *Nocardia rubra*, Tsukamura (184) Phenon 14A, Goodfellow (48)
R. rubropertinctus, Hefferan (73), comb. nov.	Phenon 14D, Goodfellow (48)
R. terrae, Tsukamura (184) emend. Tsukamura (186)	*Gordona terrae*, Tsukamura (184)

[a]Type species.

The creation of the genera *Actinomadura, Oerskovia, Rhodococcus,* and *Rothia* leave the genus *Nocardia* as a relatively homogeneous discrete taxon for the first time in its long and turbulent history. However, taxonomists working on *Nocardia* have still to agree on an acceptable definition (60, 95) and an Identikit picture is offered in light of present knowledge: aerobic, gram-positive, acid-fast to partially acid-fast actinomycetes that produce a primary mycelium that fragments into rod- and coccoid-like elements. Aerial hyphae are usually formed, strains contain mycolic acids and have a wall chemotype IV, and the G + C content of their DNA ranges from 64–69%. All nocardiae studied to date contain characteristic iron-binding compounds (152, 153) and isoprenoid quinones (27, 117), but further studies are needed to confirm these data before the genus definition can be extended. This definition would include the established taxa *N. asteroides, N. brasiliensis,* and *N. caviae,* and also *N. amarae, N. carnea, N. salmonicida, N. transvalensis,* and *N. vaccinii,* which appear to be good species (48, 59, 100, 132). *Micropolyspora brevicatena* contains mycolic acids (120) and isoprenoid quinones (117) similar to nocardiae, and its exact relationship to *Nocardia* needs to be determined; mycolic acids have also been reported in *Micropolyspora fascifera* (172). The genus *Micropolyspora* (28) is evidently heterogeneous and is in need of further study (Table 2).

The family Nocardiaceae (29) contains aerobic, gram-positive actinomycetes with a wall chemotype IV and a rudimentary-to-extensive substrate mycelium that usually fragments into rod and coccoid elements. Extensive aerial hyphae bearing spores may be formed (*Nocardia, Micropolyspora, Saccharomonospora, Saccharopolyspora*), although spores may also be formed on the substrate mycelium (*Micropolyspora*). Some strains contain mycolic acids (*Nocardia, Rhodococcus, M. brevicatena, M. fascifera*) whereas others do not (*Saccharomonospora, Saccharopolyspora, Micropolyspora faeni*); comparative studies are required to determine the relationships between these two groups of bacteria. The position of some "*Nocardia*" strains labeled *N. aerocolonigenes, N. coeliaca* (*N. autotrophica*), *N. gardneri, N. hydrocarboxydans, N. leishmanii, N. lurida, N. orientalis, N. petroleophila, N. polychromogenes, N. rugosa, N. saturnea,* and *N. tenuis* is also equivocal because most of these bacteria have a wall chemotype IV and lack mycolic acids (61, 81, 118, 149, 199–201).

THE TYPE SPECIES OF *NOCARDIA*

The taxonomic status of *Nocardia farcinica* ATCC 3318 and the presumably identical strain NCTC 4524 still has to be settled, although the two strains are clearly very different (95). Strain ATCC 3318 has many properties in common with *Nocardia asteroides* (64, 126, 164, 183), whereas strain NCTC 4524 contains isoprenoid quinones (27) and lipids (95) similar to those of mycobacteria. On the basis of comparative reciprocal intradermal sensitin tests in guinea pigs (110), strain NCTC 4524 cannot be distinguished from the authentic strain (378) of *Mycobacterium farcinogenes* var. *senegalense*; however, both strains can be separated (110) from strain ATCC 3318. In DNA reassociation assays, Bradley (18) found that strain ATCC 3318 (his 330) was more closely related to other nocardiae than to mycobacteria. It is evident from these and other studies (111, 155) that the epithet *N. farcinica* is being used to describe two groups of bacteria, a situation that can only lead to further confusion. We agree with Magnusson (110) that the use of the name *N. farcinica* for strains that cannot be distinguished from strain NCTC 4524 be discontinued; such strains should be classified as *M. farcinogenes* var. *senegalense* (25).

The group of *N. farcinica* strains with similarities to *N. asteroides* produce aerial hyphae and thereby do not conform to Nocard's original description of *N. farcinica* (see 95). In view of all of the confusion surrounding the epithet *N. farcinica,* the best course of action would seem to be the one recommended by Gordon & Mihm (64), i.e. to accept *N. asteroides* as the type species.

OCCURRENCE, DISTRIBUTION, AND PARASITISM

Actinomadurae and nocardiae cause actinomycete mycetoma and an uncommon disease of man and animals called nocardiosis. Rhodococci have not been unambiguously implicated as disease agents but are known to form symbiotic associations with a wide variety of bloodsucking arthropods (30, 49). Nocardiosis, usually caused by *Nocardia asteroides* (87) and exceptionally caused by *Nocardia brasiliensis* and *Nocardia caviae* (8), is a severe pulmonary disease that may lead to secondary and often fatal involvement with the brain, lungs, and meninges alone or in combination. The incidence of nocardiosis is rising, and it is not uncommon in patients whose resistance has been undermined by immunosuppressive drugs, corticosteroids, antimetabolites, or neoplastic disease. The bacteria live in the tissues either as acid-fast, short, hyphal elements or as bacillary and coccoid elements. *Actinomadura dassonvillei* has occasionally been isolated from preliminary infections of animals and can infect man. *Actinomadura madurae, Actinomadura pelletieri,* and *N. brasiliensis* are the primary agents of actinomycete mycetoma in man, although in rare instances *N. asteroides* and *N. caviae* may be responsible. This chronic suppurative and granulomatous disease of the subcutaneous tissues and bones is characterized by swelling, abscess production, and the formation of multiple sinuses through which pus and granules are discharged. The causal bacteria appear in the form of characteristic granules.

Schaal (163) has pointed out that in contrast to many other bacterial diseases infections by the aerobic actinomycetes have retained an unusual degree of malignancy or, at least, a doubtful prognosis. The different types of human nocardiosis are often clinically indistinguishable from other bacterial infections, nor are actinomycetomas always recognized as actinomycete in origin. Thus, in many cases only secondary considerations, such as underlying diseases or geographical distribution, prompt physicians and diagnostic bacteriologists to search for actinomycetes in etiologically obscure lesions. Since reliable and practical methods have yet to be developed for the serological or immunological diagnosis of infections resulting from actinomycetes, the recognition of the diseases depend primarily upon the isolation and identification of the etiologic agent. This is not always easily accomplished although an up-to-date manual for the demonstration, isolation, and identification of aerobic actinomycetes from clinical material now exists (163). The multitude of contradictory reports in the literature about the efficacy of antimicrobial agents against pathogenic actinomycetes reflects in part the poor taxonomy of these organisms (56). González-Ochoa (46) has found a number of drugs to be effective in the treatment of nocardiosis and actinomycete mycetoma. The possible mechanisms of nocardial pathogenesis recently have been reviewed in detail (8).

Little is known about the biology of nocardioform bacteria in natural habitats, and detailed synopses of our current knowledge already exist (30, 52). Ecologic studies on nocardioform bacteria have been severely hampered by the lack of suitable selective isolation methods and by poor taxonomy. The distribution of the pathogenic nocardiae has received the most attention, and it is generally thought that soil is the primary reservoir for these bacteria since most cutaneous infections in tropical countries occur on the feet (actinomycetoma pedis) or on the back through carrying contaminated sacks (45). It is now evident that much of the work based on the well-known paraffin wax baiting technique (173), and surveys of actinomycete communities with "nonselective" media for actinomycetes, severely underestimated populations of nocardiae. The infrequent occurrence of nocardiae on media such as chitin agar, starch-casein agar, and egg albumin is not surprising since they do not degrade chitin and rarely use egg albumin, casein, or starch (30, 132). Recently, nocardiae have been isolated in large numbers [e.g. 7.3×10^4 g^{-1} (dry wt) of soil] from both temperate and tropical soils, using Diagnostic Sensitivity Agar (Oxoid) supplemented with antifungal and antibacterial antibiotics (131, 132). A pretreatment method in combination with a selective medium was developed for the isolation of *Rhodococcus coprophilus,* and large populations of this organism have been isolated from herbivorous dung and polluted streams (30, 161). It seems likely that the development of effective isolation methods for poorly studied nocardioform taxa, such as *Micropolyspora* and *Actinomadura,* would modify our understanding of their significance in natural habitats.

CONCLUDING REMARKS

It is evident that the genus *Nocardia sensu* Waksman (194) contained several distinct taxa in addition to *Nocardia asteroides* and related species. *Actinomadura, Oerskovia,* and *Rothia* should be recognized as genera, and *Nocardia* and *Rhodococcus* should be used to describe nocardioform bacteria with wall chemotype IV and containing mycolic acids. The genera *Oerskovia* and *Rothia* appear to be homogeneous although additional work is required to determine their affinities with coryneform and nocardioform taxa. Detailed work is also necessary to establish relationships within the genera *Micropolyspora* and *Actinomadura* and between them and related genera. The genus *Rhodococcus* can be distinguished from closely related taxa such as *Nocardia, Mycobacterium,* and *Corynebacterium,* but further studies are needed to confirm the status of the 10 species classified within it. For the first time in its long history the genus *Nocardia* is relatively homogeneous; however, the same cannot be said for the *N. asteroides* taxon. Further detailed work is required to elucidate the structure of the *N. asteroides* complex, and it seems likely that numerical phenetic (164) and DNA:DNA reassociation assays (19, 126) have an important role to play here. The other vexing question concerns the taxonomic relationship of taxa such as *Nocardia coeliaca,* which have a wall type IV but which do not contain mycolic acids. There is still a dearth of simple and reliable diagnostic tests available for the identification of nocardioform bacteria. However, Sneath (170) has noted that the distribution of character frequencies is strongly U-shaped for heterogeneous taxa, and it can be anticipated with some confidence that the search for good tests to differentiate *Nocardia* and related taxa will prove fruitful. There is already evidence that this is so for chemical characters (51, 116), and given the improved classification of nocardioform bacteria, it might be timely to have a closer look at morphological criteria.

The emphasis in this review on the taxonomy of nocardioform bacteria does not imply that they are the personal preserve of a few taxonomists. However, developments in fields such as microbial ecology (52, 132), diagnostic bacteriology (163), and physiology (178) have been bedeviled by the poor state of nocardial taxonomy, and in the immediate future steady progress can now be expected in these areas. Thus, at present, little is known of the part nocardioform bacteria play in natural habitats although it seems likely that they will form an integral part of a balanced microbial community and could be involved in the degradation of complex organic substrates. Already improved methods for the recognition of nocardiae have shown that they are able to degrade rubber joints in water and sewage pipes (75).

Finally, it should be recognized that the term "nocardioform" is merely one of convenience. Since the wall structure is widely different in *Actinomadura, Nocardia, Nocardioides,* and *Oerskovia,* it is unlikely that there is a common base for fragmentation. Nocardioform bacteria should be regarded as a collection of individual genera and species and should be studied as such.

ACKNOWLEDGMENTS

Work from our laboratories received generous support from the Medical Research Council (M.R.C. project grants G973/190/B; G974/522/S).

Literature Cited

1. Adams, J. N., Brownell, G. H. 1976. In *The Biology of the Nocardiae,* ed. M. Goodfellow, G. H. Brownell, J. A. Serrano, pp. 285–309. London: Academic. 517 pp.
2. Agre, N. S., Efimova, T. P., Guzeva, L. N. 1975. *Mikrobiologiya* 44:252–57
3. Alshamaony, L., Goodfellow, M., Minnikin, D. E. 1976. *J. Gen. Microbiol.* 92:188–99
4. Alshamaony, L., Goodfellow, M., Minnikin, D. E., Bowden, G. H., Hardie, J. M. 1977. *J. Gen. Microbiol.* 98:205–13
5. Alshamaony, L., Goodfellow, M., Minnikin, D. E., Mordarska, H. 1976. *J. Gen. Microbiol.* 92:183–87
6. Ballio, A., Barcellona, S. 1968. *Ann. Inst. Pasteur Paris* 114:121–37
7. Batrakov, S. G., Pilipenko, T. V., Bergelson, L. D. 1970. *Khim. Prir. Soedin.* 1970:664–71
8. Beaman, B. L. See Ref. 1, pp. 386–417
9. Berd, D. 1973. *Ann. Rev. Resp. Dis.* 108:909–17
10. Bergelson, L. D., Batrakov, S. G., Pilipenko, T. V. 1970. *Chem. Phys. Lipids* 4:181–90
11. Bergey, D. H., Harrison, F. C., Breed, R. S., Hammer, B. W., Huntoon, F. W. 1923. *Bergey's Manual of Determinative Bacteriology.* Baltimore: Williams & Wilkins. 1st ed.
12. Bisset, K. A., Moore, F. W. 1950. *J. Gen. Microbiol.* 4:280
13. Bordet, C., Karahjoli, M., Gateau, O., Michel, G. 1972. *Int. J. Syst. Bacteriol.* 22:251–59
14. Bousfield, I. J. 1972. *J. Gen. Microbiol.* 71:441–55
15. Bousfield, I. J., Goodfellow, M. See Ref. 1, pp. 39–65
16. Bowie, I. S., Grigor, M. R., Dunckley, G. G., Loutit, M. W., Loutit, J. S. 1972. *Soil. Biol. Biochem.* 4:397–412
17. Bradley, S. G. 1971. *Adv. Front. Plant Sci.* 28:349–62
18. Bradley, S. G. 1973. *J. Bacteriol.* 113: 645–51

19. Bradley, S. G., Mordarski, M. See Ref. 1, pp. 310–36
20. Breed, R. S., Murray, E. G. D., Smith, N. R. 1957. *Bergey's Manual of Determinative Bacteriology*. Baltimore: Williams & Wilkins. 7th ed.
21. Brennan, P. J., Ballou, C. E. 1967. *J. Biol. Chem.* 242:3046–56
22. Brunchorst, J. 1886. *Bot. Inst. Tubingen* 2:151–77
23. Buchanan, R. E., Gibbons, N. E. 1974. *Bergey's Manual of Determinative Bacteriology*. Baltimore: Williams & Wilkins. 8th ed.
24. Castelnuovo, G., Bellezza, G., Duncan, M. E., Asselineau, J. 1964. *Ann. Inst. Pasteur Paris* 107:828–44
25. Chamoiseau, G. 1973. *Ann. Microbiol. Paris* 124A:215–22
26. Clark, J. E., Brownell, G. H., Bradley, S. G. 1971. *Bacteriol. Proc.* 1971:38 (Abstr.)
27. Collins, M. D., Pirouz, T., Goodfellow, M., Minnikin, D. E. 1977. *J. Gen. Microbiol.* 100:221–30
28. Cross, T. See Ref. 23, pp. 861–63
29. Cross, T., Goodfellow, M. 1973. In *Actinomycetales: Characteristics and Practical Importance,* ed. G. Sykes, F. A. Skinner, pp. 11–112. London: Academic. 339 pp.
30. Cross, T., Rowbotham, T. J., Mishustin, E. N., Tepper, E. Z., Antoine-Portaels, F. See Ref. 1, pp. 337–71
31. Cummins, C. S. 1962. *J. Gen. Microbiol.* 28:35–50
32. Cummins, C. S., Harris, H. 1956. *J. Gen. Microbiol.* 14:583–600
33. Cummins, C. S., Harris, H. 1958. *J. Gen. Microbiol.* 18:173–89
34. Davis, G. H. G., Freer, J. H. 1960. *J. Gen. Microbiol.* 23:163–78
35. Etémadi, A. H. 1967. *Bull. Soc. Chim. Biol.* 49:695–706
36. Franklin, A. A. Jr., McClung, N. M. 1976. *J. Gen. Appl. Microbiol.* 22: 151–59
37. Georg, L. K., Brown, J. M. 1967. *Int. J. Syst. Bacteriol.* 17:79–88
38. Gerber, N. N. 1971. *J. Antibiot.* 24: 636–40
39. Gerber, N. N. 1973. *J. Heterocycl. Chem.* 10:925–29
40. Gerber, N. N. 1975. *Crit. Rev. Microbiol.* 3:469–85
41. Gerber, N. N., Lechevalier, M. P. 1976. *Can. J. Microbiol.* 22:658–67
42. Gilmour, M. N., Howell, A. Jr., Bibby, B. G. 1961. *Bacteriol. Rev.* 25:131–41
43. Gledhill, W. E., Casida, L. E. Jr. 1969. *Appl. Microbiol.* 18:340–49
44. Goldfine, H. 1972. *Adv. Microb. Physiol.* 8:1–58
45. González-Ochoa, A. 1962. *Lab. Invest.* 11:1118–23
46. González-Ochoa, A. See Ref. 1, pp. 429–50
47. González-Ochoa, A., Vasquez-Hoyos, A. 1953. *Revta Inst. Salubr. Enferm. Trop.* 13:177–87
48. Goodfellow, M. 1971. *J. Gen. Microbiol.* 69:33–80
49. Goodfellow, M., Alderson, G. 1977. *J. Gen. Microbiol.* 100:99–122
50. Goodfellow, M., Brownell, G. H., Serrano, J. A. 1976. *Biology of the Nocardiae.* London: Academic. 517 pp.
51. Goodfellow, M., Collins, M. D., Minnikin, D. E. 1976. *J. Gen. Microbiol.* 96:351–58
52. Goodfellow, M., Cross, T. 1974. In *Biology of Plant Litter Decomposition,* ed. C. H. Dickinson, G. J. F. Pugh, Vol. 2, pp. 269–302. London: Academic. 775 pp.
53. Goodfellow, M., Fleming, A., Sackin, M. J. 1972. *Int. J. Syst. Bacteriol.* 22: 81–96
54. Goodfellow, M., Lind, A., Mordarska, H., Pattyn, S., Tsukamura, M. 1974. *J. Gen. Microbiol.* 85:291–302
55. Goodfellow, M., Minnikin, D. E. 1977. In *Proc. Int. Symp. Nocardia Streptomyces,* ed. M. Mordarski, W. Kuryłowicz, J. Jeljaszewicz. Berlin: Springer. In press
56. Goodfellow, M., Orchard, V. A. 1974. *J. Gen. Microbiol.* 83:375–87
57. Gordon, R. E. 1966. *J. Gen. Microbiol.* 43:329–43
58. Gordon, R. E. 1966. *J. Gen. Microbiol.* 45:355–64
59. Gordon, R. E. 1974. *Proc. Int. Conf. Biol. Nocardiae, 1st, Merida, Venezuela,* pp. 4–5
60. Gordon, R. E. See Ref. 1, pp. 66–73
61. Gordon, R. E., Barnett, D. A., Handerhan, J. E., Pang, C. H.-N. 1974. *Int. J. Syst. Bacteriol.* 24:54–63
62. Gordon, R. E., Horan, A. C. 1968. *J. Gen. Microbiol.* 50:235–40
63. Gordon, R. E., Mihm, J. M. 1957. *J. Bacteriol.* 73:15–27
64. Gordon, R. E., Mihm, J. M. 1959. *J. Gen. Microbiol.* 20:129–35
65. Gordon, R. E., Mihm, J. M. 1962. *J. Gen. Microbiol.* 27:1–10
66. Gordon, R. E., Mihm, J. M. 1962. *Ann. NY Acad. Sci.* 98:628–36
67. Gray, P. H. H. 1928. *Proc. R. Soc. London Ser. B* 102:263–80

68. Gray, P. H. H., Thornton, H. G. 1928. *Zentralbl. Bakteriol. Parasitenkd. Infektionskr. Hyg. Abt. 2* 73:74–96
69. Gross, N. M., Wayne, L. G. 1970. *J. Bacteriol.* 104:603–34
70. Hackett, J. A., Brennan, P. J. 1975. *Biochem. J.* 148:253–58
71. Hammond, B. F. 1970. *J. Bacteriol.* 103:634–40
72. Harz, C. O. 1877. *Dent. Z. Thiermed.* 5:125–40
73. Hefferan, M. 1904. *Zentralbl. Bakteriol. Parasitenkd. Infektionskr. Hyg. Abt. 2* 11:397–404
74. Holmberg, K., Hallander, H. O. 1973. *J. Gen. Microbiol.* 76:43–66
75. Hutchinson, M., Ridgway, J. W., Cross, T. 1975. In *Microbial Aspects of the Deterioration of Materials,* ed. D. W. Lovelock, R. J. Gilbert, pp. 187–202. London: Academic. 261 pp.
76. Ioneda, T., Lederer, E., Rozanis, J. 1970. *Chem. Phys. Lipids* 4:375–92
77. Jensen, H. L. 1931. *Proc. Linn. Soc. NSW* 56:345–70
78. Jones, D. 1975. *J. Gen. Microbiol.* 87:52–96
79. Kalakoutskii, L. V., Kirillova, I. P., Krassilnikov, N. A. 1967. *J. Gen. Microbiol.* 48:79–85
80. Keddie, R. M., Cure, G. L. 1977. *J. Appl. Bacteriol.* 42:229–52
81. Khuller, G. K., Brennan, P. J. 1972. *J. Gen. Microbiol.* 73:409–12
82. Komura, I., Yamada, K., Otsuka, S., Komagata, K. 1975. *J. Gen. Appl. Microbiol.* 21:251–61
83. Krassilnikov, N. A., Kalakoutskii, L. V., Kirillova, N. V. 1961. *Byull. Akad. Nauk Uzb. SSR* 1:107–12
84. Kruse, W. 1896. In *Die Mikro-organismen,* ed. C. Flügge, pp. 48–96. Leipzig: Vogel
85. Kubica, G. P., Baess, I., Gordon, R. E., Jenkins, P. A., Kwapinski, J. B. G., McDurmont, C., Pattyn, S. R., Saito, H., Silcox, V., Stanford, J. L., Takeya, K., Tsukamura, M. 1972. *J. Gen. Microbiol.* 73:55–70
86. Kurup, P. V., Randhawa, H. S., Gupta, N. P. 1970. *Mycopathol. Mycol. Appl.* 40:193–240
87. Kurup, P. V., Schmitt, J. A. 1973. *Can. J. Microbiol.* 19:1035–48
88. Kwapinski, J. B. G. 1969. *Analytic Serology of Micro-organisms,* ed. J. B. G. Kwapinski, Vol. 1. New York: Intersci. Publ. 122 pp.
89. Kwapinski, J. B. G. 1970. In *The Actinomycetales,* ed. H. Prauser, pp. 345–69. Jena: Gustav Fischer Verlag. 439 pp.
90. Kwapinski, J. B. G., Kwapinski, E. H., Dowler, J., Horsman, G. 1973. *Can. J. Microbiol.* 19:955–64
91. Lacey, J., Goodfellow, M. 1975. *J. Gen. Microbiol.* 88:75–85
92. Lacey, J., Goodfellow, M., Alderson, See Ref. 55. In press
93. Lanéelle, M.-A., Asselineau, J., Castelnuovo, G. 1968. *Ann. Inst. Pasteur Paris* 114:305–12
94. Lechevalier, M. P. 1972. *Int. J. Syst. Bacteriol.* 22:260–64
95. Lechevalier, M. P. See Ref. 1, pp. 1–38
96. Lechevalier, M. P., Gerber, N. N. 1970. *Carbohydr. Res.* 13:451–54
97. Lechevalier, M. P., Horan, A. C., Lechevalier, H. A. 1971. *J. Bacteriol.* 105:313–18
98. Lechevalier, M. P., Lechevalier, H. A. 1970. *Int. J. Syst. Bacteriol.* 20:435–44
99. Lechevalier, M. P., Lechevalier, H. A. See Ref. 89, pp. 393–405
100. Lechevalier, M. P., Lechevalier, H. A. 1974. *Int. J. Syst. Bacteriol.* 24:278–88
101. Lechevalier, H. A., Lechevalier, M. P., Gerber, N. N. 1971. *Adv. Appl. Microbiol.* 14:47–72
102. Lechevalier, M. P., Lechevalier, H., Horan, A. C. 1973. *Can. J. Mocrobiol.* 19:965–72
103. Lechevalier, H. A., Solotorovsky, M., McDurmont, C. I. 1961. *J. Gen. Microbiol.* 26:11–18
104. Lederer, E. 1976. *Chem. Phys. Lipids* 16:91–106
105. Lehmann, K. B., Neumann, R. 1896. *Atlas und Grundriss der Bakteriologie und Lehrbuch der speciellen bacteriologischen Diagnostik.* München: J J. F. Lehmann. 1st ed.
106. Lind, A., Ridell, M. See Ref. 1, pp. 220–35
107. Luedemann, G. M. 1968. *J. Bacteriol.* 96:1848–58
108. Magnusson, H. 1923. *Arch. Wiss. Prakt. Tierheilkd.* 50:22–38
109. Magnusson, M. 1973. In *Atypical Mycobacteria,* ed. J. G. Weiszfeiler, pp. 13–22. Budapest: Akademiai Kiado. 260 pp.
110. Magnusson, M. See Ref. 1, pp. 236–65
111. Magnusson, M., Mariat, F. 1968. *J. Gen. Microbiol.* 51:151–58
112. McClung, N. M. See Ref. 23, pp. 726–46
113. Metcalfe, G., Brown, M. 1957. *J. Gen. Microbiol.* 17:567–72
114. Meyer, J. 1976. *Int. J. Syst. Bacteriol.* 26:487–93

115. Michel, G., Bordet, C. See Ref. 1, pp. 141–59
116. Minnikin, D. E., Alshamaony, L., Goodfellow, M. 1975. *J. Gen. Microbiol.* 88:200–4
117. Minnikin, D. E., Collins, M. D., Goodfellow, M. See Ref. 55. In press
118. Minnikin, D. E., Goodfellow, M. See Ref. 1, pp. 160–219
119. Minnikin, D. E., Goodfellow, M. See Ref. 55. In press
120. Minnikin, D. E., Goodfellow, M., Alshamaony, L. 1977. See Ref. 55. In press
121. Minnikin, D. E., Patel, P. V., Alshamaony, L., Goodfellow, M. 1977. *Int. J. Syst. Bacteriol.* 27: In press
122. Minnikin, D. E., Pirouz, T., Goodfellow, M. 1977. *Int. J. Syst. Bacteriol.* 27: In press
123. Mordarska, H., Mordarski, M., Pietkiewicz, D. 1973. *Int. J. Syst. Bacteriol.* 23:274–77
124. Mordarski, M., Goodfellow, M., Szyba, K., Pulverer, G., Tkacz, A. See Ref. 55. In press
125. Mordarski, M., Goodfellow, M., Szyba, K., Pulverer, G., Tkacz, A. See Ref. 55. In press
126. Mordarski, M., Schaal, K. P., Szyba, K., Pulverer, G., Tkacz, A. 1977. *Int. J. Syst. Bacteriol.* 27:31–38
127. Mordarski, M., Szyba, K., Pulverer, G., Goodfellow, M. 1976. *J. Gen. Microbiol.* 94:235–45
128. Norgård, S., Aasen, A. J., Jensen, S. L. 1970. *Acta Chem. Scand.* 24:2183–97
129. Onisi, M., 1949. *Shikagaku Zasshi* 6:273–82
130. Onisi, M., Nuckolls, J. 1958. *Oral Surg. Oral Med. Oral Pathol.* 11:913–30
131. Orchard, V. A., Goodfellow, M. 1974 *J. Gen. Microbiol.* 85:160–62
132. Orchard, V. A., Goodfellow, M., Williams, S. T. 1977. *Soil Biol. Biochem.* 9:In press
133. Orla-Jensen, S. 1924. *Lait* 4:468–74
134. Overbeck, A. 1891. *Nova Acta Leopold.* 55:399–416
135. Pandhi, P. N., Hammond, B. F. 1975. *Arch. Oral Biol.* 20:399–401
136. Pier, A. C., Fichtner, R. E. 1971. *Am. Rev. Resp. Dis.* 103:698–707
137. Pine, L., Georg, L. K. 1969. *Int. J. Syst. Bacteriol.* 19:267–72
138. Pommier, M.-T., Michel, G. 1972. *C R Acad. Sci.* 275C:1323–26
139. Pommier, M.-T., Michel, G. 1973. *Biochem. Syst.* 1:3–12
140. Pommier, M.-T., Michel, G. 1976. *Biochim. Biophys. Acta* 441:327–33
141. Prauser, H. 1967. *Publ. Fac. Sci. Univ. J. E. Purkyně Brno* K40:196–99
142. Prauser, H. See Ref. 89, pp. 407–18
143. Prauser, H. 1975. In *Proc. Int. Cong. IAMS Tokyo, Vol. 1,* p. 19
144. Prauser, H. See Ref. 1, pp. 266–84
145. Prauser, H. 1976. *Int. J. Syst. Bacteriol.* 26:58–65
146. Prauser, H., Bergholz, M. 1974. *Post. High. Med. Dosw.* 28:441–57
147. Prauser, H., Falta, R. 1968. *Z. Allg. Mikrobiol.* 8:39–46
148. Prauser, H., Lechevalier, M. P., Lechevalier, H. A. 1970. *Appl. Microbiol.* 19:534
149: Pridham, T. G., Lyons, A. J. Jr. 1969. *Dev. Ind. Microbiol.* 10:183–21
150. Pulverer, G., Schütt-Gerowitt, H., Schaal, K. P. 1975. *Med. Microbiol. Immunol.* 161:113–22
151. Ratledge, C., Patel, P. V. See Ref. 59, pp. 58–59
152. Ratledge, C., Patel, P. V. See Ref. 1, pp. 372–85
153. Ratledge, C., Patel, P. V. 1976. *J. Gen. Microbiol.* 93:141–52
154. Ridell, M. 1974. *Int. J. Syst. Bacteriol.* 24:64–72
155. Ridell, M. 1975. *Int. J. Syst. Bacteriol.* 25:124–32
156. Ridell, M., Norlin, M. 1973. *J. Bacteriol.* 113:1–7
157. Rogosa, M., Cummins, C. S., Lelliott, R. A., Keddie, R. M. See Ref. 23, pp. 599–602
158. Röhrscheidt, E., Tarnok, I. 1972. *Zentralbl. Bakteriol. Parasitenkd. Infektionskr. Hyg. Abt. 1* 221:221–33
159. Roth, G. D. 1957. *Oral Surg. Oral Med. Oral Pathol.* 10:1105–17
160. Roth, G. D., Thurn, A. N. 1962. *J. Dent. Res.* 41:1279–92
161. Rowbotham, T. J., Cross, T. 1977. *J. Gen. Microbiol.* 100:123–38
162. Schaal, K. P. See Ref. 59, pp. 94–95
163. Schaal, K. P. 1977. In *CRC Handbook: Clinical Laboratory Science.* In press
164. Schaal, K. P., Reutersberg, H. See Ref. 55. In press
165. Schneidau, J. D. Jr., Shaffer, M. F. 1957. *Ann. Rev. Tuberc.* 76:770–88
166. Shaw, N. 1974. *Adv. Appl. Microbiol.* 17:63–108
167. Slack, J. M., Gerenscer, M. A. 1975. *Actinomyces, Filamentous Bacteria: Biology and Pathogenicity.* Minneapolis: Burgess Publ. Co. 158 pp.
168. Sneath, P. H. A. 1968. *J. Gen. Microbiol.* 54:1–11
169. Sneath, P. H. A. See Ref. 89, pp. 371–77
170. Sneath, P. H. A. See Ref. 1, pp. 74–101

171. Snow, G. A. 1970. *Bacteriol. Rev.* 34:99–125
172. Soina, V. S., Agre, N. S. 1976. *Mikrobiologiya* 45:329–32
173. Sönghen, N. L. 1913. *Zentralbl. Bakteriol. Parasitenkd. Infektionskr. Hyg. Abt. 2* 37:595–609
174. Staneck, J. L., Roberts, G. D. 1974. *Appl. Microbiol.* 28:226–31
175. Stees, J. L., Brown, O. R., Grigsby, R. D. 1969. *Microbios* 1:199–200
176. Šuput, J., Lechevalier, M. P., Lechevalier, H. A. 1967. *Appl. Microbiol.* 15:1356–61
177. Tabaud, H., Tisnovska, H., Vilkas, E. 1971. *Biochemie* 53:55–61
178. Tárnok, I. See Ref. 1, pp. 451–500
179. Tárnok, I., Tárnok, Z. 1970. *Tubercle* 51:305–12
180. Tárnok, I., Tárnok, Z. 1971. *Tubercle* 52:127–35
181. Thiemann, J. E., Zucco, G., Pelizza, G. 1969. *Arch. Mikrobiol.* 67:147–55
182. Trevisan, V. 1889. *I Genera e le Specie delle Battieriacee.* Milan: Zanaboni & Gabuzzi
183. Tsukamura, M. 1969. *J. Gen. Microbiol.* 56:265–87
184. Tsukamura, M. 1971. *J. Gen. Microbiol.* 66:15–26
185. Tsukamura, M. 1973. *Jpn. J. Microbiol.* 17:189–97
186. Tsukamura, M. 1974. *Jpn. J. Microbiol.* 18:37–44
187. Tsukamura, M. 1976. *Int. J. Syst. Bacteriol.* 26:409–20
188. Tsukamura, M., Mizuno, S. 1971. *Kekkaku* 46:93–98
189. Tsukamura, M., Mizuno, S., Murata, H. 1975. *Int. J. Syst. Bacteriol.* 25: 377–82
190. Turfitt, G. E. 1944. *J. Bacteriol.* 47: 487–93
191. Vacheron, M.-J., Arpin, N., Michel, G. 1970. *CR Acad. Sci.* 271C:881–84
192. Vacheron, M.-J., Guinand, M., Michel, G., Ghuysen, J. M. 1972. *Eur. J. Biochem.* 29:156–66
193. Van Saceghem, R. 1915. *Bull. Soc. Pathol. Exot.* 8:354–59
194. Waksman, S. A. 1961. *The Actinomycetes,* Vol. 11. Baltimore: Williams & Wilkins
195. Weeks, O. B., Andrewes, A. G. 1970. *Arch. Biochem. Biophys.* 137:284–86
196. Wheeler, W. C., Hanks, J. H. 1965. *J. Bacteriol.* 89:889–96
197. Williams, S. T., Sharples, G. P., Serrano, J. A., Serrano, A. A., Lacey, J. See Ref. 1, pp. 102–40
198. Willoughby, L. G. 1969. *Hydrobiologiya* 34:465–83
199. Yano, I., Furukawa, Y., Kusunose, M. 1968. *J. Biochem. Tokyo* 63:133–35
200. Yano, I., Furukawa, Y., Kusunose, M. 1969. *J. Bacteriol.* 98:124–30
201. Yano, I., Furukawa, Y., Kusunose, M. 1970. *Biochim. Biophys. Acta* 202: 189–91
202. Yribarren, M., Vilkas, E., Rozanis, J. 1974. *Chem. Phys. Lipids* 12:172–75
203. Zopf, W. 1891. *Ber. Dtsch. Bot. Ges.* 9:22–29

Ann. Rev. Microbiol. 1977. 31:181–203

ION CURRENTS AND PHYSIOLOGICAL FUNCTIONS IN MICROORGANISMS

❖1702

F. M. Harold

Division of Molecular and Cellular Biology, National Jewish Hospital and Research Center, Denver, Colorado 80206 and Department of Microbiology and Immunology, University of Colorado Medical School, Denver, Colorado 80220

CONTENTS

PUMPS, CHANNELS, CARRIERS, AND GATES 181
PROTONS AND THE METABOLIC ECONOMY OF BACTERIA 184
Energy Transduction 184
Ancillary Ion Movements 187
In Search of Novel Functions 188
ION CURRENTS IN EUKARYOTIC CELLS 189
Proton Circulation of Fungi and Algae 189
Action Potentials and Osmotic Regulation 192
Excitability, Calcium, and Locomotor Behavior 192
Electrical Control of Morphogenesis 195
Of Ions and Clocks 198
THE IMPORTANCE OF BEING ELECTRIFIED 199

> It takes a membrane to make sense out of disorder in biology . . . To stay alive you have to be able to hold out against equilibrium, maintain imbalance, bank against entropy, and you can only transact this business with membranes in our kind of world.
>
> Lewis Thomas, The Lives of a Cell.

PUMPS, CARRIERS, CHANNELS, AND GATES

That living things can generate electrical currents and potentials has been known since Galvani's day. Most bioelectric phenomena arise from the movement of ions across membranes in such a way as to produce an imbalance of electrical charge; the quantitative relationships between ion movements and electrical parameters have been thoroughly explored in systems as diverse as nerve axons, epithelial tissues, plant roots, and giant algae. As a result, electrophysiology is today one of the most sophisticated branches of biological science, but rather an arcane one, seemingly remote from the concerns of most biochemists or microbiologists. This comfortable apartheid has been shattered by developments in bioenergetics during the past decade: it has become clear that at the molecular level a central function of biological membranes is to generate gradients of ion concentration and electrical potential, and that many, though obviously not all, of the physiological roles that membranes play depend upon the controlled utilization of ion currents to perform diverse kinds of work. Electrification is not confined to squid axons and electric eels but is a fact of life for *Paramecium, Neurospora,* and even *Escherichia coli.*

A voluminous and specialized literature has grown up around the role of proton—and of sodium currents in oxidative phosphorylation and active transport [for historical perspectives (see 16, 21, 44, 84, 88, 92, 119, 124)]. But one comes to suspect that ion currents may be too important to be left entirely to students of "bioenergetics." The ubiquitous distribution of ion currents and their (presumptive) evolutionary antiquity encourages one to wonder about their involvement in other cellular activities that depend upon membranes—in sensory perception, inter- and intracellular communication, cell division, morphogenesis, differentiation, biological clocks, and other mysteries. The present essay, therefore, attempts not to review the current literature in any systematic way but to articulate a point of view: that the circulation of ions across biological membranes is at the heart of many physiological devices that allow cells and organisms to function as integrated units. In time, we may list ion currents along with membranes, genophores, and ribosomes among the essential attributes of cells.

Let us at the outset distinguish three kinds of molecular mechanisms that translocate ions across biological membranes. Simplest and best understood is passive diffusion through aqueous channels or through the lipid phase of the membrane, but ions of biological interest do not usually move in this fashion. We shall be mostly concerned with transport, processes that involve interaction of ions with specific membrane components and especially with macromolecules. Following Mitchell's terminology (86), I speak of two classes of transport, primary and secondary. *Primary* ion transport refers to movements integrally linked to some enzymic reaction; many, but not all, are electrogenic. Examples include the familiar Na^+- and K^+-stimulated ATPase of mammalian cell membranes and the translocation of protons by vectorial redox reactions. The energy required to move the ion counter to the electrochemical potential gradient is supplied by the metabolic reaction; thus, the colloquial "ion pump" properly applies to the primary transport processes that interconvert chemical, osmotic, and electrical forms of energy.

Secondary transport refers to processes that involve exchange of secondary or ionic bonds but not a concurrent chemical reaction; they provide thermodynamically passive pathways of greater or lesser specificity for the diffusion of ions in accordance with the concentration gradient, the electrical potential, or both. The driving force upon the ion in question and the physiological role of the translocation depend upon the molecular mechanism. Some secondary transport processes are electroneutral, others translocate one or more charges; in some cases the ion moves singly, in others its movement is coupled to that of another metabolite in the same direction (symport) or in the opposite one (antiport). Functions are equally varied, ranging from modulation of the transmembrane electrical potential by ion movement to the accumulation of nutrients. The translocators usually found in biological membranes are macromolecules, and their mechanism of action is in no case well understood. For that reason, much attention has been devoted to the ionophore antibiotics that exemplify many features of secondary transport: for example, valinomycin and nigericin are carrier molecules that form specific complexes with K^+, respectively charged and neutral; gramicidins and polyenes generate ion-conducting channels, respectively selective for cations and anions; and alamethicin or monazomycin form conducting channels only when a voltage is applied across the membrane and are said to exhibit "gating" (29, 48, 51, 82, 95, 96, 139).

Finally, *ion current* refers simply to the flow of an ion from a higher to a lower electrochemical potential, but in the present context, it usually involves the circulation across the membrane between two transport processes separated by some significant distance (Figure 1).

At this point, the reader may wonder why the distinction between primary and secondary ion transport has been so emphasized. The reason is that it corresponds to two kinds of physiological functions. The primary systems carry out reversible

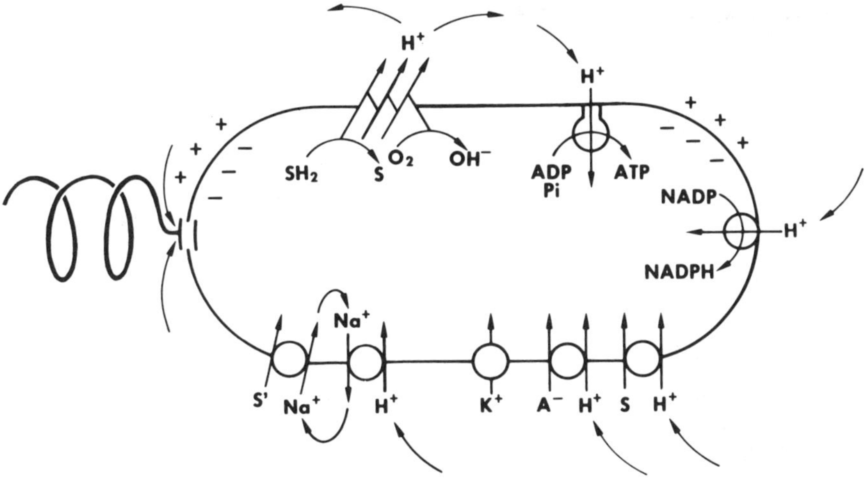

Figure 1 Energy transduction by the proton circulation in bacteria. The diagram illustrates generation of a proton current by vectorial electrogenic H^+ extrusion through the respiratory chain and completion of the current loop by several paths that perform useful work: proton-translocating ATPase (oxidative phosphorylation); pyridine nucleotide transhydrogenase; the flagellar motor; and several kinds of proton-linked transport systems. Also shown is the generation of a secondary sodium current by Na^+/H^+ antiport and an example of sodium-linked substrate transport. S, Substrate.

interconversion between the free energy of chemical reactions and that of electrical potential or concentration gradients. These are Mitchell's chemiosmotic reactions (87, 88, 91) that have an intrinsic direction in space; they generate ion currents and also utilize them for chemosynthesis. In most cases, the current loop is closed by secondary transport systems, designed to couple the electrochemical potential of the ion gradient to the performance of other kinds of work. The remainder of this article explores some of the diverse ways in which living things, and particularly microorganisms, exploit the interactions of primary and secondary ion transport.

PROTONS AND THE METABOLIC ECONOMY OF BACTERIA

Energy Transduction

Electrophysiological principles emerged largely in the context of nerves and other electrically excitable cells, but it is the bacteria that most clearly illuminate the significance of ion currents to general physiology. The work of the past decade has established that metabolizing bacteria are continuously traversed by a strong current of protons and that this is central to the conservation of metabolic energy and the performance of work.

Our growing insight into the nature, genesis, and functions of the bacterial proton circulation stems almost entirely from Mitchell's chemiosmotic theory, formulated between 1956 and 1966 (84, 85, 87, 91). The massive body of subsequent theoretical and experimental work has refined, extended, and supported the original conception but left its principles unchanged. The evidence is now so extensive that it is neither necessary nor possible to recapitulate it here. Major reviews consider in detail thc chemiosmotic theory in general (39, 85, 87, 91, 145, 146), the chemiosmotic interpretation of bacterial physiology in particular (44, 45, 46) and specific topics such as transport (41, 42, 47, 64, 126, 143), respiration and oxidative phosphorylation (40, 91, 146), and photosynthesis (22, 108, 114, 146). Here, I propose only to outline very briefly the kind of molecular machinery that is now envisaged (Figure 1).

PROTON TRANSPORT BY VECTORIAL METABOLISM The cytoplasmic membrane of bacteria always contains one or several vectorial enzymic pathways so constructed as to catalyze electrogenic transport of protons outward.[1] These are the primary pumps that generate and maintain the imbalance of the electrochemical potential of protons across the membrane, making the cytoplasm electrically negative and alkaline, and thus they drive the circulation of protons. At present, we know four quite distinct kinds of primary pumps. (*a*) One is redox chains, both aerobic and anaerobic. Although the molecular details remain in dispute, the basic principle still appears to be that of the redox loop: a vectorial dehydrogenation carries hydrogen from a donor on the inner surface to an acceptor at the outer; the electrons

[1]It is conventional to speak of proton translocation but one cannot distinguish movement of protons one way from that of hydroxyl ions the other way.

return to the cytoplasmic side; and protons are liberated at the junction of the two limbs [for recent adaptations of the principle (see 40, 90, 92, 113, 146)]. (*b*) Photosynthetic apparatus based on bacteriochlorophyll is another. Absorption of light generates the primary electric field, which redox reactions convert into an electrochemical proton gradient; this mechanism again depends on the positioning of primary acceptor and electron donor on opposite surfaces of the membrane. (*c*) Halobacteria produce a unique and chemically relatively simple proton pump comprising a single protein species and the chromophore retinal. These are so arranged that upon illumination the retinal is bleached, releasing to the outside one proton per photon absorbed; regeneration occurs with uptake of a proton from the cytoplasm. It is likely that the retinal gates a transmembrane channel. (*d*) A fourth kind is proton-translocating ATPase. The mechanism by which this sophisticated complex functions remains highly controversial (9, 10, 60, 89, 91, 115). It clearly comprises two distinct regions: a headpiece (F_1) that bears the catalytic site and a basepiece (F_0) that includes a specific proton channel spanning the membrane. The channel is normally so gated by the headpiece that protons can pass only in conjunction with the chemical reaction of ATP hydrolysis or synthesis.

PERFORMANCE OF WORK BY THE PROTON CURRENT The proton circulation serves as the driving force for the performance of chemical, mechanical, and osmotic work by bacteria. The molecular devices by which this is accomplished generally include some means of ion translocation (usually but not necessarily H^+) cunningly articulated with elements of different specificity (Figure 1).

We now recognize that a large number of transport systems couple the movement of a metabolite up its electrochemical gradient to the movement of protons down the gradient established by the proton pumps. Examples include electrogenic symport of sugars and amino acids with one or more protons, electroneutral symport of anionic metabolites, and the extrusion of sodium and calcium by antiport with protons (41, 42, 45, 46, 126, 143). From the proton's point of view, these are all secondary transport systems; little more than a beginning has been made towards understanding how they function at the molecular level (21, 129, 130, 136).

Oxidative and photosynthetic phosphorylation exemplify the coupling of one primary transport to another via the proton current (Figure 1). The ATPase is thought to catalyze a reversible chemiosmotic reaction such that ATP hydrolysis drives protons outward, and conversely, movement of protons inward (down the potential gradient established by respiration) is coupled to ATP synthesis. Pyridine nucleotide transhydrogenase is probably another enzyme that links chemical synthesis to the proton circulation. I hasten to add that this interpretation does not yet command universal assent; the molecular mechanism is particularly debatable.

Finally, a word is in order concerning the role of the proton circulation in motility and chemotaxis, a kind of energy coupling that (unlike the preceding ones) appears to be confined to the bacteria. It is now generally agreed (2, 8) that bacteria swim by rotating their flagella around the point of insertion into the cytoplasmic membrane. The energy source for the "motor" at the base of the flagellum is evidently not ATP but the proton circulation (2, 81a). Indeed, it seems increasingly likely that the proton current turns the motor in some quite direct manner, but the molecular mechanism remains totally unknown.

Chemotaxis requires modulation of flagellar rotation; evidence is beginning to accumulate that this most elementary instance of sensory perception and behavior also involves the proton circulation. Briefly, bacteria move in straight runs interrupted by a tumble, after which the cell sets off in a new direction. Tumbling results from an abrupt reversal of the sense of rotation of the flagella, and it is the frequency of tumbling that is altered by environmental signals (attractants, for example, suppress tumbling with the result that cells tend to swim up the gradient). One way in which recognition of a signal might be communicated to the flagellar motor is via fluctuations in the membrane potential or in the flux of a particular ion. Several investigators have reported findings that point in this direction (8, 110, 111, 153), but a compelling experiment has yet to be done.

POWER TRANSMISSION BY THE PROTON CURRENT The amount of work that a proton current can perform depends on the proton flux (itself determined by the metabolic rate and molecular stoichiometry of proton transport) and on the electrochemical potential of protons across the membrane. The latter is usually expressed as the protonmotive force, Δp, analogous to the electromotive force of a battery: it is the amount of work done by a single proton going once around the circuit. The expression for Δp takes account of both forces that act upon protons, the electrical potential $\Delta\psi$, and the pH gradient ΔpH:

$$\Delta p = \Delta\psi - \frac{2.3\ RT}{F}\ \Delta pH \cong \Delta\psi - 60\Delta pH,$$

where $\Delta\psi$ is the membrane potential, ΔpH is the pH gradient and Δp is the protonmotive force, all in millivolts. *R, T,* and *F* have their usual meanings.

Some representative data are collected (Table 1); more extensive compilations have been prepared by Rottenberg (128) and by Rosen & Kashket (126). In most cases, the magnitude of Δp is sufficient to perform the work attributed to it, but some doubt remains with regard to ATP synthesis in oxidative phosphorylation. The contributions of $\Delta\psi$ and ΔpH to the total protonmotive force vary with external pH and potassium content, a matter that may prove very important in the formulation of molecular mechanism to link proton flux to work functions (4, 112, 120, 129).

Less attention has been given to the flux of protons passing across the membrane, but some estimates are included (Table 1) to facilitate comparison with eukaryotic cells. The figures imply a power output of the order of 0.5 W per g (dry weight) of *Escherichia coli.*

For a membrane to sustain gradients of the order of 200 mV, it must be highly impermeable to protons and indeed to ions generally. The proton conductance is in fact of the order of 0.5 μmho cm^{-2}, comparable to that of artificial lipid bilayers. Any reagent that induces a non-physiological ion leak will short-circuit the proton circulation and dissociate metabolism from work. The ionophore antibiotics illustrate this effect, and it is at least plausible that some bacteriocins (e.g. colicins K, I, and E1) exert their effects in this manner (11a, 45, 69, 126).

Table 1 Microbial proton circulations[a]

Organism	Proton motive force, mV			Proton flux		Refs.
	ΔpH	Δψ	Δp	μeq g^{-1} sec^{-1}	peq cm^{-2} sec^{-1}	
Prokaryotes						
Escherichia coli	-100	-137	-237	(48)	(120)	20, 62
Paracoccus denitrificans				(28.6)	(72)	135
Streptococcus faecalis	-60	-150	-210	(4)	(10)	49; F. M. Harold, unpublished data
Halobacterium halobium	-40	-100	-140	(4)	(10)	4; E. Bakker, unpublished data
Mitochondria (rat liver)	-84	-139	-223	7.5	18.7	93
Eukaryotes						
Neurospora crassa	-20	-220	-240		5–30	148, 151
Nitella translucens	-60	-165	-225		20–33	155
Chara corallina		-240			(1.2)	123

[a] Selected data from the literature, figures in parenthesis were recalculated. Proton flux is given both as microequivalents of H^+ per gram of protein per second and as picoequivalents of H^+ per square centimeters of surface area. Where necessary, it was assumed that half the cell's dry weight is protein and that the surface area is 40 m^2 g^{-1} of protein.

Ancillary Ion Movements

The purpose of this section is not to discuss the many transport systems (142) that make inorganic ions available to cytoplasmic enzymes but to consider whether translocation of ions other than H^+ has a dynamic role in the operation of bacterial cells. This does appear to be the case, but movements of sodium, potassium, and calcium are ancillary in the sense of serving specialized functions that supplement the work of the proton circulation.

SODIUM The capacity to expel sodium from the cytoplasm is apparently ubiquitous among bacteria. In no case is the mechanism well defined, but it seems that bacteria have no primary sodium pumps; sodium movement occurs by antiport with one or more protons and, thus, is secondary to the proton circulation (47, 73, 142, 165).

A surprising number of bacterial transport systems require Na^+; others are inhibited by Na^+ (45, 126). In view of the role of sodium symport in mammalian transport systems, attempts have been made to determine whether or not the bacterial transport systems also translocate sodium inwards, and if so, whether or not the electrochemical potential of Na^+ contributes to the driving force upon the metabolite. Unequivocal positive results have so far been reported only for halobacteria, unique in other respects as well. According to Lanyi & MacDonald (72, 76), uptake of leucine responds both to $\Delta\psi$ and to the Na^+ gradient; glutamate responds to the Na^+ gradient alone. Sodium is expelled by electrogenic antiport for protons (73).

POTASSIUM K^+ is an essential nutrient for all cells and generally the most abundant intracellular cation. Unfortunately, the mechanism of potassium transport is not well understood. What evidence we have suggests that K^+ accumulation by *Streptococcus faecalis* is electrogenic (translocating positive charge inward) and requires both ATP and an electrical potential (interior negative). In *E. coli,* the trKA system has similar properties, whereas the Kdp system is electroneutral (47, 122, 142) (E. P. Bakker and F. M. Harold, unpublished data).

Potassium is a cofactor for many enzymes, and a high cytoplasmic K^+ level is required for protein synthesis. A more critical role for K^+ transport as such appears to be the control of the cytoplasmic pH. It has been shown repeatedly that K^+ is required to establish a pH gradient (interior alkaline), presumably because K^+ uptake compensates for the net extrusion of protons. The alkaline pH in turn appears to be involved in a number of functions, including regulation of metabolism, anion transport, and possibly osmotic adaptation (47). Indeed, Raven & Smith (121) argue that control of the cytoplasmic pH may have been the ancestral function of proton pumps in the early evolution of life. Thus, accumulation of potassium is ancillary to the proton circulation, both in terms of mechanism and of function. There is as yet no evidence for any process that depends upon the efflux of potassium from the cells.

CALCIUM Extrusion of calcium from the cytoplasm appears to be another universal attribute of bacteria, except under special circumstances such as sporulation (141). No primary pump analogous to the mammalian calcium ATPase has been described in bacteria, but there are several reports of calcium/proton antiport in response to the proton circulation (141, 161). Eukaryotic cells of various kinds make good use of calcium gradients (see below), but the role of calcium movements in bacterial physiology remains to be discovered.

In Search of Novel Functions

The continuous massive flux of protons out of and back into bacterial cells is a major feature of their physiology and may well have functions that remain to be recognized. One that comes to mind is that the proton current may serve as an index of metabolic status or as a regulatory circuit complementary to energy charge and cAMP. It is intriguing in this connection that proton conductors stimulate the phosphotransferase system and perhaps the breakdown of intracellular energy reserves by a mechanism that is quite unknown (32, 53, 61, 144).

One of the essential features of ion currents is their intrinsic direction in space. This has been emphasized in the context of transport and motility where the vector is normal to the cell membrane, but one can also ask whether bacterial cells may have an overall electrical polarity as germinating *Fucus* eggs do (see below); this would arise if either primary or secondary ion transport systems were preferentially localized in a particular region of the cell, for instance at the ends of a rod. There appears to be no information on this point, which may prove as pertinent to studies on morphological differentiation in bacteria as it has for eukaryotic cells.

Bacteria are conventionally depicted as having but a single compartment (Figure 1), but it is evident that there are exceptions. Spores, *Chlorobium* vesicles, and the membraneous lamellae so conspicuous in some chemoautotrophs and in cyanobacteria are likely to be intracellular compartments, possibly endowed with ion circulations of their own.

Finally, one can ask whether proton circulation is directly involved in DNA replication, in cell division, or in assembling the structural framework of wall, membranes, and nucleoid of bacterial cells. Recent experiments (49a) strongly suggest that the answer here is no. *S. faecalis* grows readily in the presence of ionophores under conditions so arranged that Δp, ΔpH, $\Delta\psi$, and the K^+ gradient are all zero and the membrane is freely permeable to H^+, K^+, and Na^+. To be sure, such cells are crippled; they require a rich medium, an alkaline pH, and a high level of external K^+; they are inhibited by Na^+. Yet the fact that they grow and divide at a rate comparable to that of control cells and appear morphologically quite normal sets an upper limit to the biological importance of the proton circulation. From the findings of Kopecky et al (69), it is likely that this conclusion also applies to *E. coli.*

ION CURRENTS IN EUKARYOTIC CELLS

The multiplicity of membranes and compartments is surely the most conspicuous feature of eukaryotic architecture. Nuclei, vacuoles, mitochondria, and chloroplasts define regions that differ in metabolic activity and in some cases at least segregate ion circulations that perform particular and localized tasks. It seems increasingly likely that, in principle if not in detail, chloroplasts and mitochondria operate on a proton circulation in the prokaryotic mode; the evidence has been reviewed at length by others (9, 10, 25, 34, 44, 60, 85, 91, 113, 119, 146). Whether or not other vesicular structures have private ion circuits is not clear; at least some nuclear membranes are permeable to small solutes and ions (31, 140). Interest, therefore, centers on the cytoplasmic membrane, which, released from its commitment to energy production, assumes new and extended duties. In what follows, I have selected examples from relatively simple eukaryotic microorganisms to illustrate how novel needs were met by ingenious variations on the prokaryotic theme of cation currents.

Proton Circulation of Fungi and Algae

Electrical currents and potentials across the cytoplasmic membrane of bacteria must be inferred from indirect data, but those of the fungus *Neurospora crassa* can be measured directly by use of microelectrodes. In a study that remains a landmark,

Slayman (147, 148) reported membrane potentials near –200 mV, comprised of two components. Part, amounting to some –30 to –60 mV, was sensitive to the concentration of external monovalent cations and was therefore interpreted as an ionic diffusion potential; outward diffusion of K^+ accounts for most of it. Addition of small amounts of calcium (0.1–1 mM) largely abolished the effect of external K^+ and Na^+ on the membrane potential, presumably by modifying the K^+ permeability. The major component of the membrane potential was evidently of metabolic origin as it was rapidly and reversibly abolished by cyanide, azide, or carbonylcyanide m-chlorophenylhydrazone. For example, upon addition of 1 mM sodium azide, the potential fell from –200 to –15 mV within less than a minute and recovered when the inhibitor was removed. This potential could not be accounted for as an ionic diffusion potential and was attributed to electrogenic extrusion of protons across the plasma membrane. The proton flux so generated was estimated at 5–20 pmol cm^{-2} sec, in the same range as the flux in bacteria and mitochondria (147, 148), but is subject to complex modulation (37, 150).

The energy source of the proton pump is almost certainly ATP; Slayman et al (149) estimated the stoichiometry to be about two protons per ATP hydrolyzed. Existence of the enzyme has now been confirmed by Scarborough (133), who showed that plasma membrane vesicles contain an ATPase capable of generating a potential gradient. Very little is yet known of the molecular characteristics of this proton pump, but its role in coupling transport to metabolism is well established. Slayman & Slayman (152) showed that uptake of glucose was accompanied by an inward current of protons sufficient to depolarize the membrane and inferred symport with one or two protons.

The pattern is probably much the same in yeast. Eddy and his associates have provided convincing evidence that accumulation of certain sugars, amino acids, and inorganic phosphate occurs by electrogenic symport with protons (19, 137, 138). Misra & Höfer (83) observed energy-linked electrogenic proton extrusion by *Rhodotorula,* probably mediated by an ATPase sensitive to N,N'-dicyclohexylcarbodiimide. Data on K^+ uptake (116, 127) are also consistent with the hypothesis that a primary proton pump generates a membrane potential, interior negative. To a first approximation then, we find dual proton circulations in fugal cells: a mitochondrial one, based on redox reactions, to produce ATP; and another across the plasma membrane, based on an ATPase, that functions in metabolite transport and the control of cytoplasmic pH (Figure 2).

It now appears that a pattern of this kind may be a feature also of the economy of algal cells, albeit only recently recognized. The enormous body of information on algal electrophysiology and ionic relations has been summarized by Hope & Walker (56), MacRobbie (80), and Higinbotham (54). Suffice it to mention here that an electrogenic proton pump is evidently a major contributor to the electrical potential and ion flux pattern across the plasmalemma of the freshwater algae *Nitella* (155) and *Chara* (123). The electrical potential may go as high as –200 to –240 mV; proton flux is of the order of 20 pmol cm^{-2} sec, and it is likely that the current is generated by an ATPase sensitive to dicyclohexylcarbodiimide that extrudes two protons per ATP (155, 162). A proton current is also produced by the

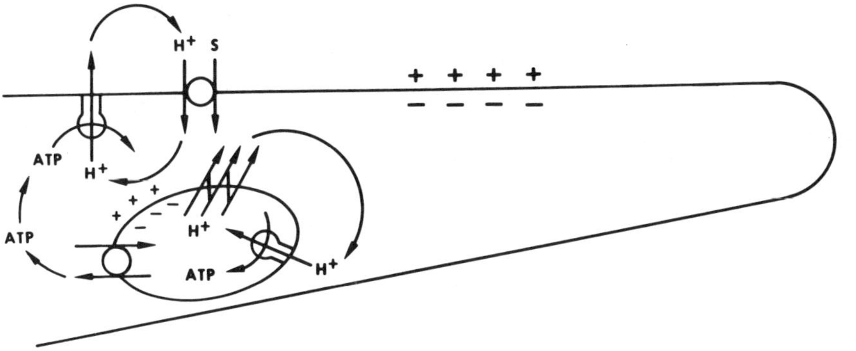

Figure 2 Dual proton circulation in *Neurospora crassa.* The diagram includes a mitochondrion, the ATP-driven proton pump in the cytoplasmic membrane, and a H^+-symport carrier.

marine alga *Acetabularia,* but it appears that in this case an ATP-driven chloride pump, directed inwards, is the chief source of the electrical potential (35). There is also evidence that K^+ transport requires ATP, but the coupling among K^+, Na^+, and H^+ fluxes is in no case clearly established. Complexity is compounded by the presence in all these algae of a second major membrane system, the tonoplast, which bounds the vacuole and thus as much as 90% of the cell's volume. Small electrical potentials have been measured between cytoplasm and vacuole, but their genesis is none too clear.

The physiological functions of algal ion currents, insofar as one can discern them now, are again related to metabolite transport. In *Chlorella,* Komor et al (65–67) have carefully characterized a system that mediates secondary glucose-proton symport. Concurrent measurements of ΔpH and $\Delta\psi$ indicate that the system is an electrogenic one (68). One would expect, however, that, in algae such as *Nitella* and *Chara* that maintain cell turgor by accumulation of salt in the central vacuole, the critical function of the proton circulation would be in the transport of inorganic ions. It has indeed been proposed that both chloride and bicarbonate are taken up by exchange for cytoplasmic OH^-, but the hypothesis remains in dispute (see 56, 80, 154).

To sum up, a proton circulation evidently is part of the metabolic economy of fungal and algal cells; at least one of its functions is to drive the secondary transport of metabolites. I have been unable to find evidence that would warrant extension of this statement to protozoa. Turning to higher organisms, there is abundant evidence from mammalian systems that a circulation of Na^+ is generated by the Na^+, K^+-ATPase and supports metabolite transport across cell membranes and epithelial tissues (e.g. 16, 21, 52). ATPases stimulated by Na^+ and K^+ have also been isolated from various plant plasmalemma preparations (55, 156), but their function is uncertain. The evidence from electrophysiology (54, 80) seems rather to point to a proton circulation as the dominant element in higher plants, and this is reinforced by recent experiments (17, 18) that implicate some kind of proton pump in growth regulation by auxin.

Action Potentials and Osmotic Regulation

It has been known for 30 years that some giant algal cells are at least mildly excitable: in response to a stimulus (usually but not necessarily electrical) that depolarizes the plasmalemma past a sharp threshold, one observes a marked further depolarization, followed by recovery of the resting potential. The duration of these action potentials is of the order of seconds (56). More recent work showed that action potentials are widespread in the plant world; they differ both in mechanism and in function from the better known and much faster action potentials of nervous tissue.

In *Chara* and *Nitella,* the action potential results from a transient rise in the permeability to chloride; there ensues a substantial efflux of Cl^- (0.5–1 nmol cm^{-2} in each action potential), accompanied by a smaller amount of K^+. Calcium ions are probably involved in triggering the response. Part of the chloride flux is electrically uncompensated, and it is this net movement of charge that accounts for depolarization of the membrane (56). A somewhat similar depolarization due to chloride efflux has been described for the single-celled alga *Acetabularia* (38, 97), but it now appears that the underlying mechanism is not a transient increase in chloride permeability but a change in the activity of the electrogenic chloride pump (36). In *Neurospora,* likewise, the sluggish action potentials appear to reflect modulation of the proton pump (150).

Quantitative studies with several organisms suggest that the function of action potentials has to do with osmotic regulation and apical growth patterns. In *Acetabularia,* the electrical potential is about –170 mV, yet the cells maintain a K^+ concentration corresponding to –90 mV. This is probably achieved by periodic release of K^+: in a single action potential the discharge of K^+ is approximately equivalent to the amount that leaks into the cell in 10 min; this fits well with a spontaneous firing rate of about six per hour (97). In embryos of the brown alga *Pelvetia,* turgor pressure is maintained by uptake of K^+ and Cl^- from the medium. Periodic current pulses during growth (see below) were shown to be carried by efflux of Cl^- from the growing tip, accompanied by efflux of K^+ elsewhere (104). Pulsing can be elicited by decreasing the external osmotic pressure, and the amounts of K^+ and Cl^- released thereby are approximately such as to restore the original turgor pressure (105). Nuccitelli & Jaffe (105) suggest that the growing tip serves as a pressure transducer that senses the turgor pressure and responds by triggering chloride release; here again, Ca^{2+} ions are somehow involved.

Excitability, Calcium, and Locomotor Behavior

Paramecium is sufficiently robust to tolerate impalement by microelectrodes with little disturbance of cell function and behavior. The union of electrophysiology and genetics, exemplified in the work of Eckert (28) and of Kung and his associates (71), revealed that a current of calcium ions plays a key role in coupling sensory perception to behavior and promises to shed light on the molecular basis of excitability.

Let us begin this brief and somewhat oversimplified summary with the classical avoidance reaction. When *Paramecium* encounters an obstacle, or a chemical stimulus such as Na^+, it backs up briefly and then resumes forward motion in a slightly different direction. This results from a temporary reversal of the direction of ciliary beating over the entire cell surface. The mechanism of ciliary beating is beyond our scope here (see 94, 157) except to note that the energy source is ATP, usually derived from oxidative phosphorylation. The direction of the power stroke is a function of the calcium concentration in the basal region: organisms whose membranes have been disrupted by detergent extraction still swim when given ATP —forward at low calcium (10^{-8}–10^{-7} M), backward at high calcium (above 10^{-6} M) (99). These and other findings suggested that calcium influx may be responsible for ciliary reversal, and electrophysiological studies implicated the membrane in controlling the calcium flux (28).

The electrical potential across the plasma membrane is normally around –20 to –40 mV; this is thought to be an ionic diffusion potential, determined primarily by the movement of K^+ out of the cells and of Na^+ inward, in accordance with the concentration gradients and the ionic conductance of the membrane (28). *Paramecium,* like other cells, accumulates K^+ and extrudes both Na^+ and Ca^{2+}, but as yet, little is known of the transport systems that generate the gradients. Suffice it to state that the cells maintain a low cytoplasmic calcium level by continuously pumping the ion out, probably via a calcium ATPase (6, 13).

Mechanical and electrical stimuli increase or reduce the membrane potential in a manner clearly related to motile behavior. Gentle tapping of the anterior of *Paramecium* with a small stylus causes it to back up and also generates an action potential: intracellular microelectrodes record transient depolarization of the membrane, sometimes an overshoot to positive readings, followed by recovery. The action potential was traced to an influx of calcium ions in amounts sufficient to raise the cytoplasmic concentration to 10^{-6} M or more. This influx is thermodynamically passive, down the gradient maintained by pumping calcium out. The sequence of events appears to be as follows: anterior stimulation causes localized depolarization of the membrane (receptor current) and increased calcium conductance; this spreads over the entire cell surface as calcium rushes in, further depolarizing the membrane; the cilia reverse in response to the elevated cytoplasmic Ca^{2+}; within 50 msec or so the original low conductance recovers, Ca^{2+} is pumped out of the cell, and forward beating resumes (28, 79).

Stimulation of the posterior end causes the organism to swim forward faster, as if to escape; this response is correlated with hyperpolarization of the membrane and an increase in the frequency of ciliary beating. The hyperpolarization was shown to reflect a transient increase in the K^+ conductance (enhanced K^+ efflux, hence a more negative potential) (98). The behavior of the organisms thus results from the interplay of physical and anatomical features: on the one hand, the electrical potential across the entire cell surface; on the other, the localization of responsive K^+ channels at the rear, Ca^{2+} channels at the front (28, 109).

One must add that the actual relationship between membrane conductance, calcium flux, and ciliary beating is rather more complex than outlined here. Just how the calcium level determines the direction of beating remains unknown, as does the role of calcium-binding plaques located at the base of the cilia (30, 118). Hyperpolarization of the membrane (posterior stimulus), as mentioned above, accelerates forward beating of the flagella; this also involves calcium. The mechanism depends on the rate of calcium influx in response to the potential gradient, rather than on the calcium level (77, 78), and again the molecular basis is unknown. These unsolved problems, however, should not obscure the fact that locomotor behavior of *Paramecium* is controlled by the current of calcium ions across the cytoplasmic membrane and particularly by the excitable transport system that mediates the entry of calcium.

To be effective, an anterior stimulus must elicit the opening of the calcium channels whose conductance varies dramatically with the potential across the membrane (that a "channel" mechanism is involved is suggested by the relatively low specificity of whatever mediates the entry of Ca^{2+}). The molecular basis of "gating" has been approached by an ingenious combination of genetic, physiological, and biochemical techniques. Kung and his associates (71) isolated and characterized a series of mutants whose markedly altered behavior could be correlated with defects in their ion gates. Most dramatic is *pawn,* which lacks calcium action potentials altogether and in consequence is unable to back up; *paranoiac* has very prolonged depolarizations resulting from excessive influx of Na^+ and exhibits excessive backward swimming; and *fast* mutants have abnormalities in the K^+ channels (14, 43, 71, 131, 132). Nelson and his co-workers (12–14) have begun to characterize the various transport pumps and channels by direct measurement of ion fluxes. At 0°C, the pump that expels Ca^{2+} from the cytoplasm is shut down but the gated Ca^{2+} channel still operates: chemical or electrical stimuli that depolarize the membrane enhance ^{45}Ca influx by tenfold and more (13, 14). The gate may also be opened by addition of certain local anaesthetics, which presumably interact with the lipids in the immediate vicinity of the channel (12).

What molecular mechanisms could account for the gating of the Ca^{2+} channel in such a way that depolarization of the membrane enhances its ion conductance? The same question arises with respect to the Na^+ and K^+ channels whose responses underlie the action potentials of nerve axons. The molecules that comprise the excitable channels are presumably proteins, as yet unidentified and not accessible to biochemical study. However, significant insight into the molecular basis of excitability stems from the studies of Mueller and his associates (95, 96) on the ionophores, alamethicin and monazomycin. These antibiotics, like gramicidin, form cation-selective channels across lipid bilayer membranes but exhibit two unusual properties: the conductance depends markedly upon the electrical potential (in one experiment with alamethicin the conductance rose by three orders of magnitude when the voltage was raised from 40–80 mV); and channel formation is an exponential function of the antibiotic concentration, suggesting that many molecules cooperate to construct each channel. Membranes doped with these ionophores generate action potentials that reproduce those of nervous tissue with remarkable fidelity. To account for the findings, Baumann & Mueller (7) proposed a model in which formation of the channel depends on the voltage across the membrane: the ionophores under consideration are all lipophilic molecules of elongated form, bearing a hydrophilic group at one end and one or more charges at the other. Under the influence of an applied voltage, the molecule would insert vertically into the lipid matrix, anchored at the surface by the hydrophilic group. Lateral diffusion would then generate channels containing three or more molecules arranged like the staves of a barrel. [For a somewhat different model see Gordon & Haydon (33)]. Models of this general kind can be constructed for macromolecular components as well (95, 96), and it is easy to conceive of situations in which abolition of a potential, rather than its imposition, is prerequisite to channel formation.

Returning again to the biological world, one must ask how general is the use of a calcium current to couple reception of a stimulus to motor response. The data are fragmentary but highly suggestive. References to work with other ciliates will be found in the papers cited above; in *Chlamydomonas* also, calcium influx appears to link a light stimulus to reversal of the flagella (134), and it is reasonable to look for an involvement of calcium in the remarkable photoresponses of *Euglena* (24). The photoreceptor here and in other systems is now thought to be riboflavin, which may function as an ion gate, perhaps across the membrane of an internal structure (23). Further afield are indications that calcium ions, possibly a flux of calcium across the plasma membrane, may be involved in chemotaxis and amoeboid movements of many kinds (26, 27, 50, 107, 160). Participation of calcium in aggregation and differentiation of *Dictyostelium* has been suggested (11, 81) but remains to be established. Finally, it is not a long step to the apparent involvement of Ca^{2+} in pinocytosis and phagocytosis, (3, 70) phenomena, which may again be mediated via the electrical properties of the cytoplasmic membrane (26, 63).

Electrical Control of Morphogenesis

Brown algae of the intertidal zone attain a length of several meters and hardly qualify as microorganisms, but their single-celled eggs deserve honorary membership, if only because of the impressive researches of Jaffe and his associates (58, 106) on the developing eggs of *Fucus* and *Pelvetia.* These studies document that differentiation into the future thallus and rhizoid is intimately related to the establishment of ion currents through and around the embryo. Moreover, they suggest possible mechanisms for the localization of morphogenetic processes and have far-reaching implications for higher plants and animals. A brief and readable review (58) summarizes the basic observations and a current one is in press (106).

During the first day following fertilization, the developing egg elongates and then divides into two unequal halves, one destined to become the rhizoid (holdfast), the other the thallus. At this stage, the rhizoid is the growing part as the embryo's first objective is to secure firm lodging. What makes this system so important is that, unlike animal eggs, the zygote of *Fucus* has no predetermined animal-vegetal axis or polarity: the site and direction of outgrowth are determined by one of a variety of external stimuli—light, an electric current, gradients of pH, or temperature (for example, the embryo grows away from the direction of incident light). The various stimuli are thought to produce a localized membrane change that confers polarity; once outgrowth has begun its direction is self-maintained.

Studies on the mechanism that determines the site of growth initiation and then maintains its direction were guided by the hypothesis that localization is a function of an ion current: the plasma membrane in the growth region would be specifically permeable to a cation that is present outside the cell at a much higher electrochemical potential than in the cytoplasm (Ca^{2+}, Na^{+}, or H^{+} are likely candidates). Movement of the ion across the membrane completes a current loop, localized in space by the positions of the pump and leak, and generates an electrical field across the cytoplasm with the positive pole at the site of cation entry (Figure 3). The field would be particularly marked for ions such as calcium, which bind strongly to anionic sites near the place of entry and thus set up a sharp gradient. The electrical field in turn may generate electrophoretic movement of negatively charged particles. Cell wall precursor vesicles, for example, would tend to be localized beneath the membrane region that admits Ca^{2+} and fuse with it, initiating localized growth. To maintain the direction, one must also envisage mechanisms to keep the growing region preferentially permeable to cations (58). Evidence in support of a scheme of this kind has accumulated rapidly in the past 2 years.

Generation of an electric current by developing *Fucus* eggs was first demonstrated by use of an ingenious arrangement that, in effect, placed about a hundred embryos

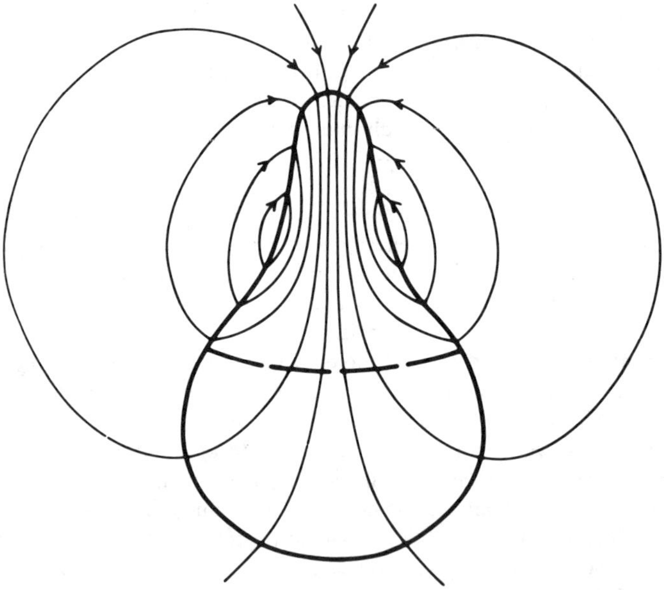

Figure 3 Current pattern around a two-cell *Pelvetia* embryo as determined by current density measurements. From Nuccitelli & Jaffe (104) with permission.

in series and thus amplified the minute voltage drop across each one (57). When the embryo begins to elongate, current begins to flow such that positive charge enters the growing (rhizoid) tip; the current persists for as long as elongation continues. Further progress became possible with the development of an ultrasensitive vibrating probe to measure the currents generated in the external fluid around a single egg. A map of the current pattern deduced from such measurements is shown (Figure 3) to illustrate that positive charges enter only at the growing tip but leave from the base of the rhizoid and the entire thallus cell. In actuality, the pattern of current flow is very much more complex because of fluctuations in time. Very briefly, there is a steady current of about 1–2 μA cm^{-2} at the tip. Superimposed on this are larger current pulses (10–30 μA cm^{-2}), which occur spontaneously several times per hour. These current pulses look like action potentials but are not elicited by changes in membrane potential; it is possible that they arise from fusion of vesicles with the plasma membrane (102, 103).

The overall pattern of current flow is established when the egg is first polarized, but the chemical composition of the current changes as development proceeds. While polarity is being established (6–12 hr after fertilization), much of the charge is carried by a flux of calcium that enters at the tip and leaves from the base of the embryo. Robinson & Jaffe (125) estimated a current density of 0.03 μA cm^{-2} corresponding to 0.15 pmol cm^{-2} of Ca^{2+}; presumably, calcium is pumped out of the egg at the base and enters passively at the tip. Polarization of the egg by an external stimulus such as light may result from a redistribution of the transport systems, such that entry channels become localized away from the illuminated region and thereby determine the future growth point (58). During this stage, the orientation of development can be influenced by external electrical fields in a manner consistent with the proposal that the ion current localizes growth (117).

Once the embryo has reached the two-cell stages and is pulsing actively, the composition of the current is quite different: calcium entry makes but a minor contribution and it is the efflux of chloride through the tip that carries most of the charge. In fact, the flux of chloride may be far larger than the current suggests since most of it is electrically balanced by efflux of K^+, and calcium ions now play a role in triggering that efflux of KCl. Nuccitelli & Jaffe (104, 105) argue persuasively that these outward pulses of KCl regulate the turgor of the growing embryo by relieving excess osmotic pressure.

Are localized and oriented electrical current a general feature of growing organisms and, indeed, a determining factor in morphogenesis? Such an assertion would be premature but support is mounting rapidly. In a recent series of papers, Jaffe and his associates (59, 163, 164) reported that germinating pollen grains of the lily are also traversed by a strong positive charge current that enters the growing pollen tube and leaves from the grain. Most of the leaving current is carried by protons, whereas K^+ ions are the main component of the entering current; calcium ions also enter the growing tip and tend to accumulate there, again pointing to a special relationship between calcium and localization of growth. In this connection, one should recall the meticulous pioneering work of Lund (75) on the generation of bioelectrical potentials by growing plants and their relationship to the pattern of growth. Curiously, in *Avena* coleoptiles and in roots, the charge current leaves the growing region rather than entering there as in the cases discussed above. The more recent literature records a growing number of observations on plants, enbryonic cells from amphibians to higher animals, sea urchin eggs, and transformed lymphocytes that implicate calcium and the electrical properties of the surface membrane in the control of differentiation (57, 58, 74). Microbiologists may wish to speculate on the role of ion currents in the apical growth of fungal hyphae (5); we may well be watching the first stirrings of a major development in biology.

Of Ions and Clocks

Circadian rhythms are ubiquitous in the eukaryotic world from protists to primates, but the chemical and physiological basis of time-keeping has remained elusive. Most authorities invoke a biological clock; a minority prefers to endow organisms with sensitivity to subtle geophysical rhythms of the earth, but until recently both views lacked plausible biochemical expression. A clue, possibly a very major one, appeared with the discovery that valinomycin shifts the phase of the circadian rhythm in beans and in the marine dinoflagellate *Gonyaulax* (15, 158). Valinomycin, a highly selective K^+ ionophore whose mode of action is intimately known, is the first reagent to affect the clock (as opposed to activities controlled by the clock) in a meaningful manner.

Unfortunately, the meaning is anything but plain. *Gonyaulax* exhibits a number of circadian rhythms (stimulated and spontaneous bioluminescence, photosynthesis, cell division, and also K^+ content), all apparently controlled by a single clock. Sweeney (158) found that exposure of the organisms to small amounts of ethanol shifts the phase of the free-running bioluminescence rhythm; the direction and magnitude of the shift depends on the time in the circadian cycle when ethanol is added. Presence of valinomycin in addition to the ethanol returns the phase of the rhythm to that of untreated control cells. An attempt to determine whether or not *Gonyaulax* undergoes oscillations of the membrane potential that might be affected by valinomycin gave ambiguous results (1) that were interpreted as indicating a rhythmic change in the structure or function of the cytoplasmic membrane. Sweeney (159) also showed that the number of intramembranous particles exposed in one fracture face of another membrane, that of the peripheral vesicle, varies as a function of circadian time.

No clear interpretation of these results is possible but they do point to a link between clocks, membranes, and ion movements. Hastings and his associates (100, 101) have constructed an explicit and very appealing model along these lines. It is based on the premise that an ion (K^+?) gradient across an unspecified membrane may oscillate in a manner determined by the interaction of pumps and leaks, modulated by ion gates sensitive to external stimuli such as light. The model accounts for many aspects of biological rhythms and has several testable features that should provoke skeptics to attempt its disproof.

THE IMPORTANCE OF BEING ELECTRIFIED

What seems to emerge from all this is that both prokaryotic and eukaryotic cells are normally enveloped in a streaming cloud of ions, moving not at random but in defined currents. The pattern of currents varies from one cell to another, fluctuates in intensity and composition as a function of time or metabolic status or developmental stage, but is rarely if ever quiescent. What makes sense and order out of the random motions of charged particles is, of course, an insulating membrane that forces the flow into loops: outward across the membrane by one path (typically but by no means always a primary electrogenic pump), back into the cytoplasm by another (often but not necessarily a secondary carrier or channel). In some organisms, the various transport pathways may be scattered over the cell's surface so that there is no overall pattern of ion flow. But it is clear that in many cases, at least in eukaryotes, current sources and sinks have particular anatomical locations that may be spaced far apart and are related to the function of the current. The ion current is thus bent into a pattern that reflects anatomy and confers upon the cell an overarching chemical or electrical polarity. This is illustrated by the flow of ions around the embryo of *Pelvetia* (Figure 3) and by the bands of acidity and alkalinity along the surface of some giant algal cells (56).

Ion currents serve two general kinds of physiological functions. One is energy transduction and the performance of work—osmotic, chemical, and even mechanical, as is so clearly exemplified by the bacterial proton circulation (Figure 1). The other is the processing and transmission of information, from environmental stimuli to the localization of growth. The special fitness of ion currents for such purposes is not far to seek. An aqueous medium is an efficient ion conductor and thus allows rapid power transmission between energy-generating and energy-consuming units that are not physically contiguous; for thermodynamic reasons, charged particles are superior to uncharged ones (87). Ion currents are intrinsically vectorial and lend themselves to modulation of intensity, coupling efficiency, and orientation in space. Finally, there may be an historical element: if it is true, as some have argued (46, 121), that ion pumps were among the necessary attributes of ancestral eobionts, they were available from the beginning for creative adaptation to the manifold purposes of life.

If ion currents play a major role in such complex physiological functions as locomotor behavior, time keeping, development, and differentiation, one may expect external electrical fields and currents to affect these processes. There is indeed a vast literature, reaching back a century and more, that describes a multitude of effects of minute currents and fields on the growth of plants and animals, the regeneration of bones and nerves, the behavior of animals high and low, even commercial and medical application [this is beyond our scope here (see 74, 75, 106); also see forthcoming papers from Jaffe's laboratory]. Among investigators with a molecular bent there has been some tendency to belittle such work, sometimes with reason; yet it may be that much of the early electrobiological research was simply premature in Stent's sense (155a) of having been performed before the results could be logically connected to the general body of biological science. Now that the molecular basis of electrobiology is beginning to emerge, a more open-minded attitude may be in order.

ACKNOWLEDGMENTS

Thanks are due to my colleagues D. S. Cummings, M. Pato, and H. V. Rickenberg for constructive criticism; to Susan Walker and Nadia de Stackelberg for help in preparing the manuscript for publication; to Lewis Thomas and the Viking Press for permission to quote from The Lives of a Cell; and to Lionel Jaffe and the Journal of Cell Biology for figure 3. There remains a larger debt to Roger Eckert, Lionel Jaffe, Peter Mitchell, and Clifford Slayman, whose insights provided much of the substance of this review. Original research in this laboratory has been supported by grant AI 03568 from the National Institutes of Health.

Literature Cited

1. Adamich, M., Laris, P. C., Sweeney, B. M. 1976. *Nature* 261:583–85
2. Adler, J. 1975. *Ann. Rev. Biochem.* 44:341–56
3. Allison, A. C., Davis, P. 1974. *Soc. Exp. Biol. Symp.* 28:249–82
4. Bakker, E. P., Rottenberg, H., Caplan, S. R. 1976. *Biochim. Biophys. Acta* 440:557–72
5. Bartnicki-Garcia, S. 1973. *Symp. Soc. General Microbiology* 23:245–67
6. Baugh, L. C., Satir, P., Satir, B. 1976. *J. Cell Biol.* 70:66a
7. Baumann, A., Mueller, P. 1974. *J. Supramol. Struct.* 2:538–57
8. Berg, H. C. 1975. *Ann. Rev. Biophys. Bioeng.* 4:119–36
9. Boyer, P. D., Chance, B., Ernster, L., Mitchell, P., Racker, E., Slater, E. C. 1977. *Ann. Rev. Biochem.* 46:In press
10. Boyer, P. D., Stokes, B. O., Wolcott, R. G., Degani, C. 1975. *Fed. Proc.* 34:1711–17
11. Brachet, P. 1976. *CR Acad. Sci. Ser. D* 282:377–79
11a. Brewer, G. J. 1976. *Biochemistry* 15:1387–92
12. Browning, J. L., Nelson, D. L. 1976. *Proc. Natl. Acad. Sci. USA* 73:452–56
13. Browning, J. L., Nelson, D. L. 1976. *Biochim. Biophys. Acta* 448:338–51
14. Browning, J. L., Nelson, D. L., Hansma, H. G. 1976. *Nature* 259: 491–94
15. Bünning, E., Moser, I. 1972. *Proc. Natl. Acad. Sci. USA* 69:2732–33
16. Christensen, H. N. 1975. *Biological Transport.* London: W. A. Benjamin. 514 pp. 2nd ed.
17. Cleland, R. 1973. *Proc. Natl. Acad. Sci. USA* 70:3092–93
18. Cleland, R. E. 1976. *Plant Physiol.* 58:210–13
19. Cockburn, M., Earnshaw, P., Eddy, A. A. 1975. *Biochem. J.* 146:705–12
20. Collins, S. H., Hamilton, W. A. 1976. *J. Bacteriol.* 126:1224–31
21. Crane, R. K. 1977. *Rev. Physiol. Biochem. Pharmacol.* In press
22. Crofts, A. R., Evans, E. H., Cogdell, R. J. 1974. *Ann. NY Acad. Sci.* 227:227–42
23. Delbrück, M., Katzir, A., Presti, D. 1976. *Proc. Natl. Acad. Sci. USA* 73: 1969–73
24. Diehn, B. 1973. *Science* 181:1009–15
25. Dilley, R. A., Giaquinta, R. T. 1975. *Curr. Top. Membr. Transp.* 7:49–107
26. Durham, A. C. H. 1974. *Cell* 2:123–36
27. Durham, A. C. H., Ridgway, E. B. 1976. *J. Cell Biol.* 69:223–26
28. Eckert, R. 1972. *Science* 176:473–81
29. Eisenman, G., ed. 1973. *Membranes, A Series of Advances: Lipid Bilayers and Antibiotics.* New York: Mancel Dekker
30. Fisher, G., Kaneshiro, E. S., Peters, P. D. 1976. *J. Cell Biol.* 69:429–42
31. Franke, W. W., Scheer, U. 1974. *Soc. Exp. Biol. Symposia* 28:249–82
32. Gilcrist, M. J. R., Konisky, J. 1975. *J. Biol. Chem.* 250:2457–62
33. Gordon, L. G. M., Haydon, D. A. 1976. *Biochim. Biophys. Acta* 436:541–56
34. Govindjee, ed. 1975. *Bioenergetics of Photosynthesis.* New York: Academic. 698 pp.
35. Gradmann, D. 1975. *J. Membrane Biol.* 25:183–208
36. Gradmann, D. 1976. *J. Membrane Biol.* 29:23–45

37. Gradmann, D., Slayman, C. L. 1975. *J. Membrane Biol.* 23:181–212
38. Gradmann, D., Wagner, G., Gläsel, R. M. 1973. *Biochim. Biophys. Acta* 323: 151–55
39. Greville, G. D. 1969. *Curr. Top. Bioenerg.* 3:1–78
40. Haddock, B. A., Jones, C. W. 1977. *Bacteriol. Rev.* In press
41. Hamilton, W. A. 1975. *Adv. Microb. Physiol.* 12:1–53
42. Hamilton, W. A. 1977. *Symp. Soc. Gen. Microbiol.* 27:In press
43. Hansma, H., Kung, C. 1976. *Biochim. Biophys. Acta* 436:128–39
44. Harold, F. M. 1972. *Bacteriol. Rev.* 36:172–230
45. Harold, F. M. 1977. *Curr. Top. Bioenerg.* 6:83–149
46. Harold, F. M. 1978. In *The Bacteria,* ed. L. N. Ornston, J. R. Sokatch, Vol. 6. New York: Academic. In press
47. Harold, F. M., Altendorf, K. H. 1974. *Curr. Top. Membr. Transp.* 5:2–50
48. Harold, F. M., Altendorf, K. H., Hirata, H. 1974. *Ann. NY Acad. Sci.* 235:149–60
49. Harold, F. M., Papineau, D. 1972. *J. Membr. Biol.* 8:27–44
49a. Harold, F. M., Van Brunt, J. 1977. *Science.* In press
50. Hato, M., Ueda, T., Kurihara, K., Kobatake, Y. 1976. *Biochim. Biophys. Acta* 426:73–80
51. Haydon, D. A., Hladky, S. B. 1972. *Q. Rev. Biophys.* 5:187–282
52. Heinz, E. 1974. *Curr. Top. Membr. Transp.* 5:137–59
53. Hernandez-Asensio, M., Ramirez, J. M., Del Campo, F. F. 1975. *Arch. Microbiol.* 103:155–62
54. Higinbotham, N. 1973. *Ann. Rev. Plant Physiol.* 24:25–46
55. Hodges, T. K., Leonard, R. T., Bracker, C. E., Keenan, T. W. 1972. *Proc. Natl. Acad. Sci. USA* 69:3307–11
56. Hope, A. B., Walker, N. A. 1975. *The Physiology of Giant Algal Cells.* New York: Cambridge Univ. 201 pp.
57. Jaffe, L. F. 1966. *Proc. Natl. Acad. Sci. USA* 56:1102–9
58. Jaffe, L. F., Robinson, K. R., Nuccitelli, R. 1974. *Ann. NY Acad. Sci.* 238: 372–89
59. Jaffe, L. A., Weisenseel, M. H., Jaffe, L. F. 1975. *J. Cell Biol.* 67:488–92
60. Jagendorf, A. T. 1975. *Fed. Proc.* 34: 1718–21
61. Jetten, A. M. 1976. *Biochim. Biophys. Acta* 440:403–11
62. Jones, C. W., Brice, J. M., Downs, A. J., Drozd, J. W. 1975. *Eur. J. Biochem.* 52:265–71
63. Josefsson, J. O., Holmer, N. G., Hansson, S. E. 1975. *Acta Physiol. Scand.* 94:278–88
64. Kaback, H. R. 1974. *Science* 186: 882–92
65. Komor, E., Tanner, W. 1974. *J. Gen. Physiol.* 64:568–81
66. Komor, E., Tanner, W. 1974. *Eur. J. Biochem.* 44:219–23
67. Komor, B., Komor, E., Tanner, W. 1974. *J. Membr. Biol.* 17:231–38
68. Komor, E., Tanner, W. 1976. *Eur. J. Biochem.* 70:197–204
69. Kopecky, A. L., Copeland, D. P., Lusk, J. E. 1975. *Proc. Natl. Acad. Sci. USA* 72:4631–34
70. Korn, E. D. 1975. In *Biochemistry of Cell Walls and Membranes,* ed. C. F. Fox, pp. 2–26. London: Butterworths
71. Kung, C., Chang, S.-Y., Satow, Y., Van Houten, J., Hansma, H. 1975. *Science* 188:898–904
72. Lanyi, J. K., MacDonald, R. E. 1976. *Biochemistry* 15:1545–603
73. Lanyi, J. K., MacDonald, R. E. 1976. *Biochemistry* 15:4608–14
74. Liboff, A. R., Rinaldi, R. A., eds. 1974. *Ann. NY Acad. Sci.* 238:1–593
75. Lund, E. J. 1947. *Bioelectric Fields and Growth.* Austin, Tex.: Univ. Tex. Press. 391 pp.
76. MacDonald, R. E., Lanyi, J. K. 1975. *Biochemistry* 14:2882–89
77. Machemer, H. 1974. *J. Comp. Physiol.* 92:293–316
78. Machemer, H. 1975. *J. Comp. Physiol.* 101:343–56
79. Machemer, H., Eckert, R. 1973. *J. Gen. Physiol.* 61:527–87
80. MacRobbie, E. A. C. 1975. *Curr. Top. Membr. Transp.* 7:1–48
81. Maeda, Y., Maeda, M. 1973. *Exp. Cell Res.* 82:125–30
81a. Manson, M., Berg, H., Tedesco, P., Harold, F. M., Van der Drift, C. 1977. *Proc. Natl. Acad. Sci. USA.* In press
82. McLaughlin, S., Eisenberg, M. 1975. *Ann. Rev. Biophys. Bioeng.* 4:335–66
83. Misra, P. C., Höfer, M. 1975. *FEBS Lett.* 52:95–99
84. Mitchell, P. 1962. *Biochem. Soc. Symp.* 22:142–68
85. Mitchell, P. 1966. *Biol. Rev. Cambridge Philos. Soc.* 41:445–502
86. Mitchell, P. 1967. *Adv. Enzymol.* 29: 33–87
87. Mitchell, P. 1970. In *Membranes and*

Ion Transport, ed. E. E. Bittar, Vol. 1, pp. 192–256. New York: Wiley
88. Mitchell, P. 1972. *J. Bioenerg.* 3:5–24
89. Mitchell, P. 1974. *FEBS Lett.* 43: 189–94
90. Mitchell, P. 1975. *FEBS Lett.* 59: 137–39
91. Mitchell, P. 1976. *Biochem. Soc. Trans.* 4:399–430
92. Mitchell, P. 1976. *J. Theoret. Biol.* 62: 327–68
93. Mitchell, P., Moyle, J. 1969. *Eur. J. Biochem.* 7:471–84
94. Mohri, H. 1976. *Biochim. Biophys. Acta* 456:85–127
95. Mueller, P. 1975. In *Energy Transducing Mechanisms,* ed. E. Racker, pp. 76–120. Baltimore: University Park Press.
96. Mueller, P. 1975. *Ann. NY Acad. Sci.* 264:247–64
97. Mummert, H., Gradmann, D. 1976. *Biochim. Biophys. Acta* 443:443–50
98. Naitoh, Y., Eckert, R. 1973. *J. Exp. Biol.* 59:53–65
99. Naitoh, Y., Kaneko, H. 1972. *Science* 176:523–24
100. Njus, D., Sulzman, F. M., Hastings, J. W. 1974. *Nature* 248:116–20
101. Njus, D., Gooch, V. D., Mergenhagen, D., Sulzman, F. M., Hastings, J. W. 1976. *Fed. Proc.* 35:2353–57
102. Nuccitelli, R., Jaffe, L. F. 1974. *Proc. Natl. Acad. Sci. USA* 71:4855–59
103. Nuccitelli, R., Jaffe, L. F. 1975. *J. Cell Biol.* 64:636–43
104. Nuccitelli, R., Jaffe, L. F. 1976. *Develop. Biol.* 49:518–31
105. Nuccitelli, R., Jaffe, L. F. 1976. *Planta* 131:315–20
106. Nuccitelli, R., Jaffe, L. F. 1977. *Ann. Rev. Biophys. Bioeng.* 6:445–76
107. Nuccitelli, R., Poo, M. M., Jaffe, L. F. 1977. *J. Gen. Physiol.* In press
108. Oesterhelt, D. 1976. *Angew. Chem. Int. Ed.* 15:17–24
109. Ogura, A., Takahashi, K. 1976. *Nature* 264:170–72
110. Ordal, G. W., Goldman, D. J. 1975. *Science* 189:802–5
111. Ordal, G. W., Goldman, D. J. 1976. *J. Mol. Biol.* 100:103–8
112. Padan, E., Zilberstein, D., Rottenberg, H. 1976. *Eur. J. Biochem.* 63:533–41
113. Papa, S. 1976. *Biochim. Biophys. Acta* 456:39–84
114. Parson, W. W., Cogdell, R. J. 1975. *Biochim. Biophys. Acta* 416:105–49
115. Pedersen, P. 1975. *J. Bioenerg.* 6: 243–75
116. Peña, A. 1975. *Arch. Biochem. Biophys.* 167:397–409
117. Peng, H. B., Jaffe, L. F. 1976. *Dev. Biol.* 53:277–84
118. Plattner, H. 1975. *J. Cell Sci.* 18:257–69
119. Racker, E. 1976. *A New Look at Mechanisms in Bioenergetics.* New York: Academic. 197 pp.
120. Ramos, S., Schuldiner, S., Kaback, H. R. 1976. *Proc. Natl. Acad. Sci. USA* 73: 1892–96
121. Raven, J. A., Smith, F. A. 1976. *J. Theor. Biol.* 57:301–12
122. Rhoads, D. B., Epstein, W. 1977. *J. Biol. Chem.* 252:1394–401
123. Richards, J. L., Hope, A. B. 1974. *J. Membr. Biol.* 16:121–44
124. Robertson, R. N. 1970. *Protons, Electrons, Phosphorylation, and Active Transport.* Cambridge: The University Press. 96 pp.
125. Robinson, K. R., Jaffe, L. F. 1975. *Science* 187:70–72
126. Rosen, B. P., Kashket, E. R. 1977. In *Bacterial Transport,* ed. B. P. Rosen. New York: Marcel Dekker. In press
127. Rothstein, A. 1974. *J. Gen. Physiol.* 64:608–21
128. Rottenberg, H. 1975. *J. Bioenerg.* 7: 63–74
129. Rottenberg, H. 1976. *FEBS Lett.* 66: 159–63
130. Rudnick, G., Schuldiner, S., Kaback, H. R. 1976. *Biochemistry* 15:5126–31
131. Satow, Y., Hansma, H. G., Kung, C. 1976. *Comp. Biochem. Physiol.* 54(A): 323–29
132. Satow, Y., Kung, C. 1976. *J. Membr. Biol.* 28:277–94
133. Scarborough, G. A. 1976. *Proc. Natl. Acad. Sci. USA* 73:1485–88
134. Schmidt, J. A., Eckert, R. 1976. *Nature* 262:713–15
135. Scholes, P., Mitchell, P. 1970. *J. Bioenerg.* 1:309–23
136. Schuldiner, S., Weil, R., Kaback, H. R. 1976. *Proc. Natl. Acad. Sci. USA* 73:109–12
137. Seaston, A., Carr, G. C., Eddy, A. A. 1976. *Biochem. J.* 154:669–76
138. Seaston, A., Inkson, C., Eddy, A. A. 1973. *Biochem. J.* 134:1031–43
139. Shamoo, A. E., ed. 1975. *Ann. NY Acad. Sci.* 264:1–490
140. Siebert, G. 1972. *Sub Cell. Biochem.* 1:277–92
141. Silver, S. 1977. In *Microorganisms and Minerals,* ed. E. D. Weinberg. New York: Marcel Dekker. In press
142. Silver, S. 1977. In *Bacterial Transport,* ed. B. P. Rosen. New York: Marcel Dekker. In press

143. Simoni, R. D., Postma, P. W. 1975. *Ann. Rev. Biochem.* 43:523–54
144. Singh, A. P., Bragg, P. D. 1976. *FEBS Lett.* 64:169–72
145. Skulachev, V. P. 1971. *Curr. Top. Bioenerg.* 4:127–90
146. Skulachev, V. P. 1975. In *Energy Transducing Mechanisms,* ed. E. Racker, pp. 31–73. London: Butterworths
147. Slayman, C. L. 1965. *J. Gen. Physiol.* 49:69–92
148. Slayman, C. L. 1965. *J. Gen. Physiol.* 49:93–116
149. Slayman, C. L., Long, W. S., Lu, C. Y.-H. 1973. *J. Membr. Biol.* 14:305–38
150. Slayman, C. L., Long, W. S., Gradmann, D. 1976. *Biochim. Biophys. Acta* 426:732–44
151. Slayman, C. L., Slayman, C. W. 1968. *J. Gen. Physiol.* 52:424–43
152. Slayman, C. L., Slayman, C. W. 1974. *Proc. Natl. Acad. Sci. USA* 71:1935–39
153. Szmelcman, S., Adler, J. 1976. *Proc. Natl. Acad. Sci. USA* 73:4387–91
154. Smith, F. A., Walker, N. A. 1976. *J. Exp. Bot.* 27:451–59
155. Spanswick, R. M. 1974. *Biochim. Biophys. Acta* 332:387–98
155a. Stent, G. S. 1972. *Sci. Am.* 227:84–93
156. Sullivan, C. W., Volcani, B. E. 1974. *Proc. Natl. Acad. Sci. USA* 71:4376–80
157. Summers, K. 1975. *Biochim. Biophys. Acta* 416:153–68
158. Sweeney, B. M. 1974. *Plant Physiol.* 53:337–42
159. Sweeney, B. M. 1976. *J. Cell Biol.* 68:451–61
160. Taylor, D. L., Condeelis, J. S., Moore, P. L., Allen, R. D. 1973. *J. Cell Biol.* 59:378–94
161. Tsuchiya, T., Rosen, B. P. 1976. *J. Biol. Chem.* 251:962–67
162. Walker, N. A., Smith, F. A. 1975. *Plant Sci. Lett.* 4:125–32
163. Weisenseel, M. H., Jaffe, L. F. 1976. *Planta* 133:1–8
164. Weisenseel, M. H., Nuccitelli, R., Jaffe, L. F. 1976. *J. Cell Biol.* 66:556–67
165. West, I. C., Mitchell, P. 1974. *Biochem. J.* 144:87–90

Ann. Rev. Microbiol. 1977. 31:205–24

BACTERIAL PHYTOTOXINS

❖1703

Gary A. Strobel
Department of Plant Pathology, Montana State University, Bozeman, Montana 59715

CONTENTS

INTRODUCTION 205
OVERVIEW 206
SYMPTOMS AND TOXIN ASSAYS 206
Wilting 207
Chlorosis 207
Blights and Necrosis 208
Water Soaking 208
Local Necrosis 208
Overgrowths 208
Hypersensitive Response 209
SOME TOXINS 209
Tabtoxin and 2-Serine Tabtoxin 209
Glycopeptides and Polysaccharides 210
Phaseotoxins 216
Rhizobitoxins 218
Toxins from Pseudomonas syringae and Pseudomonas mors-prunorum 219
Mycoplasma Toxins 219
A Proteinaceous-Enzymatic Phytotoxin? 219
PROSPECTS 220
SUMMARY 221

> When a new thought is born, or when one of the deep secrets of Nature yields to the searching scientist—in this very act of creation—there is a pure and primitive happiness deeper than anything of this kind which can ever be granted a human being to experience.
>
> Arne Tiselius

INTRODUCTION

Wheat, rice, corn, potato, barley, sweet potato, cassava, grapes, soybean, oats, sugarcane, and sorghum are the top 12 plants on which man is virtually totally dependent for his survival. All of these plants are hosts for diseases caused by plant pathogenic bacteria. As is true for many of the bacteria that cause diseases in animals and man, the plant pathogens are also known to produce toxins. Because of the relative infancy of phytotoxicology, toxins have been discovered in only two or three bacterial pathogens of these primary food plants. However, many more toxins are known from phytopathogenic bacteria that infect the minor food and fiber plants.

The best known toxins of human bacterial pathogens are proteinaceous and possess enzymatic activity, i.e. cholera toxin, diphtheria toxin, *Pseudomonas aeruginosa* toxin (16, 19, 20, 57). To date, however, the analogous situation does not exist with the bacterial or fungal phytotoxins. In fact, there is not one example of an enzymatic toxin in the plant pathological literature. The wall degradative enzymes are excluded since in a proper osmoticum they, by themselves, do not kill plant cells. Proteases and lipases have been demonstrated in cultures of some of bacterial phytopathogens, but they have not been demonstrated to act as toxins. Thus, in the broadest sense, a bacterial phytotoxin is considered as a compound of any size or chemical composition, arising from a bacterial phytopathogen, that adversely affects the normal metabolism of the plant, resulting in cell death. A review on bacterial phytotoxins was prepared by Patil (60), and various aspects of bacterial phytotoxins are mentioned in a review by Strobel (88) and in surveys by Durbin (11, 12).

OVERVIEW

Phytopathogenic bacteria cause disease symptoms, including tissue destruction, by virtue of their interference with the normal structural, physiological, or metabolic systems of the host plant. One or more toxins in the arsenal of weapons of the bacterium may hasten, enhance, and perhaps be critical for the development of the disease. Examining a diseased plant, either in the field or in a greenhouse, one looks for symptoms of wilt, chlorosis, and necrosis, any of which would be suggestive of the involvement of a toxin. A biological assay is devised to aid in the purification of the toxin from bacterial cultures. By itself, the toxin should elicit some or all of the disease symptoms in host plants. Work on the chemical structure of the toxin should eventually aid in determining mode of action and the pathway of biosynthesis. Ideally, the importance of the toxin in disease development may be assessed by using bacterial mutants unable to produce the toxin. Collectively, such information may prove useful in developing new disease control measures, the ultimate goal of the phytopathologist.

SYMPTOMS AND TOXIN ASSAYS

Throughout a toxin purification procedure, an assay based on some degree of toxin-induced symptom expression should be used. This section of the review merely summarizes some of the bioassay procedures as related to symptom production that have been used to purify bacterial phytotoxins from culture.

Wilting

Wilting of plant parts is one characteristic suggestive of the involvement of a phytotoxin. Wilts are commonly seen in diseases caused by *Corynebacterium, Xanthomonas,* and *Pseudomonas.* Obviously, an approach to be used in developing a bioassay test for toxin purification could rely on some measurement of the impairment of water flow, tissue turgidity, tissue strength, or water loss. For instance, Johnson & Strobel (36) developed a wilt-o-meter for measuring the strength of 8- to 10-day-old tomato hypocotyls treated with toxin preparations. A hypocotyl is placed in a plant holder fixed to a revolving turntable (4 rpm). As the turntable moves, a steadily increasing force is applied to the hypocotyl in contact with a needle that it deflects. The amount of deflection that occurs before the hypocotyl bends beneath the needle is related to the strength or turgidity of the hypocotyl.

Water flow (stem conductance) measurements have been used to assess the biological activity of bacterial phytotoxins. Patino-Mendez (64) used this technique in studying the toxins of *Corynebacterium michiganense,* and more recently Van Alfen & Turner (97) used it to study the biological activity of the *Corynebacterium insidiosum* wilt-inducing glycopeptide. The technique employs a pressure chamber to which a plant stem dipped into a treatment solution is attached. The time required for some given volume of water to pass through the stem is then recorded. Toxin solutions will presumably decrease the rate of water flow.

Lastly, a simple gravimetric measure of water loss in the toxin-treated tissues may suffice in lieu of the availability of other equipment. Straley, Straley & Strobel (83) used this procedure to follow the wilt reaction of various alfalfa clones to the *C. insidiosum* toxin.

Chlorosis

Another common symptom that may be suggestive of the involvement of a toxin in a bacterial disease is chlorosis. This may be especially true if these symptoms are distantly removed from the area of tissue being colonized by the bacterium. *Pseudomonas phaseolicola* produces an excellent example of this phenomenon since it releases a toxin responsible for the production of the chlorotic halos in halo blight of beans (28). The wildfire disease of tobacco caused by *Pseudomonas tabaci* (98) and halo blight of oats caused by *Pseudomonas coronafaciens* (78) are also diseases in which chlorotic symptoms are caused by toxins. A variety of other plant diseases caused by bacteria have chlorosis that is a definite part of the symptomatology, but investigative studies on the involvement of toxins have not yet begun. Tests for such toxins could be made in the classical way by direct application of extracts of cultural media to leaf surfaces topically or via a puncture wound. The degree of chlorosis in a treated leaf as a function of toxin concentration can be readily measured by extracting chlorophyll (25) or integrating the leaf area that is chlorotic (2).

Plant parts other than leaves may show bacterial-caused chlorotic symptoms. For instance, nodules in soybeans existing in symbiosis with certain strains of *Rhizobium japonicum* will eventually become chlorotic. This led Johnson, Means & Clark (35) to suspect the involvement of a toxin. Eventually, Owens and others isolated and characterized the toxins involved (55, 56). Collectively, their observations nicely illustrate a point to be learned about any biological phenomenon involving pathogenesis, i.e. one should have a good sense of the "normal situation" tempered with a genuine inquisitiveness about any deviation from it.

Blights and Necrosis

Blights produced by plant pathogenic bacteria commonly occur. They may be characterized by wilting of tissues followed by rapid extensive necrosis of leaves, stems, or flower parts. Toxins associated with blight-causing organisms may be assayed by virtue of the wilt they produce, as in the case of phytotoxic polysaccharide of *Erwinia amylovora* (13, 24), or by the extent to which necrosis occurs in toxin-treated tissues (38). Occasionally, the biological activity of a toxin may extend to microorganisms that could then be used in a bioassay test (8, 9). Pollen sensitivity has been used as a bioassay test with fungal toxins (45). Further, the inhibition of seed germination and the selective killing of seed is also a viable bioassay system (47).

Water Soaking

Increased translucence of leaf tissue is also known by the term "water clearing." This occurs as a result of water moving out of the cells into the intercellular spaces of the tissue. Many bacteria cause diseases in which one of the first symptoms is water clearing, i. e. bacterial blight of barley (*Xanthomonas translucens*), angular leaf spot of cotton (*Xanthomonas malvacearum*), and bacterial blight of rice (*Xanthomonas oryzae*). To my knowledge, no phytotoxic substances that are responsible for water-clearing symptoms in diseases caused by phytopathogenic bacteria have yet been isolated and characterized, yet several fungal pathogens produce toxins that give initial water-clearing symptoms on toxin-treated leaves (87, 88).

Local Necrosis

Many bacterial pathogens produce necrotic flecks or spots on susceptible host plants. To date, no bacterial toxin has been isolated whose initial direct action is to produce localized tissue necrosis. Diseases such as bacterial blight of soybeans (*Pseudomonas glycinea*), or any of a number caused by *Pseudomonas syringae,* may eventually lend themselves to such investigations.

Overgrowths

Overgrowth symptoms are known on a number of plants infected by pathogenic bacteria. One of the most common of these is crown gall caused by *Agrobacterium tumefaciens.* Recent reviews by Lippincott & Lippincott (48) and by Kado (37) have covered the up-to-date physiology and biochemistry of this important pathogen. There is still much debate on the arcane process of gall formation by *A. tumefaciens,* but undoubtedly, the regulatory mechanism of plant hormone production is ultimately involved and is probably ultimately directed via a bacterial plasmid. Also, for instance, galls on oleander produced by *Pseudomonas savastanoi* may be caused by an abundant production of indole acetic acid by this bacterium (42, 49).

Although an upset in the balance of phytohormones in an infected plant does result in an upset in cellular metabolism, necrosis or chlorosis of tissue does not immediately result, and therefore, the hormones are not generally considered a class of phytotoxins.

Hypersensitive Response

Hypersensitivity is a rapidly developing defense reaction induced in an incompatible host by a plant pathogen, which results in the death of a limited number of host cells and an apparent concomitant localization of the pathogen (40). Thus, whenever a pathogen attacks a resistant or uncongenial host plant, the plant responds by producing a necrotic reaction that may preclude the spread of the pathogen. In some sense, the very nature of this phenomenon is suggestive of the involvement of a phytotoxin. In this regard, at least two groups have indicated that high-molecular-weight endotoxins from pathogenic bacteria are capable of inducing the hypersensitive response (18, 76). Much more work is needed in the final isolation and characterization of such substances. Sequeira (75) and his group have shown that a high-molecular-weight protein found in *Pseudomonas solanacearum* will protect tobacco leaves from the hypersensitive response produced by infiltrating leaves with incompatible strains of *P. solanacearum.* The data collected thus far suggest that there may be some product associated with the plant pathogen that induces the hypersensitive reaction since nonpathogens do not evoke this response. Further, a receptor site could exist on the plant cell, which when combined with the bacterial product triggers a series of events leading to cellular death. Perhaps the high-molecular-weight protection protein from *P. solanacearum* competes for the receptor site, precluding the hypersensitive response.

SOME TOXINS

A review on bacterial phytotoxins would not be complete without some discussion of the paragons of the field.

Tabtoxin and 2-Serine Tabtoxin

Toxins produced by *Pseudomonas tabaci,* causal agent of wildfire disease of tobacco, have traditionally been referred to as wildfire toxin. What is now considered to be the correct structure of tabtoxin was deciphered by Stewart (81). Hydrolysis of the purified toxin yielded threonine and tabtoxinine (5-amino-2-aminomethyl-2-hydroxyadipic acid). Ultimately, tabtoxin was shown to contain a residue of the lactam of tabtoxinine linked to the amino group of L-threonine (Figure 1). Two other species of *Pseudomonas,* i.e. a pathogen on oats and another on timothy, also produce tabtoxin (60, 78, 79). Finally, it appears that all of the pseudomonads producing tabtoxin also produce 2-serine tabtoxin, which has L-serine substituted for L-threonine in the structure (96).

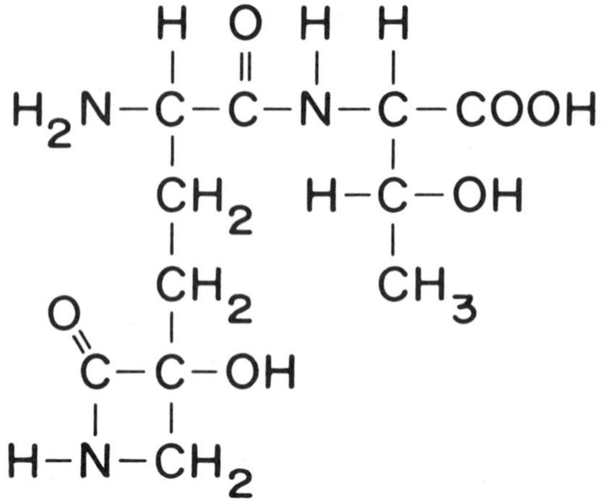

Figure 1 The structure of tabtoxin (81).

Both tabotoxin and 2-serine tabtoxin cause chlorosis in plant tissues. The toxins are not host specific and both possess relatively the same specific biological activity (95). The story on the biological activity of the tabtoxins has been beset with difficulties. The saga begins with the incorrect structural characterization of the toxin (99) and the suggestion that the toxin acts as an antagonist of L-methionine (3). From this, Carlson assumed that methionine sulfoximine (MSO), an analogue of L-methionine, was acting to produce chlorosis in a way comparable to the toxin since MSO-resistant mutants of tobacco were also resistant to chlorosis induced by *P. tabaci* (4). Carlson suggested that, therefore, MSO could be used to select *P. tabaci*-resistant plants from suspensions of tobacco protoplasts, thus introducing the beautiful concept of plant improvement via a protoplast screening technique. It is not clear why MSO-resistant mutants were also resistant to chlorosis induced by *P. tabaci* since the currently accepted structure of tabtoxin does not resemble that of MSO (Figure 1). Furthermore, the toxin does not affect reactions involving L-methionine, nor does the purified toxin affect glutamine metabolism as does methionine sulfoximine (27). Some suggestion has been made that the toxin causes a build-up of toxic concentrations of ammonia, which produces leaf chlorosis (11). Overall, it appears as though the mechanism of action of these interesting toxins is still an open question.

Glycopeptides and Polysaccharides

Extracellular high-molecular-weight polysaccharide-like compounds are produced by a number of phytopathogenic bacteria and some of these have been implicated in disease development (60). Until fairly recently, little or no work had been done to effectively isolate and chemically characterize the biologically active component(s) of such polysaccharide (slime) preparations.

CORYNEBACTERIUM SEPEDONICUM GLYCOPEPTIDE A toxic glycopeptide was isolated from cultures of *C. sepedonicum* by gel filtration techniques (85). Its molecular weight was determined by several methods to be about 22,000 (85). Utilizing the alditol acetate procedure for sugar analysis, the toxin was shown to consist primarily of glucose and mannose with lesser amounts of rhamnose, galactose, ribose, and arabinose (92). The acidic nature of the toxin is contributed by residues of 2-keto-3-deoxygluconic acid (10%), and the peptide portion of the molecule contributes only 5% of the total weight (86).

The toxin is a highly branched structure, with 1,2,6-linked glucosyl residues and 1,2,6-linked mannosyl residues occupying the majority of the branched points. Mannosyl and all of the rhamnosyl residues occupy the terminals of the branched chains (92). The peptide (which varies in amino acid composition) is connected via seryl and threonyl residues via O-glycosidic linkages to terminal reducing mannosyl residues (92).

A compound similar to the toxic glycopeptide was isolated from potato plants showing characteristic symptoms of ring-rot (56). The toxic compound from infected plants was judged to be closely related or identical to the compound from bacterial cultures when compared by infrared spectroscopy, analysis of residues, electrophoretic migration, biological assay, immunochemical procedures, and X-ray powder diffraction techniques. Thus, this work implicated the toxin in the disease process.

In young tomato and potato cuttings, the toxin causes a rapid wilt and eventually marginal necrosis of the leaves can result. Both of these symptoms are identical to those observed under field conditions. Toxin-induced ultrastructural changes in potato tissues (90) were comparable to those observed in tissues infected by *C. sepedonicum* (26). Experiments on ^{3}H-labeled toxin uptake by potato petioles, followed by autoradiography, and studies on $^{3}H_2O$ uptake and plasmolysis led Strobel & Hess (90) to conclude that the toxin ultimately interferes with the function of the plant plasma membrane. When carboxymethylated the toxin loses biological activity. Since the peptide portion of the toxin is not necessary for activity, the free carboxy group of 2-keto-2-deoxygluconic acid seems to be the biologically active site (36).

The glycopeptide toxin has antigenic properties (86), but it has not been possible to obtain highly titered antisera by using either purified or semipurified preparations of the toxin. Excellent antibody titers to the toxin and other bacterial antigens have been obtained by Claflin & Shepard (6) by using whole bacterial cells as the injected antigen. An immunochemical reaction as a diagnostic test for ring-rot was devised by Strobel & Rai (91), although the modifications on it made by Claflin & Shepard (6) have greatly improved its effectiveness. The importance of a rapid, accurate test for ring-rot is easily realized by field and lab diagnostic personnel who labor to maintain zero tolerance levels of ring-rot in certified potato seed lots.

CORNYEBACTERIUM INSIDIOSUM GLYCOPEPTIDE Ries & Strobel (69) isolated a phytotoxic glycopeptide from cultures of *C. insidiosum,* the causal agent of alfalfa wilt. The light scattering technique and column chromatography yielded molecular-weight values on the order of 5 X 10^6. Attempts to disassociate it into subunits were not successful. Nearly 40% of the toxin, by weight, consists of L-fucosyl residues. Glucosyl and galactosyl residues each constitute 20% of the weight with trace amounts of mannosyl and rhamnosyl residues. A keto-deoxy sugar acid makes up about 9% of the weight of the toxin, whereas the amino acids account for only 2.5% of its weight. The toxin, as isolated from bacterial cultures, is bright blue because of the chelation of 75 mol of copper/mol of toxin. A single peptide accounts for the amino acid composition of the toxin and there are 77 mol of peptide/mol of toxin. This stoichiometry suggests that the copper is bound to the peptide portion of the molecule. The peptide is linked O-glycosidically through the OH group of the threonyl residues. Copper is not necessary for the biological activity of the toxin (70). The toxin was isolated from alfalfa plants infected by *C. insidiosum* (70). The glycopeptide causes wilting in both leaves and stems of test plants. It is stable to wide fluctuations in pH and still retains its activity after being heated at 121°C for 2 hr.

Ries & Strobel (70) suggested that the toxin acts in some way other than a physical plugging of plant stems, since compounds bracketing the toxin in molecular weight did not have an apparent effect on stem wilt. On the other hand, Van Alfen & Turner (97) have excellent data showing that the toxin reduces stem conductance, which explains a rapid decrease in transpiration and stomatal conductance. These workers ruled out membrane damage resulting in water leakage as a factor in wilting during a 2-hr treatment. They suggest that the toxin acts by interfering with water movement through pit membranes.

Sadowski & Strobel (72) conducted experiments on the biosynthesis of the toxin. Guanosine diphosphate-L-fucosyl-transferase activity was demonstrated in this organism and was most consistently associated with the cellular membrane fraction. The best primer serving as the acceptor of L-fucosyl residues was a partial acid hydrolysis product of the toxin, with an approximate molecular weight of 50,000.

By using a critical toxin concentration of 0.05%, Straley, Straley & Strobel (83, 84) showed that the toxin has the potential to be used as a screening tool in finding wilt-resistant clones of alfalfa. A correlation coefficient of 0.62 exists between clonal resistance to the bacterium as measured by a disease score and resistance to the toxin as measured by water loss. The test has the advantage of saving time and expense in acquiring alfalfa clones resistant to *C. insidiosum.*

OTHER GLYCOPEPTIDES Several toxic glycopeptides that are primarily glucomannans have been isolated from cultures of *Corynebacterium michiganense* by Rai & Strobel (67). These compounds are antigenic and are readily taken up by cuttings of tomato, becoming localized in the petiole and leaf margins (68). Fungal pathogens including *Ceratocystis ulmi* (73) and *Phoma tracheiphila* (51) also produce phytotoxic glycopeptides. Most certainly, many of the wilt pathogens may ultimately be shown to be producers of polysaccharides and glycopeptides that cause wilt.

AMYLOVORIN One of the newly discovered and most interesting phytotoxins is amylovorin, a polysaccharide that is produced by *Erwinia amylovora,* the fireblight pathogen of apples and pears (13, 24). According to the original workers (13, 24), the polysaccharide is primarily a galactan. Critical carbohydrate analyses of amylovorin (M. McNeil, K. Johnson, and P. Albersheim, unpublished data) has shown that the toxin is galactose (68%), glucuronic acid (19%), and glucose (8%). By using the technique of methylation, hydrolysis, and reduction followed by gas chromatography-mass spectroscopy of the monomers, Albersheim's group showed that the galactosyl residues in amylovorin are primarily 1,3 linked (45%), with lesser amounts of 1,6 linkages (35%) and 1,3,4 linkages (20%). The glucuronic acid is 1,4 linked and glucose is terminal. By using the Smith degradation procedure in conjunction with methylation analyses, Albersheim's group has presented a possible structure that may serve as the basic repeating unit of the amylovorin molecule (Figure 2). The molecular weight of the toxin was originally estimated to be 165,000. It is stable to heat (100°C) for up to 1 hr, and the biological activity is completely destroyed by boiling it in 1 N H_2SO_4 for 3 hr (24). Recent evidence, however, suggests the presence of higher-molecular-weight components in toxin preparations (82).

Biological activity Goodman's group at the University of Missouri (24, 82) has made some observations on the biological activity of toxin preparations, including inactivation of the toxin, reactivation of the toxin, and the probable existence of an inhibitor of the toxin. For instance, original toxin preparations became totally inactive when standing at room temperature for 48 hr even though the toxin was present as a dried powder. However, if the toxin preparation was first precipitated with ethanol and then dried, the biological activity was stable at room temperature (82). The results suggest that the original toxin preparation contained an enzyme that was inactivating the toxin at room temperatures. Other data also suggest the presence of a toxin inhibitor. It will be interesting to see how these initial observations are extended in the next few years.

Goodman, Huang & Huang (24) showed that amylovorin possesses host specificity, meaning that it will cause symptoms (wilting) only in those rosaceous species readily attacked by *E. amylovora.* Nonrosaceous species were unaffected by a toxin concentration of 100 μg/ml. Tip cuttings (shoots) from susceptible varieties of apple

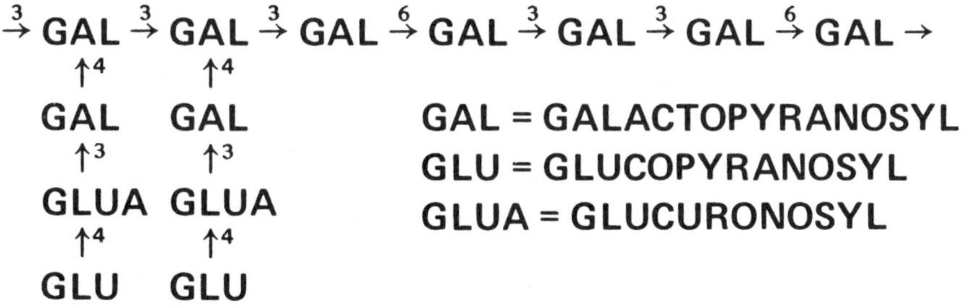

Figure 2 A likely repeating unit of amylovorin (M. McNeil, K. Johnson, and P. Albersheim, unpublished data).

and pear showed severe wilting within 1–3 hr, whereas those cuttings from resistant varieties showed no symptoms until 12–24 hr. The host specificity of amylovorin has been disputed by Sjulin & Beer (80). By using water conductance measurements on cuttings, these workers have shown that amylovorin affects two rosaceous plants, cotoneaster (a host plant) and spirea (a nonhost plant). Amylovorin treatment of these species did not alter electrolyte loss from treated tissues, but electrolyte loss was apparent in *E. amylovora*-infected tissues. They suggest that amylovorin is not important in the development of fireblight. One can argue that even though amylovorin does not cause electrolyte loss this logically does not preclude this toxin from having some role in the disease process. Other physiological and biochemical phenomena may be operating to cause electrolyte loss. No investigator has thus far shown amylovorin to cause wilting in plants, other than rosaceous ones. The disparity in results obtained by Sjulin & Beer (80) on the aberrant behavior of a rosaceous nonhost (spirea) may be related to its apparent nonsusceptibility to *E. amylovora.* On the other hand, it may truly be an exception to the rule that has been previously established by Goodman's group. It would seem that if amylovorin is host specific, it may have some potential as a screening tool for the selection of fireblight-resistant apples and pears.

Production One fascinating, and non-controversial, point about amylovorin is that it can only be obtained from *E. amylovora*-infected tissue slices or tissue cultures. It has never been recovered from cultures of *E. amylovora* grown in common laboratory media. Basically, several questions about the origin of amylovorin can be asked. Does the living host contribute any polysaccharide precursor or enzyme needed to make the final toxin product? Does the host or bacterium in any way regulate the amount of toxin made in the host-bacterium combination? Some precedent for the host regulation of fungus toxin production has been demonstrated for helminthosporoside production by *Helminthosporium sacchari.* Without sugarcane (the host) extract in cultures of *H. sacchari,* the fungus loses its ability to produce the toxin; it becomes attenuated. Serinol has been isolated and identified as one product in the susceptible host that is capable of activating attenuated cultures to produce helminthosporoside (66). Sugarcane clones, of the ones examined resistant to *H. sacchari,* do not possess activators of helminthosporoside production. It appears that other activators also are present on cane leaves susceptible to *H. sacchari* (65). Numerous plant pathogens lose their pathogenicity when cultured on common synthetic media. Perhaps many pathogens, including the bacteria, utilize key host metabolites such as the amines or alkaloids to regulate their pathogenicity?

Mode of action Huang & Goodman (31) show ultrastructural evidence for plasmolysis of xylem parenchyma cells 2 hr after treatment with 200 μg of amylovorin per ml. In *Erwinia amylovora*-infected stem tissues, plasmolysis occurred 48 hr after inoculation. Collectively, the ultrastructural changes in toxin-treated tissue closely resembled those observed in infected tissues, suggesting that some of the symptoms produced in the diseased plant may be caused by amylovorin. These authors propose that amylovorin affects the plasma membrane. When plasmolysis of xylem parenchyma occurs, there is an extrusion of the plasma membrane along with cellular contents into adjacent water conducting xylem elements through plasmodesmata (R. N. Goodman, unpublished data). Conceivably, the presence of this material in the xylem elements would greatly reduce the water conductance of the toxin-treated stem, causing the plants to wilt, as noted by Sjulin & Beer (80). However, Sjulin & Beer showed that dextran of a comparable molecular weight of amylovorin also possessed the same relative biological activity as amylovorin. They point out that amylovorin causes wilt by the nonspecific restriction of water movement. These results lead one to question the host-specific nature of amylovorin and obviously it points out a controversy in the literature. Some of these questions and others will undoubtedly be answered as the following experiments are conducted: (i) testing a wider host range of plants with the toxin by using physical measurements on water flow; (ii) blocking certain sites on the toxin to determine if biological activity is affected; (iii) examining sensitive hosts for the presence of specific toxin receptor sites; (iv) locating the ^{14}C- or ^{3}H-labeled toxin in resistant and susceptible hosts; (v) examining the total physiological effects exerted by the toxin on hosts and nonhosts and comparing these effects to those observed in infected hosts; (vi) testing inoculated resistant versus susceptible apple tissues for their relative ability to support the production of amylovorin; and (vii) developing nontoxin-producing mutants and testing their virulence on susceptible hosts.

XANTHOMONAS POLYSACCHARIDES *Xanthomonas campestris,* the causal agent of black rot of cabbage, produces an extracellular polysaccharide that normally provides the organism with a protective slime. The polysaccharide appears to be essential to the pathogenicity of the organism toward its plant host, presumably via the obstruction of water flow through the xylem (93). The polysaccharide was first isolated and characterized by Jeanes, Pittsley & Senti (34). The primary structure of the polysaccharide was recently reexamined by Jansson, Kenne & Lindberg (33) and was shown to consist of a main chain of β-1,4-linked glucopyranosyl units, as in cellulose, but with alternate glucose residues with side chains containing three glucopyranosyl units. The side chains are attached to the main chain via 1$\rightarrow$3 linkages. The estimated molecular weight of the polymer is $1.4–3.6 \times 10^6$. The polysaccharide possesses ordered secondary structure stabilized by non-ionic interactions that outweigh the repulsion between adjacent carboxyl groups in the molecule (30). The carboxyl groups are contributed by the attachment of pyranosyl residues on the terminal glucose residues in the side chains (33). With the advent of recent structural information on this compound, additional studies on the synthesis, mode of action, biologically active site, and role of this polysaccharide in the disease could commence.

One of the most destructive pathogens of rice is *Xanthomonas oryzae,* which causes leaf blight and wilting of seedlings. The seedling phase of this disease is often overlooked since infected seedlings wilt and die rapidly in the field. Kuo, Lin & Li (43) showed that cultures of *X. oryzae* produce four polysaccharides with estimated molecular weights of $\geq$200,000, 150,000, 147,000, and 29,000. The first three compounds are antigenic and phytotoxic. The largest-molecular-weight compound was reported to be a polymer of mannose and glucose. The toxic fractions are nonhost specific, and wilting in test plants was noted in 60 min at 10 $\mu g/ml$. Because of the importance of this pathogen in rice production, much more effort should be made in the structural characterization, mode of action, and practical use of its toxins in disease control.

Phaseotoxins

Pseudomonas phaseolicola is the incitant of the halo blight disease of beans. Culture filtrates of this bacterium will cause typical chlorotic symptoms that mimic those found on naturally infected plants. Hoitink, Pelletier & Coulson (28), working with crude toxin preparations, showed that the toxin is thermostable and nonspecific. Further, these workers devised a workable leaf bioassay test for the toxin. Patil et al (63) recently resolved the toxin into four biologically active components by diethylaminoethyl cellulose chromatography. Phaseotoxin A, the toxin in the first fraction eluting from the column, decomposed to yield glutamic acid and inorganic orthophosphate. The compound was chromatographically identical to synthetic N-phosphoglutamic acid (Figure 3). Their report was the first to show the natural occurrence of an N-phosphorylated primary amine. Peaks B, C, and D, from the diethylaminoethyl cellulose column, yielded several amino acids upon acid hydrolysis, among them glycine. The N-phosphoramide of glycine was synthesized and was shown to be biologically active, but only to one third the extent of N-phosphoglutamic acid. No direct evidence is presented by the authors for the presence of N-phosphoglycine in toxin preparations. Mitchell (50), however, reports the isolation and characterization of a toxin from *P. phaseolicola* that is a tripeptide composed of ornithine, alanine, and homoarginine (Figure 4). Attached to the N^{δ} of orthinine is a phosphosulfamyl group, presumably the first of its type to be reported as a natural product. The only similarity between phaseotoxin A and the toxic peptide of Mitchell (50) is the presence of an N–P bond. Conceivably, it is possible that one of the other toxic fractions reported by Patil (63) is the same compound reported by Mitchell (50). Alternatively, bacterial strain differences may account for the disparity in the structures of the toxins produced.

A suggestion has been made that the toxins of *Pseudomonas glycinea* (on soybeans) and *Pseudomonas tomato* (on tomato) are biologically and chromatographically similar to the phaseotoxins (29). Recently, R. S. Murch and S. S. Patil (unpublished data) have shown that the *P. glycinea* toxin (glytoxin) has a $v/e/v_o$ elution from Sephadex G-25 different from that of the phaseotoxins. Further, glytoxin has a much greater mobility toward the cathodic pole in high-voltage paper electrophoresis than the phaseotoxins. Glytoxin is an inhibitor of ornithine carbamoyltransferase. A suggestion is made by these workers that glytoxin and the phaseotoxins are chemically similar but not identical. Glytoxin also appears to be a phosphoramidate.

MODE OF ACTION In his review, Patil (60) summarized the available information on the mode of action of partially purified phaseotoxin. Tissues infected by *P. phaseolicola* and toxin-treated tissues accumulate ornithine (58, 59, 71). There is

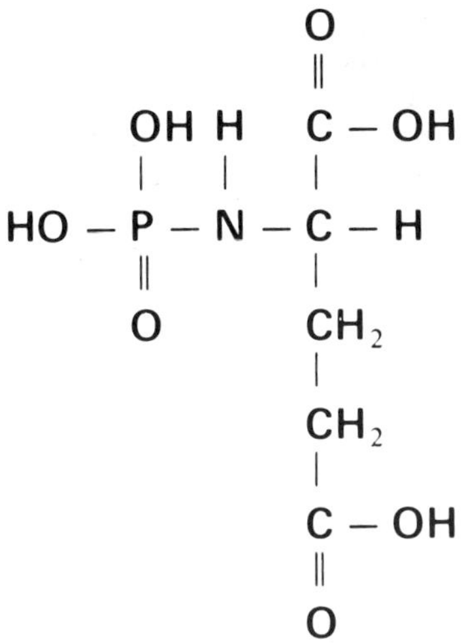

Figure 3 Phaseotoxin A *n*-phosphoglutamic acid (63).

50% less arginine in chlorotic tissues of infected plants (59) than in the healthy controls. Ornithine and arginine are both important metabolites in the urea cycle; therefore, an accumulation of ornithine and a decrease in arginine would lead one to suspect that an enzyme involved in ornithine metabolism may be inhibited by the toxin. Crude toxin preparations were inhibitory to carbamoylphosphate:L-ornithine carbamoyltransferase (EC 2.1.3.3.), the enzyme catalyzing the carbamylation of ornithine to citrulline (44). The toxic fraction eluting from Sephadex G-10 columns had the same elution volume as that of the ornithine carbamoyl transferase inhibitor. Further, Patil et al (63) have recently demonstrated that N-phosphoglutamic acid, as well as N-phosphoglycine, inhibit ornithine carbamoyltransferase, quite firmly establishing the nature of the toxin and one of its detrimental biological effects to plants.

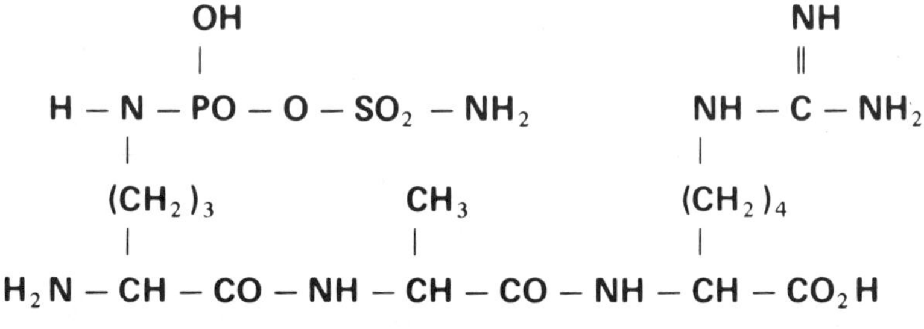

Figure 4 *Pseudomonas phaseolicola* toxin (50).

Semipurified preparations of phaseotoxin inhibit the forward reaction of ornithine carbamoyltransferase with a Michaelis constant of 5.0 mM for ornithine and 1.7 mM for carbamoylphosphate (94). The toxin preparation induces a competitive inhibition in relation to carbamoylphosphate and a noncompetitive mode of inhibition in relative to ornithine. The toxin does not inhibit the other enzymes of the urea cycle (60).

Semipurified preparations of phaseotoxin inhibited ornithine carbamoyltransferase in vivo (60), although no ornithine accumulated up to 48 hr after toxin treatment, which may have been due to toxin degradation (62). Toxin-induced chlorosis can be precluded by the prior administration of L-citrulline and can be reversed by L-arginine • hydrochloride, which supports the notion that there is a cause-effect relationship between enzyme inhibition and the induction of chlorosis in toxin-treated leaves. More credibility to the involvement of ornithine carbamoyltransferase as a toxin-sensitive site has come from the use of *P. phaseolicola* mutants (23). Isolate HB-20, which increases in number in susceptible bean tissue and does not produce phaseotoxin in infected tissue, likewise does not cause an inhibition of ornithine carbamoyltransferase. Since toxin-induced chlorosis can apparently be reversed with L-arginine, it was surmised that there would be no irreversible structural changes in bean cell organelles. Electron microscopy observations confirmed this hypothesis (62). Ultimately, it would be quite desirable for the investigators to make comparable studies with N-phosphoglutamic acid. This would effectively eliminate the possibility of contaminating compounds in toxin preparations that would compete or inhibit the effects of the toxin. The nature of toxin-induced chlorosis is not known. Patil (60) speculates that a deficiency in arginine caused by the action of the toxin may preclude the formation of chlorophyll-synthesizing enzymes.

Other effects of phaseotoxin on leaves have been reported, including starch accumulation (46), growth inhibition of bean callus tissue (1), and a decrease in cell permeability of swiss chard with a concomitant increase in the osmotic value (100).

Gnanamanickam & Patil (23) have shown that phaseotoxin plays an important role in facilitating the establishment of *P. phaseolicola* in bean tissues, since it is detected in susceptible tissues but not resistant ones in spite of substantial bacterial multiplication. This suggests that phaseotoxin production is suppressed in resistant bean tissue. Conceivably, there is a factor in resistant bean that may have something to do with the suppression of phaseotoxin production (61). Interestingly, the pretreatment of resistant cultivars of bean with phaseotoxin suppresses the hypersensitive response and phytoalexin accumulation upon subsequent inoculation with *P. phaseolicola.* Thus, the demonstration of the suppression of phytoalexin accumulation, which normally does not occur in the hypersensitive response (39, 52), by phaseotoxin offers a mechanistic explanation for the suppression of the hypersensitive response in such tissues.

Rhizobitoxins

Root nodules of some soybean plants become chlorotic and this symptom is produced by some isolates of *Rhizobium japonicum* (35). A toxic compound called rhizobitoxine was isolated from *R. japonicum* and characterized by Owens and co-workers (55, 56) as 2-amino-4-(2-amino-3 hydroxypropoxy)-*trans*-but-3-enoic acid and its saturated analogue, dihydrorhizobitoxin, *0*-(2-amino-3-hydroxypropyl)-homoserine. Rhizobitoxine blocks β-cystathionase, the enzyme in the methionine pathway that converts cystathionine to homocysteine (21, 22). The details of the toxin inhibition of this enzyme and the implications involved are summarized in previous reviews (54, 60).

Toxins from Pseudomonas syringae and Pseudomonas mors-prunorum

The symptoms of canker disease of plum and cherry caused by *P. mors-prunorum* are suspected to be caused, in part, by a phytotoxin (15). Unfortunately, the toxin was never isolated and characterized; however, because the authors implicated the host-specific nature of the toxin, investigations on it should be re-opened. *P. syringae* has been shown to produce a wide spectrum antibiotic that is also phytotoxic (9, 10). A partially purified preparation of the toxin yielded nine amino acids (77). The toxin was designated syringomycin. Other recent reviews cover the work done on its biological activity and mode of action (60, 88).

A recent outbreak of bacterial leaf blight of wheat caused by *P. syringae* in the Great Plains of the United States has caused considerable concern because the disease had not been previously reported (53). The disease caused millions of dollars in crop loss in the mid-1970s (74). Certain varieties are much more susceptible than others, which coupled with a necrotic-chlorotic fleck symptom leads one to suspect that a toxin, perhaps a host-specific one, might be involved. Some indication of this has been put forth by J. D. Otta (unpublished data). D. Sands and D. Kenfield (unpublished data) indicate that there is a phytotoxic component of the bacterial culture fluid distinct from an antibiotic component.

Mycoplasma Toxins

Of the more than 60 diseases described that may have a mycoplasma etiology, only *Spiroplasma citri,* the causal agent of stubborn disease in citrus (17), and the corn stunt mycoplasmas (5) have been cultured. Daniels & Meddins (8) have shown that cultures of *S. citri* produce a substance toxic to the single-celled green alga, *Chlorogonium euchlorium,* which was used as a bioassay test organism. The toxin also affected tobacco protoplasts and certain yeasts. It seemed to be taken up via the root system of white clover seedlings grown aseptically on an agar medium, which produces chlorosis and necrosis of the leaves. The toxin appears to be a small-molecular-weight (300 or less) neutral glycoside. This work is the first to implicate the involvement of a phytotoxin in a disease with a mycoplasma etiology.

A Proteinaceous-Enzymatic Phytotoxin?

Pseudomonas aeruginosa is probably the best-known bacterial pathogen of both plants and man (14, 41). The bacterium can cause lesions on the leaves of *Chrysan-*

themum and for this reason giving a flower to a sick friend in the hospital may not always be an act of kindness. Pathogenic human isolates of *P. aeruginosa* have been shown to produce an exotoxin that is a multisubunit protein lethal to mammalian cells. Its mechanism of action resembles that of the diphtheria toxin (57), that is, it causes the cessation of protein synthesis via the ADP-ribosylation of elongation factor II by using NAD as the substrate donor (32). Fragment A of the diphtheria toxin, which possesses the enzymatic activity, does not have antigenic reactivity with antisera to the *P. aeruginosa* toxin (32). Recently, M. Vasil (unpublished data), by using the Elek test, has demonstrated a positive reaction between an antiserum to the *P. aeruginosa* exotoxin and two *P. aeruginosa* isolates from diseased plants (isolate UB PP54 from chrysanthemum and UB PP isolate 774 from corn, supplied to me by M. N. Schroth, Univ. Calif., Berkeley). Certainly, although not conclusively since enzymatic tests have not been demonstrated, these results do suggest that further research on this problem may eventually show a proteinaceous-enzymatic exotoxin that is involved in a plant disease caused by a bacterium.

In the future, research efforts on the toxicology of plant diseases caused by *P. aeruginosa* and its close relative *Pseudomonas polycolor* on tobacco should be encouraged, since these will undoubtedly be forerunners in the development of techniques and concepts for the involvement of proteinaceous-enzymatic toxins in bacterial plant diseases. If such efforts prove fruitful, then there might be some justification for serious concern for the role of bacterial phytotoxins in human health. For instance, Cother et al (7) have described a massive outbreak of internal brown rot of onions in Australia by *P. aeruginosa.*

PROSPECTS

It seems certain that bacterial phytotoxins will prove useful as tools in furthering our knowledge of metabolic, structural, and regulatory factors of the plant or animal cell. For instance, the solution to the problem concerning the mechanism of action of the phytotoxic glycopeptides as wilt-causing agents will undoubtedly enhance our understanding of water relations in the healthy plant. Those toxins serving as metabolic inhibitors may provide information on enzyme structure and regulatory control. We have also seen at least one bacterial phytotoxin (syringomycin) possessing the properties of an antibiotic.

The structure of some phytotoxins is unique, i.e. the phosphoamide linkage of phaseotoxin (Figure 3). Furthermore, the β-lactam ring, a structural feature of tabtoxin, occurs infrequently in nature (Figure 1). These structures may provide important clues to the herbicide industry to produce more effective compounds that are environmentally safe and easily biodegradable.

It has been implicitly understood with the bacterial plant pathogens that coding for any and all of the proteins involved in toxin biosynthesis does not reside any place other than on the bacterial chromosome. However, in-depth studies may eventually show similarities to other biological systems, such as the phage in *Corynebacterium diphtheriae* that carries the *tox* gene (57). Plasmids as carriers of pathogenicity factors have been implicated in the crown gall organism, *Agrobacterium tumefaciens* (37). It would seem logical to use plasmid-curing agents on toxin-producing pathogens to determine if toxin production is related to the presence of extrachromosomal DNA.

Studies on the importance of a toxin to the pathogenicity of the bacterium have not been extensive. The nontoxin-producing nonpathogenic mutants of *Pseudomonas phaseolicola* appear to be the single recent example relating pathogenicity to toxin production (23). It seems imperative that comparable studies be done on the other known toxin-producing bacterial pathogens.

Bacteriophages are known for all of the major genera of plant pathogenic bacteria, yet there does not seem to be a single example of phage transduction of toxin production from one bacterium to another. A genetic map for toxin production in any plant pathogenic bacterium is unknown.

Fungal toxins have been extremely useful tools in studying the mechanisms of disease resistance (89). The extreme host selectivity exhibited by some of these toxins has been the primary key to their importance. Such compounds also have the potential to serve in selection for disease resistance at the protoplast level. The successful regeneration of a plant species from protoplasts coupled with phytotoxins in the regeneration medium offers a potentially useful technique for plant improvement. This feat remains to be accomplished.

The biosynthetic pathways of the bacterial phytotoxins are virtually unknown. Certainly, many are bound to be mediated by enzymes and cofactors that have been described for other systems, i.e. polysaccharide biosynthesis. Nevertheless, some are undoubtedly novel to the bacterial pathogens involved. It also seems certain that plant host factors could play an important regulatory role in toxin biosynthesis, i.e. amylovorin production by *Erwinia amylovora.* Such compounds remain to be isolated and their activity remains to be described.

Many plant pathogenic bacteria are relatively host specific, yet the toxins produced by them will affect a wide range of plant species. In some cases, even though a bacterial phytotoxin has been isolated from both bacterial cultures and the infected host, and even though it produces typical disease symptoms, it appears not to be the factor responsible for governing the host specificity of the bacterium. This is in contrast to some fungal toxins that dictate host specificity (89). Obviously, we have not made great strides in understanding the interacting factors in the plant host and the bacterial parasite that govern specificity.

SUMMARY

Representatives of all of the major genera of plant disease-causing bacteria have been shown to produce one or more phytotoxins. Toxicological studies on the bacterial diseases of the major food crops have not been extensive. Bacterial phytotoxins belong to a number of classes of organic substances, including peptide, derivatized amino acid, polysaccharide, and glycopeptide. The mechanism of action of these compounds is largely unknown, as is their origin and importance in the disease syndrome. Nevertheless, some progress has been made in these areas in isolated cases. There is a tremendous potential in the future for studies on the bacterial phytotoxins.

ACKNOWLEDGMENTS

I wish to thank David Sands, Don Mathre, and Norman Reed for helpful discussions, and Bonnie Ashley for typing the manuscript.

The work in my laboratory was supported in part by grant PCM 76-19565 from the National Science Foundation. This report is No. 744 of the Montana Agricultural Experiment Station, Journal Series.

Literature Cited

1. Bajaj, Y. P. S., Saettler, A. W. 1970. *Phytopathology* 60:1065–67
2. Barash, I., Karr, A. L., Strobel, G. A. 1975. *Plant Physiol.* 55:646–51
3. Braun, A. C. 1955. *Phytopathology* 45: 659–64
4. Carlson, P. S. 1973. *Science* 180: 1366–68
5. Chen, T. A., Granados, R. R. 1970. *Science* 167:1633–36
6. Claflin, L., Shepard, J. 1976. *Potato J.* In press
7. Cother, E. J., Darbsyshire, B., Brewer, J. 1976. *Phytopathology* 66:828–34
8. Daniels, M. J., Meddins, B. M. 1974. *Colloq. I. Inst. N. Sante R. Med. Inserm.* 33:195–200
9. DeVay, J. E., Lukezic, F. L., Sinden, S. L., English, H., Coplin, D. L. 1968. *Phytopathology* 58:95–101
10. DeVay, J. E., Strobel, G. A. 1962. *Phytopathology* 52:360 (Abstr.)
11. Durbin, R. D. 1971. In *Chlorosis-Inducing Pseudomonas Toxins: Their Mechanism of Action and Structure in Morphology and Biochemical Events in Plant-Parasite Interaction,* ed. S. Akai, S. Ouchi, pp. 369–86. Tokyo: Mochizuki. 415 pp.
12. Durbin, R. D. 1972. In *Phytotoxins in Plant Disease,* ed. R. K. S. Wood, A. Ballio, A. Graniti, pp. 19–33. New York: Academic. 530 pp.
13. Eden-Green, S. J., Knee, M. 1974. *J. Gen. Microbiol.* 81:509–12
14. Elrod, R. P., Braun, A. C. 1942. *J. Bacteriol.* 44:633–44
15. Erikson, D., Montgomery, H. B. S. 1945. *Ann. Appl. Biol.* 32:117–23
16. Finkelstein, R. A. 1973. *C. R. Microbiol.* 2:553–623
17. Fudl-Allah, A. E. A., Calavan, E. C., Igwegbe, E. C. K. 1972. *Phytopathology* 62:729–31
18. Gardner, J. M., Kado, C. I. 1972. *Phytopathology* 62:759
19. Gill, D. M. 1975. *Proc. Natl. Acad. Sci. USA* 72:2064–68
20. Gill, D. M. 1976. *Biochemistry* 15: 1242–48
21. Giovanelli, J., Owens, L. D., Mudd, S. H. 1971. *Biochim. Biophys. Acta* 227: 671–84
22. Giovanelli, J., Owens, L. D., Mudd, S. H. 1972. *Plant Physiol.* 51:492–503
23. Gnanamanickam, S. S., Patil, S. S. 1976. *Phytopathology* 66:290–94
24. Goodman, R. N., Huang, J. S., Huang, P. Y. 1974. *Science* 183:1081–82
25. Halloin, J. M., De Zoeten, G. A., Gaard, G. R., Walker, J. C. 1969. *Plant Physiol.* 45:310–14
26. Hess, W. M., Strobel, G. A. 1970. *Phytopathology* 60:1428–31
27. Hinton, J. J. C., Moran, T. 1957. *Br. J. Nutr.* 11:323–28
28. Hoitink, H. A. J., Pelletier, R. L., Coulson, J. G. 1966. *Phytopathology* 56: 1062–65
29. Hoitink, H. A. J., Sinden, S. L. 1970. *Phytopathology* 60:1236–37
30. Holzwarth, G. 1976. *Biochemistry* 15: 4333–39
31. Huang, P., Goodman, R. N. 1976. *Phytopathology* 66:269–76
32. Iglewski, B. H., Kabat, D. 1975. *Proc. Natl. Acad. Sci. USA* 72:2284–88
33. Jansson, P. E., Kenne, L., Lindberg, B. 1975. *Carbohydr. Res.* 45:275–82
34. Jeanes, A., Pittsley, J. E., Senti, F. R. 1961. *J. Appl. Polymer Sci.* 5: 519–26
35. Johnson, H. W., Means, U. M., Clark, F. E. 1959. *Nature* 183:308–9

36. Johnson, T. B., Strobel, G. A. 1970. *Plant Physiol.* 45:761–64
37. Kado, C. I. 1976. *Ann. Rev. Phytopathol.* 14:265–308
38. Karr, A. L., Karr, D. B., Strobel, G. A. 1974. *Plant Physiol.* 53:250–57
39. Keen, N. T., Kennedy, B. W. 1974. *Physiol. Plant Pathol.* 4:173–85
40. Klement, Z., Goodman, R. N. 1967. *Ann. Rev. Phytopathol.* 5:17–44
41. Kominos, S. D., Copeland, C. E., Grosiak, B., Postic, B. 1972. *Appl. Microbiol.* 24:567–70
42. Kosuge, T., Heskett, M. G., Wilson, E. E. 1966. *J. Biol. Chem.* 241:3738–44
43. Kuo, T. T., Lin, B. C., Li, C. C. 1970. *Bot. Bull. Acad. Sin.* 11:36–45
44. Lamar, C. Jr., Sinden, S. L., Durbin, R. D. 1969. *Biochem. Pharamacol.* 18: 521–29
45. Laughnan, J. R., Gabay, S. J. 1973. *Crop Sci.* 13:681–84
46. Lesemann, D., Rudolph, K. 1970. *Z. Pflanzenphysiol.* 62:108–15
47. Lim, S. M., Hooker, A. L., Smith, D. R. 1971. *Agron. J.* 63:712–13
48. Lippincott, J. A., Lippincott, B. B. 1975. *Ann. Rev. Microbiol.* 29:377–405
49. Magie, A. R., Wilson, E. E., Kosuge, T. 1963. *Science* 141:1281–82
50. Mitchell, R. E. 1976. *Nature* 260:75–76
51. Nachmias, A., Barash, I., Solel, Z., Strobel, G. A. 1977. *Physiol. Plant Pathol.* In press
52. O'Brien, F., Wood, R. K. S. 1973. *Nature* 242:532–33
53. Otta, J. D. 1974. *Plant Dis. Rep.* 58:1061–64
54. Owens, L. D. 1969. *Science* 165:18–25
55. Owens, L. D., Thompson, J. F., Fennessey, P. V. 1972. *J. Chem. Soc. Chem. Commun.* p. 715 (Abstr.)
56. Owens, L. D., Thompson, J. F., Pitcher, R. G., Williams, T. 1972. *J. Chem. Soc. Chem. Commun.* p. 714 (Abstr.)
57. Pappenheimer, A. M., Gill, D. M. 1973. *Science* 182:353–58
58. Patel, P. N., Walker, J. C. 1963. *Phytopathology* 53:855 (Abstr.)
59. Patel, P. N., Walker, J. C. 1963. *Phytopathology* 53:522–28
60. Patil, S. S. 1974. *Ann. Rev. Phytopathol.* 12:259–79
61. Patil, S. S., Gnanamanickam, S. S. 1976. *Nature* 259:5543
62. Patil, S. S., Tam, L. Q., Sakai, W. S. 1972. *Plant Physiol.* 49:803–7
63. Patil, S. S., Youngblood, P., Christiansen, P., Moore, R. E. 1976. *Biochem. Biophys. Res. Commun.* 69: 1019–27
64. Patino-Mendez, G. 1964. Studies on the pathogenicity of *Corynebacterium michiganense* and its transmission in tomatoseed. PhDthesis. Univ. Calif., Davis.53pp.
65. Pinkerton, F. 1976. Attenuation of pathogenicity of *Helminthosporium sacchari.* PhD thesis. Mont. State. Univ., Bozeman. 73 pp.
66. Pinkerton, F., Strobel, G. A. 1976. *Proc. Natl. Acad. Sci. USA* 73:4007–11
67. Rai, P. V., Strobel, G. A. 1969. *Phytopathology* 59:47–52
68. Rai, P. V., Strobel, G. A. 1969. *Phytopathology* 59:53–57
69. Ries, S. M., Strobel, G. A. 1972. *Plant Physiol.* 49:676–84
70. Ries, S. M., Strobel, G. A. 1972. *Physiol. Plant Pathol.* 2:133–42
71. Rudolph, K., Stahmann, M. A. 1966. *Phytopathology* 56:29–46
72. Sadowski, P., Strobel, G. A. 1973. *J. Bacteriol.* 115:668–72
73. Salemink, C. A., Rebel, H., Kerling, L. C. P., Tchernoff, V. 1965. *Science* 149:202–3
74. Scharen, A. L., Bergman, J. W., Burns, E. E. 1976. *Plant Dis. Rep.* 80:686–90
75. Sequeira, L. 1971. *Proc. 3rd Int. Conf. Plant Pathogen. Bacteria,* pp. 165–69
76. Sequeira, L., Ainslie, V. 1969. *Proc. 11th Int. Bot. Cong.,* p. 175
77. Sinden, S. L., DeVay, J. E., Backman, P. A. 1971. *Physiol. Plant Pathol.* 1: 199–213
78. Sinden, S. L., Durbin, R. D. 1969. *Phytopathology* 59:249–50
79. Sinden, S. L., Durbin, R. D. 1970. *Phytopathology* 60:360–64
80. Sjulin, T. M., Beer, S. U. 1976. *Phytopathol. Ann. Meet.,* p. 174 (Abstr.)
81. Stewart, W. W. 1971. *Nature* 229: 174–78
82. Stoffl, P., Karr, A. L., Goodman, R. N. 1976. *Phytopathol. Ann. Meet.,* p. 102 (Abstr.)
83. Straley, C. S., Straley, M. L., Strobel, G. A. 1974. *Phytopathology* 64:194–96
84. Straley, C. S., Strobel, G. A. 1973. *Abstr. 2nd Int. Congr. Plant Pathol.,* no. 659.
85. Strobel, G. A. 1967. *Plant Physiol.* 42: 1433–41
86. Strobel, G. A. 1970. *J. Biol. Chem.* 245:32–38
87. Strobel, G. A. 1974. *J. Biol. Chem.* 248:1321–28
88. Strobel, G. A. 1974. *Ann. Rev. Plant Physiol.* 25:541–66
89. Strobel, G. A. 1976. *Trends Biochem. Sci.* 1:247–49

90. Strobel, G. A., Hess, W. M. 1968. *Plant Physiol.* 43:1673–88
91. Strobel, G. A., Rai, P. V. 1968. *Plant Dis. Rep.* 52:502–4
92. Strobel, G. A., Talmadge, K. W., Albersheim, P. 1972. *Biochem. Biophys. Acta* 261:365–74
93. Sutton, J. C., Williams, P. H. 1970. *Can. J. Bot.* 48:645–51
94. Tam, L. Q., Patil, S. S. 1972. *Plant Physiol.* 49:808–12
95. Taylor, P. A., Durbin, R. D. 1973. *Physiol. Plant Pathol.* 3:9–17
96. Taylor, P. A., Schnoes, H. K., Durbin, R. D. 1972. *Biochem. Biophys. Acta* 286:107–17
97. Van Alfen, N. K., Turner, N. C. 1975. *Plant Physiol.* 55:559–61
98. Woolley, D. W., Pringle, R. B., Braun, A. C. 1952. *J. Biol. Chem.* 197:409–17
99. Woolley, D. W., Schaffner, G., Braun, A. C. 1955. *J. Biol. Chem.* 215:485–93
100. Zeller, W., Rudolph, K. 1972. *Z. Pflanzenphysiol.* 67:183–87

Ann. Rev. Microbiol. 1977. 31:225–74

PHOTOTROPHIC PROKARYOTES: THE CYANOBACTERIA[1]

❖1704

R. Y. Stanier and G. Cohen-Bazire
Unité de Physiologie Microbienne, Département de Biochimie et Génétique Microbienne, Institut Pasteur, Paris F 75015, France

CONTENTS

INTRODUCTION 226
MAJOR PATTERNS OF DEVELOPMENT 228
Properties of the Principal Subgroups 228
Chroococcacean Cyanobacteria 231
Pleurocapsalean Cyanobacteria 231
Oscillatorian Cyanobacteria 233
Heterocystous Subgroups 234
THE CYANOBACTERIAL VEGETATIVE CELL 235
General Organization 235
Cell Envelopes 238
Gliding Movement 240
The Photosynthetic Apparatus 241
Effect of environmental factors on synthesis and function 241
Isolation of components of the photosynthetic apparatus 242
Chlorophyll and carotenoids 242
Membrane lipids 243
PBP 244
Chromatic adaptation 245
The phycobilisome 245
Proteins of the electron transport chain 246
The Genome: Molecular Properties 246
The Machinery of Transcription and Translation 247
The control of gene expression in cyanobacteria 248
SPECIALIZED CELLS 249
The Heterocyst 249
The relation between heterocyst formation and nif gene expression 250
Heterocyst differentiation 250

[1]Dedicated to Professor C. B. van Niel.

Biochemical aspects of heterocyst differentiation 251
Patterns of heterocyst development 254
The Akinete 255
METABOLISM 255
The Relation Between Photosynthetic and Respiratory Metabolism 256
The Control of Light and Dark Metabolism 258
The Metabolic Bases of Obligate Photoautotrophy 261
Anaerobic Metabolism 262
The Assimilation of Combined Nitrogen 264
Nitrogen Fixation 264
The Synthesis and Possible Functions of Cyanophycin 265
NEW LIGHT ON THE ORIGINS OF CHLOROPLASTS 266
CONCLUDING REMARKS 267

INTRODUCTION

Cyanobacteria (blue-green bacteria) constitute the largest, most diverse, and most widely distributed group of photosynthetic prokaryotes. They can be succinctly defined as organisms that harbor, within a prokaryotic cell, a photosynthetic apparatus remarkably similar in functional, structural, and molecular respects to that contained in the eukaryotic chloroplast. To this definition, one qualification must be added: the ensemble of cyanobacterial light-harvesting pigments—chlorophyll *a* and phycobiliproteins—is specifically homologous with that of the rhodophytan (red algal) chloroplast. The cyanobacteria are accordingly distinguishable from the two other major groups of photosynthetic bacteria, purple and green bacteria, both by the nature of their photosynthetic pigment system and by their capacity to perform oxygenic photosynthesis, which confers on them the physiological character of aerobic photoautotrophs.

As for their non-photosynthetic properties, cyanobacteria belong to the great subclass of gram-negative prokaryotes, defined by the special structure and chemical composition of the cell wall. Many, but not all, cyanobacteria are motile. Motility is always of the gliding type, likewise characteristic of motile green bacteria and many groups of non-photosynthetic gram-negative bacteria.

Since their recognition as a biological group early in the 19th century, the cyanobacteria have been treated as a class or division of algae, with the common name of blue-green algae or cyanophytes. This interpretation of their taxonomic position, which was based primarily on their plantlike photosynthetic properties, became untenable about 1960, when the fundamental differences in cellular organization between prokaryotes and eukaryotes were at last fully elucidated (217, 276). The cellular properties of the blue-green algae, long known to be unlike those of any other algal group (108), are typically prokaryotic. The organisms traditionally defined as bacteria are extraordinarily diverse; their only unifying character is the prokaryotic structure of the cell (43). Hence, it is not possible to formulate a satisfactory definition of this major biological assemblage, which excludes the cyanobacteria. Continued use of the common names blue-green algae and cyanophytes perpetuates a false impression about the biological nature of cyanobacteria. This practice should be discouraged, even though some phycologists seem to find a change of name difficult to accept (e.g. 198).

In the past 20 years, it has become evident that chloroplasts are organelles with some of the attributes of prokaryotic cells (28, 66). This conceivably reflects an origin distinct from that of the cell that now encloses them: the ancestors of chloroplasts might have been photosynthetic prokaryotes, which became endosymbionts of primitive eukaryotes, and subsequently lost their genetic independence (208, 272, 274, 316). This hypothesis, although it provides a plausible evolutionary explanation for the resemblances with respect to photosynthetic structure and function between cyanobacteria and some chloroplasts, is not germane to the taxonomic problem. The only logical taxonomic treatment of the cyanobacteria is to place them in the superkingdom Prokaryotae (43), as a division, class, or order of bacteria. This raises a delicate judicial issue. Cyanobacterial nomenclature, hitherto subject to the rules of the Botanical Code (271), should in this event come under the rules of the Bacteriological Code (188). Such a change would have far-reaching consequences, since the provisions of the two codes differ in numerous respects, most importantly with regard to the nature of nomenclatural types.

In the decade since the cyanobacteria were first reviewed here (158, 186), more solid information about their properties has been acquired than in the preceding century. This is the consequence of a methodological revolution: the very tardy introduction of experimental analysis in place of the traditional descriptive analysis that previously dominated the study of these organisms. The first sustained experimental investigations were carried out between 1940 and 1950 on heterocystous cyanobacteria by Fogg (97–102), who formed and for many years led a British school of experimental botanists, which has made notable contributions to our knowledge of cyanobacterial nitrogen fixation, heterocysts, and gas vacuoles.

The availability of pure cultures is an essential precondition for effective experimental work on any microbial group. The long prevalent myth that it is exceptionally difficult, if not impossible, to isolate cyanobacteria in pure culture seems to have discouraged botanists from tackling the problem; here, the contribution of microbiologists has been paramount. The pioneering work of M. B. Allen (6) made a limited but very useful collection of pure strains available in the early 1950s. They included the unicellular organism incorrectly labeled *Anacystis nidulans,* in reality a strain of *Synechococcus* (227), which subsequently became the *Escherichia coli* of experimental cyanobacteriology. Since it will be necessary to cite repeatedly work performed with this particular strain, we refer to it here as *Synechococcus* AN. About 10 years later, other workers (10, 14, 54, 275, 297, 298) took up the job of isolation and purification where it had been left by Allen. Over 200 strains, representative of all major cyanobacterial subgroups, are now in pure culture. Many of them have been recently deposited in the American Type Culture Collection, where they are maintained under liquid nitrogen, at present the only effective method for long-term preservation of cyanobacteria. A description of the salient properties of this collection, accompanied by detailed strain histories, is in preparation (247); also, a useful summary of isolation and laboratory culture can be found (51).

The recent upsurge of interest in the cyanobacteria is reflected by the publication of two treatises on this biological group (52, 104). Numerous specialized reviews have also appeared on cell physiology (327), thermophilic cyanobacteria (53), planktonic cyanobacteria (241), differentiation (49), gas vacuoles and gas vesicles (305,

306), chromatic adaptation (29), the heterocyst (295), cyanophages (226), and the comparative properties of cyanobacteria and chloroplasts (50).

Much information, old and new, on every aspect of the biology of cyanobacteria can be found in the books and reviews cited above. The form that yet another, relatively short, review should or could take was accordingly far from obvious. We finally decided to restrict it to three themes, each of which has been close to the interests of our own research group: major patterns of development; the organization of the cyanobacterial cell; and metabolism. The choice was also dictated by our belief that these particular themes, all central to an understanding of the biology of cyanobacteria, now lend themselves to a reasonably unified and coherent presentation, despite the many obvious gaps in knowledge (which we have also attempted to pinpoint). However, a critical analysis could not be combined with a full coverage of the literature of the past 10 years. Topics that have been recently well reviewed are disposed of with references to the reviews in question. The reaction mechanisms of oxygenic photosynthesis have been excluded from the discussion of metabolism, since they do not appear to present any unusual features in this group; however, the special properties of the light-harvesting pigment system of cyanobacteria are reviewed.

In short, the reader should be warned that this is a highly selective review of certain aspects of the biology of cyanobacteria; the presentation is, perhaps unavoidably, much influenced by the experience of the authors and their associates over the past 15 years with this fascinating group of prokaryotes.

MAJOR PATTERNS OF DEVELOPMENT

The fact that cyanobacteria are a prokaryotic group of great structural diversity is evident from the perusal of phycological systematic treatises, where these organisms are divided into a bewildering array of subclasses, orders, families, and genera, all defined by structural properties (35, 77, 117). Recent studies on the structure and development of cyanobacteria in culture indicate that their diversity, although considerable, is perhaps not as great as the present taxonomic treatment of the group suggests. We use this information (still admittedly limited) to describe the cyanobacteria in terms of major developmental patterns, a subject that can be more or less divorced from the question of their formal classification.

Properties of the Principal Subgroups

Of the principal subgroups (Figures 1–7), the chroococcacean cyanobacteria are the simplest members in structural respects. They are unicellular rods or cocci, for the most part immotile, that reproduce either by binary fission or its variant, budding. Structural counterparts of these cyanobacteria exist, accordingly, in many other groups of gram-negative prokaryotes.

The pleurocapsalean cyanobacteria are also unicellular organisms, although this is not always evident from gross structure since the daughter cells produced by binary fission remain glued together through the outer wall layers to form vegetative aggregates. This subgroup is distinguished from the chroococcacean subgroup by its distinctive mode of reproduction. Small, spherical reproductive cells, termed *baeocytes* ("endospores" in the phycological literature), arise through multiple fission of a vegetative cell and are released through rupture of its outer wall layer. Gliding motility in this subgroup is displayed only by baeocytes and only for a short period following their release; however, not all members produce motile baeocytes.

In the remaining subgroups, the unit of structure is a filament of cells, or trichome. Growth leads to elongation of the trichome and to an increase, through intercalary cell division, in the number of its constituent cells. The trichome may be either motile or immotile. Reproduction occurs by breakage of the trichome into shorter chains of cells, often called *hormogonia.* The usage of this term is not very clear, but most authors appear to apply it only to short chains of cells distinguishable from vegetative trichomes by motility, or by a difference in the size or structure of the constituent cells. Except in stigonematalean cyanobacteria, the trichome is unbranched and uniseriate (one cell in width), since intercalary cell divisions occur in a plane at right angles to its long axis. The trichome is frequently surrounded by a common envelope layer (a sheath or a slime layer). Trichome breakage within the envelope and subsequent elongation of the daughter trichomes sometimes leads to a configuration termed "false branching." The end of one trichome, which breaks through the envelope in the course of elongation, may come into angular apposition within the center of another trichome, which has elongated within the envelope, suggesting (incorrectly) that a branch has been formed. Phycologists have placed considerable taxonomic weight on the presence or absence of false branching. However, this property (in any case a possible secondary consequence of the presence of an envelope layer surrounding the trichome) is highly variable in cultures; in many strains, its expression is determined by culture conditions and the phase of growth (R. Rippka, personal communication).

The trichome of oscillatorian cyanobacteria is composed exclusively of vegetative cells. The trichomes of heterocystous cyanobacteria, when grown in the absence of combined nitrogen, also contain structurally differentiated cells known as heterocysts. Removal of a combined nitrogen source triggers differentiation of a small fraction of the vegetative cells into heterocysts. Some heterocystous cyanobacteria also produced specialized resting cells, termed akinetes.

Differences in the structure of the trichome permit the recognition of three subgroups among heterocystous cyanobacteria: the nostocacean, rivularian, and stigonematalean subgroups. In nostocacean cyanobacteria, the trichome is of even width; heterocysts may be either terminal or intercalary. The rivularian trichome is characterized by its apical-basal polarity; it is tapered, and heterocysts always develop from the terminal vegetative cell at the thicker (basal) end.

Heterocystous cyanobacteria of the stigonematalean type are characterized by the formation of branched and, in part, multiseriate trichomes. Development of a hormogonium gives rise to a primary trichome that is initially unbranched and uniseriate. However, some intercalary cell divisions occur in planes that do not lie at right angles to the long axis of the primary trichome; this leads both to the development of lateral branches and to a thickening of the trichome, with certain

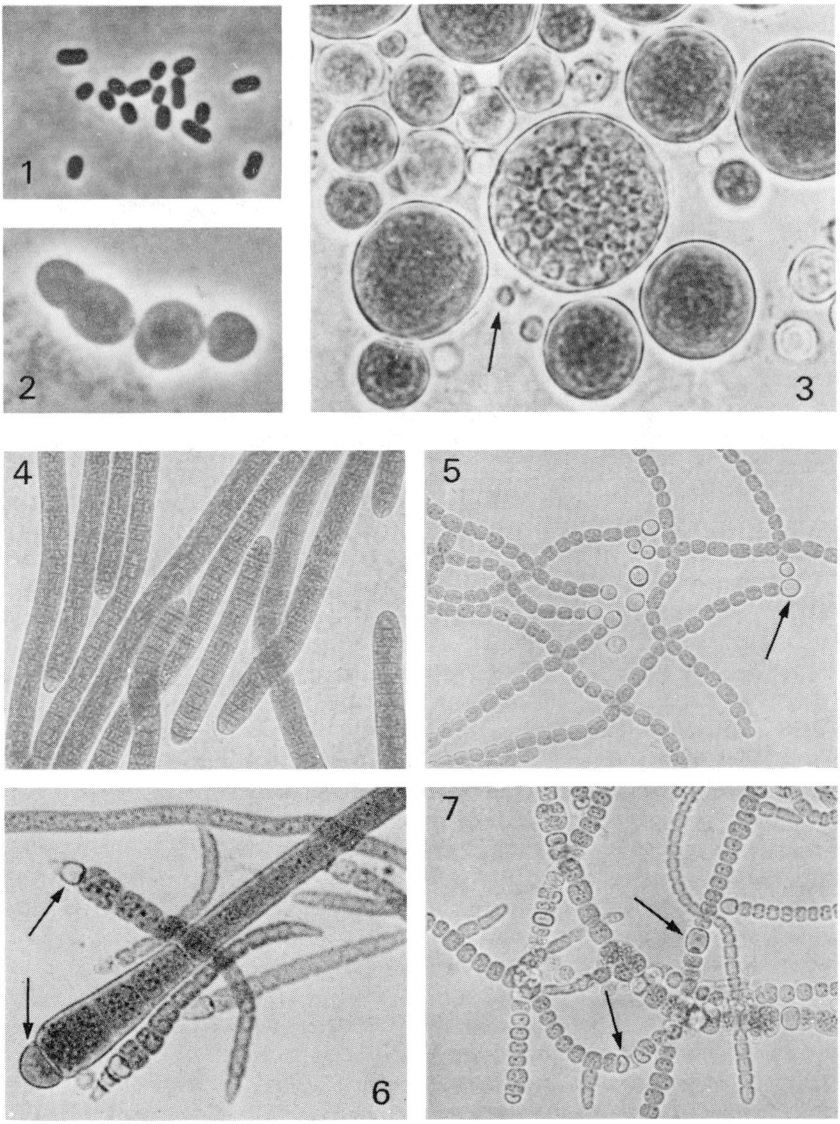

Figure 1 A small-celled chroococcacean cyanobacterium that reproduces by binary transverse fission, *Synechocococcus* ATCC 27194. X2000.
Figure 2 A budding chroococcacean cyanobacterium, *Chamaesiphon* ATCC 29397. Two cells bearing buds at different stages of development. X2000.
Figure 3 A pleurocapsalean cyanobacterium, *Dermocarpa* ATCC 29371. Vegetative cells at various stages of growth. The largest has undergone multiple fission and is filled with baeocytes. Arrow points to a free baeocyte. X1000.

regions becoming multiseriate. Heterocysts are typically intercalary; hormogonia are formed principally from the tips of lateral branches.

The six subgroups distinguishable by differences in developmental patterns correspond only in part to the major taxa now recognized by phycologists. Table 1 shows the ordinal and familial assignments of each subgroup, in the system employed by Bourrelly (35), which does not differ greatly from those of other standard treatments (77, 117).

In the following paragraphs, recent comparative cultural studies on the members of each subgroup are reviewed.

Chroococcacean Cyanobacteria

Numerous strains that reproduce by binary fission have been isolated in pure culture, and one extensive comparative study of their properties has been published (275). Some of the generic assignments proposed in this report were wrong and have been recently corrected (247). In the two genera represented by numerous strains, *Synechococcus* and *Synechocystis* [incorrectly designated *Aphanocapsa* in the initial study (275)], several different strain clusters could be distinguished by cell size, by physiological and chemical properties, and by mean DNA base composition. Although these clusters undoubtedly constitute distinct species, none could be identified unambiguously with the numerous existing nomenspecies, and no specific names were applied to them. This is a problem also encountered in the first comparative pure culture study of pleurocapsalean cyanobacteria (308, 309) and is likely to recur with the other subgroups as well.

Pure cultures of two unicellular cyanobacteria that reproduce by budding have been characterized and identified as representatives of the genus *Chamaesiphon* (308). Both reproduce by the formation of successive spherical buds from one pole of the ovoid vegetative cell. The developmental cycle of *Chamaesiphon,* thus, is analogous to that of *Nitrobacter* (333) and the budding species of *Rhodopseudomonas* (238, 315).

Pleurocapsalean Cyanobacteria

Many freshwater and marine strains have been isolated in pure culture, and a comparative study of their development by light microscopy and electron microscopy (308, 309) has revealed for the first time the properties shared by the members of this subgroup.

The vegetative cell is enclosed by a fibrous wall layer, external to but closely investing the peptidoglycan and outer membrane layers. The fibrous layer thickens

Figure 4 An oscillatorian cyanobacterium, *Oscillatoria* ATCC 29169. X500.

Figure 5–7 Heterocystous cyanobacteria. Arrows point to heterocysts. All X500. (*Figure 5*) *Anabaena* ATCC 27898 (nostocaceous subgroup). (*Figure 6*) *Calothrix* ATCC 27905 (rivularian subgroup). Basal region of one mature vegetative trichome and several smaller trichomes at early stages of development from hormogonia. (*Figure 7*) *Fischerella* ATCC 29538 (stigonematalean subgroup). Note multiseriate areas of trichome and lateral branches

Table 1 Correlation between cyanobacterial subgroups distinguishable by their developmental properties and major taxa recognized in the recent systematic treatment of Bourrelly (35)

Cyanobacterial subgroup	Order	Family
Chroococcacean		
Reproduction by binary fission	Chroococcales	Chroococcaceae
Reproduction by budding	Chamaesiphonales	Chamaesiphonaceae
Pleurocapsalean		
Dermocarpa, Dermocarpella, Chroococcidiopsis	Chamaesiphonales	Clastidiaceae
Myxosarcina	Pleurocapsales	Chroococcidiaceae
Xenococcus, Pleurocapsa	Pleurocapsales	Hyellaceae
Oscillatorian	Nostocales	Oscillatoriaceae and (in part) Scytonemataceae
Heterocystous subgroups		
Nostocacean	Nostocales	Nostocaceae and (in part) Scytonemataceae
Rivularian	Nostocales	Rivulariaceae
Stigonematalean	Stigonematales	

as the cell enlarges, attaining in extreme cases a width of 1 μm. Binary fission is never followed by a complete separation of the daughter cells, which remain enclosed by the common matrix of this wall layer. Repeated binary fissions, therefore, lead to the formation of coherent aggregates, the gross structure of which is determined by the planes of successive divisions.

The process of multiple fission, which leads to the formation and release of the reproductive cells or baeocytes, occurs through rapid, repeated binary fissions of a vegetative cell, unaccompanied by growth, to produce a uniform population of small daughter cells 2–4 μm in diameter. The number of daughter cells released from a single vegetative cell (burst size), thus, is a function of the size of the parental cell at the onset of multiple fission: it ranges from 4 to over 1000.

The introduction of the new name, baeocyte, for the pleurocapsalean reproductive cell to replace the phycological term endospore was proposed to avoid confusion in a bacteriological context, where the latter term has a well-established and different meaning.

In most pleurocapsalean cyanobacteria, synthesis of the fibrous wall layer is repressed during multiple fission, and the baeocytes at the time of their release are individually enclosed by walls that contain only peptidoglycan and outer membrane layers. They display transient gliding motility, becoming immotile as enlargement and synthesis of the fibrous wall layer begins. In the genera *Xenococcus* and *Chroococcidiopsis,* synthesis of this wall layer accompanies multiple fission; the freshly released baeocytes, each completely enclosed by a thin fibrous wall layer, are never motile.

The strains examined were assigned to six form genera: *Dermocarpa, Dermocarpella, Xenococcus, Myxosarcina, Chroococcidiopsis,* and *Pleurocapsa.* Previously recognized and distinguished primarily by their gross vegetative structure, these genera have now been redefined in terms of their characteristic developmental cycles.

Pleurocapsalean strains of marine and freshwater origin could be readily distinguished by their ionic requirements for growth. All marine strains had elevated requirements for Na^+ (not even partly replaceable by K^+), Cl^-, Mg^{2+}, and Ca^{2+}, a pattern also characteristic of indigenous marine non-photosynthetic bacteria of several different taxonomic groups (206, 240, 310, 311). One previous study of the growth responses to NaCl of several cyanobacteria isolated from marine and freshwater sources failed to reveal an absolute requirement of the marine strains for NaCl (17); this has also been observed (308) for several chroococcacean strains isolated from marine sources. The fact that these organisms were isolated from a marine source does not, of course, constitute proof that their habitat is marine.

Oscillatorian Cyanobacteria

The distinctions among genera within this large cyanobacterial subgroup at present are not clear: several mutually incompatible proposals have been advanced by phycologists (e.g. 35, 82). Our own comparative studies on many pure strains (247) have led us to recognize three genera that are accepted by some (though not all) phycologists: *Spirulina, Oscillatoria,* and *Pseudanabaena.* An oscillatorian strain that possesses the characteristics of one of these genera can be unambiguously assigned to it on the basis of light microscopy alone. However, many strains do not fall into these three pigeonholes and remain unclassifiable (at least by us). Since they display, in various combinations, the structural properties attributed by phycologists to the genera *Lyngbya, Phormidium,* and *Plectonema,* we propose to place them in a provisional category, the LPP group (247).

A property that is probably of fundamental determinative importance in the oscillatorian subgroup (and perhaps also in the heterocystous subgroups) is the mechanism of trichome breakage. There are two basically different mechanisms, one characteristic of *Oscillatoria* strains and the other characteristic of *Pseudanabaena* strains.

An elegant study by Lamont (183), who reviewed and reinterpreted earlier observations, has elucidated the mechanism of trichome breakage in *Oscillatoria.* The smooth-walled, straight trichome, often more than 1 mm long, is enclosed by a wall in which both the outer membrane and the peptidoglycan layers are continuous. Transverse walls are formed by ingrowth of the peptidoglycan layer and remain continuous with the circumferential peptidoglycan layer. The constituent cells, thus, are anchored together by the covalent bonds of an uninterrupted peptidoglycan skeleton or frame. Transverse wall formation is accompanied by the development in the peptidoglycan layer of two circumferential rows of holes (junctional pores), which flank each septum and are closely apposed to it. The peptidoglycan frame of the trichome, therefore, is perforated, like a row of postage stamps, with regularly spaced paired sets of junctional pores. Trichome breakage is initiated by the death and autolysis of an intercalary cell; the disintegrating cell is termed a necridium. The adjacent transverse walls bulge into the necridial space and thicken. Separation then occurs, by a circumferential tear, passing through one set of junctional pores in the external wall of the necridium. The newly formed terminal cells have thickened end walls, and one bears the remains of the circumferential necridial wall. Trichome breakage in *Oscillatoria,* therefore, is transcellular and involves the sacrifice of an intercalary cell converted to a necridium. After separation of the daughter trichomes, the newly formed tip regions undergo further modification, typically becoming attenuated; this process has been studied in detail in *Oscillatoria princeps* (259). The mature tip of an oscillatorian trichome, therefore, is different in structure from the central portion. The helical trichomes of *Spirulina* probably also divide by sacrificial trichome breakage, although this has not been confirmed by ultrastructural studies.

The trichome of *Pseudanabaena* is composed of a chain of identical rod-shaped cells, between which there are deep constrictions; a small gas vacuole is usually present at the poles of each cell, with new gas vacuoles appearing at the time of transverse wall formation (275). The trichomes are characteristically short; some strains are virtually unicellular and for this reason were assigned to *Synechococcus* when first described on the basis of pure culture studies (275). Transverse wall formation occurs through centripetal ingrowth of the peptidoglycan layer, followed by that of the outer membrane layer (36; G. Cohen-Bazire, unpublished observations), exactly as in chroococcacean cyanobacteria (11). The cells remain adherent only because centripetal ingrowth of the outer membrane layer is incomplete. However, the completed peptidoglycan layer is delaminated, so trichome breakage can occur easily between any two of the constituent cells; it is always intercellular.

The imprecision with which generic names have been applied to oscillatorian cyanobacteria is well illustrated by the example of the planktonic organism now known as *Oscillatoria redekei.* It produces trichomes with undifferentiated tips, the cells contain small polar gas vacuoles, and trichome breakage is intercellular (318). This organism has none of the characters of an *Oscillatoria* and resembles in most respects a typical *Pseudanabaena.*

Although the mechanism of trichome breakage can sometimes be deduced from light microscopy observations, electron microscopy is often necessary to establish it unambiguously. Therefore, a systematic comparative survey of oscillatorian cyanobacteria by electron microscopy must be conducted to determine the distribution of the two mechanisms of trichome breakage within the group.

Heterocystous Subgroups

Although the properties of the heterocyst (discussed later) have been intensively studied in a few strains of *Anabaena,* there is very little comparative cultural work on the heterocystous cyanobacteria as a group; the most extensive is a study of many strains (unfortunately only in part axenic) belonging to the *Anabaena-Nostoc* assemblage. These two genera of the nostocaceous subgroup are traditionally distinguished by a gross property often not displayed in culture: the formation by *Nostoc* strains of gelatinous aggregates containing many individual trichomes (117). This cultural study has revealed that all *Nostoc* strains produce hormogonia that are structurally distinguishable (in general, by cell size) from the vegetative trichomes, whereas *Anabaena* strains do not (172). We have confirmed this difference in the pure strains of the *Anabaena-Nostoc* group in our collection (247).

Brief reports on modifications of trichome form in strains of the rivularian subgroup (mostly nonaxenic) as a function of the nitrogen source (NO_3^- or N_2) have appeared (233, 317). Six pure strains of the stigonematalean subgroup have been compared in pure culture (209).

A heterocystous cyanobacterium that has long been in search of a home is the pure strain known as *Chlorogloea* (or *Chlorogloeopsis*) *fritschii,* which is virtually unicellular. A detailed light microscopy study has been made of its patterns of growth under photoautotrophic, photoheterotrophic, and chemoheterotrophic conditions (89). Since this organism can divide in several different successive planes, it belongs to the stigonematalean subgroup as defined here, despite the marked differences in gross structure from such stigonematalean cyanobacteria as *Fischerella* (Figure 7).

THE CYANOBACTERIAL VEGETATIVE CELL

Light microscopy, in view of the inherent limitation of its resolving power, could provide little information about the organization of cyanobacterial cells (118). Consequently, the first studies of these cells by electron microscopy, conducted between 1950 and 1960, revealed many previously unknown structures, the compositions and functions of which were established only much later by analytical work. This led to the development of a provisional terminology: for example, the successive layers of the cell envelope were identified by Roman numerals. Since it is now evident that many (though not all) elements of structure characteristic of the cyanobacterial cell are shared by the cells of other gram-negative prokaryotes, the use of a standard terminology is both possible and desirable. Accepted bacteriological terms will be used insofar as applicable; earlier synonyms peculiar to the cyanobacteriological literature will be noted in parentheses.

General Organization

The vegetative cells of most cyanobacteria have a uniform and distinctive fine structure, represented diagrammatically in Figure 8. Although many cyanobacteria synthesize additional cell envelope layers, the protoplast is always surrounded by a bilayered wall, homologous in structure and composition with that of other gram-negative prokaryotes. It consists of an inner homogeneous layer and an outer layer with the fine structure of a unit membrane. The cell membrane (plasmalemma) is usually simple; mesosomal infoldings have been observed (12, 165, 318) but appear to be rare. Much of the protoplast is occupied by the components of the photosynthetic apparatus. Except in *Gloeobacter* (discussed below), the photosynthetic apparatus is located in a series of flattened, membranous sacs or thylakoids, which are the site of the lipophilic pigments (chlorophyll *a* and carotenoids), the photochemical reaction centers, and the photosynthetic electron transport chain

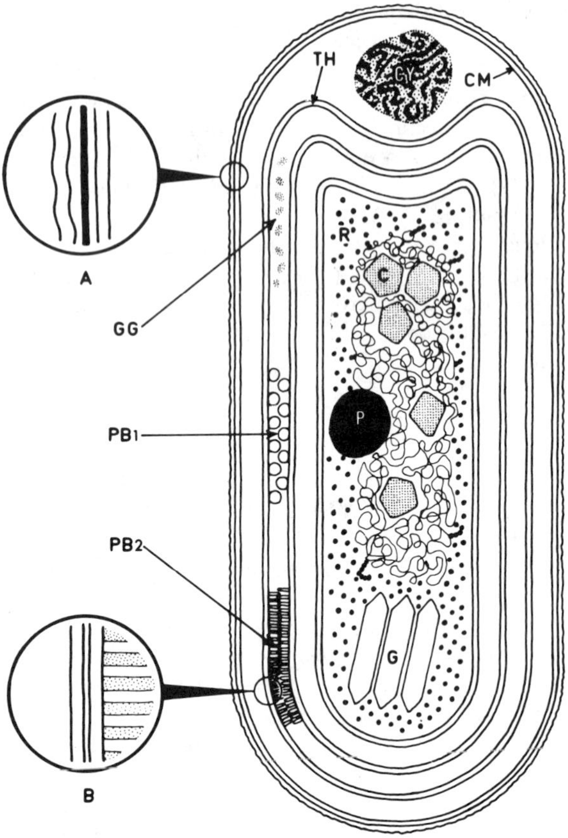

Figure 8 Schematic diagram of cyanobacterial vegetative cell. CM, Cell membrane; TH, thylakoid; PB1 and PB2, front and side views, respectively, of two rows of phycobilisomes, attached to adjacent thylakoids; GG, glycogen granules; CY, cyanophycin granule; P, polyphosphate granule; R, 70*S* ribosomes; C, carboxysome, surrounded by nucleoplasm; G, gas vesicle. (*Insert A*) Enlarged view of cell envelope, showing outer membrane and peptidoglycan wall layers and cell membrane. (*Insert B*) Enlarged view of part of a thylakoid, showing the paired unit membranes with attached phycobilisomes (drawn on one face of thylakoid only).

(179). A special feature of the cyanobacterial photosynthetic apparatus, also characteristic of that of the rhodophytan chloroplast, is the extrathylakoidal location of the phycobiliproteins, which are the major light-harvesting pigments in these two groups. These pigments are contained in organelles known as phycobilisomes, attached in regular rows to the outer surfaces of the thylakoids. In cyanobacteria where the phycobilisomes can be individually resolved (71, 88, 113, 193, 323), they are disk-shaped objects, about 40 nm in diameter. Adjacent thylakoids, therefore, are characteristically separated from one another by a space of 50 nm, occupied by contiguous rows of phycobilisomes. Individual phycobilisomes cannot be resolved in thin sections of some unicellular cyanobacteria; the interthylakoidal space is occupied by a seemingly continuous mass of electron-dense material (G. Cohen-Bazire, unpublished observations).

Several thylakoid arrangements occur. The simplest one, characteristic of *Synechococcus* (9, 87) and *Pseudanabaena* (36), is a cortical array of from two to five thylakoids, aligned parallel to another and to the long axis of the cell. In most other cyanobacteria, the thylakoids are convoluted and occupy a considerably larger fraction of the protoplast (187). The relationship, if any, between the cell membrane and the thylakoid membranes is still conjectural. In thin sections, the two membrane systems appear topologically distinct, even in *Synechococcus* and *Pseudanabaena* where interconnections, if present, should be relatively easy to detect. Phycobilisomes are never attached to the inner surface of the cell membrane; this is the best evidence now available that the two membrane systems are functionally distinct.

In the recently described unicellular cyanobacterium *Gloeobacter violaceus* (246), the photosynthetic apparatus has a unique organization. *Gloeobacter* has a typical cyanobacterial pigment complement, although the specific chlorophyll content of the cells is unusually low (about 25–30% of that in other unicellular cyanobacteria). It does not contain thylakoids: the only unit membrane is a cell membrane without intrusions, presumably the site of the components associated with the thylakoidal membranes of other cyanobacteria. Attached to the inner surface of the cell membrane is a continuous electron-dense cortical layer about 80 nm wide, which contains the phycobiliproteins.

Four classes of inclusions appear to be universally present in the vegetative cells of cyanobacteria: polyphosphate granules; glycogen granules ("α granules"); cyanophycin granules ("structured granules"); and carboxysomes ("polyhedral bodies"). Other inclusions present in the vegetative cells of some but not all cyanobacteria are poly-β-hydroxybutyrate granules and gas vesicles.

All cyanobacteria synthesize glycogen, their principal non-nitrogenous organic reserve material. In cells grown photoautotrophically, it is deposited between the thylakoids as granules too small to be resolved individually by light microscopy (36, 109, 119). Glycogen granules isolated from a *Nostoc* species have been characterized structurally and chemically (56). They are of remarkably uniform size, approximately 31 by 65 nm, and consist of highly branched polyglucosyl units, with short external chains. Poly-β-hydroxybutyrate inclusions have been demonstrated in *Chlorogloeopsis* (47, 169) and *Gloeothece* (243); this prokaryotic reserve polymer does not appear to be synthesized by most cyanobacteria.

Cyanophycin is a nitrogenous organic reserve material of unique chemical structure, probably synthesized by all cyanobacteria but not known to occur in any other biological group. It accumulates when cultures approach the stationary phase of growth, in the form of granules often large enough to be resolved by light microscopy. The tinctorial properties of these granules suggested that they contained an arginine-rich protein (100). Cyanophycin has been recently isolated and chemically characterized (260, 264). It is a highly branched polypeptide, composed of only two amino acids: a polyaspartic acid core, bearing arginyl residues attached to all free carboxyl groups of the core. The molar ratio of arginine: aspartic acid is, accordingly, 1 : 1. The correct chemical name for cyanophycin is multi-L-arginyl-poly-(L-aspartic acid).

The carboxysome, a prokaryotic organelle the existence of which was first revealed by electron microscopy, occurs in several groups of prokaryotes that fix CO_2 via the reductive pentose phosphate pathway (256). Carboxysomes have a characteristic polyhedral profile in thin sections, conferred by the thin, non-unit membrane that surrounds these organelles. The isolation and purification of carboxysomes from *Thiobacillus neapolitanus* led to the discovery that they are filled with closely packed molecules of ribulose diphosphate carboxylase, the enzyme responsible for CO_2 fixation in the reductive pentose phosphate pathway (257, 258).

A systematic survey of many strains of filamentous cyanobacteria, both heterocystous and non-heterocystous, has shown that carboxysomes are always present in vegetative cells, whether grown photoautotrophically, photoheterotrophically, or chemoheterotrophically (279). They are also invariably detectable in thin sections of chroococcacean cyanobacteria (G. Cohen-Bazire, unpublished observations) and pleurocapsalean cyanobacteria (308) grown under photoautotrophic conditions; in these subgroups, the effect of other growth conditions on the carboxysome content of the cells has not been systematically examined. Although cyanobacterial carboxysomes have not yet been purified, sucrose density gradient centrifugation of extracts of *Anabaena* has shown that a considerable fraction of the ribulose diphosphate carboxylase activity bands in a portion of the gradient that is also rich in carboxysomes (65).

The properties of gas vesicles, the structural subunits of the compound organelles known as gas vacuoles, have been recently reviewed (306).

Cell Envelopes

The basic structural and chemical homology of the cyanobacterial cell wall with that of other gram-negative prokaryotes was established by Frank et al (105). The peptidoglycan layer ("L II layer" in the older terminology) varies in width from less than 1 to over 10 nm in different cyanobacteria and, thus, is considerably thicker in many of these organisms than in other gram-negative bacteria. Thin sections often reveal an electron-transparent gap between the membrane and the peptidoglycan layer, which was construed as a distinct wall layer (LI) in early electron microscopy studies. If not an artifact of fixation, it corresponds to the periplasmic space. Compositions of isolated cyanobacterial peptidoglycans, as yet determined for few species (see 81), indicate that they have the type A structure common to nearly all gram-negative bacteria (253).

The outer membrane layer (L IV) contains both proteins and lipopolysaccharides (81). The lipopolysaccharide components of the outer membrane layer have been isolated from a considerable number of cyanobacteria and show a general chemical resemblance to those of other gram-negative bacteria; they contain a variety of sugars and amide-linked β-hydroxy-fatty acids (81a, 312, 313). Though still limited, the qualitative data on the carbohydrate composition of cyanobacterial lipopolysaccharides reveal a considerable diversity and may well provide useful chemotaxonomic markers. The two subgroups in the genus *Synechococcus* that were initially distinguished on the basis of mean DNA base composition (275) appear to be distinguishable likewise by the nature of the sugars in their lipopolysaccharides. Strains with DNA of high (66–71 mol%) guanine + cytosine (G + C) content contain rhamnose as the dominant sugar; ketodeoxyoctonate is absent. Those with DNA of low (48–55 mol%) G + C content contain mannose as the dominant sugar, as well as small amounts of ketodeoxyoctonate (81a).

The gram-negative wall of the cyanobacterial vegetative cell is often surrounded by one or more additional envelope layers, a subject of great terminological confusion. In the older phycological literature, a cell envelope that could be resolved by light microscopy (not possible, at least in living cells, for the gram-negative wall) was termed a "sheath." As far as can be determined from the descriptions of these structures, the same name was applied both to relatively dense envelopes (what the bacteriologist would call a sheath in an organism such as *Sphaerotilus*) and to slime layers (capsules). The problem was complicated by the advent of electron microscopy, for two reasons. First, it is not always easy to relate an outer envelope layer visualized in a thin section to a structure observed by light microscopy in a living cell preparation. Second, thin sections revealed, in many cyanobacteria, one (or several) envelope layer(s) external to the gram-negative cell wall that were too fine to be resolved by light microscopy; although they might be homologous with sheaths, they did not conform to the traditional definition of the light microscopist.

Surprisingly, a clear-cut discrimination in cyanobacteria between what a bacteriologist would call a sheath and a capsule seems to have been made for the first time in 1974 (210). Many cyanobacteria excrete considerable quantities of slime or mucilage; since analysis of the spent medium with the anthrone reagent reveals the presence of sugars, it is probable that most or all of these compounds are polysaccharides, although none of them has yet been well-characterized chemically (25, 26, 250). If this material is relatively soluble in water, it becomes dispersed through the surrounding medium and may make liquid cultures highly viscous, or even gelatinous; however, no technique of examination will reveal it as a discrete envelope layer. On the other hand, if it is a substance of limited water solubility, it will accumulate around cells or trichomes and can be readily revealed by negative staining in conjunction with light microscopy as a wide, homogeneous, clear area, usually with a somewhat diffuse outer boundary, enclosing the more refractile cells or filaments (210). If sufficiently abundant, the slime may unite many individual cells or trichomes into aggregates. In the phycological taxonomic treatment of cyanobacteria, the formation of such aggregates has been used as the sole criterion to separate certain genera (e.g. *Aphanothece, Aphanocapsa*) from genera composed of their non-aggregate-forming structural counterparts (118).

Cell envelopes external to the gram-negative cell wall but distinguishable from the slime layer are now considered. These envelopes appear to be diverse both in fine structure and in mode of formation: nothing is yet known about their chemical composition. In the chroococcacean genera *Gloeothece* (243), *Gloeobacter* (246), and *Microcystis* (175), very thin envelopes unite groups of cells into aggregates. As far as can be deduced from electron microscopy observations, each envelope develops initially around a single cell, in close juxtaposition to the outer membrane layer of the gram-negative wall. It remains entire after the division of the enclosing cell and becomes detached from the outer membrane, expanding to accommodate the growing population of cells that it encloses, until it is eventually ruptured. In *Gloeothece,* the enclosed cells synthesize new layers of the same material to produce characteristic multilayered aggregates.

In all pleurocapsalean cyanobacteria, the vegetative cells synthesize a fibrous outer wall layer, always closely adherent to the gram-negative cell wall and therefore rarely resolvable by light microscopy as a separate structure (308, 309). This layer thickens throughout cell growth. It does not participate in transverse wall formation and thus encloses both daughter cells. Once division is complete, each daughter cell begins to synthesize a new layer of the same material.

The sheaths of many trichome-forming cyanobacteria have a similar fibrous fine structure (135). They are usually open-ended tubes, surrounding a trichome of cells individually enclosed only by gram-negative cell walls (210). In *Fischerella,* a member of the stigonematalean subgroup, this fibrous material, initially having the form of a tubular sheath, subsequently extends inward between adjacent cells of the trichome and may eventually surround some of them completely (294).

Gliding Movement

The mechanism of gliding movement still remains one of the major unsolved problems of prokaryotic cell biology. A study by Halfen & Castenholz (137–140) on *Oscillatoria princeps* has furnished by far the most detailed phenomenological description of gliding movement in any prokaryote, as well as highly suggestive information concerning its possible mechanism (137, 138).

The very wide (35 μm) trichomes of *O. princeps* are surrounded by a thin sheath, shed as a collapsed strand behind the advancing trichome. In the absence of substrate contact, the sheath material as it is excreted is displaced over the immobilized trichome and may accumulate in rings, a phenomenon also described in *Anabaena cylindrica* (304). Both groups of observers conclude that this structure has no role in mediating movement; its displacements are a consequence, not a cause, of locomotion. Other observations support the conclusion that the locomotor system must be interior to the outer membrane layer of the wall; the short trichomes of *Pseudanabaena* strains, which glide very rapidly, are surrounded by envelopes composed only of the peptidoglycan and outer membrane layers (G. Cohen-Bazire, unpublished observations).

Gliding movement of *O. princeps* is accompanied by rotation: a surface point at any place on the circumference of the trichome describes a right-handed helix with a pitch of 60° as the trichome advances or retreats. This pitch is invariant, being unchanged by velocity, temperature, trichome length, or the consistency of the substrate. Freeze-etching reveals the presence of a continuous layer of fibrils in parallel array between the peptidoglycan and outer membrane layers of the wall, probably attached to the inner surface of the outer membrane layer (139). Each fibril is 6–9 nm in diameter, and the whole system is arranged as a right-handed helix with a pitch of 60°. Another species, *Oscillatoria animalis,* also contains such a system but is arranged as a left-handed helix with a pitch of 60°. In contrast to *O. princeps,* rotation of the trichome of *O. animalis* is left-handed with a 60° pitch. Therefore, the circumstantial evidence strongly suggests that this fibrillar system within the wall is the locomotor organelle (see also 137). As postulated by Jarosch (168), torsion-induced waves in such a fibrillar system could account for movement. The very restricted conditions under which gliding movement is possible in pleurocapsalean cyanobacteria are also worthy of note: only baeocytes that lack a continuous enclosing fibrous outer wall layer can glide (308, 309). This suggests that direct contact of the outer membrane layer with a solid substrate is indispensable for displacement of the cell.

The Photosynthetic Apparatus

EFFECT OF ENVIRONMENTAL FACTORS ON SYNTHESIS AND FUNCTION

During photosynthetic growth, a major part of the protein synthesized by the cyanobacterial cell is incorporated into the photosynthetic apparatus: the phycobiliproteins (PBPs) alone, which are specifically located in the phycobilisomes, may account for almost 50% of total protein in some cyanobacteria (291).

Growth of facultatively heterotrophic strains in the dark, even for prolonged periods, does not lead to a loss of photosynthetic function: synthesis of both chlorophyll and PBPs is maintained, and transfer to a mineral medium in the light is often followed by a resumption of photoautotrophic growth with little, if any, lag (242). Some cyanobacteria maintain PBP levels in the dark similar to that in the light; in others, they may be reduced two- to threefold (291). A much more severe reduction of PBP content (20-fold) after prolonged dark growth has been observed in *Chlorogloeopsis* (89). However, in this case, mutation and selection cannot be excluded. Indeed, there must be a very strong selective pressure against gratuitous PBP synthesis in the dark, in view of the burden it imposes on the protein-synthesizing machinery of the cell.

Under photoautotrophic growth conditions, both light intensity and light quality may affect pigment composition. Growth of *Synechococcus* AN in red light decreases the chlorophyll:PBP ratio relative to that in white light (171). Growth with high intensities of white light reduces the cellular content of both chlorophyll and phycocyanin (9, 218). However, there appears to be a relatively high threshold for the intensity effect; at lower light fluxes, both the specific chlorophyll content and the chlorophyll:PBP ratio remain constant in many cyanobacteria over a fivefold change of intensity (291). In many phycoerythrin-containing cyanobacteria, light quality specifically affects the relative differential rates of synthesis of the major PBPs: this phenomenon, chromatic adaptation, is discussed later.

Under conditions otherwise favorable for photoautotrophic growth, nitrogen starvation causes a selective and relatively rapid destruction of PBPs: after 24–30 hr in the light and in the absence of a nitrogen source, the cellular PBP content may fall to 10% of its initial level, whereas the chlorophyll content changes very little (13). Most of the cells remain viable and resynthesize PBPs when again furnished with a nitrogen source, resuming photosynthetic growth when the PBP content approaches a normal level (13). Considerable PBP synthesis will occur if the depleted cells are placed in the dark at the time they are provided with a nitrogen source, even in the absence of an exogenous carbon source (110). Under these conditions, PBP synthesis occurs at the expense of glycogen, accumulated in the cells during the preceding period of nitrogen starvation in the light (N. Tandeau de Marsac, personal communication).

Incubation of cyanobacteria in the light and in the absence of a utilizable carbon source causes a relatively rapid and eventually complete loss of both chlorophyll and PBPs. Surprisingly, the effect is reversible: reintroduction of 5% CO_2 to a suspension of fully bleached *Synechococcus* cells triggered a rapid resynthesis of both chlorophyll and PBPs by the population, with these pigments again becoming detectable as early as 3 hr later (213). Electron microscopy showed that the fully bleached cells were largely devoid of thylakoid membranes; resynthesis of the pigments was accompanied by reappearance of thylakoids. This experimental system obviously offers the best means for studying the problem of thylakoid synthesis.

ISOLATION OF COMPONENTS OF THE PHOTOSYNTHETIC APPARATUS Although phycobilisomes can be isolated in a seemingly intact state by breakage of cells in buffer of high ionic strength in the presence of a detergent and subsequently purified by sucrose density gradient centrifugation (129, 130), no procedure has yet been devised for the isolation and purification of the thylakoids. After breakage of cells in a buffer of low ionic strength, which disaggregates the phycobilisomes, a crude membrane fraction virtually free of PBPs can be obtained by differential centrifugation. It contains, in addition to thylakoid fragments, material derived from the cell wall and cell membrane. The demonstration that lipids, lipophilic pigments, and other membrane components are present in cell-free membrane fractions of this type is accordingly not a conclusive proof that they are exclusively located in the thylakoids. Some components of the photosynthetic electron transport system, presumably located in the thylakoids in the intact cell (e.g. ferredoxins, plastocyanin, and cytochrome *f*), partly or entirely pass into the soluble fraction in extracts prepared with buffers of low ionic strength (179).

CHLOROPHYLL AND CAROTENOIDS Chlorophyll and carotenoids are evidently present in the thylakoids: however, for the reason discussed above, their presence in the cell membrane as well cannot be excluded.

Chlorophyll *a* is the only species of chlorophyll synthesized by cyanobacteria (7). In cells and membrane fractions, its red absorption maximum lies at 680–685 nm (275). Refined spectrophotometric analysis of this absorption band in two cyanobacteria reveals that it is composed of a series of peaks, with absorption maxima at approximately 662, 670, 677, 683, 692, and 705 nm, probably attributable to different chlorophyll *a*-protein complexes (106). The same series of red peaks is demonstrable in chloroplast fractions from a wide diversity of algae and from higher plants (106). This is perhaps one of the most significant homologies between the photosynthetic apparatus of cyanobacteria and of chloroplasts. Some progress towards the isolation of specific chlorophyll-protein complexes from cyanobacteria has been made (reviewed in 293).

Action spectra for photosynthetic oxygen production in cyanobacteria invariably show that light absorbed by chlorophyll *a* is virtually ineffective (e.g. 194). This is a consequence of the fact that the antenna pigments for photosystems I and II are in part distinct; light harvested by chlorophyll is almost exclusively transferred to photosystem I and therefore can mediate only cyclic photophosphorylation, not revealed by the measurement of oxygen production (170).

The work of Jensen and her collaborators (151–153) has clarified the chemistry of cyanobacterial carotenoids. A summary of the carotenoid compositions of many cyanobacteria as determined by modern techniques has been published (153). β-Carotene is invariably present, usually accompanied by either or both of two oxycarotenoids, zeaxanthin and echinone. However, in addition to these three widely distributed carotenoids, most cyanobacteria synthesize group-specific pigments, notably a distinctive class of carotenoid glycosides, esterified with the methyl pentose, rhamnose: structures of several have been established (151, 152). One carotenoid glycoside, oscillaxanthin, accumulates in lake sediments and therefore provides a useful marker of the occurrence of past cyanobacterial blooms (132, 133).

MEMBRANE LIPIDS The membrane lipids of cyanobacteria are both limited in number and distinctive (see 223). There are always four major components: phosphatidyl glycerol; monogalactosyl diglyceride (MGDG); digalactosyl diglyceride (DGDG); and sulfoquinovosyl diglyceride (SQDG). Even though it lacks thylakoids, *Gloeobacter* shares this lipid pattern (B. Nichols, personal communication). The three glycolipids MGDG, DGDG, and SQDG are invariably and specifically associated with the chloroplast membrane system in eukaryotic cells; none occurs in the membranes of purple bacteria (73), and only MGDG occurs in green bacteria where it is specifically localized in the light-harvesting organelle or chlorobium vesicle (74).

In all chloroplasts, the lipids are largely esterified with polyunsaturated fatty acids, principally linolenic acids; either the α or γ insomer (C18:3α, C18:3γ) may predominate (221). These particular polyunsaturated fatty acids are restricted to the chloroplasts in eukaryotes. On the other hand, most prokaryotes (including purple and green bacteria) are unable to synthesize polyunsaturated fatty acids; their cellular lipids are esterified only with saturated and mono-unsaturated fatty acids (73). Hence, the fatty acid composition of cyanobacteria is a subject of great comparative biochemical interest, and extensive analytical data bearing on this point have been published (159, 173, 174), which reveal an extraordinary chemical diversity within the group. Certain cyanobacteria have fatty acid compositions of the chloroplast types, with a high proportion of polyunsaturated C18 fatty acids, with a predominance of either C18:3α or C18:3γ. Some do not contain C18:3 fatty acids but have a high content of linoleic acid (C18:2). Many cyanobacteria also conform more or less strictly to the general prokaryotic rule; their lipids are esterified with saturated and mono-unsaturated fatty acids, sometimes accompanied by traces of linoleic acid. A recent study of the fatty acid composition of pleurocapsalean cyanobacteria (C. Kenyon, personal communication) has revealed a high frequency in this subgroup of an unusual pattern, very rare among other cyanobacteria: a high concentration of polyunsaturated C16 fatty acids, which replace completely polyunsaturated fatty acids of the C18 series.

In cyanobacteria, the cellular complement of fatty acids is a strain (or species)-specific property little affected by changing of growth conditions (173). Therefore, it is a taxonomically useful phenotypic character (173, 174).

PBP PBPs, chromoproteins localized in phycobilisomes (129), are the major light-harvesting pigments in all cyanobacteria and also in red algae. Only wavelengths of light absorbed by the PBPs are effective in photosynthetic oxygen production; all spectral classes of PBPs in the cell are active in harvesting light energy (194). Although the light energy they absorb appears to be transferred primarily to photosystem II, it can also feed into photosystem I (170).

The chemical structure of PBPs was obscure until very recently; however, intensive studies during the past 5 years on these proteins, isolated from cyanobacteria (20, 41, 58, 72, 120, 122, 123, 136, 223), from red algae (115, 127, 302), and from cryptomonads (8, 38, 124, 125, 205, 224), have led to a much clearer understanding of their distinctive common properties. Each native PBP is built up from monomers with an $\alpha\beta$ structure, composed of two different polypeptide chains (α and β), usually of slightly different molecular weights. Each polypeptide chain carries at least one bilin chromophore, covalently attached to it. The native proteins are oligomers, with the general structure $(\alpha\beta)_n$.

All cyanobacteria contain at least three different types of PBPs (122): phycocyanin (PC; λ_{max}, 620 nm); allophycocyanin (AP; λ_{max}, 650 nm), and allophycocyanin B (APB; λ_{max}, 670 nm). The relative abundances are always PC $>$ AP $>>$ APB. Irrespective of source, each of these cyanobacterial PBPs has a constant and characteristic absorption spectrum (72, 120, 122). Many cyanobacteria also synthesize a fourth type of PBP, with an absorption maximum at shorter wavelength. This pigment is usually a phycoerythrin (PE; λ_{max}, 565 nm); cyanobacterial PEs may differ considerably in spectral character (20, 123, 246). Some *Anabaena* strains synthesize a newly discovered type of PBP, phycoerythrocyanin (PEC; λ_{max}, 565 nm, shoulder at 590 nm), which appears to have a very restricted biological distribution (41).

The red algal chloroplast contains PBPs of all classes that occur in cyanobacteria, except PEC (A. Ley, D. A. Bryant, A. N. Glazer, and W. Butler, personal communication). The close molecular homologies between cyanobacterial and red algal PBPs belonging to the same class (e.g. PEs) are shown by their invariably very strong immunological cross-reactivities (22, 27, 126). In cryptomonads, only one PBP (either a PE or a PC) is present in any given strain. These pigments are not located in phycobilisomes and do not cross-react immunologically with PEs or PCs of red algae and cyanobacteria (22, 125). Nevertheless, N-terminal amino acid sequence analyses reveal that the α and β subunits of all PBPs share some degree of homology, and that the α and β polypeptides are themselves homologous (121; A. N. Glazer and G. S. Apell, personal communication).

The recent work on PBPs has made it possible to define the different classes, originally distinguished solely by their spectral properties, in terms of molecular parameters: the molecular weights of the α and β chains and the number and nature of the chromophores attached to each; the N-terminal sequences; and the native molecular weight (i.e. the oligomeric state). In addition to its evident evolutionary interest, this work has laid the ground for studies on the synthesis of PBPs and its regulation.

CHROMATIC ADAPTATION Chromatic adaptation, recently reviewed (29), is peculiar to certain cyanobacteria that contain PE. The quality of light to which cultures are exposed during growth markedly affects the PE:PC ratio, which is far higher after growth in green light than after growth in red light; cells grown in white light usually have an intermediate PE:PC ratio.

An extensive comparative survey (291) has confirmed earlier reports that some PE-containing cyanobacteria do not show the response: in such species (a minority of the 44 strains studied), the cellular PE:PC ratio is unmodified by growth in green, red, and white light, or by growth in the dark in the case of facultative chemoheterotrophs. Among species that do adapt chromatically, two types of response can be distinguished. In some, only the differential rate of PE synthesis is modulated, being far higher in green than in red light. In others, both PE and PC synthesis are subject to photoregulation: the differential rate of PE synthesis is higher and that of PC synthesis is lower in green than in red light. In many strains of the latter group, the photoregulation of PE synthesis is stringent: synthesis ceases completely in red light. The control of PC synthesis is always relaxed, continuing at a relatively low rate in green light. The cellular PBP composition of dark-grown chromatically adapting strains that are chemoheterotrophs is identical with that after growth in red light. The effector that modulates PBP synthesis thus appears to be specifically activated by green light. A pigment that is a possible candidate for the effector has been detected, in minute quantities, in cell-free extracts, but it has not been purified (251). Radioisotopic experiments (21) show conclusively that the chromatic response reflects de novo protein synthesis: therefore, control is almost certainly transcriptional.

THE PHYCOBILISOME Purified phycobilisomes, both rhodophytan (115) and cyanobacterial (129), were originally reported to contain no proteins other than their constituent PBPs. However, analysis by sodium dodecyl sulfate-polyacrylamide gel electrophoresis has shown that purified phycobilisomes prepared from many different cyanobacteria always contain a small number of colorless proteins (four to eight polypeptides on gels), which account in toto for some 15% of the phycobilisomal protein (292). In cyanobacteria that adapt chromatically, the relative concentrations in isolated phycobilisomes of certain of these colorless polypeptides are markedly affected by the light quality to which the cells have been exposed during growth; the synthesis of these particular colorless proteins is evidently subject, like that of the major PBPs, to photoregulation.

Analysis of the fluorescence properties of isolated phycobilisomes (112, 114, 129) has confirmed the inference that the constituent PBPs constitute an energy transfer chain. Monochromatic light of short wavelength (546 nm) absorbed by the PE of the phycobilisome is re-emitted as fluorescence of a much longer wavelength (675–680 nm). At the time when this observation was made, the existence of APB was unknown, and the long wavelength fluorescence was attributed to AP; however, it corresponds much better to the fluorescence emission spectrum of APB (122).

PROTEINS OF THE ELECTRON TRANSPORT CHAIN Ferredoxins (289, 290, 303), plastocyanin (3), and cytochrome *f* (5, 15) have been characterized from cyanobacteria. Partial or complete primary structures have been determined, which reveal extensive homologies with the isofunctional proteins from photosynthetic eukaryotes (4, 141).

The Genome: Molecular Properties

The extremely wide variation of DNA base composition among cyanobacteria was shown by the first measurements, conducted on a small number of strains belonging to nearly all subgroups (86). Subsequent analyses of the DNAs of many chroococcacean strains confirmed this molecular diversity (275). The previously limited data for other subgroups have been much augmented recently (148). Moreover, the range of genome size, for which only one value had been previously published (149), has now been determined by measurements on a large number of strains belonging to all subgroups (148). Since these data have not yet been published in extenso, a summary of the results is presented in Table 2.

With respect to mean DNA base composition, wide total spans (>25 mol% G + C) are characteristic only of chroococcacean and oscillatorian cyanobacteria. The spans are remarkably narrow (less than 10 mol% G + C) both for pleurocapsalean cyanobacteria and for the heterocystous cyanobacteria in their entirety; the

Table 2 A summary of the data on cyanobacterial DNA base compositions and genome sizes[a]

Subgroup	Mean DNA base composition (mol% G + C)		Genome size ($\times 10^9$ daltons)	
	Extreme limits	Span	Extreme limits	Mean
Chroococcacean	35–71 (57)	36	1.6–4.9 (32)	2.4
Pleurocapsalean	41–47 (12)	6	2.9–4.6 (11)	3.5
Oscillatorian	41–67 (47)	26	1.9–4.6 (24)	3.6
All heterocystous subgroups[b]	38–47 (41)	9	3.0–7.6 (20)	4.6

[a] All values for genome size and many for DNA base composition are from Herdman (148; detailed reports in preparation). Other DNA base composition values are from Stanier et al (275; M. Mandel, unpublished data). The numbers in parentheses indicate the total number of strains analyzed.

[b] Subgroups: 22 nostocacean, 11 rivularian, 9 stigonematalean.

ranges for the two latter assemblages are closely similar. Somewhat surprisingly, therefore, the groups that are most complex and internally diverse in structural and developmental respects show little internal divergence in mean DNA base composition. In chroococcacean cyanobacteria, on the other hand, both the principal form genera, *Synechococcus* and *Synechocystis,* include organisms of markedly disparate mean DNA base composition. Furthermore, in these two genera, there are sharp internal discontinuities with respect to DNA base composition (275).

The data on genome size also present some interesting features. First, the total span of genome size is remarkably wide, extending from 1.6–7.6 $\times$ 10^9 daltons. Second, there are marked differences between subgroups in genome size. With few exceptions, chroococcacean cyanobacteria have comparatively small genomes (mean value, 2.4 $\times$ 10^9 daltons). The mean values for pleurocapsalean and oscillatorian cyanobacteria are considerably higher (about 3.5 $\times$ 10^9 daltons). The highest mean value (4.6 $\times$ 10^9 daltons) occurs among heterocystous cyanobacteria; this assemblage also contains two strains with exceptionally large genomes ($>7 \times 10^9$ daltons).

A histone-like protein, HU, which binds DNA nonspecifically, has been recently characterized in *Escherichia coli* (249). DNA binding proteins of closely similar amino acid composition, which cross-react immunologically with HU, have been isolated from a chroococcacean and from a nostocacean cyanobacterium (144).

The Machinery of Transcription and Translation

The DNA-dependent RNA polymerase of *Synechococcus* AN has been purified and characterized with respect to subunit composition (155). The active enzyme has been reconstituted from its subunits; interestingly, attempts at hybrid reconstitution, by using various combinations of subunits from the enzymes of *Synechococcus* AN and *E. coli,* all failed to yield a catalytically active protein (154).

Functional 30*S* and 50*S* ribosomal subunits have been isolated from *Synechococcus* AN: when added in equimolar quantities to a system containing tRNA's and the required enzymes from *E. coli,* together with polyuridylic acid, they mediate incorporation of [^{14}C]phenylalanine into trichloroacetic acid-insoluble material (131). Reconstitution experiments, with 30*S* and 50*S* subunits prepared from *Synechococcus* AN and *E. coli,* showed that both heterologous combinations are functional in the test system employed.

A cell-free system that incorporates ^{14}C-labeled amino acids into proteins has been prepared from *Anabaena variabilis* and partly characterized, with respect to amino acid activation, cofactor requirements, and antibiotic sensitivity (192). Both synthetic and natural mRNA's were effective, and the system was used to determine the mean half-life of mRNA, estimated to be 12 min.

A start has been made on the characterization of the tRNA's of *Synechococcus* AN (18, 84). The leucine, serine, and methionine tRNA's of this organism and of *E. coli* are functionally interchangeable. Like other prokaryotes, *Synechococcus* AN contains tranformylase, and its major methionine tRNA, when charged with methionine, is a substrate for this enzyme (84). The transformylase of *E. coli* will also formylate this methionyl-tRNA.

Characterization of 23*S*, 16*S*, and 5*S* ribosomal RNAs from a variety of cyanobacteria (228) has been followed by several studies on the synthesis and maturation of rRNA and post-maturational cleavage of 23*S* RNA (79, 255, 284). The most unexpected result of these studies has been the discovery of marked light effects on RNA metabolism, first (265) in *Synechococcus* AN, an obligate photoautotroph, and later in other chroococcacean strains (30), both obligate and facultative. Under nongrowing conditions in the dark, all these organisms produce one or more stable RNA species not present among the long-term-labeled RNAs of illuminated cultures; in *Synechococcus* AN, the RNA species in question undergo a rapid degradation (inhibited by chloramphenicol) when cells are re-illuminated. At least some of these RNA species are nonribosomal, and it has been suggested that they may represent stable mRNA's (30).

A start has been made on partial sequence analyses of ribosomal 16*S* RNAs from cyanobacteria; oligonucleotide catalogues are available for the 16*S* RNAs of one *Synechococcus* and three *Synechocystis* strains (31, 32). Nearly all the 26 oligonucleotide sequences previously recognized as "universal" in bacterial 16*S* RNAs (325) occur in these cyanobacterial 16*S* RNAs. The cyanobacterial 16*S* RNAs also show a high degree of homology with the 16*S* (chloroplast) RNA of the red alga *Porphyridium* and a somewhat lesser one with *Euglena* 16*S* RNA. On the other hand, the 18*S* (cytoplasmic) RNA of *Porphyridium* shows no detectable homologies either with chloroplast or with cyanobacterial 16*S* RNAs. The evolutionary implications of these findings are evident.

THE CONTROL OF GENE EXPRESSION IN CYANOBACTERIA Although end-product repression of the enzymes that mediate amino acid biosynthesis is widespread, and perhaps universal, in chemoheterotrophic bacteria, end-product repression does not seem to control the pathways of arginine (160) and valine, and leucine and isoleucine (161), biosynthesis in *Anabaena variabilis.* Moreover, most of the enzymes operative in the central pathways of carbon metabolism do not change significantly in level when cyanobacteria are shifted from photoautotrophic to chemoheterotrophic growth conditions (e.g. 237). Extrapolating from these facts, Carr (48) has postulated that gene expression in cyanobacteria is in general not regulated at the transcriptional level and suggests that this may be an important factor in determining their dependence on photoautotrophy as a dominant or exclusive mode of life.

In any microbial assemblage, the present pattern of control of gene expression—which is group specific—has been gradually molded by specific environmental pressures exerted over the whole course of its evolution. It is reasonable to expect that biological groups as different as cyanobacteria and enterobacteria, in terms of the specific evolutionary pressures to which they have been subjected, would have evolved markedly different patterns of control, governing different facets of the cellular machinery. Carr (48) was the first to emphasize this important point in the particular context of the cyanobacteria. However, it is hard to imagine that any free-living microbial group could survive if its members were wholly unable to regulate gene expression.

In fact, a fair number of proteins are now known to be subject to induction or repression in cyanobacteria. Control is probably at the transcriptional level, although this has not been directly shown in any case. The list includes nitrogenase (e.g. 220), nitrate and nitrite reductases (207), glucose-6-phosphate dehydrogenase (239), glycogen phosphorylase (266), and (in some) phycocyanin and phycoerythrin (291). Singer & Doolittle (266) have recently shown that a light-dark transition causes numerous changes in the pattern of protein synthesis in the obligate photoautotroph *Synechococcus* AN. Differential labeling with [^{14}C]- and [^{3}H]leucine of a leucine auxotroph, followed by sodium dodecyl sulfate-polyacrylamide gel electrophoresis of the soluble proteins, revealed at least 12 polypeptides that are either synthesized exclusively in the dark or synthesized at far higher rates following a light-dark transition. These results leave no doubt that the control of gene expression is extensive, even in obligately photoautotrophic strains.

SPECIALIZED CELLS

The Heterocyst

Heterocysts can be readily distinguished from vegetative cells by three structural properties, evident by light microscopy: they are enclosed by a thick outer envelope; they are weakly pigmented; and they contain, near each junction with a vegetative cell, a conspicuous refractile granule. A heterocyst that has developed from the terminal cell of a trichome consequently contains only one polar granule, whereas a heterocyst that has developed from an intercalary cell contains two. In stigonematalean cyanobacteria, rare heterocysts that have developed from a cell at a branch point contain three (167).

The ability to form heterocysts is invariably associated with a physiological property that is extremely rare in non-heterocystous cyanobacteria: the capacity for nitrogen fixation under aerobic conditions (103). The profound physiological paradox implicit in the ability of any cyanobacterium to fix nitrogen could not be recognized until the uniform and distinctive properties of nitrogenase had been established through comparative enzymological studies (75). All nitrogenases, irrespective of biological source, are rapidly and irreversibly denatured by exposure in vitro to molecular oxygen. Nitrogen fixation and oxygenic photosynthesis, therefore, are seemingly incompatible cellular processes. In 1969, Stewart et al (280) put forward a hypothesis that attempted to resolve this paradox for the particular case of heterocystous cyanobacteria. They proposed that the heterocyst, for which no function was then known, plays a special role in aerobic fixation: it has an ensemble of properties, not shared by vegetative cells, that enables it to maintain nitrogenase in an active form, even in an oxygen-rich external milieu, and thus to serve as the specific cellular site of nitrogen fixation within the trichome. A corollary of this hypothesis is that the vegetative cells become dependent upon a transfer of fixed nitrogen from the heterocyst, when the trichome grows in the absence of a combined nitrogen source.

Although based originally on relatively limited circumstantial evidence, this hypothesis had two major virtues: it accounted satisfactorily for a large number of isolated and previously unintelligible facts about heterocysts; and it immediately suggested a whole series of new experiments. Subsequent work has confirmed its essential correctness, which will be assumed throughout the following discussion. It should be noted that nearly all the critical information we now possess about heterocysts has been obtained through work on a very limited range of strains, all of the nostocacean subgroup and all belonging to one genus, *Anabaena.*

THE RELATION BETWEEN HETEROCYST FORMATION AND NIF GENE EXPRESSION The *nif* genes, which encode the machinery of nitrogen fixation, are subject in all nitrogen-fixing prokaryotes to end-product repression by ammonia (37). Removal of an exogenous combined nitrogen source, which depletes the intracellular ammonia pool, is necessary to trigger transcription and translation of the *nif* genes and thus to elicit expression of the capacity to fix nitrogen. For brevity, this treatment will be termed *induction.* As first shown by Fogg (99), heterocyst differentiation is subject to the same inductive control. Cultures of heterocystous cyanobacteria grown in the presence of an excess of nitrate or ammonia are virtually or completely devoid of heterocysts: ammonia is usually the more effective exogenous repressor of heterocyst development. Some hours after withdrawal of a combined nitrogen source from a medium otherwise favorable for growth, a fraction of the vegetative cells in the trichomes (generally 5–10%) differentiate into heterocysts. Kinetic studies on the induction of *Anabaena* strains under aerobic conditions in the light show a close correlation between the appearance of mature heterocysts and the development of nitrogenase activity (180, 220). However, when induction occurs in the light under strictly anaerobic conditions [maintained by treating the filament suspension with the herbicide dichlorophenyl methyl urea, which inhibits photosystem II activity], the results are markedly different (245). Nitrogenase becomes detectable considerably earlier than in aerobic controls, and eventually it attains a specific activity that is 10- to 20-fold greater. Although heterocysts begin to differentiate, the process is arrested at an early (proheterocyst) stage, shortly after the formation of the heterocyst envelope has started. The admission of air to the filament suspension after maximal nitrogenase activity has been attained causes rapid, total, and irreversible loss of this activity. These observations show that immature heterocysts (proheterocysts) cannot protect nitrogenase from oxygen inactivation, and also, they strongly suggest that under anaerobic conditions both vegetative cells and heterocysts synthesize nitrogenase. The ability of vegetative cells of *Anabaena* to synthesize nitrogenase has been confirmed by anaerobic induction experiments on spontaneous mutants, which are completely unable to form heterocysts. Although such mutants cannot fix nitrogen aerobically, they develop high levels of nitrogenase when induced in the absence of oxygen (R. Rippka, personal communication).

HETEROCYST DIFFERENTIATION Electron microscopy of thin sections of developing (321) and mature (186) heterocysts of *Anabaena* spp. has revealed the great complexity of the changes that occur. The heterocyst envelope, which develops outside the vegetative cell wall, is composed of three ultrastructurally distinguishable layers, a fibrous outer layer, a homogeneous middle layer, and a laminated inner layer, which appear in this temporal sequence. As the two inner envelope layers are formed, the initially rounded cell pole in contact with the adjacent vegetative cell changes into a short, narrow tubular neck, around which the two inner envelope layers are particularly thick. This modification of cell form reduces the contact with the adjacent vegetative cell to a small, flattened area at the end of the tubular neck; very fine cell-to-cell connections (microplasmodesmata) can be resolved in the contiguous walls of the two cells. These changes in the polar region are accompanied by a profound reorganization of the whole cellular system of internal membranes, which eventually leads to a concentration of heavily convoluted membranes near the base of the neck region. A large inclusion (or sometimes several smaller ones) is formed in this region, often extending into, and almost filling, the tubular neck. This is the refractile structure or "polar granule" resolvable by light microscopy. Although polar granules have not been characterized chemically by modern methods, Fogg (100) showed many years ago by cytochemical means that they are arginine rich. In the light of subsequent knowledge (260), this constitutes strong presumptive evidence that they are composed of cyanophycin. Mature heterocysts are devoid of carboxysomes (279). A schematic drawing of part of a mature heterocyst and its relation to an adjacent vegetative cell is shown in Figure 9.

BIOCHEMICAL ASPECTS OF HETEROCYST DIFFERENTIATION Thanks to their special envelopes, heterocysts are completely resistant to lysozyme, which lyses vegetative cells (92), and are also far more resistant than vegetative cells to breakage by ultrasound (93). Highly purified heterocyst suspensions, therefore, can be prepared after differential breakage of the vegetative cells by either treatment and subjected to analysis.

Heterocysts maintain a significant content of chlorophyll *a,* but they are essentially devoid of PBPs (90, 330). Under induction conditions, a major destruction of PBPs occurs in all the cells of the filament population (220); this is a universal consequence of prolonged nitrogen starvation in cyanobacteria (13). Evidently, no resynthesis takes place in the heterocysts as they mature, even though in the presence of N_2 they can replenish the internal nitrogen supply. Therefore, a total shut-down of PBP synthesis in the presence of fixed nitrogen (repression of transcription of the encoding genes?) is one major change in the normal pattern of protein synthesis that accompanies differentiation. The vegetative cells, on the other hand, begin to resynthesize PBPs as soon as they receive fixed nitrogen from the heterocyst. In the presence of N_2, therefore, the PBP content of the filament population returns to a near normal level after the onset of nitrogen fixation (221). The intense and characteristic fluorescence of phycocyanin permits the observation of resynthesis in individual filaments by fluorescence microscopy. Early in the process, the vegetative cells display a marked fluorescence gradient; those nearest the heterocysts are most highly fluorescent (301).

Isolated heterocysts do not contain the three glycolipids that are the major neutral lipids of the membranes of vegetative cells (307). A profound molecular reorganization, therefore, accompanies the restructuring of the internal membrane system revealed by electron microscopy. They do, however, contain a series of glycolipids not present in vegetative cells (42). These compounds, which appear to be located

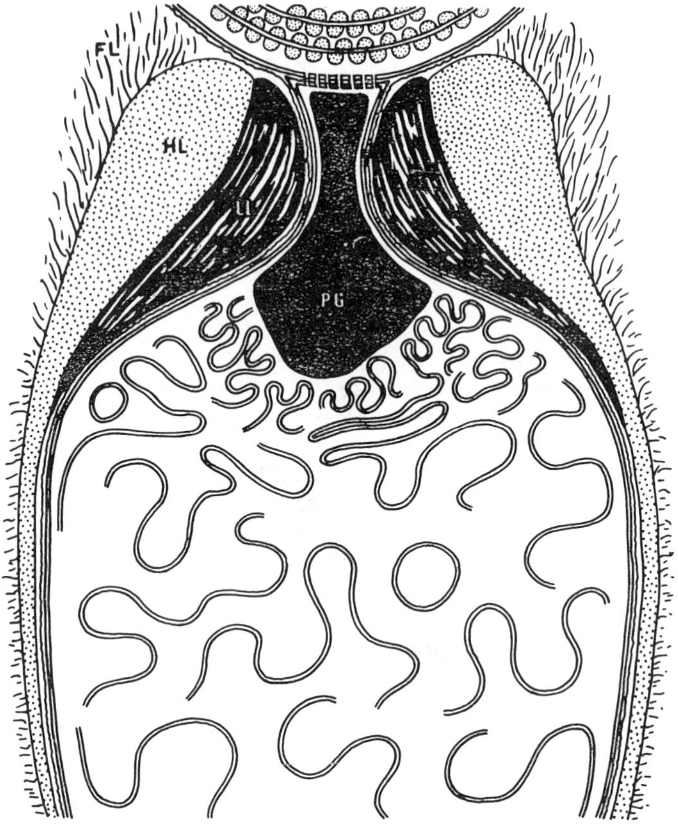

Figure 9 Schematic diagram of part of a mature heterocyst, showing the polar connection to an adjacent vegetative cell (at top) through a series of fine pores. PG, Polar granule of cyanophycin; FL, fibrous layer; HL, homogeneous layer; LL, laminated layer of the heterocyst envelope.

in the laminated envelope layer (324), have been recently characterized (182, 202). They are closely related chemically; the major species is the glycosylated derivative of a C_{26} unbranched alcohol, 3:25-hexacosanediol.

The heterocyst envelopes also have a high carbohydrate content; the constituent sugars are glucose (glc), mannose (man), galactose, and xylose (83). Structural studies on this envelope polysaccharide suggest that its chain consists of repeating units of glc→glc→glc→man, all in β-1,3 linkage, with each glycosyl residue having another sugar attached to it (45).

A first insight into the changing patterns of protein synthesis that accompany heterocyst development has been obtained by pulse-labeling and chase experiments with $^{35}SO_4^{=}$. The proteins of the vegetative cells and the heterocysts were then extracted by differential cell breakage and subjected to sodium dodecyl sulfate-polyacrylamide gel electrophoresis; the polypeptides were revealed by autoradiography and by staining (96). The synthesis of many proteins of the vegetative cell is arrested early in heterocyst development, and new classes appear. The technique employed does not permit a determination of catalytic function, but the subunits of nitrogenase have been tentatively identified from their positions on the gels. These polypeptides are synthesized throughout heterocyst development but are detectable in vegetative cells only near the beginning of induction.

The devices by which the heterocyst prevents oxygen inactivation of nitrogenase are probably multiple. Only one is now well established: loss of normal photosynthetic function and, hence, of the capacity for endogenous oxygen formation. This was first suggested by autoradiography of *Anabaena* filaments, after pulse labeling in the light with $^{14}CO_2$ (326), which showed that radioactivity is at first associated only with vegetative cells. Photosystem II activity is not detectable in heterocyst preparations (78). Nevertheless, the relatively high chlorophyll content of mature heterocysts suggests a partial retention of photosynthetic function; this has been confirmed by the demonstration that they possess photosystem I activity (283). In the light, the large amount of ATP required for nitrogen fixation, therefore, is probably generated within the heterocyst by cyclic photophosphorylation. This is also suggested by another piece of evidence: comparison of action spectra for photosynthetic oxygen production and for nitrogen fixation (measured by the rate of acetylene reduction) by intact filaments of *Anabaena* (91). The action spectrum for oxygen production, attributable only to the vegetative cells, reveals the characteristic major contribution by PBPs to light harvesting. The action spectrum for acetylene reduction, on the other hand, shows a major participation of chlorophyll in light harvesting and thus reflects principally photosystem I activity.

To put the matter succinctly, the available information suggests that the mature heterocyst retains a modified photosynthetic apparatus, which is a phenocopy of that of a purple or green bacterium.

A low potential reductant (e.g. reduced ferredoxin) is required in addition to ATP for nitrogen fixation. This cannot be generated photochemically by the heterocyst, which has lost the capacity for noncyclic electron transfer. It must either be acquired directly from adjacent vegetative cells or generated enzymatically within the heterocyst itself, at the expense of an oxidizable substrate (e.g. a sugar or sugar phosphate) furnished by the vegetative cells. With respect to carbon transfer, only two facts are now certain. As revealed by elegant autoradiographic experiments, ^{14}C initially assimilated as $^{14}CO_2$ by vegetative cells in a short pulse is subsequently transferred to heterocysts, and the transfer is intercellular (326). A further fact that has an indirect bearing on the problem of carbon transfer from the vegetative cell to the heterocyst has recently been established by short-term labeling experiments with $^{13}N_2$ (212, 331): fixed nitrogen very rapidly appears in glutamine and is exported as glutamine. To make glutamine, the heterocyst must obtain α-ketoglutarate (or a metabolic precursor of α-ketoglutarate) from the vegetative cell. One additional specific organic requirement can be pinpointed. Deposition of cyanophycin as polar granules requires a substantial supply not only of α-ketoglutarate (source of the arginine carbon skeleton) but also of oxaloacetate (the immediate precursor of aspartate).

PATTERNS OF HETEROCYST DEVELOPMENT The patterns of heterocyst development have so far been studied in a serious fashion only in strains of *Anabaena* (215, 216, 319–322, 328, 329), where heterocysts occur at regular intervals along the trichome. The observations and experiments of Wilcox et al (215, 216, 319–322) are particularly informative, and the main conclusions that emerge from their work are briefly summarized.

1. Not every vegetative cell in the trichome is competent to give rise to a heterocyst. At least in the strain studied by these workers, and under the specific environmental conditions imposed, cell division is visibly asymmetrical, with the two daughter cells differing slightly in size (319). Continuous observations show that, under otherwise favorable conditions, only the smaller daughter cell can become a heterocyst. Therefore, competence is distributed asymmetrically at each succeeding cell division, according to a rule described by Mitchison & Wilcox (215). The fact that all competent cells do not express competence is attributable to the establishment of a gradient of inhibition on either side of each heterocyst; only when a competent cell has been placed outside adjacent inhibitory zones through intercalary growth can it initiate differentiation.
2. The normal pattern of heterocyst spacing is genetically determined; it can be changed by mutation (322). It is also subject to phenotypic perturbation at the level of translation; this can be effected by treatment of cultures with 7-azatryptophan, an analog incorporated into proteins in place of tryptophan (216).
3. Up to a late stage of differentiation, maturing heterocysts can dedifferentiate and resume division, although they do not normally do so in the intact trichome. This cardinal fact was established by studying the behavior of isolated developing heterocysts and of short trichome fragments, composed of a developing heterocyst and one or more vegetative cells, obtained by micromanipulation (321). At any given stage of development, the probability of reversion is an inverse function of the number of vegetative cells to which a developing heterocyst is attached. The possibility of reversion declines as development proceeds and disappears when the heterocyst matures. A mature heterocyst, therefore, is a terminal cell; it has lost the ability to reproduce.

The ultimate irreversibility of heterocyst differentiation raises important questions that are still unanswered. What is the state of the genome in a mature heterocyst? A nucleus cannot be demonstrated by cytochemical means, including Feulgen staining, specific for DNA (100), which suggests (but does not prove) that the heterocyst may be the prokaryotic equivalent of a mammalian erythrocyte. If this is true, neither transcription nor translation can occur, and as a functional entity, the heterocyst must have a comparatively short half-life, determined by the rate of decay of its enzyme complement.

The Akinete

In contrast to the mass of information now available about the heterocyst, knowledge of the akinete is fragmentary and almost entirely descriptive (61, 185). The differentiation of the akinete is accompanied by the formation of a thick, multilayered envelope, often pigmented, around the pre-existing wall of the vegetative cell; the cell as a rule enlarges considerably and changes shape. At the time of maturation, the akinete is still unicellular. However, its germination is accompanied by rapid transverse divisions; when its emerges from the akinete envelope, the germling often consists of a short chain of cells.

Analysis of the akinete envelopes of *Anabaena cylindrica* has shown that they contain a major polysaccharide identical in composition and structure with that of the heterocyst in the same species (182). The first detailed kinetic study of akinete formation, also performed on *A. cylindrica,* was published just in time to be reviewed here (263). In this species, akinetes are almost all formed from vegetative cells adjacent to heterocysts. They are considerably longer and wider than vegetative cells; the increase in length is much greater than the increase in width. An approximate measure of the kinetics of akinete formation, therefore, can be derived from periodic measurements of the average length of cells adjacent to heterocysts; the problem is complicated, however, by the fact that heterocyst differentiation is nonsynchronous. The cell enlargement leading to akinete formation begins during the transition from the logarithmic to the stationary phase, as judged by optical density measurements, but is accompanied by little if any increase of protein in the population.

In *Cylindrospermum,* the heterocysts are almost exclusively terminal, and akinetes develop only from the adjacent, subterminal cells of the trichome. Cultures that have developed akinetes excrete into the medium an unidentified substance(s) that accelerates akinete development when added to cultures in which differentiation has not yet been initiated (95).

METABOLISM

The common nutritional properties of cyanobacteria have been recognized for many decades. All members of this group are aerobic photoautotrophs; the reactions of oxygenic photosynthesis are used to drive biosynthesis at the expense of inorganic nutrients. Some cyanobacteria of marine origin have an obligate requirement for vitamin B_{12} (296, 309); with this exception, no organic growth factor requirements have been demonstrated. In the dark, cyanobacteria display an endogenous respiratory metabolism, which is subject to immediate and severe inhibition in the light (39, 40).

The phenomenon of obligate photoautotrophy is widespread among cyanobacteria. Some are facultative chemoheterotrophs and can grow in the dark at the expense of a limited range of sugars. Dark growth is always much slower than photoautotrophic growth.

During the past 10 years, a reasonably complete explanation of the nutritional properties of cyanobacteria in metabolic terms has emerged from biochemical investigations, which have revealed the distinctive and uniform pathways of light and dark metabolism characteristic of these photosynthetic prokaryotes.

The Relation Between Photosynthetic and Respiratory Metabolism

By analogy, it appeared probable that the photoassimilation of CO_2 in cyanobacteria occurs through the reductive pentose phosphate cycle. However, this inference was not rigorously confirmed until 1972, when Pelroy & Bassham (234) applied the now classical experimental analysis developed by the Calvin School (44) to several chroococcacean cyanobacteria. In every strain examined, the kinetics of entry of radiocarbon into metabolic intermediates during short-term labeling experiments with $^{14}CO_2$ in the light, as well as the pool changes after a light-dark shift, confirmed the operation of the reductive pentose phosphate cycle as the primary pathway of net CO_2 assimilation. The first stable fixation product was identified as a water-insoluble polyglucose with the properties of glycogen.

Like other phototrophs, cyanobacteria must possess metabolic mechanisms that permit survival during the regular dark periods to which they are exposed in nature. The major reserve material accumulated by cyanobacteria in the light is glycogen, and many different types of experimental evidence indicate that maintenance energy is derived in the dark from respiratory metaoolism at the expense of the glycogen pool. Conversion of glycogen to glucose-6-phosphate is followed by oxidation of this sugar phosphate through the oxidative pentose phosphate cycle. Measurement of nucleotide pool levels during the transition from aerobiosis to anaerobiosis in the dark in the obligately photoautotrophic *Synechococcus* AN (24) first showed that endogenous respiration is accompanied by ATP synthesis, and it also suggested that NADP, not NAD, participates in respiratory electron transfer. Cyanobacteria grown under photoautotrophic conditions contain high levels of the two enzymes, glucose-6-phosphate and 6-phosphogluconate dehydrogenase (201, 231, 237, 239), which are necessary, in conjunction with the enzymatic machinery of the reductive pentose phosphate cycle, to mediate the complete oxidation of glucose-6-phosphate through the oxidative pentose phosphate cycle. Both dehydrogenases are NADP specific (237), confirming the role of this pyridine nucleotide in respiratory electron transfer. The exclusive role of the oxidative pentose phosphate cycle in cyanobacterial endogenous respiration has been established by the isolation of a double mutant of the obligate autotroph *Synechococcus* AN, which has lost both dehydrogenases of the cycle. The mutant does not consume detectable quantities of O_2 in the dark (80).

In principle, the primary oxidation of glucose-6-phosphate through the oxidative pentose phosphate pathway could be coupled with a terminal oxidation of pyruvate through the reactions of the tricarboxylic acid cycle. However, the tricarboxylic acid cycle cannot function as a respiratory pathway in cyanobacteria since these organisms do not synthesize α-ketoglutarate dehydrogenase (156, 230, 269). Although they can photoassimilate acetate (157) and convert it to acetyl-CoA (229), acetate is not respired, as a result of the blockage of the tricarboxylic acid cycle at the level of α-ketoglutarate. The remaining enzymes of the tricarboxylic acid cycle, which are synthesized by cyanobacteria (232, 269), consequently have biosynthetic roles, for example, in the formation of amino acids of the glutamate family from α-ketoglutarate (269). The cyanobacteria, like many methylotrophs (76) and chemolithotrophs (85, 269), thus belong to the category of prokaryotes that possess an incomplete tricarboxylic acid cycle.

Dark growth of facultatively chemoheterotrophic cyanobacteria is possible at the expense of a very limited range of organic substrates; glucose is the most common substrate (244), although some facultative heterotrophs cannot use it (166). Investigations of the pathway of glucose utilization by filamentous (60, 231) and unicellular (237) cyanobacteria show that it is respired, like the endogenous carbon reserve, though the oxidative pentose phosphate cycle; much of the glucose taken up in the dark is assimilated and stored as glycogen. The only other organic compounds that have been clearly shown to support dark growth of cyanobacteria are sucrose, fructose, gluconate, ribose, and glycerol (20, 21, 314). In no case has the metabolism of these exogenous substrates been investigated. Since they are all compounds readily convertible to intermediates of the oxidative pentose phosphate cycle, there is no reason to postulate the operation of any other metabolic pathway to account for their utilization.

In principle, glycogen and the carbohydrates utilizable as exogenous substrates by cyanobacteria could also be dissimilated through a fermentative pathway. However, none of the cyanobacteria so far studied appears to be capable of deriving energy by this means. In the dark, growth and sugar utilization cease in the absence of oxygen (237, 242), and under these conditions, no net synthesis of ATP can be demonstrated (235). Oxygen-linked respiration is, accordingly, the only known mechanism for dark ATP synthesis.

As discussed above, one of the distinctive metabolic properties of cyanobacteria is the exclusive role played by NADP as the primary electron acceptor in respiratory electron transport. One aspect of cyanobacterial intermediary metabolism so far completely unexplored is the pathway of electron transport between NADPH and molecular oxygen. The central role of NADP in both photosynthetic and respiratory metabolism suggests that electron transfer to oxygen might proceed largely through the carriers that operate in photosynthetic electron transport. An experimental analysis of this question is badly needed.

All facultatively chemoheterotrophic cyanobacteria can also develop as facultative photoheterotrophs, by using exogenous organic substrates that support dark growth as photosynthetic carbon sources in place of CO_2. This capacity has been revealed by several types of experiments, including the demonstration that an exogenous organic substrate can permit photosynthetic growth either in the complete absence of CO_2 (164) or at a light intensity too low to support photoautotrophic growth (225, 299). The simplest technique to demonstrate facultative photoheterotrophy (242) is to treat cultures with the herbicide, dichlorophenyl methyl urea (DCMU), which, at appropriate concentrations, completely blocks photosystem II activity but leaves photosystem I functional. Under these conditions, ATP synthesis by cyclic photophosphorylation is maintained, but the generation of the photoreductant (NADPH) necessary for CO_2 assimilation is completely arrested. The consequent inhibition of photoautotrophic growth can be overcome by providing the culture with an organic substrate capable of replacing CO_2 as a general source of cell carbon (242). Since the rate of ATP synthesis by cyclic photophosphorylation in the presence of DCMU is far higher than that of respiratory ATP synthesis at the expense of an organic substrate in the dark (235), photoheterotrophic growth of cyanobacteria in the presence of DCMU is much more rapid than dark growth at the expense of the same organic substrate (242). The demonstration of photoheterotrophic growth in the presence of DCMU is, accordingly, the most effective method of screening cyanobacteria for the ability to use organic compounds as general cellular carbon sources (244). An unambiguous demonstration of dark growth at the expense of organic compounds is often difficult, as a result of the extremely low dark growth rates characteristic of many facultatively heterotrophic cyanobacteria.

The Control of Light and Dark Metabolism

The primary pathways of carbon metabolism in the light and in the dark characteristic of cyanobacteria are shown schematically in Figure 10. The very close interconnections are evident: most of the individual step reactions are operative both in the light and in the dark. Only two enzymes, phosphoribulokinase and ribulose diphosphate carboxylase (RUDPC), are specific to the light pathway, and only two, glucose-6-phosphate and 6-phosphogluconate dehydrogenases, are specific to the dark pathway. All the enzymes that mediate the reactions shown are synthesized under both light and dark growth conditions (237). The only enzyme known to be subject to significant control at the level of gene expression is glucose-6-phosphate dehydrogenase; its specific activity often increases considerably during dark growth (237, 239). Furthermore, the machinery of photosynthesis and of respiratory electron transport is synthesized constitutively (237). Hence, the control of the pathways operative in the light and in the dark must be exerted primarily at the level of enzyme function.

Many observations show that such controls do exist and regulate the paths of carbon flow with considerable stringency. One is very old: the demonstration that dark endogenous oxygen uptake is immediately and sharply diminished in the light (40). Light has the same inhibitory effect on the respiration of exogenous glucose; this inhibition is almost completely relieved in the presence of DCMU (237). Two independent lines of evidence identify the first enzyme of the oxidative pathway, glucose-6-phosphate dehydrogenase, as the primary target of the suppression of respiration in the light. When the distribution of ^{14}C among the phosphorylated intermediates of the metabolite pool after labeling with $^{14}CO_2$ in the light has reached equilibrium, a light-dark transition provokes a rapid accumulation of ^{14}C in 6-phosphogluconate, previously undetectable in the pool. The concentration of this compound reaches a maximum after 2 min in the dark and then declines slightly (234). In the obligate photoautotroph *Synechococcus* AN, a mutant with a remarkable phenotype was isolated by Doolittle & Singer (80). It dies rapidly when placed in the dark under conditions otherwise favorable for survival; 90% of the population becomes nonviable within 1 hr. The enzymatic lesion responsible for this behavior

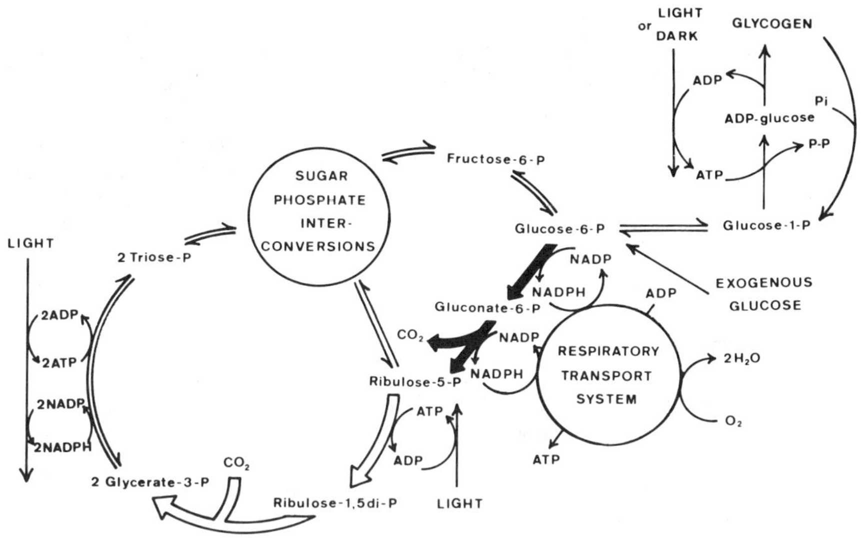

Figure 10 The pathways of light and dark metabolism in cyanobacteria, showing the central role of the pentose phosphate cycle. Heavy black arrows indicate step reactions specifically operative in the dark; heavy white arrows are those specifically operative in the light.

is loss of the second dehydrogenase of the oxidative pathway, 6-phosphogluconate. Phenotypic revertants, selected for dark survival, were all double mutants, which had also lost glucose-6-phosphate dehydrogenase activity. The severely impaired dark survival of the mutant is, accordingly, the consequence of a rapid turn on of glucose-6-phosphate dehydrogenase in the dark, which kills the cell by flooding it with the unmetabolizable product, 6-phosphogluconate.

Therefore, the properties of cyanobacterial glucose-6-phosphate dehydrogenase are of particular interest in terms of metabolic control. A preliminary attempt to identify the effectors that reduce its activity in the light led to the observation that the enzyme in crude, cell-free extracts is very markedly and specifically inhibited by low concentrations of ribulose-1,5-diphosphate (RUDP); no other sugar phosphate has this effect (237). A subsequent study with a partly purified preparation of the enzyme did not reveal any inhibition by RUDP but showed that NADPH is a potent inhibitor (134). Further detailed investigation (F. Schaeffer, personal communication) has failed to resolve the discrepancy: although the inhibition of glucose-6-phosphate dehydrogenase activity by RUDP in crude, cell-free extracts of a variety of cyanobacteria is readily demonstrable, this compound has little or no effect on partly purified preparations. However, Schaeffer's study of the enzyme, partly purified from an *Anabaena* strain, has provided many other insights into its properties. The enzyme exists in solution in three interconvertible molecular forms, probably monomer (M_1), dimer (M_2), and trimer (M_3), to judge from estimations of their respective molecular weights (120,000, 240,000, and approximately 350,000) by gel electrophoresis and sucrose gradient centrifugation. M_2 and M_3 are both catalytically active, M_3 having a higher specific activity than M_2; M_1 is virtually devoid of activity. The activity of the enzyme under any set of conditions, therefore, is determined by the equilibrium $M_1 \rightleftharpoons M_2 \rightleftharpoons M_3$. The interconversion $M_1 \rightleftharpoons M_2$ is influenced by many factors, including enzyme concentration, pH, and at least three effectors: glucose-6-phosphate, glutamine, and NADP. Simple dilution causes a rapid loss of activity, with the equilibrium shifted in favor of M_1: this can be prevented either by glucose-6-phosphate or by glutamine. At pH 7.8 (the optimum for activity), the M_1 state is also favored; the pH optimum for maintenance in an active state is about 6.7. The addition of glucose-6-phosphate to an enzyme preparation shortly after it has become totally inactive as a result of dilution leads, after a lag, to gradual restoration of full activity. Cyanobacterial glucose-6-phosphate dehydrogenase, therefore, belongs to a recently recognized category of enzymes subject to metabolic regulation, the hysteretic enzymes (107). Their catalytic function is governed not by allosteric transitions of the classical type (177) but by relatively slow transitions between forms of different molecular weight and markedly different catalytic activity (181). The glucose-6-phosphate dehydrogenase of chloroplasts appears, on the basis of rather limited information (195, 300), to have the same characteristics as the cyanobacterial enzyme. Purification of these enzymes to homogeneity, impossible until their unusual properties had been recognized, should now be feasible.

The metabolic pool changes that accompany a light-dark transition also reveal a very rapid cut-off of CO_2 fixation (162), which suggests that one of the enzymes specific to the operation of the reductive pentose phosphate cycle may be subject to metabolic regulation in cyanobacteria. A rather weak inhibition of phosphoribulokinase activity by ADP and AMP has been demonstrated in crude cell-free extracts (236); however, the extensive data on adenylate pool levels in cyanobacteria (34, 162, 236) indicate that these effects are probably not of physiological significance.

Several cyanobacterial RUDPCs have recently been purified to homogeneity (64, 176, 286–288). Their molecular weights and subunit compositions have been determined and found in some cases (64, 176, 288) to be identical with those of the chloroplast enzyme, i.e. eight small subunits (mol wt 15,000) and eight large subunits (mol wt 55,000). However, some cyanobacterial RUDPCs reportedly contain only eight large subunits (286, 287). The catalytic activity of RUDPC is reduced by 6-phosphogluconate (285), which rapidly builds up in the metabolic pool after a light-dark transition (234). More detailed study may, accordingly, show that RUDPC is the target of regulation in the reductive pentose phosphate cycle.

All RUDPCs, irrespective of biological source, possess oxygenase function. Oxygenative cleavage of RUDP produces equimolar quantities of phosphoglycerate and phosphoglycollate, instead of 2 mol of phosphoglycerate, the product of a carboxylative cleavage of the substrate (203). The phosphoglycollate is dephosphorylated and excreted as glycollate. Glycollate excretion, long believed to be intimately associated with the reactions of oxygenic photosynthesis, has been recently shown in two chemoautotrophs, *Thiobacillus thioparus* (69) and *Alkaligenes eutrophus* (62). Any organism that fixes CO_2 via the reductive pentose phosphate pathway may, accordingly, excrete part of the fixed carbon as glycollate if the environmental conditions favor oxygenative cleavage of RUDP. As in photosynthetic eukaryotes, glycollate production by cyanobacteria is favored under aerobic conditions with a limited CO_2 supply and at high light intensities (59, 63, 143, 163). This raises an interesting question: once excreted, can glycollate be re-absorbed and used as a carbon source by cyanobacteria? R. Rippka (personal communication) has shown that exogenous glycollate cannot support growth of any cyanobacteria so far examined (over 100 strains) in the presence of DCMU in the light. This does not exclude the possibility of the photoassimilation of glycollate, followed by entry of glycollate carbon into a restricted number of metabolic pathways (63). Such a process would be analogous to the photoassimilation of acetate, which can contribute approximately 10% to newly synthesized cell carbon under photoautotrophic growth conditions (269).

In view of the central role of glycogen as a cellular reserve material, the specific reactions involved in its synthesis and depolymerization are probable sites of metabolic control. One of these sites has been recently identified: ADP-glucose pyrophosphorylase, a biosynthetic enzyme subject to metabolic control in photosynthetic eukaryotes and in nearly all prokaryotes that synthesize glycogen (178). The cyanobacterial enzyme is very strongly activated (8- to 25-fold) by 3-phosphoglycerate, and to a much lesser extent by fructose-6-phosphate, fructose diphosphate, AMP, and ADP (196). Inorganic phosphate is an inhibitor. No other ADP-glucose pyrophosphorylases of prokaryotic origin are activated by phosphoglycerate; this substance, however, is a universal positive effector of the enzyme in photosynthetic eukaryotes (178).

Propionate is a potent growth inhibitor of cyanobacteria. The inhibition can be overcome by mutation, and propionate resistance is one of the most easily obtained genetic markers in cyanobacteria (270). The growth-inhibitory effect of propionate is attributable to the fact that it is a substrate for the acetokinase and phosphotransacetylase of cyanobacteria, the normal function of which is to convert acetate to acetyl-CoA. Since propionyl-CoA cannot be further metabolized, its formation causes a rapid depletion of the intracellular pool of CoA (268).

The Metabolic Bases of Obligate Photoautotrophy

Clarification of the pathways of cyanobacterial intermediary metabolism has permitted some insights into this long-standing problem. The inability of cyanobacteria to grow in the dark at the expense of all substrates normally oxidized through the tricarboxylic acid cycle is attributable to a specific enzymatic deficiency, the absence of α-ketoglutarate dehydrogenase. Acetate, even though it enters the cell and is activated, can serve only as a partial source of cell carbon, replacing endogenously synthesized acetyl-CoA in certain biosynthetic pathways (269).

Since the oxidative pentose phosphate cycle is a universal pathway of endogenous respiration and since hexokinase activity can be shown in cell-free extracts of obligately photoautotrophic cyanobacteria (237), failure to grow in the dark at the expense of any sugar, even glucose, is most plausibly attributable to the absence of sugar permeases (273). Circumstantial evidence in support of this interpretation was provided by a comparison of the dark rates of $^{14}CO_2$ formation from [U-^{14}C] glucose as a function of substrate concentration by several unicellular cyanobacteria (237). In a facultatively heterotrophic strain, *Synechocystis* 6714, the glucose concentration supporting a half-maximal rate was slightly less than 10^{-4} M. Two obligate photoautotrophs, although they produced some CO_2 from glucose, respired it at a negligible rate, which did not increase significantly at a glucose concentration of 10^{-2} M. A recent study of sugar uptake by *Synechocystis* 6714 (19) has demonstrated that it possesses a permease that concentrates free glucose in the cell and that can also transport two non-metabolizable glucose analogs, α-methylglucose and deoxyglucose. The system responsible for glucose transport, therefore, is now characterized. The patterns of utilization of glucose, fructose, sucrose, ribose, and gluconate by different facultatively heterotrophic strains of cyanobacteria (244) suggest that each sugar may be subject to transport by a specific permease; this inference is not yet supported by direct evidence. The metabolic basis of glycerol utilization also remains to be determined.

At best, chemoheterotrophic cyanobacteria grow poorly in the dark. If the initial glucose concentration exceeds 10^{-2} M, the cells of *Synechocystis* 6714 accumulate massive quantities of glycogen (242). Moreover, although *Synechocystis* 6714 grows well in liquid cultures in the dark, the growth yield at low glucose concentrations being proportional to initial substrate concentration (242), dark growth on agar media is extremely irregular, except with a large inoculum; isolated cells very rarely develop into colonies (R. Rippka, personal communication). These observations suggest that the controls that regulate biosynthesis and growth in the light become deranged in the dark. In itself, this might prevent dark growth of certain cyanobacteria even if they possessed sugar permeases. Another factor that could also lead to obligate photoautotrophy is a low rate of respiratory ATP synthesis. A direct comparison of the rates of ATP synthesis by *Synechocystis* 6714 with glucose and DCMU in the light and with glucose in the dark (235) has shown the rate under the former conditions (i.e. the rate of cyclic photophosphorylation) is slightly over four times the dark rate (i.e. the rate of oxidative phosphorylation). Yet this particular organism is a good facultative chemoheterotroph! In other members of the group, a rate of respiratory ATP synthesis sufficient to meet maintenance needs in the dark might be too low to support measurable dark growth.

Anaerobic Metabolism

Physiologically speaking, the cyanobacteria are evidently organisms that are adapted to an aerobic style of life. This is imposed on them by the fact that molecular oxygen is a major end product of their photosynthetic metabolism and becomes a required nutrient in the dark. As in other aerobes (211), the lethal effects of the superoxide free radical, produced by all organisms in the presence of molecular oxygen, are prevented by the enzyme superoxide dismutase, which has been well characterized in several cyanobacteria (204, 214). This protection, however, is not absolute (1, 2): high light intensities and O_2 concentrations, coupled with CO_2 depletion, may lead to massive photooxidative killing after a lag of some hours, during which the superoxide dismutase level in the cells drops 10-fold. In *Synechococcus* AN, the enzyme appears to be inducible by oxygen (2). As indicated by a large number of ecological observations, and first shown experimentally by Stewart & Pearson (282), many cyanobacteria can grow photosynthetically under highly reducing conditions in the presence of sulfide. However, the discovery that some cyanobacteria are capable of performing facultative anoxygenic photosynthesis was made only in 1975 (67, 68, 70).

This major discovery was an outcome of a detailed analysis of the microbial ecology of a shallow hypersaline pond, the Solar Lake, on the shore of the Gulf of Elat (67); the field work in itself set a standard of rigor and precision by which all future studies on cyanobacterial ecology will be judged. During winter stratification, a dense cyanobacterial bloom develops in the shallow but sulfide-rich hypolimnion, beneath accompanying blooms of purple and green sulfur bacteria. Isolation of the cyanobacterium, identified as *Oscillatoria limnetica,* made it possible to demonstrate that pure cultures photoassimilate CO_2, coupled with an oxidation of H_2S to elemental sulfur (68, 70). The reaction has the expected stoichiometry:

$$CO_2 + 2H_2S \xrightarrow{\text{light}} (CH_2O) + H_2O + 2S.$$

Only photosystem I is operative, as shown by the fact that the process is insensitive to DCMU inhibition, and proceeds at a high rate in red (703 nm) light, almost totally ineffective for photosystem II. In agreement with the ecological observations, the optimal sulfide concentration for anoxygenic photosynthesis is high: 3–4 mM.

A study of the kinetics of $^{14}CO_2$ assimilation in the light following sulfide addition (70) suggests that two factors operate in the switch from oxygenic to anoxygenic photosynthesis: an immediate inhibition of photosystem II by sulfide; and the subsequent induction of a sulfide-oxidizing enzyme system.

Other pure strains of cyanobacteria have now been screened by the same methods for the performance of facultative anoxygenic, sulfide-dependent photosynthesis (116). Of the 21 strains examined, no less than 11 (1 chroococcacean, 10 oscillatorian) possessed this metabolic capacity, although the maximal sulfide levels that permitted CO_2 assimilation were far below those tolerated by *O. limnetica.* Even in comparison with purple and green sulfur bacteria, this particular cyanobacterium is singularly sulfide tolerant. Facultative anoxygenic photosynthesis at the expense of sulfide has also been demonstrated in one thermophilic cyanobacterium, *Spirulina labyrinthiformis,* which is a component of the microflora of hot springs (55).

Many cyanobacteria, accordingly, are facultative anaerobes, although this physiological potentiality can be expressed only in light and in the presence of sulfide. Ecological niches where the two factors coexist are highly localized in the biosphere but are of world-wide geographical distribution. The presence of cyanobacteria as a significant component of the *sapropelische Lebewelt* was first recognized in 1915 by Lauterborn (189) in his classical study of this type of habitat. It has recently been re-emphasized by Fenchel & Riedl (94), who, apparently ignorant of Lauterborn's work, have again drawn attention to the distinctive nature of this biotic community (the thiobios), with emphasis on its importance in the marine littoral zone.

Are any other metabolic properties distinctive of an anaerobic mode of life hidden behind the aerobic facade of cyanobacteria? One has been recently discovered, although its role in cyanobacterial metabolism and its distribution within the group remain to be determined: the enzyme pyruvate ferredoxin oxidoreductase, which catalyzes a freely reversible conversion of pyruvate and CoASH to acetyl-SCoA and CO_2 (33, 191). This enzyme had hitherto appeared to be confined to prokaryotes with a fermentative type of energy-yielding metabolism and to purple and green bacteria. Another, which will be discussed below, is possessed by many non-heterocystous cyanobacteria: the ability to synthesize nitrogenase anaerobically, coupled with the inability to maintain this enzyme activity in the presence of air.

The Assimilation of Combined Nitrogen

Nitrate and ammonia will support growth of all cyanobacteria so far studied, and urea is generally also utilizable by these organisms. The pathway of ammonia assimilation has been intensively investigated, for the most part in nitrogen-fixing cyanobacteria and in the context of the problem of dinitrogen assimilation (e.g. 147). Recent kinetic studies, using short-term labeling either with $^{14}CO_2$ in the presence of NH_3 and N_2 (190) or with $^{13}N_2$ (331), indicate that ammonia assimilation proceeds through the glutamine synthetase-glutamate synthase (GOGAT) pathway. This is also supported by the finding that methionine sulfoximine, an inhibitor of the GOGAT system, provokes ammonia excretion when N_2 is the source of nitrogen (283). However, other pathways may function at high external ammonia concentrations. Enzymes potentially capable of playing a role in ammonia assimilation, which have been demonstrated in cell-free extracts of various cyanobacteria, include alanine dehydrogenase (219, 249), glutamate dehydrogenase (219), and aspartate dehydrogenase (16).

Comparatively little work has been published on nitrate and urea assimilation. Cell-free nitrate and nitrite reductases have been prepared from *Synechococcus* AN (207) and *Anabaena cylindrica* (145, 146). Reduced ferredoxin is the immediate electron donor for both reductases. In *Synechococcus* AN, the two enzymes are membrane bound in extracts but can be readily obtained in soluble form by prolonged sonication. A mutant of a *Synechococcus* sp., which has lost nitrite reductase activity and hence cannot grow with nitrate, has been described (277). The synthesis of both nitrate and nitrite reductases is repressed by ammonia (207).

Only one brief report on urea assimilation has appeared (23); urease activity was demonstrated in cell-free extracts, but no attempt was made to characterize the enzyme.

The ability of single amino acids to serve as sole nitrogen sources for cyanobacteria has not been systematically studied. Tests of the growth of a limited number of strains at the expense of L-alanine, L-glutamate, L-glutamine, and L-asparagine gave highly variable results, in some cases accompanied by evident toxic effects (219). This problem deserves further investigation.

Nitrogen Fixation

Nitrogen fixation has already been extensively discussed in the specific context of the heterocyst. Since we still do not possess detailed information about the properties of any cyanobacterial nitrogenase (278), the only aspect that merits further discussion is the distribution of nitrogen-fixing ability in non-heterocystous cyanobacteria.

The discovery that aerobic nitrogen fixation is not confined to the heterocystous representatives was made in 1969 by Wyatt & Silvey (332), who demonstrated this property in a strain of *Gloeothece* (incorrectly designated *Gloeocapsa*). This was soon confirmed for a second strain of *Gloeothece* (243) and has since been shown (245) for three other strains belonging to this genus. The only other chroococcacean cyanobacterium reported to fix nitrogen aerobically is a strain described as an *Aphanothece* (267), which resembles in structure the nitrogen-fixing *Gloeothece* strains except that it does not appear to produce the loose outer envelopes characteristic to this genus; therefore, it may be a closely related organism. Systematic tests on a large number of other pure strains of chroococcacean cyanobacteria have failed to reveal any additional cases of aerobic nitrogen fixation (245). The property, therefore, appears to be confined to a small subsection of this assemblage. Preliminary studies on the nitrogenase activity in crude cell-free extracts of a *Gloeothece* strain (111) show that the enzyme is particulate (sedimentable at 10,000 g); it is rapidly inactivated in crude extracts by exposure to 0.01 atm of O_2. The mechanism of in vivo protection, therefore, remains a total mystery.

One other plausible candidate for a non-heterocystous aerobic nitrogen fixer is the marine planktonic cyanobacterium, *Trichodesmium* (probably an *Oscillatoria* sp.). As yet, however, this organism has resisted all attempts at cultivation (let alone purification). The evidence that it can fix nitrogen aerobically (e.g. 46) is based on field studies and therefore remains presumptive.

In 1970, Stewart & Lex (281) showed that an oscillatorian cyanobacterium of the LPP group ("*Plectonema boryanum*") can synthesize nitrogenase in light, when cultures are maintained virtually anaerobic by periodic sparging with an argon-CO_2 gas mixture. No activity was detectable in parallel cultures sparged with an argon-CO_2 gas mixture containing 22% (vol/vol) of O_2; the activity was totally destroyed in 30 min when induced filaments were exposed to 10% (vol/vol) O_2. This work suggested that the latent ability to fix N_2 might be possessed by many non-heterocystous cyanobacteria, its expression being prevented under normal growth conditions by the oxygen sensitivity of the enzyme in vivo. Using techniques for the maintenance of anaerobiosis during induction more stringent than those first employed by Stewart & Lex (281), including DCMU treatment of the cultures, Rippka & Stanier (245) have screened many non-heterocystous cyanobacteria for nitrogenase synthesis in the absence of oxygen. Excluding the aerobic nitrogen fixers of the *Gloeothece* group, only 3 of 51 chroococcacean strains tested produced nitrogenase anaerobically. However, 22 of the 42 oscillatorian and 18 of the 29 pleurocapsalean strains examined synthesized the enzyme under these conditions. In all 43 positive strains, nitrogenase activity was rapidly destroyed by exposure of induced cultures to air.

The Synthesis and Possible Functions of Cyanophycin

The synthesis and breakdown of multi-L-arginyl-poly (aspartic acid) or cyanophycin is the only known aspect of cyanobacterial intermediary metabolism that is unique: no other biological group appears to synthesize this polypeptide, which is probably produced by all cyanobacteria. The observation that cyanophycin synthesis in vivo is insensitive to chloramphenicol showed that the process is nonribosomal (261). This has been confirmed (262) by the isolation and 100-fold purification of a soluble enzyme, multi-L-arginyl-poly(L-aspartic acid) synthetase, which incorporates both arginine and aspartic acid into the polymer. A primer is essential; the additional requirements are ATP, KCl, $MgCl_2$, and a sulfhydryl reagent. An interesting feature of the reaction is that incorporation of L-arginine is almost completely dependent upon the simultaneous presence of L-aspartate, whereas L-aspartate incorporation will occur, albeit to a lesser extent, in the absence of L-arginine. Since arginyl residues are attached to the β-carboxyl groups of the polyaspartic acid backbone in the native polymer (264), this finding suggests that chain elongation occurs through the addition of an aspartyl residue to the backbone, followed by the addition of an arginyl residue to the newly incorporated aspartyl residue. The biosynthetic enzyme(s) are evidently constitutive, since the addition of chloramphenicol to a culture that is growing exponentially and that has a low cyanophycin content provokes a high rate of cyanophycin synthesis (261)

Cyanophycin accumulation is a device that permits intracellular stockpiling of combined nitrogen when an exogenous nitrogen source is freely available but protein synthesis is restricted (261). One other possible metabolic role deserves study: that of an energy reserve. If cyanobacteria, like many non-photosynthetic bacteria, synthesize the enzymes arginine deiminase, ornithine carbamoyl transferase, and carbamoyl phosphokinase, a dissimilation of arginine accompanied by net ATP synthesis would be possible:

$$\text{L-arginine} + \text{ADP} + \text{Pi} + H_2O \rightarrow \text{L-ornithine} + CO_2 + NH_3 + \text{ATP}.$$

In this event, cyanophycin might provide an energy reserve, which, unlike glycogen, could be mobilized for the synthesis of ATP under strictly anaerobic conditions.

NEW LIGHT ON THE ORIGINS OF CHLOROPLASTS

Although a general discussion of the problem of chloroplast origin is outside the scope of this review, two recent discoveries deserve specific mention.

The flagellate *Cyanophora paradoxa* is a phototrophic eukaryote of indeterminate taxonomic position (142). Each cell contains two to four "cyanelles," with a typical cyanobacterial (or rhodophytan) pigment composition (57). The cyanelles have generally been interpreted as endosymbiotic cyanobacteria; they are stable in a hypotonic medium after release from the host cell and are enclosed by a thin, lysozyme-sensitive envelope (252). Cyanellar DNA has recently been purified, and its molecular complexity has been determined by the kinetics of re-association after thermal denaturation (150). The genome size is approximately 10^8 daltons, some 5–10% of the smallest genome sizes of unicellular cyanobacteria (see Table 2). The cyanellar envelopes contain both muramic acid and diaminopimelic acid (A. Aitken, personal communication). The cyanelle is accordingly an organelle (i.e. a chloroplast) in terms of its information content; however, it has retained an unmistakable vestige of prokaryotic ancestry (a peptidoglycan wall layer), which is absent from all other chloroplasts.

Lewin and his colleagues (197–200, 254) have discovered a unicellular organism of marine origin that appears to be a representative of a new class of prokaryotes able to perform oxygenic photosynthesis. It develops as an ectosymbiont of the colonial ascidian *Didemnum* and has so far not been cultivated. However, sufficient material can be detached from the body surface of the animal host to determine its salient properties. The internal organization of the cell is unmistakably prokaryotic, and the cell envelope has the typical profile of a gram-negative cell wall (254). However, pigment analyses show that PBPs are absent and that both chlorophylls *a* and *b* are present in a ratio of approximately 4.5:1 (200). The organism, therefore, possesses a light-harvesting pigment system of the chlorophytan type. Lewin initially assigned the organism to the cyanobacterial genus *Synechocystis* (197) but has later proposed to create for it a new division among the algae (!), the Prochlorophyta (198). Neither taxonomic proposal is appealing, for reasons that do not need to be spelled out.

This organism provides a heretofore missing link of the greatest evolutionary importance. The very close similarities between the light-harvesting pigment systems of the red algae and the cyanobacteria made a specifically cyanobacterial origin for the rhodophytan chloroplast an attractive evolutionary hypothesis, but they left open the question of the origin of the types of chloroplasts characteristic of other major algal groups, which have markedly different arrays of light harvesting pigments. Two possible explanations could be entertained, within the general framework of the hypothesis of an endosymbiotic origin for the chloroplast: either that other types of chloroplasts arose from a chloroplast of the rhodophytan type during the early evolution of photosynthetic eukaryotes, or that chloroplasts had polyphyletic cellular origins among photosynthetic prokaryotes capable of performing oxygenic photosynthesis. The discovery of a prokaryote with a light-harvesting pigment system of the chlorophytan type strongly favors the second explanation and suggests that the present diversity of algal pigment systems is the expression of a very ancient divergence in this respect among photosynthetic prokaryotes.

CONCLUDING REMARKS

The area of cyanobacteriology most in need of recruits is experimental taxonomy. Systematic comparative studies must be conducted on each subgroup, applying the full range of techniques—notably nucleic acid hybridizations in vitro—which have changed the face of bacterial taxonomy in the past 20 years. Such work is necessary both to recognize species and to determine intra- and intergroup relationships. However, the existing descriptive taxonomy of the cyanobacteria (35, 77, 117), which has grown up over the course of almost 150 years, coupled with the nomenclatural rules of the Botanical Code (271), is a major obstacle to the development of a modern taxonomic treatment.

The recently described chroococcacean genus *Gloeobacter* (246) is the only cyanobacterial genus defined by a type species with a living holotype—*Gloeobacter violaceus* ATCC 29802. Although *G. violaceus* is far better characterized phenotypically than any other species of cyanobacterium, the name is illegitimate under the rules of the Botanical Code (271). There are two reasons for this, one trivial and the other fundamental: a Latin diagnosis was not furnished; and cultures are not recognized as nomenclatural types. Nothing could illustrate more sharply the gulf that today separates botanical and bacteriological nomenclatural practices.

In terms of the criteria set forth in the Bacteriological Code (188), a majority of existing cyanobacterial species (including many type species, on which the recognition of genera rests) would probably qualify for rejection by the Judicial Commission. They are so incompletely described and are represented by such dilapidated type materials that they fall into the categories of *nomina dubia, nomina confusa,* and *nomina perplexa* (Rule 56a). However, most if not all are legitimate under the Botanical Code. The number of nomenspecies already proposed for cyanobacteria almost certainly far exceeds the number of biological species within the group. This puts the modern taxonomist in an impossible nomenclatural bind. Even if he characterizes fully a cyanobacterial species, the absence of solid points of nomenclatural reference will usually make it impossible to assign an existing specific name (or even in many cases a generic name) with any assurance that it is correctly chosen. This absurd situation can be remedied only by bringing cyanobacteria under the Bacteriological Code, where they evidently belong.

ACKNOWLEDGMENTS

We wish to thank many colleagues who put at our disposal data that are either unpublished or that have appeared only in the form of brief abstracts. They include Alastair Aitken, Michael Herdman, Manley Mandel, Rosmarie Rippka, Francis Schaeffer, and Nicole Tandeau de Marsac. We are also grateful to Gerard Guglielmi and Rosmarie Rippka for preparing the illustrations, and to Annick Sciot for her help in assembling the bibliography and typing the manuscript.

The work from our laboratory is supported by a grant (E.R.A. 398) from the Centre National de la Recherche Scientifique.

Literature Cited

1. Abeliovitch, A., Kellenberg, D., Shilo, M. 1974. *Photochem. Photobiol.* 19: 379–82
2. Abeliovitch, A., Shilo, M. 1972. *J. Bacteriol.* 111:682–89
3. Aitken, A. 1975. *Biochem. J.* 149: 675–83
4. Aitken, A. 1976. *Nature* 263:793–96
5. Aitken, A. 1977. *Eur. J. Biochem.* In press
6. Allen, M. B. 1952. *Arch. Mikrobiol.* 17:34–53
7. Allen, M. B. 1966. In *The Chlorophylls,* ed. L. P. Verron, G. R. Seely, pp. 511–19. New York: Academic
8. Allen, M. B., Dougherty, E. C., McLaughlin, J. J. A. 1959. *Nature* 184: 1047–49
9. Allen, M. M. 1968. *J. Bacteriol.* 96: 836–41
10. Allen, M. M. 1968. *J. Phycol.* 4:1–4
11. Allen, M. M. 1968b. *J. Bacteriol.* 96: 842–52
12. Allen, M. M. 1972. *Arch. Mikrobiol.* 84:199–206
13. Allen, M. M., Smith, A. J. 1969. *Arch. Mikrobiol.* 69:114–20
14. Allen, M. M., Stanier, R. Y. 1968. *J. Gen. Microbiol.* 51:203–9
15. Ambler, R. P., Bartsch, R. G. 1975. *Nature* 253:285–88
16. Batt, T., Brown, D. H. 1974. *Planta* 116:27–37
17. Batterton, J. C., Van Baalen, C. 1971. *Arch. Mikrobiol.* 76:151–65
18. Beauchemin, N., Larue, B., Cedergren, R. J. 1973. *Arch. Biochem. Biophys.* 156:17–25
19. Beauclerk, A. A. D., Smith, A. J. 1976. *Proc. 2nd Int. Symp. Photosynthetic Prokaryotes,* ed. G. A. Codd, W. D. P. Stewart, pp. 213–15. Dundee: Univ. Dundee. 255 pp.
20. Bennett, A., Bogorad, L. 1971. *Biochemistry* 10:3625–34
21. Bennett, A., Bogorad, L. 1973. *J. Cell Biol.* 58:419–35
22. Berns, D. S. 1967. *Plant Physiol.* 42:1569–86
23. Berns, D. S., Holohan, P., Scott, E. 1966. *Science* 152:1077–78
24. Biggins, J. 1969. *J. Bacteriol.* 99:570–75
25. Bishop, C. T., Adams, G. A., Hughes, E. O. 1956. *Can. J. Chem.* 32:999–1004
26. Biswas, B. B. 1957. *Sci. Cult.* 22:696
27. Bogorad, L. 1965. *Rec. Chem. Prog.* 26:108–19
28. Bogorad, L. 1975. *Science* 188:891–98

29. Bogorad, L. 1975. *Ann. Rev. Plant Physiol.* 26:369–401
30. Bonen, L., Allen, G. V., Dobson, P. R., Doolittle, W. F. 1976. *J. Bacteriol.* 126:1020–23
31. Bonen, L., Doolittle, W. F. 1975. *Proc. Natl. Acad. Sci. USA* 72:2310–14
32. Bonen, L., Doolittle, W. F. 1976. *Nature* 261:669–73
33. Bothe, H., Falkenberg, B., Nolteernsting, U. 1974. *Arch. Microbiol.* 96:291–304
34. Bottomley, P. J., Stewart, W. D. P. 1976. *Arch. Microbiol.* 108:249–58
35. Bourrelly, P. 1970. *Les Algues d'Eau Douce: Les Algues Bleues et Rouges, les Eugléniens, Peridiniens et Cryptomonadines.* Paris: Boubée. 512 pp.
36. Bourrelly, P., Conté, A. 1975. *Protistologia* 11:187–94
37. Brill, W. J. 1975. *Ann. Rev. Microbiol.* 29:109–29
38. Brooks, C., Gantt, E. 1973. *Arch. Mikrobiol.* 88:193–204
39. Brown, A. H. 1953. *Am. J. Bot.* 40: 719–29
40. Brown, A. H., Webster, G. C. 1953. *Am. J. Bot.* 40:753–58
41. Bryant, D. A., Glazer, A. N., Eiserling, F. A. 1976. *Arch. Microbiol.* 110:61–75
42. Bryce, T. A., Welti, D., Walsby, A. E., Nichols, B. W. 1972. *Phytochemistry* 11:295–302
43. Buchanan, R. E., Gibbons, N. E., eds. 1974. *Bergey's Manual of Determinative Bacteriology.* Baltimore: Williams and Wilkins. 1246 pp. 8th ed.
44. Calvin, M., Bassham, J. A. 1962. *The Photosynthesis of Carbon Compounds.* New York: W. A. Benjamin. 127 pp.
45. Cardemil, L., Wolk, C. P. 1976. *J. Biol. Chem.* 251:2967–75
46. Carpenter, E. J., Price, C. C. 1976. *Science* 191:1278–80
47. Carr, N. G. 1966. *Biochim. Biophys. Acta* 120:308–10
48. Carr, N. G. 1973. In *The Biology of Blue-Green Algae,* ed. N. G. Carr, B. A. Whitton, pp. 39–65. Oxford: Blackwell Sci. Publ. 676 pp.
49. Carr, N. G., Bradley, S. 1973. In *Microbial Differentiation, 23rd Symp. Soc. Gen. Microbiol.,* pp. 161–88. Cambridge, England: Cambridge Univ. Press. 450 pp.
50. Carr, N. G., Craig, I. W. 1970. In *Phytochemical Phylogeny,* ed. J. B. Harborne, pp. 119–43. London: Academic. 335 pp.
51. Carr, N. G., Komárek, J., Whitton, B. A. See Ref. 48, pp. 525–35
52. Carr, N. G., Whitton, B. A., eds. 1973. *The Biology of Blue-Green Algae.* Oxford: Blackwell Sci. Publ. 676 pp.
53. Castenholz, R. W. 1969. *Bacteriol. Rev.* 33:476–504
54. Castenholz, R. W. 1970. *Schweiz. Z. Hydrol.* 32:538–51
55. Castenholz, R. W. See Ref. 19, pp. 158–60
56. Chao, L., Bowen, C. C. 1971. *J. Bacteriol.* 105:331–38
57. Chapman, D. J. 1966. *Arch. Mikrobiol.* 55:17–25
58. Chapman, D. J. See Ref. 48, pp. 162–85
59. Cheng, K. H., Miller, A. G., Colman, B. 1972. *Planta* 103:110–16
60. Cheung, W. Y., Gibbs, M. 1966. *Plant Physiol.* 41:731–37
61. Clark, R. L., Jensen, T. E. 1969. *Cytologia* 34:439–48
62. Codd, G. A., Bowien, B., Schlegel, H. G. 1976. *Arch. Microbiol.* 110:167–71
63. Codd, G. A., Sallal, A. K. J., Stewart, R. See Ref. 19, pp. 193–95
64. Codd, G. A., Stewart, R. See Ref. 19, pp. 196–98
65. Codd, G. A., Stewart, W. D. P. 1976. *Planta* 130:323–26
66. Cohen, S. S. 1973. *Am. Sci.* 61:437–45
67. Cohen, Y. 1975. *Dynamics of prokaryotic photosynthetic communities of the Solar Lake.* PhD thesis. Hebrew Univ., Jerusalem. 125 pp.
68. Cohen, Y., Jørgensen, B. B., Padan, E., Shilo, M. 1975. *Nature* 257:489–92
69. Cohen, Y., Kuchnen, J. G. 1976. *Abstr. Annu. Meet. Am. Soc. Microbiol.,* I56, p. 120 (Abstr.)
70. Cohen, Y., Padan, E., Shilo, M. 1975. *J. Bacteriol.* 123:855–61
71. Cohen-Bazire, G. 1971. In *Biological Ultrastructure: The Origin of Cell Organelles,* ed. P. J. Harris, pp. 65–90. Corvallis: Oregon State Univ. Press. 115 pp.
72. Cohen-Bazire, G., Beguin, S., Glazer, A. N., Brown, D. M. 1977. *Arch. Microbiol.* 3:225–38
73. Constantopoulos, G., Bloch, K. 1967. *J. Bacteriol.* 93:1788–93
74. Cruden, D. L., Stanier, R. Y. 1970. *Arch. Mikrobiol.* 72:115–34
75. Dalton, H., Mortenson, L. E. 1972. *Bacteriol. Rev.* 36:231–60
76. Davey, J. F., Whittenbury, R., Wilkinson, J. F. 1972. *Arch. Mikrobiol.* 87: 359–66
77. Desikachary, T. V. 1959. *Cyanophyta.* New Delhi: Indian Council of Agricultural Research. 686 pp.

78. Donze, M., Haveman, J., Schiereck, P. 1972. *Biochim. Biophys. Acta* 256: 157–61
79. Doolittle, W. F. 1973. *J. Bacteriol.* 113: 1256–63
80. Doolittle, W. F., Singer, R. A. 1974. *J. Bacteriol.* 119:677–83
81. Drews, G. See Ref. 48, pp. 99–116
81a. Drews, G., Schmidt, W., Katz, A., Weckesser, J. See Ref. 19, pp. 69–72
82. Drouet, F. 1968. *Monogr. 16 Acad. Natl. Sci. Philadelphia,* 341 pp.
83. Dunn, J. H., Wolk, C. P. 1970. *J. Bacteriol.* 103:153–58
84. Ecarot, B., Cedergren, R. J. 1974. *Biochim. Biophys. Acta* 340:130–39
85. Eccleston, M., Kelly, D. P. 1973. *J. Gen. Microbiol.* 75:211–21
86. Edelman, M., Swinton, D., Schiff, J. A., Epstein, H. T., Zeldin, B. 1967. *Bacteriol. Rev.* 31:315–31
87. Edwards, M. R., Berns, D. S., Ghiorse, W. C., Holt, S. C. 1968. *J. Phycol.* 4:283–98
88. Edwards, M. R., Gantt, E. 1971. *J. Cell Biol.* 50:896–99
89. Evans, E. H., Foulds, I., Carr, N. G. 1976. *J. Gen. Microbiol.* 92:147–55
90. Fay, P. 1969. *Arch. Mikrobiol.* 67: 62–70
91. Fay, P. 1970. *Biochim. Biophys. Acta* 261:353–56
92. Fay, P., Lang, N. J. 1971. *Proc. R. Soc. London Ser. B* 178:185–92
93. Fay, P., Walsby, A. E. 1966. *Nature* 209:94–95
94. Fenchel, T. M., Riedl, R. J. 1970. *Marine Biol.* 7:255–68
95. Fisher, R. W., Wolk, C. P. 1976. *Nature* 259:394–95
96. Fleming, H., Haselkorn, R. 1974. *Cell* 3:159–70
97. Fogg, G. E. 1942. *J. Exp. Bot.* 19:78–87
98. Fogg, G. E. 1944. *New Phytol.* 43:164–75
99. Fogg, G. E. 1949. *Ann. Bot. London* 13:241–59
100. Fogg, G. E. 1951. *Ann. Bot. London* 15:23–35
101. Fogg, G. E. 1951. *J. Exp. Bot.* 2:117–20
102. Fogg, G. E. 1952. *Proc. R. Soc. London Ser. B* 139:373–97
103. Fogg, G. E., Stewart, W. D. P. 1965. *Sci. Prog.* 53:191–201
104. Fogg, G. E., Stewart, W. D. P., Fay, P., Walsby, A. E. 1973. *The Blue-Green Algae.* London: Academic. 459 pp.
105. Frank, H., Lefort, M., Martin, H. H. 1962. *Z. Naturforsch. Teil B* 17:262–68
106. French, S. C., Brown, J. S., Lawrence, M. C. 1970. *Carnegie Inst. Washington Yearb.* 68:487–95
107. Friden, C. 1970. *J. Biol. Chem.* 245: 5788–99
108. Fritsch, F. E. 1945. *The Structure and Reproduction of Algae,* Vol. 2. Cambridge, England: Cambridge Univ. Press. 939 pp.
109. Fuhs, G. W. 1963. *Protoplasma* 56: 178–87
110. Fujita, Y., Hattori, A. 1960. *Plant Cell Physiol.* 1:293–303
111. Gallon, J. R., Kurz, W. G. W., Larue, T. A. 1975. In *Nitrogen Fixation by Free-Living Microorganisms,* ed. W. D. P. Stewart, 6:159–73. Cambridge, England: Cambridge Univ. Press. 471 pp.
112. Gantt, E. 1975. *BioScience* 25:781–88
113. Gantt, E., Conti, S. F. 1966. *J. Cell Biol.* 29:423–34
114. Gantt, E., Lipschultz, C. A. 1973. *Biochim. Biophys. Acta* 292:858–61
115. Gantt, E., Lipschultz, C. A. 1974. *Biochemistry* 13:2960–66
116. Garlick, S., Oren, A., Padan, E. 1977. *J. Bacteriol.* 129:623–29
117. Geitler, L. 1932. Cyanophyceae. In *Kryptogamenflora von Deutschland, Österreich und der Schweiz,* ed. L. Rabenhorst, Vol. 14. Leipzig: Akademische Verlagsgesellschaft. 1196 pp.
118. Geitler, L. 1960. Schizophyceen. In *Handbuch der Pflanzenanatomie,* ed. W. Zimmermann, P. Ozenda, Band 6, Part 1. Berlin: Borntraeger. 131 pp. 2nd ed.
119. Giesy, R. M. 1964. *Am. J. Bot.* 51: 388–96
120. Glazer, A. N. 1976. *Photochem. Photobiol. Rev.* 1:71–115
121. Glazer, A. N., Apell, G. S., Hixson, C. S., Bryant, D. A., Rimon, S., Brown, D. M. 1976. *Proc. Natl. Acad. Sci. USA* 73:428–31
122. Glazer, A. N., Bryant, D. A. 1975. *Arch. Microbiol.* 104:15–22
123. Glazer, A. N., Cohen-Bazire, G. 1971. *Proc. Natl. Acad. Sci. USA* 68:1398–401
124. Glazer, A. N., Cohen-Bazire, G. 1975. *Arch. Microbiol.* 104:29–32
125. Glazer, A. N., Cohen-Bazire, G., Stanier, R. Y. 1971. *Arch. Mikrobiol.* 80:1–18
126. Glazer, A. N., Cohen-Bazire, G., Stanier, R. Y. 1971. *Proc. Natl. Acad. Sci. USA* 68:3005–8
127. Glazer, A. N., Hixson, C. S. 1975. *J. Biol. Chem.* 250:5487–95
128. Deleted in proof
129. Gray, B. H., Gantt, E. 1975. *Photochem. Photobiol.* 21:121–28

130. Gray, B. H., Lipschultz, C. A., Gantt, E. 1973. *J. Bacteriol.* 116:471–78
131. Gray, J. E., Herson, D. S. 1976. *Arch. Microbiol.* 109:95–99
132. Griffiths, M., Edmondson, W. T. 1975. *Limnol. Oceanogr.* 20:945–52
133. Griffiths, M., Perrott, P. S., Edmondson, W. T. 1969. *Limnol. Oceanogr.* 14:317–26
134. Grossman, A., McGowan, R. E. 1975. *Plant Physiol.* 55:658–62
135. Guglielmi, G. 1975. *Vie Milieu* 25:189–213
136. Gysi, J., Zuber, H. 1974. *FEBS Lett.* 48:209–13
137. Halfen, L. N. 1973. *J. Phycol.* 9:248–53
138. Halfen, L. N., Castenholz, R. W. 1970. *Nature* 225:1163–65
139. Halfen, L. N., Castenholz, R. W. 1971. *J. Phycol.* 7:133–45
140. Halfen, L. N., Castenholz, R. W. 1971. *J. Phycol.* 7:258–60
141. Hall, D. O., Cammack, R., Rao, K. K., Evans, M. C. W., Mullinger, R. 1975. *Biochem. Soc. Trans.* 3:361–68
142. Hall, W. T., Claus, G. 1963. *J. Cell Biol.* 19:551–63
143. Han, T. W., Eley, J. H. 1973. *Plant Cell Physiol.* 14:285–91
144. Haselkorn, R., Rouvière-Yaniv, J. 1976. *Proc. Natl. Acad. Sci. USA* 73:1917–20
145. Hattori, A. 1970. *Plant Cell Physiol.* 11:975–78
146. Hattori, A., Uesugi, I. 1968. *Plant Cell Physiol.* 9:689–99
147. Haystead, A., Dharmawardene, M. W. N., Stewart, W. D. P. 1973. *Plant Sci. Lett.* 1:439–45
148. Herdman, M. See Ref. 19, pp. 229–32
149. Herdman, M., Carr, N. G. 1974. *Arch. Microbiol.* 99:251–54
150. Herdman, M., Stanier, R. Y. 1977. *FEMS Microbiol. Lett.* 1:7–12
151. Hertzberg, S., Liaaen-Jensen, S. 1969. *Phytochemistry* 8:1281–92
152. Hertzberg, S., Liaaen-Jensen, S. 1969. *Phytochemistry* 9:629–35
153. Hertzberg, S., Liaaen-Jensen, S., Siegelman, H. W. 1971. *Phytochemistry* 10:3121–27
154. Herzfeld, F., Kiper, M. 1976. *Eur. J. Biochem.* 62:189–92
155. Herzfeld, F., Zillig, W. 1971. *Eur. J. Biochem.* 24:242–48
156. Hoare, D. S., Hoare, S. L., Smith, A. J. 1970. In *1st Int. Symp. on Taxonomy and Biology of Blue-Green Algae,* ed. T. V. Desikachary, pp. 501–7. Madras, India: Univ. Madras 591 pp.
157. Hoare, D. S., Moore, R. B. 1965. *Biochim. Biophys. Acta* 109:622–25
158. Holm-Hansen, O. 1968. *Ann. Rev. Microbiol.* 22:47–70
159. Holton, R. W., Blecker, H. H. 1970. In *Properties and Products of Algae,* ed. J. E. Zajic, pp. 115–27. New York: Plenum
160. Hood, W., Carr, N. G. 1971. *J. Bacteriol.* 107:365–67
161. Hood, W., Carr, N. G. 1972. *J. Gen. Microbiol.* 73:417–26
162. Ihlenfeldt, M. J. A., Gibson, J. 1975. *Arch. Microbiol.* 102:13–21
163. Ingle, R. K., Colman, B. 1976. *Planta* 128:217–23
164. Ingram, L. O., Calder, J. A., Van Baalen, C., Plucker, F. E., Parker, P. L. 1973. *J. Bacteriol.* 114:695–700
165. Ingram, L. O., Thurston, E. L. 1970. *Protoplasma* 71:55–75
166. Ingram, L. O., Van Baalen, C., Calder, J. A. 1973. *J. Bacteriol.* 114:701–5
167. Iyengar, M. O. P., Desikachary, T. V. 1953. *Curr. Sci.* 22:180–81
168. Jarosch, R. 1964. *Osterr. Bot. Z.* 111:143–48
169. Jensen, T. E., Sicko, L. M. 1971. *J. Bacteriol.* 106:683–86
170. Jones, L. W., Myers, J. 1964. *Plant Physiol.* 39:938–46
171. Jones, L. W., Myers, J. 1965. *J. Phycol.* 1:7–14
172. Kantz, T., Bold, H. C. 1969. *Phycological Studies. IX. Morphological and Taxonomic Investigations of Nostoc and Anabaena in Culture,* Publ. 6924. Austin: Univ. Texas. 67 pp.
173. Kenyon, C. N. 1972. *J. Bacteriol.* 109:827–34
174. Kenyon, C. N., Rippka, R., Stanier, R. Y. 1972. *Arch. Mikrobiol.* 83:216–36
175. Kessel, M., Eloff, J. N. 1975. *Arch. Microbiol.* 106:209–14
176. Kieras, F. J., Haselkorn, R. 1968. *Plant Physiol.* 43:1264–70
177. Koshland, D. E. Jr., Neet, K. E. 1968. *Ann. Rev. Biochem.* 37:359–410
178. Krebs, E. G., Preiss, J. 1975. *Biochem. Carbohydr.* 5:337–89
179. Krogmann, D. W. See Ref. 48, pp. 80–98
180. Kulasooriya, S. A., Lang, N. J., Fay, P. 1972. *Proc. R. Soc. London Ser. B* 181:199–209
181. Kurganov, B. L. 1975. *Symposium on Mechanism of Action and Regulation of Enzymes,* ed. T. Kelety, pp. 29–42. Amsterdam: North Holland
182. Lambein, F., Wolk, C. P. 1973. *Biochemistry* 12:791–98

183. Lamont, H. C. 1969. *Arch. Mikrobiol.* 69:237–59
184. Lang, N. J. 1968. *Ann. Rev. Microbiol.* 22:15–46
185. Lang, N. J. 1972. In *Taxonomy and Biology of Blue-Green Algae,* ed. T. V. Desikachary, pp. 6–12. Madras, India: Univ. Madras 591 pp.
186. Lang, N. J., Fay, P. 1971. *Proc. R. Soc. London Ser. B* 178:193–203
187. Lang, N. J., Whitton, B. A. See Ref. 48, pp. 66–79
188. Lapage, S. P., ed. 1976. *International Code of Nomenclature of Bacteria.* Washington, D.C.: Am. Soc. Microbiol. 180 pp.
189. Lauterborn, R. 1915. *Verh. Naturhist. Med. Ver. Heidelberg N. F.* 13:396–480
190. Lawrie, A. C., Codd, G. A., Stewart, W. D. P. 1976. *Arch. Microbiol.* 107:15–24
191. Leach, C. K., Carr, N. G. 1971. *Biochim. Biophys. Acta* 245:165–74
192. Leach, C. K., Carr, N. G. 1974. *J. Gen. Microbiol.* 81:47–58
193. Lefort, M. 1965. *CR Acad. Sci. Paris* 261:223–36
194. Lemasson, C., Tandeau de Marsac, N., Cohen-Bazire, G. 1973. *Proc. Natl. Acad. Sci. USA* 70:3130–33
195. Lendzian, K., Bassham, J. A. 1975. *Biochim. Biophys. Acta* 396:260–75
196. Levi, C., Preiss, J. 1976. *Plant Physiol.* 58:753–56
197. Lewin, R. A. 1975. *Phycologia* 14: 153–60
198. Lewin, R. A. 1976. *Nature* 261:697–98
199. Lewin, R. A., Cheng, L. 1975. *Phycologia* 14:149–52
200. Lewin, R. A., Withers, N. W. 1975. *Nature* 256:735–37
201. Lex, M., Carr, N. G. 1974. *Arch Microbiol.* 101:161–67
202. Lorch, S. K., Wolk, C. P. 1974. *J. Phycol.* 10:352–55
203. Lorimer, G. H., Andrews, T. J., Tolbert, N. E. 1973. *Biochemistry* 12:18–23
204. Lumsden, J., Hall, D. O. 1974. *Biochem. Biophys. Res. Commun.* 58: 35–41
205. MacColl, R., Habig, W., Berns, D. S. 1973. *J. Biol. Chem.* 248:7080–86
206. MacLeod, R. A. 1965. *Bacteriol. Rev.* 29:9–23
207. Manzano, C., Candau, P., Gomez-Moreno, C., Relimpio, A. M., Losada, M. 1976. *Mol. Cell Biochem.* 10:161–69
208. Margulis, L. 1970. *Origin of Eucaryotic Cells.* Princeton, N.J.: Yale Univ. Press. 349 pp.
209. Martin, T. C., Wyatt, J. T. 1974. *J. Phycol.* 10:57–65
210. Martin, T. C., Wyatt, J. T. 1974. *J. Phycol.* 10:204–10
211. McCord, J. M., Keele, B. B. Jr., Fridovich, I. 1971. *Proc. Natl. Acad. Sci. USA* 68:1024–27
212. Meeks, J. C., Wolk, C. P. See Ref. 19, pp. 110–12
213. Miller, L. S., Holt, S. C. 1976. *Abstr. Ann. Meet. Am. Soc. Microbiol,* I120, p. 131 (Abstr.)
214. Misra, H. P., Keele, B. B. Jr. 1975. *Biochim. Biophys. Acta* 379:418–23
215. Mitchison, G. J., Wilcox, M. 1972. *Nature* 239:110–11
216. Mitchison, G. J., Wilcox, M. 1973. *Nature New Biol.* 246:229–33
217. Murray, R. G. E. 1962. In *Microbial Classification,* ed. G. C. Ainsworth, P. H. A. Sheath, pp. 119–44. Cambridge, England: Cambridge Univ. Press. 483 pp.
218. Myers, J., Kratz, W. A. 1955. *J. Gen. Physiol.* 39:11–22
219. Neilson, A., Doudoroff, M. 1973. *Arch. Mikrobiol.* 89:15–22
220. Neilson, A., Rippka, R., Kunisawa, R. 1971. *Arch. Mikrobiol.* 76:139–50
221. Nichols, B. W. 1970. In *Phytochemical Phylogeny,* ed. J. B. Harbourne, pp. 105–18. New York: Academic
222. Nichols, B. W. See Ref. 48, pp. 144–61
223. O'Carra, P., Killilea, S. D. 1971. *Biochem. Biophys. Commun.* 45:1192–97
224. O'hEocha, C., Raftery, M. 1959. *Nature* 184:1049–51
225. Ohki, K., Katoh, T. 1975. *Plant Cell Physiol.* 16:53–64
226. Padan, E., Shilo, M. 1973. *Bacteriol. Rev.* 37:343–70
227. Padmaja, T. D., Desikachary, T. V. 1971. *Phykos* 7:62–89
228. Payne, P. I., Dyer, T. A. 1972. *Arch. Mikrobiol.* 87:29–40
229. Pearce, J., Carr, N. G. 1967. *J. Gen. Microbiol.* 49:301–13
230. Pearce, J., Carr, N. G. 1967. *Biochem. J.* 105:45P
231. Pearce, J., Carr, N. G. 1969. *J. Gen. Microbiol.* 54:451–62
232. Pearce, J., Leach, C. K., Carr, N. G. 1969. *J. Gen. Microbiol.* 55:371–78
233. Peat, A., Kirkby, S. M., Sinclair, C., Whitton, B. A. 1973. *Symp. Prokaryotic Photosynthetic Organisms,* p. 179 (Abstr.)
234. Pelroy, R. A., Bassham, J. A. 1972. *Arch. Mikrobiol.* 86:25–38
235. Pelroy, R. A., Kirk, M. R., Bassham, J. A. 1976. *J. Bacteriol.* 128:623–32
236. Pelroy, R. A., Levine, G. A., Bassham, J. A. 1976. *J. Bacteriol.* 128:633–43

237. Pelroy, R. A., Rippka, R., Stanier, R. Y. 1972. *Arch. Mikrobiol.* 87:303–22
238. Pfennig, N. 1969. *J. Bacteriol.* 99:597–602
239. Raboy, B., Padan, E., Shilo, M. 1976. *Arch. Microbiol.* 110:77–86
240. Reichelt, J. L., Baumann, P. 1974. *Arch. Mikrobiol.* 97:329–45
241. Reynolds, C. S., Walsby, A. E. 1975. *Biol. Rev.* 50:437–81
242. Rippka, R. 1972. *Arch. Mikrobiol.* 87:93–98
243. Rippka, R., Neilson, A., Kunisawa, R., Cohen-Bazire, G. 1971. *Arch. Mikrobiol.* 76:341–48
244. Rippka, R., Stanier, R. Y. See Ref. 233, pp. 135–38
245. Rippka, R., Stanier, R. Y. See Ref. 19, pp. 138–39
246. Rippka, R., Waterbury, J., Cohen-Bazire, G. 1974. *Arch. Microbiol.* 100:419–36
247. Rippka, R., Waterbury, J. B., Deruelles, J., Herdman, M., Stanier, R. Y. 1977. *Int. J. Syst. Bacteriol.* In press
248. Rouvière-Yaniv, J., Gros, F. 1975. *Proc. Natl. Acad. Sci. USA* 72:3428–32
249. Rowell, P., Stewart, W. D. P. 1976. *Arch. Microbiol.* 107:115–24
250. Sangar, V. K., Dugan, P. R. 1972. *Appl. Microbiol.* 24:732–34
251. Scheibe, J. 1972. *Science* 176:1037–39
252. Schenk, H. E. A. 1970. *Z. Naturforsch.* 25:656
253. Schleifer, K. H., Kandler, O. 1972. *Bacteriol. Rev.* 36:407–77
254. Schulz-Baldes, M., Lewin, R. A. 1976. *Phycologia* 15:1–6
255. Seitz, Ursula, Seitz, Ulrich, 1973. *Arch. Mikrobiol.* 90:213–22
256. Shively, J. M. 1974. *Ann. Rev. Microbiol.* 28:167–87
257. Shively, J. M., Ball, F., Brown, D. H., Saunders, R. E. 1973. *Science* 182:584–86
258. Shively, J. M., Ball, F. L., Kline, B. W. 1973. *J. Bacteriol.* 116:1405–11
259. Shukovsky, E. S., Halfen, L. N. 1976. *J. Phycol.* 12:336–42
260. Simon, R. D. 1971. *Proc. Natl. Acad. Sci. USA* 68:265–67
261. Simon, R. D. 1973. *Arch. Mikrobiol.* 92:115–22
262. Simon, R. D. 1976. *Biochim. Biophys. Acta* 422:407–18
263. Simon, R. D. 1977. *Arch. Microbiol.* 3:283–88
264. Simon, R. D., Weathers, P. 1976. *Biochim. Biophys. Acta* 420:165–76
265. Singer, R. A., Doolittle, W. F. 1974. *J. Bacteriol.* 118:351–57
266. Singer, R. A., Doolittle, W. F. 1975. *Nature* 253:650–51
267. Singh, P. K. 1973. *Arch. Mikrobiol.* 92:59–62
268. Smith, A. J., Evans, A., Lucas, C., Lewis, W. G. 1973. *Biochem. Soc. Trans.* 1:707–9
269. Smith, A. J., London, J., Stanier, R. Y. 1967. *J. Bacteriol.* 94:972–83
270. Smith, A. J., Lucas, C. 1971. *Biochem. J.* 124:23P–24P
271. Staflen, F. A. 1972. *International Code of Botanical Nomenclature.* Utrecht, Netherlands: A. Oosthock. 200 pp.
272. Stanier, R. Y. 1970. In *Organization and Control in Procaryotic and Eucaryotic Cells,* pp. 1–38. Cambridge, England: Cambridge Univ. Press. 457 pp.
273. Stanier, R. Y. See Ref. 48, pp. 501–18
274. Stanier, R. Y. 1974. *Symp. Soc. Gen. Microbiol.* 24:219–40
275. Stanier, R. Y., Kunisawa, R., Mandel, M., Cohen-Bazire, G. 1971. *Bacteriol. Rev.* 35:171–205
276. Stanier, R. Y., Van Niel, C. B. 1962. *Arch. Mikrobiol.* 42:17–35
277. Stevens, S. E. Jr., Van Baalen, C. 1973. *Plant Physiol.* 51:350–56
278. Stewart, W. D. P., Bottomley, P. J. 1976. In *Proc. 1st Int. Symp. on Nitrogen Fixation,* ed. W. E. Newton, C. J. Nyman, vol. 1, pp. 257–73. Pullman: Washington State Univ. Press. 311 pp.
279. Stewart, W. D. P., Codd, G. A. 1975. *Br. Phycol. J.* 10:273–78
280. Stewart, W. D. P., Haystead, A., Pearson, H. W. 1969. *Nature* 224:226–28
281. Stewart, W. D. P., Lex, M. 1970. *Arch. Mikrobiol.* 73:250–60
282. Stewart, W. D. P., Pearson, H. W. 1970. *Proc. R. Soc. London Ser. B* 175:293–311
283. Stewart, W. D. P., Rowell, P., Tel-Or, E. 1975. *Biochem. Soc. Trans.* 3:357–61
284. Szalay, A., Munsche, D., Wollgiehn, R., Parthier, B. 1972. *Biochem. J.* 129:135–40
285. Tabita, F. R., McFadden, B. A. 1972. *Biochem. Biophys. Res. Commun.* 48:1153–59
286. Tabita, F. R., Stevens, S. E. Jr., Gibson, J. L. 1976. *J. Bacteriol.* 125:531–39
287. Tabita, F. R., Stevens, S. E. Jr., Quijano, R. 1974. *Biochem. Biophys. Res. Commun.* 61:45–52
288. Takabe, T., Nishimura, M., Akasawa, T. 1976. *Biochem. Biophys. Res. Commun.* 68:537–44
289. Tanaka, M., Haniu, M., Yasunobu, K. T., Rao, K. K., Hall, D. O. 1975. *Biochemistry* 14:5535–40

290. Tanaka, M., Haniu, M., Yasunobu, K. T., Rao, K. K., Hall, D. O. 1976. *Biochem. Biophys. Res. Commun.* 69:759–65
291. Tandeau de Marsac, N. 1977. *J. Bacteriol.* In press
292. Tandeau de Marsac, N., Cohen-Bazire, G. 1977. *Proc. Natl. Acad. Sci. USA.* 74:1635–39
293. Thornber, J. P. 1975. *Ann. Rev. Plant Physiol.* 26:127–58
294. Thurston, E. L., Ingram, L. O. 1971. *J. Phycol.* 7:203–10
295. Tyagi, V. V. S. 1975. *Biol. Rev.* 50: 247–84
296. Van Baalen, C. 1961. *Science* 133:1922
297. Van Baalen, C. 1962. *Bot. Mar.* 4: 129–39
298. Van Baalen, C. 1965. *J. Phycol.* 1:19–22
299. Van Baalen, C., Hoare, D. S., Brandt, E. 1971. *J. Bacteriol.* 105:685–89
300. Van der Velde, H. H., Guiking, P., Van der Wulp, D. 1975. *Z. Pflanzenphysiol.* 76:95–108
301. Van Gorkom, H. J., Donze, M. 1971. *Nature* 234:231–32
302. Vaughan, M. H. Jr. 1964. *Structural and comparative studies of the algal protein phycoerythrin.* PhD Dissertation. Mass. Inst. Technol., Cambridge. 458 pp.
303. Wada, K., Hase, T., Tokunaga, H., Matsubara, H. 1975. *FEBS Lett.* 55: 102–4
304. Walsby, A. E. 1968. *Protoplasma* 65: 223–38
305. Walsby, A. E. 1972. *Bacteriol. Rev.* 36: 1–32
306. Walsby, A. E. 1975. *Ann. Rev. Plant Physiol.* 26:427–39
307. Walsby, A. E., Nichols, B. W. 1969. *Nature* 221:673–74
308. Waterbury, J. B. 1976. *Purification, developmental patterns and properties of some fresh water and marine cyanobacteria belonging to the orders Chamaesiphonales and Pleurocapsales.* PhD Thesis, Univ. Calif. Berkeley. 236 pp.
309. Waterbury, J. B., Stanier, R. Y. 1977. *Bacteriol. Rev.* In press
310. Watson, S. W. 1965. *Limnol. Oceanogr.* 10:274–89
311. Watson, S. W., Waterbury, J. B. 1971 *Arch. Mikrobiol.* 77:203–30
312. Weckesser, J., Katz, A., Drews, G., Mayer, H., Fromme, I. 1974. *J. Bacteriol.* 120:672–78
313. Weise, G., Drews, G., Jann, B., Jann, K. 1970. *Arch. Mikrobiol.* 71:89–98
314. White, A. W., Shilo, M. 1975. *Arch. Mikrobiol.* 102:123–27
315. Whittenbury, R., McLee, A. G. 1967. *Arch. Mikrobiol.* 59:324–34
316. Whitton, B. A., Carr, N. G., Craig, I. W. 1971. *Protoplasma* 72:325–57
317. Whitton, B. A., Kirkby, S. M., Peat, A., Sinclair, C. See Ref. 233, p. 180
318. Whitton, B. A., Peat, A. 1969. *Arch. Mikrobiol.* 68:362–76
319. Wilcox, M. 1970. *Nature* 228:686–87
320. Wilcox, M., Mitchison, G. J., Smith, R. J. 1973. *J. Cell Sci.* 12:707–23
321. Wilcox, M., Mitchison, G. J., Smith, R. J. 1973. *J. Cell Sci.* 13:637–49
322. Wilcox, M., Mitchison, G. J., Smith, R. J. 1975. *Arch. Microbiol.* 103:219–23
323. Wildman, R. B., Bowen, C. C. 1974. *J. Bacteriol.* 117:866–81
324. Winkenbach, F., Wolk, C. P., Jost, M. 1972. *Planta* 107:69–80
325. Woese, C. R., Fox, G. E., Zablen, L., Uchida, T., Bonen, L., Pechman, K., Lewis, B. J., Stahl, D. 1975. *Nature* 254:83–86
326. Wolk, C. P. 1968. *J. Bacteriol.* 96: 2138–43
327. Wolk, C. P. 1973. *Bacteriol. Rev.* 37: 32–101
328. Wolk, C. P. 1975. *Dev. Biol.* 46:370–82
329. Wolk, C. P. 1975. In *Spores VI,* ed. P. Gerhardt, H. Sadoff, R. Costilow, pp. 85–96. Washington: Am. Soc. Microbiol. 619 pp.
330. Wolk, C. P., Simon, R. D. 1969. *Planta* 86:92–97
331. Wolk, C. P., Thomas, J., Shaffer, P. W., Austin, S. M., Galonsky, A. 1976. *J. Biol. Chem.* 251:5027–34
332. Wyatt, J. T., Silvey, J. K. G. 1969. *Science* 165:908–9
333. Zavarzin, G., Legunkova, R. 1959. *J. Gen. Microbiol.* 21:186–90

Ann. Rev. Microbiol. 1977. 31:275–90

PHOTOTROPHIC GREEN AND PURPLE BACTERIA: A COMPARATIVE, SYSTEMATIC SURVEY[1]

❖1705

Norbert Pfennig

Institut für Mikrobiologie der Gesellschaft für Strahlen- und Umweltforschung m.b.H., Göttingen, West Germany

CONTENTS

INTRODUCTION 276
Prokaryotic Phototrophs: Basic Differences Between Cyanobacteria and the Green and Purple Bacteria 276
MAJOR CHARACTERISTICS OF THE GREEN AND PURPLE BACTERIA 277
Cytological and Biochemical Properties 277
Historical Basis of the Existing Classification 278
Legitimate Names of the Higher Taxa 279
GREEN BACTERIA (CHLOROBIINEAE) 280
Green and Brown Sulfur Bacteria (Chlorobiaceae) 280
Green-colored species 280
Brown-colored species and consortiums 280
Filamentous Gliding Green Bacteria (Chloroflexaceae) 281
Thermophilic and mesophilic Chloroflexus 281
Planctonic Chloronema 282
PURPLE BACTERIA (RHODOSPIRILLINEAE) 282
Problems of Differentiation Between Purple Sulfur and Nonsulfur Bacteria 282
Purple Sulfur Bacteria (Chromatiaceae) 283
Criteria for determinative purposes 283
Poorly studied genera and species 284

[1]Dedicated to Professor C. B. van Niel.

Purple Nonsulfur Bacteria (Rhodospirillaceae) 284
Morphological and structural diversity 284
Cell envelope lipopolysaccharides and chemotype differentiation 286
Ribosomal protein patterns and genetic relatedness 286
CONCLUSIONS 287

INTRODUCTION

Prokaryotic Phototrophs: Basic Differences Between Cyanobacteria and the Green and Purple Bacteria

Ten years ago, the term photosynthetic or phototrophic bacteria was unambiguously used to designate the green and purple bacteria performing photosynthesis without oxygen evolution (anoxygenic photosynthesis). With the advance in our knowledge of cell structure, which followed the introduction of the electron microscope, it became clear that the blue-green algae have the same prokaryotic cellular organization as the bacteria (64, 66). The blue-green algae differ from the green and purple bacteria in their possession of oxygenic photosynthesis, which they have in common with the eukaryotic phototrophs. The fundamental difference between the prokaryotic and eukaryotic cell structure must be considered of primary importance in the evaluation of the systematic position of the blue-green algae and the newly established prokaryotic prochlorophyta (27). Oxygenic photosynthesis apparently evolved in prokaryotic cells, and there are good reasons to think that eukaryotic cells acquired the capacity for oxygenic photosynthesis by the development of an endosymbiosis with prokaryotic phototrophs that became chloroplasts (62).

As a consequence of the common cellular structure, the blue-green algae, as the cyanobacteria, have recently been placed with the other bacteria into the kingdom of the Procaryotae (33, 65). Thus, the prokaryotic phototrophs or phototrophic bacteria presently comprise the green and purple bacteria as well as the cyanobacteria and prochlorophyta.

The type of photosynthesis together with the nature of the important photosynthetic pigments constitute the taxonomically significant characters for the differentiation of the groups of phototrophic bacteria. Cyanobacteria and prochlorophyta have oxygenic photosynthesis with two linked photosystems in which water is the electron donor and oxygen is the ultimate oxidation product. Their photosynthetic pigments are, in addition to carotenoids, either chlorophyll *a* and phycobiliproteins (cyanobacteria) or chlorophyll *a* and *b* (prochlorophyta). That cyanobacteria with oxygenic photosynthesis may grow and exhibit anoxygenic photosynthesis with only one photosystem when hydrogen sulfide is present as an electron donor was shown by Cohen, Padan & Shilo (3). The phototrophic green and purple bacteria possess only one photosystem and, therefore, perform anoxygenic photosynthesis exclusively; their photosynthetic pigments are the bacteriochlorophylls *a, b, c, d,* or *e* and a great variety of carotenoids. For photosynthetic electron donor, they depend on substances of a lower redox potential than water, such as reduced sulfur compounds, sulfur, molecular hydrogen, or simple organic compounds. For phototrophic growth, the green and purple bacteria depend on anaerobic conditions under which these substances are available.

MAJOR CHARACTERISTICS OF THE GREEN AND PURPLE BACTERIA

Cytological and Biochemical Properties

Green and purple bacteria have in common anoxygenic photosynthesis and bacteriochlorophyll *a* as one of several photosynthetic pigments. Cytologically, however, they represent two remarkably different groups.

All green bacteria are either nonmotile green sulfur bacteria, the Chlorobiaceae (53), or gliding filamentous green bacteria, the Chloroflexaceae (54, 69). In both families, there are genera with gas vacuoles composed of individual gas vesicles (4, 8, 72).

The photosynthetic apparatus of the green bacteria consists of the bacteriochlorophyll a_P-containing cytoplasmic membrane to which the intracellular chlorobium vesicles (5) are firmly attached. The vesicles serve a light harvesting function and contain the accessory bacteriochlorophylls *c, d,* or *e* (16). The bacteriochlorophyll a_P in the cytoplasmic membrane (39) is synthesized exclusively in one form, which is substituted with an ethyl group in position C-4 and a methyl group in position C-5 like the bacteriochlorophylls a_P, a_{Gg}, and *b* (ethylidene in C-4) in the membranes of the purple bacteria (16). In contrast, the bacteriochlorophylls *c, d,* and *e* in the chlorobium vesicles (6, 16) are synthesized with several different substituents in the positions C-4 and C-5, yielding at least six different homologues of each bacteriochlorophyll, the nature of which can be influenced by the addition of the corresponding alcohols to the medium (15). In case of bacteriochlorophyll *e,* not only those homologues have been found that are esterified at the C-7'''-side chain with farnesol (bacteriochlorophyll e_F), but also phytol (bacteriochlorophyll e_P) and cetylalcohol (hexadecanol) (bacteriochlorophyll e_C) have been identified as esterifying alcohols (15). The lower degree of structural specificity of the bacteriochlorophylls in the chlorobium vesicles must be taken as a sign of a less rigidly fixed spatial structure within the chlorobium vesicles, as compared to the structure of the cytoplasmic membrane of these bacteria as well as of the photosynthetic membranes of the purple bacteria. The chlorobium vesicles cytologically identify a particular bacterium as a member of the green bacteria, since comparable structures have not been found in other phototrophic cells (53).

In contrast to the green bacteria, most purple bacteria are flagellated and exhibit advantageous photo- and chemotactic responses to their environment; gliding motility does not occur. The photosynthetic apparatus of both groups of the purple bacteria, Chromatiaceae or purple sulfur bacteria and Rhodospirillaceae or purple nonsulfur bacteria, is located on various types of intracytoplasmic unit membrane systems that are continuous with the cytoplasmic membrane (38, 43, 53). Bacteriochlorophyll *a* is most widespread among the purple bacteria; only one species of the purple sulfur bacteria and two species of the purple nonsulfur bacteria are known to have bacteriochlorophyll *b* instead.

A great variety of different carotenoids are found in the purple bacteria; however, their taxonomic significance is rather limited and is not useful beyond the species level. The aromatic keto-carotenoid okenone is restricted to some species of the Chromatiaceae; many types of aliphatic carotenoids occur in both the Chromatiaceae and the Rhodospirillaceae (60). Gas vacuoles occur in some motile and nonmotile genera of purple sulfur bacteria but not in the purple nonsulfur bacteria.

Historical Basis of the Existing Classification

Considering the taxonomy and classification of the green and purple bacteria, it must be kept in mind that these were not established in the manner used for many bacterial groups in the past 20 years, i.e. on the basis of detailed studies of a large number of individual morphological, physiological, and biochemical characters of a large number of strains in each species. In contrast, many species and genera became known in the form of morphological descriptions of cell forms collected in nature and were assembled in physiological-ecological groups long before the growth conditions for pure cultures of representative strains of these species became known. It appears necessary, therefore, to briefly characterize the historical basis of the four physiological-ecological groups that correspond to the four existing families of the green and purple bacteria.

The basis for the taxonomy of the purple sulfur bacteria are the morphological studies of Winogradsky (79). The cell material was collected from natural enrichments and maintained in the laboratory in raw cultures that became known as the Winogradsky columns. Winogradsky followed the multiplication of the different morphological types of the purple sulfur bacteria under the microscope and gave exact descriptions of the genera and species he established. He clearly emphasized that his group of the purple sulfur bacteria is not a "natural group" but rather a physiological group of bacteria occurring together under the same conditions in nature. The common characters were the pink-to-purple color of cell accumulations and the capacity to oxidize sulfide to sulfur and further to sulfate, with the sulfur stored inside the cells in the form of globules. The task to be done since the basic physiological work of van Niel (35) consisted primarily in the isolation in pure culture and physiological characterization of purple sulfur bacteria strains resembling the morphological descriptions of Winogradsky (see 43, 53).

The taxonomy of the second family of the purple bacteria, the purple nonsulfur bacteria, was established by Molisch (32) in the same way utilized for most groups of bacteria, i.e. the study of pure cultures in organic media. Molisch described species of those purple nonsulfur bacteria best known today: *Rhodopseudomonas sphaeroides, Rhodopseudomonas capsulata, Rhodopseudomonas palustris,* and *Rhodopseudomonas gelatinosa.*

As none of the species isolated by Molisch with complex organic media formed globules of elemental sulfur inside the cells grown with sulfide, he established two physiological groups among the purple bacteria. The purple sulfur bacteria as described by Winogradsky (79) became the Thiorhodaceae Molisch (32), and the purple nonsulfur bacteria, comprising the species isolated in pure culture, was named the Athiorhodaceae Molisch (32). Molisch also postulated a new type of photosynthesis involving the photoassimilation of organic substances for these bacteria. The present taxonomy of the purple nonsulfur bacteria is based on van Niel's (36) detailed morphological and physiological studies of a large number of pure culture isolates of each species, on Giesbergers (14) studies of some *Rhodospirillum* species, and on the description of *Rhodomicrobium* by Duchow & Douglas (9).

The taxonomy of the green sulfur bacteria developed in a way similar to that of the purple sulfur bacteria. Morphological descriptions of characteristic cell forms encountered in mud and water samples of natural habitats were given by Nadson (34) for *Chlorobium limicola* and by Lauterborn (26) for a number of genera. Lauterborn separated the yellowish-green, bacteria-like cell forms of the "sapropelic" microflora from the blue-green algae and placed them in a separate family: the Chlorobacteriaceae (26). The first pure cultures of *Chlorobium* were studied by van Niel (35) and subsequently by Larsen (25) who did comprehensive physiological studies with his highly improved culture medium. The availability of adequate culture conditions allowed the cultivation and isolation of both established and new species (43, 53).

The second physiological group of the green bacteria became established in 1974 with the discovery and description by Pierson & Castenholz (54) of the thermophilic, filamentous, gliding green bacterium *Chloroflexus aurantiacus*; together with the gas vacuole containing filamentous *Chloronema* species (8), these are the only two genera of the Chloroflexaceae.

Legitimate Names of the Higher Taxa

In connection with the preparation of the eighth edition of *Bergey's Manual of Determinative Bacteriology* (53), the International Committee of Systematic Bacteriology indicated the need for legitimate names for the higher taxa of the green and purple bacteria. According to rule 3 of the International Code of Nomenclature of Bacteria (1966 ed.), the family names introduced by Molisch in 1907 for the two physiological groups of the purple bacteria were illegitimate and a request to conserve these names (48) was rejected by the Judicial Commission (50). Therefore, Pfennig & Trüper (50) proposed Chromatiaceae Bavendamm 1924 to replace the name Thiorhodaceae and Rhodospirillaceae to replace Athiorhodaceae. Both new names were based on the best known and most studied genera of the two families, the type genera *Chromatium* Perty 1852 and *Rhodospirillum* Molisch 1907.

Lauterborn's name Chlorobacteriaceae for the green sulfur bacteria was illegitimate according to rule 14a of the International Code because it was based on the type genus *Chlorobacterium symbionticum,* a symbiotic association between protozoa and green bacteria (70); the name Chlorobacteriaceae was replaced, therefore, by the correct name Chlorobiaceae Copeland 1956. The latter name is derived from the type genus *Chlorobium,* which includes the best known species of the family.

The green and purple bacteria as the phototrophic bacteria with only anoxygenic photosynthesis and with bacteriochlorophylls as indispensable photosynthetic pigments are included in the order Rhodospirillales with the suborders Rhodospirillineae, purple bacteria, and Chlorobiineae, green bacteria; the latter comprise the Chlorobiaceae and the Chloroflexaceae (51, 53, 69).

GREEN BACTERIA (CHLOROBIINEAE)

Green and Brown Sulfur Bacteria (Chlorobiaceae)

GREEN-COLORED SPECIES The studies of van Niel (35) and Larsen (25) with *Chlorobium* species established the physiological type of the green sulfur bacteria. During the past 20 years, pure culture studies confirmed for the new species and for the other species, of which the latter had been assembled in the Chlorobacteriaceae on the basis of microscopy studies by Lauterborn (26), that all are of the same physiological type. Only *Clathrochloris sulfurica* (12, 53), so far, has not been grown in enrichment or pure culture, although it occasionally has been observed in mud samples of freshwater ponds and lakes. The Chlorobiaceae are characterized by a strictly anaerobic, H_2S-, CO_2-, and light-dependent metabolism, which is different from that of the purple sulfur bacteria. In the course of CO_2 assimilation, which apparently does not proceed via the reductive pentose phosphate cycle (56, 61), elemental sulfur is formed as an intermediate oxidation product and excreted into the medium where sulfur globules form. Under conditions of limiting sulfide and depending on the strain, the elemental sulfur is then more or less completely oxidized to sulfate.

All species of the Chlorobiaceae are nonmotile. The only apparent exception to this, cultures of "*Chloropseudomonas ethylica,*" proved to be syntrophic mixed cultures of either *Chlorobium* (20) or *Prosthecochloris aestuarii* (47) with the motile *Desulfuromonas acetoxidans* (47). The latter chemoorganotrophic bacterium was shown to oxidize acetate or ethanol to CO_2 and to reduce stoichiometric amounts of elemental sulfur to sulfide (sulfur respiration). In mixed culture with any green sulfur bacterium, *Desulfuromonas* reduces the elemental sulfur, excreted by the green bacterium, back to sulfide when acetate or ethanol is present; the syntrophy, therefore, is based on a closed sulfur cycle.

The isolation of a large number of green-colored strains of the genus *Chlorobium* showed that two morphological types exist; one of them has more or less straight rod-shaped cells and the other has smaller vibrio-like curved cells that may grow as half circles, circles, coils, or spirals. The former type was recognized as *Chlorobium limicola* Nadson (34) and the latter as *Chlorobium vibrioforme* Pelsh (42, 49). Since thiosulfate-utilizing strains exist in both morphological groups, the species *Chlorobium thiosulfatophilum* (25) was not maintained. Instead, subspecies as forma specialis *thiosulfatophilum* were introduced for both *C. limicola* and *C. vibrioforme* (53). With the description of the planctonic *Ancalochloris perfilievii* by Gorlenko & Lebedeva (19), a third genus was added to the genera *Pelodictyon* and *Clathrochloris* (53) containing gas vacuoles.

BROWN-COLORED SPECIES AND CONSORTIUMS Ten years ago, the known green sulfur bacteria comprised only yellowish-green-colored species. In 1968, Pfennig described the two brown species *Chlorobium phaeobacteroides* and *Chlorobium phaeovibrioides* (44); later on, two more brown species were isolated, the gas vacuole-containing *Pelodictyon phaeum* (17) and *Prosthecochloris phaeoasteroidea* (55). In the latter two genera, green species of the same morphology were known (53). I isolated in pure culture a brown counterpart to the green, gas vacuoles-containing species *Pelodictyon clathratiforme*; however, it was lost before detailed studies were made. It should also be remembered that the motile green consortium, *Chlorochromatium aggregatum* Lauterborn (26), has a brown counterpart in the consortium *Pelochromatium roseum* Lauterborn (26, 53). Although both kinds of consortia can be grown for some time in enrichment cultures for green sulfur bacteria, they have not been obtained in pure culture and the nature of the motile nonphototrophic central bacterium is still obscure (43). The use of binomial species names for symbiotic associations of two different organisms (consortia) rather than for one of the two components violates the rules of nomenclature (70). Thus, the classical names of the consortia may be used only as trivial names, i.e. they have no standing in nomenclature.

It appears that in almost all genera of the green sulfur bacteria green- and brown-colored species exist that morphologically, cytologically, and physiologically resemble each other (55). In all cases, the brown and green species were found to differ significantly in their photosynthetic pigments. The green species regularly possess bacteriochlorophyll *c* or *d* (light harvesting), bacteriochlorophyll a_P (reaction center), and the carotenoids chlorobactene and OH-chlorobactene (53). In contrast, the brown species regularly contain bacteriochlorophyll *e* (light harvesting), bacteriochlorophyll a_P (presumably reaction center) (15, 16), and the carotenoids, isorenieratene and β-isorenieratene (28). The establishment of separate species for the green and brown counterparts in each genus, therefore, appears justified.

Filamentous Gliding Green Bacteria (Chloroflexaceae)

THERMOPHILIC AND MESOPHILIC CHLOROFLEXUS Pierson & Castenholz (54) described the new genus and species *Chloroflexus aurantiacus* on the basis of 16 pure cultures isolated from different hot springs in the United States, Guatemala, Iceland, and New Zealand. These Chloroflexaceae form a second physiological group among the green bacteria as do the Rhodospirillaceae among the purple bacteria. Like those, *Chloroflexus* is primarily photoorganotrophic and capable of chemoorganotrophic growth under aerobic conditions in the dark or light. Oxygen represses the formation of both the bacteriochlorophylls and the chlorobium vesicles but not the formation of orange-colored carotenoids. The major bacteriochlorophyll of *Chloroflexus* was shown to be a bacteriochlorophyll *c*, which is esterified at the C-7‴-side chain with stearylalcohol (bacteriochlorophyll c_S) and not with farnesol as the bacteriochlorophyll *c* of the green sulfur bacteria (15). The major carotenoids of *Chloroflexus* are the β- and γ-carotene and their derivatives (54). H_2S is used as an electron donor for autotrophic CO_2 assimilation, with the major oxidation product elemental sulfur and not sulfate (30).

Although all *Chloroflexus aurantiacus* strains of Pierson & Castenholz (54) were thermophilic, Gorlenko (18) reported the isolation of pure cultures of mesophilic

Chloroflexus strains from the mud surface of freshwater lakes. In other features, these mesophilic strains resembled *C. aurantiacus.*

PLANCTONIC CHLORONEMA Dubinina & Gorlenko (8) recently showed that species with gas vacuoles also exist in the filamentous gliding green bacteria. They established the new genus *Chloronema* with the two species *C. giganteum* and *C. spiroideum* for these planctonic forms that occurred at the chemocline of stratified freshwater lakes with very little or no H_2S in the hypolimnion. The new species were recognized as green bacteria by their chlorobium vesicles and the possession of bacteriochlorophyll *d.* These species are photoorganotrophic and facultatively aerobic like all other filamentous green bacteria.

PURPLE BACTERIA (RHODOSPIRILLINEAE)

Problems of Differentiation Between Purple Sulfur and Nonsulfur Bacteria

Molisch (32) and later van Niel (37) differentiated the two physiological groups of purple bacteria by their ability (purple sulfur bacteria) or inability (purple nonsulfur bacteria) to form globules of elemental sulfur inside the cells from sulfide. This is a readily recognizable and reliable cytological character. Physiologically, it implies that all species that form sulfur globules inside the cells are able to oxidize sulfur further to sulfate. All of these species are able to use extracellular sulfur flower as an electron donor for photosynthesis as well as the intracellular sulfur (67). Purple nonsulfur bacteria, on the other hand, either did not use sulfur or used it only very slowly (21), although under special conditions they were able to use sulfide as an electron donor for growth. When purple bacteria were described that oxidized sulfide to extracellular sulfur and this further to sulfate (24, 57, 68), problems of classification arose. Physiologically, these purple bacteria had the same capacities as the classical purple sulfur bacteria, only they did not form sulfur globules inside the cell. Should these species be considered as purple sulfur bacteria or should they be classified as purple nonsulfur bacteria in the sense of Molisch since they did not form sulfur globules inside the cells?

Those purple bacteria isolated by Trüper (68) resembled *Ectothiorhodospira mobilis* described by Pelsh in 1937 (see 53). And as the other two forms showed the same fine structure of the intracytoplasmic membrane system, stacks of lamellar membranes, they were recognized as two further species of the genus *Ectothiorhodospira,* namely *E. shaposhnikovii* (2) and *E. halophila* (57). As extracellular elemental sulfur was oxidized to sulfate by all strains, Pfennig & Trüper (53) considered *Ectothiorhodospira* as a genus of the purple sulfur bacteria and thus deviated from Molisch's definition of the group.

Views of the purple nonsulfur bacteria broadened when Hansen & Veldkamp (22) and Keppen & Gorlenko (23) described two new species able to use sulfide as an electron donor for CO_2 assimilation. Sulfate was shown to be the final oxidation product of sulfide, and no elemental sulfur was formed as an intermediate oxidation product. Except for the capacity to oxidize sulfide to sulfate, Hansen & Veldkamp's

Rhodopseudomonas sulfidophila (22) resembled in all other characteristics *Rhodopseudomonas capsulata,* and Keppen & Gorlenko's *Rhodopseudomonas sulfoviridis* (23) resembled *Rhodopseudomonas viridis.*

These results, together with the findings of Hansen & van Gemerden (21) that other purple nonsulfur bacteria could use sulfide at low concentrations as an electron donor for growth, show that the oxidation of sulfide to sulfur or even to sulfate may be more widespread in this group. Under conditions of competition with green or purple sulfur bacteria, however, this capacity appears to be of minor importance both in nature and in enrichment cultures. Otherwise, the ecological niches of these physiological groups of bacteria would not be so clearly different in most cases. The capacity of the purple sulfur bacteria for intracellular storage of sulfur, the photosynthetic electron donor, should probably be considered an indication of a more fundamental physiological and organizational difference from the purple nonsulfur bacteria than heretofore believed.

As we now know a number of typical Rhodospirillaceae species capable of growth with sulfide as an electron donor, I propose to remove the genus *Ectothiorhodospira* from the Chromatiaceae and to place it in the Rhodospirillaceae. This will allow us to reintroduce Molisch's cytological differentiation of the two groups of the purple bacteria, which proved to be useful for determinative purposes in the past. The study of nucleic acid hybridization or comparisons of ribosomal protein patterns of *Ectothiorhodospira* and certain species of the Rhodospirillaceae may yield information about the actual genetic relatedness of these genera. The closest resemblance certainly exists to the brown-colored *Rhodospirillum* species, as their photosynthetic membrane system like that of *Ectothiorhodospira* consists of lamellar membrane stacks. In this connection, it is significant to consider that the physiologically diverse species of Rhodospirillaceae possess four different types of intracellular, photosynthetic membrane systems as compared to the one vesicular type of membrane system of the Chromatiaceae forming intracellular sulfur globules; the only exception here is the bacteriochlorophyll *b*-containing *Thiocapsa pfennigii* with a unique tubular system (10, 11).

Purple Sulfur Bacteria (Chromatiaceae)

CRITERIA FOR DETERMINATIVE PURPOSES Since Winogradsky's studies (79), the characterization of most genera of the purple sulfur bacteria was based upon the mode of development of cell aggregates (37). After it was shown that the formation and development of these aggregates are influenced by the existing environmental or cultural conditions, such as sulfide concentration, light intensity, pH, and temperature, it was then necessary to use the morphological characteristics of individual cells studied under defined conditions in pure culture for identification and classification (43, 53). Although most of the species and genera described by Winogradsky were authenticated by pure culture studies, a number of new nomenclatural combinations became necessary (49, 53).

Contrary to most other groups of bacteria, nearly all cell types of the purple sulfur bacteria that can be observed in samples from nature or grown in pure culture are so characteristic that they can be identified microscopically by their morphological and cytological properties. Apart from the presence of sulfur globules inside the cells in the presence of sulfide (exception *Ectothiorhodospira*), the typical properties are shape and size of the cells, arrangement in cell aggregates, motility at low sulfide concentration and in dim light, presence or absence of gas vacuoles, and color of the cell material (60). The absorption spectra of living cells (59) and the DNA base ratios, obtained from pure cultures, are also useful.

The consistency of the species and genera has been corroborated by the DNA base compositions of the strains in each species (31) except for the genus Chromatium. This genus comprizes the species of thick, cylindrical rod-shaped, sometimes slightly curved cells with rounded ends. The nine recognized species are differentiated by the size (width) of the cells. Although uniform in shape, the DNA base ratios show that the genus is heterogenous from a genetic point of view. The mol% G + C of the species with the largest cells, *Chromatium okenii* and *Chromatium weissei,* are 48–50 whereas the values for *Chromatium gracile* with the smallest cells are 68–70; the other species range between these extremes. The overall similarity of the species within the genus makes it seem inappropriate at present to establish new genera on the basis of the known differences in the DNA base composition.

POORLY STUDIED GENERA AND SPECIES A large number of pure cultures so far have been studied for only 2 of the 26 described species of the Chromatiaceae. These are *Chromatium vinosum* and *Thiocapsa roseopersicina,* the most common species encountered in nature. Most other species were confirmed on the basis of only one or a few pure cultures. Nevertheless, the present classification is considered fairly reliable and has proved to be of practical value for determinative purposes. Only a few pure cultures of each species have been obtained, primarily because of the great effort required to isolate and maintain them. Most workers could not afford to spend the time necessary to isolate, for example, 20 strains of the beautiful platelet-forming *Thiopedia rosea* (45) primarily for taxonomic purposes. The investigator must be satisfied in most cases when he convinces himself after one or a few isolations that many pure strains of the described species can in fact be obtained.

Thiosarcina rosea, Thiospirillum sanguineum, Thiospirillum rosenbergii, and *Thiopedia sevani* have not yet been obtained in pure culture, although they were observed in enrichment cultures and in samples from nature. Workers should be encouraged to attempt pure culture studies of these forms.

Purple Nonsulfur Bacteria (Rhodospirillaceae)

MORPHOLOGICAL AND STRUCTURAL DIVERSITY The purple nonsulfur bacteria are the best studied and most diverse group of the phototrophic bacteria. All species grow best as anaerobic photoorganotrophs and have the capacity to grow also as facultatively microaerophilic-to-aerobic chemoorganotrophs, like *Chloroflexus* and *Chloronema* of the green bacteria. With the exceptions of *Rhodocyclus purpureus* (52) and *Rhodopseudomonas globiformis* (46), for which only one strain so far exists, most other species are based on the study of a large number of individual isolates (36). The variations of the DNA base ratios within each species are surprisingly small and the mol% G + C for the whole family lies between 61–70 (31).

Recent taxonomic investigations on *Rhodopseudomonas gelatinosa* (75) and *Rhodopseudomonas capsulata* (73) extend and essentially confirm earlier results with these species. In the study of 25 strains of *R. gelatinosa,* two groups that slightly differed in the utilization of substrates and the production of slime were found. Thirty three strains of *R. capsulata* were found to form a stringent taxonomic group, which is clearly differentiated from *Rhodopseudomonas sphaeroides* and *R. gelatinosa* (73). Apart from known differences, including the utilization of certain organic carbon sources, the high sensitivity to penicillin and the specific susceptibility to bacteriophages were most striking. Lytic phages were readily obtained for all strains and none of the other species of the Rhodospirillaceae was susceptible for these phages (71). Another report on a lytic phage in purple or green bacteria is that of Bosecker, Drews & Tauschel (1), who isolated a single phage that proved to be specific for a single strain of *Rhodopseudomonas palustris.*

The genera *Rhodospirillum, Rhodomicrobium,* and *Rhodocyclus* are morphologically well defined; however, the fourth genus, *Rhodopseudomonas,* comprises three morphologically different species groups. Species group 1 includes *R. capsulata, R. sulfidophila, R. sphaeroides,* and *R. globiformis,* which have spherical-to-oval cell forms and vesicular intracytoplasmic membrane systems. *R. gelatinosa,* species group 2, has slender rod-shaped-to-spirilloid cells, and the photosynthetic apparatus consists of the cytoplasmic membrane with single, small tubular or lamellar intrusions (76). *R. gelatinosa* shows the closest morphological and structural resemblance to a species of the genus *Rhodospirillum, R. tenue.* Lipid A antisera of both species cross-reacted; no cross-reaction was obtained with lipid A of *R. gelatinosa* and *R. viridis* or *R. palustris* (58). Species group 3 of *R. palustris, R. viridis, R. sulfoviridis,* and *R. acidophila* has rod-shaped-to-elongated ovoid cells that multiply by budding (77, 78). The intracytoplasmic membrane system of these species as well as that of the budding *Rhodomicrobium* consists of membranes parallel to and underlying the cytoplasmic membrane (43).

As the number of species in the genus *Rhodopseudomonas* is small and few taxonomic studies at the genetic level are available, there is at present insufficient basis to make use of the morphological differences of these species groups on a genus level. However, as more characteristics become available, it may appear justified to classify *R. gelatinosa* as a species of the genus *Rhodospirillum* and to group the budding *Rhodopseudomonas* species either in a separate genus or in the genus *Rhodomicrobium.* The genus *Rhodopseudomonas* would then be represented exclusively by species group 1.

In addition to the aforementioned three types of intracytoplasmic membrane systems of the *Rhodospirillaceae,* a fourth type exists in the brown-colored *Rhodospirillum* species, *R. fulvum, R. molischianum,* and *R. photometricum.* The cells contain several stacks of lamellar membranes forming a sharp angle to the cytoplasmic membrane with which they are continuous (13); only the *Ectothiorhodospira* species have similar membrane systems.

CELL ENVELOPE LIPOPOLYSACCHARIDES AND CHEMOTYPE DIFFERENTIATION All phototrophic green and purple bacteria are gram negative, and the main component of the outer membrane of gram negative cell envelops are the lipopolysaccharide (LPS) heteropolymers that carry the type-specific O-antigenicity (29). It was first shown by Weckesser, Drews & Ladwig (74) that a LPS similar to the O-antigens of Enterobacteriaceae could be isolated from *Rhodopseudomonas capsulata.* In later studies on LPS of a large number of strains and species of the *Rhodospirillaceae* (7, 75), it was shown that the general principle of the LPS structure is present in all species. Apart from 2-keto-3-deoxyoctonate found in all LPS samples, the sugar composition showed a large diversity of components. Strains of each species were characterized by a specific pattern of constituents, which was also reflected in the serological properties of the strains. A good example are the results obtained with the morphologically very similar budding species *Rhodopseudomonas palustris* and *Rhodopseudomonas viridis.* The 10 strains of the latter species studied all belong to a single serotype and had 7 of the 10 sugars of the LPS in common with *R. palustris* (11 strains studied). Both species contained a unique type of lipid A that differed from that of all other Rhodospirillaceae and Enterobacteriaceae. Cross-reactions of lipid A antisera occurred only between the two species and not with any other species of the Rhodospirillaceae.

The results of Drews, Weckesser & Mayer (7) supported the present species concept in the Rhodospirillaceae and in addition gave indications to a chemo- and serotype grouping of some species on the generic level. It is quite obvious that the chemical composition of the LPS provides an additional useful character for taxonomic considerations.

RIBOSOMAL PROTEIN PATTERNS AND GENETIC RELATEDNESS It was pointed out by Stanier (63) that the search for relationships rather than mere resemblances between bacterial strains will be most successfully initiated by determining whether or not the strains of a particular phenotypically defined group share a substantial degree of genetic relatedness. Basic expressions of genetic relatedness are the near identity of the DNA base compositions together with the degree of homology of the DNA, assessed by the technique of nucleic acid hybridization. Although DNA base ratios are known for many strains of all species of the phototrophic green and purple bacteria (31), DNA homology studies are needed but so far have not been carried out.

At the level of gene products, increasing information accumulates that shows that the overall relatedness of the gene compositions of phenotypically similar strains is closely correlated with the relatedness of their ribosomal protein compositions. When the elution patterns of [^{14}C]lysine-labeled ribosomal proteins of *Escherichia coli* Q13 were compared with those of [^{3}H]lysine-labeled ribosomal proteins of *E. coli* K12, they proved to be identical (41). No apparent similarities could be detected in comparisons of *E. coli* ribosomal proteins with those of several *Bacillus* species and with *Sarcina.* Later work on large numbers of strains of several species of the Enterobacteriaceae fully confirmed the usefulness of elution patterns of ribosomal proteins for taxonomic purposes (40); the genetic relationships between strains of a given species as well as of different species of the same genus may be established.

In the phototrophic green and purple bacteria, several species or even genera provide good examples for phenotypically well-defined groups. Therefore, it is interesting to see that comparisons of elution patterns of ribosomal proteins were successfully used (K. Kawaguchi and S. Taniguchi, personal communication) to establish relationships among strains and species of the Rhodospirillaceae. These authors established that of 16 *Rhodospirillum rubrum* strains from all over the world 14 showed identical ribosomal protein patterns (100% agreement) and two strains showed 92% agreement. Between *R. rubrum* and three strains of *Rhodospirillum tenue* they found about 20% agreement, and between *R. rubrum* and the brown Rhodospirillum species *R. fulvum, R. molischianum,* and *R. photometricum* they found 8–11% agreement. Of 18 *Rhodopseudomonas sphaeroides* strains from all over the world, 16 strains showed 100% and 2 strains showed 70% agreement. Not a single common ribosomal protein was detected in comparisions of *R. rubrum* and *R. sphaeroides.* Studies on ribosomal proteins by using methods similar to those of K. Kawaguchi and S. Taniguchi (personal communication) may help to solve questions concerning the taxonomic position of the genus *Ectothiorhodospira* and of the group differentiation in the genus *Rhodopseudomonas.*

Although not yet of taxonomic concern, it may be added here that the first experimental genetic research with phototrophic bacteria was recently started by Yen & Marrs (80); these authors applied Marrs' discovery of a gene transfer system of *Rhodopseudomonas capsulata* to construct a genetic map of the chromosomal region concerned with the biosynthesis of bacteriochlorophyll and carotenoids.

CONCLUSIONS

The green and purple bacteria are two clearly different physiological-ecological assemblages of phototrophic bacteria with anoxygenic photosynthesis. The species and genera—many of which were named long before pure culture studies were possible—are grouped on the basis of morphological differences, each with a high degree of shared phenotypic traits. The existing classification involves the use of readily recognizable morphological features for the differentiation of most species and genera and serves primarily determinative purposes.

The number of described species and genera of both green and purple bacteria are still increasing, and they offer great opportunities for research on many levels. As yet unknown forms as well as cell types that have been observed in samples from natural habitats, and which have not been grown in synthetic media, can probably be isolated with existing techniques. Also, our knowledge of many species and genera rests on only one or few pure cultures, and the range of variations at the species level is still unknown. The majority of isolates studied to date are freshwater forms; further careful study of marine, saline, and hypersaline environments will certainly yield new forms that will broaden our views of existing species and perhaps even extend the number of known species.

Many strains of individual species need to be well characterized in terms of their phenotypic properties and DNA base ratios before further detailed analyses on the genetic level can successfully be started. Such analyses are required for the recognition of the degree of genetic relatedness among the strains within a species, of the species within a genus, and of the genera of a family. We can then decide whether the phenotypic resemblances are expressions of genetic relationships or of convergencies under similar selective environmental conditions. The green and purple sulfur bacteria already appear to be a good example for convergence of their overall physiological-ecological features under the same, highly selective environmental conditions; these groups differ so greatly in the details of their cytological, physiological, and biochemical features that they can hardly share a substantial degree of genetic relatedness.

We already have reliable and powerful methods by which means large numbers of strains of known species—particularly among the Rhodospirillaceae—can be isolated and subjected to comparative studies. The taxonomic work (73), the bacteriophage studies (71) and the experimental genetic research with *Rhodopseudomonas capsulata* (80), the comparative studies of the LPSs of Rhodospirillaceae (7, 75), and the comparative studies on the ribosomal protein patterns of several species of the Rhodospirillaceae (K. Kawaguchi and S. Taniguchi, personal communication) are encouraging examples of detailed studies with large numbers of strains of phenotypically well-defined species.

Although many phototrophic green and purple bacteria are not as easy to handle as, e.g. the Enterobacteriaceae, they have other qualities that make them rewarding and attractive companions for the researcher—the beautiful colors of their cultures, the stimulating richness in their different cell forms—and sometimes you may feel that as colored photobacteria including the blue green bacteria they live somewhat closer than the scotobacteria to our human world, which is illuminated by the same light that they require for their development.

NOTE ADDED IN PROOF A. Abeliovich and S. Kaplan (1974. *J. Virol.* 13:1392–99) reported the isolation from sewage and characterization of a phage RS1 specifically lytic for strains of *Rhodopseudomonas sphaeroides.* The isolation and characterization of a temperate phage specific for *Rhodopseudomonas sphaeroides* was reported by R. J. Mural and D. I. Friedman (1974. *J. Virol.* 14:1288–92).

Acknowledgment

I thank Marv Bryant for reading the manuscript and for help with English usage.

Literature Cited

1. Bosecker, K., Drews, G., Tauschel, H. D. 1972. *Arch. Mikrobiol.* 87:139–48
2. Cherni, N. E., Solov'eva, Zh. V., Fedorova, V. D., Kondratieva, E. N. 1969. *Mikrobiologiya* 38:479–84
3. Cohen, Y., Padan, E., Shilo, M. 1975. *J. Bacteriol.* 123:855–61
4. Cohen-Bazire, G., Kunisawa, R., Pfennig, N. 1969. *J. Bacteriol.* 100:1049–61
5. Cohen-Bazire, G., Pfennig, N., Kunisawa, R. 1964. *J. Cell. Biol.* 22:207–25
6. Cruden, D., Stanier, R. Y. 1970. *Arch. Mikrobiol.* 72:115–34
7. Drews, G., Weckesser, J., Mayer, H. 1977. Cell envelopes. In *The Photosynthetic Bacteria,* ed. R. K. Clayton, W. R. Sistrom. New York: Plenum
8. Dubinina, G. A., Gorlenko, V. M. 1975. *Mikrobiologiya* 44:511–17
9. Duchow, E., Douglas, H. C. 1949. *J. Bacteriol.* 58:409–16
10. Eimhjellen, K. E. 1970. *Arch. Mikrobiol.* 73:193–94
11. Eimhjellen, K. E., Steensland, H., Traetteberg, J. 1967. *Arch. Mikrobiol.* 59:82–92

12. Geitler, L., Pascher, A. 1925. In *Die Süßwasserflora Deutschlands, Österreichs und der Schweiz,* ed. A. Pascher. Jena: G. Fischer
13. Gibbs, S. P., Sistrom, W. R., Worden, P. B. 1965. *J. Cell Biol.* 26:395–400
14. Giesberger, G. 1947. *Antonie van Leeuwenhoek J. Microbiol. Serol.* 13:135–48
15. Gloe, A. 1977. *Erstbeschreibung und Untersuchungen zur Struktur der neuen Bacteriochlorophyll e und c_S und ihrer Homologen.* Thesis. Univ. Göttingen, Göttingen, Germany. 171 pp.
16. Gloe, A., Pfennig, N., Brockmann, H. Jr., Trowitzsch, W. 1975. *Arch. Microbiol.* 102:103–9
17. Gorlenko, V. M. 1972. *Mikrobiologiya* 41:370–71
18. Gorlenko, V. M. 1975. *Mikrobiologiya* 44:756–58
19. Gorlenko, V. M., Lebedeva, E. V. 1971. *Mikrobiologiya* 40:1035–39
20. Gray, B. H., Fowler, C. F., Nugent, N. A., Rigopoulos, N., Fuller, R. C. 1973. *Int. J. Syst. Bacteriol.* 23:256–64
21. Hansen, T. A., van Gemerden, H. 1972. *Arch. Mikrobiol.* 86:49–56
22. Hansen, T. A., Veldkamp, H. 1973. *Arch. Mikrobiol.* 92:45–58
23. Keppen, O. I., Gorlenko, V. M. 1975. *Mikrobiologiya* 44:258–64
24. Kondratieva, E. N. 1956. *Mikrobiologiya* 25:393–400
25. Larsen, H. 1952. *J. Bacteriol.* 64: 187–96
26. Lauterborn, R. 1913. *Allg. Bot. Z.* 19: 97–100
27. Lewin, R. 1976. *Nature* 261:697–98
28. Liaaen-Jensen, S. 1965. *Acta Chem. Scand.* 19:1025–30
29. Lüderitz, O., Westphal, O., Staub, A. M., Nikaido, H. 1971. In *Microbiological Toxins,* ed. G. Weinbaum, S. Kadis, S. J. Ajl, Vol. IV, pp. 145–233. New York: Academic. 473 pp.
30. Madigan, M. T., Brock, T. D. 1975. *J. Bacteriol.* 122:782–84
31. Mandel, M., Leadbetter, E. R., Pfennig, N., Trüper, H. G. 1971. *Int. J. Syst. Bacteriol.* 21:222–30
32. Molisch, H. 1907. *Die Purpurbakterien nach neuen Untersuchungen.* Jena: Fischer Verlag. 95 pp.
33. Murray, R. G. E. 1974. In *Bergey's Manual of Determinative Bacteriology,* ed. R. E. Buchanan, N. E. Gibbons, pp. 21–22. Baltimore: Williams and Wilkins. 1246 pp.
34. Nadson, G. A. 1906. *Bull. Jard. Bot. St. Petersbourg* 6:190
35. Niel, C. B. van. 1932. *Arch. Mikrobiol.* 3:1–112
36. Niel, C. B. van. 1944. *Bacteriol. Rev.* 8:1–118
37. Niel, C. B. van. 1957. In *Bergey's Manual of Determinative Bacteriology,* ed. R. S. Breed, E. G. D. Murray, N. R. Smith, pp. 35–67. Baltimore: Williams and Wilkins. 1094 pp. 7th ed.
38. Oelze, J., Drews, G. 1972. *Biochim. Biophys. Acta* 265:209–39
39. Olson, J. M., Prince, R. C., Brune, D. C. 1976. *Abstr. Int. Conf. Primary Electron Transport Energy Transduction Photosynthetic Bacteria, Brussels*
40. Osawa, S., Itoh, T., Otaka, E. 1971. *J. Bacteriol.* 107:168–78
41. Otaka, E., Itoh, T., Osawa, S. 1968. *J. Mol. Biol.* 33:93–107
42. Pelsh, A. D. 1936. *Tr. Vses. Nauchno Issled. Inst. Galurgii* 5:49–126
43. Pfennig, N. 1967. *Ann. Rev. Microbiol.* 21:285–324
44. Pfennig, N. 1968. *Arch. Mikrobiol.* 63:224–26
45. Pfennig, N. 1973. *Abstr. Symp. Procaryotic Photosynthetic Organisms, Freiburg*
46. Pfennig, N. 1974. *Arch. Microbiol.* 100:197–206
47. Pfennig, N., Biebl, H. 1976. *Arch. Microbiol.* 110:3–12
48. Pfennig, N., Trüper, H. G. 1970. *Int. J. Syst. Bacteriol.* 20:31–33
49. Pfennig, N., Trüper, H. G. 1971. *Int. J. Syst. Bacteriol.* 21:11–14
50. Pfennig, N., Trüper, H. G. 1971. *Int. J. Syst. Bacteriol.* 21:15–16
51. Pfennig, N., Trüper, H. G. 1971. *Int. J. Syst. Bacteriol.* 21:17–18
52. Pfennig, N., Trüper, H. G. 1973. In *Handbook of Microbiology,* ed. A. I. Laskin, H. A. Lechevalier, Vol. I, pp. 17–27. Cleveland: CRC-Press. 924 pp.
53. Pfennig, N., Trüper, H. G. 1974. In *Bergey's Manual of Determinative Bacteriology,* ed. R. E. Buchanan, N. E. Gibbons, pp. 24–64. Baltimore: Williams and Wilkins Co., 1246 pp. 8th ed.
54. Pierson, B. K., Castenholz, R. W. 1974. *Arch. Microbiol.* 100:5–24
55. Puchkova, N. N., Gorlenko, V. M. 1976. *Mikrobiologiya* 45:655–60
56. Quandt, L. 1975. *Versuche zum Nachweis von Ribulose-1,5-diphosphat-Carboxylase in Chlorobium-Arten.* Thesis. Univ. Göttingen, Göttingen, Germany. 52 pp.
57. Raymond, J. C., Sistrom, W. R. 1969. *Arch. Mikrobiol.* 69:121–26
58. Roppel, J. 1975. *Chemische, immunchemische und biologische Untersu-*

chungen der Lipopolysaccharide von Rhodopseudomonas viridis Stämmen. Thesis. Univ. Freiburg, Freiburg, Germany. 169 pp.
59. Schlegel, H. G., Pfennig, N. 1961. *Arch. Mikrobiol.* 38:1–39
60. Schmidt, K., Pfennig, N., Liaaen-Jensen, S. 1965. *Arch. Mikrobiol.* 52: 132–46
61. Sirevag, R. 1974. *Arch. Microbiol.* 98: 3–18
62. Stanier, R. Y. 1970. In *20th Symp. Soc. Gen. Microbiol.*, pp. 1–38. Cambridge: University Press
63. Stanier, R. Y. 1971. In *Recent Advances in Microbiology,* ed. A. Perez-Miravete, D. Pelaez, pp. 595–604. Mexico: Asociacion Mexicana de Microbiologia. 623 pp.
64. Stanier, R. Y. 1974. In *24th Symp. Soc. Gen. Microbiol.,* pp. 219–40. Cambridge: University Press
65. Stanier, R. Y. 1974. In *Bergey's Manual of Determinative Bacteriology,* ed. R. E. Buchanan, N. E. Gibbons, p. 22. Baltimore: Williams and Wilkins. 1246 pp. 8th ed.
66. Stanier, R. Y., Niel, C. B. van. 1962. *Arch. Mikrobiol.* 42:17–35
67. Thiele, H. H. 1968. *Arch. Mikrobiol.* 60:124–38
68. Trüper, H. G. 1968. *J. Bacteriol.* 95: 1910–20
69. Trüper, H. G. 1976. *Int. J. Syst. Bacteriol.* 26:74–75
70. Trüper, H. G., Pfennig, N. 1971. *Int. J. Syst. Bacteriol.* 21:8–10
71. Wall, J. B., Weaver, P. F., Gest, H. 1975. *Arch. Microbiol.* 105:217–24
72. Walsby, A. E. 1972. *Bacteriol. Rev.* 36:1–32
73. Weaver, P. F., Wall, J. B., Gest, H. 1975. *Arch. Microbiol.* 105:207–16
74. Weckesser, J., Drews, G., Ladwig, R. 1972. *J. Bacteriol.* 110:346–53
75. Weckesser, J., Drews, G., Mayer, H., Fromme, I. 1974. *Zentralbl. Bakteriol. Parasitenkd. Infektionskr. Hyg. Abt. I Orig. Reihe A* 228:193–98
76. Weckesser, J., Drews, G., Tauschel, H.-D. 1969. *Arch. Mikrobiol.* 65: 346–58
77. Westmacott, D., Primrose, S. B. 1976. *J. Gen. Microbiol.* 94:117–25
78. Whittenbury, R., McLee, A. G. 1967. *Arch. Mikrobiol.* 59:324–34
79. Winogradsky, S., 1888. *Zur Morphologie und Physiologie der Schwefelbakterien.* Leipzig: A. Felix. 115 pp.
80. Yen, H.-C., Marrs, B. 1976. *J. Bacteriol.* 126:619–29

Ann. Rev. Microbiol. 1977. 31:291–308

ANTIFUNGAL AGENTS: RECENT DEVELOPMENTS[1]

❖1706

George S. Kobayashi and Gerald Medoff
Department of Medicine, Washington University School of Medicine,
St Louis, Missouri 63130

CONTENTS

INTRODUCTION 291
POLYENE ANTIBIOTICS 292
Chemical and Physical Properties of the Polyene Antibiotics 292
Mechanisms of Action of the Polyene Antibiotics 294
In Vitro Antibiotic Effects of the Polyenes 296
In Vivo Effects of the Polyenes 297
5-FC 298
Clinical Use of 5-FC 299
COMBINED THERAPY 300
GRISEOFULVIN 301
TOPICAL AGENTS 304
Tolnaftate 304
Haloprigin 304
Clotrimazole 304
Miconazole 305
CONCLUDING REMARKS 305

INTRODUCTION

Unlike therapy for bacterial infections, there have been relatively few therapeutic agents developed for the treatment of infections caused by fungi. There are several reasons for this. (*a*) Fungal infections are much less common than bacterial infections, so the impetus for the development of agents has been small. (*b*) The most frequent fungal infections, the superficial dermatophytoses, are nonlife threatening and in most cases trivial, again decreasing the incentive for developing new agents. (*c*) Fungi are eukaryotic, and it has been difficult to develop antifungal agents that

[1]The survey of the literature pertaining to this review was concluded in December 1976.

have the specificity for fungal structures and macromolecular synthesis that antibacterial agents have for bacteria.

The most important antifungal agents are those that affect cell membranes. The polyene macrolides and the more recently discovered imidizole derivatives are the two groups of antibiotics in this class. The other important antifungal agents are 5-fluorocytosine, which affects RNA synthesis, and griseofulvin, which interacts with microtubules and inhibits cell division in a variety of different types of cells.

In this review, we summarize what is known about the most important antifungal agents and cover only those that have been useful in clinical infections. We do not intend to present a complete review of all of the properties of these agents because several recent articles have covered the chemical and biological properties of the polyene antibiotics (105), the biology of action of polyenes in natural and artificial membrane systems (78), the pharmacology of 5-fluorocytosine and its use with amphotericin B (93), and the absorption, distribution, metabolism, and excretion of griseofulvin (70). These should be referred to for information not covered in this article.

POLYENE ANTIBIOTICS

Among the long list of polyenes that have been isolated and described are some of the most effective antifungal agents known. Problems associated with solubility, stability, absorption, and toxicity, however, have made only a few of these agents therapeutically useful. Table 1 lists the polyene antibiotics that have been the most useful clinically, some of which will be covered in detail in this review.

Chemical and Physical Properties of the Polyene Antibiotics

All of the polyene antibiotics analyzed to date have certain common structural features in addition to a conjugated double-bond system (Figure 1). They are all characterized by a macrolide ring of carbon atoms closed by the formation of an internal ester or lactone. The presence of the lactone confers a highly characteristic peak on the infrared spectra of these compounds. The ring sizes of the various polyenes vary from 12–14 up to 35–37 carbon atoms. The conjugated double-bond system is contained exclusively within the cyclic lactone. The analysis of the characteristic ultraviolet (UV) spectra of the polyene antibiotics and also the X-ray crystal-

Table 1 Clinically useful polyene antibiotics

Name	Producing organism	Chemical composition	Mol wt
Amphotericin B	*Streptomyces nodosus*	$C_{47}H_{73}NO_{17}$	924
Nystatin	*S. albulus* or *S. noursei*	$C_{47}H_{75}NO_{17}$	926
Pimaricin	*S. natalensis*	$C_{33}H_{47}NO_{14}$	666
Candicidin	*S. griseus*	$C_{63}H_{85}N_2O_{19}$	1200

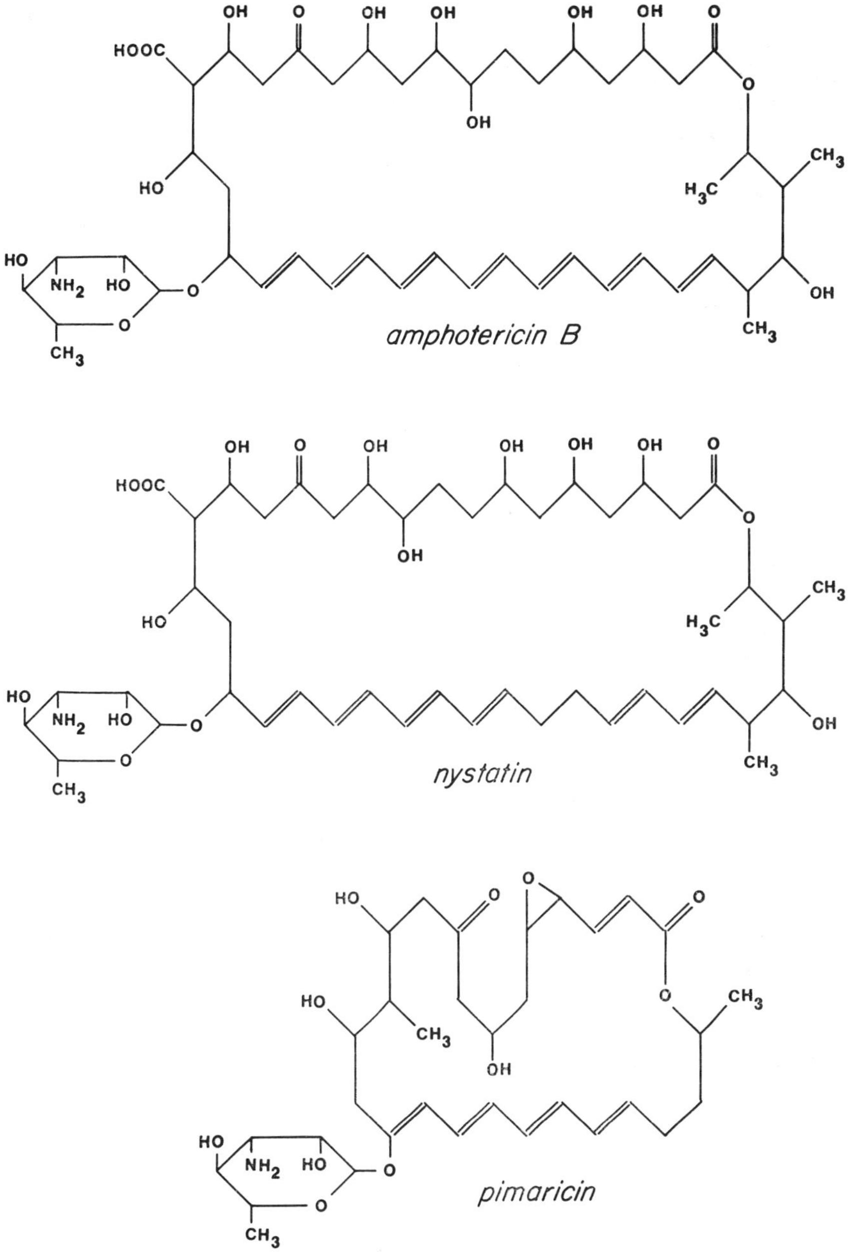

Figure 1 Chemical structures of amphotericin B, nystatin, and pimaricin.

lographic analysis of an N-iodoacetyl derivative of amphotericin B (32) indicate that all the double bonds are in the *trans* conformation.

Another highly characteristic feature of the polyene antibiotics is the large number of hydroxyls present on the molecule. The number varies between 6–14, and they are usually distributed along the macrolide ring on alternate carbon atoms. The presence of such a large number of polar hydroxyl groups and the multiple hydrophobic double bonds on the opposite side of the macrolide ring confer upon the polyene antibiotics the additional characteristic chemical property of being amphapathic. It is likely that this amphapathic feature plays an important role in the mode of action of these substances as they interact in various biological systems.

The most characteristic physical property of the polyene antibiotics is the UV absorption spectrum. The UV spectra of all the polyenes have a regular series of sharp peaks of absorption, which are separated by sharp troughs, all in the range of 400–280 nm. Oroshnik & Mebane (80) have given an extensive tabulation of the exact absorption maxima for many of the polyene antibiotics and have shown that the characteristic UV absorbing pattern is due to the conjugated double bonds. Careful analysis of the UV spectra indicates that there are several distinct classes of chromophores: tetraenes, pentaenes, hexaenes, and heptaenes. The molar extinction coefficients of the various absorption maxima range from $2\text{–}8 \times 10^4$, but it is not a simple matter to accurately measure the absorption of aqueous solutions of polyene antibiotics because there is a difference in the molar extinction coefficients when the antibiotics are dissolved in an organic or aqueous solvent. It is suspected that the differences are due to micelle or aggregate formation in water.

Mechanisms of Action of the Polyene Antibiotics

In the early 1960s, several laboratories independently presented evidence that polyene antibiotics could increase the cell membrane permeability of a number of organisms, thereby promoting a leakage of important cellular constituents and ultimately lysis and death of the cell (55, 56). Many other studies have substantiated these findings and have reinforced the belief that the other metabolic effects of the polyenes (inhibition of aerobic and anaerobic metabolism) were due to the leakage of vital cytoplasmic constituents resulting from the alteration of cell membrane permeability rather than a direct inhibition of glycolysis or some other critical metabolic events.

The antifungal effects of the polyene antibiotics are dependent upon a binding of the drugs to the cell membranes. Bacteria and protoplasts did not bind polyenes and were unaffected by them. These results led to the notion that the polyene worked by binding to membrane sterols, which are constituents of eukaryotic cells but which are not present in bacterial cell walls or membranes. Among the experiments suggesting a relationship between sterols and the action of polyenes, two series have been most convincing.

First, all organisms susceptible to polyenes contain sterols (e.g. yeasts, algae, protozoa, flatworms, and mammalian cells) and all resistant organisms do not (30, 41, 114). Second, sterols added to the medium could protect polyene-susceptible cells from these antibiotics (12, 36). This reversal of polyene effect was secondary to a physiological interaction between the polyene antibiotics and the added sterols, which prevented the antibiotic from interacting with the sterols of the organisms under study.

In addition to the indirect evidence cited above for the interaction between sterols and polyene antibiotics, direct evidence based on spectrophotometry data is also available. We have already emphasized that polyene antibiotics have characteristic UV absorption spectra with large molar extinction coefficients. Lampen, Arnow & Safferman (67) reported that when sterols were added to aqueous solutions of polyene antibiotics the UV absorbance values decreased. This suggested that a direct interaction had occurred between the added sterol and the polyene. Several other groups have confirmed these findings (62, 76, 77, 94), and more recently, Schroeder, Holland & Bieber (95) have presented strong direct evidence for binding between sterols and polyenes by use of a fluorometric technique involving the measurement of partial quantum efficiencies.

The nature of the membrane lesion resulting from the polyene-sterol interaction leading to the increase in permeability has been studied extensively by using natural and artificial membranes. Freeze-etch electron microscopy, on erythrocytes and *Acholeplasma laidlawii* treated with polyenes, have shown structural alterations such as pits, doughnut-shaped craters, and protrusions in the membranes, but there was no indication that these structural changes had resulted in holes or pores through the membrane. It has been assumed, but not proven, that these structural changes are responsible for the enhanced permeability of the membranes.

Studies have also been carried out using several different model membranes, including liposomes, black film bilayers, and monolayer systems, and have essentially confirmed the work in natural membranes. The effects of the polyenes were found to be dependent upon the presence of sterols in the membranes, and it was suggested that lipid rearrangement (58, 59) or fragmentation of the membrane caused by the presence or formation of polyene-sterol complexes was responsible for the molecular action of polyene antibiotics (22).

Freeze-etch electron microscopy of *Epidermophyton floccosum* (79) showed that amphotericin B induced profound ultrastructural changes in this fungus, which consisted of aggregation of membrane-associated particles, 85A in size, and the formation of depressions or craters on the inner faces of the membranes. No pores or holes were observed, which is in agreement with the other studies using *A. laidlawii* and artificial membranes. The absence of pores or holes in the surface membranes after polyene treatment has supported the notion that the interaction of the polyene antibiotics with the membrane increases permeability by inducing dramatic changes in the physical properties of the membranes by the avid binding of the polyenes to the membrane sterols, whose presence stabilizes membrane function and affects membrane permeability. The binding of the polyenes to membrane sterols would then mediate a phase transition from an ordered state to a melted or random state, resulting in an increased permeability (77). Although there is no direct evidence for this sequence of events, there is strong circumstantial support (31, 65, 76).

Work in our own laboratory on the nature of the membrane lesion induced by polyenes supports the idea that the changes produced are dependent upon the kind of membranes being treated and the type and concentration of polyene used. Yeast are more susceptible to amphotericin B than other polyene antibiotics because amphotericin B binds more avidly to ergosterol, the principal sterol in fungal membranes, than cholesterol, the main sterol in animal cell membranes (12). The increased susceptibility of animal cells to the other polyenes compared to amphotericin B is due to the increased binding of the former to cholesterol.

Each cell type (animal cell or fungus) also varies in susceptibility to the polyenes. For example, 3T3 and L cells are much more susceptible to amphotericin B than are HeLa cells (12). Neither the absolute cellular content of free sterol nor the amount of polyene bound to cells correlates completely with this type of differential susceptibility. Rather, we have found that the cells more susceptible to the polyene effects have a lower cholesterol: phospholipid molar ratio than the more resistant cell lines. This indicates that the sterol content in relation to phospholipid levels in cell membranes determines polyene susceptibility and is in agreement with this suggestion first made by Kinsky, Luse & Van Deenen (58) and Van Zutphen, Van Deenen & Kinsky (109).

Other factors may also play a role in the susceptibility of cells to polyenes. Hsu Chen & Feingold (50) have shown that the fatty acid composition of the phospholipids in cells is a determinant of susceptibility to amphotericin B. Because of all of these variables, it is clear that the mechanism of selective effects of the polyenes is complex.

In Vitro Antibiotic Effects of the Polyenes

The polyenes are inactive against bacteria. They exert various degrees of inhibition against many species of fungi such as yeasts (*Candida, Cryptococcus*), dimorphic fungi (e.g. *Histoplasma, Blastomyces,* and *Coccidioides*), dermatophytes (e.g. *Trichophyton, Microsporum,* and *Epidermophyton*), and molds (e.g. *Asperigillus* and *Penicillium*).

In addition to antimycotic activities, many polyenes also are toxic to protozoa of medical importance, such as trichomonads, *Entamoeba, Naeglaria,* and trypanosomes. Nystatin and amphotericin B are toxic to *Leishmania donovanii.* This effect has been shown to be a result of the loss of intracellular constituents because of its effects on membrane permeability and eventual cell lysis. Nystatin is rapidly bound to these cells and is preferentially bound to those fractions containing the highest sterol content. As with fungi, the binding is inhibited by adding digitonin or cholesterol to the incubation medium. Seneca & Bergendahl (97) and Johnson, Miller & Brumbaugh (53) have found that polyenes are toxic to snails and planaria.

As a general rule, the antifungal activity of the polyenes increases as the number of double bonds increases. This assertion is made despite the fact that accurate figures to support this widely held opinion are difficult to come by because experimentally determined minimum inhibitory concentrations (MIC) vary so much among different laboratories. Among the factors that may affect the MIC are inoculum size, temperature, and duration of incubation and medium composition

(61). Therefore, only if strictly standardized conditions are adhered to can susceptibility data from different centers be compared.

Utahara et al (106) were among the first to show that tetraenes and a pentaene (eurocidin) had about one quarter of the activity, on a weight-for-weight basis, of a hexaene (mediocidin) and heptaenes against *Candida albicans.* Table 2 is based on MIC data obtained by Athar (3) for clinically isolated strains of *C. albicans.* The heptaenes are more than one order of magnitude more active against *Candida* than filipin and pimaricin, whereas nystatin is about twice as active as the latter two compounds.

Because effective therapy for systemic fungal infection is essentially limited to the polyenes, development of resistance to these agents in fungi poses a major problem. Although fungi are intrinsically capable of giving rise to polyene-resistant variants, fortunately, the laboratory phenomenon of polyene resistance has not spread to clinical situations. The reason for this is not known, but it is probably related to the observed defectiveness of the resistant fungi. One explanation for this is that the membrane changes responsible for polyene resistance is detrimental to overall survival of these organisms in the natural environment.

In Vivo Effects of the Polyenes

The only polyene antibiotic sufficiently nontoxic and tolerated parenterally in experimental animals is amphotericin B. One cannot easily extrapolate from human dosages or in vitro studies so that the safest procedure is to be governed by a knowledge of its toxicity and measures of drug levels in serum. By using these parameters to determine drug dosage, the in vivo experiments have generally confirmed the in vitro effectiveness of amphotericin B against a variety of fungi at tolerable drug levels (61).

In any discussion of the medical uses of the polyene antibiotics, the first point to be emphasized is that these are very toxic drugs. This toxicity is well described in the literature and is probably based on the membrane effects of the polyenes on host cells (57).

Only a few of the polyenes have been developed for clinical use. The only one that is available for parenteral administration is amphotericin B. It is marketed as a bile-salt complex that forms a colloidal dispersion when hydrated. Established

Table 2 Relative activities against *C. albicans* of five polyene antibiotics

Antibiotic	Median MIC μg/ml	μM
Nystatin	3	3.3
Pimaricin	5	7.5
Filipin	5	7.4
Candicidin	0.5	0.42
Amphotericin B	0.5	0.54

protocols and therapeutic regimens for its use in a variety of different systemic fungal infections have been published (25).

Nystatin is the most frequently used topical or oral polyene antibiotic. Originally called fungicidin, this antibiotic is the product of a soil survey conducted by members of the staff of the New York State Department of Health, and the present name is a derivation of this laboratory. Nystatin is made by *Streptomyces noursei.* Its in vitro activity is highest against yeast-like fungi, but it is also effective against *Histoplasma capsulatum.* This polyene antibiotic is too toxic to be given parenterally, and there is very little or no absorption when given orally. For these reasons, its most important use is to treat topical or superficial infections by direct application. The local action of nystatin in controlling vulvovaginal candidiasis or *Candida* infections involving any part of the alimentary tract from the mouth to the anus is now so generally familiar that it does not require further discussion.

Several other polyene antibiotics, notably pimaricin, hamycin, trichomycin, and candicidin, have been used to a limited extent, topically, orally, or by inhalation for the treatment of localized and systemic mycotic infections. A colloidal preparation of hamycin when given orally (8) was found to be effective against some systemic fungal infections in animals and humans. However, the absorption of this polyene from the gastrointestinal tract has not been consistent enough to depend on it as reliable systemic chemotherapeutic agent. Pimaricin, trichomycin, and candicidin have been used to treat local fungal infections of skin, eye, and vagina by topical application or injection into infected tissue. The fact that certain of these agents combine activity against yeasts and trichomonas makes them particularly attractive antibiotics for use in vaginitis, but it is difficult to judge if they offer any real advantages over amphotericin B or nystatin.

Other uses of the polyenes are as food preservatives to prevent the growth of molds, especially on the surface of fruit, and in tissue culture media where amphotericin B is widely used with penicillin and streptomycin to suppress the growth of microorganisms.

Recently, Schaffner & Mechlinski (92) and Lawrence & Hoeprich (68) have shown that esterification of the free carboxyl group of amphotericin B or its N-acylated derivatives caused no loss of biological activity. Furthermore, the hydrochlorides of the methyl esters of amphotericin B, nystatin, pimaricin, mediocidin, candicidin, and trichomycin were highly water soluble and retained the full activity of the respective parent compounds while being of greatly decreased toxicity. It is too early to know if these preparations of polyenes will offer a therapeutic advantage, but considering the detailed information about the structure of the polyenes, it is surprising that only a few such attempts at improving the drug by molecular manipulation have been successful.

5-FC

5-Fluorocytosine (5-FC) is a synthetic oral antimycotic agent that is effective in the treatment of some deep-seated fungal infections, in particular candidiasis, cryptococcosis, and chromomycosis. It was first synthesized by Duschinsky, Pleven &

Heidelberger (26), and unlike the other compounds of this series, including 5-fluorouracil (5-FU), its riboside and deoxyriboside, as well as the riboside and deoxyriboside of 5-FC, 5-FC itself was found to lack significant cytostatic activity and toxicity in animals. In contrast to the other fluorinated pyrimidines, 5-FC exhibited practically no bacteriostatic activity in vitro but marked and rather selective antifungal activity against *Candida albicans* in vitro and in vivo. These properties suggested the clinical usefulness of 5-FC as an antifungal antibiotic.

As expected from its structure, and supported by the reversal of the in vitro inhibitory effects by cytosine, 5-FC has been considered an antagonist of cytosine. This direct function of 5-FC as an antimetabolite is probably of less importance, in regard to its antifungal properties, than a more indirect effect resulting from conversion to the antimetabolite 5-FU by organisms possessing the necessary deaminase. The evidence for this is that the antifungal effects of 5-FC correlate directly with the amount of replacement of uracil by 5-FU in rRNA and tRNA of the sensitive organisms. Polak & Scholer (88), by using many isolates of *C. albicans* with various degress and models of 5-FC sensitivity and resistance, have worked out a scheme of the pathways of 5-FC and its metabolites, which are probably responsible for its antifungal properties (Figure 2). The incorporation rates found with the various sensitive or resistant clinical isolates after exposure to 2-^{14}C-labeled 5-FC are particularly interesting because they strongly support the aformentioned hypothesis of the key role of the metabolite 5-FU in the action of the drug on RNA synthesis. It is assumed on the basis of good supporting evidence that RNA heavily substituted with 5-FU functions poorly, and abnormal proteins are synthesized, which lead to cell death.

The inhibitory effect of 5-FU on mammalian cells and certain bacteria may also be related to a block of thymidylate synthetase, leading to inhibition of DNA synthesis. There is no strong evidence for the existence of this mechanism in 5-FC-susceptible fungi, although Wagner & Shadomy (110) think this may be the mechanism of inhibition in aspergilli.

The pathway and mode of action of 5-FC proposed by Polak & Scholer (88) also explains the different mechanisms of resistance to the drug. Resistance may be produced by lack or deficiency of an enzyme at any step of the pathway, by a surplus of de novo synthesis of normal compounds competing with the fluorinated antimetabolites, or, hypothetically, by any compensation for the abnormal RNA function.

Clinical Use of 5-FC

5-FC is effective in vitro against *Candida, Cryptococcus, Torulopsis,* agents of chromomycosis, and some strains of *Aspergillus.* It has no inhibitory effects against

5-FC → (*permease*) → → 5-FC → (*deaminase*) → → 5-FU → 5-FUMP → 5-FUDP → 5-FUTP → RNA

Figure 2 Proposed metabolic pathway and mode of action of 5-FC, after Polak et al (87). 5-FUMP, 5-fluorouracil monophosphate; 5-FUDP, 5-fluorouracil diphosphate; 5-FUTP, 5-fluorouracil triphosphate.

the agents of other systemic mycosis such as *Histoplasma capsulatum* or *Blastomyces dermatitidis.* The drug has been used successfully in the treatment of clinical infections by some of these fungi, but in general its performance has been disappointing. This is probably a result of its strictly fungistatic effects and the high level of resistance present initially on some fungi or developing with continued use of the drug.

If a MIC of 16 μg/ml is used to define a sensitive organism, resistance to 5-FC was initially present in 4–67% of *Candida* species or developed in 100% of *Cryptococcus neoformans* after 7–10 days of therapy with the drug alone (102). The variability of some of these data may be due to the different media used in sensitivity testing and in the inoculum size. It has been shown that purines and pyrimidines present in most media greatly suppress the antifungal effects of 5-FC, and this has been one of the difficulties in interpreting in vivo sensitivity testing.

Toxicity of 5-FC has not been an important clinical problem. Bone marrow suppression and occasional diarrhea have been reported. The former has been thought to be secondary to conversion of 5-FC to 5-FU in the gastrointestinal tract by bacteria, but this has only been shown in animals and there is no evidence that it occurs in man (87).

COMBINED THERAPY

It is probable that the lethal effects of polyene antibiotics are separable from their permeabilizing properties. For example, Hsu Chen & Feingold (51) have been able to generate fungal mutants that are resistant to the permeabilizing effects of amphotericin B but not to its lethal effects. In addition, work done in our laboratory has shown that amphotericin B has a range of effects on the same cell types. We have determined that there are two types of binding of amphotericin B to fungi (12). One is energy dependent and reversible, and the other is irreversible and non-energy dependent. Only the latter is associated with lethality. We have also shown that very low concentrations of amphotericin B increase the permeability of eukaryotic cells to small molecules. Higher levels increase the size of the molecules transported, and finally, very high levels are lethal to the cell (11). These low concentrations of amphotericin B, which affect membrane permeability, are nonlethal, have completely reversible effects, and can be exploited to increase the therapeutic efficacy of antibiotics and antitumor agents, which normally penetrate poorly or not at all into eukaryotic cells (74). Some of these membrane effects on specific cells of the immune system are probably responsible for the adjuvant properties of amphotericin B, which we have described elsewhere (10).

We have exploited the permeabilizing nonlethal effects of amphotericin B on cells to increase the therapeutic effectiveness of several second agents (2, 60, 63, 64, 66, 72, 73). That is, at concentrations well below its MIC, amphotericin B can facilitate the entry into fungi of antibiotics that do not ordinarily affect fungi, probably because the intact cells do not take them up. Thus far, we have shown that in combination with amphotericin B the antifungal effect of 5-FC is increased against *Cryptococcus neoformans* and various species of *Candida* (72); and the effects of rifampin are increased against *Candida albicans, Saccharomyces cerevisiae, Aspergillus* sp., *Histoplasma capsulatum,* and *Blastomyces dermatitidis* (63, 64, 66, 73). We have concluded that the increased activity of the drug combinations was secondary to a potentiation of the effects of the second agents by amphotericin B, since in the presence of amphotericin B, there was an increased uptake of ^{14}C-labeled 5-FC into the fungi, and furthermore, the specificity of the second agents was maintained in the killing process. For example, when rifampin was used in combination with amphotericin B, RNA synthesis was inhibited; and when tetracycline was used, protein synthesis was inhibited. The combinations were truly synergistic because all of these effects were more than the additive effects of the two agents used alone.

These in vitro synergistic effects have been confirmed in vivo in animal models of infection (2, 60) and are presently undergoing clinical trials in patients (7). Thus far, early results of these trials are encouraging.

GRISEOFULVIN

Griseofulvin, 7-chloro-2',4,6-trimethoxy-6'-methylspiro-[benzofuran-2(3H),1'-(2) cyclohexene]-3,4'-dione, is a metabolic product of several species of *Penicillium* (14, 16, 52) and has been used for the past 18 years as the systemic drug of choice in the treatment of chronic dermatophyte (tinea, ringworm) infections. It was discovered and its chemistry was partially characterized in 1939 (81), and in 1947, the chemical structure, $C_{17}H_{17}ClO_6$ (Figure 3), was completely elucidated. The compound has UV absorption maxima at 324, 291, 252, and 236 nu (38–40), and it is possible to assay this compound spectrophotometrically in biological specimens (6, 29, 115).

Griseofulvin has been effectively used in the treatment of dermatophyte infections of the scalp and hair, nails, glaborous skin, groin, and interdigital areas of the feet caused by *Epidermophyton floccosum,* and various species in the genera *Microsporum* and *Trichophyton.* Hildick-Smith, Blank & Sarkany (46) have extensively described its pharmacological, chemical, and antimicrobial properties. It is thermostable and unaltered by autoclaving at 15 psi for 15 min unless it is in solution, when it may lose potency on heating at autoclave temperatures. The usual oral dose in adults is 500 mg per day, but this will vary according to the severity of the infection and may require starting doses as high as 1.0 g a day. In children weighing 30 to 50 pounds, a dosage of 10 mg/kg is usually adequate. Medication must be continued until the fungus is completely eradicated, as indicated by appropriate mycologic culture of specimens taken from the affected area. The duration of therapy generally depends upon the time required for normal replacement of the infected tissues and varies from 3 weeks of therapy in uncomplicated tinea infections to 12 months in the case of toenail infections (46).

In recent years, a great deal of work has been done on the absorption, distribution, metabolism, and elimination of griseofulvin in man and animals. Griseofulvin appears in the stratum corneum within 4–8 hr after oral administration (99). The degree of absorption from the gastrointestinal tract varies and depends upon particle size of the drug, fat and lipid intake, dissolution rate in intestinal fluids, and dosage

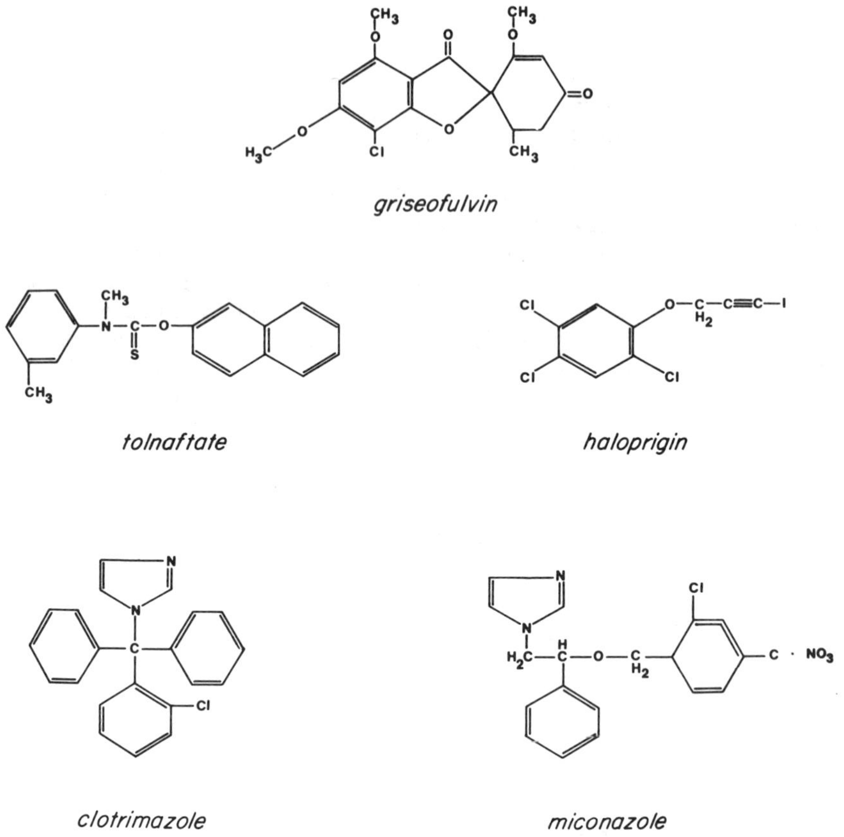

Figure 3 Chemical structures of griseofulvin, tolnaftate, haloprigin, clotrimazole, and miconazole.

regimen. In man, the major metabolites of griseofulvin are 6-desmethylgriseofulvin and 6-desmethylgriseofulvin glucuronide. The absorption and metabolism of griseofulvin have been extensively reviewed by Lin & Symchowicz (70).

The biological properties of griseofulvin were first described by Brian and his colleagues (13–15). It was termed "curling factor" because of its ability to induce stunted and aberrant growth of mycelium of *Botrytis alli.* Gentles (33) demonstrated in 1958 that experimental ringworm infection in the guinea pig could be effectively treated by oral administration of this drug. Therapeutic trials in humans followed with dramatic responses reported (9, 116). The MIC of griseofulvin against various dermatophytes ranges between 0.14–0.6 μg/ml, but the antibiotic has little or no effect against yeasts and bacteria (91). Microscopy studies on susceptible fungi have shown that, at concentrations of 0.1–0.2 μg/ml, grossly distorted growth of hyphae results (14).

The exact mechanism by which this antibiotic produces its effect against dermatophytes is unknown, but addition of griseofulvin to actively growing cultures of *Microsporum gypseum* or *Trichophyton mentagrophytes* temporarily halted protein and nucleic acid synthesis (28). El-Nakeeb & Lampen (27) demonstrated that the uptake of griseofulvin by the dermatophyte *M. gypseum* involved a two-step process similar to the process seen in plants (20). The first is an immediate uptake of small amounts of the antibiotic from the medium and does not require energy. This probably represents a simple absorption of the antibiotic to the lipids of the fungus. The second phase of uptake is prolonged and requires an energy source.

Although little is known about the antifungal mechanism of griseofulvin on dermatophytes, there is a growing fund of information on the effects of griseofulvin on microtubules of animal cells. In 1958, Paget & Walpole (82) described the striking arrest of mitosis in metaphase of bone marrow cells and intestinal epithelial cells caused by intravenous injection of griseofulvin into rats. They also reported that griseofulvin caused spindle disorientation and chromosome scattering and that the drug inhibited chromosome movement at anaphase. Although these antimitotic properties are similar to antitubulins, such as colchicine, podophilotoxin, isopropyl-N-phenyl carbamate, and vinblastine sulfate (117), the molecular action of griseofulvin is thought to be different from the other compounds that bind to the receptors on tubulin and inactivate the free subunits (118). The evidence for this is that griseofulvin does not interfere with tubulin in polymerization in vitro and that HeLa cells arrested in metaphase by griseofulvin show morphologically normal microtubules (37). It was proposed that the drug altered the function of intact microtubules in cells rather than causing them to depolymerize (37). There are data that show, however, that griseofulvin interferes with tubulin polymerization in vitro and that the observed effects of griseofulvin on microtubular assembly are dependent upon concentration of the antibiotic (113). At 10^{-5} M concentration of griseofulvin, 3T3 cells are arrested in metaphase and exhibit normal microtubules, but when the concentration of drug is increased to 5×10^{-5} M, the cytoplasmic microtubules are destroyed.

In addition to its antimitotic properties and in vitro action on tubulin, griseofulvin shares other properties with those of colchicine and the vinca alkaloids (18). It has been used in the treatment of gout (101, 111) and has some anti-inflammatory activity (21). In in vitro studies with Boyden chambers (4, 5), clinically achievable concentrations of griseofulvin (0.1–1.0 μg/ml) inhibited chemotaxis of human polymorphonuclear leukocytes. At least two possibilities have been considered to account for this inhibition. The first is that antitubulins (e.g. griseofulvin) inactive microtubules essential for the release of chemotatic substances (83), and the alternative hypothesis states that cytoplasmic microtubules are essential in conduction of chemotactic message from cell membrane to locomotor machinery of the cell (5).

Although much information has been gained about the effects of griseofulvin on microtubular structure and function in human cells, the mechanism of its action on dermatophytes remains to be elucidated. The recent isolation of tubulin from yeast (112) and filamentous fungi (100) may provide new insights into the understanding of the action of griseofulvin on fungi. Added impetus should be given to such studies in view of reports that griseofulvin specifically inhibits the mitotic spindle in various species of fungi (19, 41–43, 54).

TOPICAL AGENTS

Several topical antifungal agents are currently available for the therapeutic management of superficial mycoses, i.e. pityriasis versicolor, and the dermatomycoses, i.e. ringworm. In general, there is a paucity of information available concerning the mechanism of action of these drugs. In this section, the available information on the chemistry and mode of action of each agent is discussed.

Tolnaftate

Tolnaftate, m,N-dimethylthiocarbanilic acid O-2 naphthyl ester, synthesized and developed by Noguchi et al (75), is a colorless, odorless compound with the chemical formula $C_{19}H_{17}NOS$ (Figure 3). The antibiotic is applied topically twice a day, as a 1% solution or cream, to the affected area of skin. Tolnaftate is not very effective against dermatophyte infections of hair and nails. It is soluble in polyethylene glycol and chloroform, slightly soluble in ether and alcohol, and insoluble in water. Tolnaftate is effective against *Microsporum gypseum, Microsporum canis, Microsporum audouinii, Trichophyton mentagrophytes, Trichophyton rubrum, Epidermophyton floccocum,* and *Pityrosporum orbiculare* but not against *Candida albicans, Aspergillus fumigatus,* or *Penicillium notatum* (90). Although the drug has been used successfully in the treatment of cutaneous fungal infections, little has been published on the mechanism of its activity.

Haloprigin

Another topically active antifungal agent is haloprigin, 3-iodo-2-propynyl-2,4,5-trichlorophenyl ether, which was synthesized by Seki et al (96). It is used as a 1% solution or cream in the treatment of dermatophyte infections of the skin. It is a γ-iodopropargyl aryl ether with the formula $C_9H_4Cl_3IO$ (Figure 3). This synthetic compound is as active against dermatophytes as tolnaftate. Haloprigin, however, has a wider spectrum of action than tolnaftate because it is effective against species of *Allescheria, Alternaria, Aspergillus, Monosporium, Nigrospora,* and *Penicillium* (44). Little is known about the mechanism of action of haloprigin, but yeast cells of *C. albicans* treated with it showed an inhibition of respiration and disruption of cell membrane integrity (45).

Clotrimazole

Clotrimazole, $C_{22}H_{17}N_2Cl$ (Figure 3), [1-(O-chloro-α,α-diphenylbenzyl) imidazole], an imidazole derivative, has an extraordinarily wide range of activity against dermatophytes, yeasts, and filamentous and dimorphic fungi (84, 85). The drug has been shown to be fungistatic at 10 μg/ml but fungicidal at higher concentrations (17, 98). As with many other antibiotics, the MIC values of clotrimazole depend on the organism being tested, size of inoculum, length of incubation, temperature, and type of medium employed in the assay procedure (48, 86).

The drug is rapidly eliminated in the feces and urine of rats after oral or intravenous administration (104), and there is minimal absorption of the drug or its metabolites through the skin after topical application. Prolonged oral administration produces hepatic and adrenal changes (104), resulting in increased liver weight and cellular hyperplasia. Gastrointestinal intolerance is reported to be frequent and so severe that perbral therapy is not usually possible. Clotrimazole as a 1% solution or cream is used topically in dermatophyte infections. Suitable parenteral forms of clotrimazole for intravenous use have not as yet been developed (48).

Miconazole

Miconazole, 1-[2,4,dichloro-β-(2-4-dichlorobenzyloxy)-phenyl] imidazole nitrate (Figure 3), is a white crystalline imidazole derivative with the chemical structure $C_{18}H_{14}N_2OCl_4$. It was synthesized and shown to have antimycotic activity in 1969 (34). Miconazole nitrate is used as a 2% cream applied topically in dermatophyte infections. It is very soluble in organic solvents but practically insoluble in water. In vitro, miconazole is active against yeasts, filamentous fungi, and gram-positive bacteria (16, 34, 35, 107). It has been used in the treatment of dermatophyte infections (18, 71), candidiasis (49), aspergillosis (49), candidal vulvovaginitis (89), and coccidioidomycosis (47) with moderate to good success. In a murine model of coccidioidomycosis, Levine et al (69) have reported the effectiveness of miconazole in preventing deaths of all the infected animals whereas 60–100% of the untreated animals succumbed. Intravenous, subcutaneous, or intramuscular injection of miconazole into mice resulted in the formation of hematomas, fibrotic lesions and bleeding, and ulcerations to occur at the sites of inoculation of the drug.

It is thought that miconazole works by interacting with the cell membrane of fungi and causing leakage of cytoplasmic cations, amino acids, and proteins (103, 108). Transmission (23) and scanning (24) electron microscopy studies of yeast cells treated with miconazole support the contention that its antifungal effects are caused by a membrane effect. Similar experiments done in yeast cells of *C. albicans* treated with clotrimazole are not as convincing (1).

The recent results of the use of miconazole in the treatment of murine coccidioidomycosis (69) and the treatment of coccidioidomycosis and cryptococcal meningitis in humans (47) are encouraging, but much more experience will be necessary before its usefulness in the treatment of systemic fungal infection is known.

CONCLUDING REMARKS

It is apparent that only a small number of antibiotics are currently available for the treatment of fungus infections. Only amphotericin B is sufficiently nontoxic so that it can be given parenterally. It is presently the most useful antifungal antibiotic for systemic fungal infections. 5-FC, given orally, is most effective when given with amphotericin but its use is limited to only selected fungal infections. Griseofulvin, the other oral drug, and several different topical agents are limited to the treatment of cutaneous fungus infections.

With the exception of the polyenes and 5-FC, there is little known about the mechanism of action of the antifungal agents. The increasing occurrence of systemic fungal infections, particularly in the compromised host situation, should add impetus to the search for less toxic and more effective agents and perhaps to a greater understanding of the mechanisms of action of the ones presently available.

ACKNOWLEDGMENTS

Studies from this laboratory were supported by United States Public Health Service grants AI06213 and AI10622 and training grants AI00459 and AI07015; by the John A. Hartford Foundation, Inc.; and by the Research Corporation (Brown-Hazen Fund).

Literature Cited

1. Ansehn, S., Boquist, L., Schönbeck, J., Winblad, B. 1974. *Castellania* 2:41–44
2. Arroyo, J., Medoff, G., Kobayashi, G. S. 1977. *Antimicrob. Agents Chemother.* 11:21–25
3. Athar, M. A. 1969. *A study of the effects of some polyene antibiotics in Candida species.* PhD thesis. Univ. London, England.
4. Bandmann, U., Norberg, B., Rydgren, L. 1974. *Scand. J. Haematol.* 13:305–12
5. Bandmann, U., Norberg, B., Simmingskold, G. 1975. *Scand. J. Haematol.* 15:81–87
6. Bedford, C., Child, K. J., Tomich, E. G. 1959. *Nature* 184:364–65
7. Bennett, J. E., Dismukes, W., Duma, R., Medoff, G., Sande, M., Gallis, H., Cate, T., Cobbs, G., Haywood, H., Leonard, J., McGee, Z., Fields, B., Bradshaw, M., Williams, T., Warner, J., Alling, D. 1976. *16th Intersci. Conf. Antimicrob. Agents Chemother., Chicago,* Abstr. 308
8. Bennett, J. E., Williams, T. W., Piggott, W., Emmons, C. W. 1964. *Proc. Soc. Exp. Biol. Med.* 117:166–70
9. Blank, H., Roth, F. J. Jr. 1959. *Arch. Dermatol.* 79:259–66
10. Blanke, T. R., Little, J. R., Lynch, R., Lin, H., Medoff, G. 1975. In *Critical Factors in Cancer Immunology,* ed. J. Schultz, R. C. Lief, p. 349. New York: Academic
11. Brajtburg, J. K., Medoff, G., Kobayashi, G. S., Schlessinger, D. 1977. *Biochem. Pharmacol.* 26:705–10
12. Brajtburg, J. K., Price, H. D., Medoff, G., Schlessinger, D., Kobayashi, G. S. 1974. *Antimicrob. Agents Chemother.* 5:377–82
13. Brian, P. W. 1947. *Rep. Proc. Microbiol. 4th Internat. Congr.,* p. 153
14. Brian, P. W. 1949. *Ann. Bot. London* 13:59–77
15. Brian, P. W., Curtis, P. J., Hemming, H. G. 1946. *Trans. Br. Mycol. Soc.* 29: 173–87
16. Brugmans, J. P., Van Cutsem, J. M., Thienpont, D. C. 1970. *Arch. Dermatol.* 102:428–32
17. Burgess, M. A., Bodey, G. P. 1972. *Antimicrob. Agents Chemother.* 2:423–26
18. Burnside, B. 1975. *Ann. NY Acad. Sci.* 253:14–26
19. Crackower, S. H. 1972. *Can. J. Microbiol.* 18:683–87
20. Crowdy, S. H., Grove, J. F., Hemming, H. G., Robinson, K. 1956. *J. Exp. Bot.* 7:42–64
21. D'Arcy, P. F., Howard, E. M., Muggleton, P. W., Townsend, S. B. 1960. *J. Pharm. Pharmacol.* 12:659–65
22. De Kruyff, B., Gerritsen, W. J., Oerlemans, A., Van Dijck, P. W. M., Demel, R. A., Van Deenen, L. L. M. 1974. *Biochim. Biophys. Acta* 339:44–56
23. De Nollin, S., Borgers, M. 1974. *Sabouraudia* 12:341–51
24. De Nollin, S., Borgers, M. 1975. *Antimicrob. Agents Chemother.* 7:704–11
25. Drutz, D. J., Spickard, A., Rogers, D. E., Koenig, M. G. 1968. *Am. J. Med.* 45:405–18
26. Duschinsky, R., Pleven, E., Heidelberger, C. 1957. *J. Am. Chem. Soc.* 79:4599–609
27. el-Nakeeb, M. A., Lampen, J. O. 1965. *J. Bacteriol.* 89:564–69
28. el-Nakeeb, M. A., McLellan, W. L. Jr., Lampen, J. O. 1965. *J. Bacteriol.* 89:557–63

29. Epstein, W. L., Shah, V. P., Riegelman, S. 1972. *Arch. Dermatol.* 106:344–48
30. Feingold, D. S. 1965. *Biochem. Biophys. Res. Commun.* 19:261–67
31. Finkelstein, A., Cass, A. 1968. *J. Gen. Physiol.* 52:145–73
32. Ganis, P., Avitabile, G., Mechlinski, W., Schaffner, C. P. 1971. *J. Am. Chem. Soc.* 93:4560–64
33. Gentles, J. C. 1958. *Nature* 182:476–77
34. Godefroi, E. F., Heeres, J., Van Cutsem, J. M., Janssen, P. A. J. 1969. *J. Med. Chem.* 12:784–91
35. Godts, P., Vermylen, P., Van Cutsem, J. M. 1971. *Arzneim. Forsch.* 21:256–57
36. Gottlieb, D. H., Carter, H. E., Sloneker, J. G., Immann, A. 1958. *Science* 128:361
37. Grisham, L. M., Wilson, L., Bensch, K. G. 1973. *Nature* 244:294–96
38. Grove, J. F., Ismay, D., MacMillan, J., Mulholland, T. P. C., Rogers, M. A. T. 1951. *Chem. Ind.* 11:219
39. Grove, J. F., MacMillan, J., Mulholland, T. P. C., Rogers, M. A. T. 1952. *J. Chem. Soc.* 1952:3949–4002
40. Grove, J. F., McGowan, J. C. 1947. *Nature* 160:574
41. Gull, K., Trinci, A. P. 1973. *Nature* 244:292–94
42. Gull, K., Trinci, A. P. 1974. *Protoplasma* 81:37–48
43. Gull, K., Trinci, A. P. 1974. *Arch. Mikrobiol.* 95:57–65
44. Harrison, E. F., Zwadyk, P., Bequette, R. J., Hamlow, E. E., Tavormina, P. A., Zygmunt, W. A. 1970. *Appl. Microbiol.* 19:746–50
45. Harrison, E. F., Zygmunt, W. A. 1974. *Can. J. Microbiol.* 20:1241–45
46. Hildick-Smith, G., Blank, H., Sarkany, I. 1964. *Fungus Diseases and Their Treatment,* Chap. 49–55. Boston: Little, Brown
47. Hoeprich, P. D., Goldstein, E. 1974. *J. Am. Med. Assoc.* 230:1153–57
48. Hoeprich, P. D., Huston, A. C. 1975. *J. Infect. Dis.* 132:133–41
49. Holt, R. J. 1974. *Infection* 2:95–107
50. Hsu Chen, C. C., Feingold, D. S. 1973. *Biochem. Biophys. Res. Commun.* 51: 972–78
51. Hsu Chen, C. C., Feingold, D. S. 1974. *Nature* 251:656–59
52. Jefferys, E. G., Brain, P. W., Hemming, H. G., Lowe, D. 1953. *J. Gen. Microbiol.* 9:314
53. Johnson, W. H., Miller, C. A., Brumbaugh, J. H. 1962. *Physiol. Zool.* 35: 18–26
54. Kappas, A., Georgopoulos, S. G. 1974. *J. Bacteriol.* 119:334–35
55. Kinsky, S. C. 1961. *Biochem. Biophys. Res. Commun.* 4:353–57
56. Kinsky, S. C. 1961. *J. Bacteriol.* 82:889–97
57. Kinsky, S. C. 1967. In *Antibiotics,* ed. D. Gottlieb, P. D. Shaw, Vol. 1, p. 122–41. New York: Springer
58. Kinsky, S. C., Lusc, S. A., Van Deenen, L. L. M. 1966. *Fed. Proc.* 25:1503–10
59. Kinsky, S. C., Luse, S. A., Zopf, D., Van Deenen, L. L. M., Haxby, J. 1967. *Biochem. Biophys. Acta* 135:844–61
60. Kitahara, M., Kobayashi, G. S., Medoff, G. 1976. *J. Infect. Dis.* 133: 663–68
61. Kitahara, M., Seth, V. K., Medoff, G., Kobayashi, G. S. 1976. *Antimicrob. Agents Chemother.* 9:908–14
62. Kleinschmidt, M. G., Chough, K. S., Mudd, J. B. 1972. *Plant Physiol.* 49:852–56
63. Kobayashi, G. S., Cheung, S. C., Schlessinger, D., Medoff, G. 1974. *Antmicrob. Agents Chemother.* 5:16–18
64. Kobayashi, G. S., Medoff, G., Schlessinger, D., Kwan, C. N., Musser, W. E. 1972. *Science* 177:709–10
65. Komor, B., Komor, E., Tanner, W. 1974. *J. Membr. Biol.* 17:231–38
66. Kwan, C. N., Medoff, G., Kobayashi, G. S., Schlessinger, D., Raskas, H. 1972. *Antimicrob. Agents Chemother.* 2:61–65
67. Lampen, J. O., Arnow, P. M., Safferman, R. S. 1960. *J. Bacteriol.* 78:283–89
68. Lawrence, R. M., Hoeprich, P. D. 1976. *J. Infect. Dis.* 133:168–74
69. Levine, H. B., Stevens, D. A., Cobb, J. M., Gebhardt, A. E. 1975. *J. Infect. Dis.* 132:407–14
70. Lin, C.-C., Symchowicz, S. 1975. *Drug Metab. Rev.* 4:75–95
71. Mandy, S. J., Garrott, T. C. 1974. *J. Am. Med. Assoc.* 230:72–75
72. Medoff, G., Comfort, M., Kobayashi, G. S. 1971. *Proc. Soc. Exp. Biol. Med.* 138:571–74
73. Medoff, G., Kobayashi, G. S., Kwan, C. N., Schlessinger, D., Venkov, P. 1972. *Proc. Natl. Acad. Sci. USA* 69:196–99
74. Medoff, G., Valeriote, F., Lynch, R. G., Schlessinger, D., Kobayashi, G. S. 1974. *Cancer Res.* 34:974–78
75. Noguchi, T., Kaji, A., Igarashi, Y., Shigematsu, A., Taniguchi, K. 1962. *Antimicrob. Agents Chemother.* 1963: 259–67
76. Norman, A. W., Demel, R. A., De Kruyff, B., Geurts van Kessel, W. S.

M., Van Deenen, L. L. M. 1972. *Biochim. Biophys. Acta* 290:1–14
77. Norman, A. W., Demel, R. A., De Kruyff, B., Van Deenen, L. L. M. 1972. *J. Biol. Chem.* 247:1918–29
78. Norman, A. W., Spielvogel, A. M., Wong, R. G. 1976. In *Advances in Lipid Research,* ed. R. Paoletti, D. Kritchevsky, Vol. 14, p. 127–70. New York: Academic
79. Nozawa, Y., Kitajima, Y., Sekiya, T., Ito, Y. 1974. *Biochim. Biophys. Acta* 367:32–38
80. Oroshnik, W., Mebane, A. D. 1963. *Fortschr. Chem. Org. Naturst.* 21:17–79
81. Oxford, A. E., Raistrick, H., Simonart, P. 1939. *Biochem. J.* 33:240–48
82. Paget, G. E., Walpole, A. L. 1958. *Nature* 182:1320–21
83. Phelps, D. S. 1970. *Arthritis Rheum.* 13:1–9
84. Plempel, M., Bartmann, K., Büchel, K. H., Regel, E. 1969. *Dtsch. Med. Wochenschr.* 94:1356–64
85. Plempel, M., Bartmann, K., Büchel, K. H., Regel, E. 1970. *Antimicrob. Agents Chemother.* 1969:271–74
86. Plempel, M., Büchel, K. H., Bartmann, K., Regel, E. 1974. *Postgrad. Med. J.* 50:Suppl. 1, pp. 11–12
87. Polak, A., Eschenhof, E., Fernex, M., Scholer, H. J. 1976. *Chemotherapy* 22:137–53
88. Polak, A., Scholer, H. J. 1975. *Chemotherapy* 21:113–30
89. Proost, J. M., Maes-Dockx, F. M., Nelis, M. O., Van Cutsem, J. M. 1972. *Am. J. Obstet. Gynecol.* 112:688–92
90. Robinson, H. M. Jr., Raskin, J. 1964. *J. Invest. Dermatol.* 42:185–87
91. Roth, F. J. Jr., Sallman, B., Blank, H. 1959. *J. Invest. Dermatol.* 33:403–18
92. Schaffner, C. P., Mechlinski, W. 1972. *J. Antibiot.* 25:259–60
93. Scholer, H. J. 1976. *Chemotherapy* 22:103–46
94. Schroeder, F., Holland, J. F., Bieber, L. L. 1971. *J. Antibiot.* 24:846–49
95. Schroeder, F., Holland, J. F., Bieber, L. L. 1973. *Biochemistry* 12:4785–89
96. Seki, S., Nishihata, K., Nakayama, T., Ogawa, H. 1963. *Agric. Biol. Chem.* 27:150–51
97. Seneca, H., Bergendahl, E. 1955. *Antibiot. Chemother.* 5:737–41
98. Shadomy, S. 1971. *Infect. Immun.* 4:143–48
99. Shah, V. P., Epstein, W. L., Riegelman, S. 1974. *J. Clin. Invest.* 53:1673–78
100. Sheir-Neiss, G., Nardi, R. V., Gealt, M. A., Morris, N. R. 1976. *Biochem. Biophys. Res. Commun.* 69:285–90
101. Slonim, R. R., Howell, D. S., Brown, H. E. Jr. 1962. *Arthritis Rheum.* 5:397–404
102. Speller, D. C. E., Davies, M. G. 1973. *J. Med. Microbiol.* 6:315–21
103. Swamy, K. H. S., Sirsi, M., Rao, G. R. 1974. *Antimicrob. Agents Chemother.* 5:420–25
104. Tettenborn, D. 1974. *Postgrad. Med. J.* 50:Supp. 1, pp. 17–21
105. Thomas, A. H. 1976. *Analyst* 101:321–40
106. Utahara, R., Okami, Y., Nakamura, S., Umezawa, H. 1954. *J. Antibiot.* 7(A):120–24
107. Van Cutsem, J. M., Thienpont, D. C. 1972. *Chemotherapy* 17:392–404
108. Van den Bossche, H. 1974. *Biochem. Pharmacol.* 23:887–99
109. Van Zutphen, H., Van Deenen, L. L. M., Kinsky, S. C. 1966. *Biochem. Biophys. Res. Commun.* 22:393–98
110. Wagner, G. E., Shadomy, S. 1974. *14th Intersci. Conf. Antimicrob. Agents Chemother., San Francisco,* Abstr. 114
111. Wallace, S. L., Nissen, A. W. 1962. *N. Engl. J. Med.* 266:1099–101
112. Water, R. D., Kleinsmith, L. J. 1976. *Biochem. Biophys. Res. Commun.* 70:704–8
113. Weber, K., Wehland, J., Herzog, W. 1976. *J. Mol. Biol.* 102:817–29
114. Weber, M. M., Kinsky, S. C. 1965. *J. Bacteriol.* 89:306–12
115. Weinstein, G. D., Blank, H. 1960. *Arch. Dermatol.* 81:746–49
116. Williams, D. L., Marten, R. H., Sarkany, I. 1958. *Lancet* 2:1212–13
117. Wilson, L. 1975. *Life Sci.* 17:303–9
118. Wilson, L., Bamburg, J. R., Mizel, S. B., Grisham, L. M., Creswell, K. M. 1974. *Fed. Proc.* 33:158–66

Ann. Rev. Microbiol. 1977. 31:309–41

BIOGENESIS OF METHANE ❖1707

R. A. Mah
Division of Environmental and Nutritional Sciences, School of Public Health, University of California, Los Angeles, California 90024

D. M. Ward
Department of Geology, University of California, Los Angeles, California 90024

L. Baresi
Division of Environmental and Nutritional Sciences, School of Public Health, University of California, Los Angeles, California 90024

T. L. Glass
The Anaerobic Bacteriological Research Laboratory, Wadsworth Veteran's Administration Hospital, Los Angeles, California 90073

CONTENTS

INTRODUCTION 310
THE ROLE OF METHANOGENIC BACTERIA IN INTERSPECIES H_2 TRANSFER 310
The Methanogenic Bacterial Interaction 312
Low-molecular-weight end products 312
Carbohydrates 315
The Non-Methanogenic Bacterial Interaction 316
METHANOGENESIS FROM ACETATE 317
Acetate Enrichment 318
Methanol Enrichment 318
Benzoate Enrichment 318
PURE CULTURE ISOLATES 319
FINE STRUCTURE STUDIES 320
NUTRIENT REQUIREMENTS 322
BIOCHEMICAL AND ENZYMATIC STUDIES 323
THE ECOLOGY OF METHANOGENESIS 325
Freshwater Sediments 326
Distribution of methane and methanogenic bacteria 326
Factors affecting methanogenesis 328
Fate of methane in freshwater sediments 331

Marine and Estuarine Sediments ... 332
Methane distribution ... 332
Microbiology of methanogenesis ... 333
Fate of methane ... 334
Flooded Soils ... 335
Animal Digestive System ... 336
Anaerobic Sludge Digestors ... 336

INTRODUCTION

In anaerobic environments, the ultimate fate of the complete dissimilation of complex organic compounds such as carbohydrates, proteins, and lipids is the formation of CH_4 and CO_2 (see Figure 1). The fermentation of carbohydrates, amino acids, and long-chain fatty acids initially leads to the formation of lower volatile fatty acids, alcohols and other neutral compounds, and H_2 and CO_2. H_2 is rarely detectable (60, 167) since it is rapidly and preferentially oxidized by all known methane bacteria (168) with the reduction of CO_2 to CH_4. In the absence of H_2 removal, a mixture of products will accumulate and substrate utilization will be inhibited. The oxidation of H_2 not only yields energy for the methanogenic bacteria, it also provides an overall mechanism for terminal electron removal, thus permitting the continued breakdown of intermediates to the level of acetic acid. The oxidation-reduction state of an organic compound stoichiometrically fixes the amount of acetate that may be formed from it under anaerobic conditions; 67% or more of the starting organic carbon (66) will be converted to acetate during an active fermentation.

Acetic acid does not accumulate; it is converted directly or indirectly to CH_4 and CO_2 in aquatic sediments, black muds, marshes, swamps, anaerobic digestors, and other non-gastrointestinal environments. Its conversion to CH_4 and CO_2 removes it from solution as these less-soluble gases leave the system through diffusion and bubble formation. Hence, 67% or more (66) of the CH_4 will be derived from acetate, depending upon the type of organic substrate. In theory, only 33% (66) of the methane can be produced from CO_2 reduction by the H_2 generated during dissimilation of the starting organic substrate to the level of acetate.

In ruminants, where carbohydrates are the chief substrates, acetic acid (and propionic and butyric acids) is removed by absorption through the rumen wall and is metabolized by the host. In the rumen, methane appears to be almost exclusively produced from CO_2 reduction by H_2 (61), whereas in non-gastrointestinal habitats, methane appears to be produced chiefly from acetate (66, 140) and secondarily from CO_2 reduction by H_2 derived from the dissimilation of organic compounds. In both types of habitats, the main mechanism for electron removal is the same, namely, H_2 oxidation by methanogenic bacteria; they differ primarily in the mechanism for end product (i.e. acetate) removal.

THE ROLE OF METHANOGENIC BACTERIA IN INTERSPECIES H_2 TRANSFER

Methanogenic bacteria occupy a unique niche in those anaerobic ecosystems where light and sulfate are both limiting. In such anaerobic habitats, the methane bacteria have exploited a role for which there is little known competition by obtaining energy

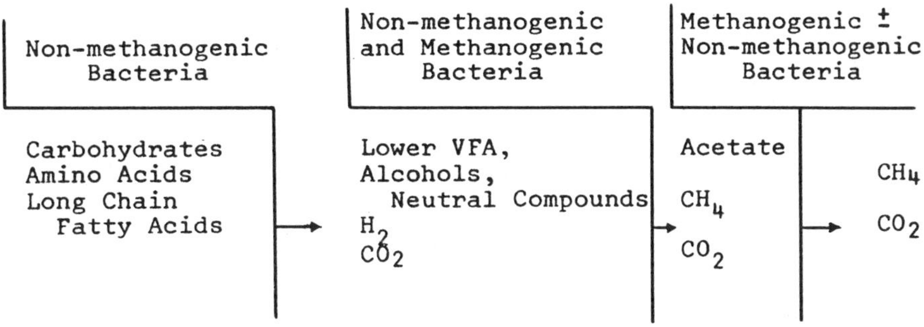

Figure 1 Dissimilation of complex organic compounds.

from the oxidation of H_2 coupled to reduction of CO_2 to methane. In fact, the H_2-oxidizing methanogenic bacteria may play an even more intimate role in the metabolism of the non-methanogenic organisms that initiate the fermentation of the complex organic compounds (Figure 1). Early evidence of this stemmed from pure culture studies of non-methanogenic rumen bacteria that formed certain reduced end products not found in the normal rumen fermentation. This contradiction led Hungate (59) to propose that H_2, which could be used as a reductant in the formation of these products, was diverted to methane formation. The metabolic interactions of the non-methanogenic and methanogenic bacteria in the anaerobic dissimilation of organic compounds has gained considerable importance, and it is in this basic area of study that a clearer understanding of the methane fermentation may lead to improved applications.

Recent investigations have established that the utilization of H_2 by methanogenic bacteria may exert a direct effect on the metabolic activities of other bacteria in the ecosystem (33, 63, 169). The non-methanogenic bacteria affected share the characteristic of H_2 formation by proton reduction, either solely or as a supplement to the formation of reduced organic end products for disposing of electrons generated during their respective fermentations. Based on an increased understanding of the organisms and mechanisms involved, the term "interspecies H_2-transfer" (63) has been used to describe the coupled oxidation-reduction reactions between two or more interacting anaerobic bacteria during fermentation of one initial substrate. Interspecies H_2 transfer provides mechanisms by which:

1. relatively unfermentable substrates (usually of low molecular weight, such as ethanol) may be used as carbon and energy sources under anaerobic conditions (22);
2. some carbohydrate-fermenting bacteria can carry out more complete oxidations of their substrates;
3. methanogenic bacteria may obtain H_2 and CO_2 from substrates such as carbohydrates, proteins, or fatty acids, which they are otherwise incapable of using. Any fermentative reactions leading to H_2 and CO_2 generation from complex substrates may satisfy this general mechanism for all known methanogenic bacteria.

Thus, interspecies H_2 transfer occurs when the flow of fermentation-generated electrons is shifted away from the formation of reduced organic end products to proton reduction. H_2 formation then becomes the major, if not sole, electron sink. Because of the thermodynamic or inhibitory properties of the reaction, such a shift in electron flow requires a mechanism for the continuous removal of the H_2 formed. This can be provided by either the methanogenic bacteria or by other non-methanogenic H_2-utilizing bacteria (63).

The Methanogenic Bacterial Interaction

LOW-MOLECULAR-WEIGHT END PRODUCTS In the first case, during methanogenesis coupled to the dissimilation of low-molecular-weight compounds, an alteration in the types of end products formed may not occur since proton reduction provides the sole mechanism for the disposal of the electrons generated. Because of the thermodynamics of the reaction, the amount of substrate fermented is critically dependent upon the removal of H_2 from the system. As Wolin (169) pointed out, the evolution of H_2 from NADH is thermodynamically unfavorable under standard conditions (1 atm of H_2, 25°C, pH 7.0): $NADH + H^+ \rightarrow NAD^+ + H_2$ $\Delta G^{o\prime} = +4.3$ kcal. However, as the partial pressure of H_2 is reduced, the free energy change becomes increasingly negative. Thus, under conditions of continuous H_2 removal, the reaction is feasible.

While the H_2-coupled reduction of NAD^+ and $NADP^+$ was demonstrated in cell-free extracts of anaerobic bacteria, recently the evolution of H_2 from $NADH_2$ was also found in extracts of *Clostridium pasteurianum, Clostridium butyricum, Clostridium acetobutylicum, Clostridium tyrobutyricum,* and S organism (70, 119, 126). Demonstration of this activity required the use of an $NADH_2$-generating system and the presence of ferredoxin or an artificial low-potential electron carrier.

The metabolism of ethanol by "*Methanobacillus omelianskii*" [see Wolfe (168) for additional details on the history of "*M. omelianskii*"] first led to the demonstration of interspecies H_2 transfer in which two organisms were mutually dependent during the formation of methane from a single substrate. "*M. omelianskii*" was mistakenly described as a pure culture of a single organism that obtained energy for growth through the oxidation of ethanol to acetate. The electrons so generated were disposed of through the reduction of externally supplied CO_2 to methane:

$$2CH_3CH_2OH + CO_2 \rightarrow 2CH_3COOH + CH_4. \qquad 1.$$

In reality, *M. omelianskii* was a mixed culture consisting of an ethanol-oxidizing, H_2-producing bacterium (S organism) and a H_2-utilizing methanogenic bacterium (*Methanobacterium* strain MOH) (22). The growth of S organism on ethanol was severely inhibited by H_2. Good growth was only obtained when S organism was cocultured with strain MOH. The relationship between the two is expressed in terms of the key intermediate, H_2:

$$2CH_3CH_2OH + 2H_2O \rightarrow 2CH_3COOH + 4H_2 \text{ (S organism)} \qquad 2.$$

$$4H_2 + CO_2 \rightarrow CH_4 + 2H_2O \text{ (\textit{Methanobacterium} strain MOH)} \qquad 3.$$

$$\text{Sum } 2CH_3CH_2OH + CO_2 \rightarrow 2CH_3COOH + CH_4 \qquad 1.$$

An enzymatic basis for H_2 production from ethanol (126) and acetaldehyde (127) by S organism has been established. H_2 may be formed via an NAD-ferredoxin-dependent (126) or NAD-independent reaction (127); an NAD-specific alcohol dehydrogenase was also demonstrated (126).

Resolution of "*M. omelianskii*" also provided an explanation for the observations of Barker (7) that "*M. omelianskii*" would not grow on formate but would convert it to CO_2 and methane only if grown in the presence of ethanol and CO_2. Neither the S organism nor strain MOH grew on formate, nor did MOH convert it to methane and CO_2 (20, 22). Reddy et al (126) demonstrated that the S organism contained an NAD-linked formate hydrogenlyase and that the $NADH_2$ formed could be oxidized by H_2 formation. These workers concluded that the growth of "*M. omelianskii*" depended upon the presence of ethanol and CO_2; if formate were also present, it was converted by the S organism to H_2 and CO_2, which could then be utilized by strain MOH.

In further studies on the S organism, Reddy et al (125) found that pure cultures of the S organism grew poorly on several short-chain alcohols (ethanol, propanol, *n*-butanol, *i*-butanol, and *n*-pentanol) with the production of varying amounts of H_2. However, when cocultured with *Methanobacterium ruminantium* on each of the above substrates, not only did growth of the methanogen occur but growth of the S organism significantly increased. The production of H_2 as calculated from the formation of methane increased 20–30 times in comparison to the amount of H_2 actually formed by S organism growing alone. This also implied an increase in substrate utilization. Presumably, each of the alcohols was oxidized to its corresponding fatty acid, but this was not reported.

In contrast to the alcohols (125), good growth of the S organism in pure culture was obtained when pyruvate was the substrate, and disposal of electrons generated during pyruvate fermentation occurred primarily by ethanol formation (125). Acetate and CO_2 were the other major end products, and H_2 was present in only trace amounts (125). The fermentation pattern changed dramatically, however, when the S organism was cocultured with *M. ruminantium.* Under these conditions, ethanol was produced in trace amounts whereas the oxidized product, acetate, was significantly increased. This change appeared to be stoichiometrically related since an increase in acetate was equivalent to the decrease in ethanol. H_2 was not detected in the mixed culture since it was oxidized by CO_2 reduction to methane. The calculated H_2 produced in the mixed system increased 30-fold over that formed by S organism growing alone. Methane production was more than predicted from the total reducing equivalents present in the end products formed by S organism in pure culture and was accounted for by increased pyruvate utilization of the mixed culture. Thus, in the presence of a methanogenic bacterium, proton reduction became the preferred pathway of electron disposal. Because of this, ethanol was not formed and the carbon that was diverted to ethanol formation in the pure culture was converted to acetate in the mixed culture. Under these conditions, acetyl-CoA would not be reduced to ethanol but instead would be converted to acetate, and the potential energy of the thioester bond could be conserved as ATP. This could allow an increase in the energy yield per mole of pyruvate fermented for S organism as well as supplying the necessary energy (as H_2) for the methanogen. However, although S organism contains phosphotransacetylase and acetate kinase (see below), the mechanism of energy generation from pyruvate is not yet known. In any case, both the methanogenic and non-methanogenic species benefitted from the interaction. These findings corroborate the earlier hypothesis of Hungate (59) that ethanol, a product of pure cultures, was not formed in the rumen because H_2 was diverted away from ethanol formation by methane production.

The rationale for increased ethanol utilization by the S organism when grown in an ethanol-containing medium with a methanogenic bacterium is similar, but not identical, to the pyruvate system. Under these conditions, proton reduction serves as the sole mechanism of electron disposal for the S organism. When cocultured with a methanogenic bacterium, there is no shift in the type of organic end products formed by the S organism, as was seen in pure and mixed culture conditions when pyruvate was the substrate. Rather, increased ethanol utilization was due to continuous removal of the inhibitory end product, H_2. Although this should also allow overall increased energy production, the means by which energy is obtained from ethanol are not known. Reddy et al (126) found that extracts of ethanol-grown S organism converted ethanol to acetaldehyde by an NAD-linked alcohol dehydrogenase. Acetaldehyde was oxidized directly to acetate and H_2 by a ferredoxin-dependent reaction that did not require CoA, NAD, or NADP. Although the extracts contained phosphotransacetylase and acetate kinase, acetyl-phosphate was not formed from acetaldehyde unless ATP was added. It is possible that the S organism is capable of producing acetyl-phosphate and thence ATP from acetaldehyde, but the reaction may require unknown cofactors or conditions different from those used.

Whether acetyl-phosphate and ATP could be produced from pyruvate by extracts of the S organism was not reported (127); thus, the mechanisms of energy generation from pyruvate and ethanol are not known. Phosphotransacetylase and acetate kinase would be expected to yield ATP and acetate via acetyl-CoA derived from pyruvate. However, when grown on ethanol, these enzymes may also function in a biosynthetic manner activating acetate for assimilatory purposes.

The type of interaction described for the S organism and a methanogenic bacterium has also been demonstrated with *Desulfovibrio* (M. P. Bryant, manuscript in preparation). Several cultures of *Desulfovibrio* isolated from anaerobic sewage enrichments grew on ethanol or lactate and produced H_2 in the presence of minimal amounts of sulfate. In the presence of adequate amounts of sulfate, the preferred route of electron disposal was via sulfate reduction, not H_2 evolution. If the concentration of sulfate was limiting, a coculture of *Desulfovibrio* with a methanogenic bacterium produced methane but not H_2. If the concentration of sulfate was not limiting, sulfate served as a terminal electron acceptor even in the presence of methanogenic bacteria, and neither methane nor H_2 were produced. This remains unexplained although, energetically, sulfate reduction is slightly more favorable than proton reduction coupled to methanogenesis and thus the energy yield may be greater with sulfate as the terminal electron acceptor.

Methanogenesis from the two-carbon end product, acetate, remains unresolved in terms of interspecies H_2 transfer. Classical labeling studies with ^{14}C and deuterium (8) have long established a unique conversion of acetate to methane and CO_2. Although evidence indicates an important role in methanogenesis from acetate via this unexplained pathway, the concept of interspecies H_2 transfer may still be applicable to special instances if acetate were first completely oxidized to H_2 and CO_2, and the gaseous end products are then used in methane formation. *Desulfuromonas acetoxidans* (120), which oxidizes acetate to CO_2 and reduces sulfur, could fit this hypothesis (if a conventional hydrogenase were present in this organism) by coupling it to a H_2-oxidizing methanogen in place of its normal electron acceptor, sulfur. Unpublished findings (M. P. Bryant and N. Pfennig, personal communication) indicate that such a coupling between *D. acetoxidans* and a H_2-oxidizing methanogen does not occur. However, indirect ecological evidence, which may involve this type of acetate catabolism, is presented later.

CARBOHYDRATES Interspecies H_2 transfer reactions involving the fermentation of carbohydrates lead to increased substrate utilization accompanying a shift to more oxidized end products because of the change in electron flow towards methane formation. This general pattern of fermentation was demonstrated with non-methanogenic rumen bacteria cocultured with *Methanobacterium ruminantium*. *Ruminococcus flavefaciens*, a major cellulolytic rumen organism, produced formate, acetate, succinate, H_2, and CO_2 when grown alone in batch culture on cellulose (169). In coculture with *M. ruminantium*, succinate decreased as acetate increased. Apparently, proton reduction was again the preferred pathway of electron disposal since acetate and methane were now the main end products. Furthermore, increased substrate utilization was also likely since more methane was formed than could be accounted for by the total reducing equivalents present in the products of the pure culture. There was no evidence presented to support an increased energy yield per mole of substrate fermented. Succinate formation may lead to ATP production by electron transport during reduction of fumarate to succinate (41, 42, 91, 92), but this has not been directly examined in *R. flavefaciens*. In fact, Hopgood & Walker (56, 57) suggested that *R. flavefaciens* may not be capable of obtaining energy from this step. If this were the case, then a shift in carbon flow from succinate to acetate via interspecies H_2 transfer may result in a net energy gain by *R. flavefaciens*.

Clostridium cellobioparum grown in batch culture on glucose produced primarily acetate, ethanol, formate, and H_2 in major amounts, with smaller quantities of lactate and butyrate (33). When cocultured with *M. ruminantium*, a shift in electron disposal was again reflected in decreased ethanol production and corresponded to an increase in acetate. In fact, methane and acetate were again the main products. A 22% increase in cell yield of *C. cellobioparum* per mole of glucose fermented was reported for the mixed culture. A 15% increase in direct microscopic counts was also observed in a separate mixed culture experiment. Removal of H_2 from pure cultures of *C. cellobioparum* via non-biological means by flushing with CO_2 or reaction with palladium black also led to increased glucose utilization and growth yield. These data support the hypothesis that electron disposal by proton reduction leads to an increased energy yield per mole of substrate fermented and benefitted the H_2 producer by an increased cell yield. The methanogen, of course, cannot metabolize glucose; it relies on the H_2 produced from glucose by *C. cellobioparum.*

Selenomonas ruminantium ferments carbohydrates to acetate, propionate, Co_2, and/or lactate as major end products. In addition, Scheifinger et al (137) recently detected H_2 in small quantities in three out of five strains of *S. ruminantium* examined. *S. ruminantium* strain HD4 produced 100 times more H_2 from glucose in coculture with *M. ruminantium*, which metabolized formate, as well as in coculture with *Methanobacterium* strain MOH, which cannot metabolize formate. Thus, the increase in H_2 formation was not a result of formate production. One strain of *S. ruminantium* produced H_2 only in the presence of *M. ruminantium*, whereas another showed no H_2 production either in the presence or absence of methanogenic bacteria. In addition to carbohydrates, *S. ruminantium* strain HD4 grew on glycerol or lactate and produced detectable H_2 (as CH_4) only when cocultured with a methanogen. Analysis of fermentation products, substrate utilization, and molar cell yields were not reported. However, these findings indicated that H_2 transfer reactions may be more widespread in natural (i.e. mixed culture) environments than indicated by pure cultures of known H_2 producers.

The Non-Methanogenic Bacterial Interaction

In addition to the methanogenic bacteria, other non-methanogenic H_2-utilizing bacteria may also participate in interspecies H_2 transfer reactions. In either case, reduced pyridine nucleotide-linked proton reduction becomes the preferred mechanism of electron disposal for the H_2-producing bacteria, allowing a more complete oxidation of their substrates. *Ruminococcus albus* grown in continuous culture on glucose produced acetate, ethanol, and H_2 (63). Formate, although produced in batch cultures of *R. albus*, was not formed in continuous culture (63, 102).

Calculations based on a fermentation balance showed that about 70% of the electrons generated by glucose fermentation were removed by ethanol formation whereas the remaining 30% were converted to H_2. In coculture with *Vibrio succinogenes* under continuous culture conditions, H_2 was not detected and a shift in end products from ethanol to acetate and succinate occurred. Since *V. succinogenes* obtains energy by the oxidation of H_2 (or formate) coupled to the reduction of fumarate to succinate (64, 170), these results are compatible with a H_2 transfer reaction bypassing ethanol formation by the H_2 producer (*R. albus*) in favor of succinate production by the H_2 utilizer (*V. succinogenes*). In fact, the amount of succinate formed in the mixed culture corresponded to the total amount of reducing equivalents present in the pure culture of *R. albus* as H_2 and ethanol. Acetate was increased in the mixed culture by an amount equal to the quantity of ethanol produced when *R. albus* was grown alone. Thus, proton reduction became the sole mechanism of electron disposal for *R. albus* in mixed continuous culture. Although cell yields were not measured, the shift in electron flow from ethanol to H_2 should again result in increased energy yield per mole of substrate fermented since *R. albus* is enzymatically capable of obtaining energy by conversion of acetyl-CoA to acetate via acetyl-phosphate (69,102).

METHANOGENESIS FROM ACETATE

In spite of the known significance of acetate as an important intermediate in non-gastrointestinal methanogenesis, especially in the anaerobic sludge digestion system (66, 140) or in lake sediment (31), there has been little advancement in knowledge about this key reaction or the organisms involved. Radioactive tracer experiments from almost 30 years ago established the origin of methane from the methyl group of acetate (24, 142, 143) and this route of methanogenesis from acetate has been confirmed in pure culture studies on *Methanosarcina barkeri* (R. A. Mah, manuscript in preparation).

Recently, ecological evidence was reported that may resurrect the "CO_2 reduction" hypothesis of van Niel (see 8) as a second possible route of methanogenesis from acetate. Conversion of the ^{14}C-labeled methyl group of acetate to $^{14}CO_2$ in natural sediments implied a possible oxidation of acetate to CO_2 and H_2. Although the pure culture studies with *Desulfuromonas acetoxidans* (120) or the earlier, unsubstantiated reports on acetate metabolism by "*Desulfovibrio rubentschickii*" (2) do not indicate H_2 production, the theoretical possibility exists that in some sediments methane might be formed from acetate by an alternative interspecies H_2 transfer route, in which the methyl group is first oxidized to CO_2 and H_2 and then the CO_2 is reduced by H_2 to form CH_4. Any other role for H_2 in acetate conversion to CH_4 and CO_2 cannot be established on the basis of existing information. The radioactive tracer experiments of Zeikus et al (179) on *Methanobacterium thermoautotrophicum* by using increasing concentrations of [UL-^{14}C] acetate in the presence of H_2/N_2 atmospheres showed at best a total conversion of 2–6% of the available acetate to CH_4 after 6.25 days of incubation. This reported requirement for H_2 (179) to metabolize acetate in experiments on *M. thermoautotrophicum* and *Methanosarcina barkeri* may be a result of pregrowing the cells in a H_2-CO_2 atmosphere in defined medium. *M. barkeri* grown under a N_2-CO_2 atmosphere in pure culture in complex organic medium containing yeast extract and Trypticase metabolized acetate to CH_4 and CO_2 at a rate sufficient to account for as much as 50% of the acetate conversion rate reported in some mixed culture enrichments and in some digesters (R. A. Mah, manuscript in preparation). Such cultures of *M. barkeri* converted [methyl-^{14}C]acetate to $^{14}CH_4$ in 24 hr without H_2 addition. Metabolically produced H_2 could not be detected. In fact, in mixed culture enrichments of *M. barkeri* growing on acetate, H_2 (and formate) was not used as a source of methane (5, 157) and may even inhibit (5) production of methane from acetate. Interspecies H_2 transfer reactions involving the intact conversion of the methyl group of acetate to CH_4 have not been found so far.

M. barkeri is the only well-described acetate-using methanogen available in pure culture. It is abundant in batch-fed enrichment cultures containing acetate as the sole organic carbon source (5) and may be readily isolated on complex medium containing methanol, H_2-CO_2, or calcium acetate (93). *Methanosarcina methanica,* which reportedly also uses acetate (23), has never been isolated. A gram-negative, acetate-using, methanogenic rod was reported by Cappenberg (28) from Lake

Vechten sediments but has not been isolated by other workers. *Methanobacterium söhngenii*, presumably present in the batch-fed acetate enrichments of Mylroie & Hungate (103), was more recently reported by Pretorius (122) but has never been isolated. It was present in a continuously fed acetate enrichment system (122) but was eventually washed out unless formate was also added. Thus, it appears likely that organisms other than *M. barkeri* are also capable of acetate metabolism but direct culture evidence is still lacking.

The following enrichment cultures are examples of mixed populations of bacteria producing methane primarily from a single organic carbon source.

Acetate enrichment When acetate served as the sole organic compound and only energy source added to a batch enrichment culture (5, 6), a certain population of bacteria developed. This population can be maintained indefinitely by weekly batch transfer into fresh medium (5). Growth of organisms in the enrichment depended upon metabolism of acetate. In the enrichments described by Baresi & Mah (5), *M. barkeri* was the only organism isolated in pure culture capable of converting acetate to methane and CO_2. The numerous other non-methanogenic organisms present in the enrichment depended completely upon the methanogenic sarcina for their nutritional requirements since none was able to use acetate as an energy source. Nutritional studies on a non-methanogenic isolate (161) showed its dependency upon the sarcina for vitamin B_{12}. The isolate also required other B vitamins, inosine, and some amino acids for optimal growth. Production of these nutrients by the sarcina has not been studied. In pure culture, *M. barkeri* grew faster in complex organic medium (R. A. Mah, manuscript in preparation), implicating a nutritional syntrophic role for non-methanogenic organisms present in the enrichment.

Methanol enrichment Trophic relationships were also reported (186) for a batch and continuous culture enrichment containing methanosarcina on methanol. Zhilina & Zavarzin (186) reported the development of a distinctive community of bacteria called a biocenosis centered around the methanogenic sarcina. One group of associates was represented by *Clostridium scatologenes* and *Catenebacterium* sp. These organisms presumably grew on the lysed cells of sarcina. The second group was thought to be dependent upon the methanosarcina for H_2 and was represented by *Desulfovibrio vulgaris*.

Benzoate enrichment Addition of benzoate as the sole organic carbon and energy source to an enrichment inoculated with sewage sludge led to the development of a microbial consortium (46), which degraded benzoate completely to CH_4 and CO_2. This enrichment was uniquely maintained by removal and replenishment of the clear culture supernatant overlying the bacterial floc. An unknown organism(s) was involved in the non-methanogenic reductive dissimilation of benzoate first to acetate, formate, H_2, and CO_2. These intermediates were then converted to CH_4 and CO_2. The only two methanogenic bacteria isolated were *Methanobacterium formicicum* and *Methanospirillum hungatii*; both used formate and H_2-CO_2 to produce CH_4 but neither fermented acetate or benzoate. Presumably, a methanogenic acetate user was present but not isolated. This benzoate enrichment appeared to fit the H_2 transfer model, as well as the requirement for end-product (acetate) removal (46) previously discussed.

PURE CULTURE ISOLATES

Since Wolfe's review (168) of the morphological types of pure methanogenic bacteria (their culture techniques, nutritional requirements, and substrate characteristics) three additional isolates have been described.

Methanobacterium thermoautotrophicum (181), a gram-positive, nonmotile, irregularly curved rod exhibited a temperature optimum of 65°–70°C and a pH optimum of 7.2–7.6 for growth. The DNA base composition was 52 mol% G + C; it was isolated from sewage sludge obtained from a waste treatment digester. *M. thermoautotrophicum* utilized H_2-CO_2 as a sole carbon and energy source and was capable of an autotrophic mode of nutrition. Other known methanogenic substrates such as methanol, formate, or acetate did not support growth or methanogenesis in the original description. Ethanol and pyruvate were not used either. However, cysteine was stimulatory for growth although vitamins were not. The addition of cysteine increased the cell yield and shortened the generation time at 65°C from 5 to 3 hr. Considering the complex organic composition of the ecological habitat from which the organism was obtained, growth stimulation by cysteine may not be surprising, though the effect of cysteine as a nutrient versus its role as a reducing agent was not established.

Methanobacterium arbophilicum (177), isolated from wetwood of a living tree, is a gram-positive, nonmotile rod, 0.53–0.75 × 1.8–3.5 μm, occurring singly, in pairs, or in chains. Its pH optimum is 7.5–8.0, and its temperature optimum is 30°–37°C. Although H_2-CO_2 served as sole carbon and energy sources, organic compounds were highly stimulatory and vitamins were required for maintenance. Generation times of 13 and 17 hr were reported for complex and mineral salts shake flask cultures, respectively. The DNA base composition was 27.5 mol% G + C.

Methanospirillum hungatii was isolated from sewage sludge in 1966 by Smith (139) and subsequently was described and named in 1974 by Ferry et al (45). The gram-negative, motile, curved rods that characterized this isolate measured 0.5 × 7.4 μm and occurred in filaments up to 100 μm in length. Tufts of polar flagella and a striated cell surface were seen under electron microscopy (45, 176). The DNA base composition was 45 mol% G + C. *M. hungatii* exhibited a temperature optimum of 30°–37°C and an optimum pH of 6.6–7.4. Formate or H_2-CO_2 served as methanogenic substrates, but benzoate, ethanol, methanol, pyruvate, and acetate did not. Growth was best in complex medium with yeast extract and Trypticase; rumen fluid was not required. The yellow colonies were distinguished by an optical pattern of regular, light and dark striations, which occurred at two-cell-length (16 μm) intervals. This colonial morphology was absent in *M. hungatii* strain GP-1 isolated by Patel et al (116) from a pear waste digestor, although other morphological and physiological properties were similar except for slight variations in DNA base composition and temperature optimum. Acetate was apparently assimilated by this latter strain.

A thermophilic methanogenic rod called *Methanobacillus kuzneceovii* (109,111) reportedly fermented methanol to methane and acetic acid (111) and produced vitamin B_{12} (111) and other corrinoid compounds (111) from methanol. Acetic acid formed from methanol was subsequently converted to methane and CO_2. Formate, formaldehyde, and CO_2 were also converted to acetate (19) and presumably to methane, but methanogenic substrates other than methanol and acetate were not reported.

The description of *M. kuzneceovii* and its purification were difficult to assess, expecially in view of the following observations.

In the earlier labeling experiments of Stadtman & Barker (142), the formation of acetate and methane in the presence of methanol took place in mixed cultures. If methanol served as a source of H_2 and CO_2, acetate could be formed via a reaction similar to that described for *Clostridium aceticum* (165), or for a new organism recently isolated by R. E. Hungate (personal communication) in which H_2 and CO_2 were converted to acetate. If this were the case, two reactions and two organisms could compete for the reducing power generated from methanol oxidation, with one reaction leading to methane and the other leading to acetate.

In *Methanosarcina barkeri,* the rate of conversion of methanol to methane and CO_2 takes place faster than the conversion of acetate to methane and CO_2, making acetate a less probable intermediate in methanol catabolism, assuming it was freely permeable to the cell.

Methanobacillus kuzneceovii should be further scrutinized because of its reported similarity (118) in morphological and physiological properties to the now defunct *Methanobacillus omelianskii*. Such properties are now widely known as the first well-described example of H_2 transfer between two co-existing bacteria (see earlier discussion). Thus, this unique report of a pure methanogenic bacterium that fermented methanol to acetate and methane and subsequently catabolized acetate to methane and CO_2 requires further verification by other workers.

FINE STRUCTURE STUDIES

The fine structure studies on a *Methanosarcina* sp. by Zhilina (183) demonstrated the presence of gas vesicles previously undescribed for methane bacteria. These vesicles appeared as hexagonal packets in cross section or as ellipses in longitudinal section (Figure 2). A recent gas-vacuolated isolate of a *Methanosarcina* sp. (R. A. Mah, unpublished findings) indicated that the absence of gas vesicles in the taxonomic description of *M. barkeri* was not a result of inadequate observations, as suggested by Zhilina (184). Gas vesicles were not present in the strains of *M. barkeri* obtained from several laboratories or in any other strains thus far examined (R. A. Mah, personal observation). Insufficient data are available to establish whether the gas-vacuolated isolate of Zhilina (183) differed from *M. barkeri* in any characteristics other than gas vesicle formation. In *Microcyclus aquaticus*, and perhaps in other organisms in general, a gas-vacuolated strain was otherwise similar in physical and biochemical properties to its non-gas-vacuolated counterpart (73, 158). In any case,

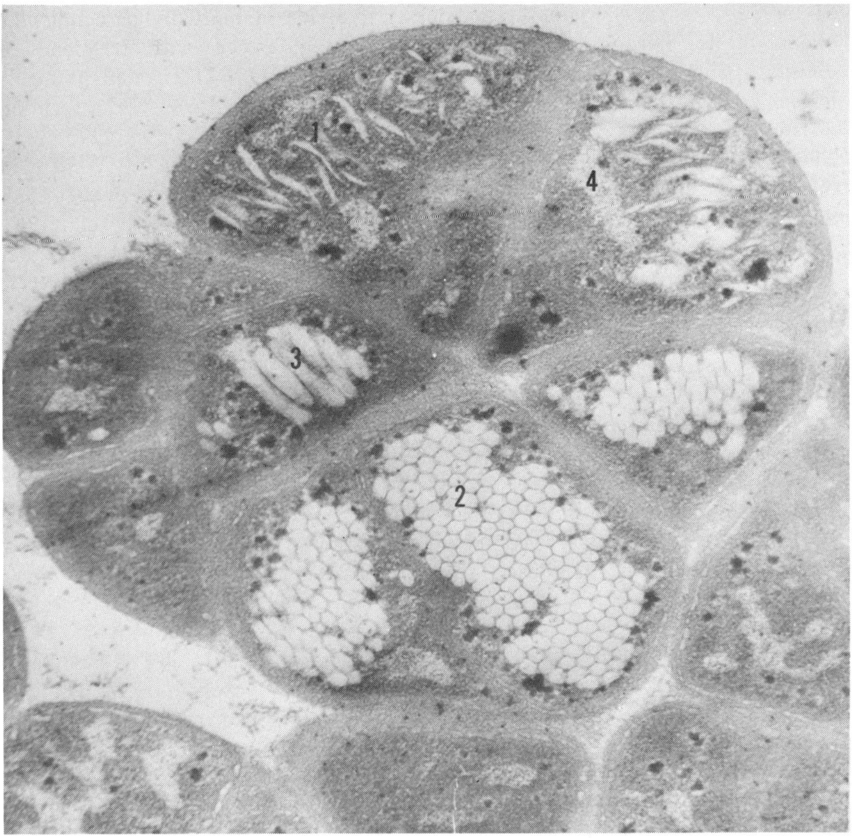

Figure 2 Electron micrograph of ultrathin section of methanosarcina (X36,000). (1) Collapsed gas vesicles; (2) cross section of gas vesicles; (3) longitudinal section of gas vesicles showing elliptical shape; (4) localized nuclear region in one of the irregular daughter cells. Note thick cell wall and delineation from cytoplasm marking boundary of cell membrane. From Zhilina (183).

the occurrence of gas vesicles in the gas-forming, strictly anaerobic methanosarcina raises questions about its functional significance in regulating buoyancy or in metabolism.

Thin sections of the methanosarcina disclosed the presence of a cell wall approximately 500 nm in thickness (175) with a tendency toward a thicker, multilayered arrangement (175, 183). The continuous, thick-layered wall surrounding aggregates of methanosarcina does not resemble the 40-nm wall surrounding each cell of *Sarcina ventriculi*, on which typically is deposited a thick outlying cellulose layer (55). Furthermore, the DNA base composition of *S. ventriculi* was 30.6 mol% G + C, and for the methanosarcina of Zhilina & Aleksandrushkina (185), it was

51 mol% G + C. Methanosarcina does not divide in mutually perpendicular planes; rather, division results in asymmetric daughter cells with the planes of division arising at various angles to the perpendicular (Figure 2). The daughter cells have their own membrane and part of the mother cell's cell wall (183), forming clusters or aggregates of cells bounded by a continuous outer cell wall (175, 183). Thus, under a light microscope, what appears as an individual cell 2–3 μm in diameter is really composed of smaller, irregular cells measuring 1 μm or less (183). Such cells were referred to as "cell segments" (183) or "segmented cocci" (175).

The cytoplasm of methanosarcina contains a large number of ribosomes and unidentified electron-dense granules of uneven size (175, 183). However, the DNA of different species or strains was either evenly distributed (175) or localized (183), as in Figure 2. Mesosomal-like structures were observed only in *M. barkeri* (175); these differences may be a result of methodological differences in culture and electron microscopy.

Methanospirillum hungatii has a well-defined, double-layered cell wall (176) not typical of either gram-positive or gram-negative bacteria, in agreement with the earlier variation of the gram reaction in this organism. Surface striations 0.1 μm apart (45, 176) indicated similarity to certain gram-negative bacteria (45). The outer wall layer, ca 9.5 nm thick, is composed of discrete subunits (176) and apparently surrounds chains of filamentous cells in a continuous sheath-like fashion; the inner wall, ca 13.6 nm thick, is more electron dense and completely surrounds individual cells within the filament (176). The ends of the cell are flattened and squared off in corners (45, 176); motile cells exhibit tufts of polar flagella (45). The cytoplasm contained internal membranes similar to those in *Methanobacterium* (176). Dark patches beneath the striated surface referred to as bag-like inclusions (81) were reported in the negatively stained cells of Ferry et al (45). In long filaments, the empty sheath-like structure of older cells observed under light microscopy (45) may be the structured spacer seen under electron microscopy by Zeikus & Bowen (176).

Electron microscopy of additional methanogenic organisms thus far have revealed no common structural features related to the methanogenic abilities of this physiological group of organisms. In fact, the ultrastructure of the cell wall illustrates the diversity of the methanogenic bacteria. In *Methanobacterium* species, a typical, sharply defined gram-positive wall and a well-delineated cytoplasmic membrane (175) were present. Numerous intracytoplasmic membranes (81, 175, 183) of unknown function occurred in *Methanobacterium* and were most numerous in *Methanobacterium formicicum* and *Methanobacterium thermoautotrophicum* (175). A dispersed, granular ribosome region and a centrally located nuclear region were also observed.

NUTRIENT REQUIREMENTS

The nitrogen requirements of *Methanobacterium* strain MOH and two strains of *Methanobacterium ruminantium* grown on H_2-CO_2 indicated NH_4^+ was the main source of cell nitrogen; amino acids or peptides were not significantly incorporated or metabolized (21). In fact, NH_4^+ may serve as a nitrogen source for all of the methanogenic organisms, although growth may be stimulated by the addition of rumen fluid, yeast extract, and Trypticase, especially in *Methanosarcina barkeri* (R. A. Mah, manuscript in preparation) and *Methanospirillum hungatii* (45). Even *M. thermoautotrophicum* was stimulated by the addition of cysteine (182), although this effect may be related to the oxidation-reduction poising capacity of this amino acid as stated above.

In rumen strains of *M. ruminantium,* N-acetylglucosamine (NAG) obtained from gram-positive or gram-negative bacteria (123) and CoM (150) were stimulatory growth factors. NAG activity from *Escherichia coli* was demonstrated only after treatment with lysozyme and/or ethylenediaminetetraacetic acid. CoM and NAG may be the two growth factors required by the rumen strain of *M. ruminantium* (19) previously presumed present only in rumen fluid and mixed rumen bacteria and not in *E. coli* or organic nitrogen sources used in bacteriological media. CoM was required at 3–5 ng/ml for half-maximal growth (150), and NAG was stimulatory at a concentration of 16 μM (123).

All known pure cultures of methanogenic bacteria utilize H_2-CO_2 as a source of energy. Even the methanol- and acetate-using *M. barkeri* preferentially metabolized H_2-CO_2 (93). *M. ruminantium* strain M1 (rumen origin) required 2-methyl butyrate. Both strain M1 and strain PS (sludge origin) required acetate for growth; however, *Methanobacterium* strain MOH utilized CO_2 as the main carbon source and was only stimulated by acetate. *M. thermoautotrophicum* does not require acetate or any other organic compounds or vitamins for growth, although it is stimulated by cysteine and shares the general requirement of all methanogens for a low oxidation-reduction potential. These findings indicate that the commonly isolated and perhaps the most numerous methanogenic bacteria depend upon other organisms in their natural habitat for essential nutrients and energy sources, as well as for the physical-chemical requirements of a low oxidation-reduction potential and pH.

BIOCHEMICAL AND ENZYMATIC STUDIES

Since Wolfe's review (168), the biochemistry of methane formation by using cell-free extracts mainly involved three methanogenic isolates: (*a*) *M. ruminantium,* a gram-positive coccus to short rod isolated from both rumen and sludge environments, used hydrogen, carbon dioxide, and formate as substrates; (*b*) *Methanobacterium* strain MOH, a gram-variable, irregularly curved rod isolated from the coculture called *Methanobacillus omelianskii,* used only hydrogen and carbon dioxide as substrates; (*c*) *Methanobacillus kuzneceovii* (see earlier discussion on purity of this isolate), a spore-forming rod, fermented methanol to acetic acid and methane (109, 112, 113).

Some of the substrates for methane production in cell-free extracts were H_2-CO_2, methylcobalamin (CH_3-B_{12}), serine, formate, formaldehyde, methanol, N^5-methyltetrahydrofolate (5-CH_3-H_4 folate), and N^5,N^{10}-methylenetetrahydrofolate (5,10-CH_2-H_4 folate) (16, 99, 109, 118, 168). Of these, methylcobalamin was the substrate of choice as a methyl donor in the generation of methane by cell-free extracts (15).

Yet, methylcobalamin was not established as a natural methyl carrier in hydrogen-grown methane bacteria (153). The failure to detect methylated derivatives of the cobamides may be a result of the lability of such compounds under normal reducing conditions (121). Analysis of cobamides formed by *M. barkeri* and "*M. omelianskii*" (presumably MOH) yielded primarily adenosyl derivatives of 5-hydroxybenzimidazolylcobamide and not CH_3-B_{12}. Nonetheless, CH_3-B_{12} as well as other corrinoids including B_{12} itself were reported in cell-free extracts of *M. kuzneceovii* (111, 114, 118). $^{14}C_1$ intermediates prior to the methyl level of reduction have not been identified.

Although aminopterin, an antagonist of folic acid, had an inhibitory effect (141) on methane production, inhibition occurred at concentrations high enough to inhibit other enzymes. Thus, the two folate compounds reported earlier as precursors of methane (168) in cell-free extracts might not be true methanogenic precursors. Furthermore, by using *M. thermoautotrophicum* in a H_2-CO_2 atmosphere, trace amounts of $H^{14}COOH$ or $H^{14}CHO$ were incorporated into histidine and purines but not methane (154). Since both 5-CH_3-H_4-folate and 5,10-CH_2-H_4-folate were well known in histidine and purine synthesis, these data tended to confirm their role in intermediary metabolism (154) rather than in methane formation from CO_2.

The characteristics of the methyl transfer coenzyme, CoM (98, 100), have been examined further and the structure has been established. The active form was identified as 2-mercaptoethanesulfonic acid, $HSCH_2CH_2SO_3^-$ (SH-CoM); the isolated form was $^-O_3SCH_2CH_2SSCH_2CH_2SO_3^-$ or $(S\text{-}CoM)_2$ or 2,2'-dithiodiethanesulfonic acid, as described by Taylor & Wolfe (151, 152). HS-CoM can be methylated under anaerobic conditions with CH_3-B_{12} as the methyl donor via methyltransferase to give 2-(methylthio)ethanesulfonic acid (CH_3-S-CoM). Following this, a methylreductase demethylates CH_3-S-CoM to yield methane (152). This reaction takes place anaerobically in the presence of H_2, ATP, and Mg^{2+} (100). Apparently, the methylation of HS-CoM via methyltransferase does not require these added cofactors. The methyltransferase also was quite stable with respect to storage and oxygen (152). Conversion of $(S\text{-}CoM)_2$ to the active HS-CoM was accomplished by an acidic protein found in the cell-free extracts of MOH by using H_2 or $NADPH_2$ as reductant. NADP was probably reduced via a F_{420}-dependent (see below) hydrogenase system (155). However, $NADPH_2$ and the acidic protein could be replaced by $NaBH_4$, which chemically reduced $(S\text{-}CoM)_2$ to HS-CoM (153).

Even though CoM was not reported in *M. kuzneceovii,* its presence was implied by the overall conversion of CH_3-B_{12} to methane, presumably by methyltransferase and methylreductase (115). Unlike MOH in which both enzymes were dialyzable, the methylreductase of *M. kuzneceovii* was reported in the particulate fraction and methyltransferase was reported in the soluble fraction (115).

CoM was reported in *Methanobacterium formicicum* strain BB, *Methanobacterium ruminantium* sewage strain, MOH, *Methanosarcina barkeri* (100, 150), and *Methanobacterium thermoautotrophicum* (38). It was also present in sewage sludge and rumen fluid but not in liver, heart, spinach, yeast extract, and various *Clostridium* spp. (100). CoM was not found in the rumen strain of *M. ruminantium* but was required for the growth of this organism in the absence of rumen fluid (150).

Cheeseman et al (32) isolated from MOH an electron carrier called factor 420 (F_{420}), a blue-green fluorescent compound with an absorption peak at 420 nm. It lost both fluorescence and absorption at 420 nm and became colorless when reduced. Hydrolysis with 6N HCl yielded a ninhydrin-positive compound identified as glutamic acid, an acid-stable chromophore, phosphate, and an ether-soluble phenolic compound. In cell-free extracts under aerobic conditions, F_{420} was freely dialyzable though irreversibly inactivated with respect to methanogenic activity. Under anaerobic conditions, it was non-dialyzable, suggesting that F_{420} was protein bound. The molecular weight of F_{420} was determined by Sephadex G-25 chromatography to be 630 ± 8% (32).

F_{420} acted as an intermediary electron carrier between H_2 or formate and NADP (Figure 3*a,b*). The hydrogenase system was also linked to FAD, FMN, methyl viologen, and Fe^{3+} but not to NAD. $NADPH_2$:NAD or $FADH_2$:NAD transhydrogenase systems were not detected (155). The fact that only NADP and not NAD could accept electrons from reduced F_{420} complements the data of McBride & Wolfe (100, 168), showing $NADPH_2$ to be the preferred reduced pyridine nucleotide necessary for the formation of HS-CoM.

The reduction of F_{420} was also linked to a formate dehydrogenase system (156). Reduced F_{420} can be linked to NADP reduction via F_{420}-NADP oxidoreductase (see Figure 3*a,b*). The formate dehydrogenase can also be linked to the formation of hydrogen through the F_{420}-dependent hydrogenase reaction (see Figure 3*c*). The production of hydrogen from formate could be accomplished by using partially purified cell extracts by addition of only F_{420}. Also, neither flavins nor crude ferredoxin from *Clostridium pasteurianum* could replace F_{420} in the reaction, and only FAD could stimulate the system when F_{420} was included (156).

In *M. ruminantium,* the enzymes involved in the transfer of electrons from formate, hydrogen, and $NADPH_2$ required F_{420} as a necessary electron carrier (156) (see Figure 3). In contrast, F_{420} may not be a required electron carrier in other organisms. Formate dehydrogenases may be linked to cytochrome reduction as in *Enterobacter* and *Escherichia coli,* or directly to NADP or NAD reduction as in *Clostridium thermoaceticum, Clostridium formicoaceticum,* and the S organism (86, 105, 156). In *Clostridium acidiurici* (72), the dehydrogenases were linked to ferredoxin. In *M. ruminantium,* the formate dehydrogenase was linked to F_{420} before NADP reduction. Extracts from *M. kuzneceovii* possessed hydrogenase activity and could reduce NAD and NADP. The involvement of such electron carriers as F_{420}, ferredoxin, or cytochromes was not reported (110). It should be emphasized that F_{420} and CoM appeared to be compounds unique to the metabolic pathways of the methanogenic bacteria.

THE ECOLOGY OF METHANOGENESIS

The distribution of methanogenic bacteria and their activity are restricted to anoxic environments where associated bacteria maintain a low E_h and produce methanogenic substrates as well as other nutrient factors. The anaerobic digestor and the gastrointestinal system, especially the rumen of herbivorous animals, have both been

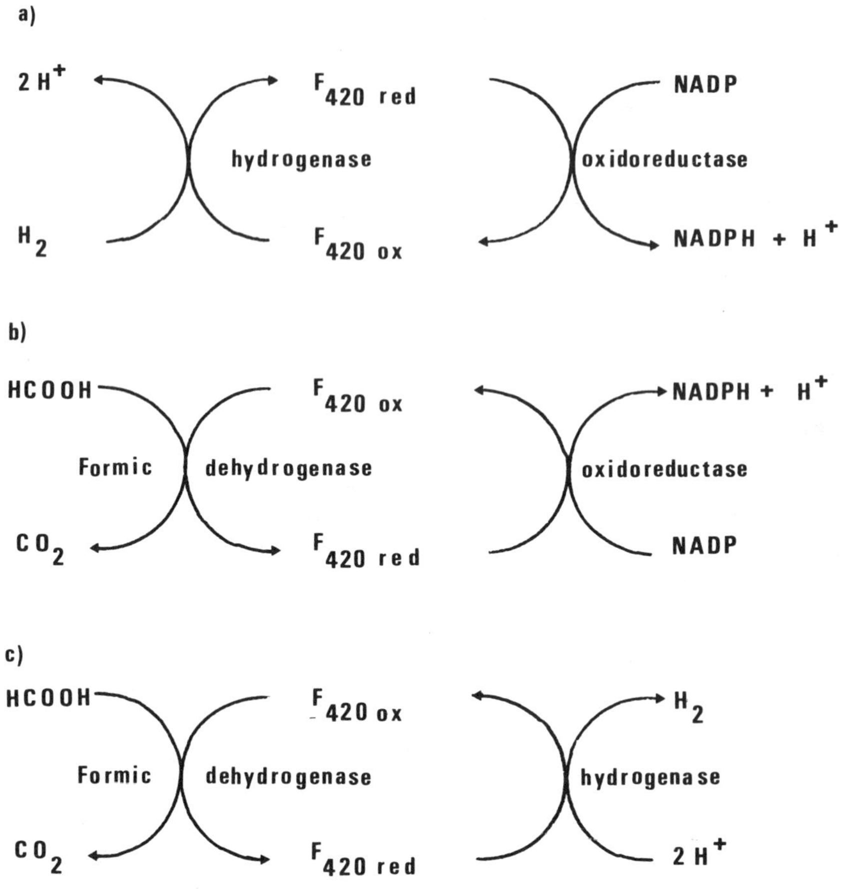

Figure 3 Electron transfer.

treated in recent reviews (54, 61) and will not be discussed in detail here. This review will focus more on freshwater and marine sediments and on flooded soils.

Freshwater Sediments

DISTRIBUTION OF METHANE AND METHANOGENIC BACTERIA The vertical distribution of methane in lake sediments has been examined by several workers (see Figure 4*a*) (26, 74, 75, 130, 133, 166). Although the relative concentrations of methane varied in different lake sediments, the vertical distribution was similar. In general, methane concentration increased with depth, reached a maximum between 2 and 17 cm, and in some cases decreased again at depths below the maximum methane concentration.

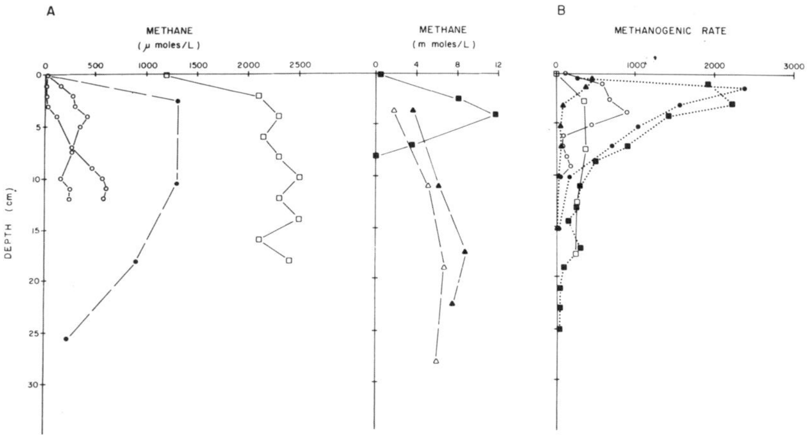

Figure 4 (*A*) Distribution of methane with depth in freshwater sediments: □ , Winfrey & Zeikus (166), Lake Mendota; ○, Rudd & Hamilton (133), Canadian Lakes; ●, Reeburgh & Heggie (130), Ace Lake; ■ , Cappenberg (26), Lake Vechten; ▲ , △ , Koyama (78), Lake Kizaki-ko and Lake Aoki-ko, respectively. (*B*) Depth distribution of methanogenic rate in freshwater sediments: ■ , Barber (4), nanomoles per milliliters of gas per week at 37°C in Lake Wingra; ▲ , ● , Zeikus & Winfrey (180), nanomoles per hour per gram at 30°C in Lake Mendota (10- and 18-m water depths, respectively); ○ , Cappenberg (27), nanomoles per milliliter per day at 8°C in Lake Vechten; □ , Belyaev et al (13), nanomoles per milliliter per day at in situ temperature in Lake Kuznechikha.

The vertical distribution of methanogenic bacteria in Lake Vechten sediments (26) was related to the distribution of methane. Despite seasonal variations in the methane profile, the maximum methane concentration was always at the depth of maximum numbers of methanogenic bacteria; viable counts ranged from 10^2–10^6 cells/ml. Viable counts of hydrogen-oxidizing methanogenic bacteria were higher than viable counts of acetate-using methanogenic bacteria in the upper sediment layers. However, viable counts of acetate-using methanogenic bacteria were higher than hydrogen-oxidizing methanogenic bacteria in lower sediment layers. This finding was difficult to reconcile since all known pure cultures of methane bacteria oxidize hydrogen (168), and hydrogen was reported as a better substrate than organic compounds for the enumeration of methanogenic bacteria (11). A range of 6×10^3–6×10^4 cells/ml was reported for Lake Kuznechikha with formate medium. A range of 25–250 cells/ml was reported for Lake Bol'shoi-Kichier and 2.5×10^2–6×10^3 cells/ml for Lakes Chernyi Kichier and Kuznechikha, with a medium containing an unspecified substrate (13, 14). In general, the viable counts did not change significantly with depth in these studies, although the lowest numbers were consistently found at the greatest sediment depth. In Lake Mendota, a viable count of 10^2–10^6 cells/g of dry sediment was reported in H_2-CO_2 medium (180). Counts were highest with seasonally warmer temperatures and with greater depth in the overlying water column. A seasonal relation was also reported in Lake Wingra sediments where the numbers ranged from less than 10^2 to greater than 10^4 cells/g of dry sediment (4). The absence of reliable methods for enumerating total counts of methanogenic bacteria and the expected variations in sampling techniques make these data, at best, rough estimates of the quantitative distribution of methanogenic bacteria. The use of UV fluorescence of methanogenic colonies (43) or examination for specific compounds of methanogenic bacteria such as F_{420} or CoM for in situ identification of methanogens may yield better distribution patterns in future ecological studies of this type.

The vertical distribution of the methanogenic activity in lake sediments may be a better measure of methanogenesis because viable counts may not be indicative of in situ methane production. Depth profiles of methanogenic activity are shown in Figure 4*B*. Because of the wide variety of methods used for measuring activity and the different incubation conditions, it is impossible to compare the specific rates from the various lakes examined. However, the general pattern was an increase in methanogenesis with depth up to a maximum point somewhere below the sediment water interface. At sediment depths below the maximum, a sharp decrease in methanogenesis was usually observed. Methanogenic activity was related to the methane distribution in freshwater sediments. In Lake Vechten (26, 27), the distribution of methane and methanogenic activity were more comparable because incubations were done at in situ temperatures. Incubation for 10 days was sufficient to reproduce the methane distribution endogenous to Lake Vechten sediments, suggesting that if methanogenesis were a continuous process the methane profile may represent a steady-state pattern in balance with mechanisms for removal of methane from the sediment.

FACTORS AFFECTING METHANOGENESIS IN NATURE

E_h Based on the characteristics of pure cultures of methanogenic bacteria, it was not surprising that the highest numbers of methanogenic organisms were found at E_h values of −200 (26) and −250 mV (12) or less. Seasonal changes in E_h also correspond to seasonal changes in methane distribution and maximum numbers of methanogenic bacteria in Lake Vechten sediments (26). Inhibition of methanogenesis in lake sediments by nitrate (4, 67, 90) may be a result of increases in sediment E_h.

Sulfate-reducing bacteria The distribution of methanogenesis in sediments may be affected by the interaction of methanogenic and sulfate-reducing bacteria. The presence of inorganic electron acceptors such as sulfate may prevent methanogenesis by encouraging development of sulfate reducers, which compete for methanogenic substrate or produce inhibitory concentrations of sulfide, although inhibition was not observed in all methanogenic environments. A mutual exclusion of these two metabolic types may be hypothesized from the following observations: sulfate inhibits methanogenesis when added to freshwater sediments (4, 26, 90, 166); maximum methane levels occur at sediment depths where sulfate is depleted (26, 166); and the population maximum of sulfate-reducing bacteria occurs nearer the sediment-water interface than the population maximum of methane-producing bacteria (26).

This separation was better defined in marine sediments where sulfate levels were higher. Sulfide, produced by sulfate-reducing bacteria, may inhibit methanogenic bacteria (25–30). [In contrast, in anaerobic digestors sulfate reduction and methane production were apparently compatible since 25 mM added $SO_4^=$ was completely reduced to sulfide (6.25 mM dissolved $S^=$) without significant effect on the rate of gas production (83).] High methane concentrations and high numbers of methanogenic bacteria occurred where sulfide concentrations were low in Lake Vechten sediments (26). Further evidence of sulfide inhibition was reported in experiments involving a two-stage continuous culture of a sulfate-reducing and a sulfide-sensitive methanogenic bacterium isolated from Lake Vechten sediments (28, 29). Manipulation of the lactate substrate in the first or sulfate-reducing stage influenced the production of sulfide that fed the second or methanogenic stage. When sulfide increased in the second stage, the methanogenic isolate washed out. The pure methanogenic isolate was inhibited by varying the sulfide concentration in a single-stage continuous culture; the yield was reduced significantly at $pS^=$ [$-\log (S^=)$] values of 12.5 or less.[1] Values of $pS^=$ sufficient to inhibit this methanogenic isolate were reported for Lake Vechten sediments (26, 27). In Lake Mendota sediments, addition of sulfide to 5 mM (0.28–0.03 mM dissolved in pore water or $pS^=$ of 9.77–10.72) stimulated methanogenesis (166). Inhibition of methanogenesis did not occur until the addition of 10 mM sulfide resulted in 3.2–4.4 mM sulfide in pore water ($pS^=$ of 8.7–8.56). Thus, some methanogenic bacteria may be extremely sensitive to $S^=$ but methanogenic bacteria of other sediment systems may be relatively resistant to high $S^=$ levels.

Competition for common substrates has also been hypothesized to account for sulfate inhibition of methanogenesis (35, 101, 166). More energy is thermodynamically available when the oxidation of hydrogen and acetate (the major methanogenic substrates) was coupled to sulfate reduction rather than carbon dioxide reduction or the conversion of acetate to methane and carbon dioxide. In fact, sulfate inhibition of methanogenesis was reversed by the addition of excess hydrogen or acetate, suggesting that both of these substrates may be competitively used by methanogenic and sulfate-reducing bacteria (166). The addition of sulfate stimulated the production of $^{14}CO_2$ from [2–^{14}C]acetate, suggesting oxidation of the methyl group linked

[1]The concentration of the various dissolved sulfide species is affected by loss of H_2S (gas) (for $H_2S \leftrightarrows H^+ + HS^-$, pK = 7.0), precipitation of sulfide minerals, or uptake of sulfide. Some confusion may arise when the $pS^=$ (which measures only the contribution of the completely unprotonated $S^=$) is compared to the amount of sulfide added to media or present in natural environments. For example, by using the following equilibrium expressions for sulfide dissociation and the pK values of Krauskopf (80), $K_1 = [(HS^-)(H^+)]/(H_2S) = 10^{-7}$, $K_2 = [(H^+)(S^=)]/(HS^-) = 10^{-12.9}$. We set up the following expression for $(S^=)$ as a function of (H^+) and the total sulfide concentration of 0.02% or 8×10^{-4} M and pH 7, as reported by Cappenberg (26), $S^=_{tot} = 8 \times 10^{-4} = [(S^=)(H^+)]/10^{-19.9} + [(H^+)(S^=)]/10^{-12.9} + (S^=)$, and calculated $(S^=) = 4 \times 10^{-8.9}$, $pS^= = 9.3$. However, note that corrections for activity coefficient were not made. This $pS^=$ would be inhibitory to the methanogenic bacterium isolated (26) on this medium.

to sulfate reduction (166, 167). $^{14}CO_2$ production from the methyl group of acetate was also observed in Lake Vechten (31) and in marine sediments (A. Warford, personal communication). Although the so-called *Desulfovibrio rubentschickii* reportedly oxidized acetate to CO_2 at the expense of sulfate reduction (2), the only known anaerobic acetate dissimilations are via the methanogenic route in *Methanosarcina barkeri* or by a complete oxidation to CO_2 coupled to the reduction of elemental sulfur to sulfide in *Desulfuromonas acetoxidans* (120).

Methanogenic substrates Methane is probably produced in nature from a limited range of substrates: acetate, formate, H_2–CO_2, and possibly methanol or some related intermediate. Carbon monoxide and other substrates metabolized by pure cultures of methane bacteria are probably not ecologically significant. Since the organic matter that enters the sediments is mainly protein, carbohydrate, and lipid polymers or heteropolymers, methanogenic bacteria are obligately associated with other bacteria that ferment these compounds to acetate, formate, and H_2–CO_2 (methanol may not be a natural fermentation product). In sedimentary environments, the availability of substrates is affected by many complex and undefined parameters, including the extent of bacterial decomposition in sediment layers above the methane production zone, the rate of burial due to sedimentation, and/or diffusion of methanogenic substrates into the methane production zone. The availability of methanogenic substrates in the methane production zone may be limited, on one hand, to extensive decomposition in the surface layers and diffusion downward into the methanogenic layer or, on the other hand, by the rate of decomposition of organic compounds to methanogenic substrates within the methanogenic zone. The second case assumes that some of the polymeric substrates subject to anaerobic decomposition are buried more rapidly than they are degraded in layers above the zone of methane production. In freshwater sediments, the zone of maximum methane production lies closer to the sediment-water interface, and diffusion of substrates may occur over smaller distances. Below the zone of maximal production, methanogenic activity decreases in freshwater sediments (Figure 4*B*). Although this decrease may relate to the availability of substrates, many other limiting factors may be involved. In contrast, the zone of maximum methane production in marine sediments may be from one to several meters below the sediment-water interface (see below), making it unlikely that diffusion could account for the transfer of methanogenic substrates produced in a layer of intense decomposition near the surface. The rate of decomposition in marine sediments is probably slow enough that burial of organic carbon occurs. Subsequent decomposition then leads to methane production at these deeper layers, provided no other factors were limiting.

The addition of known methanogenic substrates and other organic electron donors stimulated the rate of methane production in sediments (4, 26, 94, 167). As expected, bicarbonate did not increase methanogenesis in sediments (4, 167), suggesting that methane production may be limited by electron donors. Some investigators attempted to assess the relative importance of methanogenesis from H_2–CO_2 or acetate in sediments. Since the addition of acetate stimulated methyl group reduction to methane and since hydrogen, formate, ethanol, and glucose stimulated carbon dioxide reduction to methane (146, 167), endogenous methane precursors can only be identified in the absence of added electron donors. Determination of the turnover rate of acetate, its pool size, and the overall rate of methanogenesis showed that 70% of the methane may come from the methyl group of acetate (31). Furthermore, when fluoroacetate was added to inhibit acetate turnover, methane formation was 75% inhibited (27). The relative importance of acetate versus carbon dioxide reduction in methanogenesis was also reported in cores from three Russian lakes (13). In lakes Chernyi Kichier and Bol'shoi Kichier, the methyl carbon of acetate accounted for 53.5 and 67.5% of the methane, with the remainder formed from carbon dioxide. Interestingly, carbon dioxide reportedly accounted for 88.5–98.1% of the methane formed in Lake Kuznechikha.

Stable isotope data implicated reduction of carbon dioxide by hydrogen as a major source of methane in Lake Kivu (39, 40). A large preference of ^{12}C over ^{13}C in biological methane production has been used to distinguish methane of biological ($\delta^{13}C_{PDB}$ less than –50‰) or abiological ($\delta^{13}C_{PDB}$ greater than –50‰) origin.[2] In contrast to most sediments where stable isotope ratios of methane suggested a biological origin, the methane of Lake Kivu had a $\delta^{13}C_{PDB}$ of –45‰. Deuser et al (40) proposed that, if the source of methane was carbon dioxide reduced hydrogen (both gases of volcanic origin), the biological preference of ^{12}C would be conserved and the resulting methane would be unusually isotopically heavy, since the volcanic carbon dioxide is unusually isotopically heavy.

FATE OF METHANE IN FRESHWATER SEDIMENTS Methane is the most abundant gas evolved from marshes (144) and from lake sediments (4, 58, 67). Although diffusion of methane must explain some of the transport to the overlying water column, the diffusion of methane in sediments may be too slow to account for the observed flux of methane (50). Gas bubble ebullition may be a major mechanism of methane transport out of sediments (50). Gas containing 95% methane was released at a rate of 1.8 ml of CH_4/min/m^2, as estimated by collection in funnels inverted over Lake Erie sediments (58). The rates and composition of gases from

[2]See Kaplan (71) for a discussion of stable isotope fractionation. $\delta^{13}C_{PDB}$ is a measure of the relative abundance of ^{13}C to ^{12}C compared to the same ratio of a standard (PDB) carbonate. Values less than zero are enriched in ^{12}C relative to the PDB standard. Claypool & Kaplan (35) discussed the biological-versus-abiological carbon isotope fractionations in methanogenic reactions. During methanol fermentation, the methane formed was 81–94‰ (131) and 75–79‰ (53) lighter than the methanol. Heyer et al (53) found a smaller fractionation between the methyl carbon of acetate and the methane produced from acetate; the methane was only 17–20‰ lighter than the acetate methyl carbon. Games (48) studied the fractionation of methane produced from carbon dioxide reduction by hydrogen in pure cultures of *Methanosarcina barkeri*, *Methanobacterium* strain MOH, and *Methanobacterium thermoautotrophicum* and found that the methane was 31–61‰lighter than the carbon dioxide at 40°C, which he attributed either to strain differences or to differences in growth rate. Although the biological fractionation of carbon isotopes in methanogens is not well understood, no abiogenic reactions are known to produce methane of $\delta^{13}C_{PDB}$ less than about –50‰. Thus, isotopically lighter methane is probably the result of bacterial methane production.

Lake Wingra sediments were highly variable over a 2-year survey, but estimates suggested that 2–5 mmol of CH_4/day/m^2 and 0.06–0.15 mmol of CH_4/day/m^2 escaped from shallow- and deep-water sediments, respectively (4). The rate of gas collection in plastic bags suspended at the surface was approximately equal to that trapped above the sediment, suggesting that little loss of methane may occur in the aerobic water column. In the anoxic water columns of permanently stratified meromictic (162, 163) and seasonally stratified dimictic lakes (25, 117, 133, 134), methane concentrations decreased from the sediment upwards toward oxygenated water layers, where aerobic methane-oxidizing bacteria are most active (25, 65, 117, 132–135).

Methane oxidation by anaerobic, sulfate-reducing bacteria could account for $^{14}CO_2$ produced from methane derived from the methyl carbon of acetate in sediments of Lake Vechten (27), but no evidence of $^{14}CH_4$ oxidation occurred in Lake Mendota sediment incubated with or without added sulfate (166). However, the isolation of a bacterium from Lake Mendota sediments capable of methane oxidation at the expense of sulfate reduction has been reported (108). The relative amounts of methane carbon returned to the lake as a result of methane-oxidizing bacteria or lost because of outgassing are not known.

Marine and Estuarine Sediments

METHANE DISTRIBUTION Methane concentrations were determined as a function of depth in many marine and estuarine sediments, as shown in Figure 5 (9, 44, 96, 128, 129, 164). Although the environments studied were highly varied and difficult to compare, the methane profiles of the sediments were remarkably similar. Methane concentrations increased linearly with depth below the sediment-water interface. In contrast to freshwater sediments, the methane gradient does not intersect the sediment-water interface but skews to higher values at depths varying from about 10–150 cm below the sediment surface. The lack of methane in surface layers was related to a zone of sulfate reduction (decreasing levels of sulfate occurred over this depth interval) (96, 129, 138). Similar methane profiles were reported for sediments of the Labrador Shelf (160) and the Gulf of St. Lawrence (124), but the data were not included in Figure 5 because the reported levels of methane exceeded the solubility of the gas [as reported by Claypool & Kaplan (35)] under the conditions reported. The mutual exclusion of methane and sulfate was also noted in salt marshes of lower sulfate levels where methane was more abundant (164).

Methane was the predominant gas collected in cores from the Deep Sea Drilling Project at depths of 20–940 m below the sea floor (36, 49). Stable isotope determinations of the methane (range of $\delta^{13}C_{PDB}$ of –59.6 to –73.3‰) suggested that it was produced biologically (see footnote 2 above) (36, 89). Despite variations with depth, the $\delta^{13}C_{PDB}$ of bicarbonate and methane were always separated by about 70‰, suggesting the biological reduction of bicarbonate to methane over the large range of sediment depths cited. The effect of pressure and temperature on the stability of the various chemical phases of methane, including the presence of gas hydrate crystals in deep-sea environments where large pressures are possible, was discussed by Claypool & Kaplan (35).

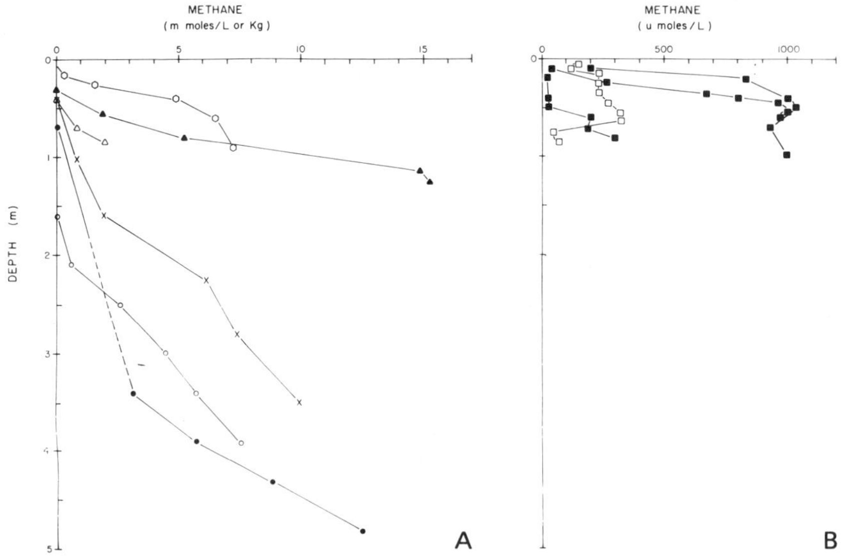

Figure 5 Distribution of methane with depth in marine and estuarine sediments: X, Emery & Hoggan (44), Santa Barbara Basin; ●, ○, Barnes & Goldberg (9), Santa Barbara Basin; ▲, △, Reeburgh (129), Cariaco Trench (east and west basin, respectively); ○, Reeburgh (128), Chesapeake Bay; ■, Martens & Berner (96), Long Island Sound; □, Whelan (164), Louisiana salt marsh.

MICROBIOLOGY OF METHANOGENESIS IN MARINE AND ESTUARINE SEDIMENTS Little information is available on the distribution of methanogenic bacteria or their activity in marine and estuarine environments. The most complete study was done in salt marshes in Georgia and South Carolina (68). In cores taken from short *Spartina* regions of the marsh, viable counts of methanogenic bacteria developed on a medium containing hydrogen and carbon dioxide ranged from about 10^2–10^7 cells/g of dry sediment. Higher numbers were present in the upper 0–7 cm, with decreasing numbers at depths down to 36 cm. In tall *Spartina* regions, the range of methanogenic bacteria was about 10^4–10^6 cells/g of dry sediment, and no depth variation was noted. The distribution of methanogenic activity in sediment from a short *Spartina* region showed a maximum rate of methanogenesis in sediment from 5–7 cm in depth. This rate was five times greater than the rate of methanogenesis from sediments taken at other depths. This pattern is similar to that in freshwater sediments (see Figure 4*B*). Hydrogen and formate stimulated methanogenesis in sediments from 5–7 cm, but acetate and lactate did not.

Nitric oxide, nitrous oxide, nitrite, and nitrate, in decreasing order of potency, inhibited hydrogen-dependent methanogenesis in Georgia salt marsh (3). However, no direct measurement of E_h was reported, and accompanying increases in oxidation-reduction potential may have occurred. Only the addition of resazurin [$E_0 = -0.042$ V at pH 6.7 for resorufin (59)] and its continued reduction under the experimental conditions tested served as an index of oxidation-reduction stability. However, a control vessel to which was added a quantity of air equal to the volume of the test nitric oxide gas was not inhibited. Furthermore, since the inhibition was inversely related to the degree of reduction of the oxides of nitrogen, Balderston & Payne (3) concluded that the effect was not a result of E_h changes. Inhibition of methanogenesis by substrate competition from denitrifying bacteria was ruled out by addition of excess substrate concentrations.

Viable counts of methanogenic bacteria from Santa Barbara Basin sediments on media containing acetate or hydrogen and carbon dioxide ranged from 10–100 cells/g of wet sediment and did not vary with depth from 0–3.5 m (A. Warford, personal communication). However, methane levels increased over this depth interval, as shown in Figure 5. This discrepancy may be attributed to inability to culture the predominant methanogenic bacteria.

The mutual exclusion of methane and sulfate is well defined in marine sediments. Methane was not produced during in vitro incubation of Long Island Sound sediments until after the depletion of sulfate (96). This agrees with environmental measurements showing separate zones of sulfate reduction and methanogenesis.

Oremland (106) studied methane production in plexiglas chambers inserted into shallow marine sediments. The results were complicated by differences in sediment E_h, plant communities, the presence of alternative electron acceptors (oxygen and sulfate), and the possible loss of methane by aerobic oxidation. The methanogenic rate increased in darkened chambers after about 40 hr, presumably because of oxygen and sulfate depletion and decreased E_h. Methane accumulated slowly in chambers exposed to light, presumably either because of high E_h or because of methane oxidation related to the photosynthetic production of oxygen. The rates ranged from 0.09–21.2 μmol/m^2/hr in reducing sediments and from 0.08–5.2 μmol/m^2/hr in oxidizing sediments. The addition of formate and acetate to one chamber significantly stimulated methanogenesis. The addition of formate to a chamber placed in an oxidizing sediment did not stimulate methanogenesis but the presence of H_2–CO_2 in laboratory-incubated sediments did. Acetylene and ethylene inhibited sediment methanogenesis (107).

FATE OF METHANE IN MARINE SEDIMENTS A methane concentration gradient exists in the anoxic water columns of many marine systems; the gradient decreases from the sediment-water interface upward toward the oxic-anoxic boundary. This observation supports a net transport of methane from the sediment to the overlying water (1, 62, 82, 87, 88, 129). In contrast to freshwater sediments, maximum methane levels occur at depths from one to several meters below the sediment-water interface. Reeburgh (128) calculated that methane concentrations in shallow marine sediments could exceed the critical concentration for bubble formation. Martens (95) observed gas ebullition in shallow marine sediments (where methanogenesis presumably occurred below a sulfate-reduction zone), whereas in deep-sea sediments, the hydrostatic pressure of the overlying water probably prevents gas ebullition. In the absence of bubble release, diffusion may be expected to control the transport of methane from sediments. A diffusion model was assumed in order to calculate a rate of methanogenesis of 2.92 and 8.45 μmol/liter/year for Western and Eastern Cariaco Trench sediments (129) and 20 μmol/liter/year (9) for Santa Barbara Basin sediments.

The skewing of the methane profile in the sulfate reduction zone may be a result of physical or biological mixing, although in the absence of biological mixing in the Cariaco Trench, the same profile was observed (129). Several investigators (9, 96, 129) have suggested that methane oxidation by sulfate-reducing bacteria would also yield the observed methane distribution. In fact, unusually low $\delta^{13}C_{PDB}$ values for bicarbonate and unusually high $\delta\ ^{13}C_{PDB}$ values of methane in the sulfate-reducing zone of Santa Barbara Basin sediments (P. Doose, personal communication) suggested the conversion of methane to bicarbonate. Biological evidence for anaerobic methane oxidation in marine sediments has not been reported.

Flooded Soils

Another habitat where rapidly decomposing organic matter leads to the development of an anoxic environment suitable for methanogenesis is flooded soils. Studies of microbial activities have assessed temporal changes in soils incubated under conditions in which anaerobiosis developed after rewetting, as might occur in nature. Electron acceptors of decreasing oxidation-reduction potential were sequentially metabolized in correspondence to the depth distribution of the same activities in sedimentary environments. Thus, oxygen, ferric iron, nitrate, and sulfate were sequentially used before methane was produced (77, 78, 147). E_h decreased to less than –200 mV before methanogenesis was observed (10, 77, 78, 146, 147, 173). Inhibition of methanogenesis by nitrate and other oxidized nitrogen compounds in flooded soils supplemented with glucose may result from an increased E_h (10, 17), in contrast to the results reported for a salt marsh (3). The specific methanogenic substrates used by these latter authors may account for this difference. However, addition of up to 500 ppm of sulfate did not significantly inhibit methane production (17), perhaps because sulfate-reducing organisms were not present in sufficient numbers to affect the methane reaction. Methanogenesis in soils may be inhibited by seawater (79), and although this was attributed to NaCl, about ten times more NaCl than is present in seawater was required for inhibition, suggesting that factors other than NaCl may be responsible.

Carbon dioxide, acetic acid, and minor amounts of formic acid accumulated after reducing conditions were established in flooded soils, but acetic and formic acids disappeared almost completely and carbon dioxide levels decreased slightly as methane was produced (76–78, 148). If anoxic paddy soils were incubated (without being dried and rewetted), the onset of methanogenesis was more rapid. Acetic and formic acids and carbon dioxide again increased initially, and the organic acids decreased to low levels when methane was produced (146). Glucose, sucrose, starch, pectic acid, cellulose, peptone, gelatin, lactate, acetate, butyrate, and propionate increased the accumulation of volatile fatty acids, H_2, and CO_2, and the consequent formation of methane (10, 149, 171–174). The fermentation of polymeric substrates was less rapid, and lignin was a poor substrate for methanogenesis (172).

Methane is produced by carbon dioxide reduction and from reduction of the methyl group of acetate in paddy soils (146). The addition of butyrate as an electron donor favored the formation of methane by $^{14}CO_2$ reduction (146). However, addition of acetate favored the formation of methane from the methyl group of [2-^{14}C]acetate (146). In the absence of extraneous electron donors, 60% of the methane formed in paddy soils (76, 78) came from reduction of the methyl group of [2-^{14}C]acetate. The remaining methane came from carbon dioxide reduction, but the endogenous pool levels of acetate and dissolved bicarbonate that diluted the added label were not accounted for.

The production of methane in paddy soils may be dependent upon environmental variables other than those that define the niche for methanogenic bacteria. Temperature limitations exist, and the maximum rate of methanogenesis for flooded soils was reported to be as high as 40°C (77, 78, 174).

The heartwood of hardwood trees located in waterlogged soils was shown to provide a suitable habitat for some methanogenic bacteria (177, 178).

Animal Digestive Systems

The best-known methanogenic animal digestive system is the rumen of herbivores. Although methane may be produced in a similar fermentation in the cecum (97) of nonruminants, a factor contributing to the lack of methanogenesis in many gastrointestinal habitats may be the rate at which the digestive contents pass through the digestive system. If the turnover of digestive contents is more rapid than the doubling time of the relatively slow-growing methanogenic bacteria, it would be difficult for these organisms to become established. Apparently only one third of human populations sampled consistently form methane as an end product of their intestinal fermentation (18, 84, 85), and a strong familial correlation was found among those who produced methane; thus, genetic and/or environmental influences (18) may be involved in distribution of methanogenic bacteria in humans.

The most significant recent developments in rumen methanogenesis have stemmed from studies on interspecies H_2 transfer between methanogenic and nonmethanogenic bacteria (see H_2 transfer section). Studies on inhibition of methane production in the sheep rumen (37a, 136) by carbon tetrachloride, trichloroethyl-pivalate, or trichloroethyl-adipate resulted in hydrogen accumulation but not in sufficient amounts to account stoichiometrically for the methane production of uninhibited controls. The formation of more reduced fermentation end products due to inhibition was reflected in an increase in the ratio of propionic to acetic acid. Thus, in the rumen where hydrogen is apparently the major substrate for methanogenesis, methanogenic bacteria play a role in establishing the fermentation balance by influencing the flow of reducing power toward methane production (60).

Anaerobic Sludge Digestors

The microbiology of anaerobic digestion as applied in waste treatment systems has been extensively reviewed (54) and will be examined only briefly here.

As in other environments, the limited substrate range of methanogenic bacteria makes them dependent upon a population of organisms that produce hydrogen, carbon dioxide, and acetate as the main substrates for methanogenesis. Factors that may affect the rate of the anaerobic digestion process include hydrolysis of polymers (47, 51, 52), the dissimilation of starting substrates to the level of acetic acid, pH changes, temperature (37, 159), the conversion of acetic acid to methane and CO_2, or even perhaps the removal of methane produced during fermentations (47). About 70% of the methane produced in digestors comes from acetate and the remainder comes from carbon dioxide reduction (66, 140). Inhibition of methanogenesis by carbon tetrachloride (34, 145) or chloroform (34) showed that H_2 may (145) or may not (34) accumulate. This contradiction may be a result of the occurrence of different populations of bacteria and different main routes of methanogenesis in the digestors sampled. It is interesting that methanogenic bacteria that metabolize acetate do not appear to be as abundant in digestors as hydrogen- or formate-using methanogenic bacteria (139). Problems in enumeration due to the slow growth rates observed on acetate (54) or the difficulty in serially diluting clumps of *Methanosarcina barkeri* may account for this paradox. Rapid methanogenesis from acetate by a *M. barkeri* culture isolated from an anaerobic digestor has been recently reported (5, 93, 161), but the rate of methanogenesis is apparently dependent upon the organic nutritional requirements of the methanogenic isolate. The stimulation of acetate fermentation in enrichments from digestor sludge by various organic growth factors, including amino acids, nucleic acid bases, and cell lysates (104; L. Baresi, unpublished results), may yield important clues to development of increased rates of anaerobic digestion and methane formation.

Varel, Isaacson & Bryant (159) demonstrated that thermophilic digestion of cattle wastes at 60°C led to shorter retention times than expected. At a feed concentration of 8.2%, a 3-day retention time was established and a volatile solids reduction of 31–37% was reported. Methane was produced at a rate of 4.5 liters/day/liter of digestor. This rate is approximately 20 times higher than a conventional mesophilic fermentation of domestic wastes.

Thermal pretreatment of secondary activated sludges for 30 min at 175°C prior to anaerobic digestion improved methane yields by more than 50% (51, 52). Other benefits included higher volatile solids reduction, pasteurization, less anaerobic sludge, and better sludge dewaterability. Thermal, chemical, or biological pretreatment of other recalcitrant substrates coupled to thermophilic digestion should be explored for future applications not only to special waste treatment problems but also to energy needs. Although waste reduction and methane formation are intimately linked, engineering efforts, until now, have focused on waste organic (BOD) reduction with methane as a byproduct rather than on methane production as the primary objective.

ACKNOWLEDGMENT

We wish to acknowledge the following individuals for their cooperation and interest in the study of methane: I. R. Kaplan, D. Kosiur, D. Toth, P. Doose, B. Simoneit, A. Warford, M. Smith, B. Mechalas, and I. Straughan. We are grateful to Southern California Edison Company for their support, without which we could not have undertaken this study.

Literature Cited

1. Atkinson, L. P., Richards, F. A. 1967. *Deep Sea Res.* 14:673–84
2. Baars, J. K. 1930. *On sulfate reduction by bacteria.* Doctor of Technical Sciences thesis. Technische Hoogeschool, Delft. 107 pp.
3. Balderston, W. L., Payne, W. J. 1976. *Appl. Environ. Microbiol.* 32:264–69
4. Barber, L. 1974. *Methane production in sediments of Lake Wingra.* PhD thesis. Univ. Wisc., Madison. 145 pp.
5. Baresi, L., Mah, R. A. 1976. *Abstr. 76th Annu. Meet. Am. Soc. Microbiol.,* Q29, p. 195
6. Barker, H. A. 1936. *Arch. Mikrobiol.* 7:420–38
7. Barker, H. A. 1941. *J. Biol. Chem.* 137:153–67
8. Barker, H. A. 1956. *Bacterial Fermentations,* pp. 1–27. New York: Wiley. 95 pp.
9. Barnes, R. O., Goldberg, E. D. 1976. *Geology* 4:297–300
10. Bell, R. G. 1969. *Soil Biol. Biochem.* 1:105–16
11. Belyaev, S. S. 1974. *Microbiology* 43: 295–98
12. Belyaev, S. S., Finkel'shtein, Z. I. 1973. *Microbiology* 42:980–85
13. Belyaev, S. S., Finkel'shtein, Z. I., Ivanov, M. V. 1975. *Microbiology* 44: 272–75
14. Belyaev, S. S., Ivanov, M. V. 1975. *Microbiology* 44:140–42
15. Blaylock, B. A., Stadtman, T. C. 1963. *Biochem. Biophys. Res. Commun.* 11: 34–38
16. Blaylock, B. A., Stadtman, T. C. 1966. *Arch. Biochem. Biophys.* 116:138–58
17. Bollag, J. M., Czlonkowski, S. T. 1973. *Soil Biol. Biochem.* 5:673–78
18. Bond, J. H. Jr., Engel, R. R., Levitt, M. D. 1971. *J. Exp. Med.* 133:572–88
19. Bryant, M. P. 1965. In *Physiology of Digestion in the Ruminant,* ed. R. W. Dougherty, pp. 411–18. Washington: Butterworths. 480 pp.
20. Bryant, M. P., McBride, B. C., Wolfe, R. S. 1968. *J. Bacteriol.* 95:1118–23
21. Bryant, M. P., Tzeng, S. F., Robinson, I. M., Joyner, A. E. 1971. *Adv. Chem. Ser.* 1971(105):23–40
22. Bryant, M. P., Wolin, E. A., Wolin, M. J., Wolfe, R. S. 1967. *Arch. Mikrobiol.* 59:20–31
23. Buchanan, R. E., Gibbons, N. E., ed. 1974. *Bergey's Manual of Determinative Bacteriology,* pp. 472–77. Baltimore: Williams and Wilkin. 1246 pp. 8th ed.
24. Buswell, A. M., Sollo, F. W. 1948. *J. Am. Chem. Soc.* 70:1778–80
25. Cappenberg, T. E. 1972. *Hydrobiologia* 40:471–85
26. Cappenberg, T. E. 1974. *Antonie van Leeuwenhoek J. Microbiol. Serol.* 40: 285–95
27. Cappenberg, T. E. 1974. *Antonie van Leeuwenhoek J. Microbiol. Serol.* 40: 297–306
28. Cappenberg, T. E. 1975. *Microb. Ecol.* 2:60–72
29. Cappenberg, T. E. 1975. *Plant Soil* 43:125–39
30. Cappenberg, T. E. 1976. In *Microbial Production and Utilization of Gases (H_2, CH_4, CO). Symp. Proc.,* ed. H. G. Schlegel, N. Pfennig, G. Gottschalk. Göttingen: Golke-Verlag. In press
31. Cappenberg, T. E., Prins, R. A. 1974. *Antonie van Leeuwenhoek J. Microbiol. Serol.* 40:457–69
32. Cheeseman, P., Toms-Wood, A., Wolfe, R. S. 1972. *J. Bacteriol.* 112: 527–31
33. Chung, K.-T. 1976. *Appl. Environ. Microbiol.* 31:342–48
34. Chynoweth, D. P., Mah, R. A. 1971. *Adv. Chem. Ser.* 1971(105):41–54
35. Claypool, G. E., Kaplan, I. R. 1974. In *Natural Gases in Marine Sediments,* ed. I. R. Kaplan, pp. 99–140. New York Plenum. 324 pp.
36. Claypool, G. E., Presley, B. J., Kaplan, I. R. 1973. *Initial Rep. Deep Sea Drill. Proj.* 19:879–84
37. Cooney, C. L. Wise, D. L. 1975. *Biotech. Bioeng.* 18:1119–35

37a. Czerkawski, J. W., Breckenridge, G. 1975. *Br. J. Nutr.* 34:447–57

38. Daniels, L., Zeikus, J. G. 1976. *Abstr. 76th Annu. Meet. Am. Soc. Microbiol.,* I58, p. 121
39. Degens, E. T., von Herzen, R. P., Wong, H., Deuser, W. G., Jannasch, H. W. 1973. *Geol. Rundsch.* 62:245–77
40. Deuser, W. G., Degens, E. T., Harvey, G. T., Rubin, M. 1973. *Science* 181: 51–54
41. de Vries, W., van Wijck-Kapteyn, W. M. C., Oosterhuis, S. K. H. 1974. *J. Gen. Microbiol.* 81:69–78
42. de Vries, W., van Wijck-Kapteyn, W. M. C., Stouthamer, A. H. 1973. *J. Gen. Microbiol.* 76:31–41
43. Edwards, T., McBride, B. C. 1975. *Appl. Microbiol.* 29:540–45
44. Emery, K. O., Hoggan, D. 1958. *Bull. Am. Assoc. Petrol. Geol.* 42:2174–88

45. Ferry, J. G., Smith, P. H., Wolfe, R. S. 1974. *Int. J. Syst. Bacteriol.* 24: 465–69
46. Ferry, J. G., Wolfe, R. S. 1976. *Arch. Microbiol.* 107:33–40
47. Finney, C. D., Evans, R. S. 1975. *Science* 190:1088–89
48. Games, L. M. 1975. *Biogeochemical and environmental applications of natural variation in carbon isotope ratios.* PhD thesis. Ind. Univ., Bloomington. 200 pp.
49. Hammond, D. E. See Ref. 35, pp. 71–90
50. Hammond, D. E., Simpson, H. J., Mathieu, G. 1975. *Am. Chem. Soc. Symp. Ser.* 18:119–32
51. Haug, R. T. 1976. *Sludge Processing to Optimize Digestibility and Energy Production.* Presented at Ann. Conf. Calif. Wtr. Poll. Contr. Assoc., 48th, South Lake Tahoe
52. Haug, R. T., Stuckey, D. C., Gossett, J. M., McCarty, P. L. 1976. *The effect of thermal pretreatment on digestibility and dewaterability of organic sludges.* Presented at Ann. Conf. Water Pollut. Control Fed., 49th, Minneapolis
53. Heyer, J., Hübner, H., Maab, I. 1976. *Isotopenpraxis* 12:202–5
54. Hobson, P. N., Bousfield, S., Summers, R. 1974. *Crit. Rev. Environ. Control* 4: 131–91
55. Holt, S. C., Canale-Parola, E. 1967. *J. Bacteriol.* 93:399–410
56. Hopgood, M. F., Walker, D. J. 1967. *Aust. J. Biol. Sci.* 20:183–92
57. Hopgood, M. F., Walker, D. J. 1969. *Aust. J. Biol. Sci.* 22:1413–24
58. Howard, D. L., Frea, J. I., Pfister, R. M. 1971. *Proc. 14th Conf. Great Lakes Res.* pp. 236–240
59. Hungate, R. E. 1966. *The Rumen and Its Microbes.* New York: Academic. 533 pp.
60. Hungate, R. E. 1967. *Arch. Mikrobiol.* 59:158–64
61. Hungate, R. E. 1975. *Ann. Rev. Ecol. Syst.* 6:39–66
62. Hunt, J. M. 1974. In *The Black Sea—Geology, Chemistry, and Biology,* ed. E. T. Degens, D. A. Ross, pp. 499–504. Tulsa: Am. Assoc. Petrol. Geol. 633 pp.
63. Iannotti, E. L., Kafkewitz, D., Wolin, M. J., Bryant, M. P. 1973. *J. Bacteriol.* 114:1231–40
64. Jacobs, N. J., Wolin, M. J. 1963. *Biochem. Biophys. Acta* 69:29–39
65. Jannasch, H. W. 1975. *Limnol. Oceanogr.* 20:860–64
66. Jeris, J. S., McCarty, P. L. 1965. *J. Water Pollut. Control Fed.* 37:178–92
67. Johnston, D. W., Holding, A. J., McCluskie, J. E. 1974. *Proc. R. Soc. Edinburgh Sect. B* 74:123–33
68. Jones, W. J. 1975. *Ecology of methanogenesis in salt marsh and estuarine sediments.* MS thesis. Clemson Univ., Clemson, S. C. 78 pp.
69. Joyner, A. E., Baldwin, R. L. 1966. *J. Bacteriol.* 92:1321–30
70. Jungermann, K., Thauer, R. K., Leimenstoll, G., Decker, K. 1973. *Biochem. Biophys. Acta* 305:268–80
71. Kaplan, I. R. 1975. *Proc. R. Soc. London Ser. B* 189:183–211
72. Kearny, J. J., Sagers, R. D. 1972. *J. Bacteriol.* 109:152–61
73. Konopka, A. E., Moore, R. L., Staley, J. T. 1976. *Int. J. Syst. Bacteriol.* 26: 505–10
74. Koyama, T. 1953. *J. Earth Sci. Nagoya Univ.* 1:107–18
75. Koyama, T. 1954. *J. Earth Sci. Nagoya Univ.* 2:5–14
76. Koyama, T. 1963. *J. Geophys. Res.* 68:3971–73
77. Koyama, T. 1964. In *Recent Researches in the Fields of Hydrosphere, Atmosphere and Nuclear Geochemistry,* ed. Y. Miyake, T. Koyama, pp. 143–79. Tokyo: Maruzen. 404 pp.
78. Koyama, T. 1964. In *Advances in Organic Geochemistry,* ed. U. Columbo, G. D. Hobson, pp. 363–76. New York: Macmillan. 488 pp.
79. Koyama, T., Hishida, M., Tomino, T. 1970. *Soil Sci. Plant Nutr.* 16:81–86
80. Krauskopf, K. B. 1967. *Introduction to Geochemistry.* New York: McGraw-Hill. 721 pp.
81. Langenberg, K. F., Bryant, M. P., Wolfe, R. S. 1968. *J. Bacteriol.* 95: 1124–29
82. Lamontagne, R. A., Swinnerton, J. W., Linnenbom, V. J., Smith, W. D. 1973. *J. Geophys. Res.* 78:5317–24
83. Lawrence, A. W., McCarty, P. L., Guerin, F. J. A. 1964. *Proc. 19th Indiana Waste Conf. Eng. Bull. Purdue Univ. Ext. Ser.* 117:343–57
84. Levitt, M. D. 1972. *J. Am. Diet. Assoc.* 60:487–90
85. Levitt, M. D., Ingelfinger, F. J. 1968. *Ann. NY Acad. Sci.* 150:75–81
86. Li, L. F., Ljungdahl, L., Wood, H. G. 1966. *J. Bacteriol.* 92:405–12
87. Linnenbom, V. J., Swinnerton, J. W. 1970. In *Symposium on Organic Matter in Natural Waters,* ed. D. W. Hood. Fairbanks: Univ. Alaska Inst. Mar. Sci. Occasional Publ. 1
88. Linnenbom, V. J., Swinnerton, J. W. 1971. *Symposium on the Investigations*

and Resources of the Carribean Sea and Adjacent Regions. Paris: UNESCO
89. Lyon, G. L. See Ref. 35, pp. 91–98
90. Macgregor, A. N., Keeney, D. R. 1973. *Water Res. Bull.* 9:1153–58
91. Macy, J., Kulla, H., Gottschalk, G. 1976. *J. Bacteriol.* 125:423–28
92. Macy, J., Probst, I., Gottschalk, G. 1975. *J. Bacteriol.* 123:436–442
93. Mah, R. A. 1976. *Abstr. 76th Annu. Meet. Am. Soc. Microbiol.* Q28, p. 195
94. Mallard, G. E., Frea, J. I. 1972. *Proc. 15th Conf. Great Lakes Res.* pp. 87–93
95. Martens, C. S. 1976. *Science* 192:998–999
96. Martens, C. S., Berner, R. A. 1974. *Science* 185:1167–69
97. McBee, R. H. 1971. *Ann. Rev. Ecol. Syst.* 2:165–76
98. McBride, B. C., Wolfe, R. S. 1970. *Fed. Proc. Fed. Am. Soc. Exp. Biol.* 29:344
99. McBride, B. C., Wolfe, R. S. 1971. *Adv. Chem. Ser.* 1971(105):1123
100. McBride, B. C., Wolfe, R. S. 1971. *Biochemistry* 10:2317–24
101. Mechalas, B. J. See Ref. 35, pp. 11–26
102. Miller, T. L., Wolin, M. J. 1973. *J. Bacteriol.* 116:836–46
103. Mylroie, R. L., Hungate, R. E. 1954. *Can. J. Microbiol.* 1:55–64
104. Novak, J. T., Ramesh, M. S. 1975. *Water Res.* 9:963–67
105. O'Brien, W. E., Ljungdahl, L. G. 1972. *J. Bacteriol.* 109:626–32
106. Oremland, R. S. 1975. *Appl. Microbiol.* 30:602–8
107. Oremland, R. S., Taylor, B. F. 1975. *Appl. Microbiol.* 30:707–9
108. Panganiban, A., Hanson, R. S. 1976. *Abstr. 76th Annu. Meet. Am. Soc. Microbiol.,* I59, p. 121
109. Pantskhava, E. S. 1969. *Doklady Biol.* 188:699–701
110. Pantskhava, E. S., Bukin, V. N. 1974. *Doklady Biochem.* 215:169–71
111. Pantskhava, E. S., Pchelkina, V. V. 1968. *Doklady Biol. Sci.* 182:552–53
112. Pantskhava, E. S., Pchelkina, V. V. 1969. *Appl. Biochem. Microbiol.* 5: 325–28
113. Pantskhava, E. S., Pchelkina, V. V. 1969. *Appl. Biochem. Microbiol.* 5: 235–38
114. Pantskhava, E. S., Pchelkina, V. V., Bukin, V. N. 1973 *Biochemistry* 38:417–23
115. Pantskhava, E. S., Syromyatnikov, E. Yu. 1973. *Doklady Biochem.* 211: 318–20
116. Patel, G. B., Roth, L. A., van den Berg, L., Clark, D. S. 1976. *Can. J. Microbiol.* 22:1404–10
117. Patt, T. E., Cole, G. C., Bland, J., Hanson, R. S. 1974. *J. Bacteriol.* 120: 955–64
118. Pchelkina, V. V., Pantskhava, E. S., Bukin, V. N. 1970. *Biochemistry* 35: 873–78
119. Petitdemange, H., Cherrier, C., Raval, G., Gay, R. 1976. *Biochem. Biophys. Acta* 421:334–47
120. Pfennig, N., Biebl, H. 1976. *Arch. Microbiol.* 110:3–12
121. Poston, J. M., Stadtman, T. C. 1975. In *Cobalamin: Biochemistry Pathophysiology,* ed. B. M. Babior, pp. 111–140. New York: Wiley. 477 pp.
122. Pretorius, W. A. 1972. *Water Res.* 6:1213–17
123. Prins, R. A. 1974. *Antonie van Leeuwenhoek J. Microbiol. Serol.* 40:585–89
124. Rashid, M. A., Vilks, G., Leonard, J. D. 1975. *Chem. Geol.* 15:83–96
125. Reddy, C. A., Bryant, M. P., Wolin, M. J. 1972. *J. Bacteriol.* 109:539–45
126. Reddy, C. A., Bryant, M. P., Wolin, M. J. 1972. *J. Bacteriol.* 110:126–32
127. Reddy, C. A., Bryant, M. P., Wolin, M. J. 1972. *J. Bacteriol.* 110:133–38
128. Reeburgh, W. S. 1969. *Limnol. Oceanogr.* 14:368–75
129. Reeburgh, W. S. 1976. *Earth Planet. Sci. Lett.* 28:337–44
130. Reeburgh, W. S., Heggie, D. T. See Ref. 35, pp. 27–46
131. Rosenfeld, W. D., Silverman, S. R. 1959. *Science* 130:1658–59
132. Rudd, J. W. M., Furutani, A., Flett, R. J., Hamilton, R. D. 1976. *Limnol. Oceanogr.* 21:357–64
133. Rudd, J. W. M., Hamilton, R. D. 1975. *Limnol. Oceanogr.* 20:902–6
134. Rudd, J. W. M., Hamilton, R. D. 1975. *Arch. Hydrobiol.* 75:522–38
135. Rudd, J. W. M., Hamilton, R. D., Campbell, N. E. R. 1974. *Limnol. Oceanogr.* 19:519–24
136. Rufener, W. H., Wolin, M. J. 1968. *Appl. Microbiol.* 16:1955–56
137. Scheifinger, C. C., Linehan, B., Wolin, M. J. 1975. *Appl. Microbiol.* 29:480–83
138. Sholkovitz, E. 1973. *Geochim. Cosmochim. Acta* 37:2043–73
139. Smith, P. H. 1966. *Dev. Ind. Microbiol.* 7:156–60
140. Smith, P. H., Mah, R. A. 1966. *Appl. Microbiol.* 14:368–71
141. Stadtman, T. C. 1967. *Ann. Rev. Microbiol.* 21:121–42
142. Stadtman, T. C., Barker, H. A. 1949. *Arch. Biochem.* 21:256–64
143. Stadtman, T. C. Barker, H. A. 1951. *J. Bacteriol.* 61:81–86

144. Swain, F. M. 1974. In *Advances in Organic Geochemistry,* ed. B. Tissot, F. Bienner, pp. 673–88. Paris: Technip. 1080 pp.
145. Sykes, R. M., Kirsch, E. J. 1972. *Water Res.* 6:41–55
146. Takai, Y. 1970. *Soil Sci. Plant Nutr.* 16:238–44
147. Takai, Y., Koyama, T., Kamura, T. 1956. *Soil Plant Food Tokyo* 2:63–66
148. Takai, Y., Koyama, T., Kamura, T. 1963. *Soil Sci. Plant Nutr.* 9:1–5
149. Takai, Y., Macura, J., Kunc, F. 1969. *Folia Microbiol. Prague* 14:327–33
150. Taylor, C. D., McBride, B. C., Wolfe, R. S., Bryant, M. P. 1974. *J. Bacteriol.* 120:974–75
151. Taylor, C. D., Wolfe, R. S. 1973. *Fed. Proc.* 32:589 (Abstr.)
152. Taylor, C. D., Wolfe, R. S. 1974. *J. Biol. Chem.* 10:4879–85
153. Taylor, C. D., Wolfe, R. S. 1974. *J. Biol. Chem.* 19:4886–90
154. Taylor, G. T. 1975. *Proc. Biochem.* 10:29–33
155. Tzeng, S. F., Wolfe, R. S., Bryant, M. P. 1975. *J. Bacteriol.* 121:154–91
156. Tzeng, S. F., Bryant, M. P., Wolfe, R. S. 1975. *J. Bacteriol.* 121:192–96
157. van den Berg, L., Patel, G. B., Clark, D. S., Lentz, C. P. 1976. *Can. J. Microbiol.* 22:1312–19
158. van Ert, M., Staley, J. T. 1971. *J. Bacteriol.* 108:236–40
159. Varel, V. H., Isaacson, H. R., Bryant, M. P. 1975. *Abstr. 75th Annu. Meet. Am. Soc. Microbiol.,* O28, p. 196
160. Vilks, G., Rashid, M. A., van der Linden, W. J. M. 1975. *Can. J. Earth Sci.* 11:1427–34
161. Ward, D. M., Kaplan, I. R., Mah, R. A. 1976. *Abstr. 76th Annu. Meet. Am. Soc. Microbiol.,* Q27, p. 195
162. Weimer, W. C., Lee, G. F. 1971. *Environ. Sci. Technol.* 5:1136–38
163. Weimer, W. C., Lee, G. F. 1973. *Limnol. Oceanogr.* 18:414–25
164. Whelan, T. 1974. *Estuarine Coastal Mar. Sci.* 2:407–15
165. Wieringa, K. T. 1936. *Antonie van Leeuwenhoek J. Microbiol. Serol.* 3:1–11
166. Winfrey, M. R., Zeikus, J. G. 1977. *Appl. Environ. Microbiol.* In press
167. Winfrey, M. R., Nelson, D. R., Klevickis, S. C., Zeikus, J. G. 1977. *Appl. Environ. Microbiol.* In press
168. Wolfe, R. S. 1971. *Adv. Microb. Physiol.* 6:107–46
169. Wolin, M. J. 1974. *Am. J. Clin. Nutr.* 27:1320–28
170. Wolin, M. J., Wolin, E. A., Jacobs, N. J. 1961. *J. Bacteriol.* 81:911–17
171. Yamane, I., Sato, K. 1963. *Soil Sci. Plant Nutr.* 9:32–36
172. Yamane, I., Sato, K. 1963. *Soil Sci. Plant Nutr.* 9:28–31
173. Yamane, I., Sato, K. 1964. *Soil Sci. Plant Nutr.* 10:35–41
174. Yamane, I., Sato, K. 1967. *Soil Sci. Plant Nutr.* 13:94–100
175. Zeikus, J. G., Bowen, V. G. 1975. *Can. J. Microbiol.* 21:121–29
176. Zeikus, J. G., Bowen, V. G. 1975. *J. Bacteriol.* 121:373–80
177. Zeikus, J. G., Henning, D. L. 1975. *Antonie van Leeuwenhoek J. Microbiol. Serol.* 41:543–52
178. Zeikus, J. G., Ward, J. C. 1974. *Science* 184:1181–83
179. Zeikus, J. G., Weimer, P. J., Nelson, D. R., Daniels, L. 1975. *Arch. Microbiol.* 104:129–34
180. Zeikus, J. G., Winfrey, M. R. 1976. *Appl. Environ. Microbiol.* 31:99–107
181. Zeikus, J. G., Wolfe, R. S. 1972. *J. Bacteriol.* 109:707–13
182. Zeikus, J. G., Wolfe, R. S. 1973. *J. Bacteriol.* 113:461–67
183. Zhilina, T. N. 1971. *Mikrobiologiya* 40:674–80
184. Zhilina, T. N. 1976. *Mikrobiologiya* 45:481–89
185. Zhilina, T. N., Aleksandrushkina, N. I. 1974. *Mikrobiologiya* 43:726–28
186. Zhilina, T. N., Zavarzin, G. A. 1973. *Mikrobiologiya* 42:266–73

Ann. Rev. Microbiol. 1977. 31:343–56

EFFECT OF PRIMARY METABOLITES ON SECONDARY METABOLISM

❖1708

Stephen W. Drew

Department of Chemical Engineering, Virginia Polytechnic Institute and State University, Blacksburg, Virginia 24061

Arnold L. Demain

Department of Nutrition and Food Science, Massachusetts Institute of Technology, Cambridge, Massachusetts 02139

CONTENTS

INTRODUCTION 344
Regulation of Primary Metabolism 344
INDUCTION IN SECONDARY METABOLITE PATHWAYS 345
FEEDBACK REGULATION IN SECONDARY METABOLISM 348
Effect on Secondary Metabolism by Feedback Regulation of Primary Precursor Biosynthesis 348
Regulation of Secondary Metabolism by Primary End Products of a Common Branched Pathway 348
CARBON CATABOLITE REGULATION OF SECONDARY METABOLISM 350
Catabolite Repression 350
Catabolite Inhibition 351
NITROGEN CATABOLITE REGULATION OF SECONDARY METABOLISM 351
ATP OR ENERGY CHARGE REGULATION OF SECONDARY METABOLISM 352
TROPHOPHASE-IDIOPHASE RELATIONSHIP 353
CONCLUDING REMARKS 354

> There are no applied sciences . . . There are only applications of science, and this is a very different matter . . . The study of the applications of science is easy to anyone who is master of the theory of it.
>
> Louis Pasteur

INTRODUCTION

As microbial cells grow, they break down complex, high-molecular-weight carbon and energy sources through the action of catabolic enzymes. The end products of catabolism are reassembled to form primary intermediates such as amino acids, nucleotides, vitamins, carbohydrates, and fatty acids. These biosynthetic intermediates are then assembled into the complex and essential metabolites that give structure and biological function to the organisms. These interdependent catabolic and biosynthetic activities comprise the pathways that make up primary metabolism. The compounds and enzymes of primary metabolism serve basic, well-defined, and often essential roles in support of growth and reproduction of microbes.

On the other hand, secondary metabolism gives rise to compounds whose functions in the welfare, development, and reproduction of the producing organisms are not readily apparent. Such compounds and the enzymatic activities unique to their synthesis appear to be of secondary importance to the organism and are apparently not essential for growth. Although secondary metabolites are both unusual in structure and metabolic activity, the separation of these compounds from primary metabolites tends to de-emphasize the complex interrelationship between primary and secondary metabolism. The metabolic pathways of primary metabolism often supply the precursors of secondary metabolism, and hence, we would expect those factors that influence primary metabolism to have some effect on secondary metabolism.

The necessity for metabolic control of primary metabolism is obvious. As in all competitive processes, efficiency is a major factor in survival of microbial species. The regulatory mechanisms that have evolved to govern the synthesis and action of the hundreds of enzymes of primary metabolism allow microbial species efficiently to compete in nature for the limited resources necessary for growth and reproduction. The list of regulatory mechanisms that control primary metabolism is extensive, and although our understanding of these mechanisms is somewhat limited, we can elaborate on several basic modes of regulatory action.

Regulation of Primary Metabolism

Some of the more important mechanisms for control of primary metabolism are substrate induction, feedback repression and inhibition, catabolite repression and inhibition, and ATP (or energy charge) regulation. In each case, regulation is a dynamic process dependent upon the local concentration of effector molecules. In the case of substrate induction, two general categories of enzymes can be identified. *Constitutive enzymes* are those whose concentrations are roughly independent of the presence of their substrates. Such enzymes are normally produced by the organism, and their concentrations are determined by the relative rates of synthesis and destruction (turnover). The rate of protein turnover during exponential growth of microorganisms is usually quite low, and therefore the concentration of constitutive enzymes is primarily controlled by gene expression. *Inducible enzymes,* on the other hand, are not produced unless their substrates or analogues of the substrates are present. Substrate induction may control the synthesis of a single enzyme or a group of enzymes. This control mechanism is dependent upon the concentration of the substrate (61).

Feedback regulation can occur by two basic mechanisms. Feedback repression acts at the genetic level to control the synthesis of an enzyme or group of enzymes. Feedback inhibition acts at the molecular level to control the activity of an enzyme(s). In both cases, feedback regulation usually involves an end product that controls the synthesis or activity of one or more enzymes in its biosynthetic pathway. Feedback regulation is dependent upon the concentration of the end product.

Occasionally, the synthesis of enzymes is repressed by the presence of rapidly used substrates for growth. This type of regulation has been termed catabolite repression (39). Inhibition of enzymatic activity by catabolites of rapidly used growth substrates has also been observed. Catabolite regulation may involve the catabolic products of several different growth substrates, including carbon- and/or nitrogen-containing compounds. Although the mechanisms of catabolite repression and catabolite inhibition are not yet totally clear, the degree of regulation seems to depend upon the rate at which the appropriate substrates are metabolized and therefore probably involves not only the concentration of specific catabolites but also the energy state of the cell. Although the mechanism of ATP (or energy charge) regulation is poorly understood, Atkinson & Walton have correlated inhibition or activation by energy charge with the regulation of metabolic pathways (2–4).

The regulation of primary metabolism by these and other mechanisms has been well studied, and excellent reviews are available (3, 6, 7). The interactions between primary and secondary metabolism must certainly involve these regulatory processes.

INDUCTION IN SECONDARY METABOLITE PATHWAYS

The response to stimulatory additives in certain secondary metabolite fermentations resembles the phenomenon of enzyme induction. One example involves tryptophan, a stimulatory precursor of ergoline alkaloid in *Claviceps.* Although the stimulatory action of tryptophan was once considered to be a result of its precursor activity, several observations indicate a second, more important role, i.e. as an inducer of one or more of the enzymes necessary for alkaloid biosynthesis. (i) Robbers & Floss (54) noted that tryptophan analogues, which are not incorporated into the alkaloids, are nevertheless stimulatory toward their production. (ii) Tryptophan must be added during the growth phase of alkaloid fermentations to stimulate alkaloid biosynthesis, even though alkaloid synthesis occurs at a later time (62). This requirement is quite rigid; failure to add the tryptophan to the fermentation results in little alkaloid production. Furthermore, if cultures are transferred to a medium lacking tryptophan during the rapid growth phase, alkaloid synthesis is severely restricted. However, if mycelia are grown in a medium containing tryptophan and then after growth has finished transferred to a medium lacking tryptophan, alkaloid is synthesized at a high rate (55). (iii) Uptake of tryptophan from the medium leads to intracellular tryptophan concentrations two- to three-fold greater than that observed in cultures from tryptophan-free media. This accumulation reaches a peak just prior to alkaloid production (55). Recently, Krupinski et al (35) made the crucial observation that dimethylallyl-tryptophan synthetase, the first unique enzyme in alkaloid synthesis, is indeed induced by tryptophan.

An inductive effect similar to that observed in alkaloid synthesis is seen in the methionine stimulation of cephalosporin C biosynthesis by *Cephalosporium acremonium* (11). The amino acid is not required for growth, although it can be used as the sole source of nitrogen or sulfur. Methionine exerts its major effect on cephalosporin C synthesis when added during growth, i.e. before antibiotic synthesis commences. Although it is clear that methionine is an efficient precursor of the sulfur atom of cephalosporin C (6, 51), other sulfur-containing compounds are without significant stimulatory effect (13, 14). These early observations suggested a regulatory role for methionine in stimulation of cephalosporin C biosynthesis.

Parenthetically, one of the more interesting findings concerning methionine supplementation is the morphological effects that result. Although mycelia grown in sufate are filamentous, methionine-grown mycelia are swollen, irregular, and more highly fragmented into arthrospores. Furthermore, it has been found that the arthrospores have a greater ability to incorporate [U-^{14}C]valine into cephalosporin C and penicillin N than do mycelia (50). Also, in a series of mutant cultures, the ability to produce high levels of cephalosporin C plus penicillin N correlates with the proportion of arthrospores (50). Whether fragmentation and antibiotic formation represent a cause-and-effect relationship or are unrelated phenomena caused by growth in methionine remains an unanswered but intriguing question.

A recent study of cephalosporin C stimulation by sulfur intermediates between methionine and cephalosporin C has confirmed the unique requirement for methionine in spite of the fact that cysteine, rather than methionine, is thought to be the more immediate precursor of sulfur in the cephalosporin nucleus. These studies (16) employed an early blocked mutant (274-1) that grows on cysteine, methionine, cystathionine, and homocysteine but not on sulfate. It was reasoned that, if methionine were acting solely as a sulfur precursor for the antibiotic, the sulfur amino acids should stimulate cephalosporin C production in the order cysteine > cystathionine > methionine. The order observed was the opposite of the above, i.e. methionine > cystathionine > cysteine. This suggested that cysteine and cystationine must be first converted via transsulfuration (Figure 1) into methionine before they can stimulate antibiotic formation, even though their activity as sulfur precursors should not involve methionine (16). To examine this point, various other types of sulfur auxotrophs were used (17, 18). For example, it was known that the early blocked auxotroph (274-1) could produce cephalosporin C when growing on cysteine. The pathway from cysteine to cephalosporin C should not involve methionine as an intermediate. An experiment was done to determine whether or not genetically blocking transsulfuration from cysteine to methionine would affect cephalosporin C production (16). A second block was added to 274-1 to produce double mutant 11-8, which grows on methionine but not on cysteine. This methionine auxotroph was grown with just enough methionine to allow normal growth in the presence of excess cysteine. Little to no antibiotic was produced unless excess methionine was added. Of crucial significance was the finding that norleucine could replace excess methionine—and norleucine contains no sulfur (15)! Like methionine, norleucine also induces fragmentation of mycelia into arthrospores (19). Thus, it appears that methionine is an inducer of cephalosporin C formation in *C. acremonium,* but elucidation of the basic mechanism involved must await the unravelling of the biosynthetic pathway to β-lactam antibiotics. Progress is being made in several laboratories (23, 33). Induction by mannan plays a role in the interconversion of streptomycins since it acts as an inducer of the α-D-mannosidase that converts mannosidostreptomycin to streptomycin (11).

Although the exact mechanisms by which primary metabolites induce the enzymes of secondary metabolism are unknown, we can assemble a set of criteria that indicate the existence of such regulation. Induction of secondary metabolism should require the effector molecule to be added to the batch fermentation prior to the synthesis of the secondary metabolite, i.e. during the growth phase of the fermentation. The primary metabolite should have a demonstrated stimulatory role divorced from any function as a precursor of the secondary metabolite in question. Nonmetabolized structural analogues of the effector should be able to replace the regulatory molecule in stimulation of secondary metabolism. Finally, since all regulatory phenomena are concentration dependent, one might expect to observe an increase in pool level concentrations of effector metabolites or their derivatives just prior to the appearance of the enzymes for secondary metabolism. Although these criteria are certainly not all-inclusive, they may be useful in searching for other examples of induction of secondary metabolism by primary metabolites. Some examples that satisfy at least one of these criteria include the stimulation of fosfomycin synthesis by methionine in *Streptomyces fradiae* (56), and the induction of virginiamycin synthesis by an unknown molecule excreted by the producer, *Streptomyces virginiae* (67).

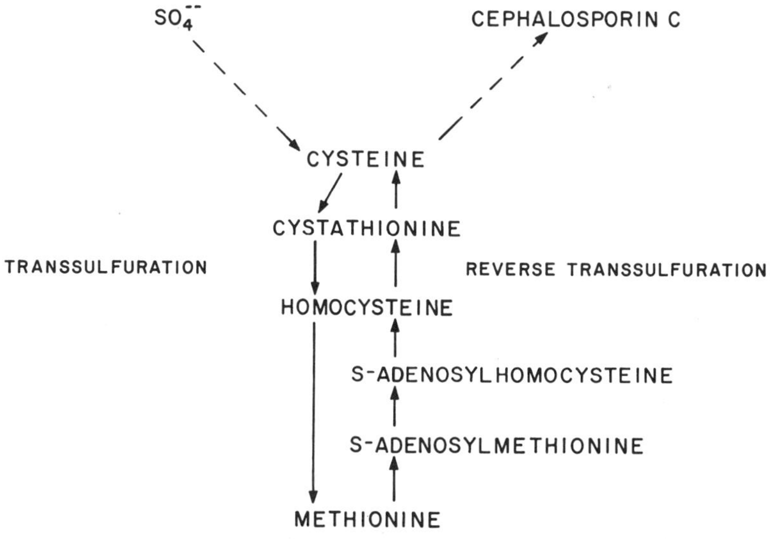

Figure 1 Probable pathway of sulfur metabolism in *Cephalosporium* sp.

FEEDBACK REGULATION IN SECONDARY METABOLISM

In some instances, feedback regulation occurs as a result of secondary metabolite accumulation rather than through the action of a primary metabolite. Chloramphenicol, ristomycin, ergot alkaloids, virginiamycin, indolmycin, cycloheximide, mycophenolic acid, aurodox, and penicillin limit their own synthesis. Chloramphenicol acts by repressing arylamine synthetase, the first enzyme of chloramphenicol biosynthesis (29). Indolmycin inhibits the first enzyme of its pathway (60). The first enzyme of alkaloid synthesis is feedback inhibited by agroclavine and elymoclavine, two alkaloid end products (26, 42). In other instances, however, primary metabolites are themselves involved in the feedback regulation. In one case, the ability of primary metabolites (which are precursors to the secondary metabolites) to regulate their own biosynthesis limits their accumulation and thus restricts secondary metabolism. In another situation, a primary metabolite formed in a branched pathway, the other branch of which leads to a secondary metabolite, can diminish the metabolic flow through the secondary branch by repressing or inhibiting an early common step(s) of the path.

Effect on Secondary Metabolism by Feedback Regulation of Primary Precursor Biosynthesis

Secondary biosynthesis often uses primary metabolite end products (as precursors) whose own pathways are feedback regulated. Penicillin synthesis by *Penicillium chrysogenum* involves valine as a direct precursor of the dihydrothiazine ring. One would expect valine to regulate its own synthesis by controlling the first enzyme of valine synthesis, acetohydroxy acid synthetase. Goulden & Chattaway (25) observed that acetohydroxy acid synthetase in a superior penicillin-producing mutant was less sensitive to feedback inhibition by valine than the ancestral and poorer penicillin-producing strain, *P. chrysogenum* Wis. Q-176. Furthermore, the enzyme content in the superior strain was twice that in Wis. Q-176.

Similar control mechanisms exist in other organisms. The production of pyrrolnitrin by early strains of *Pseudomonas aureofaciens* required the addition of the precursor tryptophan to the medium, indicating that endogenous synthesis of tryptophan was very tightly regulated. Mutants selected for resistance to 5-fluorotryptophan and 6-fluorotryptophan no longer required tryptophan supplementation. These mutants appear to be insensitive to feedback regulation by tryptophan, thus overproducing the amino acid that is incorporated into the antibiotic (21).

Regulation of Secondary Metabolism by Primary End Products of a Common Branched Pathway

Many secondary pathways share intermediates with primary pathways; taken together, they constitute branched sequences. In such cases, feedback regulation of an early enzyme by the primary end product would be expected to diminish production of the secondary metabolite. Although lysine itself is not involved in penicillin synthesis as a precursor, an intermediate in its biosynthesis, α-aminoadipic acid, is involved in the initial peptide-forming steps of penicillin biosynthesis. Thus, addition of lysine to *P. chrysogenum* reduces penicillin formation (8). α-Aminoadipic acid not only reverses the inhibitory effects of lysine but also stimulates penicillin synthesis in the absence of added lysine (59).

Lysine inhibition of penicillin formation is apparently a result of a feedback effect on its own biosynthesis, i.e. inhibition of the first enzyme of lysine biosynthesis, homocitrate synthetase (12, 45). Such an inhibition would be expected to result in a deficiency of α-aminoadipic acid needed for penicillin formation, since lysine and penicillin are end products of a branched biosynthetic pathway (Figure 2). The activity of homocitrate synthase is very important during the productive phase (idiophase). The specific activity of this enzyme drops markedly at the onset of idiophase, and addition of lysine decreases its already low activity. The expected decrease in L-α-aminoadipate in the amino acid pool would then result in the inhibition of penicillin biosynthesis. Although no penicillin production medium

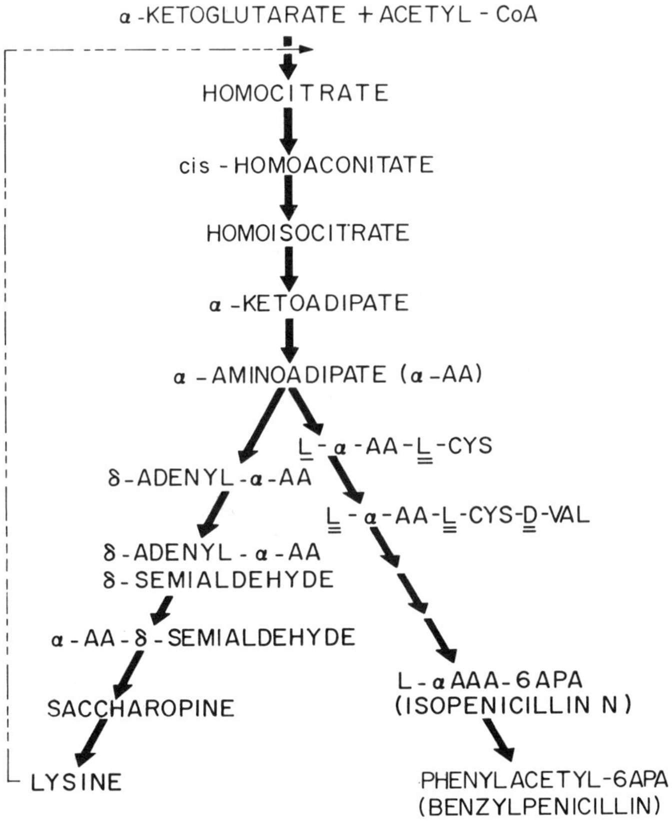

Figure 2 Probable branched pathway synthesizing lysine and penicillins in *Penicillium chrysogenum.*

contains the high level of free lysine required to inhibit penicillin production, the lysine effect appears to have physiological significance. In a series of mutants with increased ability to make lysine, there is an inverse correlation between lysine production and penicillin formation (46).

In a similar manner, aromatic amino acids inhibit production of the polyene macrolide antibiotic, candicidin, by *Streptomyces griseus* (36). The amino acids (tyrosine, tryptophan, phenylalanine) are end products of a branched pathway that also leads to *p*-aminobenzoic acid, a precursor of the aromatic moiety of candicidin. Thus, by negative feedback regulation of an enzyme of the early common pathway, the amino acids presumably inhibit candicidin formation. Based on regulatory patterns in bacterial synthesis of the aromatic amino acids, one might predict that feedback regulation involves the conversion of erythrose-4-phosphate and phosphoenolpyruvate to 3-deoxy-D-arabinoheptulosonic acid-7-phosphate (DAHP).

As information on the pathways and biochemistry of secondary metabolic synthesis becomes available, it may be possible to predict regulatory mechanisms such as branched-pathway feedback repression or inhibition based on the classical examples discussed above. Karlsson and co-workers (30) have suggested that the aromatic ring of rifamycin produced by *Nocardia mediterranei* is derived from a precursor of the aromatic amino acids. By analogy with other studies, one might expect aromatic amino acids to control and thereby regulate the synthesis of this antibiotic. Prediction is a tricky business, however, since the organism may be resistant to feedback regulation by the primary metabolite. For example, chloramphenicol is synthesized in part via the aromatic amino acid pathway, and thus, one might predict that aromatic amino acids would inhibit chloramphenicol biosynthesis; they do not. However, the amino acids have no feedback effect on DAHP synthetase in this chloramphenicol producer (38).

CARBON CATABOLITE REGULATION OF SECONDARY METABOLISM

The generality of repression or inhibition of enzymes by catabolism of rapidly utilized carbon sources is well illustrated in secondary metabolism. Although glucose is often an excellent carbon and energy source for microbial growth, it is infrequently utilized as the major carbon and energy source in secondary metabolite fermentations. Glucose and other rapidly metabolized carbon sources have been found markedly to suppress production of coumermycin, neomycin, enniatin, bacitracin, mitomycin, prodigiosin, siomycin, indolmycin, ergot alkaloids, cephalosporins, violacein, and penicillins.

Catabolite Repression

Although the preferred medium for actinomycin biosynthesis by *Streptomyces antibioticus* contains 0.1% glucose and 1.0% galactose, antibiotic synthesis is delayed until the glucose supply is depleted. If additional glucose is added prior to the initiation of actinomycin synthesis, severe repression of antibiotic synthesis occurs. Gallo & Katz (24) found that rapid growth accompanied glucose metabolism and that the formation of phenoxazinone synthetase, an enzyme unique to antibiotic synthesis, is repressed by glucose but not by galactose. They also found that other carbon sources that support rapid growth were effective in repressing phenoxazinone synthetase.

A similar phenomenon has been observed in puromycin fermentations. O-demethylpuromycin methyltransferase, presumably the final enzyme of puromycin biosynthesis, is also subject to glucose-mediated catabolite repression (53).

Although glucose is most often implicated in catabolite repression of secondary metabolism, other carbon sources can cause similar effects. In *Streptomyces niveus*, the producer of novobiocin, citrate causes catabolite repression and glucose does not. In a medium containing citrate and glucose, citrate is used first and antibiotic production is delayed until after a diauxic lag and initiation of glucose utilization (34).

Several carbon sources cause catabolite repression of N-acetylkanamycin amidohydrolase in *Streptomyces kanamyceticus*. This enzyme, presumably the last enzyme in kanamycin biosynthesis, is repressed by glucose, fructose, lactose, mannose, and maltose, with lactose and fructose causing the most severe effect. cAMP was reported to relieve glucose repression (57). It is hoped that this isolated finding of an effect of cAMP on actinomycete metabolism is confirmed in the near future.

Carbon catabolite repression is also important in the interconversion of members of an antibiotic family. Both mannosidostreptomycinase (11) and cephalosporin C acetyl hydrolase (27) are repressed by glucose.

Catabolite Inhibition

In some instances, glucose or other carbon sources appear to cause inhibition rather than repression of some enzyme of secondary metabolite biosynthesis. In the cases of neomycin (48, 41), siomycin (32), and penicillin (9), cells actively producing antibiotic are inhibited by glucose addition. Unfortunately, it is difficult to decide whether the effect is indeed a result of catabolite inhibition or instead to catabolite repression of an enzyme that is rapidly being degraded and resynthesized. Kennel (31) recently studied the production of β-lactam antibiotics (penicillin N and cephalosporin C) by resting cells of *Cephalosporium acremonium*. For many years, it was known that, in a defined medium supporting production of penicillin N and cephalosporin C, glucose was rapidly used during trophophase and sucrose was slowly used during idiophase. Kennel (31) found that rapidly used sugars (glucose, maltose, fructose) yield less β-lactam antibiotic than slowly used sugars (sucrose, galactose). He also noted that low glucose concentrations allow higher β-lactam production than higher concentrations. Although no evidence of carbon catabolite repression could be found, he did detect a type of catabolite inhibition of preformed enzymes by a combination of glucose and ammonia.

NITROGEN CATABOLITE REGULATION OF SECONDARY METABOLISM

The discovery of nitrogen catabolite regulation of primary metabolism is relatively recent and involves repression of enzymes that act on nitrogen-containing substrates, e.g. proteases, nitrate reductase, amidases, histidase, and urease, by rapidly used nitrogen sources, especially ammonia. In *Aspergillus nidulans* and yeast, repression requires the presence of the NADP-glutamate dehydrogenase. In enteric bacteria, unadenylylated glutamine synthetase is required to derepress NH_4^+-controlled enzymes.

Nitrogen catabolite repression per se has not been discussed in the literature dealing with secondary metabolites, but it certainly exists. The usefulness of soybean meal in actinomycete fermentations is probably a result of avoidance of nitrogen catabolite repression of antibiotic biosynthesis, owing to its slow breakdown into repressive amino acids and ammonia. In 1948, Dulaney (20) screened chemically defined sources of nitrogen for streptomycin formation and found proline to be best and also to be very slowly utilized as sole nitrogen source. Ammonium salts are much poorer for streptomycin production than the slowly used proline or soybean meal.

Production of acetate-derived phenolic secondary metabolites such as trihydroxytoluene by *Aspergillus fumigatus* is under nitrogen catabolite control (65). These polyketides appear in batch culture when nitrogen in the medium is exhausted, and addition of ammonium completely inhibits their production without affecting growth or pH. Cephamycin production is also under nitrogen regulation (1) as is the formation of bikaverin by *Gibberella fujikuroi* (5).

ATP OR ENERGY CHARGE REGULATION OF SECONDARY METABOLISM

Since all enzymatic reactions involve the transfer of chemical energy, it is quite logical that a regulatory mechanism based on a common form of stored energy should be active in the control of secondary pathways. Atkinson (2, 3) has characterized this type of control as activation and inhibition of enzymes of primary metabolism by the relative levels of ATP, ADP, AMP in the cell. Energy charge is quantitatively measured as ([ATP] + ½[ADP])/([ATP] + [ADP] + [AMP]) (54). High energy charge inhibits some enzymes of primary metabolism and activates others. Many secondary metabolite processes are inhibited by inorganic phosphate concentrations that are optimal or at least not inhibitory to growth (66). These processes include those for chlortetracycline, candicidin, ergot alkaloids, streptomycin, neomycin, nebramycin, vancomycin, bacitracin, gramicidin S, cephamycin, bikaverin, and corynecin.

In batch chlortetracycline fermentations, antibiotic formation begins when phosphate in the medium is exhausted. It has been suggested that the mechanism of phosphate inhibition of chlortetracycline biosynthesis might involve regulation by ATP or energy charge. A high phosphate concentration in the medium might increase intracellular ATP formation and lead to a high energy charge in the cell. [Studies with *Escherichia coli* support this hypothesis (58).] If chlortetracycline biosynthesis were inhibited by high levels of ATP or energy charge, the link between phosphate concentration and antibiotic synthesis would be established. Janglova and co-workers (28) examined the ATP content of two strains of *Streptomyces aureofaciens*: a low producer (200 μg/ml) and a high producer (2000 μg/ml) of chlortetracycline. In both strains, ATP concentration rapidly increased during growth, then rapidly decreased and remained at a lower level for most of the fermentation cycle. The low producer was found to have two to four times as much ATP as the high producer throughout.

In view of the above, some results on candicidin biosynthesis are of interest. A number of years ago, Liu and co-workers (37) reported that phosphate addition stimulates growth and inhibits antibiotic biosynthesis. Martin & Demain (43) have found that the known inhibitory effect of phosphate on candicidin fermentations can be duplicated in a short-time resting cell system. Inorganic phosphate or nucleotides inhibit net candicidin production and incorporation of labeled precursors (*p*-aminobenzoic acid and propionate) into candicidin. In the normal fermentation, the intracellular ATP concentration is high during early growth but low at the start of production. Addition of phosphate or nucleotides immediately raises the intracellular ATP concentration threefold and turns off candicidin synthesis. The nucleotides are active only because they are hydrolyzed and liberate inorganic phosphate (44). The data indicates that phosphate acts by inhibiting the action of "candicidin synthetase."

Inorganic phosphate, which totally inhibits alkaloid synthesis at high levels, has been shown to repress the first enzyme of alkaloid biosynthesis (35) and also chanoclavine cyclase in *Claviceps* SD58 (22). The addition of tryptophan or thiotryptophan (or other inducers that reverse phosphate inhibition of alkaloid biosynthesis) derepresses these enzymes.

The well-known inhibition of streptomycin biosynthesis by phosphate may involve a mechanism different from ATP or energy charge regulation, i.e. inhibition of phosphatases by inorganic phosphate (11). Since the biosynthetic intermediates of the streptomycin pathway are phosphorylated, whereas the ultimate product is not, phosphatases participate in biosynthesis. Streptomycin biosynthesis includes at least three phosphate-cleaving steps in formation of the streptidine moiety (63). The final enzymatic step in streptomycin production appears to be the cleavage of phosphate from streptomycin phosphate, and the enzyme catalyzing this reaction is inhibited by inorganic phosphate (64). Thus, conducting a streptomycin fermentation in the presence of excess phosphate leads to the accumulation of the biologically inactive streptomycin phosphate instead of streptomycin (49). Findings of a somewhat similar nature have been made in the neomycin fermentation (40).

TROPHOPHASE-IDIOPHASE RELATIONSHIP

An interesting aspect of secondary metabolism is the growth-dissociated production of many secondary metabolites during the idiophase (production phase). The interest centers on the mechanism by which formation of secondary products is usually retarded until the trophophase (growth phase) approaches completion. At the early stages of growth, most microorganisms are sensitive to their own antibiotic. It is only after the rapid growth phase that they become physiologically resistant to external antibiotic. This delay in secondary product formation is one of the major mechanisms by which antibiotic-producing microorganisms prevent suicide (10). Secondary metabolites fail to appear during growth because the enzymes responsibile for their formation are repressed during trophophase. We unfortunately know very little about the repression-derepression phenomena involved, but they undoubtedly include some of the mechanisms mentioned above. For example, carbon catabolite repression of phenoxazinone synthetase probably is important in the actinomycin fermentation.

Matteo et al (47) examined the formation of the enzymes responsible for gramicidin S synthesis. This cyclic peptide antibiotic is produced by *Bacillus brevis* by a nonribosomal synthesizing system involving two gramicidin S synthetase enzymes. As is the case with many secondary metabolites, gramicidin S is not produced until late in the cell cycle, since the gramicidin S synthetases are not formed until the latter part of the logarithmic growth phase. After reaching their peak specific activities, the enzymes rapidly disappear as the cells proceed into the stationary growth phase. The mechanism for control of synthetase formation was examined in a chemostat that allowed the study of nutritional deficiency independent of growth rate. Although gramicidin S synthetases I and II were produced under carbon, nitrogen, sulfur, or phosphorus limitation, the enzyme production was invariably low at high dilution rates (0.45–0.5 hr^{-1}) and increased as the dilution rate was lowered.

Thus, it appears that a high growth rate is incompatible with gramicidin S synthetase production. Although the mechanism responsible is unknown, it is clear that such a relationship prevents synthetase formation during exponential growth in batch culture and allows for synthetase formation as the cells leave the logarithmic growth phase.

Growth rate control is also evident in secondary metabolism of *Gibberella fujikuroi.* In batch culture, growth occurs first (maximal rate at 18 hr), then bikaverin is synthesized (40 hr), and then gibberellin is synthesized (70 hr). In the chemostat, bikaverin shows its best synthesis rate at 0.05 hr^{-1}, whereas gibberellin synthesis is optimal at 0.01 hr^{-1} where bikaverin is not produced at all.

These studies as well as earlier ones (e.g. 52) point out some important aspects of secondary metabolism that deserve special attention. First, the production of enzymes unique to secondary metabolism during logarithmic growth in the chemostat demonstrate that trophophase and idiophase are not mutually exclusive. Rather, this concept of phases is a useful, empirically derived vehicle for the study of secondary metabolism. Second, the observation that growth and antibiotic synthesis can occur simultaneously suggests still another mechanism for modifying the regulation of secondary metabolism, i.e. via control of specific growth rate. Third, the observation that no single type of nutrient controls the appearance of gramicidin S synthetases supports the hypothesis that a generalized parameter such as growth rate may be responsible for idiophase batch kinetics in certain processes of secondary metabolism.

CONCLUDING REMARKS

It seems clear that the pathways of secondary metabolisms are regulated by many of the same processes that control primary metabolism. The ways in which primary metabolites interact in secondary metabolism are evident on several levels, including roles as precursors and pathway effectors. Although comparison of the batch kinetics of primary and secondary metabolism often suggests that these two processes are separate and distinct, one must remember that the fermentation environment is constantly changing during batch operation. Because of the complexity of microbial growth and metabolism, it is difficult to study specific characteristics in batch fermentations and perhaps unwise to view primary and secondary metabolism as separate and unique events. The fact that primary and secondary metabolism can occur simultaneously under certain conditions suggests that primary and secondary metabolism may be separated only by differences in the type of regulation of their pathways. In this light, the fact that secondary metabolites have a poorly defined role in the welfare of the producing organism may simply reflect our ignorance.

Although we have identified several examples of primary metabolite regulation of secondary metabolism, our understanding of the exact mechanisms involved is remarkably sparse. Certainly the interactions of primary metabolism with secondary metabolism in batch culture are complex and difficult to understand. What factors lead to accumulation of a primary metabolite regulator of secondary metabolism? Is catabolite repression of secondary metabolism related primarily to growth rate or to a specific source of carbon or nitrogen? What are the kinetic constants associated with regulation of secondary metabolism? Are certain aspects of primary and secondary metabolism mutually exclusive and if so, can they be made compatible by altering regulatory patterns? Perhaps the continuing refinement of steady state, continuous culture production of secondary metabolites will bring us closer to answers for these and other important questions.

ACKNOWLEDGMENT

Arnold L. Demain's studies on secondary metabolism are supported by grants from the National Science Foundation (BMS75-17527) and the Bristol-Myers Co.

Literature Cited

1. Aharonowitz, Y., Demain, A. L. 1976. *Intersci. Conf. Antimicrob. Agents Chemother. 16th,* p. 49 (Abstr.)
2. Atkinson, D. E. 1969. *Ann. Rev. Microbiol.* 23:47–68
3. Atkinson, D. E. 1970. In *The Enzymes,* ed. P. D. Boyer, 1:461–89. New York: Academic. 559 pp.
4. Atkinson, D. E., Walton, G. M. 1967. *J. Biol. Chem.* 242:3239–41
5. Bu'Lock, J. D., Detroy, R. W., Hostalek, Z., Munim-al-Shakarchi, A. 1974. *Trans. Br. Mycol. Soc.* 62:377–89
6. Caltrider, P. G., Niss, H. F., 1966. *Appl. Microbiol.* 14:746–53
7. Datta, P. 1969. *Science* 165:556–62
8. Demain, A. L. 1957. *Arch. Biochem. Biophys.* 67:244–45
9. Demain, A. L. 1972. *J. Appl. Chem. Biotechnol.* 22:345–62
10. Demain, A. L. 1974. *Ann. N.Y. Acad. Sci.* 235:601–12
11. Demain, A. L., Inamine, E. 1970. *Bacteriol. Rev.* 34:1–19
12. Demain, A. L., Masurekar, P. S. 1974. *J. Gen. Microbiol.* 82:143–51
13. Demain, A. L., Newkirk, J. F. 1962. *Appl. Microbiol.* 10:321–25
14. Demain, A. L., Newkirk, J. F., Hendlin, D. 1963. *J. Bacteriol.* 85:339–44
15. Drew, S. W., Demain, A. L. 1973. *Biotech. Bioeng.* 15:743–54
16. Drew, S. W., Demain, A. L. 1975. *Antimicrob. Agents Chemother.* 8:5–10
17. Drew, S. W., Demain, A. L. 1975. *Eur. J. Appl. Microbiol.* 2:121–28
18. Drew, S. W., Demain, A. L. 1975. *J. Antibiot.* 28:889–95
19. Drew, S. W., Winstanley, D. J., De-

main, A. L. 1976. *Appl. Environ. Microbiol.* 31:143–45
20. Dulaney, E. L. 1948. *J. Bacteriol.* 56:305–13
21. Elander, R. P., Mabe, J. A., Gorman, M. 1970. *Appl. Microbiol.* 19:721–25
22. Erge, D., Maier, W., Groeger, D. 1973. *Biochem. Physiol. Pflanz.* 164:234–47
23. Fawcett, P. A., Usher, J. J., Abraham, E. P. 1976. In *Second Int. Symp. Genetics Ind. Microorganisms,* ed. K. D. Macdonald, pp. 129–38. London: Academic. 636 pp.
24. Gallo, M., Katz, E. 1972. *J. Bacteriol.* 190:659–67
25. Goulden, S. A., Chattaway, F. W. 1968. *Biochem. J.* 110:55P–56P
26. Heinstein, P. F., Lee, S. I., Floss, H. G. 1971. *Biochem. Biophys. Res. Commun.* 44:1244–51
27. Hinnen, A., Nuesch, J. 1976. *Antimicrob. Agents Chemother.* 9:824–30
28. Janglová, Z., Suchý, J., Vaněk, Z. 1969. *Folia Microbiol.* 14:208–10
29. Jones, A., Westlake, D. W. S. 1974. *Can. J. Microbiol.* 20:1599–611
30. Karlsson, A., Sartori, G., White, R. J. 1974. *Eur. J. Biochem.* 47:251–56
31. Kennel, Y. M. 1977. *Carbon source regulation of antibiotic biosynthesis in Cephalosporium acremonium.* PhD Thesis. Mass. Inst. Technol., Cambridge. 75 pp.
32. Kimura, A. 1967. *Agric. Biol. Chem.* 31:845–52
33. Kohsaka, M., Demain, A. L. 1976. *Biochem. Biophys. Res. Commun.* 70: 465–73
34. Kominek, L. A. 1972. *Antimicrob. Agents Chemother.* 1:123–34
35. Krupinski, V. M., Robbers, J. E., Floss, H. G. 1976. *J. Bacteriol.* 125:158–65
36. Liu, C. M., McDaniel, L. E., Schaffner, C. P. 1972. *J. Antibiot.* 25:116–212
37. Liu, C. M., McDaniel, L. E., Schaffner, C. P. 1975. *Antimicrob. Agents Chemother.* 7:196–202
38. Lowe, D. A., Westlake, D. W. S. 1971. *Can. J. Biochem.* 49:448–55
39. Magasanik, B. 1961. *Cold Spring Harbor Symp. Quant. Biol.* 26:249–56
40. Majumdar, M. K., Majumdar, S. K. 1971. *Biochem. J.* 122:397–404
41. Majumdar, M. K., Majumdar, S. K. 1971. *Folia Microbiol.* 16:285–92
42. Malik, V. S., Vining, L. C. 1970. *Can. J. Microbiol.* 16:173–79
43. Martin, J. F., Demain, A. L. 1976. *Biochem. Biophys. Res. Commun.* 71: 1103–9
44. Martin, J. F., Liras, P., Demain, A. L. 1976. *Int. Ferment. Symp., 5th,* p. 146 (Abstr.)
45. Masurekar, P. S., Demain, A. L. 1972. *Can. J. Microbiol.* 18:1045–48
46. Masurekar, P. S., Demain, A. L. 1974. *Antimicrob. Agents Chemother.* 6: 366–68
47. Matteo, C. C., Cooney, C. L., Demain, A. L. 1976. *J. Gen. Microbiol.* 96: 415–22
48. Maxon, W. D., Chen, J. W. 1966. *J. Ferment. Technol.* 44:255–363
49. Miller, A. L., Walker, J. B. 1970. *J. Bacteriol.* 104:8–12
50. Nash, C. H., Huber, F. M. 1971. *Appl. Microbiol.* 22:6–10
51. Nuesch, J., Treichler, H. J., Liersch, M. 1973. In *Genetics of Industrial Microorganisms: Actinomycetes and Fungi,* ed. Z. Vanek, Z. Hostalek, J. Cudlin, pp. 309–34. Prague: Academia. 511 pp.
52. Pirt, S. J., Righelato, R. C. 1967. *Appl. Microbiol.* 15:1284–90
53. Pogell, B. M., Sankaran, L., Redshaw, P. A., McCann, P. A. 1976. In *Microbiology—1976,* ed. D. Schlessinger, pp. 543–47. Washington, D.C.: Am. Soc. Microbiol. 587 pp.
54. Robbers, J. E., Floss, H. G. 1970. *J. Pharm. Sci.* 59:702–3
55. Robbers, J. E., Robertson, L. W., Hornemann, K. M., Jindra, A., Floss, H. G. 1972. *J. Bacteriol.* 112:791–96
56. Rogers, T. O., Birnbaum, J. 1974. *Antimicrob. Agents Chemother.* 5:121–32
57. Satoh, A., Ogawa, H., Satomura, Y. 1976. *Agric. Biol. Chem.* 40:191–96
58. Shechter, Y., Rafaeli-Eshkol, D., Hershko, A. 1973. *Biochem. Biophys. Res. Commun.* 54:1518–24
59. Somerson, N. L., Demain, A. L., Nunheimer, T. D. 1961. *Arch. Biochem. Biophys.* 93:238–41
60. Speedie, M. K., Hornemann, U., Floss, H. G. 1975. *J. Biol. Chem.* 250:7819–25
61. Stadtman, E. R. 1970. In *The Enzymes,* ed. P. D. Boyer, 1:397–459. New York: Academic. 559 pp.
62. Vining, L. C., 1970. *Can. J. Microbiol.* 16:473–80
63. Walker, J. B. 1971. *Lloydia* 34:363–71
64. Walker, M. S., Walker, J. B. 1971. *J. Biol. Chem.* 246:7034–40
65. Ward, A. C., Packter, N. M. 1974. *Eur. J. Biochem.* 46:323–33
66. Weinberg, E. D. 1974. *Dev. Ind. Microbiol.* 15:70–81
67. Yanagimoto, M., Terui, G. 1971. *J. Ferment. Technol.* 49:611–18

Ann. Rev. Microbiol. 1977. 31:357–77

THE GENOME OF HEPATITIS B VIRUS

❖1709

William S. Robinson
Department of Medicine, Stanford University School of Medicine,
Stanford, California 94305

CONTENTS

INTRODUCTION 357
HBV GENE PRODUCTS 358
HBsAg Forms in the Blood 358
HBcAg 360
HBeAg 360
Viral-Specified Polypeptides 361
Polypeptides of HBsAg Particles 361
Polypeptides of HBcAg Particles 364
The Possibility of Additional Viral Polypeptides 364
Current Estimate of the Total Viral-Specific Protein 364
DANE PARTICLE DNA STRUCTURE AND THE MECHANISM OF THE ENDOGENOUS DNA POLYMERASE REACTION 365
The Complexity of Dane Particle DNA 368
VIRAL GENE EXPRESSION IN INFECTED LIVER 370
SUMMARY AND CONCLUSIONS 371

INTRODUCTION

The virus that causes hepatitis B or serum hepatitis appears to infect only man in nature, and experimental infection has been achieved in only a few additional primates (9). Although highly infectious for man, hepatitis B virus (HBV) has not been propagated in tissue culture. The limited host range and failure so far to infect tissue culture cells has prevented development of convenient infectivity assays so that direct identification of the infectious form of the virus has not yet been possible.

The most important single discovery concerning this virus was of the antigen first known as Australia antigen (Au antigen) in 1964 (11). Only after several years of investigation was the antigen associated with acute hepatitis B (12, 70, 72). It was then named hepatitis-associated antigen (HAA) and currently is designated hepatitis B surface antigen (HBsAg). Much evidence now indicates that HBsAg is an HBV-specified antigen. HBsAg in the blood has proven a convenient marker for HBV infection, and studies of the antigen have provided a wealth of information about the epidemiology and course of infection, and about the structure of viral forms in the blood that bear the antigen. Among the most important discoveries arising from early investigation of HBsAg was the recognition of the relatively common occurrence of persistent or chronic HBV infection. Persistent infection is manifested by circulation for months or years of relatively high concentrations of HBsAg particles; these are mostly defective or incomplete virus forms, as well as infectious virus. The blood of persistently infected patients is a rich source of viral antigen forms for physical and chemical characterization.

Although most of the HBsAg in blood is in the form of incomplete viral antigen without nucleic acid, one form, the Dane particle (20), has several properties suggesting that it may be the complete form of HBV, and it is the only antigen form known to contain nucleic acid. Dane particles contain small circular DNA molecules with an unusual structure and a DNA polymerase that utilizes the DNA as a primer/template. The small size of the Dane particle DNA, however, has raised doubts about whether or not this could be the complete viral DNA (83). Recent studies of Dane particle DNA structure and complexity combined with evidence that different infected cells express different viral genes suggest that Dane particle DNA molecules are heterogeneous in base sequence and raise the possibility that the complete viral genome may not be contained in the DNA of a single Dane particle. Here, I review recent information: the number of viral gene products; the size, structure, and complexity of Dane particle DNA; the mechanism of the DNA polymerase reaction; the pattern of viral gene expression in infected cells; and the implications of the findings for the organization of the viral genome. Some other aspects of HBV have been recently reviewed (39, 83, 98).

HBV GENE PRODUCTS

The size of the HBV genome is not known. However, several probable viral gene products have been identified; these include HBsAg and two other antigens associated exclusively with hepatitis B virus infection. These antigens occur in the blood in several different structural forms.

HBsAg Forms in the Blood

Several particulate structures in serum are known to carry HBsAg determinants on their surfaces; the antigen has not been found in a nonparticulate or low-molecular-weight form in serum (4, 55). It is well established that the surface of the HBsAg-bearing particles is antigenically complex. At least five antigenic specificities are present on HBsAg particles. A group-specific antigen (*a*) and two pairs of subtype determinants (*d,y* and *w,r*), which, for the most part, are mutually exclusive, have been demonstrated (6, 53). The four HBsAg subtypes *adw, ayw, adr,* and *ayr* have been identified and are useful epidemiologic markers. Recent evidence suggests antigenic heterogeneity of the group-specific determinant *a* and additional minor determinants may exist (30).

Persuasive although indirect evidence suggests that HBV is a virus-specified antigen. HBsAg appears in the blood early after infection with HBsAg (90), and an antibody response after infection results in immunity (95). Immunization with highly purified HBsAg particles results in protection against HBV infection and/or disease (75), as does administration of γ-globulin with a high titer of antibody against HBsAg (anti-HBs) (33, 73, 78, 86). The antigenic subtype found in secondary cases of HBV infection is regularly the same as the subtype of the index case or of the original source used in experimental infections (54, 63), indicating that the subtype determinants are specified by the viral genome and not by the host. Finally, a large amount of serological and epidemiologic data is consistent with the concept that HBsAg is a viral antigen (90).

The HBsAg form with the most complex structure and uniform appearance is the Dane particle (20). It has an overall diameter of 42 nm (20), HBsAg on its surface (2, 20), a lipid-containing outer layer or envelope (83), a 28-nm internal core or nucleocapsid with a unique antigen [hepatitis B core antigen (HBcAg)] on its surface (2), an internal small circular DNA (81), and a DNA polymerase activity (47, 81, 82). In electron micrographs of uranyl acetate-stained preparations, the core of some Dane particles appears to have an electron-dense center and in others an electron-translucent center (45). Two populations of Dane particles and Dane particle cores (which can be prepared by detergent treatment of Dane particles) have been demonstrated by equilibrium CsCl density gradient centrifugation (42, 45). High-buoyant-density Dane particles manifest endogenously primed DNA polymerase activity and yield exclusively high-buoyant-density cores with electron microscopically "full" centers after detergent treatment. Lower-buoyant-density Dane particles do not manifest DNA polymerase activity and yield mostly low-density cores with "empty" centers by electron microscopy.

Although there is no direct demonstration that the Dane particle is infectious, several properties suggest that it may be HBV: (*a*) its surface antigen (HBsAg) induces protective antibody (anti-HBs) (75); (*b*) it contains a unique internal core antigen (HBcAg), which is probably virus specified (2); (*c*) its size (20) is consistent with estimates of the size of infectious HBV determined by ultrafiltration (61); (*d*) its concentration in most sera (1) is consistent with titrations of infectivity in serum (10); (*e*) its concentration in sera appears to correlate with the probability that patients will transmit infection to contacts (5, 69); (*f*) purified and concentrated preparations of Dane particles have been shown to be infectious at higher dilutions than previously shown for unfractionated HBsAg-positive serum (94); (*g*) it is the only viral antigen form known to contain nucleic acid (83); and (*h*) DNA reassociation experiments have shown that Dane particle DNA base sequences are only present in the DNA and RNA of infected liver and not in uninfected liver, and these sequences appear to be covalently attached to high-molecular-weight DNA (57) as are other viral DNAs when integrated into chromosomal DNA (e.g. 85).

Dane particles regularly appear in high concentrations in the blood during the late incubation period of acute hepatitis B and fall rapidly in concentration with the onset of disease (46, 50). Their concentration is variable among different chronic carriers, but for individual patients the level appears to remain fairly constant (83).

More numerous HBsAg forms in the blood are small spherical particles with diameters between 16 and 25 nm ("20-nm particles") and filamentous forms with diameters around 22 nm and variable lengths up to 1000 nm (reviewed in 83). These forms consist of protein, carbohydrate, and lipid, and no HBcAg or nucleic acid has been found. They are considered to be incomplete viral coat particles. Preparations of 20-nm particles consistently appear to contain small amounts of serum protein components (15, 62, 64) that have not been removed by extensive purification. Whether these are minor intrinsic constituents of the particles, or alternatively only avidly bound to the particle surface, or are just contaminating the preparation and copurifying with HBsAg in some cases (89) is not yet clear. Although the surfaces of these particles clearly share antigenic determinants (and thus some peptides) with the surface of Dane particles (2, 20), it is not known whether the peptide composition of the outer layer or envelope of Dane particles is identical in all respects to that in the other antigen forms.

HBcAg

HBcAg is found in the blood only as an internal component of Dane particles, as described above. No free HBcAg has been detected in serum. HBcAg-bearing particles with the electron microscope appearance of Dane particle cores have been isolated from homogenates of HBV-infected liver (37). Such particles have been shown to contain DNA polymerase activity like that of Dane particles (84). Particles with the same morphology have been seen in the nuclei of hepatocytes in electron micrographs of thin sections of HBV-infected liver (1, 16, 43). HBcAg is considered a virus-specified antigen because it appears to occur only during hepatitus B infection, there is an early and brisk antibody response to HBcAg during infection (50), and it is an internal component of one of the HBsAg forms, Dane particles (2).

HBeAg

The e antigen (HBeAg), discovered and named in 1972 (59), is physically and antigenically distinct from HBsAg. It is said to have a sedimentation coefficient of 12S and a buoyant density of 1.29 g/ml in CsCl (60). It has proven difficult to purify and is not well-characterized chemically. It occurs exclusively in HBsAg-positive sera (60), and an antibody response to HBeAg is frequently observed following HBV infection, suggesting that it may be an HBV-specified antigen. It occurs commonly in the sera of chronic HBsAg carriers who have high concentrations of Dane particles (5, 67), and thus the presence of HBeAg correlates (as do Dane particles) with a propensity for transmission of infection to patient contacts (5, 34, 69). Since carriers that produce Dane particles in high concentrations also commonly produce HBeAg, it is possible that the two antigen forms are related in some way. It has been reported that anti-HBe reacts with the surface of Dane particles (66), suggesting that HBeAg may be a surface component of Dane particles. However, the antiserum used in that study was not proven monospecific, and other investigators (e.g. 27) have failed to confirm that finding. It seems more likely that if HBeAg is a component of Dane particles it is an internal component, although it is known to be distinct from HBcAg (27). The question of its physical relationship to Dane particles remains unsettled. Recently, Neurath & Strick (65) proposed that HBeAg is an immunoglobulin, in which case it would not be a virus-specified polypeptide. The data supporting this conclusion have not yet been published. Attempts to confirm this have led others (G. L. Gerin, unpublished results; G. N. Vyas, unpublished results) to conclude that HBeAg is not an immunoglobulin. Recently, antigenic subtypes of HBeAg have been described (97).

Viral-Specified Polypeptides

As described above, there is reasonable evidence, although not direct proof, that HBV genes specify the two antigens known to be associated with HBV infection: HBsAg and HBcAg. HBeAg may also be a virus-specified antigen, although its origin is less certain than that of HBsAg and HBcAg at this time. A probable additional viral gene product is the protein of the Dane particle core with DNA polymerase activity, since the polymerase enzymes found in other viruses have been shown to be virus specified (19, 44, 56). Very little is known about the polypeptides with HBeAg reactivity and with DNA polymerase activity. Recent studies, however, have provided some information about the polypeptides with HBsAg reactivity and in HBcAg particles.

Polypeptides of HBsAg Particles

Several investigators have studied the polypeptide composition of HBsAg particles, and widely differing results have been obtained. Early studies of purified 22-nm particles by using sodium dodecyl sulfate (SDS)-polyacrylamide gel electrophoresis to separate peptides identified as few as two (96) or three (28) major polypeptides with sizes between 26,000 and 40,000 daltons (see Table 1). More recently, as many as seven (25, 87) or nine (18, 22) peptides have been identified by Coomasie blue staining of SDS-polyacrylamide gels with size ranges from 23,000–97,000 daltons and from 19,000–120,000 daltons, respectively, in two representative studies (Table 1). Two (26, 88) or three (18) polypeptides have been shown to stain with periodic acid-Schiff, suggesting they are glycoproteins. The sum of the sizes of the peptides identified in these two studies was 350,000 and 494,000 daltons, respectively.

No consistent differences in the peptides from HBsAg preparations of different subtypes have been found. Although Dreesman et al (18, 22) reported finding small amounts of two peptides (69,000 and 105,000 daltons) in HBsAg/*ayw* that were not present in HBsAg/*adw,* no difference has been found in polypeptides of different subtypes by investigators (Table 1). Shih & Gerin (88) found the same sizes, numbers, and relative amounts of polypeptides in purified preparations of HBsAg with subtypes *adw, ayw, adr* (Table 1).

To relate the polypeptides found in HBsAg preparations to the size of the HBV genome, it is important to know whether or not each peptide is unique and whether or not it is coded by the viral genome. Antigenic analysis of individual peptides has recently provided some information about these questions. Gerin (26) first reported that individual peptides from HBsAg/*ad* particles and HBsAg/*ay* particles recov-

Table 1 Polypeptides of HBsAg particle preparations[a]

Investigators	HBsAg subtype	Reported molecular weight (× 10^{-3})								
Gerin et al (28)	–	26[b]	32	(40)						
Gerin (25)	*ad*	26[b]	32	(40)	(55)		(75)	(95)		
	ay	26[b]	(32)	(40)	(55)	(65)	75	(95)		
Vyas et al (96)	–	24[b]	35							
Dreesman et al (23)	*ad*	10[c]	16	22	27	32	39	39		
Chairez et al (18)	*ad*	18.5[b]	22*	27*	32*	40	69	120		
	ay	19[b]	22*	27*	32*	40	55	69	105	120
Gerlich & May (29)	–	24[b]	28	(34)	(50)	(70)				
Rao & Vyas, (76)	–	6[d]	12	80						
Gerin (26)	*adw* [e] *ayw*	23–26[b]	30–32*	36	42	(54)*	68–72	97		
Howard & Zuckerman (40)	*ad* [e] *ay*	(30)[b]	82	90						
Chairez et al (17)	*adw*	19[b]	24*	27*	35*	40	55	120		
Dreesman et al (22)	*ayw*	19[b]	24*	27*	35*	40	55	(69)	(105)	120
Shih & Gerin (87) Gold et al (32)	*adw* [e] *ayw*	23[b]	29.5	36	41.5	53.5	72	97		
Mackay & Burrell (58)	–	(13)[b,c]	17	(23)	68					
Shih & Gerin (88)	*adw* [e] *ayw* *adr*	23[b,d,f]	29.5*	36	41.5	53.5*	72	97		

[a] ( ), Designated by investigators as minor or variable components; *, stain with PAS indicating glycosylation.
[b] Polypeptide bands detected by Coomasie brilliant blue staining after SDS-gel electrophoresis.
[c] Components detected by content of radioactivity after iodination of HBsAg particles with ^{125}I and SDS-gel electrophoresis.
[d] Components detected by absorbance at 280 nm after Sephadex G-75 chromatography.
[e] All designated subtypes had same polypeptide composition.
[f] Components detected by content of radioactivity after reductive methylation of HBsAg particles with radioactive substrate and electrophoresis in SDS-gels.

ered from SDS-gels after electrophoresis and innoculated into guinea pigs induced group-specific antibody to native HBsAg particles (anti-HBs/*a*) tested by passive hemagglutination and radioimmunoprecipitation. Most sera also contained type-specific antibody (either anti-HBs/*y* or anti-HBs/*d*). Since proteins not containing carbohydrate induced anti-HBs, it was clear that the viral-specified antigenic determinants were contained in polypeptides rather than in carbohydrate of the glycoproteins. The results also suggested that both group- and type-specific determinants reside on the same polypeptide. Because all polypeptides shared anti-HBs/*a,* they were not unique, separate primary gene products. It was not excluded, however, that the preparations used to immunize guinea pigs contained more than single peptides.

Dreesman et al (21) separated polypeptides of HBsAg particles into five fractions by preparative SDS-gel electrophoresis and used the fractions to immunize guinea pigs. Polypeptides derived from HBsAg/*adw* stimulated the production of both group- and type-specific antibodies based on preferential reaction of the antisera to ^{125}I-labeled HBsAg/*adw* over that to ^{125}I-labeled HBsAg/*ayw.* A preference for antigen of homologous subtype was not observed with antisera to *ayw* polypeptides, and some of the antisera to the *ayw*-derived polypeptides actually reacted preferentially with the *adw* subtype antigen used in the radioimmunoassays. The polypeptide separation achieved by preparative SDS-gel electrophoresis in this study resulted in fractions containing more than a single polypeptide, indicating that the antisera contained more than one antibody specificity and making it difficult to interpret the complex reactions based on preferential reactivity.

More recently, Gerin and colleagues (32, 87) have achieved more complete separation of individual peptides of highly purified preparations of HBsAg/*adw* and HBsAg/*ayw*. Each electrophoretically pure polypeptide induced antibody against the group-specific determinant *a* (87). Most or all polypeptides from the HBsAg/*adw* preparation induced antibody against the *d* determinant, and those from the HBsAg/*ayw* preparation induced anti-y (32). In another study (89), monospecific antisera to *a* and to *d* prepared from guinea pig anti-HBs/*ad* by affinity chromatography both specifically precipitated three purified and radiolabeled major polypeptides derived from a purified HBsAg/*ad* preparation. These results clearly indicate that all individual polypeptides from HBsAg preparations contain identical and multiple virus-specified antigenic determinants, and that subtype determinants are found only in polypeptides from HBsAg particles of the same subtype.

The only serum component present in large enough amounts in purified HBsAg preparations to be detected by Coomasie blue staining on SDS-gels is apparently human serum albumen, which comigrates as a separate polypeptide with the viral-specific polypeptide P-6 of Shih & Gerin (68–72 $\times$ 10^3 daltons) (Table 1) (89).

These studies suggest that HBsAg particles contain at least seven polypeptides of different apparent molecular weights, all of which contain at least in part the same or very similar virus-specific immunochemical structures and probably amino acid sequences. Furthermore, polypeptides of different HBsAg subtypes may contain a region of constant amino acid sequence specifying the group-specific determinant *a* and a variable region specifying the type-specific determinant *d* or *y*. The findings suggest that the amount of unique amino acid sequence specified by the HBV genome in HBsAg particles may be significantly less than the sum of the sizes of the individual peptides isolated by SDS-gel electrophoresis. The minimal amount of unique amino acid sequence for the protein bearing the known HBsAg determinants, thus, might be the amount in the largest polypeptide shown to contain these determinants (i.e. 97,000–120,000 daltons if these are monomeric polypeptides). Since both group- and type-specific determinants are found in even smaller polypeptides, it is possible that the amount of unique amino acid sequence in HBsAg particle polypeptides is less than the size of the largest component observed by SDS-gel electrophoresis. How the different sized polypeptides arise and their exact amino acid sequence relationship will require further study, including sequence analysis. Mackay & Burrell (58) have suggested that the presence of multiple polypeptides with different sizes but antigenic similarity could result from proteolytic degradation of one or a very few polypeptides within HBsAg particles by proteases found in serum, a process that appears to occur in human erythrocyte membranes (24). The wide variation of polypeptide sizes and number in different studies of HBsAg particles (Table 1) would be consistent with such a process. Multiple polypeptides of different sizes, which all contain the same antigenic determinants, have not been described for other viruses.

Polypeptides of HBcAg Particles

Two recent studies have examined the polypeptides of HBcAg particles. Budkowska, Shih & Gerin (14) isolated HBcAg particles from HBV-infected liver by equilibrium centrifugation in a CsCl density gradient and Bio-Gel A-5m chromatography. The particles were iodinated with ^{125}I and repurified by sedimentation in a sucrose density gradient. The ^{125}I-labeled peptides were identified by SDS-polyacrylamide gel electrophoresis of solubilized immune complexes after precipitation of ^{125}I-labeled HBcAg with anti-HBc. Two major radioactive components with apparent molecular weights of 17,000 and 35,000 and multiple minor components were found.

Hruska & Robinson (42) purified Dane particles from plasma of chronic HBsAg carriers, prepared Dane particle cores by Nonidet P-40 detergent treatment, and purified the cores by equilibrium centrifugation in CsCl density gradients. Three polypeptide bands with apparent molecular weights of 19,000, 70,000, and 80,000 were regularly detected by Coomasie blue staining after separation by SDS-polyacrylamide gel electrophoresis. The same polypeptides were detected by Coomasie blue staining after SDS-gel electrophoresis of dissociated HBcAg particles purified by equilibrium centrifugation in CsCl density gradients from HBV-infected chimpanzee liver.

The sum of the sizes of the major polypeptides reported by Budkowska et al (14) is 52,000 daltons and by Hruska & Robinson (42) is 169,000 daltons. The reason for the differences in number and sizes of polypeptides found in HBcAg particles in the two studies is not clear. It is possible that iodination of the HBcAg particle proteins altered their electrophoretic behavior. None of the polypeptides observed has been shown to possess HBcAg reactivity, and the amount of unique virus-specified amino acid sequence in Dane particle cores thus is not yet known. Clearly, however, Dane particle cores and HBcAg particles from HBV-infected liver tissue contain polypeptides distinct from those in HBsAg particles and at least some of these must be specified by viral genes.

The Possibility of Additional Viral Polypeptides

In addition to the virus-specified protein in HBsAg particles and in Dane particle cores, additional viral-specific proteins are probably necessary for the DNA polymerase activity of Dane particle cores and possibly for HBeAg. Alternatively, these viral functions could be associated with one or more of the polypeptides described for Dane particle cores and HBcAg particles from infected liver.

Current Estimate of the Total Viral-Specific Protein

The total amount of viral-specified protein is not known at this time, but a minimum estimate might be the unique polypeptide sequences found in HBsAg particles (i.e. the largest polypeptide containing type-specific and group-specific determinants) and the polypeptides in HBcAg particles. This would be more than 200,000 daltons of protein.

DANE PARTICLE DNA STRUCTURE AND THE MECHANISM OF THE ENDOGENOUS DNA POLYMERASE REACTION

The Dane particle has been shown to contain a small circular DNA molecule (81). The DNA was first detected as the endogenous template of a DNA polymerase reaction within Dane particles. In 1971, Hirschman, Vernace & Schaffner (36) described small amounts of DNA polymerase activity in crude pellets obtained by high-speed centrifugation of three HBsAg-positive sera. However, they mistakenly postulated that the endogenous template was RNA because the reaction was thought to be interrupted by RNase treatment of the enzyme preparation. They did not identify the enzyme-containing particle. Kaplan et al (47) found DNA polymerase activity in high-speed pellets from eight of eight HBsAg carriers with high concentrations of Dane particles in their serum. They found that the enzyme activity sedimented with Dane particles and with Dane particle cores after Nonidet P-40 treatment of Dane particles. Robinson & Greenman (82) found that the enzyme-containing particle was specifically immunoprecipitated by anti-HBs and not anti-HBc before Nonidet P-40 treatment and by anti-HBc and not anti-HBs after Nonidet P-40 treatment, which removes the outer HBsAg layer of Dane particles releasing the inner core. These findings were consistent with the presence of DNA polymerase activity in the core of Dane particles.

Kaplan et al (47) showed that the DNA reaction product was reasonably homogeneous and had a sedimentation coefficient of 15S. The reaction was inhibited by actinomycin D and daunomycin, suggesting that the endogenous template was DNA not RNA. The enzyme, the template, and the reaction product appeared to be internal components of the Dane particle core, since DNase (and RNase) would not attack the template or the DNA product before disruption of cores and the enzyme failed to accept a wide variety of added polynucleotides, which are accepted as primer/templates by other DNA polymerases.

Robinson, Clayton & Greenman (81) isolated DNA from purified Dane particles and showed that the same small circular molecules were present before and after a DNA polymerase reaction. Radioactive DNA reaction product sedimented with the circular molecules, indicating that these molecules served as the template for the DNA polymerases reaction. Linear DNA molecules of random length were also observed in the total DNA extracted from Dane particles. No radioactivity was incorporated into these molecules, and they were separated from the radioactive template molecules (circles) by sedimentation. The linear DNA was also eliminated by treatment of Dane particle core preparations with DNase, suggesting they were not components of the core. The circular molecules appeared to be double stranded and to have a mean length of 0.78 μm, which corresponds to approximately 1.6×10^6 daltons or 2300 nucleotide pairs (np) before a DNA polymerase reaction. No superhelical molecules were observed, suggesting that all were nicked or open circles or, alternately, had a very low superhelix density. The thermal transition curve and buoyant density of DNA molecules made radioactive in a Dane particle DNA polymerase reaction were consistent with a cytosine plus guanosine content of 48–49%. The presence of circular DNA molecules approximately 0.8 μm in length in purified preparations of Dane particles has been confirmed by other investigators (71, 74).

Several observations suggest that the circular DNA molecules from Dane particles contain a large single-stranded region heterogeneous in length, and the DNA polymerase reaction closes the single-stranded gaps. Summers, O'Connell & Millman (93) first proposed the existence of a single-stranded region in Dane particle DNA molecules because avian myeloblastasis virus (AMV) DNA polymerase, which contains no exonuclease activity and thus cannot introduce radioactive nucleotides into prexisting double-stranded DNA, successfully used Dane particle DNA as a template for DNA synthesis, presumably by using a single-stranded part of the molecule. Because the endogenous DNA polymerase activity in Dane particles introduced radioactive nucleotides into the same restriction endonuclease Hae III-generated DNA fragments as did the AMV DNA polymerase, it was concluded that the endogenous enzyme used the same single-stranded regions as a template. The data published, however, indicated that radioactive nucleotides had been incorporated into almost all Hae III fragments after a reaction with either polymerase, suggesting that DNA synthesis took place in all parts of the molecule and not only in specific regions. This result is consistent with other mechanisms for the endogenous DNA polymerase reaction, as well as with the possibility that single-stranded gaps in the circular molecules are closed during the reaction.

Hruska et al (41) showed that the electron microscope length of the circular DNA molecules from Dane particles increased by an average of 23% when DNA was spread in formamide, which extends single-stranded regions compared with the length under conditions (aqueous spreading) that do not extend such regions. This suggested that the circular DNA molecules contain single-stranded regions averaging one quarter the length of the circle. After a Dane particle DNA polymerase reaction, the mean circle length (aqueous spreading) increased by 27% and the length became more homogeneous. This suggested that single-stranded regions of variable length were closed during the endogenous DNA polymerase reaction. Most of the circular molecules must have participated in the DNA polymerase reaction because the mean length of the population of molecules increased and the length distribution was greatly narrowed. The mean length of the DNA after an endogenous DNA polymerase reaction was 1.06 μm, corresponding to a molecular weight of approximately 2.1×10^6 or 3150 np for double-stranded DNA. No superhelical forms were observed in DNA after a DNA polymerase reaction as none were before.

Landers, Greenberg & Robinson (51) showed that DNA extracted from Dane particles before a DNA polymerase reaction and detected on polyacrylamide gels by ethidium bromide staining was electrophoretically heterogeneous. Treatment with the single-strand-specific endonuclease S1 produced double-stranded linear DNA molecules ranging in length from 1700–2800 np, indicating the presence of a nick or single-stranded region susceptible to the enzyme. After an endogenous DNA polymerase reaction, the S1-resistant, double-stranded length was elongated by 15–45% (average 25%) and was made more homogeneous. The mean length of the elongated molecules was 3200 np. This length estimate is in good agreement with that determined by electron microscopy, as described above. When the DNA was analyzed by endonuclease Hae III digestion, certain double-stranded DNA fragments increased in amount or first appeared only after an endogeneous DNA polymerase reaction. These results are consistant with the existence of a single-stranded regions of varying lengths in the circular DNA molecules and closure of the single-stranded gaps during the endogenous DNA polymerase reaction.

Although the single-stranded gaps appear to be closed by the endogenous DNA polymerase reaction, the ends of the open strand do not appear to be joined to make closed circular DNA. The circular molecules after the DNA polymerase reaction as before have a nuclease S1-sensitive site (51), and no closed circular DNA has been detected by alkaline sucrose gradient sedimentation or equilibrium centrifugation in CsCl density gradients containing ethidium bromide (84).

The amount of DNA synthesis during the endogeneous Dane particle DNA polymerase reaction has also been determined in two other ways. Lutwick & Robinson (57) showed that the $Cot_{1/2}$ value for the reassociation of the DNA synthesized in an endogenous Dane particle DNA polymerase reaction corresponded to an amount of unique DNA equivalent to about one quarter of the circle length. This figure agrees with the amount of new DNA synthesis estimated by electron microscopy length change and change in electrophoretic mobility, as described above.

Hruska & Robinson (42a) carried out a Dane particle DNA polymerase reaction with Br-dUTP in place of TTP, isolated the DNA and denatured it by heating in dimethyl sulfoxide, and separated DNA strands containing BrdU from light DNA by equilibrium centrifugation in CsCl density gradients. The buoyant density of the heavy DNA indicated that approximately one third of each strand was new DNA (calculated as though 25% was Br-dUMP), in good agreement with the other estimates of the amount of new DNA synthesis. The separated DNA fractions were also tested for ability to reassociate into double-stranded DNA to determine whether new DNA was synthesized on one or both strands of Dane particle DNA (42a). None of the DNA in the heavy DNA component could be shown to reassociate into double-stranded DNA until DNA from the light component (or unfractionated Dane particle DNA) was mixed with it. This suggests that the new DNA synthesized in an endogenous Dane particle DNA polymerase reaction consists of molecules without complementary base sequences, indicating they all represent the same strand of the Dane particle DNA.

To identify the primer for DNA synthesis in the endogenous Dane particle reaction, Robinson & Lutwick (84) examined the sedimentation of the Dane particle DNA in alkaline sucrose gradients after very short reaction times (average chain growth of five to ten nucleotides). They found that the DNA product was attached to a molecule with the sedimentation coefficient (11*S*) corresponding to that of a linear DNA strand of approximately 1900 nucleotides (92). This is near the length of the double-stranded region of the circular molecule before a DNA polymerase reaction (1700–2800 np by gel electrophoresis and an average of 2300 np by electron microscopy, as described above), suggesting that the open strand of the circular

DNA molecule serves as the primer for the reaction and new DNA is covalently attached to that strand. No evidence for smaller oligodeoxynucleotides or an RNA primer was found.

Endogenous Dane particle DNA synthesis appears to be initiated at multiple sites over a large portion of the molecule. After very short reaction times (5 sec or 10 min) with a chain growth rate of 5–10 nucleotides per min under the conditions of low nucleotide concentration used, Landers et al (51) found that radioactive nucleotides had been incorporated into endonuclease Hae III fragments with sizes adding up to a total of 1600 np, or one half the length of the circular Dane particle DNA molecule. After an extensive reaction (3–4 hr with high nucleotide concentrations), the same Hae III-generated fragments were heavily labeled and all fragments contained at least some radioactive nucleotide. The wide distribution of sites for initiation of DNA synthesis suggests that the single-stranded region must exist at different sites in different molecules, or that there is more than one single-stranded region (and initiation site for DNA synthesis) per molecule, although, as described above, DNA synthesis always appears to involve only one of the two strands of Dane particle DNA. Against the possibility that individual molecules contain multiple gaps is the fact that after very short DNA polymerase reaction times the new DNA sedimented in alkaline sucrose gradients as part of a strand 1900 nucleotides in length and none appeared in shorter strands, as might be expected if there existed multiple initiation sites per molecule (84).

Another mechanism for Dane particle DNA polymerase reaction has been proposed by Overby et al (71). They observed linear "tails" joining the circular DNA molecules and proposed that such molecules represented DNA forms replicating by "rolling circle" mechanism. Hruska et al (41), however, carefully quantitated the frequency of occurence and length of such tails in Dane particle DNA before and after an endogenous polymerase reaction. No increase in frequency ($<8\%$ of circular molecules had tails) or length of tails was found after a reaction. Robinson & Lutwick (84) found no new DNA sedimenting faster than unit length Dane particle DNA strands after endogenous polymerase reactions of different durations, as observed for DNAs replicating by the rolling circle mechanism (reviewed in 49). These findings make it unlikely that the endogenous DNA polymerase reaction involves Dane particle DNA replication by this mechanism.

The biological utility of a circular DNA single stranded over approximately one third of its length and a virion enzyme that closes the single-stranded region for a virus such as HBV is not clear. Such features have not been described for other viruses.

The Complexity of Dane Particle DNA

Two studies suggest that the total complexity or the amount of unique base sequence in the circular DNA from Dane particles may exceed the amount of DNA in a single circular molecule. Summers et al (93) found that the sum of the sizes of endonuclease Hae III-generated DNA fragments, detected by autoradiography after labeling a DNA preparation from Dane particles by nick translation with *Escherichia coli* DNA polymerase I, corresponded to approximately 3900 base pairs. Landers et al (51) found the sum of the sizes of the major Hae III-generated fragments, detected by ethidium bromide staining after an endogenous Dane particle DNA polymerase reaction to fully elongate the double-stranded region, to be 3880 np (Figure 1). Two additional fragments not demonstrated with ethidium bromide were detected by autoradiography when ^{32}P-labeled deoxyribonucleotides were used in the endogenous DNA polymerase reaction mixture, indicating that these fragments were components of Dane particle core DNA since they serve as template for the endogenous enzyme; however, they were present in less than stoichiometric amounts relative to other fragments (Figure 1). The sum of the sizes of these two fragments and the major fragments detected by ethidium bromide was 4910 np. The fact that these Hae III-generated fragments are each homogeneous suggests that none of them represent random host DNA like that found in some viruses after passage at

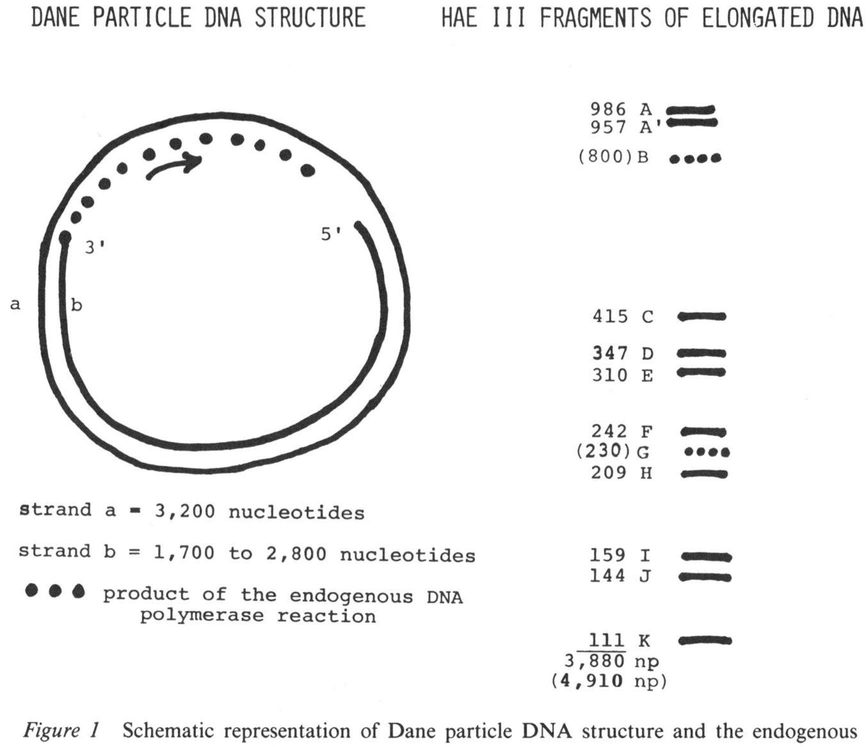

Figure 1 Schematic representation of Dane particle DNA structure and the endogenous DNA polymerase reaction (*left*), and the result of restriction endonuclease Hae III digestion of Dane particle DNA after extensive elongation of the double-stranded region by the endogenous DNA polymerase reaction (*right*). The Hae III fragments indicated by solid lines are detected by ethidium bromide, and those shown as broken lines are detected only by autoradiography after an endogenous DNA polymerase reaction with ^{32}P-labeled deoxynucleoside triphosphates. All ethidium bromide straining fragments also contain at least some radioactivity.

high multiplicity (52), which appears as a heterogeneous smear after gel electrophoresis. All of the major DNA fragments are almost certainly components of the 3200-np circular DNA molecules rather than some representing components of a larger molecule not yet detected in the DNA preparation. Electron microscope examination of Dane particle DNA (41) indicates that a molecule significantly larger than the 3200-np circles could not occur at a frequency greater than about 1 per 1000 3200-np circles. The relative amount of DNA detected in each major fragment precludes their origin in such an infrequently occurring molecule.

These measurements of the complexity suggest that the amount of unique nucleotide sequence in Dane particle DNA exceeds the amount of DNA in a single circular molecule by a significant amount. If additional minor fragments observed arose from Dane particle DNA molecules, the complexity would be even greater. This suggests that the DNA molecules in Dane particles are not all identical but are heterogeneous with respect to base sequence. The heterogeneity, however, involves a limited total amount of unique DNA (i.e. more than the DNA in a single circular Dane particle DNA molecule but less than that in two such molecules). The DNA used in both of the above studies was from Dane particles from single HBsAg carriers (both with subtype *adw*) (80), excluding the possibility that the DNA heterogeneity was due to a mixture of Dane particles specifying different HBsAg subtypes. The kind of heterogeneity that appears to occur in Dane particle DNA has not been described for other viruses.

VIRAL GENE EXPRESSION IN INFECTED LIVER

The production of 22-nm spherical HBsAg particles appears to exceed the production of other viral antigen forms, such as Dane particles, in all patients persistently infected with HBV. A concentration of 3×10^{13} 22-nm HBsAg particles per ml has been accurately measured in the serum of one patient (48). Almeida (1) estimated the concentration of Dane particles to be approximately 10^5 per ml in the serum of most chronic carriers, and a very few had concentrations as high as 10^8 or 10^9 per ml. Thus, 22-nm spheres would appear to outnumber Dane particles by as much as 10^8 to 1 in some sera and probably by as little as 10^3 or 10^4 to 1 in only a few sera. In the serum of one chronic carrier with a very high relative concentration of Dane particles, the ratio of 22-nm HBsAg spheres to Dane particles was found to be 1730 to 1 (13). Since the only known form of HBcAg in serum is as a component of Dane particle cores, the relative numbers of 22-nm HBsAg spheres and Dane particles would indicate that HBsAg production probably greatly exceeds production of HBcAg by the infected liver of most persistently infected patients. Supporting this is the finding of HBsAg/HBcAg complement fixation titer ratios on serum of several chronic HBsAg carriers with high concentrations of Dane particles to be between 32 and 512 (27). The relative amount of HBeAg production is not known, although when present in serum it is generally barely detectable by immunodiffusion.

Immunofluorescent staining of liver tissue from persistently infected humans and chimpanzees has revealed different patterns of viral antigen synthesis in different cells. Immunofluorescent staining of liver sections for HBsAg and HBcAg has shown that most infected cells synthesize only HBsAg (cytoplasmic), fewer cells synthesize only HBcAg (nuclear), and even fewer cells appear to synthesize both HBsAg and HBcAg (8, 35, 76). The number of infected cells detected by immunofluorescence can vary from less than 1% to virtually 100% of the cells in the liver, and the relative number synthesizing only HBsAg, only HBcAg, or both antigens varies widely in individual patients (8, 35, 77). In the liver of some chronic carriers, only cells synthesizing HBsAg exclusively can be found (8, 35, 77). In all chronic carriers producing relatively high concentrations of Dane particles, significant numbers of cells synthesizing HBcAg can be found in the liver (91). The observation that the number of cells synthesizing HBsAg almost always exceeds the number synthesizing HBcAg in most infected livers correlates with the fact that 22-nm spherical and filamentous HBsAg forms greatly outnumber Dane particles in sera of most infected patients. The dramatic difference in the pattern of viral antigen synthesis in individual cells of chronically infected liver indicates that different viral genes are expressed in different cells, a phenomenon not described for tissues infected with other viruses.

SUMMARY AND CONCLUSIONS

1. Several viral antigen forms are found in the blood during HBV infection. The most numerous are 22-nm spherical and filamentous HBsAg particles, which are probably incomplete virus coat particles without HBcAg or nucleic acid. Another form called the Dane particle has several properties, suggesting it may be the complete virus, although its infectivity has not been directly shown. It has HBsAg on its surface and an internal core containing a unique antigen (HBcAg), a small circular DNA, and a DNA polymerase activity. A third antigen, HBeAg, exclusively associated with HBV infection is physically and antigenically distinct from the other antigen forms. HBeAg is commonly present in sera containing Dane particles, but whether or not it is physically related to Dane particles (e.g. as an internal component) is not yet known. Claims that HBeAg is an immunoglobulin have yet to be substantiated.

2. The size of the HB genome is not certain at this time, although several probable viral gene products have been identified. The proteins containing HBsAg, HBcAg, and HBeAg reactivity, and that in Dane particles with DNA polymerase activity, are probably all specified by viral genes. The total amount of unique polypeptide involved in these functions is not yet known, but a minimum amount is probably 200,000 daltons or more (the largest polypeptide with HBsAg group and type-specific reactivity plus the polypeptides found in Dane particle cores). HBeAg and the DNA polymerase activity may be associated with additional polypeptides. Further study including purification and sequence analysis of the proteins associated with each viral function will be necessary to accurately establish the amount of protein specified by the viral genome. In theory, a DNA the size of the elongated Dane particle DNA (3200 np) could specify only about 125,000 daltons of protein. This suggests that more DNA than that in a single circular molecule from Dane

particles may be needed to specify all of the unique HBV-specific polypeptide. Whether or not the total amount of unique nucleotide sequence in the DNA from Dane particles (at least 3880 np in restriction endonuclease cleavage fragments) is sufficient to specify the HBV-specific proteins will be known only after the amount of viral-specific polypeptide is more accurately known.

3. Dane particle DNA molecules consist of one closed circular strand of constant length (strand a, 3200 nucleotides) and an open strand of variable length (strand b, 1700–2800 nucleotides) (Figure 1). Thus, 15–45% of the circle length is single stranded in different molecules. The endogenous Dane particle DNA polymerase appears to use the open strand as a primer, and the single-stranded gap is closed during the reaction, resulting in a double-stranded DNA of 3200 np. The free ends of the open strand are not joined within Dane particles to make closed circular DNA. DNA synthesis is initiated at multiple sites over a wide region (50%) of the molecule, suggesting that the single-stranded region exists at different sites in different molecules. Evidence also suggests that the same strand (strand b, Figure 1) is elongated during the endogenous DNA polymerase reaction, i.e. the single-stranded region is on the same strand in all molecules (strand a).

4. The total complexity or amount of unique nucleotide sequence in the DNA isolated from Dane particles appears to be greater than the amount of DNA in a single elongated circular molecule (3200 nucleotide pairs) (Figure 1). The sum of the sizes of the major DNA fragments resulting from restriction endonuclease Hae III cleavage of the DNA extracted from Dane particles is 3880 np. Additional minor fragments that also serve as template for the endogenous DNA polymerase of Dane particle cores make the total 4910 np. If the measure of complexity is correct, the amount of unique nucleotide sequence in the DNA from Dane particles would exceed the amount of DNA in a single circular molecule but would be less than that in two such molecules. In that case, the 3200-np circular molecules would be heterogeneous in nucleotide sequence, although no molecule would be completely different from any other. If each Dane particle contains a single circular DNA molecule, as is likely from the small size of the Dane particle core (the ratio of the elongated Dane particle DNA length to the volume of the core is nearly two times that ratio for simian virus 40), Dane particles must be genetically heterogeneous.

5. Immunofluorescent staining has revealed that in most chronic HBV infections some liver cells appear to synthesize only HBsAg, fewer cells synthesize only HBcAg, and even fewer cells synthesize both antigens. The different pattern of viral antigen synthesis in individual cells indicates that different viral genes are expressed in different cells. The expression of different viral genes in different cells could occur if individual cells contained different complements of viral genes. Alternatively, the regulation of viral gene expression could be different in individual cells containing the same complement of viral genetic information.

6. The findings described above suggest the following working model for the structure of the HBV genome (Figure 2). Four viral genes for the four functions thought to be virus specified can be designated HBsAg (although HBsAg is antigenically complex, all antigenic determinants appear to reside on the same polypeptide), HBcAg, HBeAg, and pol (the Dane particle DNA polymerase gene). Additional,

as yet unrecognized, viral genes may also exist. The base sequence heterogeneity of Dane particle DNA molecules and their small size relative to the probable amount of unique viral-specified polypeptide suggest that Dane particles have heterogeneous and incomplete genomes, and the complete viral genome may be contained in more than a single Dane particle. Liver cells synthesizing different single-viral antigens (HBsAg or HBcAg) would be infected with Dane particles possessing genes for the antigen synthesized and not genes for the other antigen. Infected cells that synthesize HBsAg and not HBcAg would be infected with Dane particles that contain the genes for HBsAg and not for HBcAg. Such cells may produce only the HBsAg forms free of HBcAg, DNA, and DNA polymerase (i.e. 22-nm spheres and filaments). Because this infected cell type is the most frequent in infected livers of most chronic carriers, greater amounts of 22-nm HBsAg particles than Dane particles appear in the blood of such patients. Cells that synthesize HBcAg and not HBsAg would be infected with Dane particles containing the HBcAg genes and not genes for HBsAg. Cells replicating virus (Dane particles) would be infected with more than one Dane particle to provide the entire complement of viral genes. Such cells would be recognized as containing both HBsAg and HBcAg by immunofluorescence. Most Dane particles in the serum of most chronic carriers probably contain HBsAg genes and not HBcAg genes because the most frequent pattern of viral antigen synthesis in cells of most persistently infected livers is synthesis of HBsAg and not HBcAg.

According to this model, infection with low doses of virus (i.e. small numbers of Dane particles) could result in infections in which the liver contains only singly infected cells. In that case, liver cells would be expected to contain only HBsAg or HBcAg genes, and none would contain the entire complement of viral genes necessary for Dane particle production, which would occur only in multiply infected cells according to the model. Such infections might result in production of incomplete HBsAg forms (22-nm spheres and filaments) exclusively and no Dane particles (i.e. infectious HBV). Infections with HBsAg production but no Dane particles might be expected to occur more frequently after experimental infection with high dilutions of infectious serum or natural transmission by routes other than blood transfusion rather than after high-dose transmission, as must occur where Dane-particle-rich blood is transfused. It is not known whether such infections occur although it has been shown that all HBsAg-positive blood units do not result in HBV infection in recipients (31). Whether such blood units actually came from donors producing only HBsAg and no infectious virus (i.e. Dane particles) or rather the recipients of the blood were immune to HBV or were not infected for other reasons is not known. Examination of serum of HBV-infected patients has also shown that Dane particles are not detectable in a significant fraction of patients. Kaplan, Gerin & Alter (46) studied nine patients who developed hepatitis B after blood transfusions for the appearance of Dane-particle-associated DNA polymerase. High levels of Dane particles appeared in the serum of seven patients during the late incubation period of the disease, but only HBsAg and no measurable Dane particles were found in two patients. Dane particles have not been detected in the serum of some HBsAg carriers by electron microscopy (20, 69, 64) or by DNA

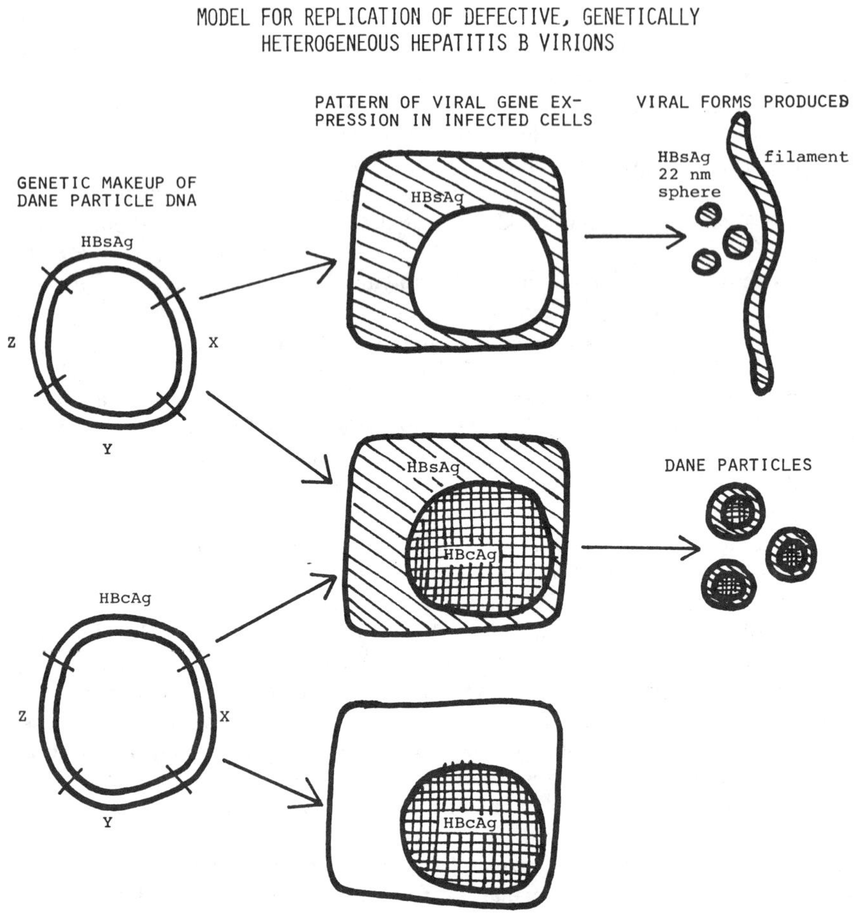

Figure 2 Model of Dane particles as defective, genetically heterogeneous hepatitis B virions, which replicate by complementation in multiply infected cells. X, Y, and Z represent unspecified hepatitis B viral genes and may include the HBeAG gene and the Dane particle DNA polymerase gene (pol).

polymerase assay (81). Whether any of these patients actually produce no Dane particles or only low levels not detectable by the assays used is not yet known. Almost all chronic HBsAg carriers appear to produce anti-HBc, indicating that they synthesize HBcAg (38). It remains to be determined, however, whether all chronic carriers actually produce Dane particles (which contain HBcAg) or whether some may produce only HBcAg within liver cell nuclei, as predicted by the model for cells singly infected by Dane particles lacking genes for HBsAg and thus the capacity to produce Dane particles.

Although the current information about HBV and Dane particles reviewed here suggests the above model, the data are also consistent with other possibilities. Until Dane particles or their 3200-np circular DNA molecules are shown directly to be infectious, it cannot be excluded that a virus particle or a nucleic acid molecule not detected in the studies to date is necessary for HBV infection. The 3200-np circular molecules might then be viral DNAs with small size and some heterogeneity because of large deletions. Under such conditions, almost all Dane particles found in serum (i.e. those containing 3200-np DNA molecules) would be defective, noninfectious virions. If a larger form of DNA does exist, it seems unlikely that it could be contained within the Dane particle core. As described above, the ratio of the 3200-np Dane particle DNA size to the volume of the Dane particle core greatly exceeds that ratio for small spherical viruses such as simian virus 40. An additional virus form not yet identified would probably be needed to contain larger DNA molecules. Further research will be needed to confirm or refute the model.

ACKNOWLEDGMENTS

Some of the work described here was supported by U.S. Public Health Service Research grant AI 13526.

Literature Cited

1. Almeida, J. D. 1972. *Am. J. Dis. Child.* 123:303–9
2. Almeida, J. D., Rubenstein, D., Stott, E. J. 1971. *Lancet* 2:1225–27
3. Almeida, J. D., Waterson, A.P., Trowell, J. M., Neale, G. 1970. *Microbios* 2:145–53
4. Alter, H. J., Blumberg, B. S. 1966. *Blood* 27:297–309
5. Alter, H. J., Seeff, L. B., Kaplan, P. M., McAuliffe, V. J., Wright, E. C., Gerin, J. L., Purcell, R. H., Holland, P. V., Zimmerman, H. J. 1976. *N. Engl. J. Med.* 295:909–13
6. Bancroft, W. H., Mundon, F. K., Russell, P. K. 1972. *J. Immunol.* 109: 842–48
7. Deleted in proof.
8. Barker, L. F., Chisari, F. V., McGrath, P. P., Dalgard, D. W., Kirschstein, R. L., Almeida, J. D., Edgington, T. S., Sharp, D. G., Peterson, M. R. 1973. *J. Inf. Dis.* 127:648–62
9. Barker, L. F., Maynard, J. E., Purcell, R. H., Hoofnagle, J. H., Berquist, K. R., London, W. T. 1975. *Am. J. Med. Sci.* 270:189–95
10. Barker, L. F., Murray, R. 1972. *Am. J. Med. Sci.* 263:27–33
11. Blumberg, B. S., Alter, H. J., Visnich, S. 1965. *J. Am. Med. Assoc.* 191:541–46
12. Blumberg, B. S., Gerstley, B. J. S., Hungerford, D. A., London, W. T., Sutnick, A. I. 1967. *Ann. Int. Med.* 66:924
13. Bond, H. E., Hall, W. T. 1972. *J. Infect. Dis.* 125:263–68
14. Budkowska, A., Shih, J. W., Gerin, J. L. Submitted for publication
15. Burrell, C. J. 1975. *J. Gen. Virol.* 27: 117–26
16. Caramia, F., De Bac, C., Ricci, G. 1972. *Am. J. Dis. Child* 123:309–11
17. Chairez, R., Hollinger, F. B., Brunschwig, J. P., Dreesman, G. R. 1975. *J. Virol.* 15:182–90
18. Chairez, R., Steiner, S., Malnick, G. R., Dreesman, G. R. 1973. *Intervirology* 1:224–28
19. Cross, R. K., Fields, B. N. 1972. *Virology* 50:799–809
20. Dane, D. S., Cameron, C. H., Briggs, M. 1970. *Lancet* 1:695
21. Dreesman, G. R., Chairez, R., Suarez, M., Hollinger, F. B., Courtney, R. J., Melnick, J. L. 1975. *J. Virol.* 16:508–15
22. Dreesman, G. R., Hollinger, F. B., Melnick, J. L. 1975. *Am. J. Med. Sci.* 270:123–29
23. Dreesman, G. R., Hollinger, F. B., Suriano, J. R., Fujioka, R. S., Brunschwig, J. P., Melnick, J. L. 1972. *J. Virol.* 10:469–76
24. Fairbanks, G., Steck, T. L., Wallach, D. F. H. 1971. *Biochemistry.* 10:2606–17

25. Gerin, J. L. 1972. In *Hepatitis and Blood Transfusions,* ed. G. N. Vyas, H. A. Perkins, R. Schmidt, pp. 205–20. New York: Grune and Stratton
26. Gerin, J. L. 1974. In *Mechanisms of Virus Disease,* ed. W. S. Robinson, C. R. Fox, pp. 215–24. Menlo Park: W. A. Benjamin
27. Gerin, J. L. Unpublished results
28. Gerin, J. L., Holland, P. V., Purcell, R. H. 1971. *J. Virol.* 7:569–76
29. Gerlich, W., May, G. 1973. *Zentralbl. Bakteriol. Parasitenkd. Infektionskr. Hyg. Abt. 1 Orig. Reihe A*
30. Gibson, P. E. 1976. *J. Infect. Dis.* 134: 540–45
31. Gocke, D. J. 1972. *J. Am. Med. Assoc.* 219:1165–70
32. Gold, J. W. N., Shih, J. W., Purcell, R. H., Gerin, J. L. 1976. *J. Immunol.* 117:1404–6
33. Grady, G. F. 1975. *N. Engl. J. Med.* 293:1067–70
34. Grady, G. F. 1976. *Lancet* 2:492–93
35. Gudat, F., Bianchi, L., Sonnabend, W., Thiel, G., Aenishaenslin, W., Stalder, G. A. 1975. *Lab. Invest.* 32:1–9
36. Hirschman, S. Z., Vernace, S. J., Schaffner, F. 1971. *Lancet* 1:1099–103
37. Hoofnagle, J. H., Gerety, R. J., Barker, L. F. 1973. *Lancet* 2:869–73
38. Hoofnagle, J. H., Gerety, R. J., Barker, L. F. 1975. *Am. J. Med. Sci.* 270:179–87
39. Howard, C. R., Burrell, C. J. 1976. *Progr. Med. Virol.* 22:36–103
40. Howard, C. R., Zuckerman, A. J., 1974. *Intervirology* 4:31–44
41. Hruska, J. F., Clayton, D. A., Rubenstein, J. L. R., Robinson, W. S. 1977. *J. Virol.* 21:666–72
42. Hruska, J. F., Robinson, W. S. 1977. *J. Med. Virol.* In press
42a. Hruska, J. F., Robinson, W. S. Submitted for publication
43. Huang, S. N. 1971. *Am. J. Pathol.* 64:483–500
44. Hunt, D. M., Wagner, R. R. 1974. *J. Virol.* 13:28–35
45. Kaplan, P. M., Ford, E. C., Purcell, R. H., Gerin, J. L. 1976. *J. Virol.* 17: 885–93
46. Kaplan, P. M., Gerin, J. L., Alter, H. J. 1974. *Nature* 249:762–64
47. Kaplan, P. M., Greenman, R. L., Gerin, J. L., Purcell, R. H., Robinson, W. S. 1973. *J. Virol.* 12:995–1005
48. Kim, C. Y., Tilles, J. G. 1973. *J. Clin. Invest.* 52:1176–86
49. Kornberg, A. 1974. *DNA Synthesis.* San Francisco: W. H. Freeman
50. Krugman, S., Hoofnagle, J. H., Gerety, R. J., Kaplan, P. M., Gerin, J. L. 1974. *N. Engl. J. Med.* 290:1331–35
51. Landers, T., Greenberg, H. B., Robinson, W. S. 1977. *J. Virol.* In press
52. Lavi, S., Winocour, E. 1972. *J. Virol.* 9:309–16
53. LeBouvier, G. L. 1971. *J. Infect. Dis.* 123:671–75
54. LeBouvier, G. L. 1972. In *Hepatitis and Blood Transfusions,* ed. G. N. Vyas, H.
54. A. Perkins, R. Schmidt, pp. 97–109. New York: Grune and Stratton
55. LeBouvier, G. L., McCollum, R. W. 1970. *Adv. Virus Res.* 16:357–96
56. Lineal, M., Masau, W. S. 1973. *Virology* 53:258–73
57. Lutwick, L. I., Robinson, W. S. 1977. *J. Virol.* 21:96–104
58. Mackay, P., Burrell, C. J. 1976. *J. Gen. Virol.* 33:181–91
59. Magnius, L. O., Espmark, J. A. 1972. *J. Immunol.* 109:1017–21
60. Magnius, L. O., Lindholm, A., Lundin, P., Iwarson, S. 1975. *J. Am. Med. Assoc.* 231:356–59
61. McCollum, R. W. 1952. *Proc. Soc. Exp. Biol. Med.* 81:157–63
62. Millman, I., Hutanen, H., Merino, F., Bayer, M. E., Blumberg, B. S. 1971. *Res. Commun. Chem. Pathol. Pharmacol.* 2:667–86
63. Mosley, J. W., Edwards, V. M., Meihaus, J. E., Redeker, A. G. 1972. *Am J. Epidemiol.* 95:529–35
64. Neurath, A. R., Prince, A. M., Lippin, A. 1974. *Proc. Natl. Acad. Sci. USA* 71:2663–67
65. Neurath, A. R., Strick, N. 1977. *Lancet* 1:146
66. Neurath, A. R., Trepo, C., Chen, M., Prince, A. M. 1976. *J. Gen. Virol.* 30:277–85
67. Nielsen, J. O., Dietrichson, O., Juhl, E. 1974. *Lancet* 2:913–15
68. Nielsen, J. O., Nielsen, M. H., Elling, P. 1973. *N. Engl. J. Med.* 288:484–87
69. Okada, K., Kamiyama, I., Inomata, M., Imai, M., Miyakawa, Y. 1976. *N. Engl. J. Med.* 294:746–49
70. Okochi, K., Murakami, S. 1968, *Vox Sang.* 15:374
71. Overby, L. R., Hung, P. P., Mao, J. C. H., Ling, C. M. 1975. *Nature* 255:84–85
72. Prince, A. M. 1968. *Proc. Natl. Acad. Sci. USA* 60:814
73. Prince, A. M., Szmuness, W., Mann, M. K., Vyas, G. N., Grady, G. F., Shapiro, F. L., Suki, W. N., Friedman, E. A., Stenzel, K. H. 1975. *N. Engl. J. Med.* 293:1063–67

74. Purcell, R. H. 1975. In *Symp. Viral Hepatitis, Washington D. C., 1975*
75. Purcell, R. H., Gerin, G. L. 1975. *Am. J. Med. Sci.* 270:395–400
76. Rao, K. R., Vyas, G. N. 1973. *Nature New Biol.* 241:240–41
77. Ray, M. B., Desmet, V. J., Bradburne, A. F., Desmyter, J., Fevery, J., De-Groote, J. 1976. *Gastroenterologia* 71: 462–67
78. Redeker, A. G., Mosley, J. W., Gocke, D. J., McKee, A. P., Pollack, W. 1975. *N. Engl. J. Med.* 293:1155–59
79. Robinson, W. S. 1975. *Am. J. Med. Sci.* 270:151–59
80. Robinson, W. S. Unpublished results
81. Robinson, W. S., Clayton, D. A., Greenman, R. L. 1974. *J. Virol.* 14: 384–91
82. Robinson, W. S., Greenman, R. L. 1974. *J. Virol* 13:1231–36
83. Robinson, W. S., Lutwick, L. I. 1976. *N. Engl. J. Med.* 295:1168–75; 1232–36
84. Robinson, W. S., Lutwick, L. I. 1976. In *Animal Virology,* ed. D. Baltimore, A. Huang, C. F. Fox, pp. 787–811. New York: Academic
85. Sambrook, J., Westphal, H., Srinivasan, P. R., Dulbecco, R. 1968. *Proc. Natl. Acad. Sci. USA* 60:1288–95
86. Seeff, L. B., Wright, E. C., Finkelstein, J. D., Greenlee, H. B., Hamilton, J., Leevy, C. M., Tamburro, C. H., Vlahcevic, Z., Zimmon, D. S., Zimmerman, H. J. 1975. *Lancet* 2:939–41
87. Shih, J. W., Gerin, J. L. 1975. *J. Immunol.* 115:634–39
88. Shih, J. W., Gerin, J. L. 1975. *J. Virol.* 21:347–57
89. Shih, J. W., Gerin, J. L. Unpublished results
90. Shulman, R. N. 1971. *Am. J. Med.* 49:669–92
91. Smith, J., Robinson, W. S. Unpublished results
92. Studier, F. W. 1965. *J. Mol. Biol.* 11: 373–90
93. Summers, J., O'Connell, A., Millman, I. 1975. *Proc. Natl. Acad. Sci. USA* 72: 4597–601
94. Thomssen, R., Gerlich, W., Stanmm, B., Biswas, R., Lorenz, P. R., Majer, M., Weinmann, E., Arnold, W., Hess, G., Wepler, W. 1976. *Zentralbl. Bakteriol. Parasitenkd. Infektionskr. Hyg. Abt. 1 Orig. Reihe A* 235:242–52
95. Trepo, C. G., Prince, A. M. 1976. *Ann. Int. Med.* 85:427–30
96. Vyas, G. N., Williams, E. W., Klaus, G. G. B., Bond, H. E. 1972. *J. Immunol.* 108:1114–18
97. Williams, A., LeBouvier, G. 1976. *Bibl. Heamatol. Basel* 42:71–74
98. Zuckerman, A. J. 1975. *Human Viral Hepatitis.* Amsterdam: North-Holland Publ.

Ann. Rev. Microbiol. 1977. 31:379–96

OIL TANKERS AND POLLUTION: A MICROBIOLOGICAL APPROACH

❖1710

David L. Gutnick and Eugene Rosenberg
Department of Microbiology, George S. Wise Center for Life Science,
Tel Aviv University, Ramat Aviv, Israel

CONTENTS

INTRODUCTION 379
CHEMICAL COMPOSITION OF CRUDE OIL 380
PHYSICAL INTERACTIONS BETWEEN MICROORGANISMS AND HYDROCARBON 381
Water-Soluble Components of Petroleum 382
Water-Insoluble Liquid Hydrocarbons 382
Emulsion formation 384
Hydrocarbon uptake into cells 385
Water-Insoluble Solid Hydrocarbons 385
PETROLEUM BIODEGRADATION: GENERAL NUTRITIONAL REQUIREMENTS 386
PETROLEUM DEGRADATION: METABOLIC SPECIFICITY 388
Initial Oxidation 388
Inducer Specificity 389
MICROBIOLOGICAL PROBLEMS ASSOCIATED WITH OIL TANKER OPERATIONS 390
Oil Tankers and the Ballast Voyage 390
Potential Applications 392
CONCLUSION 393

INTRODUCTION

During this century the demand for petroleum as a source of energy and as a primary raw material for chemical industries has resulted in an increase in world production from 29 to over 2400 million metric tons per year. This dramatic increase in the production, refining, and distribution of crude oil has also brought with it an ever-increasing problem of environmental pollution. A great part of this problem results from the fact that the major oil-producing countries are not the major oil consumers. It follows that massive movements of petroleum have to be made from areas of high production to those of high consumption. It has been estimated (71, 98) that approximately 0.5% (12 million metric tons per year) of the transported crude oil finds its way into sea water, largely through accidental spills and deliberate discharge of ballast and wash waters from oil tankers. The toxicity of crude and refined oil to marine ecology and even more directly to man is well documented (13, 72) and will not be discussed here in detail. Suffice it to mention that crude oil contains mutagenic, carcinogenic, and growth-inhibiting chemicals, and even small quantities (5–100 μg per liter) of certain petroleum fractions destroy microalgae and juvenile forms of many marine organisms. Furthermore, it has recently been reported that petroleum inhibits microbial decomposition of organic matter in sea water by interfering with chemotaxis (22). In short, oil pollution in the ocean in general and in the coastal waters in particular presents a serious problem to commercial fisheries, recreational resources, and public health.

Microbiological approaches to the problems outlined above become possible in light of emerging information concerning the specificities of interaction of microbes with their hydrocarbon substrates and some of the specific metabolic transformations that result from this interaction. Since space limitations do not permit a comprehensive discussion of the entire literature dealing with oil and microbes, the reader is referred to a number of recent reviews relating to different aspects of petroleum microbiology (1, 7, 10, 31, 90, 107, 111). This article stresses the special character of hydrocarbon-utilizing bacteria as illustrated by specific examples of both laboratory and field experiments. The latter part of the review will be devoted to the application of these principles in approaching some specific problems arising from oil tanker operations.

CHEMICAL COMPOSITION OF CRUDE OIL

Crude oil is a naturally occurring, extremely complex mixture of hydrocarbons including small quantities of oxygen-, sulfur-, and nitrogen-containing compounds and trace amounts of metallic constituents. To appreciate the complexity of crude oil, consider that the number of possible isomers of C_{30} alkanes alone exceeds 4×10^9. From the best-studied crude oil, Ponca City, Oklahoma, over 200 hydrocarbons have been isolated and positively identified (60, 82, 100), including (*a*) all of the *n*-paraffins, C_1 to C_{32}; (*b*) all four branched hexanes, six of the eight branched heptanes, and 15 out of the 17 branched octanes; (*c*) all possible C_8 isomers of alkyl cyclopentane and alkyl cyclohexane; and (*d*) all 12 C_8 and C_9 isomers of alkyl benzene. In the higher-boiling fractions of petroleum, the tremendous number of isomeric structures with very similar physical and chemical properties makes it unlikely that crude oil will ever be fully resolved.

In practice, crude oil is fractionated with regard to molecular size (e.g. distillation) and/or polarity. Table 1 summarizes the results of the fractionation of an Iranian crude oil, Agha Jari, by these two general procedures. Each of the distillate fractions contains a mixture of compounds of similar molecular weight but representing all classes of hydrocarbons. A number of different chromatographic procedures based on polarity and solubility have been used in petroleum analysis (38, 49, 50, 96, 109). The asphaltenes or heptane-insoluble fraction is poorly defined chemically; these materials have been described as sheets of condensed, aromatic rings,

Table 1 Fractionation of Agha Jari crude oil

By distillation (30)				By adsorption[a]	
Fraction	Boiling range (%)	Vol (%)	C atoms	Fraction	Vol (%)
Gasoline	40–180	30.5	5–10	Asphaltene	1.7
Kerosene	180–230	9.5	10–13	Saturates	59.5
Gas-oil	230–300	14.5	12–17	Aromatics	14.0
Lubricant	300–400	17.5	17–26	Polar aromatics	23.2
Residue	> 400	25	> 24		

[a] A. Dieber, unpublished data.

that are stacked on top of each other. The saturates contain normal and branched paraffins, cyclic paraffins, and alkyl cyclic paraffins. The aromatic fractions contain large numbers of different classes of mono-, di-, and polyaromatic hydrocarbons and related sulfur-containing analogues (26). Each of the fractions can be further resolved by gas-liquid chromatography (GLC) and high-pressure liquid chromatography (16). With proper use of internal standards, GLC allows for the quantitative determination of *n*-alkanes and to a lesser extent branched-chain paraffins. If GLC fractions are analyzed by mass spectrometry, the cycloparaffin fraction can be estimated (97).

In assessing the extent of microbial degradation of crude oil, fractionation procedures based on polarity have been widely used. The implication is that substrate specificity for microbial growth is more closely related to the type of compound than to its size or boiling point. For example, a microorganism that can degrade *n*-tetradecane (boiling point, 253.5°C) is more likely to have the enzymatic system to degrade other *n*-paraffins than to degrade biphenyl (boiling point, 255°C). Although this argument makes biochemical sense, it does not consider the problem of hydrocarbon uptake by microorganisms that may be growth-rate limiting. Although the mechanisms of hydrocarbon uptake by microorganisms are not known, it may well be that the physical state of the hydrocarbon (e.g. solid or liquid) may play an important role. In this regard, it is interesting that the interfacial tension between water and petroleum is directly related to the average carbon number of the petroleum (18).

PHYSICAL INTERACTIONS BETWEEN MICROORGANISMS AND HYDROCARBON

The chemical heterogeneity and water insolubility of crude oil define the problem and present the challenge to both microorganisms using petroleum as a growth substrate and investigators in the field of oil microbiology. In general, biological growth processes involve three phases—gas (air) phase, solid (cell) phase(s), and the liquid (aqueous) phase. Growth depends on mass transfer between these phases. When crude oil is placed in an aqueous environment, small quantities of it dissolve in the aqueous phase, lower-molecular-weight fractions transfer to the gas phase (often lost by evaporation), and the main portion constitutes an additional dispersed (oil in water) liquid phase. Furthermore, as evaporation and microbial degradation of the most susceptible components of the crude oil proceed, the oil phase tends to solidify (tar balls), leaving an additional solid phase. In considering physical interactions and uptake of petroleum by microorganisms, all of these states are important.

Water-Soluble Components of Petroleum

When one part crude oil or fuel oil is shaken with ten parts water, about 0.02% is extracted into the aqueous phase (6, 57). Although this is a minor fraction quantitatively, its importance should be emphasized because it contains the most toxic components in petroleum (6, 76). Furthermore, as is pointed out subsequently, current procedures as well as future plans for oil tanker operation involve the discharge into the sea of very large quantities of water extracts of petroleum. Compounds that have been reported in water extracts of petroleum include phenols, anilines, and alkylated derivatives of benzene and naphthalene (102, 103).

Wodzinski and co-workers (104–106) have conducted a series of carefully reasoned and quantitatively executed experiments indicating the physical state in which aromatic hydrocarbons are used by bacteria. Growth rates of bacteria on naphthalene, phenanthrene, and anthracene were directly related to the solubilities of these solid hydrocarbons in water (106); solubilities of naphthalene, phenanthrene, anthracene, and naphthacene in water are 98, 9.0, 0.45, and 0.07 μM, respectively (56). Furthermore, their attempts to isolate microorganisms on the least soluble of these compounds, naphthacene, were unsuccessful. This led to the suggestion that bacteria utilize solid aromatic hydrocarbons only in the dissolved state. This hypothesis was supported by experiments indicating that growth rates of bacteria on naphthalene (104), bibenzyl (104), and phenanthrene (105) were independent of the amount of solid present, i.e. generation times in media containing only the dissolved hydrocarbon were identical to generation times in media containing solid and dissolved hydrocarbon. Extrapolation of these data suggests that most pure polycyclic aromatic hydrocarbons would be refractory to microbial degradation, since they are highly insoluble solid materials.

As indicated above, water extracts of petroleum contain 2–20 mg of total organic material per liter. If one considers that specific compounds are present in the range 0.02–0.2 mg per liter and their molecular weights are around 200, then each would be present in initial concentrations of 0.1–10 μM. This would suggest that microorganisms utilizing the water-extracted fraction of petroleum would have to have efficient transport systems.

Water-Insoluble Liquid Hydrocarbons

The vast majority of petroleum-degrading microorganisms face the problem of growing at the expense of an immiscible liquid hydrocarbon in a system consisting of four phases: water, oil, air, and the cells themselves. The various pathways by which the microbial cell interacts with the immiscible substrate have been previously considered primarily in terms of single-cell protein production. It should be emphasized that such studies were carried out in fermentors with a view towards achieving fast growth rates and high cell yields on relatively pure substrates. Furthermore, the effects of mechanical agitation, forced aeration, continuous culture techniques, and idealized temperature, pH, and nutritional controls may not be relevant to the cell-oil interaction as it occurs in nature. Unlike the situation in open environments, fermentor experiments are generally carried out with relatively high concentrations of oil, which necessitates suitable agitation and results in the mechanical breakage of the immiscible liquid into small droplets. In spite of these reservations, such studies provide both the theoretical and experimental basis for understanding the mechanism of oil-cell interactions. Two general types of interactions have been postulated, depending upon the size of the oil droplets relative to the size of the microbial cell (28, 40): direct contact between cells and large oil droplets; and pseudosolubilization involving the uptake from the bulk phase of fine droplets of oil less than 1 μm in diameter.

In the absence of strong mechanical agitation, it seems likely that direct contact represents the main type of interaction. Phase microscopy of exponentially growing cells of *Acinetobacter* sp. (54) and the obligate marine bacterium, UP-2, growing either on pure *n*-alkane or on crude oil, has demonstrated a direct contact between the cells and the oil droplets (45). Scanning electron microscopy revealed multiple hydrocarbon spheres densely covered with bacteria (54). High affinity for oil droplets has also been demonstrated in various hydrocarbon-degrading species of yeast (28, 59, 67). In contrast, cells of *Escherichia coli, Aerobacter aerogenes,* and *Bacillus subtilis* (54), or oil-degrading yeast cells growing on glucose (51, 52, 69), showed no such affinity for oil droplets. Specific binding of microorganisms to petroleum can be measured by filtering a culture through Whatman 3mm filter paper (I. Zilber, unpublished data). In this system, bacteria bound to oil droplets do not pass through the filter, whereas cells not adhering to the oil are present in the filtrate. These results support the direct contact hypothesis and may suggest that the oil-cell interaction is mediated by specific components on the external surface of the cell.

The relationship between the size of the oil droplet and growth rate of hydrocarbon-degrading yeast has been considered theoretically (70) and experimentally (53, 75). The results of these studies have demonstrated that the growth rate can be limited by the interfacial surface area between water and oil. When the surface area becomes limiting, biomass increases arithmetically rather than exponentially (65). It has been calculated that to achieve concentrations of the bacterium UP-2 greater than 10^8 cells per ml, oil droplets would have to be reduced to less than 20 μm in diameter (45). The observed relationship between droplet size and growth rate support either the direct contact or the pseudosolubilization pathways. In the former case, increasing the surface area would be expected to increase the frequency of collisions between cells and oil, as well as to provide increased surface for growth. The rate of pseudosolubilization, however, is also a function of the interfacial surface area between oil and water and would be expected to increase with increasing surface area (39).

EMULSION FORMATION A wide variety of petroleum-degrading microorganisms have been found to bring about the formation of oil in water emulsions while growing on hydrocarbons (43, 78, 107, 111). Such emulsions are microbiological in origin and appear to be mediated either by the cells themselves or via the production of extracellular emulsifying agents.

Cell-bound activities Certain microorganisms can bring about emulsification of hydrocarbons even in the absence of cell growth (12, 108). This is presumably due to the production of specific components at the cell surface. Käppeli & Fiechter (51, 52) demonstrated the formation of a mannan-fatty acid complex at the cell surface of *Candida tropicalis* on transferring glucose-grown cells to a medium containing hydrocarbons. These unique structures may provide the basis for understanding how cell-oil interaction occurs via direct contact. Further support for this hypothesis stems from the observations of Aiba et al (4) and Mimura et al (67), who observed that growth rates of certain yeast strains actually decreased in the presence of artificial surfactants, presumably by interfering with the direct interaction between cells and hydrocarbon. It must be emphasized, however, that the relationship between emulsifying ability and optimal growth of certain cells does not necessarily imply a cause-and-effect relationship but may only be a correlation of two unrelated processes. One way to approach the problem is to isolate mutants lacking the ability to grow on hydrocarbons by virtue of lesions in the biosynthesis of these specific cell-surface components.

Extracellular emulsifying agents A number of organisms have been found to excrete emulsifying factors into the culture broth when growing on hydrocarbons. Iguchi et al (46) found that *Candida petrophilium* produced an emulsifying agent composed of peptides and fatty acid moieties. Suzuki et al (89) found trehalose lipid in the oil phase from culture broths of *Arthrobacter, Brevibacterium, Corynebacterium,* and *Nocardia.* This trehalose lipid contains about 1 mol of α,α-trehalose per 2 mol of α-branched β-hydroxy fatty acid. *Torulopsis gropengiesseri* was found to produce a sophorose lipid whereas Hisatsuka et al (44) reported a rhamnolipid produced by *Pseudomonas aeruginosa* strain S7B1. Another *P. aeruginosa* strain, KY 4025, was also found to produce rhamnolipid (47, 48). A mutant was isolated from strain KY 4025, which grew poorly on hydrocarbons and simultaneously lost the ability to produce rhamnolipid. Addition of the rhamnolipid to the medium stimulated the growth of the mutant on hydrocarbons.

Production of emulsifying agents and subsequent oil droplet formation can function to enhance pseudosolubilization of hydrocarbon. Two extreme cases of pseudosolubilization can be envisioned, occurring either in the bulk phase or in close proximity to the cell surface. In the former case, growth rate should be cell-density dependent at low cell densities (81); that is, the greater the number of cells, the higher the concentration of extra cellular product, and the faster the rate of pseudosolubilization. If emulsion occurs at or very close to the cell surface, and no mixing occurs at the microscopic level, then each cell creates its own microenvironment and no such cell-density dependence would be expected. This hypothesis could be tested by examining whether or not cells of a rhamnolipid-producing strain can stimulate the growth of the mutant *P. aeruginosa* KY 4025.

HYDROCARBON UPTAKE INTO CELLS Finnerty and co-workers (54, 84) have shown accumulation of unmodified hydrocarbons in cells of *Acinetobacter* sp. Hexadecane, heptadecane, and hexadec-1-ene were found to be localized in specific inclusion bodies within cells growing on these substrates. The inclusion bodies, contained in a smooth limit membrane, were found to be in association with an intracytoplasmic membranous system synthesized specifically during growth on the hydrocarbon (85). Such hydrocarbon inclusions were not detected in acetate-grown cells but were observed after a lag of about 75 min following transfer to a medium containing hexadecane as a sole carbon source. The same lag period was observed for growth as well as for the onset of hexadecane metabolism. Accumulation in the unmodified form as well as the fact that primary oxidation steps must occur within the cell appear to rule out substrate modifications prior to uptake. It should be noted that the localization of the hydrocarbon in restricted inclusions may alter the relation between effective concentration and activity such that the accumulation into the cell may not necessarily be an active uptake process against a concentration gradient but may be the result of diffusion. In this case, the driving force for uptake might be the higher concentration of pseudosolubilized oil outside than inside the cell. Diffusion could be facilitated by enhanced lipophilic characteristics of the cell wall and membrane. It remains to be determined as to whether or not there exist specific carriers required for hydrocarbon uptake. In this regard, *Pseudomonas aeruginosa* strain S7B1 was found to excrete a growth-stimulating protein in addition to the rhamnolipid. The weak emulsifying activity of the protein was totally inhibited by carboxyl group modification. The modified protein, however, still retained about 30% of its growth-stimulating capacity, suggesting an additional role in hydrocarbon assimilation.

Water-Insoluble Solid Hydrocarbons

Many of the arguments discussed above for uptake of water-insoluble liquid hydrocarbons by microorganisms pertain as well to uptake of hydrocarbons from the solid phase. The major difference would appear to be that uptake from the solid phase via pseudosolubilization would be harder to achieve since greater energy is required to disperse hydrophobic solids than liquids (87). Nevertheless, microorganisms may have evolved potent surface-active substances that can act both as wetting agents and as detergents.

Microbial degradation of pure solid hydrocarbons with water solubilities less than 10^{-7} M is not well documented. A recent note (42) indicates that *n*-alkanes up to 44 carbon atoms were slowly metabolized by soil microorganisms. A gram-negative rod was isolated during this study that could grow at the expense of tetracontane ($C_{40}H_{82}$) and tetratetracontane ($C_{44}H_{90}$). On the other hand, Wodzinski & Johnson (106) failed to isolate microorganisms that could grow on naphthacene. It is interesting to speculate that the general failure of investigators to isolate microorganisms on water-insoluble solid hydrocarbons may be due to the fact that the cells remain firmly bound to the substrate. Thus, standard enrichment culture procedures in which a portion of the bulk water phase is transferred would select against rather than for these microorganisms. It may be that for successful enrichments the solid phase should be used as the inoculum during the sequential transfers.

A comparison of the growth of bacteria on diphenylmethane (melting point 26°C) at 20° and 30°C clearly demonstrate the importance of the physical state of the hydrocarbon (R. S. Wodzinski, unpublished data). At 30°C, the generation time of a *Pseudomonas* sp in a medium saturated with diphenylmethane ($\sim 5 \times 10^{-4}$ M) was 2.7 hr. When additional diphenylmethane (liquid) was added, the generation time decreased to 1.6 hr. At 20°C, the generation time in a medium saturated with diphenylmethane was 4.0 hr. At this temperature, the growth rate was not altered significantly by addition of diphenylmethane (solid). Thus, at least in this special case, uptake from the liquid interface was faster than from the dissolved state, whereas substrate uptake from the solid phase is considerably slower (not measurable) than from the dilute solution.

In several regards, uptake of insoluble sulfur particles by *Thiobacillus* is analogous to uptake of petroleum by hydrocarbon-degrading bacteria. In both cases, the microorganisms must transport into the cell a highly water-insoluble hydrophobic substrate that can only be metabolized intracellularly. Unfortunately, even less is known about sulfur transport than hydrocarbon transport. Several reports indicate that the more hydrophilic forms of sulfur are oxidized more rapidly (2, 93). It has been suggested that one of the phospholipids excreted by cells during growth may act as the sulfur wetting agent (88). Direct contact between bacteria and sulfur is necessary for growth (94). Phase microscopy (95) and electron microscopy (83) reveal *Thiobacillus thiooxidans* clinging to the surface of crystals of sulfur. The area of the crystal occupied by bacteria exhibited an eroded appearance, indicating that localized contact had been maintained for a long time. Although scanning electron micrographs (3) demonstrated that *Acinetobacter* and other microorganisms were firmly attached to semisolid tar balls, no direct evidence was presented that growth had taken place on the solid substrates.

PETROLEUM BIODEGRADATION: GENERAL NUTRITIONAL REQUIREMENTS

In addition to the requirements for suitable cell-substrate interaction and specific metabolic and genetic potential, a number of general nutritional conditions must be fulfilled to achieve hydrocarbon utilization by microorganisms. The nutritional requirements stem from the fact that hydrocarbon substrates, which serve as carbon and energy for the organisms, are deficient in nitrogen, phosphorous, and oxygen, elements essential for cell growth. Since most natural aquatic environments are deficient in utilizable forms of nitrogen and phosphorous, it is necessary to add exogenous sources of these elements. This requirement is observed with all hydrocarbon substrates examined thus far in open or closed systems (3, 8, 78). In laboratory experiments, the limitation for nitrogen is generally overcome by supplementing the medium with inorganic salts of ammonia or nitrate, or with urea, whereas phosphorous is added as inorganic phosphate.

The requirement for molecular oxygen has been given much attention, particularly with respect to the maximum production of single-cell protein by hydrocarbon-degrading microorganisms (58, 66). The limitation for oxygen is easily overcome in small-scale laboratory studies, or in open systems where the oil-water interface is in direct contact with air at all times. However, biodegradation experiments in closed systems of high volume-to-surface ratio demonstrate the need for efficient aeration devices to insure adequate oxygen transfer to the water (80).

Although oxygen supply does not appear to be a problem in open systems, the water solubility of most utilizeable sources of nitrogen and phosphorous prevents their effectiveness in these environments because of rapid dilution. Atlas & Bartha (9) studied the effectiveness of several oleophilic nitrogen and phosphorous compounds with low C:N and C:P ratios. It was found that a combination of paraffinized urea and octylphosphate (pyrophosphoric acid dioctyl ester) were able to replace nitrate and inorganic phosphate, respectively. The authors stress the fact that, because of the high affinity of such oleophilic nutrients for the oil phase, these materials enhance growth of petroleum-degrading microorganisms selectively, thus minimizing their possible contribution towards algal bloom formation. Dibble & Bartha (24) have recently found that the concentration of iron may limit oil biodegradation in certain aquatic environments under conditions in which the water was supplemented with nitrogen and phosphorous. Under these conditions, an encapsulated oleophilic iron compound, ferric octoate [ferric (2-ethyl hexanoate)$_3$], was found to be as effective in stimulating biodegradation as various water-soluble iron derivations such as ferric ammonium citrate. These reports illustrate the possibility of supplementing natural environments with oleophilic nutrients to stimulate biodegradation by indigenous microbial populations.

Many investigators have discussed the advantages of artificially seeding polluted areas with pure or mixed cultures of oil-degrading microbes (e.g. see 3, 14). However, the need for supplementing the environment with essential nutrients remains unquestionable. One intriguing possibility to obviate the need for addition of nitrogen compounds to the environment is the introduction of the genetic capacity to fix molecular nitrogen into specific oil-degrading microbes. This possibility is based on recent findings concerning the genetics and regulation of the nitrogen-fixation system (*nif*) of *Klebsiella, Azotobacter,* and *Rhizobium* (15, 86). In *Klebsiella pneumoniae,* at least four genes essential for nitrogenase synthesis are located very close to the *his* region of the chromosome. Of particular interest was the finding that nitrogen-fixing recombinants of *Escherichia coli* could be constructed by transfer of the *nif* gene cluster from *K. pneumoniae* to *E. coli* (25). Furthermore, the construction of an *E. coli* hybrid with an infectious *nif* episome has been described (17) that can transfer the *his* and *nif* genes from *K. pneumoniae* to recipients lacking the ability to fix nitrogen. That certain strains of *Pseudomonas putida* can carry multiple plasmids in a compatible, stable fashion and thereby carry out petroleum degradation (20) suggests the possibility of introducing the potential for nitrogen fixation into petroleum-degrading microorganisms. One in-principle difficulty may lie in the apparent contradiction between the high oxygen requirement for oxidation of the very reduced carbon source and the low redox potential necessary for nitrogen reduction. Some of the biochemical requirements of a potential recipient for phenotypic expression of *nif* genes have been discussed (86). Two such requirements may be lacking in the highly aerobic hydrocarbon-degrading organisms: a reduced ferrodoxin or low potential electron donor, and the ability to "protect" the nitrogenase from both oxygen denaturation and competition for reductant. In fact, these constraints may account for the fact that there has been no direct demonstration of nitrogen-fixing hydrocarbon oxidizers.

PETROLEUM DEGRADATION: METABOLIC SPECIFICITY

It is beyond the scope of this review to cover the general literature dealing with metabolic transformation of hydrocarbons by microorganisms; the reader is referred to a number of reviews of the various degradative pathways for aromatic (31, 90) and aliphatic hydrocarbons (61, 62). The specificity of the process can ultimately be related to the genetic potential of the particular microorganism to introduce molecular oxygen into the hydrocarbon and, with a relatively few reactions, to generate the intermediates that subsequently enter the general energy-yielding catabolic reactions of the cell. The specific genetic capacity is expressed in the substrate specificity of the oxygenase for its substrate(s) and in the ability of the carbon source to induce the various enzyme activities necessary for its biodegradation.

Initial Oxidation

It has been clearly established that degradation of hydrocarbons proceeds with the introduction of molecular oxygen into the molecule. In the case of bacterial degradation of aromatic hydrocarbons, ring fission requires a dihydroxylation reaction, the introduction of both atoms of the oxygen molecule into the ring, and the subsequent formation of a *cis*-diol (32). The oxidation of aromatic hydrocarbons has been studied in a strain of *P. putida* that can utilize benzene, toluene, or ethylbenzene as sole sources of carbon and energy (35). Toluene-grown cells rapidly oxidized the three aromatic hydrocarbons, whereas other alkyl-substituted benzenes of longer chain length were oxidized more slowly. Furthermore, these cells were shown to catalyze the oxidation of *cis* (but not *trans*)-1,2-dihydroxy-1,2-dihydrobenzene. The *cis*-diol accumulated in the culture fluid when a mutant unable to grow on toluene, *P. putida* 39/D, was grown on glucose in the presence of benzene. The mutant oxidizes benzene (33), toluene (110), ethyl benzene (34), *p*-chloro-, *p*-fluoro-, and *p*-bromotoluene, chlorobenzene, cyanobenzene (110), *p*-xylene, and *m*-xylene (23) to the corresponding dihydrodiol derivatives. It has been pointed out that those microorganisms able to utilize dimethylated aromatic hydrocarbons for growth appear to oxidize one of the methyl groups to the carboxylic acid prior to cleavage of the aromatic nucleus. Thus, it is of interest that the *P. putida* strain can oxidize *p*- or *m*-xylene even though these compounds cannot serve as carbon sources (23). Another pseudomonad (Pxy), able to grow at the expense of *p*- and *m*-xylenes, oxidized the xylene to the corresponding toluic acid prior to ring fission (36).

Strain specificity seems to be involved in determining whether alkyl substituents are oxidized prior to ring fission. In this regard, Omori et al (68, 73) described five different strains of *Pseudomonas* capable of growth on a variety of substituted aromatic hydrocarbons. The strains could be divided into two groups on the basis of their ability to utilize *n*-alkyl and isoalkyl benzenes as carbon sources. Strains of group A showed good growth on *n*-alkylbenzenes (C_1–C_5), whereas group B organisms grew only on *n*-alkyl-substituted benzenes containing from 6–12 carbon atoms in the side chain. Of interest was the fact that only group B strains were capable of growing on *n*-alkanes such as *n*-tetradecane. Growth of group A microbes on *n*-propylbenzene yielded both β-phenylpropionic acid and 3-*n*-propylcatechol in the culture broth, suggesting that two modes of initial oxidation occur in the same organism: oxidation of the side chain and hydroxylation of the aromatic nucleus. The degradation of the *n*-alkyl substituted benzenes of higher chain length proceeds with an initial oxidation of the alkyl substituent followed by β-oxidation(s) and finally dihydroxylation of the benzene ring. Thus, it appears that in organisms of the first group the same compound can induce two different types of oxygenase systems, whereas group B strains apparently require an alkyl substituent of sufficient chain length for induction of the *n*-alkyl oxygenase. Since organisms of this class also grow on *n*-alkanes, it is possible that the initial alkylhydroxylase system is the same for *n*-alkanes and for the *n*-alkyl benzenes. This hypothesis predicts that one class of mutants unable to grow on *n*-alkanes should also be unable to grow on *n*-alkyl benzenes.

Oxidation of *n*-paraffins proceeds in general via terminal oxidation and subsequent β-oxidation to yield C_2 units (62). A species of *Corynebacterium* (55) has been shown to generate dicarboxylic acids from *n*-alkanes by ω-oxidation. Similar results were obtained with a strain of *Pseudomonas* that converted *n*-octane to *n*-octane dioic acid (5). The branched-chain derivatives also appear to be metabolized via the formation of dicarboxylic acids and subsequent β-oxidation (63). A strain of *Brevibacterium* utilized pristane (2,6,10,14-tetramethyl pentadecane) as a sole source of carbon and energy via the dicarboxylic acid pathway (74); the degradation of pristane was not observed with cells grown on a mixture of pristane and hexadecane. Furthermore, the presence of the *n*-alkane inhibited the production of $^{14}CO_2$ from [1-^{14}C]pristane. The results may explain the lower rate of biodegradation of branched-chain paraffins in nature.

This inhibitory effect may be contrasted with the phenomenon of cooxidation (77), in which nongrowth hydrocarbons are oxidized when present as cosubstrates in a medium in which a different hydrocarbon is furnished for growth. Thus, growth of a *Nocardia* sp. on hexadecane allowed for the partial oxidation of ethylbenzene to phenylacetic acid. Cooxidation was employed by using a mutant of *Beijerinckia* that oxidizes biphenyl to the corresponding *cis*-dihydroxy derivative. Cells of this organism, after growth on glucose in the presence of biphenyl, catalyzed the oxidation of benzo (a)-pyrene to the *cis*-dihydroxy compound (37). Cooxidation has also been implicated in the microbial degradation of cycloparaffins by soil microorganisms (11).

Inducer Specificity

Hydrocarbon oxidation is an inducible process. The ability of a particular substrate to serve as a sole source of carbon and energy thus will be a function of its ability to induce the necessary enzymes for its subsequent oxidation. Whole-cell alkane-oxidizing activity is inducible in a number of pseudomonads including *Pseudomonas aeruginosa* 473, in which the effective inducers include the alkanes themselves, aliphatic diols, straight-chain diethers, and dicyclopropyl compounds (91, 92). In *P. putida,* the regulation of alkane oxidation has recently been subjected to detailed genetic and physiological analysis (41). The results demonstrate that (*a*) transcription is required for induction, (*b*) induction of both alkane hydroxylase and plasmid-borne alcohol dehydrogenase is coordinate (*P. putida* also contains a chromosomal gene for a constitutive nonspecific alcohol-dehydrogenase,) (*c*) alkanes need not undergo oxidation to serve as inducers, (*d*) induction requires that one end of the chain must be without terminal hydroxyl groups [in contrast to *P. aeruginosa* (92)], and (*e*) certain substrates, such as *n*-undecane, that cannot support the growth of *P. putida* strain can be induced to do so in the presence of a gratuitous inducer, such as dicyclopropylketone. The authors suggest that failure to grow on undecane is because this compound cannot induce the oxygenase system. Since uptake of undecane was not measured directly in these experiments, an alternative explanation would be that undecane is only transported after induction by the gratuitous inducer.

Structural genes for a number of catabolic pathways in strains of *Pseudomonas* have been shown to reside on transmissible plasmids (99). Although different plasmids are generally incompatible within the same cell, it has recently been demonstrated that irradiation with UV causes plasmid fusion. This has allowed for the sequential introduction into *Pseudomonas* strains (20) of plasmids specifically coding for the octane (21), naphthalene (27), camphor (79), and salicylate (19) pathways, thereby increasing at each stage the ability of the cells to grow on crude oil (20). It has been suggested that this technique be utilized to construct specific organisms more competent genetically to catalyze effective biodegradation of petroleum. It has been noted that such strains must be capable of competing in natural environments if they are to be effective in pollution treatment. The choice of a suitable plasmid recipient therefore should take into account the importance of physical interaction between cells and oil.

MICROBIOLOGICAL PROBLEMS ASSOCIATED WITH OIL TANKER OPERATIONS

In this section, we attempt to demonstrate how some principles of petroleum microbiology can be applied to problems of oil pollution, safety, and maintenance that arise as a result of normal oil tanker operations.

Oil Tankers and the Ballast Voyage

Consider a typical very large tanker (VLT) of 250,000 tons transporting crude oil from the Persian Gulf to Japan. Such a ship is divided into about 12 large cargo compartments each with a 20,000-ton capacity; these compartments are interconnected via large pipes to two smaller compartments of 2,000 tons each, referred to as "slop" tanks. As is discussed below, these slop tanks are designed to serve as oil-water separators.

After the cargo compartments are filled with crude oil, the VLT begins its voyage of 2–3 weeks to Japan. Upon arrival, the cargo is discharged into large on-land oil storage tanks. During this operation about 99.5% of the crude oil is pumped out in about 24 hr. The residual oil remains stuck to the sides, platforms, ribs, and pipes of the compartment. As the oil is discharged, the ship rises out of the water. Before putting to sea, the VLT must take aboard large quantities of ballast water. During the return voyage to the Persian Gulf, this ballast water mixes with the residual (approximately 1,000 tons) oil. Disposal of this heavily contaminated, oily ballast water is the major contributor to chronic sea pollution. In addition, cargo compartments of oil tankers must be cleaned periodically to prevent clogging and sludge accumulation that otherwise would reduce the ship's cargo capacity, as well as inhibit discharge of crude oil. Presently, cargo compartments of oil tankers are usually cleaned with high-pressure jets of seawater; the combined ballast and wash waters are then either (*a*) discharged at sea, (*b*) transferred to separator tanks on shore where harbor facilities permit, or (*c*) transferred to the slop tanks in which the bulk water phase at the bottom is discharged, additional oily ballast water is added, and the process is repeated until the ship takes on fresh oil that is then loaded on top of the residual oil (load-on-top technique). None of these techniques is totally satisfactory either from the ecological or operational point of view.

Direct discharge at sea is still the major means of disposing of oily waters. It will remain so until pollution laws are made stricter and more enforceable or other techniques prove more economical. Direct discharge at sea requires no special equipment and, most important of all, can be carried out during the ballast voyage so that no loss of time is incurred. The 1954 International Agreement for the Prevention of Pollution at Sea, as amended in 1962, is the only international agreement regarding pollution by ships that is currently in force. This Agreement allows for unlimited discharge of oil outside of specified prohibited zones. Within the prohibited zones, discharge is restricted to a rate no greater than 1 ton of oil in 10,000 tons of water, without regard to total quantity. The 1973 Marine Pollution Convention Agreement, when ratified and if enforced, should decrease oil pollution by a factor of about ten by forcing VLTs to use the load-on-top technique.

The use of oil-water separator systems either at port or for load-on-top offers similar advantages and suffer from the same basic disadvantages. The major advantage is that the bulk of the oil is recovered rather than discharged into the sea. The quantity of recoverable petroleum from the ballast water of a VLT is a significant economic consideration. This, however, must be weighed against the costs of operating the recovery equipment. In addition, time is lost if the oily ballast water must be pumped to shore facilities. During short ballast voyages, e.g. between Mediterranean ports, insufficient time is available to apply the load-on-top technique. In our opinion, the most serious disadvantage to the use of oil-water separator systems is that the *most toxic components of petroleum are discharged into the sea,* often near shore. Water extracts of crude oil and fuel oil contain aromatic hydrocarbons, phenols, and anilines (6). The general toxicity of these compounds to marine life is well documented. More specifically, Winters and co-workers (102) have demonstrated that *p*-toluidine is toxic specifically to blue-green bacteria, whereas phenalen-1-one is particularly toxic to green algae.

Potential Applications

There has been a considerable amount of attention and publicity given to the potential use of microorganisms to combat oil slicks in the sea. In fact, several International Symposia have dealt with the subject. Nevertheless, there is no evidence to support the claim that "seeding" oil slicks with microorganisms reduces oil pollution by stimulating petroleum biodegradation. Even under the best laboratory conditions of controlled temperature, pH, nitrogen, and phosphorus supplementation, microorganisms degrade a maximum of only 60–80% of crude oil. (The residual material, consisting of those substances resistant to biodegradation, would remain a major pollution problem.) Atlas (7) has recently discussed some serious scientific, technological, and ecological problems that will have to be solved before microbes can be used for cleaning up oil spills in an open system. There are, however, at least two areas of oil tanker operation procedures involving confined volumes where microbiological processes might play an important role in the near future: (1) treatment of contaminated seawater following the oil-water separation process but before discharging; and (2) use of oil-emulsifying bacteria or their extracellular products for cleaning oil tanks and for efficient recovery of petroleum.

Studies supported by the American Petroleum Institute since 1930 have led to a body of specific information on treatment of petroleum refinery wastes (64). Generally, an oil-water separator is employed as the first step; the upper oil phase is mechanically removed and returned to the refinery. The water phase contains an average of 57 mg of emulsified oil and 27 mg of phenols per liter. After careful adjustment with nitrogen and phosphate salts, the bulk water phase is treated microbiologically by using activated sludge, trickling filters, oxidation ponds, or cooling towers. The biologically treated effluents contain around 10 mg of oil and less than 1 mg of phenols per liter. Similarly, a microbial process for treatment of waste waters rich in naphthenic acids has been described (29).

As stricter oil pollution regulations come into force and oil-water separators become the rule in oily ballast water treatment, the need for microbiological processing of the bulk seawater phase will become necessary. Although some of the experience obtained from refinery waste-treatment facilities will be useful, there are several significant differences to consider. A typical on-land separator system treats 50,000 tons of oily ballast water per day. Coming out of the separator, the sea-water contains 2–10 mg of dissolved organic matter per liter. Thus, large volumes of dilute solutions will have to be detoxified. Aeration will be unnecessary since seawater contains sufficient dissolved oxygen for the complete oxidation of such small amounts of organic matter. Additions of nitrogen and phosphorus salts as well as seed cultures will probably be necessary. The introduction of a microbiological step during the treatment of oily ballast water takes advantage of the fact that the most toxic components of petroleum are the most difficult to remove physically but are relatively simple substrates for biodegradation—both for the same reason, their water solubility.

Before an oil tanker can enter drydock for repairs, all of the cargo compartments must be cleaned and rendered gas free. Present methods for cleaning cargo compartments are time consuming, and dangerous, and they expose the worker to serious health hazards. High-pressure jets of water striking the sides of a tank containing explosive mixtures of gases have caused major explosions on oil tankers. Those regions of the tank protected by obstructions from direct exposure to the water jet must be cleaned by hand. Futhermore, if a heavy buildup of sludge has taken place, mechanical washing may not be effective.

An alternative approach to cleaning out oil tanks is the use of hydrocarbon-degrading microorganisms. The feasibility of such an approach was demonstrated in a controlled experiment aboard an oil tanker during its ballast voyage (80). One of the slop tanks containing 107 m^3 of oily ballast water over a layer of sludge was supplemented with 7.6 mM urea, 0.57 mM K_2HPO_4, and 3 m^3 of air per min. After 4 days, the tank was emptied and shown to be completely free of the thick layer of sludge that remained in the control (no aeration) tank. In this experiment, removal of the sludge was made possible by providing conditions that favored bioemulsification rather than optimum cell growth. The microbiological cleaning method had the advantage that cleaning takes place while the tank is full of ballast water, thereby decreasing the danger of explosion. All submerged components of the tank are in contact with the cleaning agent. Before this procedure can be put into routine operation, techniques will have to be developed for delivering and dispersing air throughout the cargo compartment and for disposing of the dispersed oil in an ecologically safe way.

CONCLUSION—TOWARDS A DEFINITION OF A PETROLEUM-DEGRADING MICROORGANISM

We have attempted to point out in this article that the chemical heterogeneity and water insolubility of petroleum poses special problems for microorganisms that must use these substances as nutrients. Although man-induced oil pollution is primarily a result of twentieth-century technology, natural oil seepages have been documented throughout written history (101). It is reasonable to assume, therefore, that certain microorganisms have evolved special traits to overcome these problems. Three such distinguishing traits or specificities have been discussed in order to begin to define a petroleum-degrading microorganism:

1. efficient hydrocarbon uptake system (special receptor sites for binding hydrocarbons and/or production of unique chemicals that assist in the emulsification and transport of hydrocarbons into the cell);
2. group-specific oxygenases (genetic potential of a particular microorganism to introduce molecular oxygen into the hydrocarbon and, with relatively few reactions, generate intermediates that subsequently enter common energy-yielding catabolic pathways);
3. inducer specificity (the positive response of the organism to petroleum and its constituents in inducing the first two systems; inducer specificity and substrate specificity for oxygenase need not coincide).

Scientific progress is motivated both by a desire to know and a desire to use this knowledge. Nowhere is this more evident than in petroleum microbiology.

Literature Cited

1. Abbott, B. J., Gledhill, W. E. 1971. *Adv. Appl. Microbiol.* 14:249–388
2. Adair, F. W. 1966. *J. Bacteriol.* 92:899–904
3. Ahearn, D. G., Meyers, S. P., ed. 1973. *The Microbial Degradation of Oil Pollutants.* Baton Rouge: Center for Wetland Res. Publ. No. LSU-SG-73-01
4. Aiba, S., Moritz, V., Someya, J. I., Haung, K. L. 1969. *J. Ferm. Technol.* 47:203–10
5. Ali Khan, M. Y., Hall, A. N., Robinson, D. S. 1963. *Nature* 198:289
6. Anderson, J. W., Neff, J. M., Cox, B. A., Tatem, H. E., Hightower, G. M. 1974. *Mar. Biol.* 27:75–88
7. Atlas, R. M. 1977. *Crit. Rev. Microbiol.* In press
8. Atlas, R. M., Bartha, R. 1972. *Biotechnol. Bioeng.* 14:309–17
9. Atlas, R. M., Bartha, R. 1973. *Environ. Sci. Technol.* 7:538–41
10. Atlas, R. M., Bartha, R. 1973. *Residue Rev.* 49:49–85
11. Beam, H. W., Perry, J. J. 1974. *J. Gen. Microbiol.* 82:163–69
12. Berner, N. H., Ahearn, D. G., Cook, W. L. See Ref. 14, pp. 199–219
13. Boesch, D. F., Herschner, C. H., Milgram, J. H. 1974. *Oil Spills and the Marine Environment.* Cambridge: Ballinger Publ. 114 pp.
14. Bourquin, A. W., Ahearn, D. G., Meyers, S. P., ed. 1975. *Impact of the Use of Microorganisms On the Aquatic Environment.* EPA Report 660–3–75–001. 254 pp.
15. Brill, W. J. 1975. *Ann. Rev. Microbiol.* 29:109–29
16. Camin, D. L., Raymond, A. J. 1973. *J. Chrom. Sci.* 11:625–38
17. Cannon, F. C., Dixon, R. A., Postgate, J. R., Primrose, S. B. 1974. *J. Gen. Microbiol.* 80:227–39
18. Cash, R. L., Cajias, J. L., Fournier, R. G., Jacobson, J. K., Schares, T., Schecter, R. S., Wade, W. W. 1976. *Soc. Pet.* Eng. *of AIME Pap.* SPE 5813: 217–24
19. Chakrabarty, A. M. 1972. *J. Bacteriol.* 112:815–23
20. Chakrabarty, A. M. 1974. U.S. Patent 3, 813, 316
21. Chakrabarty, A. M., Chou, G., Gunsalus, I. C. 1973. *Proc. Natl. Acad. Sci. USA* 70:1137–40
22. Chet, I., Mitchell, R. 1976. *Nature* 261:308–9
23. Davey, J. F., Gibson, D. T. 1974. *J. Bacteriol.* 119:923–29
24. Dibble, J. T., Bartha, R. 1976. *Appl. Environ. Microbiol.* 31:544–50
25. Dixon, R. A., Postgate, J. R. 1972. *Nature* 237:102–3
26. Dooley, J. E., Hirsch, D. E., Thompson, C. J. 1974. *Hydrocarbon Process.* 53: 140–46
27. Dunn, N. W., Gunsalus, I. C. 1973. *J. Bacteriol.* 114:974–79
28. Erickson, L. E., Nakahara, T. 1975. *Process Biochem.* 10:9–13
29. Ferner, R. R. 1959. *World Pet. Congr. Proc. 5th, New York,* pp. 31–41
30. Ferrero, E. P., Nidiols, D. T. 1972. *Analyser of 169 Crude Oils from 122 Foreign Oil Fields,* p. 53. Washington, D.C.: U.S. Dept. of the Interior, Bureau of Mines Information Circular 8542
31. Gibson, D. T. 1971. *Crit. Rev. Microbiol.* 1:199–223
32. Gibson, D. T. 1972. In *Degradation of Synthetic Organic Molecules in the Biosphere.* Washington, D.C.: Nat. Acad. Sci. pp. 116–36
33. Gibson, D. T., Cardini, G. E., Maseles, F. C., Kallio, R. E. 1970. *Biochemistry* 9:1631–35
34. Gibson, D. T., Gschwendt, B., Yeh, W. K., Kobal, V. M. 1973. *Biochemistry* 12:1520–28
35. Gibson, D. T., Koch, J. R., Kallio, R. E. 1968. *Biochemistry* 7:2653–62
36. Gibson, D. T., Mahadevan, V., Davey, J. F. 1974. *J. Bacteriol.* 119:930–36
37. Gibson, D. T., Mahadevan, V., Jerina, D. M., Yagi, H., Yeh, H. J. C. 1975. *Science* 189:295–97
38. Giger, W., Blumer, M. 1974. *Anal. Chem.* 46:1663–71
39. Goma, G., Al Ani, D., Pareilleux, A. 1976. *Proc. Int. Ferment. Symp. 5th.,* p. 131
40. Goma, G., Henderson, K., Ribot, D. 1976. *Proc. Int. Ferment. Symp. 5th.,* p. 88
41. Grund, A., Shapiro, J., Fennewald, M., Bacha, P., Leahy, J., Markbreiter, K., Nieder, M., Toepfer, M. 1975. *J. Bacteriol.* 123:546–56
42. Haines, J. R., Alexander, M. 1974. *Appl. Microbiol.* 28:1084–85
43. Haldom, R. S., Turner, A. G. 1969. *J. Appl. Bacteriol.* 32:448–56
44. Hisatsuka, K., Nakahara, T., Sano, N., Yamada, K. 1971. *Agric. Biol. Chem.* 35:686–92

45. Horowitz, A., Gutnick, D., Rosenberg, E. 1975. *Appl. Microbiol.* 30:10–19
46. Iguchi, J., Takeda, I., Ohsawa, H. 1969. *Agric. Biol. Chem.* 33:1657–58
47. Itoh, S., Honda, H., Tomita, F., Suzuki, T. 1971. *J. Antibiot.* 23:855
48. Itoh, S., Suzuki, T. 1972. *Agric. Biol. Chem.* 36:2233
49. Jewell, D. M., Albaugh, E. W., Davis, B. E., Ruberto, R. G. 1972. *Am. Chem. Soc.* 17:F81–F91
50. Jobson, A., Cook, F. D., Westlake, D. W. S. 1972. *Appl. Microbiol.* 23: 1082–89
51. Käppeli, O., Fiechter, A. 1976. *Proc. Int. Ferment. Symp. 5th,* p. 187
52. Käppeli, O., Fiechter, A. 1976. *Biotechnol. Bioeng.* 18:967–74
53. Katinger, H. W. D. 1973. *Biotechnol. Bioeng. Symp.* 4:485–505
54. Kennedy, R. S., Finnerty, W. R., Sudarsanan, K., Young, R. A. 1975. *Arch. Microbiol.* 102:75–83
55. Kester, A. S., Foster, J. W. 1963. *J. Bacteriol.* 85:859–69
56. Klevins, H. B. 1950. *J. Phys. Chem.* 54:283–98
57. Lee, C. C., Craig, W. K., Smith, P. J. 1974. *Bull. Environ. Contam. Toxicol.* 12:212–16
58. Linek, V., Sobotka, M., Prokop, A. 1973. *Biotechnol. Bioeng. Symp.* 4: 429–53
59. Ludvik, J., Munk, V., Dostalek, M. 1968. *Experientia* 24:1066–68
60. Martin, R. L., Winters, J. C. 1959. *Anal. Chem.* 31:1954–60
61. McKenna, E. J. 1972. In *Degradation of Synthetic Organic Molecules in the Biosphere.* Washington, D.C.: Nat. Acad. Sci., p.73–97
62. McKenna, E. J., Kallio, R. E. 1965. *Ann. Rev. Microbiol.* 19:183–208
63. McKenna, E. J., Kallio, R. E. 1971. *Proc. Natl. Acad. Sci. USA* 68:1552–54
64. McKinney, R. E. 1963. *Biological Treatment of Petroleum Refinery Wastes.* New York: Am. Pet. Inst. 73 pp.
65. McLee, A. G., Davies, S. L. 1972. *Can. J. Microbiol.* 18:315–19
66. Mimura, A., Takeda, I., Wakasa, R. 1973. *Biotechnol. Bioeng. Symp.* 4: 467–84
67. Mimura, A., Watanabe, S., Takeda, I. 1971. *J. Ferm. Technol.* 49:255
68. Minoda, Y., Omori, T. 1976. *Proc. Int. Ferment. Symp. 5th.,* p. 423
69. Miyazu, Y., Yano, T. 1974. *Agric. Biol. Chem.* 38:183–88
70. Moo-Young, M., Shimizu, T. 1971. *Biotechnol. Bioeng.* 13:761
71. Morris, B. F. 1971. *Science* 173:430–32
72. Nelson-Smith, A. 1971. In *Water Pollution by Oil,* ed. P. Hepple, pp. 273–80. New York: Elsevier. 393 pp.
73. Omori, T., Jigami, Y., Minoda, Y. 1975. *Agric. Biol. Chem.* 39:1775–79
74. Pirnik, M. P., Atlas, R. M., Bartha, R. 1974. *J. Bacteriol.* 119:868–78
75. Prokop, A., Ludvik, M. 1973. *Biotechnol. Bioeng. Symp.* 4:349–62
76. Pulich, W. M. Jr., Winters, K., Van Baalen, C. 1974. *Mar. Biol.* 28:87–94
77. Raymond, R. L., Jamison, V. W. 1971. *Adv. Appl. Microbiol.* 14:93–122
78. Reisfeld, A., Rosenberg, E., Gutnick, D. 1972. *Appl. Microbiol.* 24:363–68
79. Rheinwald, J. G., Chakrabarty, A. M., Gunsalus, I. C. 1973. *Proc. Natl. Acad. Sci. USA* 70:885–89
80. Rosenberg, E., Englander, E., Horowitz, A., Gutnick, D. See Ref. 14, pp. 157–68
81. Rosenberg, E., Keller, K., Dworkin, M. 1977. *J. Bacteriol.* In press
82. Rossini, F. D., Mair, B. J. 1951. In *Progress in Petroleum Technology,* p. 334. Washington, D.C.: Am. Chem. Soc.
83. Schaeffer, W. I., Holbert, P. E., Umbreit, W. W. 1963. *J. Bacteriol.* 85: 137–40
84. Scott, C. C. L., Finnerty, W. R. 1976. *J. Bacteriol.* 127:481–89
85. Scott, C. C. L., Makula, R. A., Finnerty, W. R. 1976. *J. Bacteriol.* 127: 469–80
86. Shanmugam, K. T., Valentine, R. C. 1975. *Science* 187:919–24
87. Shaw, D. J. 1970. *Introduction to Colloid and Surface Chemistry,* pp. 117–128. London: Butterworth. 236 pp. 2nd ed.
88. Shively, J. M., Benson, A. A. 1967. *J. Bacteriol.* 94:1679–83
89. Suzuki, T., Tanaka, K., Matsubara, I., Kinoshita, S. 1969. *Agric. Biol. Chem.* 33:1619–27
90. Treccani, V. 1974. In *Industrial Aspects of Biochemistry,* ed. B. Spencer, pp. 533–47. Berlin: Fed. Eur. Bioch. Soc.
91. Van der Linden, A. C., Huybregste, R. 1967. *Antonie van Leeuwenhoek J. Microbiol. Serol.* 33:381–85
92. Van Eyk, J., Bartels, T. J. 1968. *J. Bacteriol.* 96:706–12
93. Vogler, K. G., LePage, G. A., Umbreit, W. W. 1942. *J. Gen. Physiol.* 26:89–95
94. Vogler, K. G., Umbreit, W. W. 1941. *Soil Sci.* 51:331–37

95. Waksman, S. A. 1932. *Principles of Soil Microbiology.* Baltimore: Williams and Wilkins. 2nd ed.
96. Walker, J. D., Colwell, R. R. 1974. *Appl. Microbiol.* 27:1053–60
97. Walker, J. D., Colwell, R. R., Petrakis, L. 1975. *Can. J. Microbiol.* 21:1760–67
98. Walkup, P. C. 1971. *J. Water Pollut. Control Fed.* 43:1069–72
99. Wheelis, M. L. 1975. *Ann. Rev. Microbiol.* 29:505–24
100. Whitehead, W. L., Breger, I. A. 1963. In *Organic Geochemistry,* ed. I. Breger, pp. 248–332. New York: MacMillian. 658 pp.
101. Wilson, R. D., Monaghan, P. H., Osanik, A., Price, L. C., Rogers, M. A. 1974. *Science* 184:857–65
102. Winters, K., Batterton, J. C., O'Donnell, R., Van Baalen, C. 1976. *IDOE Workshop Meet., College Station, Tex., May 1976*
103. Winters, K., O'Donell, R., Batterton, J. C., Van Baalen, C. 1976. *Mar. Biol.* 36:269–76
104. Wodzinski, R. S., Bertolini, D. 1972. *Appl. Microbiol.* 23:1077–81
105. Wodzinski, R. S., Coyle, J. E. 1974. *Appl. Microbiol.* 27:1081–84
106. Wodzinski, R. S., Johnson, M. J. 1968. *Appl. Microbiol.* 16:1886–91
107. Zajic, J. E., Panchal, C. J. 1976. *Crit. Rev. Microbiol.* 5:39–66
108. Zajic, J. E., Supplisson, B. 1972. *Biotechnol. Bioeng.* 14:331–43
109. Zajic, J. E., Supplisson, B., Volesky, B. 1974. *Environ. Sci. Technol.* 8:664–69
110. Ziffer, H. D., Jerina, D. M., Gibson, D. T., Kobal, V. M. 1973. *J. Am. Chem. Soc.* 95:4048–49
111. Zobell, C. E. See Ref. 3, pp. 3–16

Ann. Rev. Microbiol. 1977. 31:397–419

BACTERIAL FLAGELLA ❖1711

Michael Silverman and Melvin I. Simon
Department of Biology, University of California at San Diego, La Jolla, California 92093

CONTENTS

INTRODUCTION 397
FLAGELLAR STRUCTURES 398
The Filament 398
The Hook Structure 400
The Basal Structure 401
THE GENETIC BASIS FOR FLAGELLAR FORMATION 403
Mutant Phenotypes 403
Flagellar Genes in Salmonella 405
Flagellar Genes in E. coli 405
Comparison of Flagellar Genes in E. coli and Salmonella 410
REGULATION OF FLAGELLAR SYNTHESIS 410
Phase Variation in Salmonella 410
Catabolite Repression of Flagella Formation 412
Regulation of Flagellin Synthesis 413
FLAGELLAR FUNCTION 414

INTRODUCTION

Flagella are responsible for bacterial motility and chemotaxis. They are subcellular organelles that originate in the membrane of the cell and extend 15–20 μm from the cell surface. The bacterial flagellar system has been studied from a variety of points of view, including as a model for the regulation of organelle formation and morphogenesis, as a system that transduces chemical energy into motion, and as the basic effector involved in chemotaxis. To frame precise questions in each of these areas, it is necessary that a great deal be known about the nature of the components and the behavior of the system. Recent work has led to a clearer characterization of structure and function of bacterial flagella in *Escherichia coli* and in *Salmonella*. Our objective in this review is to summarize the status of current work, as well as to identify some of the new questions this work raises. We are selective, particularly in the area of chemotaxis since comprehensive reviews of recent (4, 25, 85, 101) as well as earlier work (24) in this area have appeared. Flagellar assembly and the regulation of flagella formation have received somewhat less attention. The most recent extensive reviews were by Iino (63) and Doetsch & Hageage (47).

In this article, we describe the structure of the organelle and the genetic basis for flagellar formation and function, summarize information relating to the gene products and the mechanisms involved in regulating their synthesis, and discuss flagellar function. The discussion is limited to the *E. coli* and *Salmonella* systems.

FLAGELLAR STRUCTURES

Flagellar organelles found on intact cells and in cell lysates have been studied extensively by electron microscopy (2, 3, 35, 98). In most bacteria, the organelle was found to be composed of three morphologically distinct substructures: the filament, the hook, and the basal structure. The purification of apparently intact organelles from *E. coli* (41) and *Bacillus subtilis* (45) has resulted in a clearer picture of the structures involved in forming the base of the organelle and has revealed the relationships of the basal elements to the cell membrane.

The Filament

The filament is generally made up of a single protein subunit component, flagellin. This polypeptide is readily isolated and has been purified and characterized from a variety of strains (78). The structure of the subunit is responsible for the antigenic activity of the flagellar filament, as well as for the overall shape of the filament. This has been clearly demonstrated by the isolation of a large number of mutants that result in changes in antigenic specificity and flagellar shape (62, 67, 138). In *Salmonella,* many of these mutations have been mapped and appear to be localized in the central and terminal regions of the structural gene that codes for flagellin (58). Amino acid sequences have been determined with a view to understanding the relationship between the sequence and flagellar antigenic specificity and shape. The complete sequence of *B. subtilis* flagellin (33, 39, 110) and partial sequences of *Salmonella* flagellins have been reported (73). Although some of the peptide changes that may be involved in changing antigenic specificity have been identified, a clear-cut definition of the antigenic determinants has not been made. Nonetheless, the great serological diversity among flagellar antigens has been used for many years to type *Salmonella* and *E. coli* strains. It has been suggested that a similar system could be useful in the classification of *Bacillus* strains (49).

The flagellin subunits are capable of reassembling in vitro to form flagellar filaments that show many of the same characteristics as the filament portion of the intact organelle (1, 17). In a series of very elegant experiments, by using antibody labeling and electron microscopy, it was shown that the filament grows in a polar fashion. Filaments are elongated by adding subunits to one end (18). The same polarity of elongation was observed in vivo, i.e. the flagellar filament grows by adding subunits to its distal end. This was demonstrated in *Salmonella* by studying the incorporation of amino acid analogues, which change the shape of the flagellar filament (64). A pulse of incorporated analogue caused the shape change to occur at the tip of the filament. In experiments with *B. subtilis,* pulse labeling with radioactive leucine followed by electron microscope radioautography was used to show that the label was incorporated at the flagellar tip (50). The most reasonable hypothesis to explain this growth is that the subunits are synthesized inside the cell and then transported down the length of the flagellar filament through a central cavity. They are then incorporated into the growing tip of the organelle. This model receives support from a number of observations. First, in all situations where flagellar filament elongation has been observed, relatively high concentrations of flagellin are required (17). However, in cultures of bacteria, little or no flagellin subunit protein can be detected in the medium, thus eliminating the possibility that the subunit is excreted and then assembled from the outside of the bacterium. Second, in experiments where individual flagellar filaments on bacteria were completely coated with antibody, the filament was still able to elongate (48). Thus, the subunit is probably not transported along the outside of flagellar filament. Third, studies of the structure of the filament suggest that there is a central cavity that may be large enough to accommodate a single flagellin subunit (31). Furthermore, the rate of elongation was observed to decrease exponentially with the increasing length of the filament (65). This could readily be explained if the rate of growth was proportional to the transit time required for the subunit to reach the tip. As the filament got longer, subunits would be added more slowly. The maximal length of the filament depends upon the culture conditions, but it generally ranges from 16–22 μm.

The normal structure is 20 nm in diameter and has a wavelength of 2.3 μm. The shape of the flagellar filament depends upon conditions in the medium and upon the primary structure of the flagellin (71) subunit. Mutants have been isolated that have a variety of forms. Straight mutants have very short wavelengths or lack the helical wave entirely, and curly mutants form tighter helical waves than normal with wavelengths of 1.1 μm (68). The arrangement of flagellin subunits in the filaments of straight mutants from *Salmonella* (99) and *E. coli* (82) has been studied by optical diffraction of high-resolution electron micrographs. The subunits are arranged in a cylinder made up of 11 longitudinal rows. The subunits can also be seen as forming a helix with just under 11 subunits in two turns. Slight changes in orientation of the flagellin subunits within this basic structure can account for the superhelical forms the filament assumes (16, 32). These different forms have been observed to result from changes in the pH of the medium. For example, when the pH was decreased (77, 111), detached filaments underwent a transition from the normal superhelical form (2.3 μm) to the curly form (1.1 μm). This involved a change in helical handedness since the normal form is a left-handed superhelix and the curly form is a right-handed helix. The change has been observed to propagate along the flagellar filament (59). These kinds of transitions may also play a role in the swimming behavior of the organism. The normal-to-curly form transition of the flagellar bundle was initially observed 20 years ago and was referred to as biplicity (105). When bacteria swim smoothly in one direction, all of their flagella come together to form a single bundle, which takes on the normal helical form. Occasionally, cells stop smooth swimming and tumble (28). Tumbling appears to be correlated with a change in the shape (from normal to curly) of the flagellar filament. More recently, it has been possible to record the shape of individual filaments with dark field microscopy. By using this technique, the normal-to-curly transition has been correlated with tumbling activity (90). It has been suggested that this transition can be induced by the mechanical forces involved in rotating the flagellar filament and changing its direction of rotation (92).

The Hook Structure

The hook structure is located at the base of the flagellum. It is generally about 900 nm long and has a diameter slightly greater than that of the flagellar filament. It is composed primarily of a single polypeptide subunit with a molecular weight in *E. coli* (115) and *Salmonella* (76) of 42,000. The hook protein in *B. subtilis* has an apparent molecular weight of 33,000 (45). Both the hook polymer and the subunit have properties that are very different than those of flagellar filaments or flagellin. The hook is much more stable than the filament, so conditions of low pH, high concentrations of urea, organic solvents, or other denaturing agents that completely dissociate flagellar filaments have very little effect on the hook (1). This observation has been the basis for the separation of the hook from the filament. Specific antisera, against both the hook structure and the hook subunit protein, have been prepared. Antihook antiserum does not cross-react with flagellar filaments (45, 115). However, the antiserum shows a wider range of cross-reaction with other hook antigens (75). The hook structure may be more highly conserved than that of flagellin.

One of the difficulties involved in studying the hook subunit has been the availability of material. The hook represents only 1% of the total protein of the flagellar organelle. However, mutants have been found that cannot terminate hook formation and, therefore, overproduce the hook protein and form extended polyhook structures. These can be readily removed from the cell and purified. The mutations that cause the formation of polyhooks in *E. coli* (115) and *Salmonella* (103) do not affect the structure of the hook subunit. They probably affect the mechanism that regulates the termination of the hook structure. Hook subunits prepared from polyhook mutants and from wild-type flagella have the same antigenicity and show the same tryptic peptide maps (115; P. Matsumura, M. Silverman, and M. Simon, manuscript in preparation).

The structural gene for the hook subunit has been located on the *E. coli* genome (94). However, at present, there are no specific mutants that affect the antigenicity of the hook. Very little is known about the function of the hook. It is thought to act as a "universal joint" at the base of the filament and to allow the efficient transmission of rotational motion to the rest of the structure. The distal end of the hook structure acts as the initiation point for the growth of the filament (72), and the proximal end of the structure terminates in a rod inserted through the cell membranes to the basal structure (41, 45). The presence of the hook structure on the flagellar filament strongly stabilizes the structure of the filament (44). This observation may also add to an understanding of the role of the hook structure. Little is known about the mechanisms involved in regulating the length of the hook or assembling the hook. The discovery (94) of the structural gene that controls the hook protein may provide some insight into the role it plays in flagellar function and formation.

The Basal Structure

The basal structure accounts for about 1% of the mass of the organelle; however, it is the most complex part of the structure. The isolation of whole intact flagella from both *E. coli* and *B. subtilis* has allowed the initial exploration of the structure of the components of the base and their relationships to the cell membranes. *E. coli* and, in general, gram-negative organisms have four ringlike structures bound to the central rod, which ends in the hook structure (42). The outer rings are tightly bound to the lipopolysaccharide layer of the cell. The outer-most ring has been called the L-ring; the second ring has been called the P-ring and is presumed to be associated with the peptidoglycan layer. Figure 1 shows the insertion of the basal

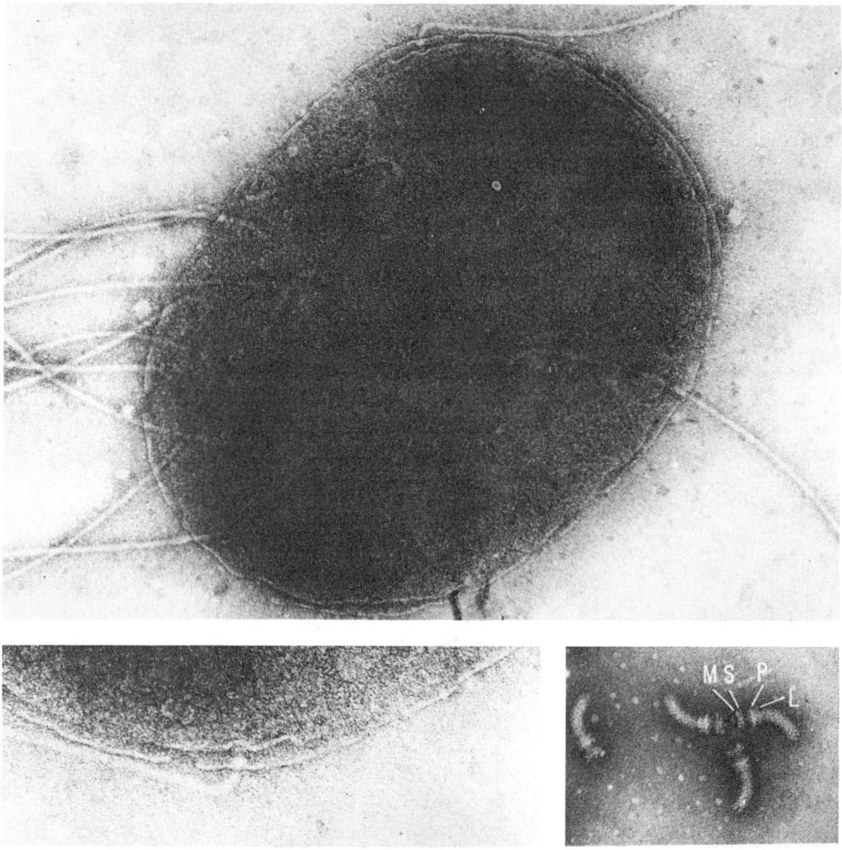

Figure 1 Insertion of the flagellar organelle of *Escherichia coli* into the cell membrane. Cells were plasmolysed to reveal attachment to inner and outer membranes (57) (*top, bottom left*). Purified isolated hook-basal structures are shown at bottom right. The apparent diameter of the hook structure is 17 nm.

complex into the membrane system and the morphology of the isolated structure. The two inner rings termed the S- and M-ring, appear to be in close contact with the plasma membrane. The M-ring is directly associated with the membrane and the S-ring is above the membrane (40, 43). In gram-positive organisms, the structure is less complex (3, 4, 45); only two rings have been found. The inner ring appears to be in contact with the plasma membrane of the cell, and the outer ring may be associated with the teichoic acid polymers on the outer surface of the cell.

The entire basal structure can be separated from the rest of the filament by using relatively mild procedures designed to dissociate the filament. The surviving hook and basal structure complex can then be separated and purified by differential centrifugation, isopycnic gradient centrifugation, and finally, by velocity gradient centrifugation (56, 57). The hook and basal structure was derived directly from bacteria by using mutants that could not make flagellin (124). These mutants make intact hook structures with no filaments (140). Membranes were isolated from the mutants, and the basal structure was released from the membranes (40) by detergent and purified. The basal complexes that were prepared by both of these procedures were dissociated, and 10 distinct polypeptide components were resolved from the dissociated structures (57). The polypeptides are listed in Table 1. They include the hook subunit with an apparent molecular weight of 42,000 and nine other polypeptides with molecular weights ranging from 60,000–9,000. The polypeptides were

Table 1 Flagellar components

Components (MW)	Location	Gene
54,000 (flagellin)	filament	*hag*
42,000	hook	*fla* region I
60,000	basal structure	*fla* region I
39,000	basal structure	*fla* region I
31,000	basal structure	*fla* region I
27,000	basal structure	*fla* region I
20,000	basal structure	not determined
18,000	basal structure	not determined
13,000	basal structure	not determined
11,000	basal structure	not determined
9,000	basal structure	not determined
31,000	inner membrane	*motA*
39,000	inner membrane	*motB*
76,000; 66,000	cytoplasm	*cheA*
12,000	cytoplasm	*cheW*
60,000; 61,000; 63,000	inner membrane	*cheM*
38,000	cytoplasm	*cheX*
28,000	cytoplasm	*cheB*
8,000	cytoplasm	*cheY*
24,000	cytoplasm	*cheZ*
64,000; 65,000	inner membrane	*cheD*

also characterized by two-dimensional polyacrylamide gel electrophoresis. Although there were clearly 10 polypeptides associated with the structure that has the morphology of the hook and basal components, there could also be other necessary structural components that were lost during the purification. For example, polypeptides with apparent molecular weights of 36,000 and 74,000 were found at early stages of the preparation but not after extensive purification (57). Furthermore, in occasional preparations, the 60,000-molecular-weight component was resolved into two bands. Thus, the structure may have as many as 13 components and as few as 10. At present, there is no functional assay for the purity of the preparation. Essentially, each of the specific polypeptides will have to be associated with the gene that regulates its structure and formation. By completely cataloguing these parts, a clearer picture of the entire structure will be obtained.

On the basis of occasional electron micrographs, it has been suggested that other structures exist that are associated with the base of the flagellum in *E. coli* (22). Evidence for these structures in other bacterial species has been obtained by electron microscopy (98). It is clear that the flagellar system in *E. coli* and *Salmonella* includes components that are localized in the cytoplasm and the cell membranes, in addition to the basal components that have been identified. These may be part of a labile structure or they may have some intermittent association with the basal structure. If such structures exist, techniques for fixing and stabilizing them will have to be developed before they can be isolated.

In recent work, the use of hybrid plasmids and phages carrying *E. coli* flagellar genes to stimulate specific synthesis of flagellar components has revealed that the synthesis of at least five of the basal complex components is controlled by genes that map in flagellar region I on the *E. coli* genome (Figure 2). The polypeptides include the hook subunit, a 60,000-molecular-weight polypeptide, a 39,000-molecular-weight subunit, and the 30,000- and 27,000-molecular-weight polypeptides (94). This approach should eventually establish all of the genes that control the structural components of the organelle. Furthermore, the isolation and characterization of the polypeptide components opens the way for partial dissociation studies to determine which of the polypeptides are concerned with the assembly of individual basal complex structures. Region I may carry most of the genes that control the structure of the basal complex. The genetic analysis of this region has not yet been completed.

THE GENETIC BASIS FOR FLAGELLAR FORMATION

Mutant Phenotypes

The isolation of mutants defective in the synthesis and function of the flagellar organelle was facilitated by the discovery of the phage chi (97). The flagellar filament acts as part of the phage receptor for this virus and similar viruses. The course of events in chi infection was inferred to involve the following steps: the attachment of the phage tail fibers to the flagellar filament; the movement of the phage down the filament to the base of the flagellum; and the injection of the phage DNA in the vicinity of the flagellar basal structure (109). An active flagellum is required for chi infection (134). This requirement may reflect the ability of the flagellum to move

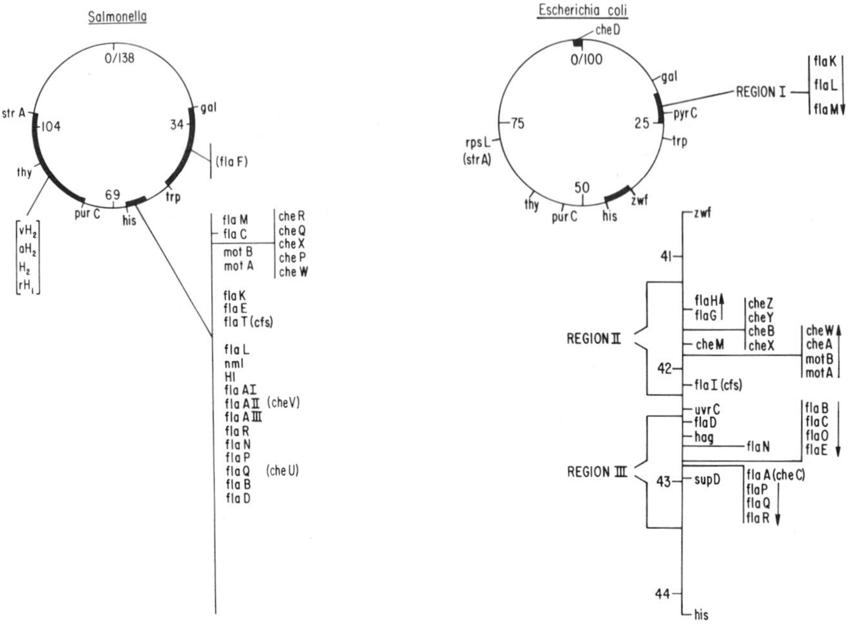

Figure 2 Distribution of flagellar genes on the genetic maps of *Salmonella* (*left*) and *Escherichia coli* (*right*).

the attached phage down the filament, or it may result from some property of a basal component necessary for phage injection. Strains of *E. coli* and *Salmonella* resistant to chi have three phenotypes: Mot⁻ strains, which have flagella that appear to be normal but that are "paralyzed" because the flagellar filaments do not rotate; Hag⁻ strains, which have flagella that are altered in configuration or antigenicity or which lack flagellar filaments entirely [these result from mutations in the structural gene for the flagellin subunit (97); in *Salmonella,* there are two genes, H1 and H2, whereas in *E. coli,* there is a single *hag* gene]; and Fla⁻ strains, which have no apparent flagellar structures, although closer scrutiny reveals partial or defective structures in some of the mutants.

Another group of mutant strains was selected by repeated propagation from the center of stabs on motility agar. In addition to Mot⁻, Fla⁻, and Hag⁻ strains, other strains that were motile but defective in chemotaxis Che⁻ were found (15). These were sensitive to chi infection and were able to swim in liquid media. However, they showed aberrant swimming behavior and did not respond to gradients of attractants or repellants. A variety of other selection procedures have been used to obtain Che⁻ mutants (20, 69, 100, 136), and their behavior has been examined extensively. They fail to show the normal change in the frequency of tumbles (abrupt changes in direction of travel) when subjected to a chemotactic stimulus (28, 100). One group of Che⁻ mutants tumbled incessantly whereas another rarely tumbled. Both classes of Che⁻ mutants are presumably defective in their ability to integrate input information and to transmit it to the flagellar organelle (101). Many mutants defective in components of the chemotaxis system have been isolated, including mutants in specific chemoreceptors. Some of the receptors correspond to components of systems for the transport of sugars and amino acids (6, 8, 55). Here, we are concerned with the chemotaxis mutants that directly impinge upon the flagellar organellar function, i.e. mutants defective in general chemotaxis.

Flagellar Genes in Salmonella

Transduction with phage P22 (51, 52, 66, 74, 130) and colicinogenic factor-mediated transfer (125) was used to establish the linkage relationships between flagellar genes and other loci in *Salmonella.* Complementation tests were performed by measuring the occurrence of abortive transductants, which appeared on semisolid growth media as trails of microcolonies emanating from the zone of inoculation of the transduction mixture. More recently, extensive analysis with overlapping deletions (58, 139) has established the order of many of the genes and their precise map positions in *Salmonella.* For the sake of discussion, it is worthwhile to consider the genes linked to H1 as being in two clusters so that they correspond to the homologous regions in *E. coli.* Region III would include the cistrons *flaD, flaB, flaQ, flaP, flaN, flaR, flaAIII, flaAII, flaAI,* H1, *nml, flaL.* Region II includes the cistrons *flaT, flaE, flaK,* (order uncertain) *motA, motB, cheW, cheP, cheX, cheQ, cheR, flaC,* and *flaM.* The analysis of region I in *Salmonella* is incomplete. There are probably a number of cistrons that map in this region (between *trp* and *gal*); however, they are only represented by *flaF* (66, 125). Finally, there is a region in *Salmonella* that has no homologue in *E. coli,* i.e. the phase 2 region. The precise map position of these genes has not been defined. They are between *purC* and *strA* (93, 125) and include the structural gene for the phase 2 antigen, H2, a gene that specifies the synthesis of a repressor of phase 1 (*rh1*) (54), a region that regulates phase transition (*vh2*) (60), as well as a regulator of the expression of the phase 2 gene product (aH2) (61).

Chemotaxis mutants were isolated and mapped between *motB* and *flaC,* as well as within the *flaAII* gene (36). More recently, a large number of Che⁻ mutants in *Salmonella* were collected by using preformed vertical gradients of chemoattractants (20, 137). Complementation tests divided these mutants into nine cistrons (137). The map positions of these genes are shown in Figure 2. Two groups have not yet been mapped. At least two of the *che* mutant groups coincide with *fla* mutants, a situation also found when *che* and *fla* mutants are compared in *E. coli* (see below).

Flagellar Genes in E. coli

Genetic experimentation to define flagellar genes in *E. coli,* in contrast to the work with *Salmonella,* began with the characterization of mutants defective in chemotaxis. In addition to the Che⁻ mutants and the Mot⁻ mutants, Fla⁻ mutants were also isolated, and three regions of the genome were defined (12–15) where all of these mutations mapped. In subsequent studies, large numbers of chi-resistant mutant strains were ordered into complementation groups, by using F factors and Rec⁻ hosts (116). Further genetic analysis with strains carrying mu phage-induced mutations defined additional *fla* cistrons and revealed the transcriptional organization of the flagellar genes (117). Two- and three-factor transductional crosses with phage P1 were used to establish the relative linkage of the genes (116). Finally, recombination tests with F' factors carrying overlapping deletions were used to establish the linear order of the genes (118). These approaches and subsequent work established 11 flagella-related genes in region III (*flaR, flaQ, flaP, flaA, flaE, flaO, flaC, flaB, flaN, hag, flaD*) and 12 in region II (*flaI, motA, motB, cheA, cheW, cheM, cheX, cheB, cheY, cheZ, flaG, flaH*). The analysis in region I is continuing; thus far, at least three cistrons (*flaK, flaL, flaM*) have been defined (56). Each flagellar gene region will be considered separately, beginning with region III (see Figure 2).

FlaA, flaP, flaQ, and *flaR* are all cotranscribed. Mutants belonging to the *flaA* complementation groups have two phenotypes: some lack flagella entirely whereas others are motile but not chemotactic. It has been suggested (117) that the *flaA* gene product has dual functions, as a structural component of the organelle as well as a part of the chemotactic pathway. A similar argument holds for the genes in region III in *Salmonella* that show both phenotypes (137). *FlaB, flaC, flaO,* and *flaE* also form a cotranscribed unit. Mutations in *flaE* lead to a distinctive phenotype. The strains have long polyhook-like structures with occasional flagellar filaments attached to the distal end. The hook subunit protein extracted from polyhooks and from hook structures on isolated flagella are identical. Deletions of *flaE* or mu-induced mutations mapping in *flaE* also result in polyhooks. This data has been taken to mean that *flaE* is involved in regulating the length of the hook rather than in specifying the structure of the hook subunit (115). A gene with a similar function, *flaR,* has been characterized in *Salmonella* (103). The function of *flaB, flaC,* and *flaO* is not known.

The *hag* gene controls the structure of flagellin and maps between *flaN* and *flaD.* Mutations that eliminate filament formation result in cells that still have the flagellar basal structures and hooks (124, 140). Some mutations that map in the *flaD* gene also appear to have hooklike structures, but not all mutations in *flaD* have the hook (M. Hilmen and M. Simon, unpublished results). The formation of flagellar filaments in many gram-negative bacteria is temperature sensitive, so cells grown at 42°C do not make flagella (95, 106). When the temperature is decreased to 33°C flagella synthesis resumes. Mutants can be isolated that are insensitive to temperature and, thus, that form flagella and swim even at 42°C. Some of these mutants appear to map in or near the *flaD* gene (M. Silverman and M. Simon, unpublished results). The characterization of flagellar mutants in region III has been repeated by using entirely different techniques (81). Lambda was inserted near the *supD* gene, and then a series of deletions were prepared that removed the genes in region III that controlled flagellar synthesis. Complementation and mapping of flagellar mutants by using these strains and a variety of other mutants agreed, on the whole, with earlier reports; there was one exception, the suggestion of a new complementation group between *hag* and *flaD.*

Ultimately, the genes have to be defined in terms of both their complementation activity and their products. The recent introduction of molecular cloning techniques has allowed this kind of analysis to be applied to the flagellar-related genes in region II. The gene products were identified by using two different systems. (*a*) Bacteriophage lambda was used as a vehicle, and Eco R1 restriction endonuclease fragments carrying flagellar genes were inserted into the vehicle in place of a dispensible region. These hybrids could then be used to infect ultraviolet-irradiated hosts that were lysogenic for lambda. Ultraviolet irradiation eliminated host DNA expression and the resident lambda repressor eliminated lambda gene expression so that the major incorporation of radioactivity was into polypeptides coded for by the inserted DNA. Deletions of the hybrid lambda generally resulted in the elimination of specific portions of the inserted piece. By using the deletions, it became possible to correlate the presence of a gene product with a specific genetic complementation activity. Finally, the *flaI* gene product appeared to be necessary for the synthesis of many of the other flagellar gene products (120). In cells that carried a *flaI* mutation, flagellar genes carried on lambda were not expressed. This allowed a further test for the specificity of a putative flagellar gene product. It should be produced in $FlaI^+$ host cells but not an $FlaI^-$ cells (112). (*b*) Colicinogenic factor E1 was used as the cloning vehicle, and sheared fragments of the *E. coli* genome were used as the inserted piece. Clarke & Carbon (34) used the enzyme terminal transferase to elongate the fragments and the vehicle with either a short polyadenylic acid chain or a polythymidylic acid chain (34). These "tails" were used to form hybrids between the Col El and the randomly sheared DNA fragments from *E. coli.* After transformation, a large number of individual clones were picked, and the colony bank was shown to contain representatives of all of the regions of the *E. coli* genome, including the flagellar genes. The hybrid plasmids carrying flagellar genes were transferred to a strain of *E. coli* that produced minicells (which lack a nucleus but retain the capacity to synthesize proteins). The hybrid plasmid segregated in to the minicells. Thus, if the minicells were purified and their expression was followed, they were found to synthesize the polypeptides directed by genes on the hybrid plasmid (107). Restriction enzymes could be used to prepare deletions of the plasmid. Furthermore, since the initial colony bank was made from fragments of DNA with random end points, different plasmids carried different subsets of genes, and again the presence or absence of a specific polypeptide could be correlated with the residual complementation activity of the plasmid in genetic tests.

In addition to identifying gene products, these techniques have also helped to clarify the genetics in region II. Initially, the results of complementation tests were interpreted in terms of the minimum number of cistrons. It was suggested that *mot* could be a single cistron with two parts showing intracistronic complementation (12). The *cheA* and *cheB* loci were also defined as single genes containing subgroups that showed intracistronic complementation (13, 102). It is now clear that the gene formerly referred to as *cheA* is made up of two genes, *cheA* and *cheW* (123). *Mot* is composed of two cistrons, *motA* and *motB,* and *motA, motB, cheA,* and *cheW* form a cotranscribed unit that has been referred to as the Mocha operon (114, 122, 123). The gene product formed by *motA* was a 31,000-molecular-weight polypeptide, and the product of the *motB* gene had an apparent molecular weight of 39,000. The *cheA* gene directed the synthesis of two polypeptides with apparent molecular weights of 66,000 and 76,000. The evidence that both gene products resulted from the *cheA* gene is twofold: physical measurements of the length of the DNA between *motA* and *cheW* indicated that it was not long enough to accommodate the synthesis of two contiguous polypeptides of 76,000 and 66,000 molecular weights; peptide map analysis of the two polypeptides indicated that they have most of their peptides in common. The *cheW* gene product has an apparent molecular weight of 12,000 (122, 123).

Studies of the polypeptides synthesized by deleted hybrid phages indicated that there was a region adjacent to the *cheW* gene responsible for the synthesis of a group of polypeptides that appeared on sodium dodecyl sulfate-acrylamide gel electrophoresis as three bands. This group of bands, called triplet, had apparent molecular weights corresponding to 63,000, 61,000, and 60,000. The region responsible for the synthesis of this group of bands has been called *cheM* (113). The multiple bands have properties on polyacrylamide gel electrophoresis that are similar to those of other polypeptides called MCP (methyl-accepting chemotaxis protein). MCP has been identified as a membrane protein that was methylated reversibly and its methylation was related to chemotaxis (84). It has been suggested that MCP is the same as triplet and that the *cheM* gene is responsible for the synthesis of these polypeptides. However, analysis of the genetic basis of the formation of MCP indicated (M. Silverman and M. Simon, manuscript in preparation) that these polypeptides were the products of two different chemotaxis genes, *cheM* and *cheD.* When strains that carried deletions in the *cheM* gene were constructed, they were found to be capable of chemotaxis toward some attractants, e.g. serine, but not toward others, e.g. aspartate. Their phenotype was that of previously described (95a) aspartate taxis mutants. Furthermore, these mutants no longer formed all of the MCP polypeptides; the lower-molecular-weight bands (60,000, 61,000) were missing. However, they were able to form methylated proteins with higher apparent molecular weights (greater than 63,000). In experiments with wild-type cells, the lower-molecular-weight MCP polypeptides were found to be preferentially methylated when the cells were stimulated with aspartate. When serine was used as attractant, the higher-molecular-weight components of MCP were preferentially methylated. The null phenotype of the chemotaxis gene *cheD,* which maps near *thr* (Figure 2), was lack of serine taxis (100), and the product of the *cheD* gene was shown to correspond to a polypeptide with an approximate molecular weight of 64,000 (M. Silverman and M. Simon, manuscript in preparation). Mutants in the *cheD* gene no longer methylated the higher-molecular-weight MCP components but were able to form the lower-molecular-weight MCP polypeptides. The double mutant *cheM, cheD* was found to be unresponsive to attractants and repellents. It formed no detectable MCP polypeptides with molecular weights in the 60,000–65,000 range. Thus, the *cheD* and *cheM* genes account for the synthesis of the MCP polypeptides (approximately 60,000- to 65,000-molecular-weight polypeptides).

Adjacent to the *cheM* gene is the *cheB* complex. This is composed of four genes, *cheX, cheB, cheY,* and *cheZ*: the product of the *cheX* gene had a molecular weight of 28,000; the *cheB* gene product had a molecular weight of 38,000, whereas *cheY,* which is adjacent to *cheB,* made a polypeptide with a molecular weight of 8000; and *cheZ* was responsible for the synthesis of a 24,000-molecular-weight polypeptide. All four of these genes may be cotranscribed, beginning with *cheX* and reading through *cheZ* (123).

There are at least three other flagellar-related genes in this region, *flaI, flaG,* and *flaH. FlaI* has associated with it a region called *cfs.* This appears to be a regulatory region that makes the synthesis of *flaI* dependent upon the presence of cAMP. The *flaI* product was clearly involved in the positive control of the entire flagellar gene complex (120). However, this polypeptide and the polypeptides corresponding to the *flaG* and *flaH* genes have not been identified. They may be synthesized at levels much lower than the level of synthesis of the *mot* and *che* gene products. Although the products of *flaG* and *flaH* are not known, they may function to influence the association of the basal structure with the outer membrane (79).

The techniques involving molecular cloning are also being applied to regions I and III in *E. coli.* It appears that many of the genes responsible for polypeptides that make up the hook and the basal structures map in region I. Experiments involving protein synthesis directed by specific plasmids segregated into minicells indicated that the 60,000-molecular-weight polypeptide, the hook subunit (42,000), and the 39,000- as well as the 30,000- and 27,000-molecular-weight subunit components of the basal structure were all synthesized when plasmids carrying region I are used (94). Initially, only three genes, *flaK, flaL,* and *flaM,* that formed a cotranscribed unit were described (56). However, more recent complementation tests suggest that there are more genes in this region. Thus far, at least six have been identified (Y. Komeda, M. Silverman, and M. Simon, unpublished results).

The polypeptides synthesized in ultraviolet-irradiated cells infected with deleted hybrid phage were able to function. Mot$^-$ or Che$^-$ host cells acquired the missing activity after infection with the phage (114, 122). In these cells, the gene products must be able to be inserted into structures and membranes so that they can function properly. The localization of the polypeptides was followed. The *cheD, cheM, motA,* and *motB* gene products are localized exclusively in the inner membrane of the cell. The products of the *cheA, cheW, cheX, cheB, cheY,* and *cheZ* genes seem to be in the cytoplasm, although it would be difficult to eliminate the possibility that they have a labile or transient association with the inner membrane (H. Ridgeway, M. Silverman, and M. Simon, manuscript in preparation). The hook, basal body complex, and flagellar filament are usually isolated with the outer membrane fraction of the cell (56). Thus, the products of the genes that direct flagellar structure and function are found in almost all of the compartments of the cell (Table 1).

We can expect that all of the products of the flagellar genes will be identified in the next few years. The gene products from region II, particularly the *mot* and *che* gene products, are synthesized in relatively large amounts. The products of many of the *fla* genes may be synthesized at lower levels. However, there are a variety of ways in which the levels of these gene products can be increased so that they may be identified. Once the gene products and their localization is known, it should be possible to determine their specific function in flagellar assembly and activity.

Comparison of Flagellar Genes in E. coli and Salmonella

It is clear from a comparison of the *E. coli* and *Salmonella* genetic maps (Figure 2) that there is a great deal of homology in the distribution of flagellar genes. However, it was not easy to make a gene by gene correspondence. Thus, for example, *flaR* in *Salmonella* and *flaE* in *E. coli* are functionally equivalent and yet are not congruent with respect to the *fla* genes on either side of them. Furthermore, *Salmonella* appeared to have gene functions that were not found in *E. coli.* For example, *nml,* the gene responsible for the methylation of flagellin, was present in *Salmonella* but not in *E. coli* (83, 129). Cross-species complementation tests between *Salmonella* and *E. coli fla* functions have been done with a number of the genes, and there is usually no difficulty in demonstrating complementation. An F' carrying *che* genes from *E. coli* complemented *che* defects in *Salmonella* (137). In two cases where *fla* genes were functionally equivalent with respect to complementation activity, their map order was reversed: *flaC* in *Salmonella* corresponded to *flaH* in *E. coli* and *flaM* in *Salmonella* corresponded to *flaG* (35a). These kinds of changes in gene positions may be very interesting in terms of the evolution of the *E. coli* and *Salmonella* genomes.

REGULATION OF FLAGELLAR SYNTHESIS

The bacterial flagellar structure is complex; it requires more than 25 specific gene products for its assembly and function. These are required in varying amounts, ranging from a minimum of 1 polypeptide per organelle to about 10,000 (flagellin). The organelle is assembled and integrated into the cell membrane system, and the distribution and number of flagella per cell appears to be regulated. However, very little is known about the coordination of flagellar gene activity, i.e. does the orderly assembly of the organelle require a specific sequence of gene expression? At present, the answer can only be a tentative yes, since our information about regulation is fragmentary. Most of the observations suggesting regulation of parts of the flagella forming pathway involve the regulation of flagellin synthesis. As information about the other gene products becomes available, the mechanisms that regulate their formation and interaction will become clearer.

Phase Variation in Salmonella

Most *Salmonella* species have been shown to possess two distinct flagellar antigens (flagellin subunit) that differ markedly from each other (9). A given bacterium generally expresses only one flagellar antigen (phase) at any time. The transition from the expression of one phase to the other occurs at a fixed frequency that ranges from 10^{-3}–10^{-5} per bacterium per generation. The frequency of transition in one direction is generally different than the frequency in the reverse direction (93, 128). Lederberg & Iino (89) showed that two loci, H1 and H2 (Figure 2), were the structural genes for phase 1 and phase 2 flagellin. They also showed that the phase expressed in the bacterium was determined by the "state" of the phase 2 gene or by some closely linked phase-determining factor. Thus, in one state, H2 was expressed and H1 repressed, whereas in the other state, H2 was not expressed and H1 was expressed. Enomoto & Stocker (53) have recently reviewed the properties of the other genetic elements involved in regulating phase transition. *rh1* is a gene thought to control the formation of a repressor substance that can act through the cytoplasm (in *trans*) to repress the synthesis of the H1 gene product. The expression of *rh1* appears to be coordinate with H2 gene expression (54, 104). Another locus, *ah2*, is defined by mutations that prevent the expression of H2 and *rh1*. Mutations in *ah2* only affect the genes that are *cis* to the mutation. Thus, *ah2* could be the promotor for the *H2* and *rh1* genes. Another *cis* acting element is *vh2*. The wild-type allele $vh2^+$ presumably allows phase variation at frequencies of 10^{-3}–10^{-5} per bacterium per generation. The $vh2^-$ allele can have two possible phenotypes. One phenotype is $H2^{on}$, in which only H2 is expressed and the frequency of transition to H1 gene expression is very low (10^{-6}–10^{-7} per bacterium per generation). In the other phenotype, $H2^{off}$, the *vh2* mutation fixes expression so that only the H1 gene is expressed (54, 60). The following facts suggest that the phase switch involves a change at the DNA level: *vh2* only acts *cis* to the H2 gene, thus it must affect a region of DNA contiguous with H2; the state of the gene can be transduced, and since the transducing phage carries the donors DNA, the state of the gene must be a function of that DNA; and no H2 mRNA can be found when H2 is off, suggesting that regulation is at the transcriptional level (131). On the other hand, it was observed that, when the H2 gene, which was not expressed in *Salmonella* because of the presence of $vh2^-$, was transferred to *E. coli*, it was expressed and showed phase transition. When it was transferred back to *Salmonella*, it again showed only low levels of phase transition (53). This observation suggests that, although the primary switch involves a change at the DNA level, the regulation of the frequency of switching (*vh2*) may involve other cytoplasmic factors.

There have been a variety of models proposed to explain the mechanism of phase variation. These were reviewed by Iino (63). Recently, evidence has developed for a model that involves the inversion of a segment of DNA adjacent to the H2 gene. The *Salmonella* H2 gene (phase 2) was cloned from an Eco R1 endonuclease digest of *Salmonella* DNA and from randomly sheared fragments of *Salmonella* DNA. When these DNA fragments were treated with endonuclease, heat denatured, and reannealed, a small region corresponding to a bubble was observed by electron microscopy (Figure 3). Furthermore, by using various restriction enzymes and retransformation with restricted plasmids, the DNA region coding for H2 formation was mapped to the segment of DNA adjoining the apparent anomaly in the DNA. The DNA was also inserted into a lambda bacteriophage vehicle (charon 1), and the expression of H2 in individual clones of lambda phage was examined. The lambda was used to transduce the H2 gene. Two kinds of lambdas were found in all single plaques: high-level transducers presumed to correspond to phase 2-on, and low-level transducers thought to represent phage particles carrying phase 2-off. When DNA from each of the populations was denatured and reannealed with itself, low levels of bubbles were found (2% for phase 2-off and 12% for phase 2-on). When they were mixed and heteroduplexed, a large fraction of the molecules showed the apparent inversion structure (34%). These experiments were interpreted as indicat-

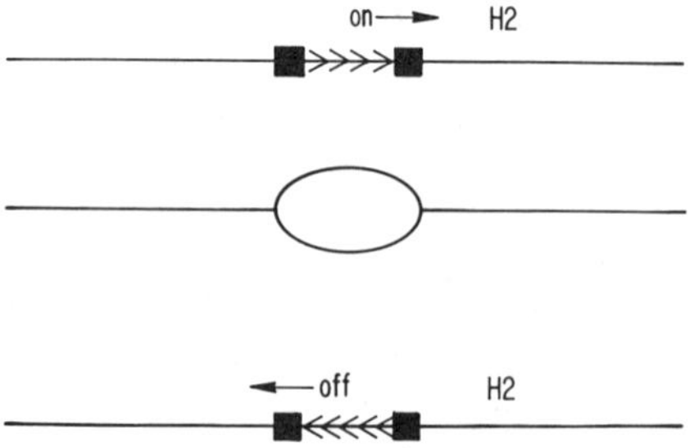

Figure 3 A model for phase variation. An inversion of the sequence between the dark blocks could result in a change in the orientation of a promotor contained within the region or it could allow read-through from a promotor outside the region.

ing that the apparent bubble structure is the result of a heteroduplex of phase 2-off and phase 2-on DNA. This suggested that phase variation resulted from an inversion in a region that controls the initiation of H2 gene transcription (142). In one orientation transcription occurs, whereas in the other it does not (see Figure 3). Molecules associated by a duplex region that corresponded to the bubble with nonhomologous single-stranded ends were observed among the heteroduplexes. These findings give strong support to the inversion hypothesis. Testable hypotheses to explain phase variation at the molecular level and the material to do the appropriate experiments now exist. There are a number of intriguing mysteries that can be addressed in this system. For example, what is the role of the *vh2* element and how does it control the rate of phase transition? Why are the frequencies of transition from phase 2-on to phase 2-off different in opposite directions? What kind of mechanism is involved in the transition itself, i.e. does it require the *rec* system of the host cell or is there an independent enzyme system for phase variation? The answers to these questions may also give some insight into the extent to which the mechanism represents a general kind of regulatory system found in both prokaryotic and eukaryotic organisms.

Catabolite Repression of Flagella Formation

Synthesis of the flagellar organelle in *E. coli* is repressed by growth in glucose and a variety of catabolites (7). The repression could be reversed by the addition of cAMP (46). Furthermore, *E. coli* and *Salmonella* strains defective in adenylcyclase (*cya*) or in the cAMP receptor protein (*crp*) were unable to synthesize that flagellar organelle (141). All of these observations suggested that cAMP exercised its regulation of flagellar formation through the binding of a cAMP-CRP complex to the flagellar genes to activate their expression. To define the site of regulation, mutants able to synthesize flagella were selected in a parent strain that was Crp$^-$. A number of these mutants were mapped. They defined a new locus designated *cfs* (constitutive flagellar synthesis), which mapped adjacent to or as part of the *flaI* gene in *E. coli.* For *cfs* to function, even when it was on an exogenotic fragment, it was necessary that the adjacent *flaI* gene were intact and functional. The *cfs* mutation had pleiotropic effects: it allowed flagellar synthesis in Cya$^-$ and Crp$^-$ strains and in cells grown under catabolite repressing conditions; it increased the number of flagella per cell by two- to threefold; it allowed some synthesis of flagella when the cells were grown at 42°C; and it allowed the intracellular synthesis of hook subunit and *hag* gene fragments in Cya^- and Crp^- strains (120).

In *Salmonella,* a mutation *flaT* similar to *cfs* was described. Although catabolites have very little effect on flagellar synthesis in *Salmonella,* H1- and H2-specific RNA were not present in Cya^- strains unless cAMP was added or the *flaT* mutation was present (80). All of these results have been interpreted to mean that *cfs* defines a site at which a CRP-cAMP complex acts to activate the expression of the *flaI* gene.

The *flaI* gene product was essential for the expression of a large variety of flagellar genes. In experiments with cloned flagellar genes on hybrid lambda in ultraviolet-irradiated cells, the synthesis of the *mot, che,* and *hag* gene products required the presence of the *flaI* gene product (112–114, 122, 123). Thus, *flaI* appeared to have an "executive" role in the management of flagellar regulation. It may function to induce the expression of all of the flagellar gene groups simultaneously, or it may have a sequential effect, i.e. *flaI* could stimulate the synthesis of one group of flagellar genes and the product of these genes could in a sequential manner induce the expression of another group.

Flagellar formation in gram-negative cells is generally temperature sensitive (106). A series of strains able to form flagella when grown at high temperatures (42°C) were isolated. Mutations in these strains were found to map at two loci in or near the *flaI* and the *flaD* genes, suggesting that an interaction between the *flaI* and *flaD* product might be necessary for temperature sensitivity (M. Silverman and M. Simon, unpublished results). The interaction of the *flaI* gene product with other *fla* genes could be necessary for the orderly assembly of the components of the organelle.

Regulation of Flagellin Synthesis

A number of attempts have been made to find intracellular pools of flagellin subunits in a variety of *hag* and *fla* mutants, as well as in the wild-type cell. *E. coli* flagellin pools were not found except in some *hag* amber mutants of *E. coli* where an immunologically active fragment has been detected (120). These results suggested that when effective *hag* subunits are synthesized they are assembled into the growing flagellar structure almost immediately. It has been observed that, when there was a temporary derepression of phase 1 flagellin synthesis in *Salmonella* that were in phase 2, the newly synthesized material appeared as a block of phase 1 flagellin on the tips of the growing phase 2 filaments (70). On the other hand, when both kinds of flagellins were synthesized simultaneously, they formed totally mixed sections of flagellar filament (119). Thus, if there were a pool of subunits, it was very small and could not sustain filament assembly for more than 2 or 3 min. The absence of pools of missense mutant subunits suggested that they are either degraded or can effectively repress their own synthesis (120).

The presence of intact hook structures on the *hag,* H1 or H2 mutants suggests that the flagellin subunit is not necessary for the synthesis of the other structural proteins (124, 140). There is evidence, however, indicating that the presence of other *fla* gene products is necessary to get *hag, mot,* and *che* gene expression. Most *fla* mutants do not make flagellin or the intracellular flagellin amber mutant polypeptide fragment (120). In *Salmonella,* 11 different *fla* mutants were tested and none of them had detectable levels of mRNA for flagellin (132). This effect was not restricted to flagellin. In many *fla* mutants, only low levels of the MCP products were found (84). Furthermore, when a *flaB* mutant was used as host for protein synthesis directed by hybrid lambda, the *mot, che,* and *hag* genes were not expressed (M. Silverman and M. Simon, unpublished results). These observations support the idea that there may be an hierarchical order of *fla* gene regulation. Thus, for example, the *flaI* gene product may be required for the expression of a number of first-tier operons, and some of the products of these genes could act to induce the expression of second-tier genes. The precise scheme of things may come clear from further studies of the expression of cloned genes in specific backgrounds.

FLAGELLAR FUNCTION

Investigation of the structure and genetics of the flagellar organelle ultimately should provide an explanation in molecular terms of the actual function of the organelle. Flagellar function can be divided into several questions. How does the flagellum propel the cell? How is this motion orchestrated to provide purposeful movement? What is the source of energy for flagellar movement? How are chemotactic signals processed to direct flagellar movement?

Flagellar filaments propel the cell by rotating. The helical filament is driven by a rotary motor at the base, part of which is the basal structure embedded in the cell membrane. Arguments for a rotary motor have been made from existing evidence (27). Conclusive evidence for this type of motion was provided by tethering experiments that measured the rotation resulting from the torque generated by the flagellar organelle. It was shown that when mutants with only polyhook structures (Hag$^-$, FlaE$^-$) were tethered to glass slides with antibody to *E. coli* hooks, the cell body rotated. This rotation was also demonstrated with cells with straight filaments. When these cells were free, they were non-motile, but when tethered, the cells spun at 10–20 revolutions per sec. Rotation could be clockwise or counterclockwise, and it was suggested that the ability to modulate the direction of rotation might be the basis for the mechanism of chemotaxis (121). The dynamic properties of flagellar motors have been extensively analyzed by using tethering experiments (23, 26).

When the paths of cells of *E. coli* swimming in an isotropic environment were measured, the motion was of two types: straight movement (runs) terminated by occasional abrupt changes in direction (twiddles, tumbles). The net result was a three-dimensional random walk. In spacial gradients of attractant (i.e. serine, aspartate), cells swimming up the gradient tumbled less, whereas cells swimming down the gradient tumbled at the same frequency as in an isotropic solution. *E. coli,* therefore, biased its random walk in a favorable direction by suppressing tumbles when movement was in that direction (28). With *Salmonella,* paths of movement were measured after rapid mixing in an apparatus, which allowed the formation of temporal gradients of attractant. A sudden decrease in attractant concentration resulted in an increased, if short lived, tumbling response, and a sudden increase in attractant concentration resulted in a long suppression of tumbling; swimming was only in long, smooth runs. The response to attractants was very similar to that of *E. coli,* and in addition, it was obvious that cells must sense attractant concentrations with time. This implied the existence of a memory of the stimuli sensed. Cells swimming in a spacial gradient sense differences in concentrations of attractant with respect to time as they move through space (91). The response of *E. coli* to temporal gradients was measured with similar results (30). Attractants and repellants had opposite effects, and the response depended upon the time rate of change of the fractional amount of chemoreceptor bound (37, 38, 96, 135). For a review of the detailed mechanism of chemotaxis, see Adler (4), Berg (25), Parkinson (101), and Koshland et al (85, 86).

Using tethered *E. coli* cells to infer the direction of filament rotation, it was shown that the direction of flagellar rotation correlated with chemotactic behavior (88). Wild-type cells stimulated with attractant rotated their filaments counterclockwise, and those stimulated by repellant rotated their filaments clockwise. Che$^-$ mutants with the ever-tumbling phenotype (uncoordinated) rotated their filaments in the clockwise direction, and Che$^-$ mutants, which swam smoothly, rotated their filaments in the counterclockwise direction. Thus, smooth swimming correlated with counterclockwise rotation and tumbling correlated with clockwise rotation. A swimming response was determined by the direction of filament rotation. Explanation of why counterclockwise rotation gave smooth swimming and clockwise rotation gave tumbly swimming has been based on the properties of filament interaction (90, 92).

Motility in eukaryotes has been shown to require ATP (108), but ATPase activity has not been demonstrated in isolated flagellar structures (43, 51). Recent isolation of mutants in *E. coli* and *Salmonella* blocked in steps in oxidative phosphorylation has allowed the definition of the source of energy for flagellar movement. By using these mutants and uncouplers of oxidative phosphorylation, it was shown that an intermediate of oxidative phosphorylation (i.e. proton motive force), not ATP, was required for bacterial motility (87, 134). This was true for clockwise or counterclockwise rotation (87), although in one report (21), ATP-depleted cells showed only counterclockwise rotation. Significantly, ATP was required for chemotaxis (21, 87). This may reflect a requirement for ATP in the formation of S-adenosylmethionine (see below). Certain components of ion flux have been shown to correlate with the application of chemotactic stimuli and to be missing in Mot$^-$ mutants (133). Since the products of the *mot* and *che* genes have been identified and their localization in the cell has been determined (113, 114, 122, 123), an examination of their properties as ion gates or regulators of ion gates will be interesting.

The phenotypes of generally nonchemotactic mutants (Che$^-$) suggested that the *che* gene products acted in the transduction of sensory information from the chemoreceptors to the flagellar motor. It has been suggested that some *che* gene products associate to act as a "tumble generator," whereas other *che* gene products integrate information from chemoreceptors and influence the activity of the tumble generator (101). A general model for sensory systems designed to account for the memory and the adaptive properties, i.e. the adjustment of the system to ranges of input signal, was proposed by Delbrück and Reichardt (39a). They postulated a bifurcation of input information so that an integrative process accumulated the signal while a second process instantaneously monitored the environment. A comparison between these information pools accounted for the responsive properties of the system. Several decision-making models have been proposed for chemotaxis (29, 91), involving two process mechanisms, i.e. comparison between a signal reservoir and an adaptation reservoir (29), or comparison between a fast and slow reaction, which is itself influenced by signal input (91).

Biochemical approaches to determining the nature of sensory information and sensory transduction have focused on the L-methionine requirement for bacterial chemotaxis (5, 19, 127). Methionine or probably S-adenosyl-L-methionine (10, 11, 21) was necessary for chemotaxis or, more specifically, for the generation of tumbles. The requirement for ATP would reflect the necessity for the activation of S-adenosyl-L-methionine, which could act as a methyl donor (21, 87). Consistent with these expectations, the methylation of a protein, MCP (methyl-accepting chemotaxis protein), was discovered in the inner membrane of *E. coli* (84). The methylation of MCP responded to chemotactic stimuli (84). MCP was found to be the product of two genes, *cheD* and *cheM* (113, 123; M. Silverman and M. Simon, manuscript in preparation). The *cheM* gene product was involved in the responses to a group of chemoeffectors including aspartate, and the *cheD* gene product was involved in response to a group of effectors including serine. A further gene product, *cheZ,* was methylated; however, its methylation was different than that of the *cheM* or *cheD* products. In *E. coli,* mutations in the *cheX* and *cheW* genes lead to a marked decrease in MCP methylation. In *Salmonella,* the product of a *che* gene has been shown to correspond to an enzyme that methylates MCP (127a). It is possible that methylation of the membrane-bound MCP could correspond to the adaptive process postulated in the models for chemotaxis, whereas the methylation of *cheZ* could be the process that is instantaneously monitoring the sensory input. The other *che* genes would be involved in translating the sensory input into methylation events. All of the pieces of the chemotaxis puzzle have not been put in place, but the outlines of a solution are emerging.

The function of the flagellar organelle is to provide the cell with motility and chemotaxis. The mechanisms involved in the processes are complex. It is not surprising, therefore, to find that the structure as well as the genetics and regulation of flagellar assembly are complex. The system has already provided interesting and novel examples of mechanisms that control gene expression, protein assembly, energy transduction into motion, and the processing of sensory information. As the nature of the components of the organelle and their interactions become clear, it should be possible to understand these mechanisms at the molecular level and to determine the extent to which they are generally applicable in other systems.

NOTE ADDED IN PROOF This review covers material available to us in April, 1977. Subsequently, we became aware of several manuscripts dealing with the genetics and function of bacterial flagella: Iino, T. 1977. *Ann. Rev. Genet.* In press; Parkinson, J. S. 1977. *Ann. Rev. Genet.* In press; Springer, M. S., Goy, M. F., Reader, R. W., Adler, J. 1977. *Proc. Natl. Acad. Sci. USA* In press.

ACKNOWLEDGMENT

This research was written during the tenure of a grant to the authors from the National Science Foundation.

Literature Cited

1. Abram, D., Koffler, H. 1964. *J. Mol. Biol.* 9:168–85
2. Abram, D., Koffler, H., Vatter, A. E. 1965. *J. Bacteriol.* 90:1337–54
3. Abram, D., Mitchen, J. R., Koffler, H., Vatter, A. E. 1970. *J. Bacteriol.* 101: 250–61
4. Adler, J. 1975. *Ann. Rev. Biochem.* 44:341–56
5. Adler, J., Dahl, M. M. 1967. *J. Gen. Microbiol.* 45:161–73
6. Adler, J., Epstein, W. 1974. *Proc. Natl. Acad. Sci. USA* 71:2895–99
7. Adler, J., Templeton, B. 1967. *J. Gen. Microbiol.* 46:175–84
8. Aksamit, R. R., Koshland, D. E. Jr. 1974. *Biochemistry* 13:4473–78
9. Andrews, F. W. 1922. *J. Pathol. Bacteriol.* 25:515–21
10. Armstrong, J. B. 1972. *Can. J. Microbiol.* 18:591–96
11. Armstrong, J. B. 1972. *Can. J. Microbiol.* 18:1695–701
12. Armstrong, J. B., Adler, J. 1967. *Genetics* 56:363–73
13. Armstrong, J. B., Adler, J. 1968. *Genetics* 61:61–66
14. Armstrong, J. B., Adler, J. 1969. *J. Bacteriol.* 97:156–61
15. Armstrong, J. B., Adler, J., Dahl, M. M. 1967. *J. Bacteriol.* 93:390–98
16. Asakura, S. 1970. *Adv. Biophys.* 1:99–146
17. Asakura, S., Eguchi, G., Iino, T. 1964. *J. Mol. Biol.* 10:42–56
18. Asakura, S., Eguchi, G., Iino, T. 1968. *J. Mol. Biol.* 35:227–36
19. Aswad, D., Koshland, D. E. Jr. 1974. *J. Bacteriol.* 118:640–45
20. Aswad, D., Koshland, D. E. Jr. 1975. *J. Mol. Biol.* 97:225–35
21. Aswad, D. W., Koshland, D. E. Jr. 1975. *J. Mol. Biol.* 97:207–23
22. Bayer, M. W. 1975. In *Membrane Biogenesis: Mitochondria, Chloroplasts, and Bacteria,* ed. A. Tzagoloff, pp. 393–427. New York: Plenum. 460 pp.
23. Berg, H. C. 1974. *Nature* 249:77–79
24. Berg, H. C. 1975. *Ann. Rev. Biophys. Bioeng.* 4:119–36
25. Berg, H. C. 1975. *Nature* 254:389–92
26. Berg, H. C. 1976. In *Cell Motility,* ed. R. Goldman, T. Pollard, J. Rosenbaum, 3:47–56. Cold Spring Harbor: Cold Spring Harbor Lab. 456 pp.
27. Berg, H. C., Anderson, R. A. 1973. *Nature* 245:380–82
28. Berg, H. C., Brown, D. A. 1972. *Nature* 239:500–4
29. Berg, H. C., Tedesco, P. M. 1975. *Proc. Natl. Acad. Sci. USA* 72:3235–39
30. Brown, D. A., Berg, H. C. 1974. *Proc. Natl. Acad. Sci. USA* 71:1388–92
31. Burge, R. E., Draper J. C. 1971. *J. Mol. Biol.* 56:21–34
32. Calladine, C. R. 1976. *J. Theor. Biol.* 57:469–89
33. Chang, J. Y., DeLange, R. J., Shaper, J. H., Glazer, A. N. 1976. *J. Biol. Chem.* 251:695–700
34. Clarke, L., Carbon, J. 1976. *Cell* 9:91–99
35. Cohen-Bazire, G., London, J. 1967. *J. Bacteriol.* 94:458–65
35a. Collins, A. L. T. 1974. *Genetic studies on generally non-chemotactic mutants of Salmonella typhimurium.* PhD thesis. Stanford Univ., Stanford, Calif. 263 pp.
36. Collins, A. L. T., Stocker, B. A. D. 1976. *J. Bacteriol.* 128:754–65
37. Dahlquist, F. W., Elwell, R. A., Lovely, P. S. 1976. *J. Supramol. Struct.* 4:329–42
38. Dahlquist, F. W., Lovely, P., Koshland, D. E. Jr. 1972. *Nature New Biol.* 236:120–23
39. Delange, R. J., Chang, J. Y., Shaper, J. H., Glazer, A. N. 1976. *J. Biol. Chem.* 251:705–11
39a. Delbrück, M., Reichardt, W. 1956. In *Cellular Mechanisms in Differentiation and Growth,* ed. D. Rudnick, pp. 3–44. Princeton, N.J.: Princeton Univ. Press
40. DePamphilis, M. L. 1971. *J. Bacteriol.* 105:1184–99
41. DePamphilis, M. L., Adler, J. 1971. *J. Bacteriol.* 105:376–83
42. DePamphilis, M. L., Adler, J. 1971. *J. Bacteriol.* 105:384–95
43. DePamphilis, M. L., Adler, J. 1971. *J. Bacteriol.* 105:396–407
44. Dimmitt, K., Simon, M. 1971. *J. Bacteriol.* 105:369–75
45. Dimmitt, K., Simon, M. I. 1971. *J. Bacteriol.* 108:282–86

46. Dobrogosz, W. J., Hamilton, P. B. 1971. *Biochem. Biophys. Res. Commun.* 42:202–7
47. Doetsch, R. N., Hageage, G. J. 1968. *Biol. Rev. Cambridge Phil. Soc.* 43: 317–62
48. Emerson, S. 1970. *Characterization and assembly of bacterial flagella.* PhD thesis. Univ. Calif., San Diego. 125 pp.
49. Emerson, S. U., Simon, M. I. 1971. *J. Bacteriol.* 106:949–54
50. Emerson, S. U., Tokyuasu, K., Simon, M. I. 1970. *Science* 169:190–92
51. Enomoto, M. 1966. *Genetics* 54:715–26
52. Enomoto, M. 1966. *Genetics* 54: 1069–76
53. Enomoto, M., Stocker, B. A. D. 1975. *Genetics* 81:595–614
54. Fujita, H., Yamaguchi, S., Iino, T. 1973. *J. Gen. Microbiol.* 76:127–34
55. Hazelbauer, G. L., Mesibov, R. E., Adler, J. 1969. *Proc. Natl. Acad. Sci. USA* 64:1300–7
56. Hilmen, M., Silverman, M., Simon, M. 1974. *J. Supramol. Struct.* 2:360–71
57. Hilmen, M., Simon, M. 1976. In *Cell Motility,* ed. R. Goldman, T. Pollard, J. Rosenbaum, 3:35–45. Cold Spring Harbor: Cold Spring Harbor Lab. 456 pp.
58. Horiguchi, T., Yamaguchi, S., Yao, K., Taira, T., Iino, T. 1975. *J. Gen. Microbiol.* 91:139–49
59. Hotani, H. 1976. *J. Mol. Biol.* 106: 151–66
60. Iino, T. 1961. *Genetics* 46:1465–69
61. Iino, T. 1962. *Annu. Rep. Natl. Inst. Genet. Japan* 13:72–73
62. Iino, T. 1962. *J. Gen. Microbiol.* 27:167–75
63. Iino, T. 1969. *Bacteriol. Rev.* 33:454–75
64. Iino, T. 1969. *J. Gen. Microbiol.* 56:227–39
65. Iino, T. 1974. *J. Supramol. Struct.* 2:373–84
66. Iino, T., Enomoto, M. 1966. *J. Gen. Microbiol.* 43:315–27
67. Iino, T., Mitani, M. 1966. *J. Gen. Microbiol.* 44:27–40
68. Iino, T., Mitani, M. 1967. *J. Gen. Microbiol.* 49:81–88
69. Iino, T., Oguchi, T. 1972. *Annu. Rep. Natl. Inst. Genet. Japan* 22:13–14
70. Iino, T., Oguchi, T., Hirano, T. 1975. *J. Gen. Microbiol.* 89:265–76
71. Iino, T., Oguchi, T., Kuroiwa, T. 1974. *J. Gen Microbiol.* 81:37–45
72. Iino, T., Suzuki, H., Yamaguchi, S. 1972. *Nature New Biol.* 237:238–40
73. Joys, T. M., Rankis, V. 1972. *J. Biol. Chem.* 247:5180–93
74. Joys, T. M., Stocker, B. A. D. 1965. *J. Gen. Microbiol.* 41:47–55
75. Kagawa, H., Asakura, S., Iino, T. 1973. *J. Bacteriol.* 113:1474–81
76. Kagawa, H., Owaribe, K., Asakura, S., Takahashi, N. 1976. *J. Bacteriol.* 125:68–73
77. Kamiya, R., Asakura, S. 1976. *J. Mol. Biol.* 106:167–86
78. Koffler, H. 1970. In *Methods in Microbiology,* ed. J. R. Norris, D. W. Ribbons, 5A:165–72. New York: Academic. 45 pp.
79. Komeda, Y., Icho, T., Iino, T. 1977. *J. Bacteriol.* 129:908–15
80. Komeda, Y., Suzuki, H., Ishidsu, J., Iino, T. 1975. *Mol. Gen. Genet.* 142:289–98
81. Kondoh, H., Ozeki, H. 1976. *Genetics* 84:403–21
82. Kondoh, H., Yanagida, M. 1975. *J. Mol. Biol.* 96:641–52
83. Konno, H., Fujita, H., Horiguchi, T., Yamaguchi, S. 1976. *J. Gen. Microbiol.* 93:182–84
84. Kort, E. N., Goy, M. F., Larsen, S. H., Adler, J. 1975. *Proc. Natl. Acad. Sci. USA* 72:3939–43
85. Koshland, D. E. Jr. 1974. In *Biochemistry of Sensory Functions,* ed. L. Jaenicke, pp. 133–60. New York: Springer-Verlag. 641 pp.
86. Koshland, D. E. Jr., Warrick, H., Taylor, B. 1976. In *Cell Motility,* ed. R. Goldman, T. Pollard, J. Rosenbaum, 3:57–69. Cold Spring Harbor: Cold Spring Harbor Lab. 456 pp.
87. Larsen, S. H., Adler, J., Gargus, J. J., Hogg, R. W. 1974. *Proc. Natl. Acad. Sci. USA.* 71:1239–43
88. Larsen, S. H., Reader, R. W., Kort, E. N., Tso, W. W., Adler, J. 1974. *Nature* 149:74–77
89. Lederberg, J., Iino, T. 1956. *Genetics* 41:744–57
90. Macnab, R. M. 1975. *Proc. 1st Int. Cong. MS Microbiol. Soc.* 1:674–83
91. Macnab, R. M., Koshland, D. E. Jr. 1972. *Proc. Natl. Acad. Sci. USA* 69:2509–12
92. Macnab, R. M., Ornston, M. K. 1977. *J. Mol. Biol.* In press
93. Mäkelä, P. H. 1964. *J. Gen. Microbiol.* 35:503–10
94. Matsumura, P., Silverman, M., Simon, M. 1977. *Nature* 265:758–60
95. McGroarty, E. J., Koffler, H., Smith, R. W. 1972. *J. Bacteriol.* 113:295–303
95a. Mesibov, R., Adler, J. 1972. *J. Bacteriol.* 112:315–16

96. Mesibov, R., Ordal, G. W., Adler, J. 1973. *J. Gen. Physiol.* 62:203–23
97. Meynell, E. W. 1961. *J. Gen. Microbiol.* 25:253–90
98. Murray, R. G. E., Birch-Andersen, A. 1963. *Can. J. Microbiol.* 9:393–401
99. O'Brien, E. J., Bennett, P. M. 1972. *J. Mol. Biol.* 70:133–52
100. Parkinson, J. S. 1974. *Nature* 252: 317–19
101. Parkinson, J. S. 1975. *Cell* 4:183–88
102. Parkinson, J. S. 1976. *J. Bacteriol.* 126:758–70
103. Patterson-Delafield, J., Martinez, R. J., Stocker, B. A. D., Yamaguchi, S. 1973. *Arch Mikrobiol.* 90:107–20
104. Pearce, U. B., Stocker, B. A. D. 1967. *J. Gen. Microbiol.* 49:335–49
105. Pijper, A., Abraham, G. 1954. *J. Gen. Microbiol.* 10:452–56
106. Quadling, C., Stocker, B. A. D. 1962. *J. Gen. Microbiol.* 28:257–70
107. Roozen, K. J., Fenwick, R. G. Jr., Curtiss, R. III. 1971. *J. Bacteriol.* 107:21–33
108. Satir, P. 1973. In *Behavior of Microorganisms,* ed. A. Perez-Miravete, pp. 214–28. New York: Plenum. 301 pp.
109. Schade, S. Z., Adler, J., Ris, H. 1967. *J. Virol.* 1:599–609
110. Shaper, J. H., DeLange, R. J., Martinez, R. J., Glazer, A. N. 1976. *J. Biol. Chem.* 251:701–4
111. Shimada, K., Kamiya, R., Asakura, S. 1975. *Nature* 254:332–34
112. Silverman, M., Matsumura, P., Draper, R., Edwards, S., Simon, M. 1976. *Nature* 261:248–50
113. Silverman, M., Matsumura, P., Hilmen, M., Simon, M. 1977. *J. Bacteriol.* In press
114. Silverman, M., Matsumura, P., Simon, M. 1976. *Proc. Natl. Acad. Sci. USA* 73:3126–30
115. Silverman, M., Simon, M. 1972. *J. Bacteriol.* 112:986–93
116. Silverman, M., Simon, M. 1972. *J. Bacteriol.* 113:105–13
117. Silverman, M., Simon, M. 1973. *J. Bacteriol.* 116:114–22
118. Silverman, M., Simon, M. 1974. *J. Bacteriol.* 117:73–79
119. Silverman, M., Simon, M. 1974. *J. Bacteriol.* 118:750–52
120. Silverman, M., Simon, M. 1974. *J. Bacteriol.* 120:1196–203
121. Silverman, M., Simon, M. 1974. *Nature* 249:73–74
122. Silverman, M., Simon, M. 1976. *Nature* 264:577–80
123. Silverman, M., Simon, M. 1977. *J. Bacteriol.* In press
124. Simon, M., Hilmen, M., Silverman, M. 1975. *Proc. 1st Int. Cong. IAMS* 1:641–55
125. Smith, S. M., Stocker, B. A. D. 1962. *Br. Med. Bull.* 18:46–51
126. Springer, M. S., Goy, M. F., Adler, J. 1977. *Proc. Natl. Acad. Sci. USA* 74:183–87
127. Springer, M. S., Kort, E. N., Larsen, S. H., Ordal, G. W., Reader, R. W., Adler, J. 1975. *Proc. Natl. Acad. Sci. USA* 72:4640–44
127a. Springer, W. R., Koshland, D. E. Jr. 1977. *Proc. Natl. Acad. Sci. USA* 74:533–37
128. Stocker, B. A. D. 1949. *J. Hyg.* 47:398–413
129. Stocker, B. A. D., McDonough, M. W., Ambler, R. P. 1961. *J. Gen. Microbiol.* 55:59–74
130. Stocker, B. A. D., Zinder, N. D., Lederberg, J. 1953. *J. Gen. Microbiol.* 9:410–33
131. Suzuki, H., Iino, T. 1973. *J. Mol. Biol.* 81:57–70
132. Suzuki, H., Iino, T. 1975. *J. Mol. Biol.* 95:549–56
133. Szmelcman, S., Adler, J. 1976. *Proc. Natl. Acad. Sci. USA* 73:4387–91
134. Thipayathasana, P., Valentine, R. C. 1974. *Biochim. Biophys. Acta* 347: 464–68
135. Tsang, N., Macnab, R., Koshland, D. E. Jr. 1973. *Science* 181:60–63
136. Vary, P. S., Stocker, B. A. D. 1973. *Genetics* 73:229–45
137. Warrick, H. M., Taylor, B. L., Koshland, D. E. Jr. 1977. *J. Bacteriol.* In press
138. Yamaguchi, S., Iino, T. 1969. *J. Gen. Microbiol.* 55:59–74
139. Yamaguchi, S., Iino, T., Horiguchi, T., Ohta, K. 1972. *J. Gen. Microbiol.* 70: 59–75
140. Yamaguchi, S., Iino, T., Kuroiwa, T. 1972. *J. Gen. Microbiol.* 70:299–303
141. Yokota, T., Gots, J. 1970. *J. Bacteriol.* 103:513–16
142. Zieg, J., Silverman, M., Hilmen, M., Simon, M. 1977. *Science* 196:170–72

Ann. Rev. Microbiol. 1977. 31:421–45

RECENT PROGRESS IN EPSTEIN-BARR VIRUS RESEARCH

❖1712

M. A. Epstein and B. G. Achong
Department of Pathology, University of Bristol, The Medical School, University Walk, Bristol BS8 1TD, England

---

CONTENTS

INTRODUCTION—GENERAL BIOLOGY OF EB VIRUS INFECTION 422
VIRUS-DETERMINED ANTIGENS 423
LYDMA 423
EBNA 423
MA 424
EA 424
VCA 425
Consequences of Antigen Expression 425
Incorporation of Antigens in the Mature Virion 425
Antigenic Relationship with Other Herpesviruses 425
VARIATIONS IN HOST ANTIBODY RESPONSES 425
Normal Seropositive Individuals 425
Primary Infection Accompanied by IM 426
African BL and NPC Patients 426
TYPES OF INFECTION AND ANTIGEN EXPRESSION IN HUMAN B CELLS IN VIVO 426
Productive Infection 426
Nonproductive Infection in BL and NPC (? Malignant Transformation) 426
Latent Infection 427
EB VIRUS DNA AND ITS RELATIONSHIP TO HOST CELL DNA 428
ORIGIN OF EB VIRUS-CARRYING HUMAN LYMPHOBLASTOID LINES 429
From BL Biopsies 429
By Infection with EB Virus In Vitro 429
From Seropositive Individuals 429
APPEARANCE OF ANTIGENS IN EB VIRUS-CARRYING HUMAN LYMPHOBLASTOID LINES 430
EB VIRUS-NEGATIVE HUMAN LYMPHOBLASTOID LINES 431
INFECTIBLE CELLS AND VIRUS RECEPTORS 431
HUMAN LYMPHOID CELLS AND TUMOR INDUCTION IN RODENTS 432
SEARCH FOR DIFFERENT STRAINS OF EB VIRUS 433

CHROMOSOME STUDIES 433
EB VIRUS AND NEOPLASIA 433
Experimental Carcinogenicity in Monkeys 433
Relationship to BL 434
Relationship to NPC 435
EB VIRUS AND INDIVIDUALS WITHOUT TUMORS 435
Relationship to IM 435
Relationship to Normal Seropositive Individuals 437
Fatal IM 437
SIGNIFICANCE OF ONCORNAVIRUSES IN EB VIRUS-TRANSFORMED CELLS 438
GENERAL DISCUSSION 438

Investigation of the Epstein-Barr (EB) virus (47) continues to accelerate year by year. The discovery and confirmation of the agent as a new human herpesvirus have already been described (41, 42, 44), and more recent reviews have dealt extensively with various aspects of its behavior (45, 46, 95, 97, 121). However, the steady flow of findings now impinges on an increasing number of different fields of study; therefore, a consideration of EB virus in relation to some of these new areas is deemed appropriate.

INTRODUCTION—GENERAL BIOLOGY OF EB VIRUS INFECTION

EB virus is transmitted horizontally and infects all human populations (33, 71, 77, 86–88, 161, 190, 223). Natural primary infection usually takes place in childhood without disease manifestations (89) and is accompanied by seroconversion and harboring the virus for the rest of the individual's life. This harboring is manifested, first, as a productive infection somewhere in the oropharynx with liberation of small amounts of infectious virus into the buccal fluid (25, 70, 76, 154), and second, as a nonproductive latent infection of a small number of circulating lymphocytes. If natural primary infection does not take place in childhood and a susceptible individual acquires such infection as a late adolescent or young adult, this event is accompanied by the clinical manifestations of infectious mononucleosis (IM) in about 50% of cases (111, 167). Delayed natural primary infection is more frequent in the more privileged classes of Western societies in comparison to lower socioeconomic groups (88), thus explaining why IM is a disease of affluence. Although usually occurring in young adults, and long known to be characteristically associated with kissing in this age group (106), IM rarely can accompany primary infection in children and in adults in later life (101). Possible reasons for EB virus infection only sometimes being accompanied by IM have been discussed elsewhere (45).

The incidence of people shedding infectious EB virus from the mouth varies in different populations and under different circumstances; in Western communities about 18–20% of healthy seropositive individuals are shedders, but this rises to 30–35% among seropositive patients on immunosuppressive therapy (140, 219) and to between 70–90% among patients with IM (69, 76, 168). Interestingly, healthy seropositives in a developing country have recently been shown to have a 45% incidence of shedders (69), probably because endemic malaria, with its immunosuppressive effects and stimulation of B-lymphocyte proliferation, activates latent EB virus infection (69). It is, of course, this infectious virus in buccal fluids that is responsible by horizontal transmission for natural primary infection, whether silent or accompanied by IM.

As regards the latent infection of lymphocytes, only B cells have been found to have receptors for the virus (113, 185), and it is now clear that the small number of such cells containing the virus genome provides the starting point for the continuous lymphoblastoid cell lines that can be established in vitro from blood or lymph node biopsies of seropositive people (39, 169). Genome-containing B cells are present in the blood in IM in higher numbers than in healthy seropositive normal subjects (95); therefore, cell lines are established more easily from the former than the latter (39, 95).

In addition to the foregoing, EB virus has a remarkable association with two human malignant tumors, African Burkitt's lymphoma (BL) and nasopharyngeal carcinoma (NPC). Thus, authenticated cases of African BL and NPC only occur in individuals infected by the virus (see 92), whereas the virus DNA is present in the tumor cells (172, 234, 247) and determines the expression of neoantigens in the cell nuclei of both types of tumor (107, 139) and in the cell membrane of BL (124, 127).

The essential postulates a putative human tumor virus must fulfill before it can be accepted as oncogenic in man have been set out by Henle (92), and it is clear that EB virus has now satisfied each of these.

VIRUS-DETERMINED ANTIGENS

With the exception of lymphocyte-defined membrane antigen (LYDMA), all currently known EB virus-determined antigens have been discovered in the course of studies with naturally occurring human antibodies. These antigens are listed below in the sequence in which they appear after infection of the human B-lymphocyte (Figure 1).

LYDMA

LYDMA (120, 224) is the only EB virus-determined antigen for which naturally occurring antibodies have not yet been demonstrated. It was discovered in the course of cytotoxicity tests using killer T cells specifically active in vitro against EB virus genome-containing B cells (224), and it now appears that it is expressed on all such cells carrying the virus genome (120).

EBNA

EB nuclear antigen (EBNA) is detected by anticomplement immunofluorescence (200) and is said to be present in all genome-containing cells (122). This antigen is produced without the necessity for virus DNA synthesis and is located in the nucleus where it associates with the chromosomes during mitosis; it is probably

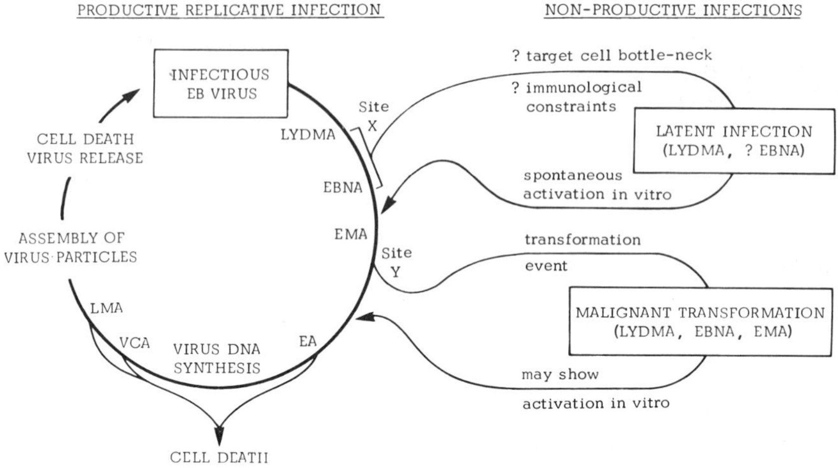

Figure 1 Antigen expression in cells during various forms of infection by EB virus in vivo.

virus-altered chromosomal protein. Available evidence suggests that EBNA represents the EB virus-associated, complement-fixing, soluble antigen (129) first described by Pope et al (194), which in turn has been shown to be identical (201) with a soluble antigen detectable by immunodiffusion (177).

MA

Membrane antigens (MA) (124) have been subtyped into two main components (54, 216). Early MA (EMA) is present in BL tumor cells in vivo and in some cells of virus-producing, continuous lymphoblastoid lines irrespective of their origin, whether established from BL, patients with IM, seropositive donors, or normal lymphocytes transformed by the virus in vitro. It is not clear why EMA has never been found in cells of nonproducer lines despite extensive search when it is so readily seen in the cells of BL tumors, which of course are also nonproducers of virus particles. Late MA (LMA) is found in the later stages of virus replication, is always preceded by virus DNA synthesis, and is accompanied by the expression of virus capsid antigen (VCA) (54, 216). Antibodies against MA appear to be closely similar to those responsible for virus neutralization (34, 35, 188, 189).

EA

Early antigens (EA) (102) are formed when a cell starts the process of virus production; EA-containing cells die even if the full productive cycle is not completed. Subtypes of EA have been recognized: the diffuse in the nucleus and cytoplasm, and the restricted occurring only as clumps in the cytoplasm (91). It is believed that EA represents a virus-coded inhibitor of cellular RNA, DNA, and protein synthesis.

VCA

VCA (86) is seen in both the nucleus and cytoplasm, and its production is always preceded by EB virus DNA synthesis (73). VCA-containing cells may either die at this stage or after the assembly and release of virus particles.

Consequences of Antigen Expression

Although expression of the early antigens (LYDMA, EBNA, EMA) is compatible with the continued viability and proliferation of the cell, production of EA, VCA, or LMA commits the cell inevitably to death whether or not the cycle is completed with assembly and release of virus (Figure 1).

Incorporation of Antigens in the Mature Virion

It has long been known that EB virus, like all other herpesviruses, replicates by the intracellular assembly of components to give immature particles, each consisting of an icosahedral capsid composed of 162 protein capsomeres that surround the nucleoid or core containing the virus DNA. These immature particles then mature by budding out through cellular membranes becoming enveloped by the latter as they pass through (see 44). Of the antigens listed above, only MA (both E and L) and VCA are known to be incorporated in the mature virus particle, the former within the cell-derived envelope and the latter as structural protein of the hollow tubular capsomeres forming the capsid; the situation as regards LYDMA has not yet been investigated.

Human leukocyte antigens are, of course, in no way related to EB virus, but it is remarkable that infection of lymphocytes by the virus leads to a 36-fold enhancement of human leukocyte antigen expression in the infected cell (145). However, despite this, human leukocyte antigens cannot be detected on the cell membrane-derived outer envelope of the mature virus particle (216).

Antigenic Relationship with Other Herpesviruses

It has been claimed, on the basis of immunodiffusion tests, that EB virus shares antigens in common with certain other herpesviruses. Such common antigens have been reported with the Lucké tumor herpesvirus (see 63), Marek's disease herpesvirus (180), infectious bovine rhinotracheitis virus (55), and herpesvirus saimiri (163).

VARIATIONS IN HOST ANTIBODY RESPONSES

Normal Seropositive Individuals

In normal seropositive individuals, after a silent primary infection (89), there are persistent anti-VCA, anti-MA (neutralizing), and anti-EBNA antibodies throughout life (89, 104). Among such people, high anti-VCA titers are sometimes seen if they subsequently develop Hodgkin's disease, leukemia, or sarcoidosis, because increased virus activation occurs during the immunosuppressive phase of the diseases (19, 96). Antibodies to EA are rarely found in healthy individuals, although the reasons for this are not fully understood.

Primary Infection Accompanied by IM

Transient immunoglobulin (Ig) M antibodies to VCA reach high titers early in the disease (5, 83, 210) followed by IgG antibodies, which reach a peak in 2 weeks and then decline to a lower level that persists throughout life (104). Antibodies to MA, the neutralizing antibodies, reach their peak somewhat later and persist at that level for life (104); there is also usually a transient response to EA of the diffuse type. In the early weeks after the onset of IM, noncomplement-fixing antibodies to EBNA reach high titers (209) followed later by complement-fixing EBNA antibodies; the latter persist at the same level for life (90). Although a short-lived appearance of heterophil antibodies in the acute phase forms the basis of the specific Paul-Bunnell test for IM, the nature of these antibodies in relation to EB virus is not understood (101).

African BL and NPC Patients

Both in African BL and in NPC, antibodies to all EB virus-determined antigens are significantly raised, and it is noteworthy that with BL it is anti-EA (restricted) that is predominant, whereas with NPC it is anti-EA (diffuse) (91); with NPC there is an almost invariable and curious production of IgA antibodies to EB virus VCA (98). The titers of the antibodies increase as BL and NPC progress from early to later stages; these increases are especially marked with NPC (100, 103). Successful treatment of NPC is followed by loss of anti-EA (diffuse) and a gradual decline in the level of antibodies to VCA (103). Changes in antibody levels also show a close and peculiar association with certain clinical events in the course of African BL. A drop in, or low, anti-EA (restricted) titer relates to a good prognosis whereas a rise in this antibody usually heralds a fatal relapse (99); furthermore, a sudden drop in antibodies to MA often precedes tumor recurrence by several months (81).

TYPES OF INFECTION AND ANTIGEN EXPRESSION IN HUMAN B CELLS IN VIVO

Productive Infection

Where infection leads to a productive cycle (Table 1), the first known antigen expression is EBNA presumably preceded or accompanied by LYDMA. This is followed by EMA expression, by the making of EA apparently to inhibit cellular synthetic activity, then by virus DNA synthesis, and finally by LMA expression and the production of VCA to provide components for the assembly and release of infectious virus particles (Figure 1).

Nonproductive Infection in BL and NPC (? Malignant Transformation)

With the tumor cells of African BL, the EB virus infection causes the expression only of the earliest antigens, namely EBNA (139), LYDMA (114), and EMA (54,

Table 1 Various forms of infection by EB virus in man

1. Productive replicative infection
virus replication leading to cell death (as in the oropharynx of some infected individuals)
2. Nonproductive infection
can be activated to productive cycle
a. Latent infection
virus genome expressed to give LYDMA and? EBNA (as in periphral B cells of all infected individuals)
b. Malignant transformation
virus genome expressed to give early antigen and ? cell changes of malignancy (as in BL showing LYDMA, EBNA, EMA, and NPC showing EBNA)
N. B. In marmosets EB virus certainly induces malignant transformation with EBNA expression to give malignant lymphomas.

124, 216), and the events of the replicative cycle are arrested at this stage (Figure 1, site Y) by some factor associated with malignant change. Here, the situation seems to resemble malignant transformation (Table 1) as seen with known oncogenic animal DNA viruses in their relationship to the cells of the tumors they cause, with EBNA perhaps corresponding to the nuclear T neoantigens, and with EMA and LYDMA corresponding to the transplantation membrane neoantigen. In the case of NPC, only EBNA so far has been found in the malignant epithelial tumor cells (107).

Latent Infection

In addition to the foregoing, EB virus can also cause a nonproductive infection different from malignant transformation (Table 1). This occurs in the few virus genome-containing B cells of all seropositive individuals. As already pointed out, such cells are considerably more frequent during the acute phase of IM than in healthy seropositive donors (95), and growing evidence supports the view that the virus is present in them in a form resembling latency. Thus, infectious virus cannot be detected when the cells are freshly removed and disrupted (203) but only becomes manifest if intact cells are cultured, when the latent infection is activated so that infectious virus is liberated into the medium where it infects and transforms coresident, uninfected B cells (204–206) (see below).

The genome-containing, nonmalignant B cells must express LYDMA on the surface since they are recognized specifically by killer T cells (109, 202, 207, 224), and the majority at least of the former have recently been found to be EBNA negative (27). Should it be confirmed that LYDMA can indeed occur in the absence of EBNA, then LYDMA clearly must be the first antigen expressed in the productive cycle (Figure 1) and the expression of LYDMA alone would then correspond to the state of latency. In this connection, it should be noted that there is conflicting evidence as to whether or not some EBNA-positive cells are also present in the virus genome-containing cell population (27, 128). It is not known what arrests and holds latently infected cells at a very early stage in the productive replicative cycle (Figure 1, site X), but this might be a result of such factors as bottlenecks in the pathway, resulting from inherent characteristics in particular B target cells that become infected, or the operation of immunological constraints. In any event, as mentioned above, the arrest breaks down when the cells are placed in culture away from host responses, with activation of infectious virus production (204–206).

The phenomenon of latency by EB virus in lymphocytes with its ability to be activated (Table 1) is paralleled by other herpesviruses that behave in a similar manner. Thus, herpes simplex type I latent in the trigeminal ganglion is activated to a productive infection when the ganglion cells are cultured (8–10, 191) and both herpes simplex type II in sacral ganglia (7, 8) and varicella-zoster virus in dorsal root ganglia (11, 214) behave in the same way. More important, since it provides an even closer parallel, is the latency behavior of lymphotropic herpesviruses; human cytomegalovirus, mouse cytomegalovirus, and herpesvirus saimiri in its natural squirrel monkey host all establish latent, nonproductive infections in lymphocytes from which infectious virus can only be recovered if the undisrupted cells are cocultivated with a susceptible monolayer (56, 64, 135, 136, 178, 179).

EB VIRUS DNA AND ITS RELATIONSHIP TO HOST CELL DNA

The double-stranded DNA of EB virus has recently been confirmed as having a molecular weight of 10^8 (13, 195); therefore, it should be able to code for over 100 proteins (196). In fact, the EB virus particle has been shown to contain at least 33 different structural polypeptides (40).

After the demonstration by nucleic acid hybridization of EB virus DNA in the cells of African BL, NPC, and continuous lymphoblastoid lines, it was evident that the virus genome had an unusual relationship to the cell, since multiple virus genome equivalents were present in each cell (36, 118, 172–174, 234, 244–247). Investigations into the state of the virus genome have revealed that a small, as yet undetermined, number of EB virus DNA molecules are linearly and covalently integrated into the host cell DNA, whereas the majority of the virus DNA is present extrachromosomally in the form of covalently closed circular molecules (1, 12, 117, 226) perhaps behaving like an episome.

The use of selective inhibitors has recently provided new insights into the replication of EB virus DNA. Phosphonoacetic acid (PAA) has been found to inhibit specifically the replication of EB virus DNA necessary for the production of progeny virus genomes in the replicative cycle of infection (175, 222, 236). By analogy with its effect on the replication of other herpesviruses (108, 137, 142, 165, 181), PAA presumably inhibits a specific EB virus DNA polymerase essential for the synthesis of new virus genomes in virus production. It is of particular interest that PAA does not affect the replication of either the integrated or the episomal EB virus DNA carried by transformed cells since, if such cells proliferate in the presence of the drug, their genome load remains constant (222), no doubt because this permanently resident DNA uses cellular synthetic mechanisms for its replication.

As regards latent infection, nothing is yet known about the state of the virus genome or its relationship to the cellular DNA.

ORIGIN OF EB VIRUS-CARRYING HUMAN LYMPHOBLASTOID LINES

From BL Biopsies

It has long been recognized that the EB virus genome-containing lymphoblastoid lines that arise when African BL biopsies are placed in culture do so by the direct outgrowth of the malignant tumor cells. This has been clearly established by studies of cytogenetic, IgM specificity and isoenzyme markers in the original tumors and the lines derived from them (60, 80, 141, 164).

By Infection with EB Virus In Vitro

It has long been known that cell lines can only be established from the B-lymphocytes of seronegative donors (including fetal cord blood) if EB virus is added in vitro (24, 72, 93, 153, 169, 193, 194). When this is done, the virus enters cells, EBNA expression can be detected within 18–24 hr (148, 235), and the virus DNA is then increased to 10–15 genome equivalents per cell, some of which is linearly integrated in the host cell DNA whereas the remainder remains free as circular molecules. At about this time, an event takes place that transforms the cell and confers on it the power of continuous proliferation in vitro; it has been speculatively suggested that the transformation event may be related either to the amplification of the genome load to 10–15 equivalents or to the integration of some of these EB virus DNA molecules (227). In any case, the resulting in vitro transformed lines with their capacity for unlimited growth maintain a steady load of 10–15 virus genome equivalents per cell, irrespective of the number of cell generations through which they have passed (227).

It has been reported that in vitro transformation by EB virus occurs more readily with fetal cells than with adult cells from seronegative donors (30, 69), and there is certainly some difference in the behavior of cell lines derived from these two sources. Thus, lines of fetal origin produce virus and late viral antigens less commonly and in smaller amounts than those of adult origin (69), suggesting that different target cells with their inherent differences in bottlenecks and pathways may to some extent be responsible for such varying reactions to EB virus (see below).

From Seropositive Individuals

As already pointed out, all seropositive individuals (whether healthy or with IM, BL, or NPC) have in their peripheral blood a few latently infected, genome-containing B-lymphocytes. Evidence from recent work with IM blood suggests that, when cell lines arise in vitro from the leukocytes of seropositive donors, they do so not by direct outgrowth but by a two-step process in which the latent infection is activated to virus production, and the resulting infectious particles infect and transform other B cells coresident in the culture (204–206). This type of activation of latent herpesviruses by an in vitro millieu has been discussed above, whereas the transformation resulting from infection by the liberated virus is exactly the same as occurs where the virus is added experimentally in vitro to B-lymphocytes from seronegative sources.

The two-step mechanism also provides an explanation for the origin of the lymphoblastoid lines that have been grown from NPC biopsies (37, 38). This squamous epithelial tumor always contains a considerable lymphocyte infiltration (212), of which a few must be latently infected B cells capable of starting lines in vitro in this way.

APPEARANCE OF ANTIGENS IN EB VIRUS-CARRYING HUMAN LYMPHOBLASTOID LINES

Although it has been known for many years that continuous B-lymphoblastoid cell lines can readily be established from BL biopsies (42), seropositive donors (169), patients with IM (39) and the cells of seronegative donors exposed to EB virus in vitro (93, 192), it has become apparent more recently that the BL-derived lines differ from those established from all other sources in cell morphology, growth characteristics, and karyotype (112, 170, 241). Nevertheless, despite these differences, continuous cell lines of whatever origin, although all containing the EB virus genome, vary widely with regard to the expression of virus antigens and the production of infectious virus.

At one extreme are those cell lines, epitomized by Raji (see 48, 197), in which every cell is in the malignantly transformed state (Figure 1) expressing only nuclear neoantigen EBNA (200) and membrane neoantigen LYDMA (224) and undergoing continuous proliferation. Although none of the cells in the populations of such lines spontaneously produces antigens of the late virus replicative cycle (MA, EA, VCA) or virus particles, treatment with halogenated pyrimidines such as bromo- or iododeoxyuridine (BUDR/IUDR) can activate a small proportion of the cells to synthesize these late antigens and virus (67, 68, 82, 220, 221).

At the other extreme are cell lines, such as EB3 (49), where at any one time most of the cells continue in the malignantly transformed state (expressing LYDMA, EBNA, EMA, and proliferating), but a variable proportion are spontaneously activated to late antigen and virus production merely by the in vitro environment (49, 85, 86, 127, 200). Furthermore, manipulation of the conditions of culture can increase the number of productively infected cells in such lines; this has usually been achieved by the use of arginine-deficient medium (94) or a lowered incubation temperature (143). Lines with a naturally occurring high proportion of late antigen and virus-producing cells have been established by cloning (P3HR-1) (105) and where EB virus has infected South American subhuman primate lymphoid cells either in vitro (B95-8) (152) or in vivo (52).

Apart from the extremes just described, variations include non-virus-producing lines, which, unlike Raji, cannot be activated by halogenated pyrimidines, non-virus-producing lines with a high incidence of cells expressing VCA, and virus-producing lines in which the majority of the EMA-positive cells continue to live and divide and only some proceed further through the virus replicative cycle. A recent review has discussed the range of possible manifestations of EB virus-host cell interaction (123). It has been suggested that the various differences are determined by a series of blocks or bottlenecks that operate at different points in the virus replicative cycle, but how or why they operate in particular cell lines, or in particular cells within a line over a period of time, is not known. Clearly, activation by halogenated pyrimidines is an example of release of a block by a chemical mediator; conversely, substances such as distamycin A, puromycin, cytosine arabinoside, and PAA have been shown to block the virus replicative cycle in different ways at various points (13, 175, 222, 227, 236, 238).

EB VIRUS-NEGATIVE HUMAN LYMPHOBLASTOID LINES

The preceding section applies to the vast majority of continuous lymphoblastoid cell lines. It has been shown by such techniques as cloning (144, 157, 240), complement fixation for soluble EB virus antigen (231), nucleic acid hybridization (173, 244–246), BUDR activation (67, 82), combined cloning and BUDR activation (220), and EBNA testing (200) that every cell in this majority of lines contains the EB virus genome, and since it is also known that only B cells have receptors for the virus (113, 185) it is hardly surprising that all such lines have been found to be of B cell origin (78, 113, 186).

However, in addition, there is a small number of exceptional lines that do not carry EB virus DNA, some of T-cell origin and some of B-cell origin. T-cell lines have been derived from the peripheral blood of leukemic patients and examples of these are MOLT (158), CCRF-CEM and HSB-2 (116), and RPMI-8402 (207); in addition, T-cell lines have been established from normal bone marrows by the use of special techniques (162). To date, the B-cell lines include U-698M and U-715M from two lymphosarcomas (171) and Ramos from an EB virus, genome-negative American BL (126) (see below). A putative EB virus, genome-negative B-cell line (BJA-B) is of equivocal status since it was established after exposure of African BL biopsy cells to EB virus in vitro (147).

INFECTIBLE CELLS AND VIRUS RECEPTORS

As already mentioned, EB virus receptors are demonstrable only on B-lymphocytes (113, 185) and all EB virus genome-containing cell lines are of B-cell origin (78, 113, 186); African BL, whose cells all contain EB virus DNA (172, 247), conforms to this pattern in being a B-cell malignant tumor. In fact, with one exception, the B-lymphocyte is the only cell currently known to be infectible by EB virus. The exception concerns the malignant tumor cells of NPC and raises interesting questions. Thus, these cells are clearly of squamous epithelial origin (66, 212, 225) and at the same time have long been known to harbor the EB virus genome (234); yet receptors for the virus have so far not been demonstrated on the surface of normal squamous epithelial cells in the nasopharynx, and the mode of entry of the virus into such cells is not understood. There is some indication that there might be virus receptors on the malignant epithelial cells of NPC (75) so that their presence on the normal epithelial cells from which the tumor originates would not be surprising; alternatively, entry of the virus might be accomplished by the formation of intercellular bridges between EB virus genome-containing lymphocytes and adjacent epithelial cells (66), or by fusion of such cells during upper respiratory tract infection with syncytium-inducing viruses. Close contact between these cell types is well known to occur in the postnasal space where the epithelium lies on cushions of lymphoid tissue (212) to form the so-called "lymphoepithelium."

Until recently, there has been no evidence that EB virus could replicate in the genome-containing malignant epithelial cells of NPC, but it has now been shown that such cells are perfectly capable of supporting a full productive replicative cycle of EB virus infection when treated in vitro with BUDR (228) and of synthesizing EA following superinfection with the virus (75).

Although the nature of the EB virus receptors is not known, a very close association has been demonstrated between them and the complement C3 receptors on the surface of the human B-lymphocyte (239).

In the context of infectible cells, some striking new experiments appear to have demonstrated the transformation by EB virus DNA of diethylaminoethyl-dextran-treated human amnion monolayers (2), although amnion cells cannot be infected by the virus itself (50) even after exposure to the polycation (2); the transformed cells contained VCA and grew as continuous lines. Only about half of the human amnions yielded transformable monolayers; the rest were completely refractory and it is possible that this was related in some way to possession of B-group 2 antigens known to occur in certain individuals (16).

Apart from the infectible human cells dealt with above, continuous lymphoblastoid lines carrying the EB virus genome have been established from the lymphocytes of a variety of sub-human primates either by transformation with EB virus in vitro or by culture from infected animals (52, 57, 152, 156, 232). As with the human lines, all the monkey lines tested are of B-cell origin (57, 199) and behave exactly like the human in producing EB virus-determined antigens and virus particles (52, 57, 152, 156).

HUMAN LYMPHOID CELLS AND TUMOR INDUCTION IN RODENTS

EB virus-containing human lymphoblastoid cells from continuous lines of various origin have been found in the past to form fatal, metastasizing tumors on inoculation into rats, mice, or hamsters (see 45); this was taken as evidence supporting the view that such lines were malignantly transformed by the virus. The compelling reasons for believing this (see 45) are still valid, although recent preliminary work has suggested that both normal fetal lymphocytes and lymphocytes from normal EB virus seronegative adults have produced "lymphoid tumors" on inoculation into antilymphocyte serum-treated newborn hamsters (160). However, this claim is tenuous in the absence of confirmation, since the same laboratory reported contrary results in an earlier paper (159) and previous investigators failed to obtain tumors in immunosuppressed newborn mice after inoculating lymphocytes from EB virus seronegative donors (31).

SEARCH FOR DIFFERENT STRAINS OF EB VIRUS

With EB virus playing such widely different roles (see 46) as etiologic agent in IM, transforming agent for human lymphocytes in vitro, suspected tumor virus in African BL and NPC, and harmless commensal in the great majority of normal human beings, efforts have been made to ascertain whether or not these different roles are associated with different strains of the virus.

So far, EB virus from every source has shown, with only minor variations, remarkably uniform properties and behavior. Only one strain of virus has been found that does not conform to the standard and this, P3HR-1, was the result of selection during cloning experiments (105). Although the P3HR-1 strain of EB virus is clearly lacking in transforming ability (155), this is best regarded as a consequence of laboratory manipulation since the parent virus, Jijoye, from which the P3HR-1 strain derived, was fully transforming (93). One might expect that virus lacking a biological activity would be defective, yet it is surprising that the P3HR-1 strain contains 15% more DNA sequences than transforming strains (149, 195). It seems probable that P3HR-1 virus represents a rare, functionally defective mutant encouraged to emerge by the manipulations of the cloning procedure. Apart from P3HR-1, the biochemical and antigenic similarities of all other EB virus isolates from whatever source (69, 118, 119, 146, 151, 174, 182) do not suggest major strain variations.

CHROMOSOME STUDIES

Early work on chromosome abnormalities associated with African BL-derived and other lymphoblastoid cell lines indicated that there might be a characteristic change on the number 10 chromosome. However, the findings were controversial even at the time, and later investigations showed that the aberration was random and nonspecific, which probably was related to cultural conditions (see 45).

More recently, the application of chromosome banding techniques has revealed a consistent marker abnormality in the number 14 chromosome in African BL tumor cells in biopsy samples and in lymphoid cell lines of African BL origin (141). Since the marker could not be found in EB virus-carrying lymphoblastoid lines from sources other than BL, it was obviously not EB virus specific and was considered, perhaps, to be specific for the malignant transformation process of BL (112). It is now known that closely similar or identical abnormalities of the number 14 chromosome occur in the malignant cells of a variety of different lymphomas of which BL is merely one example (65, 241), and it seems that number 14 chromosome abnormalities are related to malignant change in lymphoid cells in vivo in a wider, more general way.

EB VIRUS AND NEOPLASIA

Experimental Carcinogenicity in Monkeys

EB virus has been shown to cause fatal, malignant reticuloproliferative disease on inoculation into cotton top marmosets (215) and owl monkeys (51–53), and confirmation showing a dose response has been obtained with the first of these species (32). Although such experiments do not prove that the virus plays an etiologic role in human malignancy, they do demonstrate unequivocally that it can be directly oncogenic in vivo (Table 1).

In this connection, it is of interest that marmoset cells infected and transformed into continuous lines by EB virus in vitro (156) grow into malignant tumors when inoculated into autologous hosts (215). This indicates that with marmoset cells EB virus brings about truly malignant transformation in culture and suggests that the same change may occur when human cells are transformed under similar circumstances; the parallel inoculation experiments with the human material cannot, of course, be performed.

Relationship to BL

The many different kinds of evidence linking EB virus to African BL, suggesting an etiologic relationship for the virus to this malignancy, and implicating holoendemic or hyperendemic malaria as a cofactor explaining the climate dependence of the tumor in the areas of Africa and New Guinea where it is endemic, have been reviewed at length elsewhere (18, 45, 97, 121). This evidence becomes increasingly persuasive as the years go by, and EB virus looks more and more at the present time like the only convincing candidate for the role of human tumor virus.

It has long been recognized that outside the endemic areas of Africa and New Guinea, lymphomas very similar to African BL occur sporadically but rarely everywhere in the world where search has been made (17). Although even authenticated (15), nonendemic cases of this exotic tumor differ slightly from African BL in age distribution and tumor sites, nevertheless endemic and nonendemic BL appear to be indistinguishable in having a B-cell origin, in histology and cytology, and in clinical response to chemotherapy (242). These findings add point to the well-recognized problem of the relationship of EB virus to nonendemic BL. Recent studies have made it clear that a small but significant minority (8–17%) of nonendemic BL patients shows the same close association with EB virus as the endemic African cases in having serum antibodies to the virus, and both virus DNA and virus-determined nuclear and membrane neoantigens in all the tumor cells (3, 242). It is now being suggested that the condition we are currently forced to define as BL merely on histological and cytological criteria may in fact be two diseases (3, 243): on the one hand, the majority of nonendemic cases of BL that are EB virus genome negative; on the other hand, the endemic cases and the minority of nonendemic cases that have EB virus DNA in the tumor cells. That the endemic cases are relatively frequent and the genome-positive nonendemic cases are extremely rare is thought to reflect the effect, additional to that of the virus, of the climate-dependent cofactor (malaria) whose distribution determines (18) the endemic zones. The finding of a rare EB virus genome-negative case of BL in endemic areas would fit well with this view of the dual nature of the disease.

Whatever etiology EB virus genome-negative BL may ultimately prove to have, the genome-positive BL tumors are quite unlikely to have the virus DNA in the tumor cells simply as an accidental "passenger." EB virus genome-positive BL has long been recognized as a monoclonal disease (59, 60), and the presence of the virus DNA in every tumor cell indicates that the original cell undergoing malignant transformation was infected by the virus from the outset, i.e. EB virus does not simply infect some accessible tumor cells that happen to provide a suitable cellular environment. Furthermore, the occurrence of EB virus genome-negative tumors in seropositive patients (242) argues strongly against such a casual passenger infection taking place. Finally, the different characteristic patterns in antibody responses that accompany the development of African BL and NPC as well as various clinical events in the course of these malignant diseases (see above) reinforce the concept of a causally more significant role for EB virus than that of mere passenger.

Relationship to NPC

Since the first demonstration of EB virus DNA in the epithelial tumor cells of NPC (234), the presence of the viral genome and expression of viral-determined nuclear antigen has been solidly confirmed in such cells (107, 125). Although NPC has been known for many years to have its highest incidence among the Southern Chinese, in whom it is the most common tumor of men and the second most common tumor of women (211), areas with a lower yet still remarkably high incidence by comparison with the rest of the world have been recognized in Kenya (26) and North Africa (21). It is noteworthy that tumors from each of these widely different geographical regions have the EB virus genome in the malignant epithelial cells (36), and it would seem that this is the case for all NPC since no genome-negative examples have yet been reported from any continent. The presence of the virus genome in all the tumor cells of NPC has just the same implications for an etiologic relationship to the tumor as in African BL, since there is now strong evidence that NPC likewise has a monoclonal origin (58, 61).

The genetic susceptibility to NPC has recently been put on a firm basis by studies of the human leukocyte antigen types of patients and controls, which have shown an almost three times greater risk of NPC associated with particular human leukocyte antigen profiles (217, 218). On the other hand, despite extensive search for environmental cofactors, nothing specific has been identified. However, the environment must play some part since Chinese immigrants from Southeast Asia living in Australia and the United States have the same high incidence of NPC as the Chinese in China, whereas their local-born descendants have a lower incidence, which is nevertheless higher than that of the surrounding Caucasian population (26, 84). Thus, although the exact mechanisms are obscure, it would appear likely that EB virus acts with some as yet unknown environmental cofactor on a susceptible genetic constitution to bring about the malignant change of NPC.

EB VIRUS AND INDIVIDUALS WITHOUT TUMORS

Relationship to IM

It is now accepted that EB virus is the etiologic agent of IM, and it has already been pointed out that the disease accompanies primary infection in about 50% of those in whom this event is delayed until late adolescence or early adulthood (see above).

When infectious EB virus gets into the mouth of a susceptible individual, it is likely that the particles gain access to the body by infecting B-lymphocytes, with their known receptors (113, 185), probably somewhere in the lymphoid tissue of Waldeyer's ring. A productive replicative virus cycle is set up since infectious virus is shed into the buccal fluid of a high proportion of IM patients (69, 76, 168). It is also conceivable that some specialized epithelial cells of the naso- or oropharynx may be involved in this process in view of the fact that NPC squamous epithelial tumor cells carry the EB virus genome (234) and can clearly support virus replication at least under experimental conditions (228). If this should prove to be the case, productive infection with EB virus would then be strictly comparable to the situation with the herpesvirus of Marek's disease, which, although lymphotropic, replicates to give infectious virus in squamous epithelial cells of the feather follicles (20, 166).

With IM so obviously a systemic disease, EB virus must be carried throughout the body from its primary site of replication in the oropharynx via the peripheral circulation; this must occur only during the incubation or prodromal phases of IM since once the disease becomes acute antibodies develop and infectious particles cannot be recovered directly from the blood (203). During the prodromal stages, infectious virus is either carried as a viremia to infect B-lymphocytes everywhere, or B-lymphocytes already infected at the site of primary replication in the oropharynx are themselves disseminated widely to liberate virus and infect B-lymphocytes at distant sites. In either case, virus replication must lead, of course, to the death of the infected B cells with release of virus-determined antigens and the stimulation of specific immunological responses.

At the end of the prodromal period, both infectious virus and cells undergoing a productive replicative virus cycle disappear from the circulation (203), but EB virus genome-containing B-lymphocytes certainly continue to be present in appreciable numbers since continuous EB virus-carrying B-cell lines can readily be established in vitro from IM patients' blood (38, 95). As regards the nature of the infection in these B cells, there is clearly an arrest of the full cytocidal replicative cycle, and so far only LYDMA expression has been unequivocally recognized (109, 202, 207, 224), and perhaps also EBNA (128), although the latter point is not yet settled (27). As already mentioned, the arrest of the virus replicative cycle at this very early stage (Figure 1, site X) appears to correspond with the state of latency. Whatever the mechanism for the arresting of infected cells in a state of latency, latency with its continuing expression of LYDMA seems to arise at the time when immunological responses develop at the start of the disease and is clearly directly responsible for the disease manifestations. The multiplication of large numbers of specifically stimulated T cells activated against LYDMA on the latently infected B cells (109, 202, 207, 224) must be the cause of the obvious generalized lymph node hyperplasia, of the infiltration seen in internal organs, of the tonsillar and adenoidal changes giving symptoms of sore throat, as well as of the characteristic blood picture in which both the mononucleosis and the outpouring of atypical cells have been shown to consist largely of T-lymphocytes (184, 187, 213, 230, 237). Tissue necrosis due to death of cells supporting a virus replicative cycle in the oropharynx may also contribute to the symptoms of sore throat.

As the disease progresses, antibodies to all the antigens liberated by cells dying during virus replication (Figure 1) are stimulated to rise (see above), and cell-mediated responses likewise reach a peak. Virus replication in the oropharynx and the release of latently infected B cells into the circulation are brought under control, and the T-cell reaction in lymph nodes and blood subsides with consequent resolution of the disease. After convalescence, and for the rest of life, there is a low-grade virus replicative cycle in a pool of cells somewhere in the oropharynx with intermittent release of infectious virus into the mouth (25, 70, 76, 154), together with the escape of a few latently infected B cells, expressing LYDMA and perhaps also EBNA, into the peripheral circulation. The low-grade virus replication is responsible for the life-long maintenance of antibodies to VCA, MA (neutralizing), and EBNA, whereas the presence of latently infected B cells in the circulation is responsible for the ability to establish lymphoblastoid cell lines in vitro from the peripheral blood. It would appear that a few residual specific memory T cells continue to be present and destroy latently infected LYDMA-positive cells, which are then in turn replaced by others arrested in this state from the pool of virus replication situated in the oropharynx; this breakdown of latently infected cells might also contribute to the maintenance of antibodies to EBNA, if indeed they carry this antigen (27, 128).

Relationship to Normal Seropositive Individuals

Where primary EB virus infection occurs without disease manifestations, there is no information regarding the initial events involved. However, it would seem that the virus must gain access to the body via the oropharynx, and a situation exactly similar to the postconvalescent steady state described above for IM is soon established, with antibodies to VCA, MA, and EBNA (see above), rare virus genome-containing latently infected cells in the peripheral blood, which can give rise to lymphoblastoid cell lines, and infectious virus shed intermittently from the oropharynx.

Fatal IM

Up to 1966, only about 50 cases of IM dying with various complications had been reported in the world literature (62). Since that time, a fully documented fatal case showing extensive liver necrosis has been reported (23), and it is of interest that a virus with morphological features of the herpes group was observed in the liver cells. More important, a new syndrome (Duncan) has recently been recognized in which an X chromosome-linked immunological deficiency has frequently led to death in two related families as a result of primary EB virus infection accompanied by a fulminating form of IM, in which the atypical cells were exclusively B-lymphocytes (6, 198). Although the nature of the disease is not yet understood, it seems possible that death results from an unrestrained B-cell infiltration supporting virus replication in many parts of the body as a result of the absence of humoral and T-cell-mediated immunological responses.

SIGNIFICANCE OF ONCORNAVIRUSES IN EB VIRUS-TRANSFORMED CELLS

Several claims have been made that African BL and NPC show evidence for the presence of oncornavirus material in the tumor cells (132, 133). This material is said to consist of particles encapsulating a 70*S* RNA and a reverse transcriptase, both characteristic of oncornaviruses and found in suspensions of disrupted tumors by means of the simultaneous detection test (133). However, the results have only been positive in about 80% of BL and 50% of NPC, similar positive results have been obtained with each of a wide variety of other human tumors (4, 28, 29, 134, 233), and there has been no confirmatory morphological evidence for the presence of the particles either in the original tumor biopsies or in the positive fractions of the suspensions.

Apart from the foregoing, it has been found possible to activate a morphologically authenticated oncornavirus in the cells of certain EB virus genome-carrying lymphoblastoid cell lines (131), and the intermittent production of an oncornavirus by one out of eleven such lines has recently been confirmed (130).

The precise origin and significance of oncornaviruses detected in human malignant cells at present are unclear. Oncornaviruses have been found in many normal human placental and fetal tissues (22, 110, 115, 183, 229) and appear to be widespread in the normal cells of many species (138). It seems most probable that all the above oncornaviruses are examples of the well-recognized, endogenous (class I) oncornaviruses that, likewise, are widely present and that, unlike the exogenous (class II) oncornaviruses, have never been shown to be carcinogenic (14, 74).

GENERAL DISCUSSION

Although the wide-ranging progress made recently in the understanding of many aspects of the biology and behavior of EB virus is self-evident, it is also evident that the key question regarding its possible role in the causation of African BL and NPC still remains unanswered.

Much has been learned about the mechanisms involved in transformation of normal human lymphoid cells by the virus in vitro to give continuously proliferating lines, and lines produced in this way show most of the features of the malignant transformation brought about by known oncogenic animal viruses (see 45). Furthermore, although experiments in which monkey cells have been transformed by EB virus in vitro to give lines that cause malignant tumors on inoculation in autologous hosts (156, 215; see above) reinforce this view, it is nevertheless impossible to be certain that malignant change indeed takes place in the in vitro human system or to know how the changes induced relate to events in vivo in the causation of African BL and NPC.

However, some conclusions at least can be drawn from the correlation of findings from several different lines of research. If EB virus does play a part in the etiology of African BL and NPC, the nature of the transformation process in vivo seems likely to be similar to that known to occur in vitro. Thus, infection of an appropriate target cell must be followed by an increase in virus DNA molecules as happens in vitro, since the tumor cells carry a large EB virus genome load (117), some as circular episomal forms and some linearly integrated into cellular DNA. It is also known from recent studies that the details of the response to infection appear to vary with the particular target cell involved; for example, fetal B-lymphocytes behave differently in several respects after EB virus infection in vitro as compared to B-lymphocytes from adult seronegative donors (69, 182). It may well be that a target cell with special responses is involved in the malignant change of African BL and NPC. In African BL, there are persuasive arguments suggesting that holoendemic malaria may be the essential geographically restricted cofactor (18), and malaria is both immunosuppressive and a stimulator of B-lymphocyte proliferation (79, 176, 208); target cells capable of responding to EB virus by malignant change might well emerge in such conditions. It is certainly becoming clear that in the eleven cases of African BL so far studied from this point of view EB virus infection with a normal pattern of response was present in each for a considerable time before the onset of the tumor (International Agency for Research on Cancer, unpublished results). With regard to NPC, with its clear, racially determined incidence, the presence of special target cells would be likely to depend on genetic factors, although the reasons for the involvement of squamous epithelial cells of the postnasal space and for the appearance of NPC late in life many years after primary infection with EB virus are still obscure.

After the increase in the virus genome load and the integration of some genome copies, which is certainly associated with the transformation event, malignant cells in African BL show expression of EB virus-determined EBNA, LYDMA, and EMA, and killer T cells specifically activated against LYDMA have been found in the tumor (114). With NPC, only EBNA has been detected so far, but the heavy infiltration with lymphocytes that is always present suggests that LYDMA may also be expressed particularly since the majority of these infiltrating cells are known to be of the T-cell type (123).

In the context of EB virus and malignant change, it has been shown that the malignant lymphoid cells of the tumors induced by the virus in marmosets (215) exactly parallel the situation with African BL in man since they express EBNA and have the ability to grow out in vitro as EB virus-carrying continuous cell lines (150). This parallelism is even more remarkable in relation to inoculated marmosets without tumors in that some have shown a benign lymph node hyperplasia, which, like IM in man, regresses spontaneously; here the nonmalignant lymph node cells contain the EB virus genome (since they are able to give EB virus-carrying lines in vitro) but are EBNA negative (150) and thus are exactly the same as the latently infected, nonmalignant, seemingly EBNA-negative human B-lymphocytes from the peripheral circulation in IM (27). To complete the picture, inoculated marmosets showing seropositivity with a purely silent infection have also been reported (150).

Despite the reservations that remain, recent progress in EB virus research is clearly bringing us ever closer to the key problem of the role of the virus in human neoplasia. In any event, work on EB virus can be justified on the basis of the interest and biological insights it provides, but, more important, it begins to look as if more practical considerations can now enter into EB virus studies. The time is fast approaching when the planning of a vaccine program must be considered, and, as has already been pointed out (43), this should tell us in the not too distant future whether or not the virus is involved in the causation of BL and should lead in the long run to the ultimate control of EB virus-associated diseases as a whole (43).

Literature Cited

1. Adams, A., Lindahl, T., Klein, G. 1973. *Proc. Natl. Acad. Sci. USA* 70:2888–92
2. Al-Moslih, M. I., White, R. J., Dubes, G. R. 1976. *J. Gen. Virol.* 31:331–45
3. Andersson, M., Klein, G., Ziegler, J. L., Henle, W. 1976. *Nature* 260:357–59
4. Balda, B.-R., Hehlmann, R., Cho, J.-R., Spiegelman, S. 1975. *Proc. Natl. Acad. Sci. USA* 72:3697–700
5. Banatvala, J. E., Best, J. M., Waller, D. K. 1972. *Lancet* 1:1205–8
6. Bar, R. S., Delor, C. J., Clausen, K. P., Hurtubise, P., Henle, W., Hewetson, J. F. 1974. *N. Engl. J. Med.*, 290:363–67
7. Baringer, J. R. 1974. *N. Engl. J. Med.* 291:828–30
8. Baringer, J. R. 1975. In *Oncogenesis and Herpesviruses II*, ed. G. De-Thé, M. A. Epstein, H. zur Hausen, Part 2, pp. 73–77. Lyon: IARC
9. Baringer, J. R., Swoveland, P. 1973. *N. Engl. J. Med.* 288:648–50
10. Bastian, F. O., Rabson, A. S., Yee, C. L., Tralka, T. S. 1972. *Science* 178: 306–7
11. Bastian, F. O., Rabson, A. S., Yee, C. L., Tralka, T. S. 1974. *Arch. Pathol.* 97:331–33
12. Becker, Y., Shlomai, J., Weinberg, E., Ben-Zeev, A., Olshevsky, U. 1974. *Isr. J. Med. Sci.* 10:1454–57
13. Becker, Y., Weinberg, A. 1972. In *Oncogenesis and Herpesviruses*, ed. P. M. Biggs, G. De-Thé, L. N. Payne, pp. 326–35. Lyon: IARC
14. Berard, C. W., Gallo, R. C., Jaffe, E. S., Green, I., Devita, V. T. 1976. *Ann. Intern. Med.* 85:351–66
15. Berard, C., O'Conor, G. T., Thomas, L. B., Torloni, H. 1969. *Bull. WHO* 40: 601–7
16. Billing, R. J., Terasaki, P. I., Honig, R., Peterson, P. 1976. *Lancet* 1:1365–67
17. Burkitt, D. 1967. *Int. J. Cancer* 2: 562–65
18. Burkitt, D. P. 1969. *J. Natl. Cancer Inst.* 42:19–28
19. Byrne, E. B., Evans, A. S., Fouts, D. W., Israel, H. L. 1973. *Am. J. Epidemiol.* 97:355–63
20. Calnek, B. W., Adldinger, H. K., Kahn, D. E. 1970. *Avian Dis.* 14:219–33
21. Cammoun, M., Hoerner, G. V., Mourali, N. 1974. *Cancer* 33:184–92
22. Chandra, S., Liszczak, T., Korol, W., Jensen, E. M. 1970. *Int. J. Cancer* 6: 40–45
23. Chang, M. Y., Campbell, W. G. 1975. *Arch. Pathol.* 99:185–91
24. Chang, R. S. 1971. *Nature New Biol.* 233:124
25. Chang, R. S., Lewis, J. P., Abildgaard, C. F. 1973. *N. Engl. J. Med.* 289: 1327–29
26. Clifford, P. 1970. *Int. J. Cancer* 5:287–309
27. Crawford, D. H., Rickinson, A. B., Finerty, S., Epstein, M. A. 1977. Submitted for publication
28. Cuatico, W., Cho, J.-R., Spiegelman, S. 1973. *Proc. Natl. Acad. Sci. USA* 70: 2789–93
29. Cuatico, W., Cho, J.-R., Spiegelman, S. 1974. *Proc. Natl. Acad. Sci. USA* 71: 3304–8
30. Dalens, M., Zech, L., Klein, G. 1975. *Int. J. Cancer* 16:1008–14
31. Deal, D. R., Gerber, P., Chisari, F. V. 1971. *J. Natl. Cancer Inst.* 47:771–80
32. Deinhardt, F., Falk, L., Wolfe, L. G., Paciga, J., Johnson, D. 1975. In *Oncogenesis and Herpesviruses II*, ed. G. De-Thé, M. A. Epstein, H. zur Hausen, Part 2, pp. 161–68. Lyon: IARC
33. Demissie, A., Svedmyr, A. 1969. *Acta Pathol. Microbiol. Scand.* 75:457–65
34. De Schryver, A., Klein, G., Hewetson, J., Rocchi, G., Henle, W., Henle, G., Moss, D. J., Pope, J. H. 1974. *Int. J. Cancer* 13:353–62
35. De Schryver, A., Rosén, A., Gunvén, P., Klein, G. 1976. *Int. J. Cancer* 17:8–13
36. Desgranges, C., Wolf, H., De-Thé, G., Shanmugaratnam, K., Cammoun, N., Ellouz, R., Klein, G., Lennert, K., Muñoz, N., zur Hausen, H. 1975. *Int. J. Cancer* 16:7–15
37. De-Thé, G., Ambrosioni, J. C., Ho, H.

C., Kwan, H. C. 1969. *Nature* 221: 770–71
38. De-Thé, G., Ho, H. C., Kwan, H. C., Desgranges, C., Favre, M. C. 1970. *Int. J. Cancer* 6:189–206
39. Diehl, V., Henle, G., Henle, W., Kohn, G. 1968. *J. Virol.* 2:663–69
40. Dolyniuk, M., Pritchett, R., Kieff, E. 1976. *J. Virol.* 17:935–49
41. Epstein, M. A. 1970. *Adv. Cancer Res.* 13:383–411
42. Epstein, M. A. 1970. In *Burkitt's Lymphoma,* ed. D. P. Burkitt, D. H. Wright, pp. 148–57. Edinburgh: Livingstone
43. Epstein, M. A. 1976. *J. Natl. Cancer Inst.* 56:697–700
44. Epstein, M. A., Achong, B. G. 1970. In *Burkitt's Lymphoma,* ed. D. P. Burkitt, D. H. Wright, pp. 231–48. Edinburgh: Livingstone
45. Epstein, M. A., Achong, B. G. 1973. *Ann. Rev. Microbiol.* 27:413–36
46. Epstein, M. A., Achong, B. G. 1973. *Lancet* 2:836–39
47. Epstein, M. A., Achong, B. G., Barr, Y. M. 1964. *Lancet* 1:702–3
48. Epstein, M. A., Achong, B. G., Barr, Y. M., Zajac, B., Henle, G., Henle, W. 1966. *J. Natl. Cancer Inst.* 37:547–59
49. Epstein, M. A., Barr, Y. M., Achong, B. G. 1965. *Wistar Inst. Symp. Monogr.* 4:69–82
50. Epstein, M. A., Henle, G., Achong, B. G., Barr, Y. M. 1965. *J. Exp. Med.* 121:761–70
51. Epstein, M. A., Hunt, R. D., Rabin, H. 1973. *Int. J. Cancer* 12:309–18
52. Epstein, M. A., Rabin, H., Ball, G., Rickinson, A. B., Jarvis, J., Meléndez, L. V. 1973. *Int. J. Cancer* 12:319–32
53. Epstein, M. A., zur Hausen, H., Ball, G., Rabin, H. 1975. *Int. J. Cancer* 15: 17–22
54. Ernberg, I., Klein, G., Kourilsky, F. M., Silvestre, D. 1974. *J. Natl. Cancer Inst.* 53:61–65
55. Evans, D. L., Barnett, J. W., Bowen, J. M., Dmochowski, L. 1972. *J. Virol.* 10:277–87
56. Falk, L., Wolfe, L. G., Deinhardt, F. 1972. *J. Natl. Cancer Inst.* 48:1499–505
57. Falk, L., Wolfe, L., Deinhardt, F., Paciga, J., Dombos, L., Klein, G., Henle, W., Henle, G. 1974. *Int. J. Cancer* 13:363–76
58. Fialkow, P. J. 1976. *Biochim. Biophys. Acta* 458:283–321
59. Fialkow, P. J., Klein, E., Klein, G., Clifford, P., Singh, S. 1973. *J. Exp. Med.* 138:89–102
60. Fialkow, P. J., Klein, G., Gartler, S. M., Clifford, P. 1970. *Lancet* 1:384–86
61. Fialkow, P. J., Martin, G. M., Klein, G., Clifford, P., Singh, S. 1972. *Int. J. Cancer* 9:133–42
62. Finch, S. C. 1969. In *Infectious Mononucleosis,* ed. R. L. Carter, H. G. Penman, pp. 19–46. Oxford: Blackwell
63. Fink, M. A., King, G. S., Mizell, M. 1968. *J. Natl. Cancer Inst.* 41:1477–78
64. Foster, K. M., Jack, I. 1968. *Aust. Ann. Med.* 17:135–40
65. Fukuhara, S., Shirakawa, S., Uchino, H. 1976. *Nature* 259:210–11
66. Gazzolo, L., De-Thé, G., Vuillaume, M., Ho, H. C. 1972. *J. Natl. Cancer Inst.* 48:73–86
67. Gerber, P. 1972. *Proc. Natl. Acad. Sci. USA* 69:83–85
68. Gerber, P., Lucas, S. 1972. *Proc. Soc. Exp. Biol. Med.* 141:431–35
69. Gerber, P., Nkrumah, F. K., Pritchett, R., Kieff, E. 1976. *Int. J. Cancer* 17: 71–81
70. Gerber, P., Nonoyama, M., Lucas, S., Perlin, E., Goldstein, L. I. 1972. *Lancet* 2:988–89
71. Gerber, P., Rosenblum, E. N. 1968. *Proc. Soc. Exp. Biol. Med.* 128:541–46
72. Gerber, P., Whang-Peng, J., Monroe, J. H. 1969. *Proc. Natl. Acad. Sci. USA* 63:740–47
73. Gergely, L., Klein, G., Ernberg, I. 1971. *Int. J. Cancer* 7:293–302
74. Gillespie, D., Gallo, R. C. 1975. *Science* 188:802–11
75. Glaser, R., De-Thé, G., Lenoir, G., Ho, J. H. C. 1976. *Proc. Natl. Acad. Sci. USA* 73:960–63
76. Golden, H. D., Chang, R. S., Prescott, W., Simpson, E., Cooper, T. Y. 1973. *J. Infect. Dis.* 127:471–73
77. Goldman, M., Reisher, J. I., Bushar, H. F. 1968. *Lancet* 1:1156
78. Greaves, M. F., Brown, G. 1973. *Nature New Biol.* 246:116–19
79. Greenwood, B. M., Bradley-Moore, A. M., Palit, A., Bryceson, A. D. M. 1972. *Lancet* 1:169–172
80. Gripenberg, U., Levan, A., Clifford, P. 1969. *Int. J. Cancer* 4:334–49
81. Gunvén, P., Klein, G., Clifford, P., Singh, S. 1974. *Proc. Natl. Acad. Sci. USA* 71:1422–26
82. Hampar, B., Derge, J. G., Martos, L. M., Walker, J. L. 1972. *Proc. Natl. Acad. Sci. USA* 69:78–82
83. Hampar, B., Hsu, K. C., Martos, L. M., Walker, J. L. 1971. *Proc. Natl. Acad. Sci. USA* 68:1407–11

84. Henderson, B. E. 1974. *Cancer Res.* 34: 1187–88
85. Henle, G. 1971. *Proc. Int. Symp. Princess Takamatsu Cancer Res. Fund, Recent Adv. Human Tumor Virol. Immunol., 1st,* ed. W. Nakahara, K. Nishioka, T. Hirayama, Y. Ito, pp. 343–49. Tokyo: Univ. Tokyo
86. Henle, G., Henle, W. 1966. *J. Bacteriol.* 91:1248–56
87. Henle, G., Henle, W. 1966. *Trans. NY Acad. Sci.* 29:71–79
88. Henle, G., Henle, W. 1967. *Cancer Res.* 27:2442–46
89. Henle, G., Henle, W. 1970. *J. Infect. Dis.* 121:303–10
90. Henle, G., Henle, W., Horwitz, C. A. 1974. *J. Infect. Dis.* 130:231–39
91. Henle, G., Henle, W., Klein, G. 1971. *Int. J. Cancer* 8:272–82
92. Henle, W. 1971. *Proc. Int. Symp. Princess Takamatsu Cancer Res. Fund, Recent Adv. Human Tumor Virol. Immunol., 1st,* ed. W. Nakahara, K. Nishioka, T. Hirayama, Y. Ito, pp. 361–67. Tokyo: Univ. Tokyo
93. Henle, W., Diehl, V., Kohn, G., zur Hausen, H., Henle, G. 1967. *Science* 157:1064–65
94. Henle, W., Henle, G. 1968. *J. Virol.* 2:182–91
95. Henle, W., Henle, G. 1972. In *Oncogenesis and Herpesviruses,* ed. P. M. Biggs, G. De-Thé, L. N. Payne, pp. 269–74. Lyon: IARC
96. Henle, W., Henle, G. 1973. *Natl. Cancer Inst. Monogr.* 36:79–84
97. Henle, W., Henle, G. 1974. *Cancer* 34:1368–74
98. Henle, W., Henle, G. 1976. *Int. J. Cancer* 17:1–7
99. Henle, W., Henle, G., Gunvén, P., Klein, G., Clifford, P., Singh, S. 1973. *J. Natl. Cancer Inst.* 50:1163–73
100. Henle, W., Henle, G., Ho, H. C., Burtin, P., Cachin, Y., Clifford, P., De Schryver, A., De-Thé, G., Diehl, V., Klein, G. 1970. *J. Natl. Cancer Inst.* 44:225–31
101. Henle, W., Henle, G., Horwitz, C. A. 1974. *Hum. Pathol.* 5:551–65
102. Henle, W., Henle, G., Zajac, B. A., Pearson, G., Waubke, R., Scriba, M. 1970. *Science* 169:188–90
103. Henle, W., Ho, H. C., Henle, G., Kwan, H. C. 1973. *J. Natl. Cancer Inst.* 51: 361–69
104. Hewetson, J. F., Rocchi, G., Henle, W., Henle, G. 1973. *J. Infect. Dis.* 128: 283–89
105. Hinuma, Y., Konn, M., Yamaguchi, J., Wudarski, D. J., Blakeslee, J. R., Grace, J. T. 1967. *J. Virol.* 1:1045–51
106. Hoagland, R. J. 1955. *Am. J. Med. Sci.* 229:262–72
107. Huang, D. P., Ho, J. H., Henle, W., Henle, G. 1974. *Int. J. Cancer* 14: 580–88
108. Huang, E.-S. 1975. *J. Virol.* 16:1560–65
109. Hutt, L. M., Huang, Y. T., Dascomb, H. E., Pagano, J. S. 1975. *J. Immunol.* 115:243–48
110. Imamura, M., Phillips, P. E., Mellors, R. C. 1976. *Am. J. Pathol.* 83:383–94
111. Infectious mononucleosis and its relationship to EB virus antibody. A Joint Investigation by University Health Physicians and PHLS Laboratories. 1971. *Br. Med. J.* 4:643–46
112. Jarvis, J. E., Ball, G., Rickinson, A. B., Epstein, M. A. 1974. *Int. J. Cancer* 14: 716–21
113. Jondal, M., Klein, G. 1973. *J. Exp. Med.* 138:1365–78
114. Jondal, M., Svedmyr, E., Klein, E., Singh, S. 1975. *Nature* 255:405–7
115. Kalter, S. S., Helmke, R. J., Heberling, R. L., Panigel, M., Fowler, A. K., Strickland, J. E., Hellman, A. 1973. *J. Natl. Cancer Inst.* 50:1081–84
116. Kaplan, J., Shope, T. C., Peterson, W. D. 1974. *J. Exp. Med.* 139:1070–76
117. Kaschka-Dierich, C., Adams, A., Lindahl, T., Bornkamm, G. W., Bjursell, G., Klein, G., Giovanella, B. C., Singh, S. 1976. *Nature* 260:302–6
118. Kawai, Y., Nonoyama, M., Pagano, J. S. 1973. *J. Virol.* 12:1006–12
119. Kieff, E., Levine, J. 1974. *Proc. Natl. Acad. Sci. USA* 71:355–58
120. Klein, E., Klein, G., Levine, P. H. 1976. *Cancer Res.* 36:724–27
121. Klein, G. 1973. In *The Herpesviruses,* ed. A. Kaplan, pp. 521–55. London: Academic
122. Klein, G. 1975. In *Oncogenesis and Herpesviruses II,* ed. G. De-Thé, M. A. Epstein, H. zur Hausen, Part 1, pp. 293–308. Lyon: IARC
123. Klein, G. 1975. In *Oncogenesis and Herpesviruses II,* ed. G. De-Thé, M. A. Epstein, H. zur Hausen, Part 2, pp. 365–97. Lyon: IARC
124. Klein, G., Clifford, P., Klein, E., Stjernswärd, J. 1966. *Proc. Natl. Acad. Sci. USA* 55:1628–35
125. Klein, G., Giovanella, B. C., Lindahl, T., Fialkow, P. J., Singh, S., Stehlin, J. S. 1974. *Proc. Natl. Acad. Sci. USA* 71:4737–41

126. Klein, G., Giovanella, B., Westman, A., Stehlin, J. S., Mumford, D. 1975. *Intervirology* 5:319–34
127. Klein, G., Klein, E., Clifford, P. 1967. *Cancer Res.* 27:2510–20
128. Klein, G., Svedmyr, E., Jondal, M., Persson, P. O. 1976. *Int. J. Cancer* 17:21–26
129. Klein, G., Vonka, V. 1974. *J. Natl. Cancer Inst.* 53:1645–46
130. Klucis, E., Jackson, L., Parsons, P. G. 1976. *Int. J. Cancer* 18:413–20
131. Kotler, M., Balabanova, H., Weinberg, E., Friedmann, A., Becker, Y. 1975. *Proc. Natl. Acad. Sci. USA* 72:4592–96
132. Kufe, D., Hehlmann, R., Spiegelman, S. 1973. *Proc. Natl. Acad. Sci. USA* 70:5–9
133. Kufe, D., Magrath, I. T., Ziegler, J. L., Spiegelman, S. 1973. *Proc. Natl. Acad. Sci. USA* 70:737–41
134. Kufe, D. W., Peters, W. P., Spiegelman, S. 1973. *Proc. Natl. Acad. Sci. USA* 70:3810–14
135. Lang, D. J. 1975. In *Transmissible Disease and Blood Transfusion,* ed. T. J. Greenwalt, G. A. Jamieson, pp. 153–69. New York: Grune & Stratton
136. Lang, D. J., Scolnick, E. M., Willerson, J. T. 1968. *N. Engl. J. Med.* 278: 1147–49
137. Leinbach, S. S., Reno, J. M., Lee, L. F., Isbell, A. F., Boezi, J. A. 1976. *Biochemistry* 15:426–30
138. Lieber, M. M., Benveniste, R. E., Livingston, D. M., Todaro, G. J. 1973. *Science* 182:56–59
139. Lindahl, T., Klein, G., Reedman, B. M., Johansson, B., Singh, S. 1974. *Int. J. Cancer* 13:764–72
140. Lipman, M., Andrews, L., Niederman, J., Miller, G. 1975. *J. Infect. Dis.* 132: 520–23
141. Manolov, G., Manolova, Y. 1972. *Nature* 237:33–34
142. Mao, J. C.-H., Robishaw, E. E., Overby, L. R. 1975. *J. Virol.* 15: 1281–83
143. Maurer, B. A., Glick, J. L., Minowada, J. 1970. *Proc. Soc. Exp. Biol. Med.* 133:1026–30
144. Maurer, B. A., Imamura, T., Minowada, J. 1969. *Bacteriol. Proc.,* p. 154
145. McCune, J. M., Humphreys, R. E., Yocum, R. R., Strominger, J. L. 1975. *Proc. Natl. Acad. Sci. USA* 72:3206–9
146. Menezes, J., Leibold, W., Klein, G. 1975. *Exp. Cell Res.* 92:478–84
147. Menezes, J., Leibold, W., Klein, G., Clements, G. 1975. *Biomedicine* 22: 276–84
148. Menezes, J., Patel, P., Dussault, H., Bourkas, A. E. 1977. Submitted for publication
149. Menezes, J., Patel, P., Dussault, H., Joncas, J., Leibold, W. 1976. *Nature* 26:430–32
150. Miller, G. 1975. In *Oncogenesis and Herpesviruses II,* ed. G. De-Thé, M. A. Epstein, H. zur Hausen, Part 2, pp. 379–80. Lyon: IARC
151. Miller, G., Coope, D., Niederman, J., Pagano, J. 1976. *J. Virol.* 18:1071–80
152. Miller, G., Lipman, M. 1973. *Proc. Natl. Acad. Sci. USA* 70:190–94
153. Miller, G., Lisco, H., Kohn, H. I., Stitt, D. 1971. *Proc. Soc. Exp. Biol. Med.* 137:1459–65
154. Miller, G., Niederman, J. C., Andrews, L.-L. 1973. *N. Engl. J. Med.* 288: 229–32
155. Miller, G., Robinson, J., Heston, L., Lipman, M. 1974. *Proc. Natl. Acad. Sci. USA* 71:4006–10
156. Miller, G., Shope, T., Lisco, H., Stitt, D., Lipman, M. 1972. *Proc. Natl. Acad. Sci. USA* 69:383–87
157. Miller, M. H., Stitt, D., Miller, G. 1970. *J. Virol.* 6:699–701
158. Minowada, J., Ohnuma, T., Moore, G. E. 1972. *J. Natl. Cancer Inst.* 49:891–95
159. Miyoshi, I., Kubonishi, I., Hayashi, T., Abe, S., Uchida, H., Tsubota, T., Tanaka, T. 1975. *Nature* 254:272
160. Miyoshi, I., Kubonishi, I., Uchida, H., Hiraki, S., Matsuda, Y., Tanaka, T., Masuji, H., Hiraki, K. 1976. *Int. J. Cancer* 18:67–75
161. Moore, G. E., Grace, J. T., Citron, P., Gerner, R., Burns, A. 1966. *NY State J. Med.* 66:2757–64
162. Morgan, D. A., Ruscetti, F. W., Gallo, R. 1976. *Science* 193:1007–8
163. Morgan, D. G. 1977. *J. Gen. Virol.* In press
164. Nadkarni, J. S., Nadkarni, J. J., Clifford, P., Manolov, G., Fenyö, E. M., Klein, E. 1969. *Cancer* 23:64–79
165. Nazerian, K., Lee, L. F. 1976. *Virology* 74:188–93
166. Nazerian, K., Witter, R. L. 1970. *J. Virol.* 5:388–97
167. Niederman, J. C., Evans, A. S., Subrahmanyan, L., McCollum, R. W. 1970. *N. Engl. J. Med.* 282:361–65
168. Niederman, J. C., Miller, G., Pearson, H. A., Pagano, J. S., Dowaliby, J. M. 1976. *N. Engl. J. Med.* 294:1355–59
169. Nilsson, K., Klein, G., Henle, W., Henle, G. 1971. *Int. J. Cancer,* 8: 443–50

170. Nilsson, K., Pontén, J. 1975. *Int. J. Cancer* 15:321–41
171. Nilsson, K., Sundström, C. 1974. *Int. J. Cancer* 13:808–23
172. Nonoyama, M., Huang, C.-H., Pagano, J. S., Klein, G., Singh, S. 1973. *Proc. Natl. Acad. Sci. USA* 70:3265–68
173. Nonoyama, M., Pagano, J. S. 1971. *Nature New Biol.* 233:103–6
174. Nonoyama, M., Pagano, J. S. 1973. *Nature* 242:44–47
175. Nyormoi, O., Thorley-Lawson, D. A., Elkington, J., Strominger, J. L. 1976. *Proc. Natl. Acad. Sci. USA* 73:1745–48
176. O'Conor, G. T. 1970. *Am. J. Med.* 48: 279–85
177. Old, L. J., Boyse, E. A., Oettgen, H. F., de Harven, E., Geering, G., Williamson, B., Clifford, P. 1966. *Proc. Natl. Acad. Sci. USA* 56:1699–704
178. Olding, L. B., Kingsbury, D. T., Oldstone, M. B. A. 1976. *J. Gen. Virol.* 33:267–80
179. Oldstone, M. B. A., Haspel, M. V., Pellegrino, M. A., Kingsbury, D. T., Olding, L. 1976. *Transplant Rev.* 31: 225–39
180. Ono, K., Tanabe, S., Naito, M., Doi, T., Kato, S. 1970. *Biken J.* 13:213–17
181. Overby, L. R., Robishaw, E. E., Schleicher, J. B., Rueter, A., Shipkowitz, N. L., Mao, J. C.-H. 1974. *Antimicrob. Agents Chemother.* 6:360–65
182. Pagano, J. S., Huang, C.-H., Huang, Y.-T. 1976. *Nature* 263:787–89
183. Panem, S., Prochownik, E. V., Reale, F. R., Kirsten, W. H. 1975. *Science* 189: 297–99
184. Papamichail, M., Sheldon, P. J., Holborow, E. J. 1974. *Clin. Exp. Immunol.* 18:1–11
185. Pattengale, P. K., Smith, R. W., Gerber, P. 1973. *Lancet* 2:93
186. Pattengale, P. K., Smith, R. W., Gerber, P. 1974. *J. Natl. Cancer Inst.* 52: 1081–86
187. Pattengale, P. K., Smith, R. W., Perlin, E. 1974. *N. Engl. J. Med.* 291:145–48
188. Pearson, G., Dewey, F., Klein, G., Henle, G., Henle, W. 1970. *J. Natl. Cancer Inst.* 45:989–95
189. Pearson, G., Henle, G., Henle, W. 1971. *J. Natl. Cancer Inst.* 46:1243–50
190. Pereira, M. S., Blake, J. M., Macrae, A. D. 1969. *Br. Med. J.* 4:526–27
191. Plummer, G. 1973. *J. Infect. Dis.* 128:345–48
192. Pope, J. H., Horne, M. K., Scott, W. 1968. *Int. J. Cancer* 3:857–66
193. Pope, J. H., Horne, M. K., Scott, W. 1969. *Int. J. Cancer* 4:255–60
194. Pope, J. H., Horne, M. K., Wetters, E. J. 1969. *Nature* 222:186–87
195. Pritchett, R. F., Hayward, S. D., Kieff, E. D. 1975. *J. Virol.* 15:556–84
196. Pritchett, R., Pedersen, M., Kieff, E. 1976. *Virology* 74:227–31
197. Pulvertaft, R. J. V. 1964. *Lancet* 1: 238–40
198. Purtilo, D. T., Cassel, C., Yang, J. P. S. 1974. *N. Engl. J. Med.* 291:736
199. Rabin, H., Wallen, W. C., Neubauer, R. H., Epstein, M. A. 1975. In *Comparative Leukemia Research 1973, Leukemogenesis,* ed. Y. Ito, R. M. Dutcher, pp. 367–374. Tokyo: Univ. Tokyo
200. Reedman, B. M., Klein, G. 1973. *Int. J. Cancer* 11:499–520
201. Reedman, B. M., Pope, J. H., Moss, D. J. 1972. *Int. J. Cancer* 9:172–81
202. Rickinson, A. B., Crawford, D., Epstein, M. A. 1977. *Clin. Exp. Immunol.* 28:72–79
203. Rickinson, A. B., Epstein, M. A., Crawford, D. H. 1975. *Nature* 258:236–38
204. Rickinson, A. B., Finerty, S., Epstein, M. A. 1977. *Int. J. Cancer.* In press
205. Rickinson, A. B., Jarvis, J. E., Crawford, D. H., Epstein, M. A. 1974. *Int. J. Cancer* 14:704–15
206. Rickinson, A. B., Jarvis, J. E., Crawford, D. H., Epstein, M. A. 1975. In *Oncogenesis and Herpesviruses II,* ed. G. De-Thé, M. A. Epstein, H. zur Hausen, Part 2, pp. 169–77. Lyon: IARC
207. Royston, I., Sullivan, J. L., Periman, P. O., Perlin, E. 1975. *N. Engl. J. Med.* 293:1159–63
208. Salaman, M. H., Wedderburn, N., Bruce-Chwatt, L. J. 1969. *J. Gen. Microbiol.* 59:383–91
209. Schmitz, H., Kampa, D., Heidenreich, W. 1975. *Int. J. Cancer* 16:1030–34
210. Schmitz, H., Scherer, M. 1972. *Arch. Gesamte Virusforsch.* 37:332–39
211. Shanmugaratnam, K. 1967. In *Racial and Geographical Factors in Tumour Incidence,* ed. A. A. Shivas, pp. 169–88. Edinburgh: Univ. Edinburgh
212. Shanmugaratnam, K. 1971. In *Int. Rev. Exp. Pathol.,* ed. G. W. Richter, M. A. Epstein, Vol. 10, pp. 361–413. New York: Academic
213. Sheldon, P. J., Papamichail, M., Hemsted, E. H., Holborow, E. J. 1973. *Lancet* 1:1153–55
214. Shibuta, H., Ishikawa, T., Hondo, R., Aoyama, Y., Kurata, K., Matumoto, M. 1974. *Arch. Gesamte Virusforsch.* 45:382–85

215. Shope, T., Dechairo, D., Miller, G. 1973. *Proc. Natl. Acad. Sci. USA* 70: 2487–91
216. Silvestre, D., Ernberg, I., Neauport-Sautes, C., Kourilsky, F. M., Klein, G. 1974. *J. Natl. Cancer Inst.* 53:67–74
217. Simons, M. J., Wee, G. B., Chan, S. H., Shanmugaratnam, K., Day, N. E., De-Thé, G. 1975. In *Oncogenesis and Herpesviruses II,* ed. G. De-Thé, M. A. Epstein, H. zur Hausen, Part 2, pp. 249–58. Lyon: IARC
218. Simons, M. J., Wee, G. B., Day, N. E., Morris, P. J., Shanmugaratnam, K., De-Thé, G. B. 1974. *Int. J. Cancer* 13:122–34
219. Strauch, B., Andrews, L.-L., Siegel, N., Miller, G. 1974. *Lancet* 1:234–37
220. Sugawara, K., Mizuno, F., Osato, T. 1972. *Nature New Biol.* 239:242–43
221. Sugawara, K., Mizuno, F., Osato, T. 1973. *Nature New Biol.* 246:70–72
222. Summers, W. C., Klein, G. 1976. *J. Virol.* 18:151–55
223. Svedmyr, A., Demissie, A. 1968. *Acta Pathol. Microbiol. Scand.* 73:653–54
224. Svedmyr, E., Jondal, M. 1975. *Proc. Natl. Acad. Sci. USA* 72:1622–26
225. Svoboda, D. J., Kirchner, F. R., Shanmugaratnam, K. 1967. In *Cancer of the Nasopharynx,* ed. C. S. Muir, K. Shanmugaratnam, pp. 163–71. Copenhagen: Munksgaard
226. Tanaka, A., Nonoyama, M. 1974. *Proc. Natl. Acad. Sci. USA* 71:4658–61
227. Thorley-Lawson, D., Strominger, J. L. 1976. *Nature* 263:332–34
228. Trumper, P. A., Epstein, M. A., Giovanella, B. C. 1976. *Int. J. Cancer* 17: 578–87
229. Vernon, M. L., McMahon, M., Hackett, J. J. 1974. *J. Natl. Cancer Inst.* 52:987–89
230. Virolainen, M., Andersson, L. C., Lalla, M., von Essen, R. 1973. *Clin. Immunol. Immunopathol.* 2:114–20
231. Walters, M. K., Pope, J. H. 1971. *Int. J. Cancer* 8:32–40
232. Werner, J., Henle, G., Pinto, C. A., Haff, R. F., Henle, W. 1972. *Int. J. Cancer* 10:557–67
233. Witkin, S. S., Ohno, T., Spiegelman, S. 1975. *Proc. Natl. Acad. Sci. USA* 72: 4133–36
234. Wolf, H., zur Hausen, H., Becker, V. 1973. *Nature New Biol.* 244:245–47
235. Wright, J., Falk, L., Deinhardt, F. 1975. In *Oncogenesis and Herpesviruses II,* ed. G. De-Thé, M. A. Epstein, H. zur Hausen, Part 1, pp. 409–14. Lyon: IARC
236. Yajima, Y., Tanaka, A., Nonoyama, M. 1976. *Virology* 71:352–54
237. Yata, J., Desgranges, C., De-Thé, G., Tachibana, T. 1973. *Biomedicine* 19: 479–83
238. Yata, J., Klein, G., Hewetson, J., Gergely, L. 1970. *Int. J. Cancer* 5:394–403
239. Yefenof, E., Klein, G., Jondal, M., Oldstone, M. B. A. 1976. *Int. J. Cancer* 17:693–700
240. Zajac, B. A., Kohn, G. 1970. *J. Natl. Cancer Inst.* 45:399–406
241. Zech, L., Haglund, U., Nilsson, K., Klein, G. 1976. *Int. J. Cancer* 17:47–56
242. Ziegler, J. L., Andersson, M., Klein, G., Henle, W. 1976. *Int. J. Cancer* 17: 701–6
243. zur Hausen, H. 1975. *Biochim. Biophys. Acta* 417:25–53
244. zur Hausen, H., Diehl, V., Wolf, H., Schulte-Holthausen, H., Schneider, U. 1972. *Nature New Biol.* 237:189–90
245. zur Hausen, H., Schulte-Holthausen, H. 1970. *Nature* 227:245–48
246. zur Hausen, H., Schulte-Holthausen, H. 1972. In *Oncogenesis and Herpesviruses,* ed. P. M. Biggs, G. De-Thé, L. N. Payne, pp. 321–25. Lyon: IARC
247. zur Hausen, H., Schulte-Holthausen, H., Klein, G., Henle, W., Henle, G., Clifford, P., Santesson, L. 1970. *Nature* 228:1056–58

Ann. Rev. Microbiol. 1977. 31:447–71

THE ROLE OF OPPORTUNISTIC BACTERIA IN HUMAN DISEASE

❖1713

Alexander von Graevenitz
Department of Laboratory Medicine, Yale University School of Medicine, New Haven, Connecticut 06504

CONTENTS

INTRODUCTION 448
UNDERLYING CONDITIONS 449
Colonization 449
Antimicrobial treatment 449
Immunosuppressive treatment 450
BACTERIA INVOLVED IN OPPORTUNISTIC INFECTION 454
Acinetobacter calcoaceticus 454
Aeromonas hydrophila 454
Alcaligenes spp. 454
Anaerobic bacteria 455
Bacillus spp. 455
Bordetella bronchiseptica 456
Brucella spp. 456
Campylobacter fetus 456
Cardiobacterium hominis 456
Corynebacterium and Propionibacterium spp. 456
Dermatophilus congolensis 456
Eikenella corrodens 456
Enterobacteriaceae 457
Flavobacterium spp. 459
Haemophilus spp. 460
Lactobacillus spp. 460
Listeria monocytogenes 460
Moraxella spp. 460
Mycobacterium spp. 461
Mycoplasma pneumoniae 461
Neisseria spp. 462
Nocardia spp. 462
Pasteurella multocida 463

Plesiomonas shigelloides 463
Pseudomonas spp. 463
Spirillum spp. 464
Staphylococcus spp. 464
Streptococcus spp. 465
Vibrio cholerae 467
CONCLUSION 467

INTRODUCTION

As patients with generalized or local defects in antimicrobial defense mechanisms are able to survive longer now than in the past, interest has turned to infections that arise with increasing frequency in such "compromised hosts"; such infections are called "opportunistic infections." An opportunistic microorganism is one that utilizes the opportunity offered by weakened defense mechanisms to inflict damage to the host. This definition would not exclude its pathogenicity for the normal host, in whom inoculum size and virulence factors may overcome normal defenses. An opportunist may cause infection exclusively in compromised hosts (e.g. *Corynebacterium equi*), it may cause infection more frequently in compromised than in normal hosts (e.g. *Staphylococcus aureus, Salmonella* spp.), or it may cause more severe infections in compromised than in normal hosts (e.g. *Mycoplasma pneumoniae* and also *Salmonella* spp.). Organisms that cause disease only in non-immunized hosts (e.g. *Corynebacterium diphtheriae*) are not considered opportunists.

Opportunists are not identical to saprophytes (i.e. organisms that live on decaying or dead material and, as a rule, cannot compete with the normal flora of the human body); this is shown by the example of the saprophytic *Clostridium botulinum.* On the other hand, opportunists may well be saprophytic, e.g. *Nocardia* spp. They are also not identical to members of the resident flora, as *Pseudomonas aeruginosa* shows; however, opportunistic infections may be caused by members of the resident flora, e.g. diphtheroids. It must also be emphasized that the terms "nonpathogenic" and "nonvirulent" apply only (if ever) to normal hosts. For this reason, animal pathogenicity cannot be translated into human pathogenicity in opportunistic situations unless the animal experiment involves simultaneous damage to the host defense mechanisms.

Establishing a direct link between a specific defect and an opportunistic microorganism may present several problems. First, the microorganism should be isolated in several instances from clinically significant lesions in compromised hosts. Second, it must occur significantly more often under those circumstances than in an otherwise comparable population. Third, the association should not be due to one single circumstance favoring both the defect and the microbe (e.g. certain social factors favor both malnutrition and the spread of intestinal infections; a direct link between malnutrition and intestinal infection would be likely only if such infections more often affected malnourished individuals in a social setting not favoring the spread of intestinal infections). Fourth, the association must not be indirect. In one series, salmonellosis was observed significantly more often in gastrectomized patients than in an age- and sex-matched control group. Index cases of gastrectomized patients also developed more severe symptoms than their nongastrectomized contacts (72). This phenomenon, however, is not specific for *Salmonella,* gastrectomy, or surgery in general but is probably explained by hypochlorhydria following gastrectomy, which decreases the bactericidal effect of gastric juice (72). Infection with *P. aeruginosa* in Hodgkin's disease has recently been on the rise (29): formerly, typical infections in this disease resulted from organisms associated with defective cell-mediated immunity (CMI). The association between *P. aeruginosa* and Hodgkin's disease is mediated by the effect of immunosuppressive therapy and leukopenia in the late stages of the disease, with their attendant effects on opsonins and phagocytes, plus the mechanisms (antimicrobials!) that tend to select *P. aeruginosa* over *S. aureus* or *Escherichia coli* in the hospital (4).

Since the subject of opportunistic microorganisms by now has become rather extensive, this review is limited to opportunistic bacteria, excluding fungi, viruses, and parasites. Characteristics of the bacteria, pathogenicity factors, results of animal experiments, pathology, and clinical aspects of the diseases (symptomatology, diagnosis, outlook, treatment, and prevention) are not covered.

UNDERLYING CONDITIONS

Knowledge of the mechanisms that pave the way for invasion of opportunistic bacteria is incomplete. A single underlying condition may foster opportunistic infection through several mechanisms, e.g. immunosuppressive treatment. If multiple underlying conditions are present, it is often difficult to relate the emergence of an opportunist directly to any one of them. Solid tumors, for instance, may predispose to opportunistic infection through a breakdown in skin or mucosal continuity, through obstruction, or through therapeutic attempts (immunosuppression, instrumentation, and surgery) (4). Finally, there may be conditions whose opportunistic potential we cannot appreciate at present. The following are three specific conditions that have changed the spectrum of organisms involved in opportunistic infection.

COLONIZATION Colonizing microorganisms do not belong to the normal flora of a biotope, but do not inflict local damage to the host either. Colonized patients have a higher risk of infection than noncolonized patients (145). Colonization is positively correlated with the severity of the underlying illness, length of hospitalization, previous antimicrobial treatment, and incidence, as well as with the duration of manipulative medical procedures (e.g. tracheal intubation or urinary catheterization) (2, 90).

ANTIMICROBIAL TREATMENT Antimicrobial treatment alters the normal flora, facilitates colonization with abnormal organisms, and selects resistant strains that may persist in the environment. The past decades have witnessed a change in the prevalence of hospital-associated bacteria from hemolytic streptococci and penicillin-susceptible staphylococci to penicillin-resistant staphylococci and relatively susceptible gram-negative rods to resistant gram-negative rods (*P. aeruginosa, Proteus rettgeri, Providencia stuartii,* and *Serratia marcescens*) and fungi.

IMMUNOSUPPRESSIVE TREATMENT Immunosuppressive therapy is now used in a variety of conditions (post-transplantation, cancer chemotherapy, systemic lupus erythematosus, etc). Since it usually affects T cells and B cells, the organisms infecting the host will change, as was pointed out earlier for Hodgkin's disease. High risk factors in immunosuppressive treatment include the use of high doses of prednisone (often employed to treat acute rejection episodes), hyperglycemia, granulocytopenia, and renal failure (7).

Conditions predisposing to opportunistic infection have been reviewed elsewhere (4, 20, 54, 130). The following paragraphs list only the principal conditions known at present.

B-cell defects [Bruton's agammaglobulinemia, certain cases of immunoglobulin (Ig) A deficiency, transient hypogammaglobulinemia of infancy, and late-onset IgG deficiencies] affect antibody production. *Streptococcus* spp., *Staphylococcus aureus, Neisseria meningitidis, Haemophilus influenzae,* and gram-negative rods (i.e. Enterobacteriaceae except enteric pathogens and nonfermenters such as *P. aeruginosa* and *Acinetobacter calcoaceticus*) may cause pneumonia, upper respiratory tract infections, skin infections, septicemia, and meningitis (20, 54).

T-cell defects (thymic hypoplasia, DiGeorge's syndrome, and Nezelof-Allibone syndrome) affect CMI and T-cell cooperation. Infections are due to *Mycobacterium* spp., *Listeria, Nocardia,* and organisms favored by B-cell defects (20).

Combined defects (ataxia teleangiectasia, Wiskott-Aldrich syndrome, thymoma, short-limbed dwarfism, generalized hematopoietic hypoplasia, Swiss-type agammaglobulinemia, cases of hyperglobulinemia, and others) affect antibody production, CMI, and T-cell cooperation. Infections resemble those observed in T-cell defects (20).

Chronic granulomatous disease affects the bactericidal function of phagocytes. Adenitis, pneumonia, septicemia, and osteomyelitis caused by catalase-positive bacteria are observed (54, 99, 132).

Glucose-6-phosphate dehydrogenase deficiency of phagocytes affects bactericidal function. The rare infections resemble those seen in chronic granulomatous disease.

Job's syndrome, a defect in leukotaxis, is associated with "cold" abscesses, otitis, and pneumonia (but not septicemia) caused by *S. aureus* (132).

Chediak-Higashi syndrome is a defect in the number, chemotaxis, and bactericidal function of phagocytes. Upper respiratory tract infections, pneumonia, abscesses, and skin infections caused by *S. aureus, Streptococcus pyogenes, Streptococcus pneumoniae,* and gram-negative rods are reported (132).

Lazy leukocyte syndrome is a defect in leukotaxis and random mobility of granulocytes and result in stomatitis, otitis, and pneumonia (132).

Special defects (leukotaxis defects and/or T-cell defects and/or hypergammaglobulinemeia E) usually result in abscesses from *S. aureus* (31, 132).

Neutropenia (congenital or drug induced) may give rise to stomatitis and other infections resulting from *S. aureus,* gram-negative rods, and anaerobes (132).

The normal neonatal period is characterized by diminished bactericidal function of phagocytes, leukotaxis, phagocytosis, and complement, and by diminished IgM and IgA levels (54). Septicemia and meningitis are particularly conspicuous and may be caused by gram-negative rods, anaerobes, *Streptococcus agalactiae, Flavobacterium meningosepticum,* and *Listeria monocytogenes.* Enterocolitis reportedly may be caused by *P. aeruginosa* (54, 125).

Rheumatoid arthritis seems to have an associated defect in leukotaxis. Skin infections from *S. aureus* (138), as well as pneumonitis (15), are reported.

C3 deficiency and hypercatabolism result in defects in bactericidal function of leukocytes, leukotaxis, and phagocytosis. *Streptococcus* spp., *N. meningitidis, H. influenzae,* and gram-negative rods may cause skin, upper respiratory tract, and systemic infections (130).

C5 activity defects affect leukotaxis and phagocytosis. Skin and systemic infections resulting from *S. aureus* and gram-negative rods have been reported (130).

Acute myelogenous leukemia, acute lymphocytic leukemia, myelofibrosis, and myelosclerosis show a defect in the number of functioning granulocytes. In acute myelogenous leukemia, leukotaxis, mobilization, and bactericidal function of these granulocytic cells are also affected. Gram-negative rods may cause pharyngitis, rectal abscesses (often mixed with anaerobes), urinary infection, soft tissue infections, and septicemia; *Staphylococcus aureus* and pyogenic streptococci cause skin infections and septicemia (4, 81, 101). Infections are more frequent during relapse. A special risk factor is granulocytopenia below 1,000/mm^3 (101).

Lymphoproliferative disorders (chronic lymphocytic leukemia, lymphosarcoma, reticulum cell sarcoma, multiple myeloma, and macroglobulinemia) primarily affect antibody synthesis. Infections (less frequent than in acute myelogenous leukemia) are pneumonia (due to *S. aureus, Streptococcus pneumoniae,* and gram-negative rods), those of the skin (due to *S. aureus*) and urinary tract (due to gram-negative rods), and septicemia (4, 51, 101, 114).

Hodgkin's disease and sarcoidosis affect CMI; Hodgkin's disease may also affect leukocyte mobilization (4, 130, 171). Infections with mycobacteria, *Listeria monocytogenes,* nocardiae, brucellae, and salmonellae are seen in Hodgkin's disease. Infections resulting from gram-negative rods or *S. aureus* occur more often under treatment or in leukopenic patients (4, 29). Infections are considerably less frequent in sarcoidosis than in Hodgkin's disease (130).

Systemic lupus erythematosus is accompanied by defective phagocytosis, decreased leukotaxis, and impaired CMI (158, 184). Infections observed include those associated with phagocytic defects (*S. aureus,* pyogenic streptococci, and gram-negative rods), as well as those associated with defective CMI (nocardiae, salmonellae, and mycobacteria) (30, 123, 158). The infecting organism may invade independently of renal failure or steroid treatment (158).

Asplenia affects opsonization (early antibody) and bacterial clearance by the reticuloendothelial system. Septicemia, meningitis, and pneumonia are due to *S. pneumoniae, H. influenzae,* and, rarely, to *Streptococcus pyogenes* and *N. meningitidis.* The high-risk factors are portal hypertension, thalassemia major, and age under 4 years (102).

Sickle cell anemia and other hemoglobinopathies affect opsonization and clearance by the reticuloethothelial system. *S. pneumoniae, H. influenzae, Salmonella* spp., and gram-negative rods are most frequently isolated. Pneumonia, septicemia, meningitis, urinary infection (gram-negative rods), and osteomyelitis (salmonellae) are common (13, 152).

Familial lipochromic histiocytosis probably affects phagocytosis in the reticuloendothelial system. Pneumonia resulting from a variety of bacteria is observed (64).

In nephrotic syndrome, the primary defect may be in antibody production. *S. pneumoniae, H. influenzae,* and gram-negative rods may cause peritonitis and septicemia (65, 143, 174).

Renal failure shows defects in leukocyte mobilization and in CMI. Pneumonia, wound infections, urinary infections, enterocolitis, and septicemia resulting from *S. aureus,* streptococci, or gram-negative rods are observed (44, 117, 150).

Alcoholism affects the glottis reflex, leukocyte mobilization, occasionally the number of leukocytes, and (late) liver function (103, 150). Malnutrition may be an associated factor. Pneumonia and other infections resulting from *S. pneumoniae, S. aureus, H. influenzae,* anaerobes (aspiration!), gram-negative rods (*Klebsiella*), *Nocardia asteroides,* and *Listeria monocytogenes* (septicemia) may occur (48, 58, 150, 153, 178).

Cirrhosis of the liver and hemochromatosis affect bacterial clearance in the reticuloendothelial system through formation of circumhepatic shunts. Gram-negative rods (also *Yersinia* spp., *Aeromonas hydrophila*) streptococci (most often *S. pneumoniae*), and *Pasteurella multocida* may cause peritonitis and septicemia (37, 122, 124, 134).

Hepatic failure affects the bactericidal function of leukocytes and the complement level (11). Infections are those seen in cirrhosis; in addition, *S. aureus* infections are observed (95).

Diabetes mellitus affects mobilization, chemotaxis, and phagocytosis of granulocytes (15), as well as fibroblastic proliferation (54). Infecting agents are *S. aureus, Streptococcus agalactiae,* gram-negative rods, anaerobes, *H. influenzae, Listeria monocytogenes,* and *Nocardia* spp. Urinary, soft tissue, skin, and lung infections and septicemia are most common (16, 34, 58, 75, 154, 167, 178).

Malnutrition probably affects T-cell function, phagocytosis, complement activity, and bactericidal function of phagocytes. *S. aureus,* gram-negative rods, and mycobacteria cause infections of the skin, infections of the respiratory and gastrointestinal tracts, and septicemia (54).

Immunosuppression: Cytotoxic chemotherapy affects B cells more than T cells (IgG more than IgM), reduces the number of leukocytes, and causes damage to mucosal membranes (101). Radiotherapy has similar effects, plus an additional effect on phagocytosis and the bactericidal function of leukocytes (101). Corticosteroids affect phagocytosis, migration, and bactericidal power of leukocytes; and T cells are more affected than B cells (101). Any organism may cause infections. In transplant patients, pneumonia is seen mainly after renal, cardiac, and liver transplants, urinary tract infection is seen after renal transplants, and septicemia is seen after bone marrow, liver, and renal transplants (33, 68, 119, 160).

Surgery and trauma mean a break in the normal skin defense mechanisms. Wound infection may be caused by *S. aureus, Streptococcus pyogenes,* gram-negative rods, and anaerobes. The high-risk factors include a long preoperative hospitalization, prophylactic antimicrobial treatment, steroid therapy, obesity, presence of a remote infection, long duration of the operation, and presence of a drain (36).

Ischemia limits perfusion and leukocyte migration. The resulting gangrene may be infected by the same organisms causing postoperative infection.

Burns obviate the normal skin defense mechanisms and inhibit the bactericidal effects of leukocytes and leukotaxis. CMI may also be affected (54). Main agents of the resulting infection, plus pneumonia and septicemia, are gram-negative rods and, now days to a lesser degree, *S. aureus* and β-hemolytic streptococci (131).

Abacterial skin conditions like eczema or maceration mean a break in the normal skin defense mechanisms. The resulting pyoderma most often is due to *S. aureus* and gram-negative rods (6, 76, 150).

Intravenous (i.v.) cannulation (i.v. catheter, dialysis catheters, etc) breaks the normal skin defenses and causes wound infection and septicemia primarily from colonizing *S. aureus, Staphylococcus epidermidis,* enterococci, and certain gram-negative rods (*Klebsiella-Enterobacter-Serratia, Pseudomonas aeruginosa,* and *Acinetobacter calcoaceticus*) (108).

Drug abuse (i.v.) has led, through direct inoculation, to skin infections, pyomyositis, and metastatic infections (endocarditis and osteomyelitis). The main agents are now *S. aureus, P. aeruginosa,* and *Serratia marcescens* (105, 115).

Total parenteral nutrition selects (besides *Candida* ssp.) certain gram-positive bacteria (*S. aureus, S. epidermidis,* and enterococci), which may cause septicemia (67).

Cerebrospinal fluid shunts may become infected because they lack intrinsic defense mechanisms. The (mostly intraoperative) invasion may lead to meningitis and septicemia. Ventriculo-atrial shunts are predominantly infected by *S. aureus, S. epidermidis,* diphtheroids, and *Bacillus* spp., whereas ureteral shunts tend to develop gram-negative infections (146).

Prosthetic heart valves represent foreign bodies and become infected in 2–4% of patients operated on (172). The majority of early endocarditides (appearing within 2 months of the operation) is due to gram-positive bacteria (*S. aureus, S. epidermidis,* and diphtheroids) apparently acquired during surgery, whereas late-onset cases essentially reflect the pathogenetic features and bacterial spectrum of naturally occurring subacute bacterial endocarditis (172).

Heart failure, cardiopulmonary bypass, and thoracotomy affect pulmonary clearance and normal respiratory function. Pulmonary edema and inability to cough are further contributing factors; in bypass, there is also inhibition of phagocytosis (139, 160, 166). The ensuing pneumonias are mostly due to *Streptococcus pneumoniae* and *S. aureus,* and occasionally to gram-negative rods; septicemia may follow (178).

Chronic lung diseases (chronic bronchitis, bronchiectasis, emphysema, obstruction, and pulmonary alveolar proteinosis) affect pulmonary clearance and normal respiratory function. *S. pneumoniae, Haemophilus influenzae,* gram-negative rods, mycobacteria, and *Nocardia* spp. (especially in pulmonary alveolar proteinosis) are agents of pneumonia in patients with chronic lung diseases (14, 123, 164, 178).

Cystic fibrosis affects mucociliary clearance and phagocytosis in the lung (54). Colonization and infection usually are limited to the lung and are due to *S. aureus* or *P. aeruginosa* (84).

Influenza tends to damage the epithelial lining of the lower respiratory tract. The complicating pneumonia is usually due to *S. pneumoniae, S. aureus, Streptococcus pyogenes,* or *H. influenzae* (128).

Respiratory tract manipulations (tracheostomy and use of contaminated inhalation therapy equipment) and aspiration bypass the normal respiratory defense mechanisms or overwhelm them. The resulting nosocomial pneumonias are now mostly due to gram-negative rods (*Klebsiella-Enterobacter-Serratia, P. aeruginosa,* and others) (48, 90, 137) but may still be due to *S. aureus* (especially after tracheostomy) (150) or to anaerobes (particularly after aspiration) (75).

Achlorhydria (also present in gastrectomized patients) diminishes the bactericidal effect of gastric juice, thus favoring infection with *Salmonella* spp. and *Vibrio cholerae* (72).

Urinary tract manipulations (such as cystoscopy and catheterization) and obstruction tend to lead to urinary infection and septicemia resulting from gram-negative rods, enterococci, and *S. epidermidis* (12, 21, 168).

BACTERIA INVOLVED IN OPPORTUNISTIC INFECTION

ACINETOBACTER CALCOACETICUS Sources of infections with *Acinetobacter calcoaceticus* var. *anitratus* (*Herella vaginicola*) or var. *lwoffi* (*Mima polymorpha*) are exogenous (soil, water, and the hospital environment) or endogenous (skin) (82, 141). In the majority of specimens, the organisms are found in mixed culture and/or are etiologically indeterminate (71, 127). True infections do occur and may affect any organ (82). Meningitis (diplococci in the cerebrospinal fluid!) is more often due to the var. *lwoffi* and occurs predominantly in newborns and infants, whereas the rare meningitis resulting from var. *anitratus* is more often postoperative (162). Septicemia is associated with i.v. catheters (71, 108), burns, the postoperative state, and immunosuppression (45). Other infections show the usual factors predisposing to colonization or infection with gram-negative rods.

AEROMONAS HYDROPHILA *Aeromonas hydrophila,* a gram-negative rod normally found in outdoor and indoor (stagnant) water sources, may give rise to water-borne wound infections and diarrhoic disease (170); strains may be carried and not recognized because of their biochemical similarity to *Escherichia coli.* Specific opsonizing antibody and phagocytes act as defense factors (96). Septicemia, presumably of intestinal origin, is found in patients with leukemia, solid tumors under chemotherapy (96), and hepatobiliary disease (37, 156).

ALCALIGENES SPP. Because of the lack of available biochemical data, most previous reports of infections with *Alcaligenes* spp. (71) have to be questioned. These organisms may have been confused with species of *Bordetella, Moraxella,* and *Achromobacter* or with non-oxidative pseudomonads. Their ecology resembles that of pseudomonads. So far, bona fide *Alcaligenes faecalis* and *Alcaligenes odorans* strains either have been recovered from mixed cultures or were not considered etiologically significant (71, 127), with the exception of a few *A. faecalis* strains from generally benign septicemias with a variety of underlying disorders (45).

ANAEROBIC BACTERIA Anaerobes are part of the normal flora of the upper respiratory, gastrointestinal, and female genital tracts, as well as of the skin, with different species predominating at each site. Intact skin and mucosal surfaces play an important role in preventing anaerobic infections. Most infections are endogenous and mixed and originate from the above sources; exogenous anaerobic infections are mainly caused by clostridia. Breaks in skin and mucosae, impaired blood supply, tissue necrosis, and the presence of (facultatively) aerobic bacteria create favorable growth conditions for anaerobes. Thus, deep wounds, decubiti, vascular insufficiency, trauma, surgery, shock, septic abortion, malignancy, immunosuppression, rupture of a viscus, premature rupture of the fetal membranes, and aspiration pose risks for aerobic and anaerobic infection alike (58). Alcoholism, carcinoma (of the colon, uterus, or lung), leukemia, and diabetes are known to be associated with anaerobic infection (58). Diabetes favors the emergence of crepitant cellulitis (75), necrotizing fasciitis, synergistic necrotizing cellulitis (75), foot ulcers (104), anaerobic osteomyelitis, and gaseous cholecystitis (59). *Clostridium septicum* septicemia is associated with malignancies (5), and *Clostridium perfringens* septicemia is associated with septic abortion and malignancies, although it may be a benign disease (75). Many correlations can be explained by the normal habitat of the anaerobe. Thus, *Bacteroides fragilis* septicemia occurs predominantly in patients with cancer of the colon, recent abdominal surgery, gynecological disorders, premature rupture of the fetal membranes (neonatal bacteremia), and renal (58) or liver (68) homografts; besides, many of these patients have previously received antimicrobials ineffective against *B. fragilis* (59). Oropulmonary infections and brain abscess are associated with *Bacteroides melaninogenicus, Fusobacterium* spp., *Actinomyces* spp., and gram-positive cocci; gynecological infections are associated with *B. fragilis, B. melaninogenicus, Fusobacterium* spp., and gram-positive cocci; other abdominal infections are associated with *B. fragilis* and *Clostridium* spp. (58). However, practically any anaerobe may occur in any of those infections.

BACILLUS SPP. (EXCEPT B. ANTHRACIS) Bacilli are often dismissed as contaminants in cultures since they are ubiquitous and may also occur on the skin. The *Bacillus* spp. *B. subtilis, B. cereus, B. licheniformis,* and others, isolated in pure culture, have been implicated as agents of infection in the eye (after trauma), in ventriculo-atrial shunts (146), in wounds, in soft tissues, in bones, in joints (126), and as agents of systemic infections (89). The latter type and a few of the former were associated with debilitating conditions, e.g. cancer chemotherapy, surgery, and burns. In many cases, the contribution of the bacilli to the course of the underlying disease has remained unclear.

BORDETELLA BRONCHISEPTICA The source for the rare human strains may be animals who carry them in the respiratory tract. *Bordetella bronchiseptica* has usually been recovered in mixed culture and, with the exception of a very few strains causing endocarditis, has not been found to be of etiologic significance in humans (71, 127).

BRUCELLA SPP. An earlier report describes 14 cases of infection with *Brucella melitensis* in patients with Hodgkin's disease (179). A direct relationship is likely since resistance to brucellae is cell mediated (4, 29).

CAMPYLOBACTER FETUS Human infections with *Campylobacter (Vibrio) fetus* usually take the form of septicemia and are associated with malignancies, cardiovascular disorders, alcoholism, pregnancy, and prematurity (23). The strains belong chiefly to the subspecies *intestinalis*; whether or not transmission for animals to man occurs is unclear. The human intestine has been suggested as a source, although isolations from stool, difficult to accomplish, have only been made for the subspecies *jejuni,* which causes diarrhoic disease and septicemia in young children and infants (27).

CARDIOBACTERIUM HOMINIS This slow-growing, fastidious gram-negative rod, presumably an inhabitant of the upper respiratory and intestinal tracts, is known exclusively as an agent of endocarditis on previously damaged valves (172).

CORYNEBACTERIUM AND PROPIONIBACTERIUM SPP. (EXCEPT C. DIPHTHERIAE AND C. VAGINALE) *Corynebacterium* and *Propionibacterium* spp. are found on the human skin and mucous membranes. Although speciation was not attempted in every case of true infection, the aerobic *Corynebacterium* species *C. aquaticum, C. pseudodiphtheriticum, C. xerosis,* and *C. bovis* and the anaerobic *Propionibacterium acnes* have been identified as agents of human infection. Endocarditis after valvular surgery or on rheumatic valves (172), cerebrospinal fluid shunt infections (146), meningitis, osteomyelitis, and bacteremia in patients with antecedent trauma or surgery, malignancies, or abnormalities of the central nervous system have been reported (92). The soil-borne *Corynebacterium equi,* which causes disease in cattle and swine, is an agent of pneumonitis in immunosuppressed patients (28). Erythrasma, caused by *Corynebacterium minutissimum,* is significantly associated with diabetes mellitus (154).

DERMATOPHILUS CONGOLENSIS *Dermatophilus congolensis,* a facultatively anaerobic actinomycetic rod, causes streptotrichosis in animals and acute pustular dermatitis in humans. Natural habitat and mode of transmission are not known. In one patient with a deficiency of B lymphocytes bearing Fc receptors, as well as impairment of lymphokine production, chronic subcutaneous nodular disease has been observed (3).

EIKENELLA CORRODENS *Eikenella corrodens,* an occasional inhabitant of the normal oropharynx (and gastrointestinal tract?), is most commonly found in abscesses infected with saliva or feces and mixed with streptococci or staphylococci (24). Bacteremia and metastatic infections are rare. *E. corrodens* has also been isolated from abscesses following subcutaneous injection of crushed methylphenidate tablets; oral contamination played a role (24).

ENTEROBACTERIACEAE The large intestine is the main human reservoir for enterobacteriaceae; outside sources are soil, water, and occasionally the hospital environment. Systemic human defenses include bactericidal antibodies operating with the help of C8 and C9 and phagocytosis. Antibody to Re (a derivative of R) seems cross-protective, whereas O and K antibodies are associated with type-specific protection (109).

Thanks to the increased use of antimicrobials, immunosuppressive drugs, and instrumentation in hospitals, enterobacteriaceae have by now become the most frequent agents of opportunistic infection. *Escherichia coli* is the most common isolate. *Salmonella* spp. and probably *Arizona* and *Edwardsiella* spp., possibly also *Yersinia* spp., are opportunists in diseases with a defective CMI, whereas members of the other genera may infect patients with many different underlying conditions.

E. coli is the most frequent primary agent of urninary tract infection (168), neonatal meningitis (54), and peritonitis in cirrhosis (37). Bacteremia is frequently urogenic but may also originate from the intestinal tract (e.g. in leukemia) or from the biliary tract (45).

Enterobacter cloacae and *Enterobacter aerogenes* are usually supercolonizing or superinfecting bacteria in the respiratory and urinary tract (48). *Enterobacter agglomerans (Erwinia herbicola-Erwinia lathyri)*, a ubiquitous bacterium, has become known as a contaminant of i.v. fluids (56). Some recipients of such fluids did show predisposing factors—and presumably received fluids for that reason—whereas others did not. Elsewhere, *E. agglomerans* tends to occur in mixed cultures and is rarely a primary pathogen (129). Patients with septicemia not due to contaminated infusions show underlying conditions resembling those seen in patients with other gram-negative septicemias (113).

Klebsiella spp. are ubiquitous and frequent agents of hospital-acquired infections, particularly in intensive care units (49). Environmental sources include food and moist items; hand transmission is common, and intestinal colonization may precede infection (147). Urinary tract infection is more often primary than secondary (48). Primary *Klebsiella pneumoniae* (Friedlaender) pneumonia occurs usually in males over 50 years old with alcoholism, chronic lung disease, and/or diabetes (48). Septicemia may be secondary to urinary or, less often, to respiratory infection (45).

Serratia marcescens, usually resistant to many antimicrobials, has become an inhabitant of many intensive care and chronic disease units, where it may be transmitted by respiratory and other equipment and/or the hands of the personnel (57, 137). Intestinal isolates only rarely have been reported. Urinary infection after antimicrobial treatment and indwelling catheter use is common (57). Portals of entry in bacteremia may be i.v. or peritoneal catheters, burn sites, or the urinary tract (80). Recently, endocarditis has been described in heroin addicts (115).

Proteus spp. are primarily involved in urinary tract infection, *Proteus mirabilis* as a primary and the other species more often as superinfecting agents (2). Pneumonia is rare and occurs in patients with alcoholism or chronic lung disease (164). *Proteus rettgeri,* usually resistant to many antimicrobials, may cause urinary infections, particularly in males with neurogenic bladder dysfunction following catheterization and antibiotic treatment (88); nosocomial acquisition is the rule.

Providencia strains isolated from human specimens are mostly *Providencia stuartii* (57). They are often resistant to many antibiotics and are hospital acquired, although community-acquired strains have been reported (39). Predisposing factors for urinary infection resemble those seen in *Proteus rettgeri* infection (57). Colonization of burns may lead to pneumonia and septicemia; airborne transmission recently has been implicated in man-to-man spread (173).

Citrobacter freundii, found in normal stool, may be an agent of nosocomial urinary infection and a colonizer in the respiratory tract (57). Septicemia is related to intestinal disease (cancer, cirrhosis, and ulcerative colitis) or to urinary tract infection (169); these patients tend to show multiple predisposing factors. *Citrobacter diversus (Citrobacter koseri* or *Levinea malonatica*) has been isolated from the same sources (52), mostly as a superinfecting agent. Several reports of neonatal meningitis and septicemia are extant (93).

Shigella spp. infections are usually non-opportunistic; as a rule, the bacterium invades only the epithelial layer of the large intestine. A survey of bacteremia resulting from *Shigella* spp. (86) detected 110 reported cases between 1912 and 1975 as a result of *Shigella dysenteriae, Shigella flexneri,* and *Shigella sonnei* (frequency in that order); however, data on routine blood cultures from patients with shigellosis are lacking. A minority of shigella septicemias showed tissue localization, negative stool cultures, and predisposing conditions, among them sickle cell anemia, immunosuppression, and acute myelogenous leukemia (86, 120). Achlorhydria may influence susceptibility in intestinal infections (72).

Salmonella spp. are facultatively intracellular bacteria able to survive in macrophages of hosts exhibiting defective CMI (181) or hemolysis (which "overloads" the reticuloendothelial system). In such individuals, salmonellosis occurs more frequently as septicemia than in normal hosts; fatalities, although always lower than in other gram-negative septicemias, are almost always restricted to the compromised group (30). Newborns as well as persons over 60 years of age show a particularly high incidence of salmonella septicemia (30). Defective CMI, immunosuppression, and hemolysis (181) would explain the high incidence of salmonellosis in leukemia and Hodgkin's disease. The typical form encountered is *Salmonella typhimurium* septicemia, but enteritis is seen also (29, 181). Defective CMI would also account for salmonelloses in patients with kidney transplants (46), treated solid tumors (181), systemic lupus erythematosus (30), and sarcoidosis (77), although in the latter two conditions a higher than normal incidence is difficult to prove. In patients with solid tumors, the propensity for salmonellosis may also be explained by age, surgery, antimicrobial treatment, and the tendency of salmonellae to localize in tumors (18, 77). Surgery may activate a latent infection or may lead to the spread of an existing one (77); in gastrectomized patients, achlorhydria seems to be the important determinant (72). The reported cases of salmonellosis following antimicrobial treatment have been tentatively explained by the elimination of antagonistic intestinal bacteria

(*Bacteroides* sp.?) (21). Antibiotic treatment also prolongs the carrier state in salmonellosis (10). Salmonellae septicemia in cirrhosis is analogous to other septicemias in that disease (37). Hemolysis seems to be the main factor responsible for systemic salmonellosis (septicemia, pneumonitis, and, particularly, osteomyelitis) in sickle cell disease and other abnormal hemoglobin diseases (13, 152). *Salmonella* spp. cause half of all osteomyelitides in sickle cell disease, presumably because of the formation of bone infarcts (13). Hemolysis has also been blamed for the higher incidence and severity of salmonellosis in patients with malaria (18) and bartonellosis (18). The high mortality in the latter disease is almost entirely due to complicating salmonellosis (18). The reasons for the increased incidence of *Salmonella* septicemia in patients with relapsing fever (18) and schistosomiasis (*Schistosoma mansoni*) (140) have not been elucidated. In chronic granulomatous disease, *Salmonella* septicemia is a leading cause of death (99). *Salmonella* infection of the urinary tract is significantly associated with nephrolithiasis, urinary tuberculosis (112), and schistosomiasis (*Schistosoma hematobium*) (49a); tissue necrosis may favor the localization of salmonellae. Infections of aneurysms have been explained by metastatic or contiguous invasion (from an adjacent focus); there seems to be a tendency for salmonellae to localize in hematomas (21). Finally, *Salmonella* meningitis occurs predominantly in infants under 3 months old; associations with syphilitic meningitis and with relapsing meningococcal meningitis have been stressed (18).

Arizona hinshawii has its reservoir in the intestinal tract of animals, mainly turkeys and reptiles. Transmission and spectrum of the disease resemble that of salmonellae. Underlying conditions in systemic disease are similar to those of salmonellosis (sickle cell anemia, Hodgkin's disease, transplantation, and systemic lupus erythematosus) (91).

Edwardsiella tarda is found in the intestinal tract of reptiles and marine animals. The usual human infection is enteritis. Extraintestinal infections show predisposing factors that resemble those seen in salmonellosis (sickle cell anemia, systemic lupus erythematosus, and schistosomiasis) (144, 180).

Yersinia enterocolitica and *Yersinia pseudotuberculosis* occur in animals but may be carried in the human intestine. The usual diseases, mesenteric adenitis resulting from either species and enterocolitis resulting from *Y. enterocolitica,* seem to be non-opportunistic, with enterocolitis occurring predominantly in children under 4 years of age (116). Septicemia occurs mainly in individuals with cirrhosis or hemochromatosis (116, 122, 134). Thalassemia and hematological malignancies have also been predisposing factors in *Y. enterocolitica* septicemia (134). Localization in hepatic or splenic abscesses has been described (134). *Y. enterocolitica* is usually not pathogenic for laboratory animals, but significantly, "nude" (T-cell deficient) mice are susceptible (116).

FLAVOBACTERIUM SPP. Flavobacteria are found in soil, water, and the hospital environment. They are able to survive in certain disinfectants, e. g. chlorhexidine (38). In newborns, *Flavobacterium meningosepticum* causes a frequently fatal meningitis and septicemia, often traceable to throat colonization or environmental sources (1). Isolates from adults rarely have been significant (38, 127), except for a few strains reported from blood after cardiac surgery, immunosuppression, or urinary catheterization (45). The related *Flavobacterium* II-B has caused nosocomial bacteremia in patients with indwelling catheters; the source had been cooling ice (157).

HAEMOPHILUS SPP. *Haemophilus influenzae* is carried by many individuals in the upper respiratory tract. The presence of bactericidal (and possibly other) antibodies is the main (but probably not the only) factor responsible for the relatively low incidence of adult infections. Opportunistic infection in children is seen in sickle cell disease (13), agammaglobulinemia (20), and nephrosis (143) and after splenectomy (102), with septicemia and meningitis (and peritonitis in nephrosis) the most common types. In adults, meningitis is associated with cranial anatomical defects or trauma (163), diabetes mellitus, and alcoholism (153). Pneumonitis may complicate pertussis (121), influenza (128), and chronic lung disease (165). Typable as well as nontypable strains may be involved; the former have led to septicemia (133). Some patients, however, do not show any predisposing factors. Septicemia may lead to brain abscess, arthritis, and other metastatic infections. Endocarditis resulting from *H. influenzae, Haemophilus parainfluenzae,* or *Haemophilus aphrophilus* is usually superimposed on congenital or rheumatic heart disease (172).

LACTOBACILLUS SPP. Lactobacilli are part of the normal oral, intestinal, and vaginal flora. Endocarditis in previously damaged heart valves caused by *Lactobacillus casei* var. *rhamnosus* and *Lactobacillus plantarum* have been reported (149); an oral portal of entry is likely.

LISTERIA MONOCYTOGENES *Listeria monocytogenes* has been isolated from animals, from vegetation, from soil, and — with special enrichment methods — from human feces (the likely source for adult infections), as well as from the cervix (22). Immunity is cell mediated (106). Infection in babies may be an early onset, predominantly septicemic in prematures (often associated with maternal complications), or a late (2 week) onset, predominantly meningitic, associated with normal birth weight and no maternal complications (3a). Infections in early pregnancy usually result in abortion. Disease in the mother is benign. As emphasized in recent reviews (22, 70, 106), adult listeriosis, usually septicemia with or without meningitis, is seen in patients with Hodgkin's disease, immunosuppression (transplantation/steroid treatment), cirrhosis, diabetes mellitus, and, rarely, sarcoidosis. Serotypes 1b and 4b are prevalent in late-onset neonatal and adult infections, whereas early onset cases show involvement of type 1a (3a). Some patients show no predisposing factors (111).

MORAXELLA SPP. Several species of *Moraxella* probably belong to the normal flora of the upper respiratory tract, the skin, and the genitourinary tract (82). In recent years, interest has shifted from *Moraxella lacunata,* the alleged agent of angular conjunctivitis, to other species rarely found in human infections: *Moraxella liquefaciens* in endocarditis (82) and in septicemia with chronic lymphocytic leukemia (148), *Moraxella nonliquefaciens* in chronic bronchitis, endocarditis (82,

127), and meningitis (162), as well as in pneumonitis in an alcoholic with carcinoma of the larynx (142).

MYCOBACTERIUM SPP. CMI participates in the host-parasite relationship in tuberculosis (175). Various conditions have long been known to favor exogenous infection, to reactivate latent lesions, or to unfavorably influence the course of tuberculosis: diabetes mellitus, silicosis, malnutrition, and chronic alcoholism (176) (the latter condition may actually exert its effect through malnutrition). The higher incidence of tuberculosis in gastrectomized patients may be explained by malnutrition (159). Pregnancy and puerperium will aggravate existing tuberculosis and reactivate lesions only if no adequate chemotherapy has been given (42). Activation of tuberculosis by measles is not adequately supported by statistical evidence (61), and the relationship between peritoneal tuberculosis and cirrhosis of the liver is unclear (25). A combination of rheumatoid arthritis, peptic ulcer, and tuberculosis has been reported (35) but ought to be explored further. Opportunistic infection with *Mycobacterium tuberculosis* occurs in patients with defective CMI, as observed in Hodgkin's disease (94), immunosuppression (renal transplants and cancer chemotherapy) (55, 94), systemic lupus erythematosus (158), and sarcoidosis (155), although mycobacterial infections in the latter two conditions are rare. In patients with cancer of the head, neck, and lungs, pulmonary tuberculosis (usually recrudescent) was more often present when the neoplasm first appeared, whereas in patients with carcinoma elsewhere and hematological malignancies, the infection was more often present while the cancer was being treated (94). The second group also had the more severe diseases with pneumonitis and dissemination. It is not clear whether or not the tuberculous lesion was actually carcinogenic or whether or not the neoplasm was responsible for activation or increased susceptibility. The association of tuberculosis with cancer of the stomach may be mediated by gastrectomy or malnutrition (94).

So-called "atypical" mycobacteria, which are ubiquitous and do not spread from man to man, are considered clinically significant only if recovered repeatedly from a symptomatic lesion. In one series, their incidence in neoplasms was almost equal to that of *M. tuberculosis*, with 40% *Mycobacterium kansasii* and 24% *Mycobacterium fortuitum* (55); the types of cancer were similar to those associated with tuberculosis. Pulmonary disease was most common but less fulminant than in tuberculosis, and miliary spread was not observed. Association with cancer chemotherapy was more frequent than in tuberculosis. Immunosuppressive treatment also preceded *M. kansasii*, and scotochromogenic lung infection was observed in patients with myeloproliferative disorders or renal transplants (175). Atypical mycobacterial infection has been observed in thymic alymphoplasia (20) and chronic granulomatous disease (32) as well. Chronic pulmonary disease apparently predisposes to *M. kansasii* and *Mycobacterium intracellulare* infection (14).

MYCOPLASMA PNEUMONIAE Most infections transmitted among humans by the respiratory route are subclinical or mild. Resistance is correlated with the presence of antibodies and phagocytosis but may also be cell mediated (66). Pneumonia resulting from *Mycoplasma pneumoniae* is unusually severe in children with sickle cell disease (151) and in those children with antibody deficiency syndromes (66). *M. pneumoniae* may also precipitate acute exacerbations of chronic lung diseases (110).

NEISSERIA SPP. *Neisseria meningitidis* is an occasional inhabitant of the nasopharynx. Resistance is correlated with bactericidal antibodies. Children with agammaglobulinemia (20) and in the postsplenectomy state (102) have an increased incidence of meningococcal meningitis. Simultaneous outbreaks of both systemic meningococcal disease and influenza in a group (183), as well as *N. meningitidis* pneumonia complicating influenza (83), have been recorded.

Epiphytic *Neisseria* spp. *(N. subflava, N. perflava, N. mucosa,* and *Branhamella catarrhalis*) have occasionally caused opportunistic and apparent non-opportunistic infections: meningitis in children (19), endocarditis on previously damaged heart valves (172), septicemia complicating acute lymphoblastic leukemia (26), and others (54).

NOCARDIA SPP. The portal of entry for human infections with these soil-borne organisms is the lung or the skin (17); whether or not nocardiae also exist as epiphytes in humans has been controversial (123, 183). Normal body defenses seem to be cell mediated, although neutrophils may be better able to phagocytose nocardiae in vitro than monocytes (176). In the United States, 83% of *Nocardia* spp. infections observed from 1972–1974 were due to *N. asteroides,* 3% to *N. caviae,* and 7% to *N. brasiliensis*; the rest was due to "*Nocardia* spp." (17). *N. brasiliensis* infections affected mostly the skin and subcutaneous tissues, whereas *N. asteroides* and *N. caviae* mainly caused pulmonary but also central nervous system, skin, and other tissue infections (17). In at least 15% of all infections, no underlying disease was evident (17). In another series, 9 of 15 patients, among them 5 with localized extrapulmonary lesions, had no predisposing condition (74). Usually, however, nocardiosis is associated with Hodgkin's disease, sarcoidosis (rarely), alcoholism, diabetes mellitus, chronic granulomatous disease, immunosuppression (in patients with transplants, neoplasms, and systemic lupus erythematosus), chronic pulmonary disease (especially pulmonary tuberculosis and pulmonary alveolar proteinosis), and occasionally with dysgammaglobulinemic disorders (17, 74, 123, 175, 183). The bacteriologic diagnosis may be difficult, since sputum cultures may be negative, and may have to rely on multiple specimens from brush biopsies, transtracheal aspirations, percutaneous lung aspirates, or needle or open lung biopsies (175). Patients with positive cultures and without symptoms, or with symptoms referring to the upper respiratory tract only, have been seen (74, 182); thus, the significance of each isolate must be carefully evaluated, with the possibility of a mild nocardial infection of the upper respiratory tract, which may disseminate later, to be kept in mind (182). Nocardiae are practically never found in the spinal fluid, even if central nervous system disease, like brain abscess, exists (123).

Oerskovia turbata, a yellow, motile, soil-borne, aerobic, gram-positive rod, which may be confused with *Nocardia* or *Corynebacterium,* has recently been isolated from a case of endocarditis after valve replacement (136).

PASTEURELLA MULTOCIDA *Pasteurella multocida* commonly occurs in the oropharynx of domestic animals (dogs and cats) and is rarely carried on the mucous membranes of the upper respiratory tract of humans. Typical are wound infections inflicted by dog or cat bites; the organism usually does not invade beyond the local lymphnodes (41). However, in patients with liver cirrhosis, septicemia may follow the local infection (124). Invasion of the blood stream has been observed in neonates following chorioamnionitis caused by *P. multocida* and premature rupture of the fetal membranes (161). Meningitis may accompany it, but it has also been reported without apparent predisposing condition and after cranial surgery (79). Finally, *P. multocida* may lead to exacerbation of chronic lung diseases (41).

PLESIOMONAS SHIGELLOIDES Most human isolates of *Plesiomonas shigelloides*, a gram-negative rod that used to be called *Aeromonas shigelloides* (but which differs substantially from the genus *Aeromonas*), have come from stool, but a relationship to diarrheic disease has not been clearly established. Its habitat probably resembles that of *Aeromonas hydrophila*. Two stains were seen as agents of cellulitis (50, 170); one of the patients, who suffered from sickle cell anemia, had acquired the infection through a fish bone and developed fatal septicemia (50).

PSEUDOMONAS SPP. The source of human infections with *Pseudomonas aeruginosa* is rarely its natural habitat, i. e. soil and water, but usually the colonized or infected patient or moist items in the hospital environment, including certain disinfectants such as benzalkonium chloride (107). The use of antimicrobial agents has greatly contributed to the emergence of this organism as a major opportunist in the past decade. As of now, the polymyxins, very often gentamicin, tobramycin, amikacin, and often carbenicillin are effective against *P. aeruginosa*. Host defenses include specific opsonins plus complement and phagocytes (107). Infections with *P. aeruginosa* are favored by circumstances that also favor infections with enterobacteriaceae (*Salmonella/Shigella* excepted). They are often superinfections, may affect any organ, and are now particularly prevalent in patients under immunosuppression (with neoplasms or transplants) (62, 119), with acute myelogenous leukemia, with burns, and with cystic fibrosis, and also in prematures and newborns. Infections are more often hospital acquired (107) and preceded by colonization (145) and/or antimicrobial therapy (4) than most enterobacterial infections; they also lead more often to septicemia and death (62, 87). Pneumonitis may be hematogenous (in patients with leukemia, burns, or endocarditis) (87) or may follow oropharyngeal colonization, e.g. after use of contaminated suction or respiratory apparatuses (137). In cystic fibrosis, colonization and infection are most often due to mucoid strains (84), but infection remains restricted to the lung, whereas in other forms of *P. aeruginosa* pneumonia septicemia may follow (87). This latter condition, which may also originate from the urinary tract, burns, i.v. catheters, and the intestinal tract (e.g. in leukemics), has a poor prognosis (62). Endocarditis, both left and right sided, has been associated with heroin abuse (105). Burns are colonized or infected after 2–4 postburn weeks, mostly by an exogenous route (131). Application of contaminated solutions has led to wound and eye infections (107); the latter may end in panophthalmitis. Decubitus (69) and diabetic (104) ulcers may be invaded. Increased skin moisture also favors *P. aeruginosa* infections: a "green nail syndrome" after hand submersion as well as toe-web infections, pyoderma secondary to eczema and decubiti, and otitis externa have been described (76). The latter occurs after swimming, in hot, humid climates (76), and in diabetics (as "malignant external otitis" with extension into adjacent areas) (184). In newborns, *P. aeruginosa* may cause any type of infection, including severe enterocolitis and meningitis (107, 125). Meningitis in adults follows either contaminated spinal taps, trauma, or septicemia (107).

Pseudomonas spp. other than *P. aeruginosa* have been reviewed earlier (168). Their habitat is the same as that of *P. aeruginosa,* and resistance to disinfectants is observed in some. *Pseudomonas fluorescens* and *Pseudomonas putida* are primary psychrophils and as such most often are etiologically insignificant in human infections (168). *Pseudomonas cepacia* infections of the urinary and respiratory tracts have been recorded in hosts with a variety of underlying disorders (47), among them cancer, instrumentation, and chronic granulomatous disease. Some of the strains originated from contaminated disinfectants. Endocarditis caused by *P. cepacia* has been associated with heroin addiction and sickle cell anemia (168). *Pseudomonas maltophilia,* the most frequently isolated "unusual pseudomonad" in the United States, has occasionally caused infections in compromised hosts (168), but most isolates are etiologically indeterminate (71). The majority of *Pseudomonas pseudomallei* infections seem to be non-opportunistic. However, asymptomatic melioidosis, as revealed by positive serotests, is more frequent than overt disease in endemic areas, and recrudescent melioidosis has been observed long after initial exposure following diabetic ketoacidosis, surgery, burns, and pneumococcal pneumonia (168). Opportunistic infection with other *Pseudomonas* spp. is rare (73).

SPIRILLUM SPP The sparse literature on infections with *Spirillum* spp. other than *S. minus* has been reviewed earlier (98). In one patient with pancytopenia, septicemia developed; another one, an alcoholic, had meningitis. Data on the remaining four cases are too sketchy. The origin of the strains is unknown.

STAPHYLOCOCCUS SPP. Staphylococci are ubiquitous and are frequent inhabitants of the skin and the nasopharynx. Sources for human infections may be exogenous (contact transmission) or endogenous. The intact skin and polymorphonuclear leukocytes provide the most important protection and defense against infection. There are many predisposing factors for *Staphylococcus aureus* infection: (*a*) injury to the skin [wounds, incisions, decubiti (36, 69), dermatitis (150), and burns (131)]; (*b*) foreign bodies [i.v. and intraperitoneal catheters (108), sutures (150), and ventricular shunts (146); total parenteral nutrition may lead to *S. aureus* septicemia (67)]; (*c*) cardiovascular diseases [arteriosclerosis, shock (150), and previously damaged or normal (e.g. in heroin users) heart valves (105, 172)]; (*d*) lung diseases [chronic lung diseases (vide supra), cystic fibrosis (84), and the postoperative state (118); pneumonitis and septicemia (not in cystic fibrosis!) may occur]; (*e*) infectious diseases [influenza (128), measles (150), and pertussis (121) are known to predispose to staphylococcal pneumonia; *S. aureus* pneumonia in influenza shows predilection for pregnant women and patients with cardiopulmonary diseases (128)]; (*f*) diabetes mellitus [although systemic—but not wound (36)—infections with *S. aureus* are more frequent and more severe in diabetics than in a comparable population (34, 95), a direct relationship is questionable (effect of arteriosclerosis? acidosis? age?); *S. aureus* septicemia is a well-known complication (34)]; (*g*) defects in neutrophilic function (vide supra) [chronic granulomatous disease, neutropenic states, immunosuppression (transplants!), and special congenital leukocytic defects predispose to staphylococcal infections, particularly to those of the skin, lungs, and to septicemia (150); Hodgkin's disease usually shows such complications only after treatment (4, 29)]; (*h*) hepatic disease (95); (*i*) renal failure (117) [the blood urea nitrogen level usually correlates well with the severity of infection (95); wound infections, peritonitis, enterocolitis, and septicemia are observed (117), and in hemodialyzed patients, septicemia may also originate in the i.v. cannula]; and (*j*) the newborn age (vide supra). Certain staphylococcus-associated infections deserve special mention. Staphylococcal enterocolitis following surgery and antibiotic treatment now is rarely observed. Phage group III strains are most often involved. Pseudomembranous enterocolitis, however, is not specific for staphylococci (40, 107). Parotitis is seen under conditions of dehydration and renal failure (150). Polymyositis now also occurs in heroin addicts (105). Acute septic arthritis in older patients with long-standing rheumatoid arthritis has been described (138); only part of them had been treated with steroids. Finally, the predisposition of cancer patients for staphylococcal infections may be explained by several factors that were mentioned earlier.

Staphylococcus epidermidis has been incriminated as a pathogen only under few circumstances. Infections are less severe than those with *S. aureus.* They are as follows: (*a*) septicemia following i.v. cannulation (including total parenteral nutrition) (67, 108); (*b*) endocarditis, which shows a high incidence of underlying rheumatic heart disease and/or recent cardiac surgery (172); (*c*) shunt infections—ventriculo-atrial and ventriculo-peritoneal—which may also lead to bacteremia (146); (*d*) urinary tract infection in women (11); and (*e*) wound infections. A few cases with pure cultures of *S. epidermidis* in wound cultures have been reported (177), although no mention was made of anaerobic techniques used. However, deep wound infections with *S. epidermidis* after total hip arthroplasty are well documented (60). A role for *S. epidermidis* in otitis media has also been suggested (53).

STREPTOCOCCUS SPP. The sources of streptococcal infections in humans are either exogenous (i.e. infected individuals who transmit the organisms by contact or droplets) or endogenous (from colonized or infected areas). Protection against such infections is afforded by the intact skin, an antagonistic potential of normal mucosal floras, and by type-specific antibodies.

Streptococcus pyogenes (group A) infections are favored by circumstances that also favor staphylococcal infections. Primary sites are often the skin and the oropharynx. Wounds, incisions, decubiti, dermatitic areas, and burns (131) may become infected and may serve as sources for systemic infections. Puerperal infections are part of this picture. Streptococcal pneumonia may complicate influenza, rubella, rubeola, varicella, and pertussis (44, 97, 121). Hypogammaglobulinemia, asplenia, immunosuppression (transplantation/steroid therapy) (4, 44, 81, 102), cirrhosis (37), alcoholism (44), and uremia (44) predispose to systemic infection. Endocarditis of the acute variety may follow rheumatic heart disease (172). Septicemia is more often found in patients with solid tumors of the head, neck, and gastrointestinal tract than in those with hematologic malignancies; the sources often are operative sites or lymphedematous areas following lymph node dissection (81). Primary peritonitis is associated with cirrhosis (65) and nephrosis (143); however, not all cases show these predisposing factors (65).

Streptococcus agalactiae (group B) may also infect dermatitic areas, wounds, and burns (8). Primary sites are the genitourinary tract and the skin. *S. agalactiae* is a leading cause of neonatal septicemia and meningitis, transmitted either directly from the mother's genital tract (type I) or nosocomially by contact (type III) (54). High-risk factors for neonatal and maternal morbidity are a prolonged rupture-delivery interval, artificial rupture of the membranes for the mother, and prematurity for the child (135). *S. agalactiae* infections are unusually frequently associated with diabetes mellitus, in particular pyelonephritis (which is rarely caused by *S. pyogenes*), pneumonia, arthritis (16), and peripheral gangrene (8). Neoplasms under chemotherapy, liver disease, and renal failure (16) may also predispose to *S. agalactiae* infection. Types II and III are most commonly observed in adult infections; type I also occurs in newborn infections (16).

Group C and group G streptococci may be confused with *S. pyogenes* since they are sometimes bacitracin positive (9). Sources for human infections include the skin, the oropharynx, and the female genital tract. Endocarditis (44) as well as wound and systemic infections in patients with malignancies have been reported (9).

Viridans streptococci may cause disease if introduced into previously sterile areas, e.g. meningitis (100) or endocarditis of the subacute variety, especially on previously damaged valves (172).

Enterococci live in the large intestine and show a propensity to invade the urinary system. Their ability to cause wound infection must be questioned (85), although they may be found in wounds or ulcers in mixed culture (69, 85, 104). Opportunistic septicemias after renal transplantation (119), i.v. catheterization (108), and cerebrospinal fluid shunt operations (146) are known. Bacteremia and endocarditis may occur subsequent to genitourinary tract instrumentation (172) and may even lead to meningitis (100).

Streptococcus pneumoniae infections show some of the factors that predispose to *S. pyogenes* infection. The source is usually the respiratory tract; the recent tendency is towards involvement of higher serotypes (63). There are, however, certain pneumococcal diseases that are much more frequent than *S. pyogenes* infections under identical circumstances. Patients with chronic lung disease, previous surgery, influenza, pertussis, pulmonary tuberculosis, congestive heart failure, stupor, anesthesia, alcoholism (delirium tremens!), and diabetes mellitus (121, 128, 178) are particularly predisposed to pneumococcal pneumonia, which is often more severe than in patients with no discernible underlying condition. Pregnancy and cardiopulmonary disease are particular risk factors in pneumococcal pneumonia complicating influenza (128). In sickle cell anemia, fulminant and often fatal bacteremia, meningitis, pneumonia, and osteomyelitis are the most frequent infections observed (13). The risk is highest under 2 years of age; later, pneumococcal infections are seen only if previous ones have occurred (13). Hypoglobulinemic states, such as seen in multiple myeloma, macroglobulinemia (51), chronic lymphatic leukemia (51, 63), nephrosis (143, 174), and cancer under chemotherapy (63) predispose for pneumococcal pneumonia, septicemia, and, in nephrosis, peritonitis. Splenectomized patients, particularly children under 4 years old and those with high-risk factors as outlined above, may develop pneumonia, septicemia, and meningitis most often caused by *S. pneumoniae* (102). In Hodgkin's disease, the risk of infection after splenectomy is not considered high (43). Spontaneous pneumococcal peritonitis arises under similar circumstances as *S. pyogenes* peritonitis; vaginal colonization has been detected in some cases (65). Pneumococcal meningitis is often preceded by otitis media or by head trauma (163).

VIBRIO CHOLERAE A high prevalence of achlorhydria in patients with cholera has been noted (72), and experiments in volunteers suggest that subjects with achlorhydria, i.e. with a less than optimal pH for the bactericidal effect of gastric juice, might be especially susceptible to *Vibrio cholerae* infection (72).

CONCLUSION

This review has attempted to survey the spectrum of opportunistic bacteria. Some of them, like certain corynebacteria and neisseriae, have only become known as potential human pathogens through their association with compromised hosts. It is likely that more bacteria, as well as more predisposing conditions, will be added to the present list as more compromised hosts survive and as more becomes known about the intrinsic defense mechanisms of the human body.

Literature Cited

1. Abrutyn, E., Plotkin, S. 1975. In *Pathogenic Microorganisms from Atypical Clinical Sources,* ed. A. von Graevenitz, T. Sall, pp. 113–23. New York: Dekker. 229 p.
2. Adler, J. L., Burke, J. P., Martin, D. F., Finland, M. 1971. *Ann. Intern. Med.* 75:531–36
3. Albrecht, R., Horowitz, S., Gilbert, E., Hong, R., Richard, J., Conner, D. H. 1974. *Pediatrics* 53:907–12
3a. Albritton, W. L., Wiggins, G. L., Feeley, J. C. 1976. *J. Pediatr.* 88:481–83
4. Allen, J. C. 1976. In *Infection and the Compromised Host,* ed. J. C. Allen, pp. 151–71. Baltimore: Williams & Wilkins. 176 pp.
5. Alpern, R. J., Dowell, V. R. Jr. 1969. *J. Am. Med. Assoc.* 209:385–88
6. Amonette, R. A., Rosenberg, E. W. 1973. *Arch. Dermatol.* 107:71–73
7. Anderson, R. J., Schafer, L. A., Olin, D. B., Eickhoff, T. C. 1973. *Am. J. Med.* 54:453–60
8. Anthony, B. F., Concepcion, N. F. 1975. *J. Infect. Dis.* 132:561–67
9. Armstrong, D., Blevins, A., Louria, D. B., Henkel, J. S., Moody, M. D., Sukany, M. 1970. *Ann. NY Acad. Sci.* 174:511–22
10. Aserkoff, B., Bennett, J. V. 1969. *N. Engl. J. Med.* 281:636–40
11. Bailey, R. J., Cullens, H., Woolf, I. L., Williams, R. 1976. *Lancet* 2:1162–63
12. Bailey, R. R. 1973. *J. Infect. Dis.* 127:179–82
13. Barrett-Connor, E. 1971. *Medicine* 50:97–112

14. Bates, J. H. 1967. *Am. Rev. Resp. Dis.* 96:1151–57
15. Baum, J. 1971. *Arthritis Rheum.* 14:135–37
16. Bayer, A. S., Chow, A. W., Anthony, B. F., Guze, L. B. 1976. *Am. J. Med.* 61: 498–503
17. Beaman, B. L., Burnside, J., Edwards, B., Causey, W. 1976. *J. Infect. Dis.* 134:286–89
18. Bennett, I. L. Jr., Hook, E. W. 1959. *Ann. Rev. Med.* 10:1–20
19. Berger, U., Aboulkhair, I., Rottmann, W. 1974. *Infection* 2:108–10
20. Biggar, W. D. See Ref. 4, pp. 1–27
21. Black, P. H., Kunz, L. J., Swartz, M. N. 1960. *N. Engl. J. Med.* 262:811–17; 864–70; 921–27
22. Bojsen-Moller, J. 1972. *Acta Pathol. Microbiol. Scand.* 229(S):1–157
23. Bokkenheuser, V. See Ref. 1, pp. 25–32
24. Brooks, G. F., O'Donoghue, J. M., Rissing, J. P., Soapes, K., Smith, J. W. 1974. *Medicine* 53:325–42
25. Burack, W. R., Hollister, R. M. 1960. *Am. J. Med.* 28:510–23
26. Burnett, A. K., Easton, D. J., Gordon, A. M., Rowan, R. M. 1975. *Scott. Med. J.* 20:37–38
27. Butzler, J. P., Dekeyser, P., Lafontaine, T. 1974. *Antimicrob. Agents Chemother.* 5:86–89
28. Carpenter, J. L., Blom, J. 1976. *Am. Rev. Resp. Dis.* 114:235–39
29. Casazza, A. R., Duvall, C. P., Carbone, P. P. 1966. *J. Am. Med. Assoc.* 197: 118–24
30. Cherubin, C. E., Neu, H. C., Imperato, P. J., Harvey, R. P., Bellen, N. 1974. *Medicine* 53:365–76
31. Church, J. A., Frenkel, L. D., Wright, D. G., Bellanti, J. A. 1976. *J. Pediatr.* 88:982–85
32. Chusid, M. J., Parrillo, J. E., Fauci, A. S. 1975. *J. Am. Med. Assoc.* 233: 1295–96
33. Clift, R. A., Buckner, C. D., Fefer, A., Lerner, K. G., Neiman, P. E., Storb, R., Murphy, M., Thomas, E. D. 1974. *Transplant Proc.* 6:389–93
34. Cluff, L. E., Reynolds, R. C., Page, D. L., Breckenridge, J. L. 1968. *Ann. Intern. Med.* 69:859–73
35. Cobb, S., Hall, W. 1965. *J. Am. Med. Assoc.* 193:1077–79
36. Committee on Trauma. 1964. *Ann. Surg.* 160(S):1–192
37. Conn, H. O., Fessel, J. M. 1971. *Medicine* 50:161–97
38. Coyle-Gilchrist, M. M., Crewe, P., Roberts, G. 1976. *J. Clin. Pathol.* 29: 824–26
39. Curreri, P. W., Bruck, H.M., Lindberg, R. B., Mason, A. D., Pruitt, B. A. 1973. *Ann. Surg.* 177:133–38
40. Dearing, W. H., Baggenstoss, A. H., Weed, L. A. 1960. *Gastroenterology* 38: 441–51
41. DeBoer, R. G., Dumler, M. 1963. *Am. J. Clin. Pathol.* 40:339–44
42. De Marcha, P. 1975. *Chest* 68:800–5
43. Desser, R. K., Ultmann, J. E. 1972. *Ann. Intern. Med.* 77:143–46
44. Duma, R. J., Weinberg, A. N., Medrek, T. F., Kunz, L. J. 1969. *Medicine* 48:87–127
45. DuPont, H. L., Spink, W. W. 1969. *Medicine* 48:307–32
46. Dupuis, F., Vereerstraeten, P., van Geertruyden, J., Kinnaert, P., Schoutens, E., Toussaint, C. 1974. *Clin. Nephrol.* 2:131–35
47. Ederer, G. M., Matsen, J. M. 1972. *J. Infect. Dis.* 125:613–18
48. Edmondson, E. B., Sanford, J. P. 1967. *Medicine* 46:323–340
49. Eisenach, K. D., Reber, R. M., Eitzman, D. V., Baer, H. 1972. *Pediatrics* 50:395–402
49a. El-Din Hathout, S., El-Ghaffar, Y. A., Awny, A. Y. 1967. *Am. J. Trop. Med. Hyg.* 16:462–72
50. Ellner, P. D., McCarthy, L. R. 1973. *Am. J. Clin. Pathol.* 59:216–18
51. Fahey, J. L., Scoggins, R., Utz, J. P., Szwed, C. F. 1963. *Am. J. Med.* 35:698–707
52. Fauconnier, B., Cormier, M., Fabiani, G. 1974. *Nouv. Presse Med.* 3:2026
53. Feigin, R. D., Shackelford, P. G., Campbell, J., Lyles, T. O., Schechter, M., Lins, R. D. 1973. *Pediatrics* 52: 569–76
54. Feigin, R. D., Shearer, W. T. 1975. *J. Pediatr.* 87:507–14; 515–18; 852–66
55. Feld, R., Bodey, G. P., Groeschel, D. 1976. *Arch. Intern. Med.* 136:67–70
56. Felts, S. K., Schaffner, W., Melly, M. A., Koenig, G. 1972. *Ann. Intern. Med.* 77:881–90
57. Fields, B. N., Uwaydah, M. M., Kunz, L. J., Swartz, M. N. 1967. *Am. J. Med.* 42:89–106
58. Finegold, S. M., Marsh, V. H., Bartlett, J. G. 1971. In *Proc. Int. Conf. Nosocomial Infect.*, pp. 123–34. Chicago: Am. Hosp. Assoc. 334 pp.
59. Finegold, S. M., Rosenblatt, J. E. 1973. *Medicine* 52:311–22
60. Fitzgerald, R. H., Peterson, L. F., Washington, J. A., Van Scoy, R. E.,

Coventry, M. B. 1973. *J. Bone Joint Surg.* 55(A): 1242–50
61. Flick, J. A. 1976. *Am. Rev. Resp. Dis.* 114:257–65
62. Flick, M. R., Cluff, L. E. 1976. *Am. J. Med.* 60:501–8
63. Folland, D., Armstrong, D., Seides, S., Blevins, A. 1974. *Cancer* 33:845–49
64. Ford, D. K., Price, G. E., Culling, C. F. A., Vassar, P. S. 1962. *Am. J. Med.* 33:478–89
65. Fowler, R. 1957. *Aust. N. Z. J. Surg.* 26:204–13
66. Foy, H. M., Ochs, H., Davis, S. D., Kenny, G. E., Luce, R. R. 1973. *J. Infect. Dis.* 127:388–93
67. Freeman, J. B., Litton, A. A. 1974. *Surg. Gynecol. Obstet.* 139:905–8
68. Fulginiti, V. A., Scribner, R., Groth, C. G., Putnam, C. W., Brettschneider, L., Gilbert, S., Porter, K. A., Starzl, T. E. 1968. *N. Engl. J. Med.* 279:619–26
69. Galpin, J. E., Chow, A. W., Bayer, A. S., Guze, L. B. 1976. *Am. J. Med.* 61:346–50
70. Gantz, N. M., Myerowitz, R. L., Medeiros, A. A., Carrera, G. F., Wilson, R. E., O'Brien, T. F. 1975. *Am. J. Med.* 58:637–43
71. Gardner, P., Griffin, W. B., Swartz, M. N., Kunz, L. J. 1970. *Am. J. Med.* 48:735–49
72. Giannella, R. A., Broitman, S. A., Zamcheck, N. 1973. *Ann. Intern. Med.* 78:271–76
73. Gilardi, G. L., 1972. *Ann. Intern. Med.* 77:211–15
74. Goodman, J. S., Koenig, M. G. 1970. *Ann. NY Acad. Sci.* 174:552–67
75. Gorbach, S. L., Bartlett, J. G. 1974. *N. Engl. J. Med.* 290:1177–84; 1237–45; 1289–94
76. Hall, J. H., Callaway, J. L., Tindall, J. P., Smith, J. G. 1968. *Arch. Dermatol.* 97:312–24
77. Han, T., Sokal, J. E., Neter, E. 1967. *N. Engl. J. Med.* 276:1045–52
78. Deleted in proof
79. Henderson, A. 1963. *Antonie van Leeuwenhoek J. Microbiol. Serol.* 29:359–67
80. Henjyoji, E. Y., Whitson, T. C., Ohashi, D. K., Allen, B. D. 1971. *J. Trauma* 11:417–21
81. Henkel, J. S., Armstrong, D., Blevins, A., Moody, M. D. 1970. *J. Am. Med. Assoc.* 211:983–86
82. Henriksen, S. D. 1973. *Bacteriol. Rev.* 37:522–61
83. Holm, M. I., Davison, W. C. 1919. *Bull. Johns Hopkins Hosp.* 30:324–29
84. Holsclaw, D. S. 1970. *Clin. Pediatr.* 9:346–55
85. Horvitz, R., von Graevenitz, A. 1977. *Yale J. Biol. Med.* In press
86. Hubrechts, J. M., Bouton, J. M., De Coninck, P., van Beers, D., Butzler, J. P. 1976. *Med. Mal. Infect.* 6:66–69
87. Iannini, P. B., Claffey, T., Quintiliani, R. 1974. *J. Am. Med. Assoc.* 230:558–61
88. Iannini, P. B., Eickhoff, T. C., LaForce, F. M. 1976. *Ann. Intern. Med.* 85: 161–64
89. Ihde, D. C., Armstrong, D. 1973. *Am. J. Med.* 55:839–45
90. Johanson, W. G., Pierce, A. K., Sanford, J. P., Thomas, G. D. 1972. *Ann. Intern. Med.* 77:701–6
91. Johnson, R. H., Lutwick, L. I., Huntley, G. A., Vosti, K. L. 1976. *Ann. Intern. Med.* 85:587–92
92. Johnson, W. D., Kaye, D. 1970. *Ann. NY Acad. Sci.* 174:568–76
93. Juif, J.-G. Richard, C., Lavillaureix, J., Berland, H., Schneegans, P., Beauvais, P. 1974. *Arch. Fr. Pediatr.* 31:759–64
94. Kaplan, M. H., Armstrong, D., Rosen, P. 1974. *Cancer* 33:850–58
95. Keene, W. R., Minchew, B. H., Cluff, L. E. 1961. *N. Engl. J. Med.* 265: 1128–34
96. Ketover, B. P., Young, L. S., Armstrong, D. 1973. *J. Infect. Dis.* 127: 284–90
97. Kevy, S. V., Lowe, B. A. 1961. *N. Engl. J. Med.* 264:738–43
98. Kowal, J. 1961. *N. Engl. J. Med.* 264: 123–28
99. Lazarus, G. M., Neu, H. C. 1975. *J. Pediatr.* 86:415–17
100. Lerner, P. I. 1975. *J. Infect. Dis.* 131(S):9–14
101. Levine, A. S., Schimpff, S. C., Graw, R. G., Young, R. C. 1974. *Semin. Hematol.* 11:141–202
102. Likhite, V. V. 1976. *J. Am. Med. Assoc.* 236:1376–77
103. Liu, Y. K. 1973. *Am. J. Med.* 54: 605–10
104. Louie, T. J., Bartlett, J. G., Tally, F. P., Gorbach, S. L. 1976. *Ann. Intern. Med.* 85:461–63
105. Louria, D. B. 1974. *Ann. Rev. Med.* 25:219–31
106. Louria, D. B., Blevins, A., Armstrong, D. 1970. *Ann. NY Acad. Sci.* 174: 545–51
107. Lowbury, E. J. L. 1975. In *Genetics and Biochemistry of Pseudomonas,* ed. P. H. Clarke, M. H. Richmond, pp. 37–65. New York: Wiley. 366 pp.

108. Maki, D. G., Goldmann, D. A., Rhame, F. S. 1973. *Ann. Intern. Med.* 79:867–87
109. McCabe, W. R. 1976. *Ann. Rev. Med.* 27:335–41
110. McNamara, M. J., Phillips, I. A., Williams, O. B. 1969. *Am. Rev. Resp. Dis.* 100:19–24
111. Medoff, G., Kunz, L. J., Weinberg, A. N. 1971. *J. Infect. Dis.* 123:247–50
112. Melzer, M., Altmann, G., Rakowszcyk, M., Yosipovitch, Z. H., Barsilai, B. 1965. *J. Urol.* 94:23–27
113. Meyers, B. R., Bottone, E., Hirschman, S. Z., Schneierson, S. S. 1972. *Ann. Intern. Med.* 76:9–14
114. Meyers, B. R., Hirschman, S. Z., Axelrod, J. A. 1972. *Am. J. Med.* 52:87–92
115. Mills, J., Drew, D. 1976. *Ann. Intern. Med.* 84:29–35
116. Mollaret, H. H. 1976. *Med. Mal. Infect.* 6:442–47
117. Montgomerie, J. Z., Kalmanson, G. M., Guze, L. B. 1968. *Medicine* 47:1–32
118. Morgan, E. H., Lancaster, L. J., Pearsall, H. R., Lawrence, G. H. 1960. *Dis. Chest* 38:1–12
119. Myerowitz, R. L., Medeiros, A. A., O'Brien, T. F. 1972. *Am. J. Med.* 53:308–14
120. Neter, E., Merrin, C., Surgalla, M. J., Wajsman, Z. 1974. *Urology* 4:198–200
121. Olson, L. C. 1975. *Medicine* 54:427–69
122. Paff, J. R., Triplett, D. A., Saari, T. N. 1976. *Am. J. Clin. Pathol.* 66:101–10
123. Palmer, D. L., Harvey, R. L., Wheeler, J. K. 1974. *Medicine* 53:391–401
124. Palutke, W. A., Boyd, C. B., Carter, G. R. 1973. *Am. J. Med. Sci.* 266:305–8
125. Paul, R., Marget, W. 1963. *Dtsch. Med. Wochenschr.* 88:1638–43
126. Pearson, H. E. 1970. *Am. J. Clin. Pathol.* 53:506–15
127. Pedersen, M. M., Marso, E., Pickett, M. J. 1970. *Am. J. Clin. Pathol.* 54:178–92
128. Petersdorf, R. G., Fusco, J. J., Harter, D. H., Albrink, W. S. 1959. *Arch. Intern. Med.* 103:262–72
129. Pien, F. D., Martin, W. J., Hermans, P. E., Washington, J. A. 1972. *Mayo Clin. Proc.* 47:739–45
130. Provost, T., Allen, J. C. See Ref. 4, pp. 133–49
131. Pruitt, B. A. 1974. *J. Infect. Dis.* 130(S):8–13
132. Quie, P. G. See Ref. 4, pp. 81–101
133. Quintiliani, R., Hymans, P. J. 1971. *Am. J. Med.* 50:781–86
134. Rabson, A. R., Hallett, A. F., Koornhof, H. J. 1975. *J. Infect. Dis.* 131: 447–51
135. Reid, T. M. S. 1975. *Lancet* 2:533–36
136. Reller, L. B., Maddoux, G. L., Eckman, M. R., Pappas, G. 1975. *Abstr. Ann. Meet. Am. Soc. Microbiol.* p. 49
137. Rhoades, E. R., Ringrose, R., Mohr, J. A., Brooks, L., McKown, B. A., Felton, F. 1971. *Arch. Intern. Med.* 127:228–32
138. Rimoin, D. L., Wennberg, J. E. 1966. *J. Am. Med. Assoc.* 196:617–21
139. Robin, E. D., Thomas, E. D. 1954. *Arch. Intern. Med.* 93:713–24
140. Rocha, H., Kirk, J. W., Hearey, C. D. 1971. *Arch. Intern. Med.* 128:254–57
141. Rosenthal, S. L. 1974. *Am. J. Clin. Pathol.* 62:807–11
142. Rosett, W., Heck, D. M., Hodges, G. R. 1976. *Chest* 70:664–65
143. Rubin, H. M., Blau, E. B., Michaels, R. H. 1975. *Pediatrics* 56:598–601
144. Sachs, J.M., Pacin, M., Counts, G. W. 1974. *Am. J. Dis. Child.* 128:387–88
145. Schimpff, S. C., Greene, W. H., Young, V. M., Wiernik, P. H. 1974. *J. Infect. Dis.* 130(S):24–32
146. Schoenbaum, S. C., Gardner, P., Shillito, J. 1975. *J. Infect. Dis.* 131:543–52
147. Selden, R., Lee, S., Wang, W. L. L., Bennett, J. V., Eickhoff, T. C. 1971. *Ann. Intern. Med.* 74:657–64
148. Sellers, D. P., Wise, J. R., Semer, H. A. 1969. *J. Maine Med. Assoc.* 60:262
149. Sharpe, M. E., Hill, L. R., Lapage, S. P. 1972. *J. Med. Microbiol.* 6:281–86
150. Shulman, J. A., Nahmias, A. J. 1972. In *The Staphylococci,* ed. J. O. Cohen, pp. 457–81. New York: Wiley. 548 pp.
151. Shulman, S. T., Bartlett, J., Clyde, W. A., Ayoub, E. M. 1972. *N. Engl. J. Med.* 287:164–67
152. Silver, H. K., Simon, J. L., Clement, D. H. 1957. *Pediatrics* 20:439–47
153. Snyder, S. N., Brunjes, S. 1965. *Am. J. Med. Sci.* 250:658–67
154. Somerville, D. A., Lancaster-Smith, M. 1973. *Br. J. Dermatol.* 89:395–400
155. Sones, M., Israel, H. L. 1960. *Am. J. Med.* 29:84–93
156. Soussy, C. J., Squinazi, F. J., Duval, J. 1975. *Med. Mal. Infect.* 5:11–19
157. Stamm, W., Colella, J., Anderson, R., Dixon, R. 1975. *N. Engl. J. Med.* 292:1099–102
158. Staples, P. J., Gerding, D. N., Decker, J. L., Gordon, R. S. 1974. *Arthritis Rheum.* 17:1–10
159. Steiger, Z., Nickel, W. O., Shannon, G. J., Nedwicki, E. G., Higgins, R. F. 1976. *Am. J. Surg.* 131:668–71
160. Stinson, E. B., Beiber, C. P., Griepp, R. B., Clark, D. A., Shumway, N. E.,

Remington, J. S. 1971. *Ann. Intern. Med.* 74:22–36
161. Strand, C. L., Helfman, L. 1971. *Am. J. Clin. Pathol.* 55:713–16
162. Sudre, Y., Brisou, J., Lefevre, J. P., Pouget-Abadie, J. F., Becq-Giraudon, B., Gil, R., Denis, F., Talin d'Eyzac, A. 1974. *Med. Mal. Infect.* 4:479–86
163. Swartz, M. N., Dodge, P. R. 1965. *N. Engl. J. Med.* 272:779–87
164. Tillotson, J. R., Lerner, A. M. 1968. *Ann. Intern. Med.* 68:287–94
165. Tillotson, J. R., Lerner, A. M. 1968. *Arch. Intern. Med.* 121:428–32
166. Unger, P., Lundström, M., Olsson, P., Ekestrom, S. 1963. *J. Cardiovasc. Surg.* 4:664–68
167. Vejlsgaard, R. 1966. *Acta Med. Scand.* 179:173–82
168. von Graevenitz, A. 1973. *Prog. Clin. Pathol.* 5:185–218
169. von Graevenitz, A., Carrington, G. O. See Ref. 1, pp. 33–39
170. von Graevenitz, A., Mensch, A. 1968. *N. Engl. J. Med.* 278:245–49
171. Ward, P. A., Berenberg, J. L. 1974. *N. Engl. J. Med.* 290:76–80
172. Weinstein, L., Rubin, R. H. 1973. *Prog. Cardiovasc. Dis.* 16:239–74
173. Wenzel, R. P., Hunting, K. J., Osterman, C. A., Sande, M. A. 1976. *Am. J. Epidemiol.* 104:170–80
174. Wilfert, C. M., Katz, S. L. 1968. *Pediatrics* 42:840–43
175. Williams, D. M., Krick, J. A., Remington, J. S. 1976. *Am. Rev. Resp. Dis.* 114:359–94
176. Wilson, G. S., Miles, A., eds. 1975. *Topley and Wilson's Principles of Bacteriology, Virology, and Immunity,* pp. 1724–85. Baltimore: Williams & Wilkins. 2706 pp. 6th ed.
177. Wilson, T. S., Stuart, R. D. 1965. *Can. Med. Assoc. J.* 93:8–16
178. Winterbauer, R. H., Bedon, G. A., Ball, W. C. Jr. 1969. *Ann. Intern. Med.* 70:689–700
179. Wise, N. B., Poston, M. A. 1940. *J. Am. Med. Assoc.* 115:1976–84
180. Witchitz, J., Richard, C., Coulaud, J. P., Homareau, S., Pasticier, A., Saimot, G. 1975. *Med. Mal. Infect.* 5:260–62
181. Wolfe, M. S., Armstrong, D., Louria, D. B., Blevins, A. 1971. *Arch. Intern. Med.* 128:546–54
182. Young, L. S., Armstrong, D., Blevins, A., Lieberman, P. 1971. *Am. J. Med.* 50:356–67
183. Young, L. S., La Force, F. M., Head, J. J., Feeley, J. C., Bennett, J. V. 1972. *N. Engl. J. Med.* 287:5–9
184. Zaky, D. A., Bentley, D. W., Lowy, K., Betts, R. F., Douglas, R. G. 1976. *Am. J. Med.* 61:298–302

Ann. Rev. Microbiol. 1977. 31:473–505

TANDEM GENETIC DUPLICATIONS IN PHAGE AND BACTERIA

❖1714

R. Philip Anderson and John R. Roth
Department of Biology, University of Utah, Salt Lake City, Utah 84112

CONTENTS

INTRODUCTION 473
The Genetic Consequences of Tandem Duplications 474
General Methods for Detecting Tandem Duplications 477
SELECTION OF TANDEM DUPLICATIONS 478
Gene Dosage 478
Coinheritance of Allelic Markers 485
Operon Fusion 496
GENERAL CONCLUSIONS 501
Size and Frequency of Tandem Duplications 501
Mechanisms of Tandem Duplication 501
Uses of Duplications in Genetic Analysis 502
Gene Duplication as a Regulatory Mechanism 502

INTRODUCTION

Within the last several years, methods have been developed for detection and analysis of tandem duplications of genetic material in bacteria and phage. Although the mechanisms for formation of these duplications are not yet completely clear, it seems reasonable to review the accumulating literature on this phenomenon. The nature and frequency of duplications raises the possibility that this mode of gene amplification could play a significant role in bacterial adaptation. It has also been suggested that gene duplication plays an important role in evolution (47, 93, 137). The high frequency of duplications helps to explain a variety of past genetic observations involving unstable mutants and recombinants that revert to their original state with high frequency. Duplications provide a potential method for genetic analysis, including chromosome mapping and complementation testing in bacterial species that lack a conjugation system. This review considers only tandem duplications, since virtually all duplications analyzed in detail in bacteria appear to be of this type.

The Genetic Consequences of Tandem Duplications

Before discussing experimental data, it is important to consider the behavior and formal genetic aspects of tandem duplications. These considerations lead to predictions that are borne out by the experimental data.

TANDEM DUPLICATIONS GENERALLY CAUSE NO LOSS OF FUNCTION The reasons tandem duplications generally cause no loss of function can be seen in the diagram of a tandem duplication presented in Figure 1. In the chromosome carrying the duplication, the only impropriety in sequence is the marked point between the two tandemly repeated copies (*i–d*). This impropriety does not lead to a loss of function because proper versions of these sequences are present elsewhere (*c–d* and *i–j*). For this reason, one would expect no loss of function to result from the duplication mutation. Exceptions to this rule are duplications of material within a single gene, which could inactivate that gene, and duplications of several genes within a single operon, which could generate a polar effect at the join point between duplicated segments upon expression of that operon. Thus, the rule should hold as long as relatively large segments of chromosome are duplicated; this is usually found to be the case.

TANDEM DUPLICATIONS SHARE MANY PROPERTIES WITH DELETIONS Formally, both duplications and deletions can be generated by illegitimate, unequal recombination (39, 41) between nonhomologous sequences on homologous chromosomes (114). They could also be generated by legitimate, unequal recombination between identical or similar sequences located at distinct points on these chromosomes. This is illustrated in Figure 2 with recombination between daughter chromo-

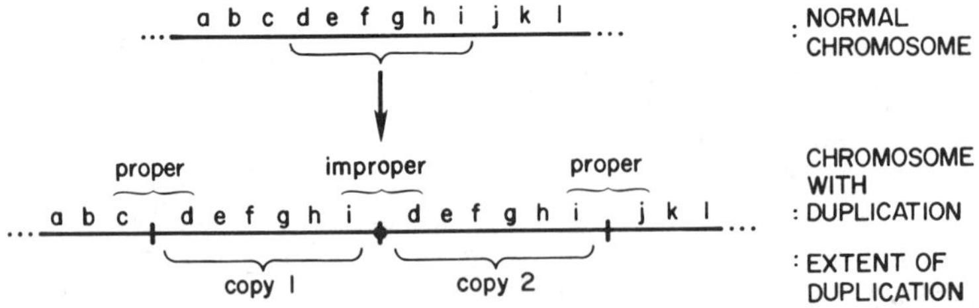

Figure 1 Tandem duplication of the chromosomal segment *defghi*. Lower case letters are nongenetic indications of hypothetical base sequences.

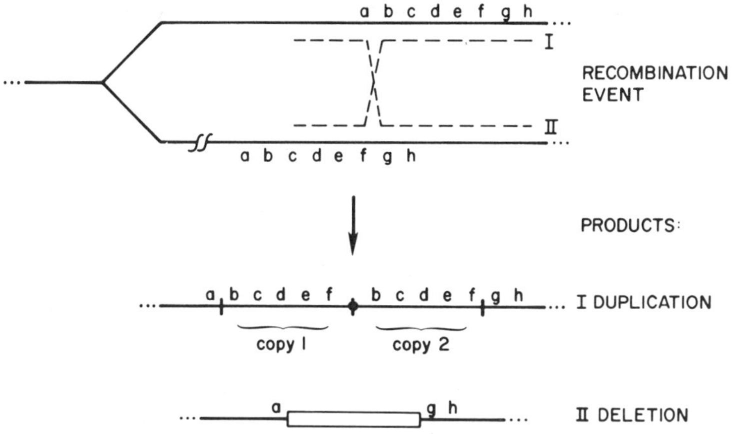

Figure 2 Illegitimate recombination resulting in duplication (I) or deletion (II) of the chromosomal segment *bcdef*. Solid lines indicate double-stranded DNA. Dashed lines represent a reciprocal recombination event.

somes. Reciprocal recombination between the sites *a–b* and *f–g* (which might not involve sequence homology) results in recombinant chromosomes (I) carrying a duplication of the sequence *b c d e f* and (II) carrying a deletion of the same sequence. It would not be surprising if at least some duplications and deletions were generated by the same mechanism.

Both duplications and deletions have a single base sequence not found in the chromosome from which they were derived (the "novel joint") (49). In deletions, extensive material has been removed at that point to make the new sequence; in duplications, material has been added at that site to generate the impropriety. These similarities should be kept in mind when considering genetic crosses involving these two mutational types.

DUPLICATIONS MAY BE OF UNLIMITED SIZE Since duplications lead to no loss of function, it seems possible that illegitimate recombination between any two points in the chromosome could give rise to a viable duplication-carrying recombinant. The corresponding deletion mutants would be unlikely to survive if the exchange points were far apart in the chromosome, since essential functions would be lost. The only restriction on the size of a duplication might be the ability of the cell to replicate and segregate this larger chromosome faithfully.

DUPLICATIONS MAY BE FREQUENT OCCURRENCES The large number of potential exchanges that yield duplication mutants and the high probability that these mutants will be viable suggest that duplications might be encountered frequently if appropriate conditions were provided for their detection. If duplications and deletions were generated by the same mechanism, one would expect that detectable duplications would be much more common than deletions, since only very small deletions would be viable.

DUPLICATIONS ARE SUBJECT TO FREQUENT LOSS AND FURTHER AMPLIFICATION The existence of a duplication should be an unstable situation. Normal recombination between the two copies should lead either to loss of the duplication or to further amplification (i.e. triplication) of the chromosomal segment. The events causing this instability are depicted in Figure 3 as recombinational events between nascent daughter chromosomes. Alternatively, loss of the duplication could also be imagined to occur by a reciprocal exchange between the tandemly located copies in a single chromosome. In Figure 3, homologous exchange is seen to give rise to either loss of the duplication (II) or to triplication of the segment (I). Since both of these events involve legitimate recombination between homologous sequences, they might be expected to occur frequently.

EXTREMELY LARGE DUPLICATIONS CAN BE TRANSDUCED As mentioned earlier, the only novel base sequence in chromosomes carrying a duplication is the join point between copies of the duplicated segment. At this point, sequences that would be widely separated in a normal chromosome are made contiguous. Transduction of this join point from a donor harboring a duplication into a normal recipient may have surprising results. It is possible to reestablish the donor's duplication state in the recipient cell. This is even possible when the region included in the duplication is much too large to be carried by a transducing phage. Recombination events that account for this behavior are depicted in Figure 4. Once a transduced fragment including the join point enters a recipient cell, recombination events between that fragment and two copies of the homologous region can serve to regenerate the duplication state. In the final recombinant, most of the duplicated material is derived from the recipient chromosome; only material adjacent to the join point is derived from the donor parent. Thus, transduction of large tandem duplications may be detected, provided the selected donor marker and the join point between duplicated material are cotransducible. Transductional events such as those described in Figure 4 were first suggested by Campbell (20). Further evidence in support of these events has been presented (4, 55).

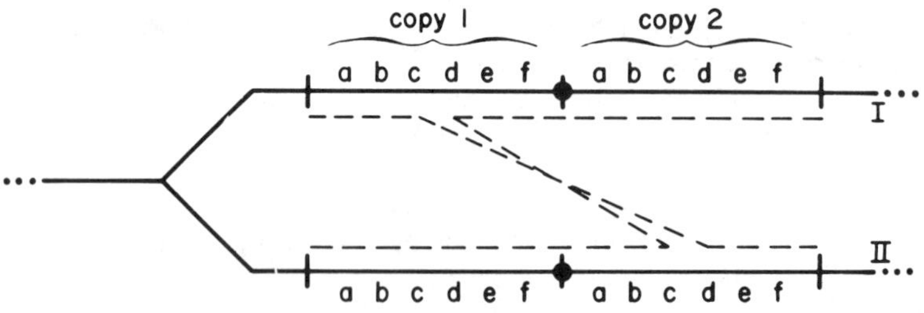

Figure 3 Legitimate recombination resulting in triplication (I) or haploidization (II) of a tandem duplication.

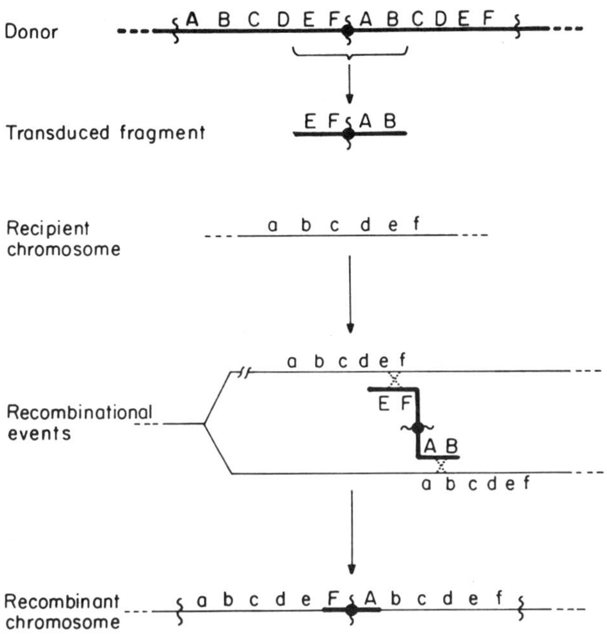

Figure 4 A mechanism for transduction of large tandem duplications. Recipient and donor DNAs are light and bold lined, respectively. Dotted lines represent reciprocal recombination events.

General Methods for Detecting Tandem Duplications

Selection schemes designed to detect tandem duplication mutants in a haploid population must capitalize upon some special property conferred by the diploid state. The merodiploid nature of tandem duplications and the sequence impropriety found at the join point between duplicated regions are often traits that lend themselves to selection. All selections described below have utilized these traits in one of three different ways. These represent three basic approaches to the selection and maintenance of tandem duplications.

GENE DOSAGE Strains merodiploid for a particular gene should produce approximately twice the amount of that gene product. If such an increase confers a selectable phenotype, strains harboring duplications may be selected from the haploid population. If appropriate selections exist, strains harboring multiple tandem copies may be selected from this merodiploid population. Selections of this general type probably make very few constraints upon the size of duplications generated. Duplication of material adjacent to the gene of interest will likely be of little consequence, provided the extra DNA may be replicated in an orderly fashion. Thus, this selection method should yield duplications that are the best indicators of the sizes and frequencies of spontaneous duplications.

COINHERITANCE OF ALLELIC MARKERS A variety of detection schemes involve genetic crosses that select for simultaneous inheritance of two alleles of a single locus. These alleles may be mutually exclusive (such as two different forms of a single gene product), such that only merodiploid strains may inherit both, or they may be complementing mutations that cannot recombine to produce true wild-type recombinants (such as overlapping complementing deletions). Coinheritance of such allele pairs is possible in heterogenotes merodiploid for the region of interest.

OPERON FUSION Analogous to fusion of genes by the deletion of intervening material (85), genes may also be fused by tandem duplication. Figure 5 shows how this may be accomplished. Tandem duplications whose end points lie within different units of transcription lead to fusion of one operon's structural genes to another operon's regulatory elements. An important feature of this selection is that neither operon is destroyed by the tandem duplication, yet a new hybrid one is created. The only requirement is that both operons have the same direction of transcription. Detection methods of this type most frequently select for turn-on of genes whose expression has been shut off, either because of polarity effects or because of inactivation of controlling elements. Unlike methods previously described, selections of this type severely restrict the permissible end points of the duplications obtained. To obtain hybrid gene expression, end points must be near the gene to be expressed and near a functional promoter oriented in the appropriate direction. Thus, sizes and frequencies observed by this method represent only a small subset of the total duplication events that occur.

SELECTION OF TANDEM DUPLICATIONS

Gene Dosage

LACTOSE OPERON Experiments by Novick et al (61, 62, 90, 91) have provided the first well-documented case of a gene dosage selection for tandem duplications. *Escherichia coli* strains capable of high rates of β-galactosidase synthesis (up to 25% of total cellular protein) were isolated following long-term growth selection in a chemostat containing limiting lactose as the sole carbon source. Such "hypersynthesizing" strains synthesize β-galactosidase constitutively at a level fourfold higher than normal strains. Apparently, initial selection in the chemostat yielded *lacI*$^-$ mutants. These were later replaced by strains harboring multiple tandem copies (up to four) of the constitutive *lac* operon. A number of observations support this conclusion. (*a*) The hypersynthesizing character is unstable. Segregation of stable haploid strains through loss of the extra gene sets is relatively frequent. Moreover, segregants of intermediate expression (indicating an intermediate number of gene copies) may be obtained. (*b*) The biochemical properties of β-galactosidase produced by hypersynthesizing strains is qualitatively identical in all respects to normal enzyme. (More, not better, enzyme is being made.) (*c*) During conjugational crosses,

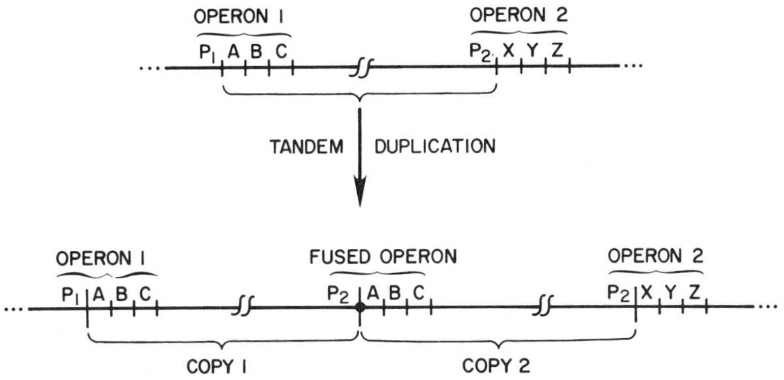

Figure 5 A mechanism for operon fusion based upon tandem duplication of intervening material.

the hypersynthesizing character is transferred at a time expected for *lac* chromosomal genes (i.e. the extra copies are closely linked to *lac*). Also, the "hyper" character is transducible by phage P1. (*d*) Diploidy for *lac* genes may be demonstrated genetically.

The duplications harbored by these strains are relatively small. Genetic tests indicate that the nearby markers *tsx* and *pro* are not duplicated. Thus, the duplicated material in these strains is less than 3 chromosomal min in length.

The nature of the selection used for isolating these duplications (optimal growth in a chemostat) makes estimation of the duplication frequency difficult. However, it is possible roughly to estimate this frequency in two ways. Data obtained by Horiuchi et al (61) indicate a spontaneous duplication rate of approximately 10^{-3}. While analyzing the recombinants obtained from conjugational crosses between haploid lac^+ donors (Hfr $lacI^-Z^+Y^+A^+$) and haploid lac^- recipients (F^- $lacI^+Z^+Y^-A^+$), one unexpected heterogenote was identified among 928 lac^+ exconjugants. This strain was concluded to contain a tandem duplication of the *lac* region, each copy of which harbored one parental allele. Since both parents in this cross were haploid, the recovery of 1 duplication per (roughly) 1000 normal haploid recombinants indicates a spontaneous duplication rate (in either the donor or the recipient) of approximately 10^{-3} (see below). The duplicated material in this strain includes both the *tsx* and *pro* loci and, thus, is considerably larger than the duplications studied in the *lac* hypersynthesizing strains.

A second estimate of the *lac* duplication frequency has been obtained more recently by Langridge (73). Sodium lactobionate is not utilized as a carbon source by *E. coli* because it is only poorly bound and hydrolyzed by β-galactosidase. Mutations conferring quantitative increases in β-galactosidase synthesis (probably analogous to hypersynthesizing strains) arise at a spontaneous frequency of approximately 10^{-4}. Most strains isolated in this manner are genetically unstable and hence are likely to be tandem duplications of *lac* genes.

RIBITOL DEHYDROGENASE Rigby, Burleigh & Hartley (106) have used a similar selection to isolate *Klebsiella aerogenes* strains, which hypersynthesize ribitol dehydrogenase. Wild-type strains will grow on ribitol as a sole carbon source because of their inducible ribitol permease and ribitol dehydrogenase (RDH) enzymes. Xylitol, which is not normally found in nature, will not support growth of wild-type strains. However, mutants constitutive for RDH will grow slowly on this unnatural pentitol. Metabolism of xylitol by these strains is due to the slight ability of RDH to catalyze dehydrogenation of the unnatural substrate (134). Continuous culture of a RDH constitutive strain, using xylitol as the sole carbon source, has yielded evolved strains that utilize xylitol much faster. The increased fitness exhibited by these strains appears to be due to quantitative increases in RDH activity. In all cases, the increased activity was due to duplication or amplification of the RDH gene, because ribitol dehydrogenase produced by these strains is qualitatively identical to wild-type strains, and because the ability to efficiently utilize xylitol is unstable. These authors suggest that under conditions in which growth is limited by an inefficient enzyme, the most frequent response by populations is amplification of the gene involved. Such amplifications occur at frequencies much higher than mutational alterations of substrate specificity. By this amplification, populations may adapt to short-term environmental stress without stably altering their genetic constitution.

GLYCYL-tRNA SYNTHETASE Folk & Berg (37) have described a class of glycine auxotrophs of *E. coli* with an altered glycyl-tRNA synthesase (*glyS*$^-$ mutants). In such strains, the K_m of the enzyme for glycine is 20-fold higher than that of wild-type enzyme. Supplying these mutants with a high concentration of exogenous glycine is thought to drive the charging reaction. Most Gly$^+$ revertants of these mutants harbor duplications (and possibly amplifications) of the *glyS*$^-$ gene (38). A compelling amount of data leads to this conclusion. (*a*) Although present in increased amounts, the glycyl-tRNA synthetase produced by these strains is qualitatively identical to parental mutant strains. (*b*) Such revertants still harbor the parental *glyS*$^-$ mutation. (*c*) Their Gly$^+$ character is unstable; segregants identical to the parental *glyS*$^-$ mutation are formed at high frequency. However, such instability is dependent upon recombination (*recA*) function. (*d*) These revertants are often diploid for the nearby loci *xyl, malA,* and *glpD,* as determined by their ability to be made heterozygous for these markers. Duplications of the *glyS* region account for most Gly$^+$ reversion events and arise at a frequency between 10^{-4} and 10^{-5}/cell.

Straus (122) has made careful measurement of the frequency of this duplication event; he estimates the spontaneous frequency to be 7×10^{-5}. The mutagens nitrous acid, ICR-372, niridazole, and ultraviolet light were seen to increase this frequency up to 25-fold.

Genetic tests for inclusion of nearby markers indicate that independent duplication isolates often include different amounts of adjacent material in their duplications. Individual Gly$^+$ revertants were seen to include various combinations of nearby markers. In two strains, both end points of the duplicated material were localized; one duplication includes less than 4.9 chromosomal min, and another includes between 4.8 and 5.6 min using the recalibrated linkage map of *E. coli* (9).

Straus & Straus (124) have described the isolation of *glyS*⁻ mutants in *Salmonella typhimurium.* As in *E. coli,* all Gly$^+$ revertants harbor chromosomal duplications, which include the *glyS*⁻ region. Such revertants occur at a spontaneous frequency of 8×10^{-5}, comparable to that observed in *E. coli.* However, tests for inclusion of nearby markers indicate that the duplications obtained by this selection are profoundly different than their *E. coli* counterparts. The majority of *Salmonella* Gly$^+$ duplications appear to include a region comprising 16% of the chromosome. A minority revertant type appears to include 22% of the genome. Thus, these duplications are considerably larger than those isolated in *E. coli.* Most duplications isolated by this technique are formed by a recombination-dependent mechanism. The Gly$^+$ reversion frequency was found to be 20-fold reduced in a recombination-deficient (*recA*$^-$) background.

HISTIDINE OPERON *Salmonella* strains harboring tandem duplications of the histidine operon may be selected as those exhibiting increased enzyme expression under conditions that prevent full derepression of the operon (R. P. Anderson and J. R. Roth, manuscript in preparation). Derepression is prevented by the use of strains harboring "down-promoter" (*hisO*^{P}) mutations. Because of a promoter defect, such strains (although His$^+$) are unable to maximally express *his* enzymes (33). From these strains, increased gene expression is selected as resistance to the histidine analog 3-amino-1,2,4-triazole (AT). This drug is a specific inhibitor of the IGP-dehydratase portion of the *hisB* enzyme (57). Wild-type strains are resistant to the growth-inhibitory properties of this compound because of their ability to derepress *hisB* expression and overcome inhibition. Down-promoter mutants are unable to derepress fully and, therefore, are sensitive to AT. Under appropriate conditions, *hisO*^{P} strains give rise to AT-resistant clones whose properties suggest that the mutational event conferring resistance is a tandem duplication of *his* genes. The appropriate conditions consist of selecting for resistance to the lowest concentration of AT necessary for growth inhibition of haploid *hisO*^{P} strains; a doubling of *hisB* activity (resulting from a duplication) is sufficient to confer AT resistance. A number of tests indicate that strains isolated by this procedure contain tandem duplications of *his* material: the AT-resistance character of such isolates is genetically unstable (such instability is completely dependent upon a functional recombination system); approximately twofold increases in *his* enzyme levels are observed in these strains; and genetic tests indicate that these strains contain at least two copies of *his* material, as demonstrated through the use of the transposable drug resistance element Tn*10* (71). The translocatable element Tn*10* is a 11,000-base-pair sequence, which confers tetracycline resistance. Normal haploid strains become His$^-$ when they inherit *his*$^-$::Tn*10* insertion mutations. However, AT-resistant strains remain phenotypically His$^+$ when they inherit such insertions. Thus, AT-resistant strains contain two (or more) copies of the histidine operon; one copy provides the His$^+$ phenotype and a second copy inherits *his*$^-$::Tn*10.* Such strains are unstable, segregating both *his*$^-$::Tn*10* and *hisO*^{P} haploid progeny.

Although selected as being resistant to an inhibitory concentration of AT, these duplication harboring strains are sensitive to higher AT levels. AT-resistant clones obtained at these higher concentrations appear to contain multiple tandem copies of the *his* operon.

The spontaneous frequency of tandem duplications isolated by this procedure is remarkably high (5×10^{-4}/cell). Moreover, this frequency is approximately 1000-fold reduced in *recA⁻hisO^P* strains. Thus, legitimate recombination appears to be involved in formation of these duplications (see below).

R-FACTOR TRANSITIONING An excellent example of the adaptive significance tandem duplications may have for bacterial populations has been provided by Rownd and co-workers (46, 100, 101, 108, 109). Drug-resistance factors (R-factors) of the Enterobacteriaceae are circular DNAs composed of two distinguishable units: the resistance transfer factor (RTF), which mediates infectious transfer of the R-factor, and the r-determinant, which harbors a variety of genes conferring drug resistance (26, 48). When harbored by *Proteus mirabilis,* one such R-factor (NR1) has the remarkable property of being able to regulate the number of identical copies of r-determinants associated with each RTF. This regulation occurs in response to drug challenge by antibiotics whose resistance genes reside on the r-determinant. When grown in the absence of antibiotics, these R-factors are composed of a single r-determinant copy attached to a single RTF (100). Following growth in the presence of the appropriate drug, the number of copies of the r-determinant attached to an RTF is seen to increase. The increased r-determinant copies are located in tandem upon the circular R-factor plasmid molecule. This combined plasmid most likely contains one copy of the RTF plus multiple tandem copies (10–15) of the r-determinant. Such selective amplification of the r-determinant portion of the R-factor leads to changes in plasmid density and size. This phenomenon is termed R-factor transitioning.

Fully transitioned cultures are more resistant to the antibiotics for which resistance determinants have been amplified (46). Thus, transitioned cells have a growth advantage over nontransitioned cells when cultured in drug-containing media. This selective advantage appears sufficient to explain how entire cultures of R-factor-containing strains become fully transitioned. By a variety of mixing and reconstruction experiments, Hashimoto & Rownd (46) were able to demonstrate selective outgrowth in drug-containing medium by the partially or fully transitioned cells in a mixed population. Furthermore, partially transitioned clones (those exhibiting increased, but not maximal, drug resistance) may be recovered spontaneously in the absence of selection at a frequency of approximately 10^{-3}. The kinetics of transitioning are consistent with selective outgrowth by this spontaneously arising subpopulation; increased amplification can occur following continued selection for increased resistance.

The response such strains make to drug challenge (transitioning) is transient. If at any time during or after the transition process cells are grown in drug-free media, the plasmid DNAs are seen to reduce the level of r-determinant amplification. After prolonged cultivation of a fully transitioned culture in drug-free media, the population will return to the nontransitioned state in which a single r-determinant is attached to a single RTF. Thus, amplification of resistance determinants is a response to environmental challenge (selection) by antibiotics. In the absence of selection, cultures return to the nontransitioned state.

The ability of R-factor populations to respond by transitioning clearly demonstrates the adaptive role gene duplication (and amplification) may play. If, under any circumstances, an increased gene dosage confers an increased fitness, then a subset of the population (the fraction that harbors a spontaneous duplication) will be able to outgrow haploid cells. Thus, they may increase their fraction of the total population. In the absence of selection, it is unnecessary to maintain the extra gene copies, and segregation events can regenerate a predominantly haploid population.

Electron microscopy of R-factor heteroduplex molecules (63, 102) reveals the presence of IS1 sequences (117, 118) at both junctions between the r-determinant and the RTF regions of the plasmid. These sequences are present as a direct (nontandem) repeat. The role these sequences play during the amplification process is currently unknown. It is attractive to speculate that such sequences are involved in recombinational exchanges and that these exchanges lead to duplication (or deletion) of intervening material (102).

MALATE UTILIZATION Most *Salmonella* strains grow extremely slowly when L-malate is provided as the sole carbon source. Large, fast-growing colonies (Mte^+) may be selected, and most of the isolates appear to contain large tandem chromosomal duplications (123). A gene dosage effect upon expression of some gene (or genes) included within the duplication is probably the basis for this selection; however, the loci responsible are obscure. Since utilization of malate appears to be limited by transport, duplication of the dicarboxylic acid permease gene (*dct*) may be the basis for this selection.

Straus & Hoffmann (123) have shown that Mte^+ mutants have a number of properties that suggest their fast growth on malate is due to a tandem duplication: the Mte^+ character is unstable; the Mte^+ character is transmissible during Hfr conjugation; and Mte^+ strains may be made heterozygous for a large number of contiguous chromosomal loci. End-point mapping of this type has shown that all duplications cover the same chromosomal region from *glpT* to *pyrE* (approximately one third of the *Salmonella* genome). Such large duplications arise spontaneously at a selected frequency of 4×10^{-5}–4×10^{-4} per plated cell. (This frequency is likely an overestimate since Mte^+ fast growers appear above a background of leaky Mte^- growth.) A second estimate of the frequency of this event has been provided nonselectively. Approximately 0.5% of His^+ recombinants arising from a standard conjugational cross (HfrB2 *metA*$^-$ $\times$ *hisG46*) have the Mte^+ phenotype. Such Mte^+ clones harbor chromosomal duplications identical to those previously described and appear nonselectively following conjugation (both parental strains are Mte^-). The detection of duplications following genetic crosses is most easily explained by the presence of preexisting duplications in a fraction of the recipient population (see below). Consistent with this explanation, it was observed that most of the duplicated material in Mte^+ strains isolated as above was of recipient origin. Thus, a duplication frequency of 5×10^{-3} is indicated.

BACTERIOPHAGE LAMBDA Lambda phages harboring tandem duplications of portions of their genome may be selected both genetically and physically from parental phages carrying large deletions of nonessential material (13, 19, 34, 35, 40). Genetic selections are based upon the finding that there is a minimal genome length (about 75–77% of normal lambda) required for phage viability. Deletion mutants of lambda whose genome is very near this critical length have extremely low burst sizes. Large plaque-forming revertants of such deletions usually harbor tandem duplications of an amount of DNA required to confer viability. More recent genetic selections have capitalized upon an *E. coli* host (GL1) that restricts the growth of deletion phages. This strain strongly selects against the growth of such phages and can be used to select addition derivatives arising from them. Physical selections are based upon measurements that relate lambda DNA length to phage buoyant density in CsCl (130). Since lambda phage heads are of approximately fixed volume, the buoyant density of DNA-filled heads depends upon the length of DNA encapsulated. Deletion mutants of phage lambda band at a density characteristically lighter than normal. DNA additions to these deletion phages may be detected on the phage density profile as a shoulder of increased density. Subsequent genetic and physical characterization of the phages found in this shoulder confirm that the majority contain tandem duplications.

One advantage to studying duplications arising on phage genomes is that identification of tandemly duplicated material may be done by both genetic and physical means. Tandem duplications detected by the selections described above have been identified genetically by their instability. Propagation of such strains (in $recA^+$ hosts) yields many progeny phages identical to the parental deletion plus many phages harboring triplication of the region. However, this genetic instability is absent when duplication phages (int^-red^-) are grown on $recA^-$ hosts. Physical identification of duplicated regions has been provided by DNA-DNA heteroduplex analysis. Heteroduplexes involving duplicated and nonduplicated DNAs exhibit a characteristic single-stranded loop (equal to the length of duplicated material), which may be located anywhere along the region that has been repeated. Based upon similar heteroduplex analysis, Emmons & Thomas (36) have mapped the end points of 24 spontaneously occurring duplications. The distribution of such end points was found to be random.

Duplications of the type described above arise at a spontaneous frequency of 10^{-4}–10^{-5} during a single cycle of infection. Furthermore, this frequency is independent of known recombination functions, because identical frequencies were measured under conditions that eliminate all known homologous recombination systems ($int^-red^-recA^-$). The measured frequencies of duplication in the above two experiments are likely to be underestimates of total duplication events, since each isolated duplication must be large enough to confer viability, yet not large enough to prevent packaging of the entire genome.

Coinheritance of Allelic Markers

It is standard practice in bacterial genetics to set up conditions that select for cells carrying a particular allele of a given gene. In selecting for a mutant allele the conditions permit loss of the wild-type allele. It is expected that this allele will be converted by mutation to the new selected form. Similarly, in genetic crosses, one selects for inheritance of a particular donor allele under conditions that permit the recipient's copy to be lost and replaced by donor material. Contrary to this standard practice, it is sometimes possible to establish conditions that require both acquisition of the new allele and maintenance of the original allele. One can then select cells having two copies of the gene in question. Only recipient cells carrying a duplication of that gene can acquire the new allele (in one copy) and still maintain the other gene copy in its original form. This general method has been used in a variety of guises to detect gene duplications in bacteria. Several examples are presented below.

glyT SUPPRESSORS The *glyT* gene of *E. coli* codes for a species of glycine tRNA reading the codons GGA and GGG. Missense suppressor mutations can arise in the *glyT* gene, which cause the mutant tRNA to read the arginine code words AGA and AGG. Work on these suppressor mutations and the tRNA produced has been reviewed by Hill (50).

Strains carrying only the suppressor allele grow poorly on minimal medium, presumably because they lack sufficient tRNA to read the normal glycine codons GGA and GGG. Strains carrying both a *glyT* suppressor mutation and a second, wild-type copy of the *glyT* gene grow well on minimal medium. When selection is made for new *glyT* suppressor mutants (on minimal medium), most arise as slow-growing haploids carrying one (mutant) copy of the *glyT* gene. Approximately 0.1%, however, arise as fast-growing merodiploids carrying a duplication including the *glyT* gene; one copy is wild type, the other is the suppressor allele (53). Following ultraviolet irradiation, as many as 10% of the *glyT* suppressor mutations arise in strains harboring a duplication (51). It appears that strains carrying duplications of the *glyT* gene are frequent (0.1%) in a normal cell population and that their frequency is greatly stimulated by ultraviolet irradiation. Several lines of evidence indicate that the merodiploid strains carry tandem duplications of a chromosomal region including the *glyT* locus: the merodiploid strains are unstable (clones lacking the suppressor arise frequently); this instability is dependent upon recombination ability (introduction of a $recA^-$ mutation allows the stable maintenance of both wild-type and suppressor alleles of *glyT,* which suggests that loss of the suppressor occurs by recombination between duplicate copies; see Figure 3); by construction of appropriate heterozygotes, it can be shown that the unstable suppressor carrying strains are also diploid for one or more chromosomal genes near the *glyT* locus (the extent of several duplications is presented in Figure 6); and the duplication state is cotransducible with chromosomal markers (55). As outlined above (see Figure 4), if one transduces the join point between two copies of a duplicated region into a haploid recipient, the donor's duplication state can be reestablished. When such crosses are done by using donor strains harboring a *glyT* duplication, it can be shown that the duplication join point is genetically linked to chromosomal markers and to the *glyT* gene. This is very strong evidence that the merodiploid region is a tandem duplication that is part of the chromosome and not plasmid borne.

As can be seen from the *glyT* case, suppressors represent an ideal situation for detection of duplications. The wild-type allele can be selected if it is vital or required for optimal growth. The suppressor allele can be selected by requiring suppression of an appropriate auxotrophic mutation.

Recently, Hill, Grafstrom & Hillman (54) have reported convincing evidence concerning the mechanism of formation of the *glyT* duplications. They propose that these duplications arise by recombination between ribosomal RNA genes (*rrn*) located at distinct points in the chromosome. Their proposal is strongly supported by the isolation and characterization of closed circular DNA formed in duplication strains following recombination between the duplicate copies. These circles are of the size expected if they arose by recombination between *rrn* genes. Furthermore, each class of circles possesses the expected number of *rrn* sequences (54; see Figure 6; C. W. Hill, personal communication). The existence of the *rrnD* gene between *purD* and *metA* was inferred from this work and has been independently demonstrated by Nomura and co-workers (81, 89, 135). If the *glyT* duplications of class IV and V also involve *rrn* sequences, their structure predicts that another *rrn* gene will be found located clockwise from the *metA* gene.

It is striking to note that four or possibly five *rrn* gene copies are located in this rather small region of the genetic map and that all are placed in the same orientation. Thus, they can provide the nontandem, direct sequence repeats needed for *rec*-dependent duplication formation. This arrangement may be of adaptive significance to *E. coli*, since it permits amplification of the number of *rrn* gene copies. Cells carrying such *rrn* amplifications might have a selective advantage under conditions of extremely rapid growth. Duplications of the *glyT* locus are possibly by-products of this amplification process.

trpT SUPPRESSORS Another example of the use of suppressors to detect duplications is the case of lethal amber and UGA suppressor mutations that arise by mutations in the *trpT* gene of both *E. coli* and *Salmonella.* The *trpT* gene codes

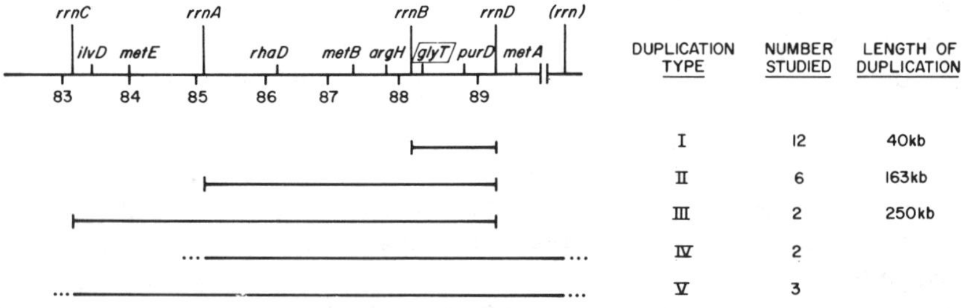

Figure 6 End points of tandem duplications that include that *glyT* region of *Escherichia coli* (54).

for the single tryptophan tRNA and, thus, is essential (58, 115, 136). The first description of mutations at this locus is probably that of Schwartz, who studied unstable suppressors of certain *lac* mutations (111, 112). The *lac* mutations used by Schwartz proved to be UGA mutations (107). Later *trpT* mutations suppressing either amber or UGA mutations were studied in both *Salmonella* and *E. coli*. In these later studies, suppressor mutations were selected in F'-merodiploid strains possessing two copies of the wild-type *trpT* gene. Suppressor mutations could convert one of the two *trpT* gene copies to an amber or UGA suppressor form and still leave the cell with one wild-type copy of the *trpT* gene. Since *trpT* codes for an essential tRNA, it is vital that the cells maintain this wild-type allele. When attempts were made to transduce these recessive lethal suppressor mutations into a haploid recipient strain, it was expected that no transductants would be recovered, since no extra copy of the *trpT* gene was provided. In practice, however, transductants were obtained with surprisingly high frequency. In both *E. coli* (116) and *Salmonella* (84), haploids show less than a fivefold reduction in the frequency of transductants carrying the lethal suppressor (compared to F'-merodiploid recipients with two copies of the relevant region). In both species, all such suppressor-carrying transductants obtained with haploid recipients harbor duplications including both the *ilv* and the *trpT* genes. Since neither the donor nor the recipient in these crosses was known to carry a duplication, it is unclear how these transductants were formed. It seems possible that 20% of the recipient cell population carried a pre-existing duplication, and that transductants arose in this subpopulation by recombination into one of the two copies of the duplicated region. Such a high frequency of duplications seems surprising. However, the *trpT* gene, like the *glyT* gene discussed above, is located between copies of the rRNA cistrons (9). These neighboring genes might provide homologous sequences that could recombine to generate the duplications detected. A high level of duplications for this region might account for the unstable UGA suppressors isolated by Schwartz (111, 112). It seems likely that these are lethal suppressors at the *trpT* locus, which arose in strains carrying a pre-existing duplication of that gene.

Many other examples of unstable suppressor mutations have been reported (28, 30, 43, 56). Like the *glyT* and *trpT* cases described above, these unstable suppressors are likely to be deleterious or lethal when haploid, but they can arise in strains that carry pre-existing duplications. These duplications permit the cells to maintain both the suppressor mutation and its wild-type allele.

T4rII Crosses between complementary mutations with limited opportunity for recombination provide another way of detecting duplications. This method has been exploited extensively in the *r*II region of phage T4. Here, because of a peculiarity of the *r*II region, overlapping deletion mutations exist that are unable to recombine but that can complement to provide an rII^+ phenotype. Crosses between such mutants cannot yield wild-type progeny but, at low frequency, can yield phenotypically rII^+ progeny that carry a duplication of the *r*II region; one of the complementing *r*II mutations is carried by each copy of the duplicated region. Such partially diploid heterozygotes are unstable and generate segregants of the two parental *r*II⁻ genotypes. This selection method is made possible by the fact that a portion of the *r*IIB cistron is not essential for *r*IIB function (21, 29). Deletions affecting *r*IIA and the nonessential region of *r*IIB still provide *r*IIB function. Deletions that affect both essential and nonessential portions of *r*IIB provide *r*IIA function. Thus, *r*IIA and *r*IIB deletions that overlap in the nonessential portion of the *r*IIB cistron complement, yet are unable to recombine. Crosses between such deletions (selecting $r\text{II}^+$) yield tandem duplications, each copy of which harbors one of the parental mutations. It is inferred that these duplications are formed by illegitimate recombination between the two mutant T4 genomes.

The increased genome size of such duplications may have serious consequences for T4 viability, if the "headful" packaging mechanism can no longer generate a terminal redundancy. For this reason, most duplications in T4 must be accompanied by a deletion mutation that removes nonessential material elsewhere in the genome (97, 131). This permits formation of the terminal redundancy. The necessity for this second event reduces the apparent frequency of duplication formation.

This selection method for T4 duplications was first described by Weil, Terzaghi & Crasemann (132). Since then, these duplications have been studied by Symonds and co-workers (27, 125, 128, 129), with special emphasis on analysis of T4 recombination pathways, and by Van de Vate & Symonds (127) and Homyk & Weil (59), with emphasis on the non-essential regions affected by the associated deletion mutations. The nature of the duplications themselves has been investigated in most detail by Parma and co-workers (97–99), who have made the following observations. (*a*) Duplication heterozygotes segregate triplication mutants at a frequency approximating the frequency of $r\text{II}^-$ segregants. This supports the tandem nature of the duplications and suggests that duplications segregate by recombination between different genomes rather than between copies of the duplicated region in a single genome (see Figure 3). (*b*) There is a direct relationship between size of the duplicated region and the frequency of $r\text{II}^-$ segregant formation. (*c*) The end points of over 50 duplications are located at a wide variety of sites, suggesting that many different illegitimate exchanges are capable of generating duplications. However, the distribution of end points is not random; given the map region of one end of a duplication, it is possible to predict the region of the map in which the other end is most likely to fall. There seems to be a tendency of duplicated regions to terminate within structural genes. No explanation for either of these observations is currently available. (*d*) The size of the duplications appear to be on the order of 1000–5000 base pairs. The spectrum of duplication types is limited by the requirement that both copies of the *r*II region must function and that the duplications cannot exceed a size that can be compensated by a deletion of nonessential material. (*e*) Constraints upon the nature of detectable duplications make it difficult to estimate their frequency, as discussed by Parma et al (97). However, it has been estimated that the minimum frequency of duplications per genome in T4 is between 2.5×10^{-6} and 5×10^{-4}.

HISTIDINE OPERON. Crosses between closely linked, complementary mutations have also provided a way of identifying chromosomal duplications in *Salmonella typhimurium* (4). For example, when two closely linked but complementing histidine-requiring mutations are crossed, two distinct types of His$^+$ recombinants result. The first type is the expected wild-type recombinant, which arises following a genetic exchange in the small region between the two *his* mutations. The second type of recombinant arises when the recipient cell carries a duplication of the *his* region. In such a cell, the donor's mutant *his* operon can be inherited in one copy of the duplicated region whereas the recipient *his* region is retained in the other copy. Since the two mutations involved complement, the resulting recombinant is a phenotypically His$^+$ merodiploid, harboring a different *his*$^-$ mutation in each of its two *his* regions.

The relative frequency of His$^+$ merodiploid and true *his*$^+$ recombinants depends upon the frequency of recombination between the two mutations involved and the frequency of duplication-carrying cells in the recipient population. By choosing extremely closely linked mutations, the frequency of true recombinants can be made quite low. In such cases, almost all His$^+$ recombinants recovered are the complementing merodiploids. The frequency of this recombinant type can be used to estimate the frequency of duplications in the recipient culture. By this means, the frequency of cells carrying duplications of the *Salmonella his* region has been estimated to be approximately 10^{-3}–10^{-4}. The segments of chromosome included in such duplications can be extremely large; several have been estimated to include as much as 25% of the chromosome (4).

UNSTABLE RECOMBINANT CLONES If one assumes that duplications are frequent events and that they can include large segments of the bacterial chromosome, it is clear that whenever complementary auxotrophic mutations are crossed and selection is made for phototrophic recombinants, unstable merodiploids can be expected.

There are many reports of unstable and mixed recombinant clones arising following conjugational crosses (5, 17, 24, 76, 77, 80, 96, 133). Frequently these findings have been discussed as evidence for several rounds of recombination between the recipient chromosome and the transferred chromosomal segment. It seems likely that many reports of unstable recombinant clones can be accounted for in terms of the phenomenon described above. Such cases could be due to inheritance of the donated segment in one of two copies of a duplicated region carried by the recipient cell. The resulting merodiploid cell could then divide repeatedly before undergoing recombination between copies. Eventually, recombination would lead to a mixed clone composed of several haploid segregant types.

GALACTOSE OPERON One example of an unstable conjugational recombinant has been analyzed by Campbell (20). He found recombinant clones that were heterozygous for the *gal* region. Subsequent analysis suggested that the merodiploidy was not associated with an F'-factor but was likely to be maintained as a tandem duplication. The two *gal* regions, present in the partially diploid cell, were not cotransduced by P1 phage. Thus, if tandem duplication is involved, the duplicated segment is larger than a P1 genome. However, the unstable characteristic of the duplication was found to be cotransducible with the *gal* region. Campbell suggested that transduction of the join point between tandem copies of the duplicated region would be sufficient to re-establish the duplication state of the donor (20). Such recombination events must occur between the transduced fragment and each of two copies of the recipient chromosome. His model (outlined in Figure 4) has been used by Hill, Schiffer & Berg (55) to explain their transduction results with the *glyT* duplications. Recombination events such as those depicted in Figure 4 account for many instances in which the merodiploid state of unstable strains has been found to be transducible.

HETEROCLONES IN STREPTOMYCES Partially diploid conjugational progeny are frequently encountered in *Streptomyces coelicolor.* Extensive use has been made of these progeny (termed *heteroclones*) in mapping and complementation testing of this organism (see 60). The means of obtaining heteroclones is exactly parallel to one of the methods described above for obtaining duplications of the histidine region of *Salmonella*. Strains carrying closely linked, complementing auxotrophic mutations are crossed, and selection is made for prototrophy. Such crosses yield two recombinant types. Wild-type recombinants result from a genetic exchange between the selected markers; such recombinants are recovered in low yield because of the small region in which the exchange must occur. In addition to these standard recombinants, clones are frequently encountered that have inherited two copies of the entire region. These heteroclones maintain both donor and recipient alleles of the two genes under selection and are often diploid for large segments of chromosome extending well beyond the immediate neighborhood of the selected markers. The structure and segregation behavior of these merodiploids has been used to infer the map order and intervening map distances of widely separated genes in the *Streptomyces* chromosome. The structure and mode of inheritance of these added chromosomal segments has never been fully explained. It seems possible, in view of the high frequency of duplications in other bacteria, that heteroclones result from recombination events occurring in recipient cells that carry pre-existing tandem duplications. The size of the merodiploid region would be determined by the pre-existing duplication, and the heterozygosity would result from replacement of material in one of the two copies by material inherited from the donor parent.

TRANSFORMATION STUDIES Transforming systems have also provided examples of unstable recombinants that may represent tandem duplications. These have been observed in *Haemophilus* (78) and *Streptococcus* (8, 15) in situations involving unstable but simultaneous inheritance of two capsular types. Hotchkiss and coworkers (69, 70, 74, 75) have analyzed an unstable mutation in *Streptococcus* conferring sulfonamide resistance (*sul*^{r}–*c*). The resistance property is lost with rather high frequency. During transformation, this unstable resistance characteristic can be transferred by a single DNA fragment, suggesting that the duplicated region may be small or that the duplication state can be re-established by a mechanism such as that outlined in Figure 4. The reasons this drug resistance mutation must be carried as a duplication are not clear. It seems possible that the mutation has a recessive lethal effect and that selection is being made for simultaneous maintenance of both a wild-type and a mutant copy of the gene involved. Another possibility is that drug resistance is dependent upon the simultaneous presence of two mutant forms of the locus. This seems less likely but could account for the behavior of these strains.

Ravin et al (103, 104) have described erythromycin and streptomycin mutations of *Streptococcus* that behave similarily to the *sul*^{r}*–c* mutations. The erythromycin resistance mutations (*ery*^{R}) have been most extensively analyzed. When particular *ery*^{R} mutations are transferred into recipient strains by transformation, the resulting recombinants are unstable and segregate both stably resistant clones and fully sensitive clones. Similar to *sul*^{r}*–c*, it is not clear why these particular mutations are inherited frequently as merodiploids. The high efficiency with which merodiploid transformants arise suggests that something in the structure of the donor chromosome promotes duplication formation. Existence of a duplication in the donor could explain this efficiency (see Figure 4). Stable *ery*^{r} segregants also give rise to merodiploid transformants when used as donor strains. It is possible that these stable strains still carry a duplication, but its instability is not apparent because of the acquisition of a recessive lethal mutation within one copy of the duplicated region. Most haploid segregants would be nonviable and, thus, not detected.

Although a full explanation of the above phenomena is not yet available, they are likely to involve tandem duplications, since recombination is essential to their segregation and since the unstable state can be cotransferred with chromosomal markers.

An additional case of duplication in a transforming system is the work of Anagnostopoulos and co-workers in *Bacillus subtilis* (6, 7, 126). This is discussed later.

CROSSES INVOLVING LOW HOMOLOGY For unknown reasons, unstable recombinants are frequently recovered from crosses in which there is reduced homology for recombination. One example of this situation is interspecies crosses in which the two DNAs involved share little sequence homology. Another example is seen in crosses involving recipient strains carrying large deletions. If selection is made for inheritance of a donor gene by a recipient strain that carries a large deletion removing material homologous to that donor gene, then available sites for recombination between donor and recipient DNA are severely limited. In such situations, unstable recombinant clones are often recovered. These two examples are discussed below, and a model is presented that we feel can explain these observations in terms of tandem duplications present in the donor DNA.

In conjugational crosses between *E. coli* and *Salmonella,* recombinants are recovered with greatly reduced frequency. The genetic maps of these organisms are virtually identical (9, 110), but at the base sequence level most regions of the chromosome show greatly reduced homology. From such crosses, unstable recombinants are frequently recovered. Some of these probably carry F' episomes. Other recombinants, however, seem to have inherited the selected markers by addition at a chromosomal site near the normal map location of the selected marker. The nature of such interspecies crosses has been reviewed by Middleton & Mojica-a (83). Additional reports of similar findings have appeared (67, 68, 86).

One of the best documented cases is the report of Johnson et al (68). Crosses were made between a *Salmonella* Hfr and an *E. coli* F⁻ recipient strain. Selection was made for inheritance of the donor's *argH*$^+$ gene. Many of the Arg$^+$ recombinants seemed to have inherited the *argH*$^+$ gene at a chromosomal site independent of the F-factor. Analysis of these recombinants indicated that a block of *Salmonella* material including the *rha*$^+$, *metB*$^+$, and *argH*$^+$ genes were inserted near the *E. coli* *argH* gene, possibly generating a tandem repeat of this chromosomal region. One possible explanation of the occurrence of such insertions is discussed below.

Homology between donor and recipient can also be reduced by use of a deletion mutation. In several cases, unstable recombinants have been observed following transductional crosses in which the recipient strain carries a large deletion of the region whose inheritance was selected. The large size of the deletion reduces the extent of homology shared by the recipient and the transduced fragment. In such cases, transductants arise with greatly reduced frequency and, in some cases, seem to have inherited the selected material by unstable addition to the chromosome at a site near the recipient's deletion. It is likely that these unstable recombinants carry tandem duplications.

Two examples of the above situation have been described in detail. One example, discussed below, involves the *lac* operon of *E. coli* (119–121). Another involves a threonine deaminase mutant of *B. subtilis* studied by Anagnostopoulos and coworkers (65, 66).

Stodolsky, Rae & Mullenbach (121) used a large *lac* deletion (Δ111) as recipient in transductional crosses. This deletion removes the *proA* and *proB* genes as well as the entire *lac* operon. Since no stable *lac*$^+$ recombinants are formed in these crosses, it is thought that the deletion is too large to be spanned by a single transducing fragment. Thus, standard recombination events at the ends of the deletion cannot account for inheritance of the donor *lac* region. The few *lac*$^+$ recombinants that arise appear to inherit the donor *lac*$^+$ region by addition to a site near the end of the recipient deletion. The transductants are unstable and segregate *lac*$^-$ clones that are not distinguishable from the original parent deletion mutant (Δ111). The transductants become stable after introduction of a *rec*$^-$ mutation. It seems likely that these strains carry tandem duplications of the *lac* region; one copy carries the recipient's deletion and the other copy carries the functional *lac*$^+$ operon. The duplicated segment can also include the *proC, lon,* and *purE* loci. Since *purE* is not contransducible with *lac,* much of the duplicated material must be of recipient origin.

Stodolsky proposes a novel model to account for these findings (120). This model involves replication of a partially completed recombinational intermediate followed by illegitimate fusion of two DNA ends. Although the model is plausible and accounts neatly for the observations, we would like to propose a slightly different mechanism, which involves more standard events. We propose that some transductional events depend upon the existence of tandem duplications in the *donor* population. In Figure 7, the transductional data of Stodolsky is interpreted in this way. This interpretation requires that duplications are present at a low but detectable level in the donor strain. (Evidence that duplications are present at such frequency has been discussed previously.) When a duplication event generates a linkage between *lac* and a sequence to the right of *purE,* the resulting sequence *jk-de* (see Figure 7) is formed. Transduction of this novel chromosome fragment into a recipient can permit regeneration of the donor duplication and provide a means of inheriting the lac^+ region. The resulting Lac^+ transductants carry a duplication of recipient chromosomal material extending from *lac* to a point to the right of *purE*; from the donor, they have inherited only lac^+ and material immediately adjacent to the join point of the donor duplication (heavy lines in Figure 7). The only requirement for this sort of transductional event is a duplication in the donor strain, which leaves the lac^+ gene cotransducible with the duplication join point. The other end of the duplication (*j–k* in Figure 7) can be anywhere in the chromosome to the right of the *lac* region. This mode of inheritance of lac^+ is nearly identical to transductional behavior of duplications described earlier; the only difference is that in this case the duplication would be carried by relatively rare individuals in the donor population.

Events described above may permit inheritance of genes in many cases of restricted homology. If the donor and recipient share few regions of homology, duplication events in the donor can serve to bring these regions close to the selected donor markers. Such rearrangements may be necessary to permit inheritance of that marker. Events of this sort may help to explain the frequent recovery of unstable recombinant clones following crosses between distantly related species.

Transductional shortening of F' episomes can also be accounted for in terms of events similar to those outlined above. The basic observation has been made that F' episomes can be transduced into F^- recipients by P1 phage (92, 94). Frequently F' transductants so obtained carry episomes that are shorter than the donor F' episome. It appears that only a portion of the donor F' episome is transduced into the recipient. Yet, this portion is able to circularize to generate a new, smaller F' plasmid. The events that lead to circularization are unclear. One possible explanation is that duplications in the donor F' episome provide a terminal redundancy, which allows for circularization of the transduced F' fragment by means of recombination. The only requirement for this would be existence of duplications in the F' episome that are transducible and that include genes essential to plasmid replication. If the transduced fragment included all of one copy of such a duplicated region and a small portion of the second copy, a terminal redundancy would be generated. Recombination between these terminal redundancies would allow circularization of the fragment in the recipient. If this explanation were correct, then the structure of the shortened episome would reflect duplication events that occurred in the donor strain. This mechanism for transductional shortening should require recombination. In the experiments of Ohtsubo (94), shortened F' episomes were formed at 50-fold higher frequency in $recA^+$ than in $recA^-$ recipients. This recombination dependence supports the idea that shortened F' episomes circularize by means of terminal redundancy. The above explanation of F' shortening gains credibility from the observed high frequency of duplication mutations in bacteria. We have recently measured the frequency of tandem duplications of the *his* region on an F'*his* episome (R. P. Anderson and J. R. Roth, manuscript in preparation); 1 in 1000 F'

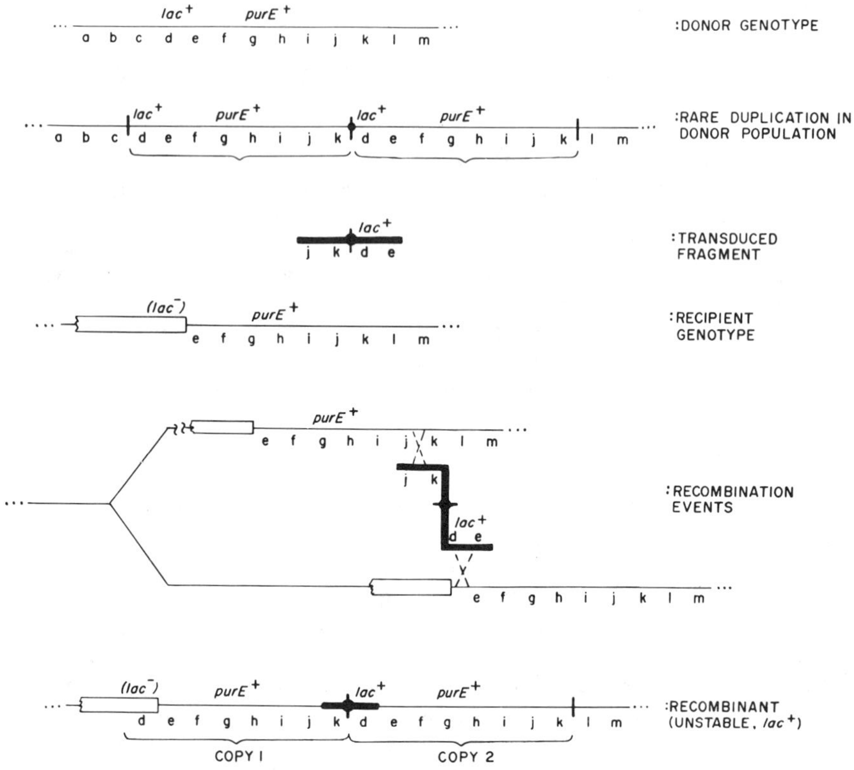

Figure 7 Tandem duplications in a donor population allow the formation of *lac*$^+$ merodiploid recombinants using a nontransducible *lac*$^-$ recipient deletion (116). Recipient and transduced donor DNAs are light and bold lines, respectively.

episomes carries such a duplication. This high frequency is sufficient to provide an explanation for transductional shortening of F' episomes.

DUPLICATION FORMATION IN STRAINS WITH TRANSPOSITIONS Anagnostopoulos et al (6, 7, 126) have described a novel strain of *Bacillus subtilis* in which duplications are formed with high efficiency following transductional or transformational crosses. The unique properties of this strain are associated with a particular mutation (*trpE26*). When strains carrying this mutation are used as recipients in transduction or transformation crosses, the Trp$^+$ recombinants obtained are unstable and can be shown to carry a large duplication including one quarter to one third of the entire chromosome. The *trpE*$^+$ gene is included in the duplicated segment.

The unusual behavior of this strain has been shown to be a result of a transposition that generates the *trpE* mutation. The transposition moves a segment of the chromosome (including part of the *trpE* gene) from one point on the chromosome to another; this rearrangement leaves a haploid cell with a disrupted *trpE* gene (*trpE26*). Any wild-type *trpE*$^+$ chromosomal segment transduced or transformed into this recipient is homologous to widely separated sequences in the *trpE26* chromosome. The *trpE*$^+$ fragment must recombine with both of these homologous sequences to permit inheritance of *trpE*$^+$. The situation is diagrammed in Figure 8. The events are completely analogous to those described earlier (20, 55); the only difference is that now the illegitimate join point is carried by the recipient.

Duplications such as those described above can now be generated for virtually any region of the chromosome of *Salmonella* and *E. coli* (72). This is made possible through the use of transposable drug resistance genes such as the Tn10 element (14, 71). A translocation situation analogous to that described above for *B. subtilis* can be provided by use of strains carrying Tn10 insertions at different points on the chromosome, thus providing homology at these separated sites. Recombination between these separated homologies yields duplications that include all material between the sites of Tn10 insertion. This method has been tested for the *his* region

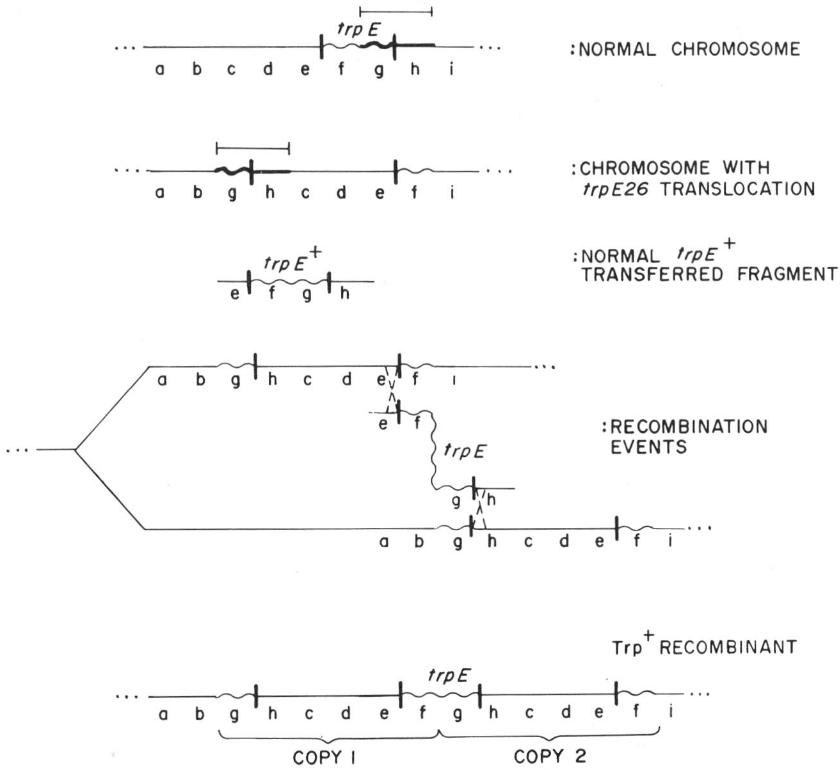

Figure 8 The *trpE26* mutation results from transposition of the chromosomal segment *gh* (bold lined) and promotes tandem duplication when used as a recipient (122).

of *Salmonella* (F. Chumley; unpublished results). Duplications of predetermined extent can be constructed by such transductional crosses. Formation of these duplications is completely analogous to the situation described by Anagnostopolous and coworkers (6, 7, 126).

Operon Fusion

A variety of selections involving what we term "operon fusion" have allowed detection of tandem duplications. Figure 5 depicts the basic scheme. Tandem duplications whose end points lie within different units of transcription lead to formation of a hybrid operon in which genes of one transcriptional unit are fused to promoter elements of another. The only restriction on such fusions is that both operons must have the same direction of transcription. Since no material is destroyed by the duplication event, widely separated operons may be subject to such fusion. This is quite unlike deletion fusions (85), in which the preservation of essential genetic material requires that the operons to be fused must be in rather close proximity.

In most cases, selections of this type demand expression of genes that are structurally intact but that have been turned off either by polarity effects or by inactivation of natural promoters. Thus, the selections detect tandem duplication events that fuse unexpressed genes to functional promoters. In the following sections, details of individual selections are considered.

HISTIDINE OPERON Operon fusions in the *his* region of *Salmonella* may be selected as follows: mutation *his-203* deletes the entire operator-promoter region and a portion of the first structural gene of the *his* operon. In this strain, the remaining *his* genes are structurally intact, yet unexpressed. Selection is made for turn-on of one of these remaining genes (*hisD*); strains with a functional *hisD*$^+$ gene are able to utilize the intermediate histidinol as a source of histidine. These *hisD*$^+$ revertants arise in *his-203* at a spontaneous frequency of approximately 10^{-9}. It appears that many of these strains harbor tandem duplications, which fuse the *hisD* gene to foreign regulatory elements. Figure 9 shows how this may be accomplished. At some distance from the histidine operon are promoters (termed P') capable of expressing the *hisD* gene. Tandem duplication of material from a point within the *his* operon to a point within the transcription unit P' leads to expression of the duplicated *hisD* gene by this foreign promoter. Of 21 independent, unstable histidinol-utilizing revertants of *his-203* that we have investigated, all may be accounted for by duplication events such as that shown here (R. P. Anderson and J. R. Roth, manuscript in preparation).

Transducibility As discussed above, transduction of the merodiploid state of large tandem duplications may be detected, provided the selected donor marker and the join point between duplicated segments are cotransducible (20, 55). According to Figure 9, the *hisD*$^+$ gene is necessarily located at the join point between duplicated regions. Thus, the *hisD*$^+$ character of all such unstable strains is transducible. All transductants obtained in this manner are unstably *hisD*$^+$ and segregate *hisD*$^-$ clones of the recipient genotype. Thus, the merodiploid state of these revertants is transducible (see Figure 4).

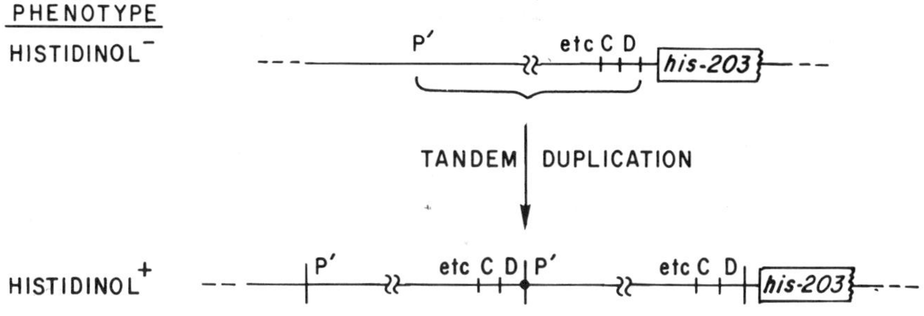

Figure 9 The selection for operon fusions of the *his* region of *Salmonella.*

Stability The instability of these strains is dependent upon recombination; *recA*⁻ derivatives of the unstable revertants are stably *hisD*⁺. When such stable *recA*⁻ strains are used as donors, the *hisD*⁺ recombinants obtained with recipient *his-203* are all unstable. Thus, the stable (*recA*⁻) strains still harbor the duplication, and recombination is required for instability of the *hisD*⁺ activity.

Merodiploidy Unstable strains isolated by this procedure may be shown genetically to be diploid for large chromosomal regions. The extent of duplicated material in 21 independent *hisD*⁺ unstable revertants of *his-203* is shown in Figure 10. These different classes of revertants are evident. Class I revertants (5 of 21 isolates) are merodiploid for the nearby loci *metG* and *udk* but not for *cysA.* Class II revertants (15 of 21 isolates) are merodiploid for each of 10 loci tested in the region from *his* through *argB.* Thus, these strains harbor duplications of approximately 16% of the *Salmonella* genome. The join point in class II duplications may be shown to be linked to the *argB* gene by the following experiment: when any class II strain is used as a donor and *argB*⁻ *his-203* is used as a recipient, 25% of Arg⁺ recombinants inherit *hisD*⁺ nonselectively. Such recombinants are unstable for both their *hisD*⁺ and their *argB*⁺ characters. The most likely explanation for these observations involves inheritance of a tandem duplication by events such as those outlined in Figure 4. The single class III isolate is merodiploid for each of 14 markers tested in the region from *his* through *argE.* Thus, this strain harbors a duplication of approximately 26% of the chromosome.

The selection system and unstable *hisD*⁺ revertants discussed above were originally described by Ames, Hartman & Jacob (3). The phenomenon was further studied by Levinthal & Yeh (79). Instability of *hisD*⁺ revertants was originally interpreted as evidence that the functional *hisD*⁺ gene was translocated to an extrachromosomal element (termed the pi-histidine plasmid). The more recent results outlined above suggest strongly that the unstable revertants carry tandem duplications that fuse the *hisD*⁺ gene to a functional chromosomal promoter. The most convincing evidence for this conclusion is that recombination is required for both instability and inheritance of the *hisD*⁺ character and that the *hisD*⁺ gene in class II revertants is cotransducible with a chromosomal *argB*⁻ gene. These properties would not be expected of a plasmid-borne *hisD*⁺ gene (10, 94).

Class II revertants of *his-203* appear to be generated by a recombination-dependent mechanism, since duplications of this type are not found when the selection is performed in a *recA*⁻ background (see below).

ARGININE OPERON A number of chromosomal duplications carrying one or more of the four genes clustered in the *argECBH* bipolar operon have been isolated by selecting for reversal of the polar effect caused by certain *arg* mutations (12, 23, 31, 32, 44). Strongly polar *argC*⁻ or *argB*⁻ mutants are unable to utilize ornithine as an arginine source because of polar effects upon the *argH* (argininosuccinase) enzyme. At a frequency of 10^{-7}–10^{-8}, strains able to utilize ornithine may be selected. Approximately 10% of these are unstable for their Orn⁺ phenotype and are concluded to contain tandem duplications that fuse the *argH* gene to unrelated promoter elements. This conclusion is based upon observed recombination dependence for segregation of the Orn⁺ character and upon genetic tests, which demonstrate chromosomal merodiploidy of nearby genes. Cotransduction of Orn⁺ with the nearby chromosomal markers *ppc* and *purD* indicate that some *arg* duplications are relatively short (1–2 genes), whereas others are somewhat larger (10–30 genes). The formation of such tandem duplications occurs by a recombination-independent mechanism, since the observed frequency is approximately the same in Rec⁺ and Rec⁻ genetic backgrounds.

TRYPTOPHAN OPERON Jackson & Yanofsky have described the isolation of duplications that fuse the *trp* operon to nearby promoters (64). Such duplications arise from a selection designed to provide relief from the polar effects of *trpE* nonsense mutations. The selection is as follows: the tryptophan synthetase β_2 enzyme found in *trpA*⁻ strains has but 3% of the activity of the tryptophan synthetase $\alpha_2\beta_2$ complex in conversion of indole to tryptophan. However, because of the ability of cells to derepress *trpB* (β_2) activity, such *trpA*⁻ strains will grow on indole media. A strain such as *trpE*⁻ (amber) *trpE*⁻ (ochre) *trpA*⁻, which contains two strong polar mutations in the *trp* operon operator-proximal to *trpB*, is unable to grow on indole media. Selection for indole growers from this strain selects for mutations that relieve the polar effect of the *trpE* nonsense mutations. In addition to indole growth, selection was made for 5-methyltryptophan resistance. Since this analog represses expression of a wild-type *trp* operon, growth in its presence indicates constitutive expression of the *trp* enzymes.

The majority of mutants isolated by this procedure (which arise at a frequency between 10^{-7} and 10^{-8}) are unstable for their selected phenotype. They are concluded to contain duplications (or translocations) of the *trp* operon, which lead to constitutive expression of *trpB* activity. This conclusion is based upon the instability exhibited by such mutants and a demonstration that these strains are merodiploid for the *trp* operon. In each case, the *trpB*⁺ character of these strains does not exhibit the tight linkage to *cysB* found for wild-type strains. Rather, in most cases *trpB*⁺ is rather weakly linked to *cysB.* Thus, the *trpB* gene has been moved to a location nearby (but at some distance from) the *trp* locus. Genetic tests indicate that the *trpC, trpB,* and *trpA* genes (but not *trpD*) are included in the duplicated region.

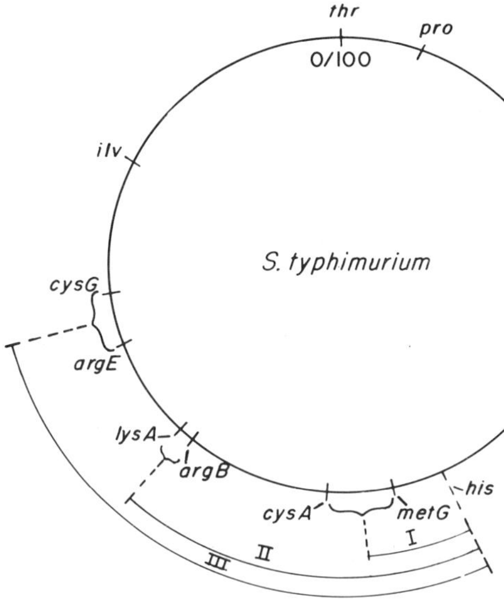

Figure 10 End points of tandem duplications selected by operon fusion in the *his* region of *Salmonella.*

One anomalous behavior of these strains is not easily explained by the simple sort of tandem duplication depicted in Figure 5. In addition to being unstable for their *trpB*$^+$ character, these strains may also be unstable for other unselected markers; *trpB*$^-$ segregants are often (but not always) Cys$^-$, or they require other unidentified supplements. The simplest duplication and/or translocation models for *trpB*$^+$ reversion do not account for these results.

Strains harboring tandem duplications of the *trp* operon may be similarly selected in *Salmonella typhimurium* (10a, 11, 82). Positive selection for *supX* deletions (88) has yielded a large collection of strains in which all or part of the *trp* operon has been deleted. Some of these deletions appear to remove only the operator-promoter region of the operon (leaving the structural genes intact), whereas others extend varying amounts into the structural genes. For many of these deletions, expression of "silent" genes may be selected as Trp$^+$ revertants (in the former case) or as strains able to utilize anthranilic acid or indole as a tryptophan source (in the latter cases). In each instance, some of the revertants are unstable for their selected phenotype. Fusion of remaining *trp* genes to nearby promoters appears the most likely explanation for such strains. Preliminary evidence has been presented that indicates this event occurs by a recombination (*recA*)-dependent process (11).

GALACTOSE OPERON The *E. coli* mutation *gal3* results from the linear insertion of an 1100-base-pair insertion sequence into the operator-promoter region of the *gal* operon (2). As a result, genes *galETK* are unexpressed. Among the Gal$^+$ revertants of *gal3* is a class that is unstable and that synthesizes constitutive levels of the enzymes (52, 87). It seems likely that these unstable strains are the result of tandem duplications that fuse the *gal* enzymes to unrelated promoters (1): instability of these strains is dependent upon recombination (*recA*) function; unstable revertants are merodiploid for *gal*; LFT lysates prepared from revertants lysogenic for phage lambda contain few λ*gal*$^+$ transducing particles. However, P1 generalized transduction indicates linkage between *gal*$^+$ in these strains and the lambda prophage site. Thus, the *gal*$^+$ character of these strains is located near the original *gal3* site but not close enough to be packaged by a single λd*gal* particle.

A rough estimate of the size of the duplicated region can be obtained from this data. Since λd*gal*$^+$ particles cannot be formed, yet phage P1 can cotransduce *gal*$^+$ with the lambda prophage, it appears the duplications include 1–3 min of chromosomal material.

T4rIIB Tandem duplications that fuse the bacteriophage T4rIIB region to secondary promoters may be selected as pseudorevertants of frameshift mutations occurring in the promoter proximal region of the *r*IIB cistron (42). The amino acid sequence coded by the first part of the *r*IIB cistron is not critical for gene function (21, 29). Thus, revertants of frameshift mutations need not preserve this sequence. Rather, events that restore the reading frame suffice to confer the *r*IIB$^+$ phenotype. Among such revertants are strains whose *r*IIB$^+$ phenotype is genetically unstable; *r*IIB$^-$ segregants identical to the parental strain accumulate in stocks of these revertants. Genetic tests indicate that these unstable strains are merodiploid for the *r*IIB cistron. Thus, they are concluded to contain tandem duplications that fuse the essential region of *r*IIB to more distal promoters. This event must occur such that the correct reading frame for the *r*IIB cistron is encountered at the join point between duplicated regions. Segregation data indicate that these duplications are relatively small, including very little material beyond the *r*IIB cistron. Headful packaging of DNA necessitates this (see above).

BACTERIOPHAGE P2 An unusual clear-plaque mutant of bacteriophage P2 (P2*vir37*) has been shown to result from tandem duplication of a small portion of the phage genome (16, 22). This event leads to expression of the early genes *A* and *B* in a manner insensitive to immunity repressor. Thus, it is similar to the types of operon fusions discussed above in that expression of these early genes is no longer under normal control elements. The nature of this mutational event is well documented. (*a*) The virulent nature of P2*vir37* is unstable. Turbid (wild type) plaques are present in lysates of this mutant at high frequency, despite repeated plaque purification. These segregants appear to arise by a recombinational mechanism, since ultraviolet irradiation of P2*vir37* leads to an increased proportion of turbid segregants. (*b*) P2*vir37* contains additional DNA. This is indicated by increased phage buoyant density in CsCl and increased heat lability of phage particles. (*c*) Merodiploidy for gene *B* can be demonstrated genetically. (*d*) Electron microscope analysis of heteroduplex molecules reveals a tandem duplication of 2.8% of the genome in strain P2*vir37*. This duplication occurs in the genome at a site very near the early functions *A* and *B*.

It is not possible to distinguish whether the duplication event has attached the early genes to a new repressor-insensitive promoter or whether the event has merely separated the normal promoter from its adjacent operator site. In either case, events analogous to operon fusion are involved.

GENERAL CONCLUSIONS

Size and Frequency of Tandem Duplications

Duplications have been observed in a wide variety of situations. Common to most of these cases is the finding that duplications occur with an unexpectedly high frequency and can include rather large segments of the bacterial chromosome. In retrospect, these properties may not be so surprising. The fact that large duplications cause no loss of function means that there may be virtually no limit to the extent of the duplicated segment. This, in turn, means that a large number of sites may be available for the illegitimate exchanges that lead to duplication. It is likely that the high frequency and large size of duplications reflect these considerations.

Mechanisms of Tandem Duplication

Based upon the cases described above, it seems likely that duplications can be formed by at least two distinct mechanisms. We have termed these legitimate and illegitimate duplications.

Legitimate duplications are those thought to arise by normal recombination between identical or nearly identical sequences located at distinct points in the chromosome. Events of this sort depend upon a functional recombination system and show strong preference for particular end points. Since homologous recombination occurs at a fairly high frequency, it is not surprising that duplications of this type are quite common. It will be interesting to learn what sorts of sequences provide the homology for these events. In the case of *glyT,* it seems clear that the several *rrn* genes are sites for recombination. In other regions of the chromosome, identical or nearly identical tRNA genes may serve. It is also possible that some fortuitous homologies could be sufficient to permit recombination. The possible role of IS sequences will be discussed below.

Illegitimate duplications are those that arise independent of the *rec* system. These include many of the duplications that fuse genes to new promoters. Since it is unlikely that a sequence within a given gene will be repeated elsewhere in the genome, duplications with end points within genes would most likely require an illegitimate recombination, but such events appear to be rare; therefore, one would expect that illegitimate duplications might be rare. In general, this is confirmed by the cases studied. High frequency illegitimate exchange has been observed, however, in cases of site-specific recombination (45). Illegitimate exchanges catalyzed by IS sequences may be examples of such events. In these situations, *rec*-independent duplications might arise at high frequency.

Over the last several years, data has accumulated on a series of transposable base sequences, the IS sequences (18, 117, 118). These sequences can transpose from place to place in the genome and generate, with high frequency, deletions of material adjacent to the site of insertion (25, 105). Wild-type bacterial strains are thought to carry multiple copies of these IS sequences in their genomes. The sites of such sequences are largely unknown, but some have been identified as points of F-factor insertion (25, 95, 113). IS sequences have many properties that could allow them to play an important role in the formation of both legitimate and illegitimate duplications. For legitimate duplications, IS elements could provide the homology necessary at separated sites on the chromosome. Normal (*rec* dependent) recombination between IS sequences at distant chromosomal positions could be an important contribution to the high frequency of *rec*-dependent duplication formation.

For illegitimate duplications, IS specific events could provide the source of illegitimate exchange. The deletion-generating property of IS elements can be thought of as resulting from an illegitimate exchange between the IS element and a different point in the same chromosome; such exchanges loop out and remove the segment of chromosome between these sites. If such events occur between the IS element and a point on a sister chromosome (see Figure 2), then IS-generated events could form illegitimate duplications.

Uses of Duplications in Genetic Analysis

Theoretically, duplications provide a means of performing complementation testing and chromosome mapping in bacterial species for which no conjugation system is available.

Mapping is possible since each duplication includes a contiguous block of genes in the chromosome, and since some of the duplications are quite large. Generation of a set of duplications by any of the methods outlined above and determination of what genes are located within the duplicated segment should allow the construction of chromosomal maps. The resolution of this technique is limited only by the number of duplication end points available. If the heteroclones described in *Streptomyces* (see above) are, in fact, the result of duplications, the efficacy of this mapping method may have already been demonstrated.

The use of duplications in complementation testing requires maintaining the duplication state while moving desired mutations into each of the two copies. This could be a problem in some situations, but the use of transposable drug resistance elements as dominant selective markers (72) should provide a means of circumventing such difficulties. Again, the work in *Streptomyces* (see above) may have already provided a demonstration of the general method.

Gene Duplication as a Regulatory Mechanism

The high frequency of duplication suggests the possibility that cells might use this process as a form of gene amplification. Cells carrying duplications of various regions of the chromosome are present as a reasonably high fraction of the population. Therefore, any environmental condition that favored cells with two (or more) copies of a particular chromosome segment would permit those cells to outgrow the rest of the population in a short time. If the conditions that favored a particular duplication changed, the cell population would not be committed to its new genotype, since the instability of the duplication would permit return to a predominantly haploid state. The kinetics of these populational responses have been described in theoretical terms (72a). In a sense, this might be thought of as a rather crude regulatory mechanism, which gains its specificity from natural selection. Although we know of no direct evidence demonstrating that such amplification is important to bacterial chromosomes, its role in R-factor transitioning has been clearly demonstrated (see above). A more widespread use of this process for amplification of chromosomal genes would not seem surprising. The finding of Hill et al (54) that many rRNA cistrons are located close together and in the same orientation is suggestive. Duplications arising between these cistrons would amplify rRNA genes; some such duplications would also amplify the ribosomal protein genes that lie between rRNA genes. Amplification of this region might be of selective advantage under conditions of fast growth rate. The findings of Nomura and co-workers (81, 89, 135) that essential tRNA genes are located within some of the *rrn* transcripts could be interpreted as a mechanism of preventing loss of *rrn* loci following unequal recombination events.

Literature Cited

1. Ahmed, A. 1975. *Mol. Gen. Genet.* 136: 243–53
2. Ahmed, A., Scraba, D. 1975. *Mol. Gen. Genet.* 136:233–42
3. Ames, B. N., Hartman, P. E., Jacob, F. 1963. *J. Mol. Biol.* 7:23–42
4. Anderson, R. P., Miller, C. G., Roth, J. R. 1976. *J. Mol. Biol.* 105:201–18
5. Anderson, T. F. 1958. *Cold Spring Harbor Symp. Quant. Biol.* 23:47–58
6. Audit, C., Anagnostopoulos, C. 1973. *J. Bacteriol.* 114:18–27
7. Audit, C., Anagnostopoulos, C. 1975. *Mol. Gen. Genet.* 137:337–51
8. Austrian, R., Bernheimer, H. P. 1959. *J. Exp. Med.* 110:571–84
9. Bachmann, B. J., Low, K. B., Taylor, A. L. 1976. *Bacteriol. Rev.* 40:116–67
10. Bastarrachea, F., Willetts, N. S. 1968. *Genetics* 59:153–66

10a. Basu, S. K., Margolin, P. 1972. *Genetics* 71:Suppl., p. 3

11. Basu, S. K., Margolin, P. 1973. *Abstr. Annu. Meet. Am. Soc. Microbiol.*, p. 71
12. Beeftinck, F., Cunin, R., Glansdorff, N. 1974. *Mol. Gen. Genet.* 132:241–53
13. Bellett, A. J. D., Busse, H. G., Baldwin, R. L. 1971. *The Bacteriophage Lambda*, pp. 501–13. Cold Spring Harbor, N.Y.: Cold Spring Harbor Lab.
14. Berg, D. E., Davies, J., Allet, B., Rochaix, J. D. 1975. *Proc. Natl. Acad. Sci. USA* 72:3628–32
15. Bernheimer, H. P., Wermundsen, I. E. 1969. *J. Bacteriol.* 98:1073–79
16. Bertani, G., Bertani, L. E. 1974. *Proc. Natl. Acad. Sci. USA* 71:315–19
17. Bresler, S. E., Lanzov, V. A., Blinkova, A. A. 1967. *Genetics* 56:105–16
18. Bukhari, A. I., Shapiro, J. A., Adhya, S., eds. 1977. *DNA Insertion Elements, Plasmids, and Episomes.* Cold Spring Harbor, N.Y.: Cold Spring Harbor Lab. 450 pp.
19. Busse, H. G., Baldwin, R. L. 1972. *J. Mol. Biol.* 65:401–12
20. Campbell, A. 1965. *Virology* 27:329–39
21. Champe, S. P., Benzer, S. 1967. *J. Mol. Biol.* 4:288–301
22. Chattoraj, D. K., Inman, R. B. 1974. *Proc. Natl. Acad. Sci. USA* 71:311–14
23. Cunin, R., Elseviers, D., Glansdorff, N. 1970. *Mol. Gen. Genet.* 108:154–57
24. Curtiss, R. III. 1964. *Genetics* 50: 679–94
25. Davidson, N., Deonier, R. C., Hu, S., Ohtsubo, E. 1975. *Microbiology* 1: 56–71
26. Davies, J. E., Rownd, R. 1972. *Science* 176:758–68
27. Davis, K. J., Symonds, N. 1974. *Mol. Gen. Genet.* 132:173–80
28. Dawson, G. W. P., Smith-Keary, P. F. 1963. *Heredity* 18:1–20
29. Drake, J. W. 1963. *Genetics* 48:767–76
30. Eggertsson, G., Adelberg, E. A. 1965. *Genetics* 52:319–40
31. Elseviers, D., Cunin, R., Glansdorff, N. 1969. *FEBS Lett.* 3:18–20
32. Elseviers, D., Cunin, R., Glansdorff, N., Baumberg, S., Ashcroft, E. 1972. *Mol. Gen. Genet.* 117:349–66
33. Ely, B. 1974. *Genetics* 78:593–606
34. Emmons, S. W. 1974. *J. Mol. Biol.* 83:511–25
35. Emmons, S. W., MacCosham, V., Baldwin, R. L. 1975. *J. Mol. Biol.* 91:133–46
36. Emmons, S. W., Thomas, J. O. 1975. *J. Mol. Biol.* 91:147–52

37. Folk, W. R., Berg, P. 1970. *J. Bacteriol.* 102:193–203
38. Folk, W. R., Berg, P. 1971. *J. Mol. Biol.* 58:595–610
39. Franklin, N. C. 1967. *Genetics* 55:699–707
40. Franklin, N. C. 1967. *Genetics* 57:301–18
41. Franklin, N. C. 1971. *The Bacteriophage Lambda,* pp. 175–82. Cold Spring Harbor, N.Y.: Cold Spring Harbor Lab.
42. Freedman, R., Brenner, S. 1972. *J. Mol. Biol.* 69:409–19
43. Gallucci, E., Garen, A. 1966. *J. Mol. Biol.* 15:193–200
44. Glansdorff, N., Sand, G. 1968. *Genetics* 60:257–68
45. Gottesman, M. F., Weisberg, R. A. 1971. *The Bacteriophage Lambda,* pp. 113–38. Cold Spring Harbor, N.Y.: Cold Spring Harbor Lab.
46. Hashimoto, H., Rownd, R. H. 1975. *J. Bacteriol.* 123:56–58
47. Hegeman, G. D., Rosenberg, S. L. 1970. *Ann. Rev. Microbiol.* 24:429–62
48. Helinski, D. R. 1973. *Ann. Rev. Microbiol.* 27:437–70
49. Hershey, A. D. 1970. *Carnegie Inst Washington Yearb.* 69:717–22
50. Hill, C. W. 1975. *Cell* 6:419–27
51. Hill, C. W., Combriato, G. 1973. *Mol. Gen. Genet.* 127:197–214
52. Hill, C. W., Echols, H. 1966. *J. Mol. Biol.* 19:38–51
53. Hill, C. W., Foulds, J., Soll, L., Berg, P. 1969. *J. Mol. Biol.* 39:563–81
54. Hill, C. W., Grafstrom, R. H., Hillman, B. S. 1977. *DNA Insertion Elements, Plasmids, and Episomes.* Cold Spring Harbor, N.Y.: Cold Spring Harbor Lab. 450 pp.
55. Hill, C. W., Schiffer, D., Berg, P. 1969. *J. Bacteriol.* 99:274–78
56. Hill, R. F. 1963. *J. Gen. Microbiol.* 30:289–97
57. Hilton, J. L., Kearney, P. C., Ames, B. N. 1965. *Arch. Biochem. Biophys.* 112:544–47
58. Hirsh, D. 1971. *J. Mol. Biol.* 58:439–58
59. Homyk, T., Weil, J. 1974. *Virology* 61:505–23
60. Hopwood, D. A. 1967. *Bacteriol. Rev.* 31:373–403
61. Horiuchi, T., Horiuchi, S., Novick, A. 1963. *Genetics* 48:157–69
62. Horiuchi, T., Tomizawa, J., Novick, A. 1962. *Biochim. Biophys. Acta* 55:152–63
63. Hu, S., Ohtsubo, E., Davidson, N., Saedler, H. 1975. *J. Bacteriol.* 122:764–72
64. Jackson, E. N., Yanofsky, C. 1973. *J. Bacteriol.* 116:33–40
65. Jamet, C., Anagnostopoulos, C. 1969. *Mol. Gen. Genet.* 105:225–42
66. Jamet-Vierney, C., Anagnostopoulos, C. 1975. *Genetics* 81:437–58
67. Johnson, E. M., Craig, W. G. Jr., Wohlhieter, J. A., Lazere, J. R., Synenki, R. M., Baron, L. S. 1973. *J. Bacteriol.* 115:629–34
68. Johnson, E. M., Placek, B. P., Snellings, N. J., Baron, L. S. 1975. *J. Bacteriol.* 123:1–6
69. Kashmiri, S. V. S., Hotchkiss, R. D. 1975. *Genetics* 81:9–19
70. Kashmiri, S. V. S., Hotchkiss, R. D. 1975. *Genetics* 81:21–31
71. Kleckner, N., Chan, R. K., Tye, B.-K., Botstein, D. 1975. *J. Mol. Biol.* 97:561–75
72. Kleckner, N., Roth, J., Botstein, D. 1977. *J. Mol. Biol.* In press
72a. Koch, A. L. 1977. *Genetics.* In press
73. Langridge, J. 1969. *Mol. Gen. Genet.* 105:74–83
74. Ledbetter, M. S., Hotchkiss, R. D. 1975. *Genetics* 80:667–78
75. Ledbetter, M. S., Hotchkiss, R. D. 1975. *Genetics* 80:679–94
76. Lederberg, J. 1949. *Proc. Natl. Acad. Sci. USA* 35:178–84
77. Lederberg, J. 1957. *Proc. Natl. Acad. Sci. USA* 43:1060–65
78. Leidy, G., Hahn, E., Alexander, H. E. 1953. *J. Exp. Med.* 97:467–82
79. Levinthal, M., Yeh, J. 1972. *J. Bacteriol.* 109:993–1000
80. Lotan, D., Yagil, E., Bracha, M. 1972. *Genetics* 72:381–91
81. Lund, E., Dahlberg, J. E., Lindahl, L., Jaskunas, S. R., Dennis, P. P., Nomura, M. 1976. *Cell* 7:165–77
82. Margolin, P., Bauerle, R. H. 1966. *Cold Spring Harbor Symp. Quant. Biol.* 31:311–20
83. Middleton, R. B., Mojica-a, T. 1971. *Adv. Genet.* 16:53–76
84. Miller, C. G., Roth, J. R. 1971. *J. Mol. Biol.* 59:63–75
85. Miller, J. H., Reznikoff, W. S., Silverstone, A. E., Ippen, K., Signer, E. R., Beckwith, J. R. 1970. *J. Bacteriol.* 104:1273–79
86. Mojica-a, T., Middleton, R. B. 1972. *Genetics* 71:491–505
87. Morse, M. L. 1967. *Genetics* 56:331–40
88. Mukai, F. H., Margolin, P. 1963. *Proc. Natl. Acad. Sci. USA* 50:140–48
89. Nomura, M. 1976. *Cell* 9:633–44
90. Novick, A. 1961. *Purdue Growth Sym-*

posium. Growth in Living Systems, New York: Basic Books
91. Novick, A., Horuichi, T. 1961. *Cold Spring Harbor Symp. Quant. Biol.* 26:234–45
92. Novick, R. P. 1969. *Bacteriol. Rev.* 33:210–63
93. Ohno, S. 1970. *Evolution by Gene Duplication,* p. 160. New York: Springer-Verlag.
94. Ohtsubo, E. 1970. *Genetics* 64:189–97
95. Ohtsubo, E., Deonier, R. C., Lee, H. J., Davidson, N. 1974. *J. Mol. Biol.* 89:565–84
96. Ou, J. T. 1975. *Genetics* 80:401–19
97. Parma, D. H., Heath, G. T., Che, C.-C., Annest, J. L. 1977. *Genetics.* In press
98. Parma, D. H., Ingraham, L. J., Snyder, M. 1972. *Genetics* 71:319–35
99. Parma, D. H., Snyder, M. 1973. *Genetics* 73:161–83
100. Perlman, D., Rownd, R. H. 1975. *J. Bacteriol.* 123:1013–34
101. Perlman, D., Twose, T. M., Holland, M. J., Rownd, R. H. 1975. *J. Bacteriol.* 123:1035–4
102. Ptashne, K., Cohen, S. N. 1975. *J. Bacteriol.* 122:776–81
103. Ravin, A. W., Ma, M. 1975. *Genetics* 80:421–43
104. Ravin, A. W., Takahashi, E. A. 1970. *J. Bacteriol.* 101:38–52
105. Reif, H. J., Saedler, H. 1975. *Mol. Gen. Genet.* 137:17–27
106. Rigby, P. W. J., Burleigh, B. D., Hartley, B. S. 1974. *Nature* 251:200–4
107. Roth, J. R. 1970. *J. Bacteriol.* 102: 467–75
108. Rownd, R., Mickel, S. 1971. *Nature New Biol.* 234:40–43
109. Rownd, R., Perlman, D., Hashimoto, S., Mickel, S., Appelbaum, E., Taylor, D. 1973. *Cellular Modification and Genetic Transformation,* pp. 115–28. Baltimore: Johns Hopkins Univ. Press
110. Sanderson, K., Hartman, P. E. 1977. *Bacteriol. Rev.* In press
111. Schwartz, N. M. 1965. *J. Bacteriol.* 89:712–17
112. Schwartz, N. M. 1967. *Genetics* 57:505–12
113. Sharp, P. A., Hsu, M.-T., Ohtsubo, E., Davidson, N. 1972. *J. Mol. Biol.* 71: 471–97
114. Smithies, O., Connell, G. E., Dixon, G. H. 1962. *Nature* 196:232–36
115. Soll, L., Berg, P. 1969. *Nature* 223: 1340–42
116. Soll, L., Berg, P. 1969. *Proc. Natl. Acad. Sci. USA* 63:392–99
117. Starlinger, P., Saedler, H. 1972. *Biochemie* 54:177–96
118. Starlinger, P., Saedler, H. 1976. *Curr. Top. Microbiol. Immunol.* 75:111–23
119. Stodolsky, M. 1973. *Genetics* 73:Suppl. pp. 65–66
120. Stodolsky, M. 1974. *Genetics* 78:809–22
121. Stodolsky, M., Rae, M. E., Mullenbach, E. 1972. *Genetics* 70:495–510
122. Straus, D. S. 1974. *Genetics* 78:823–30
123. Straus, D. S., Hoffmann, G. R. 1975. *Genetics* 80:227–37
124. Straus, D. S., Straus, L. D. 1976. *J. Mol. Biol.* 103:143–54
125. Symonds, N., Van den Ende, P., Durston, A., White, P. 1972. *Mol. Gen. Genet.* 116:223–38
126. Trowsdale, J., Anagnostopoulos, C. 1975. *J. Bacteriol.* 122:886–98
127. Van de Vate, C., Symonds, N. 1974. *Genet. Res. Cambridge* 23:87–105
128. Van de Vate, C., Van den Ende, P., Symonds, N. 1974. *Genet. Res. Cambridge* 23:107–13
129. Van den Ende, P., Symonds, N. 1972. *Mol. Gen. Genet.* 116:239–47
130. Weigle, J., Meselson, M., Paigen, K. 1959. *J. Mol. Biol.* 1:379–86
131. Weil, J., Terzaghi, B. 1970. *Virology* 42:234–37
132. Weil, J., Terzaghi, B., Crasemann, J. 1965. *Genetics* 52:683–93
133. Wood, T. H. 1967. *Science* 157:319–21
134. Wu, T. T., Lin, E. C. C., Tanaka, S. 1968. *J. Bacteriol.* 96:447–56
135. Yamamoto, M., Strycharz, W. A., Nomura, M. 1976. *Cell* 7:179–90
136. Yaniv, M., Folk, W. R., Berg, P., Soll, L. 1974. *J. Mol. Biol.* 86:245–60
137. Zipkas, D., Riley, M. 1975. *Proc. Natl. Acad. Sci. USA* 72:1354–58

Ann. Rev. Microbiol. 1977. 31:507–33

PHAGOCYTE LYSOSOMES: INTERACTIONS WITH INFECTIOUS AGENTS, PHAGOSOMES, AND EXPERIMENTAL PERTURBATIONS IN FUNCTION[1]

❖1715

Mayer B. Goren
Division of Molecular and Cellular Biology, National Jewish Hospital and Research Center and Department of Microbiology, University of Colorado School of Medicine, Denver, Colorado 80206

CONTENTS

INTRODUCTION 508
Transition 509
MICROBICIDAL MECHANISMS IN PHAGOCYTIC CELLS 510
Metabolism 510
Reduced pyridine nucleotides in the metabolic burst 510
Superoxide anion 511
The Peroxidase Paradox 513
ANTAGONISM OF HOST DEFENSES BY MICROORGANISMS 514
Mycobacteria 514
Mycobacterium lepraemurium 515
Mycobacterium tuberculosis 515
Chlamydia and Rickettsia 516
Toxoplasma and Besnoitia 517
Aspects of toxoplasma-induced cellular or humoral immunity 518
Macrophages in immunity to Toxoplasma and Besnoitia 519
Miscellaneous Parasitic Agents 520
Streptococci and a Digression 521
Streptolysins and leucocidin 521

[1]This paper is dedicated to Professor Robert Burns Woodward on the occasion of his sixtieth birthday.

INFLAMMATORY PROCESSES AND MEMBRANE FUSION 522
Cyclic Nucleotides and Fusion Phenomena 522
PERTURBATION OF PHAGOLYSOSOME FORMATION 523
Cyclic Nucleotides 523
Glucocorticosteroids and Concanavalin A 523
Sulfatides of Mycobacterium tuberculosis 524
Sulfatide-macrophage interactions 524
Suramin 525
Death and the Membrane: Fact or Artifact? 525
Extrapolations to Polyanionics 527
Dextran sulfate and Carrageenan 527
CONCLUSIONS AND SPECULATIONS 528

INTRODUCTION

A brief motion picture, a phase-contrast cinematographic demonstration of leukocytes engulfing bacteria [Cohn, Hirsch & Wiener (22); see also Robineaux and Frederic (140)] portrayed the long-sought link between Metchnikoff's phagocytes, Ehrlich's leukocyte granules, and the ubiquitous lysosome of de Duve (see 37). The explosive disappearance of the cytoplasmic granules by a process of fusion with the intact phagosome (110) exposed a mechanism of intracellular killing and digestion that had long been an enigma. This process, its ready "acceptance" on the one hand or antagonism on the other by intracellular pathogens, and in experimental manipulations, is the central theme of this review; however, it is embellished by a mass of modifying details, which must at the least be summarized as an introduction (see 60, 159). Many of the succeeding citations are for comprehensive reviews; indeed, within the body of the paper series of related studies will be cited by one or two representative references.

Two lines of professional phagocytes derived from hemapoietic stem cells proliferate, differentiate, and largely mature within the bone marrow—the cells of the Mononuclear Phagocyte System (170) and the neutrophil or heterophil of the granulocytic series. The processes as recognized in humans are shown [Figure 1, freely adapted from (13) and (173)]. During their maturation process, the cells synthesize, secrete, and store a complement of digestive and even killing enzymes (see 79, 134) packaged as granules or lysosomes (13, 21).

Within the tissues, the phagocytes are attracted to sites of microbial invasion or inflammation (184) by responding to stimuli generated by a diversity of agents, which encompass, for example, the complement-derived C5b67, the anaphylatoxins C5a and C3a of much lower molecular weight (124, 156, 177), microbial secretion products (48, 178), and, experimentally, the highly potent synthetic N-formylmethionyl di- and tripeptides (152). The resemblance of the latter to bacterial proteins in process of synthesis (187) may reflect sensu stricto an exquisitely selective recognition mechanism (cf also 185).

These directed migrations, and movements in phagocytosis as well, appear to depend upon submembranal and cytoplasmic cytoskeletal and muscular structures composed of microtubules and actomyosin-like microfilaments, which have been

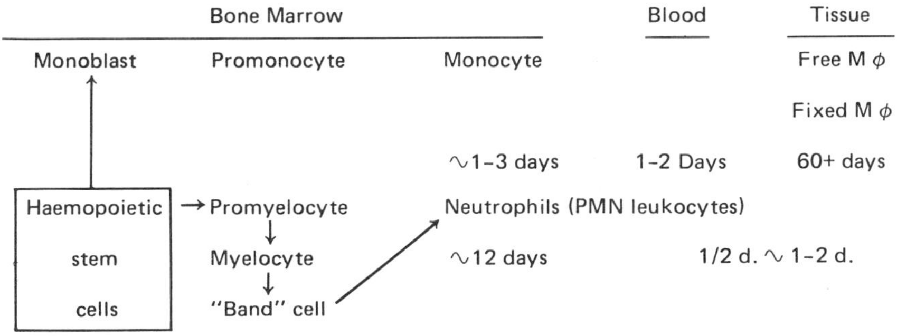

Figure 1 Differentiation, maturation, and life span of phagocytic cells.

recognized in ultrastructural studies (58, 138) and from the isolation, identification, and properties of actin, myosin, and cofactors recovered from phagocytic cells (17, 160, 164). A variety of surface membrane receptors participate either independently or cooperatively in the recognition and engulfment of targets for phagocytosis. The process involves a sequential or "zipper" mechanism, which is effected by successive membrane receptor and target-ligand interactions (67, 68). Thereafter, microtubules and microfilaments may serve to guide and propel the internalized phagosome and lysosomes to their collision, to merge and form the phagolysosome (115, 123, 182).

Metabolic changes elicited by contact and phagocytosis serve to generate superoxide and H_2O_2. In neutrophils and monocytes, H_2O_2 participates with lysosomal myeloperoxidase and halides in potent microbicidal activities (99). These agents probably also mediate killing through generation of singlet molecular oxygen $^1O_2^*$ (3). In neutrophils, which appear surfeited with antimicrobial activity, oxygen-linked killing is further augmented by a battery of cationic bactericidal proteins (108, 128, 189); however, hard evidence respecting killing mechanisms in macrophages is meager. Finally, within the phagolysosome, the destroyed organisms then are almost completely digested by the variety of acid hydrolases provided to the vacuole by the lysosomes (21).

Transition

Although the remainder of this review begins with microbicidal mechanisms, it is principally concerned with the interactions of phagosomes and lysosomes. Mutual antagonisms in aggression and defense have evolved between phagocytes and pathogens, and select examples illustrate at least some of the variety; however, my bias respecting antagonism of phagosome-lysosome fusion as a ploy of several successful intracellular pathogens is manifest. This extends to processes in inflammation and thus directly leads to experimental systems for testing agents putatively involved in fusion phenomena. The conclusion is undeniably devoted to speculation. There are, of course, important omissions. Abundant excellent reviews are cited, as in the preceding overview, in an effort to fill some of these lacunae.

MICROBICIDAL MECHANISMS IN PHAGOCYTIC CELLS

Metabolism

Dramatic metabolic changes are stimulated in leukocytes, in some monocytes, and in certain stimulated macrophages (review 93) when they are challenged with particulate material. In its most exquisite expression, the induced burst of metabolic activity is elicited merely by contact of the cell with the target or with surface stimulant, e.g. detergents, concanavalin A, phospholipase C, phorbol myristate-acetate, etc [summarized in (146)] (see also 36, 59, 144, 148, 153).

Polymorphonuclear (PMN) leukocytes depend upon glycolysis for metabolic energy and for the energy necessary for the ingestion process in phagocytosis (91). Still, the engulfment process in PMN leukocytes and in some classes of macrophages is accompanied by a marked surge in oxygen consumption, an increased utilization of glucose, especially in the conversion of 1-^{14}C to $^{14}CO_2$ (i.e. stimulation of the hexose monophosphate shunt), and an increased production of H_2O_2 (reviewed in 93, 100, 146); Root et al describe sensitive methodology (see 143). Our present understanding of the metabolic events is summarized in a simplified scheme of Karnovsky (92) (reproduced with permission in Figure 2).

REDUCED PYRIDINE NUCLEOTIDES IN THE METABOLIC BURST Figure 2 depicts the participation of both NADH and NADPH in the metabolic flow leading to hydrogen peroxide, which has assumed a central role in the elucidation of specific microbicidal activities. According to Rossi and collaborators (141, 145, 146), the most likely candidate whose activation (by an increased affinity for the substrate) could be responsible for the enhanced oxygen uptake in the metabolic burst is a particulate granule-associated NADPH oxidase, originally described by Iyer & Quastel (86). This hypothesis has the appeal of simplicity in directly linking respiration to the stimulation of the hexose monophosphate pathway by providing $NADP^+$; it has been considerably strengthened by recent studies of Hohn & Lehrer (83), DeChatelet et al (34), and Babior et al (9). The alternative hypothesis of Karnovsky and others (11, 92) favors activation of NADH oxidase to increase H_2O_2 production, which in turn stimulates the shunt by providing $NADP^+$ via GSH-GSSG. The disagreement has not generated unrestrained polemics, but neither has it led to a unique resolution, for the latter hypothesis has also been buttressed by the recent provocative demonstration of NADH oxidase localized on the membrane surface of human PMN leukocytes. This enzyme, when internalized during phagocytosis, retains its peroxide-generating capacity (19). New evidence from both groups (25, 132) suggests that the granule-associated NADPH oxidase may function to produce superoxide anion (see below), possibly as an intermediate in H_2O_2 generation, so that the convictions of all protagonists may yet be upheld. (The exciting resolution in these latter studies of a curious Mn^{2+} dependence of the isolated granule oxidase, which specifically implicates superoxide, is intriguingly detailed.)

The importance of oxygen in microbicidal activity is inferred on the one hand from an attenuation in killing induced by anaerobiosis (116, 121) and on the other

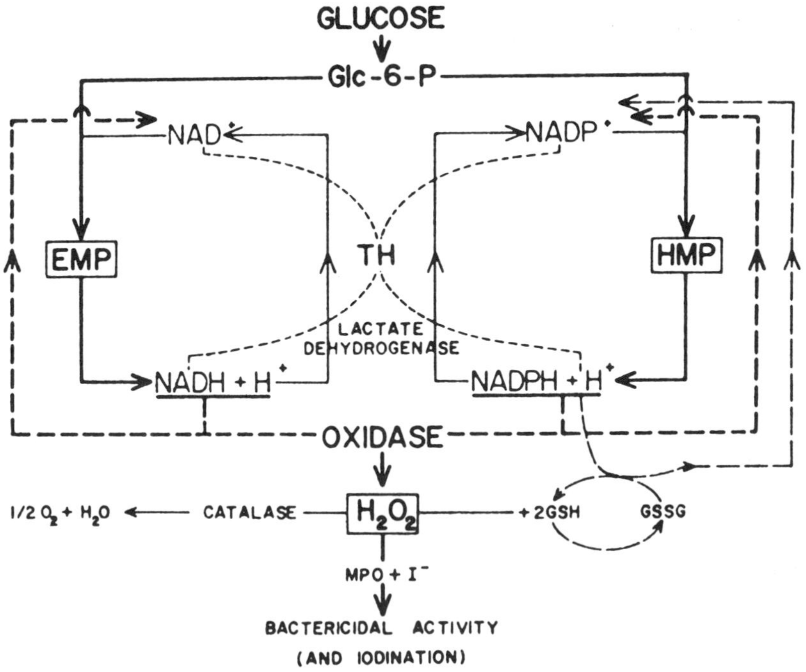

Figure 2 Oxygen uptake, peroxide production, and the hexose monophosphate shunt pathway during phagocytosis in granulocytes. Reprinted from *Federation Proceedings* 32:1527–33 (1973).

hand from the impaired microbicidal activity of phagocytic cells defective in oxidative metabolism—as from patients with chronic granulomatous disease (9, 11, 26, 27, 83, 87, 92, 142, 154). Powerful amplification processes exist for the utilization of H_2O_2 in bactericidal activity. These encompass especially the myeloperoxidase-H_2O_2-halide systems of Klebanoff (99), singlet molecular oxygen ($'O_2^*$) (3), and superoxide anion (10; see below). These subjects have been reviewed recently by Klebanoff & Hamon (99, 100). More recent studies on superoxide, however, require elaboration.

SUPEROXIDE ANION The biological ubiquity of superoxide dismutase (SOD), save for the notable exception of strict anaerobes (120), suggests that this enzyme protects cells from the highly reactive and toxic free radical superoxide anion O_2^- (reviewed in 51). O_2^- is generated in many chemical reactions involving molecular oxygen, owing to a preferred univalent pathway of reduction; it is generated in biochemical systems as well, e.g. the granule NADPH oxidase (preceding). Superoxide can be specifically detected through inhibition of its chemical reactivities by SOD. O_2^- behaves both as a powerful oxidant and as a reducing agent: it reduces cytochrome *c* or nitroblue tetrazolium to yield oxygen and formazan; and in its behavior as an oxidant, O_2^- is reduced to H_2O_2. In accord with these properties, it undergoes a rapid disproportionation in aqueous solution, a reaction catalyzed some 10^4-fold by SOD, e.g. as the conjugate acid. $HO_2 + HO_2 \rightarrow H_2O_2 + O_2$. O_2^- also reacts with H_2O_2 to yield hydroxyl radical, hydroxide ion, and O_2—an interpretation now modified to embrace singlet molecular oxygen (97). Superoxide, therefore, can provide cytotoxic $'O_2^*$ on the one hand and H_2O_2 on the other for stimulating hexose monophosphate shunt activity or to participate in the myeloperoxidase-halide system.

The heuristic discovery of Babior, Kipnes & Curnutte (10) that phagocytizing leukocytes produce superoxide has elicited a response of investigatory activities that rivals the metabolic burst. As examples, O_2^- production is stimulated in leukocytes, monocytes, and some classes of macrophages by phagocytosis (35, 43, 125), by minute levels of phorbol myristate acetate (36), or (in human cytochalasin-inhibited leukocytes) by opsonized zymosan, heat-aggregated immunoglobulin G, or C5a in the absence of phagocytosis (59); in several of these studies, O_2^- production by chronic granulomatous disease cells was demonstrably defective. According to Tsan & McIntyre (165), membrane sialic acid residues of putative receptors are stringently required: thus, neuraminidase treatment of human PMN leukocytes, resulting in desialylation of 40–60% of accessible sialic acid, had no adverse influence on phagocytosis but inhibited the associated O_2^- production by 90%.

The often-expressed dilemma about myeloperoxidase-independent bactericidal mechanisms in macrophages (see below) has stimulated much of the activity to delineate possible roles for superoxide. A serious and frustrating inherent limitation in the methodology, however, is that only the fraction of O_2^- released from the cells is discernible. Still, some intriguing results have emerged (35, 43). Phagocytosis induces an incremental O_2^- release, which may range from zero (guinea pig or rabbit alveolar macrophages) to a tenfold increase for mouse alveolar cells. Thus, there are wide ranging species differences and equally wide ranges within a species according to cell type: mouse PMN leukocytes and mouse or guinea pig peritoneal cells, "activated" by caseinate elicitation, respond to phagocytosis with only an apparent doubling or trebling of O_2^- release; the increment accounts for only 3–6% of the increased oxygen consumption (ΔO_2). In striking contrast, the resident mouse peritoneal macrophage exhibits a similar incremental release of O_2^-, but this is equivalent to 80% of ΔO_2 (43)! For this cell, superoxide, therefore, may play a (extracellular?) role in a killing ability that is undeniable despite an almost total absence of myeloperoxidase (154, 171) [see especially Discussion in (100)]. However, in the absence of an internal probe for estimating total O_2^- production relative to the respiratory burst, the increased bactericidal capacity of "activated" macrophages cannot yet be explained by superoxide.

The evidence for direct O_2^- mediated microbicidal activity on the part of phagocytes is meager. Johnston et al (87) described inhibition by SOD of intracellular killing by human PMN leukocytes. The SOD, adsorbed onto latex particles, was phagocytosed simultaneously with the target bacteria and, according to electron microscopy (EM) documentation, acted from within the phagolysosomes. This system is exceptional in that the intravacuolar consequence of dismutation did not lead to the amplified killing effects that in fact would be expected (cf 98). It is also difficult to reconcile with the results of a succeeding study (12), in which SOD presented in the same fashion stimulated H_2O_2 production, hexose monophosphate shunt activity, and intracellular iodination of ingested particles. In my interpretation, the numerous investigations in which iodination was studied suggest that, although "killing is not necessarily dependent upon iodination" (12), nevertheless increased iodination usually presages functional and increased killing.

In sum, the role of superoxide is still elusive. Its production during phagocytosis seems unequivocal, but not so any manifestation of a direct major participation in microbicidal activity. In the absence of any compelling evidence surfacing in the interim, Occam's razor would dictate that, as Karnovsky (92a) suggested several years ago, "superoxide may simply be an intermediate on the way to H_2O_2, which is the key antimicrobial agent."

The Peroxidase Paradox

The secretory granules in promonocytes of human bone marrow contain both peroxidase and lysosomal enzymes. However, in more mature cells, peroxidase secretion in rough endoplasmic reticulum (RER) and Golgi apparatus is terminated while a second coexistent population of storage granules lacking peroxidase appears. As reviewed by Bainton et al (13, 126), this cell was recognized as the least mature monocyte, in its closer resemblance to the blood cell.

As with the human promonocyte, that of the mouse is endowed with numerous peroxidase-containing granules; however, the monocyte has fewer and the mature macrophage essentially has none (154, 171). The need for an understanding of this state of affairs seems colored with an immediate urgency. It is paradoxical that the functional cell (macrophage) is apparently deprived of a killing potential that is abundantly bestowed upon less- or nonfunctional progenitors. Daems and colleagues (28) have compiled evidence from their own studies and from those of others that cytochemically demonstrated peroxidatic activity in tissue macrophages of various animal species—distributed in the RER, in the nuclear envelope, and in the Golgi apparatus, but evidently not in lysosomes. By contrast, the blood monocytes are evidently devoid of peroxidase activity in these sites but instead, in most animal species, retain this enzyme in a portion of their lysosomal granules. In Daems' interpretation (28), this and still other evidence strongly suggests that monocytes and tissue macrophages are different types of cells, and it contradicts the argument that all tissue macrophages are derived from monocytes [the "Paradigm of the proposed 'Mononuclear Phagocyte System' " (see also 175)]. Lepper & Hart (109) have also recently reported cytochemical/EM studies in which peroxidase (or peroxidatic) reaction product was recognized in the nuclear envelope, in the RER, and in occasional Golgi vesicles of unelicited mouse peritoneal macrophages. It is possible that these enzymatic entities in toto may (with H_2O_2) contribute to the bactericidal activities of mononuclear phagocytes (see 100). Nevertheless, the failure of cultured mouse peritoneal macrophages to iodinate phagocytosed particles may deny a functional capacity for these peroxidatic enzymes (154; see also 15).

Perhaps it is ghoulish to participate in raising the debris of myriads of dead granulocytic cells as a not insignificant source of peroxidase for the macrophage in vivo. This notion is by no means new (78a, 100), and it may be buttressed by reports that mouse peritoneal macrophages elicited with thioglycollate (162) or caseinate (93) have significant levels of peroxidase activity. Although monocytes migrate into inflammatory sites independently, still they are ordinarily preceded by an influx of suicidally programmed neutrophils and may be accompanied by other granulocytes as well. Their "funeral bak'd meats (may thriftily) coldly furnish forth the (macrophage) table" with a delicacy, excepting horseradish peroxidase (23), which has not been provided for the resident mouse peritoneal macrophage matured in a Leighton tube and engorged with endocytosed serum. It seems plausible that results of in vitro studies with these cells may be notably influenced if they first consumed a dying population of homologous granulocytes.

ANTAGONISM OF HOST DEFENSES BY MICROORGANISMS

Evolutionary processes have provided various pathogens with an array of protective or aggressive responses to host defense mechanisms: surface capsules that prevent attachment and phagocytosis; the assumption of a mask of host-derived antigens by adult schistosomes and thus escape of recognition (57); impairment of host humoral immunity in malaria and trypanosomiasis (66); and the chameleon-like alterations in glycoprotein surface antigens with which the trypanosome responds to host humoral antagonists (174).

The spectrum of bacterial toxins reviewed by Allen (2) may now be augmented by surface envelope lipids of certain mycobacteria and corynebacteria. According to extensive studies by Kato, "cord factor" (6,6'-trehalose dimycolate) of *Mycobacterium tuberculosis* and simpler analogs elaborated by *Corynebacterium diphtheriae* exert a destructive physical attack both in vivo and in vitro on mitochondrial and submitochondrial membranes. (62, 94, 95). Aqueous dispersions of cord factor also appear to be potently toxic for mouse peritoneal macrophages in culture (M. B. Goren and P. D. Hart, unpublished data). Studies by Hard (72) demonstrated necrotizing effects of both *Corynebacterium ovis* organisms and of extracted *C. ovis* lipids on phagocytic cells, the lipids on the one hand providing a protective barrier for the intact organisms within phagolysosomes (see below) and on the other inducing acute lethal injury in phagocytic cells by a membrane disruptive process. The succeeding sections elaborate on some intracellular and extracellular defense mechanisms that have evolved for a limited selection of pathogenic microorganisms.

Mycobacteria

H. B. Fell kindly informed me—respecting her collaborative studies with Brieger (18)—of their astonishment at the unchecked multiplication of virulent tubercle bacilli within tissue culture cells. To elucidate the intracellular survival mechanisms, studies at Mill Hill [recently reviewed (40)] have long been concerned with several mycobacterial species.

MYCOBACTERIUM LEPRAEMURIUM Ultrastructural studies with tissues from infected mice, cultured rat fibroblasts, or mouse peritoneal macrophages (see 2, 40, 74) revealed a uniform picture of bacteria harbored within vacuoles clearly recognizable as phagolysosomes. This was the case regardless of whether the bacilli appeared viable or dead, as judged by well-established morphological criteria (139). *Mycobacterium lepraemurium,* therefore, is well adapted to survival within the ordinarily hostile environment of the phagolysosome. (*Mycobacterium leprae* has a more complex life cycle, only a part of which is spent within the phagosomal system.) A prominent electron transparent zone (41; see also 72) around the intracellular bacteria, as seen in EM profiles, was recognized as resulting from a fibrillar or tape-like wrapping in which the bacteria, gently removed from liver lesions, were enclosed (42). The principal substance of this capsular material is the peptidoglycolipid "mycoside C," many variants of which have been described among several species of mycobacteria (review 61). Relatively inert chemically, the mycoside seems a suitable candidate for an encapsulating substance to provide passive protection to its resident bacterium, but which because of its fibrillar construction would still be permeable to small molecules of nutrients (41). *M. lepraemurium* therefore seems especially adapted to and in fact may require the lysosomal environment for survival. A closely related mycoside C has also been obtained as an adherent substance from in vitro harvests of *Mycobacterium avium* 357 (39), for which the mycoside may perform a similar passive function, a question which may presently be under study.

MYCOBACTERIUM TUBERCULOSIS An entirely different mode of survival has evolved for the facultative intracellular parasite *Mycobacterium tuberculosis.* By actively interfering with or antagonizing phagosome-lysosome fusion, a microorganism may evade the lysosomal armamentarium and therefore avoid potential digestion, if not killing. Following documentation of the fusion phenomenon, scattered reports appeared, which inferred or recognized this dysfunction vis-a-vis specific microorganisms (see 40, 107). Phase-contract studies of mouse peritoneal macrophages following ingestion of virulent microorganisms (*M. tuberculosis, Listeria monocytogenes*) capable of intracellular multiplication suggested to Fauve & Delaunay (50) that phagosomes containing the pathogens did not fuse with lysosomes; they advanced an early hypothesis to account for the aberration in fusion.

Ultrastructural studies with cultured mouse peritoneal macrophages infected with various tubercle species have confirmed these early inferences (7, 73, 74). The electron opaque marker, ferritin, which accumulates in secondary lysosomes, was routinely used in these studies to allow quantitation of the incidence of phagosomal-lysosomal fusion. After infection with the virulent strain H37Rv, phagolysosome formation was almost universal for vacuoles containing damaged bacteria (quite certainly present in the original inoculum) but was relatively infrequent for phagosomes containing intact and presumably viable organisms. With intact but inactivated (^{60}Co irradiated) H37Rv, a high incidence of fusion prevailed. Quite similar results were obtained with *Mycobacterium microti* (virulent for the mouse). Strains of intermediate virulence, BCG and H37Ra (73), which remain viable within cultured macrophages (mouse peritoneal) for a limited period of time, showed a progressive pattern of fusion as the viability of the intracellular organisms declined. With H37Ra in the intermediate stage of infection, or somewhat later with BCG, the incidence of fusion, even with phagosomes containing apparently intact organisms, increased—as if the lysosomes were responding to an increasingly nonviable population.

Two hypotheses were considered: that many bacilli are intact and alive because of a failure of fusion; or conversely, that fusion does not occur because the bacilli are intact and alive. The weight of evidence in toto seems strongly in favor of the second alternative—fusion by the secondary lysosomes is somehow "dependent on recognition of the status of the intraphagosomal organisms" (7).

If the bacteria were preincubated with either normal or specifically immune rabbit serum, and presumably "coated," prior to phagocytosis (8), the majority of phagosomes containing intact bacilli fused with ferritin-labeled lysosomes; however, the consequences had no effect on subsequent intracellular survival and growth: lysosome contents manifestly failed to exert an antibacterial effect on *M. tuberculosis.*

Can the kind of evasion demonstrated in vitro be maintained in vivo in healing tuberculosis lesions or in an immunized host? In these, cooperative interactions between specifically sensitized lymphocytes and activated macrophages evidently provide the factors necessary to overcome the parasitic onslaught (31, 113, 114, 176). Some of these factors may be in the form of tuberculocidal free fatty acids (90, 101), or they may be associated with the richness in content of macrophage lysosomal enzymes (31). Thus, the intracellular behavior of *M. tuberculosis* as seen with mixed cultures of activated cells (see 133) may yield information on whether the host cells adapt to overcome the specific lysosomal antagonism or whether extracellular killing must first intervene.

Chlamydia and Rickettsia

Member of the genus *Chlamydia* are obligate intracellular parasites whose intricate developmental cycle is consummated entirely within phagocytic vacuoles of the host cell. After endocytic entry (as into L cells), the infectious elementary body differentiates during about 8 hr into vegetative, non-infectious reticulate forms, which divide by binary fission within the inclusion membrane. The latter balloons to accommodate the growth, presumably by incorporation of membrane components present within the host cell (157). The structural composition of the membrane appears to be modified via glycosylations (158) and by alterations in lipid fatty acid components (49)—both evidently parasite induced. Extensive multiplication during 30 hr or more is followed by the re-emergence in several intermediate stages (52) of a new population of infectious elementary bodies and a concomitant lysis of the host cell —a cytopathic effect associated with lysosomal enzyme release (102, 167) and remarkably similar to that seen in certain virus infections (see 29). Studies by Kordová and collaborators (102–104) have distinguished between an early cytotoxic and agglutinating effect (TE) on mouse peritoneal macrophages, which is elicited by high doses of viable or even heat-inactivated *Chlamydia psittaci,* and a cytopathic effect of productive infections; in both effects massive lysosomal enzyme release is implicated. The toxic agent associated with TE is also recoverable in culture medium from infected L cells. Both TE and cytopathic effect (and chlamydia multiplication) are abolished if the infectious agent is preincubated with immune serum.

The cytocidal mechanisms in lysis resulting from productive infection have been studied (167). At various postinfection stages, EM examination consistently revealed absence of lysosomal markers within both the original phagocytic vacuoles and the inflated inclusion bodies into which these transformed as the infection progressed. Coincident with the enormous increase in inclusion volume and the reorganization to the infectious elementary bodies, the host cell lysosomes are displaced to the cell periphery. This is succeeded by progressive lysosomal rupture, cytoplasmic distribution of the acid phosphatase activity, and cytoplasmic disintegration. At these stages, increasing fractions of latent lysosomal enzyme activities appeared in released form in supernates of cell homogenates. Even at the penultimate stage, amid a picture of total disintegration of host cell cytoplasm, the massive, centrally located inclusions may still retain a brief integrity before the (inferred) protective membrane and host cell plasmalemma rupture to release the infectious progeny.

To account for the characteristics of the phagosome and its evolved inclusion body as an obviously privileged site, Friis (52) postulated that the chlamydial cells prevent the lysosomal responses owing to some intrinsic feature of the parasite's architecture already present at the time of entry. This activity was not expressed by killed cells nor by infectious bodies in even a loose association with specific antibody, which may simply "cover" or perhaps neutralize the postulated architectural feature (52).

Preincubation of *Rickettsia mooseri* with immune serum and complement, which are not rickettsiacidal, renders these organisms susceptible to destruction within human monocyte-derived macrophages (53). But the related, more resistant *Coxiella burnetii* is not destroyed after similar treatment. [In the presence of immune lymphocytes, however, or of lymphocyte-antigen culture supernatants, at least multiplication is suppressed (78).] This pattern, or variants, is seen in other systems as well and is consistent with the masking by the adsorbed antiserum of some peripherally located substance(s) of the pathogen, which may be involved in inducing the fusion dysfunction.

Toxoplasma and Besnoitia

Hirsch, Jones & Len (80) have described infection of a host by the obligate intracellular protozoan *Toxoplasma gondii* as a "near-perfect parasitic onslaught." Toxoplasma are capable of infecting a wide variety of animals to produce, in those surviving the acute stage, a latent infection in which the persistence of the parasites in cysts produces an effective and prolonged cellular immunity (16, 82, 89). With both professional phagocytes and nonphagocytic cells, entry of the parasite appears to be by a phagocytic process (80) evidently induced by the parasite—as for example in fibroblasts or HeLa cells, either by some secreted substance or by a select surface property. However, Zaman & Colley also documented direct penetration processes (188).

About half the parasitic cells of a viable inoculum, or toxoplasma killed by glutaraldehyde and exposed to normal mouse peritoneal macrophages, elicit a vigorous lysosomal fusion response with the endocytic vacuole. This is demonstrated in the striking electron micrographs kindly provided by J. G. Hirsch and T. C. Jones (Figure 3*a*). In this study, the secondary lysosomes were prelabeled with Thorotrast; abundant fusion is evident, as indicated by the electron opaque marker within the phagocytic vacuole. With intact live organisms (Figure 3*b*), however, no lysosomal marker intrudes within the phagocytic vacuole despite an abundance of thorotrast-labeled, secondary lysosomes in the vicinity. This correlation appeared to be absolute; frequently, single cells with adjacent vacuoles containing dead and viable organisms, respectively, and distinguished by the marker were noted.

ASPECTS OF TOXOPLASMA-INDUCED CELLULAR OR HUMORAL IMMUNITY Immunization of mice with a few cysts of a low-virulent strain of *T. gondii* elicits both a humoral and cellular immunity, which manifests itself in a resistance to intraperitoneal challenge with a virulent strain after about 11 days (80, 89, 151). Elevated antibody titers, detectable by the Sabin-Feldman dye test (147), are then evident throughout the life of the animal. Effective neutralization of toxoplasma [and the morphologically similar besnoitia (82)] by antibody requires a complement-

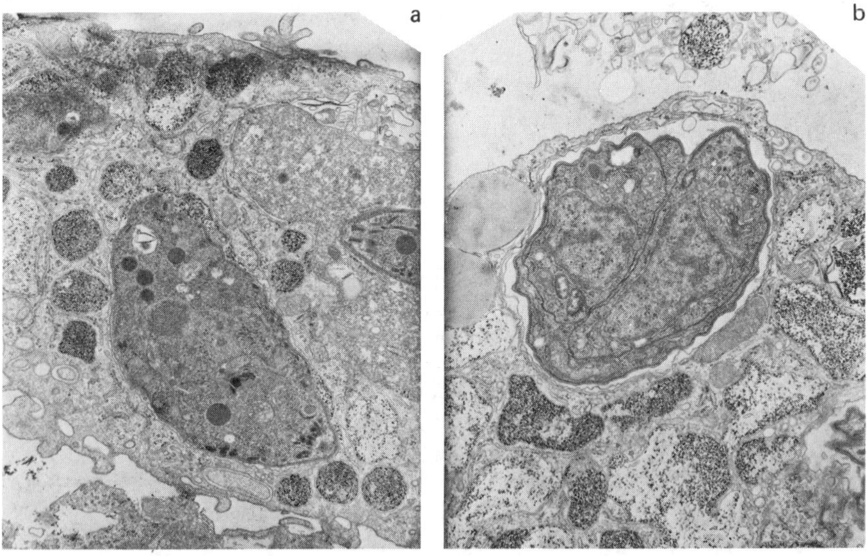

Figure 3 Thorotrast-labeled macrophages after ingestion of (*a*) glutaraldehyde-killed *Toxoplasma gondii* and (*b*) viable toxoplasma [after Jones & Hirsch (88)].

like "accessory factor," which is most abundant in human immune serum and absent in heat-inactivated serum (82, 147). Complete but not heat-inactivated antiserum will kill the parasites in vitro (6), by lysis, and it seems likely that such direct humoral intervention may play a role in acquired immunity. Although committed lymphoid cells, but not serum, can adoptively transfer to normal recipients immunity against *T. gondii* and *Besnoitia jellisoni* (82), still, after exposure of toxoplasma to heat-inactivated antitoxoplasma antibody—either human or murine, over 90% of the inoculum phagocytosed by normal mouse peritoneal macrophages was killed and digested within phagolysosomes (80, 89). In a reversal of the ordinary nonfusion pattern, these viable toxoplasma now elicited a prompt and destructive lysosomal fusion response, as betrayed by the presence of lysosomal markers within the phagocytic vacuoles. A comparable pattern has been described with human peripheral blood monocytes (16) or matured macrophages (6). Once untreated organisms were intracellular, however, even complete immune serum added to the medium was without effect. In contrast, besnoitia merely treated with inactivated immune serum proliferated in casein-elicited normal or toxoplasma-immune hamster peritoneal macrophages in culture (82). Investigation of this system by ultrastructural and/or cytochemical methods such as have been described for toxoplasma seems desirable for elucidating the lysosomal response to serum-treated besnoitia.

MACROPHAGES IN IMMUNITY TO TOXOPLASMA AND BESNOITIA The behavior of immune murine macrophages as effectors of cellular immunity to toxoplasma appears to involve the lysosomal system only indirectly. In the absence of specific antibody, even macrophages from immune mice were incapable of destroying toxoplasma during some 28 hr in culture. Nevertheless, the ordinary 5- to 6-hr generation time of the agent was prolonged about fourfold (89). The maximum effect was achieved when a mixed population of peritoneal cells was incubated for 24 hr with toxoplasma antigen prior to challenge of the adherent population. The stasis was not associated with any evident delivery of lysosomal constituents to the phagocytic vacuole and could be induced in macrophages exposed to supernates from lymphocyte-antigen incubations. Jones et al (89) speculate that these slowly dividing organisms may evolve into a toxoplasma cyst—the "hallmark of the immune state." Although in this study only macrophages from immune mice suppressed multiplication, Sethi et al (151) reported instead that thioglycollate-stimulated peritoneal exudate cells from either normal or immune mice destroyed *T. gondii* if infection was followed by co-culturing the cells with T lymphocytes from immune animals. Supernates from toxoplasma-immune lymphocytes exposed to specific antigen also induced antitoxoplasma activity in non-immune macrophages.

In the *Besnoitia* system of Hoff & Frenkel (82), peritoneal macrophages elicited from immune hamsters with a combination of caseinate and disrupted homologous organisms were directly inhibitory or cidal for the pathogen in culture. Specifically committed peritoneal exudate cell lymphocytes also "instructed" casein-elicited normal or toxoplasma-immune macrophages to limit growth or to destroy besnoitia in vitro, but only in co-cultivation systems involving intimate contact between lymphocytes and effector cells. Thus, caseinate or thioglycollate elicitation evidently provide an additional increment of resistance to lymphocyte-induced specific activation against toxoplasma and besnoitia.

Borges & Johnson (16) and Anderson et al (5, 6) described inhibition of *T. gondii* multiplication and even killing within human monocytes and macrophages, which is mediated in either normal or specifically immune cells by sensitized lymphocytes [T cells (16)] and toxoplasma lysate antigen or by appropriate supernates (16). Nonsensitized lymphocytes from Sabin-Feldman dye test negative subjects and toxoplasma lysate antigen were ineffective. However, incubation of macrophages with lymphocytes and streptokinase-streptodornase or concanavalin A also induced a significant but lesser activation (5, 6). Thus, human monocytes/macrophages may respond more efficiently to lymphocyte activation, whereas some form of "contact language" seems required for effectively stimulating mouse or guinea pig cells (82).

The sustained stimulation of macrophages in animals chronically infected with *T. gondii* or *Besnoitia* species induces powerful and prolonged resistance to various intracellular pathogens and antitumor activity. Since approximately 50% or more of the world's adult population is estimated to be chronically infected with toxoplasma, the agent is potentially useful for tumor immunotherapy (105).

Miscellaneous Parasitic Agents

Two recent studies provide evidence that amastigotes of *Leishmania mexicana* and *Leishmania donovani* persist and multiply within phagolysosomes of cultured macrophages (1, 20). In both studies, EM profiles showed that 80–95% of vacuoles containing living amastigotes also contained the electron opaque markers used to prelabel the secondary lysosomes. Moreover, when nonlabeled macrophages ingested the parasite and were then later exposed to marker, the label subsequently appeared in the pre-existing parasitophorus vacuoles. Explants of hamster spleen infected in vivo exhibited a similar distribution of marker to these vacuoles following uptake of Thorotrast (20). Accordingly, the indifference to or perhaps requirement for the lysosomal environment resembles that described for *Mycobacterium lepraemurium.* Because of this ongoing fusion, the system seems an excellent model to study the behavior of appropriately designed drugs, rendered lysosomotropic in accordance with the concepts recently advanced by de Duve et al (38).

As an example of yet another ploy for escaping host defenses, *L. donovani* thwarts humoral processes by aggregating surface antigen-antibody complexes into polar caps, which are removed from the cell surface by both endocytosis and shedding (45).

Trypomastigotes and transition forms of *Trypanosoma cruzi* [but not epimastigotes (127)] resist intracellular killing in non-immune macrophages by escaping from phagocytic vacuoles into the cytoplasm (163). A number of animal viruses exhibit a similar escape behavior (30). Cells of the inoculum that do not escape are rapidly destroyed in phagolysosomes and this process is notably enhanced in activated macrophages from specifically immunized mice, or from mice stimulated by BCG or *Listeria* infection (81, 163) but not in thioglycollate-stimulated cells (127).

This may be attributable to a more extensively developed or more efficiently delivered lysosomal armamentarium (see 31).

The parasitophorus vacuole of *Encephalitozoon cuniculi,* a small parasitic eukaryote, grows to enormous size in mouse peritoneal macrophages parasitized in vivo. Continuous growth is at the expense of host cell cytoplasm, which is incorporated into blebs and vesicles formed at the parasitophorus vacuole boundary and which is interiorized by pinocytosis. A similar phenomenon has been described for toxoplasma (88). Lysosomal markers, on the other hand, are rigidly excluded (179).

Streptococci and a Digression

STREPTOLYSINS AND LEUCOCIDIN Elaboration of the potent toxins streptolysin O and S equips the group A β-hemolytic streptococci for a formidable onslaught against phagocytic cells. The destructive effects are almost instantly demonstrable against intact cells. Invariably, the topic provokes comparisons with the staphylococcal toxin, leucocidin, which superficially at least expresses equally devastating effects on (only) leukocytes and macrophages of rabbits and humans. Nevertheless, there are differences, e.g. leucocidin does not affect isolated lysosomes or alter their permeability.

Leucocidin has been studied in a prodigious series of investigations by A. M. Woodin and A. A. Wieneke (reviewed in 186). The leucocidins act at the membrane surface by a nonadsorptive, nonlytic process in which the agents are inactivated and participate no further in the subsequent events. In Woodin's interpretations, a membrane nitrophenyl phosphatase and/or its local environment are implicated as the specific target(s). This enzyme behaves as a potassium pump and its phosphatase activity is stimulated by potassium (prevented by ouabain), leucocidin, or phospholipase A. After potassium stimulation, an incremental enhancement is induced by leucocidin, but not after phospholipase activation. The result of leucocidin activity on the intact leukocyte is an immediate loss of potassium from the cell, possibly by the opening of a K^+ channel. In its behavior, it then resembles a permanently depolarized, uncoupled, and potentially secretory cell.

Morphologically, whether Ca^{2+} is present or not, the granules of the treated cell show only an alteration from their normal streaming motions to a random Brownian movement. In the presence of Ca^{2+}, the granules adhere to and evidently fuse with the inner membrane surface and discharge their contents externally. Thus, degranulation is by an exocytic mechanism and not by an overall increase in membrane permeability.

The degranulation requires presence of both Ca^{2+} and ATP; however, both in excess inhibit secretion. Woodin & Wieneke (186) propose that, when Ca^{2+} and ATP are optimally present at specific sites in the cell membrane, these become available for granule adherence. For fusion and exocytosis to follow, both Ca^{2+} and ATP must then be removed from the contact site. This would be accommodated by hydrolysis of the ATP by a proximate ATPase to give a localized concentration of calcium-depleting orthophosphate. The displacement of membrane ATP and

Ca^{2+}, by decreasing cross-linking between phospholipids or between phospholipid and acidic proteins, produces areas in the apposed membranes of increased motional freedom and so allows for enhancement of molecular interactions across the gap between the membranes. When these become as strong as the interactions within the individual membranes, fusion occurs (see also 137).

The streptolysins have been treated in several recent reviews (14, 54, 71). As summarized further by Duncan & Schlegel (44), only those cells that contain cholesterol in their membranes are susceptible to streptolisin O (SLO). The speed with which sensitive cells are affected suggests that the cell membrane is the primary site of attack; neither membrane proteins nor lipids are significantly altered by SLO, and cell lysis must be due to actual holes produced in the membrane rather than to an osmotic mechanism. In the current studies (44), SLO induced ring- and C-shaped structures in the surface of erythrocytes and in cholesterol-containing liposomes; identical structures are formed from the reaction of SLO and cholesterol dispersions. Similar structures are induced by *Clostridium perfringens* θ toxin (155). Based upon their uniformity, the identity in lengths of thc C-shaped structures and the circumference of rings, and the calculated length of unfolded α-helix SLO, Duncan & Schlegel (44) propose that interaction with and adsorption of cholesterol by SLO results in an unfolding of the toxin molecule and stabilization of the α-helix: "sticky" ends of the C-shaped structures close to produce rings; dimers produce S-shaped forms as well. The resultant high concentrations of cholesterol at these loci on a membrane surface, therefore, may weaken the site sufficiently to produce holes.

Because of an unusual resistance of group A streptococcal cell walls (106, 119) to enzymatic degradation (55, 129, 149, 150), their persistence in macrophages has been found causative in inflammatory processes (33), which are the subject of the succeeding section.

INFLAMMATORY PROCESSES AND MEMBRANE FUSION

The path from our present knowledge in this area to its source would lead the searcher to Ehrlich's confident declaration (see 37) that "the leukocyte granules are true products of secretion which the cell, according to the needs, dissolves and pours around itself." Seven decades later, the endocytosis of immune complexes by both leukocytes and macrophages and the accompanying selective release of lysosomal enzymes into the extracellular milieu have been abundantly documented and are recognized as a much more generalized phenomenon (32, 76, 84, 181). In some of these exocytic processes, the phagocytes behave like secretory cells and lysosomes fuse directly with the plasma membrane as if to a phagocytic vacuole.

Cyclic Nucleotides and Fusion Phenomena

From the groups of Weissmann (181, 190) and Ignarro (84), the salutary, or on the other hand exacerbating, effects of a host of pharmacologic agents in inflammatory processes are seen to relate to the immediate intracellular concentrations of cAMP or of the guanosine analog cGMP, which these agents stimulate or depress. The bidirectional or Yin/Yang modulation of particle ingestion (24, 85) and of lysosomal enzyme secretion is stimulated by cholinergic agonists, which raise the intracellular level of cGMP, and is antagonized by those agents that instead elevate cAMP concentrations. The interpretations in Weissmann's group suggest that the signal for cells to secrete or to abrogate release of lysosomal hydrolases is in part associated with the transient assembly or diassembly of microtubules (58, 181, 190). Supportive evidence for antagonism involves a cAMP-dependent protein kinase isolated from human PMN leukocytes, for which tubulin may be a substrate (166). However, for lysosomal secretion, microtubule assembly, although necessary, is not in itself sufficient. A sufficient stimulus can instead be provided by interaction of a humoral agent (C5a, for example) at a membrane receptor and by the presence of stringently required levels of intracellular calcium.

PERTURBATION OF PHAGOLYSOSOME FORMATION

Cyclic Nucleotides

The accumulating evidence concerning their influence on lysosome-limiting membrane fusions has prompted consideration that cyclic nucleotides may influence phagosome-lysosome fusions as well (118, 182). It is not clear that the extrapolation is stringently valid. Still, a careful study by Lowrie et al (111) examining this thesis indicated that, in phagocytosing mouse peritoneal macrophages in culture, intracellular levels of cAMP were significantly raised following ingestion of living *Mycobacterium microti* (virulent for mice), an organism that ordinarily inhibits phagolysosome formation (74). However, monolayers ingesting objects that elicit a prompt fusion response showed little or no increase in cAMP. The results may be interpreted in two ways: either phagocytosis of the viable organisms stimulates the cell to produce more of the cyclic nucleotide, or the pathogen itself may generate and secrete cAMP from within the phagosome; the latter alternative was favored (111).

If the influence of cAMP is on microtubule assembly, then perhaps aberrations specifically associated with individual phagosomes may be sufficient for inhibition (cf, for example, 88). However, it has been documented in recent studies (135, 136, 161), in disagreement with earlier reports (reviewed in 115, 180, 182), that microtubule-disrupting colchicine does not induce lysosome-phagosome fusion dysfunctions. Still, since chemically defined agents with such properties have now been recognized (see below), their influence on intracellular cAMP levels and a possible antagonism of their activity by cholinergic agents would seem important to examine.

Glucocorticosteroids and Concanavalin A

The stabilizing influence of hydrocortisone on lysosomal membranes has prompted speculation that this steroid may also interfere with intracellular phagolysosome formation. However, several studies discerned only minor influences of hydrocortisone on phagocytosis and intracellular killing or digestion (183) and essentially no influence on phagolysosome formation following ingestion of killed toxoplasma (172).

The plant lectin concanavalin A (conA) has also been intensively investigated. Studies by Goldman & Raz (56) and Edelson & Cohn (46, 47) showed that macrophages endocytose conA extensively in the form of minute pinocytic-like vesicles, which appear to fuse and grow in size until they occupy most of the cell cytoplasm. In Goldman's interpretation (56), the attendant extensive membrane internalization was responsible for a subsequent inhibition in phagocytosis of erythrocytes. Edelson & Cohn (46, 47), on the other hand, described an abolition of lysosome fusion with the conA-containing vacuoles but no inhibition of phagocytosis. The lesion in fusion was inferentially ascribed to a binding of conA to carbohydrate residues of glycoprotein exposed at the membrane surface, for it could be alleviated by incubation with mannose. They speculate further that interaction of surface components of *Mycobacterium tuberculosis* and *Toxoplasma gondii* may also involve carbohydrate membrane receptors and may similarly be susceptible to antagonism by the correct sugar. However, Goldman & Raz (56) reported uninhibited fusion of the swollen conA phagosomes with lysosomes, as detected cytochemically. How these contradictory results can be reconciled is presently uncertain.

Sulfatides of Mycobacterium tuberculosis

Virulent strains of tubercle bacilli adsorb the cationic phenazine dye neutral red, whereas avirulent *M. tuberculosis* strains and most saprophytic mycobacteria do not. The cytochemical staining is principally attributable to a group of high-molecular-weight, strongly acidic glycolipid sulfates [sulfatides, "sulfolipid" (SL)] (63, 122), which may be implicated in virulence of *M. tuberculosis* (64). As plausible roles for SL in contributing to pathogenesis (compatible with their anionic and amphipathic properties), the authors speculated that surface-active behavior, directed against phagosomal or lysosomal membranes, could express itself disruptively, as demonstrated with isolated mitochondrial preparations (96); more cryptically, as by orientation within membranes, the glycolipid might alter their functional properties. Specifically within phagocytic cells, this might lead to interference with the intracellular fusion of lysosomes and phagosomes containing tubercle bacilli (vide supra).

SULFATIDE-MACROPHAGE INTERACTIONS In pulse or prolonged exposure of mouse peritoneal macrophage monolayers to fine aqueous dispersions of SL, the lipid is readily endocytosed. Although accumulation of relatively high levels is cytotoxic, lower levels—from 0.001–0.1 ng/cell—are well tolerated and the cells survive for several weeks. After uptake of intermediate-to-higher nontoxic levels, the cells assume a swollen grainy appearance owing to accumulation and sequestration of SL in secondary lysosomes, as confirmed with ferritin-prelabeled cells. Unlike control monolayers, cells exposed to SL are intensely stained by neutral red, suggesting that at least some SL is also adsorbed at the surface of the macrophage membrane, where it mimics the adsorption of dye by tubercle bacilli.

Antagonism of phagolysosome formation Accumulation of even very low levels of mycobacterial sulfatides in macrophage secondary lysosomes renders them almost entirely incompetent for fusing with phagosomes (65). The desulfated glycolipid did not provoke a similar dysfunction (M. B. Goren, unpublished data). The specific behavior of the sulfatides was confirmed at the ultrastructural level with ferritin-labeled cells, and also by dark field vital-fluorescence microscopy after acridine orange prelabeling of lysosomes (4), and with viable baker's yeast as targets. Phagolysosome formation in normal cells is discerned under blue-violet irradiation from the slow and colorful influx of acridine orange marker into yeast-containing phagosomes (75) (Figure 4*a*). This is completely abolished in cells previously exposed to SL (Figure 4*b*), in which the phagosomes appear as dark spaces amid a background of fluorescent lysosomes. Although this dysfunction seems to be induced by the lysosomal sequestration, SL adsorbed to the macrophage membrane surface [neutral red activity (see above)] and subsequently internalized with the yeasts may also contribute. Thus, fusion was almost totally inhibited by exposing acridine orange-labeled cells for 0.5 hr to 10^{-6} M SL at ice temperature (to suppress endocytosis), followed immediately (or 24 hr later) by yeast feeding, and was significantly but incompletely suppressed by yeasts to which discrete microdroplets of SL were attached and, thus presumably, were acting from within the phagosome. However, in the latter system, both EM and fluorescence examination showed that lysosomes, especially in close proximity to yeast-containing phagosomes, contained lipid droplets inferred to be SL; some EM profiles strongly suggested the possibility of a transportation of SL droplets from phagosomes into cytoplasm and to proximate lysosomes. Perhaps the amphipathic, undiluted SL droplets at the yeast-phagosome boundary can directly penetrate and traverse the phagosomal membrane to accumulate in nearby lysosomes. Still, it seems plausible that the sulfatides, whether alone or reinforced by other agents, may well be associated with antagonism of phagolysosome formation by viable *M. tuberculosis*. However, it is by no means clear in the experimental model whether the dysfunction is induced in lysosomal or phagosomal membrane, or in both.

Suramin

Suramin (Bayer 205) is a polyanionic (hexasulfonate) drug that is actively lysosomotropic and probably enters cells in combination with plasma proteins (i.e. by piggyback endocytosis) and thus becomes localized in lysosomes (see 38). Accumulation of marginally subtoxic doses of suramin in macrophage lysosomes over several days also renders these incompetent for fusion with phagosomes containing viable yeasts (75). The structural similarities between suramin and the mycobacterial sulfatides, which may underlie a common mechanism in inducing lysosomal dysfunction, are considered below.

Death and the Membrane: Fact or Artifact?

The choice of viable yeast cells for the vital-fluorescence studies was based on the discrete separation of intracellular events that these phagocytosed targets allowed in normal macrophages (75). With boiled yeast cells as targets, lysosomal fusion was evidently too rapid to allow the sequential psychedelic display to develop. Quite surprisingly, with suramin-loaded cells, uptake of killed boiled yeast followed a

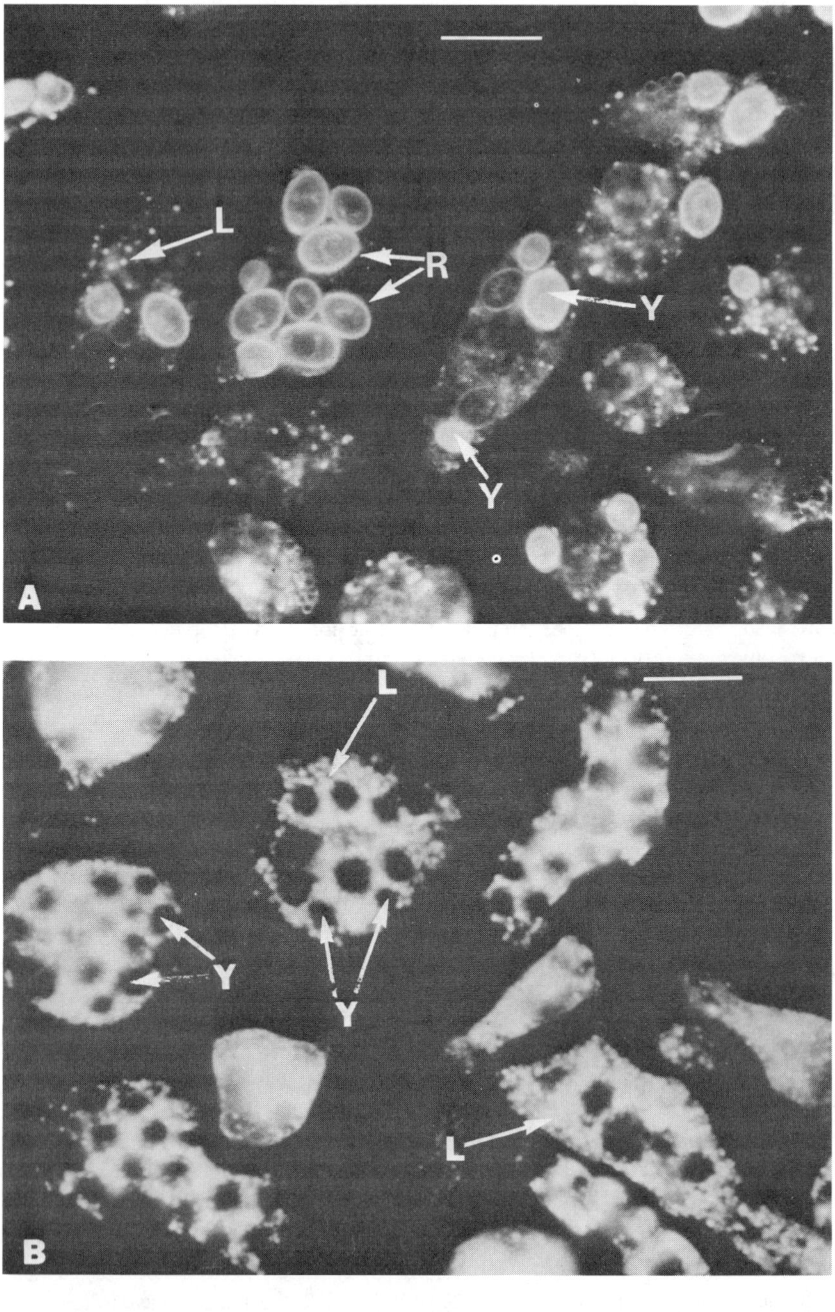
L
R
Y
Y
A
L
Y
Y
L
B

similar fusion pattern: there was little evidence of lysosomal dysfunction. SL-loaded macrophages exhibited a similar, but in slow motion (M. R. Young, personal communication), behavior with phagosomes containing the dead yeasts. So far as I am aware, this presumed fusion has not been examined by electron microscopy with ferritin-labeled cells subsequently rendered nonfunctional with suramin or mycobacterial SL.

Does the evidence from fluorescence microscopy unequivocally implicate fusion, or do the killed yeast cells by virtue of surface alterations successfully compete with lysosomes for only the acridine orange marker? If the status of cell death can in fact, from within the confines of a phagocytic vacuole, provide the agonist for initiating phagolysosome formation in normal cells or for overwhelming the potent aberrational influences induced by SL or suramin at the lysosomal membrane, then its recognition and identification are clearly of significance. Relief of the dysfunction induced by certain classes of viable pathogens from within the phagosome would seem, according to de Duve et al (38), to require an agent with the right kind of tropism—a "phagosomotropic drug," admittedly much more difficult to achieve than a lysosomotropic drug. Still, if the presumed necrogenous agents are as potent as might be implied from the preceding, perhaps an adequate delivery of such substances to functional lysosomes would alleviate a counterpart dysfunction even in the phagosomal membrane. However, the recognition within the same cell of *phagosomes* enclosing viable organisms adjacent to *phagolysosomes* containing dead ones (88) may deny a productive delivery for the presumed agent. Still, in the event the inferred behavior of killed yeast cells is unequivocally confirmed at the ultrastructural level, then a search for the eliciting agonists is nevertheless important.

Extrapolations to Polyanionics

From the results with suramin and mycobacterial SL, an immediate extrapolation could be drawn that polyanionic character may provide a structural common denominator of at least one type, which provokes the specific membrane dysfunction, possibly through sustained distortions dependent upon interactions of the polyanionics with multiple cationic sites in membrane proteins. The mycobacterial sulfatides are embraced in this category owing to the micellar configuration (thus, a particulate polysulfate), which they assume in an aqueous environment.

DEXTRAN SULFATE AND CARRAGEENAN Testing the polyanion hypothesis has already provided support for its probable validity as briefly reported (65). Thus, the high-molecular-weight species of dextran sulfate, like mycobacterial SL and

Figure 4 (A) Living macrophages (controls) with acridine-stained lysosomes (L) after incubation with live yeasts. Some yeasts are surrounded by a bright intraphagosomal rim (R) and others show overall fluorescence (Y) from diffusion of marker into the phagosome. Bar represents 10 μm. (B) Living macrophages pretreated with sulfatide (SLI) before acridine staining and yeast uptake. Dark spaces (Y) are unstained yeast in nonfused phagosomes.

suramin, interfere with phagolysosome formation (viable yeast targets) in cultured macrophages. A similar induction of the dysfunction in vivo has been recognized as a result of the accumulation of iota carrageenan in colonic submucosal macrophages of monkeys (117). Aside from direct toxic effects of dextran sulfate on macrophages, this specific fusion dysfunction may provide in part an explanation for the devastating abrogation by dextran sulfate of cell-mediated defense mechanisms in normal and in specifically immunized mice to a challenge with *Listeria monocytogenes* (69, 70). One may ask further whether the long-exploited, virulence-enhancing activity of hog gastric mucin may not at least in part be attributable to a similar property! This, of course, is subject to testing, and it is anticipated that the catalog of polyanionics that antagonize phagosome-lysosome fusion will grow.

CONCLUSIONS AND SPECULATIONS

The reality of page limitations has necessitated omission of prepared, but lengthy, sections devoted to (*a*) activation of macrophages (see 169), (*b*) aspects of membranal and submembranal structures and their implication in alleviation of the Chediak-Higashi syndrome (see 130, 131), and (*c*) mechanisms and theories in membrane fusion phenomena (see 37, 112, 137). Respecting the topics discussed, important questions remain unanswered about microbicidal mechanisms in macrophages, the ultimate significance of superoxide, and the undeniable influence of cell death on phagosome-lysosome fusion (7, 88).

To indulge in speculations may be a compensation for the effort expended in preparation of a review. My enthusiasm, of course, is in the association of polyanionic agents with antagonism of phagolysosome formation. Whether these have wide-spread validity remains to be established—and at the present state, essentially nothing is known about how they function.

The potent activity of at least some polyanionics raises important questions about natural analogs that are ordinarily considered innocuous. Can these be inferentially implicated in other lysosomal dysfunctions? The question may be particularly germane to those genetic storage diseases associated with lysosomal accumulation of, for example, sulfatides, hyaluronic acids, mucosulfatides, chondroitin sulfate, etc (see 77). It may be speculated that the accumulation of these polyanionics or pseudoanalogs (clusters of cerebroside sulfates, for example) might exacerbate the effects of the specific enzymatic lesion by interfering with what otherwise should be normal functions of the affected lysosomes. These may be unable to fuse with newly internalized endocytic vacuoles, or the undegraded charged storage compounds may inactivate otherwise normally functional hydrolases that share the same vesicle. The in vitro intracellular events following endocytosis of suitable markers or substrates by fibroblasts, as from patients with metachromatic leukodystrophy, may provide meaningful information.

Important questions must also be confronted about the phenomenon as it concerns, for example, viable tubercle, *Toxoplasma gondii,* and chlamydiae. What agents or secretion products, if any, of the latter two microorganisms are involved in antagonizing fusion? It would indeed be most remarkable if these had evolved the mycobacterial SL for promoting their survival within phagosomes. In fact, the toxoplasma or chlamydial agents, if they exist, may function by an entirely different mechanism. Still, the ubiquity of polyanionics in nature tempts the speculative inference that such substances with potential antifusion activity might be found in these and other microorganisms as well.

Finally, the implicit recognition of polyanionics as at least one class of substances endowed with functions that may promote intracellular survival of specific pathogens raises questions about how this behavior may be antagonized or abrogated. The problem was alluded to briefly in a preceding section, and as de Duve et al have inferred (38), relief of the dysfunction may require delivery of specific antagonists to phagosomes. Perhaps lysosomes may be valid targets as well. I hope the association of particular structural features with this function may lend more than empirical direction to studies dedicated to its antagonism in vivo.

Epilogue

Having no recollection of a picture of Metchnikoff, I substitute in my mind's eye a well-known photograph of the portly Johannes Brahms, seated in solitude and contemplatively gazing out on an autumnal scene. Transpose to Messina, and Brahms selects a tiny wooden splinter and delicately inserts it into a star-fish larva.

Acknowledgment

Cited original work of mine was supported by Public Health Service grant AI-08401 from the U.S.-Japan Cooperative Medical Science Program administered by the National Institute of Allergy and Infectious Diseases.

Literature Cited

1. Alexander, J., Vickerman, K. 1975. *J. Protozool.* 22:502–8
2. Allen, J. M. 1969. In *Lysosomes in Biology and Pathology,* ed. J. T. Dingle, H. B. Fell, 2:41–69. Amsterdam: North Holland. 668 pp.
3. Allen, R. C. 1975. *Biochem. Biophys. Res. Commun.* 63:675–83
4. Allison, A. C., Young, M. R. See Ref. 2, pp. 600–28
5. Anderson, S. E. Jr., Bautista, S., Remington, J. S. 1976. *J. Immunol.* 117: 381–87
6. Anderson, S. E. Jr., Remington, J. S. 1974. *J. Exp. Med.* 139:1154–74
7. Armstrong, J. A., Hart, P. D. 1971. *J. Exp. Med.* 134:713–40
8. Armstrong, J. A., Hart, P. D. 1975. *J. Exp. Med.* 142:1–16
9. Babior, B. M., Curnutte, J. T., McMurrich, B. J. 1976. *J. Clin. Invest.* 58: 989–96
10. Babior, B. M., Kipnes, R. S., Curnutte, J. T. 1973. *J. Clin. Invest.* 52:741–44
11. Baehner, R. L. 1975. In *The Phagocytic Cell in Host Resistance,* ed. J. A. Bellanti, D. H. Dayton, pp. 173–200. New York: Raven. 348 pp.
12. Baehner, R. L., Murrmann, S. K., Davis, J., Johnston, R. B. Jr. 1975. *J. Clin. Invest.* 56:571–76
13. Bainton, D. F., Nichols, B. A., Farquhar, M. G. 1976. In *Lysosomes in Biology and Pathology,* ed. J. T. Dingle, R. T. Dean, 5:3–32. Amsterdam: North Holland. 404 pp.
14. Bernheimer, A. W. 1974. *Biochim. Biophys. Acta* 344:27–50
15. Biggar, W. D., Buron, S., Holmes, B. 1976. *Infect. Immun.* 14:6–10
16. Borges, J. S., Johnson, W. D. Jr. 1975. *J. Exp. Med.* 141:483–96
17. Boxer, L. A., Stossel, T. P. 1976. *J. Clin. Invest.* 57:964–76
18. Brieger, E. M., Fell, H. B., Smith, B. R. 1951. *J. Hyg.* 49:189–200
19. Briggs, R. T., Drath, D. B., Karnovsky, M. L., Karnovsky, M. J. 1975. *J. Cell Biol.* 67:566–86

20. Chang, K.-P., Dwyer, D. M. 1976. *Science* 193:678–80
21. Cohn, Z. A., Fedorko, M. E. 1969. In *Lysosomes in Biology and Pathology,* ed. J. T. Dingle, H. B. Fell, 1:43–63. Amsterdam: North Holland. 543 pp.
22. Cohn, Z. A., Hirsch, J. G., Wiener, E. 1963. In *Lysosomes,* ed. A. V. S. de-Reuck, M. P. Cameron, pp. 126–50. Boston: Little, Brown. 446 pp.
23. Cotran, R. S., Litt, M. 1970. *J. Immunol.* 105:1536–46
24. Cox, J. P., Karnovsky, M. L. 1973. *J. Cell Biol.* 59:480–90
25. Curnutte, J. T., Karnovsky, M. L., Babior, B. M. 1976. *J. Clin. Invest.* 57:1059–67
26. Curnutte, J. T., Kipnes, R. S., Babior, B. M. 1975. *N. Engl. J. Med.* 293:628–32
27. Curnutte, J. T., Whitten, D. M., Babior, B. M. 1974. *N. Engl. J. Med.* 290:593–97
28. Daems, W. Th., Wisse, E., Brederoo, P., Emeis, J. J. 1975. In *Mononuclear Phagocytes in Immunity Infection and Pathology,* ed. R. van Furth, pp. 57–77. London: Blackwell. 1062 pp.
29. Dales, S. See Ref. 2, pp. 69–86
30. Dales, S. 1973. *Bacteriol. Rev.* 37:103–35
31. Dannenberg, A. M. Jr., Ando, M., Shima, K., Tsuda, T. See Ref. 28, pp. 959–80
32. Davies, P., Allison, A. C. See Ref. 13, pp. 61–98
33. Davies, P., Page, R. C., Allison, A. C. 1974. *J. Exp. Med.* 139:1262–81
34. DeChatelet, L. R., McPhail, L. C., Mullikin, D., McCall, C. E. 1975. *J. Clin. Invest.* 55:714–21
35. DeChatelet, L. R., Mullikin, D., McCall, C. E. 1975. *J. Infect. Dis.* 131:443–46
36. DeChatelet, L. R., Shirley, P. S., Johnston, R. B. Jr. 1976. *Blood* 47:545–54
37. de Duve, C. See Ref. 21, pp. 3–40
38. de Duve, C., de Barsy, T., Poole, B., Trouet, A., Tulkens, P., Van Hoof, F. 1974. *Biochem. Pharmacol.* 23:2495–531
39. Draper, P. 1974. *J. Gen. Microbiol.* 83:431–33
40. Draper, P., Hart, P. D. See Ref. 28, pp. 575–94
41. Draper, P., Rees, R. J. W. 1970. *Nature* 228:860–61
42. Draper, P., Rees, R. J. W. 1973. *J. Gen. Microbiol.* 77:79–87
43. Drath, D. B., Karnovsky, M. L. 1975. *J. Exp. Med.* 141:257–62
44. Duncan, J. L., Schlegel, R. 1975. *J. Cell Biol.* 67:160–73
45. Dwyer, D. M. 1976. *J. Immunol.* 117:2081–91
46. Edelson, P. J., Cohn, Z. A. 1974. *J. Exp. Med.* 140:1364–86
47. Edelson, P. J., Cohn, Z. A. 1974. *J. Exp. Med.* 140:1387–403
48. Engel, D., Van Epps, D., Clagett, J. 1976. *Infect. Immun.* 14:548–54
49. Fan, V. S. C., Jenkin, H. M. 1974. *Infect. Immun.* 10:464–70
50. Fauve, R. M., Delaunay, J. 1966. *Ann. Inst. Pasteur* 111:Suppl. 5, pp. 78–84
51. Fridovich, I. 1975. *Ann. Rev. Biochem.* 44:147–59
52. Friis, R. R. 1972. *J. Bacteriol.* 110:706–21
53. Gambrill, M. R., Wisseman, C. L. Jr. 1973. *Infect. Immun.* 8:631–40
54. Ginsburg, I. 1970. In *Microbial Toxins,* ed, T. C. Montie, S. Kadis, S. Ajl, 3:99–171. New York: Academic. 548 pp.
55. Ginsburg, I., Sela, M. 1976. *Crit. Rev. Microbiol.* 4:249–332
56. Goldman, R., Raz, A. 1975. *Exp. Cell Res.* 96:393–405
57. Goldring, O. L., Clegg, J. A., Smithers, S. R., Terry, R. J. 1976. *Clin. Exp. Immunol.* 26:181–87
58. Goldstein, I., Hoffstein, S., Gallin, J., Weissmann, G. 1973. *Proc. Natl. Acad. Sci. USA* 70:2916–20
59. Goldstein, I. M., Roos, D., Kaplan, H. B., Weissmann, G. 1975. *J. Clin. Invest.* 56:1155–63
60. Gordon, S., Cohn, Z. A. 1973. *Int. Rev. Cytol.* 36:171–214
61. Goren, M. B. 1972. *Bacteriol. Rev.* 36:33–64
62. Goren, M. B. 1975. *Tubercle* 56:65–71
63. Goren, M. B., Brokl, O., Roller, P., Fales, H. M., Das, B. C. 1976. *Biochemistry* 15:2728–34
64. Goren, M. B., Brokl, O., Schaefer, W. B. 1974. *Infect. Immun.* 9:142–49
65. Goren, M. B., Hart, P. D., Young, M. R., Armstrong, J. A. 1976. *Proc. Natl. Acad. Sci. USA* 73:2510–14
66. Greenwood, B. M. 1974. In *Parasites in the Immunized Host: Mechanisms of Survival,* ed. R. Porter, J. Knight, pp. 137–46. Amsterdam: Assoc. Sci. Publ. 280 pp.
67. Griffin, F. M. Jr., Griffin, J. A., Leider, J. E., Silverstein, S. C. 1975. *J. Exp. Med.* 142:1263–82
68. Griffin, F. M. Jr., Griffin, J. A., Silverstein, S. C. 1976. *J. Exp. Med.* 144:788–809

69. Hahn, H. 1974. *Infect. Immun.* 10:1105–9
70. Hahn, H., Bierther, M. 1974. *Infect. Immun.* 10:1110–19
71. Halbert, S. P. See Ref. 54, pp. 69–99
72. Hard, G. C. 1975. *Infect. Immun.* 12:1439–49
73. Hart, P. D., Armstrong, J. A. 1974. *Infect. Immun.* 10:742–46
74. Hart, P. D., Armstrong, J. A., Brown, C. A., Draper, P. 1972. *Infect. Immun.* 5:803–7
75. Hart, P. D., Young, M. R. 1975. *Nature* 256:47–49
76. Henson, P. M. See Ref. 13, pp. 99–126
77. Hers, H. G., Van Hoof, F. See Ref. 2, pp. 19–40
78. Hinrichs, D. J., Jerrells, T. R. 1976. *J. Immunol.* 117:996–1003
78a. Hirsch, J. G. See Ref. 168, p. 48
79. Hirsch, J. G. 1971. In *The Inflammatory Process,* ed. B. W. Zweifach, L. Grant, R. T. McCluskey, 1:411–47. New York: Academic. 647 pp. 2nd ed.
80. Hirsch, J. G., Jones, T. C., Len, L. See Ref. 66, pp. 205–23
81. Hoff, R. 1975. *J. Exp. Med.* 142:299–311
82. Hoff, R. L. Frenkel, J. K. 1974. *J. Exp. Med.* 139:560–80
83. Hohn, D. C., Lehrer, R. I. 1975. *J. Clin. Invest.* 55:707–13
84. Ignarro, L. J. 1975. In *Lysosomes in Biology and Pathology,* ed. J. T. Dingle, R. T. Dean, Vol. 4. Amsterdam: North Holland. 614 pp.
85. Ignarro, L. J., Cech, S. Y. 1976. *Proc. Soc. Exp. Biol. Med.* 151:448–52
86. Iyer, G. Y. N., Quastel, J. H. 1963. *Can. J. Biochem. Physiol.* 41:427–34
87. Johnston, R. B. Jr., Keele, B. B. Jr., Misra, H. P., Lehmeyer, J. E., Webb, L. S., Baehner, R. L., Rajagopalan, K. V. 1975. *J. Clin. Invest.* 55:1357–72
88. Jones, T. C., Hirsch, J. G. 1972. *J. Exp. Med.* 136:1173–94
89. Jones, T. C., Len, L., Hirsch, J. G. 1975. *J. Exp. Med.* 141:466–82
90. Kanai, K., Kondo, E. 1970. *Jpn J. Med. Sci. Biol.* 23:295–302
91. Karnovsky, M. L. 1968. *Semin. Hematol.* 5:156–65
92. Karnovsky, M. L. 1973. *Fed. Proc.* 32:1527–33
92a. Karnovsky, M. L. 1974. In *Progress in Immunology II: Clinical Aspects I,* ed. L. Brent, J. Holborow, 4:83–93. Amsterdam: North Holland. 407 pp.
93. Karnovsky, M. L., Lazdins, J., Drath, D., Harper, A. 1975. *Ann. NY Acad. Sci.* 256:266–74
94. Kato, M. 1970. *Arch. Biochem. Biophys.* 140:379–90
95. Kato, M. 1971. *J. Bacteriol.* 107:746–52
96. Kato, M., Goren, M. B. 1974. *Infect. Immun.* 10:733–41
97. Kellogg, E. W. III, Fridovich, I. 1975. *J. Biol. Chem.* 250:8812–17
98. Klebanoff, S. J. 1974. *J. Biol. Chem.* 249:3724–28
99. Klebanoff, S. J. 1975. *Semin. Hematol.* 12:117–41
100. Klebanoff, S. J., Hamon, C. B. See Ref. 28, pp. 507–31
101. Kochan, I., Golden, C. A. 1974. *Infect. Immun.* 9:249–54
102. Kordová, N., Wilt, J. C. 1972. *Can. J. Microbiol.* 18:457–64
103. Kordová, N., Wilt, J. C., Martin, C. 1975. *Can. J. Microbiol.* 21:323–31
104. Kordová, N., Wilt, J. C., Sadiq, M. 1971. *Can. J. Microbiol.* 17:955–59
105. Krahenbuhl, J. L., Lambert, L. H. Jr., Remington, J. S. 1976. *Immunology* 31:837–46
106. Krause, R. M. 1963. *Bacteriol. Rev.* 27:369–80
107. Leake, E. S., Myrvik, Q. N. 1966. *J. Reticuloendothel. Soc.* 3:83–100
108. Lehrer, R. I., Ladra, K. M., Hake, R. B. 1975. *Infect. Immun.* 11:1226–34
109. Lepper, A. W. D., Hart, P. D. 1976. *Infect. Immun.* 14:522–26
110. Lockwood, W. R., Allison, F. 1963. *Clin. Res.* 11:34
111. Lowrie, D. B., Jackett, P. S., Ratcliffe, N. A. 1975. *Nature* 254:600–2
112. Lucy, J. A. See Ref. 2, pp. 313–41
113. Lurie, M. B. 1964. *Resistance to Tuberculosis.* Cambridge: Harvard Univ. 391 pp.
114. Mackaness, G. B. 1968. *Am. Rev. Respir. Dis.* 97:337–44
115. Malawista, S. E. 1975. *Ann. NY Acad. Sci.* 253:738–49
116. Mandell, G. L. 1974. *Infect. Immun.* 9:337–41
117. Mankes, R., Abraham, R. 1975. *Proc. Soc. Exp. Biol. Med.* 150:166–70
118. May, C., Levine, B. B., Weissmann, G. 1970. *Proc. Soc. Exp. Biol. Med.* 133:758–63
119. McCarty, M. 1971. *Harvey Lect.* 65:73–96
120. McCord, J. M., Keele, B. B. Jr., Fridovich, I. 1971. *Proc. Natl. Acad. Sci. USA* 68:1024–27
121. McRipley, R. J., Sbarra, A. J. 1967. *J. Bacteriol.* 94:1417–24
122. Middlebrook, G., Coleman, C., Schaefer, W. B. 1959. *Proc. Natl. Acad. Sci. USA* 45:1801–4

123. Moore, P. L., Bank, H. L., Brissie, N. T., Spicer, S. S. 1976. *J. Cell Biol.* 71:659–66
124. Müller-Eberhard, H. J. 1975. *Ann. Rev. Biochem.* 44:697–724
125. Nelson, R. D., Mills, E. L., Simmons, R. L., Quie, P. G. 1976. *Infect. Immun.* 14:129–34
126. Nichols, B. A., Bainton, D. F. See Ref. 28, pp. 17–55
127. Nogueira, N., Cohn, Z. 1976. *J. Exp. Med.* 143:1402–20
128. Odeberg, H., Olsson, I. 1975. *J. Clin. Invest.* 56:1118–24
129. Ohanian, S. H., Schwab, J. H., Cromartie, W. J. 1969. *J. Exp. Med.* 129:37–44
130. Oliver, J. M., Berlin, R. D. 1976. In *Immunobiology of the Macrophage,* ed. D. J. Nelson, pp. 259–73. New York: Academic. 633 pp.
131. Oliver, J. M., Zurier, R. B. 1976. *J. Clin. Invest.* 57:1239–47
132. Patriarca, P., Dri, P., Kakinuma, K., Tedesco, F., Rossi, F. 1975. *Biochim. Biophys. Acta* 385:380–86
133. Patterson, R. J., Youmans, G. P. 1970. *Infect. Immun.* 1:600–3
134. Pearsall, N. N., Weiser, R. S. 1970. *The Macrophage.* Philadelphia: Lea & Febiger. 204 pp.
135. Pesanti, E. L., Axline, S. G. 1975. *J. Exp. Med.* 142:903–13
136. Pesanti, E. L., Axline, S. G. 1975. *J. Exp. Med.* 141:1030–46
137. Poste, G., Allison, A. C. 1973. *Biochim. Biophys. Acta* 300:421–65
138. Reaven, E. P., Axline, S. G. 1973. *J. Cell Biol.* 59:12–27
139. Rees, R. J. W., Valentine, R. C., Wong, P. C. 1960. *J. Gen. Microbiol.* 22: 443–57
140. Robineaux, J., Frederic, J. 1955. *CR Soc. Biol.* 149:486–92
141. Romeo, D., Zabucchi, G., Marzi, T. Rossi, F. 1973. *Exp. Cell Res.* 78: 423–32
142. Root, R. K. See Ref. 11, pp. 201–26
143. Root, R. K., Metcalf, J., Oshino, N., Chance, B. 1975. *J. Clin. Invest.* 55:945–55
144. Root, R. K., Stossel, T. P. 1974. *J. Clin. Invest.* 53:1207–15
145. Rossi, F., Romeo, D., Patriarca, P. 1972. *J. Reticuloendothel. Soc.* 12: 127–49
146. Rossi, F., Zabucchi, G., Romeo, D. See Ref. 28, pp. 441–62
147. Sabin, A. G., Feldman, H. A. 1948. *Science* 108:660–63
148. Schell-Frederick, E., Paridaens, R., Dubois, L. 1975. *J. Reticuloendothel. Soc.* 18:38a
149. Schwab, J. H. 1965. *J. Bacteriol.* 90: 1405–11
150. Schwab, J. H., Smialowicz, R. 1975. *Z. Immunitaetsforsch. Exp. Klin. Immunol.* 149:283–88
151. Sethi, K. K., Pelster, B., Suzuki, N., Piekarski, G., Brandis, H. 1975. *J. Immunol.* 115:1151–58
152. Showell, H. J., Freer, R. J., Zigmond, S. H., Schiffmann, E., Aswanikumar, S., Corcoran, B., Becker, E. L. 1976. *J. Exp. Med.* 143:1154–69
153. Simberkoff, M. S., Elsbach, P. 1971. *J. Exp. Med.* 134:1417–30
154. Simmons, S. R., Karnovsky, M. L. 1973. *J. Exp. Med.* 138:44–63
155. Smyth, C. J., Freer, J. H., Arbuthnott, J. P. 1975. *Biochim. Biophys. Acta* 382:479–93
156. Snyderman, R., Mergenhagen, S. E. See Ref. 130, pp. 323–48
157. Stokes, G. V. 1973. *Infect. Immun.* 7:173–77
158. Stokes, G. V. 1974. *Infect. Immun.* 9:497–99
159. Stossel, T. P. 1974. *N. Engl. J. Med.* 290:717–23; 774–80; 833–39
160. Stossel, T. P., Hartwig, J. H. 1976. *J. Cell Biol.* 68:602–19
161. Stossel, T. P., Mason, R. J., Hartwig, J., Vaughan, M. 1972. *J. Clin. Invest.* 51:615–24
162. Strauss, R. R., Friedman, H., Mills, L., Zayon, G. 1975. *Nature* 255:343–44
163. Tanowitz, H., Wittner, M., Kress, Y., Bloom, B. 1975. *Am. J. Trop. Med. Hyg.* 24:25–33
164. Tatsumi, N., Shibata, N., Okamura, Y., Takeuchi, K., Senda, N. 1973. *Biochim. Biophys. Acta* 305:433–44
165. Tsan, M.-F., McIntyre, P. A. 1976. *J. Exp. Med.* 143:1308–16
166. Tsung, P.-K., Sakamoto, T., Weissmann, G. 1975. *Biochem. J.* 145:437–48
167. Todd, W. J., Storz, J. 1975. *Infect. Immun.* 12:638–46
168. van Furth, R., ed. 1970. *Mononuclear Phagocytes.* Philadelphia: Davis. 654 pp.
169. van Furth, R., ed. 1975. Mononuclear Phagocytes. In *Immunity, Infection and Pathology.* London: Blackwell. 1062 pp.
170. van Furth, R., Cohn, Z. A., Hirsch, J. G., Humphrey, J. H., Spector, W. G., Langevoort, H. L. 1972. *Bull. WHO* 46:845–52
171. van Furth, R., Hirsch, J. G., Fedorko, M. E. 1970. *J. Exp. Med.* 132:794–812

172. van Furth, R., Jones, T. C. 1975. *Infect. Immun.* 12:888–90
173. van Furth, R., Langevoort, H. L., Schaberg, A. See Ref. 28, pp. 1–15
174. Vickerman, K. See Ref. 66, pp. 53–80
175. Volkman, A. 1976. *J. Reticuloendothel. Soc.* 19:249–68
176. Wagner, W.-H. 1975. *Infect. Immun.* 12:1295–306
177. Ward, P. A. 1968. *J. Exp. Med.* 128:1201–21
178. Ward, P. A., Lepow, I. H., Newman, L. J. 1968. *Am. J. Pathol.* 52:725–36
179. Weidner, E. 1975. *Z. Parasitenkd.* 47:1–9
180. Weissmann, G. See Ref. 21, pp. 276–95
181. Weissmann, G., Goldstein, I., Hoffstein, S., Chauvet, G., Robineaux, R. 1975. *Ann. NY Acad. Sci.* 256:222–32
182. Weissmann, G., Goldstein, I., Hoffstein, S., Tsung, P.-K. 1975. *Ann. NY Acad. Sci.* 253:750–62
183. Wiener, E., Marmary, Y., Curelaru, Z. 1972. *Lab. Invest.* 26:220–26
184. Wilkinson, P. C. 1974. *Chemotaxis and Inflammation.* Edinburgh: Churchill-Livingstone. 214 pp.
185. Wilkinson, P. C. 1976. *Clin. Exp. Immunol.* 25:355–67
186. Woodin, A. M. 1973. In *Lysosomes in Biology and Pathology,* ed. J. T. Dingle, 3:395–422. Amsterdam: North Holland. 577 pp.
187. Yoshida, A., Watanabe, S., Morris, J. 1970. *Proc. Natl. Acad. Sci. USA* 67:1600–7
188. Zaman, V., Colley, F. C. 1972. *Trans. R. Soc. Trop. Med. Hyg.* 66:781–82
189. Zeya, H. I., Spitznagel, J. K. 1971. *Lab. Invest.* 24:229–36
190. Zurier, R. B., Weissmann, G., Hoffstein, S., Kammerman, S., Tai, H. H. 1974. *J. Clin. Invest.* 53:297–309

Ann. Rev. Microbiol. 1977. 31:535–47

BEHAVIORAL GENETICS OF *PHYCOMYCES*

❖1716

Enrique Cerdá-Olmedo
Departamento de Genética, Facultad de Ciencias, Universidad de Sevilla, Sevilla, Spain

CONTENTS

BEHAVIOR 535
Effects of Light on Growth of the Mature Sporangiophore 537
Other Stimuli and Responses 538
BEHAVIORAL GENETICS 539
Mutants 539
Heterokaryons 541
Crosses 542
NATURE OF THE SENSORY TRANSDUCERS 543
Photoreceptor 543
Adaptation 544
Intermediate Steps 544
The Regulation of Growth 545

The contrast between the relative simplicity of the fungus *Phycomyces* and the relative complexity of its reactions to several environmental stimuli has attracted the attention of various groups of researchers attempting to understand the mechanisms of cellular sensitivity and behavior. Early work, chiefly concerned with the nature of the stimuli and the relationships between stimuli and responses, has been critically examined in an extensive review (5). Recent research has been marked by the availability of mutants and the introduction of sophisticated methods for the study of the responses. The biochemical aspects are the least developed, but they should become more important in the future. This review considers these several facets, with emphasis on the application of genetics to the study of behavior and on the recent literature. General introductions to the organism's biology and behavior have been written in English (17), German (27), and Spanish (28).

BEHAVIOR

The different stages in the life cycle of *Phycomyces* are sketched in Figure 1. During vegetative growth, the whole mycelium is a large, coenocytic cell. Most of our

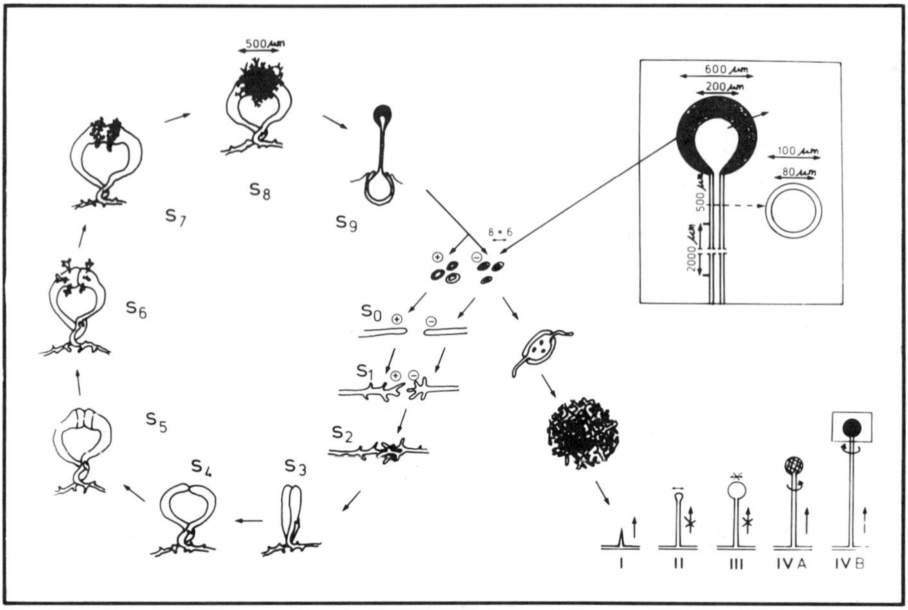

Figure 1 The life cycles and the schematic appearance of *Phycomyces blakesleeanus.* Sizes in micrometers. Each spore (center) originates a branching, nonseptate mycelium. After 3 or 4 days, the mycelium develops aerial, usually unbranched sporangiophores, which grow to several centimeters. Four stages are recognized in sporangiophore development (16, 36). Elongation occurs in stages I and IV; radial growth, with formation of the sporangium, occurs in stage II. The twist of the sporangium defines substages IVa and IVb. The mature sporangium contains about 10^5 spores, which are able to reinitiate the asexual cycle.

The proximity of mycelia of the two sexes, (+) and (–), under suitable conditions, triggers off the sexual cycle, stages S_0 through S_9 (76). After a dormancy of at least 2 months, the zygospore (stage S_8) produces a germsporangiophore, whose germspores enter the asexual cycle.

attention centers on its aerial parts, the sporangiophores, in stage IVb, when they have already formed the sporangium and grow at about 1 μm/sec. As the sporangiophore sprouts out of decaying organic matter in natural environments, the behavioral responses probably allow it to avoid the surrounding obstacles, thus facilitating spore dispersal.

The stimuli include light, gravity and centrifugal forces, mechanical stretch, wind, defined chemicals, and proximity of objects or barriers. The sensitive zone approximately coincides with the growing zone and occupies the upper 3-mm section of the sporangiophore, just below the sporangium. When the stimuli are symmetrically distributed around the sporangiophore, the responses are *mecisms,* i.e. changes in growth velocity; asymmetrically distributed stimuli give rise to *tropisms,* i.e. changes in the direction of growth.

Effects of Light on Growth of the Mature Sporangiophore

Phycomyces is able to respond to an enormous range of light intensities, similar to that of our own eyes. Photomecism is described in Figure 2. The traditional study of photomecism with incandescent lamps and simple optical devices, including a small horizontal microscope, is relatively time consuming and imprecise. The automatic tracking machine has permitted a refined study of this response (43), including the application of the Wiener-Lee-Schetzen method of nonlinear system analysis to the relationship between a random light program or "white noise" and the instantaneous growth of the organism (53, 54). The result is a comprehensive mathematical statement of the relationship between stimulus and response, hard to express, alas, in intuitive terms.

Growth velocity at a given moment is found to depend upon the succession of previous stimuli: the system exhibits a certain degree of "memory." Photomecism is usually a transient response, even if the stimulus is kept constant. The sporangiophore thus adapts to changes in light intensity. It is possible to define an internal variable, the level of adaptation, measurable in light intensity units, such that the growth velocity depends upon the comparison between the light intensity and that internal variable. The level of adaptation approaches external light intensity following exponential kinetics, with a time constant of about 6 min in the case of adaptation to the dark. Upward changes are much faster, with a time constant of about 1 min (30, 56; E. D. Lipson and S. M. Block, unpublished data).

The sporangiophore is phototropic (grows toward blue and near-ultraviolet light sources, away from ultraviolet light sources) and geotropic (grows upwards in the dark). Quantitatively, phototropism can be described by the tropic rate or angular velocity, once the light and the precise geometry of the situation have been defined. The compromise between phototropism and geotropism can be expressed by the

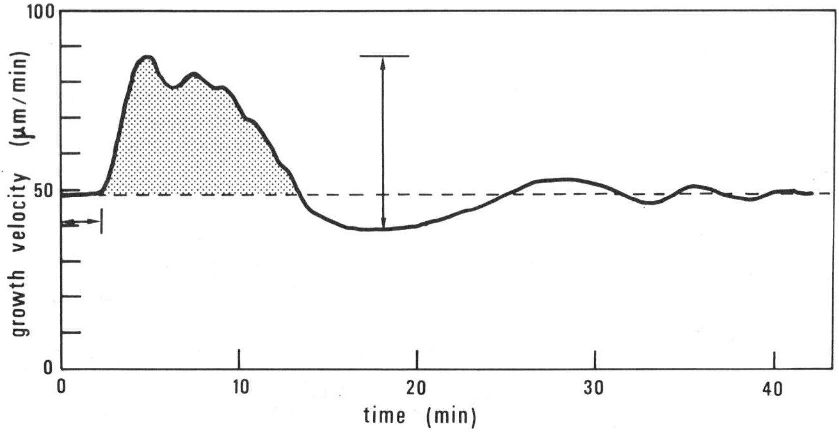

Figure 2 Positive photomecism. Growth velocity of the sporangiophore after an increase in light intensity for 30 sec. The size of the response is measured by the shaded area, or by the peak-to-peak amplitude (vertical arrow). The latency is indicated by the horizontal arrow.

photogeotropic equilibrium angle, i.e. the angle with the vertical finally reached by a sporangiophore exposed to a horizontal light beam (6, 81). The wild type's photogeotropic equilibrium angle is about 75° for blue light intensities between 1 $\mu W/m^2$ and 0.2 W/m^2. Outside that range, the photogeotropic equilibrium angles are smaller than 75° and depend upon light intensity; they become 0° at the lower threshold of about 1 nW/m^2 and at the upper threshold of about 10 W/m^2.

It has long been suspected that phototropism is the result of many localized photomecisms, asymmetrically distributed around the sporangiophore, and many early experiments were designed to prove this hypothesis. The sensitive zone constitutes a cylindrical lens, and local light intensities are mainly determined by refraction, with minor contributions from reflections, absorption, and scattering. The precise light distribution in a laterally illuminated sporangiophore is unknown, but it may be inferred from the study of a large glass and liquid model (42). A simpler situation is found with ultraviolet illumination, since the sporangiophore then becomes opaque, chiefly because of its high gallic acid content.

The situation is further complicated by the continuous twist of the sporangiophore's surface around the sporangiophore axis. The sporangium and the upper part of the sensitive zone turn at about 12° per min, but the rotation slows down in the lower part of the sensitive zone and disappears at its border with the inert sporangiophore (70). The importance of this rotation in phototropism is made clear in experiments combining artificial rotation of the whole organism with different illumination programs (32, 33).

The current theory of phototropism (32, 33, 59) assumes that the elements involved in photoreception and growth regulation turn around the sporangiophore, adapting to local light intensities. The optical properties of the sporangiophore, the latency, and the adaptation kinetics conspire to yield maximal photomecisms on the side required for tropism.

Other Stimuli and Responses

A sudden increase in the concentration of ethylene or ethane in the air produces a positive mecism (75); similarly, *n*-heptanol and many other chemicals induce a negative mecism (R. J. Cohen, unpublished information). The very small concentrations needed in these experiments are suggestive of specific olfaction, but it is important to demonstrate tropisms in chemical concentration gradients since chemomecisms alone are unlikely to be useful to the organism.

The sporangiophore is anemotropic (grows into the wind) and mysteriously avoids hitting obstacles and barriers, even in total darkness. The considerable attention devoted to these phenomena (22, 23, 50, 52, 75) has led to the refutation of many hypotheses on the nature of the immediate stimuli, but not to the decisive confirmation of any. Perhaps the sporangiophore emits a growth-stimulating chemical whose distribution is disturbed by barriers and wind (23). Ethylene could be such a chemical (75) since it induces positive mecism and suppresses avoidance, but the quantities produced by the sporangiophore are very small in comparison with those needed to induce experimental effects. On the other hand, recent and ingenious experiments with different combinations of wind and obstacles (J. F. LaFay and J.

Matricon, unpublished information) suggest that anemotropism and avoidance involve basically different stimuli.

The sensory responses are by no means limited to mature sporangiophores. Tropisms and mecisms occur in other stages of sporangiophore growth, and a peculiar radial photomecism has been described during sporangium formation (51). The formation of sporangia, and thus the end of stage I in sporangiophore development, is influenced by the rate of ventilation and by the illumination program (T. Ootaki and V. E. A. Russo, unpublished information). Sporangiophores are uniformly distributed over the mycelium with either constant light or constant darkness, but when the mycelium is grown on certain media in a cycle of 23 hr of dark/1 hr of light, circles of sporangiophores, reminiscent of fairy rings in the forests, appear at the sites reached by the edge of the mycelium at the time of illumination (4). This phenomenon can be called photophorogenesis. On other media, dwarf sporangiophores may be formed instead of the usual giant ones; development of the sporangiophore primordia into one or the other kind is determined by absolute light intensity (79).

Light induces the synthesis of β-carotene (photocarotenogenesis) resulting in a 20-fold difference in pigment concentration from darkness to bright light (6). The study of carotene biosynthesis has recently made some progress: an in vitro system has been developed (8); the results of quantitative complementation have defined an enzyme aggregate carrying out the conversion of phytoene into β-carotene (3, 26, 41); and the pathway regulation has been studied with the help of mutants (38, 62). Photocarotenogenesis is being actively investigated with other microorganisms, particularly *Fusarium aquaeductum* and *Neurospora crassa* (25, 73).

Light appears to have additional effects on mycelial growth in the presence of riboflavin (14), on cell contents (77), and on structure and development (78, 80).

BEHAVIORAL GENETICS

Mutants

Phycomyces was the subject of early studies on mutants, both spontaneous (9, 10, 13) and radiation induced (35). Its multinucleate nature throughout the asexual life cycle, however, complicates the isolation of recessive mutants. This is usually circumvented by combining mutagenesis with nuclear killing of the spores, so that an appreciable fraction of the survivors becomes effectively uninucleate (19). Most of the available mutants have been obtained after treatment with N-methyl-N'-nitro-N-nitrosoguanidine. Ultraviolet light, X radiation, ethyl methanesulfonate, and ICR-170 have been used to a lesser extent.

Mutations commonly used as genetic markers result in color changes, nutritional requirements, or resistance to inhibitory drugs. The color mutants, carrying various alterations in carotene biosynthesis, differ widely in intracellular light absorption and are useful to investigate the role of this parameter in behavior; albino strains are convenient when the presence of visible pigment is undesirable.

No selective procedure is known for the isolation of behavioral mutants and only a few screening procedures are rapid and reliable enough for large-scale application.

The procedure originally introduced by M. Heisenberg (see 6) involves growing cultures from mutagen-treated spores in a glass-bottomed box where all light comes from below. The spores from erect sporangiophores are picked out and retested. Mutations resulting in abnormal phototropism are termed *mad,* followed by the appropriate capital letter for the gene (or a hyphen if the gene is not known) and an isolation number. J. F. LaFay and J. Matricon (unpublished data) have recently used a laminar wind flow to isolate a mutant gravely deficient in anemotropism but largely responsive to barriers and light. The mere existence of this mutant indicates that the avoidance of barriers is not just a consequence of their effects on wind distribution.

Mutants isolated because of their deficient phototropism belong in two main phenotypic classes (6, 43, 55, 74; I. M. López-Díaz and R. Mercurio, unpublished information). The night-blind mutants are normal in their responses to all stimuli other than light. At most light intensities, their responses are, approximately, the same as those the wild type would exhibit at intensities *m* times lower. The value of *m* differs from one mutant to another, often being from 10^4–10^5. Consequently, their lower threshold is increased by the same factor in relation to the wild type. This may be due to a very scarce supply of a gene product involved in the responses to light, or a normal supply of a very ineffective one. A small amount of active gene product is expected from suppression and reversion of simple base pair changes. Totally blind mutants would then result only from changes involving many base pairs, such as large deletions or insertions. In fact, the available mutants all respond normally at sufficiently high light intensities, and all have the same upper threshold as the wild type.

This class of mutants can be divided into three sub-classes after consideration of the responses of the mycelium to light: those exhibiting defective photocarotenogenesis and photophorogenesis, those defective only for photophorogenesis, and those normal for both.

A very different class of mutants, the "stiff" mutants, is characterized by defective mecisms and tropisms to all stimuli, suggesting that these responses share common mechanisms, presumably those responsible for growth regulation. They exhibit smaller mecisms and slower tropisms than the wild type in the same conditions. It seems that their light thresholds and their photogeotropic equilibria are those of the wild type, but their slowness makes them appear largely or totally blind.

The phenotypic study of *mad* mutants can be summarized in a diagram (Figure 3), which attempts to relate the receptors to the responses, indicating the sites where the connection between them is broken by different mutations. The diagram is simultaneously a summary of the available information and a proposal to guide further research, but it should not be taken too literally. Some genes may not specify actual sensory transducers, i.e. molecules involved in the flow of information, but their products may play an indirect role, such as physically interacting with these transducers or intervening in their synthesis.

The relationships in Figure 3 are consistent with unrelated observations on the possibility of sensory responses after saturating light stimuli in the wild type and the mutants (66; V. E. A. Russo, unpublished information).

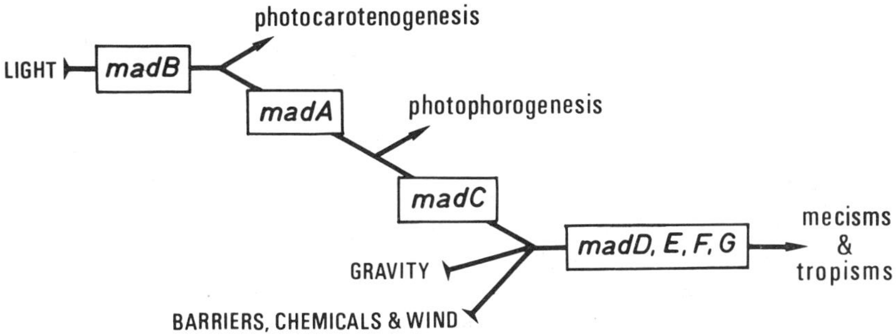

Figure 3 The flow of information between the stimuli (capitals) and the responses (lower case roman type). In italics, the genes responsible for specific steps in sensory transduction. The diagram does not attempt to establish the true nature of the stimuli nor the number of distinct receptors for barriers, chemicals, and wind.

The behavioral mutants do not appear as varied and diversified as might be expected from the relative complexity of *Phycomyces* responses. It is, of course, possible that further studies along the same lines may yield new mutant classes, although recent work (T. Ootaki and H. I. Yazán, unpublished information) has not revealed any. Certain kinds of mutants will probably be recognized only after the application of selective procedures, or at least new screening methods. The frequencies of behavioral mutants are comparable to the frequencies of color mutants that have lost certain enzyme activities. This suggests that the available *mad* mutants involve losses, rather than specific modifications, of active gene products. Certain mutations, such as those leading to an altered regulation of sporangiophore growth by sensory information, may occur very rarely and may not yet be represented in our strain collections.

Heterokaryons

Multinucleate cells lend themselves to heterokaryosis, i.e. the coexistence of nuclei with different genotypes. *Phycomyces* heterokaryons may arise from spontaneous mutation during the asexual cycle or from exceptional germspores in the sexual cycle, but the heterokaryons normally used in research have to be made by one of several surgical procedures (10, 64, 82–84). Most heterokaryons are now made by Ootaki's technique (64) based on the joint regeneration of two sporangiophores of different strains; its rate of success is high when carried out by persons of exceptional manual dexterity. Protoplasts, obtained by enzymatic digestion of cell walls, fuse spontaneously but rarely (7), so that heterokaryons may be isolated only with appropriate selective markers. Gauger (44; W. Gauger, unpublished information) has taken advantage of the fact that zygospores are natural heterokaryons for the parental genotypes. Immature zygospores, dissected and transplanted to solid medium, produce heterokaryotic vegetative mycelia. This method is convenient, but it is limited to making intersexual heterokaryons.

The study of the heterokaryon phenotype is the basis of complementation analysis and the assignment of mutations to genes. Seven genes involved in phototropism thus have been identified (40, 55, 65); they are called *madA* through *madG*. Mutants in each gene belong to the same phenotypic group. The relationship between genes and phenotypic classes is indicated in Figure 3.

Phycomyces heterokaryons, at least when made from strains with similar genetic backgrounds, are very stable and maintain their nuclear proportions during prolonged vegetative subcultivation. Nuclear proportions may be calculated from the proportions of different types of spores produced by the heterokaryons (47). This permits the correlation of quantitative phenotypic traits with allelic proportions at genes responsible for those traits. The application of this method to the color mutants led to a precise model for the biosynthesis of carotene (3, 26).

The photogeotropic equilibria of heterokaryons carrying wild-type and *mad* mutant nuclei are similar to those of the wild type over most of the nuclear proportion range. This observation has been made with representative mutant alleles of genes *madA* through *madE* (58). The results were compatible with the idea that the products of wild-type and mutant alleles act independently so that the capacity to transduce information is proportional to the number of active gene products. The only exception is that *madB* heterokaryons had higher thresholds than expected from this assumption, suggesting an interaction between the products of this gene.

Crosses

Work on experimental crosses, started at the beginning of this century (9, 11–13), was continued only recently, with well-marked mutant strains. Multinucleate parental cells, the gametangia, fuse to form zygospores. The germination of each zygospore gives rise to several thousand germspores, morphologically similar to the vegetative spores. Each germspore carries several haploid nuclei, but it is homokaryotic, except for a variable, generally low, proportion of heterokaryons. Usually, all the germspore nuclei are formed by mitotic amplification of the meiotic products of a single diploid nucleus from the zygospore. When the parents derive from different natural isolates, the number of viable germspores per germsporangium is highly variable, often zero; the four possible meiotic products are represented by unequal numbers of germspores and some may fail to be present at all. Most germsporangia contain incomplete tetrads (18, 37, 39). A. P. Eslava (unpublished data) has now obtained (+) strains largely isogenic with the standard (–) strain, NRRL1555. When these strains are crossed, most of the germsporangia contain complete tetrads that can be classified as parental ditypes, nonparental ditypes, or tetratypes for each pair of genetic markers. The genetics of *Phycomyces* thus becomes formally similar to that of yeast, with the option of studying random germspore pools or carrying out tetrad analysis.

Since the differences in genetic backgrounds cause irregularities in the crosses and incompatibility in heterokaryons, it is highly recommended that all future work be restricted to the standard wild-type, NRRL1555, and isogenic strains.

Genes involved in phototropism are not linked with each other, as has recently been shown by random germspore analysis (40). This confirms the conclusions reached from the study of mutant phenotypes and from complementation analysis. It is interesting to note that one of the mutants turned out to contain two unlinked *mad* mutations, one of them representing a new complementation group, *madG*. Thus, the possibility must be kept in mind that the phenotype of strains isolated after strong mutagen treatment is due to more than one mutation.

NATURE OF THE SENSORY TRANSDUCERS

The biochemical identification of the molecules involved in *Phycomyces* behavior is barely commencing. Both photoreception and response, conceivable starting points for this aspect of the research, present great difficulties to investigators.

Photoreceptor

The action spectra (24, 31) for photomecism and phototropism suggest that the photoreceptor is a complex of a protein and either a carotene or a flavin. The action spectra might not exactly match the absorption spectra of isolated flavins or carotenes, since the conjugation of these chromophores with proteins may alter their absorption.

Some of the carotene-deficient mutants exhibit defective phototropism, but these two traits are due to different mutations that can be separated by crossing (6; M. I. G. Roncero and D. Presti, unpublished information). The normal responses to light of color mutants indicate that carotene is not essential for photoreception.

A flavin photoreceptor is suggested by the closeness of the calculated extinction coefficient for photoreceptor inactivation at high light intensities and the known extinction coefficent of oxidized riboflavin (54). Stronger evidence is provided by the recent addition of a small, 595-nm peak to the action spectrum (29). The discovery of this peak, a billion times lower than the main 454-nm peak, was made possible by the enormous light intensity range and the low noise level of phototropism. Absorption at 595 nm corresponds to the direct transition from the ground state to the lowest triplet state of riboflavin and is consistent with the idea that the relevant physiological photochemistry occurs with a high quantum yield from the triplet state.

The sporangiophore exhibits about 20% greater sensitivity to light polarized transversally than longitudinally (15). The explanation for this effect caused an interesting controversy. Jesaitis (49) has concluded that the photopigment is linearly dichroic and has a fixed orientation in the sporangiophore. The usual assumption is that it is located at the outer cell membrane. When the sporangiophore is illuminated with visible laser microbeams not passing through its axis, it grows away from the illuminated side (60); these experiments indicate that the pigment cannot be confined to the vacuole or the vacuole membrane and must extend to the cell membrane, but they do not fully agree with its presence at the cell membrane alone.

The photoreceptor has not yet been identified among the flavoproteins in the cell. It is not even clear how it could be recognized. One possibility is to compare flavoproteins isolated from the wild-type and *mad* mutants; another one (82) is to inject wild-type cell extracts into mutant sporangiophores and hope for restoration of phototropism. Gene *madB* is the best candidate for specifying the protein moiety of the photoreceptor, since *madB* mutants are defective for all light responses, but we are not sure that any known mutants lack the photoreceptor or contain an altered one.

All responses to light are probably mediated by the same flavoprotein. This is suggested by the common effectiveness of blue light, the normal behavior of color mutants, and the pleiotropy of certain *mad* mutants. A detailed action spectrum for photocarotenogenesis in *Neurospora,* on the other hand, has been interpreted as evidence for a carotene photoreceptor (25). The participation of a carotene photoreceptor in the regulation of carotene biosynthesis cannot yet be excluded in *Phycomyces.*

The absorption spectra of living cells of *Phycomyces* and other microorganisms change after exposure to a bright flash of light (61, 72). The action spectrum for this phenomenon suggests a flavin photoreceptor and the resulting absorbance changes indicate reduction of a *b*-type cytochrome. It is unlikely, however, that these events are relevant to the early steps of sensory transduction, since they occur with a very low quantum efficiency in the wild-type and *mad* mutants of *Phycomyces,* and even in human HeLa cells (57). In the investigation of the effects of light, particularly at high intensities, one must always consider the possibility of physiologically spurious photochemical events, unrelated to the specific processes involved in sensory transduction.

Adaptation

Adaptation makes the organism sensitive to changes, rather than absolute values, of the stimuli. Adaptation must be present at an early step in the sensory transducing pathway, most likely in the same section as gene *madA* (see diagram in Figure 3), since only photocarotenogenesis depends upon absolute light intensities. Gene *madA* itself is probably not concerned with adaptation, as a mutant in this gene exhibits normal adaptation kinetics (E. D. Lipson and S. M. Block, unpublished data).

Lipson (54) has proposed that adaptation occurs at the photoreceptor itself: the adaptation level would be proportional to the ratio of light-inactivated to active pigment. This is supported by the similarity of the time constants for both adaptation and pigment regeneration. His results would be consistent with the existence of three successive elements in the early part of the sensory pathway: the photoreceptor; a logarithmic transducer, whose signal would be proportional to the logarithm of the proportion of light-inactivated molecules; and a rate-sensitive or adaptative transducer.

Intermediate Steps

Photomecism is accompanied by transient changes in the concentration of the cyclic nucleotides cAMP and cGMP (20; R. J. Cohen, unpublished work). These responses occur immediately after the stimulus; the minimum cAMP concentration is reached in less than 1 min. The transient change in cyclic nucleotide concentration could be the signal for growth control, but the possibility that these changes are side effects irrelevant to the sensory responses has not been excluded.

Little else is known that might be relevant to the intermediate steps in sensory transduction. When sporangiophores are exposed to light in the cold, the stimulus is stored, presumably as a relatively stable chemical intermediate, producing a response after warming up (71). Sporangiophore growth depends upon a chemical produced by the spores, so that growth ceases upon removal of the sporangium and resumes after replacement of a spore mass (45). This chemical has not been identified, but it is not auxin and it is not known whether it is in any way connected with the growth responses.

The transmembrane potential of −120 mV (negative inside) does not change as a result of a light stimulus or during adaptation to the dark (46). There is no firm evidence of electrical activity related to behavioral responses.

The Regulation of Growth

Two general and not mutually exclusive proposals have been made for the mechanism of the growth responses: variations in the rate of cell wall synthesis and loosening of the cell wall, accompanied by cellular extension resulting from internal pressure.

Since the major structural components of the cell wall are chitin and chitosan, chitin synthetase might be regulated by a signal from the sensory transducers. *Phycomyces* chitin synthetase bound to the plasma membrane is present in all stages of mycelial and sporangiophore development. In sporangiophores, its activity is greatest at the growing zone, but it is noticeable in the nongrowing part. Its activity was increased by 30% after exposure of crude homogenates to high intensities of blue light—a very suggestive result in view of the first proposal above (48).

Cell wall loosening would presumably be mediated by a chitinolytic enzyme. *Phycomyces* chitinase is soluble and apparently requires a small, dialyzable activator (21).

The stages in sporangiophore development are characterized by differences in the rate and the site of growth and in the twist of the sporangium. The varied and seemingly unrelated features of sporangiophore growth, including recent observations on the mechanical properties of the cell wall, the disposition of chitin microfibers, and the local rates of elongation and rotation (1, 2, 63, 70), are consistent with a relatively simple model (67). In stage IVb, used most in behavioral studies, the cell wall is basically a plastic structure, composed of stiff microfibers imbedded in a viscous matrix. The microfibers newly deposited at the top of the growing zone are predominantly transversal to the sporangiophore. The internal turgor pressure of 2–3 atm drives the elongation of the growing zone cell wall and causes the microfibers to become largely longitudinal.

Photomecism is accompanied by an increased extensibility of the growing zone cell wall (69), following approximately similar time courses (68). A signal from the sensory pathway could weaken the cell wall, perhaps by activating chitinase or another chitinolytic enzyme, and result in an acceleration of growth. To prevent thinning and breaking of the cell wall, an increase in cell wall synthesis, perhaps by activation of chitin synthetase, must be assumed. The cell wall becomes stronger, its extensibility increases, and growth velocity slows down, thus accounting for the transient nature of mecisms. It is interesting to note that, conversely, artificial stretch of the sporangiophore leads to a negative mecism (34).

The mechanisms underlying *Phycomyces* behavior do not appear forbiddingly complex. The convergence of physiological, genetical, and biochemical studies is soon expected completely to unravel the behavior of this simple, but clever, low eukaryote.

Literature Cited

1. Ahlquist, C. N., Gamow, R. I. 1973. *Plant Physiol.* 51:586–87
2. Ahlquist, C. N., Iverson, S. C., Jahsman, W. E. 1975. *J. Biomech.* 8:357–62
3. Aragón, C. M. G., Murillo, F. J., de la Guardia, M. D., Cerdá-Olmedo, E. 1976. *Eur. J. Biochem.* 63:71–75
4. Bergman, K. 1972. *Planta* 107:53–67
5. Bergman, K., Burke, P. V., Cerdá-Olmedo, E., David, C. N., Delbrück, M., Foster, K. W., Goodell, E. W., Heisenberg, M., Meissner, G., Zalokar, M., Dennison, D. S., Shropshire, W. 1969. *Bacteriol. Rev.* 33:99–157
6. Bergman, K., Eslava, A. P., Cerdá-Olmedo, E. 1973. *Mol. Gen. Genet.* 123:1–16
7. Binding, H., Weber, H. J. 1974. *Mol. Gen. Genet.* 135:273–76
8. Bramley, P. M., Davies, B. H. 1975. *Phytochemistry* 14:463–69
9. Burgeff, H. 1912. *Ber. Dtsch. Bot. Ges.* 30:679–85
10. Burgeff, H. 1914. *Flora Jena* 107:259–316
11. Burgeff, H. 1915. *Flora Jena* 108:353–448
12. Burgeff, H. 1925. *Flora Jena* 118/119: 40–46
13. Burgeff, H. 1928. *Z. Indukt. Abstamm. Vererbungsl.* 49:26–94
14. Carlile, M. J. 1962. *J. Gen. Microbiol.* 28:161–67
15. Castle, E. S. 1934. *J. Gen. Physiol.* 17: 751–62
16. Castle, E. S. 1942. *Am. J. Bot.* 29: 664–72
17. Cerdá-Olmedo, E. 1974. In *Handbook of Genetics,* ed. R. C. King, 1:343–57. New York: Plenum. 676 pp.
18. Cerdá-Olmedo, E. 1975. *Genet. Res.* 25:285–96
19. Cerdá-Olmedo, E., Reau, P. 1970. *Mutat. Res.* 9:369–84
20. Cohen, R. J. 1974. *Nature* 251:144–46
21. Cohen, R. J. 1974. *Life Sci.* 15:289–300
22. Cohen, R. J. 1976. *J. Theor. Biol.* 58:207–17
23. Cohen, R. J., Jan, Y. N., Matricon, J., Delbrück, M. 1975. *J. Gen. Physiol.* 66:67–95
24. Curry, G. M., Gruen, H. E. 1959. *Proc. Natl. Acad. Sci. USA* 45:797–804
25. De Fabo, E. C., Harding, R. W., Shropshire, W. 1976. *Plant Physiol.* 57: 440–45
26. de la Guardia, M. D., Aragón, C. M. G., Murillo, F. J., Cerdá-Olmedo, E. 1971. *Proc. Natl. Acad. Sci. USA* 68: 2012–15
27. Delbrück, M. 1974. *Anfänge der Wahrnehmung. Untersuchungen über den Mechanismus der Wandlung von Sinnessignalen bei Phycomyces.* Wiesbaden: Franz Steiner. 48 pp.
28. Delbrück, M., Cerdá-Olmedo, E. 1977. In *Genética Microbiana,* ed. E. Cerdá-Olmedo, pp. 298–311. Madrid: Alhambra. 311 pp.
29. Delbrück, M., Katzir, A., Presti, D. 1976. *Proc. Natl. Acad. Sci. USA* 73: 1969–73
30. Delbrück, M., Reichardt, W. 1956. In *Cellular Mechanisms in Differentiation and Growth,* ed. D. Rudnik, pp. 3–44. Princeton: Princeton Univ. Press
31. Delbrück, M., Shropshire, W. 1960. *Plant Physiol.* 35:194–204
32. Dennison, D. S., Bozof, R. P. 1973. *J. Gen. Physiol.* 62:157–68
33. Dennison, D. S., Foster, K. W. 1977. *Biophys. J.* 18:103–23
34. Dennison, D. S., Roth, C. C. 1967. *Science* 156:1386–88
35. Dickson, H. 1932. *Ann. Bot.* 46:389–405
36. Errera, L. 1884. *Botan. Zh.* 42:497–566
37. Eslava, A. P., Alvarez, M. I., Burke, P. V., Delbrück, M. 1975. *Genetics* 80: 445–62
38. Eslava, A. P., Alvarez, M. I., Cerdá-

Olmedo, E. 1974. *Eur. J. Biochem.* 48:617–23
39. Eslava, A. P., Alvarez, M. I., Delbrück, M. 1975. *Proc. Natl. Acad. Sci. USA* 72:4076–80
40. Eslava, A. P., Alvarez, M. I., Lipson, E. D., Presti, D., Kong, K. 1976. *Mol. Gen. Genet.* 147:235–41
41. Eslava, A. P., Cerdá-Olmedo, E. 1974. *Plant Sci. Lett.* 2:9–14
42. Foster, K. W. 1972. *The photoresponses of Phycomyces.* PhD thesis, Calif. Inst. Technol., Pasadena. 244 pp.
43. Foster, K. W., Lipson, E. D. 1973. *J. Gen. Physiol.* 52:590–617
44. Gauger, W. 1977. *J. Bacteriol.* In press
45. Goodell, E. W. 1971. *Planta* 98:63–75
46. Groves, P. M., Gamow, R. I. 1975. *Plant Physiol.* 55:946–47
47. Heisenberg, M., Cerdá-Olmedo, E. 1968. *Mol. Gen. Genet.* 102:187–95
48. Jan, Y. N. 1974. *J. Biol. Chem.* 249: 1973–79
49. Jesaitis, A. J. 1974. *J. Gen. Physiol.* 63:1–21
50. Johnson, D. L., Gamow, R. I. 1971. *J. Gen. Physiol.* 57:41–49
51. Johnson, D. L., Gamow, R. I. 1972. *Plant Physiol.* 49:898–903
52. LaFay, J. F., Matricon, J., Bodéré, C. 1975. *Physiol. Veg.* 13:259–63
53. Lipson, E. D. 1975. *Biophys. J.* 15:989–1011
54. Lipson, E. D. 1975. *Biophys. J.* 15: 1013–31
55. Lipson, E. D. 1975. *Biophys. J.* 15: 1033–45
56. Lipson, E. D., Block, S. M. 1976. *Biophys. J.* 16:33
57. Lipson, E. D., Presti, D. 1977. *Photochem. Photobiol.* 25:203–8
58. Medina, J. R. 1975. *Complementación cuantitativa entre mutantes del comportamiento en Phycomyces.* PhD thesis. Univ. Sevilla, Seville, Spain. 100 pp.
59. Medina, J. R., Cerdá-Olmedo, E. *J. Theor. Biol.* In press
60. Meistrich, M. L., Fork, R. L., Matricon, J. 1970. *Science* 169:370–71
61. Muñoz, V., Butler, W. L. 1975. *Plant. Physiol.* 55:421–26
62. Murillo, F. J., Cerdá-Olmedo, E. 1976. *Mol. Gen. Genet.* 148:19–24
63. Oort, A. J. P., Roelofsen, P. A. 1932. *K. Ned. Akad. Wet. Proc.* 35:898–908
64. Ootaki, T. 1973. *Mol. Gen. Genet.* 121:49–56
65. Ootaki, T., Fischer, E. P., Lockhart, P. 1974. *Mol. Gen. Genet.* 131:233–46
66. Ortega, J. K. E., Gamow, R. I. 1970. *Science* 168:1374–75
67. Ortega, J. K. E., Gamow, R. I. 1974. *J. Theor. Biol.* 47:317–32
68. Ortega, J. K. E., Gamow, R. I. 1976. *Plant Physiol.* 57:456–57
69. Ortega, J. K. E., Gamow, R. I., Ahlquist, C. N. 1975. *Plant. Physiol.* 55:333–37
70. Ortega, J. K. E., Harris, J. F., Gamow, R. I. 1974. *Plant Physiol.* 53:485–90
71. Petzuch, M., Delbrück, M. 1970. *J. Gen. Physiol.* 56:297–308
72. Poff, K. L., Butler, W. L. 1974. *Nature* 248:799–801
73. Rau, W. 1975. *Ber. Dtsch. Bot. Ges.* 88:45–60
74. Russo, V. E. A. 1977. *J. Bacteriol.* In press
75. Russo, V. E. A., Halloran, B., Gallori, E. 1977. *Planta* 134:61–67
76. Sutter, R. P. 1975. *Proc. Natl. Acad. Sci. USA* 72:127–30
77. Thornton, R. M. 1969. *Plant Physiol.* 44:861–65
78. Thornton, R. M. 1973. *Plant Physiol.* 51:570–76
79. Thornton, R. M. 1975. *Am. J. Bot.* 62:370–78
80. Tu, J. C., Malhotra, S. K. 1975. *Cytobios* 13:217–28
81. Varjú, D., Edgar, L., Delbrück, M. 1961. *J. Gen. Physiol.* 45:47–58
82. Villet, R. H. 1972. *Plant Physiol.* 49:273–74
83. Weide, A. 1939. *Arch. Exp. Zellforsch.* 23:299–337
84. Zalokar, M. 1969. *J. Cell Biol.* 41:494–509

Ann. Rev. Microbiol. 1977. 31:549–95

BACTERIAL BIOLUMINESCENCE

❖1717

J. Woodland Hastings
The Biological Laboratories, 16 Divinity Avenue, Cambridge, Massachusetts 02138

Kenneth H. Nealson
Scripps Institution of Oceanography, La Jolla, California 92093

CONTENTS

SUMMARY 550
INTRODUCTION 551
PROPERTIES OF THE ORGANISMS: ECOLOGICAL AND TAXONOMIC RELATIONSHIPS 552
BIOCHEMISTRY 557
Luciferase Structure and Chemistry 557
Substrates and Stoichiometry 560
Reaction Pathway and Intermediates 561
Reaction Mechanism, Products, and Emitter 564
Quantum Yield 567
NADH:FMN-Coupled Assay 568
Photoexcitable Luciferase 569
PHYSIOLOGY AND CONTROL 570
Transcriptional Control 570
Inhibition of luciferase synthesis 570
Autoinduction 571
Minimal medium: arginine and salt effects 573
Catabolite repression 574
Oxygen and the synthesis of the bioluminescence system 575
Ecological implications 575
Pathway And Metabolism 576
Oxygen 576
Reducing power 577
Aldehyde 577
Inhibitors 578
Anaesthetics 579
Membranes 580

Energetics 580
Acid Production 581
Color 582
MUTANTS 584
Induced Mutants 584
Spontaneous and Natural Isolates 586
Dark (K) variants 586
Natural isolates 588
PHAGE AND GENETICS 588
FUNCTIONS OF BACTERIAL LUMINESCENCE 589

SUMMARY

The possible functions of light emission in bacteria that live as symbionts in special organs of higher organisms such as fish and squid have long been appreciated. But in luminous bacteria that occur elsewhere, such as free in the seawater, in the guts of fish, or in saprophytic or parasitic modes, the functional importance of light emission has been questioned. One answer, which we put forward here, is that luminous bacteria may be nonluminous under certain circumstances. The bacterial luminescent system is both inducible and subject to repression. Moreover, spontaneous (but revertible) variation to a dark (dim) form allows for one or the other of the alternate forms to be selected under particular circumstances. A second answer that we have proposed is that as an alternate to the light organ mode luminous bacteria are involved in other forms of symbiosis in which the light may also have a specific function. For example, parasitic symbiosis of crustacea by luminous bacteria may allow the infected organism to be more readily detected and ingested by a predator at night. Within the gut of the predator, the bacteria can then act as enteric symbionts.

Of the three major groups of luminous bacteria, two (*Photobacterium*) have now been found to occur as light organ symbionts. The third, the *Beneckea* species, has not been found in specific association and may actually not occur as such. Instead, they may engage more extensively in the alternate symbiotic and saprophytic modes proposed.

The light-emitting reaction itself involves a diversion of electrons directly to oxygen at the level of flavin. In fully induced cells, an appreciable fraction of the total electron flow may be utilized for luminescence, with the overall oxygen uptake per cell remaining about the same as in cells prior to induction and luminescence. Evidence concerning the involvement of membranes in the reaction suggests that the possibility that control mechanisms involved in the channelling of electrons may be membrane related. The reaction itself, catalyzed by bacterial luciferase, involves the mixed function oxidation of reduced flavin mononucleotide and long-chain aldehyde by molecular oxygen. The slow turnover rate of the reaction, which is unusual, together with its ability to react with reduced flavin and oxygen without aldehyde, has allowed for the isolation and characterization of an enzyme substrate intermediate, and for detailed postulates concerning the reaction mechanism and emitting chromophore. The many mutants now available have provided additional insight concerning the reaction mechanism. An understanding of the details of regulation awaits the development of a versatile genetic system.

INTRODUCTION

Fifteen or twenty years ago, when the subject was last reviewed (133, 134), knowledge concerning bacterial luminescence was scanty. Activity of bacterial luciferase in cell-free extracts had only recently been achieved (198), and physiological phenomena involving the control of the light emitting system, its repression and induction, were unknown. Taxonomy was in a confused state, and ideas concerning the ecological and functional aspects of the system were not supported by adequate knowledge of the physiology and biochemistry of the system.

The past 20 years have witnessed great progress in these and other facets of our knowledge concerning luminous bacteria (37, 38, 79, 97). Of particular importance has been the development of easy diagnostic methods for unambiguous species determination so that the identification of an organism is routine. With the advent of these methods, it has become apparent that important differences with regard to bioluminescence and its control exist among the major groups of luminous bacteria.

Mutants have been exploited extensively as tools for understanding bioluminescence. Studies with temperature-sensitive (conditional) and nonconditional mutants have provided clues to the understanding of luciferase activity, luciferase structure, and the regulation of the luminescent system.

Many of the structural and functional details of bacterial luciferase have been elucidated. The substrates and their order of reaction in vitro have been established. Luciferase and its subunits are now well described, along with the mechanism of the light-emitting reaction. The turnover is unusually slow: three times per minute at 20°C. A significant recent achievement is the isolation and purification at subzero temperatures of an intermediate in the reaction, characterized as the peroxy adduct of luciferase-bound reduced flavin. Postulates concerning the reaction mechanism and the emitting chromophore have been proposed. Recently, different lines of evidence have indicated that the in vivo functioning of luciferase involves membrane interaction.

With regard to the physiology and ecology of luminous bacteria, a variety of regulatory mechanisms controlling bioluminescence have been elucidated. All of the findings are not yet firmly established, but, in effect, it seems clear that the bacteria enjoy more than one "life-style," luminous and nonluminous, and that different mechanisms can provide for this. Repression of the synthesis of luciferase by glucose and its reversal by cAMP indicates that, under certain conditions, the luminescence system may be classed as nonessential, similar to inducible systems in other bacteria. Indeed, the luminescence system is inducible, but the inducer (termed autoinducer) is synthesized by the cells themselves. It then accumulates in the medium and triggers the development of the system. Autoinduction predicts that cells growing in nonconfined conditions such as in the ocean or in a medium subjected to continuous dialysis should neither synthesize luciferase nor emit light. This has been shown to be so. There appears to exist, in addition, a control of the luminescence system at the genetic level, which may also be viewed as a mechanism providing for the alternative luminous and nonluminous life-styles.

Advances in knowledge of the physiology and biochemistry of the luminous bacteria have led to a developing appreciation of their biological properties and capabilities, permitting the formulation and testing of specific hypotheses concerning their ecology.

PROPERTIES OF THE ORGANISMS: ECOLOGICAL AND TAXONOMIC RELATIONSHIPS

In 1889, Beijerinck (19) proposed that all bacteria that emit light should be placed in a single genus, *Photobacterium.* Over the years, and especially with the advent of numerical taxonomy, it became clear that this was a mistaken view, and that bioluminescence (or any other weighted character) might occur in species that are otherwise quite different (133). In the case of bioluminescence, its occurrence in physiologically distinct groups might imply that light emission would have functional importance under more than one specific ecological situation or, conversely, that different species can adapt to similar niches. Also, the character of bioluminescence might have more than one specific function. Finally, the present taxonomic view allows for the recognition that a specific bacterial group may have some members that possess bioluminescence and others that lack it. With the inclusion of nonluminous species in the genus *Photobacterium* (177), we have now come clearly to the opposite pole from Beijerinck's original suggestion.

Three recent studies (28, 98, 174) concerning the classification of luminous bacteria have cleared up much of the confusion and mistaken identifications. Although the specific epithets used by various workers differ, the major conclusion is the same, namely that there are three major groups of luminous bacteria (26) (Table 1) and that these share a large number of morphological, physiological, and biochemical properties (12) with the genera in the *Enterobacteriaceae* and the *Vibrionaceae* (35). In addition to light emission, there are many other properties common to all luminous bacteria. They are all gram-negative, motile rods, facultative anaerobes capable of growth at 25°C on glucose, mannose, galactose, fructose, glycerol, and N-acetylglucosamine. This last character may be significant in relation to the fact that all the luminous bacteria also produce an extracellular chitinase.

Although the specific generic assignments of these species have not been fully settled, the separation into three groups is based most firmly on (*a*) the mode of flagellation, (*b*) the moles percent guanine plus cytosine (% G + C) composition of the DNA (174), and (*c*) in vitro DNA/DNA and DNA/rRNA hybridization (11a, 177). Diagnostically, the three groups may be classified unambiguously on the basis of certain nutritional and enzymatic properties (177, 178).

The *Photobacterium* (*Vibrio*) *fischeri* group consists of rod-shaped cells with a light yellow, cell-associated pigment and a tuft of sheathed flagella (2, 98, 174). The species is restricted to the marine environment and has a specific requirement for

200 mM sodium ion for growth (175). It occurs both free-living in seawater (183) and as the specific luminous symbiont of the monocentrid fishes, *Monocentris japonica* (183) and *Cleidopus gloriamaris* 61, 70a). *P. fischeri* shows a phenotypic (174) and genotypic (177) relationship to a nonluminous strain, ATCC 15382.

Photobacterium phosphoreum and *Photobacterium leiognathi* are in a second group, which consists of very short rods (coccobacilli) with one to three unsheathed polar flagella and (when grown on glucose) bright refractile granules of poly-β-hydroxybutyric acid (23, 51, 98, 174, 176). *P. phosphoreum,* the type species of the genus *Photobacterium,* has a specific requirement for the sodium ion and can be reliably isolated from seawater by enrichment cultures at low temperatures (174). It also occurs symbiotically in the argentinoid fish *Opisthoproctus* (100) and in a number of other specific hosts (Table 1). *P. leiognathi,* which is also marine with a specific requirement for 250 mM sodium for growth (175), has been isolated directly from seawater (91, 98, 174), from the intestines of nonluminous marine fish (174), and as the specific luminous symbiont of a wide variety of leiognathid fishes (23, 91, 178). *P. leiognathi* is phenotypically and genotypically closely related to the nonluminous marine species *Photobacterium angustum* (13, 177).

Insofar as is known, there is absolute specificity with regard to the bacterial species cultured in the light organs of a given species of fish. Also, closely related species of fish, even when living or maintained in very different locations, appear to carry the same bacterial species. This is exemplified by the different Leiognathidae from different locales (11, 91) and by the Monocentridae. All the luminous leiognathid fishes thus far reported contain *P. leiognathi* as their symbionts (11, 91, 178); in a given host a single predominating strain of *P. leiognathi* occurs (178); and a similar specificity occurs in *M. japonica* and in several hosts carrying *P. phosphoreum. M. japonica* from Japan and others of the same species maintained in the San Francisco aquarium for 15 years, along with *C. gloriamaris* from Australia, all carry *P. fischeri* (61, 183).

The third group includes *Beneckea* (*Lucibacterium*) *harveyi, Beneckea* (*Photobacterium*) *splendida,* and *Vibrio cholerae.* They have rod-shaped cells—straight rods in *B. harveyi* and curved rods in *B. splendida* and *V. cholerae*—with one to three sheathed polar flagella (43, 174). *B. harveyi,* in addition, has inducible unsheathed peritrichous flagella (98, 174). *B. harveyi* has a specific requirement for 300 mM sodium ion for optimal growth (175) and occurs in coastal seawater in relatively high concentrations (174).

In contrast to the two *Photobacterium* groups, no members of this third group have yet been found in specific association with a higher organism. *B. harveyi,* as previously described, has recently been shown by in vitro DNA/DNA hybridization studies (177) to include two distinct species, *B. harveyi* and *B. splendida.* Chumakova et al (28) named a species *Photobacterium belozerski,* which closely resembled *B. harveyi*; however, the degree of relationship has not been determined. Nonluminous strains genetically indistinguishable from *B. harveyi* have been isolated from seawater and fish surfaces (13, 177). *B. harveyi* has been found to be very closely related to several well-studied species of marine bacteria, namely *Vibrio* (*Beneckea*) *parahaemolytica, Vibrio* (*Beneckea*) *alginolytica,* and *Vibrio* (*Beneckea*)

Table 1 Affinities and properties of luminous bacteria

	Currently used and proposed epithets[a]				DNA (mol% G + C)[b]
	RB	H	C	BM	
A	*Photobacterium fischeri*[f]	*Vibrio fischeri*	*Photobacterium fischeri* Group I[g]	*Vibrio fischeri*	39.0–40.5
B	*Photobacterium phosphoreum*	*Photobacterium phosphoreum*		*Photobacterium phosphoreum*	41.2–41.8
	Photobacterium leiognathi[h]	*Photobacterium mandapamensis*	Group II[g]	*Photobacterium mandapamensis*	42.8–43.8
C	*Beneckea splendida*	*Lucibacterium harveyi*[i]	*Lucibacterium harveyi*[i]		45.0–45.9
	Beneckea harveyi	*Lucibacterium harveyi*[i]		*Lucibacterium harveyi*[i]	46.0–47.2
			Group III *Photobacterium belozerskii*[j]		46.1–48.2
	Vibrio cholerae	*Vibrio albensis*		*Vibrio cholerae* (biotype albensis)	47.8

[a] RB, Reichelt & Baumann (11a, 174, 176, 177); H, Hendrie et al (98); C, Chumakova et al (28); and BM, *Bergey's Manual* (26).

[b] Ordered according to the increasing mol% G + C content in DNAs (28, 174, 177).

[c] Earlier synonyms with references are provided in *Bergey's Manual* (26).

[d] Group A: *Monocentris japonica* (Japan), *Cleidopus gloriamaris* (Australia) (61, 183). Group B: *Nezumia stelgidolepis* (US, west coast), *Nezumia aequalis, Winteria telescopa, Opisthoproctus grimaldi, Opisthoproctus soleatus,* and *Sphagemacrurus hirundo* (Atlantic) (100; E.G. Ruby, personal communication).

[e] Not necessarily applicable to 100% of the strains of a given species. Consult original studies for details (174, 177).

[f] These authors agree that this group deserves separate status, but because it differs in several diagnostic traits they do not concur with its assignment in *Vibrio* (11a, 174, 177).

[g] Group I was assigned to *Photobacterium fischeri* by these authors. Group II was recognized (28) as closely resembling both *Photobacterium phosphoreum* and *Photobacterium mandapa-*

Table 1 *(Continued)*

Recently published epithets[c]	Specific hosts[d] with light organs	Major distinguishing features[e]	
Achromobacter fischeri (93, 186, 187) *Vibrio luminosus* (113, 114)	*Monocentris* *Cleidopus*	Polar tuft of 2–8 sheathed flagella Yellow cell-associated pigment Fast luciferase kinetics	
Photobacterium WSU (127)	*Nezumia* *Winteria* *Opisthoproctus* *Sphagemacrurus*	No extracellular lipase Growth at 4°C	1–3 unsheathed polar flagella Acetoin and/or diacetyl production PH accumulation Fast luciferase kinetics
	Leiognathus *Secutor* *Gazza*	No pyruvate excretion	
		Curved rods Single, sheathed polar flagellum Nutritionally more versatile than A and B Slow luciferase kinetics	
MAV (71, 96) *Photobacterium fischeri* (MAV) (157, 162) *Achromobacter fischeri* (34)	Not known to be cultured in light organs	Single, sheathed polar flagellum Inducible unsheathed peritrichous flagella Extracellular amylase Extracellular gelatinase Growth at 40°C Nutritionally more versatile than A and B Slow luciferase kinetics	
Vibrio phosphorescens (133)		Nonmarine isolate 1–3 sheathed polar flagella Curved rods Growth at 40°C Slow luciferase kinetics	

mensis, but the distinction between these two species could not be justified on the basis of their own work at that time. More recent studies (personal communication) place group II with *Photobacterium leiognathi.*

[h]Originally designated as *Photobacterium mandapamensis* by these authors (174) revised to *Photobacterium leiognathi* (176).

[i]The new genus *Lucibacterium* was erected largely on the basis of peritrichous flagellation (26, 98). Since this feature relates to growth on solid medium (174) and since other nutritional properties indicate that they have characteristics of the genus *Beneckea* (13), the group was transferred to *Beneckea* and the definition of the genus was altered to include luminous strains (174). Both groups of worker (98, 177) recognize affinities with the genus *Vibrio*.

[j]Group III was recognized (28) as being similar to *Lucibacterium* (*Photobacterium*) *harveyi* except for the nature of the flagellation. Since that character can be different depending on the medium (see footnote i), it seems likely that *Photobacterium belozerskii* is a *Beneckea* (*Lucibacterium*) species.

natriegens (12). These marine bacterial species have specific requirements for 50–150 mM sodium ion for optimal growth (175). *B. splendida* has a similar close relationship to a nonluminous species, which has been provisionally designated *B. splendida* biotype II (177, 178).

A single luminous strain, *Vibrio cholerae,* biotype *albensis,* ATCC 14547, has been found to be phenotypically (98) and genotypically (177) indistinguishable from nonluminous strains of *V. cholerae* (including the type strain). Both the luminous and nonluminous strains of *V. cholerae* were able to grow on media without added sodium. The growth rate and the cell yield of the latter strains, however, were stimulated by addition of low amounts of NaCl (optimum at 2.5–5.0 mM) (175). *V. cholerae* var. *albensis* was isolated from the Elbe River (Germany) and is the only luminous species known to occur outside the marine environment. A recent study of the DNA/rRNA homology between marine and terrestrial enterobacteria has indicated that *V. cholerae* differs substantially from *Photobacterium* and *Beneckea* but is nevertheless more closely related to these genera than to the terrestrial isolates (11a).

As mentioned above, there have been no reports of any of the three luminous species in the *Vibrio-Beneckea* group occurring as the specific symbiont in the luminous organs of a fish, whereas all species of *Photobacterium* have been isolated as such. This raises the interesting possibility, as pointed out by Hastings & Mitchell (91), that luminous members of the genus *Beneckea* may be classed as "free-living." Both their ubiquity and frequency of occurrence in temperate coastal waters suggests this. So does their nutritional profile, which, compared to the *Photobacterium* species, is far more versatile, indicative of a more cosmopolitan species. Although members of the other two groups can utilize about 20 different organic compounds as carbon and energy sources, *Beneckea harveyi* strains can use about 40 (174).

But the view that they are simply free-living seems unnecessarily restrictive. *B. harveyi,* and members of the other two groups as well, occur both as gut symbionts and as symbionts parasitic on shrimp and other crustacea (K. H. Nealson and E. G. Ruby, unpublished data). Since fish feed on crustacea, and since all groups of luminous bacteria produce an extracellular chitinase and utilize the product N-acetyl glucosamine, this can be viewed as a second type of symbiosis for the luminous bacteria. For the light organ symbionts, this niche might also be exploited as an alternate type of symbiosis and provide for survival and propagation during the phase outside the light organ.

For *B. harveyi,* which is not known to occur in light organs, this might represent a major and exhaustively exploited way of life. If so, the question as to the specific ecology and function of the luminescence must be addressed. In particular, the fact that their bioluminescence is subject to autoinduction must be explained. One possibility is that as marine enterobacteria their propagation might be favored if they could incubate on potential food material that would be seen at night and thereby ingested by the host. For example, shrimp infected by luminous bacteria should be more subject to predation at night by virtue of the luminescence. Studies of feeding habits and gut microflora of marine fish, especially those feeding at night, might provide evidence concerning this idea.

Thus, it appears that many light organ symbionts are capable of host-independent survival, and that, in fact, gut and parasitic symbioses may represent a light organ-independent ecology for the same bacterial species. This could also provide an inoculum for infection of the light organ of the developing host (if indeed such a route is involved). But if one regards nutritional versatility (metabolic adaptability) as a measure of an organism's host independence, then a pattern can be seen among the groups of luminous bacteria. *Beneckea* (group C) is the most host-independent group, whereas group B, especially *P. phosphoreum*, many strains of which are auxotrophs, is the least. In fact, some luminous bacteria may be "obligate" symbionts; the cultivation of the "bacteroids" from some light organs has not been accomplished (73, 74, 169). Electron micrographs of these organs reveal bacteria with poly-β-hydroxybutyrate-like granules characteristic of the *Photobacterium*. Similar granules are seen in hosts carrying *Photobacterium leiognathi* (75).

In the above cases, a function and positive selection for luminescence can be postulated. It seems likely that the luminous bacteria are also capable of exploiting habitats where there is no positive selection for the ability to emit light. We say this primarily because there exists a control of the luminescence system at the genetic level giving rise to spontaneous dark "K" variants (see below) at a reasonable frequency. If there are conditions, possibly growth as a saprophyte, under which bioluminescence is not selected for, then these dark K variants can take over. Since reversion to bright forms also occurs, the propagation of either form acts as a potential inoculum for either.

BIOCHEMISTRY

Bacterial luciferase catalyzes the bioluminescent oxidation of $FMNH_2$ and a long-chain aliphatic aldehyde (RCHO) by molecular oxygen. The enzyme may be viewed as a mixed function oxidase (83, 159), since the reaction involves the concomitant oxidation of $FMNH_2$ and RCHO according to the following overall stoichiometry:

$$FMNH_2 + O_2 + RCHO \xrightarrow{\text{luciferase}} 0.1\ h\nu + FMN + H_2O + RCOOH.$$

The reaction is closely analogous to certain flavoprotein hydroxylases (monooxygenases). The reduced flavin-enzyme complex can react with oxygen, even in the absence of the second substrate, to give an oxygenated form of the reduced flavin, an intermediate that may be designated as the active oxidizing species (82, 130). A difference is, of course, that the luciferase reaction emits light, with a reasonably high bioluminescence quantum yield (~10%). Another notable feature of the luciferase reaction is its slowness: at room temperature, the oxygenated intermediate referred to above may have a lifetime of 10 or 20 sec. At lower temperatures, it has been isolated, purified, and characterized (84).

Luciferase Structure and Chemistry

Structurally, bacterial luciferase seems to be simple: no metals, prosthetic groups, or non-amino acid residues appear to be involved (38, 93). Only recently, however, luciferase from one species, *Photobacterium leiognathi,* has been reported to be a membrane-bound glycoprotein whose activity is labile to lysozyme (4).

Beneckea harveyi luciferase is a heterodimer of molecular weight 79,000 whose two non-identical subunits, α (molecular weight 42,000) and β (molecular weight 37,000), can be isolated in quantity by diethylaminoethyl cellulose-Sephadex chromatography in 5 M urea (71, 96). Individual subunits are inactive, but when recombined under appropriate conditions they recover nearly full activity. For both *Photobacterium fischeri* and *B. harveyi* luciferases, there is evidence that the two subunits have some degree of homology (9, 63, 141), and for *B. harveyi,* that their synthesis is induced and concerted (143, 209). For any given luciferase, the two subunits are functionally distinct. Substrate binding ($FMNH_2$ and aldehyde) and catalytic properties appear to reside on the α subunit; the function of the β subunit, which is absolutely required for luminescence activity, remains undefined.

Succinylation of luciferase results in a nearly complete inactivation and an altered rate of turnover (138, 139). Hybrid luciferases formed with native α and succinylated β have the unmodified turnover rate, whereas luciferases with a native β and succinylated α show the same altered turnover rate as the succinylated dimer (α_s β_s). These results indicate that the two subunits are functionally distinct and suggest that α is the catalytic subunit. This interpretation has been confirmed by mutant enzyme analysis (30, 31). Mutations affecting the catalytic center were obtained by screening for luciferase activity in vitro, showing altered rates of turnover; all of these mutations resided exclusively on the α subunit and had various concomitant changes, including altered $FMNH_2$ or aldehyde binding affinities and/or emission spectral shifts. On the other hand, screening for mutants with thermally unstable luciferase yielded proteins modified in either the α or the β subunit.

B. harveyi luciferase contains a particularly reactive sulfhydryl group in or near the active center of the enzyme whose modification results in a loss of activity; the substrates aldehyde and $FMNH_2$ and the product FMN protect the reactive sulfhydryl from modification (166, 167). Studies with N-[^{14}C]ethylmaleimide have shown it to be located on the α subunit in a tryptic peptide with the sequence phe-gly-ile-cys-arg (85). However, a direct involvement of this reactive sulfhydryl in catalytic function was not shown; its pK_a was found to be 9.4, which did not correlate with the pH dependence of $FMNH_2$ binding, the stability of the intermediate, or quantum yield of the reaction. *P. fischeri* contains a similar but less reactive sulfhydryl group (7).

Luciferase also has a single binding site for the fluorescent probe, 8-anilino-1-naphthalenesulfonate (ANS). ANS acts as a luciferase inhibitor competitive with $FMNH_2$, but it does not significantly displace FMN from binding to luciferase (206). This provides a distinction between the FMN and $FMNH_2$ binding by luciferase. Also, the $FMNH_2$ binding affinity of luciferase, which has been 99.7% inactiviated by reaction with 1.0 Meq of N-octylmaleimide, is decreased at least 10-fold (167), whereas that of FMN is almost unchanged (165) even though, as mentioned above, FMN protects the sulfhydryl against alkylating reagents. From fluorescence energy transfer studies, the distance between the "essential" sulfhydryl group and the ANS site was calculated to be about 20 Å (207).

A histidyl residue on the α subunit has also been implicated as playing an essential role in the mechanism of the luciferase reaction (39). Luciferase is inactivated by ethoxyformic anhydride with a concomitant increase in ethoxyformylhistidyl derivatives. Substrates protect against chemical inactivation; in hybrid luciferases, modification of two histidyl residues on the β subunit is without effect on activity, whereas modification of a single histidyl on the α causes inactivation.

Sequential modification of these "essential" residues, cysteinyl and histidyl, showed that modification of one did not affect the reactivity of the remaining one, suggesting that chemical modification had not caused a major change in protein conformation (40). However, after modification of the histidyl residue, $FMNH_2$ and aldehyde no longer protected the cysteinyl residue against modification, whereas after modification of the cysteinyl residue, substrates still protected the histidyl residue against modification. The results were taken as evidence that the histidyl and not the cysteinyl residue of luciferase is essential for the binding of substrates.

Although luciferase activity is highly specific for $FMNH_2$, other flavins and flavin analogues do exhibit a low but authentic activity (140, 147), and binding of oxidized forms to luciferase can be measured by fluorescence quenching (6, 8). Studies of the structural requirements for interacting with luciferase indicate a broader specificity for the oxidized than for the reduced forms of the flavins and differences in the nature of the interactions of the two forms (208).

Bacterial luciferases from *Beneckea harveyi* and *Photobacterium fischeri* appear to have a specific binding site for phosphate associated in some fashion with the flavin binding site. The turnover rate of the enzyme is significantly affected by phosphate concentration (146). Meighen & MacKenzie (140) have shown that a negative charge at least four methylene groups removed from the isoalloxazine ring is required for strong binding of the flavin to luciferase. This negative charge is provided by the phosphate of $FMNH_2$, but a carboxylate will also suffice. Furthermore, Meighen & MacKenzie found that the quantum yield of the bioluminescence reaction with reduced riboflavin as substrate is dramatically enhanced by the presence of high inorganic phosphate concentrations in the buffer, although the binding affinity for reduced riboflavin is not altered.

Phosphate (as well as several other anions) has a dramatic effect upon the structure and stability of the luciferase as well. The enzyme is rapidly inactivated by all proteases tested (168); the rate of inactivation is paralleled by loss of the α subunit, which is converted from 42,000 daltons to about 28,000 daltons plus several smaller fragments. The β subunit is not attacked by proteases under nondenaturing conditions (5). The rate of proteolytic inactivation is decreased at least 20-fold upon binding of FMN, phosphate, sulfate, or certain other anions (165). In addition, anion binding has been found to stabilize the protein to inactivation by heat or urea (T. O. Baldwin, S.-C. Tu, P. L. Riley, and J. W. Hastings, unpublished observations). These results suggest that phosphate binding, either inorganic or the group on FMN, is accompanied by a change in the structure of the protein, which results in an enhanced bioluminescence quantum yield and an increased stability to denaturation. A more definitive statement regarding the nature and magnitude of this change must await further experiments. It is interesting that the reactivity of the "essential" sulfhydryl with N-ethylmaleimide is not altered by phosphate binding (T. O. Baldwin, personal communication).

Luciferase is reversibly denatured by heat, urea, guanidine, and sodium dodecyl sulfate (62). A mild reducing agent (dithiothreitol) is required for efficient renaturation and also for long-term stability during storage. Luciferase that has been heat denatured by boiling can be restored to activity by dissolving it in 8 M urea and subsequent dilution to decrease the urea concentration (62).

Luciferases from other bacterial species are distinct yet similar in many ways to *B. harveyi* luciferase. The recent report that *Photobacterium leiognathi* luciferase is a glycoprotein that requires solubilization by treatment of extracts with deoxycholate (4) is in contrast to earlier reports that its purification and properties were essentially similar to *P. fischeri* luciferase (55, 116). It seems possible that there may be strain differences in this regard. The properties of both *P. fischeri* (71, 93, 96) and *Photobacterium phosphoreum* (129, 153, 215, 216, 218, 219, 229, 230, 232) luciferases have been described.

All luciferases described possess the $\alpha\beta$ heterodimeric structure with molecular weights in the range of 76,000 ± 4,000. All exhibit specificity for $FMNH_2$, the requirement for aldehyde, and the slow turnover feature indicative of a long-lived intermediate. The exact turnover rate is dependent upon the chain lengths of the aldehydes used and may differ significantly and characteristically with different luciferases.

Finally, all the luciferases appear to possess a special type of contaminating protein (see below), an inactive luciferase possessing a bound flavin (146). In *B. harveyi* and *P. fischeri,* this protein has been shown to possess bioluminescence activity, which can only be initiated by photoexcitation of the bound flavin (no added flavin is needed). This protein appears to be a product of luciferase turnover in vivo, since dark aldehyde mutants that possess luciferase do not have photoexcitable luciferase. Such mutants, if supplied with exogenous aldehyde so that they emit light during growth, do possess photoexcitable luciferase (148).

Substrates and Stoichiometry

Although it was earlier postulated by Strehler (199, 200) that two reduced flavins were involved in the reaction, and that aldehyde might have only a catalytic function, these possibilities now appear to have been ruled out. As shown by both binding and activity measurements, only a single flavin is required for bioluminescence (15, 137) and several laboratories have shown that long-chain aldehyde is oxidized to the corresponding acid in the light-emitting reaction (48, 131, 186, 214).

A more recent "two-flavin" hypothesis (37, 117–119) based on the relative quantum yields of $FMNH_2$ and aldehyde also appears to be incorrect (6, 8, 14, 15, 137, 215, 218). A two-flavin mechanism requires that the two flavins bind either simultaneously or sequentially to the same or different sites on luciferase during a catalytic cycle. Measurements by using equilibrium techniques have shown that the luciferase dimer has only a single binding site for both oxidized and reduced flavin. Quantum yield results demonstrate that bioluminescence requires only one reduced flavin per luciferase, ruling out mechanisms involving either two $FMNH_2$ molecules or one $FMNH_2$ plus one FMN per catalytic cycle.

With *P. phosphoreum* luciferase, the K_D for $FMNH_2$ binding was 1–6 $\times$ 10^{-7} M, whereas its affinity for FMN was more than 10^5 times less (218). Binding of FMN to *P. fischeri* luciferase is also weak (K_D between 5 $\times$ 10^{-4} and 5 $\times$ 10^{-3} M), but with *B. harveyi* binding is stronger; the K_D at 2°C is 2 $\times$ 10^{-4} M (6, 8, 222). With these two luciferases, K_m values of 9.7 $\times$ 10^{-7} M and 8 $\times$ 10^{-7} M, respectively, have been reported for $FMNH_2$ by using a kinetic method (137). The equilibrium value for *B. harveyi* luciferase based on circular dichroism measurements is consistent with the kinetic value (15). A similar value was reported for $FMNH_2$ binding to *P. phosphoreum* luciferase (215). There is no apparent explanation for the much (100X) higher values reported by Lee & Murphy (119).

Luciferase is quite specific for $FMNH_2$, but as mentioned above, some luminescence occurs upon reaction of luciferase with various flavin isomers and analogues in their reduced form (147), and added inorganic phosphate and sulfate increase the activity of reduced riboflavin, presumably by interaction with a phosphate binding site (140).

The requirement for aldehyde is also specific; only aliphatic aldehydes of chain lengths above about eight carbons (depending upon the type of luciferase) are effective (94, 96). Substitution or unsaturation interferes with the aldehyde effectiveness only if it is close to the carbonyl group (88, 195). Long-chain hydrocarbons (ketones, acids, alcohols, or thiols) are in general without activity with luciferase; however, some are competitive inhibitors (88). The report (21) that decylnitrite is active as an aldehyde analogue has not been confirmed (130). The chain length of the aldehyde used in the reaction has a profound effect upon the kinetics of the reaction (turnover rate) but much less effect upon the photon yield (94, 186). The specific relationships between aldehyde chain length and enzyme turnover rate are not the same for luciferases from different species (96).

With *P. phosphoreum* luciferase, the values of K_m for aldehyde are 280, 180, and 120 μM for aldehydes with 10, 12, and 13 carbon chain lengths, respectively (232). With *P. fischeri* over the range from 8–16 carbon atoms, the K_m values were 30, 15, 10, 3, 1.5, 1, 0.75, 0.3, and 0.05 μM, respectively (194). Values are higher in the presence of bovine serum albumin, with both *P. fischeri* and *B. harveyi* (86, 159).

Reaction Pathway and Intermediates

The bacterial luciferase reaction is unusual because its turnover rate is extremely slow, involving an enzyme intermediate with a half-life of about 20 sec at 20°C (86). The fact that the free substrate ($FMNH_2$) is rapidly autoxidized ($<$1 sec) (67) means that the substrate is offered as a pulse whose duration is short compared to the lifetime of the intermediate(s). The assay in vitro, therefore, involves only a single turnover of enzyme. Furthermore, an enzymatic reaction that results in little or no light emission, but that also involves the long-lived intermediate, can occur with $FMNH_2$ and O_2 alone, i.e. without aldehyde. There is now a substantial body of evidence for the detailed scheme for the reaction pathway (Figure 1), similar in its key respects to the one originally proposed (86).

The reaction of reduced flavin with luciferase results in the formation of luciferase-bound $FMNH_2$, designated as intermediate I. This has been detected and

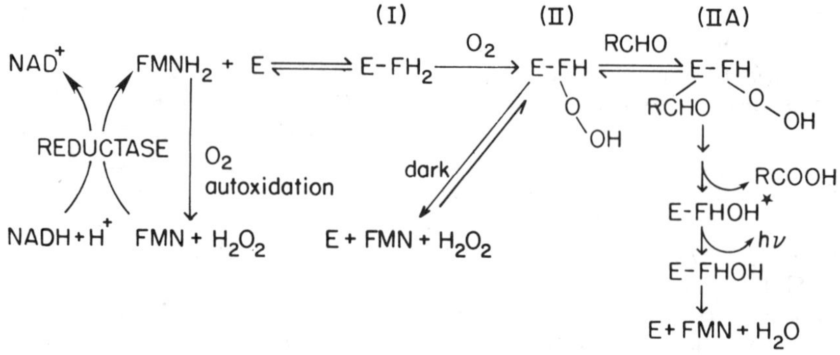

Figure 1 Reaction sequence and intermediate hypothesized for the reaction of bacterial luciferase with $FMNH_2$.

studied by circular dichoism spectroscopy in the presence of excess reducing agent and is shown to involve a 1:1 reduced flavin-luciferase complex for *P. fischeri* and *B. harveyi* luciferases (14, 15). A similar stoichiometry was found for the *P. phosphoreum* enzyme (215). In initial studies (86, 93), we reported evidence leading to the postulate that this step involved the reduction of an enzyme disulfide to a dithiol with concomitant flavin oxidation. Subsequent attempts to repeat these experiments failed. This, together with the observation that renaturation of luciferase activity after treatment with 8 M urea required the presence of a reductant (62, 63), led us to specifically abandon the hypothesis (79). However, the disulfide-to-dithiol hypothesis was again incorporated in a postulated reaction mechanism, but without additional evidence in support of it (118, 119). Recent experiments have reconfirmed that it is not valid: intermediate I prepared without excess reducing agent is in fact a reduced flavin-luciferase complex involving no flavin oxidation, and the native enzyme contains no disulfide bonds (203).

Reaction of I with one molecule of oxygen (215) is extremely rapid, forming a second intermediate (II), which because of its relatively long lifetime can be accumulated, purified, and studied by using low-temperature techniques (84). After isolation and purification by column chromatography at low temperatures (–20° to –30°C), it can be made to give rise to bioluminescence, with a quantum yield equal to that of the overall reaction, simply by injection into buffer-containing aldehyde at +22°C. Oxygen is not required for this reaction (18). This oxygen-containing intermediate of *B. harveyi* luciferase differs spectrally from both oxidized and reduced flavin; it has absorption in the visible range, peaking at 372 nm, and fluroescence emission centered at about 490 nm. In its color, the fluorescence corresponds closely to the bioluminescence emission (10), and although the intermediate cannot itself be the emitter (the aldehyde has not yet reacted), its structure may provide a clue to that of the emitter. Similar properties and absorption spectra have been reported both for the intermediate from *P. fischeri* (in aqueous solution at 2°C) (16, 57a) and for that from *P. phosphoreum* (3a), retracting an earlier report (231).

The intermediate is postulated to be the 4a-peroxy adduct of $FMNH_2$ (84). Spectral properties (absorption and fluorescence) of 4a-substituted flavins resemble those of the luciferase intermediate. Moreover, a 4a-substituted flavin hydroperoxide recently synthesized by Bruice's laboratory does, in fact, emit light when reacted with aldehyde (27, 106). Their more recent experiments (107) suggest that the reaction mechanism involves the reaction of aldehyde with the peroxyreduced flavin, as earlier postulated (50).

Bioluminescence initiated by H_2O_2 and FMN in lieu of $FMNH_2$ has been reported for both *B. harveyi* and *P. phosphoreum* (17, 216) due, it is postulated, to the direct formation of the luciferase 4a-peroxy flavin intermediate by attack of H_2O_2 on FMN (the latter may be bound to luciferase).

The report (151) that chromatography of intermediate II in aqueous buffers at 0°C produced an active intermediate, but one nearly devoid of flavin, has not been substantiated. In fact, the intermediate so prepared does possess a flavin moiety and has an activity potential strictly proportional to the amount of the flavin intermediate (16).

In the absence of aldehyde, intermediate II breaks down to yield H_2O_2 and FMN (Figure 1); the pathway may be viewed essentially as an enzyme-mediated flavin oxidation, which is much slower than the same reaction in the absence of enzyme. By using purified intermediate II, the identity and stoichiometry of the products via this pathway were determined. The decay of II in the absence of aldehyde produces a very small amount of bioluminescence [between 10^{-2} and 10^{-4} of that with aldehyde (85, 88), and 1 mol each of H_2O_2 and FMN per mol of enzyme intermediate (10, 82)]. There is no satisfactory explanation for the emission in the absence of aldehyde. An increase in the yield of "non-aldehyde" emission after freezing the intermediate (89) was attributed to "puddling" (53), but since the luminescence with and without aldehyde differs with regard to the temperature at which peak emission occurs, such an explanation seems inadequate.

In the presence of aldehyde, an intermediate (IIA) is formed whose continued reaction via several additional intermediates results in a high quantum yield emission (86). An important feature of the aldehyde interaction is the effect of chain length on the turnover time in vitro: some aldehydes cause the enzyme to turn over much faster and others cause it to be even slower than the "dark" pathway (88, 94, 96, 187, 219, 232). Over the range of 8–14 carbon atoms, different fatty aldehydes nevertheless result in comparable quantum yields with perhaps a few exceptions and some differences, depending upon the bacterial species from which the luciferase is obtained (see below).

The formation of the enzyme-aldehyde intermediate complex has been detected by optical absorption spectroscopy at –30°C (82). The reversibility of aldehyde binding in this complex (88) has been questioned (29, 119), based on the biphasic nature of decay curves in reaction mixtures containing aldehydes of two different chain lengths. A more definitive experiment utilizing RCHO and RCDO (which have different decay constants but similar binding constants) has demonstrated that the aldehyde binding is indeed reversible, both early and late in the decay (P. Shannon, R. Spencer, J. Becvar, S.-C. Tu, C. Walsh, and J. W. Hastings, unpublished results).

With *P. fischeri* luciferase, it was reported in 1966 (88) that there was no isotope effect (k_H/k_D) with decanal. Later, a deuterium isotope effect of 1.7 was reported for *B. harveyi* luciferase with dodecanal (21). More recent studies have confirmed an isotope effect of about 1.7 for both aldehydes with *B. harveyi* and have demonstrated that there is an effect, but somewhat smaller (~1.2), with *P. fischeri* luciferase (P. Shannon, R. Spencer, J. Becvar, S.-C. Tu, C. Walsh, and J. W. Hastings, unpublished results.)

For the reaction in vitro, the conversion of aldehyde to acid concomitant with light emission has been shown by several workers (48, 131, 186, 214). The other product of the reaction, starting with intermediate II and aldehyde at –30°C and warming to obtain light emission, has been shown to be FMN but not H_2O_2 (82).

The identity and reaction of the aldehyde factor in vivo is not well established. Shimomura et al (187) extracted endogenous aldehydes from both *Achromobacter fischeri* and *P. phosphoreum* and, by converting to acids, identified chain lengths of predominantly 12, 14, and 16 carbon atoms. Lesser amounts were obtained from a mutant that was dark without exogeneously added aldehyde (see Table 2). It would be useful to have similar determinations with temperature-sensitive aldehyde mutants (30, 32).

An alternative substrate for the luciferase intermediate was reported by McCapra & Hart (130), who showed that long-chain dialkyl sulfides are oxidized by one of the intermediates of the reaction with *P. phosphoreum* luciferase. They concluded that intermediate II is an active peroxide for which the sulfide is a specific reductant, exhibiting also chain-length specificity.

Reaction Mechanism, Products, and Emitter

Several specific mechanisms have been proposed for the bacterial luciferase reactions (50, 123, 131). Lowe et al (123) suggested that aldehyde reacts with the dihydroperoxy flavin at the N-5, that a four-membered flavin-oxazetidine ring is an intermediate, and that the product FMN is the emitter (see below). In the McCapra-Hysert mechanism (131), aldehyde is postulated to react with $FMNH_2$ prior to the entry of oxygen. This does not conform to the observation that $FMNH_2$ reacts with oxygen first (86). Eberhard & Hastings (50) postulated that intermediate II is the luciferase-bound 4a-hydroperoxide of $FMNH_2$ and that the light-emitting steps involve the reaction of II to form a mixed flavin-aldehyde peroxide followed by a Baeyer-Villiger type rearrangement. Model 4a-hydroperoxy dihydroflavins have recently been synthesized (106, 107). The spectrum of 4a-hydroperoxy-5-ethyl-3-methyllumiflavin was shown to be virtually superimposable upon that of the luciferase intermediate II, as reported by Hastings et al (84), and to be chemiluminescent upon reaction with aldehyde. Evidence supporting the intermediacy of the proposed peroxyhemiacetal has been reported (107).

In the scheme of Figure 2, at least one additional intermediate must be involved between breaking of the aldehyde C–H bond and production of the emitter, as deduced from the following observations (R. P. Presswood and J. W. Hastings, unpublished observations). Upon reacting decanal with intermediate II at 2°C, a rapid absorbance increase (complete within 0.1 sec after mixing) is observed at 380

Table 2 Mutants affecting bioluminescence or its control in bacteria[a]

Type of lesion or character affected	Conditional	Nonconditional
Luciferase structure	TSL- (α) (30, 31) TSL-10 (β) (30, 31)	AK-1 (α, fast) (31) AK-6 (α, slow) (31) FB-1 (β) (29) FB-2 (α) (29)
Aldehyde synthesis	TSAS-1 (30, 32) TSAS-F1 (30, 32)	M-16, M-17, M-18 (15)[b] N-25 (161)
Synthesis of entire luminescent system	TSLS-1 (30) UY-437 (cAMP) (212)	PTS-EnzI; PTS-HPr (122) ACR-1 (161) ACF-1[c] N-1 (161)
Control elements		MB-4 (arginine) (220) BG-1 (glucose) (122) BG-5 (glucose, PEP carboxylase$^-$) (122)
Inducer synthesis	MJ-1 (bright, Nat) (156) B-61 (dim, Nat) (156)	S-1 (Nat) (bright, constitutive) (4)[c]
Nutritional	Flavin (Nat)	
Color of emission	Y-1 (Nat) (163)[d]	Y-1 (Nat) AK-6 (α) (33)

[a] All mutants were isolated after mutagenesis except those designated as natural isolates (Nat). Conditional mutants include those that are temperature sensitive (TS) and also those whose luminescence is conditional upon some substance in the medium; the two whose brightness relates to the level of autoinducer are included here. PTS, Phosphotransferase system.

[b] M-16, M-17, and M-18 were isolated by T. Cline in 1971 following mutagenesis with n-methyl-n-nitro-n′-nitrosoguanidine.

[c] S. Ulitzur, personal communication.

[d] Cells grown at 30°C emit blue light only (λ_{max}, 500 nm); those grown at 15°C emit mostly yellow light (λ_{max}, 550 nm).

nm; this is followed by two phases of absorbance decrease (the first complete within 1 sec and the second continuing with a half-time for decay of about 10 sec). When this reaction is examined by using [^{2}H]decanal, only the slower second phase of absorbance decrease is altered in rate; a kinetic isotope effect (k_H/k_D) of about 4 is apparent for this absorbance change, in contrast to the isotope effect of 1.7 for the decay of light intensity. The magnitude of the former isotope effect makes it reasonable to associate the C–H bond breaking with this particular absorbance change. Since the half-time for the decay of light intensity at this temperature is about 60 sec, the rate-limiting step for the formation of the emitter occurs subsequent to breaking of the C-H bond of the aldehyde.

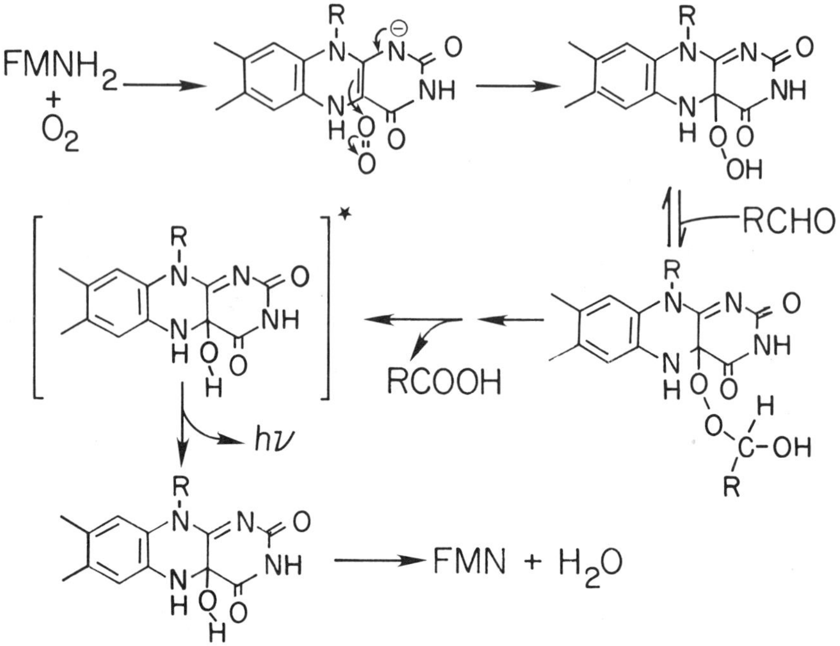

Figure 2 Postulated reaction mechanism and intermediates, including the emitting flavin chromophore in bacterial bioluminescence.

The emitter is, of course, an intermediate of special interest. It has always seemed that excited FMN could be the emitter in a reaction where oxidized FMN—a highly fluorescent molecule—is the product.

However, there are substantial arguments against FMN itself as the emitter (37, 147). Its fluorescence emission is centered at 530 nm whereas the bioluminescence peaks aroung 490 nm, a difference difficult to attribute solely to environmental effects. A more recent and more compelling observation is the fact that luciferase-bound FMN is actually nonfluorescent (8).

However, there is considerable evidence that some form of the flavin, presumably as a chemical intermediate in the reaction, is the emitter. Thus, the emitting species is designated as (E-FHOH)* (Figure 1). Certain flavin analogues with different fluorescence emissions exhibit low but authentic activity with bacterial luciferase, and the color of the resulting bioluminescence is different with different analogues (147). The fluorescence emission spectrum of flavin can be altered by substitution or by protonation (54, 66). Most important, the isolated luciferase intermediate II exhibits a fluorescence emission attributable to its flavin moiety, which exactly matches the bioluminescence emission (10). The emitting species in the mechanism proposed, designated E-FHOH* (Figure 1), is postulated to be the 4a-hydroxy-substituted flavin (Figure 2). In this mechanism, which is similar to the one proposed earlier (50), intermediate II reacts with aldehyde to generate the enzyme-bound, excited flavin, E-FHOH*. As described above, analysis of the kinetic isotope effect in the reaction of II with decanal indicates that the C–H bond breaking of the aldehyde precedes the formation of the emitter, so that in the scheme of Figure 2 at least one additional intermediate must be involved. Since the proposed emitter is the 4a-hydroxy-substituted flavin, it should have essentially the same emission properties as the 4a-peroxy compound. Upon light emission, H_2O and FMN are formed as the chemical products. The latter, because of its low affinity for luciferase, dissociates.

Over the years there have been suggestions that the actual emitter in bacterial bioluminescence might not be the flavin that participates in the reaction (201, 202). The possibility that energy transfer might occur to some other group within the luciferase complex, suggested many years ago (36) but no longer considered likely (37), can be ruled out on the basis of experiments with flavin analogues (147). Similarly, the idea that two flavins are involved, one of which might serve as the emitter, has been ruled out (15, 84).

The idea that emission might occur by energy transfer from the flavin intermediate to some other molecule must also be carefully considered, especially for cases such as the recently discovered "yellow" emitting strain of *Photobacterium fischeri* (163). Moreover, energy transfer has been shown to be involved in coelenterate bioluminescence (37, 150), and extracts of luminous bacteria do contain a protein-bound fluorescent substance whose emission closely matches bioluminescence (129, 148, 205). This material has been shown to be luciferase with a bound, substituted flavin (see below). A material with similar properties has been isolated from cell extracts and postulated to serve as the emitting species by means of an energy transfer mechanism (64). It seems quite likely that this latter material is identical with photoexcitable luciferase, and that it has no such involvement in bioluminescence emission by energy transfer. Actually, the general proposition of energy transfer to some other molecule appears to be ruled out for *Beneckea harveyi* by the properties of mutants with altered emission spectra (33). These mutants (five different ones were characterized) have lesions in the luciferase molecule, resulting in an alteration of the color of luminescence to the same extent both in vivo and in vitro. If energy transfer to another molecule were involved, then a mutation in the luciferase should not result in a color change in vivo; if the lesion were in the proposed secondary emitter, then the purified luciferase should not have its emission in vitro shifted. It would be valuable to obtain similar mutants in other species where the luciferases differ (4).

Quantum Yield

The overall bioluminescence quantum yield (Q_B) is an expression of the number of quanta emitted per molecule of substrate utilized, enzyme turned over, or product formed. The yield can be expressed as a function that takes into account side reactions, efficiency of populating the excited state, and efficiency of emission from the excited state, which may be designated as Q_C, Q_{Ex}, and Q_F, respectively (37). Thus, the product of these terms gives the overall bioluminescence quantum yield $Q_B = Q_C \times Q_{Ex} \times Q_F$.

Considering the various reports and the different values for light standards, as detailed below, we believe that the bioluminescent quantum yield per enzyme turned over under optimum conditions is, within a factor of two, 0.1.

In the bacterial system, Q_B values of 0.3 for $FMNH_2$ (86) and 0.28 for *P. fischeri* luciferase (93) were reported by using a radioactive light standard prepared by Hastings & Weber (95). Nakamura & Matsuda (152), by using a similar standard (153), recorded a quantum yield of 0.2 per molecule of *Photobacterium phosphoreum* luciferase. Lee (117), by using a luminol light standard (121), which should result in lower values [about 40% of the radioactive standard (92)], reported yields of 0.10, 0.047, and 0.12 for dodecanal, $FMNH_2$, and H_2O_2, respectively, with *P. fischeri.* These differences were taken as evidence of the involvement of two flavins in the reaction. McCapra & Hysert (131), also by using the luminol standard, determined a photon yield of 0.13 per molecule of decanoic acid formed with *Achromobacter fischeri* enzyme. Shimomura et al (186) reported quantum yields of about 0.16 per molecule of aldehyde with *A. fischeri.* They used yet another standard, which can be traced to the photomultiplier of Reynolds (92), which should give values about 40% higher.

Hastings et al (84), by using *B. harveyi* luciferase, isolated and purified the actual enzyme intermediate at subzero temperatures and then determined its yield by injecting it into buffer-containing aldehyde (dodecanal) at 22°C. From their data, a value of 0.16 quanta per molecule of intermediate based on flavin content can be calculated; a value of about 0.2 was reported per molecule of intermediate isolated at 0°C (16). One molecule of H_2O_2 is produced via the dark pathway per molecule of intermediate (82). Becvar and co-workers (14, 15) determined the bioluminescence quantum yield in the overall reaction at 21°C, utilizing different relative amounts of $FMNH_2$ and luciferase, and found a quantum yield of about 0.18, invariant over a millionfold range of the ratio of the two and calculated with respect to the amount of the limiting reagent. This result argues against a two-flavin mechanism for the reaction. At the very low $FMNH_2$ and high luciferase concentrations, the probability that a single luciferase molecule could capture more than one $FMNH_2$ molecule becomes very low; so if two flavins were required, many unproductive complexes should be formed, thereby lowering the measured quantum yield.

With regard to the differences in light standards, a fourth determination of the photon emission of standards (142) agrees closely with the luminol standard. The relative differences between this and the radioactive standard were also confirmed (92).

NADH:FMN-Coupled Assay

In the bioluminescence reaction catalyzed by bacterial luciferase, the $FMNH_2$ may be supplied in vitro by NAD(P)H and FMN via the following reaction (69, 93).

$$\text{NAD(P)H} + \text{H}^+ + \text{FMN} \xrightarrow[\text{reductase}]{\text{FMN}} \text{NAD(P)}^+ + \text{FMNH}_2.$$

The enzyme catalyzing the reaction may be referred to as NAD(P)H:FMN oxidoreductase, or by the trivial name FMN reductase or NAD(P)H dehydrogenase. The reduced flavin produced is not tightly bound to the reductase, thus providing $FMNH_2$ for luciferase and allowing the reductase to turn over. Reductases active in such a "coupled" reaction have been studied in four species by five laboratories (47, 60, 65, 103a, 172, 217). Gerlo & Charlier (65) resolved NADH- and NAD(P)H-specific activities in *B. harveyi* and found that the efficiency of coupling to luciferase is about 2.4 times greater with NADH. A similar resolution was achieved by Jablonski & DeLuca (103a) with *B. harveyi* by using affinity chromatography; no such resolution was obtained with *P. fischeri* activities.

In the coupled assay, the light emission from luciferase should be directly related to the product of the concentrations of the two enzymes if the $FMNH_2$ is produced as a free intermediate. This has been found to be so (93). There are several lines of evidence that suggest that the two enzymes are capable of a more specific coupling in this reaction (47), especially the report that added reductase protects luciferase against thermal denaturation (69). Altogether, the evidence is not very strong; the protective effect may have been due to the presence of phosphate in the reductase preparation. Phosphate is now known to protect luciferase against heat denaturation (S.-C. Tu, T. O. Baldwin, and J. W. Hastings, unpublished results).

The coupled system has been used as an assay for NADH and FMN (25, 103, 120, 184, 196, 197), and in principle, luciferase can be coupled to any reaction that produces NAD or FMN or the reduced forms thereof (1a). Jablonski & DeLuca (103) have attached luciferase and FMN reductase to glass rods, thus providing a sensitive and reusable system for assaying low concentrations of NADH and NADPH. Luciferase can also be used to detect and quantitate aldehydes and molecular oxygen (170).

With *P. fischeri* reductase, the addition of NADH prior to FMN in the assay, instead of conversely, results in a markedly lower (20 X) activity (47). The reason for this is not known. Recent kinetic studies (204) indicate that a ping-pong reaction mechanism is involved in *P. fischeri* reductase function such that a reduced enzyme intermediate is formed by reaction with NADH. The NAD^+ product is released prior to reaction of the reduced enzyme with FMN. A similar analysis shows that a sequential mechanism is involved instead in the reaction catalyzed by *B. harveyi* flavin reductase (65). This, along with the fact that the soluble flavin reductase is not coinduced with luciferase (47, 217) underscores the still unresolved question as to whether or not the soluble reductase studied actually is the molecular species responsible for feeding electrons to luciferase in vivo.

Photoexcitable Luciferase

An interesting feature of bacterial bioluminescence is the existence of two types of activity in vitro. In addition to luciferase, there exists photoexcitable luciferase (PL) in both *B. harveyi* and *P. fischeri*; its bioluminescent light emission can be induced only by flash irradiation, and its activity has no dependence upon exogenous FMN or $FMNH_2$ (68). The photoinduced reaction is aldehyde and oxygen dependent (87); these substrates react in the same sequence as in the $FMNH_2$-induced luminescence.

PL has been shown to be a luciferase molecule modified by a firmly but noncovalently bound flavin chromophore, designated B (148), which possesses spectral and photochemical properties characteristic of substitute reduced flavins. PL lacks luciferase ($FMNH_2$ induced) activity. A reconstituted PL (referred to as LB) can be prepared by combining chromophore-free (active) luciferase with the isolated B. PL and LB appear similar in all respects studied (210). It is postulated that B is a substituted reduced flavin that resembles but is not identical with the normal flavin intermediate in II and, thus, is a false intermediate of the bacterial bioluminescence reaction, which remains bound to and inactivates luciferase (205, 206a). The photochemical step is postulated to result in the conversion of B to $FMNH_2$ and thus to generate intermediate I photochemically. In the presence of oxygen and aldehyde, normal bioluminescence then occurs.

Photobacterium phosphoreum preparations also possess a firmly bound flavin-like chromophore in the ratio of about one chromophore per five luciferases (129, 229). The pigment, designated p-flavin, is different from the B of *B. harveyi.* It contains isoalloxazine nucleus and phosphoric acid in a ratio of 1:4, is more hydrophobic than FMN or riboflavin, and does not correspond chromatographically to known flavin derivatives. Although the authors compare this protein to the PLs of *P. fischeri* and *B. harveyi,* its bioluminescence potential in either the chemical or photoinduced assay was not determined. However, "stripped" luciferase in which the p-flavin was removed by denaturation, gel filtration, and renaturation was reported to have the same properties and activity as the native enzyme.

PHYSIOLOGY AND CONTROL

Bioluminescent bacteria provide a unique experimental system in which to correlate activities in vivo with those in vitro. Luminescence, reflecting in vivo luciferase activity, can be followed with ease and accuracy and without perturbing the cells. One has merely to monitor with a light measuring device to obtain instantaneous and quantitative values. In fact, the light emission of single cells can readily be measured in fully induced cells by using the most sensitive photometric instruments (24). For determinations in vitro, small aliquots are removed for later analysis, with the time resolution limited by pipetting. Even with a relatively insensitive photometer ($\sim 10^5$ times less) (148a), only 10^6 cells are required for a single luciferase assay in fully induced cells, i.e. containing maximum luciferase. More cells are required, of course, when the specific luciferase content is less.

Transcriptional Control

INHIBITION OF LUCIFERASE SYNTHESIS Luminous bacteria grown in a complex medium (peptone, yeast extract) exhibit a lag in the development of bioluminescence relative to growth. Kempner & Hanson (108) attributed this lag to an inhibitor (present primarily in the yeast extract), and Eberhard (49) distinguished its action from that of an activator (autoinducer). The phenomenon is notable for its lack of specificity: all (luminous) species apparently respond to inhibitor, and many different bacteria are able to "condition" a medium, presumably by removing it. The inhibitor has a low molecular weight (<1000); it is stable to autoclaving, hot 1 N NaOH or 1 N HCl, and prolonged treatment with H_2O_2. It is soluble in several organic solvents including ethanol.

AUTOINDUCTION An unusual—perhaps unique—mechanism, termed autoinduction, controls the synthesis of the bioluminescence system in the luminous bacteria (162). Autoinduction (illustrated in Figure 3) apparently occurs in all luminous species but nevertheless is quite specific. The luminous bacteria produce a specific substance, termed autoinducer, which accumulates in the culture medium and induces the synthesis of the components of the luminous system. Identification of autoinducer has been plagued by instability of the molecule and the small amounts available. It has been purified from *Photobacterium fischeri*; its mass spectral characteristics compare favorably with those of indole-3-acetaldehyde (molecular weight 159). However, no biological activity can be obtained from an authentic sample of this compound; some other other candidates, isomeric compounds, are being synthesized (B. Fenical and K. Nealson unpublished results).

Several natural isolates of *P. fischeri* have been found that differ in the amount of autoinducer produced (156). A bright strain, MJ-1, produces ten times the normal levels of autoinducer and has been used as a source for its isolation, whereas a dim

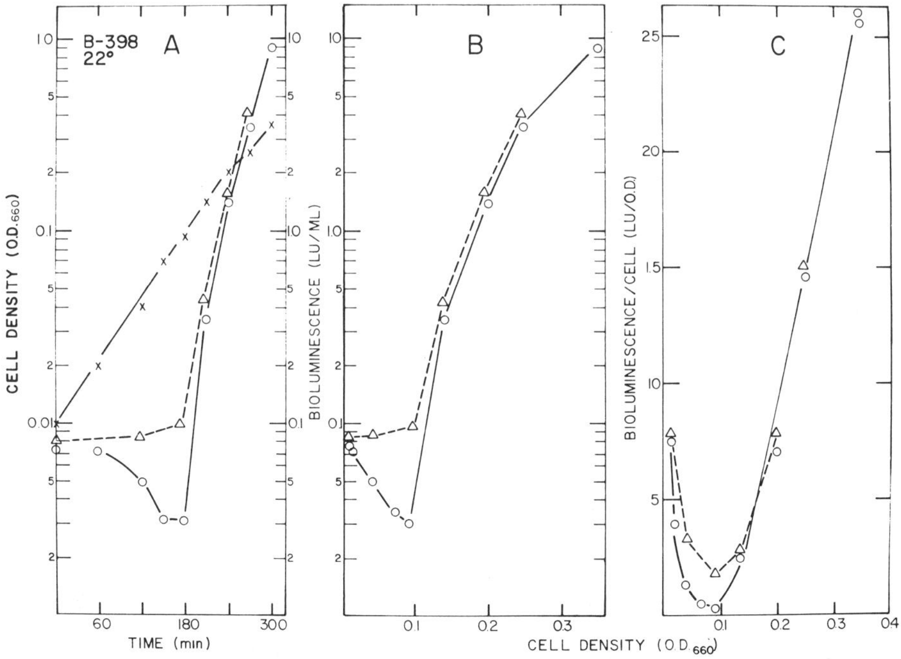

Figure 3 These graphs illustrate the phenomenon of autoinduction, plotted in three different ways, showing that the luminescence per cell is much greater in cells in denser cultures. Symbols: X, cell density; O, bioluminescence in vivo; Δ, bioluminescence in vitro.

strain (B-61) produces very low levels and has been used as a sensitive bioassay for the compound (Figure 4). By using this bioassay, it has been shown that autoinducer is produced continuously and constitutively during growth and accumulates in the medium but not preferentially within the cells. The action of autoinducer can be detected within 10 min at a final concentration as low as 10^{-12} M and is blocked by inhibitors of either protein or mRNA synthesis. This molecule might be viewed as a bacterial pheromone: a small molecule with a specific biological target acting from without at very low concentrations.

The inducer from *Beneckea harveyi,* where autoinduction was first described, has not been purified or studied. However, autoinduction appears to be similar in the different species (49, 162), even though the inducer molecules appear to be species specific (49, 126).

In *Photobacterium phosphoreum* (127, 217), *Photobacterium leiognathi* (91), and *Vibrio albensis* (126), autoinduction has been reported but not carefully studied. Two reports suggest that under some conditions luciferase synthesis may be constitutive for bright strains of *Photobacterium* species (217; R. Katzenelson and S. Ulitzur, personal communication), but detailed knowledge concerning the physiology of control in these cases is lacking.

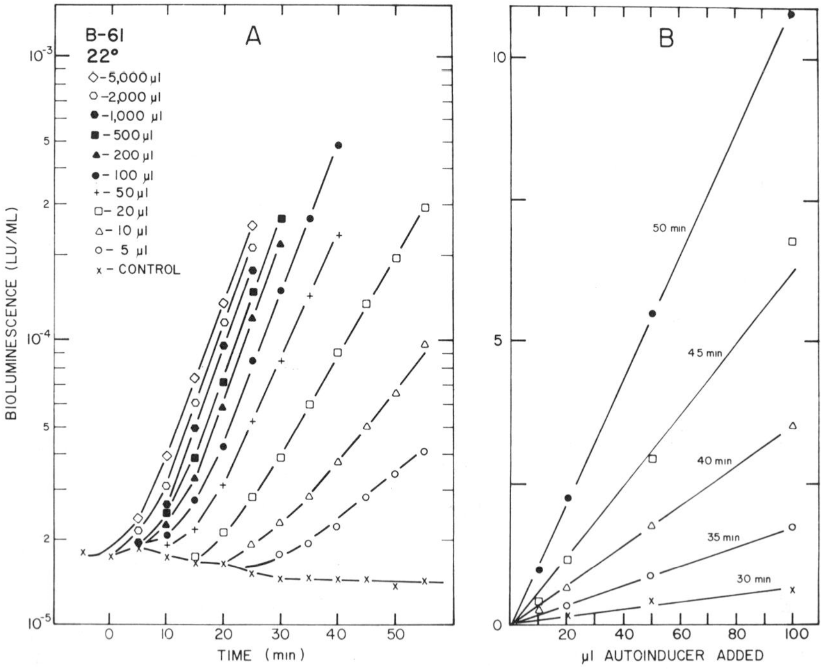

Figure 4 This shows the effect of autoinducer isolated from *Photobacterium fischeri* strain MJ-1 upon the development of luminescence in strain B-61.

MINIMAL MEDIUM: ARGININE AND SALT EFFECTS In a minimal medium, the components are defined and the inhibitors present in complex medium are absent. For these reasons, considerable effort has been made to examine the phenomenon of autoinduction in a minimal medium (154, 162). However, the minimal medium of Farghaly (58), which has been used for all or most of the studies reported, appears to stress the cells and may itself contribute to certain unusual responses. J. Reichelt (personal communication) suggests that this stress may be due to magnesium and/or iron limitation. This might also explain why at least some of the *Photobacterium* species, which have a higher magnesium requirement (175), usually fail to grow in the medium of Farghaly.

Irrespective of the cause, the growth of *Beneckea* species is limited in this minimal medium and the bioluminescence is severely repressed. Although autoinduction occurs, only very low levels of luciferase are actually produced (162). Additional autoinducer does not stimulate additional luminescence in this medium, but arginine and salt (NaCl) have pronounced stimulatory effects on bioluminescence and luciferase synthesis.

Added arginine dramatically stimulates the development of luminescence of *B. harveyi* (MAV) growing in a minimal medium. In the first report of this enhancement, it was concluded that arginine is an inducer of luciferase synthesis (34). Later experiments (162) demonstrated that arginine alone has no stimulatory effect if added prior to autoinduction; the substance thus was viewed as a coinducer or stimulator. Certain compounds structurally and metabolically related to arginine are also capable of stimulating or inhibiting the development of luminescence. Citrulline and argininosuccinate (the immediate biosynthetic precursors of arginine) stimulate, as does proline (34, 220). The mode of action of arginine in its stimulation of bioluminescence is not clear.

Mutants that have "escaped" the arginine requirements have been isolated by selecting those that are brighter (about 100 times more) than wild type on minimal medium (223). These are called minimal bright (MB) mutants and possess correspondingly greater amounts of luciferase. In fact, MB mutants are also overproducers of luciferase (by 50–100%) when grown on a complete medium. The reason for the escape from the arginine requirement is not known. MB mutants apparently do not overproduce arginine, are not altered in cAMP levels, and produce normal levels of autoinducer (221; J. C. Makemson and J. W. Hastings, unpublished results).

B. harveyi grown in a minimal medium is not only sensitive to stimulation by arginine, it also exhibits a great sensitivity to the NaCl concentration of the medium (154, 220). Kössler (115) describes effects of salt concentration on oxygen consumption and luminescence in *Vibrio luminosus* cells transferred into a buffered glucose medium. *B. harveyi* cells grown with 1% instead of 3% NaCl are considerably brighter, because of the synthesis of more luciferase and other components of the luminescent system (154, 220). Although the salt effect has not been investigated in detail, it may be related to the arginine effect discussed above. Cells grown in 1% NaCl exhibit appreciably less arginine stimulation, and MB mutants, which have escaped the arginine requirement, exhibit very little stimulation of the luminous system upon growth in a low salt medium. Neither the salt nor the arginine effect occurs in a complete medium (154, 220). If, as Reichelt suggests, the minimal medium used in these experiments is magnesium limited, one should be cautious in drawing conclusions.

When the minimal medium of Reichelt & Baumann (174) is used, most strains of *B. harveyi, P. leiognathi,* and *P. fischeri* grow well, and specific growth factor requirements can be demonstrated for the more fastidious strains of *P. phosphoreum.* In this medium, the luminescence of *B. harveyi* is not so severely repressed (J. C. Makemson, and J. W. Hastings, unpublished results), but studies of autoinduction, arginine, or salt effects have not been reported. In addition, salt and arginine effects have not been examined in relationship to autoinduction or catabolite repression for the other species of luminous bacteria in this medium. It would be especially interesting to study these effects in *Vibrio albensis,* which has a low salt requirement.

CATABOLITE REPRESSION One of the more intriguing recent findings is that the synthesis of the luminescent system of *B. harveyi* is subject to catabolite repression; glucose represses luciferase synthesis and cAMP reverses this repression (157). This system is analogous to catabolite-sensitive systems in other bacteria in the sense that the control operates over and above induction; in the luminous bacteria, glucose repression occurs even in the presence of adequate autoinducer. Furthermore, Anderson & Pastan (3) have isolated the cAMP binding protein from *B. harveyi* and have shown that it is immunologically homologous with that of *Escherichia coli* and several other enterobacteria. Thus, by analogy with other known catabolite repressible systems, luciferase was proposed to be a "nonessential" enzyme, capable of functioning (presumably to the end of nutrient acquisition) (124, 125) under certain advantageous conditions while being repressed under other conditions (157).

Mutants resistant to (escaped from) catabolite repression have been isolated as "bright on glucose" (BG) phenotypes. One type of lesion that might be expected to result in the BG phenotype is a glucose transport mutant, but none of the BG mutants have been identified as such (158). In fact, sugar transport mutants of *B. harveyi* also do not exhibit the BG phenotype on glucose. When "tight" phosphotransferase system mutants were isolated, all of those tested were found to be less bright, about 10–50% of the wild-type level (122). It seems possible that such an effect could be exerted through changes in intracellular cAMP, but this possibility was not examined.

Standard negative selection techniques were used by Ulitzur & Yashphe (212) to isolate a mutant (UY-437) that is nonluminous unless supplied with exogenous cAMP. The mutant is pleiotropic for a variety of other characters; as expected, it is deficient for a variety of other functions for which cAMP is normally required in enteric bacteria (125). Although UY-437 can be used to assay cAMP, it is not ideal; the lower limit of detection is only about 0.5 nM, and the mutant itself exhibits a high rate of reversion. The isolation of similar mutants by using deletion mutagens might allow for a more suitable sensitive cAMP bioassay.

In the absence of added cAMP, UY-437 is stimulated by low concentrations of cGMP (213). At higher cGMP levels inhibition occurs; in the presence of added cAMP, cGMP has an inhibitory effect only. The results indicate complicated interactions between the cyclic nucleotides in these procaryotes.

For other species of luminous bacteria, catabolite repression is less well understood. Henry & Michelson (99) reported that a strain of *P. leiognathi* displays a strong permanent glucose repression that is not reversed by cAMP. As expected, growth of these organisms in a glucose-limited chemostat allows continuous bright luminescence. In *P. phosphoreum,* strain WSU, Makemson (127) reported that glucose repression occurs, but he was unable to demonstrate its reversal by cAMP. *P. fischeri,* on the other hand, exhibits a transient repression when transferred to a glucose medium. This repression is not reversed by cAMP, and once the cells are glucose adapted, no further effect of glucose is seen, even in batch culture (183).

There are other reports of diverse effects of added nutrients, inhibitors, and metabolites upon the development of the luminous system (34, 44, 45, 52, 58, 101, 127, 157, 162, 179, 190). Many of these effects might now be capable of interpretation in terms of our current knowledge of the physiology of the bacteria. In other cases, it might be that the differences reported are simply a characteristic of the different bacterial species and thus related to the specific physiology associated with the niches the different species occupy.

OXYGEN AND THE SYNTHESIS OF THE BIOLUMINESCENCE SYSTEM Oxygen is important not only as a substrate for the reaction but as a controlling element in the synthesis of the luminous system. Because oxygen has an extremely high affinity for luciferase (78), it can limit the aerobic growth of luminous bacteria at concentrations where it is still fully active as a substrate for the luminous reaction (160). At these low oxygen concentrations, where growth is limited, the synthesis of luciferase is similarly limited in some species but not in others. In the latter, cells develop with a high specific luciferase content.

The first group, in which there is a tight coupling between growth and luciferase synthesis, includes *B. harveyi* and *P. leiognathi.* When growth is limited by low oxygen levels, synthesis of luciferase is likewise limited. Thus, oxygen-limited cultures develop as much luciferase per cell as nonlimited ones. For *P. phosphoreum* and *P. fischeri,* quite a different response to oxygen limitation is observed. At concentrations where growth is limited by low oxygen, luciferase synthesis is not, resulting in cells with very high levels of luciferase. The extreme differences in conditions that allow maximum synthesis of the luminescent system for different species suggest that these species may occupy niches that are fundamentally different with regard to oxygen concentration and/or the necessity for the presence of the luminescent system (160).

ECOLOGICAL IMPLICATIONS It is apparent that control of the synthesis of the luminous system at the level of transcription is a major factor relating to many aspects of the biology and ecology of the luminous bacteria. If one considers all of the factors (inhibitors, autoinducer, catabolite repression, arginine, and oxygen), then the regulation of the synthesis of the luminous system can involve a multiplicity of controls in a given species. It is possible to envisage different conditions under which some of the factors might come into play and that certain factors might be significant in some species and not in others. For example, for bacteria free in seawater, autoinducer could not accumulate, whereas with bacteria living as symbionts within a light organ it would. Thus, autoinduction could be viewed as an "environmental sensing" mechanism, which functions to turn off the synthesis of the luminescent system when the cell density is low, when bioluminescence may have no functional importance. Under certain nutrient-rich conditions, possibly in the gut of fish, where luminescence as such may not be functional, catabolite repression might operate and repress luciferase synthesis. The species in which low oxygen inhibits growth but not luciferase synthesis might inhabit a niche, perhaps some type of luminous organ, where oxygen is poised at this level, permitting luciferase synthesis with little or no cell growth. The elucidation of mechanisms controlling transcription and their applicability for the different species will be of utmost importance in building models to explain the ecology of the luminous bacteria and to understand their physiology under various life-styles. Differences in species may offer clues regarding both their versatility and their role(s) in the marine environment.

Pathway and Metabolism

The bioluminescent system can be viewed as a branch of the electron transport pathway in which electrons are shunted to oxygen at the level of flavin, essentially as postulated by van Schouwenburg in 1938 (see 76).

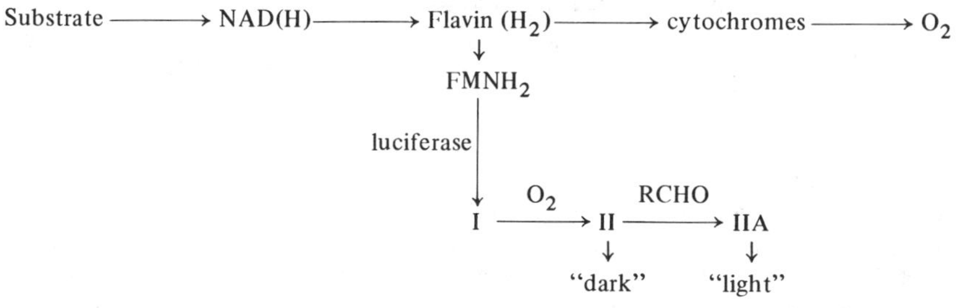

Assuming that the several luciferase intermediates elucidated from studies in vitro occur also in vivo, controls and limitations could operate at a variety of sites, some involving luciferase and its intermediates, others in the associated electron transport system. The expression of luciferase in vivo may be less than maximal if substrates are limiting. This occurs during the eclipse period, that is, prior to the induction of the luminescent system when both aldehyde, and possibly reduced flavin, are limiting (162).

OXYGEN In 1668, Boyle demonstrated the requirement of air for bioluminescence, which, as is now known, is a result of the participation of oxygen as a substrate in the luciferase reaction itself. It has also been known for a long time that luminous bacteria provide an unusually sensitive test for oxygen, which has found recent application (170). The bacteria continue to emit light at a maximum intensity at oxygen concentrations where the respiratory oxygen uptake rate of the bacteria is less than 10% of normal (77, 188). During strict anaerobiosis, luminescence ceases, and upon reoxygenation, an excess flash of luminescence occurs (105). This can now be interpreted in terms of an accumulation of intermediate I, the luciferase-$FMNH_2$ complex. Similarly, van Schouwenburg's (see 76) demonstration that electron transport through the luciferase system can occur without light emission can be interpreted as involving flow through intermediate II, the dark pathway. No contemporary studies have reevaluated this matter, especially with regard to possible control points in vivo for electron flow. For example, if luciferase is not fully expressed in vivo, as when aldehyde is lacking, do electrons nevertheless flow through luciferase unabated, or is there some control mechanism?

REDUCING POWER The system for the production of luciferase-$FMNH_2$ in vivo and its possible localization have not been elucidated. As described earlier, soluble flavin reductases coupling to luciferase in vitro have been isolated, but their role in vivo may still be considered questionable. The reductases studied are not coinduced with luciferase, and since there are a considerable number of proteins that are coinduced [five soluble (143) and four membrane polypeptides (164)], one of these may couple electron flow to luciferase (see below).

ALDEHYDE During the early phase of growth in a batch culture (the eclipse phase, where no new luciferase is synthesized), the luminescence in vivo actually decreases, whereas the luciferase already present stays constant (162). This decrease is due in part to aldehyde limitation; exogenously added long-chain aldehydes stimulate luminescence during this period. In general, any growth situation or genetic lesion that results in repression of luciferase synthesis also leads to aldehyde limitation, as demonstrated by stimulability of luminescence of cells by exogenous aldehyde. One implication of such results is that the synthesis of aldehyde is closely coupled to that of luciferase, a view supported by studies on different classes of aldehyde mutants (32). After aldehyde synthesis, it is no longer limiting and luciferase is expressed maximally. Aldehyde limitation might be thought of as a mechanism to turn off the system more rapidly than occurs by dilution and loss of luciferase. However, it could also be viewed as nothing more than the consequence of the genetic organization of the system, and as such of no particular significance in terms of the control of luminescence in vivo.

Although the identity of the in vivo aldehyde is not definitively proven, there has been some progress in our understanding. The report of the occurrence of nonanal (59) must be discounted because the cells used were harvested in late stationary phase, long after luciferase-specific aldehyde synthesis has ceased. Shimomura et al (187), by using both *Photobacterium phosphoreum* and *Achromobacter fischeri*, isolated small quantities of endogenous aldehydes, mostly of chain lengths of 12, 14, and 16 carbons, in relative abundance of 5, 63, and 30%, respectively, in *P. phosphoreum* (total about 600 nmol from 40 g of cell paste) and of 36, 32, and 20% (total 90 nmol) in *A. fischeri.* Smaller amounts of other chain lengths were found. The quantity was estimated to be sufficient to sustain maximum in vivo luminescence for only about 1 sec. The involvement in bioluminescence of the compounds isolated was suggested by the fact that by similar procedures less than 10% of this amount was isolated from a dark aldehyde mutant of *A. fischeri.* The relationship of that mutant to the wild type used was not specified; a study utilizing temperature-sensitive aldehyde mutants (see below) would be desirable.

Aldehyde-deficient mutants (30, 32, 161, 180) are very dim (10^{-2}–10^{-5} of wild type) but contain normal amounts of luciferase, so that a near normal level of luminescence in vivo will occur with exogenously added aldehyde. In the early studies, attention was directed to the penetration time of the different aldehydes (181, 182), and it was concluded that decanal was not the in vivo aldehyde for *Beneckea harveyi* because the stimulation was transitory (161). More recent studies have provided insight into the nature of the natural aldehyde, its synthesis and control (32, 187). In several independently isolated aldehyde mutants (of both *B. harveyi* and *Photobacterium fischeri*), the bioluminescence has been found to be stimulated by exogenously added long-chain fatty acid (S. Ulitzur and J. W. Hastings, unpublished results). In contrast to aldehyde, where different chain lengths are all reasonably effective, the 14 carbon acid is far more effective than any other chain length. This is consistent with the results of Shimomura et al (187) and the postulate that the natural aldehyde is tetradecanal, and it can be explained by assuming specificity of a putative enzyme converting acid to aldehyde for bioluminescence.

INHIBITORS Inhibitors have been effectively used as a way to deduce the pathways involved in bacterial bioluminescence (76, 133). The view that luciferase acts essentially as a shunt of the electron transport system has been generally confirmed and accepted but not further elaborated. It would be valuable to know the effects of many of the different classes of inhibitors now available, especially those related to energy metabolism, particularly in relation to autoinduction, repression, and salt effects. Some recent studies have been concerned with inhibitors of macromolecular synthesis during the induction of the luminescent system (34, 162).

With the isolated coupled system (NADH initiated), a few studies of the effects of inhibitors of electron transport and phosphorylation have been reported (47). The results were difficult to interpret, suggesting the existence of more than one reductase in the preparation. An isolated system more assuredly related to the pathway of electron flow in vivo is needed.

Not many inhibitors have been reported that block the luciferase reaction itself. Exceptions are two inhibitors reported to be specific for mixed function oxidases (159); however, their inhibitory effects on luciferase do not seem to relate to that. One interferes with the binding of $FMNH_2$ to luciferase (formation of intermediate I) whereas the other competes with aldehyde. A large variety of other compounds, mostly long-chain aliphatics, also compete with aldehyde without causing any decrease in the quantum yield (88). A substrate alternative to aldehyde (long-chain dialkyl sulfide), which can be hydroxylated, does dissipate the enzyme intermediate and thus reduces its potential for light emission (130).

The possibility for the utilization of luminous bacteria as sensitive detection agents for noxious or even contraband chemical substances has been widely discussed in newspapers and periodicals and from at least one laboratory (112, 113). It seems possible that some such substances might interfere with the aldehyde interaction with luciferase.

A final class of compounds that are effective inhibitors are those that react directly with luciferase. Amino acid residues whose modification has been found to cause inactivation include lysine (succinic anhydride) (138, 139), cysteine (*p*-hydroxymercuribenzoate iodoacetamide, N-ethylmaleimide, sodium tetrathionate) (40, 166, 167), and histidine (ethoxyformic anhydride) (39).

ANAESTHETICS Recent studies from several laboratories (144, 145, 224, 227) have confirmed and extended knowledge concerning the inhibition of the luminescence of bacteria by anaesthetic agents (76, 104). The relative potencies of a variety of different anaesthetics when acting on luminous bacteria parallel their relative potencies in causing general anaesthesia in humans (72, 225, 226). Anaesthetic sensitivity in vivo varies during the growth cycle in liquid cultures, with the lowest during the eclipse period, prior to the onset of new luciferase and aldehyde syntheses (144). The sensitivity during this time may be increased by small amounts of exogenously added aldehyde (decanal), whereas higher aldehyde concentrations reverse the inhibition. This could be interpreted by assuming that some bioluminescence (which is less sensitive to anaesthetics) occurs in the absence of aldehyde, whereas with aldehyde-dependent luminescence anaesthetics are competitive with aldehyde. Indeed, the low level of luminescence of an aldehyde mutant (see Table 2) is insensitive to concentrations of anaesthetic that are usually inhibitory and is actually stimulated many-fold at high concentrations (e.g. 4% halothane or 1.5% methoxyflurane; D. C. White, personal communication). Might this aldehyde- and anaesthetic-independent luminescence be attributable to some fraction of the luciferase that has a different type of association with the cell membrane (see below)?

With purified *B. harveyi* luciferase, all anaesthetic agents studied (methoxyflurane, halothane, chloroform, diethyl ether, and cyclopropane) were shown to be inhibitors competitive with aldehyde (1, 145, 224). This is probably the first demonstration of a competitive inhibition by general anaesthetics in any enzyme system and provides a model for the way in which anaesthetics may exert their effects via proteins. With shorter chain-length aldehydes, anaesthetics may actually stimulate bioluminescence intensity, perhaps being similar in this regard to isobutanol and certain organic solvents (88).

An especially interesting new finding is that the effectiveness of halothane in inhibiting bacterial luminescence in vivo depends upon the growth temperature as compared to the temperature at which the anaesthetic is tested (111). If the test temperature is more than 2°C below the growth temperature, the effective anaesthetic dose required increases abruptly by more than 25%, implicating a phase change in membrane lipids in anaesthetic action. The results are consistent with the suggestion that luciferase in vivo is membrane associated, and that anaesthetics act on proteins in membranes.

MEMBRANES Bacterial luciferase is a very soluble protein, and until recently there has been no evidence that its activity might be associated with membranes. However, the biochemical link of luminescence with electron transport, its aldehyde requirement, and its sensitivity in vivo to anaesthetics had suggested this possibility. Two lines of research now provide clear indications of the involvement of membranes.

In all previous reports with all the different species and strains, luciferase activity was associated exclusively with the soluble fraction, and all attempts to demonstrate membrane-related activity were negative. But Balakrishnan & Langerman (4) have reported that treatment with deoxycholate is needed to achieve the solubilization of luciferase activity in extracts of the S-1 strain of *P. leiognathi,* and that the purified material is a glycoprotein whose activity is lost upon treatment with lysozyme.

The second line of evidence is that there are membrane polypeptides implicated in the bioluminescence system (164). Cells lacking the system were obtained by two independent means (harvesting prior to induction and mutation). Cells harvested prior to induction were compared to induced cells. Temperature-sensitive (conditional) mutants were compared at permissive and nonpermissive temperatures. At least four membrane polypeptides appear to be associated with luminescence; they are absent in cells prior to induction and also in certain dark mutants at the nonpermissive temperature. Clear differences between such luminous and nonluminous cells were also observed by electron microscopy of replicas of freeze-cleaved membranes.

Energetics

The energies involved in bioluminescent reactions are considerably higher than those encountered in other biological reactions; photons at 500 nm are equivalent to about 50 kcal (210 kJ) per einstein. Such light-emitting reactions thus are highly exergonic (128), the equivalent of perhaps 6 ATP per photon. However, if the quantum yield is only about 0.1, and if a luciferase cycle that fails to emit a photon is equally costly energetically, then the cell foregoes the production of about 60 ATP molecules per photon.

The question as to what this apparently significant energy expenditure (both photic and biosynthetic) represents to the cellular economy has often been raised, especially in connection with the possible selective advantage of dark strains.

Fully induced bioluminescent bacteria (with maximum luciferase) emit light at an appreciable rate, somewhere between 10^3 and 10^5 photons per sec per cell, depending upon the strain (76, 79). Eymers & Van Schouwenburg (56, 57) were able to deduce from KCN inhibition studies that 20% of oxygen taken up was utilized in the luminescent system. Although no primary data was provided, Watanabe et al (217) reported that 0.045 photons were emitted per O_2 consumed in *Photobacterium phosphoreum.* Based on a bioluminescence quantum yield of 0.2, they thus estimated that 23% of the total cellular O_2 uptake was due to the luciferase system. In our own laboratories, oxygen consumption and light emission of different species were compared, both before induction and at peak luminescence (S. Ulitzur, D.

Karl, K. H. Nealson, and J. W. Hastings, unpublished observations). Assuming a bioluminescence quantum yield of 0.1 per O_2 consumed, we also find that a highly significant portion (~10%) of the oxygen consumed goes via the light-emitting reaction. But in these experiments, no appreciable change in oxygen consumption per cell occurred over the course of the growth cycle, although luminescence differed by a factor of 1000. Dim and dark mutants of *P. phosphoreum* (217) and also of *Photobacterium fischeri* and *Beneckea harveyi* consume oxygen at the same rate as the wild-type strains. Thus, finely tuned control mechanisms must operate if, as would be deduced, the amount of oxygen utilized by the light-emitting system varies relative to that consumed in the respiratory pathway over the course of the growth cycle, whereas total consumption remains constant.

In view of this apparently major energy commitment to luminescence, Ulitzur & Hastings (211) measured ATP levels per cell and found a significant (>10X) drop prior to and during the period of induction of the luminescence system. The dip did not occur in those mutants that fail to synthesize the luminescence system, including the cAMP mutant UY437. The fact that the activity per se of the luminescent system is not wholly responsible was indicated by the fact that mutants with a temperature-sensitive luciferase still showed a dip in ATP at the restrictive temperature. Aldehyde-deficient mutants fell into two classes: in some (M-17) there was no dip, showing that it is also not the synthesis of the luciferase that is responsible; in others (TSAS-1) the dip was even more pronounced than in the wild type. The results suggested that a metabolite belonging to the pathway of aldehyde synthesis is involved in the dip in the ATP pool.

A phenomenon that may be related is the decrease in CO_2 evolution reported to occur just prior to induction (114). Although no O_2 consumption data was presented, the decrease in CO_2 evolution was interpreted as a metabolic shift that diverts electrons to the luminescence system. Still another indication of the shift in energy utilization along with the induction of luminescence is the recent calorimetric investigation of *B. harveyi* and *Photobacterium leiognathi* (135). It was demonstrated that there seems to be a pause in the rate of metabolic heat production at the same point in time that luciferase begins to be synthesized.

A question asked more than once is whether the emission of the 10^3–10^5 photons per sec per bacterium occurs randomly in time or in some pulsative or discontinuous fashion. Hagins et al (71a) concluded that emission was random; a Russian group has reported that individual bacteria emit light in pulses (22).

Acid Production

In 1928, Hill (101) stated that "the most characteristic activity of luminous bacteria seems to be that of acid production." Indeed, all groups of luminous bacteria, when grown anaerobically on glucose, prove to be respectable facultative anaerobes (102; Ruby and Nealson, unpublished experiments), as was demonstrated in 1942 (46) for *P. phosphoreum.* They are fermentors of the "mixed acid" type, producing a mixture of formic, acetic, lactic, and succinic acids.

Except for one species, *P. leiognathi,* an unusual metabolic feature is that pyruvic acid is produced during aerobic growth (E. G. Ruby and K. H. Nealson, unpublished data). With *B. harveyi, P. fischeri,* and *P. phosorpheum,* glucose carbon is inefficiently utilized, and for some strains as much as 50% appears in the growth medium as pyruvate. Pyruvate is not a usual excretion product in bacteria; it occurs only in cases of apparently unbalanced growth resulting from pH stress, oxygen limitation, or metabolic inhibition (R. Hungate, personal communication). One reported exception, which is interesting, is *Pseudomonas natriegens* (171), an estuarine isolate subsequently reclassified as *Beneckea natriegens* and shown to be closely related to *B. harveyi* (177). The fact that *P. leiognathi* apparently does not form pyruvate suggests that its ecology, especially its specific symbiotic relationship, might be distinctly different from that of other luminous bacteria.

The luminous bacteria can metabolize a wide variety of carbohydrates and amino acids (175); however, pyruvate excretion occurs only during the metabolism of glucose, glucose-6-phosphate, N-acetylglucosamine, fructose, and mannose. Utilization of 17 other carbohydrates such as glycerol, mannitol, maltose, glucose-1-phosphate, ribose, or glucosamine is not accompanied by pyruvate production (E. G. Ruby and K. H. Nealson, unpublished observations). A similar pattern of specificity is observed with *B. harveyi.* It is interesting to note that although glucose and galactose are metabolized at the same rate by *P. fischeri,* over five times as much pyruvate is excreted per mole of glucose than per mole of galactose. Thus, pyruvate production is not a general phenomenon of carbohydrate metabolism. Growth on amino acids (peptone or tryptone) leads to the excretion of a small amount of acetate, but no pyruvate.

It is possible that the inefficient substrate utilization with acid excretion has functional importance in the specific association of these bacteria in the light organs of luminous fishes (183). For example, the pyruvate excreted may be utilized by the cells of the host. Such a relationship may very well represent an example of nutrient exchange, a phenomenon now considered common in symbiotic relationships (189) and as such may be a reflection of a specific physiological adaptation of these luminous bacteria that is compatible with a symbiotic life-style.

Color

Prior to the discovery this year of a yellow-emitting strain of *P. fischeri* (163), the emission spectra of all luminous bacteria have been characterized by a single broad band peaking in the vicinity of 490 nm (185, 193) with a tail well into the red (183a). Although consistent species-related differences have not been established, *P. phosphoreum* appears to be blue shifted compared to other species [λ_{max} 465 nm (193) or 478 nm (132)]. Seliger & Morton (185) reported on 18 strains whose peak emissions ranged from 478–505 nm, with *Achromobacter fischeri* and *P. fischeri* (origin of strains not specified) at 497 and 505 nm, respectively. *P. leiognathi* was reported to emit maximally at 491 nm (91).

Although the color of light emission in vitro from the reaction with purified luciferase is tolerably close to that of the living cell (93), the really surprising and still unexplained fact is that it may differ, and substantially so in some instances. Thus, although the wavelength of the peak luminescence in vivo may differ by up to 25 nm in the different strains, the color of the luminescence from luciferases isolated from the different strains is the same, or nearly so (132, 185), meaning that in some cases there is a big difference between in vivo and in vitro. With luciferase isolated from 11 of the 18 Seliger & Morton (185) strains, the peak emissions were at 497 ± 2 nm and not far away for four others (491, 491, 493, and 500 nm). These differences in vivo are not due to different aldehydes, as judged by the fact that aldehyde mutants respond to exogenous aldehydes of different chain lengths with the same color of light as the wild type. It is probably not due to different flavins; the light is the same in crude extracts utilizing endogenous flavin. Seliger & Morton (185) suggested that it could be due to self-absorption effects within the bacterial cell.

Since the specific conformation of the luciferase at the site where the emitter is bound may have significant effects upon the color of the emission, as documented for firefly luciferase (185), the differences observed for the different bacterial strains in vivo might be attributed to luciferase conformation in vivo. If the functional luciferase is membrane bound in vivo, then its specific conformation in different strains could easily differ, causing the differences of the magnitude observed.

The yellow-emitting strain (Y-1; Table 2) is different in that it possesses a discrete band at 545 nm along with a shoulder or second peak in the blue at 500 nm (163). The relative proportions of the energy in these two bands may be variable, depending upon experimental conditions, especially temperature. In cells grown at about 30°C the yellow band is virtually completely absent (S.-C. Tu, K. H. Nealson, and J. W. Hastings, unpublished observations). The occurrence of the yellow band is also dependent upon the intact cell; the reaction in vitro with luciferase isolated from the yellow strain exhibits only a single band in the blue, peaking at 500 nm (163). An aldehyde dark mutant of Y-1 responds to exogenous aldehyde by exhibiting bioluminescence with both bands represented.

The phenomenon might be explained in terms of energy transfer, resulting, for example, from a second pigment that acts as an acceptor and that, in the intact cell, is associated with the luciferase. Upon cell lysis, dissociation and dilution result in loss of transfer efficiency. Attempts to isolate such a pigment have been unsuccessful. A second possibility is similar to the one discussed earlier, namely that the luciferase localization in vivo determines a conformation, as compared to that in solution, such that the environment of the excited state is different than it is with luciferase in aqueous solution. The two discrete bands suggest a mechanism involving two alternate forms of the emitter, which could result from its ionization. An ionization of the emitter or the ionization of a group on the protein near the emitter might occur in the excited state where it is known that the pK values can be radically different from those in a corresponding ground state. Again, there is precedent for this in firefly bioluminescence where there are two emitting species of the product molecule, the dianion (λ_{max} 560 nm) and the ketoanion (λ_{max} 610 nm) (228).

Assuming that Y-1 is not simply a singly occurring, nonselected, natural mutant, its existence has interesting implications, ecological and otherwise. Taxonomically Y-1 is classed as *P. fischeri,* which occurs as a symbiont (Table 1). However, the known hosts harbor only blue-green, not yellow, species, so the specificity of symbiosis must be more sophisticated than the taxonomic characters used to define the species.

If Y-1 itself occurs as a symbiont, it may be in some organism that emits yellow light (76). Without specific association with such an organ, its light-emitting capability would not seem to have much selective advantage, since blue light is more readily transmitted in seawater and more commonly utilized in photoreception by marine organisms. An alternate possibility is that this is an instance where the light-emitting capability is associated with some biochemical function where the reception of the emitted photons by some other organism has no functional importance (79). If so, the color of the light would be irrelevant.

MUTANTS

Induced Mutants

A variety of mutants altered with regard to bioluminescence have been isolated after mutagenesis with n-methyl-n-nitro-n'-nitrosoguanidine, ICR 191, acridine dyes, or ultraviolet light (30–33, 161, 180, 212, 220). Most studies have been carried out with *Beneckea harveyi,* and with the exception of two classes selected for increased brightness, all mutants have been selected originally as dim or dark. No selective or enrichment method for obtaining darks is available, so they are located by tedious visual screening of surviving clones under dim red light. Luminous colonies emit green and reflect the red light and thus look white; dim mutants only reflect and thus look red. All dark mutants emit a very dim luminescence.

The general classes of luminescence mutants are listed in Table 2 (p. 565), which shows the characteristics that have been examined. The temperature-sensitive mutants (selected initially as darks at 35°C, which are luminescent at 25°C) have been of particular value. At the different temperatures they display different luminescence phenotypes, attributable to luciferase structure, luminescent system synthesis, and aldehyde synthesis.

Temperature-sensitive luciferase mutants are selected as those whose luminescence is extinguished rapidly ($<$1 min) upon transfer from a permissive to a nonpermissive temperature. Of about 35 cases examined, selection on this basis invariably yielded clones producing luciferases, which after isolation were confirmed to be more thermolabile (ranging from 22°–42°C) than that of the wild type (30). The location of the lesion was not confined to one of the two subunits, and different specific residue(s) within the subunit in question might be involved in any particular mutant. Such mutants appeared "renaturation" deficient and could presumably be used to map the residues responsible for the structural integrity of the protein molecule.

Nonconditional luciferase mutants were obtained in two ways (31). The most powerful method involved screening the residual luciferase activity of dark mutants for changes in turnover rate. As described above, luciferase activity can be measured in a nonturnover ($FMNH_2$ initiated) assay, so irrespective of the quantity (or absolute activity) the turnover rate can be readily determined. Altered kinetics

(AK), fast or slow, mutant luciferases thus could be obtained for study; over 50 were obtained, and 16 of these were examined in detail. As a class they were not thermally unstable, although a few were. In general, they exhibited altered binding towards one or the other or both substrates, although two (AK-9 and AK-16) showed no alterations in this regard. For most, substrate binding was less avid, though in one case (AK-20) the affinity for $FMNH_2$ was greater than that of the wild type. Without exception, the lesions were located in the α subunit; all of these different lesions have in common the ability to alter the turnover rate and thus must be at or near the active center, so that either directly or indirectly (as for example by a conformational change) the rate constants or stabilities of intermediates in the reaction can be altered.

FB-1 is another luciferase mutant that illustrates the power of selection with this system and provides the exception to the rule that all mutants concerned with the active center are located on the α subunit. By using the dithionite assay (137) and two different flavin concentrations, it is possible to detect flavin binding mutants. This allows one to select for substrate binding mutants independent of the constraint that the turnover rate be altered. Of the three selected, two were located on the α subunit and one on the β, illustrating that substrate binding can be affected by residues on an adjacent subunit (29).

Aldehyde mutants have been referred to in an earlier section. They are selected as those darks that become bright when the colonies are exposed to aldehyde vapor. Both temperature-sensitive aldehyde synthesis (TSAS) (30) and non-temperature-sensitive mutants (161, 180, 181) have been studied.

In TSAS-F1, the onset of the decline or rise following a temperature shift occurs without a lag, with a half-time for the response in either direction of about 3 min. In TSAS-1 on the other hand, there is a 10-min lag after transfer from 36°–23°C, and in the converse direction, there is a 40-min lag before appreciable loss of luminescence begins. Assuming that the aldehyde factor itself is not temperature sensitive, then the fact that there are "rapid out" mutants indicates that there cannot be a large aldehyde pool, as has also been concluded by Shimomura et al (187). TSAS-1 was postulated to involve one of the factors controlling the synthesis of an enzyme involved in aldehyde synthesis, whereas in TSAS-F1 the lesion was postulated to be in a structural gene for such an enzyme, making the enzyme thermally unstable (32).

Among the non-temperature-sensitive dark aldehyde mutants of *Beneckea harveyi,* M-16, M-17, and M-18 (Table 2) were found to respond not only to aldehyde but also to tetradecanoic acid (S. Ulitzur and J. W. Hastings, unpublished results). Aldehyde mutants of *Photobacterium fischeri* have been found to respond similarly. Luciferase has long been known to be relatively nonspecific in its aldehyde requirement over the range of 8–16 carbon chain length, thus explaining why aldehyde mutants respond (though to varying degrees) to different chain-length aldehydes (181). The fact that, of the different chain-length acids, tetradecanoic acid is by far the most effective in the mutants suggests that there is a higher degree of specificity in the enzyme, which converts the acid to the aldehyde. This putative enzyme has not been isolated. Meighen et al (136) have isolated an aldehyde dehydrogenase (molecular weight 120,000, two 60,000-molecular-weight subunits), which is coinducible with luciferase and exhibits a specificity for long-chain aldehydes similar to that of luciferase. However, attempts to demonstrate its reversibility and possible involvement in the conversion of acid to aldehyde have not been successful.

Assuming that a long-chain acid is the precursor of aldehyde, then the M16-type mutant must be blocked prior to acid formation, whereas the temperature-sensitive mutants (which do not respond to exogenous acid) must have lesions after the acid-forming step. The possibility that the acid produced in the luminescent reaction is recycled has been discussed (32).

Mutants in which very low levels of luciferase are synthesized (but with wild-type properties) may be classed as luminescent system (LS) mutants. In one temperature-sensitive LS mutant examined (TSLS-1), the defect involves also a number of membrane peptides as deduced from gel electrophoresis of isolated solubilized membranes of TSLS-1 compared at permissive and nonpermissive temperatures. The results implicate membrane polypeptides in the bioluminescence system (164). An LS-type mutant conditional upon added cAMP for luminescence has also been reported (212). Nonconditional LS mutants have also been obtained in large numbers after mutagenesis with n-methyl-n-nitro-n'-nitrosoguanidine and with acriflavin. In the latter case, relatively large numbers of this class are obtained, and they are pleiotropic in nature, involving also capsular and flagellar alterations. Indeed, they may be the same type as the spontaneous K variants (see below) (109, 161).

As described previously, luminescence and luciferase synthesis are repressed in *B. harveyi* cells grown in a minimal salts medium. Added arginine is known to increase the luminescence in vivo and in vitro in such cells (34, 162). Mutants that are bright in such a medium without added arginine have been isolated and classed as minimal bright (MB) mutants (220, 223). These mutants, such as MB-4, produce higher levels of luminescence than the wild type both in vivo and in vitro, and in both complex and minimal media both with and without arginine. This is attributed to the production of an increased amount of luciferase, which itself is wild type in terms of its specific activity.

BG mutants are those that are brighter than the wild type when grown on a complete medium with added glucose. BG-1 may be representative of a class of phosphotransferase system-negative mutants that are visibly luminous on glucose but actually less bright than the wild type in the absence of glucose. Actually, all phosphotransferase system-negative mutants thus far isolated are less bright than the wild type (122). Other BG mutants are truly bright on glucose, and they are apparently normal with regard to glucose transport. In only one, BG-5, has a specific lesion been shown; it is defective in pyruvate carboxylase.

Another type of chemically induced mutant is the color shift mutant reported by Cline & Hastings (33). This mutant was one of several identified because of its (kinetically) altered luciferase and later was shown to be altered spectrally in its emission, both in vivo and in vitro.

Spontaneous and Natural Isolates

DARK (K) VARIANTS Luminous bacteria kept under laboratory conditions display an instability in their light-emitting capacity; they commonly give rise to dark variants. Actually none of these dark variants are truly dark: all exhibit a dim luminscence, the exact level of which may vary between 10^{-2} and 10^{-5} of the wild type. Thus, they do not lack the luciferase genes; they simply express these genes at extremely low levels. They will be referred to as K variants. Although the phenomenon was reported long ago by Beijerinck (19, 20), it has not yet been well described.

K variants are low in luciferase and luciferase cross-reacting material. All or many of the other components of the luminescent system are also lacking. Failure to produce the luminescent system is not attributable to a lack of inducer, nor is synthesis stimulated by cAMP. K variants are stable and heritable and are pleiotropic. In addition to their deficiencies in bioluminescence, they are altered in colonial morphology (more oblate and translucent) and flagellation and show decreased phage sensitivity. On solid medium (but not in liquid), flagellation in the *B. harveyi* K variant is peritrichous as compared to the characteristic sheathed polar flagellation in the luminescent forms. In *B. harveyi,* the efficiency of plating of phage hν-1 is 10^{-2} with the K variant as compared to the luminescent form (K. H. Nealson and J. W. Hastings, unpublished results). The presence of peritrichous flagella is evidently not correlated with the phage resistance since the K variant is also not sensitive to phage in a liquid medium where, like the wild type, it possesses only one sheathed polar flagellum.

As was first observed by Beijerinck, revertants occur and the brightly luminescent form can be readily reisolated (see 109). All of the altered characters revert at the same time.

Neither the conditions that favor the appearance of K variants nor those that favor reversion are understood. In cultures of either all brights or all darks, maintained under conditions of rapid growth and/or vigorous aeration, changes to the alternate form have not been observed, whereas partial anaerobiosis (as in dense cultures without aeration) and higher temperatures appear to favor variant forms. Neither genetic transfer between brights and darks nor specific inhibitory or toxic factors produced by either form could be demonstrated (154). Strains freshly isolated from nature as symbionts readily mutate (91), whereas laboratory strains repeatedly selected for luminescence form spontaneous darks less readily (155). However, treatment of such laboratory strains with acridine dyes allows dark mutants (which appear to be indistinguishable from the K variants) to be more readily isolated (161). These are called ACR or ACF mutants (Table 2).

Although the mechanisms involved in the generation of these variants are not clear, it may be postulated that the possibility for losing and gaining in a reversible fashion the capacity to transcribe the elements controlling the quantitative production of the luminescent system has ecological significance. In effect, this allows the species to enjoy two life-styles and to maintain cells with the genetic reservoir capable of forming variants with a distinct physiology—one compatible with the demands of an alternate niche. Under some conditions, where light emission presumably has no particular functional advantage, the nonluminous K variants do outgrow the luminous types (109). In fact, such dark cells may "take over" a culture, which is a repeated source of irritation to those who maintain culture collections of luminescent bacteria.

The very existence of K variants, and the ease with which they appear and revert, raises several interesting questions. What are the natural conditions under which luminous forms are favored? How does selection act? If oxygen is involved, do symbiotic hosts use this to advantage? How many naturally occurring apparently dark marine isolates are actually K variants of luminous bacteria? An understanding of the phenomenon of dark variation will be a key to a better appreciation of the biology and ecology of luminous bacteria.

NATURAL ISOLATES To our knowledge, a K variant has never been isolated from nature and identified as such; but it is not clear that an effort to do so has been made. However, natural isolates do exhibit a wide range of luminescence intensities, and for more than one reason. For instance, the requirement for flavin in luminescence was predicted based on the stimulation of light emission by lactoflavin (riboflavin) in naturally occurring dim strains (44). Nealson (156) has demonstrated that among natural isolates of *Photobacterium fischeri* one strain (B-61) is virtually dark because of failure of autoinducer production, whereas another (MJ-1) is ten times brighter than typical isolates and produces ten times more autoinducer. Actually, such super bright strains are frequently isolated in all of the *Photobacterium* species (but not in *Beneckea*), but no other studies of the mechanism(s) responsible have been reported.

Nealson & Ruby (163) obtained a natural isolate of *P. fischeri* that exhibits a uniquely different property: it emits a yellow luminescence. The biochemical and ecological explanations for this are not known (see above).

PHAGE AND GENETICS

Bacteriophages active against luminous bacteria were reported in the early 1960s (90, 191, 192). Indeed, it is a routine matter to obtain such phages from nearly any marine environment (42, 70).

A phage isolated in 1964 by A. Keynan and J. W. Hastings is the only one that has been extensively studied (110). It is a DNA phage, which has a specific sodium ion requirement for stability, and is similar in size, morphology, and burst size to phage lambda. The phage, called hν-1, was originally isolated on *Beneckea harveyi*, strain MAV, and exhibits a narrow host range, infecting only a few *Beneckea* strains, all of which were isolated from the Atlantic Ocean (K. H. Nealson and J. W. Hastings, unpublished results). Although the phage is apparently lytic, and stable lysogeny has not been demonstrated, it nevertheless has been shown to be genetically active as a specialized transducing phage for the tryptophan region (110). Later and continuing studies by Crawford & Nealson (41), who have mapped and characterized many independent tryptophan mutants, indicate that the trp region of *B. harveyi* is very similar, possibly identical, to that of other enteric bacteria. This is reflected both in the enzymology of the operon and in its genetic organization and arrangement (41). These studies represent the first documentation of a successful transducing system in a marine bacterium and indicate that techniques and approaches used for genetic analysis of other bacteria are compatible with these marine forms. Despite these encouraging developments, no transfer of the genetic elements involved in bacterial bioluminescence has been achieved. Genetic manipulation should be considered to be of high priority in terms of our future understanding of the physiology and molecular biology of the luminous bacteria.

FUNCTIONS OF BACTERIAL LUMINESCENCE

The light emission of bioluminescent organisms may be used in many different specific ways, which, for the most part, fall under three major rubrics: to assist in predation (offense), to aid in avoiding predators (defense), and for intraspecific communication (149). The bioluminescence of higher luminous organisms may be shown to have one or more such functions.

For bacteria, the case is less straightforward, since their behavior can less easily be considered in the above categories. For the symbiont, however, the symbiotic habitat does involve conditions that correspond to the first two: nutrient acquisition is favored, and both predators and competitors are excluded. For the host, the light of luminous bacteria that are carried in a special organ can indeed be used in any or all of the ways mentioned (80, 149); the light emitted therefore is functional. Moreover, the autoinduction of the luminescent system has significant physiological and ecological implications, in the sense that the bacteria may be imagined to have both a symbiotic stage in a host (luminescent) and a free-living stage in the seawater (nonluminescent). This free-living situation could allow for the propagation outside the host and provide for the inoculum presumably required to reinfect the young of the host. Thus, two life-styles, one with and one lacking the luminescent system, appear to exist for these bacteria. Indeed, a question frequently posed, namely what function does the luminescence in these bacteria serve when they are free living in sea-water, is no longer a real question. The bacteria under these conditions are not luminescent (24).

But pursuit of this idea brings another question. Are there luminous bacterial species that do not occur as symbionts in light organs? If so, what about their luminescence? Although we cannot be certain (on the basis of the present limited data), it appears that one of the three groups, namely the *Beneckea,* may not occur as a symbiont in a light organ. However, their luminescence, like that of the other groups, is also subject to autoinduction, implying that in this group also the luminescence has functional importance under some specific condition that favors the accumulation of autoinducer. One seeks some kind of niche (which is perhaps less specific since the species is nutritionally far more versatile) where light emission would have positive selection value. One possibility is that as marine enterobacteria (digestive tract symbionts) their propagation might be favored if they could incubate (either by a parasitic or saprophytic mode) on potential food material of the host. Actually, parasitic symbioses of luminous bacteria on small crustacea (amphipods, shrimps) are well known (76); the luminescence could serve to attract a higher organism to ingest the material. Luminescence would presumably not have a positive function within the gut, but there is an interesting report of the occurrence of luminous fecal pellets of Antarctic fishes (cod) (173).

In support of a postulate concerning this kind of role for luminous bacteria, all species produce chitinase and utilize its breakdown product, N-acetylglucosamine (174), and all except *Photobacterium leiognathi* excrete pyruvate, which, in contrast to N-acetylglucosamine, could presumably be utilized by a fish. As gut symbionts, their contribution to the host thus is a nutritional rather than a light-emitting one, whereas their light-emitting capability is exploited to enhance their own propagation, the acquisition of food by their hosts, and possibly also the further cycling of fecal pellets.

ACKNOWLEDGMENTS

Our research reviewed and reported here has been supported in part by grants from the National Science Foundation, BMS 74-23651 (J. W. H.) and PCM 74-13788 (K. H. N.). We are grateful to many colleagues for providing data prior to publication and for critical comments concerning this review, especially A. Keyman, P. Baumann, J. Reichelt, J. Morin, E. Ruby, N. Langerman, and S. Ulitzur.

Literature Cited

1. Adey, G., Wardley-Smith, B., White, D. 1976. *Life Sci.* 17:1849–54
1a. Agren, A., Berne, C., Brolin, S. E. 1977. *Anal. Biochem.* 78:229–34
2. Allen, R. D., Baumann, P. 1971. *J. Bacteriol.* 107:295–302
3. Anderson, W. B., Pastan, I. 1973. *Biochim. Biophys. Acta* 32:577–87
3a. Ashizawa, N., Nakamura, T., Watanabe, T. 1977. *J. Biochem.* 81:1057–62
4. Balakrishnan, C. V., Langerman, N. Submitted for publication
5. Baldwin, T. O. 1974. *Fed. Proc.* 33:1441
6. Baldwin, T. O. 1974. *Biochem. Biophys. Res. Commun.* 57:1000–5
7. Baldwin, T. O., Currie, M. S., Nicoli, M. Z., Cline, T. W. 1975. *Fed. Proc.* 34:681
8. Baldwin, T. O., Nicoli, M. Z., Becvar, J. E., Hastings, J. W. 1975. *J. Biol. Chem.* 250:2763–68
9. Baldwin, T. O., Nicoli, M. Z., Powers, D. A., Hastings, J. W. 1975. *Biophys. J.* 15:55a
10. Balny, C., Hastings, J. W. 1975. *Biochemistry* 14:4719–23
11. Bassot, J. M. 1975. *Arch. Zool. Exp. Gen.* 116:359–73
11a. Baumann, L., Baumann, P. 1976. *Microbios Lett.* 3:11–20
12. Baumann, P., Baumann, L. 1977. *Ann. Rev. Microbiol.* 31:39–61
13. Baumann, P., Baumann, L., Mandel, M. 1971. *J. Bacteriol.* 107:268–94
14. Becvar, J. E., Baldwin, T. O., Nicoli, M. Z., Hastings, J. W. 1976. In *Flavins and Flavoproteins*, ed. T. P. Singer, pp. 94–100. Amsterdam: Assoc. Sci. Publ. 813 pp.
15. Becvar, J. E., Hastings, J. W. 1975. *Proc. Natl. Acad. Sci. USA* 72:3374–76
16. Becvar, J. E., Tu, S.-C., Hastings, J. W. 1976. *Biophys. J.* 16:100a
17. Becvar, J. E., Tu, S.-C., Hastings, J. W. 1976. *Fed. Proc.* 35:163
18. Becvar, J. E., Tu, S.-C., Hastings, J. W. 1977. *Biophys. J.* 17:146a
19. Beijerinck, M. W. 1889. *Neerl. Sci. Exact. Naturelles* 23:401–15
20. Beijerinck, M. W. 1916. *Folia Microbiol. Delft* 4:15–40
21. Bentley, D., Eberhard, A., Solsky, R. 1974. *Biochem. Biophys. Res. Commun.* 56:865–68
22. Berzhanskaya, L. Y., Gitel'zon, I. I., Fish, A. M., Chumakova, R. I., Shapiro, V. Ye. 1973. *Biofizika* 18: 285–92
23. Boisvert, H., Chatelain, R., Bassot, J. M. 1967. *Ann. Inst. Pasteur Paris* 112: 520–24
24. Booth, C. K., Nealson, K. H. 1975. *Biophys. J.* 15:56a
25. Brolin, S. E., Borglund, E., Tegner, L., Wettermark, G. 1971. *Anal. Biochem.* 42:124–25
26. Buchanan, R. E., Gibbons, N. E., eds. 1975. *Bergey's Manual of Determination Bacteriology*, pp. 345–52. Baltimore: Waverly Press. 8th ed. 1246 pp.
27. Chan, T. W., Williams, R. F., Bruice, T. C. 1977. *J. Am. Chem. Soc.* In press
28. Chumakova, R. I., Vanyushin, B. F., Kokurina, N. A., Vorob'eva, T. I.,

Medvedeva, S. E. 1972. *Microbiology USSR* 41:613–20
29. Cline, T. W. 1973. *Mutational alteration of the bacterial bioluminescence system*. PhD thesis. Harvard Univ., Cambridge, Mass. 322 pp.
30. Cline, T. W., Hastings, J. W. 1971. *Proc. Natl. Acad. Sci. USA* 68:500–4
31. Cline, T. W., Hastings, J. W. 1972. *Biochemistry* 11:3359–70
32. Cline, T. W., Hastings, J. W. 1974. *J. Bacteriol.* 118:1059–66
33. Cline, T. W., Hastings, J. W. 1974. *J. Biol. Chem.* 249:4668–69
34. Coffey, J. J. 1967. *J. Bacteriol.* 94: 1638–47
35. Cohen, G. N., Stanier, R. Y., Le Bras, G. 1969. *J. Bacteriol.* 99:791–801
36. Cormier, M. J., Eckroade, C. B. 1962. *Biochim. Biophys. Acta* 64:340–44
37. Cormier, M. J., Lee, J., Wampler, J. E. 1975. *Ann. Rev. Biochem.* 44:255–72
38. Cormier, M. J., Totter, J. R. 1964 *Ann. Rev. Biochem.* 33:431–58
39. Cousineau, J., Meighen, E. A. 1976. *Biochemistry* 15:4992–5000
40. Cousineau, J., Meighen, E. A. 1977. *Can J. Biochem.* 55:433–38
41. Crawford, I. P., Nealson, K. H. 1976. *Fed. Proc.* 35:1541
42. Curtis, P., Nealson, K. 1973. *Biol. Bull.* 145:431
43. Das, J., Chatterjee, S. N. 1966. *Indian J. Med. Res.* 54:330–38
44. Doudoroff, M. 1938. *Enzymologia* 5: 239–43
45. Doudoroff, M. 1942. *J. Bacteriol.* 44: 451–59
46. Doudoroff, M. 1942. *J. Bacteriol.* 44: 461–67
47. Duane, W., Hastings, J. W. 1975. *Mol. Cell. Biochem.* 6:53–64
48. Dunn, D. K., Michaliszyn, G. A., Bogacki, I. G., Meighen, E. A. 1973. *Biochemistry* 12:4911–18
49. Eberhard, A. 1972. *J. Bacteriol.* 109: 1101–5
50. Eberhard, A., Hastings, J. W. 1972. *Biochem. Biophys. Res. Commun.* 47: 348–53
51. Eberhard, A., Rouser, G. 1971. *Lipids* 6:410–14
52. Eley, M. H. 1972. *J. Gen. Microbiol.* 72:415–17
53. Eley, M., Cormier, M. J. 1968. *Biochem. Biophys. Res. Commun.* 32: 454–60
54. Eley, M., Lee, J., Lhoste, J.-M., Lee, C. V., Cormier, M. J., Hemmerich, P. 1970. *Biochemistry* 9:2902–8
55. Erlanger, B. F., Isambert, M. F., Michelson, A. M. 1970. *Biochem. Biophys. Res. Commun.* 40:70–76
56. Eymers, J. G., Van Schouwenburg, K. L. 1936. *Enzymologia* 1:328–40
57. Eymers, J. G., Van Schouwenburg, K. L. 1937. *Enzymologia* 1:328–40
57a. Faini, G. J., DeSa, R. J., Lee, J. 1976. In *Flavins and Flavoproteins,* ed. T. P. Singer, pp. 82–86. Amsterdam: Assoc. Sci. Publ.
58. Farghaly, A. H. 1950. *J. Cell Comp. Physiol.* 36:165–83
59. Ferrell, W. J., Kessler, R. J., Drouillard, M. 1971. *Chem. Phys. Lipids* 6:131–34
60. Fisher, J., Spencer, R., Walsh, C. 1976. *Biochemistry* 15:1054–64
61. Fitzgerald, J. M. 1977. *Arch. Microbiol.* 112:153–56
62. Friedland, J., Hastings, J. W. 1967. *Biochemistry* 6:2893–900
63. Friedland, J. M., Hastings, J. W. 1967. *Proc. Natl. Acad. Sci. USA* 58:2336–42
64. Gast, R., Lee, J. 1976. *Proc. Int. Congr. Photobiol. Rome,* p. 324
65. Gerlo, E., Charlier, J. 1975. *Eur. J. Biochem.* 57:461–67
66. Ghisla, S., Massey, V., Lhoste, J.-M., Mayhew, S. G. 1974. *Biochemistry* 13:589–97
67. Gibson, Q. H., Hastings, J. W. 1962. *Biochem. J.* 83:368–77
68. Gibson, Q. H., Hastings, J. W. Greenwood, C. 1965. *Proc. Natl. Acad. Sci. USA* 53:187–95
69. Gibson, Q. H., Hastings, J. W., Weber, G., Duane, W., Massa, J. 1966. In *Flavins and Flavoproteins,* ed. T. P. Singer, pp. 341–59. Amsterdam: Elsevier
70. Gill, M. L., Nealson, K. 1972. *Biol. Bull.* 143:463–64
70a. Graham, P. H., Paxton, J. R., Cho, K. Y. 1972. *Arch. Mikrobiol.* 81:305–8
71. Gunsalus-Miguel, A., Meighen, E. A., Nicoli, M. Z., Nealson, K. H., Hastings, J. W. 1972. *J. Biol Chem.* 247:398–404
71a. Hagins, W. A., Hanseon, F. E., Buch, J. B. 1966. In *Bioluminescence in Progress,* ed. F. H. Johnson, Y. Haneda, pp. 475–85. Princeton, N.J.: Princeton Univ. Press
72. Halsey, M. J., Smith, E. B. 1970. *Nature* 227:1363–65
73. Haneda, Y., Tsuji, F. I. 1971. *Science* 173:143–45
74. Haneda, Y., Tsuji, F. I. 1971. *Sci. Rep. Yokosuka City Mus. Yokosuka Shi Hakabutsukan Kenkyu Hokoku* 9:18–28

75. Haneda, Y., Tsuji, F. I. 1976. *J. Morphol.* 150:539–52
76. Harvey, E. N. 1952. *Bioluminescence.* New York: Academic
77. Hastings, J. W. 1952. *J. Cell. Comp. Physiol.* 39: 1–30
78. Hastings, J. W. 1955. *Anat. Rec.* 122: 458
79. Hastings, J. W. 1968. *Ann. Rev. Biochem.* 37:597–630
80. Hastings, J. W. 1971. *Science* 173: 1016–17
81. Hastings, J. W. 1975. In *Energy Transformation in Biological Systems,* ed. G. E. W. Wolstenhilme, D. W. Fitzsimons, pp. 125–46. Amsterdam: Assoc. Sci. Publ.
82. Hastings, J. W., Balny, C. 1975. *J. Biol. Chem.* 250:7288–93
83. Hastings, J. W., Balny, C., Douzou, P. 1976. In *Flavins and Flavoproteins,* ed. T. P. Singer, pp. 53 61. Amsterdam: Assoc. Sci. Publ.
84. Hastings, J. W., Balny, C., Le Peuch, C., Douzou, P. 1973. *Proc. Natl. Acad. Sci. USA* 70:3468–72
85. Hastings, J. W., Eberhard, A., Baldwin, T. O., Nicoli, M. Z., Cline, T. W., Nealson, K. H. 1973. In *Chemiluminescence and Bioluminescence,* ed. M. J. Cormier, D. H. Hercules, J. Lee, pp. 369–80. New York: Plenum
86. Hastings, J. W., Gibson, Q. H. 1963. *J. Biol. Chem.* 238:2537–54
87. Hastings, J. W., Gibson, Q. H. 1967. *J. Biol. Chem.* 242:720–26
88. Hastings, J. W., Gibson, Q. H., Friedland, J., Spudich, J. 1966. In *Bioluminescence in Progress,* ed. F. H. Johnson, Y. Haneda, pp. 151–86. Princeton, N.J.: Princeton Univ. Press
89. Hastings, J. W., Gibson, Q. H., Greenwood, C. 1964. *Proc. Natl. Acad. Sci. USA* 52:1529–35
90. Hastings, J. W., Keynan, A., McCloskey, K. 1961. *Biol. Bull.* 121:375
91. Hastings, J. W., Mitchell, G. 1971. *Biol. Bull.* 141:261–68
92. Hastings, J. W., Reynolds, G. T. 1966. In *Bioluminescence in Progress,* ed. F. H. Johnson, Y. Haneda, pp. 45–50. Princeton, N.J.: Princeton Univ. Press
93. Hastings, J. W., Riley, W. H., Massa, J. 1965. *J. Biol. Chem.* 240:1473–81
94. Hastings, J. W., Spudich, J. A., Malnic, G. 1963. *J. Biol. Chem.* 238:3100–5
95. Hastings, J. W., Weber, G. 1963. *J. Opt. Soc. Am.* 53:1410–15
96. Hastings, J. W., Weber, K., Friedland, J., Eberhard, A., Mitchell, G. W., Gunsalus, A. 1969. *Biochemistry* 8:4681–89
97. Hastings, J. W., Wilson, T. 1976. *Photochem. Photobiol.* 23:461–73
98. Hendrie, M. S., Hodgkiss, W., Shewan, J. M. 1970 *J. Gen. Microbiol.* 64:151–69
99. Henry, J. P., Michelson, A. M. 1970. *CR Acad. Sci.* 270:1947–49
100. Herring, P. J. 1975. *Proc. 9th Eur. Mar. Biol. Symp.,* pp. 563–72
101. Hill, S. E. 1928. *Biol. Bull.* 55:143–50
102. Hill, S. E., Shoup, C. S. 1929. *J. Bacteriol.* 18:95–99
103. Jablonski, E., DeLuca, M. 1976. *Proc. Natl. Acad. Sci. USA* 73:3848–51
103a. Jablonski, E., DeLuca, M. 1977. In press
104. Johnson, F. H., Eyring, H., Polissar, M. J. 1954. In *The Kinetic Basis of Molecular Biology.* New York: Wiley
105. Johnson, F. H., Van Schouwenburg, K. L., Spruit van der burg, A. 1939. *Enzymologia* 7:194–224
106. Kemal, C., Bruice, T. C. 1976. *Proc. Natl. Acad. Sci. USA* 73:995–99
107. Kemal, C., Chan, T. W., Bruice, T. C. 1977. *Proc. Natl. Acad. Sci. USA.* 74:405–9
108. Kempner, E. S., Hanson, F. E. 1968. *J. Bacteriol.* 95:975–79
109. Keynan, A., Hastings, J. W. 1961. *Biol. Bull.* 121:375
110. Keynan, A., Nealson, K. H., Sideropoulos, H., Hastings, J. W. 1974. *J. Virology* 14:333–40
111. King, S. M., White, D. C. 1976. *Br. J. Anaesth.* 48:814–15
112. Kössler, F. 1967. *Stud. Biophys.* 2: 173–80
113. Kössler, F. 1968. *Arch. Mikrobiol.* 64: 146–57
114. Kössler, F. 1970. *Z. Allg. Mikrobiol.* 10:475–86
115. Kössler, F. 1970. *Z. Allg. Mikrobiol.* 10:615–25
116. Lavelle, F., Henry, J.-P., Michelson, A. M. 1970. *CR Acad. Sci. Paris* 270: 2126–27
117. Lee, J. 1972. *Biochemistry* 11:3350–59
118. Lee, J., Murphy, C. L. 1973. *Biochem. Biophys. Res. Commun.* 53:157–63
119. Lee, J., Murphy, C. L. 1975. *Biochemistry* 14:2259–68
120. Lee, J., Murphy, C. L., Faini, G. J., Baucom, T. L. 1974. In *Liquid Scintillation Counting,* pp. 403–20. New York: Academic
121. Lee, J., Wesley, A. S., Ferguson, J. F. III, Seliger, H. H. 1966. In *Bioluminescence in Progress,* ed. F. H. Johnson, Y. Haneda, pp. 35–43. Princeton, N.J.: Princeton Univ. Press

122. Lin, P., Saier, M. H., Nealson, K. H. 1976. *Fed. Proc.* 35:1361
123. Lowe, J. N., Ingraham, L. L., Alspach, J., Rasmussen, R. 1976. *Biochem. Biophys. Res. Comm.* 73:465–69
124. Magasanik, B. 1962. *Cold Spring Harbor Symp. Quant. Biol.* 26:249–56
125. Magasanik, B. 1970. In *The Lac Operon,* ed. J. R. Beckwith, D. Zipser, pp. 182–219. New York: Cold Spring Harbor
126. Magner, J., Eberhard, A., Nealson, K. 1972. *Biol. Bull.* 143:469
127. Makemson, J. C. 1973. *Arch. Microbiol.* 93:347–58
128. Mangold, A., Langerman, N. 1975. *Arch. Biochem. Biophys.* 169:126–33
129. Matsuda, K., Nakamura, T. 1972. *J. Biochem.* 72:951–55
130. McCapra, F., Hart, R. 1976. *J. Chem. Soc. D* 8:273–74
131. McCapra, F., Hysert, D. W. 1973. *Biochem. Biophys. Res. Commun.* 52:298–304
132. McCloskey, K. R. 1960. *The role of aldehyde in bacterial bioluminescence as determined by emission spectra.* BS thesis. Univ. Ill., Urbana. 42 pp.
133. McElroy, W. D. 1961. In *The Bacteria,* ed. I. C. Gunsalus, R. Y. Stanier, Vol. II, pp. 479–508. New York: Academic
134. McElroy, W. D., Strehler, B. L. 1954. *Bacteriol Rev.* 18:177–94
135. McIlvaine, P., Langerman, N. 1977. *Biophys. J.* 17:17–25
136. Meighen, E. A., Bogacki, I. G., Bognar, A. 1976. *Biochem. Biophys. Res. Commun.* 69:423–30
137. Meighen, E. A., Hastings, J. W. 1971. *J. Biol. Chem.* 246:7666–74
138. Meighen, E. A., Nicoli, M. Z., Hastings, J. W. 1971. *Biochemistry* 10: 4062–68
139. Meighen, E. A., Nicoli, M. Z., Hastings, J. W. 1971. *Biochemistry* 10: 4069–73
140. Meighen, E. A., MacKenzie, R. E. 1973. *Biochemistry* 12:1482–91
141. Meighen, E. A., Smillie, L. B., Hastings, J. W. 1970. *Biochemistry* 9: 4949–52
142. Michael, P. R., Faulkner, L. R. 1976. *Anal. Chem.* 48:1188–92
143. Michaliszyn, G. A., Meighen, E. A. 1976. *J. Biol. Chem.* 251:2541–49
144. Middleton, A. J., Smith, E. B. 1976. *Proc. R. Soc. London Ser. B* 193:159–71
145. Middleton, A. J., Smith, E. B. 1976. *Proc. R. Soc. London Ser. B* 193:173–90
146. Mitchell, G. W. 1969. *Light induced proteins: a distinct bioluminescent species isolated from luminous marine bacteria.* PhD thesis. Harvard Univ., Cambridge, Mass. 89 pp.
147. Mitchell, G. W., Hastings, J. W. 1969. *J. Biol. Chem.* 244:2572–76
148. Mitchell, G. W., Hastings, J. W. 1970. *Biochemistry* 9:2699–707
148a. Mitchell, G. W., Hastings, J. W. 1971. *Anal. Biochem.* 39:243–50
149. Morin, J. G., Harrington, A., Krieger, N., Nealson, K. H., Baldwin, T. O., Hastings, J. W. 1975. *Science* 190: 74–76
150. Morin, J. G., Hastings, J. W. 1971. *J. Cell. Physiol.* 77:313–81
151. Murphy, C. L., Faini, G. J., Lee, J. 1974. *Biochem. Biophys. Res. Commun.* 58:119–25
152. Nakamura, T. 1972. *J. Biochem.* 72: 173–77
153. Nakamura, T., Matsuda, K. 1971. *J. Biochem.* 70:35–44
154. Nealson, K. H. 1969. *Mutational and biochemical studies of bacterial bioluminescence.* PhD thesis. Univ. Chicago, Chicago, 149 pp.
155. Nealson, K. 1972. *Biol. Bull.* 143: 471–72
156. Nealson, K. H. 1977. *Arch. Microbiol.* 112:73–79
157. Nealson, K., Eberhard, A., Hastings, J. W. 1972. *Proc. Natl. Acad. Sci. USA* 69:1073–76
158. Nealson, K. H., Hastings, J. W. 1970. *Bacteriol. Proc.* pp. D-6 (Abstr.)
159. Nealson, K. H., Hastings, J. W. 1972. *J. Biol. Chem.* 247:888–94
160. Nealson, K. H., Hastings, J. W. 1977. *Arch. Microbiol.* 112:9–16
161. Nealson, K. H., Markovitz, A. 1970. *J. Bacteriol.* 104:300–12
162. Nealson, K., Platt, T., Hastings, J. W. 1970. *J. Bacteriol.* 104:313–22
163. Nealson, K. H., Ruby, E. G. 1977. *Science* 196:432–34
164. Ne'eman, Z., Ulitzur, S., Branton, D., Hastings, J. W. 1977. *J. Biol. Chem.* In press
165. Nicoli, M. Z., Baldwin, T. O., Becvar, J. E., Hastings, J. W. 1976. In *Flavins and Flavoproteins,* ed. T. P. Singer, pp. 87–93. Amsterdam: Assoc. Sci. Publ.
166. Nicoli, M. Z., Hastings, J. W. 1974. *J. Biol. Chem.* 249:2392–96
167. Nicoli, M. Z., Meighen, E. A., Hastings, J. W. 1974. *J. Biol. Chem.* 249:2385–92
168. Njus, D., Baldwin, T. O., Hastings, J. W. 1974. *Anal. Biochem.* 61:280–87
169. O'Day, W. T. 1974. *Contributions in*

Science No. 255. Los Angeles: Natural History Museum

170. Oshino, R., Oshino, N., Tamura, M., Kobilinsky, L., Chance, B. 1972. *Biochim. Biophys. Acta* 272:5–17
171. Payne, W. J., Eagon, R. G., Williams A. K. 1961. *Antonie von Leeouwenhoek J. Microbiol. Serol.* 27:121–28
172. Puget, K., Michelson, A. M. 1972. *Biochimie* 54:1197–204
173. Raymond, J. A., DeVries, A. L. 1976. *Limnol. Oceanogr.* 21:599–602
174. Reichelt, J. L., Baumann, P. 1973. *Arch. Mikrobiol.* 94:283–330
175. Reichelt, J. L., Baumann, P. 1974. *Arch. Microbiol.* 97:329–45
176. Reichelt, J. L., Baumann, P. 1975. *Int. J. Syst. Bacteriol.* 25:208–9
177. Reichelt, J. L., Baumann, P., Baumann, L. 1976. *Arch. Microbiol.* 110:101–20
178. Reichelt, J. L., Nealson, K. H., Hastings, J. W. 1977. *Arch. Microbiol.* 112:157–61
179. Rodicheva, E. K., Kharuk, V. I., Kuznetsov, A. M., Fish, A. M., Chumakova, R. I., Scherbakova, G. Ya. 1973. *Mikrobiologiya* 42:65–69
180. Rogers, P., McElroy, W. D. 1955. *Proc. Natl. Acad. Sci. USA* 41:67–70
181. Rogers, P., McElroy, W. D. 1958. *Arch. Biochem. Biophys.* 75:87–105
182. Rogers, P., McElroy, W. D. 1958. *Arch. Biochem. Biophys.* 75:106–16
183. Ruby, E. G., Nealson, K. H. 1976. *Biol. Bull.* 151:574–86

183a. Ruby, E. G., Reynolds, G. T., Walton, A. J., Hardy, C. J. 1976. *Biol. Bull.* 151:428

184. Schroeder, H. R., Carrico, R. J., Boguslaski, R. C., Christner, J. E. 1976. *Anal. Biochem.* 72:283–92
185. Seliger, H. H., Morton, R. A. 1968. In *Photophysiology,* ed. A. C. Giese, Vol. IV, pp. 253–314. New York: Academic
186. Shimomura, O., Johnson, F. H., Kohama, Y. 1972. *Proc. Natl. Acad. Sci. USA* 69:2086–89
187. Shimomura, O., Johnson, F. H., Morise, H. 1974. *Proc. Natl. Acad. Sci. USA* 71:4666–69
188. Shoup, C. S. 1929. *J. Gen. Physiol.* 13:27–45
189. Smith, D., Muscatine, L., Lewis, D. 1969. *Biol. Rev.* 44:17–90
190. Soli, G. 1970. *Atti. Soc. Peloritana Sci. Fis. Mat. Nat.* 16:159–78
191. Spencer, R. 1960. *J. Bacteriol.* 79:614
192. Spencer, R. 1963. In *Symposium on Marine Microbiology,* ed. C. H. Oppenheimer, pp. 350–65. Springfield, Ill.: Thomas
193. Spruit, van der burg, A. 1950. *Biochim. Biophys, Acta* 5:175–78
194. Spudich, J. A. 1963. *The effects and function of aldehyde in the in vitro bioluminescent reaction of Achromobacter fischeri.* BS thesis. Univ. Illinois, Urbana. 63 pp.
195. Spudich, J. A., Hastings, J. W. 1963. *J. Biol. Chem.* 238:3106–8
196. Stanley, P. E. 1974. In *Liquid Scintillation Counting,* ed. M. A. Cook, P. Johnson, pp. 253–72. London: Heyden
197. Stanley, P. E. 1971. *Anal. Biochem.* 39:441–53
198. Strehler, B. L. 1953. *J. Am. Chem. Soc.* 75:1264–65
199. Strehler, B. L. 1955. In *The Luminescence of Biological Systems,* ed. F. H. Johnson, pp. 209–44. Washington, D.C.: AAAS
200. Strehler, B. L. 1961. In *Light and life,* ed. W. D. McElroy, B. Glass, pp. 306–8. Baltimore: Johns Hopkins Univ. Press
201. Terpstra, W. 1962. *Biochim. Biophys. Acta* 60:580–90
202. Terpstra, W. 1963. *Biochim. Biophys. Acta* 75:355–64
203. Tu, S.-C., Baldwin, T. O., Becvar, J. E., Hastings, J. W. 1977. *Arch. Biochem. Biophys.* 179:342–48
204. Tu, S.-C., Becvar, J. E., Hastings, J. W. 1976. *Biophys. J.* 16:55a
205. Tu, S.-C., Hastings, J. W. 1975. *Biochemistry* 14:1975–80
206. Tu, S.-C., Hastings, J. W. 1975. *Biochemistry* 14:4310–16

206a. Tu, S.-C., Hastings, J. W. 1976. In *Flavins and Flavoproteins,* ed. T. P. Singer, pp. 101–7. Amsterdam: Assoc. Sci. Publ.

207. Tu, S.-C., Hastings, J. W. 1977. *Biophys. J.* 17:146
208. Tu, S.-C., Hastings, J. W., McCormick, D. B. 1977. *Fed. Proc.* 36:722
209. Tu, S.-C., Makemson, J. C., Becvar, J. E., Hastings, J. W. 1977. *J. Biol. Chem.* 252:803–5
210. Tu, S.-C., Waters, C. A., Hastings, J. W. 1975. *Biochemistry* 14:1970–74
211. Ulitzur, S., Hastings, J. W. 1976. *Proc. Am. Soc. Microbiol.*, pp. 138.
212. Ulitzur, S., Yashphe, J. 1975. *Biochim. Biophys. Acta* 404:321–28
213. Ulitzur, S., Yashphe, J., Hastings, J. W. 1976. *Proc. Natl. Acad. Sci. USA* 73:4454–56
214. Vigny, A., Michelson, A. M. 1974. *Biochimie* 56:171–76
215. Watanabe, T., Nakamura, T. 1972. *J. Biochem.* 72:647–53

216. Watanabe, T., Nakamura, T. 1976. *J. Biochem.* 79:489–95
217. Watanabe, H., Mimura, N., Takimoto, A., Nakamura, T. 1975. *J. Biochem.* 77:1147–55
218. Watanabe, T., Tomita, G., Nakamura, T. 1974. *J. Biochem.* 75:1249–55
219. Watanabe, T., Yoshida, K., Takahashi, M., Tomita, G., Nakamura, T. 1976. In *Flavins and Flavoproteins,* ed. T. P. Singer, pp. 62–76. Amsterdam: Assoc. Sci. Publ.
220. Waters, C. A. 1974. *Studies on the cellular control of bacterial bioluminescence.* PhD thesis. Harvard Univ., Cambridge, Mass. 133 pp.
221. Waters, C. A., Hastings, J. W. 1977. *J. Bacteriol.* In press
222. Waters, C. A., Murphy, J. R., Hastings, J. W. 1974. *Biochem. Biophys. Res. Commun.* 57:1152–58
223. Waters, C. A., Nealson, K. H., Hastings, J. W. 1973. *Proc. Am. Soc. Microbiol.,* pp. 64.
224. White, D. C. 1974. In *Molecular Mechanisms in General Anaesthesia,* ed. M. J. Halsey, R. A. Miller, J. A. Sutton, pp. 209–23
225. White, D. C., Dundas, C. R. 1970. *Nature* 226:456–58
226. White, D. C., Dundas, C. R. 1972. In *Cellular Biology and Toxicity of Annesthetics,* ed. B. R. Fink, pp. 168–81. Baltimore: Williams and Wilkins
227. White, D. C., Wardley-Smith, B., Adey, G. 1975. *Progr. Anaesthesiol.* 1:583–93
228. White, E. H., Rapaport, E., Hopkins, T. A., Seliger, H. H. 1969. *J. Am. Chem. Soc.* 91:2178–80
229. Yoshida, K., Nakamura, T. 1973. *J. Biochem.* 74:915–22
230. Yoshida, K., Nakamura, T. 1974. *J. Biochem.* 76:985–90
231. Yoshida, K., Takahashi, M., Nakamura, T. 1973. *Biochem. Biophys. Res. Commun.* 52:1470–74
232. Yoshida, K., Takahashi, M., Nakamura, T. 1974. *J. Biochem.* 75:583–89

Ann. Rev. Microbiol. 1977. 31:597–629

CELL DIFFERENTIATION IN *NAEGLERIA GRUBERI*

❖1718

Chandler Fulton
Department of Biology, Brandeis University, Waltham, Massachusetts 02154

CONTENTS

INTRODUCTION 597
NAEGLERIA GRUBERI 598
Amebae 600
Encystment and Excystment 601
Differentiation to Flagellates 601
Place in Nature 602
Genome 604
ASPECTS OF METHODOLOGY 604
Strains 605
Cultivation and Growth of Amebae 606
Control and Measurement of Differentiation to Flagellates 607
Biochemical Methods 611
Prospects for Genetic Analysis 611
EVENTS DURING DIFFERENTIATION 612
Assembly of the Flagellar Apparatus 613
Cell Cycle and Competence to Differentiate 614
Initiation of Differentiation 616
Environmental Manipulation of Differentiation 618
Transcription and Translation 620
A Specific Synthesis and Assembly: Flagellar Tubulin 621
Control of Flagellum Number 623
Cell Shape Morphogenesis 624
Reversion of Flagellates to Amebae 624
Timetable of Events 625
PROSPECTS 626

INTRODUCTION

My colleague, Still Waters, a physicist recently wooed by molecular biology, is always asking questions.

"What do you do?" he asked one day.

"I work on cell differentiation," I replied. He looked puzzled.

"I'm not sure exactly what that is."

"Well, neither is anyone else, I guess. Each developmental biologist is sure he knows instinctively what the process is, but none of us understand it at all. When the term is applied to the differentiation of cells during the development of vertebrate embryos, it often includes both the process through which a cell becomes committed or determined to have a certain specialized phenotype or repertory of phenotypes, and the process of phenotypic expression through which the permitted phenotypes are expressed. Most biologists studying vertebrate cell differentiation are concerned with the latter process, with phenotypic expression in already determined cells."

"The process by which a cell becomes determined, as you call it, sounds very interesting, at least from the viewpoint of a geneticist."

"It is extremely interesting, but no one seems to know how to study it effectively."

"But isn't the study of phenotypic expression during differentiation simply the study of β-galactosidase induction in eukaryotic cells?"

"Not at all, Still. In the phenotypic expression that occurs during cell differentiation, it is not just the expression of one gene or operon that is involved. In most if not all cases of cell differentiation, a whole constellation of characteristics change in a temporally and spatially programmed sequence, culminating in a differentiated cell that has specific macromolecules but also has a different morphology and behavior."

Still picked up the manuscript I was writing and began to read.

At the present time, no more than a half-dozen laboratories are using *Naegleria gruberi* to study developmental problems. As a consequence, a review of the relevant literature for the past few years would be an easy task, but it would serve little useful purpose. On the other hand, the ameba-to-flagellate transformation of *Naegleria* has special attributes that recommend its use to investigate particular aspects of cell differentiation. This essay offers a general introduction to the developmental biology of *N. gruberi,* and especially to the use and potential utility of this "system" for studying phenotypic expression and cell morphogenesis.

This essay spans work from 1899, when Schardinger discovered *Naegleria* (86), to the present. A comprehensive 1970 monograph on *Naegleria* (33) is referred to frequently to minimize unnecessary duplications. The perspectives of several of the recent investigators of differentiation in *Naegleria* may be found in symposium papers (24, 37, 41, 79, 127).

NAEGLERIA GRUBERI

Naegleria is a Jekyll-and-Hyde organism (59), entirely appropriate for studying a frankenstein problem like cell differentiation. In Robert Louis Stevenson's tale, Dr. Jekyll spent brief periods entirely transformed into the terrible other half of his personality. Similarly, *Naegleria* spend most of their life as amebae, feeding on bacteria and reproducing by fission. When amebae are transferred from a growth environment to a dilute aqueous solution, without nutrients, they transform rapidly into swimming flagellates with two anterior flagella and an elongate, streamlined body shape. In the laboratory, the conversion of cell phenotype, from an organism that would be placed in the class Sarcodina to one that would be placed among the Mastigophora, can easily be made to occur quickly, synchronously, and temporally reproducibly (38). Flagellates are not an obligatory part of the laboratory life cycle; amebae may be grown for thousands of generations without ever differentiating. The flagellates are temporary; they do not feed and eventually revert to amebae. Only amebae are known to feed or reproduce.

N. gruberi has been found in soil and freshwater samples from all over the world, from the South Sea islands to the Arctic to Massachusetts, and everywhere in between (33). On the basis of its worldwide distribution, and the frequency with which it is recovered from samples of soil and water, in numbers this organism is among the most prevalent nonmarine eukaryotes on Earth. Yet its habits in nature are unknown. It grows out of samples of soil and water brought into the laboratory, and only in the laboratory has the organism been observed or studied. Thus, the role of the ameba-to-flagellate transformation in nature is anyone's guess. The flagellates might be useful for dispersal; perhaps they are (as yet undiscovered) gametes.

In the laboratory life cycle of *Naegleria,* amebae decide among three choices: they can remain amebae, they can encyst, or they can transform into flagellates (Figure 1). Both encystment and transformation are differentiations; in this essay, unless otherwise qualified, differentiation refers to the phenotypic change of amebae to flagellates.

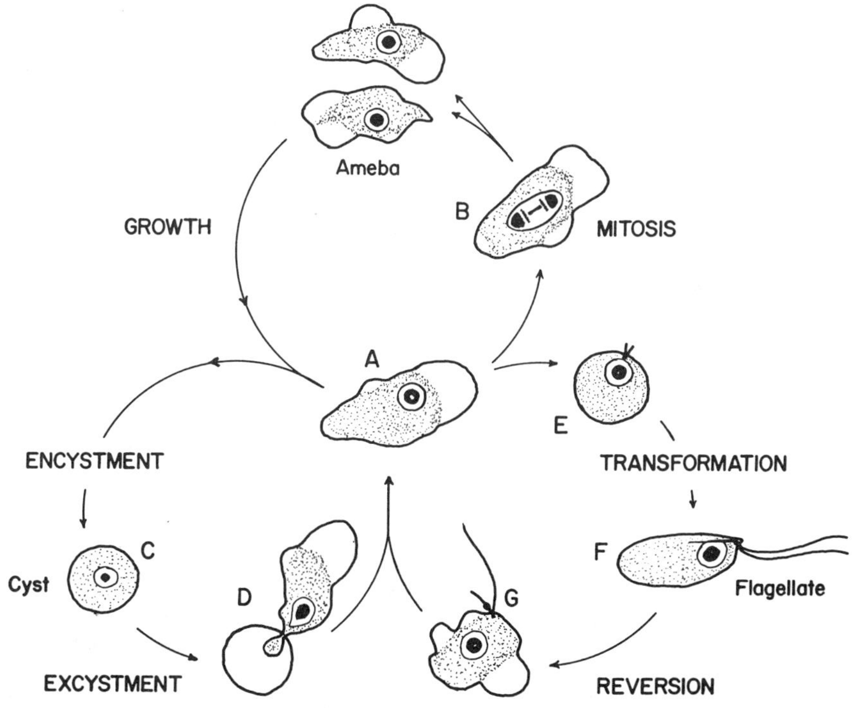

Figure 1 Life cycle of *Naegleria gruberi* as it is known in the laboratory. [After (33)].

Amebae

The amebae of *N. gruberi* are "small," at least by comparison to the familiar giants *Amoeba* and *Chaos*; they have a diameter of roughly 15 μm when rounded. They move along a substratum with a single leading blunt pseudopodium that is free of large cytoplasmic organelles (Figure 1*A*). Their motion is not slug-like; rather, a pseudopodium erupts, the ameba flows in that direction for a moment, and then another pseudopodium erupts, usually near the anterior end but frequently elsewhere, in which case the direction of movement changes (33, 69). The nucleus with its prominent nucleolus (Figure 1*A*) rolls about in the cytoplasm as amebae move and is frequently deformed. The amebae move quite rapidly; at room temperature they progress 50–100 μm, or several times their diameter, per min (69). Amebae in suspension usually have several pseudopodia and no obvious polarity (e.g. Figure 1*G*).

The fine structure of *Naegleria* amebae is basically similar to other amebae and to eukaryotic cells in general (25, 33, 89). The plasma membrane, nuclear envelope, nucleolus, and mitochondria all have the expected morphologies. The cell surface has some polysaccharide (69), suggesting the presence of a glycocalyx. The contractile vacuole seems to form through the coalescence of several small vacuoles (124), and its contents are expelled to the outside by fusion of the vacuole membrane with the plasma membrane (89). The amebae are phagotrophs, usually fed bacteria, and in their cytoplasm are intricate lamellar food vacuoles containing bacteria in various stages of digestion (33). Exhausted food vacuoles, basically consisting of whorls of membranes, are expelled from the cell. Ribosomes are very abundant in the cytoplasm, often in clusters; only small fragments of endoplasmic reticulum are found. No structures that can be correlated with ameboid movement, such as arrays of microfilaments, have been observed so far. Actomyosin (62) and actin (J. Sellers and C. Fulton, manuscript in preparation) have been isolated from *Naegleria* amebae, so the major proteins that have been implicated in motility in other eukaryotes are present in *Naegleria.*

Amebae fed bacteria can grow with a doubling time of as little as 1.7 hr (38); in axenic cultures grown in nonparticulate media, the minimum observed doubling time is 7–8 hr (33, 36).

Mitosis is intranuclear, which means that the nuclear envelope remains intact throughout the process (33, 92). The Feulgen-positive chromosomes go through conventional movements during karyokinesis (69, 80, 98). Although chromosome counts have been published, in my experience the chromosomes are too minute and close together to count accurately (33). The mitotic apparatus contains typical microtubules, but they do not focus to the poles and no centrioles are present (33, 39, 92). The nucleolus does not disassemble during mitosis but instead becomes dumbbell shaped and separates as two masses, usually leaving a piece, the interzonal body, between the separating groups of chromosomes (Figure 1*B*). In late telophase, the interzonal body breaks in half, then cytokinesis occurs and the nuclei reorganize their interphase morphology. Karyokinesis takes 15–20 min (40, 80, 86); the amebae remain motile during most of this time (69, 124).

This pattern of nuclear division has caused confusion and controversy, and it has been suggested that the pattern indicates that *Naegleria* is an atypical eukaryote. My own conclusion is that there is nothing extraordinary about the pattern of karyokinesis (reviewed in 33). The behavior of the chromosomes is orthodox. Intranuclear mitosis is common among protists. Persistence of the nucleolus through division is less common but has been found in organisms scattered throughout the protists. Many protists, and higher plant cells as well, divide without centrioles. Perhaps the most unusual feature of mitosis in *Naegleria* is that the chromosomes cannot be recognized in electron micrographs of mitotic nuclei (33, 39, 92), even though we know from light microscopy where they should be. In most eukaryotes, fixed and stained by using procedures similar to those used with *Naegleria,* mitotic chromosomes are readily recognized in electron micrographs.

Encystment and Excystment

After amebae reach stationary phase, if conditions are otherwise favorable, they form resting cysts (Figure 1*C*) that can survive in environments that would be lethal to amebae—temperature, drying, pH, and so forth. The cysts are enclosed in a double wall pierced by three or more plugged pores (33, 70, 90, 93); the wall has been reported to contain cellulose (118). During encystment, the size of the nucleolus is reduced and RNA-containing bodies appear in the cytoplasm (95). The process of encystment has barely been studied in *Naegleria* (18), even though this differentiation should be as amenable to experimental analysis as it is in other small amebae, such as *Acanthamoeba* (117).

Excystment occurs when cysts are inoculated into fresh culture medium with bacteria. There are strain differences in the factors controlling excystment. In one strain, there is an absolute dependence on an increased pCO_2 (0.8% CO_2 is sufficient) (6). In another strain, some cysts excyst in water alone, although the percentage is increased by increased pCO_2; in a third, there is an additional requirement that can be met by factor(s) in yeast extract (33). Excystment has been reported to be induced by brief exposure of cysts to high hydrostatic pressure (109). In all cases, it appears likely that an early event of excystment is an inflow of water. Excystment can occur within 80 min after initiation, and changes have been observed within 20 min (6). The amebae emerge through one of the pores, apparently after digesting its plug. The contortions that amebae undergo in crawling through the pores are dramatic to watch (Figure 1*D*); the nuclei, for example, have a diameter of 4–5 μm and the pores are only about 0.6 μm in diameter (90). The empty walls remain after excystment.

Differentiation to Flagellates

Ameboid motility, mitosis, encystment, and excystment could all be studied in *Naegleria,* but this organism offers no obvious advantages (or disadvantages) over amebae such as *Acanthamoeba* or *Dictyostelium* for such studies. The unique feature of *Naegleria* is the transformation of amebae to flagellates. Schardinger described the wonder of it (see 33, 86):

> From the beginning of my culture studies, flagellate nuisances appeared occasionally in the condensation water of the cultures. I took these to be contaminants. . . . The matter remained confused, until a fortunate 'accident' brought enlightenment. A 'hanging drop' inoculated with amebae was left in the incubator at about 25–30° . . . for two hours and then observed. The amebae were almost completely replaced with lively swimming flagellates.

During differentiation, there is a "covert period" during which the amebae remain motile and no obvious morphological changes occur. Then, in rapid sequence, the cytoplasm seems to gel, the cells round up to spheres, and flagella, usually two, appear next to one another on the rounded cells (Figure 1*E*). As the flagella elongate they are active, causing the cells to tremble, then to spin, and suddenly to swim, with the flagella leading. As the flagellates swim, they elongate to their flagellate contour (Figure 1*F*).[1] The phenotypic conversion can be completed within as little as 60 min after transfer of amebae from growth medium to dilute buffer (33). The flagellates are good swimmers; at room temperature they progress at 90–140 μm per sec—nearly 100 times as rapidly as amebae (37).

The flagellates are temporary and always revert to amebae after a few minutes, hours, or days, depending upon the environmental conditions (33). In reversion they lose their shape, then resorb their flagella (37). The morphological events of reversion occur very rapidly: suddenly a cell loses its smooth contour and begins ameboid movement (Figure 1*G*); suddenly the flagella cease to move and are retracted into the cell.

After flagellates revert to amebae, the amebae can redifferentiate to flagellates again—in the same environment, without intervening growth (38). In some strains, reversion and redifferentiation can occur repeatedly until the amebae begin to encyst; in others, very few cells redifferentiate after the first reversion (33).

Place in Nature

TAXONOMY *N. gruberi* is uniquely defined by (*a*) the size and gross morphology of its amebae; (*b*) mitosis, including intranuclear karyokinesis in which the nucleolus divides, forming polar masses and usually leaving an interzonal body between the separating chromosomes; (*c*) rounded cysts with a double wall and three to ten exit pores, through which the amebae excyst, leaving empty walls behind; and (*d*) amebae that transform readily, when suspended in water or dilute buffer, to temporary flagellates that have an elongated contour and two to four equal, anteriorly directed flagella.

Numerous isolates share these properties. *N. gruberi* has had many names [six generic and seven specific names are listed in reference (33)]; in the past this caused much confusion. *N. gruberi* is generally accepted as correct (33, 69, 70, 99). Other species of *Naegleria* have been described but, with one notable exception, little studied.

[1]A time-lapse movie of this differentiation, filmed by Joseph Durden at the Education Development Center, is available commercially from BFA Educational Media, 2211 Michigan Ave., Santa Monica, Calif. 90404.

The exception is *Naegleria fowleri* (=*Naegleria aerobia*), which is pathogenic to mammals, including humans, causing meningoencephalitis, which is usually fatal. It apparently infects individuals swimming in polluted water, enters the brain through the nasal passage, and there destroys the nervous system. Although not more than 100 deaths have been attributed to *N. fowleri* since the first case was discovered in 1966, as opposed to malaria, for example, which causes over a million deaths a year,the pathogenic *Naegleria* has been extensively studied and several hundred papers have appeared [bibliography in (120)] (see also 17, 20, 21, 26, 33). *N. fowleri* differs from *N. gruberi* in several respects: its cysts have thinner walls, and pores are not visible with the light microscope (70, 93); it is immunochemically distinct, although the two species share some antigenic determinants (e.g. 4, 21, 99, 110, 119, 121); it tolerates higher temperatures (45); and it is pathogenic. Isolates of *N. fowleri,* whether from human infections or from water, readily infect and kill mice. By the same criteria, *N. gruberi* appears to be nonpathogenic (21, 33, 45, 99).

Several isolates of both *N. gruberi* and *N. fowleri* contain an infectious agent that can kill vertebrate cells in culture (27). One strain also carries virus-like particles (94), but these are independent of the infectious agent (27).

N. gruberi is found everywhere that people live, and we must come in contact with it often in our lives, especially if we swim or garden. It has been worked with casually in laboratories for 80 years. I know of no case where *N. gruberi* (as opposed to *N. fowleri*) has caused a human disease. Yet the organism deserves to be treated with some respect, especially by those of us who regularly handle large quantities in the laboratory. Amebae of *N. gruberi* can grow at 37°C; there is no question that *N. gruberi* and *N. fowleri* are related organisms; and many if not all isolates of *Naegleria* appear to contain an infectious agent. On the other hand, with the two strains we use regularly in this laboratory—both authentic *N. gruberi* (33)—we have not always been cautious. We routinely handle up to 4.5×10^{10} cells at a time, and before we were aware of the possible risks, we did not hesitate to get the cells on our hands and many of us inadvertently swallowed large inocula. We are more careful now, but still we do not hesitate to work with the organism, including in laboratory exercises for students.

PHYLOGENY *Naegleria* occupies a special position among the eukaryotic protists (33). It can change from an ameba to a flagellate; each form, by itself, would be unhesitatingly placed in a separate class of the phylum Protozoa. It is generally classified with the amebae, but there is no indication that it is closely related to other organisms in that class, such as *Acanthamoeba. Naegleria* is closely related to another amebo-flagellate, *Tetramitus rostratus,* which is usually classified among the flagellates. It is likely also to be related to the true slime molds, Myxomycetes, which are usually classified among the fungi, but there is no evidence that it is related to the cellular slime molds, such as *Dictyostelium.*

The related organism, *T. rostratus,* is worthy of comment. *T. rostratus* was first described, in 1852, as a flagellate with four flagella, a beaklike anterior projection or rostrum, and a trough running from the anterior end to midbody—the oral groove, cytostome, or mouth. These flagellates, studied by protozoologists for 70 years, feed on bacteria and reproduce by fission. In 1922, Bunting isolated a strain of amebae, and from these, flagellates arose that were indistinguishable from *T. rostratus* (13). Her studies established *T. rostratus* as an amebo-flagellate. Its amebae are much like those of *Naegleria* in size, morphology, and even detailed pattern of nuclear division (33, 81). These amebae form cysts that, unlike those of *N. gruberi* or any known species of *Naegleria,* have thin walls that disappear when the amebae excyst. The amebae also transform, slowly and not readily, into flagellates. Differentiation to flagellates is favored by a reduced oxygen concentration in the environment (32, 33). Flagellates of *T. rostratus* can revert to amebae shortly after they form, but they also can form a mouth, feed on bacteria, reproduce, and form cultures in which only flagellates are found. Brent studied a stable strain of flagellates, and the only way he could obtain amebae was to treat the flagellates with nitrogen mustard (11). Although *T. rostratus* is an extraordinary organism, in which both amebae and flagellates can reproduce as stable phenotypes, it has received very little attention in recent years.

Genome

A haploid strain of *N. gruberi,* strain NEG, contains about 0.17 pg of DNA per cell (33), an amount similar, for example, to that found in *Dictyostelium discoideum* (106). The DNA has been isolated and characterized as to buoyant density (33; C. Walsh, I. Mahler, and C. Fulton, manuscript in preparation). It contains a main component (1.693 g/cm^3; 69% of DNA), and two satellites (1.683, 14% and 1.702, 17%). The main component, with a G + C of 34%, is nuclear. The heavy satellite is also nuclear but is not separated from the main band when nucleolus and nucleoplasm are fractionated, even though this procedure cleanly separates RNA species (113). The light satellite is mitochondrial DNA. The base compositions of the DNA components of *N. gruberi* more closely resemble those of the true slime mold *Physarum* (50) than those of *Acanthamoeba* (1, 10) and *Dictyostelium* (30, 106). If the satellite DNA is excluded, the DNA content of *N. gruberi* is about 30 times the DNA content of the genome of *Escherichia coli* and 0.03 times that of mammals.

Three apparently unrelated amebae—*Naegleria* (33), *Acanthamoeba* (63), and *Dictyostelium* (22)—are all extremely resistant to ionizing radiation. This has been interpreted to indicate that these amebae possess unusually efficient repair mechanisms. *Naegleria* amebae are quite sensitive to ultraviolet radiation (33, 66, 127).

ASPECTS OF METHODOLOGY

Still suddenly spoke, reminding me he was still in the room.

"You started out by defining vertebrate cell differentiation, and now you are telling me about a protist. Should the term differentiation be used at all in reference to developmental changes in microorganisms?"

"I could skirt your question, Still, and say it's a question of semantics, that it is just a phrase, and that I like it. But there are other reasons. One reason is that other names seem less suitable to me. In his beautiful first description of *Naegleria,* Schardinger called the change transformation (*Umgestaltung*), and this is also a good descriptive term. However, cell transformation has come to have a special meaning to those biologists—most of us—interested in the spontaneous or virus-induced transformation of vertebrate cells to tumor cells, or 'transformed' cells. In this sense of transformation, or in the sense that one refers to DNA-mediated genetic transformation, the change of amebae to flagellates is certainly more like differentiation than 'transformation.' There is a protozoological term sometimes used for the process, enflagellation, but that sounds more like a flogging than a differentiation to me. The process has even been called AFT, for ameba-to-flagellate transformation, in which case reversion to amebae becomes FAT. To me, in 1977, differentiation fits best."

"It doesn't seem to matter much what you call it as long as you know what you are studying, why you are studying it, and how to study it."

"True."

Still departed, leaving me in peace. But I knew he would be back.

In general, working with *N. gruberi* as a microorganism is as easy and as quantitative as working with *E. coli* or yeast.

Strains

Several of the laboratories engaged in developmental studies are using one or both of two strains that have been described in detail (33). Strain NEG was derived from an isolate by F. L. Schuster, designated EG, and comes from California. Its advantages are that it differentiates well and is haploid, and a derivative strain, NEG-M, can be grown in one of the simplest axenic media available (36). Strain NEG has been tested for pathogenicity in mice and was found to be nonpathogenic (33). The strain tends to go from haploid to diploid (presumably through mitotic errors), and diploids are selected for by faster migration on agar, so maintaining haploid NEG requires regular checking and recloning (33). Unfortunately, strain NEG-M is a diploid. Strain NB-1 is a clonal derivative of strain 1518/1a isolated in England by E. G. Pringsheim; it is a stable diploid. It is especially easy to maintain, transform, and use to examine encystment and excystment; it recommends itself for classroom use. Strains NEG and NEG-M are deposited in the American Type Culture Collection as 30223 and 30224, respectively; strain NB-1 is in the Culture Center of Algae and Protozoa as 1518/1d. Although strains NEG and NB-1 originated at opposite corners of the world and differ in many respects, they are both typical *N. gruberi* and they share some surface antigenic determinants in common (33).

Since *N. gruberi* is so readily isolated, there are literally thousands of strains mentioned in the literature, usually only once and often so ambiguously as to be without meaning. For example, as Page (70) pointed out, for the Culture Center of Algae and Protozoa strains, 1518/1 does not identify the strain and 1518 does not identify the species, yet both appear frequently in the literature. Although much use can be made of strain differences, the advantages of using well-characterized strains are also obvious, and it would help if those using *N. gruberi* for analytical studies would standardize on a few strains rather than using each strain for one or two papers and then discarding it.

Those who isolate *Naegleria* from soil and water should remember that *N. fowleri* may be included among the isolates and should take appropriate precautions.

In this and most other laboratories, amebae are grown on *Klebsiella pneumoniae.*[2] They will grow on other bacteria as well (5, 16).

Strains can be maintained on agar with bacteria, where the cysts remain viable for months (33, 69). Axenic strains can be maintained in the same way, in association with bacteria, and returned at will to axenic culture by using antibiotics (33). Otherwise, the axenic cultures must be subcultured soon after they reach stationary phase, since they do not encyst well and lose viability rapidly. Strains can be preserved by freezing amebae and storing them at −150°C (87, 96, 121).

Cultivation and Growth of Amebae

Happily, the days are past when the amebae are grown on undefined bacterial flora supported by irreproducible nutrients, such as cabbage and crackers (124) or human feces (80). Several methods are available for growing quantities of healthy amebae.

The simplest method is cultivation on dilute nutrient agar in association with *K. pneumoniae* or other suitable bacteria. At 34°C, cultures can be grown overnight; the doubling time is 1.7 hr (38) and yields of 4×10^7 amebae per 100-mm petri dish (33) or 10^9 amebae per baking tray (60) are obtained. Amebae will grow at temperatures to nearly 40°C (33, 45), but the rate is maximal between 30° and 34°C. Agar media can also be used for eliminating unwanted contaminants or changing the host bacterium, and for cloning by plating dilute suspensions of cells so that the offspring of individual amebae form clear plaques in the lawn of bacteria, in a little over 24 hr (33).

Amebae can also be grown in suspension culture in buffer containing a dense suspension of bacteria. Under these conditions, amebae grow with a doubling time of about 2 hr at 30°C to a stationary phase yield of about 2×10^6 amebae per ml (40). Such suspension cultures permitted development of a method for obtaining synchronous mitosis. When log phase cultures, growing at 30°C, are shifted to 39°C, division ceases and the amebae increase in size. After 100 min at 39°C, the cell

[2]This is the same organism that we and many others have used for years under the name *Aerobacter aerogenes.* We received the strain we use from M. Sussman (see 103); this strain is widely used as food for *Dictyostelium discoideum* as well as other phagotrophs. The generic name *Aerobacter* caused confusion and has been formally rejected (12). Since then, several new names for this organism have appeared in the ameba literature, including *Enterobacter aerogenes, Klebsiella aerogenes* (there is no such species in the United States) (12), and *Klebsiella pneumoniae.* In an effort to reduce this confusion, I had the strain we and others are using carefully identified by the Center for Disease Control in Atlanta, Ga. (through the courtesy of Don Brenner and Mary Alyce Fife-Asbury). The strain is a typical *K. pneumoniae* in every respect, and in the United States at least, that is the only correct name for it. Amebae of *N. gruberi* also grow well on *Enterobacter aerogenes* (C. Fulton, unpublished observations), as they do on *Escherichia coli* and numerous other species of bacteria, but *K. pneumoniae* remains a particularly convenient food source (33). The widely used strain of "*A. aerogenes,*" hereafter designated *K. pneumoniae* strain BS (Brandeis-Sussman), has been deposited in the American Type Culture Collection.

volume has nearly doubled. If the cultures are returned to 30°C, a single burst of division occurs, during which 80–90% of the amebae divide within 30 min and 60–70% of the amebae are in karyokinesis (metaphase to telophase) simultaneously (40). Suspension cultures also have been used to grow large quantities of amebae (62). Growth of amebae in nutrient liquid media containing bacteria has not proved very satisfactory, since usually the byproducts of bacterial growth render the environment inhospitable for the amebae (33).

The first successes at axenic cultivation involved growth of amebae in media containing heat-killed bacteria (88). A breakthrough came when Balamuth developed a bacteria-free axenic medium that would support the growth of strain EG (7). We modified Balamuth's medium so that it would support the growth of several strains of amebae, including strains NB-1 and NEG, in suspension cultures (33). One of these media has been simplified to a partially defined, particulate-free medium that supports the growth of strain NEG-M, but not NEG or NB-1 (36). This medium, medium M7, contains 0.3 mM L-methionine, 30 mM dextrose, 7 mM phosphate buffer, pH 6.8, 10% (vol/vol) dialyzed fetal calf serum (the "macromolecular fraction" after exhaustive dialysis against water), and 0.5% yeast extract. This medium has supported vigorous growth for more than 6000 generations. Cultures shaken at 32°C grow with a doubling time of 8 hr to a stationary phase yield of 2–5 $\times 10^6$ amebae per ml.

Band & Balamuth succeeded in replacing the serum component in their axenic medium with hemin (9), and similar replacement has been achieved in an axenic medium for *N. fowleri* (52). So far we have been able to obtain growth of NEG-M in medium M7 containing hemin instead of dialyzed serum only if proteose peptone is added to the medium (C. Webster and C. Fulton, unpublished observations).

Control and Measurement of Differentiation to Flagellates

Straightforward microbiological procedures allow one to control and measure differentiation (38). The method is formally analogous to the one-step growth experiment that proved so useful in the analysis of bacteriophage reproduction. Growing or early stationary phase amebae are suspended in non-nutrient buffer at time zero, the bacteria or growth medium is washed away by differential centrifugation, and the cells are incubated in buffer at a defined temperature and maintained in suspension by gentle agitation. The progress of differentiation is evaluated by fixing samples in Lugol's iodine, a one-step fixative stain, and by counting the percentage of cells that have a given property, such as cells with flagella, independent of body shape, or cells with a flagellate body shape, independent of flagella (Figure 2). By careful attention to details, the conversion of cell phenotype can be made to occur synchronously, rapidly, and temporally reproducibly.

This method of measuring the phenotypic change separates the continuum of morphological changes into a series of quantal changes. The rise portion of curves such as those in Figure 2 indicates the population heterogeneity in time of each quantal change; if the population were totally synchronous the curve would appear as a step. The population heterogeneity in time of each change approximates a summed normal distribution, and the standard deviation may be determined by

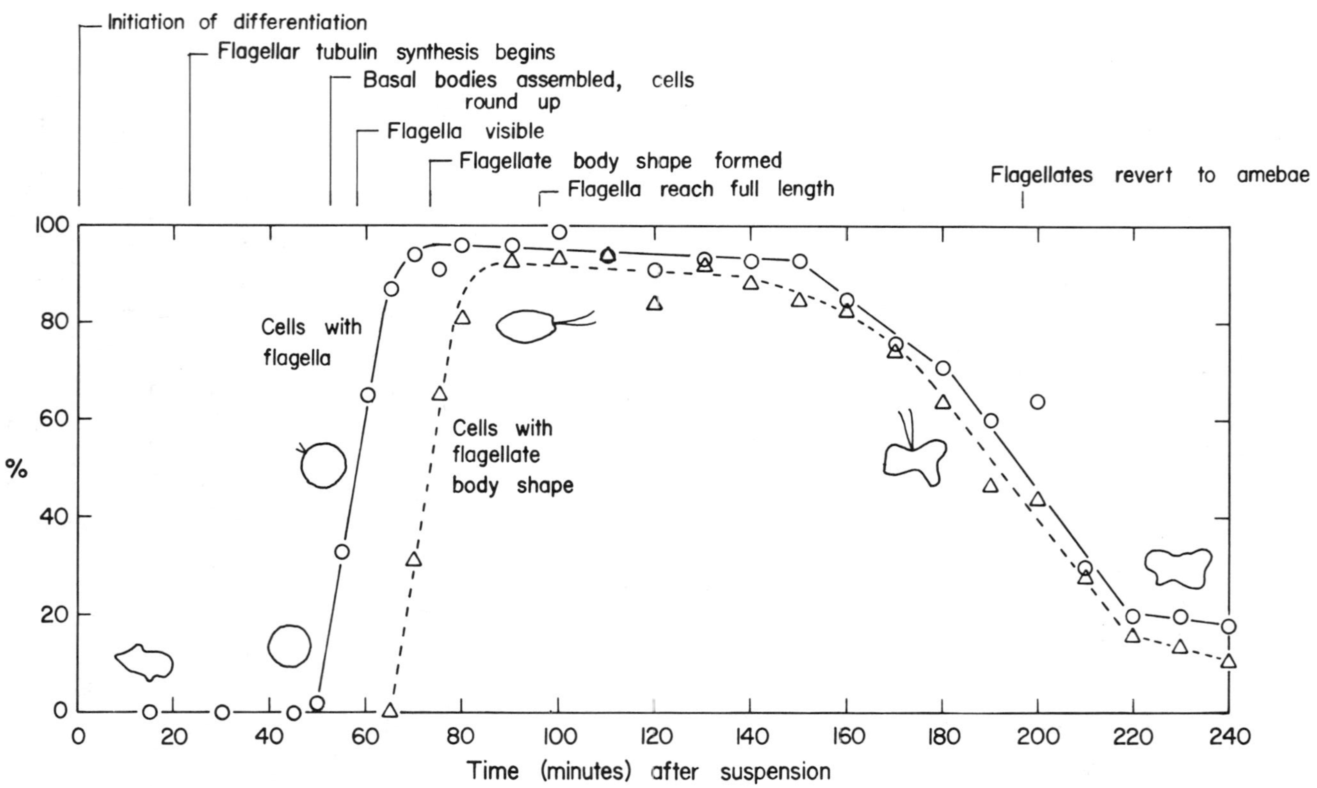

Figure 2 Differentiation of amebae to flagellates. Amebae of *Naegleria gruberi* NEG were grown at 33°C on NM agar (38) in association with *Klebsiella pneumoniae.* At time zero, the cells were suspended in T buffer [2 mM tris(hydroxymethyl)aminomethane-HCl, pH 7.2], washed relatively free of bacteria by a rapid procedure for differential centrifugation at room temperature, and then incubated in T buffer at 10^7 cells per ml, at 25°C with gentle shaking. Samples were taken at intervals to Lugol's iodine, and two independent counts were made: for percentage of cells with flagella and for percentage of cells with flagellate body shape. Some of the major events of differentiation are shown above the graph.

probit analysis (38). To the best of my knowledge, the synchrony routinely obtained is as good as that observed in any phenotypic change.

It is convenient to express the time of differentiation as the time that 50% of the population has completed a given phenotypic change. The time that 50% of the cells have flagella is specifically defined as the T_{50}. The times to 50% can be used to compare the relative rates of differentiation if the population heterogeneity in time of differentiation is similar among the samples examined, as it often is (38).

Differentiation can be completed very rapidly. At 28°C, 60 min after suspension more than 95% of the population has differentiated to flagellates. We usually use 25°C. At this temperature, for strain NEG, flagellates (cells with flagella) are first seen 50 min after suspension, and by 70 min more than 90% of the cells have flagella (Figure 2). The T_{50} is about 60 min, with a range, in hundreds of recent experiments, of from 58–63 min. For strain NB-1, differentiation takes 3–5 min longer than it does for strain NEG under the same conditions (33). Axenically grown cells differentiate more slowly (see Figure 3). In 50 successive differentiations of axenic cells at 25°C, the T_{50} averaged 79 min, with a standard deviation of ±1.7 min (36).

Although it is easy to obtain reproducible differentiation of this quality, the details of procedure are important. For those who may be interested in using this system, the following lists the major details we have found to be important, and unimportant, during the past decade. Our standard conditions, for bacteria-grown and axenically grown cells, respectively, are summarized (see Figures 2 and 3) and have been described in detail (33, 36, 38).

1. *Cells* In our experience, if one is working with a good clonal strain of *Naegleria* and encounters difficulties, the cells usually are not at fault. Chang (15) reported that after growth at high temperature the capacity to differentiate was lost, but we have been unable to confirm this (33). No spontaneous mutants have been found.

2. *Growth conditions* For bacteria-grown cells, the nutrient agar medium should have dilute nutrients, since otherwise differentiation is delayed and heterogeneous. Wet plates or droplets of water of condensation on the agar can cause the appearance of flagellates at time zero; if water is avoided, flagellates are never seen until the proper time during differentiation. Growing or early stationary phase cells can be harvested for differentiation, but late stationary phase cells, that have started to encyst, do not differentiate reproducibly. We usually incubate petri dishes at 34°C and baking trays at 28°C, but this is for convenience, and over the range of 22°–34°C, the growth temperature is not an important variable for differentiation. In contrast, the differentiation of axenically grown cells is profoundly influenced by the prior growth temperature (36), and also by the pH and the conditions of agitation during growth [proper conditions are described in reference (36)]. Since a decrease in temperature can initiate the differentiation of both bacteria-grown and axenic cells, as described below, cultures should be maintained at the growth temperature until one is ready to start differentiation.

3. *Suspension buffer* A wide variety of buffers (or just water) give comparable results; for convenience, we frequently use 2 mM tris(hydroxymethyl)aminomethane-HCl, pH about 7.2. Axenic cells differentiate more synchronously if a little

electrolyte is present; 10 mM KCl or NaCl is adequate, but if NaCl is used the flagellates are somewhat more stable than in KCl (C. Fulton, unpublished observations). Two important variables are the purity of the water (we use distilled-demineralized water) and the cleanliness of the glassware. In our experience traces of detergents, heavy metals, etc, are the most frequent cause of difficulties.

4. *Centrifugation* We wash both bacteria-grown and axenic amebae by three cycles of centrifugation and resuspension. The amebae are adversely affected by being incubated as pellets and their subsequent differentiation is retarded (38). A rapid centrifugation procedure in which each centrifugation takes 45 sec and washing can be completed in 3–5 min reduces this damage to a minimum (33). One need not worry about being too rough with the cells; we pipet them vigorously and agitate them by using a Vortex Genie mixer without any signs of cell damage. Routine differential centrifugation of bacteria-grown cells removes 99% of the bacteria (38). Some of the remaining bacteria are carried along, stuck to the amebae; the number of these can be reduced by vortexing the cells between each centrifugation.

5. *Population density* The differentiation of strain NB-1 was found to be independent of cell population density (38). The time course of appearance of cells with flagella is similarly independent of population density in strain NEG, over at least a 10^3-fold range, but for this strain the formation of the flagellate shape and stability of flagellates are favored by high population density (37). At very high population densities, agitation for aeration becomes especially crucial, but synchronous differentiation at cell densities as great as 10^8 per ml can be obtained with 25 ml of suspension in a 250-ml flask (C. Fulton and E. Y. Lai, unpublished data).

6. *Temperature and agitation* The rate of differentiation is very dependent upon temperature (15, 38, 71, 86). Differentiation does not occur below 10°C, the rate increases to a plateau at about 28°C, and differentiation above about 34°C is unreliable. We usually work at 25°C, which is a compromise between obtaining rapid differentiation and rapid reversion. The T_{50} at 25°C is about 60 min; at 28°C it is 47 min. Most commercial water baths do not hold temperature adequately for reproducible differentiation and should be modified with a regulator that permits control to within 0.2°C. Because of the importance of temperature control it is also crucial that the containers be adequately submerged in the water bath.

Agitation should be sufficient to maintain the cells in suspension and to provide sufficient gas exchange (depending upon the cell population density), but excessive mechanical agitation can cause reversion during differentiation. We use reciprocating shaker water baths, with 100 oscillations per min and 2.5-cm strokes. Under these conditions, excellent differentiation can be obtained with 3 ml per 25-ml Erlenmeyer flask, 15 ml per 125, and 25–40 per 250, or with 500 ml per 2500-ml Corning Low Form flask.

Differentiation is initiated by transferring cells to non-nutrient buffer; this defines the zero time. For cells grown on an agar substratum, this equals the moment buffer (at room temperature or, for critical experiments, 25°C) is added to suspend the cells. For cells grown in a liquid medium (with bacteria or axenically), the cells are sedimented and then resuspended in buffer at time zero. Three other procedures have been used successfully to defer time zero until after centrifugation is completed.

The cells can be maintained below 10°C until washing is completed (38), they can be maintained at a low pH (126), or they can be maintained in buffer containing 0.1 M NaCl (35; C. Fulton, unpublished data). We have obtained excellent control of the initiation of differentiation by rapid washing in ice-cold buffer or by initially suspending the cells in high salt and then washing them in the cold. Yuyama obtained synchronous differentiation by using low pH buffer to wash the cells (126, 127), but with our strains the low pH treatment damages the cells and results in heterogeneous differentiation.

Biochemical Methods

During the past few years, many of the standard methods of cellular biochemistry and molecular biology have been adapted for use with *N. gruberi.* These include labeling of DNA (19), RNA (113), and protein (43, 61) with radioactive precursors and isolation of DNA (33), RNA (113), and specific proteins, especially outer doublet tubulin (60). Cell fractionation has been used to obtain flagella (60), nuclei, nucleoli, and polysomes (113). RNA polymerase (101) and translatable mRNA (114; E. Lai, C. Walsh, and C. Fulton, manuscript in preparation) have been isolated. *Naegleria* is easy to label, lyse, fractionate, and study biochemically. In cultures grown in association with bacteria, one must guard against possible contributions of bacteria to the results (e.g. 33). One must also use precautions to avoid the effects of degradative enzymes. Amebae are bacteria eaters, and we have found that the cells have formidable nucleases and proteases (J. D. Kowit, I. Mahler, J. Sellers, P. A. Simpson, C. Walsh, and C. Fulton, unpublished data). Similar problems have been reported in other bacteria eaters, such as cellular slime molds (104).

Prospects for Genetic Analysis

In strain NEG, which apparently is haploid, methods have been developed for mutagenesis and for selection of mutants altered with respect to differentiation, and mutants of several phenotypes have been obtained (33). These include mutants that remain amebae under all conditions tested, ones that form paralyzed flagella or flagella that only tremble, ones that form normal flagella but remain ameboid throughout, and so forth. Mutants resistant to drugs have also been isolated. Okubo & Inoki (67) reported the isolation, in another strain, of mutants that are temperature sensitive for growth. None of these mutants have been extensively studied as yet. In strain NB-1, apparently diploid, no mutants were found after extensive mutagenesis and selection (33).

So far, all searches for mating have been unsuccessful (33). I am encouraged to hope that mating will be found. Many organisms use flagellated cells as gametes, from algae to primates and including the Myxomycetes and possibly also *Tetramitus* (33). Perhaps the right conditions for *Naegleria* have not yet been found, or the right mating types. Mating was unknown in *Dictyostelium discoideum* until a few years ago, but recently both a parasexual system for genetic analysis (54, 58) and a bonafide sexual cycle (28) have been discovered. The challenge, I believe, is not whether *Naegleria* has a sexual cycle but rather how to find it.

EVENTS DURING DIFFERENTIATION

Later, Still stopped by my laboratory.

"I've asked a couple of other biologists what differentiation is, and they both got annoyed with me. Why do people get so passionate about what is, after all, a term?"

"I don't know, Still. But they certainly do. Let me tell you about conversations I had with two outstanding vertebrate embryologists, both worthy of respect.

"The first embryologist, Professor Hill, came to my university in the early 1960s to give a seminar course on cell differentiation, which I had the pleasure to attend. The topic of the first session was the 'attributes' of differentiation. Attributes began to accumulate on the blackboard: a constellation of phenotypic changes, ordered in space and time, involving the synthesis of specialized 'luxury' products, especially proteins. All the examples were vertebrate cells. I noted that *Naegleria,* in changing from an ameba to a flagellate, appeared to do all these things as dramatically as any cell. 'Yes,' said Professor Hill, 'but that change is reversible and therefore not differentiation.' This idea, Still, comes from an old dictum of Paul Weiss that differentiation, by definition, is an irreversible, unidirectional phenotypic change. Anyway, I was not to be so easily dismissed by Professor Hill, and pointed out that *Tetramitus* did all the things that *Naegleria* did in changing from an ameba to a flagellate, but that the change could be considered 'irreversible' in that the product of the change was stable, reproducing flagellates. Thus *Tetramitus,* sister (or brother) to *Naegleria,* accomplishes as irreversible a phenotypic change as most vertebrate cells are known to do. It took me a long time to make this argument, because of course I had to introduce *Tetramitus.* When I finished, Professor Hill, obviously perturbed, said: 'All right. But we will restrict our discussion to the differentiation of vertebrate cells.' The sessions were interesting, and at the end of the series Professor Hill summed them all up by describing how the revolutionary Jacob-Monod model for the regulation of gene activity, then new, might be used to explain cell differentiation."

While I was talking, Still had become restless.

"Now you really have me confused. Are you telling me that the term differentiation applies to the *lac* operon of *E. coli* and to vertebrate cells but not to eukaryotic protists?"

There was nothing I could say to Still, so I just stood there. Soon he had another question.

"You know, the reversibility of differentiation, or whatever you call it, in *Naegleria,* and the stability of the two phenotypes in *Tetramitus,* raises all sorts of questions about the meaning of 'irreversible' phenotypic changes. Why don't you study *Tetramitus* instead of *Naegleria?*"

"Because for studying phenotypic change, the rapid and synchronous differentiation of *Naegleria* is much more suitable than *Tetramitus.* But certainly the alternation of stable phenotypes in *Tetramitus* is a very challenging problem, and it is amazing to me that no one is studying it."

Still picked up the manuscript again.

Each system—event in the life cycle of an organism—used for studying differentiation has attributes that encourage exploration of particular aspects of the process. Those aspects that so far have proved attractive in the differentiation of *Naegleria* amebae to flagellates are summarized here. It will be evident to the reader that some doors have been opened toward understanding specific events during differentiation, but in each case we are still standing in the vestibule.

Assembly of the Flagellar Apparatus

The flagellar apparatus—the flagella, their basal bodies, associated cytoplasmic microtubules, and a rootlet—can be isolated more-or-less intact by lysis of flagellates under various conditions (24, 25; C. Allen and D. E. Larson, unpublished observations).

The synchronous differentiation of *Naegleria* provides an advantageous basis for description of the morphogenesis of the flagellar apparatus.

Flagella are first seen with the light microscope when they are about 1 μm long (38). At 25°C they elongate at an initial rate of about 0.5–1 μm per min, and the rate steadily decelerates as they elongate (C. Fulton, unpublished data). The pattern of growth at a decelerating rate is similar to what has been observed during the regeneration of flagella in other organisms (e.g. 83, 107).

Flagellum development as observed in the electron microscope is very straightforward (25). Basal bodies assume a position just beneath the plasma membrane, with their microtubules perpendicular to the cell surface. The microtubules of the flagella are assembled beginning at the distal end of the basal bodies, with the outer doublet microtubules continuous with the A and B tubules of the basal bodies. The outer doublet and central pair microtubules of the flagellar axoneme are assembled simultaneously inside a ballooning continuation of the cell membrane. The flagellar membrane elongates to accommodate the elongation of the axoneme; outgrowth occurs simultaneously with assembly. The sequence of development was verified by quantitative study of samples fixed at intervals during differentiation. Many observers have since found this simple sequence of flagellum development in other organisms, including in *Tetramitus rostratus* (68).

Flagellar microtubules are probably assembled by adding subunits to the distal end of the elongating microtubules. Witman has obtained direct evidence for this in regenerating flagella of *Chlamydomonas* (125). In *Naegleria,* the flagella are functional as they elongate, and it is difficult to imagine intercalation of subunits into intact, continuous outer doublet microtubules between the distal end of the basal body and the distal tip of the elongating axoneme.

The basal bodies of *Naegleria* flagellates have the typical centriole-like structure observed in other organisms (25, 89). Since centriole-like structures have been thought to be self-replicating (34), we expected that basal bodies would be present in amebae. However, a quantitative search with the electron microscope allows confidence that centriole-like structures are absent in amebae (39). At 25°C, centriole-like structures appear in differentiating cells 10 min before the appearance of flagella. Even the mitotic apparatus of dividing amebae does not have any associated centriole-like structures (39, 92). Since this study, increasing evidence has been obtained in other organisms, suggesting that the de novo formation of centriole-like structures may not be unusual (e.g. 14, 46, 49). In the Myxomycetes, no centrioles are found during intranuclear mitosis in the plasmodial stage, but in myxamoebae, centrioles are present at the poles during mitosis (3, 47, 91).

The flagellar rootlet, or rhizoplast, is a periodically banded fiber that runs from the basal bodies along the nucleus and tapers to end free in the cytoplasm (Figure

1*F*) (25). The association with the nucleus appears to be reasonably firm, and in lysed cells, the flagellar apparatus and nucleus often isolate together (25). It has been suggested that the function of the rootlet, found in many flagellated and ciliated cells, is to serve as an anchor for the flagellar apparatus; this is plausible but conjectural. The rootlet in *Naegleria* has been found to have a variable periodicity in situ but not in isolation, suggesting that the variations "are related to some function (either contractile or elastic) of the organelle" (97). No trace of the rootlets has been found in amebae, and Dingle has estimated that the rootlets are assembled concurrently with the assembly of flagella (24).

Associated with the flagellar apparatus there is a complex array of microtubules; these might have a role in determining the shape of flagellates. Only those nearest the basal bodies, which are preserved by osmium tetroxide, have been adequately described (25). The cortical microtubules, which are preserved when glutaraldehyde is used as the primary fixative, have been documented (23, 33), but their arrangement awaits study. Under conditions of fixation that preserve the cortical microtubules in flagellates and the mitotic apparatus microtubules in amebae, no microtubules have been found in the cytoplasm of amebae (A. D. Dingle, C. Fulton, and P. A. Simpson, unpublished observations).

It is noteworthy that every component of the flagellar apparatus is assembled during differentiation. The events of assembly appear to occur rapidly. At 25°C, there is a "covert period" of about 50 min before any structures are assembled. Then the basal bodies are assembled, apparently rapidly since intermediate stages have been very hard to find (24, 39). Ten minutes later, the flagella begin to elongate and the rootlets begin to be assembled, and within 40 min after that the definitive flagellate-shaped cell with full-length flagella has formed.

All the components of the flagellar apparatus also appear to be assembled during differentiation of *Tetramitus* amebae to flagellates (68). In Myxomycetes, the myxamoebae already have basal bodies and some of the accessory cytoplasmic microtubules, and when they form flagellated swarm cells, the major structure assembled is the flagellum (2, 91). In this case, the phenotypic change from amebae to amebae with flagella (swarm cells) occurs without a lag (48, 51, 55, 56), and in many respects this change appears more analogous to flagellar regeneration than to the more major reorganization undergone by *Naegleria* and *Tetramitus* (33).

Cell Cycle and Competence to Differentiate

When amebae are suspended in non-nutrient buffer, all of the population (regularly >95%) differentiate synchronously to flagellates. This differentiation is a 1:1 conversion of cell phenotype, and there is no change in cell number during the process (38, 43). Each cell responds to the environmental change as an individual, independent of interaction with its neighbors, as is indicated by the observation that the rate of differentiation is independent of cell population density (37, 38). Individual cells in microdrops also differentiate (38, 64). Cell volume decreases during differentiation (24, 53).

All healthy amebae are competent to differentiate, whether they are growing exponentially or are in stationary phase. Even the kinetics of differentiation is unaffected by the growth phase of the amebae at the time they are sampled, unless the amebae are in late stationary phase and have begun to encyst. Unpublished experiments have verified the independence of competence and growth phase for both bacteria-grown and axenic cells. In one such experiment (Figure 3), axenic cells were grown in a series of replicate flasks. Each day the cells from one flask were harvested and suspended in buffer. As can be seen in Figure 3, each culture differentiated synchronously. For the five cultures, the T_{50} averaged 79 min with a standard deviation of ±2.3 min. There is a hint in this experiment that cells in exponential growth (days 1 and 2) differentiated slightly faster than stationary phase cells (inoculum and days 3 and 4), but this is not always reproducible and comparable variability has been observed in replicate flasks tested on the same day. Experiments such as this one indicate that cells are competent to differentiate all through their growth cycle.

Is the capacity to differentiate influenced by the position of a cell in the cell cycle at the time it is sampled for differentiation? Attempts to determine this by using amebae in synchronized mitosis were unsuccessful, because the amebae "primed" for mitosis at high temperature tended to complete mitosis during washing and differentiation (40). Thus, although these amebae differentiated, the events of differentiation did not reflect the mitotic state of the cells at the time of sampling.

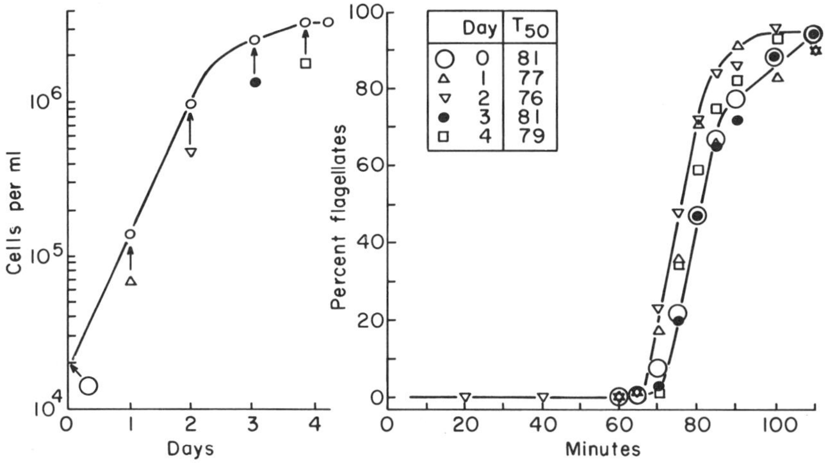

Figure 3 Differentiation is independent of the precise growth state of the amebae. Stationary phase amebae of *Naegleria gruberi* NEG-M were inoculated into a series of replicate flasks of medium M7, 20 ml per 125-ml flask, and incubated at 32°C with gentle shaking. Three flasks were counted each day, and the counts agreed with an average variation of 4.4%. The growth curve (*left*) yielded a doubling time of 8 hr and a stationary phase yield of 3.3×10^6 amebae per ml. At the time of inoculation, and each subsequent day, a portion of the cells was tested for differentiation under standard conditions: the cells were sedimented, resuspended in TK buffer (T buffer with 10 mM KCl) at time zero, washed by two more centrifugations, and incubated in TK buffer at 25°C with gentle shaking. The population density during differentiation ranged from $3.5–7.0 \times 10^5$ cells per ml. Samples fixed in Lugol's iodine were counted for the percentage of cells with flagella; the results are shown (*right*).

However, for axenic cells, the population heterogeneity in time of differentiation is only about 20 min for cells with an 8-hr doubling time, so cells at any time in an 8-hr cell cycle can differentiate within a few minutes of one another. Corff & Yuyama have estimated the timing of events in the cell cycle under these growth conditions: G_1, 180 min; S, 180 min; G_2, 90 min; and M, 30 min (19). Bacteria-grown cells, harvested during exponential growth at 34°C, where the doubling time is 100 min, differentiate with a temporal heterogeneity of about 15 min. Therefore, the amebae initiate differentiation as a result of suspension, without having to get out of, or into, any major part of their cell cycle.

When cysts are induced to excyst in an aqueous environment suitable for differentiation of amebae to flagellates, encystment and transformation occur simultaneously (see 33). Thus, even cysts are "competent."

Suspension in non-nutrient buffer causes each ameba to begin to differentiate to a flagellate, independent of the ameba's precise position in the growth cycle or cell cycle. Thus, aspects of differentiation that are controversial, and difficult to determine, in many cultured cells, especially vertebrate cells (82), are easily settled in *Naegleria.*

Suddenly Still interrupted again.

"You told me you were going to tell me about two conversations, but so far you have only told me one. Will the other make the meaning of differentiation clearer?"

"I doubt it, Still, but I will tell you the story. I was sunning on the beach at Cold Spring Harbor, in 1975, when Professor Wood came down for a swim. As he passed by he remarked 'I like your work, as long as you don't call it cell differentiation.' When he emerged from the water, we had a good talk. His point was that every true cell differentiation is preceded by a crucial, or quantal, mitosis, and therefore *Naegleria* did not qualify."

"You're beginning to lose me again. Are you saying that a quantal mitosis is part of every differentiation?"

"No, I'm not. Professor Wood was."

Initiation of Differentiation

One research opportunity offered by *Naegleria* is that it should be possible to learn about events at the beginning of this cell differentiation. Time zero for differentiation is not an arbitrary time point. At any time during thousands of generations of growth, amebae only begin to differentiate when treated appropriately. Conversely, they do not begin unless treated appropriately. In this sense, the moment of initiation is under the experimenter's control. This is similarly true, for example, for the initiation of development of cellular slime molds or for the initiation of encystment in various amebae.

The environmental signal that causes amebae to begin to differentiate must, in some way, give direction. The amebae are not prepared cells, waiting for a start signal (as an unfertilized egg or a cyst or spore), but are growing and would continue to grow unless directed, by a suitable change in their external environment, to either encyst or to transform.

In most studies of *Naegleria,* differentiation to flagellates has been initiated by transferring amebae from an agar substratum to an aqueous solution. This led us, as well as others, to think that the initial stimulus for differentiation must somehow involve the flow of water and ions (e.g. 73, 74, 122, 123). Other observations suggested that the emphasis on water and ions might be misleading. In particular, amebae growing in buffer with washed *Klebsiella* differentiate if diluted into the same buffer without *Klebsiella* (40). In this case, the only environmental alteration is the removal of washed *Klebsiella*; the major ionic composition of the aqueous environment is unchanged. Such experiments suggest that starvation might be involved in the initiation of differentiation. However, in both agar and buffer cultures with *Klebsiella,* the presence of living bacteria makes an analysis of the controlling environmental signals difficult. Analysis of the environmental signals became possible with the development of particulate-free axenic media. In suspension cultures in media such as M7, only amebae are found, and transfers from medium M7 to fresh medium M7 do not cause differentiation. One component of the medium, yeast extract, controls whether differentiation occurs (35). Transfer of amebae from medium M7 to the same medium without yeast extract is sufficient to cause differentiation. Only the removal of yeast extract has this effect. In reciprocal experiments, in which individual components of medium M7 are added to buffer, only the addition of yeast extract prevents differentiation. Fractionation of the yeast extract yielded two components that control differentiation: electrolytes and an unidentified Factor. Electrolytes alone prevent differentiation if present above a certain concentration. For NaCl and KCl, for example, the critical concentration is 0.08 M. The effect is not specific to particular ions, nor is it due simply to ionic strength. Osmotic pressure produced by nonpenetrating nonelectrolytes like sucrose can also inhibit differentiation, but the effect of electrolytes is not due solely to osmotic pressure. The unidentified Factor, a small molecule, can prevent differentiation at a concentration that does not increase the osmotic pressure of the solution, and that is estimated to be not more than 0.001 M. The action of Factor in controlling differentiation is much potentiated by electrolytes, such that a combination of one eighth the electrolyte concentration needed to prevent differentiation with one fourth the Factor concentration completely prevents differentiation. Factor and osmotic pressure do not act synergistically.

Axenically grown amebae somehow measure the concentration of Factor-electrolyte in their environment, and if either or both of these are decreased sufficiently they change their metabolism from growth to differentiation. The cells measure the relative, rather than the absolute, concentrations. For example, amebae grown in the presence of extra Factor adapt to it and will differentiate in concentrations of Factor and of electrolyte that prevent the differentiation of unadapted cells. These adapted cells also differentiate if transferred to regular growth medium (35).

Factor probably is the crucial member of this synergistic pair. Concentrations of electrolyte sufficient to prevent differentiation by themselves have an adverse effect on the incorporation of radioactive amino acids into proteins, whereas suitable mixtures of Factor-electrolyte prevent differentiation without any adverse effect on protein synthesis or RNA synthesis (C. Fulton and C. Walsh, unpublished data). The results to date suggest that electrolytes act to potentiate the action of Factor.

Differentiation can be initiated simply by lowering the temperature of cultures growing in medium M7—about 3°C is sufficient—or by violently agitating such cultures (C. Fulton, manuscript in preparation). The combination of temperature shift and agitation acts synergistically, and agitation followed by a decrease of 10°C causes at least 80% of the cells to differentiate to flagellates right in their growth medium. Factor and temperature also act synergistically in controlling differentiation. As with Factor and electrolytes, the synergism is quite pronounced. For example, 16 times as much Factor is required to prevent differentiation of cells shifted from 32° to 22°C as is required to prevent differentiation of cells shifted from 32° to 29°C.

Four initiating stimuli have been found, any one of which is enough to trigger at least a few minutes of differentiation: (*a*) lowering electrolyte concentration, (*b*) lowering concentration of Factor, (*c*) lowering temperature, and (*d*) increasing mechanical agitation. Probably still other stimuli could be found. Pairwise combinations of the environmental signals are synergistic, suggesting the possibility that they all affect a common cellular start signal.

A most useful byproduct of this work is the ability to manipulate the environment of axenic cells in relation to differentiation. One can obtain differentiation in a nutritionally sufficient environment (by reducing the concentration of Factor or by temperature downshifts), and one can starve the cells without differentiation (in buffer with Factor). This provides powerful means to distinguish, for example, between events that are induced by differentiation and those induced by starvation in non-nutrient buffer.

The environmental signals for bacteria-grown cells remain obscure. Plate-grown cells will begin to differentiate on the plate if exposed to a temperature downshift (C. Fulton, manuscript in preparation). However, attempts to control differentiation of bacteria-grown cells with concentrations of Factor-electrolyte sufficient to prevent differentiation of axenic cells have been unsuccessful, as have been attempts to isolate Factor from *Klebsiella* (C. Fulton, unpublished data). High concentrations of electrolytes alone will prevent differentiation (116, 122), but such high concentrations are required that it is questionable whether this inhibition has anything to do with normal regulation.

Todd & Kitching (109) reported that brief exposure to high hydrostatic pressure (45 min at 3500 psi) would cause amebae to differentiate to flagellates without any other change in their environment.

In many developing systems, diverse environmental signals lead to a specific response. The situation in *Naegleria* is not unusual—nor is the obscurity of the cellular start signal.

Environmental Manipulation of Differentiation

Still stood up and began to pace.

"I seem to be getting lost in semantics. Is differentiation irreversible?"

"Depends on your definition."

"Does it require a quantal mitosis?"

"That depends on your hypothesis."

"Then what is it?"

"There have been many attempts at definition. Consider one by Paul Gross: 'Cytodifferentiation, simple or complex, involves an actinomycin-sensitive step.' Here, at least, *Naegleria* qualifies."

Events during differentiation have been explored by altering the environment of differentiating cells.

PHYSICAL ENVIRONMENT Differentiation does not occur at temperatures below 10°C, but after an unknown "critical event," differentiation can be completed (i.e. the formation and elongation of flagella can occur) at 10°C (38). This critical event is accomplished about 5–10 min prior to the appearance of flagella. Ultraviolet light (260 nm) inhibits differentiation, and there is a decline in sensitivity as differentiation progresses (127).

INHIBITORS OF TRANSCRIPTION AND TRANSLATION Does the differentiation of amebae to flagellates require the synthesis of new RNA and protein? Many observers have found that either actinomycin D or cycloheximide prevents differentiation (8, 33, 44, 77, 79, 85, 111, 126). Recently, the effects of these inhibitors have been investigated more thoroughly (43). Experiments with radioactive precursors revealed that both RNA and protein are synthesized throughout differentiation but, not surprisingly since the cells are in non-nutrient buffer, synthesis is approximately balanced by degradation. Actinomycin D (120 μg/ml) and daunomycin (250 μg/ml) selectively inhibit RNA synthesis, and cycloheximide (100 μg/ml) selectively inhibits protein synthesis, throughout the time required for differentiation. These inhibitors prevent differentiation if added soon after the amebae are transferred to non-nutrient buffer but cease to block specific events of differentiation at specific times, the transition points. After each transition point, morphogenesis can occur in the presence of the inhibitor and in the relative absence of transcription or translation. For both axenic and bacteria-grown cells, RNA synthesis is required until half-way through the temporal process from initiation to flagellum assembly, and protein synthesis is required until three fourths of the way through. Even after flagellum outgrowth can occur in the presence of cycloheximide, the length of the flagella formed is determined by the extent of synthesis of an unknown "limiting precursor."

Temporally separate periods of transcription and translation are required for (*a*) the loss of ameba shape (rounding up), (*b*) the formation of flagella, and (*c*) the formation of the elongated flagellate shape (37; C. Fulton, manuscript in preparation).

A temporal sequence of requirements for transcription and translation has been observed in many developing systems, from cellular slime molds (105) to pancreas (84). The absolute times are much shorter in *Naegleria.*

These inhibitor experiments suggest that differentiation in *Naegleria* involves not only a rearrangement of pre-existing cell components but also a redirection of cell metabolism to produce, in a programmed sequence, new RNA and protein molecules that are required for differentiation. The experiments also make it possible to use these inhibitors to separate synthesis from morphogenesis, and thus to obtain, for example, the assembly of flagella or the formation of the flagellate shape in the virtual absence of concurrent protein synthesis.

OTHER INHIBITORS Many other inhibitors have been tested for their effects on differentiation, especially by Yuyama (126). A few warrant mention. 2-Mercaptoethanol reversibly inhibits differentiation (24, 111, 126); the significance of this is not obvious since its oxidation product, dithiodiglycol (2-hydroxyethyl disulfide), is even more effective (126). Concanavalin A inhibits differentiation (65, 75), but I have found that at effective concentrations this lectin damages the cells, as is evident from their swollen, vacuolated morphology (C. Fulton, unpublished data), so it is unclear whether the inhibition of differentiation is a direct effect or a secondary consequence of more general cell damage. Preston & O'Dell (77) reported that polymyxin B, itself an inhibitor, increases the sensitivity of *Naegleria* to certain other inhibitors. Okubo & Inoki (67) reported that cAMP reversibly inhibits differentiation, but we were unable to confirm this observation, and S. Okubo (personal communication) wrote that they are also unable to confirm their first experiment.

Transcription and Translation

RNA SYNTHESIS The RNA synthesized by cells differentiating in buffer versus amebae in axenic growth medium has been compared (113). There is proportionally more synthesis of messenger-like RNA and less of rRNA in differentiating cells than in growing cells. The messenger-like RNA synthesized during differentiation is heterogeneous in size. A careful search failed to reveal any giant heterogeneous nuclear RNA in *Naegleria*; this class of RNA also appears to be absent from *Dictyostelium* (29, 57). In differentiating *Naegleria,* the rapidly labeled RNA is first present in the nucleoplasm and moves rapidly to the cytoplasm, reaching equilibrium (nucleus/cytoplasm) within 10 min. Recently, Walsh et al (115) described changes in poly(A)-containing RNA during differentiation.

The pattern of RNA synthesis observed during differentiation is similar to that observed in other eukaryotic cells subjected to a nutritional stepdown. The conditions used for differentiation—shift from axenic medium to buffer—certainly involve a stepdown, and it was possible to demonstrate that the change in pattern of RNA synthesis is due to the stepdown and is independent of differentiation (112). When differentiation was obtained under conditions where there is little or no nutritional stepdown, rRNA synthesis continued at a level approximating that in growing cells. In contrast, amebae tranferred to Factor-electrolyte did not differentiate, but they showed a reduced proportion of rRNA synthesis. These experiments provide useful possibilities for manipulating RNA synthesis during differentiation.

Differentiating cells, under stepdown conditions where there are gross changes in the pattern of RNA synthesis, were examined to see if there were any changes in DNA-dependent RNA polymerases (101). Three major RNA polymerases were separated by chromatography; one appears to be the rRNA polymerase and the other two probably represent two forms of the same enzyme. The polymerases were extracted at three times during differentiation of axenic cells: 0 min (amebae), 30 min (near the end of the actinomycin D-sensitive period for flagellum formation), and 90 min (flagellates). No changes were found in the quantities of each polymerase, in their chromatographic behavior, or in the sensitivities to α-amanatin or to ions. It was concluded that the gross changes in RNA synthesis are not accompanied by any significant fluctuations in the major DNA-dependent RNA polymerases.

PROTEIN SYNTHESIS Differentiation occurs in a nutrient-free environment, and the amino acids for protein synthesis must come from intracellular pools or turnover of pre-existing protein. Stationary phase cells differentiate well in the absence of nutrients, and J. Mar and I (manuscript in preparation) are studying protein synthesis in these cells. Stationary phase, axenically grown amebae have about 25% of their cellular ribosomes in polysomes. When such amebae are transferred to non-nutrient buffer, the proportion of ribosomes in polysomes increases rapidly after a 20-min lag; by 60 min, about 75% of the ribosomes are in polysomes. During differentiation in buffer, pre-existing protein is degraded at the rate of about 6% per hr. Several different inhibitors of serine proteases reduce the rate of degradation to about 1% per hr and also prevent differentiation. These results suggest that differentiation in buffer may depend upon protein degradation, and that perhaps this degradation is catalyzed by serine proteases. However, these effects occur as a result of the nutritional stepdown and are independent of differentiation. Increased protein degradation occurs in cells starving in the presence of Factor-electrolyte, under conditions where differentiation does not occur. Cells differentiating in growth medium (in response to agitation and reduced temperature) do so without showing the increased rate of protein degradation. Under some conditions, cells can differentiate in growth medium in the presence of serine protease inhibitors.

The usefulness of the ability to manipulate the differentiation of *Naegleria* is evidenced by these experiments. In both the case of the change in pattern of RNA synthesis and of increased protein degradation, it was possible to show that these changes occur because of the nutritional stepdown rather than as an obligatory or programmed part of the differentiation process (although they may still be necessary for differentiation to occur under starvation conditions). In many other systems, if one observed comparable changes—indeed they have been observed—it would be difficult to determine whether or not the changes were part of the differentiation program.

OTHER SYNTHESES Corff & Yuyama have described experiments with [^{3}H]thymidine and autoradiography, which suggest that nuclear DNA synthesis ceases quickly after the initiation of differentiation (19). Surprisingly, there have been no studies of intermediary metabolism in *Naegleria,* during either growth or differentiation.

A Specific Synthesis and Assembly: Flagellar Tubulin

Many eukaryotes develop flagella during parts of their life cycles, especially when forming gametes. Flagella are favorable organelles to study: they can be isolated readily because of their peninsular location, they have a precise fine structure, and useful information about their biochemistry is available from studies in diverse organisms (100). The major structural protein of flagella, tubulin, has been extensively studied (102). For these reasons we decided to focus on the study of the synthesis and assembly of flagellar tubulin during differentiation. Tubulin was isolated from outer doublets and characterized; it was found similar to the tubulins of other organisms (60). An antiserum was prepared by using outer doublet tubulin as immunogen, and this antitubulin was found to recognize flagellar tubulin but not the tubulin found in amebae (60). Contrary to our expectation, the tubulin that formed the outer doublets was found to be synthesized de novo during differentiation (61).

Definitive isotope dilution experiments are possible because of the closed system aspect of this differentiation, i.e. the absence of any dependence on exogenous nutrients. Amebae are prelabeled during growth with a radioactive amino acid, such as [^{35}S]methionine, and then washed to buffer and divided into two aliquots. One aliquot, the control, is allowed to differentiate in buffer. In this control, all methionine would have to come from endogenous sources, and the specific activity of outer doublet tubulin would be the same whether or not it were synthesized. The other aliquot is incubated in buffer containing unlabeled L-methionine at the highest concentration that does not interfere with differentiation. In these chased cells, the specfic activity of newly synthesized proteins would be reduced to the extent of incorporation of exogenous unlabeled methionine. The outer doublet tubulin from the chased cells has only 30% as much radioactivity in methionine as that from the control cells, indicating that at least 70% of the outer doublet tubulin is synthesized de novo during differentiation. These results have been confirmed and extended to include both subunits of outer doublet tubulin (42), and also to demonstrate that the tubulin of flagellar central pair microtubules is also synthesized de novo, to the same extent (P. A. Simpson, D. Larson, J. Sellers, A. D. Dingle, and C. Fulton, manuscript in preparation).

In both axenic and bacteria-grown cells, synthesis of flagellar tubulin begins about one third of the way through differentiation, so synthesis and assembly are temporally separate (41, 61). Although there is abundant tubulin in amebae, this preexisting tubulin is not used in assembling the flagella (41). In fact, little nonflagellar tubulin is synthesized during differentiation (42). Both synthesis and utilization of flagellar tubulin is selective, in that most if not all of the tubulin incorporated into flagellar microtubules is newly synthesized in spite of the presence, in the cells, of a 20- to 50-fold excess of total cell tubulin. These results raise many questions about the synthesis and assembly of flagellar tubulin that provide a challenge for future work (41, 42).

Since flagellar tubulin synthesis can be detected as soon as 20 min after the initiation of differentiation, this programmed synthesis is an appealing one to examine regulation. An obvious first question is whether the mRNA for flagellar tubulin pre-exists in amebae. The in vitro synthesis of flagellar tubulin in heterologous cell-free systems programmed with mRNA from differentiating cells has been obtained (114; E. Y. Lai, C. J. Walsh, and C. Fulton, manuscript in preparation). The antigenic determinants unique to flagellar tubulin are present on flagellar tubulin that is synthesized in these cell-free systems, supporting the hypothesis that flagellar tubulin differs in primary structure from the bulk of the cellular tubulin, and leading to the "multi-tubulin hypothesis" (42). mRNA extracted from amebae does not program the synthesis of flagellar tubulin in vitro (114; C. J. Walsh, E. Y. Lai, and C. Fulton, manuscript in preparation). This result, together with the observation that the synthesis of flagellar tubulin by differentiating cells is prevented by early addition of actinomycin D (41), suggests the possibility that flagellar tubulin synthesis depends upon transcription of flagellar tubulin mRNA early in differentiation.

The flagellar rootlet of *Naegleria* has been isolated and appears to be composed primarily of a single protein with a molecular weight of 165,000 (D. E. Larson and A. D. Dingle, manuscript in preparation). Isotope dilution experiments have shown that the rootlet protein is synthesized during differentiation to approximately the same extent as is outer doublet tubulin (D. E. Larson, P. A. Simpson, A. D. Dingle, and C. Fulton, manuscript in preparation).

Control of Flagellum Number

Naegleria flagellates usually have two flagella, side by side, but they do not count perfectly and cells with one, three, and four flagella are not uncommon (33). What controls the number of flagella that develop on a cell? One possibility is that two flagella is the normal number, that four flagella are found on cells in which some entity has replicated or increased in anticipation of division, and that one and three flagella are errors of production or observation. Much work has failed to elucidate whether or not this hypothesis has validity. Several conclusions do emerge from these studies.

Flagella are never seen without basal bodies, in this or any eukaryote, so at least part of the counting mechanism is the number of basal bodies produced.

Ploidy itself does not directly determine flagellum number (33). Both strains NEG (haploid) and NB-1 (diploid) tend to form the same number of flagella. When strain NEG changes from haploid to diploid, the 2X cells tend to have three to four flagella, but after a number of generations these cells restore the original number of flagella while remaining diploid. In addition, mutants of haploid NEG have been obtained that produce three to four flagella, but these mutants are metastable and after sufficient growth they tend to revert to the wild-type phenotype. These observations suggest that there might be some nucleus-independent counting entity, which determines the number of flagella that will develop, but if so the cellular control mechanism tends to restore a one nucleus-two flagella relationship regardless of whether the nucleus is haploid or diploid.

Binucleate cells tend to produce two pairs of flagella (40, 76). This situation is metastable, since binucleate cells do not produce binucleate offspring.

Treatment of strain NB-1 with a sublethal temperature shock during the early part of differentiation causes the uninucleate cells to produce substantially increased numbers of flagella (23, 24). Under optimal treatment conditions, these "hairy" cells had a mean of nearly six basal bodies and flagella per flagellate, with a range of from 1 to 27. Most remarkable, when these hairy cells reverted to amebae and then redifferentiated again, without intervening growth, the flagella per flagellate on the second-cycle flagellates was completely normal. Whatever was perturbed by the temperature shock in the first cycle that caused the production of excess organelles did not leave behind an increased number of "entities" to produce the same result in the second cycle. A similar temperature shock treatment also causes strain NEG to produce excess flagella, but so far the increases obtained are less dramatic (C. Fulton and A. D. Dingle, unpublished data).

Cell Shape Morphogenesis

During differentiation, the cells progress through a temporally reproducible series of shape changes: amebae to spheres to streamlined flagellates. The first results of our attempt to study the intracellular regulation of these changes in shape and motility, including a working hypothesis, were presented recently (37).

Naegleria appears to approach cell motility and shape in a "yin-yang" fashion: amebae with a functioning actin-based motility system and no cytoplasmic microtubules, alternating with flagellates with a microtubule cytoskeleton and no functioning actin-based motility system. The intermediate shape, spheres, is postulated to result from an intermediate state: no functioning motility system and no cytoskeleton.

A cell-produced chemical factor, designated ψ, can be extracted from flagellates and, when added to the environment of fresh flagellates, causes a reproducible sequence of rapid shape changes (31, 37). Cells give an obvious morphological reaction in response to ψ only when they are flagellate shaped. The response requires environmental Ca^{2+} and can be mimicked by the divalent cation ionophore A23187. ψ is a small molecule, normally intracellular. It appears to be controlled in the cell by other molecules that regulate its activity, including a putative enzyme that destroys ψ. The total amount of ψ in cells does not change very much during differentiation, but the extractability of ψ changes in a manner that suggests "compartmentalization." This change in extractability occurs at about the same time cells form flagella.

Four elements are postulated in the working hypothesis: Ca^{2+}; an actin-based ameboid motility system that depends upon free Ca^{2+} for functioning; a tubulin-based cytoskeleton that assembles and remains assembled only when free Ca^{2+} is low; and ψ. ψ is postulated to regulate the intracellular release of Ca^{2+}. According to the hypothesis, intracellular free Ca^{2+} is constantly swept up into Ca reservoirs. Motility of amebae depends upon local release of Ca^{2+} from these reservoirs, which in turn is caused by the intracellular release of ψ. During differentiation, ψ is compartmentalized as part of the differentiation program, and as a consequence, intracellular Ca^{2+} is swept up into Ca reservoirs but not released. As free Ca^{2+} becomes limiting, ameboid movement stops and the cells round up. Subsequently, in a process that depends upon low free Ca^{2+}, the microtubular cytoskeleton is assembled and the flagellate shape is formed.

Reversion of Flagellates to Amebae

Many observers have agreed that, in individual cells, reversion of flagellates to amebae occurs very rapidly, and it can be made to occur almost instantly by mechanical or surface tension forces (33, 76, 86). This rapid reversion to motile amebae indicates that the ameboid motility system remains latent in flagellates (37). In the working hypothesis, it is postulated that during reversion, release of ψ from its compartments permits local intracellular release of Ca^{2+}, which then causes both disassembly of the flagellate cytoskeleton and immediate resumption of ameboid movement.

Rapid reversion of flagellates to amebae can be induced by many treatments, including high and low temperatures (38, 86), treatment with D_2O (78) or high hydrostatic pressure (72), and many other physical and chemical treatments.

Willmer (122, 123) reported that Mg^{2+} specifically inhibited the differentiation of *Naegleria* and that Ca^{2+} reversed this inhibition. In contrast, we found that Mg^{2+} has no effect on the kinetics of differentiation of amebae to flagellates, but that the flagellates revert rapidly to amebae (37). The addition of small amounts of Ca^{2+} prevented these effects of Mg^{2+}. Willmer reached the conclusion that Mg^{2+} inhibited differentiation because he made single observations to determine the extent of differentiation (122). In our experiments, if we returned to the cultures after 2 hr, it would have appeared that Mg^{2+} had prevented differentiation, but during that interval the cells had differentiated and reverted.

Timetable of Events

Still began to pace again, interrupting my work.

"You are still going back and forth with definitions," Still said, "and it is becoming obvious to me that everyone has a conviction about differentiation. Using the word is bound to provoke argument, so why insist on using it?"

"Now you are getting to the substance of the matter. The term differentiation, applied to the phenotypic change of amebae to flagellates, expresses my own convictions, or hopes. At the present time, we don't know whether the study of 'differentiation' in diverse 'systems' will yield one or a few important general mechanisms, or will become a study in comparative biology, with each case unique. We certainly do not know enough about *Naegleria* or vertebrate cells to know whether differentiation of these involves common or different mechanisms. I work with the optimistic conviction that, if we understand anything fundamental about the sequence of events by which genetic information is converted to orderly, sequential phenotypic expression in *Naegleria,* or slime molds, or hydra, or vertebrate cells, we might have understood one aspect of the regulation of 'differentiation' in eukaryotic cells in general. In other words, I hope there is (or are) such a process as cell differentiation, and that such a process can be studied in *Naegleria* or in any other favorable 'model system.' At the very least, I believe that if we obtain any substantive insight in one system it should allow a test of its generality in other systems."

"Now I think I'm beginning to understand." Still smiled. "You use the term differentiation because it makes you feel good about your work."

"Yes, but better because it expresses a belief, a conviction. We are in the stage where 'differentiation' is a black box that provokes polemic as well as provides a great challenge for investigation. Those of us studying the problem in diverse systems have made great progress, but have been notoriously unsuccessful at elucidating mechanism. So I persist, and use a loaded term."

"That seems reasonable enough to me. But the whole argument reminds me of the great polemic about the meaning of the term 'gene' that raged from about 1915 until 1953, and now seems so irrelevant. Once you people studying differentiation break the barrier of system-specific results, the polemic you are engaged in will disappear—though if the history of 'gene' is any indication people probably will never use the term 'differentiation' in a consistent fashion."

I could only agree with Still.

Table 1 Timetable of events during differentiation

Time	Measured event
0	Initiation of differentiation (by one of several external signals)
<0.1	Nutritional stepdown leads to a change in RNA synthesis
0.25	Polysomes begin to increase
0.4	Flagellar tubulin synthesis begins
0.45	Ability to round up becomes insensitive to actinomycin D
0.5	Ability to form flagella becomes insensitive to actinomycin D
0.55	Optimum time to temperature shock for production of hairy flagellates
0.75	Ability to round up and ability to form flagella become insensitive to cycloheximide
	Ability to form flagellate body shape becomes insensitive to actinomycin D
0.9	Basal bodies appear
	Cells round up
	Flagellum assembly can occur at 10°C
	Intracellular rearrangement of ψ occurs
1.0	Flagella are first seen
	Flagellar rootlets are first seen
1.1	Synthesis of limiting precursor is complete
	Ability to form flagellate body shape becomes insensitive to cycloheximide
1.3	Flagellate body shape forms
	Cells are sensitive to ψ
1.6	Flagella reach full length

A summary of the major events of differentiation, and the approximate time at which each event occurs in the "average" cell, are listed in Table 1; some also are indicated above Figure 2. It is convenient to express the times as the fraction of the time required for the formation of visible flagella (T_{50}). The time at which several events occur are proportional to the total time for differentiation, independent of the temperature at which differentiation occurs and whether axenic or bacteria-grown cells are used (43, 61; C. Fulton, unpublished data). Of course, this is not known for all of the events listed. All the events have been described in the text.

PROSPECTS

"Tell me one more thing, and then I have to get back to my gradients."

"What is it, Still?" I was beginning to tire of his questions.

"Why do you use the ameba-to-flagellate change—I'm not sure what word to use—to study cell differentiation?"

"That's easy. Because *Naegleria* is so cooperative. Because large numbers of cells can be caused to change rapidly from one homogeneous population to a dramatically different one. Because environmental control of the moment of initiation gives us hope of understanding the cellular start signal. Because each cell undergoes the change as an individual, and populations go through the change synchronously, and in suspension. Because the organism has a small genome, and also because some strains are haploid, allowing us to isolate mutants. I dream of a system for genetic analysis someday. Because the change includes a major reorganization of cell metabolism, a gross change in cell morphology, the making of new organelles, the synthesis of new proteins. Because the cells are rugged, and as easy to work with as *E. coli* K12: overnight cultures, cloning, differentiation in an hour after initiation, reproducible to within a couple of minutes from year to year. Because specific structural proteins are synthesized. Because of certain glorious morphogenetic aspects: the regulation of cell shape, of flagellum number and position. Because I know of no eukaryotic differentiation that is more accessible to experimental analysis. Because . . ."

"Sorry, I've got to go," said Still, looking at his stopwatch, "but it sounds like a fantastic system. I've got some ideas about the DNA; perhaps we could collaborate, or you'd teach me how to work with *Naegleria.*"

"I'd be delighted. You know, only a few labs are using *Naegleria* to study differentiation."

"I don't believe it. That's the strangest thing you've told me," said Still, as he ran off to his centrifuge.

Acknowledgment

The unpublished research cited herein was supported by grants from the National Science Foundation. I am grateful to Peter Simpson for a helpful reading of the manuscript.

Literature Cited

1. Adam, K. M. G., Blewett, D. A., Flamm, W. G. 1969. *J. Protozool.* 16:6–12
2. Aldrich, H. C. 1968. *J. Gen. Microbiol.* 50:217–22
3. Aldrich, H. C. 1969. *Am. J. Bot.* 56:290–99
4. Anderson, K., Jamieson, A. 1972. *Pathology* 4:273–78
5. Anderson, K., Jamieson, A. 1974. *Pathology* 6:79–84
6. Averner, M., Fulton, C. 1966. *J. Gen. Microbiol.* 42:245–55
7. Balamuth, W. 1964. *J. Protozool.* 11: Suppl., pp. 19–20
8. Balamuth, W. 1965. In *Progress in Protozoology, Abstr. 2nd Intern. Conf. Protozool.,* p. 40. Amsterdam: Excerpta Medica
9. Band, R. N., Balamuth, W. 1974. *Appl. Microbiol.* 28:64–65
10. Bohnert, H. J., Herrmann, R. G. 1974. *Eur. J. Biochem.* 50:83–90
11. Brent, M. M. 1957. *Nature* 179:1029
12. Buchanan, R. E., Gibbons, N. E., eds. 1974. *Bergey's Manual of Determinative Bacteriology.* Baltimore: Williams & Wilkins. 8th ed.
13. Bunting, M. 1926. *J. Morphol.* 42: 23–81
14. Cavalier-Smith, T. 1974. *J. Cell Sci.* 16:529–56
15. Chang, S. L. 1958. *J. Gen. Microbiol.* 18:579–85
16. Chang, S. L. 1960. *Can. J. Microbiol.* 6:397–405
17. Chang, S. L. 1974. *CRC Crit. Rev. Microbiol.* 3:135–59
18. Chiovetti, R. Jr. 1976. *J. Protozool.* 23:24a
19. Corff, S., Yuyama, S. 1976. *J. Protozool.* 23:587–93
20. Culbertson, C. G. 1971. *Ann. Rev. Microbiol.* 25:231–54
21. Cursons, R. T. M., Brown, T. J. 1976. *NZ J. Mar. Freshwater Res.* 10:245–62
22. Deering, R. A. 1968. *Science* 162: 1289–90
23. Dingle, A. D. 1970. *J. Cell Sci.* 7: 463–81
24. Dingle, A. D. 1977. In *Eucaryotic Microbes as Model Developmental Systems,* ed. D. H. O'Day, P. A. Horgen, pp. 96–129. New York: Marcel Dekker
25. Dingle, A. D., Fulton, C. 1966. *J. Cell Biol.* 31:43–54
26. Duma, R. J., Rosenblum, W. I., McGehee, R. F., Jones, M. M., Nelson, E. C. 1971. *Ann. Intern. Med.* 74: 861–69

27. Dunnebacke, T. H., Schuster, F. L. 1974. *J. Protozool.* 21:327–29
28. Erdos, G. W., Raper, K. B., Vogen, L. K. 1973. *Proc. Natl. Acad. Sci. USA* 70:1828–30
29. Firtel, R. A., Baxter, L., Lodish, H. F. 1973. *J. Mol. Biol.* 79:315–27
30. Firtel, R. A., Bonner, J. 1972. *J. Mol. Biol.* 66:339–61
31. Fuller, M., Fulton, C. 1974. *J. Gen. Physiol.* 64:4a
32. Fulton, C. 1970. *Science* 167:1269–70
33. Fulton, C. 1970. In *Methods in Cell Physiology,* ed. D. M. Prescott, 4:341–476. New York: Academic
34. Fulton, C. 1971. In *Origin and Continuity of Cell Organelles,* ed. J. Reinert, H. Ursprung, pp. 170–221. New York: Springer-Verlag
35. Fulton, C. 1972. *Dev. Biol.* 28:603–19
36. Fulton, C. 1974. *Exp. Cell Res.* 88: 365–70
37. Fulton, C. 1977. *J. Supramol. Struct.* 6:In press
38. Fulton, C., Dingle, A. D. 1967. *Dev. Biol.* 15:165–91
39. Fulton, C., Dingle, A. D. 1971. *J. Cell Biol.* 51:826–36
40. Fulton, C., Guerrini, A. M. 1969. *Exp. Cell Res.* 56:194–200
41. Fulton, C., Kowit, J. D. 1975. *Ann. NY Acad. Sci.* 253:318–32
42. Fulton, C., Simpson, P. A. 1976. *Cell Motility,* ed. R. Goldman, T. Pollard, J. Rosenbaum, pp. 987–1005. Cold Spring Harbor: Cold Spring Harbor Lab.
43. Fulton, C., Walsh, C. 1977. *J. Cell Biol.* In press
44. Gong, T., Balamuth, W. 1973. *J. Protozool.* 20:498
45. Griffin, J. L. 1972. *Science* 178:869–70
46. Grimes, G. W. 1973. *J. Cell Biol.* 57:229–32
47. Guttes, S., Guttes, E., Ellis, R. A. 1968. *J. Ultrastruct. Res.* 22:508–29
48. Haskins, E. F. 1968. *Can. J. Microbiol.* 14:1309–15
49. Hepler, P. K. 1976. *J. Cell Sci.* 21:361–90
50. Holt, C. E., Gurney, E. G. 1969. *J. Cell Biol.* 40:484–96
51. Jacobson, D. N., Adelman, M. R. 1975. *J. Cell Biol.* 67:188a
52. Josephson, S. L., John, D. T. 1976. *J. Protozool.* 23:23a
53. Kahn, A. J., Boroff, R., Cutler, R. W. 1968. *J. Protozool.* 15:Suppl., p. 29
54. Katz, E. R., Sussman, M. 1972. *Proc. Natl. Acad. Sci. USA* 69:495–98
55. Kerr, N. S. 1960. *J. Protozool.* 7:103–8
56. Kerr, S. J. 1972. *J. Gen. Microbiol.* 72:419–27
57. Kessin, R. H. 1973. *Dev. Biol.* 31: 242–51
58. Kessin, R. H., Williams, K. L., Newell, P. C. 1974. *J. Bacteriol.* 119:776–83
59. Kofoid, C. A. 1915. *Science* 42:937–40
60. Kowit, J. D., Fulton, C. 1974. *J. Biol. Chem.* 249:3638–46
61. Kowit, J. D., Fulton, C. 1974. *Proc. Natl. Acad. Sci. USA* 71:2877–81
62. Lastovica, A. J., Dingle, A. D. 1971. *Exp. Cell. Res.* 66:337–45
63. Little, J. B., Chang, R. S. 1968. *Radiat. Res.* 35:132–46
64. Napolitano, J. J., Smith, B. H., Persico, F. J. 1967. *J. Protozool.* 14:108–9
65. O'Dell, D. S., Preston, T. M., King, C. A., Gardiner, P. R. 1976. *Biochem. Soc. Trans.* 4:124–25
66. Okubo, S. 1976. *Jpn. J. Genet.* 51: 207–11
67. Okubo, S., Inoki, S. 1973. *Biken J.* 16:181–84
68. Outka, D. E., Kluss, B. C. 1967. *J. Cell Biol.* 35:323–46
69. Page, F. C. 1967. *J. Protozool.* 14:499–521
70. Page, F. C. 1975. *Protistologica* 11:195–204
71. Pearson, J. L., Willmer, E. N. 1963. *J. Exp. Biol.* 40:493–515
72. Perkins, D. L., Babb, S. E. Jr. 1973. *J. Protozool.* 20:520
73. Perkins, D. L., Eckert, R. 1976. *J. Protozool.* 23:11a
74. Perkins, D. L., Jahn, T. L. 1970. *J. Protozool.* 17:168–72
75. Perkins, D. L., Morris, G. S. 1974. *J. Protozool.* 21:445
76. Pietschmann, K. 1929. *Arch. Protistenk.* 65:379–425
77. Preston, T. M., O'Dell, D. S. 1971. *Exp. Cell Res.* 68:465–66
78. Preston, T. M., O'Dell, D. S. 1973. *J. Gen. Microbiol.* 75:351–61
79. Preston, T. M., O'Dell, D. S. 1974. *Ann. Soc. Belge Med. Trop.* 54:279–86
80. Rafalko, J. S. 1947. *J. Morphol.* 81:1–44
81. Rafalko, J. S. 1951. *J. Morphol.* 89: 71–90
82. Reinert, J., Holtzer, H., eds. 1975. *Cell Cycle and Cell Differentiation.* New York: Springer-Verlag
83. Rosenbaum, J. L., Moulder, J. E., Ringo, D. L. 1969. *J. Cell Biol.* 41: 600–19
84. Rutter, W. J., Kemp, J. D., Bradshaw, W. S., Clark, W. R., Ronzio, R. A., Sanders, T. G. 1968. *J. Cell. Physiol.* 72(2, pt. II):1–18

85. Satir, P. 1965. *Protoplasmatologia* 3E: 1–52
86. Schardinger, F. 1899. *Sitzungsber. Akad. Wiss. Wien Math. Naturwiss Kl. Abt. 1* 108:713–34
87. Scharf, J. F. 1954. *Biodynamica* 7: 225–28
88. Schuster, F. L. 1961. *J. Protozool.* 8: Suppl., p. 19
89. Schuster, F. L. 1963. *J. Protozool.* 10: 297–313
90. Schuster, F. L. 1963. *J. Protozool.* 10: 313–20
91. Schuster, F. L. 1965. *Protistologica* 1: 49–62
92. Schuster, F. L. 1975. *Tissue Cell* 7:1–12
93. Schuster, F. L. 1975. *J. Protozool.* 22:352–59
94. Schuster, F. L., Dunnebacke, T. H. 1971. *J. Ultrastruct. Res.* 36:659–68
95. Schuster, F. L., Svihla, G. 1968. *J. Protozool.* 15:752–58
96. Simione, F. P. Jr., Daggett, P.-M. 1976. *J. Parasitol.* 62:49
97. Simpson, P. A., Dingle, A. D. 1971. *J. Cell Biol.* 51:323–28
98. Singh, B. N. 1952. *Phil. Trans. R. Soc. London Ser. B* 236:405–61
99. Singh, B. N., Das, S. R. 1970. *Phil. Trans. R. Soc. London Ser. B* 259: 435–76
100. Sleigh, M. A., ed. 1974. *Cilia and Flagella.* London: Academic
101. Soll, D. R., Fulton, C. 1974. *Dev. Biol.* 36:236–44
102. Stephens, R. E., Edds, K. T. 1976. *Physiol. Rev.* 56:709–77
103. Sussman, M. 1951. *J. Exp. Zool.* 118:407–17
104. Sussman, M. 1966. In *Methods in Cell Physiology,* ed. D. M. Prescott, 2:397–410. New York: Academic
105. Sussman, M., Sussman, R. 1969. *Symp. Soc. Gen. Microbiol.* 19:403–35
106. Sussman, R. R., Rayner, E. P. 1971. *Arch. Biochem. Biophys.* 144:127–37
107. Tamm, S. L. 1967. *J. Exp. Zool.* 164:163–86
108. Deleted in proof
109. Todd, S. R., Kitching, J. A. 1973. *J. Protozool.* 20:421–24
110. Visvesvara, G. S., Healy, G. R. 1973. *J. Protozool.* 20:522
111. Wade, J., Satir, P. 1968. *Exp. Cell. Res.* 50:81–92
112. Walsh, C., Fulton, C. 1971. *Am. Soc. Cell Biol. Abstr. 11th Ann. Meeting,* p. 317
113. Walsh, C., Fulton, C. 1973. *Biochim. Biophys. Acta* 312:52–71
114. Walsh, C., Fulton, C. 1975. *J. Cell Biol.* 67:444a
115. Walsh, C., Nakazato, H., Hickey, C., Edmonds, M. 1976. *J. Cell Biol.* 70:136a
116. Wasielewski, T. V., Hirschfeld, L. 1910. *Abh. Heidelberger Akad. Wiss., Math. Natur. Kl.* 1:1–31
117. Weisman, R. A. 1976. *Ann. Rev. Microbiol.* 30:189–219
118. Werth, J. M., Kahn, A. J. 1967. *J. Bacteriol.* 94:1272–74
119. Willaert, E. 1974. *Ann. Soc. Belge Med. Trop.* 54:395–404
120. Willaert, E. 1974. *Ann. Soc. Belge Med. Trop.* 54:429–40
121. Willaert, E., Le Ray, D. 1973. *Protistologica* 9:417–26
122. Willmer, E. N. 1956. *J. Exp. Biol.* 33:583–603
123. Willmer, E. N. 1958. *J. Embryol. Exp. Morphol.* 6:187–214
124. Wilson, C. W. 1916. *Univ. Calif. Publ. Zool.* 16:241–92
125. Witman, G. B. 1975. *Ann. NY Acad. Sci.* 253:178–91
126. Yuyama, S. 1971. *J. Protozool.* 18: 337–43
127. Yuyama, S. 1971. In *Developmental Aspects of the Cell Cycle,* ed. I. L. Cameron, G. M. Padilla, A. M. Zimmerman, pp. 41–66. New York: Academic

AUTHOR INDEX

A

Aasen, A. J., 168
Abbott, B. J., 380, 392
Abe, S., 432
Abeliovitch, A., 262, 288
Abildgaard, C. F., 422, 437
Aboulkhair, I., 462
Abraham, E. P., 347
Abraham, G., 399
Abraham, R., 528
Abram, D., 398, 400, 402
Abrams, G. D., 109, 126
Abrutyn, E., 460
ACHONG, B. G., 421-45; 422, 425, 430, 432-34, 438
Adair, F. W., 386, 392
Adam, K. M. G., 604
Adamich, M., 198
Adams, A., 428, 439
Adams, G. A., 239
Adams, J. N., 169
Adelberg, E. A., 40, 41, 114, 128, 487
Adelman, M. R., 614
Adey, G., 579
Adhya, S., 501
Adldinger, H. K., 436
Adler, J., 91, 185, 186, 397, 398, 400-5, 407, 408, 412, 414-17
Adler, J. L., 449, 457
Aenishaenslin, W., 371
Agre, N. S., 164-66, 171, 173
Agren, A., 569
Aharonowitz, Y., 352
Ahearn, D. G., 384, 386, 387
Ahlquist, C. N., 545
Ahmed, A., 499, 500
Aiba, S., 71, 77, 83, 384
Ainslie, V., 209
Aitken, A., 246
Akama, K., 119
Akasawa, T., 260
Akin, D. E., 111
Aksamit, R. R., 405
Al Ani, D., 383
Albaugh, E. W., 380
Albersheim, P., 211
Albrecht, R., 456
Albrink, W. S., 454, 460, 464-67
Albritton, W. L., 460
Alderson, G., 160-63, 165-67, 169, 171, 172, 174
Aldrich, H. C., 613, 614
Aleksandrushkina, N. I., 321
Alexander, A. D., 94, 95, 100
Alexander, H. E., 490
Alexander, J., 520
Alexander, M., 64, 66, 70, 71, 108-11, 119, 385
Alexander, T. J. L., 96
Ali Khan, M. Y., 389
Allen, B. D., 457
Allen, G. V., 248
Allen, J. C., 449-51, 456, 463, 465, 466
Allen, J. M., 514, 515
Allen, M. B., 227, 242, 244
Allen, M. M., 227, 234, 235, 237, 241, 251
Allen, R. C., 509, 511
Allen, R. D., 40, 41, 43, 44, 47, 48, 53, 55, 56, 195, 552
Allet, B., 482, 495
Alling, D., 301
Allison, A. C., 195, 522, 525, 528
Allison, F., 508
Almeida, J. D., 359, 360, 370, 371
Al-Moslih, M. I., 432
Alp, M. H., 123
Alpern, R. J., 455
Alshamaony, L., 163-67, 171, 173, 176
Alspach, J., 564
Altendorf, K. H., 27, 183, 184, 187, 188
Alter, H. J., 357-60, 373
Altmann, G., 459
Alvarez, M. I., 539, 542
Amano, T., 52
Ambler, R. P., 246, 410
Ambrosioni, J. C., 430
Ames, B. N., 481, 497
Ames, G. F., 153
Amonette, R. A., 453
Amoss, H. L., 6
Anagnostopoulos, C., 491, 492, 494, 496
Andersen, S., 96
Anderson, D. L., 90-92
Anderson, J. W., 382, 391
Anderson, K., 603, 606
Anderson, R., 460
Anderson, R. A., 414
Anderson, R. J., 450
ANDERSON, R. P., 473-505; 476, 488, 489
Anderson, R. S., 52, 54
Anderson, S. E., 84
Anderson, S. E. Jr., 519, 520
Anderson, T. F., 489
Anderson, W. B., 574
Andersson, L. C., 436
Andersson, M., 434, 435
Ando, M., 516, 521
Andrewes, A. G., 168
Andrews, F. W., 410
Andrews, L.-L., 422, 437
Andrews, T. J., 260
Annest, J. L., 488
Ansehn, S., 305
Anthony, B. F., 452, 466
Antoine-Portaels, F., 174, 175
Aoyama, Y., 428
Apell, G. S., 244
Appelbaum, E., 482
Aragón, C. M. G., 539, 542
Arbuthnott, J. P., 522
Arcamone, F., 31
Archer, D. B., 14
Aris, R., 66
Arita, M., 48
Armstrong, D., 451, 454, 455, 458, 460-62, 466, 467
Armstrong, J. A., 515, 516, 523, 525, 527, 528
Armstrong, J. B., 404, 405, 407, 416
Arnold, W., 359
Arnow, P. M., 295
Arpin, N., 168
Arroyo, J., 300, 301
Asakura, S., 398-400
Asano, T., 126
Aserkoff, B., 459
Ash, M. M., 96
Ashcroft, E., 498
Ashizawa, N., 562
Ashworth, J. M., 137, 143
Asselineau, J., 165, 170
Aswad, D. W., 404, 405, 415, 416
Aswanikumar, S., 508
Aszalos, A., 15
Athar, M. A., 297
Atkinson, D. E., 345, 352
Atkinson, L. P., 334
Atlas, R. M., 380, 386, 387, 389, 392
Attebery, H. R., 112, 119, 125
Audit, C., 491, 494, 496
Auran, N. E., 90-93, 102
Austin, S. M., 253, 264
Austrian, R., 490
Averner, M., 601
Avery, O. T., 10, 11
Avitabile, G., 14, 294
Awaya, J., 23
Awny, A. Y., 459
Axelrod, J. A., 451
Axline, S. G., 509, 523
Ayoub, E. M., 462
Azuma, I., 92

B

Baars, J. K., 317, 330
Babb, S. E. Jr., 625
Babior, B. M., 510-12
Babudieri, B., 94
Bacha, P., 390
Bacher, A., 27
Bachmann, B. J., 481, 487, 491
Backman, P. A., 219
Bader, F. G., 69, 77, 79
Baehner, R. L., 510-13
Baer, H., 457
Baess, I., 161
Baggenstoss, A. H., 465
Bailey, R. J., 452, 465
Bailey, R. R., 454
Bainton, D. F., 508, 513
Bajaj, Y. P. S., 218
Baker, C. N., 52, 53
Baker, H. J., 100
Baker, M. F., 100
Bakker, E. P., 186, 187
Balabanova, H., 438
Balakrishnan, C. V., 558, 560, 565, 567, 580
Balamuth, W., 607, 619
Balda, B.-R., 438
Balderston, W. L., 333-35
Baldwin, R. L., 316, 482, 484
Baldwin, T. O., 558-63, 566, 568, 589
Balish, E., 112, 116, 123
Ball, F. L., 238
Ball, G., 430, 432, 433
Ball, G. H., 95
Ball, M. G., 102
Ball, W. C. Jr., 452-54, 466
Ballio, A., 165
Ballou, C. E., 166
Balny, C., 557, 562-64, 566-68
Balows, A., 97
Bamburg, J. R., 303
Banatvala, J. E., 426
Bancroft, W. H., 358
Band, R. N., 607
Bandmann, U., 303
Bank, H. L., 509
Bar, R. S., 437
Barash, I., 207, 212
Barber, L., 327-32
Barcellona, S., 165
BARESI, L., 309-41; 317, 318, 337
Baringer, J. R., 428
Barker, H. A., 313, 315, 317, 318, 320
Barker, L. F., 357, 359, 360, 371, 374
Barnes, E. M., 125
Barnes, R. O., 332, 333, 335
Barnett, D. A., 173
Barnett, J. W., 425
Barnum, D. A., 120
Baron, L. S., 491, 492
Barr, Y. M., 422, 430, 432
Barrett-Connor, E., 452, 459, 460, 467
Barrow, G. I., 40
Barsilai, B., 459
Bartels, T. J., 390
Bartha, R., 380, 386, 387, 389
Bartlett, J., 462
Bartlett, J. G., 452, 454, 455, 464, 466
Bartmann, K., 304
Bartnicki-Garcia, S., 198
Bartsch, R. G., 246
Barua, D., 58
Baseman, J. B., 102
Bassham, J. A., 256-58, 260, 262
Bassot, J. M., 553
Bastarrachea, F., 482, 497
Bastian, F. O., 428
Basu, S. K., 482, 499
Bates, J. H., 454, 461
Batrakov, S. G., 167
Batt, T., 264
Batterton, J. C., 233, 382, 391
Bauchop, T., 112, 117
Baucom, T. L., 569
Bauerle, R. H., 499
Baugh, L. C., 193
Baum, J., 451, 452
Baumann, A., 195
BAUMANN, L., 39-61; 39-41, 43-45, 47, 48, 51-56, 58, 552-56, 582
BAUMANN, P., 39-61; 39-45, 47, 48, 51-56, 58, 233, 552-56, 573, 574, 582, 590
Baumberg, S., 498
Bautista, S., 520
Baxter, L., 620
Bayer, A. S., 452, 464, 466
Bayer, M. E., 360
Bayer, M. W., 403
Beam, H. W., 389
Beaman, B. L., 174, 462
Beauchemin, N., 247
Beauclerk, A. A. D., 262
Beauvais, P., 458
Becker, E. L., 508
Becker, V., 423, 428, 431, 435, 436
Becker, Y., 428, 431, 438
Beckwith, J. R., 478, 496
Becq-Giraudon, B., 454, 461
Becvar, J. E., 558-63, 565-69
Bedford, C., 301
Bedon, G. A., 452-54, 466
Beeftinck, F., 482, 498
Beer, S. U., 214, 215
Beerens, H., 128
Beguin, S., 244
Behal, V., 20
Beiber, C. P., 452, 453
Beijerinck, M. W., 552, 587
Bell, R. G., 139, 335
Bellanti, J. A., 450
Bellen, N., 451, 458
Bellett, A. J. D., 482, 484
Bellezza, G., 170
Belousova, I. I., 16, 17, 20, 22
Belyaev, S. S., 327, 328, 331
Bender, R. A., 150
Ben-Hamida, F., 147
Bennett, A., 244, 245, 257
Bennett, I. L. Jr., 458, 459
Bennett, J. E., 298, 301
Bennett, J. V., 457, 459, 462
Bennett, P. M., 140, 142, 399
Benno, Y., 119
Bensch, K. G., 303
Benson, A. A., 386
Bentley, D., 561, 564
Bentley, D. W., 451, 464
Benveniste, R. E., 438
Ben-Zeev, A., 428
Benzer, S., 488, 500
Bequette, R. J., 304
Berard, C., 434
Berard, C. W., 438
Berd, D., 163
Berenberg, J. L., 451
Berg, D. E., 482, 495
Berg, H. C., 185, 186, 397, 399, 404, 414-16
Berg, P., 476, 480, 485, 487, 490, 494-96
Berg, R. D., 123, 124
Bergelson, L. D., 167
Bergendahl, E., 296
Berger, J., 113, 115, 117
Berger, U., 462
Bergey, D. H., 172
Bergholz, M., 159
Berghuis-de Vries, J. M., 121, 126
Bergman, J. W., 219
Bergman, K., 535, 538-40, 543
Bergter, F., 71
Berland, H., 458
Berlin, R. D., 528
Berne, C., 569
Berner, N. H., 384
Berner, R. A., 332-35
Bernhardt, H., 113
Bernheimer, A. W., 522
Bernheimer, H. P., 482, 490
Bernlohr, R. W., 138, 141-43, 148, 152
Berns, D. S., 237, 244, 264
Berquist, K. R., 357
Bertani, G., 500

Bertani, L. E., 500
Bertolini, D., 382
Berzhanskaya, L. Y., 581
Best, J. M., 426
Bethke, H., 28
Betts, R. F., 451, 464
Betz, H., 143, 146
Beuscher, N., 138, 142, 145, 151
Bey, R. F., 91
Beynon, P., 28
Bharier, M. A., 91
Bianchi, L., 371
Bianchi, M., 14, 20
Bibby, B. G., 96, 160
Bieber, L. L., 14, 295
Biebl, H., 280, 315, 317, 330
Bierther, M., 528
Biggar, W. D., 450, 460-62, 513
Biggins, J., 256
Billing, R. J., 432
Binder, H. J., 122
Binding, H., 541
Birch, A. J., 16, 20, 31
Birch-Andersen, A., 90-92, 97, 398, 403
Birnbaum, J., 20, 26, 347
Bishop, C. T., 239
Bisset, K. A., 162, 171, 172
Biswas, B. B., 239
Biswas, R., 359
Bittman, R., 14, 20
Bjursell, G., 428, 439
Black, P. H., 454, 459
Black, S. H., 90-92
Blake, J. M., 422
Blakeslee, J. R., 430, 433
Bland, J., 332
Blank, H., 301, 302
Blanke, T. R., 300
Blau, E. B., 452, 460, 466, 467
Blaylock, B. A., 323
Blecker, H. H., 243
Blevins, A., 451, 458, 460, 462, 466, 467
Blewett, D. A., 604
Blinkova, A. A., 489
Bloch, K., 23, 24, 26, 243
Block, S. M., 537
Blom, J., 456
Bloom, B., 520
Blumauerova, M., 20, 31, 33, 34
Blumberg, B. S., 357, 358, 360
Blumbergs, P., 30, 31
Blumer, M., 380
Blumershine, R. V. H., 112, 113
Bocker, H., 22
Bodéré, C., 538
Bodey, G. P., 304, 461
Boesch, D. F., 380
Boezi, J. A., 428
Bogacki, I. G., 560, 564, 585
Bogert, M. T., 1, 3
Bognar, A., 585
Bogorad, L., 227, 228, 244, 245, 257
Boguslaski, R. C., 569
Bohlmann, F., 28
Bohlool, B. B., 94
Bohnert, H. J., 604
Boisvert, H., 553
Bojsen-Moller, J., 460
Bokkenheuser, V., 456
Bold, H. C., 235
Boll, M., 140, 142, 149
Bollag, J. M., 335
Bolte, H., 101
Bond, H. E., 361, 362, 370
Bond, J. H. Jr., 336
Bonen, L., 248
Bonner, J., 604
Bonomi, A., 77, 78
Booth, C. K., 570, 589
Boquist, L., 305
Bordet, C., 162, 163
Borgers, M., 305
Borges, J. S., 517, 519, 520
Borglund, E., 569
Borg-Petersen, C., 90-92
Bornkamm, G. W., 428, 439
Boroff, R., 614
Bosecker, K., 285
Bothe, H., 263
Botstein, D., 481, 495, 502
Bottomley, P. J., 260, 264
Bottone, E., 457
Boulding, E. T., 123, 124
Bouma, J. M. W., 147
Bounous, G., 125
Bourgin, D. G., 80
Bourkas, A. E., 429
Bourquin, A. W., 387
Bourrelly, P., 228, 231-34, 237, 267
Bousfield, I. J., 161, 162, 169, 170
Bousfield, S., 326, 336, 337
Bouton, J. M., 458
Bovee, E. C., 91
Bovet, D., 8
Bowden, G. H., 163, 164, 171
Bowen, C. C., 236, 237
Bowen, J. M., 425
Bowen, V. G., 319, 321, 322
Bowie, I. S., 166
Bowien, B., 260
Box, B., 139, 143, 145
Boxer, L. A., 509
Boyd, C. B., 452, 463
Boyer, P. D., 185, 189
Boyse, E. A., 424
Bozof, R. P., 538
Brabson, J. S., 138, 139, 143, 146, 152
Bracha, M., 489
Brachet, P., 195
Bracker, C. E., 191
Bradburne, A. F., 371
Bradley, S., 227
Bradley, S. G., 139, 161, 162, 169, 172, 173, 175
Bradley-Moore, A. M., 439
Bradshaw, M., 301
Bradshaw, W. S., 619
Bragg, P. D., 188
Brajtburg, J. K., 295, 296, 300
Bramley, P. M., 539
Brandis, H., 518, 519
Brandt, E., 257
Brandt, R., 28
Branton, D., 577, 580, 586
Braun, A. C., 207, 210, 219
Braun, J. L., 94
Breckenridge, G., 336
Breckenridge, J. L., 452, 465
Brederoo, P., 513
Breed, R. S., 45, 159, 172
Breger, I. A., 380
Brenchley, J. E., 150
Brendle, J. J., 95
Brennan, P. J., 166, 167, 173
Brenner, D. J., 43
Brenner, S., 500
Brent, M. M., 604
Bresler, S. E., 489
Brettschneider, L., 452, 455
Brewer, G. A., 25
Brewer, G. J., 186
Brewer, J., 220
Breznak, J. A., 94, 95, 101, 102
Brian, P. W., 301, 302
Brice, J. M., 187
Brieger, E. M., 514
Briggs, M., 358-60, 373
Briggs, R. T., 510
Brill, W. J., 250, 387
Brillinger, G. U., 32
Brisou, J., 454, 461
Brissie, N. T., 509
Brock, D. J. H., 24
Brock, T. D., 25, 64, 66, 67, 70, 127, 281
Brockmann, H. Jr., 277, 281
Broitman, S. A., 449, 454, 458, 467
Brokl, O., 524
Brolin, S. E., 569
Brooker, B. E., 113
Brooks, C., 244
Brooks, G. F., 457
Brooks, L., 454, 457, 463
Brostrom, C. O., 147
Brown, A. H., 255, 258

Brown, C. A., 515, 523
Brown, D. A., 399, 404, 414, 415
Brown, D. E., 65
Brown, D. H., 238, 264
Brown, D. M., 244
Brown, G., 431
Brown, H. D., 140, 149, 153
Brown, H. E. Jr., 303
Brown, J. M., 160, 162, 163
Brown, J. S., 242
Brown, M., 172
Brown, M. S., 154
Brown, O. R., 168
Brown, T. J., 603
Brown, W. H., 7
Brown, W. R., 123
Brownell, G. H., 161, 169
Browning, J. L., 193, 194
Bruce, M. A., 96
Bruce-Chwatt, L. J., 439
Bruck, H.M., 458
Brugmans, J. P., 301, 305
Bruice, T. C., 563, 564
Brumbaugh, J. H., 296
Brunchorst, J., 160, 161
Brune, D. C., 277
Brunjes, S., 452, 460
Brunschwig, J. P., 362
Bryant, D. A., 244, 246
Bryant, M. P., 75, 95, 111, 117, 127-29, 311-14, 316, 320, 322-25, 337
Bryce, T. A., 251
Bryceson, A. D. M., 99, 439
Buch, J. B., 581
Buchanan, R. E., 57, 160, 170, 226, 227, 317, 552, 554, 555, 606
Büchel, K. H., 304
Buckner, C. D., 452
Budkowska, A., 364
Bukhari, A. I., 501
Bukin, V. N., 320, 323-25
Bull, C. G., 6
Bull, M. J., 138
Bulock, J. D., 20, 352
Bungay, H. R. III, 64-66, 69, 71, 74, 76, 81, 83, 84
Bünning, E., 198
Bunting, M., 604
Burack, W. R., 461
Burgdorfer, W., 99, 100
Burge, R. E., 399
Burgeff, H., 539, 541, 542
Burgess, M. A., 304
Burke, J. P., 449, 457
Burke, P. V., 535, 542
Burkholder, P. R., 39
Burkitt, D. P., 434, 439
Burleigh, B. D., 480
Burnett, A. K., 462
Burns, A., 422
Burns, E. E., 219
Burnside, B., 303, 305
Burnside, J., 462
Buron, S., 513
Burrell, C. J., 358, 360, 362, 363
Burrows, W., 58
Burt, S. J., 122, 130
Burtin, P., 426
Burton, G. C., 125
Bushar, H. F., 422
Busse, H. G., 482, 484
Buswell, A. M., 317
Butler, K., 1, 10
Butler, W. L., 544
Buttiaux, R., 48
Butzler, J. P., 456, 458
Byrne, E. B., 426

C

Cabib, E., 137
Cachin, Y., 426
Cajias, J. L., 381
Calavan, E. C., 219
Calder, J. A., 257
Caldwell, D. R., 41
Calladine, C. R., 399
Callaway, J. L., 453, 464
Calnek, B. W., 436
Caltrider, P. G., 345, 346
Calvin, M., 256
Cameron, C. H., 358-60, 373
Camin, D. L., 381
Cammack, R., 246
Cammoun, M., 435
Cammoun, N., 428, 435
Campbell, A., 476, 489, 490, 495, 496
Campbell, J., 465
Campbell, N. E. R., 332
Campbell, W. G., 437
Canale, R. P., 76, 77
Canale-Parola, E., 90-94, 101, 102, 321
Candau, P., 249, 264
Cannon, F. C., 387
Caplan, S. R., 186, 187
Cappenberg, T. E., 317, 326-32
Caramia, F., 360
Carbon, J., 407
Carbone, P. P., 449, 451, 456, 458, 465
Cardemil, L., 252
Cardini, G. E., 388
Carlile, M. J., 539
Carlson, P. S., 210
Carlton, B. C., 146, 150
Carpenter, E. J., 265
Carpenter, J. L., 456
Carr, G. C., 190
Carr, N. G., 227, 228, 235, 237, 241, 246-48, 256, 257, 263
Carrera, G. F., 460
Carrico, R. J., 569
Carrillo, C., 119, 120
Carrington, G. O., 458
Carter, G. R., 117, 452, 463
Carter, H. E., 295
Carter, J. H., 126
Casazza, A. R., 449, 451, 456, 458, 465
Cash, R. L., 381
Casida, L. E. Jr., 160, 161
Cass, A., 295
Cassel, C., 437
Cassinelli, G., 31
Castelnuovo, G., 165, 170
Castenholz, R. W., 227, 240, 263, 277, 279, 281
Castle, E. S., 543
Cate, T., 301
Cato, E. P., 126, 129
Causey, W., 462
Cavalier-Smith, T., 613
Cech, S. Y., 523
Cedergren, R. J., 247
Celesk, R. A., 126
Celikkol, E., 137
CERDÁ-OLMEDO, E., 535-47; 535, 538-40, 542, 543
Chairez, R., 361, 362
Chakrabarty, A. M., 387, 390
Chamoiseau, G., 173
Champe, S. P., 488, 500
Chan, R. K., 481, 495
Chan, S. H., 435
Chan, T. W., 563, 564
Chance, B., 185, 189, 510, 569, 577
Chandra, S., 438
Chang, J. Y., 398
Chang, K.-P., 520
Chang, M. L., 80
Chang, M. Y., 437
Chang, R. S., 422, 429, 436, 437, 604
Chang, S. L., 603, 606, 609, 610
Chang, S.-Y., 192, 194
Chang, T. S., 80
Chao, C.-C., 71, 72
Chao, L., 237
Chapman, D. J., 244, 266
Chapman, G. B., 40
Chappelka, A. R., 115
Charlier, H., 113, 117
Charlier, J., 569
Charney, J., 25
Charon, N. W., 95

Chase, D. B., 124
Chatelain, R., 553
Chattaway, F. W., 348
Chatterjee, A. K., 40
Chatterjee, S. N., 553
Chattoraj, D. K., 500
Chauvet, G., 522, 523
Che, C.-C., 488
Cheeseman, P., 325
Chen, J. W., 351
Chen, M., 360
Chen, M. S. K., 80, 81
Chen, T. A., 219
Cheng, K. H., 261
Cheng, L., 266
Cherni, N. E., 282
Chernukha, Y. G., 100
Cherrier, C., 312
Cherubin, C. E., 451, 458
Chet, I., 380
Cheung, S. C., 300, 301
Cheung, W. Y., 257
Chichester, C. O., 40
Chick, M., 14, 24, 25, 31, 32
Child, K. J., 301
Chiovetti, R. Jr., 601
Chisari, F. V., 371, 432
Cho, J.-R., 438
Cho, K. Y., 553
Chopin, A., 125
Chou, G., 390
Chough, K. S., 295
Chow, A. W., 452, 464, 466
Christensen, H. N., 182, 191
Christiansen, P., 216, 217
Christiansen, S., 90
Christner, J. E., 569
Chumakova, R. I., 43, 552-55, 575, 581
Chung, K.-T., 311, 315
Church, J. A., 450
Chusid, M. J., 461
Chynoweth, D. P., 337
Ciardi, J. E., 152
Cinco, M., 94
Citron, P., 422
Claffey, T., 463
Claflin, L., 211
Clagett, J., 508
Clark, A., 97
Clark, D. A., 452, 453
Clark, D. S., 317, 319
Clark, F. E., 207, 218
Clark, J. E., 169
Clark, R. L., 255
Clark, W. R., 619
Clarke, F. E., 207, 218
Clarke, L., 407
Clarke, R. T. J., 112, 117
Claus, G., 266
Clausen, K. P., 437
Claypool, G. E., 329, 331-33
Clayton, D. A., 359, 365, 366, 368, 370, 374
Clegg, J. A., 514
Cleland, R. E., 192
Clement, D. H., 452, 459
Clements, G., 431
Clemmons, G., 83
Cleverdon, R. C., 39, 48
Clifford, P., 423, 424, 426-31, 434, 435
Clift, R. A., 452
Cline, T. W., 558, 563-65, 567, 577, 578, 584-86
Cluff, L. E., 452, 463, 465
Clyde, W. A., 462
Cobb, J. M., 305
Cobb, S., 461
Cobbs, G., 301
Cockburn, A., 78, 79
Cockburn, M., 190
Codd, G. A., 238, 251, 260, 261, 264
Coffey, J. J., 555, 573, 575, 578, 586
Cogdell, R. J., 184
Cohen, G. N., 40, 552
Cohen, R. J., 538, 544, 545
Cohen, S. N., 483
Cohen, S. S., 227
Cohen, Y., 260, 263, 276
COHEN-BAZIRE, G., 225-74; 227, 231, 234, 236, 237, 239, 242-47, 265, 267, 277, 398
Cohn, M., 136, 137
Cohn, Z., 520
Cohn, Z. A., 508, 509, 524
Cole, G. C., 332
Colella, J., 460
Coleman, C., 524
Coleman, G. S., 83
Colley, F. C., 518
Collins, A. L. T., 405, 410
Collins, M. D., 163-65, 167, 171, 173, 176
Collins, P. A., 53
Collins, S. H., 187
Colman, B., 261
Colwell, R. R., 40, 45, 52, 53, 380, 381
Combriato, G., 485
Comfort, M., 300
Concepcion, N. F., 466
Condeelis, J. S., 195
Conn, H. O., 452, 454, 457, 459, 466
Connell, G. E., 474
Conner, D. H., 456
Conolly, B. W., 80
Constantopoulos, G., 243
Conté, A., 234, 237
Conti, S. F., 236
Contois, D. E., 71, 77
Contopoulou, R., 45, 57
Cook, F. D., 380
Cook, W. L., 384
Cooney, C. L., 337, 354
Coope, D., 433
Cooper, T. Y., 422, 436, 437
Coote, J. G., 149
Copeland, C. E., 219
Copeland, D. P., 186, 189
Coplin, D. L., 208, 219
Corcoran, B., 508
Corcoran, J. W., 14, 24-26, 31, 32
Corff, S., 611, 616, 621
Cormier, M., 458
Cormier, M. J., 40, 551, 557, 560, 563, 566-68
Cosenza, B. J., 39, 48
Costello, R., 108-10, 112-15, 117, 120, 123
Costerton, J. W., 41
Cother, E. J., 220
Cotmore, J., 97
Cotran, R. S., 514
Cotta, E., 14, 20
Coulaud, J. P., 459
Coulson, J. G., 207, 216
Counts, G. W., 459
Courtney, R. J., 362
Cousineau, J., 559, 579
Cove, D. J., 141, 143
Coventry, M. B., 465
Cox, B. A., 382, 391
Cox, C. D., 90, 91, 102
Cox, G. B., 26
Cox, J. P., 523
Cox, P. J., 91
Coyle, J. E., 382
Coyle-Gilchrist, M. M., 459, 460
Crackower, S. H., 304
Craig, I. W., 227, 228
Craig, W. G. Jr., 491
Craig, W. K., 382
Crane, R. K., 182, 185, 191
Crasemann, J., 488
Craven, J. A., 120
Crawford, D. H., 427-29, 436, 437, 439
Crawford, I. P., 27, 41, 588
Creevy, D. C., 139
Creswell, K. M., 303
Crewe, P., 459, 460
Crifo, C., 14
Crofts, A. R., 184
Cromartie, W. J., 522
Cross, R. K., 361
Cross, T., 160-64, 169, 171-76
Crowdy, S. H., 303
Cruden, D. L., 243, 277
Crumpton, M. J., 152
Cuatico, W., 438

Cudlin, J., 31, 33, 34
Culbertson, C. G., 603
Cullens, H., 452, 465
Culling, C. F. A., 452
Cummins, C. S., 163, 169, 171
Cunin, R., 482, 498
Curds, C. R., 77-79
Cure, G. L., 163
Curelaru, Z., 523
Curnutte, J. T., 510-12
Curreri, P. W., 458
Currie, M. S., 558
Curry, G. M., 543
Cursons, R. T. M., 603
Curtis, P., 588
Curtis, P. J., 302
Curtiss, R. III, 407, 489
Cutler, J. C., 97, 98
Cutler, R. W., 614
Czerkawski, J. W., 336
Czlonkowski, S. T., 335

D

Daems, W. Th., 513
Daggett, P.-M., 606
Dahl, M. M., 404, 405, 416
Dahlberg, J. E., 486, 503
Dahlquist, F. W., 415
Dalens, M., 429
Dales, S., 516, 520
Dalgard, D. W., 371
Dalton, H., 249
Dane, D. S., 358-60, 373
Daniels, L., 317, 324
Daniels, M. J., 208, 219
Daniher, F. A., 31
Dannenberg, A. M. Jr., 516, 521
Daoust, V., 31
Darbsyshire, B., 220
Darby, F. J., 26
D'Arcy, P. F., 303
Das, B. C., 524
Das, J., 553
Das, S. R., 602, 603
Dascomb, H. E., 427, 436
Datta, P., 141, 143, 145, 345
Davey, J. F., 257, 388
David, C. N., 535
Davidson, N., 483, 502
Davies, B. H., 539
Davies, J., 141, 143, 146, 152, 482, 495
Davies, J. E., 482
Davies, M. G., 300
Davies, P., 522
Davies, S. L., 383
Davis, B. D., 80
Davis, B. E., 380
Davis, C. L., 95
Davis, C. P., 96, 112, 116, 117, 120-23
Davis, G. H. G., 162
Davis, H. T., 77
Davis, J., 513
Davis, K. J., 488
Davis, P., 195
Davis, S. D., 461, 462
Davison, W. C., 462
Dawson, G. W. P., 487
Day, N. E., 435
Deal, D. R., 432
Dearing, W. H., 465
De Bac, C., 360
Debanne, M. T., 141, 143, 146, 152
de Barsy, T., 520, 525, 527, 529
DeBoer, R. G., 463
de Boer, W. E., 48, 51
Dcchairo, D., 433, 434, 438, 439
DeChatelet, L. R., 510, 512
Decker, J. L., 451, 461
Decker, K., 312
De Coninck, P., 458
Decuypere, J., 113-15, 117, 120
de Duve, C., 508, 520, 522, 525, 527-29
Deering, R. A., 604
De Fabo, E. C., 539, 544
Degani, C., 185, 189
Degens, E. T., 331
DeGroote, J., 371
De Harven, E., 424
Dehmlow, E. V., 28
Deinhardt, F., 428, 429, 432, 433
Dekeyser, P., 456
de Kruyff, B., 14, 295
de la Guardia, M. D., 539, 542
DeLange, R. J., 398
Delaunay, J., 515
Delbrück, M., 195, 416, 535, 537, 538, 542, 543, 545
Del Campo, F. F., 188
Delektorskii, V. V., 90
DeLeo, A. B., 150
Delor, C. J., 437
DeLuca, M., 569
DEMAIN, A. L., 343-56; 16, 34, 346, 347, 349-54
De Marcha, P., 461
Demel, R. A., 14, 295
Demissie, A., 422
DeMoss, R. D., 128
Denis, F., 454, 461
Dennis, P. P., 486, 503
Dennison, D. S., 535, 538, 546
De Nollin, S., 305
Deonier, R. C., 502
DePamphilis, M. L., 91, 398, 400-2, 415
Derge, J. G., 430, 431
Deruelles, J., 227, 231, 233, 235
DeSa, R. J., 562
De Schryver, A., 424, 426
Desgranges, C., 428, 430, 435, 436
Desikachary, T. V., 227, 228, 231, 249, 267
Desmet, V. J., 371
Desmyter, J., 371
Desser, R. K., 467
De-Thé, G., 426, 428, 430-32, 435, 436
De-Thé, G. B., 435
Detroy, R. W., 352
Deuser, W. G., 331
Deutscher, M. P., 138, 142, 143, 147, 150
DeVay, J. E., 208, 219
Devita, V. T., 438
DeVries, A. L., 589
de Vries, W., 315
Devroede, G. J., 125
Dewey, F., 424
De Zoeten, G. A., 207
Dharmawardene, M. W. N., 264
Dharmgrongartama, B., 137
Dibble, J. T., 387
Dice, J. F., 136, 137, 147
Dickinson, A. B., 113, 117
Dickman, M. D., 115
Dickson, H., 539
Diehl, V., 423, 426, 428-31, 433
Diehn, B., 195
Diesch, S. L., 94
Dietrichson, O., 360
Dietzler, D. N., 31
Dilley, R. A., 189
Dimitroff, V. T., 95
Dimmick, R. L., 65
Dimmitt, K., 398, 400, 402
Dimroth, P., 24, 25
Dingle, A. D., 598-602, 606-11, 613, 614, 619, 620, 623, 625
Dismukes, W., 301
Dive, D., 78
Dixon, G. H., 474
Dixon, R., 460
Dixon, R. A., 387
Djerassi, C., 16, 20, 31
Dmochowski, L., 425
Dobrogosz, W. J., 412
Dobson, P. R., 248
Dobzhansky, T., 107
Dochez, A. R., 10
Dodge, P. R., 460, 467
Dodge, R. W., 101

Doelle, H. W., 128
Doetsch, R. N., 91, 398
Doi, R. H., 45, 146
Doi, T., 425
Dolyniuk, M., 428
Dombos, L., 432
Donze, M., 251, 253
Dooley, J. E., 381
Doolittle, W. F., 248, 249, 256, 258
Dostalek, M., 383
Doudoroff, M., 41, 42, 45, 55, 57, 264, 575, 581, 588
Dougherty, E. C., 244
Douglas, H. C., 279
Douglas, R. G., 451, 464
Douzou, P., 557, 562-64, 567, 568
Dowaliby, J. M., 422, 436
Dowell, V. R. Jr., 455
Dowler, J., 170
Downs, A. J., 187
Drake, J. F., 68-72, 76-78, 82, 84
Drake, J. W., 488, 500
Drapeau, G. R., 41
Draper, J. C., 399
Draper, P., 514, 515, 523
Draper, R., 407, 413
Drasar, B. S., 108, 113, 115, 117-23, 125, 127, 128, 130
Drath, D. B., 510, 512, 514
Dreesman, G. R., 361, 362
Drew, D., 453, 457
DREW, S. W., 343-56; 346, 347
Drews, G., 238, 239, 277, 285, 286, 288
Dri, P., 510
Drouet, F., 233
Drouillard, M., 577
Drozd, J. W., 187
Drutz, D. J., 298
Duane, W., 568, 569, 578
Dubes, G. R., 432
Dubinina, G. A., 277, 279, 282
Dubnau, D., 45
Dubois, L., 510
Dubois, R. S., 123
Dubos, F., 125, 126
Dubos, R., 108-15, 117, 120, 123, 128
Duchow, E., 279
Ducluzeau, R., 113, 120-22, 124-26, 128
Dugan, P. R., 239
Dulaney, E. L., 352
Dulbecco, R., 80, 359
Duma, R., 301
Duma, R. J., 452, 466, 603
Dumler, M., 463
Duncan, J. L., 522
Duncan, M. E., 170
Dunckley, G. G., 166
Dundas, C. R., 579
Dunn, D. K., 560, 564
Dunn, J. H., 252
Dunn, N. W., 390
Dunn-Coleman, N. S., 141
Dunnebacke, T. H., 603
Duntze, W., 136, 139, 140, 142-45, 148, 149
DuPont, H. L., 454, 455, 457, 460
Dupuis, F., 458
Durbin, R. D., 206, 207, 209, 210, 217
Durham, A. C. H., 195
Durston, A., 488
Duschinsky, R., 299
Dussault, H., 429
Dutcher, J. D., 16, 20, 28, 30, 31
Duval, J., 454
Duvall, C. P., 449, 451, 456, 458, 465
Dworkin, M., 384
Dwyer, D. M., 520
Dyer, T. A., 248

E

Eagle, H., 101
Eagon, R. G., 41, 53, 582
Earnshaw, P., 190
Easton, D. J., 462
Eberhard, A., 55, 553, 555, 558, 560, 561, 563, 564, 567, 570, 572, 574, 575
Ebner, E., 146
Ecarot, B., 247
Eccleston, M., 257
Echols, H., 137, 500
Eckert, R., 192, 193, 195, 617
Eckman, M. R., 462
Eckroade, C. B., 567
Edds, K. T., 621
Eddy, A. A., 190
Edelman, M., 246
Edelson, P. J., 524
Eden-Green, S. J., 208, 213
Ederer, G. M., 464
Edgar, L., 538
Edgington, T. S., 371
Edmonds, M., 620
Edmondson, E. B., 452, 454, 457
Edmondson, W. T., 243
Edwards, B., 462
Edwards, M. R., 236, 237
Edwards, S., 407, 413
Edwards, T., 328
Edwards, V. M., 359
Efimova, T. P., 166, 171
Egan, R. S., 33
Eggebraten, L. M., 93, 102
Eggertsson, G., 487
Eguchi, G., 398, 399
Eickhoff, T. C., 450, 457, 458
Eimhjellen, K. E., 283
Eisen, H. N., 80
Eisenach, K. D., 457
Eisenberg, M., 183
Eisenman, G., 183
Eiserling, F. A., 91, 244
Eitzman, D. V., 457
Ekestrom, S., 453
Elander, R. P., 348
Elbein, A. D., 32
El-Din Hathout, S., 459
Eley, J. H., 261
Eley, M. H., 563, 566, 575
Elgart, R. E., 16, 17, 20, 22
El-Ghaffar, Y. A., 459
Elkington, J., 428, 431
Ellinghausen, H. C., 90, 94, 102
Elliott, A. M., 83
Elliott, W. H., 32
Ellis, R. A., 613
Ellison, D., 100
Ellner, P. D., 463
Ellouz, R., 428, 435
el-Nakeeb, M. A., 303
Eloff, J. N., 239
Elrod, R. P., 219
Elsbach, P., 510
Elseviers, D., 498
Elson, H. E., 92
Elsworth, R., 64, 65
Elwell, R. A., 415
Ely, B., 481
Emeis, J. J., 513
Emerson, S. U., 398, 399
Emery, K. O., 332, 333
Emmons, C. W., 298
Emmons, S. W., 484
Engel, D., 508
Engel, R. R., 336
Engelbrecht, H. L., 137
Englander, E., 387, 393
English, H., 208, 219
Enomoto, M., 405, 411, 415
Epstein, H. T., 246
EPSTEIN, M. A., 421-45; 422, 425, 427-30, 432-34, 436-40
Epstein, W., 188, 405
Epstein, W. L., 301
Erdos, G. W., 611
Erge, D., 353
Erickson, L. E., 65, 383
Eriksen, L., 96
Erikson, D., 219
Erlandson, S. L., 124
Erlanger, B. F., 560

Ernberg, I., 424-26
Ernster, L., 185, 189
Eschenhof, E., 299, 300
Eslava, A. P., 538-40, 542, 543
Espmark, J. A., 360
Etémadi, A. H., 165
Evans, A., 261
Evans, A. S., 422, 426
Evans, D. L., 425
Evans, E. H., 184, 235, 241
Evans, L. B., 94, 100
Evans, M. C. W., 246
Evans, R. S., 337
Eymers, J. G., 580
Eyring, H., 579

F

Fabiani, G., 458
Fahey, J. L., 451, 467
Faine, S., 92
Faini, G. J., 562, 563, 569
Fairbanks, G., 363
Fales, H. M., 524
Falk, L., 428, 429, 432, 433
Falkenberg, B., 263
Falta, R., 169
Fan, L. T., 65
Fan, V. S. C., 516
Farghaly, A. H., 573, 575
Farquhar, M. G., 508, 513
Farrand, R. J., 137
Fauci, A. S., 461
Fauconnier, B., 458
Faulkner, L. R., 568
Fauve, R. M., 515
Favre, M. C., 430, 436
Fawcett, P. A., 347
Fay, P., 227, 250, 251, 253
Fedorko, M. E., 508, 509, 512, 513
Fedorova, V. D., 282
Feeley, J. C., 97, 460, 462
Fefer, A., 452
Feigin, R. D., 450-54, 457, 462, 465, 466
Fein, J. E., 41
Feingold, D. S., 294, 296, 300
Feld, R., 461
Feldman, D. A., 141, 143, 145
Feldman, H. A., 518, 519
Fell, H. B., 514
Felsenfeld, O., 99, 100
Felter, R. A., 40
Felton, F., 454, 457, 463
Felts, S. K., 457
Fenchel, T. M., 263
Fennessey, P. V., 208, 219
Fennewald, M., 390
Fensom, A. H., 139
Fenwick, R. G. Jr., 407
Fenyö, E. M., 429
Ferguson, A. R., 139, 143
Ferguson, J. F. III, 568
Ferguson, J. J., 140, 142, 149
Ferner, R. R., 392
Fernex, M., 299, 300
Ferni, G., 14, 20
Ferrell, W. J., 577
Ferry, J. G., 318, 319, 322, 323
Fessel, J. M., 452, 454, 457, 459, 466
Fevery, J., 371
Fialkow, P. J., 429, 434, 435
Fichtner, R. E., 170
Fiechter, A., 140, 383, 384
Fields, B., 301
Fields, B. N., 361, 457, 458
Filburn, B., 122
Filer, D., 138, 143
Finch, S. C., 437
Fincham, J. R. S., 141, 143
Finegold, S. M., 112, 119, 125, 452, 455
Finerty, S., 427-29, 436, 437, 439
Fink, M. A., 425
Finkel'shtein, Z. I., 327, 328, 331
Finkelstein, A., 14, 295
Finkelstein, J. D., 359
Finkelstein, R. A., 206
Finland, M., 449, 457
Finn, M. A., 101
Finnerty, W. R., 383, 385
Finney, C. D., 337
Firtel, R. A., 604, 620
Fischer, E. H., 137
Fischer, E. P., 542
Fischkoff, S. A., 14, 20
Fish, A. M., 575, 581
Fisher, G., 194
Fisher, J., 569
Fisher, R. W., 255
Fisher, W. P., 25
Fitzgerald, G. B., 130
Fitzgerald, J. M., 553, 554
Fitzgerald, R. H., 465
Fitzgerald, T. J., 101
Flamm, W. G., 604
Fleming, A., 162
Fleming, H., 253
Flett, R. J., 332
Flick, J. A., 461
Flick, M. R., 463
Flick, P. K., 26
Floch, M., 122
Floch, M. H., 108, 112
Flora, D. J., 112, 119, 125
Floss, H. G., 345, 346, 348, 352, 353
Flury, U., 140
Fogg, G. E., 227, 237, 249-51, 254
Folger, C., 101
Folk, W. R., 480, 487
Folland, D., 466, 467
Foo, M. C., 123, 124
Foor, F., 150
Ford, D. K., 452
Ford, E. C., 359
Fordtran, J. S., 58
Fork, R. L., 543
Forsberg, C. W., 41
Forsyth, M. P., 41
Fosset, M., 137
Foster, J. W., 389
Foster, K. M., 428
Foster, K. W., 535, 537, 538, 540
Foulds, I., 235, 241
Foulds, J., 485
Fournier, R. G., 381
Fouts, D. W., 426
Fowler, A. K., 438
Fowler, C. F., 280
Fowler, R., 452, 466, 467
Fox, G. E., 248
Foy, H. M., 461, 462
Fraenkel, D. G., 41
Franceschi, G., 31
Francis, B. S., 45
Frank, H., 238
Franke, W. W., 189
Franklin, A. A. Jr., 169
Franklin, M. A., 114, 121
Franklin, N. C., 474, 484
Frato, J., 137
Frazier, W. R., 25
Frea, J. I., 330-32
Frederic, J., 508
FREDRICKSON, A. G., 63-87; 66, 68-74, 76-79, 82, 84
Freedman, R., 500
Freeman, J. B., 453, 464, 465
Freeman, M. J., 101
Freer, J. H., 162, 522
Freer, R. J., 508
French, S. C., 242
Frenkel, J. K., 517-20
Frenkel, L. D., 450
Freter, R., 109, 121, 122, 124, 126, 127
Fribourg-Blanc, A., 99
Friden, C., 260
Fridovich, I., 262, 511, 512
Friebe, G., 139, 148
Friedberg, E. C., 137
Friedland, J. M., 555, 558, 560-64, 578, 579
Friedman, D. I., 288
Friedman, E. A., 359
Friedman, H., 514

Friedmann, A., 438
Friis, R. R., 516, 517
Fritsch, F. E., 226
Fromme, I., 238, 285, 286, 288
Frost, G. M., 42
Fudl-Allah, A. E. A., 219
Fuhs, G. W., 237
Fujino, T., 40, 48
Fujioka, R. S., 362
Fujisawa, A., 41
Fujita, H., 405, 410, 411
Fujita, Y., 242
Fukuhara, S., 433
Fukumi, H., 52, 54
Fulghum, R. S., 95
Fulginiti, V. A., 452, 455
Fuller, M., 624
Fuller, R., 113
Fuller, R. C., 280
FULTON, C., 597-629; 598-611, 613-17, 619-26
Furukawa, Y., 164-67, 173
Furutani, A., 332
Fusco, J. J., 454, 460, 464-67

G

Gaard, G. R., 207
Gabay, S. J., 208
Gabriel, O., 32
Gage, V., 146
Galanos, C., 31
Gallin, J., 509, 523
Gallis, H., 301
Gallo, G. G., 28
Gallo, M., 350
Gallo, R., 431
Gallo, R. C., 438
Gallon, J. R., 265
Gallori, E., 538
Gallucci, E., 487
Galonsky, A., 253, 264
Galpin, J. E., 464, 466
Galpin, J. V., 113
Gambrill, M. R., 517
Games, L. M., 331
Gamow, R. I., 538-40, 545
Gancedo, C., 138, 141, 142, 146, 149-51
Ganesan, A. K., 137
Gani, J., 80
Ganis, P., 14, 294
Ganju, P. L., 30
Gantt, E., 236, 242, 244-46
Gantz, N. M., 460
Gardiner, P. R., 620
Gardner, J. M., 209
Gardner, P., 453-56, 464-66
Garen, A., 487
Gargus, J. J., 415, 416
Garlick, S., 263
Garnier, J., 113, 115, 117
Garrott, T. C., 305
Gartler, S. M., 429, 434
Gartner, K., 114, 121
Garver, J., 76
Gary, N. D., 102
Gast, R., 567
Gateau, O., 163
Gatenbeck, S., 24
Gaudiano, G., 16
Gauger, W., 541
Gause, G. F., 63, 65, 75
Gaworowska-Michalik, J., 24, 34
Gay, R., 312
Gazzolo, L., 431, 432
Gealt, M. A., 303
Gebhardt, A. E., 305
Gee, D. L., 41
Geering, G., 424
Geigy, R., 100
Geitler, L., 228, 231, 234, 235, 239, 267, 280
Gemmell, E., 120, 124, 126
Gentles, J. C., 302
Georg, L. K., 160, 162, 163
Georgopoulos, S. G., 304
Gerber, N. N., 163, 164, 168, 171
Gerber, P., 422, 423, 429-33, 436, 437, 439
Gerding, D. N., 451, 461
Gerenscer, M. A., 161
Gerety, R. J., 360, 374
Gergely, L., 425, 431
Gerin, J. L., 359-65, 370, 373
Gerlich, W., 359, 362
Gerlo, E., 569
Gerner, R., 422
Gerritsen, W. J., 295
Gerstley, B. J. S., 357
Gest, H., 285, 288
Geurts van Kessel, W. S. M., 295
Gewitz, H. S., 141, 143, 145
Ghiorse, W. C., 237
Ghisla, S., 566
Ghuysen, J. M., 163
Giannella, R. A., 449, 454, 458, 467
Giaquinta, R. T., 189
Gibbons, N. E., 57, 160, 170, 226, 227, 317, 552, 554, 555, 606
Gibbons, R. J., 96, 97
Gibbs, M., 257
Gibbs, S. P., 285
Gibson, D. T., 380, 388, 389
Gibson, F., 26, 27, 29, 30
Gibson, J., 260
Gibson, J. L., 260
Gibson, M., 26
Gibson, P. E., 359
Gibson, Q. H., 561-64, 568, 569, 578, 579
Giddon, D. B., 97
Giesberger, G., 279
Giesy, R. M., 237
Giffhorn, F., 138, 142, 145, 151
Giger, W., 380
Gil, J. A., 27
Gil, R., 454, 461
Gilardi, G. L., 464
Gilbert, E., 456
Gilbert, S., 452, 455
Gilch, B., 27
Gilcrist, M. J. R., 188
Gill, D. M., 206, 220
Gill, M. L., 588
Gillespie, D., 438
Gillmore, J. D., 125
Gilmour, M. N., 160
Ginger, C. D., 92
Ginsberg, H. S., 80
Ginsburg, A., 136, 137, 139, 143-45, 148, 151, 154
Ginsburg, I., 522
Giovanella, B. C., 427, 428, 431, 432, 435, 436, 439
Giovanelli, J., 219
Girolami, R. L., 33
Gitel'zon, I. I., 581
Glansdorff, N., 482, 498
Gläsel, R. M., 192
Glaser, L., 32
Glaser, R., 431, 432
GLASS, T. L., 309-41
Glazer, A. N., 244, 246, 398
Gledhill, W. E., 160, 161, 380, 392
Gleiser, C. A., 100
Glick, J. L., 430
Glinski, R. P., 30
Glock, R. D., 96
Gloe, A., 277, 281
Glosser, J. W., 91
Gnanamanickam, S. S., 218, 221
Gocke, D. J., 359, 373
Godefroi, E. F., 305
Godts, P., 305
Goebel, W. F., 11
Gold, J. W. N., 362, 363
Gold, M. H., 137
Goldberg, A. L., 136, 137, 147
Goldberg, E. D., 332, 333, 335
Goldberg, I., 23
Golden, C. A., 516
Golden, H. D., 422, 436, 437
Goldfine, H., 166
Goldhaber, P., 97
Goldman, D. J., 186
Goldman, M., 139, 143, 147, 149, 153, 422

Goldman, P., 126
Goldman, R., 524
Goldmann, D. A., 453, 454, 464-66
Goldring, O. L., 514
Goldspink, D. F., 147
Goldstein, A. W., 33
Goldstein, E., 305
Goldstein, I., 509, 522, 523
Goldstein, I. M., 510, 512
Goldstein, L. I., 422, 437
Golten, C., 48, 51
Goma, G., 383
Gomez-Moreno, C., 249, 264
Gong, T., 619
Gonzalez, C., 153
González-Ochoa, A., 170, 174, 175
Gooch, V. D., 198
Good, I. J., 112, 119, 125, 127
Goodell, E. W., 535, 545
GOODFELLOW, M., 159-80; 160-76
Goodman, J. S., 462
Goodman, R. N., 208, 209, 213, 214
Gorbach, S. L., 108, 115, 122, 452, 454, 455, 464, 466
Gordon, A. M., 462
Gordon, F. B., 125
Gordon, H. A., 107, 119, 123, 124, 127, 130
Gordon, H. W., 15, 16
Gordon, J., 96, 111, 117
Gordon, J. H., 111, 117
Gordon, L. G. M., 195
Gordon, R. E., 161, 162, 172-74
Gordon, R. S., 451, 461
Gordon, S., 508
GOREN, M. B., 507-35; 514, 515, 524, 525, 527
Gorlenko, V. M., 277, 279-83
Gorman, M., 348
Görts, C. P. M., 139, 140
Gossett, J. M., 337
Gossling, J., 119
Gots, J., 412
Gottesman, M. F., 501
Gottlieb, D. H., 295
Gottschalk, G., 138, 142, 145, 151, 315
Goulden, S. A., 348
Govindjee, 189
Goy, M. F., 408, 414, 416, 417
Grace, J. T., 422, 430, 433
Gracey, M., 113, 114
Gradmann, D., 190-92
Grady, G. F., 359, 360
Graefe, U., 22
Grafstrom, R. H., 486, 503
Graham, H. D., 40
Graham, P. H., 553
Granados, R. R., 219
Grandgenett, D. P., 138, 143
Graw, R. G., 451, 452
Gray, B. H., 138, 141-43, 148, 242, 244-46, 280
Gray, J. E., 247
Gray, P. H. H., 162, 172
Greaves, M. F., 431
Green, I., 438
Greenberg, E. P., 94, 101
Greenberg, H. B., 366-69
Greene, W. H., 449, 463
Greenlee, H. B., 359
Greenman, R. L., 359, 365, 374
Greenwood, B. M., 439, 514
Greenwood, C., 563, 569
Grein, A., 14, 20
Greville, G. D., 184
Griepp, R. B., 452, 453
Grieves, R. B., 65
Griffin, F. M. Jr., 509
Griffin, J. A., 509
Griffin, J. L., 603, 606
Griffin, T. B., 41, 53
Griffin, W. B., 454-56, 464
Griffiths, M., 243
Grigor, M. R., 166
Grigsby, R. D., 168
Grimes, G. W., 613
Gripenberg, U., 429
Grisebach, H., 25, 32
Grisham, L. M., 303
Groeger, D., 353
Groeschel, D., 461
Grosiak, B., 219
Gross, N. M., 169
Grossman, A., 259
Groth, C. G., 452, 455
Grove, J. F., 301, 303
Groves, P. M., 545
Gruber, M., 147
Gruen, H. E., 543
Grunberg, E., 15
Grund, A., 390
Gschwendt, B., 388
Gudat, F., 371
Guerin, F. J. A., 329
Guerrini, A. M., 600, 606, 607, 615, 617, 623
Guglielmi, G., 240
Guiking, P., 260
Guinand, M., 163
Gull, K., 294, 304
Gunsalus, A., 555, 558, 560, 561, 563
Gunsalus, I. C., 390
Gunsalus-Miguel, A., 555, 558, 560
Gunvén, P., 424, 426
Gupta, S. K., 30
Gurney, E. G., 604
Gustafson, G. L., 137, 143, 148
Guthe, T., 97
GUTNICK, D. L., 379-96; 383, 384, 386, 387, 393
Guttes, E., 613
Guttes, S., 613
Guze, L. B., 452, 464-66
Guzeva, L. N., 166, 171
Gysi, J., 244

H

Haarasilta, S., 141, 142
Habig, W., 244
Hackett, C. J., 98
Hackett, J. A., 166
Hackett, J. J., 438
Haddock, B. A., 184, 185
Haff, R. F., 432
Hageage, G. J., 398
Hageman, J. H., 146, 150
Hager, L. P., 25
Hagino, H., 30
Hagins, W. A., 581
Haglund, U., 430, 433
Hahlbrock, K., 28
Hahn, E., 490
Hahn, H., 528
Haines, J. R., 385
Hake, R. B., 509
Halbert, S. P., 522
Haldom, R. S., 384
Halfen, L. N., 234, 240, 241
Hall, A. N., 389
Hall, D. O., 246, 262
Hall, H. E., 52
Hall, J. H., 453, 464
Hall, W., 461
Hall, W. T., 266, 370
Hallander, H. O., 162, 171
Hallett, A. F., 452, 459
Halloin, J. M., 207
Halloran, B., 538
Halsey, M. J., 579
Halvorson, H. O., 139, 140, 150
Hamer, G., 65, 70, 71, 75, 78
Hamilton, J., 359
Hamilton, P. B., 412
Hamilton, R. D., 76, 78, 326, 327, 332
Hamilton, W. A., 184, 185, 187
Hamilton-Miller, J. M. T., 13, 14
Hamlow, E. E., 304
Hammer, B. W., 172
Hammond, B. F., 164, 167, 171
Hammond, D. E., 332
Hamon, C. B., 510-14
Hampar, B., 426, 430, 431
Hampp, E. G., 97

Han, T., 458
Han, T. W., 261
Hanaoka, M., 52
Handerhan, J. E., 173
Haneda, Y., 557
Haniu, M., 246
Hanks, J. H., 167
Hansen, T. A., 282, 283
Hanseon, F. E., 581
Hansma, H. G., 192, 194
Hanson, A. W., 102
Hanson, F. E., 570
Hanson, L. E., 94, 100
Hanson, R. S., 332
Hansson, S. E., 195
Harada, S., 17
Hard, G. C., 514
Harder, W., 68
Hardie, J. M., 163, 164, 171
Hardin, G., 70
Harding, R. W., 539, 544
Hardy, C. J., 582
Hardy, P. H., 90, 97, 98
Harland, W. A., 96, 117
HAROLD, F. M., 181-203; 182-89, 199
Harper, A., 510, 514
Harrington, A., 589
Harris, D. L., 96, 101
Harris, H., 163
Harris, J. F., 538, 545
Harris, M. A., 117
Harris, V. G., 102
Harrison, E. F., 304
Harrison, F. C., 172
Hart, P. D., 513-16, 523, 525, 527, 528
Hart, R., 557, 561, 564, 578
Harter, D. H., 454, 460, 464-67
Hartley, B. S., 480
Hartman, P. E., 491, 497
Hartmann, U., 141, 145
Hartwig, J. H., 509, 523
Harvey, E. N., 40, 576-80, 584, 589
Harvey, G. T., 331
Harvey, R. L., 451, 454, 462
Harvey, R. P., 451, 458
Harz, C. O., 159, 160
Hase, T., 246
Haselkorn, R., 247, 253, 260
Hashimoto, H., 482
Hashimoto, S., 482
Hasilik, A., 146
Haskins, E. F., 614
Haslam, E., 29
Haslam, E. A., 137
Haspel, M. V., 428
HASTINGS, J. W., 549-95; 40, 41, 198, 551-53, 555-82, 584-89
Hato, M., 195
Hattori, A., 242, 264
Hattori, Y., 92
Haug, R. T., 337
Haung, K. L., 384
Haveman, J., 253
Haxby, J., 295
Hayakawa, K., 119-21
Hayashi, M., 40
Hayashi, T., 432
Haydon, D. A., 183, 195
Haystead, A., 249, 264
Hayward, S. D., 428, 433
Haywood, H., 301
Hazelbauer, G. L., 405
Head, J. J., 462
Healy, G. R., 603
Hearey, C. D., 459
Heath, E. C., 32
Heath, G. T., 488
Heberling, R. L., 438
Heck, D. M., 461
Heer, B., 140
Heeres, J., 305
Hefferan, M., 172
Hegeman, G. D., 473
Heggie, D. T., 326, 327
Hehlmann, R., 438
Heidelberger, C., 299
HEIDELBERGER, M., 1-12; 1-3, 5-11
Heidenreich, W., 426
Heineken, F. G., 83
Heinstein, P. F., 348
Heinz, E., 191
Heisenberg, M., 535, 542
Helfman, L., 463
Helinski, D. R., 482
Hellman, A., 438
Helmke, R. J., 438
Hemmerich, P., 566
Hemming, H. G., 301-3
Hemmings, B. A., 139, 143, 145, 148, 149, 151
Hemsted, E. H., 436
Henderickx, H. K., 113
Henderson, A., 463
Henderson, B. E., 435
Henderson, K., 383
Hendler, S., 27
Hendlin, D., 346
Hendrie, M. S., 43, 48, 55, 552-56
Henjyoji, E. Y., 457
Henkel, J. S., 451, 466
Henle, G., 422-36
Henle, W., 422-37
Henneberry, R. C., 102
Henning, D. L., 319, 336
Henrichsen, J., 51, 52
Henrici, A. T., 67
Henriksen, S. D., 454, 460
Henry, J.-P., 560, 575
Henry, R. A., 94, 95, 102
Henson, P. M., 522
Hentges, D. J., 108, 122, 126
Hepler, P. K., 613
Herbert, D., 64, 65
Herdman, M., 227, 231, 233, 235, 246, 266
Hermans, P. E., 457
Hermodsson, S., 24
Hernandez-Asensio, M., 188
Herring, P. J., 553, 554
Herrmann, R. G., 604
Hers, H. G., 528
Herschner, C. H., 380
Hershey, A. D., 475
Hershko, A., 147, 149, 352
Herson, D. S., 247
Hertzberg, S., 243
Herzfeld, F., 247
Herzog, W., 303
Heskett, M. G., 209
Hespell, R. B., 101
Hess, G., 359
Hess, W. M., 211
Heston, L., 433
Hewetson, J. F., 424-26, 431, 437
Heyer, J., 331
Heylings, R. T., 97
Hickey, C., 620
Hidaka, T., 41
Higgins, R. F., 461
Hightower, G. M., 382, 391
Higinbotham, N., 190, 191
Hildick-Smith, G., 301
Hill, C. W., 476, 485, 486, 490, 495, 496, 500, 503
Hill, L. R., 460
Hill, M. J., 108, 113, 115, 117-23, 125, 127, 128, 130
Hill, R. F., 487
Hill, S. E., 575, 581
Hillman, B. S., 486, 503
Hilmen, M., 401-3, 406, 408, 409, 412, 413, 415, 416
Hilton, J. L., 481
Hinnen, A., 351
Hinrichs, D. J., 517
Hinton, J. J. C., 210
Hinuma, Y., 430, 433
Hinze, H., 146
Hiraki, K., 432
Hiraki, S., 432
Hirano, T., 413
Hirata, H., 183
Hirner, E. A., 33
Hirsch, D. E., 381
Hirsch, J. G., 508, 512-14, 517-19, 521, 523, 527, 528
Hirschfeld, L., 618
Hirschman, S. Z., 365, 451, 457
Hirsh, D., 487

Hisatsuka, K., 384
Hishida, M., 335
Hixson, C. S., 244
Hladky, S. B., 183
Ho, H. C., 426, 430-32, 436
Ho, J. H., 423, 427, 435
Ho, J. H. C., 431, 432
Hoagland, R. J., 422
Hoare, D. S., 256, 257
Hoare, S. L., 256
Hobson, P. N., 326, 336, 337
Hochstein, F. A., 20
Hodges, G. R., 461
Hodges, T. K., 191
Hodgkiss, W., 43, 48, 55, 56, 552-56
Hoeprich, P. D., 298, 304, 305
Hoerner, G. V., 435
Hoet, P., 108-10, 112-15, 117, 123
Höfer, M., 190
Hoff, R., 520
Hoff, R. L., 517-20
Hoffmann, G. R., 483
Hoffstein, S., 509, 522, 523
Hofmann, R. R., 117
Hogg, R. W., 415, 416
Hoggan, D., 332, 333
Hogness, D. S., 136, 137
Hohn, D. C., 510, 511
Hoitink, H. A. J., 207, 216
Holbert, P. E., 386
Holborow, E. J., 436
Holdeman, L. V., 112-19, 125-27, 129, 130
Holding, A. J., 328, 331
Holland, J. F., 14, 295
Holland, M. J., 482
Holland, P. V., 359-62
Holldorf, A. W., 139, 148
Hollinger, F. B., 361, 362
Hollis, D. G., 52, 53
Hollister, R. M., 461
Holm, M. I., 462
Holmberg, K., 162, 171
Holmer, N. G., 195
Holmes, B., 513
Holm-Hansen, O., 227
Holms, W. H., 140, 142
Holohan, P., 264
Holsclaw, D. S., 454, 463, 464
Holt, C. E., 604
Holt, R. J., 305
Holt, S. C., 90-93, 102, 237, 242, 321
Holton, R. W., 243
Holtzer, H., 616
Holz, R., 14
Holzapfel, C. W., 16, 20, 31
Holzer, H., 136, 139, 140, 142-49
Holzwarth, G., 215
Homareau, S., 459
Homyk, T., 488
Honda, H., 384
Honda, T., 48
Hondo, R., 428
Hong, R., 456
Honig, R., 432
Hood, W., 248
Hoofnagle, J. H., 357, 360, 374
Hook, E. W., 458, 459
Hooker, A. L., 208
Hope, A. B., 187, 190-92, 199
Hopgood, M. F., 315
Hopkins, T. A., 583
Hopwood, D. A., 490
Horan, A. C., 161-65, 169
Hori, T., 34
Horiguchi, T., 398, 405, 410
Horiuchi, I., 96
Horiuchi, S., 478, 479
Horiuchi, T., 478, 479
Hornc, M. K., 424, 429, 430
Hornemann, K. M., 345, 346
Hornemann, U., 348
Horowitz, A., 383, 387, 393
Horowitz, S., 456
Horsman, G., 170
Horuichi, T., 478
Horvitz, R., 466
Horwitz, C. A., 422, 426
Hoskins, L. C., 123, 124
Hostalek, Z., 20, 352
Hotani, H., 399
Hotchkiss, R. D., 490
Hovind-Hougen, K., 90-93, 97
Hovorkova, N., 34
Howard, C. R., 358, 362
Howard, D. L., 331, 332
Howard, E. M., 303
Howell, A. Jr., 160
Howell, D. S., 303
Howie, J. G. R., 96, 117
Hruska, J. F., 359, 364, 366-68, 370
Hsu, K. C., 426
Hsu, M.-T., 502
Hsu Chen, C. C., 296, 300
Hu, S., 483, 502
Huang, C.-H., 423, 428, 431, 433, 439
Huang, D. P., 423, 427, 435
Huang, E.-S., 428
Huang, J. C.-C., 80
Huang, J. S., 208, 213
Huang, K.-P., 137
Huang, M., 27
Huang, P. Y., 208, 213, 214
Huang, S. N., 360
Huang, Y. T., 427, 433, 436, 439
Huber, F. M., 346
Hubersak, C., 96, 97
Hübner, H., 331
Hubrechts, J. M., 458
Hudson, R. F., 41
Hughes, E. O., 239
Huisman, W., 147
Humphrey, A. E., 69, 80, 81
Humphrey, J. H., 508
Humphreys, R. E., 425
Hung, P. P., 33, 366, 368
Hungate, R. E., 110, 111, 117, 128, 310, 311, 314, 318, 326, 334, 336
Hungerford, D. A., 357
Hunt, D. M., 361
Hunt, J. M., 334
Hunt, R. D., 433
Hunting, K. J., 458
Huntley, G. A., 459
Huntoon, F. W., 172
Hurlbert, R. E., 141
Hurtubise, P., 437
Huston, A. C., 304, 305
Hutanen, H., 360
Hutchinson, M., 176
Hutt, L. M., 427, 436
Huybregste, R., 390
Hylemon, P. B., 45
Hymans, P. J., 460
Hynes, M. J., 139, 141, 143
Hysert, D. W., 560, 564, 568

I

Iannini, P. B., 458, 463
Iannotti, E. L., 129, 311, 312, 316
Icho, T., 409
Igarashi, R. T., 45
Igarashi, Y., 304
Iglewski, B. H., 220
Ignarro, L. J., 522, 523
Iguchi, J., 384
Igwegbe, E. C. K., 219
Ihde, D. C., 455
Ihlenfeldt, M. J. A., 260
Iino, T., 398-400, 402, 404-6, 409-11, 413, 414, 417
Imai, M., 359, 360, 373
Imamura, M., 438
Imamura, T., 431
Immann, A., 295
Imperato, P. J., 451, 458
Inamine, E., 346, 347, 351, 353
Ingelfinger, F. J., 58, 336
Ingle, R. K., 261
Ingraham, J. L., 40, 41, 114, 128
Ingraham, L. J., 488
Ingraham, L. L., 564
Ingram, L. O., 235, 240, 257
Inkson, C., 190

Inman, R. B., 500
Inoki, S., 611, 620
Inomata, M., 359, 360, 373
Ioneda, T., 168
Ippen, K., 478, 496
Isaacson, H. R., 337
Isambert, M. F., 560
Isbell, A. F., 428
Ishidsu, J., 413
Ishikawa, T., 428
Ismay, D., 301
Israel, H. L., 426, 461
Issaly, A. S., 141
Issaly, I. M., 141
Ito, Y., 295
Itoh, S., 384
Itoh, T., 286
Iuchi, S., 41
Ivanov, M. V., 327, 328, 331
Iverson, S. C., 545
Iwanami, S., 52, 54
Iwarson, S., 360
Iyengar, M. O. P., 249
Iyer, G. Y. N., 510

J

Jablonski, E., 569
Jack, I., 428
Jackett, P. S., 523
Jackson, E. N., 498
Jackson, L., 438
Jackson, S., 90-92
Jacob, F., 497
Jacobs, N. J., 316
Jacobs, W. A., 6-9
Jacobson, D. N., 614
Jacobson, J. K., 381
Jaffe, E. S., 438
Jaffe, H., 97
Jaffe, L. A., 197
Jaffe, L. F., 192, 195-99
Jagendorf, A. T., 185, 189
Jahn, T. L., 91, 617
Jahsman, W. E., 545
Jamet, C., 492
Jamet-Vierney, C., 492
Jamieson, A., 603, 606
Jamison, V. W., 389
Jan, Y. N., 538, 545
Janglová, Z., 352
Jann, B., 31, 238
Jann, K., 31, 238
Jannasch, H. W., 42, 45, 64, 68-70, 331, 332
Janssen, F. G. J., 126
Janssen, K. A., 150
Janssen, P. A. J., 305
Jansson, P. E., 215
Jarosch, R., 241
Jarvis, J. E., 427-30, 432, 433
Jaskunas, S. R., 486, 503
Jeanes, A., 215
Jeffay, H., 147
Jefferys, E. G., 301
Jenkin, H. M., 93, 101, 102, 516
Jenkins, P. A., 161
Jennings, H. S., 83
Jensen, E. M., 438
Jensen, H. L., 171
Jensen, H. S., 97
Jensen, R. A., 30, 40
Jensen, S. B., 96
Jensen, T. E., 237, 255
Jerina, D. M., 388, 389
Jeris, J. S., 310, 317, 337
Jerrells, T. R., 517
Jervis, H. R., 96
Jesaitis, A. J., 543
Jetschmann, K., 141
Jetten, A. M., 188
Jewell, D. M., 380
Jigami, Y., 388
Jindra, A., 345, 346
Jobson, A., 380
Johanson, W. G., 449, 454
Johansson, B., 423, 426
John, D. T., 607
John, P. C. L., 140, 146, 147, 149, 153
Johnson, D., 433
Johnson, D. L., 538, 539
Johnson, D. W., 100
Johnson, E. M., 491, 492
Johnson, F. H., 48, 52, 56, 555, 560, 561, 563, 564, 568, 577-79, 585
Johnson, H. W., 207, 218
Johnson, J. L., 45
Johnson, M. J., 382, 385
JOHNSON, R. C., 89-106; 90-95, 101, 102
Johnson, R. H., 459
Johnson, T. B., 207, 211
Johnson, W. D., 456
Johnson, W. D. Jr., 517, 519, 520
Johnson, W. H., 296
Johnston, D. W., 328, 331
Johnston, J., 122
Johnston, R. B. Jr., 510-13
Joncas, J., 433
Jondal, M., 423, 426-28, 430-32, 436, 437, 439
Jones, A., 30, 348
Jones, C. W., 184, 185, 187
Jones, D., 162, 167, 171, 172
Jones, L. W., 241, 243, 244
Jones, M. M., 603
Jones, R. H., 101
Jones, T. C., 517-19, 521, 523, 527, 528
Jones, W. J., 333
Jorgensen, B. B., 263
Josefsson, J. O., 195
Joseph, R., 92, 93
Josephson, S. L., 607
Jost, J. L., 68, 70, 76-78, 82, 84
Jost, M., 252
Joyner, A. E., 316, 322
Joys, T. M., 398, 405
Juhl, E., 360
Juif, J.-G., 458
Julita, P., 14, 20
Jungermann, K., 312
Jusic, M., 146

K

Kaback, H. R., 184-86
Kabat, D., 220
Kado, C. I., 208, 209, 221
Kafkewitz, D., 129, 311, 312, 316
Kagawa, H., 400
Kahn, A. J., 601, 614
Kahn, D. E., 436
Kaiser, G. E., 91
Kaji, A., 304
Kakinuma, K., 510
Kalakoutskii, L. V., 160, 161
Kallio, R. E., 388, 389
Kalmanson, G. M., 452, 465
Kalter, S. S., 438
Kamiya, R., 399
Kamiyama, I., 359, 360, 373
Kammerman, S., 522, 523
Kampa, D., 426
Kamura, T., 335
Kanai, K., 516
Kandler, O., 238
Kane, J. F., 27
Kaneko, H., 193
Kaneko, T., 53
Kaneshiro, E. S., 194
Kantz, T., 235
Kaplan, H. B., 510, 512
Kaplan, I. R., 318, 329, 331-33, 337
Kaplan, J., 431
Kaplan, M. H., 461
Kaplan, P. M., 359, 360, 365, 373
Kaplan, S., 288
Kappas, A., 304
Käppeli, O., 383, 384
Karahjoli, M., 163
Karaseva, E. V., 100
Kariyama, R., 51
Karlsson, A., 28, 350
Karnovsky, M. J., 510
Karnovsky, M. L., 510-14, 523
Karr, A. L., 207, 208, 213

Karr, D. B., 208
Karu, A. E., 137
Kaschka-Dierich, C., 428, 439
Kashket, E. R., 184-87
Kashmiri, S. V. S., 490
Katinger, H. W. D., 383
Kato, M., 514, 524
Kato, S., 425
Kato, Y., 52
Katoh, T., 257
Katz, A., 238, 239
Katz, E., 350
Katz, E. R., 611
Katz, S. L., 452, 467
Katzir, A., 195, 543
Kaufmann, A. F., 100
Kawai, Y., 113, 115, 117, 128, 428, 433
Kaye, D., 456
Kearney, P. C., 481
Kearny, J. J., 325
Keddie, R. M., 163, 171
Keele, B. B. Jr., 262, 511, 512
Keen, N. T., 218
Keenan, T. W., 191
Keene, W. R., 452, 465
Keeney, D. R., 328, 329
Kehrberger, P. M., 77
Kelleher, M. F., 100
Kellenberg, D., 262
Keller, K., 384
Kellogg, E. W. III, 512
Kelly, D. P., 257
Kelly, R., 93, 101, 102
Kemal, C., 563, 564
Kemp, J. D., 619
Kempner, E. S., 570
Kenne, L., 215
Kennedy, B. W., 218
Kennedy, R. S., 383, 385
Kennedy, S. F., 40
Kennel, Y. M., 351
Kenney, E. B., 96
Kenny, G. E., 461, 462
Kenyon, C. N., 243, 244
Keppen, O. I., 282, 283
Kerkenaar, A., 138, 150
Kerling, L. C. P., 212
Kern, F. Jr., 115, 119, 122, 123
Kerr, N. S., 614
Kerr, S. J., 614
Keryer, E., 146, 150
Keshin, J. G., 15
Kessel, M., 48, 51, 239
Kessin, R. H., 611, 620
Kessler, R. J., 577
Kester, A. S., 389
Ketover, B. P., 454
Kevy, S. V., 466
Keynan, A., 41, 586-88
Kharuk, V. I., 575
Khuller, G. K., 166, 167, 173
Kieff, E., 422, 423, 428, 429, 433, 436, 439
Kiely, M. L., 153
Kieras, F. J., 260
Killick, K. A., 137, 143, 148
Killilea, S. D., 243, 244
Kim, C. Y., 370
Kimura, A., 351
Kimura, N., 119-21
Kindler, S. H., 138, 143
King, C. A., 620
King, G. S., 425
King, S. M., 579
King, W. R., 65
Kinghorn, J. R., 139, 143
Kingsbury, D. T., 428
Kinnaert, P., 458
Kinoshita, S., 384
Kinsky, S. C., 14, 294-97
Kinumaki, A., 34
Kinyon, J. M., 96, 101
Kiper, M., 247
Kipnes, R. S., 511, 512
Kirchner, F. R., 431
Kirillova, I. P., 160
Kirillova, N. V., 160, 161
Kirk, J. W., 459
Kirk, M. R., 257, 258, 262
Kirkby, S. M., 235
Kirsch, E. J., 337
Kirschstein, R. L., 371
Kirsten, W. H., 438
Kishi, T., 17
Kitahara, M., 297, 300, 301
Kitajima, Y., 295
Kitao, C., 17
Kitching, J. A., 601, 618
Klaus, G. G. B., 361, 362
Klaviter, E. C., 90-92
Klebanoff, S. J., 509-14
Kleckner, N., 481, 495, 502
Klein, E., 423, 424, 426, 427, 429, 430, 434, 439
Klein, G., 422-37, 439
Klein, H. P., 26
Kleiner, D., 141, 143
Kleinschmidt, J. A., 141, 143
Kleinschmidt, M. G., 295
Kleinsmith, L. J., 303
Klement, Z., 209
Klevickis, S. C., 310, 330, 331
Klevins, H. B., 382
Kline, B. W., 238
Klucis, E., 438
Kluss, B. C., 613, 614
Knee, M., 208, 213
Knight, S. T., 101
Knowles, C. J., 53
Kobal, V. M., 388
Kobatake, Y., 195
KOBAYASHI, G. S., 291-308; 15, 295-97, 300, 301
Kobayashi, K., 77
Kobilinsky, L., 569, 577
Koch, A. L., 70, 82, 136, 137, 503
Koch, J. R., 388
Kochan, I., 516
Kodama, T., 42
Koenig, G., 457
Koenig, M. G., 298, 462
Koffler, H., 398, 400, 402, 406
Kofoid, C. A., 598
Kohama, Y., 555, 560, 561, 564, 568
Kohn, G., 423, 429-31, 433
Kohn, H. I., 429
Kohsaka, M., 347
Kokurina, N. A., 43, 552-55
Kollins, E. L., 31
Komagata, K., 166
Komárek, J., 227
Komeda, Y., 409, 413
Komersova, I., 31, 33, 34
Kominek, L. A., 351
Kominos, S. D., 219
Komor, B., 191, 295
Komor, E., 191, 295
Komura, I., 166
Kondo, E., 516
Kondo, W., 96
Kondoh, H., 399, 406
Kondratieva, E. N., 282
Kong, K., 542
Konisky, J., 188
Konn, M., 430, 433
Konno, H., 410
Konopka, A. E., 320
Koopman, J. P., 126
Koornhof, H. J., 452, 459
Kopecky, A. L., 186, 189
Kordová, N., 516
Korn, E. D., 195
Kornberg, A., 138, 142, 143, 147, 150, 368
Korol, W., 438
Kort, E. N., 408, 414-16
Koshland, D. E. Jr., 260, 397, 404-6, 410, 415, 416
Kössler, F., 555, 573, 579, 581
Kosuge, T., 209
Kotiuszko, D., 22-24, 33
Kotler, M., 438
Kourilsky, F. M., 424-26
Kowal, J., 464
Kowit, J. D., 598, 606, 611, 621-23, 626
Koyama, T., 326, 327, 335, 336
Kozuka, Y., 40
Krahenbuhl, J. L., 520
Krassilnikov, N. A., 160, 161
Kraszewski, A., 96, 117
Kratz, W. A., 241
Krause, R. M., 522

Krauskopf, K. B., 329
Krebs, E. G., 261
Kress, Y., 520
Kreuzaler, F., 28
Krick, J. A., 461, 462
Krieg, N. R., 45, 74
Krieger, N., 589
Krogmann, D. W., 236, 242
Krugman, S., 360
Krupinski, V. M., 346, 353
Kruse, W., 172
Kubica, G. P., 161
Kubonishi, I., 432
Kuchnen, J. G., 260
Kuehn, G. D., 141, 149
Kuenen, J. G., 65
Kufe, D. W., 438
Kuhn, D. A., 95
Kujomoto, A., 31
Kulasooriya, S. A., 250
Kulla, H., 315
Kunc, F., 335
Kung, C., 192, 194
Kunisawa, R., 45, 57, 227, 231, 234, 237, 239, 242, 246, 247, 249-51, 265, 277
Kunstyr, I., 113, 114, 121
Kunz, L. J., 452, 454-60, 464, 466
Kuo, T. T., 215
Kurata, K., 428
Kurganov, B. L., 260
Kurihara, K., 195
Kuroiwa, T., 399, 402, 406, 413
Kurowski, W. M., 139
Kurup, P. V., 161, 174
Kurz, W. G. W., 265
Kushner, D. J., 41
Kusunose, M., 164-67, 173
Kuznetsov, A. M., 575
Kwan, C. N., 15, 300, 301
Kwan, H. C., 426, 430, 436
Kwapinski, E. H., 170
Kwapinski, J. B. G., 161, 169, 170

L

Lacey, J., 160, 162, 163, 171
Ladire, M., 120, 125
Ladra, K. M., 509
Ladwig, R., 286
LaFay, J. F., 538
Lafontaine, T., 456
LaForce, F. M., 458, 462
Lalla, M., 436
Lamar, C. Jr., 217
Lambein, F., 252, 255
Lambert, L. H. Jr., 520
Lamont, H. C., 233
Lamontagne, R. A., 334
Lampen, J. O., 14, 295, 303
Lancaster, L. J., 464
Lancaster-Smith, M., 452, 456
Lancini, G., 28
Landers, T., 366-69
Landsteiner, K., 9
Lanéelle, M.-A., 165
Lang, D. J., 428
Lang, N. J., 227, 237, 250, 251, 255
Langenberg, K. F., 322
Langerman, N., 558, 560, 565, 567, 580, 581
Langevoort, H. L., 508
Langridge, J., 479
Lanyi, J. K., 187, 188
Lanzov, V. A., 489
Lapage, S. P., 227, 267, 460
Laris, P. C., 198
Larsen, D. H., 65
Larsen, H., 41, 279, 280
Larsen, S. H., 408, 414-16
Larue, B., 247
Larue, T. A., 265
Lascelles, J., 138, 141
Lastovica, A. J., 600, 607
Laughnan, J. R., 208
Lauterborn, R., 263, 279-81
Lavelle, F., 560
Lavi, S., 370
Lavillaureix, J., 458
Lawrence, A. W., 329
Lawrence, G. H., 464
Lawrence, M. C., 242
Lawrence, R. M., 298
Lawrie, A. C., 264
Lazarus, G. M., 450, 459
Lazdins, J., 510, 514
Lazere, J. R., 491
Leach, C. K., 247, 257, 263
Leach, W. D., 96, 117
Leadbetter, E. R., 284-86
Leahy, J., 390
Leake, E. S., 515
Leatherwood, J., 31
Lebedeva, E. V., 280
LeBouvier, G., 361
LeBouvier, G. L., 358, 359
Le Bras, G., 40, 552
Lechevalier, H. A., 159-65, 168, 169, 171, 173
Lechevalier, M. P., 159-65, 168, 169, 171-74
Ledbetter, M. S., 490
Lederberg, J., 405, 410, 489
Lederer, E., 168
Lee, A., 96, 111, 117, 120, 123, 124, 126
Lee, C. C., 382
Lee, C. H., 30
Lee, C.-J., 111, 117
Lee, C. Y., 566
Lee, F. D., 96, 117
Lee, G. F., 332
Lee, H. J., 502
Lee, I. H., 71, 72
Lee, J., 40, 551, 560-63, 566-69
Lee, L. F., 428
Lee, S., 457
Lee, S. I., 348
Leevy, C. M., 359
Lefevre, J. P., 454, 461
Lefort, M., 236, 238
Legunkova, R., 231
Lehman, I. R., 138
Lehmann, K. B., 160
Lehmeyer, J. E., 511, 512
Lehrer, R. I., 509-11
Leibold, W., 431, 433
Leider, J. E., 509
Leidy, G., 490
Leifson, E., 39, 48, 51
Leimenstoll, G., 312
Leinbach, S. S., 428
Leithead, C. S., 99
Leitzmann, C., 141, 143, 152
Lekkerkerk-van der Wees, J. E. C., 121, 126
Lelliott, R. A., 171
Lemasson, C., 243, 244
Len, L., 517-19
Lendzian, K., 260
Lennert, K., 428, 435
Lenoir, G., 431, 432
Lentz, C. P., 317
Leonard, J., 301
Leonard, J. D., 332
Leonard, R. T., 191
LePage, G. A., 386
Le Peuch, C., 557, 562-64, 567, 568
Lepow, I. H., 508
Lepper, A. W. D., 513
Le Ray, D., 603, 606
Lerche, M., 115
Lerner, A. M., 454, 458, 460
Lerner, K. G., 452
Lerner, P. I., 466
Lesemann, D., 218
Levaditi, C., 97
Levan, A., 429
Levi, C., 261
Levin, A. P., 139
Levine, A. S., 451, 452
Levine, B. B., 523
Levine, G. A., 260
Levine, H. B., 305
Levine, J., 433
Levine, L., 153
Levine, P. H., 423
Levinthal, M., 497
Levis, D. G., 100
Levitt, M. D., 336

Levy, H. R., 136, 137
Levy, S. B., 130
Lewin, R. A., 226, 266, 267, 276
Lewis, B. J., 248
Lewis, C. M., 141, 143
Lewis, D., 582
Lewis, D. W., 97
Lewis, J. P., 422, 437
Lewis, W. G., 261
Lex, M., 256, 265
Lhoste, J.-M., 566
Li, C. C., 215
Li, L. F., 325
Liaaen-Jensen, S., 168, 243, 278, 281, 284
Liboff, A. R., 198, 199
Lieber, M. M., 438
Lieberman, P., 462
Liedtke, M. P., 141
Liersch, M., 346
Light, R. J., 20, 25, 28
Likhite, V. V., 451, 460, 462, 466, 467
Lim, S. M., 208
Lin, B. C., 215
Lin, C.-C., 292, 302
Lin, E. C. C., 139, 480
Lin, H., 300
Lin, P., 41, 565, 574, 586
Lind, A., 161, 162, 169, 170, 172
Lindahl, L., 486, 503
Lindahl, T., 423, 426, 428, 435, 439
Lindberg, B., 215
Lindberg, R. B., 458
Lindholm, A., 360
Lindquist, L. C., 32
Lineal, M., 361
Linehan, B., 127, 316
Linek, V., 387
Ling, C. M., 366, 368
Lingens, F., 27
Linke, H. A. B., 16, 17
Linn, S., 137
Linnenbom, V. J., 334
Lins, R. D., 465
Linscott, W. D., 102
Lipman, M., 422, 430, 432-34, 438
Lippin, A., 360, 373
Lippincott, B. B., 208
Lippincott, J. A., 208
Lipschultz, C. A., 242, 244-46
Lipson, E. D., 537, 540, 542-44
Liras, P., 14, 16, 17, 26, 27, 353
Lisco, H., 429, 432, 434, 438
Lishnevskaya, E. B., 16, 17, 20, 22
Listgarten, M. A., 90, 96, 97
Liszczak, T., 438
Litt, M., 514
Little, J. B., 604
Little, J. R., 300
Litton, A. A., 453, 464, 465
Liu, C. M., 16, 26, 28, 30, 34, 350, 353
Liu, Y. K., 452
Livermore, B. P., 90, 93, 94, 102
Livingston, D. M., 438
Livoni, J. P., 137
Ljungdahl, L. G., 325
Lockhart, P., 542
Lockwood, W. R., 508
Lodish, H. F., 620
Löe, H., 96
Loesche, W. J., 96, 102
London, J., 256, 257, 261, 398
London, W. T., 357
Long, W. R., 125
Long, W. S., 190, 192
Lorch, S. K., 252
Lorenz, P. R., 359
Lorimer, G. H., 141, 143, 145, 260
Losada, M., 141, 143, 249, 264
Lotan, D., 489
Lotter, L., 117
Louie, T. J., 455, 464, 466
Louria, D. B., 453, 458, 460, 463-66
Loutit, J. S., 166
Loutit, M. W., 166
Lovely, P. S., 415
Low, K. B., 481, 487, 491
Lowbury, E. J. L., 463-65
Lowe, B. A., 466
Lowe, D., 301
Lowe, D. A., 30, 350
Lowe, J. N., 564
Lowrie, D. B., 523
Lowy, K., 451, 464
Lu, C. Y.-H., 190
Lucas, C., 261
Lucas, S., 422, 430, 437
Luce, R. R., 461, 462
Luckey, T. D., 107, 108, 112
Luckinbill, L. S., 65
Lucy, J. A., 528
Lüderitz, O., 31, 32, 286
Ludvik, J., 383
Ludvik, M., 383
Luedemann, G. M., 160
Lukacs, G., 17
Lukezic, F. L., 208, 219
Lumsden, J., 262
Lund, E., 486, 503
Lund, E. J., 197, 199
Lundberg, A. M., 100
Lundin, P., 360
Lundström, M., 453
Lurie, M. B., 516
Luse, S. A., 295, 296
Lusk, J. E., 186, 189
Lust, G., 26
Lustig, T. D., 77
Lutwick, L. I., 358-60, 367, 368, 459
Lyengar, M. R. S., 30
Lyles, T. O., 465
Lynch, R. G., 300
Lynen, F., 20, 24-26
Lyon, G. L., 332
Lyons, A. J. Jr., 163, 173

M

Ma, M., 491
Maab, I., 331
Mabe, J. A., 348
MacColl, R., 244
MacCosham, V., 484
MacDonald, J. B., 96, 97
MacDonald, R. E., 187, 188
Macgregor, A. N., 328, 329
Machemer, H., 193, 194
Mackaness, G. B., 516
Mackay, P., 362, 363
MacKenzie, R. E., 559, 561
MacLeod, R. A., 41, 233
MacMillan, J., 301
Macnab, R. M., 400, 415, 416
Macone, A. B., 130
Macrae, A. D., 422
MacRobbie, E. A. C., 190, 191
Macura, J., 335
Macy, J., 315
Maddoux, G. L., 462
Madigan, M. T., 281
Maeda, M., 195
Maeda, Y., 195
Maes-Dockx, F. M., 305
Maezawa, I., 34
Maffei, H. V. L., 121
Magasanik, B., 139, 150, 345, 574
Magie, A. R., 209
Magner, J., 572
Magnius, L. O., 360
Magnusson, H., 172
Magnusson, M., 169, 170, 173
Magrath, I. T., 438
MAH, R. A., 309-41; 310, 317, 318, 323, 337
Mahadevan, V., 388, 389
Mahadik, S. P., 137
Maier, W., 353
Mair, B. J., 380
Maisey, C. W., 100
Majer, J., 31
Majer, M., 359
Majumdar, M. K., 351, 353

Majumdar, S. K., 351, 353
Mäkelä, P. H., 405, 410
Makemson, J. C., 555, 558, 572, 575
Maki, D. G., 453, 454, 464-66
Makula, R. A., 385
Malawista, S. E., 509, 523
Malhotra, S. K., 539
Malik, V. S., 348
Mallard, G. E., 330
Mallory, A., 115, 119, 122, 123
Malnic, G., 561, 563
Malnick, G. R., 361, 362
Maloiy, G., 117
Mandel, M., 39-41, 43-45, 47, 48, 51, 53-55, 102, 227, 231, 234, 239, 242, 246, 247, 284-86, 553, 555
Mandell, G. L., 510
Mandelstam, J., 136, 140, 145, 149
Mandy, S. J., 305
Mangold, A., 580
Mankes, R., 528
Mann, M. K., 359
Manolov, G., 429, 433
Manolova, Y., 429, 433
Manson, M., 185
Manwaring, D. G., 16
Manzano, C., 249, 264
Mao, J. C. H., 366, 368, 428
Marget, W., 451, 464
Margolin, P., 482, 499
Margulis, L., 227
Mariat, F., 173
Markbreiter, K., 390
Markovitz, A., 565, 578, 584-87
Marks, C. L., 33
Marmary, Y., 523
Marmur, J., 45
Marr, A. G., 66
Marriapan, M., 100
Marrs, B., 287, 288
Marsh, V. H., 452, 455
Marshall, K. C., 84
Marso, E., 454-56, 460, 461
Marten, R. H., 302
Martens, C. S., 332-35
Martin, C., 516
Martin, D. F., 449, 457
Martin, G. M., 435
Martin, H. H., 238
MARTÍN, J. F., 13-38; 13, 14, 16, 17, 21, 23-28, 31, 33, 34, 353
Martín, J. R., 33
Martin, R. L., 380
Martin, T. C., 235, 239, 240
Martin, W. J., 457
Martinelli, E., 28
Martinez, R. J., 398, 400, 406
Martos, L. M., 426, 430, 431
Marzi, T., 510
Masau, W. S., 361
Maseles, F. C., 388
Mason, A. D., 458
Mason, R. J., 523
Massa, J., 555, 557, 560, 562, 568, 569, 582
Massey, V., 566
Masuji, H., 432
Masurekar, P. S., 349, 350
Mata, L. J., 119, 120
Mateju, J., 31, 33, 34
Mateles, R. I., 64
Matern, H., 32, 146
Matern, U., 32
Mathieu, G., 332
Matricon, J., 538, 543
Matsen, J. M., 464
Matsubara, H., 246
Matsubara, I., 384
Matsuda, K., 560, 567, 568, 570
Matsuda, Y., 432
Matsuhashi, M., 31, 32
Matsuhashi, S., 32
Matsumoto, K., 41
Matsumura, P., 400, 403, 407-9, 413, 415, 416
Matteo, C. C., 354
Matula, T. I., 41
Matumoto, M., 428
Maurer, B. A., 430, 431
Maurizi, M. R., 148
Maxon, W. D., 351
May, C., 523
May, G., 362
Mayer, F., 138
Mayer, H., 238, 285, 286, 288
Mayhew, J. W., 122
Mayhew, S. G., 566
Maynard, J. E., 357
Mayo, H. E., 96, 97
Mazzoleni, R., 14, 20
McAllister, J. S., 96, 112, 117, 120
McAuliffe, V. J., 359, 360
McBee, R. H., 110, 128, 129, 336
McBride, B. C., 313, 323-25, 328
McCabe, W. R., 457
McCall, C. E., 510, 512
McCann, P. A., 351
McCapra, F., 557, 560, 561, 564, 568, 578
McCarthy, D. H., 48, 53
McCarthy, F. J., 25
McCarthy, L. R., 463
McCarty, M., 80, 522
McCarty, P. L., 310, 317, 329, 337
McCloskey, K., 588
McCloskey, K. R., 582, 583
McClung, N. M., 160, 169, 171
McCluskie, J. E., 328, 331
McCollum, R. W., 358, 359, 422
McCord, J. M., 262, 511
McCormick, D. B., 559
McCrumb, F. R. Jr., 100
McCulloch, W. F., 94
McCullough, W. G., 102
McCune, J. M., 425
McDaniel, L. E., 13, 14, 16, 17, 21, 23-26, 28, 30, 31, 33, 34, 350, 353
McDonough, M. W., 410
McDurmont, C. I., 160, 161
McElroy, W. D., 551, 552, 555, 578, 584, 585
McFadden, B. A., 141, 149, 260
McGee, Z., 301
McGehee, R. F., 603
McGowan, J. C., 301
McGowan, R. E., 259
McGrath, P. P., 371
McGroarty, E. J., 406
McIlvaine, P., 581
McIntyre, P. A., 512
McIntyre, W. I. M., 100
McKee, A. P., 359
McKenna, E. J., 388, 389
McKinney, R. E., 392
McKnight, G. S., 153
McKown, B. A., 454, 457, 463
McLaughlin, J. J. A., 244
McLaughlin, S., 183
McLee, A. G., 231, 285, 383
McLellan, W. L. Jr., 303
McMahon, M., 438
McMurrich, B. J., 510, 511
McNamara, M. J., 462
McPhail, L. C., 510
McRipley, R. J., 510
McSeveney, D., 96, 117
Means, U. M., 207, 218
Mebane, A. D., 13, 14, 294
Mechalas, B. J., 329
Mechlinski, W., 14, 16, 17, 294, 298
Mecke, D., 140, 146, 152
Meddins, B. M., 208, 219
Medeiros, A. A., 452, 460, 463, 466
Medina, J. R., 538, 542
MEDOFF, G., 291-308; 15, 295-97, 300, 301, 460
Medrek, T. F., 452, 466
Medvedeva, S. E., 43, 552-55
Meeks, J. C., 253
Meers, J. L., 64, 66, 68, 71, 72

Megee, R. D. III, 65, 66, 68, 69, 71, 72, 79
Meighen, E. A., 555, 558-61, 564, 577, 579, 585
Meihaus, J. E., 359
Meissner, G., 535
Meistrich, M. L., 543
Meléndez, L. V., 430, 432, 433
Mellors, R. C., 438
Melly, M. A., 457
Melnick, J. L., 361, 362
Melo, A., 32
Melzer, M., 459
Menezes, J., 429, 431, 433
Mensch, A., 454, 463
Mergenhagen, D., 198
Mergenhagen, S. E., 97, 508
Merino, F., 360
Merkel, J. R., 41, 53
Merrin, C., 458
Meselson, M., 484
Mesibov, R. E., 405, 408, 415
Metcalf, J., 510
Metcalfe, G., 172
Metzger, F. J., 2
Metzger, M., 90
Meyer, F., 93
Meyer, H., 93
Meyer, J., 160, 161, 163, 164, 171
Meyer, J. S., 69, 73-75, 84
Meyers, B. R., 451, 457
Meyers, D. M., 94, 102
Meyers, S. P., 386, 387
Meynell, E. W., 403, 404
Michael, P. R., 568
Michaels, R. H., 452, 460, 466, 467
Michaliszyn, G. A., 558, 560, 564, 577
Michel, G., 162, 163, 165-68
Michelson, A. M., 560, 564, 569, 575
Mickel, S., 482
Midak, B., 24
Middlebrook, G., 524
Middleton, A. J., 579
Middleton, R. B., 491
Mifuchi, I., 92
Mihm, J. M., 161, 162, 173, 174
Miles, A., 462
Milgram, J. H., 380
Miller, A. G., 261
Miller, A. L., 353
Miller, C. A., 296
Miller, C. G., 476, 487-89
Miller, G., 422, 429-34, 436-39
Miller, J. H., 478, 496
Miller, J. N., 101
Miller, L. S., 242
Miller, M. H., 431
Miller, M. W., 20
Miller, T. L., 316
Millet, J., 146
Millman, I., 360, 366, 368
Mills, E. L., 512
Mills, J., 453, 457
Mills, L., 514
Mimura, A., 383, 384, 387
Mimura, N., 569, 572, 580, 581
Minchew, B. H., 452, 465
Minio, F., 117
MINNIKIN, D. E., 159-80; 161, 163-68, 171, 173, 176
Minoda, Y., 388
Minowada, J., 430, 431
Minton, K., 137
Mishustin, E. N., 174, 175
Misra, H. P., 262, 511, 512
Misra, P. C., 190
Mitani, M., 398, 399
Mitchell, G. W., 553, 555, 556, 558-61, 563, 566, 567, 570, 572, 582, 587
Mitchell, P., 182, 184, 185, 187, 189, 199
Mitchell, R., 42, 380
Mitchell, R. E., 216, 217
Mitchen, J. R., 398, 402
Mitchison, G. J., 250, 254
Mitsuhashi, O., 23
Mitsuoka, T., 111, 119-21, 123
Miwatani, T., 48, 51
Miyakawa, Y., 359, 360, 373
Miyazawa, J., 17
Miyazu, Y., 383
Miyoshi, I., 432
Mizel, S. B., 303
Mizell, M., 425
Mizuno, F., 430, 431
Mizuno, S., 171, 172
Mocquot, G., 113, 117
Moebus, K., 42
Mohr, J. A., 454, 457, 463
Mohri, H., 193
Mojica-a, T., 491
Molano, J., 138, 146, 150
Molisch, H., 278, 279, 282
Mollaret, H. H., 99, 459
Monaghan, P. H., 393
Mondelli, R., 31
Mondovi, B., 14
Monod, J., 64, 136, 137
Monroe, J. H., 429
Montgomerie, J. Z., 452, 465
Montgomery, H. B. S., 219
Moody, M. D., 451, 466
Moore, F. W., 162, 171, 172
Moore, G. E., 422, 431
Moore, P. L., 195, 509
Moore, R. B., 256
Moore, R. E., 216, 217
Moore, R. L., 320
Moore, W. E., 95
Moore, W. E. C., 112-19, 125-27, 129, 130
Moo-Young, M., 383
Moran, T., 210
Morawaska, H., 22-24, 33
Mordarska, H., 162, 165, 170-72
Mordarski, M., 161, 168, 169, 172, 173, 175
Moreau, M.-C., 122, 128
Morell, P., 45
Morgan, D. A., 431
Morgan, D. G., 425
Morgan, E. H., 464
Morin, J. G., 567, 589
Morise, H., 555, 563, 564, 577, 578, 585
Morishita, Y., 113, 115, 117, 120, 123, 125
Moritz, V., 384
Morotomi, M., 113, 115, 117, 128
Morris, B. F., 379
Morris, G. S., 620
Morris, J., 508
Morris, J. C., 42
Morris, N. R., 303
Morris, P. J., 435
Morse, M. L., 500
Mortenson, L. E., 249
Morter, R. L., 101
Morton, R. A., 582, 583
Moser, I., 198
Mosley, J. W., 359
Moss, D. J., 424
Moulder, J. E., 613
Mourali, N., 435
Moyle, J., 187
Mudd, J. B., 295
Mudd, S. H., 219
Mueller, P., 183, 194, 195
Mueller, S. L., 33
Muggleton, P. W., 303
Muir, L. W., 137
Mukai, F. H., 499
Mukerjee, B. B., 41, 53
Mulcahy, D., 96
Mulholland, T. P. C., 301
Mullenbach, E., 492
Müller, H., 146
Müller-Eberhard, H. J., 508
Mullikin, D., 510, 512
Mullinger, R., 246
Mumford, D., 427, 431
Mummert, H., 192
Mundon, F. K., 358
Munim-al-Shakarchi, A., 352
Munk, V., 383
Muñoz, N., 428, 435
Muñoz, V., 544
Munsche, D., 248

Murakami, S., 357
Mural, R. J., 288
Murata, H., 172
Murchelano, R., 39, 48
Murillo, F. J., 539, 542
Murphy, C. L., 560-63, 569
Murphy, J. R., 561
Murphy, M., 452
Murray, E. G. D., 45, 159
Murray, R., 359
Murray, R. G. E., 92, 226, 276, 398, 403
Murrmann, S. K., 513
Muscatine, L., 582
Muschel, L. H., 90, 95, 101
Musser, W. E., 15, 300, 301
Mutai, M., 113, 115, 117, 128
Myerowitz, R. L., 452, 460, 463, 466
Myers, J., 241, 243, 244
Mylroie, R. L., 318
Myrvik, Q. N., 515

N

Nachmias, A., 212
Nadkarni, J. J., 429
Nadkarni, J. S., 429
Nadson, G. A., 279, 280
Nagai, S., 80, 81
Nahas, L., 115
Nahmias, A. J., 452-54, 464, 465
Naito, M., 425
Naitoh, Y., 193
Nakagawa, A., 17
Nakagawa, M., 119
Nakahara, T., 383, 384
Nakamura, S., 297
Nakamura, T., 560-63, 567-70, 572, 580, 581
Nakayama, K., 30
Nakayama, T., 304
Nakazato, H., 620
Nakazawa, H., 96
Namba, K., 119
Napolitano, J. J., 614
Nardi, R. V., 303
Nash, C. H., 346
Nauman, R. K., 90, 91
Nazerian, K., 428, 436
NEALSON, K. H., 549-95; 40, 41, 56, 552-58, 560, 561, 563, 565, 567, 570-78, 582-88
Neauport-Sautes, C., 424, 425
Nedwicki, E. G., 461
Neeff, J., 140, 146, 152
Ne'eman, Z., 577, 580, 586
Neet, K. E., 260
Neff, J. M., 382, 391
Neidhardt, F. C., 138, 153
Neilsen, L. D., 137
Neilson, A., 237, 239, 249-51, 264, 265
Neilson, A. H., 141, 143
Neiman, P. E., 452
Nelis, M. O., 305
Nell, E. E., 90
Nelson, D. L., 193, 194
Nelson, D. R., 310, 317, 330, 331
Nelson, E. C., 603
Nelson, R. D., 512
Nelson-Smith, A., 380
Neter, E., 458
Neu, H. C., 450, 451, 458, 459
Neubauer, R. H., 432
Neuhahn, H. J., 28
Neumann, D., 140, 142, 149
Neumann, R., 160
Neurath, A. R., 360, 361, 373
Newell, P. C., 611
Newhook, J. C., 112, 117
Newkirk, J. F., 346
Newman, L. J., 508
Nichols, B. A., 508, 513
Nichols, B. W., 243, 251
Nickel, W. O., 461
Nicolella, V., 16
Nicoli, M. Z., 555, 558-63, 566, 568, 579
Nieder, M., 390
Niederman, J. C., 422, 433, 436, 437
Niel, C. B. van., 276, 278-80, 282, 283, 285
Nielsen, J. O., 360
Nikaido, H., 286
Niles, E. G., 138
Nilsson, K., 423, 429-31, 433
Nishida, S., 119
Nishihata, K., 304
Nishimura, M., 260
Niss, H. F., 345, 346
Nissen, A. W., 303
Nitti, F., 8
Njus, D., 198, 559
Nkrumah, F. K., 422, 423, 429, 433, 436, 439
Noack, D., 71, 81
Nobrega, F. J., 121
Noguchi, T., 304
Nogueira, N., 520
Nolteernsting, U., 263
Nomura, M., 486, 503
Nomura, S., 23
Nonoyama, M., 422, 423, 428, 431, 433, 437
Norberg, B., 303
Nordlund, S., 141, 143
Norgard, S., 168
Norlin, M., 170
Norman, A. W., 14, 292, 295
North, M. J., 140
Northrop, J. H., 84
Novak, J. T., 337
Novick, A., 478, 479
Novick, R. P., 493
Nozawa, Y., 295
Nuccitelli, R., 192, 195-99
Nuckolls, J., 162
Nuesch, J., 346, 351
Nugent, N. A., 280
Nunheimer, T. D., 349
Nurmikko, V., 75, 84
Nyormoi, O., 428, 431

O

O'Brien, E. J., 399
O'Brien, F., 218
O'Brien, H. D., 27
O'Brien, R. W., 42
O'Brien, T. F., 452, 460, 463, 466
O'Brien, W. E., 325
O'Carra, P., 243, 244
Ochs, H., 461, 462
O'Connell, A., 366, 368
O'Connor, R. J., 83
O'Conor, G. T., 434, 439
O'Day, D. H., 148
O'Day, W. T., 557
Odeberg, H., 509
O'Dell, D. S., 598, 619, 620, 625
O'Donell, R., 382
O'Donnell, R., 382, 391
O'Donoghue, J. M., 457
Odum, E. P., 67, 73
Oelze, J., 277
Oerlemans, A., 295
Oesterhelt, D., 184
Oettgen, H. F., 424
O'Farrell, P. H., 153
Ogata, M., 113, 115, 117, 120, 125
Ogawa, H., 304, 351
Ogawa, M., 51
Oguchi, T., 399, 404, 413
Ogura, A., 193
Ohanian, S. H., 522
Ohashi, D. K., 457
Ohashi, H., 32
O'hEocha, C., 244
Ohki, K., 257
Ohmann, E., 141
Ohno, H., 23
Ohno, K., 119
Ohno, S., 473
Ohno, T., 23, 438
Ohnuma, T., 431
Ohsawa, H., 384
Ohta, K., 405

Ohtsubo, E., 483, 493, 497, 502
Ohwaki, K., 117
Okada, K., 359, 360, 373
Okami, Y., 297
Okamura, Y., 509
Okazaki, R., 31
Okazaki, T., 31
Okochi, K., 357
Okubo, S., 604, 611, 620
Old, L. J., 424
Olding, L. B., 428
Oldstone, M. B. A., 428, 432
Olin, D. B., 450
Oliver, G., 113
Oliver, J. M., 528
Olshevsky, U., 428
Olson, J. M., 277
Olson, L. C., 460, 464, 466
Olsson, I., 509
Olsson, P., 453
Omori, T., 388
Omura, S., 17, 23
Onderdonk, A. B., 122
Onisi, M., 96, 162
Ono, H., 17
Ono, K., 425
Oort, A. J. P., 545
Oosterhuis, S. K. H., 315
Ootaki, T., 541, 542
Orchard, V. A., 161, 163, 170, 173-76
Ordal, E. J., 52, 54
Ordal, G. W., 186, 415, 416
Oremland, R. S., 334
Oren, A., 263
Orezzi, P., 31
Orkin, L. A., 15
Orla-Jensen, S., 160
Orlowski, M., 139, 140, 143, 147, 149, 153
Ornston, M. K., 400, 415
Oroshnik, W., 13, 14, 294
Ortega, J. K. E., 538, 540, 545
Ortman, R., 32
Osanik, A., 393
Osato, T., 430, 431
Osawa, S., 286
Oshino, N., 510, 569, 577
Oshino, R., 569, 577
Osterman, C. A., 458
Ostrowska-Krysiak, B., 22, 34
Otaka, E., 286
Otani, S., 119
Otsuka, S., 166
Otta, J. D., 219
Otterbach, D. H., 31
Ou, J. T., 489
Oura, E., 141, 142
Outka, D. E., 613, 614
Ovchinnikov, N. M., 90
Overbeck, A., 172
Overby, L. R., 366, 368, 428
Owaribe, K., 400
Owens, L. D., 208, 211, 219
Oxford, A. E., 301
Oyama, V. I., 101
Ozeki, H., 406

P

Paciga, J., 432, 433
Pacin, M., 459
Packter, N. M., 352
Padan, E., 186, 228, 249, 256, 258, 263, 276
Padmaja, T. D., 227
Paff, J. R., 452, 459
Pagano, J. S., 422, 423, 427, 428, 431, 433, 436, 439
Page, D. L., 452, 465
Page, F. C., 600-3, 605, 606
Page, R. C., 522
Paget, G. E., 303
Paigen, K., 484
Painter, P. R., 66
Palacios, R., 153
Palit, A., 439
Palleroni, N. J., 42, 45, 55, 57
Palmer, D. L., 451, 454, 462
Palutke, W. A., 452, 463
Panchal, C. J., 380, 384
Pandhi, P. N., 164, 167
Panem, S., 438
Pang, C. H.-N., 173
Panganiban, A., 332
Panigel, M., 438
Pantskhava, E. S., 320, 323-25
Papa, S., 185, 189
Papamichail, M., 436
Pape, H., 17, 32
Papineau, D., 187
Pappas, G., 462
Pappenheimer, A. M., 206, 220
Pareilleux, A., 383
Paridaens, R., 510
Paris, G. G., 150
Parker, P. L., 257
Parkinson, J. S., 397, 404, 405, 407, 408, 415, 417
Parle, J. N., 113
Parma, D. H., 488
Parrillo, J. E., 461
Parry, E. H. O., 99
Parson, W. W., 184
Parsons, P. G., 438
Parthier, B., 248
Pascher, A., 280
Pastan, I., 574
Pasticier, A., 459
Patel, G. B., 317, 319
Patel, P., 429
Patel, P. N., 216, 217
Patel, P. V., 163, 166, 167, 171, 173
Pateman, J. A., 139, 141, 143
Patil, S. S., 206, 209, 210, 216-19, 221
Patino-Mendez, G., 207
Patriarca, P., 510
Patt, T. E., 332
Pattengale, P. K., 423, 431, 436
Patterson, R. J., 516
Patterson-Delafield, J., 400, 406
Pattyn, S., 162, 170, 172
Pattyn, S. R., 161
Paul, R., 451, 464
Paulsen, H., 32
Paxton, J. R., 553
Payne, P. I., 248
Payne, W. J., 333-35, 582
Paynter, M. J. B., 81, 84
Pchelkina, V. V., 320, 323, 324
Pearce, J., 256, 257
Pearce, L., 7
Pearce, U. B., 411
Pearsall, H. R., 464
Pearsall, N. N., 508
Pearson, G., 424
Pearson, H. A., 422, 436
Pearson, H. E., 455
Pearson, H. W., 249, 262
Pearson, J. L., 610
Peat, A., 234, 235
Pechman, K., 248
Pedersen, M., 428
Pedersen, M. M., 454-56, 460, 461
Pedersen, P., 185
Pelizza, G., 163
Pellegrino, M. A., 428
Pelletier, R. L., 207, 216
Pelroy, R. A., 248, 256-62
Pelsh, A. D., 280
Pelster, B., 518, 519
Pena, A., 190
Peng, H. B., 197
Pereira, M. S., 422
Periman, P. O., 427, 431, 436
Perine, P. L., 99
Perkins, D. L., 617, 620, 625
Perlin, E., 422, 427, 431, 436, 437
Perlman, D., 16, 482
Perrott, P. S., 243
Perry, J. J., 389
Perry, M. B., 31
Persico, F. J., 614
Persson, P. O., 428, 436, 437
Perun, T. J., 33
Pesanti, E. L., 523
Pesetsky, B. R., 98

Pesti, L., 107, 119, 123, 124, 127, 130
Peters, K., 114, 121
Peters, P. D., 194
Peters, W. P., 438
Petersdorf, R. G., 454, 460, 464-67
Peterson, L. F., 465
Peterson, M. R., 371
Peterson, P., 432
Peterson, W. D., 431
Petitdemange, H., 312
Petrakis, L., 381
Petzuch, M., 545
PFENNIG, N., 275-90; 68, 231, 277-86, 315, 317, 330
Pfister, R. M., 39, 331, 332
Phaff, H. J., 114
Phelps, D. S., 303
Phibbs, P. V. Jr., 102
Phillips, I. A., 462
Phillips, P. E., 438
Pickett, M. J., 454-56, 460, 461
Piekarski, G., 518, 519
Pien, F. D., 457
Pier, A. C., 170
Pierce, A. K., 449, 454
Pierson, B. K., 277, 279, 281
Pietkiewicz, D., 172
Pietschmann, K., 623, 624
Piggott, W., 298
Pijper, A., 399
Pilipenko, T. V., 167
Pillot, J., 90, 92, 93, 95
Pine, L., 160
Pine, M. J., 136, 137, 147
Pinkerton, F., 214
Pinto, C. A., 432
Piriou, F., 17
Pirnik, M. P., 389
Pirouz, T., 164-67, 171, 173
Pirt, S. J., 139, 354
Piskunova, L. A., 100
Pitcher, R. G., 208, 211, 219
Pittard, J., 26, 27, 29, 30
Pittsley, J. E., 215
Placek, B. P., 491, 492
Platt, T., 555, 571-73, 575-78, 586
Plattner, H., 194
Plaut, A. G., 115
Plempel, M., 304
Pleven, E., 299
Plotkin, S., 460
Plucker, F. E., 257
Plummer, G., 428
Podojil, M., 20
Podwinska, J., 90
Poff, K. L., 544
Pogell, B. M., 351
Polak, A., 299, 300
Polissar, M. J., 579
Pollack, W., 359
Pollock, M. R., 137
Pommier, M.-T., 165-67
Pontén, J., 430
Poo, M. M., 195
Poole, B., 520, 525, 527, 529
Pope, J. H., 424, 429-31
Porter, K. A., 452, 455
Poste, G., 522, 528
Postgate, J. R., 387
Postic, B., 219
Postma, P. W., 184, 185
Poston, J. M., 324
Poston, M. A., 456
Pouget-Abadie, J. F., 454, 461
Powell, E. O., 64, 68
Powers, D. A., 558
Prauser, H., 159-63, 169, 171
Preiss, J., 261
Prescott, J. M., 41, 53
Prescott, W., 422, 436, 437
Preslan, J. E., 76, 78
Presley, B. J., 332
Presti, D., 195, 542-44
Prestidge, L., 146
Preston, T. M., 598, 619, 620, 625
Pretorius, W. A., 318
Price, A. R., 137
Price, C. A., 141
Price, C. C., 265
Price, G. E., 452
Price, H. D., 295, 296, 300
Price, L. C., 393
Pridham, T. G., 163, 173
Primrose, S. B., 285, 387
Prince, A. M., 357, 359, 360, 373
Prince, R. C., 277
Pringle, R. B., 207
Prins, R. A., 317, 323, 330, 331
Pritchett, R., 422, 423, 428, 429, 433, 436, 439
Prival, M. J., 150
Probst, I., 315
Prochownik, E. V., 438
Prokop, A., 383, 387
Proost, J. M., 305
Proper, G., 76
Provost, T., 450, 451
Pruitt, B. A., 453, 458, 463-65
Ptashne, K., 483
Puchkova, N. N., 281
Puget, K., 569
Pulich, W. M. Jr., 382
Pulverer, G., 168, 169, 173, 175
Pulvertaft, R. J. V., 430
Purcell, R. H., 357, 359-63, 365, 366
Purtilo, D. T., 437
Putnam, C. W., 452, 455

Q

Quadling, C., 406, 413
Quandt, L., 280
Quastel, J. H., 510
Quie, P. G., 450, 512
Quijano, R., 260
Quintiliani, R., 460, 463

R

Rabin, H., 430, 432, 433
Raboy, B., 249, 256, 258
Rabson, A. R., 452, 459
Rabson, A. S., 428
Racker, E., 182, 185, 189
Raczynska-Bojanowska, K., 20, 22-26, 33, 34
Rae, M. E., 492
Rafaeli-Eshkol, D., 149, 352
Rafalko, J. S., 600, 604, 606
Rafalski, A., 20, 22, 23, 25, 26, 33
Raftery, M., 244
Rai, P. V., 211, 212
Raibaud, P., 113, 115, 117, 120-22, 124-26, 128
Raistrick, H., 301
Rajagopalan, K. V., 511, 512
Rakowszcyk, M., 459
Ramesh, M. S., 337
Ramirez, J. M., 188
Ramos, S., 186
Rangan, A., 80
Rankis, V., 398
Rao, G. R., 305
Rao, K. K., 246
Rao, K. R., 362, 371
Rapaport, E., 583
Raper, K. B., 611
Rashid, M. A., 332
Raskas, H., 300, 301
Raskin, J., 304
Rasmussen, R., 564
Ratcliffe, N. A., 523
Ratledge, C., 163, 167, 173
Rau, W., 539
Raval, G., 312
Raven, J. A., 188, 199
Ravin, A. W., 491
Ray, M. B., 371
Raymond, A. J., 381
Raymond, J. A., 589
Raymond, J. C., 282
Raymond, R. L., 389
Rayner, E. P., 604
Raz, A., 524

Reader, R. W., 415-17
Reale, F. R., 438
Reau, P., 539
Reaven, E. P., 509
Rebel, H., 212
Rebello, J. L., 30, 40
Reber, R. M., 457
Record, B. R., 10
Reddy, C. A., 117, 312-14
Redeker, A. G., 359
Redmond, J. W., 31
Redshaw, P. A., 351
Reeburgh, W. S., 326, 327, 332-35
Reedman, B. M., 423, 424, 426, 430, 431
Rees, R. J. W., 515
Regel, E., 304
Reichardt, W., 416, 537
Reichelt, J. L., 40-45, 47, 48, 51-56, 233, 552-56, 573, 574, 582, 590
Reid, J., 30
Reid, T. M. S., 466
Reif, H. J., 502
Reilly, P. J., 71, 72
Reiner, J. M., 138, 149
Reinert, J., 616
Reisfeld, A., 384, 386
Reisher, J. I., 422
Relimpio, A. M., 249, 264
Reller, L. B., 462
Remington, J. S., 452, 453, 461, 462, 519, 520
Rengaraju, S., 30
Renneboog-Squilbin, C., 68, 83
Reno, J. M., 428
Reuter, G., 112, 115, 116, 118
Reutersberg, H., 161, 169, 173, 175
Revel, M., 141, 146
Reynolds, C. S., 227
Reynolds, G. T., 568, 582
Reynolds, R. C., 452, 465
Reysset, G., 146
Reznikoff, W. S., 478, 496
Rhame, F. S., 453, 454, 464-66
Rheinwald, J. G., 390
Rhoades, E. R., 454, 457, 463
Rhoads, D. B., 188
Ribot, D., 383
Ricci, G., 360
Richard, C., 458, 459
Richard, J., 456
Richards, F. A., 334
Richards, J. L., 187, 190
Rickards, R. W., 16, 20, 31
Ricketts, T. R., 83
Rickinson, A. B., 427-30, 432, 433, 436, 437, 439
Ridell, M., 161, 169, 170, 173
Ridgway, E. B., 195
Ridgway, J. W., 176
Riedl, R. J., 263
Riegelman, S., 301
Ries, S. M., 211, 212
Rigano, C., 141, 143
Rigby, P. W. J., 480
Righelato, R. C., 354
Rigopoulos, N., 280
Riley, M., 473
Riley, W. H., 555, 557, 560, 562, 568, 569, 582
Rimoin, D. L., 451, 465
Rimon, S., 244
Rinaldi, R. A., 198, 199
Ringelmann, E., 25
Ringo, D. L., 613
Ringrose, R., 454, 457, 463
Riottot, M., 125
Rippka, R., 227, 231, 233, 235, 237, 239, 241, 243, 244, 248-51, 256-59, 261, 262, 265, 267
Ris, H., 403
Rissing, J. P., 457
Ritchie, A. E., 90, 93
Rittenberg, M. B., 102
Rittenberg, S. C., 91
Ritzi, D. M., 90-92
Robbers, J. E., 345, 346, 352, 353
Roberts, G., 459, 460
Roberts, G. D., 163
Robertson, J. J., 139, 140, 150
Robertson, L. W., 345, 346
Robertson, R. N., 182
Robin, E. D., 453
Robineaux, J., 508
Robineaux, R., 522, 523
Robinson, D. M., 96
Robinson, D. S., 389
Robinson, H. M. Jr., 304
Robinson, I. M., 322
Robinson, J., 433
Robinson, K., 303
Robinson, K. R., 195-98
Robinson, L. H., 100
ROBINSON, W. S., 357-77; 358-60, 364-71, 374
Robishaw, E. E., 428
Rocchi, G., 424-26
Rocha, H., 459
Rochaix, J. D., 482, 495
Rodicheva, E. K., 575
Roelofsen, P. A., 545
Rogers, D. E., 298
Rogers, M. A., 393
Rogers, M. A. T., 301
Rogers, P., 94, 102, 578, 584, 585
Rogers, T. O., 347
Rogosa, M., 171
Röhrscheidt, E., 168
Roller, P., 524
Rollins, E. L., 31
Romeo, D., 510
Ronzio, R. A., 619
Roos, D., 510, 512
Root, R. K., 510, 511
Roozen, K. J., 407
Roper, M. M., 84
Roppel, J., 285
Roscoe, D. H., 137
Rosebury, T., 97
Rosén, A., 424
Rosen, B. P., 184-88
Rosen, P., 461
Rosenbaum, J. L., 613
ROSENBERG, E., 379-96; 138, 143, 383, 384, 386, 387, 393
Rosenberg, E. W., 453
Rosenberg, S. L., 473
Rosenblatt, J. E., 455
Rosenblum, E. N., 422
Rosenblum, W. I., 603
Rosenbrook, W., 33
Rosenfeld, W. D., 331
Rosenthal, S. L., 454
Rosett, W., 461
Rossi, A., 25
Rossi, F., 510
Rossini, F. D., 380
Roszkowski, J., 22-24, 33, 34
Roth, C. C., 546
Roth, F. J. Jr., 302
Roth, G. D., 162
Roth, J., 495, 502
ROTH, J. R., 473-505; 476, 487-89
Roth, L. A., 319
Rothstein, A., 190
Rotman, B., 136
Rottenberg, H., 185-87
Rottmann, W., 462
Rouser, G., 55, 553
Rouvière-Yaniv, J., 247
Rowan, R. M., 462
Rowbotham, T. J., 172, 174, 175
Rowell, P., 247, 253, 264
Rownd, R. H., 482
Royston, I., 427, 431, 436
Rozanis, J., 167, 168
Rubenstein, D., 359, 360
Rubenstein, J. L. R., 366, 368, 370
Ruberto, R. G., 380
Rubin, H. M., 452, 460, 466, 467
Rubin, M., 331
Rubin, R. H., 453, 456, 460, 462, 464-66
Rubin, S. J., 52

Ruby, E. G., 56, 553, 554, 565, 567, 575, 582, 583, 588
Ruczaj, Z., 20, 24, 34
Rudd, J. W. M., 326, 327, 332
Rudnick, G., 185
Rudolph, K., 216, 218
Rueter, A., 428
Rufener, W. H., 336
Rüger, H.-J., 45
Ruscetti, F. W., 431
Ruseler-van Embden, J. G. H., 126
Russell, P. K., 358
Russo, V. E. A., 538, 540
Rutter, W. J., 619
Ryder, D. N., 65, 69
Rydgren, L., 303
Ryser, M., 113-18
Ryter, A., 90, 93, 95

S

Saari, T. N., 452, 459
Sabin, A. G., 518, 519
Sachs, J.M., 459
Sackin, M. J., 162
Sacquet, E., 113, 115, 117
Sadiq, M., 516
Sadoff, H. L., 137
Sadowski, P., 212
Saedler, H., 483, 501, 502
Saettler, A. W., 218
Safferman, R. S., 295
Sagers, R. D., 325
Saheki, T., 146
Saier, M. H., 41, 565, 574, 586
Saimot, G., 459
Saito, H., 161
Sakaguchi, G., 40
Sakai, M., 41
Sakai, W. S., 218
Sakaki, Y., 137
Sakamoto, T., 523
Sakazaki, R., 40, 43, 45, 52, 54
Salaman, M. H., 439
Salemink, C. A., 212
Sallal, A. K. J., 261
Sallman, B., 302
Salo, J. E., 77
Salt, G. W., 75, 78, 79, 83
Saltza, M. von, 30
Sambrook, J., 359
Samoilenko, V. A., 81
Sand, G., 498
Sande, M., 301
Sande, M. A., 458
Sanders, T. G., 619
Sanderson, K., 491
Sanderson, K. E., 52, 54
Sandok, P. L., 101
Sanford, J. P., 99, 100, 449, 452, 454, 457
Sangar, V. K., 239
Sankaran, L., 351
Sano, N., 384
Santesson, L., 423, 428, 431
Santoro, A. S., 14
Sarkany, I., 301, 302
Sartori, G., 28, 350
Satir, B., 193
Satir, P., 193, 415, 619, 620
Sato, K., 335, 336
Satoh, A., 351
Satomura, Y., 351
Satow, Y., 192, 194
Satyanarayana, T., 26, 140, 149, 153
Saunders, R. E., 238
SAVAGE, D. C., 107-31; 96, 107, 110-28
Sawnor-Korszynska, D., 20, 24, 34
Sawula, R. V., 27
Sazerac, R., 97
Sbarra, A. J., 510
Scarborough, G. A., 190
Schaal, K. P., 161, 168-70, 173-76
Schaberg, A., 508
Schade, S. Z., 403
Schaedler, R. W., 108-15, 117, 120, 123, 128
Schaefer, W. B., 524
Schaeffer, W. I., 386
Schafer, L. A., 450
Schaffner, C. P., 14-17, 26, 28, 30, 34, 294, 298, 350, 353
Schaffner, F., 365
Schaffner, G., 210
Schaffner, W., 457
Schamhart, D. H. J., 138, 150
Schardinger, F., 598, 600, 601, 610, 624, 625
Scharen, A. L., 219
Schares, T., 381
Scharf, J. F., 606
Schechter, M., 465
Schecter, R. S., 381
Scheer, U., 189
Scheffers, W. A., 48, 51
Scheibe, J., 245
Scheifinger, C. C., 127, 316
Schell-Frederick, E., 510
Schenk, H. E. A., 266
Scheps, R., 141, 146
Scherbakova, G. Ya., 575
Scherer, M., 426
Schiereck, P., 253
Schiff, J. A., 246
Schiffer, D., 476, 485, 490, 495, 496
Schiffmann, E., 508
Schimke, R. T., 153
Schimpff, S. C., 449, 451, 452, 463
Schlegel, H. G., 68, 260, 284
Schlegel, R., 522
Schleicher, J. B., 428
Schleifer, K. H., 238
Schlessinger, D., 15, 147, 295, 296, 300, 301
Schmidt, E. L., 94
Schmidt, J. A., 195
Schmidt, K., 278, 284
Schmidt, W., 238, 239
Schmitt, J. A., 161, 174
Schmitz, H., 426
Schneegans, P., 458
Schneidau, J. D. Jr., 170
Schneider, R. P., 139
Schneider, U., 428, 431
Schneierson, S. S., 457
Schnoes, H. K., 209
Schoenbaum, S. C., 453, 455, 456, 464-66
Scholer, H. J., 292, 299, 300
Scholes, P., 187
Schönbeck, J., 305
Schonebeck, J., 113, 114
Schoutens, E., 458
Schroeder, F., 14, 295
Schroeder, H. R., 569
Schuelke, L. M., 69
Schuldiner, S., 185, 186
Schulte-Holthausen, H., 423, 428, 431
Schultz-Haudt, S., 96
Schulz-Baldes, M., 266, 267
Schuster, F. L., 600, 601, 603, 607, 613, 614
Schütt-Gerowitt, H., 169
Schwab, J. H., 522
Schwartz, N. M., 487
Schwerzmann, N., 141, 142, 151
Scoggins, R., 451, 467
Scolnick, E. M., 428
Scott, C. C. L., 385
Scott, E., 264
Scott, W., 429, 430
Scraba, D., 499
Scriba, M., 424
Scribner, R., 452, 455
Seaston, A., 190
Seeff, L. B., 359, 360
Segal, A., 154
Segel, I. H., 137
Seides, S., 466, 467
Seiler, H. E., 100
Seitz, Ulrich, 248
Seitz, Ursula, 248
Seki, S., 304
Sekiya, T., 295
Sela, M., 522

Selden, R., 457
Seliger, H. H., 568, 582, 583
Sellers, D. P., 460
Semar, J. B., 16
Semer, H. A., 460
Senda, N., 509
Seneca, H., 296
Senti, F. R., 215
Sequeira, L., 209
Serrano, A. A., 171
Serrano, J. A., 161, 171
Seth, V. K., 297
Sethi, K. K., 518, 519
Shackelford, P. G., 465
Shadomy, S., 299, 304
Shaffer, M. F., 170
Shaffer, P. W., 253, 264
Shah, P. S., 65
Shah, V. P., 301
Shamoo, A. E., 183
Shanmugam, K. T., 387, 388
Shanmugaratnam, K., 428, 430-32, 435
Shannon, G. J., 461
Shaper, J. H., 398
Shapiro, D. J., 153
Shapiro, F. L., 359
Shapiro, J., 390
Shapiro, J. A., 501
Shapiro, V. Ye., 581
Sharp, D. G., 371
Sharp, P. A., 502
Sharpe, M. E., 460
Sharples, G. P., 171
Shaw, D. J., 385
Shaw, N., 166
Shearer, W. T., 450-54, 457, 462, 466
Shechter, Y., 149, 352
Shedlofsky, S., 124
Sheir-Neiss, G., 303
Sheldon, P. J., 436
Shenberg, E., 102
Shepard, J., 211
Shewan, J. M., 43, 48, 55, 56, 552-56
Shibata, N., 509
Shibuta, H., 428
Shifrine, M., 114
Shigematsu, A., 304
Shih, J. W., 360-64
Shillito, J., 453, 455, 456, 464-66
Shilo, M., 228, 249, 256-58, 262, 263, 276
Shima, K., 516, 521
Shimada, K., 399
Shimizu, T., 383
Shimomura, O., 555, 560, 561, 563, 564, 568, 577, 578, 585
Shindala, A., 71
Shinjo, T., 120
Shinoda, S., 48, 51
Shipkowitz, N. L., 428
Shirakawa, S., 433
Shirley, P. S., 510, 512
Shively, J. M., 238, 386
Shlomai, J., 428
Shoda, M., 71
Sholkovitz, E., 332
Shope, T., 432-34, 438, 439
Shope, T. C., 431
Shortman, K., 138
Shoup, C. S., 577, 581
Showalter, R., 123
Showell, H. J., 508
Shropshire, W., 535, 539, 543, 544
Shukovsky, E. S., 234
Shulman, J. A., 452-54, 464, 465
Shulman, R. N., 359
Shulman, S. T., 462
Shumway, N. E., 452, 453
Shunk, I. V., 52
Sicko, L. M., 237
Sideropoulos, H., 41, 588
Siebert, G., 189
Siegel, N., 422
Siegelman, H. W., 243
Siejko, D., 24
Siess, E. A., 141, 145
Signer, E. R., 478, 496
Silcox, V., 161
Silver, H. K., 452, 459
Silver, S., 187, 188
SILVERMAN, M., 397-419; 400, 402, 403, 406-9, 412-16
Silverman, S. R., 331
Silverstein, S. C., 509
Silverstone, A. E., 478, 496
Silvestre, D., 424-26
Silvey, J. K. G., 264
Simberkoff, M. S., 510
Simione, F. P. Jr., 606
Simmingskold, G., 303
Simmons, R. L., 512
Simmons, S. R., 511-13
Simon, J. L., 452, 459
Simon, M., 400-3, 406-9, 412-16
SIMON, M. I., 397-419; 398-400, 402
Simon, R. D., 237, 251, 255, 265, 266
Simonart, P., 301
Simoni, R. D., 184, 185
Simons, M. J., 435
Simpson, E., 422, 436, 437
Simpson, H. J., 332
Simpson, P. A., 614, 622
Sims, A. P., 139, 143, 145
Sinclair, C., 235
Sinclair, C. G., 65, 69
Sinden, S. L., 207-9, 216, 217, 219
Sinderman, C. J., 54
Singer, R. A., 248, 249, 256, 258
Singh, A. P., 188
Singh, B. N., 600, 602, 603
Singh, P. K., 265
Singh, S., 423, 426, 428, 431, 434, 435, 439
Sinnwell, V., 32
Sirevag, R., 280
Sirsi, M., 305
Sistrom, W. R., 282, 285
Sjulin, T. M., 214, 215
Skoryna, S. C., 114, 121
Skulachev, V. P., 184, 185, 189
Slack, J. M., 161
Slater, E. C., 185, 189
Slayman, C. L., 187, 190, 192
Slayman, C. W., 187, 190
Sleigh, M. A., 621
Sleight, S. D., 100
Sloneker, J. G., 295
Slonim, R. R., 303
Smadel, J. E., 100
Smialowicz, R., 522
Smibert, R. M., 101, 102
Smillie, L. B., 558
Smith, A. J., 241, 251, 256, 257, 261, 262
Smith, B. H., 614
Smith, B. R., 514
Smith, D., 582
Smith, D. R., 208
Smith, E. B., 579
Smith, F. A., 188, 190, 191, 199
Smith, H. W., 120, 121, 130
Smith, I., 45
Smith, I. W., 54
Smith, J., 371
Smith, J. G., 115, 119, 122, 123, 453, 464
Smith, J. L., 98
Smith, J. M. B., 113, 120
Smith, J. W., 457
Smith, N. R., 45, 159
Smith, P. H., 310, 317, 319, 322, 323, 337
Smith, P. J., 382
Smith, R. J., 250, 254
Smith, R. W., 406, 423, 431, 436
Smith, S. M., 405
Smith, W. D., 334
Smithers, S. R., 514
Smithies, O., 474
Smith-Keary, P. F., 487
Smyth, C. J., 522
Sneath, P. H. A., 161, 162, 169, 170, 175

Snellings, N. J., 491, 492
Snow, G. A., 167
Snyder, M., 488
Snyder, S. N., 452, 460
Snyderman, R., 508
Soapes, K., 457
Sobotka, M., 387
Socransky, S. S., 90, 96, 97, 102
Soderberg, F. B., 126
Soina, V. S., 164, 165, 173
Sokal, J. E., 458
Solel, Z., 212
Soli, G., 575
Soll, D. R., 611, 620
Soll, L., 485, 487, 494
Sollo, F. W., 317
Solomonson, L. P., 141, 143, 145
Solotorovsky, M., 160, 161
Solov'eva, Zh. V., 282
Solsky, R., 561, 564
Somerson, N. L., 349
Somerville, D. A., 452, 456
Someya, J. I., 384
Sones, M., 461
Sönghen, N. L., 175
Sonnabend, W., 371
Sorger, G. J., 141, 143, 146, 152
Soussy, C. J., 454
Spalla, C., 14, 20
Spanswick, R. M., 187, 190
Spaulding, P. L., 52
Spector, W. G., 508
Speedie, M. K., 348
Speller, D. C. E., 300
Spencer, R., 569, 588
Spicer, S. S., 509
Spickard, A., 298
Spiegelman, S., 136, 138, 149, 438
Spielvogel, A. M., 292
Spink, W. W., 454, 455, 457, 460
Spitznagel, J. K., 509
Spizizen, J., 146
Springer, M. S., 416, 417
Springer, W. R., 416
Spruit van der burg, A., 577
Spudich, J., 561, 563, 564, 578, 579
Spudich, J. A., 561, 563
Squinazi, F. J., 454
Srinivasan, P. R., 26, 27, 137, 359
Srinivasan, S. K., 80
Stacey, M., 1, 10
Stadler, P., 32
Stadtman, E. R., 136, 137, 139, 143-45, 148, 151, 152, 154, 345
Stadtman, T. C., 317, 320, 323, 324
Stafford, K., 95
Staflen, F. A., 227, 267
Stahl, D., 248
Stahly, D. P., 138, 142, 143
Stahmann, M. A., 216
Stajner, K., 31, 33, 34
Stalder, G. A., 371
Staley, J. T., 320
Staley, T. E., 52
Stalheim, O. H. V., 102
Stamm, W., 460
Stanaszek, R. S., 33
Staneck, J. L., 163
Stanford, J. L., 161
STANIER, R. Y., 225-74; 40-42, 55, 57, 114, 128, 226, 227, 231, 233-35, 239-44, 246-48, 250, 255-59, 261, 262, 265, 266, 276, 277, 286, 552
Stanley, P. E., 569
Stanmm, B., 359
Staples, P. J., 451, 461
Starlinger, P., 483, 501
Starr, M. P., 40, 80
Starzl, T. E., 452, 455
Staub, A. M., 31, 32, 286
Steck, T. L., 363
Steed, P., 92
Steensland, H., 283
Stees, J. L., 168
Stehlin, J. S., 427, 431, 435
Steiger, Z., 461
Steinberg, D., 147
Steiner, S., 361, 362
Steinerova, N., 31, 33, 34
Steinman, H. G., 101
Stent, G. S., 199
Stenzel, K. H., 359
Stephens, R. E., 621
Sterkin, V. E., 81
Stern, J. R., 42
Stevens, C. E., 110, 111, 114, 115
Stevens, C. L., 30, 31
Stevens, D. A., 305
Stevens, S. E. Jr., 260, 264
Stewart, R., 260, 261
Stewart, W. D. P., 227, 238, 247, 249, 251, 253, 260, 262, 264, 265
Stewart, W. W., 209, 210
Stinson, E. B., 452, 453
Stitt, D., 429, 431, 432, 434, 438
Stjernswärd, J., 423, 424, 427
St. John, A. C., 136, 137, 147
Stockard, C. R., 100
Stocker, B. A. D., 400, 404-6, 410, 411, 413
Stodolsky, M., 492
Stoenner, H. G., 102
Stoffl, P., 213
Stokes, B. O., 185, 189
Stokes, G. V., 516
Stolp, H., 80
Stone, D. E., 113, 114
Storb, R., 452
Storz, J., 516, 517
Stossel, T. P., 508-10, 523
Stott, E. J., 359, 360
Stouthamer, A. H., 315
Straley, C. S., 207, 212
Straley, M. L., 207, 212
Strand, C. L., 463
Strauch, B., 422
Straus, D. S., 480, 481, 483, 495
Straus, L. D., 481
Strauss, R. R., 514
Strehler, B. L., 551, 560
Streicher, S. L., 150
Strick, N., 361
Strickland, J. E., 438
STROBEL, G. A., 205-24; 206-8, 211, 212, 214, 219, 221
Strom, R., 14
Strominger, J. L., 31, 32, 425, 428, 429, 431
Strycharz, W. A., 486, 503
Stuart, R. D., 465
Stubbs, R. P., 96, 117
Stuckey, D. C., 337
Studier, F. W., 367
Suarez, M., 362
Subrahmanyan, L., 422
Subramanian, K. N., 141, 143
Suchy, J., 352
Sudarsanan, K., 383, 385
Sudo, R., 77, 83
Sudre, Y., 454, 461
Suegara, N., 113, 115, 117
Sugawara, K., 430, 431
Sugimoto, K., 31
Suharjona, S., 113, 114
Sukany, M., 466
Suki, W. N., 359
Sullivan, C. W., 191
Sullivan, J. L., 427, 431, 436
Sullivan, N. D., 100
Sulzer, C. R., 91
Sulzman, F. M., 198
Summers, J., 366, 368
Summers, K., 193
Summers, R., 326, 336, 337
Summers, W. C., 428, 431
Sundström, C., 431
Supplisson, B., 380, 384
Suput, J., 163
Surgalla, M. J., 458
Suriano, J. R., 362

Sussman, M., 137, 143, 606, 611, 619
Sussman, R., 137, 143, 619
Sussman, R. R., 604
Sutnick, A. I., 357
Sutter, R. P., 536
Sutter, V. L., 112, 119, 125
Sutton, J. C., 215
Suzuki, H., 400, 411, 413, 414
Suzuki, K., 119
Suzuki, M., 16, 20, 31, 34
Suzuki, N., 518, 519
Suzuki, S., 31
Suzuki, T., 384
Svedmyr, A., 422
Svedmyr, E., 423, 426-28, 430, 436, 437, 439
Svihla, G., 601
Svoboda, D. J., 431
Swain, F. M., 331
Swamy, K. H. S., 305
Swartz, M. N., 454-60, 464, 467
Sweeney, B. M., 198
Swinnerton, J. W., 334
Swinton, D., 246
SWITZER, R. L., 135-57; 138, 139, 142, 143, 145-50, 152
Swoveland, P., 428
Syed, S. A., 109
Sykes, J. A., 101
Sykes, R. M., 69, 337
Symchowicz, S., 292, 302
Symonds, N., 488
Synenki, R. M., 491
Syrett, P. J., 140, 146, 147, 149, 153
Syromyatnikov, E. Yu., 324
Szalay, A., 248
Szmelcman, S., 186, 415
Szmuness, W., 359
Szulmajster, J., 146, 150
Szwed, C. F., 451, 467
Szyba, K., 168, 169, 173, 175

T

Tabaud, H., 165, 167
Tabita, F. R., 260
Tachibana, T., 436
Tai, H. H., 522, 523
Taira, T., 398, 405
Takabe, T., 260
Takahashi, E. A., 491
Takahashi, I., 137
Takahashi, K., 193
Takahashi, M., 560-63
Takahashi, N., 400
Takai, Y., 331, 335, 336
Takeda, I., 383, 384, 387
Takeda, Y., 40, 48, 51
Takeshima, H., 17, 23
Takeuchi, A., 96, 112, 117
Takeuchi, K., 509
Takeya, K., 161
Takimoto, A., 569, 572, 580, 581
Talin d'Eyzac, A., 454, 461
Tally, F. P., 455, 464, 466
Talmadge, K. W., 211
Tam, L. Q., 218
Tamburro, C. H., 359
Tamm, S. L., 613
Tamura, M., 569, 577
Tanabe, S., 425
Tanaguchi, S., 42
Tanaka, A., 428, 431
Tanaka, K., 384
Tanaka, M., 246
Tanaka, S., 41, 480
Tanaka, T., 432
Tanaka, Y., 120
Tandeau de Marsac, N., 241, 243-45, 249
Taniguchi, K., 304
Taniyama, T., 92
Tanner, W., 191, 295
Tannock, G. W., 113, 114, 116, 117, 120, 125
Tanowitz, H., 520
Tardrew, P. L., 33
Tarizzo, M. L., 99
Tarnok, I., 168, 176
Tárnok, Z., 168
Tatem, H. E., 382, 391
Tatsumi, N., 509
Tauschel, H.-D., 285
Tavormina, P. A., 304
Tax, J., 31, 33, 34
Taylor, A. L., 481, 487, 491
Taylor, B. F., 334
Taylor, B. L., 405, 406, 410, 415
Taylor, C. D., 323, 324
Taylor, D., 482
Taylor, D. J., 96
Taylor, D. L., 195
Taylor, G. T., 324
Taylor, J. M., 153
Taylor, K. G., 30
Taylor, P. A., 69, 209, 210
Tchernoff, V., 212
Tecson, E. M., 138, 146
Tedesco, F., 510
Tedesco, P. M., 185, 416
Tegner, L., 569
Tellez-Inon, M. T., 137
Telling, R. C., 64, 65
Tel-Or, E., 253, 264
Templeton, B., 412
Tepper, E. Z., 174, 175
Terada, A., 111
Terasaki, P. I., 432
Tereshin, I. M., 20, 22, 25
Terpstra, W., 567
Terry, R. J., 514
Terui, G., 347
Terzaghi, B., 488
Tettenborn, D., 305
Thauer, R. K., 312
Theilade, E., 96
Thiel, G., 371
Thiele, H. H., 282
Thiemann, J. E., 163
Thienpont, D. C., 301, 305
Thipayathasana, P., 403, 415
Thomas, A. H., 292
Thomas, E. D., 452, 453
Thomas, G. D., 449, 454
Thomas, H. W., 6
Thomas, J., 253, 264
Thomas, J. J., 101
Thomas, J. O., 484
Thomas, L. B., 434
Thomas, R., 16, 20, 31
Thompson, C. J., 381
Thompson, J., 41
Thompson, J. F., 208, 211, 219
Thomssen, R., 359
Thorley-Lawson, D. A., 428, 429, 431
Thornber, J. P., 242
Thornsberry, C., 52, 53
Thornton, H. G., 162, 172
Thornton, R. M., 539
Thrum, H., 22
Thurn, A. N., 162
Thurston, C. F., 136, 140, 146, 147, 149, 153
Thurston, E. L., 235, 240
Tilles, J. G., 370
Tillotson, J. R., 454, 458, 460
Tilton, R. C., 52
Tindall, J. P., 453, 464
Tinelli, R., 92
Tisnovska, H., 165, 167
Titman, D., 68, 69
Titsworth, E., 15
Tkacz, A., 168, 169, 173, 175
Todaro, G. J., 438
Todd, S. R., 601, 618
Todd, W. J., 516, 517
Toepfer, M., 390
Tokunaga, H., 246
Tokyuasu, K., 399
Tolbert, N. E., 260
Tomich, E. G., 301
Tomino, T., 335
Tomita, F., 137, 384
Tomita, G., 560, 561, 563
Tomizawa, J., 478
Tomkins, G. M., 147
Toms-Wood, A., 325
Tonietti, G., 117
Toone, J., 139, 143, 145

Topiwala, H. H., 65, 70, 71, 75, 78
Torloni, H., 434
Torres, H. N., 137
Torsoli, A., 117
Totter, J. R., 551, 557
Toussaint, C., 458
Townsend, S. B., 303
Traetteberg, J., 283
Traganza, E. D., 41, 53
Tralka, T. S., 428
Treccani, V., 380, 388
Tréfouel, J., 8
Tréfouel, T. J., 8
Treichler, H. J., 346
Tremblay, R., 96, 97
Trepo, C. G., 359, 360
Trevisan, V., 159-61
Trinci, A. P., 294, 304
Tripathy, D. N., 94
Triplett, D. A., 452, 459
Tronick, S. R., 152
Trouet, A., 520, 525, 527, 529
Trowitzsch, W., 277, 281
Trowsdale, J., 491, 494, 496
Truffa-Bachi, P., 40
Trumper, P. A., 432, 436
Trüper, H. G., 277-86
Tsai, B. I., 65
Tsan, M.-F., 512
Tsang, N., 415
Tso, W. W., 415
Tsubota, T., 432
Tsuchiya, H. M., 66, 68-74, 76-79, 82, 84
Tsuchiya, T., 188
Tsuda, T., 516, 521
Tsuji, F. I., 557
Tsukamura, M., 161, 162, 165, 170-73
Tsung, P.-K., 509, 523
Tu, J. C., 539
Tu, S.-C., 558, 559, 562, 563, 567-70
Tubiash, H. S., 45
Tucker, R. G., 137
Tulkens, P., 520, 525, 527, 529
Tumilowicz, J. J., 95
Tuominen, F. W., 148
Turfitt, G. E., 172
Turnbough, C. L., 138, 139, 142, 143, 145-47, 150, 152
Turner, A. G., 384
Turner, L. H., 94, 100
Turner, N. C., 207, 212
Turner, W. B., 20
Twedt, R. M., 52
Twigg, G. I., 91
Twose, T. M., 482
Tyagi, V. V. S., 228
Tye, B.-K., 481, 495
Tyler, B. M., 150
Tyson, G. E., 94, 95
Tytell, A., 25
Tzeng, S. F., 322, 324, 325

U

Uchida, H., 432
Uchida, K., 111, 120
Uchida, T., 248
Uchino, H., 433
Uchiyama, Y., 96
Udris, Z., 102
Ueda, T., 195
Uesugi, I., 264
Ulitzur, S., 48, 51, 565, 574, 577, 580, 581, 584, 586
Ultmann, J. E., 467
Umbarger, H. E., 140, 149, 153
Umbreit, W. W., 386
Umezawa, H., 297
Unemoto, T., 40
Unger, P., 453
Uphill, P. F., 113, 115, 117
Usher, J. J., 347
Utahara, R., 297
Utz, J. P., 451, 467
Uwaydah, M. M., 457, 458

V

Vacheron, M.-J., 163, 168
Vagelos, P. R., 20, 26
Valentine, R. C., 387, 388, 403, 415, 515
Valeriote, F., 300
Van Alfen, N. K., 207, 212
Van Baalen, C., 227, 233, 255, 257, 264, 382, 391
van Beers, D., 458
Van Brunt, J., 189
Vance, D., 23
Van Cutsem, J. M., 301, 305
Van Deenen, L. L. M., 14, 295, 296
van den Berg, L., 317, 319
Van den Bossche, H., 305
van den Ende, P., 77, 84, 488
van de Poll, K. W., 138, 150
van der burg Spruit, A., 582
Van der Drift, C., 185
Van Der Heyde, H., 113-15, 117, 120
Van der Holden, J., 94
Van der Linden, A. C., 390
van der Linden, W. J. M., 332
Van der Velde, H. H., 260
van der Waaij, D., 121, 122, 126
Van der Wulp, D., 260
Van de Vate, C., 488
Van Dijck, P. W. M., 295
Van Druten, J. A. M., 126
Vanek, Z., 20, 31, 33, 34, 352
Van Epps, D., 508
van Ert, M., 320
VanEseltine, W. P., 91, 93, 102
Van Eyk, J., 390
van Furth, R., 508, 512, 513, 523, 528
van Geertruyden, J., 458
van Gemerden, H., 69, 70, 282, 283
Van Gorkom, H. J., 251
Van Hoof, F., 520, 525, 527-29
van Houte, J., 96
Van Houten, J., 192, 194
Van Niel, C. B., 226
van Rijn, J., 140
Van Saceghem, R., 160
Van Schouwenburg, K. L., 577, 580
Van Scoy, R. E., 465
van Uden, N., 66
Van Vunakis, H., 153
van Wijck-Kapteyn, W. M. C., 315
van Wijk, R., 140
Vanyushin, B. F., 43, 552-55
Van Zutphen, H., 14, 296
Varel, V. H., 337
Varela-Diaz, V. M., 102
Varjú, D., 538
Vary, P. S., 404
Vasquez-Hoyos, A., 170
Vassar, P. S., 452
Vatter, A. E., 398, 402
Vaughan, M., 147, 523
Vaughan, M. H. Jr., 244
Vejlsgaard, R., 452
Veldkamp, H., 64, 65, 68-70, 282, 283
Venkov, P., 15, 300, 301
Vennesland, B., 141, 143, 145
Vereerstraeten, P., 458
Vermylen, P., 305
Vernace, S. J., 365
Vernon, M. L., 438
Vervaeke, I., 113
Vickerman, K., 514, 520
Vigny, A., 560, 564
Vilkas, E., 165, 167
Vilks, G., 332
Villatoro, E., 119, 120
Villet, R. H., 541, 543
Vining, L. C., 13, 345, 348
Vinopal, R. T., 41
Virolainen, M., 436
Visnich, S., 357
Visvesvara, G. S., 603
Vlahcevic, Z., 359
Voelker, W., 141, 143, 145
Vogen, L. K., 611
Vogler, K. G., 386

Voisin, C., 48
Volcani, B. E., 191
Volesky, B., 380
Volk, W. A., 31
Volkman, A., 513
Volpe, J. J., 20, 26
von Essen, R., 436
VON GRAEVENITZ, A., 447-71; 454, 457, 458, 463, 464, 466
von Herzen, R. P., 331
Vonka, V., 424
Vorob'eva, B. F., 43
Vorob'eva, T. I., 552-55
Vosti, K. L., 459
Vuillaume, M., 431, 432
Vukotich, D., 99
Vyas, G. N., 359, 361, 362, 371

W

Wachter, M. S., 90-92
Wada, K., 246
Wade, J., 619, 620
Wade, W. W., 381
Wagner, G., 192
Wagner, G. E., 299
Wagner, M., 126
Wagner, R. R., 361
Wagner, W.-H., 516
Wahl, H. P., 32
Waindle, L. M., 138, 139, 142, 143, 146, 147, 149, 150, 152
Wajsman, Z., 458
Wakasa, R., 387
Waksman, S. A., 161, 162, 169, 170, 175, 386
Walby, J. K., 93, 102
Walden, W. C., 122, 126
Walker, D. J., 315
Walker, J. B., 353
Walker, J. C., 207, 216, 217
Walker, J. D., 380, 381
Walker, J. L., 426, 430, 431
Walker, J. R., 23
Walker, M. S., 353
Walker, N. A., 190-92, 199
Walkup, P. C., 379
Wall, J. B., 285, 288
Wallace, S. L., 303
Wallace, W., 141
Wallach, D. F. H., 363
Wallen, W. C., 432
Waller, D. K., 426
Walpole, A. L., 303
Walsby, A. E., 227, 228, 238, 240, 251, 277
Walsh, C., 569, 604, 611, 614, 619, 620, 622, 626
Walter, H., 24, 25
Walters, D. R., 30
Walters, M. K., 431
Walton, A. J., 582
Walton, G. M., 345
Wampler, J. E., 40, 551, 560, 566-68
Wang, C. H., 41, 53
Wang, S.-L., 65
Wang, W. L. L., 457
Ward, A. C., 352
WARD, D. M., 309-41; 318, 337
Ward, J. C., 336
Ward, P. A., 451, 508
Wardley-Smith, B., 579
Warner, J., 301
Warrell, D. A., 99
Warren, G., 48, 56
Warrick, H. M., 405, 406, 410, 415
Waser, E., 4
Washington, J. A., 457, 465
Wasiclewski, T. V., 618
Wasserman, E., 153
Watanabe, H., 569, 572, 580, 581
Watanabe, S., 383, 384, 508
Watanabe, T., 113, 115, 117, 560-63
Water, R. D., 303
Waterbury, J. B., 227, 231, 233, 235, 237-41, 244, 255, 267
Waters, C. A., 561, 565, 570, 573, 574, 584, 586
Watson, S. W., 233
Waubke, R., 424
Wayne, L. G., 169
Weathers, P., 237, 266
Weaver, P. F., 285, 288
Weaver, R. E., 52, 53
Webb, L. S., 511, 512
Weber, G., 568, 569
Weber, H. J., 541
Weber, K., 303, 555, 558, 560, 561, 563
Weber, M. M., 294
Webster, G. C., 255, 258
Weckesser, J., 238, 239, 285, 286, 288
Wedderburn, N., 439
Wee, G. B., 435
Weed, L. A., 465
Weeks, O. B., 168
Wehland, J., 303
Weide, A., 541
Weidner, E., 521
Weigle, J., 484
Weil, J., 488
Weil, R., 185
Weimer, P. J., 317
Weimer, W. C., 332
Weinberg, A., 428, 431
Weinberg, A. N., 452, 460, 466
Weinberg, E., 428, 438
Weinberg, E. D., 352
Weinmann, E., 359
Weinstein, G. D., 301
Weinstein, L., 115, 453, 456, 460, 462, 464-66
Weisberg, R. A., 501
Weise, G., 238
Weisenseel, M. H., 197
Weiser, R. S., 508
Weiser, U., 143
Weisman, R. A., 601
Weiss, B., 26
Weissmann, G., 509, 510, 512, 522, 523
Wells, J. S., 45
Welti, D., 251
Wennberg, J. E., 451, 465
Wensinck, F., 126
Wenzel, R. P., 458, 466
Wepler, W., 359
Wermundsen, I. E., 482, 490
Werner, J., 432
Werth, J. M., 601
Wesley, A. S., 568
West, I. C., 187
Westhead, E. W., 138, 146
Westlake, D. W. S., 30, 348, 350, 380
Westley, J., 16, 20, 31
Westmacott, D., 285
Westman, A., 427, 431
Weston, J. A., 53
Westphal, H., 359
Westphal, O., 31, 32, 286
Wettermark, G., 569
Wetters, E. J., 424, 429
Whang-Peng, J., 429
Wheat, R. W., 31
Wheeler, J. K., 451, 454, 462
Wheeler, L. A., 126
Wheeler, W. C., 167
Wheelis, M. L., 390
Wheelwright, P., 1
Whelan, T., 332, 333
White, A. W., 257
White, D., 140, 143, 149, 579
White, D. C., 579
White, E. H., 583
White, P., 488
White, R. J., 28, 350, 432
Whitehead, W. L., 380
Whitson, T. C., 457
Whitt, D. D., 128
Whitten, D. M., 511
Whittenbury, R., 231, 257, 285
Whitton, B. A., 227, 234, 235, 237
Wiame, J. M., 136, 141, 142, 145
Wieland, O. H., 141, 145
Wiener, E., 523

Wiener, L. E., 508
Wieringa, K. T., 320
Wiernik, P. H., 449, 463
Wiggins, G. L., 460
Wilcox, M., 250, 254
Wilde, J. K. H., 113, 115, 117
Wildman, R. B., 236
Wiley, W. R., 139
Wilfert, C. M., 452, 467
Wilkins, T. D., 125
Wilkinson, J. F., 257
Wilkinson, P. C., 508
Wilkinson, T. G., 71, 75
Willaert, E., 603, 606
Willcox, R. R., 97, 98
Willecke, K., 24
Willerson, J. T., 428
Willetts, N. S., 137, 482, 497
Williams, A., 361
Williams, D. L., 302
Williams, D. M., 461, 462
Williams, E. W., 361, 362
Williams, F. M., 65, 66
Williams, K. L., 611
Williams, L. S., 138, 153
Williams, O. B., 462
Williams, P. H., 215
Williams, P. J. LeB., 69
Williams, R., 452, 465
Williams, R. C., 123
Williams, R. D., 101
Williams, R. F., 563
Williams, S. T., 161, 163, 171, 173, 175, 176
Williams, T., 208, 211, 219, 301
Williams, T. W., 298
Williams A. K., 582
Williamson, B., 424
Willmer, E. N., 610, 617, 618, 625
Willoughby, L. G., 172
Willstätter, R., 4, 5
Wilson, C. W., 600, 606
Wilson, E. E., 209
Wilson, G. S., 462
Wilson, J. B., 102
Wilson, L., 303
Wilson, R. D., 393
Wilson, R. E., 460
Wilson, T., 551
Wilson, T. S., 465
Wilt, J. C., 516
Winblad, B., 305
Winfrey, M. R., 310, 326-32, 336
Winkenbach, F., 252
Winocour, E., 370
Winogradsky, S., 278, 279, 283
Winstanley, D. J., 347
Winterbauer, R. H., 452-54, 466
Winters, J. C., 380
Winters, K., 382, 391
Wintersteiner, O., 30
Wise, D. L., 337
Wise, J. R., 460
Wise, N. B., 456
Wisse, E., 513
Wisseman, C. L. Jr., 517
Witchitz, J., 459
Withers, N. W., 266, 267
Witkin, S. S., 438
Witman, G. B., 613
Witter, R. L., 436
Wittner, M., 520
Wodzinski, R. S., 382, 385
Woese, C. R., 248
Wohlhieter, J. A., 491
Wolcott, R. G., 185, 189
Wolf, H., 423, 428, 431, 435, 436
Wolfe, L., 432
Wolfe, L. G., 428, 433
Wolfe, M. S., 458
Wolfe, R. S., 75, 310-13, 318, 319, 322-25, 327
Wolin, E. A., 75, 311-13, 316
Wolin, M. J., 75, 127, 129, 311-16, 336
Wolk, C. P., 227, 251-55, 264
Wollgiehn, R., 248
Wong, H., 331
Wong, P. C., 515
Wong, P. T. S., 41
Wong, R. G., 292
Wood, D. A., 149
Wood, H. G., 325
Wood, R. K. S., 218
Wood, T. H., 489
Wood, W. B. Jr., 80
Woodin, A. M., 521
Woods, D. R., 122, 130
Woolf, I. L., 452, 465
Woolley, D. W., 207, 210
Worden, P. B., 285
Wright, B. E., 137, 143, 148
Wright, D. G., 450
Wright, E. C., 359, 360
Wright, J., 429
Wu, T. T., 480
Wudarski, D. J., 430, 433
Wyatt, J. T., 235, 239, 240, 264

Y

Yabuuchi, E., 48
Yagi, H., 389
Yagil, E., 489
Yajima, Y., 428, 431
Yale, C. E., 112, 116, 123
Yalpani, M., 24
Yamada, K., 166, 384
Yamaguchi, J., 430, 433
Yamaguchi, S., 398, 400, 402, 405, 406, 410, 411, 413
Yamamoto, M., 486, 503
Yamamura, Y., 92
Yamane, I., 335, 336
Yanagawa, R., 92
Yanagida, M., 399
Yanagihara, Y., 92
Yanagimoto, M., 347
Yang, J. P. S., 437
Yang, R. D., 69
Yango, L. D., 71, 77
Yaniv, M., 487
Yano, I., 164-67, 173
Yano, T., 383
Yanofsky, C., 498
Yao, K., 398, 405
Yashphe, J., 565, 574, 584, 586
Yassky, D., 80
Yasuda, S., 92
Yasunobu, K. T., 246
Yata, J., 431, 436
Yee, C. L., 428
Yefenof, E., 432
Yeh, H. J. C., 389
Yeh, J., 497
Yeh, W. K., 388
Yen, H.-C., 287, 288
Yeoh, H. T., 74
Yocum, R. R., 425
Yokota, T., 412
Yokoyama, M. T., 95
Yoshida, A., 508
Yoshida, K., 560-63, 570
Yosipovitch, Z. H., 459
Youmans, G. P., 516
Young, L. S., 454, 462
Young, M. R., 525, 527
Young, R. A., 383, 385
Young, R. C., 451, 452
Young, V. M., 449, 463
Youngblood, P., 216, 217
Yribarren, M., 167
Yuyama, S., 598, 604, 611, 616, 619-21

Z

Zablen, L., 248
Zabucchi, G., 510
Zafriti, D., 138, 143
Zajac, B., 430
Zajac, B. A., 424, 431
Zajic, J. E., 380, 384
Zaky, D. A., 451, 464
Zalokar, M., 535, 541
Zaman, V., 518
Zamcheck, N., 449, 454, 458, 467
Zavarzin, G., 231

Zavarzin, G. A., 318
Zayon, G., 514
Zech, L., 429, 430, 433
Zeigler, J. A., 91
Zeikus, J. G., 310, 317, 319, 321-24, 326-32, 336
Zeldin, B., 246
Zeller, J. A., 96, 112, 117
Zeller, W., 218
Zeya, H. I., 509
Zhilina, T. N., 318, 320-22
Zieg, J., 412
Ziegler, J. L., 434, 435, 438
Ziffer, H. D., 388
Zigmond, S. H., 508
Zilberstein, D., 186
Zillig, W., 247
Zimmerman, H. J., 359, 360
Zimmon, D. S., 359
Zinder, N. D., 405
Zipkas, D., 473
Zobell, C. E., 380, 384
Zopf, D., 295
Zopf, W., 171, 172
Zuber, H., 244
Zucco, G., 163
Zuckerman, A. J., 358, 362
zur Hausen, H., 423, 428-31, 433-36
Zurier, R. B., 522, 523, 528
Zwadyk, P., 304
Zworykin, N., 48, 56
Zygmunt, W. A., 304

SUBJECT INDEX

A

Acanthamoeba
comparative analysis of the DNA from, 604
differentiation in, 601
encystment, 601
relationship to Naegleria, 603
Acetabularia
electrical potential of, 192
proton pump of, 191
Acetyl-CoA:carbon dioxide ligase
involvement in synthesis of polifungin, 23
Acetyl-CoA:orthophosphate acetyltransferase
involvement in polyene macrolide synthesis, 20
Acetyl-CoA synthase
involvement in polyene macrolide synthesis, 20
Achlorhydria
opportunisitic bacterial diseases associated with, 453
Acholeplasma laidlawii
effect of polyene antibiotics on, 295
Achromobacter fisheri
characteristics, 555
characterization of the luciferase from, 564
isolation of the bioluminescence aldehyde from, 577
light-bearing specific hosts of, 555
wavelength of luminescent light emitted from, 582
Acidaminococcus
isolation from the feces of nonruminant animals, 119
Acinetobacter
attachment to semisolid tar balls, 386
effect on mixed cultures, 75
growth on n-alkane or crude oil, 383
hydrocarbon uptake by, 385
Acinetobacter calcoaceticus
involvement in opportunistic infections, 450, 454
Actinobacillus
isolated from
the large bowels of nonruminant animals, 117
the small bowels of nonruminant animals, 115
the stomach of nonruminant mammals, 113
Actinomadura
chemotaxonomic studies of, 163, 165, 168
current taxonomic position, 170-73
distribution of chemical characters in, 164
DNA analysis and genetic study of, 169
earlier designations and synonyms, 160
numerical phenetic studies of, 162
taxonomic classification, 160-80
Actinomadura africana
chemotaxonomic studies of, 163
Actinomadura dassonvillei
chemotaxonomic studies of, 163, 166-68
current name and synonyms, 160
current taxonomic position, 171-73
distribution of chemical characters in, 164
isolated from infections, 174
numerical phenetic studies of, 162
Actinomadura longispora
chemotaxonomic studies of, 163
Actinomadura madurae
chemotaxonomic studies of, 166-68
current taxonomic position, 171-73
distribution of chemical characters in, 164
numerical phenetic studies of, 162
as primary agent of actinomycete mycetoma, 174
serotaxonomic studies of, 170
Actinomadura pelletieri
chemotaxonomic studies of, 166-68
current taxonomic position, 171-73
distribution of chemical characters in, 164
numerical phenetic studies of, 162
as primary agent of actinomycete mycetoma, 174
serotaxonomic studies of, 169-70
Actinomyces
earlier designations and synonyms, 160
involvement in opportunistic infections, 455
serotaxonomic studies of, 170
taxonomic classification, 159-80
Actinomyces dentocariosus
current name and synonyms, 160
numerical phenetic studies of, 162
Actinomyces propionicus
current name and synonyms, 160
Actinomyces viscosus
chemotaxonomic studies of, 167
Actinomycete mycetoma
primary agents of, 174
Actinomycin
catabolite regulation of synthesis of, 350
Actinomycin D
inhibition of DNA reaction of Dane particles by, 365
use in enzyme inactivation studies, 149
Acute lymphocytic leukemia
opportunistic bacterial diseases associated with, 451
Acute myelogenous leukemia

opportunistic bacterial diseases associated with, 451
Acute necrotizing ulcerative gingivitis, 97
Aerobacter aerogenes
glyceraldehyde dehydrogenase
in vivo inactivation, 139
lack of affinity for oil in, 383
taxonomic classification, 606
see also Klebsiella aerogenes
Aeromonas hydrophila
involvement in opportunistic infections, 452, 454, 463
Aeromonas shigelloides
involvement in opportunistic infections, 463
Agha Jardi crude oil
fractionation, 381
Agrobacterium tumefaciens
glucoside-3-dehydrogenase inactivation in vivo, 139
overgrowths caused by, 208
pathogenicity-conferring plasmid of, 220, 221
Agromyces
taxonomic classification, 160-80
Akinete, 255
Alcaligenes
involvement in opportunistic infections, 454
Alcaligenes eutrophus
glycollate extraction by, 260
Alcaligenes faecalis
involvement in opportunistic infections, 455
Alcaligenes odorans
involvement in opportunistic infections, 455
Alcoholism
opportunistic bacterial diseases associated with, 452
Alfalfa wilt, 211
Allescheria
haloprigin sensitivity, 304
Allogenic succession, 108
Altermonas haloplanktis
sodium requirement, 41
Alternaria
haloprigin sensitivity, 304
Alternaria tenuis
synthesis of alternariol by, 24
Alternariol, 24
Amensalism, 68, 70-71
Amino acids
usé by gastrointestinal tract bacteria, 128
Aminoacyl-tRNA synthetases
inactivation in vivo, 138
δ-Aminolevulinic acid synthetase
inactivation in vivo, 138
Amphotericin B
chemical structure, 19, 293
effect on Candida albicans, 297
precursors, 16-17
source and properties, 15-17, 292
Amylovorin, 212-15
mode of action, 214-15
structure, 213
Anabaena
carboxysomes in, 238
heterocyst differentiation in, 250
nitrogenase regulation in, 250
protection of nitrogenase from oxygen in, 253
taxonomic classification, 234-35
Anabaena cylindrica
akinetes in, 255
gliding motility of, 240
nitrite and nitrate reductases from, 264
Anabaena variabilis
cell-free protein synthesizing from, 247
control of gene expression in, 248-49
Anacystis nidulans
chemostat study of, 79
study of, 227
Anaerobic bacteria
involvement in opportunistic infections, 455
Ancalochloris perfilievii
taxonomic classification, 280
Angular leaf spot of cotton, 208
Antagonism, 67
Antibiotics
amphotericin B, 292-93
antifungal agents, 291-308
arenomycin, 18
ascosin, 15, 26
aureofacin, 15
aureofungin, 15, 26
axenomycin, 14, 25
ayfactin, 15, 26
azacolutin, 26
candicidin, 16-17, 23, 297-98, 350
candidin, 15, 292
candihexin, 15, 33
candimycin, 26
carrageenan, 22
caudicidin, 15, 292
cerulenin, 23
chainin, 15-19
clotrimazole, 302-4
concanavalin A, 523-24
corynecin, 352
cyanophycin, 265
cycloheximide, 149
daunomycin, 365
dermostatin, 15
erythromycin, 14-34
etruscomycin, 17-18
eurocidin, 15, 31, 297
filipin, 15-18, 297
flavofungin, 15-17
5-fluorocytosine, 102, 298-300
fosfomycin, 347
fungichromin, 15
fungimycin, 15-18, 28
of gastrointestinal flora, 126
gramicidin, 354
griseofulvin, 301-4
haloprigin, 302-4
hamycin, 15, 26
heptafungin A, 15
heptamycin, 26
lagosin, 15
leucocidin, 521-22
leucomycin, 23
levorin, 65
lucensomycin, 15-18
magnamycin, 17
maridomycin, 17
mediocin, 397-402
miconazole, 305
moldcidin B, 15
mycoheptin, 15
mycoticin A, B, 15-19
nebramycin, 352
neomycin, 102, 351-52
nocobactins, 167-68
nystatin, 17-24, 31, 292-93, 298
penicillin, 348-51
pentamycin, 15
perimycin 15, 26-30
phytotoxins, 205-24
pimaricin, 17-18
polifungin, 15-26
polyene antibiotics, 13-38,

292-98
pyrrolnitrin, 348
rhizobitoxine, 218-19
rifampin, 149, 301, 350
rifamycin, 28
rimocidin, 15
siomycin, 351
streptomycin, 32, 352-53
suramin, 525
tabatoxin, 209-10
telrin A, B, 15
tennectin, 15-18
tolnaftate, 302-4, 553
trichomycin, 298
turimycin, 22
tylosin, 17, 32
valinomycin, 198
vancomycin, 352
virginiamycin, 347
Aphanocapsa
aggregation, 239
generic assignments, 231
Aphanothece
aggregation, 239
Arachnia
earlier designations and synonyms, 160
serotaxonomic studies of, 170
taxonomic classification, 160-80
Arenomycin
chemical structure, 18
Argas (tick)
as vectors of avian borreliosis, 100
Arginine dihydrolase system
in Beneckea, 47, 53
Arginine operon
genetic duplication in, 498
Arizona hinshawii
involvement in opportunistic infections, 459
Aromatic amino acid pathway
involvement in synthesis of polyene macrolides, 27
Aromatics
crude oil fractionation product, 381
Artemia salina
association with spirochete-like organism, 95
Arthrobacter
numerical phenetic studies of, 162
production of extracellular emulsifying agents by, 162
Ascosin, 15, 26
Aspartate transcarbamylase
inactivation in vivo, 138
Aspartokinase
inactivation in vivo, 138
lysine sensitive
inactivation in vivo, 138
regulation, 40
Aspergillus
effect of 5-fluorocytosine on, 299
effect of polyene antibiotics on, 296
haloprigin sensitivity of, 304
use of combined therapy for diseases caused by, 301
Aspergillus fumigatus
nitrogen catabolite repression in, 352
tolnaftate sensitivity in, 304
Aspergillus nidulans
glutamate dehydrogenase-NADP dependent
inactivation in vivo, 139-43
nitrate reductase, 141
nitrogen catabolite repression in, 352
Asphaltene
crude oil fractionation product, 381
Asplenia
opportunistic bacterial diseases associated with, 451
Atoxia teleangiectasia
opportunistic bacterial diseases associated with, 450
Aureofacin, 15
Aureofungin, 15, 26
Australia antigen, 357
Autogenic succession, 108
Avena
charge current of, 198
Avian borreliosis, 100
Axenomycins, 14, 25
Ayfactin, 15, 26
Azacolutin, 26
Azotobacter
nitrogen-fixation genetic studies of, 387
Azotobacter vinelandii
chemostat competition study of, 82
nitrogen-fixing activity in
inactivation in vivo, 141
as prey, 17

B

B-cell defects
opportunistic bacterial diseases associated with, 450
Bacillus
DAHP synthase regulation in, 29
involvement in opportunistic infections, 455
ribosomal proteins of compared with those of E. coli, 286
Bacillus brevis
gramicidin S synthesis in, 354
Bacillus cadaveris
lysine decarboxylase
inactivation in vivo, 140, 145
Bacillus cereus
fructose biphosphate aldolase modification, 137
glucose-6-phosphate dehydrogenase
inactivation in vivo, 139, 153
involvement in opportunistic infections, 455
Bacillus licheniformis
in vivo inactivation of enzymes in, 138, 147-48
involvement in opportunistic infections, 455
threonine dehydratase
inactivation in vivo, 141
Bacillus polymyxa
syntropism study, 74
Bacillus proteolytica
taxonomic classification, 53
Bacillus subtilis
aspartate transcarbamylase
inactivation in vivo, 138, 146, 149, 152
characterization of structure and function of the flagella of, 398, 401
effect of rifampin on, 149
genetic duplication in, 491-95
glutamine PRPP amidotransferase
inactivation in vivo, 139, 145
inosine monophosphate dedrogenase
inactivation in vivo, 148
isolated from the large bowels of nonruminant animals, 117
isolation from the feces of

nonruminant animals, 119
lack of affinity for oil in, 383
ornithine transcarbamylase
inactivation in vivo, 141
PABA synthase of, 27
proteinases
role in enzyme inactivation, 147
Bacitracin
inhibition of synthesis by inorganic phosphate, 352
Bacterial blight
of barley, 208
of rice, 208
of soybeans, 208
Bacteriocins
of gastrointestinal flora, 126
Bacteriological Code, 227, 267
Bacterionema
chemotaxonomic studies of, 163, 166-67
current taxonomic position, 171-73
distribution of chemical characters in, 164
DNA analysis and genetic study of, 168-69
earlier designations and synonyms, 160
serotaxonomic studies of, 170
taxonomic classification, 160
Bacterionema matruchotii
chemotaxonomic studies of, 166
Bacteriophage
activity against luminescent bacteria, 588-89
Bacteroides melaninogenicus
in human oral flora, 96
isolated from
the feces of nonruminant animals, 119
the large bowels of nonruminant animals, 117
the small bowels of nonruminant animals, 115
the stomach of nonruminant mammals, 113
Baeocytes, 229
Barodamycin, 30
Basidiomycete
β-1,3-glucanase
inactivation in vivo, 139
Bdellovibrio
predation by, 80-81
Behavioral genetics of phycomyces
effects of light on, 537
environmental stimuli in, 538
genetic crosses, 542
heterokaryons, 541
mutants, 539-41
photoreceptros, 543-44
regulation of growth of, 545
Beijerinckia
petroleum degradation mechanism of, 389
Bejel, 97-98
Beneckea
diaminopimelate decarboxylase
inactivation in vivo, 138
flagellation, 48
genus properties, 47-52
host dependence of luminescent members of, 557
pathogenic characteristics, 52
relation to Lucibacterium and Vibrio, 57-58
species, 52-54
swarming in, 57
Beneckea alginolytica
characteristics, 52
source, 42
Beneckea anguillara
pathogenic characteristics, 54
source, 42
taxonomic properties, 53
Beneckea campbelli
characteristics, 52
source, 42
Beneckea harveyi
the bioluminescence-associated acid production in, 582
characteristic of the luciferase from, 558-69
characteristics, 41, 553
currently used and proposed epithets, 553
DNA homology group of, 52
energetics of bioluminescence in, 581
factors influencing pyruvate excretion, 582
guanine plus cytosine DNA base composition of, 553
luminescence in, 553
luminosity, 56
mutants in the luminescence system of, 584-87
source, 42
specialized transducing bacteriophage of, 588-89
Beneckea natriegens
characteristics, 52
growth rate, 53
nutritional versatility, 53
pyruvate excretion by, 582
source, 42
Beneckea nereida
source, 42
Beneckea nigrapulchrituda
pigment, 53
source, 42
Beneckea parahaemolytica
characteristics, 52
source, 42
Beneckea pelagia I
characteristics, 53
source, 42
Beneckea splendida
characteristics, 553
DNA homology group of, 53
guanine plus cytosine DNA base composition of, 553
luminescence, 553
source, 42
tolnaftate sensitivity of, 553
Beneckea vulnifica
characteristics, 53
source, 42
Besnoitia
antagonism of host defenses by, 520
Bifidobacterium
earlier designations and synonyms, 160
in gastrointestinal tract of babies, 120
isolated from
the feces of nonruminant animals, 119
the large bowels of nonruminant animals, 117
the small bowels of nonruminant animals, 115
the stomach of nonruminant animals, 113
taxonomic classification, 160
Bikaverin
inhibition of synthesis by inorganic phosphate, 352
nitrogen regulation of synthesis of, 352
Bile acids
effect on flora of gastrointestinal tract, 122-23
Black rot of cabbage, 215
Blastomyces

effect of polyene antibiotics on, 296
Blastomyces dermatidis
effect of 5-fluorocytosine on, 300
use of combined therapy for diseases caused by, 301
Blue-green bacteria
see Cyanobacteria
Bordetella bronchiseptica
involvement in opportunistic infections, 454
Borrelia
effect of dodecyl sulfate on, 90
fermentation end products of, 102
flagella, 91
lipid composition, 93
Borrelia anserina
nutrition and growth requirements, 101-2
role in avian borreliosis, 100
Borrelia duttonii
role in East African relapsing fever, 100
Borrelia hermsii
role in endemic relapsing fever, 100
Borrelia hispancia
nutrition and growth requirements, 102
Borrelia melainogenicus
role in acute necrotizing ulcerative gingivitis, 97
Borrelia parkeri
nutrition and growth requirements, 101
Borrelia recurrentis
as causal agent of epidemic relapsing fever, 99
proton circulation measurements in, 101-2
Borrelia turicatae
nutrition and growth requirements, 101
role in endemic relapsing fever, 100
Borrelia venezuelensis
role in endemic relapsing fever, 100
Botanical Code, 227, 267
Botrytis alli
griseofulvin used in effective treatment of disease caused by, 302
Branhamella catarrhalis
involvement in opportunistic infections, 462
Brevibacterium
petroleum degradation mechanism in, 389
production of extracellular emulsifying agents by, 384
Bronchiectasis
opportunistic bacterial diseases associated with, 453
Brucella
involvement in opportunistic infections, 456
Brucella melitensis
involvement in opportunistic infections, 456
Bruton's agammaglobulinemia
opportunistic bacterial diseases associated with, 450
Burns
opportunistic bacterial diseases associated with, 453
Butyrivibrio
isolated from the feces of nonruminant animals, 119

C

C-5 activity defects
opportunistic bacterial diseases associated with, 451
C-3 deficiency
opportunistic bacterial diseases associated with, 451
Calcium
role in
flagella reversal of Chlamydomonas, 195
phagocytosis and pinocytosis, 195
photoresponses of Euglena, 195
sodium sparing in marine enterobacteria, 41
transport, 188
Campylobacter fetus
involvement in opportunistic infections, 456
Cancer
Epstein-Barr related causation in monkeys, 433-34
Candicidin
effect on Candida albicans, 297
inhibition of synthesis by inorganic phosphate, 342
precursors, 16-17
regulation of synthesis of, 350
synthesis inhibition by cerulenin, 23
use, 298
Candida
combined therapy for diseases caused by, 300
effect of 5-fluorocytosine on, 300
effect of polyene antibiotics on, 296
fructose biphosphatase
inactivation in vivo, 138
isolated from the stomach of nonruminant animals, 113
nystatin treatment of diseases caused by, 298
Candida albicans
effect of 5-fluorocytosine on, 298
effect of polyene antibiotics on, 297
haloprigin sensitivity of, 304
tolnaftate sensitivity of, 304
use of combined therapy for diseases caused by, 301
Candida petrophium
excretion of emulsifying agents by, 384
Candida stellatoidea
α-glucosidase
inactivation in vivo, 139
Candida tropicalis
cell-bound hydrocarbon emulsification activity in, 384
Candida utilis
glutamate dehydrogenase-NAD dependent
inactivation in vivo, 139-46
glutamate dehydrogenase NADP dependent
inactivation in vivo, 139
glutamine synthetase
inactivation in vivo, 139
Candidin, 15, 292
Candihexin A, B, 15, 33
Candihexin E, F, 15
Candimycin, 26
Carboxysomes, 238
Cardiobacterium hominis
involvement in opportunistic infections, 456
Cardiopulmonary bypass

opportunistic bacterial diseases associated with, 453
Carotenoids
of cyanobacteria, 242
Carrageenan
membrane dysfunction caused by, 527-28
Catabolite inactivation, 142
Catabolite regulation
of flagella formation, 412-13
of synthesis of the bioluminescence system, 574-75
Catenabacterium
isolated from the feces of nonruminant animals, 119
methanol enrichment in, 318
Cellulomonas
numerical phenetic studies of, 162
Cellulose
hydrolysis by bacteria in gastrointestinal tracts, 128
Cephalosporin C
synthesis, 346
Cephalosporium acremonium
methionine-stimulated synthesis of cephalosporin C by, 346-47
pathway of sulfur metabolism in, 350
regulation of β-lactam antibiotics in, 351
Cephamycin
inhibition of the synthesis of by inorganic phosphate, 352
Ceratocystis ulmi
phytotoxin glycopeptide from, 212
Cerebrospinal fluid shunts
opportunistic bacterial diseases associated with, 453
Cerulenin, 21-28
mode of action, 23
Chainia
antibiotics produced by, 15
Chainin, 15-19
chemical structure, 19
precursors, 17
Chamaesiphon
generic assignments, 231
micrograph, 230
Chamaesiphonaceae
taxonomic classification, 232
Chamaesiphonales
taxonomic classification, 232
Chara
proton pump of, 190-92
Chara corallina
proton circulation measurements in, 187
Chediak-Higashi Syndrome, 450
Chemical characters of nocardiform bacteria, 164
Chemiosmotic theory, 181-203
Chemotaxis, 186
Chlamydia
antagonism of host defenses by, 516-17
Chlamydia psittaci
antagonism of host defenses by, 517
Chlamydomonas
flagellar microtubule assembly in, 613
mechanism of flagella reversal, 195
Chlamydomonas reinhardii
nitrate reductase
inactivation in vivo, 141
Chloramphenicol
synthesis, 30
use in enzyme inactivation studies, 149
Chlorella
glucose-proton symport in, 191
isocitrate lyase
inactivation in vivo, 146-47, 153
nitrate reductase
inactivation in vivo, 141
Chlorella fusca
isocitrate lyase
inactivation in vivo, 140
Chlorella pyrenoidosa
isocitrate lyase
inactivation in vivo, 140
Chlorobacterium symbionticum
taxonomic classification, 279
Chlorobiaceae, 280
Chlorobiineae
see Green bacteria
Chlorobium
early studies, 279
as member of syntropic mixture, 280
Chlorobium limicola
characteristics, 280
taxonomic classification, 279
Chlorobium phaeobacteroides
taxonomic classification, 281
Chlorobium phaeovibriodes
taxonomic classification, 281
Chlorobium thiosulfatophilum
taxonomic classification, 280
Chlorobium vibrioforme Pelsh
characteristics, 280
Chlorochromatium aggregatum
taxonomic classification, 281
Chloroflexaceae, 281
Chloroflexus
pigments, 281
taxonomic classification, 281
Chloroflexus aurantiacus
taxonomic classification, 279-81
Chlorogloea fritschii
characteristics, 235
Chlorogloeopsis
effect of prolonged dark growth on, 241
poly-β-hydroxybutyrate inclusions in, 237
Chlorogloeopsis fritschii
characteristics, 235
Chlorogonium euchlorium
use in toxin assay, 219
Chloronema
taxonomic classification, 279-82
Chloronema giganteum
taxonomic classification, 282
Chloronema spiroideum
taxonomic classification, 282
Chlorophyll
of cyanobacteria, 242
Chloroplast origin, 266
Chloropseudomonas ethylica, 280
Chlortetracycline
inhibition of synthesis by inorganic phosphate, 352
Cholera toxin, 206
Chromatiaceae, 283
Chromatic adaptation in cyanobacteria, 245
Chromatium
naming of, 279
ribulose-1, 5-diphosphate carboxylase

inactivation in vivo, 141
Chromatium gracile
taxonomic classification, 284
Chromatium okenii
taxonomic classification, 284
Chromatium vinosum
taxonomic classification, 284
Chromatium weissei
taxonomic classification, 284
Chrombacterium violaceum
sugar amine of, 31
Chronic bronchitis
opportunistic bacterial diseases associated with, 453
Chronic granulomatous disease
opportunistic bacterial diseases associated with, 450
Chronic lymphocytic leukemia
opportunistic bacterial diseases associated with, 451
Chroocarccean cyanobacteria, 231
Chroococcaeae
genome size, 246
guanine plus cytosine DNA base composition of, 246
taxonomic classification, 232
Chroococcales
taxonomic classification, 232
Chroococcidiacea
taxonomic classification, 232
Chroococcidiopsis
taxonomic classification, 232-33
Chrysanthemum
disease of, 219-20
Cirrhosis of the liver
opportunistic bacterial diseases associated with, 451
Citrate lyase
inactivation in vivo, 138
Citrobacter diversus
involvement in opportunistic infections, 458
Citrobacter freundii
involvement in opportunistic infections, 458
Citrobacter koseri
involvement in opportunistic infections, 458
Clathrochloris
taxonomic classification, 280
Clathrochloris sulfurica
pure culture growth of, 280
Claviceps SD 58
inorganic phosphate repression of alkaloid synthesis in, 353
Cleiodopus gloriamaris
luminescent symbionts of, 553-54
Clostridia
isolated from
the feces of nonruminant animals, 119
the large bowels of nonruminant animals, 117
the small bowels of nonruminant animals, 115
the stomach on nonruminant animals, 113
Clostridium acetobutylicum
hydrogen evolution by, 312
Clostridium acidiurici
electron transfer in, 325
Clostridium botulinum
involvement in opportunistic infections, 448
Clostidium butyricum
hydrogen evolution by, 312
Clostridium cellobioparum
coculturing with Methanobacterium ruminantium, 315-16
Clostridium formicoaceticum
electron transfer in, 325
Clostridium pasteurianum
enzymatic studies of methane biogenesis in, 325
hydrogen evolution by, 312
Clostridium perfringens
effects of toxin from, 522
involvement in opportunistic infections, 455
Clostridium scatologenes
methanol enrichment in, 318
Clostridium septicum
involvement in opportunistic infections, 455
Clostridium thermoaceticum
electron transfer in, 325
Clostridium tyrobutyricum
hydrogen evolution by, 312
Clotrimazole
properties, 304
structure, 302
Coccidioides
effect of polyene antibiotics on, 296
Coliform bacteria
isolated from
the feces of nonruminant animals, 119
the large bowels of nonruminant animals, 117
the small bowels of nonruminant animals, 115
the stomach of nonruminant animals, 113
Colpoda steinii
encystment, 79
as predator, 76, 83
Commensalism, 66, 71-72
Competition, 67-68
Concanavalin A
involvement in perturbation of phagolysosome formation, 523-24
Coprococcus
isolated from the feces of nonruminant animals, 119
Corynebacterium
chemotaxonomic studies of, 167-68
current taxonomic position, 171-72
distribution of chemical characteristics in, 164
involvement in opportunistic infections, 456
mechanism of petroleum degradation in, 389
production of extracellular emulsifying agents by, 384
serotaxonomic studies of, 169-70
wilting disease of, 207
Corynebacterium aquaticum
chemotaxonomic studies of, 166
involvement in opportunistic infections, 456
Corynebacterium bovis
involvement in opportunistic infections, 456
Corynebacterium diphtheriae
antagonism of host defenses by, 514
numerical phenetic studies of, 162
serotaxonomic studies of, 170
toxigenic phage, 220
Corynebacterium equi

currently accepted name, 172
involvement in opportunistic infections, 448, 456
Corynebacterium fascians
chemotaxonomic studies of, 166
Corynebacterium glutamicum
numerical phenetic studies of, 162
Corynebacterium insidiosum
phytotoxid glycopeptide from, 211
toxin assay for, 207
Corynebacterium michiganense
toxic glycopeptide from, 212
toxin assay for, 207
Corynebacterium minutissimum
involvement in opportunistic infections, 456
Corynebacterium ovis
antagonism of host defenses by, 514
Corynebacterium pseudodiphtheriticum
involvement in opportunistic infections, 456
Corynebacterium sensu stricto
chemotaxonomic studies of, 163, 166
DNA analysis and genetic study of, 168-69
numerical phenetic studies of, 161-62
Corynebacterium sepedonicum
toxic glycopeptide from, 211
Corynebacterium xerosis
involvement in opportunistic infections, 456
Corynecin
inhibition of synthesis by inorganic phosphate, 352
Coxiella burnetii
antagonism of host defenses by, 517
Cristispira
cellular inclusions in, 93
distribution, 95
flagella, 91
nutrition and growth requirements, 101
Crown gall, 208, 221
Cryptococcus
effect of 5-fluorocytosine on, 299
effect of polyene antibiotics on, 296
Cryptococcus neoformis
combined therapy for diseases caused by, 300
effect of 5-fluorocytosine on, 300
Curling factor, 302
Cyanidium caldarium
nitrate reductase
inactivation in vivo, 141
Cyanobacteria
Chroocaccean cyanobacteria, 231
differences between green and purple bacteria and, 276
heterocystous subgroups, 234
metabolism, 255-65
anaerobic metabolism, 262-64
assimilation of combined nitrogen, 263
control of light and dark metabolism, 258-61
cyanophycin, 265
metabolic bases of obligate photoautotrophy, 261
nitrogen fixation, 264
relation between photosynthetic and respiratory metabolism, 256-57
micrographs, 230
origin of chloroplasts in, 266
oscillatorian cyanobacteria, 233
pleurocapsalean cyanobacteria, 231-32
properties of principal subgroups, 228-31
specialized cells, 249-55
the akinete, 255
the heterocyst, 249-54
vegetative cell, 235-49
cell envelopes, 238-40
general organization, 235-38
genome, 246
gliding movement, 240
machinery of transcription and translation, 247-48
photosynthetic apparatus, 241-46
schematic diagram, 236
Cyanophora paradoxa
taxonomic classification, 266
Cyanophycin, 265
Cyclic nucleotides
involvement in perturbation of phagolysosome formation, 523
Cycloheximide
use in enzyme inactivation studies, 149
Cylindrospermum
akinetes in, 255
Cystic fibrosis
opportunistic bacterial diseases associated with, 454

D

DAHP synthase
comparative regulation, 29
Dane particle, 358-77
complexity of the DNA of, 368-70
schematic representation, 369
DNA structure, 365
mechanism of the endogenous DNA polymerase reaction, 365-68
see also Hepatitis B virus
Daunomycin
inhibition of the DNA reaction of Dane particles by, 365
Dendogram
of marine enterobacteria, 44
DNA analysis and genetic studies of nocardiform bacteria, 168-69
DNA/DNA hydrization studies
of marine enterobacteria, 43-46
DNA/rRNA hybridization studies
of marine enterobacteria, 45, 50
Dermatophilus
taxonomic classification, 160-80
Dermatophillus congolensis
involvement in opportunistic infections, 456
Dermocarpa
micrograph, 230
taxonomic classification, 232-33
Dermocarpella
taxonomic classification, 232-33
Dermostatin, 15
Desulfovibrio
coupled growth with the S organism, 314-15
hydrogen production studies

in, 317
interspecies hydrogen transfer in, 315
Desulfovibrio acetoxidans
association with methanogenic bacteria, 330
Desulfovibrio rebent-schickii
association with methanogenic bacteria, 330
hydrogen production studies in, 317
Desulfovibrio vulgaris
methanol enrichment, 318
Desulfuromonas acetoxidans
as syntropic member of Chloropseudomonas ethylica, 280
Dextran sulfate-caused membrane dysfunction studies, 527-28
Diabetes mellitus
opportunistic bacterial diseases associated with, 450
Diaminopimelate decarboxylase
inactivation in vivo, 138
Dichlorophenyl methyl urea (DCMU), 257-58
Dictyostelium
DNA comparative analysis of, 604
pinocytosis and phagocytosis mechanisms in, 195
relationship to Naegleria, 603
study of, 601
Dictyostelium discoideum
food bacteria for, 606
glycogen synthetase of
inactivation in vivo, 148
as predator, 77
the sexual cycle, 611
Didemnum
taxonomic classification, 266
Didinium-Paramecium predator-prey system, 65, 83
Differentiation in Naegleria gruberi, 597-629
DiGeorge's syndrome
opportunistic bacterial diseases associated with, 450
Diphtheria toxin, 206
DJ-400 B_1, 15, 26
DJ-400 B_2, 15, 26
Drug abuse
opportunistic bacterial diseases associated with, 453
Durhamycin, 15

E

East African relapsing fever
causal agent, 100
Ectothiorhodospira
chemical structure, 18
ribosomal protein analysis of, 287
taxonomic classification, 282
Ectothiorhodospira halophila
taxonomic classification, 282
Ectothiorhodospira mobilis
taxonomic classification, 282
Ectothiorhodospira shaposhnikovii
taxonomic classification, 282
Eczema
opportunistic bacterial diseases associated with, 453
Edwardsiella
involvement in opportunistic infections, 457
Edwardsiella tarda
involvement in opportunistic infections, 459
Eikenella corrodens
involvement in opportunistic infections, 456
Electron transport proteins
of cyanobacteria, 246
Emphysema
opportunistic bacterial diseases associated with, 453
Encephalitozoon cuniculi
antagonism of host defenses by, 521
Endemic relapsing fever, 99-100
Endemic syphilis (bejel), 97-98
Endonuclease I
inactivation in vivo, 138
Entamoeba
effect of polyene antibiotics on, 296
Enterobacter
aspartokinase regulation in, 40
electron transfer in, 325
Enterobacter aerogenes
involvement in opportunistic infections, 457
taxonomic classification, 606
Enterobacter agglomerans
involvement in opportunistic infections, 457
Enterobacter cloacae
involvement in opportunistic infections, 457
Enterobacteriaceae
involvement in opportunistic infections, 457-58
lipopolysaccharide sugars of, 31
Entodinium caudatum
predation by, 83
Enzyme inactivation, 135-57
in differentiation, 143-44
effects of inhibitors, 149
examples, 138-41
fate after inactivation, 151-53
mechanisms of
chemical, 145
physical, 144, 145
methods of study, 147-54
physiological conditions leading to, 137, 142
reactivation in vivo and in vitro, 151
use of mutant strains, 149-51
Epidemic relapsing fever, 99
Epidermophyton
effect of polyene antibiotics on, 296
tolnaftate sensitivity of, 304
Epidermophyton floccosum
effect of amphotericin B on, 295
griseofulvin used in effective treatment of disease caused by, 301
Epstein-Barr virus, 421-45
antigenic relationship with other herpesviruses, 425
antigens determined by, 423-25
chromosome studies of, 433
Epstein-Barr virus-negative lymphoblastoid lines, 431
general biology, 422
human lymphoid cells and tumor induction in rodents, 432-33
in individuals without tumors, 438-39
infectible cells and virus receptors, 431

and neoplasia, 433-35
oncornaviruses in cells transformed by, 438
origin of Epstein-Barr virus-carrying human lymphoblastoid lines, 429-39
relationship of DNA from with that from host cell, 428
search for different strains of, 433
types of infection in human B cells, 426-28
variations in host antibody responses, 425
Ergot alkaloids
inhibition of synthesis by inorganic phosphate, 352
Erwinia
aspartokinase regulation in, 40
Erwinia amylovora
necrosis produced by, 208
toxin produced by, 212-13, 221
Erwinia herbicola
involvement in opportunistic infections, 457
Erwinia lathyri
involvement in opportunistic infections, 457
Erythromycin, 14-34
precursors, 17, 31
Escherichia
aspartokinase regulation in, 40
Escherichia coli
aminoacyl-tRNA synthetases of
inactivation in vivo, 138, 153
aromatic pathway of, 27
aspartokinase-lysine sensitive
inactivation in vivo, 138, 146
aspartokinase regulation in, 40
characterization of structure and function of the flagella of, 397-414
chemostat competition study of, 82
cytoplasmic membrane of, 92
DAHP synthase regulation in, 29
distribution of flagella gene compared with that of Salmonella, 404
DNA binding protein from, 247
DNA comparative analysis of, 604
effect of H_2S on in gastroenteric tract, 126
effect of nutrition on in mice cecums, 126
electrical power output of, 186
electron transfer in, 325
endonuclease I of
inactivation in vivo, 138
energy charge studies, 352-53
fatty acid synthesis in, 24
in gastrointestinal tract, 111
in gastrointestinal tract of babies, 120
glutamine synthetasc modification, 137-39
interstrain comparison of ribosomal proteins, 286
involvement in opportunistic infections, 457
isocitrate dehydrogenase
inactivation in vivo, 140, 145
lack of affinity for oil in, 383
lipopolysaccharide sugar amine in, 31
N-acetylglucosamine as a growth factor for, 323
nitrogen-fixation genetic studies of, 387
as prey, 76-77
protein synthesis initiation factor IF-3
inactivation in vivo, 146
proton circulation measurements in, 187
ribosomal subunit complementation study in, 247
RNA polymerase subunit complementation study, 247
role in ridding gastrointestinal tract of oxygen, 128
synthesis of unique TDP-sugars in, 32
tandem duplication selection in, 478-81
tRNA study, 247
Etruscomycin, 17-18
precursors, 17
Eubacterium
isolated from
the feces of nonruminant animals, 119
the large bowels of nonruminant animals, 117
Euglena
mechanism of photoresponses, 195
study of 16S RNA from, 248
Euglena gracilis
phosphomonesterase
inactivation in vivo, 141
Eurocidin, 15, 31, 297

F

Familial lipochromic histiocytosis
opportunistic bacterial diseases associated with, 452
Fatty acid synthesis
pathway, 21
Feces
microbial composition, 118
Filipin
characteristics, 15-18
chemical structure, 18
effect on Candida albicans, 297
precursors, 17
Fire blight of apples and pears, 212-13
Fischerella
taxonomic classification, 235
Flagella of bacteria
function, 414
genetics of formation, 403-10
comparison of flagellar genes in E. coli and Salmonella, 410
E. coli flagellar genes, 405-10
mutant phenotypes, 403-5
Salmonella flagellar genes, 405
map of genes, 404
regulation of synthesis, 410-14
catabolite repression, 412-13
phase variation in Salmonella, 412
regulation of flagellin synthesis, 413-14
structures, 398-403
the basal structure, 401-3
the filament, 398-400

the hook structure, 400-1
Flavacid, 15
Flavobacter
protocooperation in, 75
Flavobacterium
involvement in opportunistic infections, 459
Flavobacterium meningosepticum
involvement in opportunistic infections, 451, 459
Flavofungin, 15-17
precursors, 17
5-Fluorocytosine
as antifungal agent, 299
pathway of incorporation, 299
use in isolation of leptospires, 102
Fosfomycin
synthesis, 347
Frankia
taxonomic classification, 160-80
Fructose biphosphate aldolase
modification, 137
Fructose-1,6-bisphosphatase
inactivation in vivo, 138, 142
Fucus
differentiation in, 195-96
Fungichromin, 15
Fungimycin, 15-18, 28
chemical structure, 18
precursors, 16
Fusarium aquaeductum
photocartenogenesis in, 539
Fusobacteria
involvement in opportunistic infections, 455
isolated from the large bowels of nonruminant animals, 113
role in acute necrotizing ulcerative gingivitis, 97

G

Galactose operon
genetic duplication in, 499-500
unstable recombinants of, 489-90
Galactozymase
inactivation in vivo, 138
Galls on oleander, 209
Gas-oil
crude oil fractionation product, 381
Gasoline
crude oil fractionation product, 381
Gastrointestinal tract microbial ecology, 107-33
Gemminger
isolated from the feces of nonruminant animals, 119
Gene expression
control in cyanobacteria, 248-49
Generalized hematopoietic hypoplasia
opportunistic bacterial diseases associated with, 450
Genome sizes
of cyanobacterial subgroups, 246
Geodermatophilius
taxonomic classification, 160-80
Gibberella fujikuroi
growth rate control of secondary metabolism in, 354
nitrogen regulation of bikaverin synthesis in, 352
Gingivitis
spirochete involvement, 96
Glands of Luberkuhn
spirochetes in, 96
Gliding motility
of cyanobacterial cell, 240
of green bacteria, 281-82
Gloeobacter
cell envelope of, 239
lipid pattern, 243
taxonomic classification, 267-68
Gloeobacter violaceus
photosynthetic apparatus, 235-37
taxonomic classification, 267
Gloeothece
cell envelope of, 239
nitrogen fixation in, 264
poly-β-hydroxybutyrate from, 237
β-1,3-Glucanase (extracellular)
inactivation in vivo, 139
Glucocorticosteroids
involvement in perturbation of phagolysosome formation, 522-24
Glucose-6-phosphate dehydrogenase
inactivation in vivo, 139
Glucose-6-phosphate dehydrogenase deficiency
opportunistic bacterial diseases associated with, 450
Glucose transport system II
inactivation in vivo, 139
α-Glucosidase
inactivation in vivo, 139
Glucoside-3-dehydrogenase
inactivation in vivo, 139
Glutamate dehydrogenase
inactivation in vivo, 139
Glutamine auxotrophy
gln A, B, D, E mutants, 150
Glutamine PRPP amidotransferase
inactivation in vivo, 139
Glutamine synthetase
modification, 137-39
Glycerol dehydrogenase
inactivation in vivo, 139
Glycerol kinase
inactivation in vivo, 140
Glycogen phosphorylase
modification, 137
Glycogen synthetase
inactivation in vivo, 148
modification, 137
Glycollate excretion in chemoautotrophs, 260
GOGAT pathway
in cyanobacteria, 264
Gonyaulax
effect of valinomycin on, 198
Gordona
chemotaxonomic studies of, 165
current name and synonyms, 160
current taxonomic position, 171-73
numerical phenetic studies of, 162
Gordona aurantiaca
chemotaxonomic studies of, 166
current taxonomic position, 171-73
Gordona bronchialis
currently accepted name, 172
Gordona lentifragmenta
currently accepted name, 172
Gordona rosea
currently accepted name, 172

Gordona rubra
currently accepted name, 172
Gordona rubropertincta
currently accepted name, 172
Gordona terrae
currently accepted name, 172
Gout
use of griseofulvin in the treatment of, 303
Gramicidin S
inhibition of synthesis by inorganic phosphate, 352
synthesis of, 354
Green bacteria
comparison with cyanobacteria, 276
cytological and biochemical properties, 277
filamentous gliding, 281
green and brown sulfur bacteria, 280
historical basis of existing classification, 278
legitimate names of the higher taxa, 279
Griseofulvin, 301-3
mechanism of action, 303-4
structure, 302
Guanine plus cytosine DNA base composition
of chroococcaceans, 246
of heterocystous subgroups of cyanobacteria, 246
of marine enterobacteria, 43-47
of methanosarcina, 321
of Naegleria gruberi, 604
of oscillatorians, 246
of pleurocapsaleans, 246
of purple nonsulfur bacteria, 284
of purple sulfur bacteria, 284
of Sarcina ventriculi, 321
of Synechococcus, 238
use in taxonomic studies of luminescent bacteria, 552

H

Haemophilus
genetic duplications in, 490-91
involvement in opportunistic infections, 460
Haemophilus aphrophilus
involvement in opportunistic infections, 460
Haemophilus influenzae
involvement in opportunistic infections, 450, 459
Halo blight
of beans, 207
of oats, 207
Halobacterium halobium
proton circulation measurements in, 187
Haloprigin
organisms sensitive to, 304
properties, 304
structure, 302
Hamycin, 15, 26
Heart failure
opportunistic bacterial diseases associated with, 453
Helminthosporium sacchari
regulation of toxin production studies, 214
Hemochromatosis
opportunistic bacterial diseases associated with, 452
Hepatic failure
opportunistic bacterial diseases associated with, 452
Hepatitis B virus, 357-77
Dane particle DNA studies, 365-70
gene products, 358-65
model for replication of defective virions, 374
viral gene expression in infected liver, 370
Heptafungin A, 15
Heptamycin, 26
Heteroclones
selection of in Streptomyces, 490
Heterocyst, 249-55
differentiation, 250
formation of and NIF gene expression, 250
schematic diagram, 252
Heterocystous subgroups of cyanobacteria, 234-36
genome size, 246
guanine plus cytosine DNA base composition of, 246
Histoplasma
effect of polyene antibiotics on, 296
Histoplasma capsulatum
effect of 5-fluorocytosine on, 300
effect of nystatin on, 298
use of combined therapy for diseases caused by, 301
Hodgkin's disease
opportunistic infection involving, 449
Hormogonia, 229
Hydrogenomonas
DAHP synthase regulation in, 29
ribulose-1, 5-diphosphate carboxylase
inactivation in vivo, 141
Hyellaceae
taxonomic classification, 232
Hypercatabolism
opportunistic bacterial diseases associated with, 451
Hyperglobulinemia
opportunistic bacterial diseases associated with, 450
Hyphomicrobium
mixed culture studies of, 75

I

Immunoglobulin A deficiency
opportunistic bacterial diseases associated with, 450
Immunosuppressive treatment
in hospitals, 450
Inactivation of enzymes in vivo, 135-57
Influenza
opportunistic bacterial diseases associated with, 454
Inosine monophosphosphate dehydrogenase
inactivation in vivo, 148
Intrasporangium
taxonomic classification, 160-80
Intravenous cannulation
opportunistic bacterial diseases associated with, 453
Ion currents in eukaryotic cells
action potential and osmotic regulation, 192
electrical control of morpho genesis, 195-97
excitability and locomotor

behavior calcium effects, 192-94
of ions and clocks, 198
proton circulation of fungi and algae, 189-91
Ion currents in microorganisms
ancillary ion movements, 187
energy transduction, 184-86
novel functions, 188
pumps and carriers, 181-83
Ion transport
primary, 182
secondary, 182-83
Ischemia
opportunistic bacterial diseases associated with, 453
Isocitrate dehydrogenase
inactivation in vivo, 140
Isocitrate lyase
inactivation in vivo, 140
Isoprenoid quinones
use in classification of nocardioform bacteria, 167
Isopropylmalate synthase
inactivation in vivo, 140

J

Jensenia
current name and synonyms, 160
current taxonomic position, 171-73
numerical phenetic studies of, 162
Jensenia canicruria
currently accepted name, 172
Job's syndrome
opportunistic bacterial diseases associated with, 450

K

Kerosene
crude oil fractionation product, 381
Klebsiella
inactivation in vivo, 139, 150
nitrogen-fixation genetic studies of, 387
Klebsiella aerogenes
as food for amebae, 606
isocitrate dehydrogenase inactivation in vivo, 140
tandem duplication selection in, 480
taxonomic classification, 606
see also Aerobacter aerogenes
Klebsiella pneumoniae
involvement in opportunistic infections, 457
nitrogen-fixation genetic studies of, 387
taxonomic classification, 606

L

Lactic acid bacteria
isolated from the stomach of nonruminant animals, 113
Lactobacillus
chemostat studies of, 60
in gastrointestinal tract of babies, 120
involvement in opportunistic infections, 460
isolated from
the feces of nonruminant animals, 119
the large bowels of nonruminant animals, 117
the small bowel of nonruminant animals, 115
in stomach of nonruminant mammals, 113
Lactobacillus bifidus
current name and synonyms, 160
Lactobacillus casei
commensalism study of, 72
involvement in opportunistic infections, 460
Lactobacillus plantarum
commensalism study of, 72
involvement in opportunistic infections, 460
lagosin, 15
Lambda bacteriophage
tandem duplications in, 484-85
Late-onset IgG deficiencies
opportunistic bacterial diseases associated with, 450
Lazy leukocyte syndrome
opportunistic bacterial diseases associated with, 450
Leishmania donovanii
antagonism of host defenses by, 520
effect of polyene antibiotics on, 296
Leishmania mexicana
antagonism of host defenses by, 520
Leptospira
composition of outer envelope, 90-91
effect of sodium dodecyl sulfate on, 90
flagella, 91
isolation techniques for, 102
lipid composition, 93
motility model, 91
nutrition and growth requirements, 102
pathogenic members, 100
Leptospira interrogans
complexes involving, 94
Leptospirosis, 100
Leptospiruria
duration, 100
Leptothrichia buccalis
current name and synonyms, 160
Leptothrichia dentium
current name and synonyms, 160
Leucocidins, 521-22
Leucomycin
synthesis inhibition by cerulenin, 23
Leukemia
acute lymphocytic
opportunistic bacterial diseases associated with, 451
acute myelogenous
opportunistic bacterial diseases associated with, 451
Levinea malonatica
involvement in opportunistic infections, 458
Levorin
precursors, 16-17
regulation of synthesis, 25
Lipids
of cyanobacterial membrane, 243
of nocardiform bacteria, 163-68
Listeria monocytogenes
antagonism of host defenses by, 515, 528
involvement in opportunistic

infections, 460
Louse-borne fever, 99
Lubricant
crude oil fractionation product, 381
Lucensomycin, 15-18
chemical structure, 18
precursors, 16
Lucibacterium
relation to Beneckea, 57
Lucibacterium harveyi
currently used and proposed epithets, 554
guanine plus cytosine DNA base composition of, 554
Luciferase
inhibition of synthesis of, 570
photoexcitable, 568
reaction mechanism, 564-67
reaction pathway and intermediates, 561-64
structure and chemistry, 557-60
substrates and stoichiometry, 560
Luminescence in bacteria, 550-95
associated acid production in, 581-82
color of light emitted by, 582-84
ecological implications, 575-76
effect of anaesthetics on, 579
energetics of, 580-81
inhibitors, 578-79
mutants affecting, 565, 584-88
NADH:FMN-coupled assay, 567-68
pathway and metabolism, 576-77
postulated reaction mechanism, 566
quantum yield, 567-68
Luminous bacteria
in luminous organ of fish, 56
marine enterobacteria, 40, 55-56
Lymphoproliferative disorders
opportunistic bacterial diseases associated with, 451
Lymphosarcoma
opportunistic bacterial diseases associated with, 451
Lysine decarboxylase
inactivation in vivo, 140

M

Macroglobulinemia
opportunistic bacterial diseases associated with, 451
Magnamycin
precursors, 17
Magnesium
sodium sparing in marine enterobacteria, 41
Malate dehydrogenase
association with sulfate-reducing bacteria, 328-29
inactivation in vivo, 140-42
Malnutrition
opportunistic bacterials diseases associated with, 452
Maltose permease
inactivation in vivo, 140
Maridomycin, 17
Marine enterobacteria
characteristics and comparative evolution, 39-61
numerical analysis of phenotypic similarities, 44
source of specific strains, 42
Mediocidin, 397-402
griseofulvin used in effective treatment of disease caused by, 301
structure, 302
Megasphaera
isolated from the feces of nonruminant animals, 119
Merodiploidy, 497-98
Methane biogenesis, 309-41
by anaerobic sludge digestors, 336-37
in animal digestive systems, 336
distribution of freshwater sediments, 327-33
distribution of methane in marine and estuarine sediments, 332-33
electron transfer diagram, 326
factor affecting in nature, 328
fate of methane in marine sediments, 334-35
in flooded soils, 335-36
microbiology of in marine and estuarine sediments, 333-34
substrates, 330-31
Methanobacillus kuzneceovii
characteristics, 319
electron transfer in, 325
enzymatic studies of methane biogenesis in, 323-24
Methanobacillus omelianskii
enzymatic studies of methane biogenesis in, 323
interspecies transfer in, 312-13
similarity with Methanobacillus kuzneceovii, 320
taxonomic classification, 25
Methanobacterium
enzymatic studies of methane biogenesis in, 323
fine structure studies of, 322
nutrient requirements, 322-23
Methanobacterium arbophilicum
characteristics, 319
nutrient requirements, 323
Methanobacterium formicum
benzoate enrichment, 318
enzymatic studies of methane biogenesis in, 324
fine structure studies of, 322
Methanobacterium ruminantium
coculturing with Ruminococcus flavefaciens, 315
coupled growth with the S organism, 312-14
electron transfer in, 325
enzymatic studies of methane biogenesis in, 323-25
nutrient requirements, 322
Methanobacterium söhngenii
methanogenesis studies involving, 318
Methanobacterium thermoautotrophicum
characteristics, 319
enzymatic studies of methane biogenesis in, 324
fine structure studies of, 322
isotope fractionation by, 331
methanogenesis by, 317
Methanosarcina
electron micrograph, 321
fine structure studies of, 320
Methanosarcina barkeri

acetate enrichment with, 318
association with sulfate-reducing bacteria, 330
enzymatic studies of methane biogenesis in, 324
fine structure studies of, 320-22
isotope fractionation by, 331
methanogenesis by, 317-20
methanogenesis tracer studies in, 317
nutrient requirements, 323
Methanosarcina mathanica
methanogenesis studies of, 317
Methanospirillum hungatii
benzoate enrichment of, 318
characteristics, 319
fine structure studies of, 322
nutrient requirements, 323
Methyl malonyl-CoA:pyruvate carboxyltransferase
in synthesis of polifungin, 22
Miconazole
properties, 305
Microbacterium flavum
numerical phenetic studies of, 162
Microbial ecology of the gastrointestinal tract
generation times of resident bacteria, 127
influential conditions imposed by the animal, 122
of the large bowel, 116
of the small bowel, 115
of the stomach and esophagus, 112-14
succession in babies, 119-21
Microbispora
chemotaxonomic studies of, 165, 168
Microcyclus aquaticus
fine structure studies of, 320
Microcystis
cell envelope of, 239
Micromonospora
DAHP synthase regulation in, 30
Micromonospora rubra
current name and synonyms, 160
Micropolyspora
current taxonomic position, 173
taxonomic classification, 160-80
Micropolyspora brevicatena
chemotaxonomic studies of, 165
current taxonomic position, 173
distribution of chemical characters in, 164
Micropolyspora faeni
chemotaxonomic studies of, 165-67
current taxonomic position, 173
distribution of chemical characteristics, 164
Micropolyspora fascifera
chemotaxonomic studies of, 165
current taxonomic position, 173
serotaxonomic studies of, 164
Microsporum
effect of polyene antibiotics on, 296
Microsporum andouinii
tolnaftate sensitivity of, 304
Microsporum canis
tolnaftate sensitivity of, 304
Microsporum gypseum
effect of griseofulvin on, 303
sensitivity to tolnaftate, 304
Mitochondria
proton circulation measurements in, 187
Mixotricha paradoxa
in association with spirochetes, 95
Moldcidin B, 15
Monocentris japonica
luminescent symbionts of, 553-54
luminosity, 56
Monosporium
haloprigin sensitivity of, 304
Moon blindness, 101
Moraxella
involvement in opportunistic infections, 460
Moraxella lacunata
involvement in opportunistic infections, 460
Moraxella liquefaciens
involvement in opportunistic infections, 460
Moraxella nonliquefaciens
involvement in opportunistic infections, 460
Multiple myeloma
opportunistic bacterial diseases associated with, 451
Mutualism, 67, 73-75
Mycobacterium
chemotaxonomic studies of, 163-68
distribution of chemical characters in, 164
DNA analysis and genetic study of, 168-69
involvement in opportunistic infections, 461
numerical phenetic studies of, 161
serotaxonomic studies of, 169-70
taxonomic classification, 160-80
Mycobacterium avium
antagonism of host defenses by, 515
Mycobacterium fortuitum
involvement in opportunistic infections, 461
Mycobacterium intracellulare
involvement in opportunistic infections, 461
Mycobacterium kansasii
involvement in opportunistic infections, 461
Mycobacterium leprae
antagonism of host defenses, by, 515
Mycobacterium lepraemurium
antagonism of host defenses by, 515
Mycobacterium microti
antagonism of host defenses by, 515-16
Mycobacterium paratuberculosis
chemotaxonomic studies of, 167
Mycobacterium rhodochrous
current name and synonyms, 160
numerical phenetic studies of, 162
Mycobacterium tuberculosis
antagonism of host defenses by, 515-16
cord factor, 514
involvement in opportunistic

infections, 452
involvement in perturbation of phagolysosome formation, 524
sulfatides of, 524
Mycoheptin, 15
Mycoplasma
toxins of, 219
Mycoplasma pneumoniae
involvement in opportunistic infections, 461
Mycosamine, 30-31
Mycoses
treatment, 14
Mycoticin A, B, 15-19
chemical structure, 19
precursors, 17
Myelofibrosis
opportunistic bacterial diseases associated with, 451
Myelosclerosis
opportunistic bacterial diseases associated with, 451
Myxobacteria
exoenzymes of, 70
Myxococcus xanthus
aspartokinase
inactivation in vivo, 138
isocitrate lyase
inactivation in vivo, 140
Myxosarcina
taxonomic classification, 232-33

N

Naeglaria
effect of polyene antibiotics on, 296
Naegleria fowleri
isolation, 606
Naegleria gruberi, 597-629
amebae, 600
control of differentiation, 607-11
cultivation, 606
differentiation to flagellates, 601
encystment and excystment, 601
events during differentiation, 612-26
genetic analysis, 611
genome, 604
life cycle, 599
phylogeny, 603
reversibility of differentiation in, 612
sequence of flagella assembly in, 613-14
sexual cycle research in, 611
strains, 605-6
taxonomic classification, 602-3
Nalidixic acid
in isolation of leptospires, 102
Nebramycin
inhibition of synthesis by inorganic phosphate, 352
Neisseria meningitidis
involvement in opportunistic infections, 450
Neisseria mucosa
involvement in opportunistic infections, 462
Neisseria perflava
involvement in opportunistic infections, 462
Neisseria subflava
involvement in opportunistic infections, 462
Neomycin
catabolite regulation of synthesis of, 351
inhibition of synthesis by inorganic phosphate, 352
in isolation of leptospires, 102
Neonatal period
opportunistic bacterial diseases associated with, 451
Nephrotic syndrome
opportunistic bacterial diseases associated with 452
Neurospora crassa
aromatic pathway, 27
dual proton circulation in, 191
glucose transport system II
inactivation in vivo, 139
glycerol kinase
inactivation in vivo, 140
microelectrode measurements of membrane potenials in, 189-90
nitrate reductase
inactivation in vivo, 141
photocarotenogenesis in, 539
proton circulation measurements in, 187
pyruvate dehydrogenase of
inactivation in vivo, 141, 145
Neutropenia
opportunistic bacterial diseases associated with, 450
Nezelof-Allibone syndrome
opportunistic bacterial diseases associated with, 450
Nezumia cequalis
luminescent symbiotic bacteria of, 554
Nezumia stelgidolepic
luminescent symbiotic bacteria of, 554
NIF genes
in cyanobacteria, 250
Nigrospora
haloprigin sensitivity of, 304
Nitella
proton pump of, 190-92
Nitella translucens
proton circulation measurements in, 187
Nitrate reductase
in cyanobacteria, 264
inactivation in vivo, 141
missing in mutant Synechococcus species, 264
Nitrobacter
developmental cycle, 231
Nitrogen-fixation
in cyanobacteria, 250, 264-65
inactivation in vivo, 141
Nocardia
chemotaxonomic studies of, 166-68
current taxonomic position, 171-73
DNA analysis and genetic study of, 168-69
involvement in opportunistic infections, 462
petroleum degradation mechanism in, 389
production of extracellular emulsifying agents by, 384
serotaxonomic studies of, 164, 169-70
taxonomic classification, 159-80
type species, 173-74
Nocardia aerocolonigenes
current taxonomic position, 173
Nocardia amarae
current taxonomic position, 173

numerical phenetic studies of, 161
Nocardia asteroides
chemotaxonomic studies of, 163-68
current taxonomic positions, 173
disease caused by, 174
DNA analysis and genetic study of, 169
numerical phenetic studies of, 161
as primary agent of actinomycete mycetoma, 173-74
serotaxonomic studies of, 170
as type species of Nocardia, 173-74
Nocardia autotrophica
current taxonomic position, 173
Nocardia brasiliensis
chemotaxonomic studies of, 167
current taxonomic position, 173
disease caused by, 174
involvement in opportunistic infections, 462
numerical phenetic studies of, 161
as primary agent of actinomycete mycetoma, 174
serotaxonomic studies of, 170
Nocardia calcarea
current taxonomic position, 171-73
currently accepted name, 172
Nocardia carnea
current taxonomic position, 173
numerical phenetic studies of, 173
Nocardia caviae
chemotaxonomic studies of, 163, 167
current taxonomic position, 173
disease caused by, 174
involvement in opportunistic infections, 462
numerical phenetic studies of, 161
as primary agent of actinomycete mycetoma, 174
serotaxonomic studies of, 170
Nocardia cellulans
involvement in opportunistic infections, 452, 462
numerical phenetic studies of, 162
Nocardia coeliaca
chemotaxonomic studies of, 165-66
current taxonomic position, 173
distribution of chemical characters in, 164
Nocardia corallina
chemotaxonomic studies of, 168
current taxonomic position, 171-73
DNA analysis and genetic study of, 169
Nocardia dassonvillei
current name and synonyms, 160
numerical phenetic studies of, 162
Nocardia dentocariosus
current name and synonyms, 160
distribution of chemical characters in, 164
Nocardia erythropolis
current taxonomic position, 171-73
currently accepted name, 172
DNA analysis and genetic study of, 169
Nocardia farcinica
chemotaxonomic studies of, 167
numerical phenetic studies of, 161
serotaxonomic studies of, 170
Nocardia gardneri
chemotaxonomic studies of, 165
current taxonomic position, 173
Nocardia globerula
current taxonomic position, 171-73
currently accepted name, 172
Nocardia hydrocarboxydans
current taxonomic position, 173
Nocardia kirovani
chemotaxonomic studies of, 163
current taxonomic position, 171-73
Nocardia leishmanii
chemotaxonomic studies of, 165-66
current taxonomic position, 173
Nocardia lurida
current taxonomic position, 173
Nocardia madurae
current name and synonyms, 160
numerical phenetic studies of, 162
Nocardia mediterranei
chemotaxonomic studies of, 165
regulation of rifamycin synthesis in, 350
Nocardia opaca
current taxonomic position, 171-73
Nocardia orientalis
current taxonomic position, 173
Nocardia otitidis-caviarum
numerical phenetic studies of, 161
Nocardia pellegrino
currently accepted name, 172
Nocardia pelletieri
current name and synonyms, 160
numerical phenetic studies of, 162
Nocardia petroleophila
current taxonomic position, 173
Nocardia polychromogenes
chemotaxonomic studies of, 167
current taxonomic position, 173
Nocardia restrictas
current taxonomic position, 171-73
currently accepted name, 172
Nocardia rhodochrous
chemotaxonomic studies of, 168
Nocardia rubra
current taxonomic position, 171-73
currently accepted name, 172
DNA analysis and genetic study of, 167
Nocardia rubropertincta

current taxonomic position, 171-73
Nocardia rugosa
current taxonomic position, 173
Nocardia salivae
current name and synonyms, 160
numerical phenetic studies of, 162
Nocardia salmonicida
current taxonomic position, 173
numerical phenetic studies of, 161
Nocardia salmonicolor
current taxonomic position, 171-73
Nocardia saturnea
current taxonomic position, 173
Nocardia sensu stricto
chemotaxonomic studies of, 163-69
DNA analysis and genetic study of, 168-69
numerical phenetic studies of, 161, 162
serotaxonomic studies of, 169-70
Nocardia tenuis
current taxonomic position, 173
Nocardia transvalensis
current taxonomic position, 173
numerical phenetic studies of, 161
Nocardia turbata
current name and synonyms, 160
numerical phenetic studies of, 162
Nocardia vaccinii
current taxonomic position, 173
numerical phenetic studies of, 161
Nocardioform bacteria, 159-
taxonomy, 161-70
chemotaxonomic studies, 162-68
DNA analysis and genetic studies, 168-69
numerical phenetic studies, 161
occurrence, distribution, and parasitism of, 174-75
serology, 169
Nocardioides
DNA analysis and genetic study of, 169
taxonomic classification, 160-61
Nocardiopsis
current taxonomic position, 171-73
distribution of chemical characters in, 164
earlier designations and synonyms, 160
taxonomic classification, 160-80
Nocobactins and related compounds
use in classification of nocardioform bacteria, 167-68
Nostoc
glycogen granules from, 237
taxonomic classification, 234-35
Nostocaceae
taxonomic classification, 232
Nostocacean
taxonomic classification, 232
Nostocales
taxonomic classification, 232
Nucleic acid hybridization studies
of marine enterobacteria, 43-47
use in taxonomic study of luminescent bacteria, 552-56
Nystatin
chemical structure, 18
precursors, 17, 31
structure, 293

O

Obligate photoautotrophy, 261
Odontomyces
current name and synonyms, 160
Oerskovia
chemotaxonomic studies of, 163-66
current taxonomic position, 170-73
distribution of chemical characters in, 164
DNA analysis and genetic study of, 169
earlier designations and synonyms, 160
numerical phenetic studies of, 162
taxonomic classification, 160-80
Oerskovia turbata
chemotaxonomic studies of, 165-67
involvement in opportunistic infections, 462
Oerskovia xanthineolytica
numerical phenetic studies of, 162
Oil
biodegradation, 386-88
chemical composition of crude oil, 380
microbiological problems associated with oil-tanker operations, 390-93
water-soluble components, 381
Opisthoproctus grimaldi
luminescent symbiotic bacteria of, 554-55
Opisthoproctus soleatus
luminescent symbiotic bacteria of, 554
Opportunistic bacteria
in human diseases, 448-71
Ornithine transcarbamylase
inactivation in vivo, 141
Ornithodoros (tick)
role in endemic relapsing fever, 99-100
Ornithodorus moubata
role in East African relapsing fever, 100
Oscillatoria
taxonomic classification, 233
Oscillatoria animalis
gliding motility, 240-41
Oscillatoria limnetica
facultative anoxygenic photosynthesis in, 263
Oscillatoria princeps
gliding motility, 240
Oscillatoria redekei
characteristics, 234
Oscillatoriaceae
taxonomic classification, 232
Oscillatorian
genome size, 246
guanine plus cytosine DNA base composition of, 246

Oscillatorian cyanobacteria, 233-34

P

P-2 bacteriophage
genetic duplications in, 500-1
PABA synthase, 27
Paneth cells
influence on intestinal flora, 124
Paracoccus denitrificans
proton circulation measurements in, 187
Paramecium
electrical control of behavior, 192-95
Paramecium aurelia
encystment, 79
Parasitism, 79-82
Pasteurella
synthesis of unique TDP sugars in, 32
Pasteurella multocida
involvement in opportunistic infections, 463
PBP, 244
Pediculus humanus humanus
role in epidemic relapsing fever, 99
Pelochromatium roseum
taxonomic classification, 281
Pelodictyon
taxonomic classification, 280
Pelodictyon clathratiforme
taxonomic classification, 281
Pelodictyon phaeum
taxonomic classification, 281
Pelvetia
current pattern, 196, 199
differentiation, 195
Penicillin
catabolite regulation of synthesis of, 351
pathway of synthesis, 349
regulation of synthesis of, 348
Penicillium
effect of polyene antibiotics on, 296
haloprigin sensitivity of, 304
production of griseofulvin by, 301
Penicillium chrysogenum
regulation of penicillin synthesis in, 348-49
Penicillum notatum
tolnaftate sensitivity of, 304
Pentamycin, 15
Peptococcus
isolated from the feces of nonruminant animals, 110
Peptostreptococcus
isolated from
the feces of nonruminant animals, 119
the stomach of nonruminant animals, 113
Periodontal disease
etiologic role of spirochetes, 97
Perimycin, 15, 26-30
Perosamine, 30-31
Peroxidase
paradox, 513-14
Petroleum-degrading organism definition, 393
Phagocyte lysosomes
antagonism of host defenses by microorganisms, 514-22
Chlamydia and Rickettsia, 516
miscellaneous parasitic agents, 520
mycobacteria, 514
streptococci, 521
Toxoplasma and Besnoitia, 517
inflammatory processes and membrane fusion, 522
microbicidal mechanisms in, 510-14
peroxidase paradox, 510-14
perturbation of phagolysome formation, 523-28
Phaseotoxins
mode of action, 216-17
properties, 216
structure, 217
Phenylmethysulfonyl fluoride (PMSF)
use in enzyme inactivation studies, 149
Phoma tracheiphila
toxic glycopeptide from, 212
Phosphoenolpyruvate carboxykinase
inactivation in vivo, 141
in the synthesis of polyene macrolides, 22
Phosphomonesterase
inactivation in vivo, 141
Phosphoribulokinase
from cyanobacteria, 258-59
Phosphotransferase ATP:acetate
in polyene macrolide synthesis, 20
Photobacterium
characteristics, 555
genus properties, 54-55
homology groups, 55-56
as light organ symbionts, 550
specific hosts with light organ, 555
taxonomy, 552
Photobacterium angustum
characteristics, 553
electron micrograph, 49
source, 42
Photobacterium belozerski
characteristics, 553
currently used and proposed epithets, 554
guanine plus cytosine DNA base composition of, 554
luminescence in, 553
Photobacterium fischeri
the bioluminescence-associated acid production in, 582
catabolite repression of synthesis of the luminescence system of, 575
characteristics, 552-55
characteristics of the luciferase from, 558-69
currently used and proposed epithets, 554
DNA homology group of, 55-56
electron micrograph, 49
energetics of bioluminescence in, 581
factors influencing pyruvate excretion, 582
growth media for, 574
luciferase autoinducer from, 571
luminescent symbiosis in, 56
photoexcitable luciferase of, 569-70
sodium requirement, 41
yellow light-emitting strain of, 582-84
Photobacterium leignathi
the bioluminescence-associ-

ated acid production in, 581
characteristics, 553
characteristics of the luciferase from, 558-60
currently used and proposed epithets, 554
distinct symbiotic relationship with, 582
energetics of bioluminescence in, 581
growth media for, 574
guanine plus cytosine DNA base composition of, 554
luminescent symbiosis in, 56
luminescent system synthesis autoinduction in, 572
poly-β-hydroxybutyrate-like granules in, 557
source, 42
wavelength of luminescent light from, 582
Photobacterium maudapamensis
currently used and proposed epithets, 554
guanine plus cytosine DNA base composition of, 554
Photobacterium phosphoreum
blue-shifted luminescence color of, 582
catabolite repression of synthesis of the luminescence system of, 575
characteristic of the luciferase from, 560-70
characteristics, 553
currently used and proposed epithets, 554
DNA homology group, 55
energetics of bioluminescence, 580
enrichment, 55
growth media, 574
guanine plus cytosine DNA base composition of, 554
host dependence, 557
isolation of the bioluminescence aldehyde from, 577
luminescent symbiosis, 56
luminescent system synthesis autoinduction in, 572
mutants in the luminescent system of, 584, 588
mutants incapable of making the bioluminescence aldehyde, 578
source, 42
wavelength of luminescent light from, 582
Photobacterium splendida
see Beneckea splendida
Photosynthesis
cyanobacterial apparatus, 241-46
cyanobacterial faculatative anoxygenic photosynthesis, 263
of green and purple bacteria, 275-90
pathways of light and dark metabolism in cyanobacteria, 259
Phycobilisome, 245
Phycomyes
behavioral genetics, 535-47
the bioluminescence-associated acid production in, 581-82
Phycomyces blakesleeanus
schematic life cycle, 536
Physarum
DNA comparative analysis of, 604
Phytotoxins, 205-24
blights and necrosis, 208
chlorosis, 207-8
hypersensitive response, 209
local necrosis, 208
overgrowths, 208-9
symptoms and assay, 206-8
water soaking, 208
wilting, 207
Pimaricin, 15, 292-93, 297
effect on Candida albicans, 297
use, 292
Pinta, 97
Pityrosporum orbiculare
tolnaftate sensitivity of, 304
Plectonema boryanum
synthesis of nitrogenase in the light by, 265
Plesiomonas shigelloids
involvement in opportunistic infections, 463
Pleurocapsa
taxonomic classification, 232-33
Pleurocapsalean cyanobacteria, 231-33
genome size, 246
guanine plus cytosine DNA base composition of, 246
Pleurocapsales
taxonomic classification, 232
Polar aromatics
crude oil fractionation product, 381
Polifungin, 15-26
chemical structure, 18
Poly-β-hydroxybutyrate
in Beneckea, 47, 55
Polyene macrolide antibiotics, 13-38, 292-97
effect of fatty acids on, 25
list of, 15
mode of action, 14
pathway of, 21-33
aromatic pathway of, 29
regulation of, 22
Polyketide pathway, 17-20
Porphyridium
study of 16S RNA from, 248
Potassium
transport, 188
Predator-prey studies, 68-79
Primaricin, 17-18
chemical structure, 18
precursors, 17
Promicromonospora
DNA analysis and genetic study of, 169
taxonomic classification, 160-80
Propionibacterium
involvement in opportunistic infections, 447
isolated from
the feces of nonruminant animals, 119
the large bowels of nonruminant animals, 113
Propionibacterium acnes
involvement in opportunistic infections, 456
Propionibacterium shermanii
chemotaxonomic studies of, 166
commensalism, 72
Propionyl-CoA synthase
in polyene macrolide synthesis, 20
Prostatic hypertrophy
treatment, 15
Prosthecochloris aestuarii
as syntropic member of Chloropseudomonas ethylica, 280
Prosthecochloris phaeoastdroidea
taxonomic classification, 281

Prosthetic heart valves
opportunistic bacterial diseases associated with, 453
Protein synthesis factor IF-3
inactivation in vivo, 141
Proteus
aspartokinase regulation in, 40
swarming, 51
Proteus mirabilis
involvement in opportunistic infections, 457
R-factor transitioning in, 482-83
Proteus rettgeri
in hospitals, 450
Proteus vulgaris
syntropism study of, 74
Protocooperation, 73-75
Providencia stuartii
in hospitals, 450
involvement in opportunistic infections, 457-58
Pseudanabaena
gliding motility, 240
taxonomic classification, 233
thylakoid arrangement in, 237
trichome of, 234
Pseudomonas
in hospitals, 450
induction of alkane degradation enzymes in, 390
involvement in opportunistic infections, 463
mixed culture studies, 75
petroleum degradation mechanism in, 389
wilting diseases of, 207
Pseudomonas aeruginosa
hydrocarbon uptake by, 385
induction of alkane degradation enzymes in, 390
involvement in opportunistic infections, 448, 463-64
production of extracellular emulsifying agents by, 384-85
proteinaceous-enzymatic toxin from, 219-20
toxin from, 206
Pseudomonas aureofaciens
regulation of pyrrolnitrin synthesis in, 348
Pseudomonas cepacia
involvement in opportunistic infections, 464
Pseudomonas coronafaciens
chlorosis produced by, 207
Pseudomonas fluorescens
involvement in opportunistic infections, 464
Pseudomonas glycinea
local necrosis produced by, 208
toxin from, 216
Pseudomonas maltophila
involvement in opportunistic infections, 464
Pseudomonas mors-prunorum
toxin from, 219
Pseudomonas natriegens
pyruvate excretion by, 582
Pseudomonas phaseolicola
chlorosis produced by, 207
nontoxin-producing mutant of, 221
phaseotoxin from, 216-17
Pseudomonas polycolor
tobacco disease caused by, 220
Pseudomonas pseudomallei
involvement in opportunistic infections, 464
Pseudomonas putida
induction of alkane degradation enzymes in, 390
involvement in opportunistic infections, 464
mechanism of petroleum degradation in, 388
petroleum-degrading plasmids in, 387
Pseudomonas savastanoi
disease cause by, 209
Pseudomonas solanacearum
hypersensitive response study, 209
Pseudomonas syringae
diseases caused by, 208
toxin from, 219
Pseudomonas tabaci
chlorosis produced by, 207
tabtoxin from, 209-10
Pseudomonas tomato
toxin from, 216
Pseudonocardia
distribution of chemical characters in, 164
Pulmonary alveolar proteinosis
opportunistic bacterial diseases associated with, 453
Purple bacteria
comparison with cyanobacteria, 276
cytological and biochemical properties, 277
historical basis of existing classification, 278
legitimate names of the higher taxa, 279
purple nonsulfur bacteria
cell envelope lipopolysaccharide, 284-85
morphogical and structural diversity, 284
ribosomal protein patterns and genetic relatedness, 286
purple sulfur bacteria, 283
chemostat studies of, 70
determinative criteria, 283
poorly studied genera and species, 284
Pyrrolnitrin
regulation of synthesis of, 348
Pyruvate dehydrogenase
inactivation in vivo, 141
in polyene macrolide synthesis, 20

R

R-factors
transitioning, 482-83
Recurrent uvlitis, 101
Relapsing fever
East African
causal agent, 100
endemic
causal agent, 100
epidemic
causal agent, 99
Renal failure
opportunistic bacterial diseases associated with, 452
Reticulum cell sarcoma
opportunistic bacterial diseases associated with, 451
Rheumatoid arthritis
opportunistic bacterial diseases associated with, 451
Rhizobitoxine, 218-19
Rhizobium
nitrogen-fixation genetic studies of, 387
Rhizobium japonicum
chlorosis produced by, 207
toxin from, 219

Rhodococcus
chemotaxonomic studies of, 163-67
composition of genus, 161-62
current taxonomic position, 170-73
distribution of chemical characters in, 164
DNA analysis and genetic study of, 168-69
earlier designations and synonyms, 160
numerical phenetic studies of, 162
serotaxonomic studies of, 169-70
taxonomic classification, 160-80
Rhodococcus bronchialis
chemotaxonomic studies, 166-67
current taxonomic position, 172
Rhodococcus coprophilus
chemotaxonomic studies of, 165-67
current taxonomic position, 172-73
previous designation, 172
selective medium for, 175
Rhodococcus corallinus
chemotaxonomic studies of, 167
current taxonomic position, 172-73
previous designation, 172
Rhodococcus equi
chemotaxonomic studies of, 165-66
current taxonomic position, 172
previous designation, 172-73
Rhodococcus erythropolis
chemotaxonomic studies of, 165-67
current taxonomic position, 172-73
DNA analysis and genetic study of, 169
previous designation, 172
Rhodococcus rhodnii
chemotaxonomic studies of, 165
current taxonomic position, 172-73
previous designation, 172
Rhodococcus rhodochrous
chemotaxonomic studies of, 165-67
current taxonomic position, 172-73
DNA analysis and genetic study of, 169
numerical phenetic studies of, 162
previous designation, 172
Rhodococcus rubropertinctus
chemotaxonomic studies of, 165-67
current taxonomic position, 172-73
previous designation, 172
Rhodococcus rubrus
chemotaxonomic studies of, 165-67
current taxonomic position, 172-73
previous designation, 172
Rhodococcus terrae
chemotaxonomic studies of, 166
current taxonomic position, 172-73
previous designation, 172
Rhodocyclus
taxonomic classification, 285
Rhodocyclus purpureus
taxonomic classification, 284
Rhodomicrobium
DAHP synthase regulation in, 29
taxonomic classification, 279, 285
Rhodopseudomonas
developmental cycle, 231
ribosomal protein analysis of, 287
taxonomic classification, 285
Rhodopseudomonas capsulata
cell envelope composition of, 286
taxonomic classification, 278-85
Rhodopseudomonas gelatinosa
citrate lyase
inactivation in vivo, 138-42
taxonomic classification, 278-85
Rhodopseudomonas globiformis
taxonomic classification, 284-85
Rhodopseudomonas palustris
cell envelope composition of, 286
taxonomic classification, 278-85
Rhodopseudomonas spheroides
δ-aminolevulinic acid synthetase
inactivation in vivo, 138
ribosomal protein analysis of, 287
taxonomic classification, 278-85
Rhodopseudomonas sulfidophila
taxonomic classification, 283-85
Rhodopseudomonas sulfoviridis
taxonomic classification, 283-85
Rhodopseudomonas viridis
ribosomal protein analysis of, 286
taxonomic classification, 283-85
Rhodospirillaceae
cell envelope composition of, 286
taxonomic classification, 824-85
Rhodospirillum
taxonomic classification, 279-85
Rhodospirillum acidophila
taxonomic classification, 285
Rhodospirillum fulvum
ribosomal protein analysis of, 287
taxonomic classification, 285
Rhodospirillum molischianum
ribosomal protein analysis of, 287
taxonomic classification, 285
Rhodospirillum photometricum
ribosomal protein analysis of, 287
taxonomic classification, 285
Rhodospirillum rubrum
nitrogen-fixing activity
inactivation in vivo, 141
ribosomal protein analysis of, 287
Rhodospirillum tenue
ribosomal protein analysis of, 287
taxonomic classification, 285
Rhodotorula
electrogenic proton extrusion by, 190

Riboflavin
as a photoreceptor, 195
Ribonucleic acid
from cyanobacteria, 247-48
Ribulose-1, 5-diphosphate carboxylase
from cyanobacteria, 258-60
inactivation in vivo, 141
Rickettsia
antagonism of host defenses by, 516-17
Rickettsia mooseri
antagonism of host defenses by, 517
Rifampin
effect on Bacillus subtilis, 149
pathway of synthesis of, 350
use in combined antifungal therapy, 301
use in enzyme inactivation studies, 149
Rifamycin
synthesis, 28
Rimocidin, 15
Rivularian
taxonomic classification, 232
Rothia
chemotaxonomic studies of, 163-65
current taxonomic position, 170-73
distribution of chemical characters in, 164
earlier designations and synonyms, 160
numerical phenetic studies of, 162
taxonomic classification, 160-80
Rothia dentocariosa
chemotaxonomic studies of, 167
Ruminococcus
isolated from the feces of nonruminant animals, 119
Ruminococcus albus
involvement in intergeneric hydrogen transfer, 316
Ruminococcus flavefaciens
coculturing with Methanobacter ruminantium, 315

S

Saccharomonospora
current taxonomic position, 173
distribution of chemical characters in, 164
Saccharomyces
fructose biphosphatase
inactivation in vivo, 138
malate dehydrogenase
inactivation in vivo, 140
ornithine transcarbamylase
inactivation in vivo, 141
Saccharomyces carlsbergenesis
isolated from
the feces of nonruminant animals, 119
the large bowels of nonruminant animals, 117
maltose permease
inactivation in vivo, 140
Saccharomyces cerevisiae
commensalism study of, 72
fructose-1, 6-bisphosphatase
inactivation in vivo, 142, 150
galactozymase
inactivation in vivo, 138
α-glucosidase
inactivation in vivo, 139
glutamate dehydrogenase
NAD dependent
inactivation in vivo, 139
α-isopropylmalate synthase
inactivation in vivo, 140
malate dehydrogenase
inactivation in vivo, 142-50
maltose permease
inactivation in vivo, 140, 150
ornithine transcarbamylase
inactivation in vivo, 141
phosphoenolpyruvate carboxykinase
inactivation in vivo, 141-51
use of combined therapy for diseases caused by, 301
Saccharopolyspora
chemotaxonomic studies of, 163
current taxonomic position, 173
distribution of chemical characters in, 164
taxonomic classification, 160-80
Salmonella
aspartokinase regulation in, 40
characterization of structure and function of the flagella of, 397-414
distribution of flagellar genes compared with that of E. coli, 404
glutamine synthetase
inactivation in vivo, 139
involvement in opportunistic infections, 458-59
lipopolysaccharide sugar amine in, 31
synthesis of unique TDP sugars in, 32
Salmonella typhimurium
detection of genetic duplication in, 488-505
involvement in opportunistic infections, 458
isocitrate dehydrogenase
inactivation in vivo, 140
tandem duplication selections in, 481
Sapropelische Lebewelt
cyanobacteria in, 263
Sarcina
ribosomal proteins compared with those from E. coli, 286
Sarcina ventriculi
fine structure studies of, 321
guanine plus cytosine base composition of, 321
Sarcoidosis
opportunistic bacterial diseases associated with, 451
Saturates
crude oil fractionation product, 381
Sch 16656, 26
Schistosoma hematobium
involvement in opportunistic infections, 459
Schistosoma mansonii
involvement in opportunistic infections, 459
Schizosaccharomyces pombe
malate dehydrogenase
inactivation in vivo, 140
Scytonemataceae
taxonomic classification, 232
Secondary metabolism
carbon catabolite regulation of, 350-51
energy charge regulation of, 352
feedback regulation in, 348-50
induction, 345-48

nitrogen catabolite regulation of, 351
trophosphase-idiophase relationship of, 353
Selenomonas ruminantium
coculture production of methane by, 316
Serology
in Epstein-Barr virus research, 423-26
of nocardioform bacteria, 169-70
Serratia
aspartokinase regulation in, 40
Serratia marcescens
isocitrate dehydrogenase inactivation in vivo, 140
Shigella
glutamine synthetase inactivation in vivo, 139
Shigella dysenteriae
involvement in opportunistic infections, 458
Shigella flexneri
involvement in opportunistic infections, 458
Short-limbed dwarfism
opportunistic bacterial diseases associated with, 450
Sickle cell anemia
opportunistic bacterial diseases associated with, 452
Siomycin
catabolite regulation of synthesis of, 351
Sodium
requirements in marine enterobacteria, 41-42
transport, 187-88
Sphagemacrurus hirundo
luminescent symbiotic bacteria of, 554
Spirillum
involvement in opportunistic infections, 464
Spirillum minus
involvement in opportunistic infections, 464
Spirochaeta
cytoplasmic membrane of, 91
cytoplasmic tubules of, 92
distribution, 94
fermentation end products, 102
flagella of, 91
isolation techniques for, 102
lipid composition of, 93
in mammalian gastrointestinal tracts, 117
peptidoglycan layer of, 91-92
Spirochaeta aurantia
distribution, 94
nutrition and growth requirements, 101
Spirochaeta halophila
distribution, 94
nutrition and growth requirements, 101
Spirochaeta litoralis
nutrition and growth requirements, 101
Spirochaeta plicatilis
nutrition and growth requirements, 101
Spirochaeta stenostrepta
nutrition and growth requirements, 101
Spirochaeta zuelzerae
nutrition and growth requirements, 101
Spirochetes, 89-106
cytoplasmic membrane of, 91
cytoplasmic tubules of, 92
distribution, 94
etiologic role in acute necrotizing ulcerative gingivitis, 97
flagella of, 91
general description, 90
in human oral flora, 96
isolation techniques, 102
lipid composition of, 93
microfibrils of, 92
nutrition and growth requirements, 101
outer envelope, 90
peptidoglycan layer of, 91
perimural fibrils of, 92
slime layer of, 90
Spiroplasma citri
toxin from, 219
Spirulina
taxonomic classification, 233
Spirulina labyrinthiformis
facultative anoxygenic photosynthesis in, 363
Staphylococcus
involvement in opportunistic infections, 464
isolated from
the small bowels of nonruminant animals, 115
the stomach of nonruminant animals, 113
Staphylococcus aureus
involvement in opportunistic infections, 448, 464-65
Stigonematalean
taxonomic classification, 232
Stigonematales
taxonomic classification, 232
232
Streptococcus
chemostat studies of, 69
genetic duplications in, 490-91
involvement in opportunistic infections, 464
isolated from
the feces of nonruminant animals, 119
the large bowels of nonruminant animals, 117
the small bowels of nonruminant animals, 115
the stomach of nonruminant animals, 113
Streptococcus agalactiae
involvement in opportunistic infections, 451, 466
Streptococcus faecalis
in gastrointestinal tract of babies, 120
proton circulation measurements in, 187
Streptococcus pneumoniae
involvement in opportunistic infections, 450, 466-67
Streptococcus pyogenes
involvement in opportunistic infections, 450, 465-66
Streptolysins, 521-22
Streptomyces
antibiotics produced by different species, 15
chemotaxonomic studies of, 167-68
chloramphenicol synthesis in, 30
DAHP synthase regulation in, 30
distribution of chemical characteristics in, 164
serotaxonomic studies of, 170
Streptomyces albulus
antibiotic produced by, 292
Streptomyces antibioticus
catabolite regulation of actinomycin synthesis in, 350
Streptomyces aureofaciens
energy charge regulation of

chlortetracycline synthesis in, 352
glycosylation of pyrromycinone by, 34
Streptomyces coelicolor
heteroclone selection in, 490
Streptomyces erythreus
erythromycin synthesis by, 25
Streptomyces fradiae
methionine-stimulated synthesis of fosfomycin by, 347
Streptomyces griseus
antibiotic produced by, 292
regulation of candicidin synthesis in, 350
synthesis of candicidin, 15, 17, 25-26
Streptomyces kanamyceticus
catabolite regulation of kanamycin synthesis in, 351
Streptomyces levoris
levorin synthesis by, 22
Streptomyces luteofluorescens
current name and synonyms, 160
Streptomyces mediterranei
chemotaxonomic studies of, 163
Stretomyces narboensis
glycosylation studies of, 34
Streptomyces natalensis
antibiotic produced by, 292
Streptomyces nodosus
antibiotic produced by, 292
Streptomyces noursei
nystatin from, 20-24, 292, 298
carboxylating systems involved in synthesis of, 22
in vitro effects, 296
properties, 292
synthesis, 20-24
synthesis in mutants, 22-23
Streptomyces rimosus
TDP-mycarose synthesis by, 32
Streptomyces somaliensis
regulation of polyene macrolide synthesis in, 26
serotaxonomic studies of, 170
synthesis of polifungin by mutants of, 33
Streptomyces virginiae
virginiamycin synthesis induction in, 347
Streptomyces viridoflavus
activity of candihexan subcomponents from, 33
mutant with altered polyene macrolide synthesis, 24
Streptomycin
characterization of structure and function of the flagella of, 352-53
epimerase in synthesis of, 32
precursor, 32
Streptosporangium amethystogen
chemotaxonomic studies of, 168
PABA synthase regulation in, 30
streptomycin synthesis by, 32
synthesis of candicidin by mutants of, 27-30
Streptoverticillium
antibiotics produced by different species, 15
chemotaxonomic studies of, 168
Succinivibrio
isolated from the feces of nonruminant animals, 119
Sulfatides
involvement in perturbation of phagolysosome formation, 524
Superoxide
phagosome involvement, 511-13
Superoxide dismutase
in Synechococcus AN, 262
Suppressors
use in detecting genetic duplication, 486-88
Suramin, 525
Surgery
opportunistic bacterial diseases associated with, 453
Swarming, 51
Swiss-type agammaglobulinemia
opportunistic bacterial diseases associated with, 450
Symbiosis, 73
Synechococcus
cell envelope of, 238
control of chlorophyll and PBP synthesis, 242
control of gene expression in, 249
generic assignments, 231
guanine plus cytosine content, 238-47
micrograph, 230
mutant devoid of nitrite reductase, 264
16S RNA study of, 248
thylakoid arrangement in, 237
Synechoccus AN
growth in red light, 241
light-regulated stable RNA synthesis, 248
mutant studies, 256-58
nitrate and nitrite reductases in, 264
nucleotide pool measurements, 256
ribosomal subunit complementation study in, 247
RNA polymerase complementation study in, 247
study of, 227
tRNA characterization in, 247
Synechocystis
generic assignments, 231
glucose uptake in, 261-62
guanine plus cytosine DNA base composition of, 247
study of 16S RNA from, 248
Syphilis, 97-98
Systemic lupus erythematosus
opportunistic bacterial diseases associated with, 451

T

T4 bacteriophage
genetic duplication in, 500
T-cell defects
opportunistic bacterial diseases associated with, 450
Tabtoxin
organisms that produce it, 209-10
structure, 210
Tandem genetic duplications
genetic consequences of, 474-77
mechanisms of formation, 501
methods for detecting, 477
as a regulatory mechanism, 503
selection for, 478-501

coinheritance of allelic markers, 485-96
gene dosage, 478-85
operon fusion, 496-501
size and frequency of, 501
uses in genetic analysis, 502
Tennecetin, 15-18
chemical structure, 18
Tetrahymena pyriformis
chemostat studies, 79-82
as predator, 77-83
Tetramius
flagellated gamete stage in, 611
irreversibility of differentiation, 612
Tetramitus rostratus
relationship to Naegleria, 603-4
sequence of flagella assembly in, 613-14
Tetrin A, B, 15
Thermoactinomyces
chemotaxonomic studies of, 165
Thermomonospora
chemotaxonomic studies of, 165
Thermopolyspora flexieosa
current name and synonyms, 160
Thiobacillus
uptake of insoluble sulfur particles by, 386
Thiobacillus reapolitanus
carboxysomes from, 238
Thiobacillus thiooxidans
sulfur crystals clinging to the surface of, 386
Thiobacillus thioparus
glycollate excretion by, 260
Thiocapsa pfennigii
taxonomic classification, 283
Thiocapsa roseopersicina
taxonomic classification, 283
Thioesterases
in regulation of polyene macrolide synthesis, 22
Thiopedia rosea
taxonomic classification, 284
Thiopedia sevani
taxonomic classification, 284
Thiosarcina rosea
taxonomic classification, 284
Thiospirillum rosenbergii
taxonomic classification, 284
Thiospirillum sanguineum
taxonomic classification, 284
Thoracotoma
opportunistic bacterial diseases associated with, 453
Threonine dehydratase
inactivation in vivo, 141
Thymic hypoplasia
opportunistic bacterial diseases associated with, 450
Thymoma
opportunistic bacterial diseases associated with, 450
Ticks
Argas
as vector of avian borveliosis, 100
role in endemic relapsing fever, 99-100
Tolnaftate
organism sensitive to, 304
properties, 304
structure, 302
Torulopsis
effect of 5-fluorocytosine on, 299
isolated from the stomach of nonruminant animals, 299
Torulopsis gropengiesseri
production of extracelluar emulsifying agents by, 384
Total parenteral nutrition
opportunistic bacterial diseases associated with, 453
Toxoplasma gondii
antagonism of host defenses by, 517-20, 528
involvement in perturbation of phagolysosome formation, 524
Tracheostomy
opportunistic bacterial diseases associated with, 454
Transcription
cyanobacterial machinery, 247
in Naegleria differentiation, 619
Transformation
in genetic duplication studies, 490-91
Transient hypogammaglobulinemeia of infancy
opportunistic bacterial diseases associated with, 450
Translation
cyanobacterial machinery, 247
inhibitors in Naegleria, 619
Trauma
opportunistic bacterial diseases associated with, 453
Trench mouth
role of spirochetes in, 97
Treponema
distribution, 94
effect of sodium dodecyl sulfate on, 90
fermentation end products of, 102
flagella of, 91
isolation techniques, 102
lipid composition of, 93
Treponema carateum
as etiologic agent of pinta, 98
nutrition and growth requirements, 101
Treponema denticola
in human oral flora, 97
Treponema genitalis
cytoplasmic tubules of, 93
Treponema hyodysenteriae
disease caused by, 96
nutrition and growth requirements, 101
Treponema macrodentium
in human oral flora, 97
Treponema oralis
in human oral flora, 97
Treponema pallidum
diseases caused by, 97
nutrition and growth requirements, 101
slime layer of, 90
Treponema paraluis-caniculi
as causal agent of rabbit venereal disease, 98
nutrition and growth requirements, 101
Treponema pertenue
as etiologic agent of yaws, 98
nutrition and growth requirements, 101
Treponema phageodonis
isolation techniques, 101
Treponema vincentii

in human oral flora, 97
Trichodesmium
non-heterocystous aerobic nitrogen fixation in, 265
Trichomycin
chemical components, 15
producer species, 15
synthesis, 26
use, 298
Trichophyton
effect of polyene antibiotics on, 296
griseofulvin used in effective treatment of disease caused by, 301
Trichophyton mentagrophytes
effect of griseofulvin on, 303
tolnaftate sensitivity of, 304
Trichophyton rubrum
tolnaftate sensitivity of, 304
Trypanosoma cruzi
antagonism of host defenses by, 520
Tryptophan operon
genetic duplication in, 499
Turimycin, 22
Turnover of protein, 137, 145-47
Tylosin
precursors, 17
sugar nucleotide diphosphate intermediates, 32

U

Urinary tract manipulations
opportunistic bacterial diseases associated with, 454
Ustilago maydis
nitrate reductase
inactivation in vivo, 141

V

Valinomycin
effect on circadian rhythm, 198
Vancomycin
inhibition of synthesis by inorganic phosphate, 352
Veillonella
isolated from
the feces of nonruminant animals, 119
the large bowels of nonruminant animals, 117
the small bowels of nonruminant animals, 117
the stomach of nonruminant animals, 113
Vibrio
relation to Beneckea, 57
Vibrio albensis
currently used and proposed epithets, 554
guanine plus cytosine DNA base composition of, 554
luminescent system synthesis autoinduction in, 572
Vibrio alginolytica
characteristics, 553
Vibrio cholerae
colonization of small intestine, 124
currently used and proposed epithets. 554
guanine plus cytosine DNA base composition of, 554
involvement in opportunistic infections, 467
lipopolysaccharide sugar amine in, 31
luminescence in, 556
similarity with members of Beneckea, 43-45, 556
Vibrio fischeri
currently used and proposed epithets, 554
Vibrio luminosus
characteristics, 555
effects of sodium chloride concentration on the luminescence of, 573
specific hosts with light organs, 555
Vibrio natriegens
characteristics, 553-56
guanine plus cytosine DNA base composition of, 554
Vibrio parahaemolytica
characteristics, 553
Vibrio phosphorescens
characteristics, 555
Virginiamycin
induction of synthesis of, 347
Vorticella
chemostat studies of, 83

W

Water-clearing diseases, 208
Wildfire disease of tobacco, 207
Winteria telescopa
luminescent symbiotic bacteria of, 554
Wiskott-Aldrich syndrome
opportunistic bacterial diseases associated with, 450
Woodruffia metabolica
predator study of, 79

X

Xanthomonas
polysaccharides of, 215-16
wilting diseases of, 207
Xanthomonas campestris
polysaccharide from, 215
Xanthomonas malvacearum
water clearing caused by, 208
Xanthomonas oryzae
polysaccharides from, 215
water-clearing disease caused by, 208
Xanthomonas translucens
water clearing produced by, 208
Xenococcus
taxonomic classification, 232-33

Y

Yaws, 97-98
Yeast
chemostat studies of, 69
glucose-induced inactivation of enzymes in, 142
isolated from
the feces of nonruminant animals, 119
the large bowels of nonruminant animals, 117
the small bowels of nonruminant animals, 115
the stomach of nonruminant animals, 113
use of mutant in enzyme inactivation study, 149
Yersinia
involvement in opportunistic infections, 457
Yersinia enterocolitica
involvement in opportunistic infections, 459
Yersinia pseudotuberculosis
involvement in opportunistic infections, 459

CUMULATIVE INDEXES

CONTRIBUTING AUTHORS VOLUMES 27-31

A

Achong, B. G., 27:413-36; 31:421-45
Adler, H. E., 30:147-68
Anderson, R. P., 31:473-505
Anderson, T. F., 29:1-18
Andrewes, C. H., 27:1-11
Arden, S. B., 28:265-99
Armstrong, J. A., 29:131-61

B

Barer, R., 28:371-89
Baresi, L., 31:309-41
Barksdale, L., 28:265-99
Baumann, L., 31:39-61
Baumann, P., 31:39-61
Bray, R. S., 28:189-217
Breinig, M. C., 29:131-61
Brenchley, J. E., 29:251-74
Brener, Z., 27:347-82
Brill, W. J., 29:109-29
Bryan, B. A., 30:241-62
Bulla, L. A. Jr., 29:163-90

C

Cabib, E., 29:191-214
Calhoun, D. H., 29:275-99
Cameron, D. S., 27:243-59
Cashel, M., 29:301-18
Cerdá-Olmedo, E., 31:535-47
Chet, I., 30:221-39
Cohen-Bazire, G., 31:225-74
Curtiss, R. III, 30:507-33

D

Delwiche, C. C., 30:241-62
Demain, A. L., 31:343-56
DeVay, J. E., 30:147-68
Diener, T. O., 28:23-39
Dondero, N. C., 29:407-28
Dressler, D., 29:525-59
Drew, S. W., 31:343-56

E

Epstein, M. A., 27:413-36; 31:421-45

F

Fraenkel, D. G., 27:69-100
Fredrickson, A. G., 31:63-87
Fuccillo, D. A., 28:231-64
Fulton, C., 31:597-629

G

Gander, J. E., 28:103-19
Gibbons, R. J., 29:19-44
Glass, T. L., 31:309-41
Glenn, A. R., 30:41-62
Goldman, J. C., 29:429-43
Goldstein, S., 27:13-26
Goodfellow, M., 31:159-80
Goren, M. B., 31:507-33
Grunberg, E., 27:317-46
Gutnick, D. L., 31:379-96

H

Haines, T. H., 27:403-11
Handmaker, S. D., 27:189-204
Harold, F. M., 31:181-203
Harris, R. H., 27:27-50
Hastings, J. W., 31:549-95
Hatfield, G. W., 29:275-99
Hausmann, R., 27:51-67
Heidelberger, M., 31:1-12
Helinski, D. R., 27:437-70
Henning, U., 29:45-60
Henriksen, S. D., 30:63-83
Hirsch, P., 28:391-444
Ho, M., 29:131-60
Hotchkiss, R. D., 28:445-68
Huang, A. S., 27:101-17
Hylemon, P. B., 30:303-25

I

Inniss, W. E., 29:445-65
Irons, E. S., 29:319-32
Isenberg, H. D., 30:483-505

J

Jensen, R. A., 30:409-25
Jernelöv, A., 29:61-77
Johnson, R. C., 31:89-106

K

Killick, K. A., 28:139-66
Kingsbury, D. W., 30:21-39
Kobayashi, G. S., 31:291-308
Krieg, N. R., 30:303-25
Kurent, J. E., 28:231-64

L

Lemke, P. A., 30:105-45
Levinthal, M., 28:219-30
Lin, E. C. C., 30:535-78
Lindberg, A. A., 27:205-41
Lippincott, B. B., 29:377-405
Lippincott, J. A., 29:377-405
Lipps, J. H., 27:471-88
London, J., 30:279-301

M

MacLowry, J. D., 30:483-505
Mah, R. A., 31:309-41
Maramorosch, K., 28:301-24
Martin, A.-L., 29:61-77
Martín, J.-F., 31:13-38
McElroy, W. D., 30:1-20
McKeever, W. G., 29:215-50
Medoff, G., 31:291-308
Miller, C. G., 29:485-504
Miller, R. C. Jr., 29:355-76

Minnikin, D. E., 31:159-80
Mitchell, R., 27:27-60; 30:221-39
Mosbach, K., 28:61-83
Mrak, E. M., 28:1-22
Müller, M., 29:467-83

N

Nealson, K. H., 31:549-95
Neidhardt, F. C., 29:215-50

O

Ottow, J. C. G., 29:79-108
Owen, P., 30:451-82

P

Parker, J., 29:215-50
Parson, W. W., 28:41-59
Pfennig, N., 31:275-90
Pirie, N. W., 27:119-32

Q

Quigley, J. P., 28:325-51

R

Raghow, R., 30:21-39
Rhodes, R. A., 29:163-90
Rickenberg, H. V., 28:353-69
Rifkin, D. B., 28:325-51
Robinson, W. S., 31:357-77
Rosenberg, E., 31:379-96
Rosenkranz, H. S., 27:383-401
Roth, J. R., 31:473-505
Ryther, J. H., 29:429-43

S

Sack, R. B., 29:333-53
Sadoff, H. L., 27:133-53
St. Julian, G., 29:163-90
Salton, M. R. J., 30:451-82
Sanderson, K. E., 30:327-49
Savage, D. C., 31:107-33
Schaechter, M., 27:261-82
Scott, W. A., 30:85-104
Sears, M. H., 29:319-32
Sever, J. L., 28:231-64
Shapiro, L., 30:377-407
Shively, J. M., 28:167-87
Siegel, P. J., 27:261-82
Silverman, M., 31:397-419
Simon, M. I., 31:397-419
Soriano, S., 27:155-70
Srere, P. A., 28:61-83
Stanbridge, E. J., 30:169-87
Stanier, R. Y., 31:225-74
Steinfeld, J. L., 30:427-50
Stewart, W. D. P., 27:283-316
Strobel, G. A., 31:205-24
Suzuki, I., 28:85-101
Switzer, R. L., 31:135-57

T

Taber, W. A., 30:263-77
Tachibana, D. K., 30:351-75
Taylor, D. L., 27:171-87
Taylor, G. R., 28:121-37
Taylor, I. E. P., 27:243-59
Titsworth, E. H., 27:317-46

V

van Houte, J., 29:19-44
Vinopal, R. T., 27:69-100
von Graevenitz, A., 31:447-71

W

Ward, D. M., 31:309-41
Weisman, R. A., 30:189-219
Wheelis, M. L., 29:505-24
White, R. G., 30:579-600
Williams, L. S., 29:251-74
Wishnow, R. M., 30:427-50
Wright, B. E., 28:139-66

CHAPTER TITLES VOLUMES 27-31

PREFATORY CHAPTERS

Fifty Years with Viruses	C. H. Andrewes	27:1-11
A Microbiologist Turned Administrator—How It Happened	E. M. Mrak	28:1-22
Some Personal Memories of Research	T. F. Anderson	29:1-18
From the Precise to the Ambiguous: Light, Bonding, and Administration	W. D. McElroy	30:1-20
A "Pure" Organic Chemist's Downward Path	M. Heidelberger	31:1-12

ANIMAL PATHOGENS AND DISEASES

Algal Symbionts of Invertebrates	D. L. Taylor	27:171-87
Biology of Trypanosoma cruzi	Z. Brener	27:347-82
Aspects of Microbiology in Cancer Research	H. S. Rosenkranz	27:383-401
Viroids: The Smallest Known Agents of Infectious Disease	T. O. Diener	28:23-39
Leishmania	R. S. Bray	28:189-217
Slow Virus Diseases	D. A. Fuccillo, J. E. Kurent, J. L. Sever	28:231-64
Bacterial Adherence in Oral Microbial Ecology	R. J. Gibbons, J. van Houte	29:19-44
Bacteria as Insect Pathogens	L. A. Bulla Jr., R. A. Rhodes, G. St. Julian	29:163-90
Human Diarrheal Disease Caused by Enterotoxigenic Escherichia coli	R. B. Sack	29:333-54
A Reevaluation of the Role of Mycoplasmas in Human Disease	E. J. Stanbridge	30:169-87
Microbiology of the Foot	D. K. Tachibana	30:351-75
The Conquest of the Major Infectious Diseases in the United States: A Bicentennial Retrospect	R. M. Wishnow, J. L. Steinfeld	30:427-50
Automated Methods and Data Handling in Bacteriology	H. D. Isenberg, J. D. MacLowry	30:483-505
Recent Progress in Epstein-Barr Virus Research	M. A. Epstein, B. G. Achong	31:421-45
The Role of Opportunistic Bacteria in Human Disease	A. von Graevenitz	31:447-71

APPLIED MICROBIOLOGY AND ECOLOGY

The Role of Polymers in Microbial Aggregation	R. H. Harris, R. Mitchell	27:27-50
Algal Symbionts of Invertebrates	D. L. Taylor	27:171-87
Nitrogen Fixation by Photosynthetic Microorganisms	W. D. P. Stewart	27:283-316
Microscopes, Microscopy, and Microbiology	R. Barer	27:371-89
A Microbiologist Turned Administrator—How It Happened	E. M. Mrak	28:1-22
Fungal Cell Wall Glycoproteins and Peptido-Polysaccharides	J. E. Gander	28:103-19
Space Microbiology	G. R. Taylor	28:121-37
Bacterial Adherence in Oral Microbial Ecology	R. J. Gibbons, J. van Houte	29:19-44
Ecological Implications of Metal Metabolism by Microorganisms	A. Jernelöv, A.-L. Martin	29:61-77
Ecology, Physiology, and Genetics of Fimbriae and Pili	J. C. G. Ottow	29:79-108
Bacteria as Insect Pathogens	L. A. Bulla Jr., R. A. Rhodes, G. St. Julian	29:163-90

Patents in Relation to Microbiology	E. S. Irons, M. H. Sears	29:319-32
The Sphaerotilus-Leptothrix Group	N. C. Dondero	29:407-28
Microbes as Food in Mariculture	J. H. Ryther, J. C. Goldman	29:429-44
Interaction of Temperature and Psychrophilic Microorganisms	W. E. Inniss	29:445-65
Production of Extracellular Proteins by Bacteria	A. R. Glenn	30:41-62
Antigens Common to Hosts and Parasites	J. E. DeVay, H. E. Adler	30:147-68
Ecological Aspects of Microbial Chemotactic Behavior	I. Chet, R. Mitchell	30:221-39
Denitrification	C. C. Delwiche, B. A. Bryan	30:241-62
Wastewater Microbiology	W. A. Taber	30:263-77
The Ecology and Taxonomic Status of the Lactobacilli	J. London	30:279-301
Automated Methods and Data Handling in Bacteriology	H. D. Isenberg, J. D. MacLowry	30:483-505
Genetics Manipulation of Microorganisms: Potential Benefits and Biohazards	R. Curtiss III	30:507-33
Biology of the Marine Enterobacteria: Genera Beneckea and Photobacterium	P. Baumann, L. Baumann	31:39-61
Behavior of Mixed Cultures of Microorganisms	A. G. Fredrickson	31:63-87
Microbial Ecology of the Gastrointestinal Tract	D. C. Savage	31:107-33
The Inactivation of Microbial Enzymes In Vivo	R. L. Switzer	31:135-57
Biogenesis of Methane	R. A. Mah, D. M. Ward, L. Baresi, T. L. Glass	31:309-41
Effect of Primary Metabolites on Secondary Metabolism	S. W. Drew, A. L. Demain	31:343-56
Oil Tankers and Pollution: A Microbiological Approach	D. L. Gutnick, E. Rosenberg	31:379-96
Bacterial Bioluminescence	J. W. Hastings, K. H. Nealson	31:549-95
CHEMOTHERAPY AND CHEMOTHERAPEUTIC AGENTS		
Chemotherapeutic Properties of Heterocyclic Compounds: Monocyclic Compounds with Five-Membered Rings	E. Grunberg, E. H. Titsworth	27:317-70
Plasmid Determined Resistance to Antibiotics: Molecular Properties of R Factors	D. R. Helinski	27:437-70
Patents in Relation to Microbiology	E. S. Irons, M. H. Sears	29:319-32
The Conquest of the Major Infectious Diseases in the United States: A Bicentennial Retrospect	R. M. Wishnow, J. L. Steinfeld	30:427-50
Biosynthesis of Polyene Macrolide Antibiotics	J.-F. Martin	31:13-38
Antifungal Agents: Recent Developments	G. S. Kobayashi, G. Medoff	31:291-308
DIVERSITY AND SYSTEMATICS		
Zoosporic Marine Fungi (Thraustochytriaceae and Dermocystidiaceae)	S. Goldstein	27:13-26
Flexibacteria	S. Soriano	27:155-70
Algal Symbionts of Invertebrates	D. L. Taylor	27:171-87
Nitrogen Fixation by Photosynthetic Microorganisms	W. D. P. Stewart	27:283-316
Biology of Trypanosoma cruzi	Z. Brener	27:347-82
Test Structure in Foraminifera	J. H. Lipps	27:471-88
Inclusion Bodies of Prokaryotes	J. M. Shively	28:167-87
Budding Bacteria	P. Hirsch	28:391-444
Determination of Cell Shape in Bacteria	U. Henning	29:45-60
The Genus Agrobacterium and Plant Tumorigenesis	J. A. Lippincott, B. B. Lippincott	29:377-405
The Sphaerotilus-Leptothrix Group	N. C. Dondero	29:407-28
Moraxella, Neisseria, Branhamella, and Acineto-		

bacter	S. D. Henriksen	30:63-83
The Taxonomy of the Chemoheterotrophic Spirilla	N. R. Krieg, P. B. Hylemon	30:303-25
Genetic Relatedness in the Family Enterobacteriaceae	K. E. Sanderson	30:327-49
Biology of the Marine Enterobacteria: Genera Beneckea and Photobacterium	P. Baumann, L. Baumann	31:39-61
The Spirochetes	R. C. Johnson	31:89-106
Nocardioform Bacteria	M. Goodfellow, D. E. Minnikin	31:159-80
Phototrophic Prokaryotes: The Cyanobacteria	R. Y. Stanier, G. Cohen-Bazire	31:225-74
Phototrophic Green and Purple Bacteria: A Comparative, Systematic Survey	N. Pfennig	31:275-90
GENETICS		
The Genetics of T-Odd Phages	R. Hausmann	27:51-67
Hybridization of Eukaryotic Cells	S. D. Handmaker	27:189-204
Plasmid Determined Resistance to Antibiotics: Molecular Properties of R Factors	D. R. Helinski	27:437-70
Bacterial Genetics Excluding E. coli	M. Levinthal	28:219-30
Models of Genetic Recombination	R. D. Hotchkiss	28:445-68
Ecology, Physiology, and Genetics of Fimbriae and Pili	J. C. G. Ottow	29:79-108
Regulation and Genetics of Bacterial Nitrogen Fixation	W. J. Brill	29:109-29
Molecular Aspects of Yeast Morphogenesis	E. Cabib	29:191-214
Function and Regulation of Aminoacyl-tRNA Synthetases in Prokaryotic and Eukaryotic Cells	F. C. Neidhardt, J. Parker, W. G. McKeever	29:215-50
Transfer RNA Involvement in the Regulation of Enzyme Synthesis	J. E. Brenchley, L. S. Williams	29:251-74
Autoregulation of Gene Expression	D. H. Calhoun, G. W. Hatfield	29:275-99
Regulation of Bacterial ppGpp and pppGpp	M. Cashel	29:301-18
Replication and Molecular Recombination of T-Phage	R. C. Miller Jr.	29:355-76
The Genetics of Dissimilatory Pathways in Pseudomonas	M. L. Wheelis	29:505-24
Recent Excitement in the DNA Growing Point Problem	D. Dressler	29:525-59
Biochemical Genetics of Morphogenesis in Neurospora	W. A. Scott	30:85-104
Genetic Relatedness in the Family Enterobacteriaceae	K. E. Sanderson	30:327-49
Enzyme Recruitment in Evolution of New Function	R. A. Jensen	30:409-25
Genetic Manipulation of Microorganisms: Potential Benefits and Biohazards	R. Curtiss III	30:507-33
Tandem Genetic Duplications in Phage and Bacteria	R. P. Anderson, J. R. Roth	31:473-505
Behavioral Genetics of Phycomyces	E. Cerdá-Olmedo	31:535-47
GROWTH AND NUTRITION		
Production of Extracellular Proteins by Bacteria	A. R. Glenn	30:41-62
Behavior of Mixed Cultures of Microorganisms	A. G. Fredrickson	31:63-87
IMMUNOLOGY		
Antigens Common to Hosts and Parasites	J. E. DeVay, H. E. Adler	30:147-68
The Adjuvant Effect of Microbial Products on the Immune Response	R. G. White	30:579-600
Phagocyte Lysosomes: Interactions with		

Infectious Agents, Phagosomes, and Experimental Perturbations in Function	M. B. Goren	31:507-33
METABOLISM, BIOCHEMISTRY, AND REGULATION		
The Role of Polymers in Microbial Aggregation	R. H. Harris, R. Mitchell	27:27-50
Carbohydrate Metabolism in Bacteria	D. G. Fraenkel, R. T. Vinopal	27:69-100
Preparation and Quantitative Analysis of Fungal Cell Walls: Strategy and Tactics	I. E. P. Taylor, D. S. Cameron	27:243-59
Nitrogen Fixation by Photosynthetic Microorganisms	W. D. P. Stewart	27:283-316
Halogen- and Sulfur-Containing Lipids of Ochromonas	T. H. Haines	27:403-11
Bacterial Photosynthesis	W. W. Parson	28:41-59
Metabolic Compartmentation: Symbiotic, Organellar, Multienzymic, and Microenvironmental	P. A. Srere, K. Mosbach	28:61-83
Mechanisms of Inorganic Oxidation and Energy Coupling	I. Suzuki	28:85-101
Fungal Cell Wall Glycoproteins and Peptido-Polysaccharides	J. E. Gander	28:103-19
Regulation of Enzyme Activity During Differentiation in Dictyostelium discoideum	K. A. Killick, B. E. Wright	28:139-66
Cyclic AMP in Prokaryotes	H. V. Rickenberg	28:353-69
Determination of Cell Shape in Bacteria	U. Henning	29:45-60
Ecological Implications of Metal Metabolism by Microorganisms	A. Jernelöv, A.-L. Martin	29:61-77
Regulation and Genetics of Bacterial Nitrogen Fixation	W. J. Brill	29:109-29
Function and Regulation of Aminoacyl-tRNA Synthetases in Prokaryotic and Eukaryotic Cells	F. C. Neidhardt, J. Parker, W. G. McKeever	29:215-50
Transfer RNA Involvement in the Regulation of Enzyme Synthesis	J. E. Brenchley, L. S. Williams	29:251-74
Autoregulation of Gene Expression	D. H. Calhoun, G. W. Hatfield	29:275-99
Regulation of Bacterial ppGpp and pppGpp	M. Cashel	29:301-18
Interaction of Temperature and Psychrophilic Microorganisms	W. E. Inniss	29:445-65
Biochemistry of Protozoan Microbodies: Peroxisomes, α-Glycerophosphate Oxidase Bodies, Hydrogenosomes	M. Müller	29:467-83
Peptidases and Proteases of Escherichia coli and Salmonella typhimurium	C. G. Miller	29:485-504
The Genetics of Dissimilatory Pathways in Pseudomonas	M. L. Wheelis	29:505-24
Production of Extracellular Proteins by Bacteria	A. R. Glenn	30:41-62
Ecological Aspects of Microbial Chemotactic Behavior	I. Chet, R. Mitchell	30:221-39
Denitrification	C. C. Delwiche, B. A. Bryan	30:241-62
Enzyme Recruitment in Evolution of New Function	R. A. Jensen	30:409-25
Glycerol Dissimilation and Its Regulation in Bacteria	E. C. C. Lin	30:535-78
The Inactivation of Microbial Enzymes In Vivo	R. L. Switzer	31:135-57
Ion Currents and Physiological Functions in Microorganisms	F. M. Harold	31:181-203
Biogenesis of Methane	R. A. Mah, D. M. Ward, L. Baresi, T. L. Glass	31:309-41
Effect of Primary Metabolites on Secondary Metabolism	S. W. Drew, A. L. Demain	31:343-56
Oil Tankers and Pollution: A Microbiological		

Approach	D. L. Gutnick, E. Rosenberg	31:379-96
MORPHOLOGY, ULTRASTRUCTURE, AND DIFFERENTIATION		
"On Being the Right Size"	N. W. Pirie	27:119-32
Comparative Aspects of Morphogenesis in Three Prokaryotic Genera	H. L. Sadoff	27:133-53
Preparation and Quantitative Analysis of Fungal Cell Walls: Strategy and Tactics	I. E. P. Taylor, D. S. Cameron	27:243-59
The Role of the Host Cell Membrane in the Replication and Morphogenesis of Bacteriophages	P. J. Siegel, M. Schaechter	27:261-82
Test Structure in Foraminifera	J. H. Lipps	27:471-88
Metabolic Compartmentation: Symbiotic, Organellar, Multienzymic, and Microenvironmental	P. A. Srere, K. Mosbach	28:61-83
Fungal Cell Wall Glycoproteins and Peptido-Polysaccharides	J. E. Gander	28:103-19
Regulation of Enzyme Activity During Differentiation in Dictyostelium discoideum	K. A. Killick, B. E. Wright	28:139-66
Inclusion Bodies of Prokaryotes	J. M. Shively	28:167-87
Microscopes, Microscopy, and Microbiology	R. Barer	28:371-89
Some Personal Memories of Research	T. F. Anderson	29:1-18
Determination of Cell Shape in Bacteria	U. Henning	29:45-60
Ecology, Physiology, and Genetics of Fimbriae and Pili	J. C. G. Ottow	29:79-108
Molecular Aspects of Yeast Morphogenesis	E. Cabib	29:191-214
Biochemical Genetics of Morphogenesis in Neurospora	W. A. Scott	30:85-104
Differentiation in Acanthamoeba castellanii	R. A. Weisman	30:189-219
Ecological Aspects of Microbial Chemotactic Behavior	I. Chet, R. Mitchell	30:221-39
Differentiation in the Caulobacter Cell Cycle	L. Shapiro	30:377-407
Bacterial Membrane Structure	M. R. J. Salton, P. Owen	30:451-82
Bacterial Flagella	M. Silverman, M. I. Simon	31:397-419
Cell Differentiation in Naegleria gruberi	C. Fulton	31:597-629
PLANT PATHOGENS AND DISEASES		
Viroids: The Smallest Known Agents of Infectious Disease	T. O. Diener	28:23-39
Mycoplasmas and Rickettsiae in Relation to Plant Diseases	K. Maramorosch	28:301-24
Bacteria as Insect Pathogens	L. A. Bulla Jr., R. A. Rhodes, G. St. Julian	29:163-90
The Genus Agrobacterium and Plant Tumorigenesis	J. A. Lippincott, B. B. Lippincott	29:377-405
Antigens Common to Hosts and Parasites	J. E. DeVay, H. E. Adler	30:147-68
Bacterial Phytotoxins	G. A. Strobel	31:205-24
VIROLOGY		
Fifty Years with Viruses	C. H. Andrewes	27:1-11
The Genetics of T-Odd Phages	R. Hausmann	27:51-67
Defective Interfering Viruses	A. S. Huang	27:101-17
Bacteriophage Receptors	A. A. Lindberg	27:205-41
The Role of the Host Cell Membrane in the Replication and Morphogenesis of Bacteriophages	P. J. Siegel, M. Schaechter	27:261-82
The EB Virus	M. A. Epstein, B. G. Achong	27:413-36
Viroids: The Smallest Known Agents of Infectious Disease	T. O. Diener	28:23-39
Slow Virus Diseases	D. A. Fuccillo, J. E. Kurent, J. L. Sever	28:231-64
Persisting Bacteriophage Infections, Lysogeny, and Phage Conversions	L. Barksdale, S. B. Arden	28:265-99
Virus-Induced Modification of Cellular Mem-		

branes Related to Viral Structure	D. B. Rifkin, J. P. Quigley	28:325-51
Interferon	M. Ho, J. A. Armstrong	29:131-61
Replication and Molecular Recombination of T-Phage	R. C. Miller Jr.	29:355-76
Endogenous Viral Enzymes Involved in Messenger RNA Production	R. Raghow, D. W. Kingsbury	30:21-39
Viruses of Eukaryotic Microorganisms	P. A. Lemke	30:105-45
The Genome of Hepatitis B Virus	W. S. Robinson	31:357-77
Recent Progress in Epstein-Barr Virus Research	M. A. Epstein, B. G. Achong	31:421-45